THE REFORM OF THE LITURGY

The Reform of the Liturgy
1948–1975

by

Annibale Bugnini
Titular Archbishop of Diocletiana

Translated by
Matthew J. O'Connell

THE LITURGICAL PRESS
Collegeville, Minnesota

The Reform of the Liturgy (1948–1975) is the authorized English translation of *La riforma liturgica (1948–1975),* published by Centro Liturgico Vincenziano—Edizioni Liturgiche, Rome, 1983.

Printed in the United States of America.

Library of Congress Cataloging-in-Publication Data

Bugnini, Annibale.
   [Riforma liturgica, 1948–1975. English]
   The reform of the liturgy, 1948–1975 / by Annibale Bugnini ;
translated by Matthew J. O'Connell.
        p.   cm.
   Translation of: La riforma liturgica, 1948–1975.
   Includes bibliographical references and index.
   ISBN 0-8146-1571-6 (hardcover)
   1. Catholic Church—Liturgy—History—20th century. 2. Bugnini,
Annibale.   I. Title.
BX1970.B77   1990
264'.02'00904—dc20
                                      90-36986
                                         CIP

Table of Contents

FOREWORD   xix
PREFACE   xxiii
EDITORIAL NOTE   xxxi
ABBREVIATIONS   xxxiii

Part I

THE MAIN STAGES

I. THE BEGINNING OF THE REFORM

Chapter 1. THE KEY TO THE LITURGICAL REFORM   5
1. The Movement for Reform **6** — 2. The "Pian" Commission (1948–1960) **7** — 3. Liturgical Publications **10** — 4. The Assisi Congress (1956) **11**

Chapter 2. THE PREPARATORY COMMISSION   14
1. Formation of the Commission **14** — 2. First Meeting: Autumn 1960 **17** — 3. Second Meeting: Spring 1961 **18** — 4. Third Meeting: Winter 1962 **21** — 5. Sacred Music **21** — 6. Latin **22** — 7. *Via Purgativa* **25** — 8. *In pace cum sanctis* **27**

Chapter 3. THE LITURGICAL CONSTITUTION AT THE COUNCIL   29
I. History **30**
II. Amendments and Changes **32**
III. Promulgation **37**

Chapter 4. "FUNDAMENTAL PRINCIPLES"   **39**

    I. Guiding Principles **39**
    1. The Liturgy Is "An Exercise of the Priestly Office
    of Jesus Christ" (no. 7) **39** — 2. The Liturgy as "Sum-
    mit and Fount" of the Church's Life **40** — 3. Full,
    Conscious, Active Participation **41** — 4. Manifestation
    of the Church (no. 26) **41** — 5. "Substantial Unity,"
    Not "Rigid Uniformity" (no. 38) **42** — 6. "Sound Tra-
    dition" and "Legitimate Progress" (no. 23) **43**

    II. Operational Principles **45**
    1. Language **45** — 2. The Word of God **46** — 3. Cat-
    echetical Instruction **46** — 4. Singing **47** — 5. Reform
    of the Liturgy **48**

Chapter 5. THE "CONSTITUENT ASSEMBLY" OF THE
CONSILIUM   **49**

Chapter 6. THE MOTU PROPRIO *SACRAM LITURGIAM*   **54**

    I. History **54**
    II. Content **56**
    III. Agreements and Disagreements **58**

Chapter 7. ORGANIZATION OF THE WORK   **60**

    I. Preparation **60**
    II. General Plan of Liturgical Reform **63**
    III. Explanation of the Plan **65**

Chapter 8. THE SACRED CONGREGATION FOR DIVINE
WORSHIP   **69**

    I. The Consilium and the Congregation of Rites **71**
    II. Attempts at Organizing the Consilium **73**
    III. The Consilium in the Reform of the Curia **78**
    IV. The Congregation for Divine Worship **80**

II. First Accomplishments

Chapter 9. MARCH 7, 1965: SHIFT FROM LATIN TO VERNACULAR   **99**

    1. First Steps **101** — 2. The Preface in the Vernacular
    104 — 3. The Roman Canon **105** — 4. Against the
    Mind of the Council? **110**

Chapter 10. CHANGES IN THE MISSAL   114
    I. *Ordo Missae* and *Ritus Servandus* 114
    II. Changes in Holy Week 116
    III. Chant 119

Chapter 11. CONCELEBRATION   123
    I. Preparation of the Rite 123
    II. Experiments 124
    III. The Definitive Rite 127
    IV. Content 129
    V. Interritual Concelebration 132
    VI. Communion Under Both Kinds 133

III. Two Areas of Activity

A. Preparation of the Liturgical Reform

Chapter 12. MEETINGS   137
    I. Preliminary Meetings 137
    II. Ordinary Meetings 137
    III. General Meetings 139
    IV. Plenary Meetings 192

Chapter 13. OBSERVERS AT THE CONSILIUM   199

B. Encouragement of a Pastoral Approach to the Liturgy

Chapter 14. LETTERS TO THE PRESIDENTS OF THE EPISCOPAL
    CONFERENCES   205
    I. General Letters 206
    II. Particular Interventions 215

Chapter 15. CONFERENCES   219
    I. Conference of Translators of Liturgical Books 219
    II. Meetings with the Presidents of the National Liturgical Commissions 222
    III. Relations with the Directors of Liturgical Periodicals 225
    IV. Conference of the Secretaries of the National Commissions 230

Chapter 16.   TRANSLATIONS   **233**
            1. Joint Commissions **233** — 2. Instruction on the
            Translation of Liturgical Texts **236** — 3. Interim Trans-
            lations **239** — 4. Integrity of the Liturgical Books **240** —
            5. Translation of the Sacramental Formulas **241** —
            6. Publication of Liturgical Books **244**

Chapter 17.   NOTITIAE   **247**

IV. TRIALS AND TRIBULATIONS OF THE REFORM

Chapter 18.   EXPERIMENTS   **257**
            I. Unauthorized Experiments **257**
            II. Statements on Experiments **259**
            III. Experiments Authorized by the Consilium **262**

Chapter 19.   ADAPTATION   **267**

Chapter 20.   OPPOSITION   **277**
            1. *Una voce* **277** — 2. Organization of the "Counter-
            reform" **278** — 3. The "Heretical" Mass **284** — 4. The
            Challenge to Papal Authority **290** — 5. Attitude of the
            Holy See **295** — 6. A Binding Missal **298**

Part II

SECTIONS COMMON TO THE NEW LITURGICAL BOOKS

Chapter 21.   THE CALENDAR   **305**
            I. History **305**
            1. First Report to the Consilium (1965) **306** — 2. Sec-
            ond Report (1966) **308** — 3. Examination by the Curia
            309 — 4. Papal Approval and Publication **313** —
            5. New Revisions **315**
            II. Contents **318**
            1. Proper of the Seasons **318** — 2. Proper of the Saints
            321
            III. Special Questions **322**
            1. Holy Days of Obligation **322** — 2. Sanctification of
            Sunday **324**

Chapter 22. THE LITANY OF THE SAINTS   327

    1. Principles of the Revision **327** — 2. Elimination of
    Doublets **328** — 3. Plurality of Forms **329** — 4. List
    of the Saints **330**

Chapter 23. COMMONS   331

Part III

THE MISSAL

Chapter 24. THE ORDER OF MASS   337

    I. The "Normative" Mass **337**
    1. First Phase of the Work (April 1964–October 1965)
    338 — 2. Continuation of the Work **341** — 3. First
    Schema of the "Normative" Mass **342**

    II. The Normative Mass at the Synod of Bishops **346**
    1. Papal Queries **351** — 2. The Queries on the Mass
    352

    III. The Normative Mass in the Presence of the Pope **359**
    1. Performance of the Celebrations **361** — 2. Scrutiny
    of the Experiment **364** — 3. Observations of the Pope
    364 — 4. Observations of the Churchmen **365** —
    5. Observations of the Laity **367** — 6. "The Pope's
    Wishes" **369**

    IV. Critique by the Prefects of the Curial Agencies **372**

    V. The Final Stage **377**
    1. New Study by the Pope **377** — 2. Changes in the
    Roman Canon **381**

    VI. Publication of the Order of Mass **383**
    1. Apostolic Constitution *Missale Romanum* **385** —
    2. General Instruction of the Roman Missal **386** —
    3. Effective Date of Use **391**

Chapter 25. THE NEW ROMAN MISSAL   393

    I. Documents **394**

    II. The Sacramentary **396**
    1. Euchological Riches **396** — 2. Commons **398** —
    3. Masses for Various Needs **399** — 4. Some Special
    Rites **402** — 5. General Intercessions (Prayer of the
    Faithful) **402** — 6. Songs **405**

Chapter 26. THE LECTIONARY OF THE ROMAN MISSAL   **406**

    I. Experimental Lectionary for Weekdays **406**
    1. The German Plan **406** — 2. The French Plan **408** — 3. The Consilium Plan **408** — 4. Special Lectionaries **409**

    II. Lectionary for Mass **409**
    1. Goal **410** — 2. Principles **410** — 3. Collection of Materials **412** — 4. Discussion at the Seventh General Meeting (1966) **414** — 5. Report to the Pope **418** — 6. Consultation **419** — 7. Papal Approval **420** — 8. Publication **420** — 9. Festal Lectionary **421** — 10. Weekday Lectionary **422** — 11. Lectionary for the Saints **423** — 12. Masses for Various Occasions **423** — 13. Songs Between the Readings **423** — 14. Initial Use **424**

Chapter 27. MASSES WITH SPECIAL GROUPS   **426**

    I. Precedents **426**
    II. Study of the Problem **429**
    III. Reception of the Instruction **436**

Chapter 28. THE DIRECTORY FOR MASSES WITH CHILDREN   **438**

    I. History **438**
    II. Contents **445**

Chapter 29. THE EUCHARISTIC PRAYERS   **448**

    I. New Eucharistic Prayers **448**
    1. Return to Authentic Tradition **448** — 2. Preliminary Questions **450** — 3. Eucharistic Prayer II **456** — 4. Eucharistic Prayer III **456** — 5. Eucharistic Prayer IV **458** — 6. Alexandrian Anaphora of St. Basil **458** — 7. A Long Journey **460**

    II. The Circular Letter *Eucharistiae Participationem* **465**
    1. Work of the Study Group **467** — 2. Discussion at the Plenary Meeting **471** — 3. Final Phase **473** — 4. The Circular Letter **475**

    III. Special Eucharistic Prayers **476**

Part IV

THE LITURGY OF THE HOURS

Chapter 30. THE GENERAL STRUCTURE OF THE LITURGY OF THE
HOURS   491
I. First Phase (1964–1965) **491**
1. The Problem of the Psalms **493** — 2. Second
Thoughts **495** — 3. Intervention of the Pope **497**—
4. Back to the Consilium **498**
II. Second Phase (1966–1967) **501**
1. A New Approach **501** — 2. Specimen of a Week
505 — 3. At the Synod of Bishops **507** — 4. Final Decision of the Pope **508**
III. Final Phase (1968–1972) **512**
1. Consultation of the Bishops **513** — 2. Experimental Psalter **514** — 3. Obligation **517**

Chapter 31. COMPOSITION OF THE LITURGY OF THE HOURS   520
I. General Instruction of the Liturgy of the Hours **522**
II. Psalter **524**
1. Psalms **524** — 2. New Testament Canticles **525** —
3. Latin Text of the Psalms **526**
III. Biblical Readings **533**
1. Relation of Mass and Office **537** — 2. Short Read-
ings **537**
IV. Patristic Readings **538**
V. Hagiographic Readings **545**
VI. Hymns **547**
VII. Chants **551**
VIII. Intercessions in Lauds and Vespers **555**

Chapter 32. RELIGIOUS AND THE LITURGY OF THE HOURS   558
I. The Hour of Prime **559**
II. The Vernacular **559**
III. The Notification of August 6, 1972 **565**
IV. Experiments **566**

Chapter 33. DIOCESAN AND RELIGIOUS PROPERS   571
1. Instruction of 1965 **571** — 2. Instruction of 1970 **572**
— 3. Particular Rites **575**

Part V

THE SACRAMENTS

Chapter 34. THE ROMAN RITUAL   **579**
    1. Relation Between the Future Ritual and Particular
    Rituals **581** — 2. Extent of Adaptations **581** — 3. In-
    structions to Be Prefixed to Each Rite **582** — 4. General
    Norms **582**

Chapter 35. CHRISTIAN INITIATION OF ADULTS   **584**
    I. History **584**
    II. Contents **591**
    1. Introduction **591** — 2. A Complete Catechumenate
    593 — 3. Special Cases **594** — Rite of Reception of Bap-
    tized Christians into Full Communion with the
    Catholic Church **595**

Chapter 36. INFANT BAPTISM   **598**
    I. History **598**
    II. Contents **602**
    1. Introductions **602** — 2. Structure of the Rite **605** —
    3. Other Forms **609**

Chapter 37. CONFIRMATION   **613**
    I. History **613**
    1. First Phase **613** — 2. Second Phase: Preparation of
    the Rite **618** — 3. Publication **618**
    II. The Main Questions **620**
    1. Sponsors **621** — 2. Minister **621** — 3. Matter and
    Form **622** — 4. The Sacramental Formula **625**

Chapter 38. HOLY COMMUNION   **626**
    I. Communion Under Both Kinds **626**
    1. The Liturgical Constitution **626** — 2. Preparation
    of the Rite **627** — 3. First Extension (1967) **629** —
    4. Second Extension (1969) **629** — 5. Third Extension
    (1970) **630**
    II. Communion Twice in One Day **634**
    III. Extraordinary Minister of Communion **636**

IV. Communion in the Hand **640**
1. Consultation of the Bishops **641** — 2. Result of the Consultation **647** — 3. Comments and Suggestions **647** — 4. Results and Reflections **655** — 5. The Instruction *Memoriale Domini* **656** — 6. Later Developments **659**

V. Communion Outside Mass and Worship of the Eucharist **661**

Chapter 39. RECONCILIATION   664

I. History **664**
1. First Stage (1966–1969) **664** — 2. Second Stage (1972–1973) **670**

II. Contents **677**
1. Title **677** — 2. Introduction **678** — 3. The New Rites **679** — 4. Penitential Celebrations **681** — 5. Essential Elements **682**

Chapter 40. RITES FOR THE SICK   684

I. History **684**

II. Contents **690**
1. Apostolic Constitution **690** — 2. Introduction **692** — 3. Visitation and Communion of the Sick **692** — 4. Anointing of the Sick **692** — 5. Viaticum **694** — 6. Continuous Rite **694**

Chapter 41. MARRIAGE   696

I. History **697**

II. Contents **699**
1. Introduction **699** — 2. A Special Question **699** — 3. Marriage During Mass **701** — 4. Marriage Outside Mass **705** — 5. Marriage of a Catholic and an Unbaptized Person **705**

Chapter 42. HOLY ORDERS   707

I. History **707**
1. Approval by the Consilium **710** — 2. To the Curial Agencies **711** — 3. Final Revision **712** — 4. Approval **717**

II. Contents **717**
1. Apostolic Constitution **718** — 2. Rite of Ordination **719**

III. A New Undertaking **721**

Part VI

BLESSINGS

Chapter 43. MINISTRIES   **727**

    I. First Phase (1965–1966) **727**
    1. Study of the Question **727** — 2. Presentation to the
    Consilium **731**

    II. Second Phase (1967–1971) **736**
    1. Intervention of the Secretariat of State (1967) **736**
    — 2. At the Congregation for the Sacraments
    (1968–1972) **739** — 3. At the Plenary Meeting of the
    Congregation for Divine Worship **745**

    III. Final Stage (1972) **748**

Chapter 44. THE LAITY AND THE LITURGY   **752**

    1. Eucharistic Ministries **752** — 2. Sacraments and
    Sacramentals **753** — 3. Sunday Worship **753** —
    4. Catechists **757** — 5. A New Study of Ministries **758**
    — 6. Draft of a Directory for Lay Ministries **760**

Chapter 45. RELIGIOUS PROFESSION   **763**

    I. History **763**

    II. Contents **766**
    1. Introduction to Religious Life **766** — 2. Temporary
    Profession **766** — 3. Perpetual Profession **767** —
    4. Renewal of Vows **769** — 5. Texts **769** — 6. Rite of
    a Religious Promise **769** — 7. Appendix **770** —
    8. Adaptations **770**

Chapter 46. FUNERALS   **771**

    I. History **771**

    II. Contents **773**
    1. Introduction **773** — 2. Prayer Vigil at the Home of
    the Deceased **774** — 3. Three Forms for the Celebra-
    tion of the Funeral **775** — 4. The Final Commenda-
    tion **776** — 5. Funerals of Children **776** — 6. Collection
    of Texts **777**

Chapter 47. BLESSINGS OF THE RITUAL AND THE PONTIFICAL   **778**

    I. Blessings of the Ritual **778**
    1. First Phase **778** — 2. Second Phase **780**

    II. Blessings of the Pontifical **782**

Chapter 48. BLESSING OF AN ABBOT AND AN ABBESS   **784**
     I. History **784**
     II. Contents **785**

Chapter 49. CONSECRATION OF VIRGINS   **787**
     I. History **787**
     II. Contents **789**

Chapter 50. DEDICATION OF A CHURCH AND AN ALTAR   **792**
     I. History **792**
     II. Publication **795**
         1. Dedication of a Church **795** — 2. Dedication of an Altar **796** — 3. Blessing of a Church and an Altar **797** — 4. Blessing of a Chalice and Paten **797**

Chapter 51. BLESSING OF THE OILS   **798**
     I. History **798**
     II. Contents **799**

Part VII

SIMPLIFICATION OF PONTIFICAL RITES

Chapter 52. PAPAL CHAPEL   **805**
     I. Plan of Reform **805**
         1. Need of Reform **805** — 2. Directing Principles **806**
     II. First Results: The Liturgy at the Council **808**
     III. Papal Altar **812**
     IV. Oversight of Papal Ceremonies **814**

Chapter 53. EPISCOPAL CEREMONIAL   **818**
     I. First Phase **818**
         1. Motu Proprio *Pontificalia insignia* **820** — 2. Simplification of Pontifical Rites **820**
     II. Second Phase **821**

Part VIII

SPECIAL DOCUMENTS

Chapter 54. INSTRUCTIONS ON THE CARRYING OUT OF THE
LITURGICAL CONSTITUTION   825

A. First Instruction: *Inter Oecumenici* 825

   I. History 825
     1. Beginnings 825 — 2. The Foundational Schema 826
     — 3. Presentation to the Pope 827 — 4. Final Text 829
     — 5. Taking Effect 831

   II. Contents 832
     1. General Norms 832 — 2. Mass 833 — 3. Sacraments
     834 — 4. Divine Office 834 — 5. Art and Liturgy 825

B. Second Instruction: *Tres abhinc annos* 836

   I. History 836

   II. Contents 838
     1. Mass 838 — 2. Divine Office 839 — 3. Vernacular
     839

C. Third Instruction: *Liturgicae instaurationes* 839

   I. History 840

   II. Contents 844

Chapter 55. INSTRUCTION ON WORSHIP OF THE EUCHARISTIC
MYSTERY   848

   I. History 848

   II. Contents 852
     1. Part I: Pastoral Principles 853 — 2. Part II: Celebra-
     tion of the Memorial of the Lord 854 — 3. Part III:
     Worship of the Eucharist Outside Mass 856

Chapter 56. LITURGY AND SEMINARIES   859

   I. Instruction on Liturgy in Seminaries 859
     1. First Phase: 1965 860 — 2. Second Phase: 1966–1967
     862 — 3. Third Phase: 1970–1972 864 — 4. Fourth
     Phase: 1974–1975 867

   II. Concelebration in Seminaries 869

Chapter 57. VENERATION OF MARY   873

   I. History 873

   II. Contents 878

Part IX

SACRED MUSIC AND THE LITURGY

Chapter 58.   SONG AND LITURGY   **885**
1. Preconceptions **886** — 2. Labors of the Consilium
for Music and Song **890** — 3. The Difficult Path of the
Graduale simplex **892**

Chapter 59.   THE INSTRUCTION ON SACRED MUSIC   **898**
I. History **898**
1. Origin of the Document **898** — 2. The Instruction's
Way of the Cross **900** — 3. Within the Consilium **902**
— 4. The Musicians Behind the Scenes **903** — 5. Four
Points Made to the Pope **905** — 6. Harmonization of
Texts **909**
II. Contents **911**
1. General Norms **911** 2. Those with a Role in the
Celebration **911** — 3. Singing at Mass **912** — 4. The
Divine Office **913** — 5. Other Celebrations **913** —
6. Language **913** — 7. Musical Settings for Vernacular Texts **913** — 8. Sacred Instrumental Music **914** —
9. Commissions for Sacred Music **914**

Part X

VARIA

Chapter 60.   THE LITURGICAL REFORM AT SPECIAL EVENTS   **917**
I. International Eucharistic Congresses **917**
1. Eucharistic Congress of Bombay **917** — 2. Eucharistic Congress of Bogotá **919** — 3. Eucharistic Congress
of Melbourne **920**
II. Jubilees
1. Extraordinary Jubilee **922** — 2. Holy Year 1974–1975
923

Conclusion.   "WE TRIED TO SERVE THE CHURCH"   **931**

Appendix.   MEMBERS AND CONSULTORS OF
              THE ORGANIZATIONS FOR LITURGICAL REFORM   937
                I. Commission for Liturgical Reform 937
                II. Preparatory Conciliar Commission 938
                III. Conciliar Commission on the Liturgy 940
                IV. The Consilium 942
                V. Sacred Congregation for Divine Worship 953

BIBLIOGRAPHY OF ANNIBALE BUGNINI   957
INDEX OF PERSONS   968

Foreword

"They who sow amid tears shall reap rejoicing" (Ps 126:6). Such is the thought, and the hope, that comes to mind as I entrust to the press a volume conceived, developed, and finally brought to birth in moments of great suffering.

In mid-July 1975, after gathering up his papers and casting a final nostalgic glance at the setting of his daily work—a setting he had loved and looked after as "the house of the liturgy"—Archbishop Bugnini retired, on tiptoe as it were, to his two modest rooms in the Mission House at San Silvestro al Quirinale. His service to the liturgy thus came to an unexpected and almost dramatic end, without any plausible explanation being given to him. Months of utter silence followed during which no one but a very few faithful friends caught so much as a glimpse of him. These were days of bitter affliction for him and gave others an opportunity to admire his strong faith, which was modeled on the grain of wheat that must die in order to bear fruit.

But they were also days of intense work that helped to soften the blow inflicted on him. As he compiled recollections, notes, and varied writings, the years spent in implementing the liturgical reform willed by the Council gradually came to vivid life again, almost as if by magic: the first steps, the successive accomplishments, the schemas, meetings, undertakings, contacts—and struggles.

By December, when his departure for Iran was imminent, the pile of manuscript pages was already tall. He entrusted it to me as a precious treasure to be protected and completed. The outline and framework were clearly defined, but not all of the parts were equally developed. The needed development took place over the next two years, in the midst of various occupations. Then came a pause for reflection. Meanwhile Archbishop Bugnini threw himself headlong into the new service that had been asked of him; not only did he deal with the ordinary business of any papal delegation, but he also studied and acquired knowledge of the country, its history, and its cultural, religious, and social traditions. The result was his book *La Chiesa in Iran.*

Once this book had been completed, he turned back to his manuscript on the liturgical reform. A first revision was finished in Tehran during the summer of 1979, while the Islamic revolution was raging. A further revision was made in 1980–81. At each revision harsh expressions that still conveyed something of the author's original bitterness were toned down, and the exposition was made as serene and objective as possible.

Though far distant and absorbed by quite different concerns, Archbishop Bugnini continued to follow the course of the liturgical reform: the reactions to it, the more or less correct application of it, and the not infrequently distorted or misinformed interpretations given of it. The experience deepened his conviction that the book he had written needed to be published. There was no letter from him in which he did not come back, explicitly or indirectly, to this undertaking.

Here are a few references taken from the letters of his last years: "Upon my word, on my first visit to Italy we shall send it to the printer. Without delay, and without second thoughts" (December 14, 1980). "At the first opportunity I shall send you the manuscript, which has been revised and reread, and is in my opinion ready for printing" (September 10, 1981). "We must publish the book. . . . If the reform is well-grounded, as indeed it is, and if it was carried out in an honorable way, as indeed it was, then this must be made clear. . . . Prepare the book for the press as quickly as possible" (January 10, 1982).

Archbishop Bugnini was waiting to be relieved of further direct service to the Holy See. He had twice asked for his release as he approached his seventieth birthday, but his plea was not heard. During his final illness he used to voice his conviction that he would soon be retired and would be able for the first time to devote himself to bringing the book on the liturgical reform to a successful end. During his daily visits to the Pius XI Clinic, his exhortation became increasingly urgent: "I implore you to publish the book." I accepted his plea as though it were part of his last will and testament, and indeed I made it my primary task during the days of fresh bitterness that followed his death (July 3, 1982). The volume appears here as Archbishop Bugnini wanted it and prepared it and corrected it, and with the introduction he had written for it a year earlier.

Why did Archbishop Bugnini attach so much importance to this book? The reason was certainly not a desire to defend himself. The purification effected by exile, deepening as it did his faith and his love of the Church, had brought him serenity and had almost wholly detached him from all human aspirations, even the longing to see justice done. He felt liberated and at peace with his conscience. He had at first trusted in the Holy See to defend his honor as a bishop and faithful servant of the Church (see pp. 92ff.). Then he realized that he could rely on God alone: "Otherwise, why do we so often say with the psalmist and the evangelist that God is mindful of us, that we put our trust in him, that not a hair of our head falls without his willing it . . . ? Well, then, all the more do we leave our present and our future in his hands" (September 9, 1979).

The main thing he was anxious to show by means of this book was that the liturgical reform had been carried out in an honest and honorable way. By this he meant that it had been based on lengthy reflection and careful study and had been closely examined by all the agencies legitimately concerned. Even more, however, he meant that it had been carried out *cum Petro et sub Petro* ("with Peter and under Peter")—an expression he would have wanted to include in a further revision of his introduction. He was emphatic on this point: "People must know how much the reform is the work of Pope Paul VI and how much that of his humble faithful followers" (November 2, 1981). Toward the end especially it consoled him to be able to say: "I have *faithfully carried out* the will of Paul VI and the Council." It was this that convinced him he had acted properly, although he admitted that "perfection is not to be found in this world": "The work I did in the area of the liturgy was an important undertaking. I am happy that I saw it through; if I had to start all over again, I would do the same things in the same way. I tried to follow the 'ways' of God" (February 1982, on the tenth anniversary of his episcopal ordination).

This book is neither a diary nor a set of memoirs. Personal recollections are integrated into the treatment of the subject, which is presented in the almost impersonal style of a chronicler. Only at two crucial points does the account take a personal turn, as Archbishop Bugnini tries to explain the events which, in his person, attacked the very aims of the liturgical reform, halted a promising course of action, extinguished a new spirit, and suppressed a working method that had been proven valid by the results achieved and by the applause of the episcopate.

Nor is the book a history, for this is too ambitious a title, since a full history of the subject cannot be encompassed in a single volume nor written by one who did not have all the documentation at his disposal.

What the book does provide is a picture that is complete, even if only in its broad lines, of what was done in composing and then implementing the Constitution on the Sacred Liturgy. Some aspects that are less fully developed because of the lack of sources are nonetheless included precisely in order to give a comprehensive vision of the vast work accomplished. These comments can serve as subjects for further studies.

Archbishop Bugnini looked upon the book as "the finest memorial to Paul VI," and he let the Pope know of it. In my opinion, it is also the most eloquent testimony to the part played by Archbishop Bugnini in the history of the liturgical reform associated with Vatican II. If the renewal of the liturgy has become a reality, it is due above all to Pope Paul VI and Archbishop Bugnini. But the book is also a proof of Archbishop Bugnini's love of the Church. He was content to be able to say of himself: "I have served the Church, I have loved the Church, I have suffered for the Church" (September 9, 1979).

The simple words he wanted on his tombstone—"He served the Church"—characterized his life and explain his unwearying activity and unqualified obedience. They are his claim to glory.

GOTTARDO PASQUALETTI, I.M.C.

Preface

The following pages bring together notes and recollections accumulated during the years I spent in charge of the liturgical reform, first as secretary of the commission that prepared for the Council (1959–62); then as secretary of the Consilium (*Consilium ad exsequendam Constitutionem de sacra liturgia* = Council for the Implementation of the Constitution on the Sacred Liturgy; 1964–69); and finally as secretary of the Sacred Congregation for Divine Worship (1969–75). To complete the picture, I have thought it appropriate to call attention also to the work of the commission for general liturgical reform that Pius XII established in 1948. The Lord willed that from those early years a whole series of providential circumstances should thrust me fully, and indeed in a privileged way, *in medias res*, and that I should then remain there in charge of the secretariat. This volume thus embraces in a measure the entire history of liturgical reform in the period from 1948 to 1975—twenty-seven years devoted to restoring splendor and charm, youthful beauty, trenchancy, and a sweet fragrance to the public prayer of the Church.

In addition to personal notes taken during my labors, I have made extensive use of the articles I wrote for *Notitiae* or other periodicals and those I published in *L'Osservatore Romano*. Ever since the reform began to yield its first fruits, it was thought useful for the secretary to present the innovations in the official journal of the Holy See from time to time and to explain their spirit, intention, and, if need be, limits. The aim was to guide and control, stimulate and encourage, put on guard and prevent illusions. These articles gradually became an institution; they were read and extensively reprinted in daily and weekly newspapers, in the national and international press, and, above all, in diocesan bulletins;

they became a continuing and expected source of guidance, especially for the clergy.

The other writings were occasional. At times they were suggested or called for by the Pope, who in some cases (for example, the article on communion in the hand) gave me an outline to follow. As a rule Pope Paul VI read them all in manuscript (he loved to be given them) and tactfully made known his observations and corrections. If it happened that he had not seen the manuscript in advance, he provided me with his notes later on; then, on the first occasion offered me, I did not fail to make it known that he had not seen the text before publication. This paternal assistance from the Pope was not only a superlative honor but a great encouragement and source of strength for the reform—and for me.

I have made use of two further sources. One may be called sentimental: my recollections of incidents that I did not want simply to omit and have therefore inserted in footnotes. They are admittedly of only relative value, but at times they bring out the real point of what happened. The other source is literary: the periodicals, especially liturgical, that have dealt with the reform. My twenty years as editor-in-chief of *Ephemerides Liturgicae* gave me a certain familiarity with literature on the liturgy and, of course, with liturgists, who are the most idealistic and inoffensive people to be found in holy Mother Church.

The first draft of these pages was written almost uninterruptedly between the end of my "service" as secretary of the Congregation for Divine Worship and the beginning of my "service" as a diplomat, that is, between July 15, 1975, and January 5, 1976. These were six months of solitude but not of spiritual repose (on the contrary, they were *dies amaritudinis*). Above all, they were months of restless energy that went into the sustained work of recollecting and organizing the tesserae that would make up a mosaic depicting eleven years of intense work, months in which I relived, from the beginning, the luminous journey on which the prayer of the Church was transformed and transfigured.

Once written down, the notes went into hibernation for some years. They were then retouched, revised, weeded out, and sifted, thanks to the intelligent, affectionate, balanced, and prudent work of Father Gottardo Pasqualetti, who had first been my student at the Pontifical Urban University and then a faithful and judicious collaborator during the entire period of the reform. When I reread these pages years later and in a far different setting, at a time when I was engaged in quite dissimilar labors and living in an atmosphere far different in warmth and innocence, they seemed to belong to an unreal world, almost a dream world; they seemed to be lacking in earthly solidity, like projections on the picture screen of eternity.

Another detail: I composed these notes at San Silvestro al Quirinale, the religious house of the Vincentians. This house is very dear to me because I resided there for most of my life in Rome. But it is dear also and above all because within those walls, in that little church ("all golden and embroidered with fretwork," as Fra Mariano, a Dominican, described it in the sixteenth century), and in the very rooms where I lived, I seemed to feel the presence still of Cardinal Guglielmo Sirleto (d. October 7, 1585) and the liturgical commission, made up mostly of Theatines, that from 1566 on carried out the liturgical reform decreed by the Council of Trent and known as the reform of St. Pius V. San Silvestro had been the motherhouse of the Theatines for only about ten years (since 1555), but they had made it a center of biblical and liturgical studies and spirituality. The missal which Cardinal Sirleto used and which he annotated for the reformed Mass is now kept in the Vatican Library, but it is still stamped "Bibliotheca sancti Silvestri."[1] All these small details were very dear to me, for I could look upon myself as continuing, in my modern circumstances, a tradition as precious as any in the life of the Church.

In this book I simply describe the picture frame. I do not attempt even to sketch the picture itself, that is, the reform, in its conception, its main lines, its many hues, and its most striking effects, which make it a work that challenges the centuries and, more importantly, will have a profound effect on the interior life of our communities, and thereby on the life of the Church. Who today can deny that our liturgical assemblies, provided they are properly prepared and directed, can become high points in the life of the ecclesial community? In every place and at all levels, even in that maze of peoples that is Iran, when Catholics, those *rari nantes*, gather on Sundays or join their fellow believers for an ecumenical celebration, or when on Corpus Christi they wind their way around the gardens of the Italian embassy in a joyously devout procession with songs and prayers in various languages, the heart knows that these rites speak to human beings and effectively unite them, that grace descends upon the faithful and turns the many into a single body with one heart and one soul.

The purpose of the reform was to rejuvenate and update the expression of the Church's prayer in gestures, rites, words, and forms. The resto-

---

1. See A. P. Frutaz, "Sirleto e la riforma del Messale Romano di s. Pio V," *Regnum Dei. Collectanea Theatina a Clericis Regularibus edita* 30 (1974; published 1976) 86–111, with sixteen plates.

ration was to be sensitive and careful, its organization rational but also fully human. At times there were to be new creations; at times existing forms were to be used, with an eye to continuity and the avoidance of sharp breaks; at times the foundation was to be laid for an intelligent adaptation that would satisfy the sensibilities of diverse peoples. Eleven years of work, to which some hundred *periti* and many pastors, as well as commissions and study groups, all made their contribution; four hundred general schemas and several hundred more specialized schemas: all these were concealed behind the little volumes that from time to time presented the Church with a rite, an instruction, a constitution, or a motu proprio—in short, a polished stone for the building or rebuilding of the wonderful sanctuary that is the prayer of the Church.

The liturgical reform was a "movement of the Holy Spirit in the Church" (Pius XII), a great work that all who took part in approached with humility, faith, intense love, and prayer; they "put off their shoes," as Moses did on approaching the burning bush, because they knew that everything they touched was sacred. All of us had constantly before our eyes a vision either of the divine Majesty whose earthly praise we were providing with new expressions and new emphases, or of the Church, which would be putting this new song on the lips of the faithful.

All this work, moreover, was being accomplished in harmonious continuity by a multitude of individuals with their variety of tendencies, opinions, characters, and mentalities. All of them were endeavoring to accomplish the *opus Dei* under the unvarying sign of charity, which alone gives things human their eternal value. Of what use would anything be, however sublime and fascinating ("If I speak in the tongues of angels. . ."—1 Cor 13:1), without this "divine seal"?

Those who have the patience to persevere through these pages will see a continual alternation of green, yellow, and red lights, like the circling beams of a lighthouse at sea; I mean the expectations, oppositions, second thoughts, forward thrusts, and setbacks, and finally the home-stretch and joyous arrival—just like a small boat on the open sea. Such was the course usually followed by all the rites and documents that issued from the reform. And it could not have been otherwise. Unfortunate indeed would we have been if the contrary had occurred—if changes in treasured forms of devotion or the elimination of one or other sacred gesture that age-old tradition loved so much and regarded as untouchable had met with disinterest or widespread apathy. The immediate and strong reaction to everything we did forced us to reflect, think twice, wait, and proceed cautiously.

In the final analysis, it was a good thing that the publication of a reformed rite was accompanied by a whole series of articles, pamphlets, and other demonstrations for and against; this was tangible evidence that the people were following the reform with alert and growing love, and that the work of the experts needed to be ratified in the minds of ordinary folk if the change was to find acceptance in the soul of the people.

During the period of hottest debate on the Mass, an Italian comic weekly published a series of lighthearted articles. From these I learned that the head of the Roman office of the journal wanted to see for himself what was going on and therefore came incognito to my Mass at San Silvestro al Quirinale. He saw to his surprise that I was celebrating at an altar over which towered a picture of St. Pius V (chapel of the Madonna delle Catene), and in Latin (this was at a time when those celebrating private Masses still had to use Latin). He wrote, therefore, that in his opinion the celebrant was celebrating "with faith." He concluded, however, by asking: "But how is it possible for this priest to celebrate in the morning before St. Pius V, in Latin, and using the Tridentine Missal, and then in the afternoon to impose on the Church a reformed Mass in the vernacular, thus betraying the Council of Trent?"

In 1973 I was invited to give some lectures in Latin America. When I arrived on the scene, a leaflet was being distributed that contained on its two interior pages a lengthy poem entitled "Stone Archbishop Bugnini!" Initially the friends who had invited me hid the leaflet from me, fearing that I would be offended; they told me about it during the final days of my stay. I reassured them that I found the poem amusing. The only stoning that took place was that contained in the four clandestinely printed little pages. I myself saw neither stones nor stoners but only a fine gathering of bishops who had been won over to the reform and throngs of the faithful who sang and prayed their faith with an enthusiasm that moved me to tears.

Not all of the opposition, however, was "academic" in kind. There was also the war against the Council that used the liturgy as its pretext, on the grounds that the latter blazed the way, so to speak, at that solemn gathering and was the first exemplification of its working methods. The liturgy therefore became, later on, the scapegoat blamed for various deviations, for example, the theological errors and aberrant doctrines, or at least the stubborn positions, of some headstrong people in the Church. In fact, of course, the liturgy had and has nothing at all to do with any of this.

Then there was the war against the president of the Consilium that ended with his being dismissed in circumstances known to everyone. Finally, there was the war against the secretary of the Consilium. It did me too much honor! The truth is, of course, that those carrying on the war were trying to strike at the liturgical movement itself through these representatives. The Pope warned me of this in my first audience after the retirement of Cardinal Lercaro: "Now you alone are left. I urge you to be very patient and very prudent. I assure you once again of my complete confidence." These words were a source of strength to me, but I could not help replying: "Holy Father, the reform will continue as long as Your Holiness retains this confidence. As soon as it lessens, the reform will come to a halt."

This attack was underhanded and the fruit of ignorance, but there was another that was more malicious, although always disguised as a claim to be defending and safeguarding traditional values of the Church. I never took offense. Only once did calumny wound me deeply: when I was accused of infidelity to the Church, and the accusation was backed by the authority of a fellow bishop. Then I took my pen and wrote: "Nothing in this world is dearer to me than my episcopal cross. But if my slanderers are able, in an honest way, to prove the truth of even a smidgeon of what they claim, I am ready to surrender that cross."

This book is intended as a homage of filial gratitude to Pope Paul VI, the man who really brought about the liturgical reform. If ever a Pope devoted all his energies to a specific task, it was Paul VI and the task of the liturgical renewal. I have attempted to make this clear in the pages that follow and to give the lie to those who, due to ignorance or superficiality or to censoriousness or prejudice, have claimed, and perhaps still think, that a handful of rash individuals were able to impose their own ideas on the Pope. In fact, the Pope saw, followed, tested, and approved everything.

How many evenings I spent with him studying the many and often lengthy files heaped on his table! He read and reflected on them all, line by line, word by word, annotating everything in black, red, and blue pencil and criticizing it if need be with a logical mind that could formulate ten questions on a single point.

Pope Paul told me that he found discussion of the liturgy restful; for that reason he put it off to the end of the day. And while the pages passed before his eyes, recollections of his pastoral activity in Milan came thronging to his lips and interrupted the work from time to time. Whether the subject was confirmation or penance or ministries or the needs of young people, it elicited personal memories. The idea of postponing confirmation until after compulsory schooling, and his insistence on holding to it despite the firm opinion of the theologians and amid the studies carried out by three successive commissions, were due to his pastoral experience in the capital city of Lombardy.

Pope Paul's lively intelligence and wide knowledge of persons and affairs made him less vulnerable to the inevitable snares laid by those around him. One time, during the summer, when holidays made it necessary to shift work from one office to another, he was presented with a statement from the Consilium on the Mass. We in the Consilium had just finished examining the schema on the *Missa normativa* and, as was customary, were asking permission for the bishops belonging to that body to experiment with it. The *minutante* who presented the statement to the Pope had added a note: "Be careful! Father Bugnini is asking for this permission so that superiors will be faced with a *fait accompli.*"

The Pope summoned me to an audience, read me this note, and asked me: "Is that what you were trying to do?" "Why, of course not!" I answered in surprise. "By no means!" The Pope read to me in a low voice the name of the man who had drawn up the statement, and told me: "Go to this individual and tell him he has misunderstood; explain to him the usual procedure followed by the Consilium. Then go also to this other person and explain to him, too, the true situation. These people need instruction." Those were the early and still lightsome years of a pontificate that produced such a marvelous crop of works. The renewed liturgy had a place of honor in the mind, heart, and words of the Pope. The Wednesday homilies and addresses of that period often dealt with matters liturgical.

Pope Paul VI liked that kind of immediate—I might even say fraternal—collaboration, and it became habitual with him. Only twice did I find him stubbornly resolved and unmovable: when it was a question of approving the bylaws of the Consilium (see below, Chapter 8) and again, at the end, when he combined the Congregation for Divine Worship with the Congregation for the Sacraments. In the first case, he had been skillfully led to believe that his authority was at stake. He did not have the strength to reexamine the question calmly; if he had, he would doubtless have discovered the pitfall. In the second case, I never found out his reason for taking the serious and oddly unusual step of suppressing an institution which he himself had established and by which he set so much store.

After that I saw Pope Paul VI only twice more. On both occasions he gave evidence of great good will in action, gesture, and tone. The second time, he himself turned the conversation, somewhat timidly but with real interest, to the liturgy.

His preference was to let the mystery of God silently cast its veil over the mystery of human beings.

✛ Annibale Bugnini

Tehran
August 6, 1981
Third anniversary of the
godly death of Pope Paul VI

Editorial Note

For those readers and/or scholars who would like to learn more about Annibale Bugnini and the part he played in the reform of the Roman liturgy, we offer on pages 957–967 a complete bibliography of his writings. This bibliography appeared in a collection entitled *Liturgia opera divina e umana: Studi sulla riforma liturgica offerti a S.E. Mons. Annibale Bugnini in occasione del suo 70° compleanno*, published in 1982 and edited by Pierre Jounel, Reiner Kaczynski, and Gottardo Pasqualetti. We are grateful to the publisher, Centro Liturgico Vincenziano—Edizioni Liturgiche, Rome, for permission to reprint it.

The Reform of the Liturgy was translated from the Italian edition, entitled *La riforma liturgica 1948–1975* and also published by Centro Liturgico Vincenziano (Rome, 1983). Monsignor Frederick R. McManus, professor of canon law at The Catholic University of America and a member of the preparatory, conciliar, and postconciliar liturgical commissions, reviewed the original Italian edition in *Worship*, Vol. 60, No. 3 (May 1986) 194–200, under the title "Roman Liturgical Reform 1948–1975." Excerpts of that review are reproduced on the dust jacket of this volume with the gracious permission of Monsignor McManus.

This book has also been translated into German under the title *Die Liturgiereform 1948–1975: Zeugnis und Testament*, edited by Johannes Wagner and François Raas, and translated by Heinrich Venmann, O.M.I. (Freiburg im Breisgau, 1988). Reviews of the German edition have been written by Angelus Häussling, O.S.B., *Archiv für Liturgiewissenschaft*, Vol. 30, No. 1/2 (1988) 141, and by L. Legardien, *Questions Liturgiques* 70 (1989/3) 196–97.

La Chiesa in Iran (Rome, 1981) was written by Archbishop Bugnini while he served as apostolic pro-nuncio to Iran from 1976 to 1982. Reviews may be found in *Apollinaris*, Vol. 55 (1982) 236–38, and in *Orientalia Christiana Periodica*, Vol. 48 (1982) 232–34.

An informative account of Annibale Bugnini's career, by Monsignor Frederick R. McManus, appears in the *New Catholic Encyclopedia*, Vol. 18, Supplement 1978–1988 (Washington, 1989) 46–48. An editorial by Daniel Callam, C.S.B., in the *Canadian Catholic Review*, Vol. 3 (1985) 122–23, and an article by Emil Lengeling in *Theologische Revue*, Vol. 80 (1984) 265–84, also deal with Bugnini's contribution to liturgical reform.

A tribute to Archbishop Bugnini by Carlo Braga, C.M., was published in *Notitiae*, Vol. 18 (1982) 441–52 under the title "Ricordo di Mons. Annibale Bugnini." The periodical *Worship* also published a brief tribute by Columba Stewart, O.S.B., in Vol. 57, No. 2 (March 1983) 157–58.

Finally, mention must be made of the monumental collection entitled *Documents on the Liturgy 1963–1979: Conciliar, Papal, and Curial Texts*, translated, compiled, and edited by the International Commission on English in the Liturgy (ICEL) and published by The Liturgical Press, Collegeville, Minnesota, in 1982. Dedicated to Archbishop Bugnini, this volume provides 554 official texts that document the reform of the liturgy, to which Archbishop Bugnini devoted the major part of his life. In *The Reform of the Liturgy*, Archbishop Bugnini provides an extraordinarily detailed account of the history and content of the revised rites, as well as fascinating historical notes about the persons and events involved in the process of their revision.

The reader will note that the translator has provided, wherever pertinent, references to *Documents on the Liturgy 1963–1979* (abbreviated *DOL*), despite the anachronism and without further editorial indication. Unless otherwise noted, the numbers following the *DOL* abbreviation refer to the number of the document and the number in the margin, not to page numbers. References are likewise made to *The Rites of the Catholic Church*, *The Pope Speaks*, and a few other English titles that do not appear in the Italian original. These citations in the footnotes have been made to provide scholars and researchers with immediate and practical reference to standard English texts that might be useful for their work. We hope that at least a few of our readers will find this information useful.

Abbreviations

AAS	*Acta Apostolicae Sedis* (Vatican Polyglot Press, 1909ff.)
DOL	*Documents on the Liturgy. 1963–1979: Conciliar, Papal, and Curial Texts* (Collegeville, 1982)
DS	Henry Denzinger and Adolf Schönmetzer (eds.), *Enchiridion symbolorum*, 32nd ed. (Barcelona, 1963)
EDIL	*Enchiridion documentorum instaurationis liturgicae I*, ed. R. Kaczynski (Turin, 1976)
EL	*Ephemerides Liturgicae* (Rome, 1887ff.)
GILH	General Instruction of the Liturgy of the Hours
GIRM	General Instruction of the Roman Missal
Neuner-Dupuis	J. Neuner and J. Dupuis (eds.), *The Christian Faith in the Doctrinal Documents of the Catholic Church* (Staten Island, N.Y., 1982)
Not	*Notitiae* (Vatican City, 1965ff.)
RL	*Rivista Liturgica* (Turin-Leumann, 1913ff.)
SC	*Sacrosanctum Concilium:* Constitution of Vatican II on the Sacred Liturgy
SCDF	Sacred Congregation for the Doctrine of the Faith
SCDW	Sacred Congregation for Divine Worship
SCR	Sacred Congregation of Rites
SCSDW	Sacred Congregation for the Sacraments and Divine Worship

Part I

The Main Stages

I. The Beginning of the Reform

1

The Key to the Liturgical Reform

The reform that the Second Vatican Council inaugurated is differentiated from all others in the history of the liturgy by its pastoral emphasis. The participation and active involvement of the people of God in the liturgical celebration is the ultimate goal of the reform, just as it was the goal of the liturgical movement.[1] This involvement and participation is not limited to externals but reaches to the very root of things: to the mystery being celebrated, to Christ himself who is present. "Ceremonies," St. Vincent de Paul used to say, "are only a shadow, but they are the shadow of the most magnificent realities."[2]

In the course of time, however, a kind of intellectual separation occurred between rites and their theological content. This tendency derived some support from the Council of Trent, which dealt with doctrinal liturgical questions in dogmatic decrees[3] while putting off from session to session anything relating to "rites and ceremonies," and leaving it finally to the decision of the Holy See and its revision of the liturgical books. This distinction made its way down the centuries, was incorporated into the Code of Canon Law (1917), and is still to be found in the administrative arrangements of the Church and in the outlook of many.

---

1. A. Bugnini, " 'Movimento liturgico' o 'pastorale liturgico'?"*Not* 19 (1974) 137–38.
2. St. Vincent de Paul, *Conferenze ai Preti della Missione* (Rome, 1959) 336.
3. I am thinking of, for example, the questions concerning the Canon of the Mass, the language to be used, and Eucharistic worship that were introduced in the acts of the well-known twenty-second session on the Holy Sacrifice of the Mass.

1. *The Movement for Reform*

The liturgical movement was an effort to reunite rites and content, for its aim was to restore as fully as possible the expressiveness and sanctifying power of the liturgy and to bring the faithful back to full participation and understanding. The process was begun by Abbot Prosper Guéranger, O.S.B. (d. 1875), who spread his love of the liturgy in the Benedictine monasteries he founded, while his publications disseminated the spirituality of the liturgy among more alert and receptive Christians.

Reliable directives and decisive stimuli were given by St. Pius X, who saw the active participation of the faithful in the liturgy as "the foremost and indispensable fount" of "the true Christian spirit,"[4] and therefore of interior renewal in the Church.

The thinking of St. Pius X was especially welcome in the Abbey of Mont-César, where Dom Lambert Beauduin (d. 1960) started the organized liturgical movement in 1909. He was followed by the Benedictines of Maria Laach in Germany, who went more deeply into the theological, biblical, and patristic aspects of the liturgy, although always with pastoral effectiveness as the goal. Liturgical associations, periodicals, weeks, and congresses multiplied everywhere at the diocesan, national, and international levels. Finally, the Holy See gave the movement its support and favor, and then took it under its own direction.

In his encyclical *Mediator Dei* of November 11, 1947, Pope Pius XII put the seal of his supreme authority on this movement, which by now was to be found everywhere in the Church. The liturgy had entered upon its true course, that of pastoral concern, and was thus returning to the ideal it had had in the beginning.

The reforms that would follow from 1951 to 1960 were primarily concerned with this pastoral aspect. The norms, structures, and laws of a pastoral liturgy were formulated during those years. People throughout the world and at all levels of society became interested. The most perceptive among the Church's pastors saw in the liturgy the means best fitted—sometimes the only means—for bringing the faithful back to the practice of Christian life or for deepening that life in them.

Only two years before *Mediator Dei* there was another event of considerable importance for the liturgical reform: the publication of the new Latin version of the Psalms, which the Pontifical Biblical Institute finished in 1945 under commission from Pius XII. This work, which had been

---

4. Pius X, motu proprio *Tra le sollecitudini* (November 22, 1903), in A. Bugnini (ed.), *Documenta Pontificia ad instaurationem liturgicam spectantia* (Rome, 1953) 12–13. English translation in J. J. Megivern (ed.), *Worship and Liturgy* (Wilmington, N.C., 1978) 17–18 (n. 28).

brought to completion by the tenacious determination of the rector, Father (later Cardinal) Augustin Bea, helped to ripen in the Pope's mind the idea of a reform of the entire liturgy; the new Psalter would be simply the first building block in the new edifice.

I say "ripen the idea" because Pius XII had already been thinking of reform some years earlier. A project for liturgical reform—or, more accurately, liturgical codification—was later found among the papers of Father Pio Alfonzo, a Benedictine, who taught liturgy at the College of the Propaganda and was a consultor of the Sacred Congregation of Rites. The document is dated "The Purification of Mary, 1942." It is clear that the proposal (the author calls it "General Norms"), which occupies two typewritten pages, was not simply a literary exercise but had been requested by the so-called "Wednesday Commission" of the Congregation of Rites, of which Alfonzo was a member. But the experiment was not followed up.

2. The "Pian" Commission (1948–1960)

The idea of a reform acquired definite shape when the historical section of the Sacred Congregation of Rites—the organization best equipped for a work of this kind—was assigned to undertake it. Its members were to prepare a basic plan that should serve as a guide for discussion of the various problems with which a special commission was to deal.[5]

In October 1946 the vice-relator general of the historical section, Father Joseph Löw, an Austrian Redemptorist, began the drafting of a plan. The composition took about two years; three hundred copies of it were published as a *Positio* (No. 71) of the historical section, under the title *Memoria sulla riforma liturgica* (342 pp.).

While the approach taken in the *Memoria* was quite general, two points were somewhat developed: the liturgical year and the Divine Office. For the rest, it was explicitly stated that studies of other points would gradually be prepared. And in fact about forty such were composed, the majority of them cyclostyled and with only a few copies made for the use of the commission. Four that were of greater importance were published in the form of supplements to the *Memoria*.

---

5. In an audience granted to Cardinal Carlo Salotti, prefect of the Sacred Congregation of Rites, on May 10, 1946, Pope Pius XII expressed his wish that a start be made on studying the problem of a general reform of the liturgy. In another audience, granted to Archbishop Alfonso Carinci, secretary of the same Congregation, on July 17, 1946, it was determined "that a special commission of experts should reflect on the general reform of the liturgy and offer concrete proposals"; see SCR, Sectio historica 71: *Memoria sulla riforma liturgica* (Vatican Polyglot Press, 1948) 6.

The first of these[6] had to do with the ranking of feasts. Father Anselmo Albareda, O.S.B., consultor of the commission, prefect of the Vatican Library, and later a cardinal, started the discussion by proposing a "ranking of feasts on theological grounds." The plan was complicated, artificial, and practically impossible to implement.

The second supplement contained the judgments and observations of Fathers Capelle and Jungmann and Monsignor Righetti on the *Memoria*.[7]

The third and most important supplement brought together the historical, hagiographical, and liturgical material needed for a reform of the calendar. It had two parts. The first reproduced the calendar then used in the Church of the Roman Rite, along with other liturgical anniversaries that might be of interest on each date. The second part, which was a kind of alphabetical dictionary of feasts with relevant liturgical, historical, and hagiographical information, was intended as a basis for the composition of a new calendar. And in fact it was used in preparing the calendar of the "Pauline" reform.[8]

The fourth supplement contained the results of the consultation (completed in 1956–57) of the episcopate on reform of the Roman Breviary, together with the conclusions drawn from these results. The questionnaire had been sent on May 17, 1956, to the metropolitans and the bishops "directly subject" to them, or to four hundred prelates in all. The questions were phrased in general terms; six months were allowed for replies, but the period was extended for another six months. The cards on which the replies were organized numbered eighteen hundred, with forty-seven main headings. The study groups subsequently charged with the reform of the Office made use of this valuable material.[9]

Meanwhile, on May 28, 1948, a commission for liturgical reform was appointed. Its president was Cardinal Clemente Micara, prefect of the Sacred Congregation of Rites. Its members were: Archbishop Alfonso Carinci, secretary of the same Congregation; Father Ferdinando Antonelli, O.F.M., relator general of the historical section; Father Joseph Löw,

6. SCR, Sectio historica, no. 75: *Memoria sulla riforma liturgica*, Supplemento I. *Intorno alla graduazione liturgica* (Vatican Polyglot Press, 1950). 38 pp.

7. Idem, no. 76: Supplemento II. *Annotazioni alla "Memoria," presentate su richiesta, dai Rev.mi Dom Capelle, O.S.B., P. Jungmann, S.J., Mons. Righetti* (Vatican Polyglot Press, 1950). 64 pp.

8. Idem, no. 79: Supplemento III. *Materiale storico, agiografico, liturgico per la riforma del Calendario* (Vatican Polyglot Press, 1951). 204 pp.

9. Idem, no. 97: Supplemento IV. *Consultazione dell'Episcopato intorno alla riforma del Breviario Romano (1956–1957). Risultati e deduzioni* (Vatican Polyglot Press, 1957). 140 pp.

C.SS.R., vice-relator; Father Anselmo Albareda, O.S.B., prefect of the Vatican Library; Father Augustin Bea, S.J., rector of the Pontifical Biblical Institute; Father Annibale Bugnini, C.M., editor of *Ephemerides Liturgicae*, who was appointed secretary, a position he held until the commission was dissolved when the conciliar preparatory commission was set up in 1959. In 1951 Monsignor Enrico Dante, *sostituto* for the Sacred Congregation of Rites, was added; and in 1960 Monsignor Pietro Frutaz, relator general; Don Luigi Rovigatti, pastor of the Church of the Nativity on Via Gallia in Rome; Monsignor Cesario D'Amato, Abbot of St. Paul's; and Father Carlo Braga, C.M. This last named group took part in only four meetings. In 1953 Cardinal Micara, who had become Vicar for Rome, was replaced as president by Cardinal Gaetano Cicognani, who had been appointed prefect of the Congregation of Rites.

The first meeting of the commission was held on June 22, 1948, at the Pontifical Ecclesiastical Academy in Piazza della Minerva, where Cardinal Micara, recently created a cardinal, was then living. The other meetings took place in the afternoon, either in the apartment of the Cardinal President or in the meeting room of the Congregation of Rites.

In the beginning not everyone grasped the importance of the issues or realized that the work would be long and demanding. The Cardinal President thought the work might take a few months or at most a year. The disillusionment began when Father Bea gave his opinion on this point: A revision of the Scriptures for liturgical use would take at least five years if the criteria adopted for the Psalter were applied universally. The disillusionment was completed when the majority accepted this forecast and added that five years was an absolute minimum.

In the twelve years of its existence (June 28, 1948, to July 8, 1960) the commission held eighty-two meetings and worked in absolute secrecy. So secret, in fact, was their work that the publication of the *Ordo Sabbati Sancti instaurati* at the beginning of March 1951 caught even the officials of the Congregation of Rites by surprise. The commission enjoyed the full confidence of the Pope, who was kept abreast of its work by Monsignor Montini and even more, on a weekly basis, by Father Bea, confessor of Pius XII. Thanks to them, the commission was able to achieve important results even during periods when the Pope's illness kept everyone else from approaching him.

It must be honestly acknowledged that the work accomplished despite the limitations of personnel and business[10] was enormous. Almost all the

---

10. In addition to work on the general reform, all the problems of any importance that reached the Congregation had to be dealt with. Furthermore, of the members of the com-

liturgical books were revised, including the Ritual, which was corrected and set in type but not published, because the Vatican bookstore was afraid it would not be able to sell it with the Council on the horizon.

Also surprising was the pastoral sense shown by the "Pian" reform, despite the fact that the commission was composed exclusively of scholars. Its success in this respect was due chiefly to Father Joseph Löw, a man of extremely flexible and versatile intellect who was capable of devising a whole range of concrete proposals, from which the best model could be developed.

The first fruit of the commission's work was the restoration of the Easter Vigil (1951), which elicited an explosion of joy throughout the Church. It was a signal that the liturgy was at last launched decisively on a pastoral course.

The same reforming principles were applied in 1955 to the whole of Holy Week[11] and in 1960, with the Code of Rubrics, to the remainder of the liturgy, especially the Divine Office. Two years later the new typical editions of the Breviary and the Roman Pontifical were published. But once the Council was announced and new reforming currents of thought exerted their superior pressure, the Johannine liturgical renewal lost a good deal of its energy.

3. *Liturgical Publications*

Attention should be called, at least in passing, to two other factors that played a part in the expectation of reform and in preparation for it: the publications issued from time to time by the Roman periodical *Ephemerides Liturgicae*, and the international congress held at Assisi in 1956.

On January 28, 1948, the editors of *Ephemerides Liturgicae* sent a questionnaire on reform of the Missal, Breviary, calendar, Martyrology, and other liturgical books to almost a hundred liturgical experts in all parts of the world. This questionnaire, sent as it was by the editorial staff of a periodical regarded as the semi-official voice of Roman liturgical circles, was the first alarm signal that something was stirring. In those days it

---

mission only the three full-time workers had a real desire for reform and a considerable knowledge of the liturgy; the other members took part in the meetings more from a sense of duty than from conviction. Once the expectation of any lightning-quick reform disappeared, some lost interest completely. Two meetings a month were scheduled; due to the demands of the Holy Year, only two were held in all of 1950. When the acts of the commission are finally published, it will be possible to relive all the phases of one of the most interesting chapters in the history of the liturgy.

11. See SCR, Sectio historica, no. 90: *De instauratione liturgica maioris hebdomadae. Positio* (Vatican Polyglot Press, 1955). 110 pp.

was unheard of for anyone to challenge even a rubric or to use the word "reform." The questionnaire was therefore a bold move. In this case the proverb was proved true: "Fortune favors the brave." For the question- naire was not a front for secret maneuvering but simply a free—and risky—undertaking by the young editor-in-chief of the periodical.

The questionnaire roused a very great deal of interest. Above all, it encouraged scholars to direct their researches to the goal of practical reform.

A few months later, when the editors set about drafting the article "Verso una riforma liturgica generale,"[12] in which they would systema- tize and evaluate the responses received, they were able to profit by the approach taken in the *Memoria* that had meanwhile been prepared by the reform commission.

This Roman periodical continued to publish articles on reform in the years that followed; these were everywhere read, commented on, praised, and criticized. They always had an international influence on other litur- gical publications and publications directed at the clergy, and were fre- quently reprinted in their entirety. The reason for this was that these writings stayed on sure ground and were quite balanced; they contributed to the creation of a climate of expectant trust and scholarly reexamina- tion. They were generally respectful and calm, even if also at times quite lively. When the new Easter Vigil was published in 1951, the mystery behind this series of trenchant liturgical publications gave up its secrets to some extent. This did not, however, lessen interest but rather intensi- fied it.

4. *The Assisi Congress (1956)*

The second force operative in ensuring the coming of liturgical reform found its mature expression at Assisi. This International Congress of Pas- toral Liturgy was, in God's plan, a dawn announcing a resplendent day that would have no decline. Who would have predicted at that time that three years later the greatest ecclesial event of the century, Vatican Council II, would be announced, in which the desires expressed at Assisi would be fulfilled, and this by means of the very men who were present at Assisi?

The theme of the congress was the pastoral nature of the liturgy; it is this that gives the liturgy a determining role in the Church's life and in promoting the encounter of souls with God. Two lectures were basic from this point of view: that of Josef Andreas Jungmann, "The Pastoral

---

12. *EL* 62 (1948) 3ff.; 63 (1949) 166–84.

Idea in the History of the Liturgy,"[13] and that of Augustin Bea, "The Pastoral Value of the Word of God in the Sacred Liturgy."[14] The principles set forth in these addresses would be found again in the Constitution on the Liturgy.

Two subjects aroused special interest at Assisi and were the subject of lively debate: the problem of the vernacular and the reform of the Divine Office. Interest in the use of the vernacular, which large groups of the participants called for openly, was intensified by a hitch at the beginning. The organizers of the congress had installed a system for simultaneous translation into the various languages; the translators had been given the papers in advance. At the last moment, however, Cardinal Cicognani introduced into his opening address a few rather strong pages on the need of keeping Latin as the language of the liturgy. The translators were taken by surprise and fell silent at this point. The assembly, which was listening through headphones, waited a while for something to be said; this only intensified interest in these pages, which were perhaps (it was said) "inspired," and gave rise to many lively discussions in the course of the congress.

A further circumstance made the situation even more tense. On the second day Cardinal Cicognani departed for Rome, leaving Cardinal Lercaro to serve as president. The latter read a general statement on the premature departure of the prefect of the Sacred Congregation of Rites, but it convinced no one. The rumor spread that Cardinal Cicognani had been annoyed at the reception of his statement about Latin and had gone to tell the Pope and persuade him to issue a stern rebuke in his coming address to the congress on September 22.

The rumor was in fact baseless. Pope Pius XII gave a fine address, although because of his illness he read only part of it. In his introduction he made this historic remark: "The liturgical movement is . . . a sign of the providential dispositions of God for the present time [and] of the movement of the Holy Spirit in the Church."[15]

The real reason for the Cardinal's early departure from Assisi was quite different.[16]

---

13. In *The Assisi Papers. Proceedings of the First International Congress of Pastoral Liturgy, Assisi-Rome, September 18-22, 1956* (Collegeville, Minn., 1957) 18–31.

14. *Ibid.*, 74–90.

15. *Ibid.*, 224.

16. What happened was this: The revered Bishop of Assisi, Placido Niccolini, who lived quite simply in a few rooms of the episcopal palace, wished at any cost to have the Cardinal as his guest; he therefore ordered the reopening of the cardinalatial apartment, which had been closed for some time. But an army of parasites had invaded the premises and

Cardinal Lercaro discussed the reform of the Office in a lecture that was very well received: ''The Simplification of the Rubrics and the Breviary Reform.''[17] It is interesting to read the Cardinal's suggestions in light of the reform that did come about in the Liturgy of the Hours, especially with regard to the selection and distribution of the psalms, readings, and hymns. It is clear today that the reform was the fruit of a long period of maturation, a fruit produced by the thought and prayer of elite minds and then gradually shared with ever wider circles of the faithful.

---

during the night tormented the guest to the point of causing swelling and a fever; medical help could bring no relief. The guest endured it for one more day and then decided to return to Rome in order to free himself from this intolerable plague and get some rest.

17. *The Assisi Papers*, 203-19; on the same subject see *RL* 48 (1961) 353-56.

The Preparatory Commission

On January 25, 1959, in the Basilica of St. Peter, Pope John XXIII announced the Second Vatican Ecumenical Council. On June 6, 1960, Cardinal Cicognani was appointed president of the preparatory commission on the liturgy, and on July 11 Father Annibale Bugnini, C.M., was appointed secretary. The planning of the work began immediately.

1. *Formation of the Commission*

The full commission consisted of sixty-five members and consultors, about thirty advisors, and the personnel of the secretariat. The appointed members included some bishops and some acknowledged scholars and experts in pastoral liturgy. The consultors and advisors, on the other hand, included both men of action and scholars as well as directors of diocesan liturgical centers and commissions. All these were professional workers who could make an effective contribution when there was need of research and information.

There were further considerations at work in the formation of the commission. One was nationality: every part of the world in which the liturgical movement was active and prospering had to be represented on the commission, and this in a real and not a fictitious way. It would in fact have been quite possible to form an international commission right in Rome itself, but the "international" element would have been purely formal. The witness given by those living and working here and now in their native environment has quite a different value from that of persons from foreign nations who actually live and work in Rome. Due to the application of this criterion, twenty-five nations from the five continents were represented on the commission; they included various young nations. Such a selection seemed indispensable if the work was to be truly ecclesial in character.

Another criterion was competence. The area of historical studies provided a sizable number of first-rate experts, but other, no less important aspects of the liturgy had also to be taken into account: theology, pastoral activity, music, law, and art.

A fourth element could not be overlooked: the contribution of the various spiritualities that flourish in the Church. The monastic orders, which had proved their surpassing merit in the area of the liturgy, could have furnished the majority of the commission's members, but the commission decided to profit also from the very valuable contribution to be made by the other religious families of antiquity, the Middle Ages, the fifteenth and sixteenth centuries, and more recent times. As a result, the Benedictines, Premonstratensians, Dominicans, Franciscans, Jesuits, Oratorians, Vincentians, Redemptorists, and some modern congregations were all represented on the commission. And because by the express will of the Holy Father the pastoral outlook was to be predominant in the preparatory work, about ten parish priests, various directors of pastoral liturgical centers, and twelve bishops ensured the presence of this outlook on the commission.

The following outline shows the structure of the preparatory commission:

President: Cardinal Gaetano Cicognani
Secretariat: A. Bugnini, secretary; C. Braga, archivist and scribe; G. Tautu, scribe

SUBCOMMISSIONS

I. *The mystery of the sacred liturgy and its relation to the life of the Church*
 Relator: G. Bevilacqua
 Secretary: C. Vagaggini
 Consultors: H. Jenny, J. A. Jungmann, G. Cannizzaro, I. Oñatibia, H. Schmidt, A. Dirks

II. *The Mass*
 Relator: J. A. Jungmann
 Secretary: T. Schnitzler
 Consultors: H. Jenny, A. Chavasse, P. Borella, P.-M. Gy, H. Kahlefeld, V. Kennedy

III. *Sacramental concelebration*
 Relator: B. Capelle
 Secretary: B. Botte
 Consultors: J. Gogué, A.-G. Martimort, A. Hänggi

IV. *Divine Office*
    Relator: J. Pascher
    Secretary: H. Schmidt
    Consultors: J. Walsh, M. Righetti, J. O'Connell, J. Wagner, P. Siffrin

V. *Sacraments and sacramentals*
    Relator: M. Righetti
    Secretary: I. Oñatibia
    Consultors: K. Calewaert, J. Wagner, A. Chavasse, P. Jounel, C. Vagag-
    gini, B. Luykx

VI. *Revision of the calendar*
    Relator: J. O'Connell
    Secretary: A. Dirks
    Consultors: J. Gogué, F. McManus, G. Pizzoni

VII. *Use of Latin*
    Relator: P. Borella
    Secretary: L. Brinkhoff
    Consultors: J. Malula, P. Radó, B. Botte, F. McManus

VIII. *Liturgical formation*
    Relator: C. Kniewald
    Secretary: A. Hänggi
    Consultors: F. Muthappa, J. Mejia, I. Oñatibia, H. Schmidt, P.-M. Gy

IX. *Participation of the faithful in the sacred liturgy*
    Relator: G. Cannizzaro
    Secretary: P. Jounel
    Consultors: C. Rossi, L. Brinkhoff, G. Diekmann, M. Pfliegler, G.
    Bevilacqua

X. *Linguistic adaptation to the tradition and ethos of peoples*
    Relator: J. Quasten
    Secretary: G. Diekmann
    Consultors: J. Malula, F. Muthappa, C. Vagaggini, J. Hofinger, B. Luykx

XI. *Simplification of liturgical vestments*
    Relator: G. Martinez de Antoñana
    Secretary: G. Schiavon
    Consultors: K. Kowalski, J. Nabuco, M. Dubois

XII. *Sacred music*
    Relator: I. Anglés
    Secretary: E. Cardine
    Consultors: J. Hervas, C. Kniewald, P. Jones, P. Jounel, L. Brinkhoff

XIII. *Sacred art*
    Relator: J. Nabuco
    Secretary: V. Vigorelli
    Consultors: H. Jenny, G. Fallani, J. O'Connell, T. Klauser, J. Wagner

2. First Meeting: Autumn 1960

The commission met for the first time on November 12 and 15, 1960. At this meeting the program was formulated and the work divided up among the members. From among the proposals regarding liturgy that had reached the Holy See, twelve basic ones were chosen that in practice included all the others; these were assigned to twelve subcommissions, each made up of seven to nine individuals. One member was appointed by the president to be relator, and one consultor to be secretary. Each of the twelve bishops was likewise appointed to a subcommission.

The gathering on November 12 was open to members only, that of November 15 to members and consultors.

The subcommissions planned by the president were twelve in number; a thirteenth, which was given first place on the list, was suggested on November 15 by G. Bevilacqua, who became its relator. His idea was that the entire document should be introduced by a theologico-ascetical chapter on the mystery of the liturgy in the life of the Church.[1] Little by little, however, the chapter grew more substantial and became the most important part of the entire Constitution; to the theological and ascetical aspects were added the pastoral and the normative. The gradual evolution of the chapter is also reflected to some extent in the successive new titles given to it.[2]

The subcommissions had five months to prepare drafts on their own subjects. It was a time of astonishingly intense work. What was being called for was concrete, documented, substantial presentations. Local meetings were held in Rome, Milan, Freiburg, and Washington; meanwhile there was constant correspondence between the center and the periphery and among the members of each subcommission. The work, both collective and individual, was done with a strong sense of responsibility and also—this must be emphasized—with a generosity and self-sacrifice that in some cases reached the level of heroism, and without regard to time, personal expense, and necessary travel. A young Colombian priest, for example, arranged with the airline to pay for his travel

---

1. This was the suggested outline of the chapter: "The broad principles on the importance of the sacred liturgy in the life of the Church are to be set forth, and specifically: (a) the central place of the mysteries of Christ; (b) the latreutic value of the liturgy in itself; (c) its soteriological value; (d) its ascetical and instructional value."

2. The Latin titles were as follows: November 1960: "De mysterio sacrae liturgiae in vita Ecclesiae"; April 1961: "De sacra liturgia fovenda atque instauranda in genere"; November 1961: "De principiis generalibus pro instauranda atque fovenda sacra liturgia"; January 1962: "De principiis generalibus ad liturgiam instaurandam atque fovendam."

over a two-year period simply in order not to miss any of the general meetings. A single controlling thought galvanized everyone and inspired enthusiasm: to show a common love for the Church, to serve the Church, to renew the Church's liturgy.

3. Second Meeting: Spring 1961

The members and consultors gathered in the spring of 1961 to discuss the drafts of the subcommissions. All were present in the meeting room of the Congregation of Rites, and all shared with loving interest in the work. The contribution being made by cultural background and by experience was quite clear. Local views and local situations evoked the sensitivity of others and helped refine thinking, expression, and emphases. A real family was gradually formed in which the sense of the Church was keen and palpable.

The men who took part in those study meetings will never forget the effort to find solutions that would strike a balance between past and future, between the call of tradition and pastoral needs. They will never forget the relief felt when the desired formula was at last found, or the alert, prudent wisdom that the great masters of the liturgy, all of them gathered there, showed in solving the most difficult problems with lovable simplicity and naturalness—a wisdom that was the fruit of long intellectual labors and, at times, of hard-earned experience.

Study of the drafts showed that the whole of the material handled by the thirteen subcommissions was being restructured and reorganized. The first chapter, as I said earlier, had for its function to emphasize the importance of the liturgy in the life of the Church and to set down the principles and norms that must govern the entire reform. One advantage of this procedure was that the same points did not have to be repeated in chapter after chapter. This was the case, for example, with the problem of Latin (Subcommission VII), liturgical formation (VIII), participation of the faithful in the liturgy (IX), and adaptation to the traditions and distinctive character of the various peoples (X).

When the plenary meetings ended, some thousands of typewritten cards were heaped on the table of the secretariat. The moment had come to combine the various elements into a single whole. This the secretariat did in three months of intensive editorial work.

The first thing to be considered was the general approach. Each number of the Constitution, called a *votum* (statement of something desired), had three parts: a *text*, approved by the Fathers and provided with a suitable short title in square brackets that gave the gist of the passage; a *declaratio voti*, that is, an explanation in terms more intelligible to those not familiar with liturgical terminology; and finally *notae*, in which each statement was duly documented.

In order to be sure that this approach reflected the thinking of the commission, Chapter II, on the Mass, was composed in May and sent to the members and consultors for inspection and study. The replies were encouraging; the document was satisfactory. The right path had been found. The work continued through June and July and was completed in the first days of August.

The result was a volume of 250 pages, duplicated and put together entirely by the three members of the secretariat in order to ensure absolute secrecy. The volume was sent to the members of the commission on August 10, 1961, along with a letter asking them to submit their observations to the secretariat as soon as possible. The following schedule was drawn up: August 10, sending of the volume; September 10, deadline for observations; October 10, secretariat sends revised draft for a second examination; November 1, deadline for sending observations on the revised draft to the secretariat; November 15–16 (probably), meeting of the commission for final approval of the text; December 15, presentation of the Constitution to the secretariat of the Council.

This schedule, which was certainly too tight, was fairly well met. There was a delay of a month and a half because of material difficulties in preparing and sending out on time the final corrected drafts. A certain haste was required by pressure from the central secretariat and from the Council to meet deadlines and by the need of having the responses back in time so that the Constitution might pass through all the preliminary stages required if it was to be examined during the first session of the Council, as the Holy Father desired.

The early responses showed that from a redactional standpoint the first chapter was the weakest of all. Since four others depended on it, a more careful development of the text had to be undertaken with the help of the more important representatives on the commission. For this purpose a meeting of the first subcommission, together with some other consultors, was called. It was held in the Domus Mariae (Rome), October 11–12, 1961. Those asked to attend were: G. Bevilacqua (relator), H. Jenny, J. A. Jungmann, I. Oñatibia, C. Vagaggini, A.-G. Martimort, J. Pascher, H. Schmidt, and A. Dirks. Also present were the secretary of the commission and C. Braga, or eleven persons in all.[3]

---

3. This meeting at the Domus Mariae gave rise to a misunderstanding that had unpleasant consequences. The complete secrecy governing the preparatory work led some to think that this group of ten *periti*, led by the secretary of the commission, had gathered secretly to

From these days of intense work in which study and prayer alternated, there emerged the splendid first chapter of the Constitution on the Sacred Liturgy.

But its journey was not yet over. On receiving the revised text, Father Herman Schmidt, S.J., found that the first nine numbers were "wordy" and that their "oratorical" style contrasted with that of the other chapters; he offered an alternative text that reduced the nine numbers of the official text to three. The secretariat took his remarks under advisement and called Subcommission I, enlarged by some other *periti*, to meet again on the afternoon of January 10, 1962. The discussion was frank and lively; the text was touched up but not substantially changed. The *periti* did not, of course, limit their skilled examination to the first chapter only. The other parts of the Constitution were also extensively annotated.

The observations on the first draft numbered about fifteen hundred. Some were repetitions; others raised new problems; by and large they were most useful in improving the text. There was a general desire that the draft be further reduced in length. This was a wise suggestion. It was true that most of the text contained very useful *declarationes*; it was also true that the extensive programs coming in from other preparatory groups made the commission fear, at one point, that its draft was overly modest. But calmer reflection persuaded the commission to be decisive in following the path of moderation. This was in fact the salvation of the document. The second draft was 150 pages long instead of 250. It was sent to all the members for examination, and new observations soon came in: 750, to be exact, or half as many as for the first draft. A third version was prepared (November 15, 1961) and was to have been sent to each member's address. Time was pressing, however, and it was necessary

---

interfere with the work of the other groups and revise it along "progressive" lines. As a matter of fact, the meeting was simply a normal study session employing the best qualified consultors, who had been chosen because the material was especially involved and the available time very limited.

The same strange inference was also spread abroad with regard to the work that followed. There was a good deal of talk to this effect when the secretary of the preparatory commission was not kept on as secretary of the conciliar commission in October 1961, and there was even an echo of the rumor at the Council. The preparatory commission was specifically accused of not having taken into account the observations approved by a very large majority of the central commission, and this "because of a real itch for innovations in matters where they are not only not necessary or useful but can even become harmful" (see the intervention of Cardinal Alfredo Ottaviani at the tenth plenary session, October 25, 1962, in *Acta synodalia sacrosancti Concilii oecumenici Vaticani II*, Vol. I, Periodus prima. Pars II [Vatican Polyglot Press, 1970] 18–21). The conduct of those who had prepared and corrected the schemas was firmly and authoritatively defended by the president of the subcommission for changes, Cardinal Carlo Confalonieri, on November 5, 1962 (*ibid.*, 106–8).

to rely on a collegial examination of the draft. A meeting of the commission was therefore called for January 1962.

4. *Third Meeting: Winter 1962*

In four days of intensive work (January 11–14) the Constitution was revised for the last time. Each article was read, discussed, corrected, and finally approved. Rarely was there disagreement. In fact, an effort was made to find conciliatory formulations without sacrificing substance, for all were convinced that the variety of opinions manifested at the microcosmic level in the preparatory commission would surface again in the Council. For practical purposes the Constitution received unanimous approval from the preparatory commission. For this reason, the forty pages of text (the remainder being *declarationes* and *notae*)[4] that emerged fresh and luminous from only three plenary meetings may be said to have been the result of the joint work of the commission.

Two problems aroused special interest in the course of the preparatory work: sacred music and the use of Latin.

5. *Sacred Music*

The relator appointed for the subcommission on sacred music was Monsignor Anglés, dean of the Pontifical Institute of Sacred Music in Rome. Persons representing the various branches of music were assigned to him as consultors. Only one of these, however, was acceptable to him, and he asked that all the others be substitutes. The Cardinal President did not agree with him; the most he would do was to approve the request of a bishop who did not wish to work in this group.

On December 22 Monsignor Anglés asked that Monsignor Johannes Overath of Cologne and Monsignor Jean Beilliard of France be assigned to him as "advisors"; later on he asked also for Father Smits van Waesberghe, a Dutch Jesuit. The requests were granted, although Monsignor Anglés was obviously trying to rid himself of members of the commission and to work with others whom he himself chose.

The first meeting, held at Monsignor Anglés' home with the Ursuline Sisters on the Via Nomentana, ended in a quarrel when he openly accused the French (Father Jounel was present) of being chauvinist and opposed to the spirit of the Church. The consultors of the subcommission were kept in the dark about all this. Bishop Kowalski of Poland wrote that he had never received any information from the presiding officer of

---

4. In its final redaction the complete text had ix + 79 pages.

the group. When Monsignor Anglés was told of this, he answered, "How do I know that he's not a Communist bishop?" The rumor then spread through Roman circles that the music question was being poorly handled and that Monsignor Anglés had had no one to help him in the work.

At the meeting in April 1961, Monsignor Anglés read a very lengthy paper and asked that the greater part of it be inserted into the Constitution. When this was refused, he took two steps. To circles in the Sacred Congregation of Seminaries he painted a picture of the preparatory commission as "the number one enemy of Latin"; and he presented the International Congress on Sacred Music, which was to be held in Cologne in June of that year, as the body that was really doing the preparatory work for the Council in the area of music. And, in fact, a single refrain was constantly to be heard in the reports and interventions at the congress and in the bulletins on it in periodicals: that the members must make themselves heard at the Council and must do the preparatory work for the Council. An expression of wishes to this effect was even introduced into the acts of the congress, which were read at the Abbey of Maria Laach on June 30.

When Cardinal Cicognani was informed of all this, he had a rather cold letter sent to Monsignor Anglés. It elicited from the latter a very stubborn answer, but one based on weak or inconsistent arguments. This answer in turn received from the secretariat of the preparatory commission a lengthy and fully argued reply, which it placed at the disposal of the Cardinal President.

This was the state of affairs when the final meeting was held on January 11-13, 1962. Monsignor Anglés took part in the discussion during the first day and a half but then left the meeting room with threatening mien.

These details show how sacred music was unfortunately the most unsettled area of the reform both before and after the Council. The hostile attitude of music directors and distinguished composers prevented the reform from introducing renewal and pastoral participation into sacred music. This background of negative reaction explains the confusion of the postconciliar period, which saw a mushrooming of compositions that were not always inspired works of art and yet were widely received because they were more in keeping with the reform spirit of the postconciliar liturgy.

6. *Latin*

The use of Latin was another problem that caused difficulties in the work of the preparatory commission. The echoes of the debate enkindled

at the Assisi Congress (1956) had not yet died out when they were revived by various articles in *L'Osservatore Romano* and even more by Pope
John XXIII when on February 22, 1962, at the tomb of St. Peter and amid
great pomp, he signed the constitution *Veterum sapientia* on the preservation of Latin. The preparatory liturgical commission was being depicted
in the Curia as the number one enemy of Latin. Musical circles made their
contribution to the growing uneasiness. The secretariat of the preparatory commission had already been called on the carpet and had had to
defend itself against this manifest calumny. Here is a memorandum of
March 4, 1961:

> The "language" problem comes up in almost all the questions to be stud-
> ied by the Pontifical Liturgical Commission. Since the individual subcom-
> missions to which areas have been assigned have not yet formulated all
> their definitive conclusions, and since each of these conclusions will have
> to be examined at the plenary meeting of the commission in April, it is dif-
> ficult to say what direction will be taken in this matter.
>
> From the discussions thus far it seems clear that two principles will have
> to be respected by any solution:
>
> a) Latin must, without qualification, continue to be used by the clergy;
>
> b) the vernacular is to be introduced into the liturgy for the sake of the
> faithful, in accordance with the principles set down by Pius XII in *Mediator
> Dei (AAS* 39 [1947] 545) and in his address to the participants in the Assisi
> Congress (*AAS* 48 [1956] 724), as well as with the line followed in succes-
> sive concessions by the Supreme Sacred Congregation of the Holy Office.
>
> On February 14, a "joint commission"[5] of members from the liturgical
> commission and the commission for seminaries also took up the problem
> of Latin. The delegates from both areas were in agreement on the need of
> maintaining and intensifying the study of Latin in the seminaries.
>
> Also suggested was the application of a kind of scale meant to take into
> account the mission countries in particular. It was hoped that the seminar-
> ies, ecclesiastical universities, and theological faculties of the Romance-
> language countries would demand a solid humanistic formation based on
> both the classical and the Christian authors. But the possibility was consid-
> ered that in countries further removed from Western culture, such as Asia
> and Africa, the study of Latin, which would continue through the four years
> of theology, might be more functional in character; the goal would be to
> have the young clerics be able to read with ease at least the Bible, the holy
> Fathers, the Breviary, the Missal, the liturgical sources, and the documents
> of the Church. On this point, too, there was unanimous agreement.

---

5. During the preparation some problems required the work of joint commissions, that
is, the liturgical commission along with commissions dealing with other areas to be handled
at the Council: seminaries, religious, the missions. Rather than being "joint commissions"
in the true and proper sense, these were study meetings to handle common problems.

The reports of the subcommissions on the liturgy are to be so drawn up that in more important or more controversial questions two or three solutions of greater importance will always be offered in order to respect the freedom of those representing divergent tendencies. The liturgical commission will then have to decide among these solutions at a plenary session. In the case of problems for which not even the liturgical commission can agree on a solution, it will set forth the various solutions and leave the decision to the Fathers of the Council.

On the other hand, some questions are to be treated from varying points of view by several preparatory commissions. Since all the resolutions arrived at by the commissions are to be examined by the central commission, the latter will coordinate the various problems, choose the position it thinks most opportune, and present it to the Fathers of the Council for their consideration.

Meanwhile, a subcommission under the presidency of Monsignor Pietro Borella was charged with studying the problem of Latin in the liturgy. But as the plenary meeting of April 12–24, 1961, drew near, the secretariat thought it more opportune to remove the question of Latin from the agenda and leave it to be dealt with under particular headings. Two factors suggested this decision: the rising tide of disagreement, which could have a negative effect on the entire work of the commission, and the rather muddled text that was being presented to the commission for its examination. Some of the *periti* and members were dissatisfied with this decision; they wanted a public debate of a general kind. Some of them appealed to the president against the secretariat, which they accused of favoring the vernacular. Cardinal Cicognani decided that the question should be discussed at the meeting and prepared a personal statement on it.

For more than two hours on the appointed day, the *periti*, one from each country, pleaded—some of them in sorrowful tones, including Father Godfrey Diekmann, an American Benedictine, and Professor Frederick McManus of the Catholic University in Washington, D.C.—that the door be opened to the mother tongues. It was an evening of deep emotion; all were shaken, being deeply moved by what had been said and heard. Finally, the Cardinal spoke. He had collected from the Book of Leviticus all the passages describing the Ark, the temple, and the liturgical services, in order to bring out the beauty of the liturgy and the need of being faithful to tradition. His exposition was itself given in a rather unusual mixture of Latin, Italian, and Spanish, and was thus the most eloquent possible proof of the position taken by the commission that the vernaculars should be used.

The conclusion reached in this debate was ultimately set forth in Chapter I of the Constitution on the Liturgy, where the question is answered in a way that reconciles the rights of Latin and the need of the vernaculars in celebrations with the people.

7. *Via Purgativa*

After the plenary meeting of January 11-14, 1962, the secretariat of the commission undertook the redaction and transcription of the definitive text. On January 22 the official copy was on the table of Cardinal Gaetano Cicognani, president of the commission, where it awaited his signature. He received it with joy and trepidation. As always when he had to make a binding decision, he hesitated and wanted to reread the text. A week passed. He finally signed it on February 1, 1962, and had it passed on to the secretariat of the Council. It was his last official act. Four days later, on February 5, he returned silently and peacefully to "the Father's house." Thus he, the president of the preparatory commission, went to join the three members who had preceded him, there to serve as "good patrons" of the work they had accomplished together.[6]

The text was printed in five fascicles, making a total of 125 pages containing 127 articles, along with detailed *declarationes* for each. A copy was sent to all the members and consultors.[7]

On February 22, 1962, Cardinal Arcadio M. Larraona, C.M.F., new prefect of the Congregation of Rites and a great jurist of conservative bent, was appointed to succeed Cardinal Cicognani as president of the preparatory commission. That same day saw the publication of the apostolic constitution *Veterum sapientia*, which confirmed the need of intensifying the study of Latin. Not a few people interpreted this document as an admonition to those liturgists who favored the introduction of the vernaculars into worship. It certainly influenced the atmosphere in which prepara-

---

6. If Cardinal Cicognani had not signed the Constitution, the result, humanly speaking, would have been a real disaster. Everything would have had to be discussed all over again. But "who knows the ways of God?" We can see here one of the many presences of the Spirit during the sometimes difficult and unforeseeable course of reform.

7. Pontificia Commissio Centralis Praeparatoria Concilii Vaticani II, *Quaestiones de sacra liturgia. Schema Constitutionis de sacra Liturgia a Commissione liturgica propositum Em.mo ac Rev.mo Domino Cardinali Commissionis Praeside Relatore* (Vatican Polyglot Press, 1962). The bland wording and lack of a proper name in the last part of the title were due to the fact that the document was printed while the position of president was vacant. The text was subsequently reprinted in *Acta et Documenta Concilio Oecumenico Vaticano II apparando*, Series II (Praeparatoria), Vol. III. *Acta Commissionum et Secretariatuum praeparatoriorum Concilii Oecumenici Vaticani II*, Pars II (Vatican Polyglot Press, 1969) 9-68.

tion for the Council was carried out. The *via purgativa* was beginning for the Constitution on the Liturgy.[8]

In preparation for the Council, John XXIII had also established, on June 5, 1960, a central commission that was to oversee the work of the particular commissions. This central commission was a kind of microcosmic council. At its fifth meeting (March 26 to April 3, 1962) it examined the schema on the liturgy. Several speakers said that this was the best of the schemas thus far examined.[9]

The central commission passed an overall judgment on the schemas and suggested some changes that were made by a special subcommission; this was the third of the conciliar subcommissions, the "subcommission for changes," and had Cardinal Carlo Confalonieri as its president. The subcommission began by asking the preparatory commission for a report on the schema; it then passed on to it the changes requested by the Fathers of the central commission. There was a continuous exchange of explanations and memoranda, but on some points, even important ones, the secretariat had to agree to the requests of the subcommission for changes.

The Constitution in its amended form was published in the volume of schemas to be discussed at the Council; the Pope approved these on July 13, 1962, and they were sent to all the Council Fathers.[10]

The members and consultors of the preparatory liturgical commission were in possession of the schema they had approved and could gauge the changes that had been made: the *declarationes*, so useful in helping nonspecialists to understand the text, had been completely eliminated; the decentralization so ardently sought was "watered down" (local authorities could only make suggestions to the Holy See); nothing was said of communion under both kinds for the laity; concelebration was limited to a few occasions; no reference was made to the use of the vernacular by priests in celebrating the Divine Office. The title page (page 155 of the volume) carried the statement: "The sole purpose of this Constitution is to provide general norms and 'the fundamental principles

---

8. See H. Schmidt, S.J., *La Costituzione sulla sacra liturgia. Testo–Genesi–Commento–Documentazione* (Rome, 1966) 166.

9. The Introduction and Chapters I and II were studied on March 26–27: *Acta et Documenta* (note 7, above), Vol. II, Pars III: *Acta Pontificiae Commissionis Centralis Praeparatoriae Concilii Oecumenici Vaticani II* (Vatican Polyglot Press, 1968) 96–144.

Chapters II–V were reviewed by the central commission on March 29–30 (*ibid.*, 275–368), and Chapters VI–VII on March 30–April 2 (*ibid.*, 460–92).

10. Sacrosanctum Oecumenicum Concilium Vaticanum Secundum, *Schemata Constitutionum et Decretorum, de quibus disceptabitur in Concilii sessionibus*, Series prima (Vatican Polyglot Press, 1962) 155–201.

governing general liturgical reform' (see John XXIII, motu proprio *Rubrica-rum instructum* of July 25, 1960). The practical application to particular cases is to be left to the Holy See.''

Someone copied out in two columns the text composed by the preparatory commission and the text printed in the volume of schemas, and called attention to the differences between the two; he then circulated this among the Fathers of the Council, who were thus able to see what had happened. The text of the Constitution that Cardinal Gaetano Cicognani had signed did not please the new president, who had therefore appointed a secret small committee to correct it. One member of this committee was Father Antonelli, who entrusted the task to Father Joseph Löw. Thus two ''secretariats'' were working simultaneously on the Constitution, one of them unknown to the other: a legitimate secretariat entrusted with introducing the corrections required by the central commission, and working with the subcommission for changes; and a ''secret'' secretariat whose task was to restructure the Constitution according to the intentions of the new president. The latter then juggled the two, anxious that the game not be discovered.

Father Löw, who was doing most of the work of revision, died unexpectedly on September 23, 1962. This event introduced confusion into the opposition.

Then came the Council itself, which restored the text to its original form. It can be said, therefore, that although the Constitution was reviewed by four appointed ''courts''—the central commission, the subcommission for changes, the Council itself, and the conciliar commission—no substantial changes were made in the text that emerged from the preparatory commission on January 13, 1962, and was approved by Cardinal Gaetano Cicognani on February 1, 1962.

8. *In pace cum sanctis*

The preparatory commission, too, had its dead:

Bishop Tadeusz Pawel Zakrzewski, president of the Polish liturgical commission, was able to take part in the work only by letter. But his letters disclosed a moving enthusiasm, love, and interest. He joined the holy pastors of heaven on November 7, 1961.

Bernard Capelle, O.S.B., Abbot of Mont-César (Louvain), a splendid scholar and religious, departed for the homeland of heaven on October 19, 1961.

Giovanni Bruno Cannizzaro, O.S.B., Abbot of S. Andrea in Genoa, left this world on March 14, 1961, at the age of only fifty-eight. He was a Calabrian by birth and combined gentleness and refinement of spirit with a lively mind and an uncommon theological formation; these two gifts he was able to use to great advantage with the aid of an ardent and inspiring eloquence. He was relator of the subcommission on the participation of the faithful in the liturgy, which had Professor Jounel as its secretary. Father Cannizzaro was "tormented" by the thought of the "priesthood of the faithful," which he would have liked to study thoroughly with a group of theologians, liturgists, and members of the commission on the laity.

March 15 was the final deadline for submitting the reports of the subcommissions to the secretariat. Professor Jounel traveled to Genoa to join Abbot Cannizzaro in composing the final version of the text. The two men worked hard for two days, and the work was completed by noon of March 14. At four o'clock, before his departure, Professor Jounel wanted to say goodbye to the Abbot. They knocked on the latter's door but there was no answer. The Abbot's heart had not been up to the intense work; he had died in the breach. It can indeed be said that the Constitution on the Liturgy had its own special "martyr."

A month later, on April 14, the entire commission, led by its president, Cardinal Gaetano Cicognani, went to the Aventine and the abbatial church of Sant' Anselmo, where a solemn "month's mind" funeral Office was celebrated with the entire monastic community. It was a homage paid by the liturgical commission to an unforgettable fellow worker who had died in the field, where his death became a seed of blessing and hope.

3

The Liturgical Constitution at the Council

Of the seven drafts contained in the first volume of *Schemata* to be examined at the Council, the first four, which were doctrinal in nature, found little favor. The fact that the Council began by discussing these schemas meant that it had to enter into, and get lost in, a maze of theological discussions.[1] It was precisely this that the bishops, in agreement with the intention of Pope John XXIII, wanted to avoid, in order to give an essentially pastoral stamp to the great ecumenical meeting.

The members of the presidency and many bishops told the Pope of their misgivings. As a result, it was announced at the second general congregation on October 16, 1962, that the sacred liturgy was the first item on the agenda for examination by the Fathers.[2]

This action was an implicit acknowledgment of the maturity and importance of the theme. But this new agenda also had its risks, since being the first document also meant being a test case for the procedures of the Council. The Constitution passed the test. The large number of interventions showed the interest that the schema aroused among the Council Fathers.

---

1. The first four subjects were, in this order: the sources of revelation; the preservation of the deposit of faith in its purity; the Christian moral order; chastity, marriage, family, virginity. These were followed by the schemas on the liturgy and on the communications media. See Sacrosanctum Oecumenicum Concilium Vaticanum Secundum, *Schemata Constitutionum et Decretorum, de quibus disceptabitur in Concilii sessionibus*, Series prima (Vatican Polyglot Press, 1962).

2. The documentation for this chapter owes much to H. Schmidt, S.J., *La Costituzione sulla sacra liturgia* (Rome, 1966) 115–209.

I. History

The first task of the Council was to establish conciliar commissions. On October 20, 1962 (third plenary session), the Fathers elected the sixteen members of the liturgical commission, to whom were added eight members appointed by the Pope. When the Pope decided to include in the commissions the secretaries of the relevant Roman agencies, Archbishop Enrico Dante, secretary of the Congregation of Rites, was added to the liturgical commission on October 29.

At the first meeting, on October 21, the president, Cardinal Arcadio Larraona, appointed Cardinals Paolo Giobbe and André Jullien as vice-presidents. Surprisingly, Cardinal Giacomo Lercaro was passed over, even though he was the senior cardinal there, the only one elected a member of the liturgical commission by the Council Fathers, and a man with a reputation as a liturgist.[3] At this same meeting the president announced the appointment of Father Ferdinando Antonelli, O.F.M., as secretary.[4]

On September 22, 1962, the Pope had appointed 201 *periti* to assist in the work of the Council; the number would be greatly augmented in

---

3. The first six meetings were spent dealing with trifling matters of juridical procedure. The Fathers wanted to give definitive approval to the Constitution on the Liturgy at the end of the first session, but the slow pace of the work quickly made it clear that this was impossible. There were those who seemed to be using delaying tactics to gain time, and this finally gave rise to a latent discontent, which Bishop Malula, Auxiliary Bishop of Kinshasa, expressed in a rather unrestrained way at the seventh meeting.

4. Of all the secretaries of the preparatory commissions, Father Bugnini was the only one not appointed secretary of the corresponding conciliar commission. This was the first sign that the new president of the liturgical commission, Cardinal Arcadio Larraona, was following a different course from that of the commission that had drawn up the schema; this last, meanwhile, was continuing the normal course leading to presentation at the Council. To achieve his purpose, Cardinal Larraona began by dismissing the secretary, who was the pivotal figure in the entire preparatory work. This was Father Bugnini's first exile.

At the same time that Father Bugnini was dismissed from the secretariat of the conciliar commission, he was also discharged from his post as teacher of liturgy in the Pontifical Pastoral Institute of the Lateran University, and an attempt was made to take from him the chair of liturgy at the Pontifical Urban University. This repressive activity emanated directly from Cardinal Larraona and was very kindly seconded by some fellow workers who wanted to better serve the Church and the liturgy. The basis for the dismissals was the charge of being a "progressivist," "pushy," and an "iconoclast" (innuendos whispered half-aloud), accusations then echoed in turn by the Congregation of Rites, the Congregation of Seminaries, and the Holy Office. But no proof was offered, no clear justification for such serious measures.

Some friends—Cardinals Lercaro and Bea, for example—who knew Father Bugnini well were the good angels who blazed a direct path, first to Pope John, who made a few gestures but accomplished nothing in face of the strict intransigence of Cardinal Larraona, and then to Cardinal Montini, one of whose first acts as Pope was to make reparation by appointing Father Bugnini secretary of Consilium (January 3, 1964).

the coming months. In October 1962 the liturgical commission, too, had its *periti;* at the beginning they numbered twenty-six, of whom only twelve had taken part in the work of the preparatory commission. Others were added in 1963.

The task of the commission was to revise the Constitution on the basis of the amendments *(emendationes)* and changes *(modi)* proposed by the Council Fathers. From October 21 to December 12, 1962, twenty-one meetings were held, during which the Introduction and Chapter I were revised. The other chapters were revised in meetings running from April 23 to May 10 and from September 27 to September 30, 1963. Still other meetings were held after October 14, 1963, in order to put the finishing touches on the definitive version.

From October 22 to November 13, 1962, the Fathers discussed the schema on the liturgy at fifteen general congregations. They devoted about fifty hours to it; there were 328 oral interventions and another 297 submitted only in written form.

The Fathers were able to study the schema in depth with the aid of many liturgists gathered in Rome from various parts of the world. These experts held conferences, lectures, and dialogues. For example, Herman Schmidt, S.J. (October 25), Salvatore Marsili, O.S.B. (November 3), and Pierre-Marie Gy, O.P. (November 15) spoke in the pressroom of the Holy See to the journalists accredited to the Council.

Even more important were the direct contacts with bishops desirous of deriving information from reliable sources. In their interventions the Fathers frequently repeated the same points. But even this drawback was eliminated after November 6, when the moderators received permission to put an end to the interventions when they thought a subject had been exhaustively dealt with.

On November 14, 1962, at the nineteenth general congregation, the discussion of the liturgical schema was complete and a vote was taken on the following points:

> (1) The Second Ecumenical Council of the Vatican has studied the schema on the liturgy and has approved its guiding norms, which are intended in a prudent and comprehensive way to give the various parts of the liturgy a more vital and effective form that will meet contemporary pastoral needs.
> (2) The amendments proposed during the conciliar debate, after being examined and classified by the liturgical commission, are to be proposed for a vote at a general congregation; the result of the vote will serve in drawing up the definitive text.

The vote was as follows: number voting: 2215; in favor: 2162; against: 46; void: 7. This result showed that the schema reflected the liturgical sense and expectations of the universal Church and that it deserved confidence and was a valid tool for a liturgical reform in harmony with the best traditions of the Church.

The schema had struck the right note, enabling the Council to express its own pastoral desires. Its language was that of the Bible and the Fathers, and could be easily understood by the practicing faithful and by other Christians as well; it bridged the gap between doctrine and pastoral practice. One *peritus* finely observed that in this vote "the creaking of an opening door had been heard in the two-thousand-year-old Church."[5]

II. AMENDMENTS AND CHANGES

The secretariat of the Council immediately passed on to the liturgical commission the interventions of the Fathers on the schema. There were 625 interventions in all, which the secretary of the commission distributed according to the chapters of the schema.

Fifteen subcommissions were formed: one for theological questions, one for juridical questions, and one for general matters; three were to deal with Chapter I; the others dealt with the remaining seven chapters. A final subcommission was to see to the Latin of the document.

The first task of the conciliar commission was to correct the text in accordance with the amendments requested by the Fathers so that the revised passages might be submitted to a new vote. Eighty-six amendments were voted on at twenty-two general congregations. Before each vote the Fathers heard an explanation from the relator. The documentation for the work that had been done was contained in a series of printed fascicles bearing the title *Emendationes a Patribus conciliaribus postulatae a Commissione Conciliari de sacra Liturgia examinatae et propositae.*[6] The eleven fascicles (224 pages in all) contained the explanations of the relators, the amendments on which the vote was to be taken, and, in two columns, the unamended text and the amended text, together with the more important *declarationes* offered by the preparatory commission and expounded by the conciliar commission.

In the first session of the Council, votes were taken on all the amendments for Chapter I. This chapter was approved on December 7, 1962, except for very minor revisions *(modi)* that were to be presented during

---

5. Schmidt, *La Costituzione*, 140.

6. Vatican Polyglot Press, 1962, for the amendments in the Introduction and Chapter I; 1963 for the others. The first fascicle, which deals with the Introduction, is entitled *Emendationes a Commissione Conciliari de sacra Liturgia propositae.*

the second session. Pope John XXIII was therefore able to say on December 8, 1962, as he brought the first session to a close:

> It was no accident that the first *schema* to be considered was the one dealing with the sacred liturgy.The liturgy has to do with man's relationship with God. This relationship is of the utmost importance. It must be based on the solid foundation of revelation and apostolic teaching, so as to contribute to man's spiritual good; and that, with a broadness of vision which avoids the superficiality and haste often characterizing relationships among men.[7]

In the second session (1963) the examination of the *emendationes* continued, and votes were then taken on the *modi*, which were contained in five fascicles numbering 144 pages in all and entitled *Modi a Patribus conciliaribus propositi a Commissione Conciliari de sacra Liturgia examinati.*[8] Here are the principal amendments passed by the Council.

Introduction

No. 1: Instead of "separated brethren" read "all who believe in Christ."

No. 2: The expression "visible and invisible," referring to the Church, is changed to "visible yet endowed with invisible resources."

No. 3: Instead of "to the Eastern and Western rites" read "both to the Roman Rite and also to all the other rites."

No. 4: The phrase "all rites lawfully in force" has been replaced by "all lawfully acknowledged rites," which can also refer to the future, in case new rites are in fact approved.

Chapter I. *General Principles*

No. 5: "Holy Spirit": there was a widespread sense that the schema spoke too little of him. He has been named in a larger number of sections. "His [Christ's] humanity was the *cause* of our salvation": "cause" was used in order to follow Scholastic terminology; the Fathers chose "instrument" instead.

No. 6: "The sacrifice and the sacraments" replaces the single word "sacraments" of the original schema, which included the sacrifice among the sacraments.

No. 7: On the presence of Christ in liturgical celebrations: the text of the schema took as its basis a passage in *Mediator Dei* (no. 20) and added a phrase about the presence of Christ in the reading of Sacred Scripture. The expression "and in the explanation [of Scripture]" has been omitted

---

7. John XXIII, Address *Prima sessio* at the end of the first session of Vatican II (December 8, 1962), in *The Pope Speaks* 8 (1962–63) 400.

8. Vatican Polyglot Press, 1963.

as being a doctrinal development not sufficiently advanced for a conciliar document.

No. 10: The liturgy as "summit and fount": the entire statement has been set in a much more effective context. The Fathers who had asked for its omission probably did not realize that the same statement was to be found in the encyclical *Mediator Dei* of Pius XII, the encyclical *Mirae caritatis* of Leo XIII, and the Catechism of the Council of Trent.

No. 14: Active participation "by reason of their baptism" and not by an ecclesiastical concession.

No. 16: The liturgy is to be included "among the compulsory and major courses in seminaries."

No. 22: On competent ecclesiastical authorities: the second paragraph on bishops is completely new.

No. 25: Bishops and not just experts are to play a part in the reform of the liturgy.

No. 27: On the public and social value of every Mass: the second paragraph is new.

No. 32: On acceptance of persons: the final words in the schema, "customs approved by the Ordinary of the place being safeguarded," have been omitted so as not to undermine the entire article.

No. 35: On the word of God: paragraph 4 on the approval of translations into the vernacular is new. One hundred forty-five votes on this point were void. The next day (December 6, 1962) Archbishop Felici explained this by the fact that many Fathers had already left the hall to join in the *Angelus*, which the Pope was once again reciting with the people after several days of illness.

No. 36: On Latin and the vernaculars: (a) an exception to the use of Latin is granted in paragraph 1, in the phrase "particular law remaining in force."—(b) In paragraph 2 an addition, "in the Mass, etc.," lists the occasions on which the vernacular is acknowledged as useful. The same paragraph had previously said "let greater room be given *(tribuatur)*; this has been replaced by the milder "may be extended" *(tribui valeat)*.— (c) Territorial ecclesiastical authorities need not "make proposals to the Holy See" but are "empowered to decide" *(statuere)*. A condition is added, however: "The enactments of the competent authority are to be approved, that is, confirmed by the Holy See" (= *actis ab Apostolica Sede probatis seu confirmatis*; the earlier text had read *recognitis*); the word *probatis* (approved) is further explained (*seu* = that is) by *confirmatis* (confirmed). The whole phrasing grants much more to the local authorities, since they now have the right to decide, while higher authority reserves only the right to examine and confirm decisions.—(d) Paragraph 4 is new.

No. 37: Admission of local usages into the liturgy: here there is a new addition: "provided they are in keeping with the true and authentic spirit of the liturgy."

At the thirty-sixth general congregation (December 7, 1962), the Introduction and Chapter I were approved. There were, however, 108 *modi*. Since in the commission's judgment none of these touched anything essential, the question was asked on November 18, 1963, if there was agreement on the way the conciliar commission had dealt with the *modi* for the Introduction and Chapter I. The response was favorable: only 20 negative out of 2066.

Chapter II. *The Eucharist*

No. 47: New wording.

No. 49: The Council issues regulations concerning *"Masses celebrated with the assistance of the faithful*, especially on Sundays and holydays of obligation.''

No. 50: The second paragraph is new.

No. 52: On the homily: redone.

No. 54: On the vernaculars: (a) a suitable place "may be allotted" *(tribui potest)*, instead of "is to be allotted" *(tribuatur)*, to the vernaculars.—(b) addition: "but also, as local conditions may warrant, to those parts belonging to the people."—(c) The second paragraph on the possibility of the people saying or singing texts in Latin is an addition.—(d) The third paragraph, on a more extended use of the vernacular, has been added.

No. 55: The first paragraph, on communion at Mass, is new. In the second paragraph the words "to avoid all danger to faith" have been changed to: "the dogmatic principles laid down by the Council of Trent remain intact." The change was suggested by the fact that talk of "dangers" was offensive to the Easterners.

In the amended schema "the professed" and "the newly baptized" were added to "the ordained." A group of Fathers asked that "newlyweds" be added, but the suggestion was not accepted because it was not clear how communion under both kinds was to be given.

No. 57: Concelebration: the article was almost completely revised. "Unity of the Church" was replaced by "unity of the priesthood." There was a lively debate as to what authority was to regulate concelebration: the Ordinary *(Ordinarius)* or the Ordinary of the place *(Ordinarius loci)?* The problem discussed at length in the preparatory commission thus arose again at the Council. The definitive formulation, which distinguishes between "permission" (the Ordinary) and "regulation" (the Ordinary of the place, or bishop), was a happy compromise.

A vote was taken on Chapter II on October 14, 1963, and the definitive vote (after the examination of the *modi*) on November 23, 1963.

Chapter III. *Sacraments and Sacramentals*

No. 60: The introduction is new, as is the first paragraph, which ensures greater room for the vernacular even in the sacramental formula.

No. 68: Baptism: the first sentence is new.

No. 73: Anointing of the sick: the most important revision was in the second
sentence, where the words "as soon as any one of the faithful is seriously ill" were replaced by "as soon as any one of the faithful begins
to be in danger of death from sickness or old age."

No. 76: Episcopal ordination: the second paragraph, on the imposition of hands
by all bishops present, is new.

No. 78: Marriage: the paragraph on the blessing of the spouses even in a celebration without a Mass is new.

No. 79: Sacramentals: the final paragraph, on sacramentals administered by laypersons, is new.

> A vote on Chapter III was taken on October 18, 1963, and the defini-
tive vote on November 12, 1963.

Chapter IV. *The Divine Office*

No. 86: New.

No. 89: The words "it (Matins) shall be made up of fewer psalms and longer
readings" are new.

No. 91: Psalter: the second paragraph was changed.

No. 97: Commutations and dispensations: new.

No. 99: The paragraph on recitation of the Divine Office in common is new.

> A vote on Chapter IV was taken on October 24, 1963, and the defini-
tive vote on November 22, 1963.

Chapter V. *The Liturgical Year*

> The amendments were unimportant. The entire chapter was submitted
to a vote on October 29, 1963, and the definitive vote was taken on
November 22, 1963.

Chapter VI. *Sacred Music*

No. 113: Solemn liturgies: the wording is new and is more general than in the
original text.

No. 115: Musical training: the original text emphasized not only musical training but liturgical formation both for the singers and musicians and for
the congregation. The recommendation has largely been omitted.

No. 120: Organ: the term "organ" has been replaced by "pipe organ."

No. 121: Compositions: the article is partly new.

> A vote was taken on the entire chapter on October 30, 1963, and
the definitive vote on November 22, 1963.

Chapter VIII. *Sacred Art and Sacred Furnishings*

> Chapter VI, on furnishings, was combined with Chapter VIII, on sa-
cred art. New are the first paragraph of article 122, and article 125 on
sacred images. Other amendments were of lesser importance.

A vote was taken on Chapter VIII on October 31, 1963, and the definitive vote on November 22, 1963.

Appendix: *Declaration on the Revision of the Calendar*

The text was taken from Chapter V on the liturgical year and approved on October 30, 1963.

On Wednesday, November 22, 1963, during the seventy-third general congregation, the entire schema was put to a vote and approved with only twenty nays; the date was the sixtieth anniversary of the publication of the motu proprio *Tra le sollecitudini* of St. Pius X.

Cardinal Tisserant, who was presiding that day, thanked the liturgical commission for its excellent work. He remembered Cardinal Gaetano Cicognani, who had directed the work of the preparatory commission, and expressed the hope that the example of the liturgical commission would encourage other commissions and be a spur to them.

III. PROMULGATION

The definitive approval and promulgation of the Constitution on the Sacred Liturgy took place on December 4, 1963, in the presence of Pope Paul VI. The secretary general of the Council, Archbishop Felici, read the beginning and end of each chapter. A vote was then taken; the result was 2147 for, 4 against. The Pope then proceeded to the solemn approval and promulgation "together with the Fathers of the Council."

When the secretary general, Archbishop Felici, announced the results of the vote, his ritual formula was greeted by endlessly prolonged applause that ran from tribune to tribune and throughout the broad naves and vast spaces of the basilica, while a restrained but festive joy was reflected in face after face. "Holy Father, the Constitution on the Liturgy is acceptable to two thousand one hundred forty-seven Fathers, with four against." It was an emotional moment, a historical moment.

The date was exactly four centuries from the day, December 4, 1563, when the Council of Trent, anxious to conclude its work, left to the Holy See the task of effecting a liturgical reform. Such a reform had been called for in many quarters; in the overall plan of the Council of Trent, however, it was regarded as of secondary interest and so ended up as one of the problems the Council left untouched.

Four centuries had passed. What seemed a marginal problem at Trent had become the number one problem at Vatican II and was the first to be dealt with there. Divine providence had played a part in securing it this priority.

In the Pope's name, Archbishop Felici announced that the norms promulgated in the new Constitution would not take effect until the first Sunday of Lent (February 16) in 1964.

In his closing address the Pope spoke as follows of the liturgy:

> The arduous and intricate discussions have certainly borne fruit, for one of the topics—the first to be discussed and, in a certain sense, the first in order of intrinsic excellence and importance for the life of the Church, the schema on the sacred liturgy—has been brought to a happy conclusion. Today We have solemnly promulgated it, and We rejoice at this accomplishment.
>
> We may see in this an acknowledgment of a right order of values and duties: God in the first place; prayer our first duty; the liturgy the first school of spirituality, the first gift which we can bestow on Christians who believe and pray with us. It is the first invitation to the world to break forth in happy and truthful prayer and to feel the ineffable lifegiving force that comes from joining us in the song of divine praise and of human hope, through Christ Our Lord and in the Holy Spirit.
>
> We cannot here pass over in silence the great honor shown to divine worship by the faithful of the Eastern Church, and their accurate and diligent observance of the sacred rites. To these faithful the sacred liturgy has always been a school of truth and a flame of Christian charity.
>
> It would be good to treasure this fruit of our Council as something that should animate and characterize the life of the Church. For the Church is a religious society, a community at prayer. It is composed of people with a flourishing interior life and spirituality that is nourished by faith and grace. If now we wish to simplify our liturgical rites, if we wish to render them more intelligible to the people and accommodated to the language they speak, by so doing we certainly do not wish to lessen the importance of prayer, or to subordinate it to other concerns of the sacred ministry or pastoral activity, or to impoverish its expressive force and artistic appeal. On the contrary, we wish to render the liturgy more pure, more genuine, more in agreement with the source of truth and grace, more suitable to be transformed into a spiritual patrimony of the people.
>
> To attain these ends it is necessary that no attempt should be made to introduce into the official prayer of the Church private changes or unusual rites, nor should anyone arrogate the right arbitrarily to interpret the Constitution on the Liturgy before proper and authoritative instructions are published. Furthermore, the reforms to be prepared by postconciliar bodies must receive official approbation. The nobility of ecclesiastical prayer and its melodious expression throughout the world is something no one would wish to disturb or to damage.[9]

---

9. Paul VI, Address *Tempus iam advenit* at the end of the second session of Vatican II (December 4, 1964), in *The Pope Speaks* 9 (1963–64) 224–25.

4

"Fundamental Principles"

After a lengthy journey in which love, sweat, and suffering played their part, the Constitution on the Sacred Liturgy emerged from the Council to serve as a guide in the renewal of the liturgy of God's people.

In the motu proprio *Rubricarum instructum*, with which Pope John XXIII had promulgated the new code of rubrics on July 25, 1960, the Pope had said that the purpose of the publication was eminently practical: to simplify the rubrics of the Mass and the Divine Office. It would be for the coming ecumenical council to establish the "fundamental principles" *(altiora principia)* of a comprehensive liturgical reform.

The preparatory commission endeavored to search out these principles and set them down in the Constitution. Without attempting an exhaustive inventory, I shall identify two series of principles—guiding and operational—in the constitution *Sacrosanctum Concilium* that was approved by Vatican II.

I. Guiding Principles

1. The Liturgy Is "An Exercise of the Priestly Office of Jesus Christ" (no. 7)

The liturgy is theology in the form of prayer. In its sensible signs the sanctification of human beings is signified and brought about, and at the same time the whole public worship of the Mystical Body of Christ, head and members, is carried out.

At the center of the liturgy is Christ, who by passing from this world to the Father through his death and resurrection became the Lord, the giver of life. This pasch, or passage, of Christ lives on in the sacrament that is the Church, where it has become a mystery of worship, in the celebration of which "the victory and triumph of his death are again made present" (no. 6) and continued in time. The liturgy in its entirety, therefore, is simply the varied celebration of the paschal mystery, according to several aspects of the latter; by means of this celebration Christ is constantly present to the Church, his beloved bride, "who calls to him and through him offers worship to the eternal Father" (no. 7).

The paschal mystery is thus the heart of the entire liturgy. This truth is recalled in nine articles of the Constitution. Only by entering ever anew into this mystery (or, as Tertullian would say, "immersing" itself in it) and drawing all the practical conclusions from this relationship will the world find salvation; only thus will Christian life be radically renewed.

All this begets a new attitude toward liturgical actions and sacramentals. These should increasingly become a "celebration," that is, the glorification of God for the salvation which Christ has accomplished and which the Church makes present and operative for us in the Holy Spirit. Attention is no longer focused on the minimum required for the validity of liturgical actions nor simply on their outward form considered in isolation, but on the congregation that has gathered to hear and respond to God's word, share in the sacrament, remember the Lord Jesus, and give thanks to God the Father, by whose great mercy "we have been reborn to a living hope through the resurrection of Jesus Christ from the dead" (1 Pet 1:3).

2. The Liturgy as "Summit and Fount" of the Church's Life

A liturgical celebration is the supreme sacred action of the Church. At the heart of the Constitution is a profound meditation on the mystery of the Church, which is looked upon as being a flood of love pouring from the open side of the crucified Christ (no. 5). The liturgy is the sign that offers the truest and fullest image of the Church: a worshiping community gathered around a single altar, under the presidency of its lawful pastors. But the symbol also becomes the reality, for the Eucharist feeds the Church; the Church continually grows and renews itself through the celebration of the Eucharist and the administration of the sacraments.

No other ecclesial action, therefore, is as efficacious as the celebration of the liturgy. The latter is the culmination toward which all evangelizing and pastoral activity are aimed; at the same time it is the source of the supernatural life that nourishes the Church's being and activity.

The celebration of the liturgy is the exercise of Christ's priestly power by which God is glorified and human beings are sanctified.

The liturgy is thus the unifying center of all of the Church's activity. Evangelization and catechetical instruction are not ends in themselves but have for their purpose to help human beings attain to full communion with God and participation in the salvation which Christ has accomplished and which is made present in liturgical celebrations. The song that is the liturgy kindles love of God in the hearts of the faithful and brings them to a full realization of his interventions in their behalf; it inspires them to tell others what they themselves have seen and contemplated, and to bear witness by their lives to what they have received through faith (see no. 10). The centrality of the liturgy must be kept in mind in teaching, catechetics, and pastoral practice.

3. *Full, Conscious, Active Participation*

The very nature of the liturgy, as well as the baptismal character that makes of the faithful "a chosen race, a royal priesthood, a holy nation, a people God has made his own to praise his wonders," requires that they be led to a "full, conscious, and active participation in liturgical celebrations" (no. 14). This participation is both their right and their duty. The full and active participation of all the people has been a special concern in the reform and promotion of the liturgy, for the liturgy is the primary and indispensable source from which the faithful can derive the true Christian spirit. This thought has been the basic motive at work in the modern liturgical renewal and the conciliar document.

No article in the Constitution is unaffected by the idea that the liturgy, which is the worship and adoration of God, also effects the sanctification of human beings and must therefore be understood, followed, and shared by the entire community of the faithful. That thought returns over and over, whatever the subject—liturgical formation and instruction; the adaptation of the liturgy to the mentalities and customs of the various peoples; communal celebration; language; the more extensive reading of the Sacred Scriptures; the Mass; the sacraments; the Divine Office, which should be a form of prayer that the faithful also love; the liturgical year; sacred music and sacred art. Everything is presented with an eye on the conscious and devout participation that should result from the properly organized instruction of the faithful and, even before that, from the development in priests and seminarians of a strong and comprehensive sense of the liturgy.

4. *Manifestation of the Church* (no. 26)

The celebration of the liturgy—when the whole people of God gathers for full and active participation in the same action, around the same altar, in the unity of prayer—is the supreme manifestation of the Church. And because the Church is the "sacrament of unity," liturgical actions belong to the whole Body of Christ (no. 26). Communal celebration is therefore always to be preferred to individual celebration. Communal celebrations show forth the nature of the Church as a hierarchically organized community; all play a part, but each member has his or her task, depending on the ministry received, the nature of the rite, and the principles of liturgy (see nos. 27-30).

The path opened up by the Council will surely bring a radical change in the very appearance of traditional liturgical assemblies, for in these the liturgical action, in keeping with age-old custom, has been carried out almost exclusively by the clergy, while the people have too often "attended" as mute spectators from outside. Patient education will be needed to make it understood that the liturgy is the action of the people of God. This education will not affect the liturgy alone; it will also have a beneficial influence on the development of a sense of the Church and will give rise to a variety of ministries in the service of the community.

5. "Substantial Unity," Not "Rigid Uniformity" (no. 38)

This principle represents a momentous departure from past practice. For centuries the Church willed that all worship in the Roman Rite should everywhere show perfect uniformity. The two liturgical reforms which history has recorded—that of the eighth century and that promoted by the Council of Trent in the sixteenth century—had precisely that aim. The six liturgical books published in typical, or normative, editions from 1568 to 1614 became the rule book for the Church's prayer for four centuries; no one was allowed to "add or subtract" from it. Bishops were the watchful guardians who saw to it that whatever the Holy See, the sole legislator in matters liturgical (Code of 1917, can. 1257), decreed was in fact faithfully observed. In 1587 Pope Sixtus V established the Sacred Congregation of Rites as the supreme agency "for protecting the sacred rites," and the seven volumes containing the approximately five thousand decrees issued by that agency down to our time are so many witnesses to the scrupulous care with which the supreme authority in the Church defended the law of a single form of prayer for the entire Church.

Social, religious, cultic, and cultural conditions, and indeed the entire psychological climate, have changed radically in our day. The peoples in the developing countries who are opening themselves to the light of the gospel feel an urgent need not to abandon the many things that are an authentic expression of the national soul and constitute their cultural patrimony, even if one that is at times in a pristine state, still bound up with deeply rooted usages and customs.

For this reason the Constitution, echoing the thinking in recent magisterial documents, makes the following statement:

> Even in the liturgy the Church has no wish to impose a rigid uniformity in matters that do not affect the faith or the good of the whole community; rather the Church respects and fosters the genius and talents of the various races and peoples. The Church considers with sympathy and, if possible, preserves intact the elements in these peoples' way of life that are not indissolubly bound up with superstition and error. Sometimes in fact the Church admits such elements into the liturgy itself, provided they are in keeping with the true and authentic spirit of the liturgy (no. 37).

And in the next article it goes on to say:

> Provision shall also be made . . . for legitimate variations and adaptations to different groups, regions, and peoples, especially in mission lands, provided the substantial unity of the Roman Rite is preserved; this should be borne in mind when rites are drawn up and rubrics devised (no. 38).[1]

This principle is in fact applied throughout the Constitution, thus giving new meaning to the word "unity" and new vigor to the word "catholicity," two notes or marks that must remain inviolable characteristics of liturgical prayer, just as they are of the Church itself.[2]

The attention given to catholicity within basic unity also has legislative consequences. The complete centralization effected by the Council of Trent now makes way, in matters liturgical, to three levels of authority: the Holy See, episcopal conferences, and diocesan bishops. Regulation of the liturgy now depends on all three, even if in varying degrees (no. 22). In particular, the Constitution reminds the local bishop that as "high priest of his flock," he has an obligation to foster the liturgical life by his example and by the use of all necessary means.

6. *"Sound Tradition" and "Legitimate Progress"* (no. 23)

The liturgy has two dimensions: one invisible, unchanging, and everlasting; the other, human, visible, and changeable. What is of divine institution is evidently untouchable and unchangeable. The same cannot

---

1. The principle of adaptation is applied to the various subjects as they come up: see no. 65 (baptism), no. 77 (marriage), no. 81 (funerals), no. 119 (sacred music), no. 123 (sacred art).

2. See A. Bugnini, "La liturgia fonte e culmine della vita della chiesa," *Fede e Arte* 12 (1964) 6–11.

be said of what the Church, whose action extends through time and covers the entire world, has established in order to clothe the divine elements of worship in signs and rites that will bring to light the riches and hidden meaning of the mystery.

Signs and rites are likely to become incrusted by time, that is, to grow old and outmoded. They may therefore need to be revised and updated, so that the expression of the Church's worship may reflect the perennial youthfulness of the Church itself.

This kind of change is vitally necessary for a living organism. The liturgy feeds the Church's life; it must therefore remain dynamic and not be allowed to stagnate or become petrified. Pius XII said as much in 1947 in this lapidary sentence: "The liturgy is something lasting and alive."[3] And John XXIII: "The liturgy must not become a relic in a museum but remain the living prayer of the Church."

This is not to deny that the visible and human part of the liturgy may contain priceless elements that have been sanctified by age-old tradition and are therefore to some extent untouchable and to be approached only with respect, love, and veneration. Tradition thus gives protection. But, apart from the properly theological content of the liturgy, what else in it can be called "traditional"? It has been said that "in important matters authentic tradition consists not in restoring what others have done, but in rediscovering the spirit that brought those things into existence and that would do other, completely different things at other times."

"To rediscover the spirit": this requires research and review; a scrupulously careful and diligent determination of what makes up the sacred patrimony so that a valid appraisal may emerge objectively and, as it were, naturally and spontaneously from study, meditation, and prayer:

> That sound tradition may be retained and yet the way remain open to legitimate progress, a careful investigation is always to be made into each part of the liturgy to be revised. This investigation should be theological, historical, and pastoral. Also the general laws governing the structure and meaning of the liturgy must be studied in conjunction with the experience derived from recent liturgical reforms and from the indults conceded to various places. Finally, there must be no innovations unless the good of the Church genuinely and certainly requires them; care must be taken that any new forms adopted should in some way grow organically from forms already existing (no. 23).

---

3. Bugnini, *Documenta*, 95.

In light of what is said here, the only legitimate attitude is uncompromising defense of what is truly an untouchable patrimony because it is in some way inherent in the nature of the rites, and a diligent and scrupulously careful evaluation—based on thorough study, meditation, and prayer—of the other elements of the liturgy, in order to adapt them to the teaching, mission, and mystery of the Church, which today, as in every age, must bring the message of salvation to souls by appropriate means.

Rediscovery of the spirit, then, and the effort to make the rites speak the language of our own time so that the men and women of today may understand the language of the rites, which is both mysterious and sacred. Needed is a process of research and revision. This does not meaning putting the liturgy on trial, as it were; there are no accused, much less guilty, parties here. The aim is simply to look at elements which may have come down to us as the fruit of a particular setting and a particular occasion and which may no longer be, or be only with difficulty, visible witnesses to the reign of grace.[4]

II. Operational Principles

1. *Language*

The problem most keenly felt in the area of liturgy was that of the language to be used. It was a difficult and touchy problem with two sides, both of which raised many questions. On the one hand, there was the tradition of the Latin Church and the advantages of using a single, sacred language that was also sufficiently technical from the liturgical and juridical points of view. On the other hand, there was the fact that use of a language unintelligible to many weakened the message itself and made divine realities less trenchantly present. The alternatives were to abandon to a great extent the Latin that was an age-old patrimony of the Church or to reduce the effectiveness of what is the most natural, spontaneous, and expressive of all signs—the language we use. Given these alternatives, the Council did not hesitate but decreed the introduction of the vernaculars into the liturgy. As Pope Paul VI was to say with St.

---

4. See G. Fallani, "In preparazione al Concilio Vaticano II. L'Arte sacra e la liturgia," *Fede e Arte* 10 (1962) 18–25. This article was the opening address at the ninth Settimana di Arte Sacra in Italia, held at Rome, October 23–28, 1961. The author brings out well the relations between sacred art and liturgy, and the requirements of an artistic kind that a pastoral liturgy brings into focus.

Augustine: "It is better to have the learned reproach us than to have the liturgy remain unintelligible to the people."

The mother tongues in the liturgy do not replace but accompany the traditional Latin with its melodious beauty and special genius, a language at once sturdy and austere, radiant and seductive, a language in which countless generations of Christians have prayed. The vernaculars will not impoverish the liturgy but enrich it; they will make it easier to converse with God, especially in parochial communities. Nonetheless, even where the vernacular is used most of the time, vestiges are to be kept, in all times and places, of the enduring primitive liturgy. Thus, the Council decreed that the Latin songs for Mass should be everywhere known. This will facilitate great international gatherings that are united under the sign of common prayer.

2. The Word of God

After centuries of neglect, the word of God is regaining its place as alive and life-giving in all the liturgical rites. First the word, then the sacrament or blessing. This pedagogical approach, used even by God, changed over the centuries and reached us in a defective, distorted, and skeletal form. We have returned to the principle: no liturgical action without the word as part of it.

It was objected both in the central commission and at the Council that the majority of the faithful are not prepared to absorb large amounts of the Scriptures. Some thought it enough to make full use of what is given in the Tridentine Roman Missal. The Council, however, put its trust in the ability of the word to form Christians. Above all, it believed what it approved in the Constitution: that Christ "is present in his word, since it is he himself who speaks when the holy Scriptures are read in the Church" (no. 7); that he "is still proclaiming his Gospel" (no. 33).

The Council therefore urged that Scripture be given a place "of greatest importance in the celebration of the liturgy" and that pastors foster "a warm and living love" for it (no. 24); that preaching be based on it, that Bible services be encouraged (no. 35), and that the treasures of the Bible be opened up more lavishly and with greater variety (nos. 51; 35).

3. Catechetical Instruction

The liturgical renewal that the Constitution expects and promotes cannot be achieved by a more or less mechanical observance of a certain number of prescriptions, norms, and ceremonial regulations. It requires a spirit, a mentality, a soul. It requires an "initiation" or education in the liturgy. The need for instruction based on the liturgy is attested in even the earliest patristic tradition. Even today we are amazed as we read the instructions that the Fathers gave the newly baptized and the sermons they preached on the liturgical feasts. What we find there is a whole catechetical method that is based on the word of God and on the "rites and prayers" used in the celebrations.

That same method is inculcated by the Constitution, namely, that the faithful are to be brought to an understanding of the liturgy through "the rites and prayers" (no. 48); through instruction in the Bible, especially the psalms (no. 90); and, indirectly, through the training of those who are more immediately involved in the celebrations: singers, servers, readers, commentators (no. 29). Only an ongoing, tireless catechesis can help the faithful enter into the world of the liturgy.

No results may be expected, however, unless priests themselves are first given a liturgical formation. The Constitution therefore insists on the teaching of liturgy in seminaries, on the formation of priests, and on the thorough training of professors (nos. 15-18). It also emphasizes the need for liturgical commissions at the diocesan, interdiocesan, and national levels, made up of experts in liturgy, music, sacred art, and pastoral practice (nos. 44-46). The Constitution thus calls for the efforts of the entire Church structure; without these efforts the prospects opened up by the Constitution will remain simply words on a page.

4. Singing

The communal nature of the liturgy and the beauty it should have require the presence of song. Song gives sweetness to the expression of prayer, promotes the union of minds, and makes rites more solemn. Song is not something added on from outside; it springs from the very nature of the celebration. A celebration is always a feast, a glorification of God, a commemoration of the Easter victory of Christ. Profound participation in such a celebration is inconceivable apart from its joyous expression in song. The Constitution regards singing as "a necessary or integral part of the solemn liturgy" (no. 112). The liturgy will therefore always be marked by the presence of song.

The priceless musical heritage of the past is to be preserved. In addition, the adoption of the vernaculars marks the beginning of a laborious work—the creation of new songs whose text and music will be worthy of the worship of God. The work will take years and will call for continual improvement, but it is indispensable if the liturgy is to be alive and touch the heart, and if the people are to take an active part in it.

5. *Reform of the Liturgy*

The directives and principles set down in the Constitution amount to a general mobilization of the entire Church. The pastors of local Churches, along with all their pastoral workers, are urged to start the process of educating the faithful in the liturgy, familiarizing them with the Scriptures, and getting them actively involved in the celebration through listening and singing and through acclamations, prayers, and responses. In addition, they are to begin the work of translating the liturgical books; this a completely new field, full of difficulties and responsibilities.

At the same time, the Holy See pledges itself to undertake a general reform of the liturgy (no. 21) according to the principles set down by the Council in the Constitution on the Sacred Liturgy. The reform will be a labor of sensitive, intelligent renewal, in which "elements that, with the passage of time, came to be duplicated or were added with but little advantage are now to be discarded; other elements that have suffered injury through accident of history are now, as may seem useful or necessary, to be restored to the vigor they had in the tradition of the Fathers" (no. 50). It will be a work of simplification, so that the rites may radiate what the Constitution calls "a noble simplicity" and be "short, clear, and unencumbered by useless repetitions; they should be within the people's powers of comprehension and as a rule not require much explanation" (no. 34). It will be a work that concentrates on essentials, while not neglecting what is secondary if it is cohesive with the essentials and has a useful pastoral purpose.

These various areas of activity will require a considerable effort and will bring the Church's best powers into play for a number of years. Neither the revision of the liturgical books nor their translation can be simply improvised. Nor can the training of the faithful be accomplished by a few brief instructions, but only by a slow, persevering, intelligent, and prolonged effort.

The principles set down by the Council will be reduced to practice in a gradual process. The road will be long and difficult, but also sure. At the end the Church will have a renewed liturgy that will give God's people once again a sense of the sacred mystery and help them to enter into it.

The "Constituent Assembly" of the Consilium

The practical implementation of the liturgical Constitution began immediately. Delay was indefensible in view of the importance and extent of the undertaking, the lively expectations that discussion of the conciliar document had aroused everywhere in the Church, and the ferment of renewal that was beginning to give rise in some places to arbitrary initiatives. Even during the second session some bishops and experts were already interested in how the program of renewal was to be organized and in the first concrete applications of the Constitution.

On the morning of January 3, 1964, Cardinal Amleto G. Cicognani, Secretary of State, summoned Father Bugnini and told him that the Holy Father had appointed him secretary of the commission that was to implement the Constitution. The message was only verbal. The official appointment came in a letter from the Secretariat of State, dated January 13. It read:

> The Holy Father has graciously deigned to establish a "Council for the Implementation of the Constitution on the Sacred Liturgy"[1] and at the same

---

1. *Consilium* (Council) was chosen by the Latinists as being "more classical" than *Commissio* (Commission). The meaning, however, was the same. In fact, among the postconciliar bodies we find a "Council for the Laity" and a "Cor Unum Council," but also a "Commission for Justice and Peace," a "Commission for the Revision of the Code of Canon Law," and a "Commission for Social Communications."

A different view was taken, however, by those who interpreted a *consilium* as being a body whose purpose was to do research, prepare projects, and offer opinions, thus making room for a second commission that would evaluate this material and make timely decisions. Such a commission could only be located within the Congregation of Rites. And in fact such a commission was set up in February 1964, and the deputy of the Congregation

time is pleased to number among its members Their Eminences Cardinals
Giacomo Lercaro, Archbishop of Bologna, Paolo Giobbe, and Arcadio Larraona, and to appoint the Reverend Annibale Bugnini, of the Congregation of the Mission, as its secretary.

This act established what Pope Paul VI liked to call the "constituent assembly" for the Consilium.

The announcement of the new entity came on January 25, 1964, in
the motu proprio *Sacram Liturgiam*, while the announcement of the membership was made in *L'Osservatore Romano* for January 28. The motu
proprio did not give the commission a name, nor did it specify its competence. It said only that the commission was established to see that the
prescriptions of the liturgical Constitution were put into effect.[2] Meanwhile, however, the Consilium had already begun its labors and was continuing them by establishing its organization and defining its task.

The "constituent assembly" held its first meeting on January 15. On
its agenda were a communication from Cardinal Lercaro; an examination of the draft of the motu proprio; a working program; a discussion
of possible members. The Cardinal President limited himself to some general remarks on the goals of the Consilium, "which the Holy Father has
established for implementing the entire program set down in the conciliar Constitution on the Sacred Liturgy," and on the serious nature of
the task assigned. The secretary presented a first outline of the work to
be done.

A month later, on February 15, the second meeting took place, this
time, as a mark of respect, in the apartment of Cardinal Larraona, Via
Serristori, 10. The group examined the list of suggested members of the
Consilium that was to be presented to the Holy Father. The list was unanimously approved and, after being confirmed by the Holy Father, was published in *L'Osservatore Romano* on March 5, 1964.

At that same meeting, March 11 was chosen as the date for the first
general meeting of the Consilium. In addition, a first study group was
established, this one for the revision of the Psalter; it was made up of
six of the best qualified biblical experts living in Rome. The priority given
to the appointment of this group was justified by the fact that revision

---

of Rites was put in charge of it. But it was short-lived. When the Pope was informed of
its existence, he firmly supported the full authority of the Consilium and suppressed the
commission.

The remainder of the name—"ad exsequendam Constitutionem de sacra Liturgia"—
was thought up by Archbishop Felici, secretary of the Council, who wished to express the
purpose of the body by means of this somewhat baroque title.

2. *AAS* 56 (1964) 140. Translated in *DOL* 20 nos. 276-89; see no. 278.

of the Psalms would take a long time and that delay in this work might interfere with the orderly rhythm and progress of the other groups.

In taking these steps, the "constituent assembly" of the Consilium had accomplished its mandate, and it therefore ceased to exist. The Secretariat of State had set forth the tasks of the Consilium as follows in a letter of February 29, 1964, to Cardinal Lercaro:

> I have the honor of communicating to Your Eminence, in keeping with the directives of Pope Paul VI, the responsibilities of the Consilium for the Carrying out of the Constitution on the Liturgy, of which Your Eminence is President. They are as follows:
>
> a. to suggest the names of the persons charged with forming study groups for the revision of rites and liturgical books;
>
> b. to oversee and coordinate the work of the study groups;
>
> c. to prepare carefully an instruction explaining the practical application of the Motu Proprio *Sacram Liturgiam* and clearly outlining the competence of territorial ecclesiastical authorities, pending the reform of the rites and liturgical books;
>
> d. to apply, according to the letter and spirit of the Council, the Constitution it approved, by responding to the proposals of the conferences of bishops and to questions that arise involving the correct application of the Constitution.
>
> Appeals of decisions of the Consilium as well as the solution of particularly sensitive and grave or completely new problems will be referred by the Consilium to the pope.[3]

This document, which has always been regarded as the constitutional charter of the Consilium, gave the new entity a recognizable face. There had in fact been no little uncertainty about its juridical status. Some thought it should be simply a consultative body or a study group, with any administrative functions being left entirely to the Congregation of Rites. But this conception of it was rejected.

It was next proposed that the Consilium be a joint commission headed by the prefect of the Congregation of Rites. But this again was not agreeable.

The outcome of the discussion was the letter cited above, which made the Consilium an authoritative study group that also had temporary administrative functions and was directly dependent on the Pope. The Consilium was therefore closer in structure to an agency of the Curia than to a commission.

The final sentence of the letter: "Appeals of decisions . . . as well as the solution of particularly sensitive and grave or completely new prob-

---

3. Letter *Mi onoro di communicare: EDIL* 191 = *DOL* 77 no. 613.

lems will be referred by the Consilium to the pope," was both the strength and the weakness of the Consilium.[4]

Once the appointment of members was completed, the Consilium was fully established. It had forty-two members: cardinals, archbishops and bishops, a Benedictine abbot, three priests. Later on the number was increased, to a maximum of fifty-one, in order to allow for better representation of countries, situations, and problems.[5]

Now that the Consilium was organized, the first question was where it was to be located. When Father Bugnini asked where he should make arrangements for the new body, Cardinal Cicognani answered tersely: "Wherever you wish, but not at the Congregation of Rites." With this possibility excluded, Father Bugnini looked elsewhere. Each of the conciliar commissions had been assigned a location of its own on the fourth floor of the pontifical Ospizio di Santa Marta, but none of them had in fact moved there, each preferring to remain at its respective curial agency.[6] The Consilium settled initially for the two rooms that had been assigned to the liturgical commission; gradually, however, it took over the entire floor. It was in these small rooms, isolated as it were between heaven and earth, and in the hall for pilgrims on the ground floor, which the Consilium shared, that the liturgical reform was carried out until Novem-

---

4. "Strength" because of the security given by the trust and support of the Holy Father; "weakness" because the juridical formula used was novel and weak. On the one hand, the Sacred Congregation of Rites regarded itself as the juridical organ of the Holy See for handling liturgical matters, and it tended to look upon the Consilium as simply a study group, and therefore as having no autonomy. On the other hand, the lack of a more detailed set of regulations for its functioning did not help a continually growing body to act flexibly.

The reluctance to accept not simply the competence but even the very existence of the Consilium was also shown by the fact that despite repeated requests, the letter of February 29 was never published in the *Acta Apostolicae Sedis*, and the list of members, which had appeared in *L'Osservatore Romano*, was not published in the *Acta* until June, and then only after the obituaries (see *AAS* 56 [1964] 479). Mere coincidence?

A second letter from the Secretariat of State, dated January 7, 1965, further clarified the respective competencies of the Congregation of Rites and the Consilium by giving to the latter the duty of overseeing and regulating the experimental phase of new rites, and to the former the duty of giving juridical force to the definitive publication of these rites; see *EDIL* 379 = *DOL* 82 no. 625, and the address of the Holy Father to the Consilium on October 13, 1966, in *AAS* 58 (1966) 1145-50 = *DOL* 84 nos. 630-36. Other responsibilities were given to the Consilium as the work proceeded. At the psychological level, however, a good deal of water still had to pass under the bridge!

5. See the list on pp. 942ff. (and, in slightly different form, in *DOL* 78 no. 614).

6. Hardly had the news spread that the Consilium had settled in at S. Marta than all the commissions hurried to occupy their own locations there, and we had a good deal of difficulty in persuading them to let us have a little room to move in. "Don't stand on ceremony; just take over," a high-ranking prelate suggested.

ber 1969, when the Consilium, now transformed into the Congregation for Divine Worship, was assigned the bright and airy fourth floor of the Palazzo delle Congregazioni, 10 Piazza Pio XII, for its offices.

While the intense work of liturgical reform went on, we looked down from above, between the presbytery of St. Peter's, the Camposanto Teutonico, and the stern palace of the Holy Office, on the great scaffolding for the splendid audience hall. This was the period when the old irregular buildings around the Chapel of St. Peter were being razed; pneumatic drills were thrusting sixty to seventy meters down for the mighty pillars of reinforced concrete that would support the prodigious vault of architect Nervi. Day after day for five years we watched the steel, at once slender and strong, rise into the air for this gigantic building. Here were two workyards in close proximity: both intended for the people of God, both of them eloquent symbols and consoling realities.

After the location, the personnel. The secretariat was kept to a minimum. In fact, for a year it consisted of only three persons.[7] Then a few were added, but the total number was never more than nine or ten.[8] There was a reason for the limitation. We did not want too many people at the center, since the reform was to be brought about chiefly by bishops and experts who would be drawn "from various parts of the world" according to the liturgical Constitution (no. 25) and would represent the thinking, hopes, and desires of the local Churches. The secretariat's role would be to organize the work and serve as a liaison.

In compensation, the people working in the secretariat were always young; they were specialists; and they formed an international group, with the principal languages being represented: French, English, Spanish, German, and, of course, Italian.

---

7. In addition to the secretary, there were Father Carlo Braga, C.M., editor of *Ephemerides Liturgicae* and assigned to the Congregation of Rites, and Father Gottardo Pasqualetti, of the Missionari della Consolata, who had recently gotten his doctorate in theology at the Pontifical Urban University.

8. Those who worked (some only briefly) in the secretariat included: Don Piero Marini, of the diocese of Bobbio; Father Gaston Fontaine, of the Canons Regular of the Immaculate Conception, founder and director of the liturgical movement in French-speaking Canada; Franz Nikolasch, at that time professor of liturgy in the University of Salzburg; Father John Rotelle, O.S.A., at that time secretary of the liturgical commission of the United States bishops and of the International Commission for English in the Liturgy; Monsignor Peter Coughlan, of England; Geri Broccolo, of the archdiocese of Chicago; Father Ignacio Calabuig, O.S.M., professor at the Marianum; D. Carmelo García del Valle, a Spaniard; Father Hermann Gräf, of the Divine Word Fathers, a missionary in the Philippines. All of them, in addition to theological studies in the universities, had attended the courses in liturgy at the Pontifical Institute of San Anselmo in Rome, or in Paris or Trier. Among the laypersons: Dr. Roman Rus, a Slovene; Marcello Olivi and Domenico Santolamazza.

6

The Motu Proprio Sacram Liturgiam

I. History

When Pope Paul VI received the four cardinal moderators of the Council in an audience on October 10, 1963, he told them that he wanted to mark the end of the second session with a document indicating those norms in the liturgical Constitution that could be immediately applied. It would be a kind of partial law that would be given to the Fathers before they left Rome. The Pope gave Cardinal Lercaro the responsibility of preparing such a document.

The next day, October 11, Cardinal Lercaro summoned Father Bugnini and asked him to offer a list of people who would help him in this task. The list was ready on October 12, and that afternoon nine experts gathered with Cardinal Lercaro, who was staying with the Benedictine Sisters at S. Priscilla on the Via Salaria. The work was divided up as follows: Canon Martimort was charged with studying what the Pope's undertaking might signify for Chapter I of the Constitution; J. A. Jungmann for Chapter II (Mass); C. Vagaggini and F. McManus for Chapter III (sacraments); H. Schmidt for Chapter IV (Divine Office); Monsignor Wagner for Chapters VII and VIII (sacred art and sacred music); Monsignor E. Bonet was to look to the juridical aspect; A. Bugnini, finally, would act as secretary for the group.

The experts were urged not to include too much, however attractive; they were to limit themselves to essentials. The suggestions were to be formulated as a series of paragraphs. Extreme reserve was requested, of course; the experts could consult with one another but not with anyone outside of the group.

A schedule was then set up: October 19 and 20: meeting at San Gregorio al Celio (at C. Vagaggini's); October 25 and 26, at Cardinal Lercaro's; October 30: final meeting.

The work proceeded rapidly. On October 20 a first sketch of the document was ready; it began with the words "Constitutio de sacra Liturgia." On the following days Monsignor Bonet completely recast the document on the basis of the examination of it by the experts. It was divided into two parts: a motu proprio (entitled "Primitiae"), which determined the juridical aspects, and an instruction, which gave practical norms for implementation.

Both parts were examined at length by Father Giulio Bevilacqua during the early days of November. Further revisions were made until the definitive draft was given to the Holy Father on November 21. It was now too late, however, for the document to undergo necessary revisions and still be ready on time. The end of the session was at hand, and the document on the liturgy that the Pope announced in his closing address (December 4, 1963) was put off until later.[1]

In the first days of January the secretariat of the Council, which was in charge, and the Congregation of Rites took a hand. It was decided to go back to the original plan of a single document that would be juridical in character.

The three cardinals who had recently been appointed members of the Consilium had received a copy of the proposed document from Archbishop Felici. They studied it at a meeting on January 15 and decided that it should be revised. The beginning and end of the draft sent to them by Archbishop Felici should be kept, but in the part containing the regulations fuller use was to be made of the draft that the experts had prepared back in October. But these proposals had no great influence on the final redaction.

L'Osservatore Romano for January 29, 1964, published the awaited motu proprio *Sacram Liturgiam*, which was dated January 25, feast of the Conversion of St. Paul and anniversary of the announcement of a council by Pope John XXIII five years earlier.[2]

---

1. The Pope announced that "proper and authoritative instructions" would be published before the end of the *vacatio legis* (February 16, 1964) and that postconciliar bodies would by then have made preparations for the reform; see his address at the end of the second session (December 4, 1963) in *AAS* 56 (1964) 34; English translation in *The Pope Speaks* 9 (1963–64) 225.

2. *AAS* 56 (1964) 139–44; *DOL* 20 nos. 276-89.

II. CONTENT

After an introduction in which the liturgy was described as a source of spiritual life for priests and faithful, the document listed those provisions of the Constitution on the Liturgy that were to go into effect at the end of the *vacatio legis* period. In this list the simple but noble language of the Constitution was able from time to time to infuse into the dry legal statements the warmth of ascetical and spiritual motivation that was to be found in almost every article of the conciliar document.

The first condition for a liturgical renewal is the formation of the clergy, both diocesan and religious, in seminaries, religious institutes, and theological faculties. The motu proprio specified that with the beginning of the next academic year (1964–65), the pertinent articles of the Constitution (nos. 15-17) were to be implemented—that is, qualified professors were to be trained at suitable institutions specializing in liturgy (no. 15); the liturgy was to be taught under its theological, historical, ascetical, and pastoral aspects and its harmonious connection with the other main disciplines (no. 16); the life of the seminary was to be grounded in the spirit of the liturgy (no. 17).

It is clear that if the liturgy was to be introduced among the "compulsory and major" or "principal" courses (no. 16) and time was to be allowed for the changes this would necessitate in the number of hours for various subjects, the years of instruction in them, and other organizational matters, then the competent agency of the Holy See would have to publish appropriate norms in good time. Only thus could the new regulations be introduced in an orderly way *(ordinate)* and with the generous and intelligent cooperation and good will *(diligenter)* of all concerned (Motu Proprio I).

The second norm (II) has to do with the diocesan, interdiocesan, and regional liturgical commissions, for which provision had already been made in *Mediator Dei* (1947) and which were again emphasized in the Instruction on Sacred Music and Sacred Liturgy of September 3, 1958 (no. 118). In those two documents the liturgy was closely linked, from the organizational viewpoint, with sacred music and sacred art. The conciliar Constitution and the motu proprio carried this harmonization still further. Worship of the Lord should take place amid the delightful beauty provided by the arts, in sacred edifices that welcome and uplift, amid unobtrusive and invigorating harmonies, and with texts, formulas, songs, and gestures that invite the faithful to raise their hearts in prayer. Music, art, and liturgy retain their autonomy as far as the techniques of each are concerned, but they ought to be constantly working together, from the organizational standpoint, so as better to achieve their common purpose: the worship of the Lord, which emerges like a delicate flower from the synchronous operation of this indivisible sacred trio.

The third provision (III), on the homily, is simply a reminder; of itself it adds nothing to the corresponding article 52 of the Constitution, which in turn fully reflects existing legislation and is the echo of an age-old tradition.

But the emphasis on the reminder highlights the spirit at work in the conciliar norms and the Church's desire that the homily at Mass be a stable and indispensable part of the pastoral ministry. The priest is not to be easily excused from speaking to the "holy assembly" the living word that elucidates what has been read, that exhorts and enlightens, that strengthens and inspires and nourishes the Christian life. The priest who acts thus is God's spokesperson for the gathered faithful, the minister of the Church and authoritative commentator.

The next two articles of the motu proprio (IV and V) deal with confirmation and marriage. They contain some interesting, though expected, details. Confirmation can be administered within Mass, after the gospel and the homily.

Marriage is normally (*de more*) to be celebrated within Mass, again after the gospel and homily. If for good reasons it is celebrated without a Mass, it is to be preceded by a short instruction, as provided and advised for all rites in article 35, §3 of the Constitution. For this reason, the epistle and gospel of the wedding Mass are to be read in the vernacular at these ceremonies without a Mass; at the end of the rite the blessing provided in the Roman Ritual is to be given. This blessing is always given, even if the marriage is celebrated, under proper dispensation, during the "closed seasons." In this case—and this is something to be emphasized in instructions—there must be none of the pomp, display, and ostentation that are out of keeping with the penitential character of Lent and Advent. The Church does not, however, wish to deprive the spouses of the special blessing reserved for them, so that they may not lack the Lord's help at the moment when they stand before the altar and take upon themselves such demanding and solemn duties for the rest of their lives.

The next four articles (VI-IX) have to do with the clergy and the fulfillment of their first obligation: the prayer of the Divine Office. Article VI decrees that those not obliged to choral recitation may omit the Hour of Prime and may say only one of the other Little Hours, selecting the one that best suits the time of day at which it is celebrated. The omission of Prime went beyond the provisions of the Constitution, which called for the suppression of Prime when the Office was reformed and for the use of some individual prayers in the other parts of the liturgy of praise. This regulation of the motu proprio was therefore a benign concession, in the true and proper sense, by the Pope.

In like manner, a reason which the letter of the Constitution (no. 97) describes simply as "just" but which its spirit would describe also as "exceptional," can—but only in particular cases—justify Ordinaries in dispensing their subjects, in whole or in part, from the Divine Office or replacing it with another form of prayer (VII).

Religious families of whatever rank or kind which say all or part of the Divine Office or which are obliged by their constitutions to recite Little Offices modeled on the Roman Breviary form part of the joyful choir of the Church at prayer. Their prayer, whether communal or individual, counts as the prayer of the mystical bride (VIII).

Finally, the pontifical document more clearly defines (IX-X), on the basis of article 36 of the Constitution on the Liturgy, the competence of territorial ecclesiastical authorities (for the moment this meant national episcopal conferences) in regard to use of the vernacular. Furthermore, when these assemblies make decisions on liturgical matters, coadjutor and auxiliary bishops may be invited to attend. To be lawful, these decisions require two-thirds of the votes in a secret balloting.

III. AGREEMENTS AND DISAGREEMENTS

In substance, the motu proprio granted little of the much that the Constitution had promised. But we must keep in mind the principle of gradualness that had to be followed in the practical implementation of the conciliar document, as well as an admitted mistrust and concern in face of the impatience of some who were already launching into rash courses of action without adequate preparation of clergy or faithful.

This concern explains the reminder given in article 22 of the Constitution and frequently repeated from 1964 on. Pope Paul VI had already emphasized it in his closing address of December 4, 1963: "No attempt should be made to introduce into the official prayer of the Church private changes or unusual rites. . . . The nobility of ecclesiastical prayer and its melodious expression throughout the world is something no one would wish to disturb or damage."[3]

The much-awaited document was joyously received at the beginning. Disagreements developed, however, as soon as liturgists and pastors had the text in their hands and could read it carefully. The strongest criticisms came from Italy, Germany, Austria, France, and Spain. A chief objection

---

3. *The Pope Speaks* 9 (1963–64) 225.

was the limitation to episcopal conferences of the right to approve translations in the vernacular;[4] this was interpreted as a first maneuver of the Curia to block the conciliar Constitution. Thus, Bishop Franz Zauner of Linz wrote:

> We bishops and Council Fathers are distressed that so soon after the official approval of the Constitution, the Curia and parties within it are still insisting on centralization and resisting decentralization by every means at their disposal. Approval of biblical and liturgical texts in the vernacular has always been a prerogative of the bishops. . . . In the future, we bishops cannot be confident that this right will not be changed by the Curia, even though it has been clearly defined by the Council.

The problem was thus primarily one of trust. The uneasiness was increased by a series of imprecise wordings and liturgical and historical inaccuracies which made it clear, at the very least, that the final editors of the document lacked familiarity with the style of the Constitution. At the suggestion of the secretariat of the Consilium, twenty corrections were introduced when the motu proprio was published in the *Acta Apostolicae Sedis*. This was the first of the "subsidiary" tasks the Consilium was called upon to accomplish in the context of the liturgy, and sometimes on its periphery, in the course of its history.

---

4. In Section IX of the original text, the motu proprio said that vernacular versions were to be *proposed* by the competent territorial authority, while the Holy See was to *review and approve* them. The definitive text, on the contrary, repeats the liturgical Constitution, article 36, §4, and says that the conferences are to *approve* the translations and submit them to the Holy See for *confirmation*.

7

Organization of the Work

I. Preparation

In December 1963 the Pope sent separate requests to the secretariat of the conciliar liturgical commission and to Cardinal Lercaro to offer a plan for the organization of a postconciliar commission that would implement the liturgical Constitution. Cardinal Lercaro asked Father Bugnini to draft such a plan, while the conciliar commission left the task to its secretariat.

The plan drawn up by the secretariat of the conciliar commission reflected, by and large, the organization of the preparatory commission. It had fourteen study groups attached to a commission; the latter was not to be identified either with the Congregation of Rites or with the conciliar commission, but was in fact to be a minor commission. Father Antonelli suggested that it might be composed, for example, of five bishops and eight experts. The secretariat, it was said, could be identical with that of the conciliar commission. Finally, a list was given of the individuals best qualified to serve on each study group. This plan was forwarded to the Pope on December 19, 1963.

The Bugnini plan dwelt first of all on the identifying marks of the commission to be established. It should be: (1) autonomous and concerned solely with the reform, after the model of the preparatory commission; (2) active, so as to carry out the reform in a reasonable period of time; therefore—this point was emphasized—as in the case of the preparatory commission, it should exclude any persons engaged full-time in other offices or tasks, such as those of the curial agencies; (3) international, in order to voice and interpret in an authentic manner the needs of the entire Church and bring about a reform that would, as far as possible, be acceptable to all.

The structure of the commission was therefore rather complex. According to the plan, it should be made up of: (a) a secretariat that would be aided by a group of *periti;* (b) the commission proper, composed of a cardinal president and twenty to thirty bishops; and (c) a "super-commission" of cardinals.

The basic work, to be assigned by the central commission, would be done by two sets of study groups: one set of groups would deal with the liturgical books, one to a group; the other set would do the work of revision, examining each schema from the doctrinal, biblical, theological, ascetical, and pastoral viewpoints.

The anticipated method of operation: the central commission would divide up the work among the various study groups. As each piece of work was ready, it would be examined by the commission of bishops; from them it would go to the commission of cardinals; from the cardinals to the episcopal conferences; and finally to the Pope for definitive approval.

The time required for the reform: five years, "on the assumption that the executive commission set to work in a decisive, active, and completely organized way." A chart displayed the pyramidal structure of the commission and the division of the basic work.

The kind of reception given to each of the two plans was never made public. The simple fact is that on January 3, 1964, Father Bugnini was given the responsibility of organizing the Consilium; he set to work immediately. As the new secretary knew from twenty years' experience of the liturgical world, it was no simple matter to determine in a short time the tasks, limits, and possible interlocking of the study groups and to mobilize some hundred scholars while identifying their specializations, tendencies, abilities, and readiness to be assigned to the most appropriate group. The Pope was anxious to see the reform get under way, and now and then urged that the machinery be set in motion.

Once the problem of the overall structure of the organization, that is, of the Consilium responsible to the Pope for the work of reform, had been resolved, and once the secretary had a large group of experts who would do the research and the technical work, the plan to be followed had to be improved and made functional. In this area the Consilium could draw on the experience of the preconciliar preparatory commission.

At the first meeting of the "constituent assembly," on January 15, 1964, the secretary presented a first formula for the work. It allowed for two phases. The first would be devoted to the liturgical books: Breviary, Missal, Pontifical, Ritual, Martyrology (calendar); the second to the Ceremonial of Bishops and to a code of liturgical law.

The plan provided five study groups for the Breviary, five for the Missal, and three for the Breviary and Missal jointly. With regard to the Pontifical and the Ritual, it said, in general terms, that the "appropriate committees" were to be set up, but that precedence would have to be given to work on the Breviary and Missal. With regard to the Martyrology, it emphasized that with the suppression of the Hour of Prime, this lost much of its immediate urgency, and that the calendar was a more urgent matter.

For the second phase, only a very general approach was sketched. The *Caeremoniale Episcoporum* should rather become a *Caeremoniale Romanum* that would take all forms of liturgical celebration into account. The liturgical code, for its part, would be "the natural crown set on the entire work of reform. The subcommission to be entrusted with it would be appointed only when the overall reform had reached an advanced stage."

The work was to be organized as follows:

1) The six liturgical books and the code would be assigned to corresponding subcommissions; as the complexity of the work required, these would in turn be subdivided into a suitable number of sections. All the sections would set to work at the same time.

2) Once the experts in an area had put a schema through a number of redactions and finally achieved the structure they wanted, the schema was to be given in succession to the following subcommissions: theological, pastoral, stylistic, and musical, and then to a supercommission of experts, who would subject it to an inclusive examination.

3) Only then was it to be handed on to the liturgical commission.

4) If the Holy Father thought it appropriate, each schema would then be sent to the episcopal conferences.

The sketch thus presented a few days after the Consilium was created contained a set of perspectives and programs that would appear, substantially unchanged, in the definitive redaction of the "General Plan for Liturgical Reform," a booklet of fifty-three pages that was presented to the Holy Father on March 15, 1964.

I shall here reproduce the complete plan in schematic form, without stopping to describe the work programs of the individual groups; these programs will be described later on.

II. General Plan of Liturgical Reform[1]

FIRST SECTION: COMPOSITION

I. CALENDAR

1. Revision of the calendar

II. BREVIARY[2]

2. Revision of the Psalter
3. Distribution of the psalms
4. Scripture readings of the Office
5. Patristic readings
6. Hagiographical readings
7. Hymns
8. Songs of the Office
8bis [12bis]. Intercessions *(preces)* at Lauds and Vespers[3]
9. Overall structure of the Divine Office

III. MISSAL

10. Ordinary of the Mass
11. Scripture readings in the Mass
12. "Common prayer, or prayer of the faithful"[4]
13. Votive Masses
14. Songs in the Mass
15. Overall structure of the Mass
16. Concelebration and communion in two kinds

IV. ELEMENTS COMMON TO BREVIARY AND MISSAL

17. Special rites in the liturgical year
18. Revision of the Commons
18bis. Prayers and prefaces[5]
19. Rubrics of the Breviary and the Missal

---

1. The plan is set forth according to its logical order. The study groups for the various subjects were given numbers that in general corresponded to those of the subjects in the following plan. When this correspondence was lacking, the number of the group is given here in parentheses.

2. I have retained the original wording. In the course of the reform even the terminology underwent a gradual evolution before reaching its definitive form.

3. The corresponding group was established on April 25, 1967, and given the number 12bis.

4. This was the original title; to avoid ambiguity—since every liturgical prayer is "common" and "of the faithful"—"common" was changed to "general" (Latin: *universalis*) because of the nature of *this* prayer.

5. This group was put under Number IV because the prayers (i.e., *orationes*) are common to Office and Mass.

V. PONTIFICAL

20. Revision of Book I
20bis. Consecration of virgins and religious profession[6]
21. Books II and III
21bis. Dedication of church and altar[7]

VI. RITUAL

22. Sacraments
23. Sacramentals
23bis. Penance[8]

VII. MARTYROLOGY

24. Revision of the Martyrology

VIII. CHANT BOOKS

25. Revision of the chant books

IX. EPISCOPAL CEREMONIAL

26. Revision of the Ceremonial of Bishops

X. NON-ROMAN RITES

27. Elements that might be used by the other rites

XI. CODE OF LITURGICAL LAW

28 [38]. Preparation of a Code of Liturgical Law

XII. PAPAL CHAPEL

29 [39]. Rites of the papal chapel[9]

SECOND SECTION: REVISION

30 [28]. Theological revision
31 [29]. Scriptural revision
32 [30]. Juridical revision
32bis. Translation of the liturgical books[10]
33 [31]. Historical revision
34 [32]. Stylistic revision

---

6. Group established in May 1966.
7. Established in 1970.
8. Established on October 14, 1966.
9. Established on February 26, 1965, and in the beginning given the number 39.
10. Established on April 26, 1967.

35 [33]. Musical revision
36 [34]. Revision in light of pastoral principles
37 [35]. Revision in light of pastoral applications
38 [36]. Revision for adaptation
39 [37]. Artistic revision

It is clear that to the original set of groups others were subsequently added to supply an area previously lacking or to effect a better distribution of work that had originally been assigned to a single group. The added groups are indicated by a "bis."[11]

III. EXPLANATION OF THE PLAN

The plan was accompanied by an explanation of the overall plan and of the particular groups. The point of the departure for the whole was the six liturgical books of the Roman Church: Missal, Breviary, Pontifical, Ritual, Martyrology, and Ceremonial of Bishops.

Each liturgical book was divided up into two or more areas according to the various elements found in it; for example, the Breviary was divided into nine areas, the Missal into eight, and so on. Each area was assigned to a study group.

The study groups were of two kinds: (a) study groups that were to prepare and draft schemas (first section: composition); and (b) study groups entrusted with conceptual revision (second section: revision).

The groups in the first set were to do the "horizontal" work of preparing and drafting schemas; those in the second set were to do "vertical" revision in the area of their competence. Ideally, this twofold sifting of the schemas by qualified scholars would provide a security net guaranteeing the seriousness and worth of the work.

a) *Compositional Section*

Each group had a relator, a secretary, and five or six members, rarely more. The choice of members (= consultors) followed three criteria:

---

11. The habit of working in groups in which experts in various areas were included was also followed in examining other questions that arose apart from, or concomitantly with, the work of reform but were not strictly connected with the revision of the liturgical books. This was true, for example, of the instructions on sacred music and on the worship of the Eucharist, and, in the Congregation for Divine Worship, of the Eucharistic Prayers, the Directory for Masses with Children, the Eucharistic Prayers for Masses with children and for Masses of reconciliation, the celebrations for the Holy Year, and so on. Even if these groups were drawing up general documents connected with the liturgical reform, they were not given a special number. An account of the schemas developed by the various groups can be found in *Not* 18 (1982) 543–762.

(a) specialization; (b) nationality; and (c) availability to meet and work together. The total number of consultors was rather high, in order that all the areas might set to work simultaneously, except for the few areas involving joint work.

For each particular subject or for special problems "advisors" were then appointed—either on a regular basis or for a single occasion—who would make their contribution in writing, without having to take part in the meetings, except in rare instances that the president authorized as they arose. The consultors were appointed by the Pope; the advisors were appointed by the president of the Consilium.

The guidelines, or criteria, for the work of each group were based on the data provided by the liturgical Constitution, the material gathered for the preparatory commission, the desires of the bishops and clergy, and liturgical studies.[12] On the basis of the criteria and the material supplied, each group would compose a first schema for its area. This would be sent for examination to the consultors and to a suitable number (twenty to thirty) of advisors in various parts of the world. The observations that came in from the advisors within a certain period of time and those made by the consultors of the Consilium would serve as the basis for a second draft of the schema, which would in turn be sent to the same persons for examination. This method would produce a formulation that would at a very early stage win a majority of votes. This was the system followed by the preparatory commission in drafting the Constitution itself.

When all the schemas for a liturgical book had passed through the sieve and were ready to be used, the group entrusted with the "overall structure" of the books was to prepare a comprehensive schema for the entire book; all the consultors who had worked on the individual schemas would take part in this work. The schema resulting from this work would be sent for examination to the members of the Consilium and then to the Holy Father.

To facilitate the work of the Consilium, it was decided that rather than present it with whole books that are overly vast (for example, the entire Missal or the entire Breviary), it would be given homogeneous and self-contained parts (Scripture readings, patristic readings, and so on).

---

12. The secretariat also undertook to provide the groups with the bibliography for their subject, and to this end it contacted the Centre Bibliographique at Mont-César, which is the one best organized for matters liturgical. The Centre made a serious commitment to the work by assigning six monks and a layperson to list all the useful material. By March 15, 1964, it had already sent to the Consilium all the slips concerned with the Order of Mass. In practice, however, this undertaking did not prove useful because the consultors were all professionals and each had the suitable tools at hand.

b) *Revisory Section*

The plan provided that after the schemas had been produced by the experts in a particular area, they would be given to various study groups for conceptual, that is, theological, juridical, historical, stylistic, musical, pastoral (principles and application), cultural (problems of adaptation), and artistic revision.

This was to be revision at the "horizontal" or synthetic level. What it meant was that after the analytical work of the area groups, these further groups, made up of scholars who were specialists but had had no part in the work and were therefore not influenced by the difficulties or problems encountered at the compositional level, would carefully inquire whether the various, separately composed parts showed continuity and accuracy of thought, a homogeneous approach, logical progress, a uniform style, an equal breadth of vision, and accuracy of juridical expression; whether a text that was cited several times was being used with different meanings; above all, whether that which was theoretically perfect would likewise be useful and effective in pastoral practice. Only after this complex process, which we intended to streamline as much as possible, would the schemas be submitted to the members of the Consilium.

As the work actually proceeded, only the procedure indicated in Section I of the plan was followed. The study groups in the second set, which were to engage in what I have called the horizontal process of conceptual revision, were not activated. The chief reason for this was that it did not seem necessary. The experts were on the whole scholars of distinction. Furthermore, in each group were to be found not only liturgists but a theologian, an exegete, a patrologist. Then, too, all the schemas passed through the sieve of the general meetings of the consultors, thus in large measure ensuring the correctness of the doctrinal content.

In like manner, the pastoral aspect was validated by the presence in the Consilium of a good number of parish priests (about twenty) and by the contributions of the bishops, who are authoritative pastors. Finally, the pastoral validity was ensured because the Consilium could profit by the experiments, which, although they brought not a few complaints and expressions of annoyance, provided a broad basis of experience on which to polish and enrich the schemas before introducing them into the current practice of the Church.

For the stylistic aspect we were able to profit, in the final stage of the various schemas, by the expertise of A. Lentini and the Latinists of the Secretariat of State, especially the skillful Abbot Karl Egger, who with great care and respect polished almost all the restored rites.

The juridical aspect, on the other hand, proved weaker. This was not because the Consilium did not have its own first-rate jurists, such as Archbishop Felici and the unforgettable Monsignor Bonet. The reason was rather that because of the sacred sciences, law was at that time in the most precarious situation. The Consilium preferred, therefore, to embark, in a balanced way, on the formation of a new liturgical law. That was why the plan allowed for a group whose task would be to prepare a "code of liturgical law."

Ground, plans, structures, workers—all were now ready. It was time to begin to build.

8

The Sacred Congregation for Divine Worship

In order to complete the organizational picture, I insert here a chapter on the difficult road that had to be traveled in creating an agency for the promotion of liturgical worship. It seems to me like news from only yesterday, and yet it is already part of history! It was a long-cherished dream, but, like all dreams, it vanished in a moment.

For the time being.

Human beings go their way, but ideas remain. If they are valid, because they reflect compelling needs that cannot be suppressed, they continue on and sooner or later find their definitive embodiment.

When Pope John XXIII established the preparatory commissions for Vatican II, he was creating what were in a way duplicates of the agencies and offices of the Roman Curia, a (temporary) curia within the Curia. The commissions had the advantage that, since their directives came from the Pope, they could organize their work with complete freedom, in the sense of not having to respect the competencies of the various agencies in the same areas. This was a blessing, because only thus could serious problems on which several curial agencies had a say be handled in a complete and rounded manner. It even seems that Pope John intended to follow the same pattern in reforming the Curia after the Council; his death prevented this.

To avoid interferences and dissensions, the commissions were all assigned a common location on the fourth floor of Santa Marta. But in fact, as I pointed out earlier, each commission managed with the few, sometimes small rooms set up for it on the premises of the corresponding Congregation. It was really more comfortable working there because the cardinal president, who was always the prefect of the corresponding agency, was within easy reach and because archives and sources of information were at hand. But there were also disadvantages: secrecy was harder to maintain, and interferences multiplied. The liturgical commission did not seek to avoid the common lot with its good and less good sides. Once the preparatory period had ended and the examination by the Council had been passed (with full marks!), the period of implementation arrived. In dealing with a liturgical constitution such as the one adopted by Vatican II, it was impossible to go back to the methods, limitations, and spirit of the Congregation of Rites. The Congregation reflected its origin in 1587; *Sacrosanctum Concilium* belonged to 1963. Four centuries had not passed without leaving their mark.

In order to implement a constitution that involved the competencies of almost all the Roman Congregations, it was necessary in the nature of things to establish contacts, to be attentive and circumspect, and to engage in prudent and submissive exchanges with the age-old legal "owners" of the various "pieces of property" that the Constitution assigned to the liturgy. The Consilium did not immediately realize the real state of affairs; it even expected something quite different, as it continued (so it thought) along the lines of the preparatory commission. Keenly aware that the Pope was its real "president" and that its cause was just, the Consilium set to work as though it were completely free to act as it wished.

The first agency that felt its rights were being infringed upon was the Congregation of Rites, which for four centuries had been writing the laws for the subject now assigned to the Consilium. Here were two agencies working in the same field and dealing with the same problems. Were they parallel, or was one subordinate to the other? The secret wish of the officials of the Consilium was that they might be parallel. The Congregation of Rites evidently thought the Consilium should be subordinate and said as much: the Consilium should be simply a consultative commission within the Congregation of Rites (*audito Consilio*, "having heard the views of the Consilium"), while the Congregation should continue to be the agency for giving legal form to all decisions in liturgical matters. In theory everything worked perfectly; in practice the Congregation interfered in many ways,[1] and unless some radical solution could be found, it would end up hindering and stalling the work of the Consilium.

---

1. For example, in the introduction to a decree dealing with various liturgical problems presented by the French Episcopal Conference, this contorted and casuistic statement is made: "Sacra haec Rituum Congregatio, per sectionem competentem, quae motui liturgico poctconciliari praeest, ex consulto Consilii ad exsequendam Constitutionem de sacra

I. The Consilium and the Congregation of Rites

a) April 22, 1964, brought a resolution of the juridical problem involved in *the publication of liturgical documents,* a problem Cardinal Lercaro had brought to the Pope's attention. After a rush of plans and counterplans in search of an approved formula that would respect the wishes of all parties, the Secretary of State decided that the Congregation of Rites and the Consilium should be associated "in the promulgation of the decrees issued by the Ecumenical Council." As for the decisions reached by the Consilium, the Pope had determined that the two agencies should come to terms on "an agreed formula" to accompany their publication.[2]

About fifteen proposals were made, and finally the two agencies agreed on the statement found at the end of the first instruction and used, in substance, in all subsequent documents. The procedure to be followed was this: General documents having juridical status were to be published by the Congregation of Rites; approval was always to be given by the Pope. In the preparation of documents, the two agencies were to consult with one another, and this collaboration was to find expression in the formula of approval. The documents were to be signed by the prefect of the Congregation, the president of the Consilium, and the secretary of the Congregation.[3]

Liturgia (Motu Proprio *Sacram Liturgiam,* 25 ianuarii 1964), et audita Deputatione Commissionis conciliaris de sacra Liturgia, necessariis facultatibus munita ad normam can. 244, 1 et 2 CIC, actis a te missis rite expensis, circa dispositiones ab Episcopatu gallico die 14 ianuarii 1964 latas, cum interim in lucem prodierit Motu Proprio *Sacram Liturgiam* suum esse duxit tibi patefacere . . . ." ("This Sacred Congregation of Rites, through the competent section in charge of the postconciliar liturgical movement, having consulted the Council for the Implementation of the Constitution on the Sacred Liturgy [Motu Proprio *Sacram Liturgiam,* January 25, 1964], and having heard the deputation from the conciliar commission on the sacred liturgy, and being provided with the necessary faculties in accordance with Canon 244, 1 and 2, of the Code of Canon Law, and having duly weighed the documentation you sent regarding the measures taken by the French episcopate on January 14, 1964, and in view of the fact that the Motu Proprio *Sacram Liturgiam* has appeared in the interim— this Congregation has thought it necessary to declare to you . . . .").

2. Letter of the Secretary of State, May 19, 1964 (No. 2656/64). The solution of the problem, which in the terminology of the Consilium was described as *quaestio spinosa* (a "thorny question"), was received toward the middle of June (Letter from the Secretariat of State, June 16, 1964, Prot. n. 3324/64), after a thorough examination of the entire question and after the juridical acumen of the secretary of the Council had been brought to bear.

3. More precisely: the signature of the president of the Consilium was to be placed at the left and preceded by the word *visum* ("seen"); this word was subsequently omitted. The secretary of the Consilium was not to sign. The omission was deliberate—four signatures seemed too many, and, in addition, there was a desire to make the relative juridical positions of the two agencies clear: two signatures to one!

A further codicil was added after the publication of the instruction *Inter Oecumenici.* At

b) On July 3 and again on October 1, 1964, a second problem then causing difficulty, the problem of *concelebration*, was resolved. In a faculty given on July 3 and completed on October 1, the president of the Consilium was authorized to grant indults for experiments until such time as a definitive description of the rite should be achieved.

This was agreed upon and done in an orderly manner: the indult was granted, and at the same time the rite to be followed was prescribed. But within the Curia the rumor kept circulating that there was "disorder, confusion, abuses" (Archbishop Enrico Dante) and that too many different rites were being practiced. Meanwhile, all the reports reaching the Consilium were consoling. But there came a point when the Pope himself was influenced by the negative rumors, and he even thought of withdrawing the faculty given to the Cardinal President.

The Consilium put up a strong resistance. Such a step would be an extraordinarily serious one; it would rouse the indignation of the bishops; there would be no objective justification for it. Then, too, there was the question of principle: the rite of concelebration was in the experimental stage, and it was agreed that this phase should be under the control of the Consilium, which had prepared the rite, allowed the experiments, and was asking for reports on it so that it might have the concrete information needed in order, if necessary, to complete, modify, and put the finishing touches on the rite itself. Only in the final phase should the whole matter then be handed over to the juridical agency of the Holy See for promulgation. The experiments—which are the constant cross of any reform—continued.

In order to relieve some of the pressure being exerted by the Congregation of Rites, it too was allowed to grant the indult for concelebration. It issued the decree and then sent the petitioner to the Consilium for the rite to be followed.

c) *Texts in the vernacular.*—Here again there seemed to be agreement. The instruction *Inter Oecumenici* (no. 29) had determined that texts approved by the episcopal conferences should be sent to the Consilium for approval. But when printed liturgical books began to appear, accompa-

---

first the Congregation of Rites accepted the fact that possible doubts arising about the interpretation of the document should be examined by the Consilium, and this procedure was approved by the Pope on October 1. But then the question immediately arose: "Who is to publish the answers?" The Congregation of Rites asked the Secretariat of State that it might publish the answers in the *Acta Apostolicae Sedis* with the notation that it "had consulted the Consilium." The Secretariat of State accepted this proposal (November 3, 1964, No. 31126), but nothing to this effect was ever published. The Consilium preferred to publish official explanations in *Notitiae*.

nied by a decree from the Consilium and the signatures of its president and secretary, without any reference to the Congregation of Rites, there was another commotion (November 30, 1964). But the conduct of the Consilium was finally approved (December 17, 1964).[4]

d) *Clarification.*—On this occasion, however, a request was made for a further clarification of competencies so that the work might not be continually hindered by procedural questions. The clarification came in a letter from the Secretariat of State, dated January 7, 1965 (No. 36624), and addressed to the prefect of the Congregation of Rites and, for his information, to the president of the Consilium. The letter clearly distinguished three phases of the work, as the Consilium had suggested: preparation of liturgical books and study of the questions involved; experimentation; promulgation. The first two phases belonged to the Consilium, the third to the Congregation.

> To the Consilium will fall attention either to issues or to liturgical texts that application of the Constitution on the Liturgy now requires. To the Congregation of Rites will fall, with consultation of the Consilium, promulgation of the documents that will put into effect norms and liturgical texts as they become available. It seems advisable to reserve to the critical evaluation of the Consilium those conditions required for the applications of the Constitution now in the process of testing. The Consilium will thus have a basis for deciding what forms may be best for definitive and authoritative approval by the Congregation of Rites.
>
> Promulgation of liturgical books of an official, permanent, and universal character, will naturally be reserved to the same Congregation. At the same time, it is clearly appropriate that the decree of promulgation also bear the signature of the Cardinal President of the Consilium, as was the case with publication of the recent Instruction [*Inter Oecumenici*].[5]

II. Attempts at Organizing the Consilium

Once calm was restored on the subject of competencies, the Consilium could go about its work with greater tranquility. But even here there were difficulties, due chiefly to the weak juridical basis of the Consilium itself. The latter was an extensive and complex organism with a presidency

---

4. The occasion for the approval was the publication of the Missal in English in the United States: *The Roman Missal—Missale Romanum.* The situation was made stickier by the fact that the book contained only the English text without the Latin, although the inclusion of the Latin had been prescribed. See *Not* 1 (1965) 163.

5. See *EDIL* 379 = *DOL* 84 no. 625. The same norms were repeated by the Pope in his address to the Consilium on October 13, 1966 (*DOL* 84 nos. 630-36).

and a secretariat, about fifty members who held general meetings once or twice a year, and consultors and advisors distributed into study groups. It held both limited and general meetings, and dealt with liturgical commissions, institutes of liturgy, and periodicals devoted to liturgy and pastoral practice. Everything was done with great good will but without a controlling set of regulations.

The difficulties in various relationships began to make themselves felt and, with this, the need for specific norms that would regulate the course of meetings and clarify the roles of the presidency and the secretariat. Another reason why norms were needed was that the Consilium could not be brought together for a meeting to discuss every question that arose. When, for example, the various documents were published, the Consilium had to consult with the other concerned agencies of the Holy See, or was itself consulted. Unexpected questions arose that required a prompt answer and could not wait for the members of the Consilium to be brought together. How was it possible in these cases for the presidency or the secretariat to commit the Consilium or interpret its mind? It had been anticipated that in these cases a limited group of members might be summoned for an "ordinary" meeting, but after early experiences of this procedure, everyone agreed that it would be better not to go this route.

Care was usually taken to make inquiries of at least some of the consultors and members who were at hand; nothing more could be done. Nevertheless, the people making up the Consilium voiced their disappointment at not being called upon in some situations.[6] Two efforts were made to eliminate these drawbacks.

1. A "Presidential Council"

It was thought that the presidency and the secretariat could be aided in their work by having available a group of six persons chosen from within the Consilium by all the members. This group would be able to meet more often—every three months on the average. Cardinal Lercaro

---

6. For concrete instances see below, p. 154, n. 32. But as early as the beginning of 1965 (January 23) Canon Martimort gave voice to a sore point with the consultors when he wrote: "The changes made in the *Ritus servandus* for the celebration of Mass, above and beyond the rubrical details foreseen in the first instruction, have two defects: they were not submitted for discussion by the experts at their meeting, even though the pros and cons ought always to be carefully weighed. The second defect in such a procedure is often prejudicial to further reform. Without discussion, without mature reflection, without any vote of the bishops, a definitive solution is imposed. What is the role of the bishops of the Consilium under these conditions? And what responsibility is being allowed to the experts?"

showed this plan to the Pope on September 22, 1966, and received his approval for it.

On October 8, at a meeting attended only by the members of the Consilium, the purposes and tasks of the "presidential council" were decided. The group was to:

a) examine and settle, by mandate of the Consilium itself, urgent problems that did not come under ordinary administration (for example, the examination of certain documents; the solution to special situations described by the episcopal conferences) and could not be put off until the next general meeting;

b) participate in the work of the groups, as far as possible,[7] especially the group of relators, so that they might then act as a link between the groups and the Fathers;

c) judge whether the schemas prepared by the study groups were advanced enough to be usefully and fruitfully discussed at the general meetings.

The seven members were elected on October 11.[8] But despite good intentions, the presidential council had difficulty in operating. The principle that its members should be residential bishops from a variety of cultural areas ensured that the group was representative, but it also made it difficult for these members to take part in the meetings of the study groups; this was possible only now and then. The majority of the members lived far from Rome; almost all their meetings (five out of eight), therefore, had to be held concomitantly with the general meetings. This defeated, at least in part, the very purpose of the council and its meetings. Furthermore, it must be kept in mind that the Pope was personally interested in the work of the Consilium and gave it timely directives. He thought of the Consilium as directly dependent on himself; his personal freedom of operation might have been hindered if the agency were to be given a more rigid juridical form.

2. A Constitution and Regulations for the Consilium

Another attempt to strengthen the operational structure of the Consilium took the form of an effort to draw up a constitution and a set of regulations for internal operation. Of this, too, Cardinal Lercaro spoke

---

7. The groups had expressed a desire to have a representative of the members join them. It was thought that this would facilitate discussion with the Fathers. In fact it was sometimes necessary to stop and give the Fathers lengthy explanations of the solutions proposed by the experts.

8. The names are given below on p. 160.

to the Pope at the audience of September 22. The Holy Father gave his consent. At their meeting on October 8, the members of the Consilium decided: (1) It is time to revise the few guidelines set down for the work of the groups and to incorporate them into a real set of internal regulations that will control the functions and responsibilities of the relators, consultors, individual study groups, and the group of relators. (2) The time also seems ripe for establishing with greater clarity some constitutional articles that will better define the organizational structure of the Consilium—presidency, presidential council, and meetings—and the guidelines for meetings, both general and limited. Cardinal Lercaro communicated these decisions to the Holy Father on November 10.

At the first meeting of the presidential council, on October 14, 1966, a commission of consultors was appointed to prepare the set of regulations. Its relator, Monsignor Bonet, was assigned to sketch out the general lines of the constitution, which would then serve also as a basis for the set of regulations.[9] This commission met in Rome on December 7-8, 1966, and January 10-12, 1967. It discussed the constitution and the general criteria to be followed in redacting the set of regulations. The presidential council studied the general lines of the constitution on January 13, 1967. The text of the draft introduced no novelties; it summarized the documents that had to do with the Consilium and sought to show the agency's nature, composition, and duties, but always on the basis of what had already been decided. The set of regulations, on the other hand, were to consider the procedure to be followed in the work of the study groups, in the meetings, and in voting.

The group met again at Nemi on March 7, 1967, in order to clarify the constitution in response to the observations of the presidential council. The resultant text was to be scrutinized by the members of the Consilium at their general meeting on April 15, 1967.[10]

After the Consilium had given its approval, the document was to be presented to the Pope. In the meantime, however, another document had reached him which depicted the constitution as a weapon that would do away with every other authority:

> This constitution seems to describe an agency that is stable and permanent, possessing almost unlimited legislative powers and full and complete executive authority in the area of liturgy. In practice, it would throttle even the governmental effectiveness of the Congregation of Rites and turn the

---

9. Monsignor E. Bonet had also been relator of the group that had prepared the bylaws of the conciliar commission of the liturgy. The appointed members of the group were: B. Fischer, A. Hänggi, J. Cellier, C. Vagaggini, P. Gy, and H. Schmidt.

10. See *Res secretariae*, no. 27 (March 18, 1967).

latter into a decrepit, formal tool that is kept in existence for reasons of mere expediency and convenience. . . . At the same time, however, the Consilium would not become an instrument of the Holy Father, as the existing Congregations are, but would have powers unqualifiedly greater than those of any Congregation whatsoever. The Consilium itself would in fact appoint the vast majority of its own members, cardinals included.[11] Other provisions of the constitution make it clear that its authors see the Consilium no longer as an agency that acts with delegated authority in the name of the Holy Father but as a continuation of the Council, and therefore as invested with supreme conciliar authority.

Such an arrangement is obviously a complete novelty in the Church, something without precedent in ecclesiastical law, and, in addition, an anomaly in the true and proper sense, inasmuch as the Church cannot exist in a state of permanent council. It is clear, too, that such an arrangement would be utterly unique and unparalleled, making the Consilium an agency radically different from all the other agencies of the Church and from the other Congregations or tribunals that are presently concerned with the application of the conciliar decisions. The Congregation of Rites would be the only exception, for it would be an agency subordinated to another.

Inasmuch as these plans are so radically at odds with what we were given to understand was involved in the transformation of the Consilium into an institute of experts whose function would be to prepare for the liturgical renewal according to the norms of the constitution *Sacrosanctum Concilium*, the aforementioned draft leaves us somewhat at sea. Our perplexity is deepened by the fact that although this is presented as a *definitive* draft of a new constitution, the Consilium has thus far not called upon the Congregation of Rites or asked it to express its views on the draft, even though the matter is of direct and vital concern to it.

The document ended by asking the Pope to prevent the creation of another *fait accompli* and to turn the matter over to the commission studying the reform of the Curia before any disagreeable situations should arise.

It has always been a mystery how Pope Paul VI could have been brought to believe such outrageous and grotesque claims. The fact remains that although he had previously given his approval in every case, after reading this document he took a sheet of paper and wrote "April 13, 1967: Approved." On April 14, before the Consilium was to begin its discussion of the draft of a constitution, the facts were explained to the Pope and all the documentation presented to him. But he was not to be moved from his decision. He called the secretary of the Consilium

---

11. This was really a mendacious inference. The document simply pointed out the practice followed everywhere in the Curia: proposal by the Cardinal President (and, in the case of the Consilium, in agreement with the presidential council) and appointment by the Pope.

to an audience and told him there was to be no more talk of the constitution. During the audience he read the document cited above and stopped, convinced and distressed, at the words that cleverly brought out the—completely fanciful—danger to his authority. Every attempt to prove the accusation unfounded was in vain. The constitution and regulations ended up in the archives for good, and we continued to move forward . . . with good will.

III. The Consilium in the Reform of the Curia

On August 15, 1967, the apostolic constitution *Regimini Ecclesiae* on the reform of the Roman Curia was published. Its coming had been spoken of for some time. A memorandum of September 30, 1966, on the definitive reorganization of the Congregation of Rites had been "prepared for presentation to the Holy Father as soon as he indicated his desire for it" and would, it was hoped, "be acceptable to him."[12] We may think that the memorandum was given to him when the agencies were questioned with a view to their reform.

The plan started with the assumption that the Congregation of Rites was to retain its twofold jurisdiction over the liturgy and the causes of saints. It reached these conclusions: (1) It is appropriate that the name "Sacred Congregation for Worship" be adopted; (2) the Congregation keeps its twofold competence and is to have two sections—one for the liturgy, the other for the causes of saints—with a subsecretary presiding over each; but the Congregation continues to have a single prefect and a single secretary; (3) in the liturgical section, after the appointment of a subsecretary back on October 25, 1965, no need can be seen for further changes. One problem, however, remains to be resolved—that of the relationship of the Consilium to the Congregation of Rites. It is decided, therefore, that the Consilium should continue to be a technical agency for preparing the revision of the liturgical books, while the major decisions regarding the reform are to be discussed and approved by the congregation of the cardinals "in charge of defending the sacred rites," in plenary sessions in which not only the cardinals of the Curia but also suitable cardinals from outside the Curia are to take part; (4) in addition to the existing office for the settlement of the numerous ordinary affairs of the Congregation, there are to be two new offices: one for overseeing liturgi-

---

12. There were two redactions: a more prolix one (38 pp.) and another, in contorted Italian, that was shorter (27 pp.), clearer, and more graceful in its exposition.

cal developments around the world, and the other for overseeing non-liturgical forms of devotion.

The Consilium, meanwhile, had not been asked for its views. It was the only agency in the entire Curia that had been forgotten until the final stage of the planning. Recourse was had to the Pope, who arranged that the Consilium, too, should have its place in the document on curial reform. As a result, it figures among the—temporary—agencies. If no one had gone to the Pope, the Consilium would have been simply annexed by the Congregation of Rites.[13]

Facing this prospect, the Consilium took the further step of proposing a different organization "in case the idea of dividing the Congregation be accepted." In fact, although the proposal reflected a longstanding wish, it seemed premature.[14] It served nonetheless to keep the idea alive and give it a more mature form. The point made was that the two sections of the Congregation of Rites are completely independent and have nothing to do with one another. The procedure used in the causes of saints is nothing more than a trial and has nothing to do with worship. Steps are also taken at the diocesan level in the causes of saints, but in the judicial branch of the local curia, and no one has ever thought of linking them with the liturgical commission.

The idea of linking worship and the procedures for beatification and canonization arose in a period when the true concept of liturgy had been lost and the cult of the saints was predominant. Today the Church has rediscovered the true face of the liturgy, which is centered in Christ, the paschal mystery, and the history of salvation, and has made the faithful

---

13. The plan for the reform of the Congregation of Rites was evidently based on the statement cited in the text. Thus, in the printed draft of *Regimini Ecclesiae* the Consilium was spoken of as follows: "No. 61, 4. The Consilium appointed to apply the liturgical Constitution has for its task to revise the liturgical books and carry out the liturgical reform. Its decisions, however, are to be submitted to the plenary assembly of this section [i.e., the liturgical section of the Congregation of Rites]. The members of the Consilium, moreover, are automatically *periti* of the Sacred Congregation of Rites." The authors of the document had no understanding of the Consilium. How could they think that cardinals and bishops should become *periti* of the Congregation of Rites? And how could the decisions reached by the Consilium be submitted to a similar agency, the plenary meetings of the Congregation?

14. A note made for the audience of March 16, 1965, reads: "The directors of the Consilium are quite content; the members and consultors less so. The latter are puzzled, for they would have liked a more 'functional' organization [the reference is to the letter of January 7 on the respective competencies of the Consilium and the Congregation of Rites]. The impression is abroad that this represents the first step toward an agency for the sacred liturgy that is distinct from the tribunal for the causes of beatification and canonization. Experience has shown that these two sections, while theoretically not remote from one another, are in practice at odds in their conception and type of work."

aware of their role as participants in the sacred action. Both the liturgical Constitution and the entire pastoral approach to the contemporary renewal require that the cult of the saints be located within this new vision.

IV. THE CONGREGATION FOR DIVINE WORSHIP

The idea proposed by the Consilium had an unexpectedly quick success. It is probable that the Pope himself already had the same idea. In order to pave the way, on January 9, 1968, he accepted Cardinal Lercaro's resignation as president of the Consilium[15] and asked Cardinal Larraona to resign as prefect of the Congregation of Rites. On that same day he appointed Cardinal Benno Gut, a member of the Consilium, as head of both agencies. This step helped to relax tensions, and relations between the two organizations became truly cordial and cooperative.

1. *Establishment of the Congregation*

Not a year had passed since the publication of *Regimini Ecclesiae* when an urgent communication asked whether it was not time to divide the Congregation of Rites into two independent agencies—one for divine worship and the other for the canonization of saints. The norms governing the worship section of the Congregation of Rites were to govern the new Congregation, together with any additions, changes, or omissions that might seem advisable.

---

15. On this occasion Pope Paul VI sent a letter of thanks to Cardinal Lercaro (*DOL* 90 no. 667); the Secretary of State sent another, which is printed in *Not* 4 (1968) 4–5.

Before sending in his letter of resignation, Cardinal Lercaro asked the secretary of the Consilium to come to Bologna so that he could read the letter. It was an autograph in his unmistakable aristocratic script that was a reflection of his transparent soul.

On this occasion the Consilium sent a circular letter to all the members, consultors, and *periti* to tell them of the event and introduce the new president. On January 13 Cardinal Lercaro replied: ''Reverend and dear Father. I have received the circular letter sent to all the advisors and co-workers of the Consilium, and with it your greetings and those of all my friends in the secretariat.

''To you and all of them I return my own affectionate and devoted greetings; at the same time, with a lively sense of deep gratitude I thank them all and especially you, Father, for the work that you carried out at my side in the Consilium in such a conscientious and intelligent way, with so much dedication and sacrifice, and with such profit—I dare say it—for the holy Church of God, whose first task is certainly to offer perfect praise to the Lord.

''I am sure that the secretariat of the Consilium will continue at the same pace and in the same spirit on the road still to be traveled in implementing fully the directives and dictates of the conciliar Constitution. This brotherly union of intentions and life that characterizes collaboration within the secretariat of the Consilium is a guarantee of success, for where 'brothers dwell in unity,' there 'the Lord has commanded the blessing' (Ps 132[133]).''

Everyone was taken by surprise. No one expected an initiative of this kind so soon upon the heels of the general reorganization of the Curia.

That was on April 5, 1969. Twenty-three days later (April 28) the Pope made the following announcement at a consistory:

> To carry out the great work of facilitating the Church's office of guiding and furthering the prayer-life of the faithful we have accepted the argument and the desire for dividing the Sacred Congregation of Rites into two separate congregations. The one will be concerned with divine worship; the other, with handling the causes of saints. We have judged this to be very necessary. In the case of the first congregation, the one principal agency will thereby have as its sole responsibility the strengthening and preservation everywhere of the Church's life of prayer, especially since Vatican II has done so much to advance the cause of liturgy in all its aspects. In the case of the second, there will thus be an agency, distinct by a name having a historical connotation, that will specifically deal with the causes of saints, since this work is both so extensive and so difficult. We have thoroughly weighed the arguments for the advisability of this change and therefore will promulgate the norms for the newly established congregations in an apostolic constitution soon to be published. In this we will describe the nature of these congregations, outline their organization, and specify their duties and competence.[16]

The reason for the step is given by the Pope: the importance which the liturgical life has acquired in the Church since the Council requires that there be a central agency whose sole function is to oversee and promote the Church's prayer and worship of God.

The apostolic constitution *Sacra Rituum Congregatio* appeared on May 8; it ratified what the Pope had announced, and determined the roles of the Congregation for Divine Worship and the Congregation for the Causes of Saints.[17] The Consilium now became part of the Congregation for Divine Worship "as a special intra-Congregational Commission for the duration of the work begun on the liturgical books."

Since Cardinal Gut had been both prefect of the Congregation of Rites and president of the Consilium, the Pope allowed him to choose the one or the other position for the future. After some hesitation the Cardinal chose the Congregation for Divine Worship and became its first and certainly best-loved prefect. The members of the new Congregation were chosen according to the norms set down in *Sacra Rituum Congregatio*.[18]

---

16. *DOL* 93 no. 677.

17. *DOL* 94 nos. 678-79.

18. The cardinals who were members of the Consilium automatically became members of the new Congregation. These were: Cardinals Lercaro, Agagianian, Gracias, Giobbe, Con-

Father Bugnini, already secretary of the Consilium, was appointed secretary of the Congregation for Divine Worship.

On that same day, May 8, at the first meeting of the new Congregation, the Cardinal Prefect, acting in the name of all the officials,[19] sent a message of devoted and grateful homage to the Holy Father:

> The Sacred Congregation for Divine Worship, meeting for the first time, in reverence and filial devotion turns its first thought to Your Holiness for having given to the Church the gift of this new Congregation. Our hope is that it will be a source of blessing and grace for souls and of consolation to yourself. We thank you also for having called on us to continue the work that we have been able to develop so far with such enthusiasm, total dedication, and joy.
>
> May you be sure, Holy Father, that we revere the Consilium ad exsequendam Constitutionem de Sacra Liturgia, born out of your own heart. It was like a banner heralding the ideal of renewal and youth in the field of liturgy.
>
> We will hold just as dear this new Congregation, in which today we begin our ecclesial service, humbly yet moved by an equal and, if possible, a greater dedication. Holy Father, we implore a special apostolic blessing on all of us, your workers, on this Congregation, on all the members and *periti* of the Commission that is the special heir of the Consilium.[20]

On May 12 the Pope answered with an autograph letter:

> To the esteemed Lord Cardinal Benno Gut,
> Prefect of the Sacred Congregation for Divine Worship:
>
> We hasten to reply to the letter which you, together with Father Bugnini and his co-workers in the Consilium, have sent us today at the beginning of the activity of your Congregation. The Congregation's purpose is to make ever more effective the incomparably important work that the Holy See, following its own centuries-old traditions and in keeping with the norms and mind of Vatican II, directs to the practice and advancement of the Church's prayer. We thank you profoundly for the sentiments and resolve expressed, from which we derive the surest promise for the successful con-

---

falonieri, Rugambwa, Silva Henríquez, Conway, Pellegrino, Cody, Gray, Enrique y Tarancón, and Felici; to them were added newly created cardinals Baggio and Willebrands.

The diocesan bishops who were to be members of the Consilium had to be elected this time by their colleagues. The election was held on November 7, 1969; those elected were: D. Hurley, O. Spülbeck, R. Boudon, L. Nagae, C. Isnard, G. Carter, and A. Hänggi. The Pope confirmed the election on January 5, 1970.

19. The employees of the Consilium went over as a group to the new agency. To their number was added Monsignor S. Laboa, who came from the Congregation of Rites, and Monsignor V. Noè as subsecretary assigned by higher authority; see "Compositio novae Congregationis," *Not* 5 (1969) 133.

20. *DOL* 96 no. 686.

tinuation and fruitful increase of the work already in progress and already of such distinguished merit. Surely the Lord will come to the aid of such activity, since it centers completely on his glory and the spread of his Spirit among the people of God. We confirm these good wishes with our apostolic blessing.[21]

The Congregation for Divine Worship moved its offices from the Palazzo di S. Marta to that of the Congregations, at 10 Piazza Pio XII. The new location was officially opened on April 9, 1972, during the final general meeting of the glorious Consilium, which had now become the "Commission for the duration of the work begun on the liturgical books." A tablet was unveiled, along with a bronze bust of Paul VI, sculpted by Professor Molteni of Milan. They were placed in the airy atrium of the Congregation. The dedication was an act of devotion to the Pope who had understood the place given to the liturgy by the Council and had done so much to apply the liturgical Constitution. The inscription read as follows:

> In his wholehearted zeal
> for promoting the splendor and dignity of divine worship
> in accordance with the desires
> of the Second Ecumenical Council of the Vatican,
> the Supreme Pontiff Paul VI, after the Council
> for Implementing the Liturgical Constitution,
> which he established,
> had already yielded a rich harvest,
> in 1970 providentially created this new Sacred Congregation,
> adorned it with new ordinances,
> and gave it more extensive quarters.

Speeches were given by Cardinal Gut, Bishop Boudon for the members; Professor Pascher for the *periti*, Canon Ronald Jasper for the observers; Father Lentini, who had composed a Latin poem for the occasion; and, finally, Cardinal Lercaro. The singing of the Alleluia brought this memorable ceremony to a close.[22]

---

21. *DOL* 97 no. 687.

22. See "Inauguratio novarum Aedium Sacrae Congregationis pro Cultu Divino," *Not* 6 (1970) 230-31.

Professor Pascher used a particularly felicitous image. In the past, he said, the Popes maintained splendid fountains in Rome to slake the thirst of the Romans; Pope Paul VI has unsealed the joyous fountain of the reformed liturgy, from which the water of everlasting life flows out for the entire Church. On the following day the secretariat of the Congregation rewarded Professor Pascher for these words by giving him an illustrated volume on the "fountains of Rome."

2. *Second Thoughts?*

Strange to say, the joy did not last long. On December 8, 1970, Cardinal Gut unexpectedly ended his earthly sojourn. For some unknown reason, his death brought a flood of suggestions for the future of the Congregation. Some proposed that it be reunited with the Congregation for the Causes of Saints. Other proposals: leave it directly dependent on the Pope for the time being, or, more logically, appoint a new prefect.

The first suggestion was quickly rejected. Not even nineteen months had elapsed since the new Congregation was established. A return to the previous state of affairs would make a negative impression.

The second suggestion was, of course, an attractive one, because it would give a great deal of support to the liturgical renewal and would set a crown on the seven years during which the Pope had effectively presided over it. As everyone knew, the reform had in fact been successful and the Consilium, despite all the attacks against it, had been able to hold out, because the Holy Father's gestures of kindness and interest had made it clear to all both far and near that behind the Consilium stood the Pope. But the idea was too startling to be practical, and so the suggestion was dropped.

The third proposal was adopted. The qualities desired in the new prefect were: the strength to maintain unity amid variety; the perspicacity to welcome legitimate aspirations; pastoral experience and knowledge of the liturgical situation throughout the world; knowledge of the liturgy in its various aspects. And because the reform was already being carried out by an active organization in which pastors and experts were giving a new look to the prayer of the Church, it seemed suitable that the new prefect be chosen from among those who had taken an active part in either the Consilium or the Congregation. If such a choice were not possible, then (it was pointed out) it would be a step in the right direction to choose the president of one of the national liturgical commissions.

These desires were fulfilled on February 20, 1970, when Cardinal Arturo Tabera, a Spanish Claretian and Archbishop of Pamplona, was appointed the new prefect. He was a member of the Congregation, president of the Basque liturgical commission, and had been involved in the pastoral life. He had taken part only once in the meetings of the Congregation, but in other sporadic contacts he gave the impression of being a man who was open to liturgical problems and sensitive to pastoral problems.

All these facts recommended him. The two and a half years of his term as prefect were years of fervent work. They were also the period in which the Congregation, at the instigation of the prefect, sought out the national liturgical commissions through direct contacts in the various countries.

On September 15, 1973, Cardinal Tabera was appointed prefect of the Congregation for Religious.[23] An interim followed during which it was necessary to report "to the Holy Father, through the Secretariat of State, regarding all matters that called for a resolution, a direction, a decision" and "then to submit the interventions in question for the signature of the Cardinal Secretary of State."[24] And in fact during this period before the last prefect, Cardinal James Knox, Archbishop of Melbourne, was appointed (March 24, 1974), all the documents issuing from the Congregation carried the signature of Cardinal Jean Villot, Secretary of State, "by special mandate of the Supreme Pontiff."

3. *Other Difficulties*

The insertion of the Congregation for Divine Worship among the agencies of the Roman Curia was not accomplished smoothly. The following factors can be given as the reasons for the difficulty:

a) *Working methods*

While desirous of following the procedures of the curial agencies, the Congregation for Divine Worship also wanted to continue working in the spirit, and according to the method, that had been tried and tested in the years of the Consilium—all the more so since the material it would deal with was the same and the same persons would still be doing the work.

A difficulty immediately arose in the method to be followed at meetings. In the meetings of the Consilium it was possible to go into a subject exhaustively and on a broad front; there was open discussion, and the experts were able to make their contributions and bring clarity on the scientific, liturgical, and pastoral aspects of each issue. The method of the cardinalatial Congregations—a "position" was presented by a cardinal or bishop; this was followed by a reading of the "wishes" (*vota*) of

---

23. This transfer seemed to be a normal step in view of the specific competence of Cardinal Tabera. In the Curia the usual "well-informed sources" claimed that the reason was quite different, with certain complaints or confidences of the Cardinal as the basis for the conjectures. And in fact, despite all the attention paid him and all the clarifications given, there came a point when the Cardinal grew impatient; he felt isolated and had the impression that there was an effort to oust him. Unfortunately, there were those who treacherously made their way in "in sheep's clothing," tried to undermine the unity of the Consilium, and managed to influence the Cardinal; they did not do him a good service!

24. Letter of the Secretary of State, September 27, 1973 (No. 221699).

the members—did away completely with a tradition that had yielded good results in the Consilium, even if at times it had also created difficulties.

For this reason, on the occasion of the first plenary meeting of the Congregation for Divine Worship, the Secretariat of State was asked whether the consultors might also take part and whether, in view of the often technical character of the material, the relator might be the consultor who had overseen the preparatory work. The answer was: "Not by any means."

The working method also became a subject of lively dispute. In the Consilium the investigation of questions was entrusted to a study group that looked at the matter from every angle—doctrinal, liturgical, pastoral, disciplinary. When a draft was thought to be sufficiently advanced, it was submitted to the members to ascertain whether the approach taken or the solutions envisaged were acceptable. On one and the same subject several different presentations might be made in succession. In this way the Fathers were able to judge how the work was being done and to give their opinions or decisions regarding points on which their views were asked. Even a definitive approval allowed for the continuation of the work and, in every case, for its presentation to the Pope and its examination by the other curial agencies that had an interest in the subject. As a matter of fact, some of the schemas approved by the Consilium had to wait some years before being published, precisely because of the several subsequent examinations that had to be made of them by the Pope and the other curial agencies. Moreover, the final text did not always agree fully with the text that had emerged from the general meetings of the Consilium.[25]

This system, which was applied in a broadminded way and allowed for freedom of movement, ensured both respect for the competencies of all the individuals involved and a thorough and complete study of the material. But it was not accepted. During the five years of the Congregation's existence, there was constant opposition to this method of working. The agencies that regarded themselves as having any competence in a particular subject demanded the right to take part from the very out-

---

25. The following pages will make it quite clear that the accusation sometimes leveled at the Consilium of having acted independently was utterly groundless. Not only did the Pope see and carefully examine everything, but the other agencies were also called upon at every point, with some exceptions in the very early days.

In the beginning the Consilium was directly dependent on the Pope and therefore sent its work to be examined only by persons or agencies expressly indicated by the Pope himself. Subsequently application was made to all the agencies that it was thought might be interested in the subject under discussion. Some, however, who did not understand the Consilium's working methods and were presented with well-advanced schemas were afraid that they were being confronted with a *fait accompli*.

set in any meeting on it and discussion of it. Only the final schemas were to be presented at general meetings, which were regarded as the occasion for decisions that could not be altered except by the Pope.[26]

Experience shows, however, that this system requires years for the resolution of a problem, or even that no resolution will ever be reached. On the other hand, the method followed by the Consilium is proof that a streamlined procedure can accomplish something worthwhile.

b) *Competencies*

Connected with the preceding problem was a disagreement over competencies. The difficulties that the Consilium had originally had with the Congregation of Rites arose again here. In most instances the disagreements were over forms, but behind these lay divergent conceptions of the liturgy and of the role to be played by the central agencies of the Church.

The liturgy is "an exercise of the priestly office of Jesus Christ. In the liturgy, by means of signs perceptible to the senses, human sanctification is signified and brought about in ways proper to each of these signs; in the liturgy the whole public worship is performed by the Mystical Body of Jesus Christ" (Constitution on the Liturgy, no. 7). The liturgy is therefore not simply an outward garment but involves teaching, Sacred Scripture, law, pastoral practice, art, music, action, and contemplation. To break all these up into isolated parts is to mutilate the liturgical action.

The unity of the various elements also requires that the treatment of liturgical questions not be portioned out among various agencies with their different methods and mentalities but that it be carried out in a unitary way. This fact perhaps inspired the need Pope Paul VI felt at one point of establishing an appropriate agency that would deal solely with the sacred liturgy. In the mind of the Curia, however, the liturgy was still a matter of "rites and ceremonies" that drew support from discipline, pastoral practice, and doctrine, these in turn being entrusted to as many different agencies.[27]

---

26. See, in this context, the objections raised in connection with penance (p. 671, n. 21, and p. 672, n. 22), the anointing of the sick (p. 689), minor orders (pp. 739ff.), and the Eucharistic Prayers (pp. 483–84).

27. The same viewpoint emerged in the schema for the new Code of Canon Law that was presented to the SCDW in order that it might study the part dealing with the sacraments. Only the sanctification aspect of the sacraments was taken into account, while the cultic element, or the element of worship, was treated elsewhere, as though sanctification and worship did not form a unity. The SCDW prepared a study of 219 pages on the subject; it was drawn up in June 1975 by a study group comprised of G. Agustoni, P. Jounel, J. Manzanares, and M. Lessi. It was one of the last efforts of the Congregation.

By long tradition, therefore, before liturgical texts can be used in worship they have to have a verdict of "no objection" *(nihil obstat)* from the Congregation for the Doctrine of the Faith. And this is only right, since the liturgy is "faith in the state of prayer" that must be expressed with all possible purity. Yet how unsatisfactory it is to stop at the doctrinal aspect and not go on to judge opportuneness, especially if there is question of new rites and formulas, adaptations, and special concessions! In the first period of the Consilium's existence things went fairly well. In the later period doctrinal examination often infringed upon the areas of ritual, pastoral practice, and discipline, without taking into account the studies and investigations carried out by the agency whose competence was the liturgy.

c) *Divergence in "pastoral" outlook*

The Congregation for Divine Worship was continually accused of causing the evils that were afflicting the Church, of fostering a lack of discipline, of yielding to arrogant pressures from some circles or countries, and of being unable to put down abuses. There were points at which these outbursts of anger became rather violent: translations,[28] permission to distribute communion in the hand,[29] and the Eucharistic Prayers.[30] The Congregation was forced continually to justify its actions.

Different mentalities were at work here. On one side were people who believed that good government required repression. The Congregation for Divine Worship, on the other hand, maintained that it had to listen to the legitimate desires of pastors, prudently study them case by case, and anticipate problems by taking steps and making concessions that were equitable and reasonable. "There are those who think that authority is exercised by saying 'No.' Sometimes this is true. Most of the time, however, authority should be exercised by saying 'Yes' and preventing abuses rather than having to suppress them."[31]

Because of its outlook, the Congregation addressed itself to problems and requests that arose over the years: the participation of children in

---

28. See pp. 241ff.

29. A letter of Cardinal Šeper on the subject was a deadly blow to Cardinal Gut, who was personally against the concession and signed the decree allowing it only because he knew he was obeying the Pope. His reply of June 9, 1970, clearly brings out the divergent perspectives in treating problems.

30. See pp. 80ff. and 485–86. On this occasion, as on others, the recurring accusation that "evils" and "scandals" were rife in the Church "because of the weakness of superiors, even in the Roman Congregations," was a clear reference to the SCDW.

31. Letter of Cardinal Gut, June 9, 1970.

the Mass and the sacraments; creativity in the liturgy; the use of audio-visual media; and so on. But some circles and individuals in the Curia systematically labeled all this as "weakness," a giving in to the undisciplined and a desire for never-ending "reform."

4. Sunset

These attacks, like the other difficulties caused by circles opposed to the reform, could be overcome only by the Pope's support of the Congregation and his great confidence in it. His personal interventions enabled the work to go on and from time to time removed obstacles, even the most treacherous.

On June 20, 1974, the Pope received Archbishop Bugnini in order to learn from him, as he had so many times in the past, how the work was going and what problems were being faced. On this occasion the Pope gave another of his countless signs of friendliness and trust. He took a copy of his recently published apostolic exhortation *Marialis cultus*, with which, he said, he was very satisfied, and wrote on it in his own hand: "To our esteemed brother, Annibale Bugnini, Titular Bishop of Diocletiana and Secretary of the Sacred Congregation for Divine Worship, with gratitude for his labors on behalf of the sacred liturgy, and praying that he and his activity will enjoy the maternal help of the Blessed Virgin Mary, with our apostolic blessing. — Pope Paul VI, July 29, 1974."

This was our last face-to-face meeting. During the following year the Eucharistic Prayers for Masses with children and for Masses of reconciliation were published "as an experiment."

Other proposals by the Congregation almost inevitably received a negative answer. The question arose of granting special Eucharistic Prayers for Holland and Belgium, and an ordinary meeting of the Congregation was held to discuss it on June 19, 1975. The Congregation for Divine Worship, while accepting the negative judgment of the cardinals, also presented its thinking to the Pope with its usual frankness and receptivity. The Pope accepted the proposal of the Congregation for Divine Worship, which favored granting an anaphora to each of the two episcopal conferences.

On July 8, 1975, Cardinal Knox let the secretary of the Consilium know that it was proposed to "combine the Congregation for the Sacraments and the Congregation for Divine Worship." This was not something new in the thinking of Pope Paul VI; it was well known that he had been considering it for some time. On July 12 Cardinal Knox presented the Pope with a final statement on the subject that had been drawn up by some of the Congregation's experts. The best thing, said the plan, would be to create an agency for sacred worship that would have all the competencies required by a comprehensive conception of the liturgy; to other agencies would be left questions of dispensation from marriages that are ratified but not consummated, from the obligations attaching to holy orders, and so on. The Pope expressed his thanks for the statement but said that for the moment the plan could not be carried out.

On July 16, the apostolic constitution *Constans nobis studium*, dated July 11, 1975, made known the decision to combine the Congregations for the Sacraments and for Divine Worship.[32] Within a few days the plan had been carried out. The Congregation for Divine Worship, with a reduced personnel, became a section of the Congregation for the Sacraments and was banished to a corner of that agency's premises. It had had a life long enough only to produce some first blossoms—six years, two months, and thirteen days.

Even though some time later the Pope emphasized in one of his addresses the importance of the liturgy and of liturgical renewal, everyone had a sense that something had changed and that the fusion of the two Congregations was an attempt to rein back and to turn the work in a different direction. The facts were to show that the feeling was justified.[33]

What were the reasons that led the Pope to such a drastic decision, which no one expected and which lay so heavily on the Church? I said in the Preface to this book that I myself never knew any of these reasons for sure, even though, understandably in the distress of the moment, I knocked on many doors at all levels. When the opportunity arose of learning the reasons, I preferred the "discretion" that the philosopher says is the outer colonnade of the temple of wisdom. Everything has remained hidden in the secret recesses of human hearts. God keep me, therefore, from lifting now the veil that covers this "mystery." With the bureaucratic detachment of a country lawyer, I choose, nonetheless, to set down for the record some points picked up in the heat of the moment itself.

The majority looked for the source of the change in the regular meeting of the cardinals on June 19; news of the heated and hostile atmosphere

---

32. DOL 101 nos. 702-8. See *Not* 11 (1975) 209-11; *L'Osservatore Romano*, July 18, 1975.
33. The Pope's address of August 6, 1975, appeared in *L'Osservatore Romano* for August 8 (DOL 57 nos. 550-51); on the same day (August 8) an article of L. Spadini, "Lo sfratto della Liturgia," appeared in *Paese sera*. See also: A. Haug, "Ein zu geratener Reformschritt," *Gottesdienst*, August 12, 1975; B. Testacci, "Ammainata una bandiera," *Settimana del Clero*, no. 30 (August 3, 1975); S. Marsili, "Dove va la liturgia?" *Rivista Liturgica*, no. 5 (1975) 198-201; P. Gy, "La nouvelle Congrégation pour les Sacrements et le Culte divine," *La Maison-Dieu*, no. 124 (1975) 7-13; Anonymous, "La nuova Congregazione per i Sacramenti e il Culto Divino," *L'Osservatore Romano*, July 20, 1975, reprinted in *Not* 11 (1975) 217-19; F. D., "La fin d'une Congrégation. Hommage à Mgr. Bugnini," *La Libre Belgique*, December 15, 1975.

there leaked even to the outside world.[34] There were those who ascribed the change to the "authoritarian," "almost dictatorial" way in which the secretary of the Congregation supposedly managed the agency, not allowing freedom of movement to his own co-workers and limiting the role even of the cardinal prefects.[35]

But when all is said and done, all this seems to be the stuff of ordinary administrative life. There must have been something more earth-shaking. Toward the end of the summer a cardinal who was usually no enthusiast for liturgical reform told me of the existence of a "dossier" which he had seen on (or brought to?) the Pope's desk and which proved that Archbishop Bugnini was a Freemason.[36] The knowledge was com-

---

34. S. M., "In Latino est veritas, e così sia," *L'Espresso*, no. 30 (August 3, 1975) 16; L. Capovilla, "Rivolta di 19 Cardinali contro un potente Monsignore," *Tempo*, no. 37 (September 12, 1975) 21.

35. Human deficiencies are always possible, of course, but the accusation reflects a mentality that was periodically revived among officials of the Congregation who, out of ambition or defects of character, were determined to create difficulties for the secretary. Despite this, the general atmosphere in the Congregation for Divine Worship was "homelike." The Pope, moreover, was kept informed of certain attitudes and difficulties, and several times exhorted the secretary to "be patient" (audiences of July 26 and November 6, 1971, and June 20, 1974).

36. E. Catania, "Il no di Paolo VI ai comunisti conclude una guerra segreta," *Tempo*, no. 47 (November 21, 1975) 22–26, where reference is made to the famous "dossier" that was presented to the Pope. Cardinal Sebastian Baggio was charged with being a Freemason, along with Archbishop Bugnini.—See: Lo Svizzero, "Monsignore dica 'trentatrè,'" *Il Borghese*, no. 27 (July 4, 1976) 739; idem, "Una 'loggia' senza Raffaelo," *ibid.*, no. 30 (July 25, 1966) 943; idem, "I 'dossier neri' per una 'congiura,'" *ibid.*, no. 33 (August 15, 1976) 1141.

The enemies of the liturgical reform did not fail to take advantage of the situation, hoisting the flag of Marcel Lefèbvre's claim that "until 1975 the principal director of liturgical reform at the Vatican was a Freemason" (in: *Lettre aux amis et bienfaiteurs [d'Ecône]*, no. 10: *Itinéraires*, May 15, 1976).

Next came the accusations in *Sì, sì, no, no*, which gave a list of the highest authorities in the Church, all of whom were supposedly infected by Modernism or associated with the Freemasons. For Archbishop Bugnini see no. 6 (June, 1976); see also T. Casini, *Nel fumo di Satana. Verso l'ultimo scontro* (Florence, 1976) 94; as proof of the claims, *La Contro-réforme catholique*, no. 119 (October, 1976) 14, cited the fact that Archbishop Bugnini had been dismissed from his office and bundled off to Iran. See also *Minute*, no. 744 (July, 1976). Finally: "Caccia al Massone," *Panorama*, no. 538 (August 10, 1976), gave the names of 114 supposed Freemasons.

The "bomb" thus fizzled out, but in the ensuing years there was still a desire, especially on the part of the authorities, to conduct a thorough examination of the charges. It was not possible, after all, simply to let doubts, hesitations, and suspicions stand unchallenged; justice and love of truth could not accept that. V. Levi's denial, "Riflessioni di fine settimana," *L'Osservatore Romano*, October 10, 1976, elicited further charges in *Sì, sì, no, no*. (The question arises of how such a poisonous, anti-conciliar publication, filled with lies and calumnies, could have prospered, even if directed by a priest, at Grottaferrata, so close to Rome.)

municated with the utmost secrecy, but it then became known that the rumor was already abroad in curial circles. The charge was absurd, a malignant calumny. The weapon chosen for this new attack on the liturgical reform was to bespatter the moral purity of the secretary of the reform. Therefore Archbishop Bugnini wrote as follows to the Pope (October 22, 1975):

> I have never had any interest in Freemasonry; I do not know what it is, what it does, or what its purposes are. I have lived as a religious for fifty years, as a priest for forty; for twenty-six my life has been limited to school, home, and office, and for eleven to home and office alone. I was born poor and I live as a poor man . . . . Anyone interested could learn that for eleven years I have traveled to and from my office by public transportation. I live in my community, in two small rooms, which barely contain what for me are the necessities of life.

This last sentence alludes to the charge that I had been abundantly supplied with luxuries by the Freemasons.

Hardly a month later the same report began to spread in the press, becoming increasingly persistent and including other individuals as well. The silence of the official organs of the Holy See was interpreted as proof that the "rumors" were well-founded. But the charges were inflated to the point where in the course of 1976 they were extended to include a good number of the higher authorities in the Roman agencies, as well as eminent representatives of the worldwide episcopacy. The nonsense thus proved its own undoing. But repeated calumnies leave lingering suspicions. And in fact suspicion did linger, at least for the former secretary of the Congregation for Divine Worship.

In January 1980 a friend in the United States told me that the *Homiletic and Pastoral Review* was stirring up the old mud in the form of two letters from readers. This time I decided to give myself the pleasure of writing to the editor, Kenneth Baker, S.J., in New York:

> *Editor:* I was shown p. 8 of *Homiletic and Pastoral Review*, [*August*] *1979* (*sic*) (actually, HPR, January 1980—Ed.) where two references are made in which I am personally concerned. You know without doubt that when in 1976 polemics on freemasonry spread in the ecclesiastical circles, and at first 2, then 17 and then 114 names were paraded around, I preferred to retreat in absolute silence, the calumny being so brazen and insensible. Only upon the insistence of my French friends did I make a brief declaration which read thus: "Mgr. Bugnini leaves to the Holy See the task of defending him, if it deems it useful. But he categorically denies ever having the least contact, direct or indirect, with freemasonry or any other society of the kind" (*Le Figaro*, Oct. 8, 1976).

Some wrote that I was too "discreet" (Jean Bourdarias, in *Le Figaro*, Oct. 8, 1976).[37] Perhaps with reason. I had to keep in mind that being in the service of the Holy See, it was the concern of the Holy See to defend the honour and credibility of its officials. And the Holy See intervened with a note in the *Osservatore Romano*, Oct. 10, 1976, in which it declared: "A consideration comes to us from the reading of a sheet of paper of the very worst clericalism, entitled 'Yes, Yes, No, No,' and written by people who lack courage to sign their names and surnames. They defend a type of purity of faith, which consists in shouting Attack them! at all those who do not think like them, i.e. in terms of the most squalid conservative thinking: they may be cardinals, archbishops, theologians, men of the Curia, journalists and so on. They spend their time in accusing the official and institutional Church of being guided by prelates affiliated to freemasonry. They write their names and dates of membership, with the presumption of a treacherous official who writes falsehood in public documents. There would be only one way to silence them: a sharp denunciation for calumny and defamation, through the press, with all the ample availability of proof. They would end behind bars. Should we adhere to legal channels? It would be to give too much importance to people who behave in a shameless way.

"This firm and decisive protest is enough, at least for now. Not one, we write, not one of the prelates pointed out by them has ever had anything to do with freemasonry. This must be said to reject the probable accusation that the one who keeps silent shows his consent. For the rest it is too evident that the Yes, Yes, No, No gospel preacher hides in this case mean and base morality, and it is not clear whether also doubtful and ignoble interests."

I ended my response to the first of the periodical's "readers" by saying that all this would be enough of an answer. Then I added:

But for him and his colleagues, calumniators by profession, (how sad, that also a bishop [Marcel Lefèbvre] should indulge himself in such miserable intrigues against a fellow bishop!), I repeat what I wrote [to the Pope] in 1976: "I do not own anything in this world more precious than the pectoral cross: if one is able to prove, honestly and objectively, an iota of truth of what they affirm, I am ready to return back the pectoral cross."

The other reader accused me and the liturgical reform of not believing in the Eucharist and of having emptied the churches. I answered simply:

---

37. The writer of the article said: "To have written these lines [in *Le Figaro*], Archbishop Bugnini, whom some seem to blame for being overly discreet, must have been deeply wounded and bruised by a course of action that will in the final analysis turn against those who adopted it."

1) By the grace of God my faith in the Holy Eucharist was and is that of the Holy Catholic Church. I challenge . . . to find a single expression in the liturgical reform that puts in doubt faith in the Holy Eucharist. 2) As for the "liturgical revolution," which would have alienated "millions" of people from the faith, he makes a gratuitous claim. The author knows very well that the causes of the weakening of faith in our time are many and complex. The liturgical reform not only [has] not deviated from the faith, but has been the most valid factor to give the faithful a faith more convincing, strong and operative in charity.[38]

I ended by saying how surprised I was to see such obvious falsehoods being still reprinted in 1980 and such well-known lies being given a semblance of truth and offered to the readers of a respectable publication. The periodical did not have the courage to reply to my clarification, although some readers did write approvingly in a later issue.

It is worth recalling here another in the flood of rumors and hypotheses that surrounded the suppression of the Congregation for Divine Worship. The secretary, it was said, had permitted experiments that created confusion and disorder in the liturgy. This rumor was echoed at the meeting of June 19, 1975, which discussed the request of the episcopal conferences of Holland and Belgium for one or two Eucharistic Prayers of their own. In a preliminary statement the prefect of the Congregation for the Doctrine of the Faith blamed the Congregation for Divine Worship for having allowed the Eucharistic Prayers for Masses with children and Masses of reconciliation, another on the occasion of a synod (Switzerland), and still others for special circumstances. But in fact all these prayers had been authorized by the Pope in general or particular concessions. No Eucharistic Prayer was ever authorized by the Congregation before it had been examined by competent agencies and had received papal approval.[39]

The Consilium did make extensive use of a permission granted by the far-sighted Paul VI from the very beginning of the reform—permission for experiments prior to the redaction of the official documents. It had every right to do so. But, as we shall see, it allowed these experiments with restrictions of time and place and to carefully defined persons.

Such experiments were a necessity. The whole body of individuals working on the reform were fully aware of their responsibility in proposing formulas and rites that were sometimes entirely new. No one possessing even a minimum of intelligence could have opposed a procedure

38. *Homiletic and Pastoral Review* 80 (May 1980) 4–6.
39. See below, pp. 465–66 and 477, nn. 36-38.

that helped to obviate surprises, triviality, and a lack of spiritual inspiration or pastoral appropriateness. The Pope realized this and unhesitatingly allowed us to enter upon the path of experimentation. Others regarded this route as less advisable. There were those who opposed it in a systematic way. The Pope, however, was convinced of it, and the experiments continued.

The problem gradually bulked larger, of course, and caused even greater hesitation as it became a question of attempting adaptations in each region of the world to the genius, customs, usages, and needs of the various peoples. Here, too, we proceeded in the same spirit and within carefully defined limits.

There were some drawbacks, of course, and excesses and unauthorized ventures. But this does not justify saying that the "authorized" experiments sowed "confusion and disorder," even if perfection is not to be found in this sad world.

II. First Accomplishments

March 7, 1965: Shift from Latin to Vernacular

Once the work of the study groups preparing for the reform was under way, the Consilium began to concern itself with the principles, norms, and aids for regulating the initial practical applications.

Some episcopal conferences had already been asking permission to use the language of their countries in some parts of the liturgy. Others were preparing to make decisions in liturgical matters. According to its charter of February 29, 1964, one responsibility of the Consilium was to prepare an "instruction" that would, among other things, "clearly outline the competence of territorial ecclesiastical authorities, pending the reform of the rites and liturgical books."[1]

In a letter of March 25, 1964, addressed to the papal representatives in the various countries, the Consilium hastened to communicate the contents of the February 29 document to the presidents of the episcopal conferences. It explained that decisions in liturgical matters had to be carried by a two-thirds majority; that for the time being it did not seem right to request "modifications, omissions, or variations in the present arrangement of the liturgical celebrations"; and that requests for introduction of the vernacular had to specify the parts in which the vernacular was desired and the texts that were to be used. With regard to introduction of the vernaculars, the letter added: *"Doing one part at a time* seems appropriate, as does the principle of *proceeding gradually.* The point is to avoid an excessively abrupt transition from the present arrangement of almost

---

1. Letter of Cardinal A. Cicognani to Cardinal A. Lercaro, president of the Consilium, in *DOL* 77 no. 613.

complete fidelity to Latin to the new arrangement that provides for bringing in the vernacular more extensively."[2]

The first of these two principles was called for by the conciliar Constitution, which had wanted to ensure a peaceful coexistence of Latin and the vernaculars.[3] The second reflected the need of allowing the faithful to be introduced gradually to the new rites. By and large, with the exception of some countries that had been better prepared by the liturgical movement, the Church was not ready for a sudden complete change in the liturgy. A period was needed during which the principles of the liturgical Constitution could be assimilated in a concrete way through a gradual renewal of forms.

The principle of gradualness was also the basis of the Consilium's concern to introduce first those changes which were indispensable for a more intense liturgical participation and which at the same time would not prejudice the future reform. It limited itself to those changes that it could be fairly sure would also be adopted in the subsequent reform.

The first application of the liturgical Constitution was defined and regulated by the Consilium in the instruction *Inter Oecumenici*, which was the fruit of six months of intense work and was published on September 26, 1964, the Holy Father's birthday.[4] It was to take effect on March 7, 1965, the First Sunday of Lent.

March 7 thus became a historical date and a milestone in the history of liturgical reform. It was the first tangible fruit of a Council that was still in full swing and the beginning of a process in which the liturgy was brought closer to the assemblies taking part in it and, at the same time, acquired a new look after centuries of inviolable uniformity.

The day of the change was preceded by feverish activity in every country—instructions to the faithful, practical explanations,[5] hard work

---

2. *EDIL* 192-96; *DOL* 79 nos. 615-19. The text as given in *EDIL* is incomplete; missing are the part of no. 4 that explains the criteria governing gradualness in implementing the reform, and the whole of nos. 5-8.

3. The early regulations for the use of the vernacular, especially at the very beginning, reflected a "prudence" that was in fact almost a fear of taking too much away from Latin. Extreme reserve was also shown in the regulations of those bishops who limited the use of the vernacular to well-defined circumstances, for example, to Masses on Sundays and holydays of obligation and to one or two Masses on weekdays.

4. SCR, instruction (first) *Inter Oecumenici*: *AAS* 56 (1964) 877-900 (*EDIL* 199ff. = *DOL* 23 nos. 293-391). See below, pp. 825ff., on this document.

5. As March 7 drew closer, some conferences that were alert to the situation, and some individual bishops, asked permission to prepare their clergy and the faithful by celebrating some Masses according to the new norms, *ad experimentum*. The first requests came from Spain and Italy in November 1964. There was a difficulty in granting the requests, since

by experts to turn out the first translations, and the printing of the liturgical books.[6] The Consilium, for its part, was focusing its attention on three areas in particular: language, the Missal, and concelebration.

1. *First Steps*

On April 21, 1964, the Holy Father had approved the criteria established by the Consilium for use of the vernaculars in the liturgy.[7] These norms defined in a clear and distinct way the parts of the Mass and of the celebration of the sacraments and sacramentals in which the vernaculars could be used. Before being codified in the first instruction, these criteria provided the content of a "normative decree" to be used in approving the decisions of episcopal conferences, which sometimes asked for everything that could possibly be granted!

The normative decree[8] provided that:

The vernacular can be used:
1. In sung and recited Masses that are celebrated with a congregation:
   a) in the lessons, epistle, and gospel;
   b) in the prayer of the faithful;
   c) in the chants of the Ordinary of the Mass,
       namely, the *Kyrie, Gloria, Credo, Sanctus-Benedictus,* and *Agnus Dei;*
   d) in the chants of the Proper of the Mass: the introit, offertory, and communion antiphons with their psalms, and the chants between the readings;
   e) in the acclamations, greetings, and dialogues;
   f) in the Our Father, as well as in its introduction and in the embolism;
   g) in the formulas for the communion of the faithful;
   h) in the collect, prayer over the gifts, prayer after communion, and prayer "over the people."

---

the relevant liturgical books were still not ready. But it was stated that a good master of ceremonies who had only the regulations in the instruction as a guide could prepare a dignified ceremony. On this basis the Holy Father gave his consent (via Cardinal Lercaro in an audience of December 17, 1964). A letter from the Consilium (December 21, 1964) communicated the permission to the presidents of the national liturgical commissions and made them responsible for the experiments. There had to be a legitimate reason for the experiments, and the clergy, faithful, servers, and singers had to be given a careful pastoral, technical, and ceremonial preparation. The letter ended by saying that it would be better not to make the experiments than to have an imperfect and inadequate celebration.

6. The printing of liturgical books required a technical training that until then only the pontifical publishers had. In this area too the different countries had to create an organization, some of them from scratch.

7. See below, Chapter 12, on General Meeting II (pp. 142–44).

8. See *Not* 1 (1965) 9.

2. In the administration of the sacraments and sacramentals:
   a) in the rites of baptism, confirmation, penance, marriage, and anointing of the sick, including the sacramental formulas; and in the distribution of communion outside of Mass;
   b) in the conferring of holy orders: in the address that begins each ordination or consecration; in the examination of the candidate in an episcopal consecration; and in the admonitions;
   c) in the sacramentals;
   d) in funerals.

Then began one of the tasks that the Consilium was specifically charged with performing: the confirmation of decisions made by the episcopal conferences and of the vernacular liturgical texts that they had approved.[9] The first decrees were signed by the Cardinal President on April 25, 1964. The very first gave approval to use of the Sango language for Scripture readings in the Republic of Central Africa.[10] A year later (April 13, 1965), 87 conferences had requested approval of texts in the vernacular, 187 texts had been approved, 205 languages had been allowed. Thirty-three conferences had asked for a normative decree for the Mass, 60 for the sacraments.

In order that translations might be made without the pressure of hurry, it was accepted that approval might initially be given to use translations already in use among the faithful, whether in missalettes or in small rituals. The number of such texts that could be used "until the competent territorial ecclesiastical authority had provided an official translation" varied from country to country. Italy, for example, adopted six of them; fourteen missalettes were presented for approval by the Spanish-speaking countries, although not all were in fact used.

In general, all the conferences wanted to have a single text for the Ordinary of the Mass. The principle of uniformity was then extended to the other parts of the Mass. In a short time the larger nations had an altar Missal for Sundays and feastdays.[11] The first was the United States conference with its *Roman Missal—Missale Romanum*, published by the Catholic

---

9. There is a list in *Notitiae* of all the decrees issued and the vernacular liturgical books approved by the Consilium and later by the SCDW. For an overview of the Consilium's vast activity in this area, together with a detailed listing of the decrees issued for the individual countries and religious families, see *Not* no. 113, which contains the general indexes for 1965–75; see also "Le lingue parlate nella liturgia dopo il Concilio Vaticano II," *Not* 15 (1979) 387–520.

10. See *Not* 1 (1965) 277. The first issue (nos. 1-4, 1965) lists all the decrees granted in a year.

11. See C. Braga, C.M., "Il lavoro finora compiuto: metodi, difficoltà incontrate," in *Le traduzioni dei libri liturgici. Atti del Congresso tenuto a Roma il 9–13 novembre 1965* (Vatican City, 1966) 57–72.

Book Publishing Company of New York. It was the first in line, but it also brought the first difficulty: despite its bilingual title, the Missal did not contain the Latin text, contrary to the provision in no. 57 of the instruction *Inter Oecumenici*. The publishers were able to show, however, that the Missal had been almost completely printed by the time the instruction appeared.[12] Use of the Missal was therefore allowed until the supply ran out; at that point the bishops would be obliged to complete the book by including the new Ordinary of the Mass and the *Ritus servandus*, as well as any corrections introduced in the meantime,[13] and by printing the complete Latin text along with the English.

Next was the Latin-French Missal in two volumes, with a third that contained the readings; all the French-speaking countries were obliged to use it. The Latin-German Missal was also in three volumes; the Latin-English Missal for England and Wales was in five. In April 1965, Italy published a "Latin-Italian Roman Missal for Sundays and Feastdays." Since the national liturgical commission of Italy had taken no action in this matter, the Pope commissioned the Consilium, "as a last resort," to produce the needed book; the task took three months of intense work (February to April).[14]

The criteria for introducing the vernacular into the sacraments allowed this to be done on a rather extensive scale. The only area excluded was holy orders, except for the addresses and admonitions.

Almost universally, recourse was had to "manual" editions already in use. The alternative was to risk introducing translations that would be short-lived; for this reason approval of existing versions was sought. But there were also some courageous attempts, as, for example, that of the Canadian bishops with their *Rituel des sacrements*,[15] and, on a more modest scale, that of the Italian bishops with their *Rituale dei sacramenti e dei sacramentali.*[16]

---

12. The plea was regarded as having been made in good faith. As a matter of fact, the regulation in no. 57 of the instruction *Inter Oecumenici* was not originally included; it was added with the final corrections proposed by the SCR. Therefore, even the members and consultors of the Consilium who had the drafts in their possession were not informed on this point.

13. See below, pp. 114–15.

14. These Missals are described in *Not* 1 (1965) 161, 163, 164, 165, 166, 281.

15. See *ibid.*, 162.

16. See *ibid.*, 2 (1966) 267.

2. The Preface in the Vernacular

The normative decree certainly allowed a great deal, but the resultant Mass, partly in Latin, partly in the vernacular, was a hybrid, lacking in continuity.

The part in which the clash was most evident was the preface, in which the Latin text was framed by a dialogue and a *Sanctus* that could be and in fact were recited in the vernacular. The Consilium discussed this problem at length at its meeting of April 1964, which established the criteria for approving the decisions of the episcopal conferences. It finally seemed better, however, to leave the preface in Latin, both because it was part of the Canon and because of the impressive Gregorian melodies provided for it. These were the two official arguments. There was a further and perhaps more persuasive reason: Some Fathers thought that if the vernacular were allowed for the preface, too much would have been conceded, and they were therefore opposed. The problem came up again in the following autumn (fourth meeting) because of pressure from various conferences for permission to have the preface in the vernacular.

The two "official" reasons proved on re-examination to be easily countered. It is true that the preface is part of the Canon; in practice, however, the Canon has begun with the *Te igitur* since as far back as the eighth century. In light of this fact, greater emphasis could rightly be put on the discomfort of shifting from vernacular to Latin and back to vernacular and on the value of having the congregation understand texts of such lyrical beauty and profound theological content. The argument from the Gregorian melodies could be applied to other texts that were now being recited in the vernacular, such as the Our Father. A different solution should therefore be found that would apply to all these texts: adapt the existing melodies or compose others better suited to texts in the vernacular. The proposal was put to a vote on November 16; of the 25 Fathers voting, 21 were in favor and only 4 against.

Because the vote in this case had to do with texts for which the Consilium could not grant use of the vernacular, the Cardinal President submitted the matter to the Holy Father on December 17, 1964. On January 4, 1965, the Pope let it be known that the decision should be postponed. But pressure from the conferences was increasing. The experience of the vernacular that began on March 7, 1965, only intensified from day to day the malaise felt at placing a Latin text in a vernacular framework.

The problem was again presented to the Holy Father on March 22, 1965, along with requests from twenty-seven episcopal conferences. A letter from the Secretariat of State (No. 36624), dated April 27, communicated the Pope's answer: "that the resolution of this matter be left to the decision of each conference of bishops."[17]

On May 14, hardly twenty days later, the first formal request came in from India. Next came requests from Malaya, Jamaica, Panama, Peru, and Venezuela, and then gradually from all the other countries.

3. *The Roman Canon*

The welcome given by the faithful to the introduction, even if only partial, of the vernaculars into the liturgy was so great that the question of language could not be shelved on March 7 or even on April 27, when the translation of the preface was allowed.

The settlement of problems in this area of the reform was to occupy the Consilium for years to come. Various measures would clarify specific questions about translations, provisional texts, the competent authorities in this area, the use of the vernacular by religious, and editions of liturgical books. I shall take up all these matters as I proceed, but they can all be called peripheral in comparison with the fundamental principle of allowing the vernaculars into the liturgy. But the vernaculars had to stop at the threshold of the Roman Canon and the sacrament of holy orders. Many thought or hoped that this threshold would not be crossed, or at least not in the near future.

But a need was very quickly felt for having the entire liturgy in the vernacular. It was felt with special intensity in certain parts of the world, particularly in the Netherlands, where translations of the Canon were beginning to circulate, along with texts of new Eucharistic Prayers. In order to retain control of liturgical development, the Dutch episcopal conference presented requests to the Holy See via Bishop Jean Bluyssen, of 's-Hertogenbosch, president of the national liturgical commission and a member of the Consilium. These requests were for permission to develop and revise the presidential prayers of the Mass, to translate the Canon and the rites of holy orders, to use other Eucharistic Prayers that would be approved by the Holy See, to allow the laity to distribute communion, and to let them do so by placing the sacred host in the hand of the faithful.[18]

---

17. See *ibid.*, 1 (1965) 149 (*DOL* 110 no. 766).

18. Some instances of violations of liturgical discipline came to the attention of the public and required the Holy See to step in; see the declaration of the SCR and the Consilium (December 29, 1966) on "family eucharistic meals," in *Not* 3 (1967) 37ff. (*DOL* 35 nos. 433-34).

By order of the Holy Father, Cardinal Amleto Cicognani, Secretary of State, on October 21, 1966 (No. 81223), commissioned the Consilium, together with the Congregation of Rites, to conduct an urgent review of this sensitive question "in order to establish a norm that would apply not only to the request of the Dutch episcopate but to other similar requests that might be presented."

After study of the Dutch problem, a "mission" composed of Monsignor Amato Pietro Frutaz, relator general of the historical section of the Congregation of Rites, Father Annibale Bugnini, secretary of the Consilium, and Bishop Jan Willebrands (subsequently replaced by Bishop Petrus Canisius Van Lierde) was sent to the Netherlands.[19] The program for the visit was drawn up in direct consultation with the Holy Father on December 9 and was carried out from December 15 to December 20. It included discussing the liturgy with Cardinal Alfrink and all the bishops, hearing the views of the provincials of the Franciscans and Jesuits, and taking part in several celebrations in a variety of environments.

On January 7 the mission, along with Archbishop Dell'Acqua and Father Antonelli, was received by the Holy Father for the purpose of drawing appropriate conclusions from the visit. It was agreed that some requests of the Dutch Conference had to be granted: the translation of the Canon and the entire rite of ordination, the study and eventual approval of three new anaphoras, the preparation of new texts for the presidential prayers of the Mass, and more copious cycles of readings for Sundays and weekdays.

The Holy Father asked that a hearing be given first to the views of a special commission of curial cardinals and bishops and that it be seriously considered whether "it is not appropriate to extend the concessions foreseen for the Netherlands to other countries or even to the entire Church." The reason for this second point was that requests had meanwhile come in from various episcopal conferences for the same concessions.[20]

---

19. The secretary of the Consilium had already paid a visit to the Netherlands in September 1965 in order to become directly acquainted with the situation. The results of his visit were communicated to Cardinal Alfrink in a letter from the president of the Consilium (October 12, 1965), but without perceptible impact.

The secretary paid a third visit from December 8 to 13, 1973, when he had become secretary of the SCDW. At that time he met with the episcopal conference and the national liturgical commission to discuss the main aspects of the liturgical situation in the Netherlands and the steps that were to be taken on the basis of a note that he had sent, with the Pope's approval, to the bishops concerned on November 20 of that same year.

20. In the early days of January alone, South Africa, Jamaica, France, and the United States had asked for the Canon in the vernacular.

The commission met on January 17, 1967, in the meeting room of the Congregation of Rites. All those invited were present.[21] Two days later, on the 19th, the secretary of the Consilium conveyed to the Holy Father the views expressed by each member of the commission on each point.

On January 31, 1967 (No. 89147) the Holy Father approved the letter of concession to be sent to Cardinal Bernard Alfrink from the Consilium. In the same communication from the Secretariat of State to the Consilium, all the conferences that had requested it were given permission to introduce the vernacular into the Canon and the rite of ordinations and to adopt weekday Lectionaries approved by the Consilium. The desire was expressed that in sacred orders the essential formula for the ordination of deacons, priests, and bishops remain in Latin, but the decision was left to the conferences. In addition, the preparation of new Eucharistic Prayers was requested; meanwhile a special commission would be examining those submitted by the Netherlands. The Consilium was also asked to work on a general decree regarding concessions available to the entire Church.[22]

Some time was to pass before approval was actually given to the translations of the Roman Canon that had been presented by the episcopal conferences. The Consilium was in fact somewhat fearful of the responsibility and difficulty of translating such a venerable text in a manner at once dignified and accurate. Therefore, on February 13 it directed joint commissions of members from the various language areas to prepare translations that would be literal and faithful. The commissions did a careful job in collaboration with the national liturgical commissions. In May and June the episcopal conferences concerned in the matter approved the texts and sent them to the Consilium for its confirmation.[23]

---

21. Those invited were: Cardinals Giacomo Lercaro, Arcadio M. Larraona, and Charles Journet; Bishops Pietro Parente, secretary of the Congregation for the Doctrine of the Faith; Giacomo Violardo, secretary of the Congregation for the Sacraments; Father Ferdinando Antonelli, secretary of the SCR. The members of the commission were Bishop Van Lierde, Monsignor Frutaz, and Father Bugnini.

22. Notice of the concession was given in *Not* 3 (1967) 154 (*DOL* 117 nos. 816-19). The regulations issued by the Pope were confirmed in another letter from the Secretariat of State on February 13, 1967.

The decree, preparation of which was under way, would take the form of a second instruction on the implementation of the liturgical reform: *Tres abhinc annos* (May 4, 1967) (*DOL* 39 nos. 445-74). The instruction speaks in no. 28 of the possibility of using the vernacular in the Canon of the Mass, all the rites of ordination, and the readings of the Divine Office (*EDIL* 837; *DOL* no. 474).

23. By August 14 the following translations had come in: English, French, Spanish, Portuguese, Flemish, Sango (Central Africa), Tumbuka (Malawi), Gujarati (India), Lingala (Congo), Tshiluba (Congo), and Bulu (Cameroons).

But the texts did not survive the revisional examination of the Congregation for the Doctrine of the Faith; the reason given was that the translations were overly free and oversimplified. The Congregation proposed as a temporary measure the use of existing translations to be found in the missalettes. The Consilium was puzzled by the suggestion,[24] but it agreed in order not to postpone a solution indefinitely. Therefore, on August 10, 1967, it sent to all the episcopal conferences a communication that had been approved by the Pope on August 4. This included the following practical directives:

1. The version which is in the process of preparation, the sole version for the languages spoken in the several countries, is to render faithfully the text of the Roman Canon, without variations, omissions, or insertions which would make it different from the Latin text.

2. The language is to be that normally used in liturgical texts, avoiding exaggerated classical and modern forms.

3. The style is to display a certain rhythm, making the text easy to speak and sing.

4. Since it is expected that a considerable period will be needed for the revision and confirmation of the versions prepared by the episcopal conferences, and since, while there is no official translation, provision should be made to supply the necessary uniformity between the various texts, the episcopal conferences may, *in the meantime*, approve and permit one of the translations already in use with the permission of ecclesiastical authority.[25]

There is to be no more than a single translation adopted by any nation during the interim period.

5. It is the desire of the Holy Father that missals, whether they are for feast days or for daily use, in complete or partial editions, should always carry the Latin text next to the vernacular version, in double columns, or facing pages, and not [be] in pamphlet form or separate books. This is in accordance with the Instruction *Inter Oecumenici* of 26 September 1964, nos. 57 and 98 and with the Decree of the Sacred Congregation of Rites *De editionibus librorum liturgicorum* of 27 January 1966, no. 5.[26] Any official approval was put off until the end of the summer holidays.

The conferences, and especially the liturgical commissions, were not very enthusiastic about this communication; they interpreted it as a sign

---

24. The reasons for the Consilium's opposition to this practice had been communicated to the presidents of the episcopal conferences in a letter of June 21, 1967: *Not* 3 (1967) 296 (*DOL* 41 nos. 477-86; see no. 486).

25. The wording "already in use with the permission of ecclesiastical authority," instead of "found in hand missals for the faithful," was suggested by the Holy Father.

26. *Not* 3 (1967) 326 (*DOL* 118 nos. 820-25). The other documents referred to are in *DOL* 23 nos. 349 and 390; 134 no. 913.

of distrust of their work, which was found less acceptable than the translations in the missalettes, though these were often inferior from a literary standpoint.

The main reason for the refusal of the Holy See to issue an approval was omissions found in the new versions. The Holy See was insisting on a "faithful and complete" translation and was requiring specifically:

—the preservation of Alcuin's insert, "pro quibus tibi offerimus," in the memento of the living;

—the retention of the conclusions "Per (eundem) Christum Dominum nostrum";

—the preservation, without addition or omission, of the lists of the saints in the *Communicantes* and the *Nobis quoque*.

Agreement was finally reached on the French translation. The Congregation for the Doctrine of the Faith approved this, and on October 31, 1967, the Consilium sent it to the conferences as a model, urging that the other translations be complete and entirely faithful, especially at the points just indicated.

Thus, little by little, the vernacular also came to be heard in the Canon of the Mass.[27]

---

27. The emphasis on accurate and faithful translation was certainly legitimate, but it also had its drawbacks. This was brought home to the secretariat of the Consilium in connection with the Italian translation it had prepared. When the translation was introduced by the episcopate, some persons raised a fruitless question about the translation of *enim* in the words of consecration. The discussion continued for a long time; it had its dramatic moments and stimulated research and study by experts in theology and philology; doubts were raised about the validity of the consecration. It was said that the translation "Take and eat, *because (poichè)* this is my body" was "grammatically inaccurate and theologically unfortunate," inasmuch as it might cast doubt on the validity of the formula used for the consecration. The Latin *enim*, it was said, should be translated by an asseverative "in fact" *(infatti)* and not by an explicative and consequential "because."

The Secretariat of State became so alarmed that it decided "to suspend the circulation of this Canon for the time being, with the agreement of the Italian Episcopal Conference" (February 14, 1968; No. 112468). Others suggested that the best solution would be to leave the formula of consecration in Latin.

After various consultations and exchanges of letters, the secretariat of the Consilium succeeded, on April 4, 1968, in allaying the fears of the papal Secretariat by deciding that: (1) the *enim* is rhetorical and can be omitted; it was not omitted in the Italian translation, despite the vote to this effect in the Italian Episcopal Conference, because the Congregation for the Doctrine of the Faith had already decided that *enim* should be translated in the French, German, English, and Spanish versions; (2) a change could not be made in the Italian version alone; (3) the words of consecration would eventually be made uniform in all the Eucharistic Prayers, and the same would hold for the translations of these, permission being given not to translate *enim*.

The translation of *pro multis* created a similar incident, with wide international participation. The secretariat of the Consilium became so weary of explaining the same thing over

4. Against the Mind of the Council?

The movement officially begun on March 7, 1965, led for practical purposes to all parts of the liturgy being translated into the vernacular, in a process that, while gradual, was also quite swift. Did this represent a simple yielding to pressure, or was it a downright distortion of the Council's decrees? Some said, and still say, that the latter was the case.

It cannot be denied that the principle, approved by the Council, of using the vernaculars was given a broad interpretation. But this interpretation did not spring from a desire to take risks or from an itch for novelty; it was adopted after deliberation, with the approval of competent authority, and in line with the spirit of the conciliar decrees.

It is the prerogative of the Holy See and, within the limits set by law, of the episcopal conferences and individual bishops to regulate the sacred liturgy. These various authorities saw it as a pastoral necessity that the faithful should understand the Canon of the Mass; they simply extended the principle of intelligibility that had already been admitted for the other parts of the Mass. They examined the problem in their plenary meetings, made their decisions, and presented these to the Holy See for approval. The Pope, as we have seen, engaged in lengthy consultation with the competent Roman agencies, studied the concrete situation and needs and the spirit of the Council, and finally approved the requests of the episcopal conferences.

The latter decided that it was legitimate and pastorally useful, if not necessary, to put the Canon of the Mass into the vernacular. If the rest of the Mass were to be celebrated in the vernacular while the Canon remained in Latin, it would have been like opening all the doors of the house to a guest and then excluding him from its heart. It is in the heart that the life is to be found; it is in the Canon that the mystery resides. The Canon is a vital part of a living liturgy. It did remain in Latin for over two years from the beginning of the reform, but pastoral experience showed that a situation in which the celebration was half in the vernacular and half in Latin was intolerable. This, then, is a classic example of a legitimate postconciliar development. It was a logical consequence of premises set down by the Council itself. In fact, even if the extension of the vernacular to the entire liturgy can be called a broad interpretation (though made by one with the right to make it), it cannot be said to contradict the Constitution on the Sacred Liturgy.

---

and over to individual correspondents that it commissioned M. Zerwick to write an article, "Pro vobis et pro multis effundetur," *Not* 6 (1970) 138.

In article 54 the Constitution says that a *suitable* place may be allowed to the mother tongue in Masses celebrated with the people, *especially* ("in the first place") in the readings and the prayer of the faithful and, depending on local conditions, also in the parts belonging to the people. The wording is vague. What is a "suitable" place? What is the point of the words "in the first place"? And what does "parts belonging to the people" include?

In the third paragraph of this same article 54, the Council leaves it to the episcopal conferences to judge whether "a more extended use of the mother tongue" is desirable. What limits, then, did the Council intend to set? If we judge solely on the basis of the text, no one will ever be able to answer with certainty. The situation changes if we turn to the acts of the Council.[28]

In his report to the Council on article 54, Bishop Jesús Enciso Viana of Mallorca, a member of the conciliar liturgical commission, had this to say:

> We have formulated the article in this manner so that those who wish to celebrate the entire Mass in Latin may not be able to force their viewpoint on others, while those who wish to use the vernacular in some parts of the Mass may not be able to compel others to do the same. . . . The door is not closed against anyone. . . .
>
> In regard to the various parts of the Mass in which the vernacular may be used—and we have expressly not decided to exclude any part, even though persons entirely deserving of respect wanted to exclude the Canon—we have decided on the following method of achieving the goal stated above:
>
> a) for the readings and the prayer of the faithful, where there are very special reasons for using the vernacular, the territorial authorities will have competence in accordance with the norm set down in article 36. The peculiar nature of these parts is suggested by the adverb *praesertim* ["in the first place"];
>
> b) for the other parts of the Mass, both in the Proper and in the Ordinary, we make a double distinction, according as these parts are sung or recited by the faithful or are sung or recited by the celebrant. In the former case the territorial authorities have competence, again in accordance with the norm in article 36. In the latter case, the norm set down in article 40 is to be followed.

Bishop Enciso ended by saying that only one obligation is imposed— that of taking steps "enabling the faithful to say or sing together in Latin those parts of the Ordinary of the Mass belonging to them."

---

28. Concilium Vaticanum II, *Schema Constitutionis de Sacra Liturgia: Emendationes a Patribus Conciliaribus postulatae, a Commissione Conciliari de sacra Liturgia examinatae et propositae* VI, Caput II Schematis de Sacrosancto Eucharistiae Mysterio, p. 18.

The Council's intention was to open the treasures of the table of the Word and of the Eucharistic table to the people. Is there anything that is not part of the liturgical action of God's people? No! Everything belongs to them. Nothing is excluded from their attention and their participation. They are to take part in the singing with minds and voices; in the readings through hearing and understanding, for the first thing a speaker wants is to be understood; in the presidential prayers and Eucharistic Prayer through understanding, since they are to ratify with their "Amen" what the priest has done and asked of God in the assembly's name. If, then, the purpose of using the vernacular in the liturgy is to enable the assembly to participate consciously, actively, and fruitfully, there is no justification for using in any part of the sacred action a language that the people do not understand.[29]

Time will show the validity of these principles. The question of Latin was raised again as late as the eighties. A questionnaire sent to the bishops of the entire world showed that in their view, if the vernaculars had not been introduced, "the liturgical reform would have been much less fruitful; that the demand for Latin is almost nonexistent; and that Latin is more and more disappearing from use as a liturgical language of the Church."[30]

In the view of some, this disappearance is to be blamed on the Consilium and the Congregation for Divine Worship. The charge is unjust; these bodies never discouraged the use of Latin. They even issued regulations in favor of Latin: Every Missal in a national language is to have an appendix with at least a minimum number of formularies in Latin.[31] They several times urged that "the faithful" be able "to say or to sing together those parts of the Ordinary of the Mass belonging to them."

29. See A. Bugnini, "Restaurare la linea autentica del Concilio?" Not 10 (1974) 217–21; idem, "Il Canone in volgare," Avvenire, March 23, 1968. The latter article was prepared at the request of the Holy Father and revised by him personally. After the first draft of it had been submitted and observations on it had been made by individuals whom the Pope asked to read it, the Pope wrote on a sheet of paper: "3. 19. 68. It is good that an authoritative article should prepare the faithful and public opinion for the introduction of the Canon of the Mass in Italian. Father Bugnini is a suitable person to write it; he has the competence and inclination for the task. The observations made on the first draft of the article are nevertheless legitimate and deserve to be taken into consideration. The article should be more expository and explanatory than apologetic in tone, justifying the innovation from the view of the bishops and from its pastoral aims and calling to mind the norms that are intended to maintain the use of Latin even by the faithful and, much more, in the choral Office of religious."

30. See "Investigatio de usu linguae latinae in liturgia romana et de missa quae 'Tridentina' appellari solet," Not 17 (1981) 589–611.

31. See pp. 107–9 and 246.

They even prepared a suitable little book, *Iubilate Deo*, which the Pope gave to all the bishops.[32] In large cities and in places popular with tourists, the bishops were asked to consider whether it might be appropriate to have one or more Latin Masses in some churches.[33] Religious were several times exhorted to retain the Latin liturgy, in whole or at least in part.[34]

Serious pastoral reasons opened the door to the vernaculars everywhere in the liturgy. If the vernaculars gained the upper hand, it was clearly because authenticity required them and there was a real need for them.

---

32. See below, pp. 236f. (and n. 27).

33. This point was made in a letter from the president of the Consilium, dated January 25, 1967, and repeated in the instruction *Musicam sacram* of March 5, 1967 (*DOL* 508 nos. 4122ff.) and other documents.

34. See the instruction *In edicendis normis* of November 23, 1965 (*DOL* 114 nos. 791-811); epistle *Sacrificium laudis* of Paul VI, August 15, 1966 (*DOL* 421 nos. 3402-4); instruction *Musicam sacram*, no. 49 (*DOL* 508 no. 4170). For a more complete view of the documents urging the use of Latin in the liturgy, see *EDIL*, Index analyticus, pp. 1111-12 and *DOL*, General Index, p. 1470.

10

Changes in the Missal

The introduction of the vernacular into the liturgy was accompanied by some rubrical adaptations and simplifications.[1] This first adjustment in the rubrics had to do with some points in the Mass, Holy Week, and the chants.

I. ORDO MISSAE AND RITUS SERVANDUS

There were changes, first of all, in the *Ordo Missae* and the two short treatises that for centuries had come at the head of the Roman Missal: the *Ritus in celebratione Missae servandus*, which went back to John Burchard (d. 1506), master of ceremonies to Pope Alexander VI, and the *De defectibus in Missae celebratione occurrentibus*.

Some would have preferred to see the rite completely revised. The Consilium was of this opinion at the beginning, and it had even prepared a draft. But this idea was then rejected when it was realized that the disadvantages would outweigh the advantages, both in regard to the rite, the rubrics, the habits and education of the clergy, and in relation to the reform, which might be jeopardized by such a complete revision. There was unanimous agreement at this point that there should instead be a careful revision of the *Ordo Missae* so as to include in it whatever could be introduced without difficulty.

Study group 19[2] provided various schemas for the work. A valuable and substantial contribution was made by Father Braga, who had assisted

---

1. These were listed in Chapter II of the instruction *Inter Oecumenici* of September 26, 1964 (*DOL* 23 nos. 340ff.).

2. *Relator:* S. Famoso; *secretary:* A. Franquesa; *members:* T. Schnitzler, R. Pilkington, J. O'Connell, F. Laroque, L. Trimeloni, J. Pfab.

114

in the redaction of the 1962 code of rubrics and prepared the "Johannine" editions of the liturgical books, and was thus more than ordinarily experienced in this area. Help was also requested from the consultors to the other study groups, especially group 10, which was then working on the schema for the new *Ordo Missae*.

The whole work was finally reviewed at a joint session of the Consilium and the Congregation of Rites in order to settle any remaining difficulties by common agreement. The *Ordo* was published on January 27, 1965.[3]

But how difficult it is to take an ancient building in hand and make it functional and habitable without changing the structure! Peripheral alterations are not enough; there has to be a radical restoration. All this applied to the Ordinary of the Mass. Just as the introduction of the vernacular into some parts of the Mass brought home the need of extending it to the entire rite, so the changes made in 1965 only showed up more clearly certain inconsistencies in rites, signs, and ceremonies that had become anachronistic. As a result, the further extension of the vernacular was accompanied by a further revision of some details of the Mass in the second instruction on the implementation of the liturgy, *Tres abhinc annos*, dated May 4, 1967.

In keeping with this instruction, a little volume containing changes in the rite of Mass was published on May 18, 1967. It gave the old and new texts on facing pages so that the changes could be easily seen.[4]

The selection of texts was simplified, since there was now to be but a single "oration" (first presidential prayer) and no commemorations; use of the experimental biblical Lectionary for weekdays was encouraged; the number of genuflections, signs of the cross, and kissings of the altar was reduced; wearing of the maniple was made optional. All this represented a truly courageous step in the direction of a complete reform.[5]

---

3. *Ordo Missae. Ritus servandus in celebratione Missae et de defectibus in celebratione Missae occurrentibus* (Vatican Polyglot Press, 1965). See *EDIL* 380; *Not* 1 (1965) 101–2. The decree of promulgation is in *DOL* 196 no. 1340.

4. *Variationes in Ordinem Missae inducendae ad normam Instructionis S.R.C. diei 4 maii 1967* (Vatican Polyglot Press, 1967). The complete text of the little book is also given in *Not* 3 (1967) 195–211. The decree of promulgation is in *DOL* 201 no. 1356.

5. Earlier, and still in the context of getting the reform started, the Consilium had published some norms, accompanied by some models, for the preparation of the prayer of the faithful. These were published first *pro manuscripto* on January 13, 1965, in the booklet *De oratione communi seu fidelium. Eius natura, momentum ac structura. Criteria atque specimina ad experimentum Coetibus territorialibus Episcoporum proposita* (32 pp.), and then, on April 17, 1966, in the volume *De oratione communi seu fidelium. Natura, momentum ac structura. Criteria ac specimina Coetibus territorialibus Episcoporum proposita* (Vatican Polyglot Press, 1966; 182 pp.). The introductory part of this book is in *DOL* 239 nos. 1890-1928.

What criteria did the revision follow?

1) The Mass according to the revised *Ordo* was to become more truly a "celebration," that is, an organically and hierarchically organized sacred action in which each participant plays his or her proper part; there was thus a return to the specific roles of reader, deacon, and priest.

2) The basic distinction between the forms of celebration was no longer to depend on the presence or absence of singing but on the participation of the faithful. The only distinction now was to be between Mass with a congregation and Mass without a congregation.

3) A clear and natural distinction was made between the two main parts of the Mass: the liturgy of the Word and the liturgy of the Eucharist. This distinction involved a distinction of places: the first part was to take place preferably at the celebrant's chair or the lectern, the second at the altar, the place of sacrifice and the table of the Eucharistic banquet.

4) Some rubrics ceased to be rigidly uniform and became flexible.

5) Although the revision was intended as an application of the norms given by the liturgical Constitution and the instruction *Inter Oecumenici*, it sometimes went beyond these documents, which obviously could not go into details. Not all inconsistencies were eliminated, however; that was to be one specific task of the reform itself.

II. Changes in Holy Week

For the time being no changes were made in the liturgical year, except for two details of Holy Week: the Chrism Mass of Holy Thursday and some of the prayers on Good Friday.

a) *The Chrism Mass* came into existence as the morning Mass of Holy Thursday in cathedral churches, in the days when the Mass *in Cena Domini* was still celebrated at its natural time, that is, in the evening. When this evening Mass was transferred to the morning, the Chrism Mass disappeared, and the consecration of the oils was made part of the one Holy Thursday Mass, for which the formulary *in Cena Domini* was still used. When the Mass of the Lord's Supper was moved back to the evening in 1955, it became necessary to reconstruct the formulary for a Chrism Mass.

Two ideas controlled the development of the formulary at that time: the consecration of the oils, and the day itself, prior to the sacred Triduum, on which the consecration took place.

Of the texts that were selected in 1955 and introduced into the Roman Missal, some were classical and beautifully constructed; others were less satisfactory. The liturgists were rather critical of the formulary as a whole.

They found fault with its poverty of ideas; for example, three of the texts (epistle, gospel, and communion antiphon) emphasized the oil of the sick, although this is the lowest in the hierarchy of oils, and its blessing had for centuries not even been reserved to the bishop but had been delegated to simple priests, who would give it on each occasion as need required.

Greater emphasis was subsequently put on a later conceptual development; I refer to the ritual or quasi-ritual presence of a good part of the diocesan clergy around the bishop in the cathedral church. In the afternoon the clergy are fully involved in their parishes or local churches as they prepare for and celebrate the Mass of the Lord's Supper with their own parish families. But in the morning the one Mass in the cathedral can be the occasion for a real feast of the priesthood on the day when the priesthood was originally instituted. Moreover, the Chrism Mass can embody in a vivid and effective way the true image of a bishop as described in article 41 of the Constitution on the Liturgy: "The bishop is to be looked on as the high priest of his flock, the faithful's life in Christ in some way deriving from and depending on him. Therefore all should hold in great esteem the liturgical life of the diocese centered around the bishop, especially in his cathedral church." The idea of transforming the Chrism Mass into a "feast of the priesthood" came from the Pope, who as Archbishop of Milan had annually emphasized this special meaning of Holy Thursday to the clergy of St. Ambrose's diocese.

The more austere liturgists were vexed by the new turn. They reluctantly resigned themselves to saying farewell to the centuries-old liturgy that had focused the Chrism Mass on the consecration of the oils as the foundation of all consecrations in the Church and as an immediate preparation for the baptism of catechumens during the Easter Vigil. Gradually, however, the new approach made its way, and finally everyone acknowledged that the pastoral reasons for it were persuasive and justified the sacrifice of a cherished tradition. A new and attractive element was added in 1965—Eucharistic concelebration, which could be freely chosen in every cathedral, according to the rite which in that same year, after lengthy preparation and ten months of experimentation, made its radiant entrance into the liturgical practice of the Church on the very anniversary of the institution of the Eucharist and the priesthood.

The other Mass texts were left unchanged, except for the offertory, where the hymn *O Redemptor, sume carmen* was introduced to accompany the procession, while the offertory verse *Diligis iustitiam* became the communion antiphon, the text being slightly altered to make it correspond to the Gradual.

The concept of priestly service for the regeneration of humankind and for the growth and sanctification of the people of God found expression in the collect (taken from the Gelasian Sacramentary), the prayer over the gifts, the preface, and the prayer for the consecration of the chrism. The blessing of the oils was mentioned in the rite and the chants. The sense of renewal was linked to the atmosphere of Holy Thursday itself and the closeness of Easter, which is the source of rebirth for human beings and of their passage from death to life.

The rites and texts of the Roman Pontifical continued in use for the blessing of the oils and the consecration of the chrism. Only brief indications were given for the course of the celebration, including the adaptations required by concelebration.[6]

One last pearl in the liturgical crown that is the Chrism Mass was included in the definitive texts of the Roman Missal, making its appearance shortly before the book was published.

On November 4, 1969, a circular letter from the Congregation for the Clergy on the continuing formation of the clergy said that in order to strengthen the spiritual life of God's ministers and their sense of their priesthood, it was recommended that on Holy Thursday every priest should renew his dedication to Christ the Lord and his priestly promises, especially those concerning celibacy and obedience to the bishop.[7] The Congregation for Divine Worship was asked to integrate this proposal into the texts of the Mass and to have the new texts ready for Holy Week of the following year. On March 6, 1970, the Congregation circulated the texts for the promises and for the proper preface of the Mass.[8] The former contains three questions addressed by the bishop to his priests regarding their commitment to celibacy, priestly service, and obedience, and two appeals to the faithful to pray for their priests and their bishop. The preface tells of the excellence and functions of the ministerial priesthood, its character as service, and its place in relation to the mission of Christ and the priesthood of the faithful.

Thus, in three stages, the liturgy of the Chrism Mass acquired a new appearance that is more responsive to the spiritual needs of the Church in our times.

---

6. The little book containing these changes and those in the Good Friday prayers was published by the SCR and the Consilium on March 7, 1965: *Variationes in Ordinem Hebdomadae sanctae inducendae* (Vatican Polyglot Press, 1965). The decree of promulgation is in *DOL* 454 no. 3853.

7. See *AAS* 62 (1970) 127; *EDIL* 1993; *DOL* 333 nos. 2762-64.

8. See *Not* 6 (1970) 87–89; *EDIL* 2059; *DOL* 315 nos. 2556-58.

b) *The "General Intercessions (Orationes sollemnes)" of Good Friday.* In the ecumenical climate of Vatican II, some expressions in the *Orationes sollemnes* of the Good Friday service had a bad ring to them. There were urgent requests to tone down some of the wording.

It is always unpleasant to have to alter venerable texts that for centuries have effectively nourished Christian devotion and have about them the spiritual fragrance of the heroic age of the Church's beginnings. Above all, it is difficult to revise literary masterpieces that are unsurpassed for their pithy form. It was nevertheless thought necessary to face up to the task, lest anyone find reason for spiritual discomfort in the prayer of the Church.

The revisions, limited to what was absolutely necessary, were prepared by study group 18bis. In Intercession I: "For the Church," the phrase "subiciens ei principatus et potestates" ("subjecting principalities and powers to it [the Church]") was omitted; even though this was inspired by what St. Paul says about the "angelic powers" (Col 2:15), it could be misinterpreted as referring to a temporal role which the Church did indeed have in other periods of history but which is anachronistic today.

Intercession VII was given a new title: "For Unity Among Christians" (instead of "For the Unity of the Church"). The text was changed so that it no longer referred to "heretics" and "schismatics" but to "all our brothers and sisters who share our faith in Christ."

Intercession VIII: "For the Jewish People" (instead of "For the Conversion of the Jews") was completely rewritten.

Intercession IX: "For Those Who Do Not Believe in Christ" (instead of: "For the Conversion of Unbelievers") was likewise completely rewritten.

III. CHANT

In order to adapt the chants to the requirements of the initial revision of the Missal, group 25 prepared three aids:[9]

a) *Kyriale simplex*

This was a little anthology of very simple Gregorian chants,[10] drawn from the authentic sources of the Roman, Ambrosian, and Mozarabic Rites. There were thirty-eight compositions in all, of which sixteen were

---

9. *Relator:* E. Cardine; *secretary:* L. Agustoni; *members:* J. Harmel, J. Claire, J. Hourlier, L. Kunz, M. Altisent.

10. Published by the SCR and the Consilium on December 14, 1964, under the title *Kyriale simplex* (Vatican Polyglot Press, 1965). The Introduction is in *DOL* 530 no. 4254.

being used in the Roman Church for the first time. The book was a practical implementation of article 117 of the Constitution on the Liturgy, which said it was desirable that a collection of Gregorian chants with simpler melodies be prepared.

b) *Chants of the Missal*

This was a collection of chants regarded as useful or necessary in a sung Mass,[11] in compliance with the new norms for Mass and for concelebration. The instruction *Inter Oecumenici*, which took effect on March 7, 1965, allowed for the singing of the prayer over the gifts, the Our Father and its embolism, and part of the Canon in concelebration. Melodies therefore had to be provided for the Latin texts.

The little book had six parts: (1) melody for the prayer over the gifts: this was the ancient solemn melody for orations, as found in the Vatican edition. It was used here because its conclusion harmonized better with the beginning of the dialogue before the preface; (2) melodies for the Canon: two melodies for the singing of the main part of the Canon; singing not only lends solemnity but serves to unite the concelebrants; (3) melodies for the doxology at the end of the Canon: two were provided, one simple and one solemn; (4) melodies for the Our Father: those found in the Missal had been composed for singing by the celebrant alone, not by the people; the melodies provided here were better adapted to group singing; one was from the Mozarabic liturgy, the other from ancient recitatives; (5) melody for the embolism: this was inspired by the old melody for orations; it might have been taken from the liturgy of Lyons and Milan, but it was decided to use a Roman melody, even if this required adaptation, in order to give melodic unity to the entire ceremony; (6) an appendix containing the variants in the *Hanc igitur* for Holy Thursday, the octaves of Easter and Pentecost, and the consecration of bishops. Finally, some melodies were provided for the prayer of the faithful.

c) *Graduale simplex*

The third aid, which involved a greater effort and was published only some years later, was the *Graduale simplex*,[12] a final attempt to lend solem-

---

11. Published by the SCR and the Consilium with a decree of December 14, 1964: *Cantus, qui in Missali Romano desiderantur, iuxta instructionem ad exsecutionem Constitutionis de sacra Liturgia recte ordinandam et iuxta ritum concelebrationis* (Vatican Polyglot Press, 1965). The decree is in *DOL* 531 no. 4255.

12. *Graduale simplex in usum minorum ecclesiarum* (Vatican City: Libreria Editrice Vaticana, 1967; xii + 432 pp.). It was published by decree of the SCR, September 3, 1967, but it was not presented as an *editio typica* (decree in *DOL* 532 no. 4256). This was in order not to offend the sensitivities of some composers who did not look favorably on it. See *Not* 3 (1967) 311–25.

nity to the Latin liturgy and prevent a complete loss of the priceless patrimony of traditional Latin chant. The Gradual is concerned with the proper parts of the Mass. There was a period of very laborious and absorbing work, and therefore I shall deal with this later on in a special section.[13] The book deserves mention here, however, because its publication was certainly another step toward a new form of celebration. By making it easier to sing the proper parts of the Mass (introit, offertory, communion, responsorial chant between the readings)—singing often neglected in the past because of the difficulty of the chants in the *Graduale Romanum*—the new book helped to make the value of this chant understood. In addition, it offered a selection of texts for each chant in the Proper, created Commons for the seasons, and revived the responsorial psalm—innovations very useful for participation.

The Council Fathers themselves were given a preview of all this during the Council's own celebrations, which owed some of their renewed form to the melodies of the *Graduale simplex*. Later on, the book became the usual source for the Latin celebrations in the papal chapel. This is evidence that the need for such a book was not felt solely in "smaller churches."[14] In fact, the *Graduale simplex* was very successful. Two printings were sold out in a short time. Many conferences asked permission to produce vernacular editions; the Consilium took up these requests in November 1967 and established some norms that the Pope approved on January 25, 1968:

1) The conferences have permission to translate the chants of the *Graduale simplex* in whole or in part and to adapt its texts.

2) The chants for each part of the Mass must respect the character of the liturgical action: a duly approved translation of the psalms may be used; suitable adaptations may be made of the antiphons to fit them for singing in the vernacular; the types of chant may be adapted to the type of music and song peculiar to the various peoples.

3) Whenever a text or melody cannot be adapted, the episcopal conference may substitute other chants, provided they are in harmony with the principles set forth in the Introduction to the *Graduale simplex*.[15]

---

13. See pp. 892ff.

14. The extent to which the need was felt may also be gauged from the fact that back in 1962 Prof. Hermann Kronsteiner of Linz had already published a Latin-German *Proprium simplex* (Vienna: Verlag Veritas, 1962; 402 pp.). Its publication is perhaps to be explained in part by the encouragement of Bishop Franz Zauner of Linz, who was well informed about the work of the commission preparing the liturgical Constitution, which was to call for such a work.

15. Text in *Not* 4 (1968) 10; DOL 120 nos. 831-34.

After the publication of the *Missale Romanum* in 1970, the *Graduale simplex* was revised to make it fit the new situation. At the same time, the contents of the other two little volumes described earlier were incorporated into it.[16]

16. Published by decree of the SCDW on November 22, 1974: *Graduale simplex in usum minorum ecclesiarum*, editio typica altera (Vatican Polyglot Press, 1975; 516 pp.). The decree and the Introduction are in *DOL* 536–37 nos. 4303-10. See "De editione typica altera Gradualis simplicis," *Not* 11 (175) 290–96.

11

Concelebration

I. Preparation of the Rite

The first completely new rites of the reform were those of concelebration and of communion under both kinds. The decree of publication was dated March 7, 1965; the rites were to go into effect on Holy Thursday, April 15, of that year.[1]

Study group 16[2] was in charge of preparing the rite of concelebration. But even before the Constitution on the Sacred Liturgy was promulgated in November 1963, Father Cipriano Vagaggini had been studying an earlier draft of a rite of concelebration. He felt it urgently necessary to restore dignity and meaning to the Eucharistic celebration, especially at gatherings of priests.

On March 15, 1964, the secretariat of the Consilium sent the following note to the study group:

> There are many technical studies of concelebration; on the practical side, the Consilium already has in its possession a first draft that is sufficiently "polished." This must be discussed, sent for examination to a group of experts in various parts of the world, and then given a definitive form.

---

1. *Ritus servandus in concelebratione Missae et ritus communionis sub utraque specie*, editio typica (Vatican Polyglot Press, 1965; 104 pp.). Published by the SCR and the Consilium. See the presentation of the document by A. Bugnini in *L'Osservatore Romano*, March 28, 1965. The decree of promulgation is in *DOL* 222 nos. 1788-93; the Introduction to the rite of concelebration is in *DOL* 223 nos. 1794-1810; the Introduction to the rite of communion under both kinds is in *DOL* 268 nos. 2105-7.

2. *Relator:* C. Vagaggini; *secretary:* A. Franquesa; *members:* J. Wagner, A.-G Martimort, B. Fischer, B. Botte, B. Neunheuser, A. Dirks, R. Falsini.

After the commission has approved it, it will be sent out, with the consent of the Holy Father, for "experimentation," in order to make sure that what seems good at the ideal level is also good in practice. The experiments will be made in some abbeys of various countries and perhaps at some gatherings of priests.

After studying the existing schema, the group composed six others[3] and, in addition to consulting experts, profited by extensive experimentation. After some further work, the schema approved by the Consilium at its second general meeting was presented to the Holy Father by the Cardinal President at an audience on June 26, 1964, and the Pope gave permission for it to be used in experimental celebrations.

II. Experiments

The first official experiment was conducted in six abbeys: Sant' Anselmo (Rome), Montserrat (Spain), Encalcat (France), Maredsous (Belgium), Maria Laach (Germany), and St. John's (United States), and in Le Saulchoir, the Dominican house of studies in France.

The permission was for concelebration several times a month and for all forms of Eucharistic celebration. The conditions were: (1) that the consent of the Ordinary of the place be obtained; (2) that the rite established by the Consilium and accompanying the decree of concession be faithfully followed; (3) that the concelebrants be no more than twenty in number and stand around the altar; (4) that one person be in charge of the concelebration and submit a report on it to the Consilium, listing any difficulties that may have arisen and suggesting a solution; (5) that if possible some photographs be sent to the Consilium as proper documentation.

The liturgical centers that had been chosen prepared to carry out a mandate that they had welcomed with great joy and enthusiasm. There was painstaking preparation: repeated practices of the ceremonies and

---

3. Schema 1, April 2, 1964 (17 pp.), sent for inspection by about thirty experts around the world;

Schema 2, May 30, 1964 (13 pp.), drawn up after examination by the relators and the members of the Consilium in the sessions of April 14–20;

Schema 3, June 14, 1964 (13 pp.), again studied by the members of the Consilium during the third general meeting (June 18–20);

Schema 4, June 20, 1964 (14 pp.), given to the Holy Father;

Schema 5, December 20, 1964 (29 pp.), prepared on the basis of the observations suggested by the experiments;

Schema 6, January 20, 1965 (28 pp.): the definitive text, given to the Holy Father and approved by him on March 4, 1965.

chants; use of graphics; courses of lectures to the community and to the faithful who were to participate. The drafted rite was usually recopied or even printed in elegant booklets so that all might have it in hand.

After the concelebrations there was usually a general meeting of all, religious and laity, and each participant was asked to give his or her impressions and to make any suitable observations. These general meetings were the source of the reports sent to the Consilium. The reports were lively, intelligent, filled with pastoral good sense, and of incalculable value for the correcting, polishing, clarifying, and preparing of the final version of the rite.

Cardinal Gracias asked that at the International Eucharistic Congress in Bombay groups of priests attending be permitted to concelebrate daily, since it was impossible to supply enough altars for the celebration of "private" Masses. The Pope gave his permission, with the proviso that the number of concelebrants in each group be limited and that there be someone in charge to lead the celebrations. The broad outline of the rite was printed in the congress program, again by special permission of the Pope.

On July 3, 1964, Cardinal Lercaro received permission to allow concelebration "in particular cases." Three such cases received special attention. First and foremost, there was the case of sick priests, some of them in extremely trying circumstances, who asked that they might concelebrate at least on Sundays. Among such requests was a moving one from a parish priest who was paralyzed and limited to receiving communion; he was a missionary Oblate of Mary Immaculate and had been unable to celebrate for the past year after a fall into a ravine in Alaska. The Pope granted the indults for these sick priests and ordered the Consilium to prepare an appropriate rite.

Some bishops at the Council asked that they might concelebrate in the colleges or religious houses in which they were staying. The Pope gave the permission but ordered them to see to it that all the conditions for a seemly concelebration were present.

From several quarters came requests that concelebration might also take place in St. Peter's. This petition, too, was granted. The concelebrations at which the Holy Father himself presided in the Vatican Basilica at the opening of the third session (September 14),[4] during it, and at its

---

4. The first concelebration by the Pope in St. Peter's was a historic event, not only by reason of the expectations it aroused throughout the ecclesiastical world but also by reason of difficulties caused by customs that would have to be revised or abandoned. There was even an amusing incident. Since the event was a "first Mass," the secretary of the Consi-

close intensified the desire for this new rite. Requests from bishops multiplied.

How many concelebrations were allowed as experiments? From July 3, 1964, to March 21, 1965, 720 indults for concelebration were granted to bishops and diocesan clergy. In addition, for special reasons a collective indult was granted to the episcopal conferences of various countries (three in Europe, five in Africa, eight in the Americas); the conference communicated the indult to individual bishops in specific cases and under the usual conditions.

During the same period 206 religious families (in addition to the six centers named at the beginning) asked for an indult for concelebration. Here again, for reasonable cause, eight communities received a collective indult, which the major superior then communicated to his own religious provinces.

In all, then, there were over fifteen hundred concelebrations. Eight albums of photographs and about a thousand reports in the archives of the Consilium give evidence of the atmosphere of lively and holy enthusiasm, intense feeling, and profound spirituality that everywhere marked the preparation and the ceremonies themselves.

The conditions laid down were always the same. The occasions were extremely varied, but pastoral reasons were always at work. Only one kind of concelebration was allowed in order to foster individual devotion—that of sick priests who found it impossible to celebrate individually.

In the beginning, concelebration was a privilege. This is sufficiently clear from the fact that a particular, authoritative decree of the Consilium was required and that while the Consilium was generous and magnanimous, it carefully examined the circumstances and possibilities.

---

lium wanted to see from close up how the ceremony went, and he obtained from Archbishop Enrico Dante, papal master of ceremonies, special permission to stand near the altar as a "chapel cleric." Before the ceremony began, one of the guards approached him and asked: "Excuse me, but are you eligible to stand here?" The secretary showed his card to the man, who then went away. Shortly after, when Mass had begun, another gentleman, a short fellow loaded down with decorations, well known in those circles for . . . his extremely courteous manners, passed back and forth and finally issued an order: "Withdraw, hide yourself, don't be seen here!" Since the person being commanded did not leave, our much-decorated gentleman returned in great excitement, accompanied by a guard, and without mercy forced the secretary of the Consilium to leave. Documents, explanations, pleas were useless. He had already been taken outside when a prelate, moved to pity and disgusted by the scene, intervened so that the poor unfortunate secretary might at least remain in the benches of the transept.

III. THE DEFINITIVE RITE

While this experiment was being conducted on a grand scale throughout the world, the reports daily reaching the Consilium provided valuable information for revising and perfecting the rite.

The rite had meanwhile been sent on to the Congregation of Rites for its expert examination. The Congregation issued its observations in August 1965.[5] The prefecture for papal ceremonies also drafted a series of remarks. Both sources[6] raised the same difficulties, which were the product of a frame of mind bent on curbing rather than promoting the renewal.

The chief objections had to do with:

a) *the number of concelebrants.* The Consilium schema suggested about fifteen, but this number was found to be too large. The criterion desired was "that all the concelebrants be able to stand around the altar during all their actions and to concelebrate on it."[7]

There was a gradual evolution in regard to the number of concelebrants. In the beginning the Pope had directed that the number be limited to between twenty and twenty-five. At that time, before experience of concelebration, it was feared that a larger number would keep the celebration from proceeding in an orderly and dignified manner. Outside of Rome it was urged that the number not be limited. The number fifty took both views into account. The definitive solution left the number undetermined and simply decreed that "in each case the number of concelebrants is to be settled by considering how many the church and the altar of concelebration can accommodate, even if all the concelebrants are not right next to the table of the altar."[8]

b) *Parts that the concelebrants are to recite.* The objectors asked that "all the concelebrants recite the whole Canon in Latin, from the *Te igitur* to the communion inclusive."[9]

---

5. The Consilium's reply to the observations of the SCR on the instruction *Inter Oecumenici,* on the rite of concelebration, and on communion under both kinds was delivered to the Holy Father on August 31, 1965, in a fifty-page foolscap booklet.

6. As a matter of fact, there was only one source, since the secretary of the SCR was also the papal master of ceremonies.

7. The idea that the concelebrants should stand around the altar and touch it was rather widespread and resisted dying out. The phenomenon can be seen in the photographs of the first concelebrations, for which at times enormous altars were set up so that all the concelebrants could stand around them in the most literal sense.

8. *DOL* 223 no. 1797. This solution enabled hundreds of priests and bishops to concelebrate at congresses, synods, and conferences. The problem gradually disappeared, so that there was no longer any reference to it in the definitive norms that were eventually incorporated into the Roman Missal.

9. It had to be noted, among other things, that the Canon ends with the final doxology, not with the communion!

This was another *idée fixe*. The final solution, which assigned different parts to the principal concelebrant and to the other concelebrants, either as a group or singly, was not only based on the earliest tradition and on the more recent tradition of the Eastern Churches but was also a balanced one. It made the concelebration more harmonious by allowing a suitable variety of voices to be heard. The simultaneous, prolonged recitation of many prayers by many concelebrants makes for monotony and dullness. Another advantage of diversified recitation is that it gives the sense of a concelebration in which there is a variety of roles even among the priests themselves.

c) *Extension of hands over the gifts* during the consecratory epiclesis and the words of consecration. The objectors wanted this to be "absolutely forbidden." They failed to grasp the meaning of the gesture and confused it with the Roman greeting. The Consilium, however, took into consideration both the importance of the meaning conveyed by the gesture and varying local sensibilities; it therefore made the gesture optional.

d) *Use of a paten by each concelebrant*. This would have been an unnecessary complication and without any expressive value. In all rites the priest receives the Lord's body in his hand.

Other observations had to do with the exclusion of any concelebrants besides the bishop and ordinands at an ordination; communion by drinking directly from the chalice; bination in anticipated cases (Holy Thursday, Easter, Christmas, November 2, a diocesan synod[10]); the obligation of all concelebrants to wear all the vestments. In the view of the prefect of papal ceremonies, these points were to be the basis "for drawing up the rite of concelebration."[11]

In the early days of December, the Pope summoned the secretary of the Consilium and asked him to put an end to the period of experimental concelebration and prepare the definitive rite for publication. On December 20 the revised rite was sent to twenty-eight experts, with a request that they submit any observations by January 5. The accompanying let-

---

10. In the first three cases, bination or trination was already provided for in the rubrics; in the other two it was provided for in the liturgical Constitution, no. 57.

11. The opposition was subjectively motivated rather than based on objective arguments. The master of ceremonies claimed, for example, during preparation of the rite of concelebration for the third session of the Council, that the Pope "wants to put an end to all the confusion and disorder going on just now" and wants the rite to be based on "the rite in the Pontifical." The Pope evidently issued no such order, since he had already approved for experimentation the rite drawn up by the Consilium, and since he knew there was no rite of concelebration in the Pontifical! And, in fact, after all his "rubrical" prancing, the good Archbishop Dante yielded with a minimum of argument and ended by going along with the Consilium.

ter explained why the text was so full: in addition to the general norms (which in the subsequent *Ordines* would become the *Praenotanda generalia*, or General Introduction), the schema contained the full rite for a pontifical Mass and the elements peculiar to all the other forms of Mass, reference being made to the pontifical Mass for the parts common to all. In addition, there were the elements peculiar to concelebrations at the ordination of priests, the consecration of a bishop, and the blessing of an abbot. Finally, there was the rite of concelebration with a sick priest.

IV. CONTENT

The decree promulgating the rite of concelebration duly highlights the basic principles that justify, improve, and condition concelebration. In substance they are as follows.

In guiding or reforming the celebration of the sacred mysteries, the Church has always taken care that the rites should manifest as effectively as possible the inexhaustible riches of Christ which they contain and communicate to those who are well-disposed. For then they will more readily influence the life and outlook of those who take part in them.

This is especially true of the celebration of the Eucharist. The various forms of this celebration are meant to express and convey to the faithful the various aspects of the Eucharistic sacrifice. In every form of the Mass, even the simplest, all the marks and properties that belong to the Eucharistic sacrifice by its nature are contained. Specifically:

1) *the unity of the sacrifice* of the cross, inasmuch as a plurality of Masses represent the one sacrifice of Christ and derive their sacrificial character from the fact that they are the memorial of Christ's sacrifice on the cross;

2) *the unity of the priesthood*, in the sense that although many celebrate, each is a minister of Christ, who exercises his own priesthood through these priests and indeed gives them a special share of his priesthood via the sacrament of orders. Therefore, even when they offer the sacrifice individually, they always do it in virtue of the one priesthood that they all share, and they act in the person of the one High Priest, who confects the sacrament of his body and blood, whether through one priest or through many;

3) *the joint action* of the entire people of God appears more clearly; in fact, every Mass, being a celebration of the sacrament to which the Church owes its continual growth and life, and in which it chiefly manifests its true nature, is, more than any other liturgical action, an action of the entire, hierarchically organized, holy people of God.

These three characteristics, which belong to every Mass, become more evident in the rite of concelebration. For in this form of celebration a number of priests act together with one will and one voice, in virtue of the same priesthood and in the person of the same High Priest; they celebrate the one sacrifice with a single sacramental act and participate in it together.

Therefore this way of celebrating Mass, in which the faithful take a conscious and active part as a community, is—especially if the bishop presides—the supreme manifestation of the Church in the unity of sacrifice and priesthood and in a single act of thanksgiving around one altar with the ministers and the holy people. The rite of concelebration presents and conveys in a striking way truths of the greatest importance that nourish the spiritual and pastoral life of priests and promote the Christian training of the faithful.

For these, rather than for purely practical reasons, Eucharistic concelebration in a variety of styles and forms has been accepted in the Church since antiquity; though it has developed along different lines, it has always remained in use in both East and West.

The *Ritus concelebrationis* begins by recalling the pertinent articles in the Constitution on the Liturgy and some general norms.

1. Concelebration is allowed *only* in the following cases:
a) Holy Thursday in both the Chrism Mass and the evening Mass;
b) during councils, synods, and meetings of bishops;
c) in the Mass for the blessing of an abbot;
d) with the permission of the Ordinary, in the conventual Mass and the principal Mass in a church or oratory, when the needs of the faithful do not require the priests to celebrate separately;[12]
e) on the occasion of meetings of priests, of whatever kind.
2. It is for the bishop to regulate concelebration in his own diocese. It is for the Ordinary, on the other hand, to decide whether it is opportune and to determine its formalities.[13]

---

12. This directive left the door open to use of the rite on many occasions and contributed, in fact, to the growth of the view that concelebration is the proper and preferred form of celebration for the priestly community. This view was also conveyed in the instruction *Eucharisticum mysterium* (May 25, 1967), no. 47, which even empowers superiors of communities having a large number of priests to permit two or more concelebrations on the same day (*DOL* 179 no. 1276).

13. Some clarification was needed on this point and was officially given by the SCR for the diocese of Rome. It said that it is for the religious superior to grant permission for concelebration in his own houses. This means: to judge the opportuneness, decide the number of concelebrants, and give the permission.

It is for the Ordinary of place to regulate concelebration and to determine the schedule, churches, rite, and prayer of the faithful. Practice would brilliantly resolve all these questions, and without any great difficulties. See *Not* 2 (1966) 265–66.

In this area, one special problem was raised (still in the Vicariate of Rome) about con-

3. At ordinations and the blessing of an abbot, the bishops can also allow others to concelebrate.

4. No one may be admitted as a concelebrant once the Mass has begun.

5. A priest can celebrate or concelebrate more than once: on Holy Thursday, at the Chrism Mass and the evening Mass; on Easter, at the Vigil and during the day; on Christmas, at the three Masses that are celebrated at appropriate hours; at synods, pastoral visits, or meetings of priests with the bishop or his delegate, if in the bishop's judgment they are required to celebrate again to meet the needs of the faithful.[14]

6. Concelebrants must wear all the vestments prescribed for individual celebration. The color is to be that of the day, except in case of need; then the principal celebrant is to wear the color of the day, but the others can wear white.[15]

7. The principal celebrant is to recite all the formulas and perform the actions prescribed for him by the rubrics. Concelebrants are to say only the formulas and perform only the actions explicitly prescribed for them; the formulas which they do not say aloud in accordance with the rubrics they are to say mentally or simply listen to them.[16]

8. Deacons and subdeacons at solemn Masses may receive communion in both kinds. If the deacon or subdeacon is in fact a priest, he may not concelebrate but he can receive communion, even if he already has said Mass or is to say it later.

Next come specific directives on stipends for a concelebrated Mass and for the instruction of the faithful. There follows a detailed description of

---

celebration in the international colleges and seminaries of the city. It led to a sustained examination of the question; I shall return to this in Chapter 56, pp. 869–72.

14. Here again, practice and understanding of the significance of concelebration brought about an evolution. Requests came in asking that those members of chapters or religious communities who were obliged to attend the conventual or community Mass and also had to celebrate individually for the faithful might be allowed to binate so that they might take part in the concelebration. At the time, GIRM 76 allowed them only to receive communion under both kinds at the concelebrated Mass. The same request was made by priests for special gatherings of priests (*ibid.,* no. 158). The question was taken up at an "ordinary" meeting of the SCDW, and bination was allowed in the declaration *In celebratione Missae,* which the SCDW issued on August 7, 1972: *AAS* 64 (1972) 561–63 (*DOL* 226 nos. 1813-16). See also *Not* 8 (1972) 327–28, with the commentary of G. P., 329–32. GIRM 76 was corrected in the 1975 edition to conform to the declaration.

15. On this point, too, the law evolved. The obligation that all the concelebrants wear all the vestments proved burdensome. The second instruction for the application of the liturgical Constitution (May 4, 1967) laid this obligation only on the principal concelebrant; the others could wear only an amice, chasuble, and stole; see the instruction *Tres abhinc annos* 27: *AAS* 59 (1967) 448 (*DOL* 29 no. 473).

16. The Missal of 1970 gave an even better solution when it recommended that the parts common to all be said by the concelebrants in a low voice so that the voice of the principal concelebrant can be clearly heard (see GIRM 170).

each type of Mass as well as of special cases: conferral of orders, blessing of an abbot, concelebration of sick priests.

The norms of 1965, revised in their juridical parts, stripped of what had been provisional and brought up to date in relation to documents published later, have in their substance become part of the Roman Missal that emerged from the Pauline reform.[17]

V. Interritual Concelebration

Once concelebration was reintroduced as a normal rite in the Latin Church, the problem arose of Latin Rite and Eastern Rite priests concelebrating together. Once questions of this kind began to be presented, they were resolved case by case in the manner that seemed most satisfactory but was not always felicitous from the liturgical standpoint.[18]

The Congregation for the Eastern Churches took up the matter at a plenary meeting in the early months of 1969 and asked for the views of the Consilium, even extending it an invitation to participate in the meeting. The problem was taken up by a special study group in the Consilium.[19]

The questions to be answered were these:

a) whether and for what reasons and with what reservations bishops and priests were to be granted permission to concelebrate in another rite, the equality and integrity of the separate rites being maintained;

b) whether, and if so which, elements of their own rite (dress, insignia, language, readings, prayers, etc.) could be kept and introduced into a concelebration in a different rite;

c) whether concelebrants from different rites could be allowed to recite in synchrony each their own Canon, or at least its words of consecra-

---

17. See GIRM 153-60.

18. On July 15, 1965, the Ukrainian Eparch (Gabro) of St. Nicholas in Chicago was given permission to concelebrate with the Archbishop (Cody) of that city on the occasion of his enthronement; on September 5, 1966, on the other hand, Latin Rite priests on pilgrimage in the Holy Land were refused an indult for concelebrating with the Melkites; on December 12, 1967, the Ukrainian Eparch in France was allowed "in special circumstances" and "in case of necessity" to concelebrate "in another rite"; in 1968 concelebration in another rite "on Sundays and some other days of greater solemnity, with each concelebrant preferably wearing the vestments of his own rite," was granted to seminaries with students from different rites: Poona (July 2, 1968), Kurseong (December 6, 1968), Alwaye (December 18, 1968).

During the concelebration of the new cardinals in February 25, 1965, with the Pope presiding, Cardinals Saigh and Slipyi used their own Byzantine anaphora, timing it (especially at the words of consecration) to harmonize with the Latin Canon.

19. This group consisted of G. Arrighi, P. Jounel, E. Lanne, and L. Ligier.

tion, or whether a special anaphora should be composed for such concelebrations.

Here was the opinion of the Consilium on each question:

a) Interritual celebration should be permitted, but according to the rite of the Church that issued the invitation, and provided the authorities of that Church judged that the invited priest knew how to concelebrate according to that rite and was familiar with the anaphora being used.

b) Concelebrating priests should wear the garb of their own rite; as for language, they could use their own or that of the majority of the concelebrants. In no other respect was the rite of liturgical concelebration to be altered; concelebrants from other rites were to follow the rite of the inviting Church.

c) Interritual concelebration is a legitimate desire of many priests, especially of the younger generation, and ought not to be prevented. Synchronization of different Canons is to be utterly avoided, since this would militate against the deeper meaning of concelebration as a "sign of unity." Therefore, it was suggested that an agreed choice be made of one of the Eastern anaphoras (the value of Eucharistic Prayer II in this context was underscored) or that the Latin Church adopt the Alexandrine Anaphora of St. Basil.

The Consilium had had this last-named anaphora in mind all along and wanted to adopt it together with the three new Eucharistic Prayers, but the Congregation for the Doctrine of the Faith would not allow it.[20] The plenary meeting of the Congregation for the Eastern Churches also favored the idea, but nothing seems to have come of it.[21]

VI. COMMUNION UNDER BOTH KINDS

Norms for the distribution of communion under both kinds were issued along with the norms for the rite of concelebration. The ceremonial was that used in the rite of concelebration, but with necessary adaptations for the faithful. Four methods of receiving the blood of Christ were envisaged: drinking directly from the chalice, intinction, use of a straw, use of a spoon.[22]

---

20. See pp. 461–62.

21. At least nothing more is known of it. On other questions as well no results were seen. Perhaps the directives given were enough to let the Congregation for the Eastern Churches handle concrete cases. But since the regulations were not made known, who knows to what extent it acted on its own initiative?

22. No one seems to have used the third and fourth methods, which were perhaps kept at the insistence of a few archeologists or people with an exaggerated concern for "hygiene." Certainly these two methods did not become common.

Of greater interest are the cases in which, in accordance with the liturgical Constitution, communion under both kinds was allowed.[23] The directives here were dictated by pastoral and disciplinary considerations; there would be a subsequent development that merits separate treatment.[24]

---

23. See *SC* 55.
24. See pp. 626ff.

III. Two Areas of Activity

A. Preparation of the Liturgical Reform

12

Meetings

I. Preliminary Meetings

The official beginning of the Consilium's activity was preceded by two preliminary meetings of the appointed members.[1] The organization had hardly been established when meetings in the true and proper sense began. The purpose of these was to discuss and evaluate the labors of the various study groups that were preparing the documents for implementing the liturgical reform and, even more important, were revising the liturgical books. These meetings were therefore the basic focal points in the activity of the Consilium and the Congregation of Rites.

In keeping with curial tradition, the meetings were to be of two kinds: ordinary and plenary.

II. Ordinary Meetings

These were to be meetings of the members who were present in Rome, along with seventeen consultors from the Congregation of Rites, Propaganda, and the Consilium. Two meetings a month were planned, to be held on Thursdays. The purpose of the ordinary meetings was to deal with matters of regular administration, to draw up the agenda for plenary meetings and prepare the material to be submitted for approval at these meetings, to clear up uncertain points in the liturgical Constitution, and to approve the decisions of the episcopal conferences.

The idea was a good one, but it did not work out in practice. The work of the study groups was so demanding that it produced its results barely

---

1. January 15 and February 15, 1964. See p. 50.

in time to organize the material and send it to the Fathers who were invited to the plenary meetings. It was not possible, therefore, to have it examined in advance at ordinary meetings. Moreover, the problems raised were chiefly of a pastoral kind: new situations, difficulties, suggestions, petitions—all of them matters which the participants in the ordinary meetings did not feel capable of settling and which they therefore sent on to the plenary meetings. As for approving the decisions of episcopal conferences, the problem here was to establish criteria. Once these were in place, it would have been a waste of time to bring the members together for an ordinary meeting in order to give their approval; this would only have caused extensive delays in replying to the episcopal conferences. At the first plenary meeting, therefore, the Consilium would decide to entrust to the president the task of confirming the decisions of the conferences, provided these decisions were in accord with the approved criteria.

The ordinary meetings of the Consilium had but a brief history—only two were held.

Ordinary Meeting I (March 20, 1964)

This first meeting was held at Santa Marta on March 20, 1964, with fourteen members and four consultors in attendance. It approved the schedule of meetings for the coming months and discussed the text of the letter to be sent, via the pontifical representatives, to the presidents of the episcopal conferences.[2] Also brought up for discussion was a first schema of "points to be considered in studying the decisions of the episcopal conferences." But the task immediately proved to be very demanding and was referred to a plenary meeting.

Ordinary Meeting II (April 13, 1964)

The second—and final—ordinary meeting was likewise held at Santa Marta, on April 13, 1964. It dealt chiefly with questions raised about the interpretation of the motu proprio Sacram Liturgiam.

The questions had to do with:

1) The votive Mass of marriage and the nuptial blessing during the forbidden seasons. The reply was that the Mass could always be celebrated and the blessing always given; the parish priest was obliged, however, to urge the couple to keep in mind the special character of the liturgical season.

---

2. The reference is to the letter of March 25, 1964. See p. 99.

2) The instruction to be given at a marriage without a Mass.[3] It was explained that this referred to an introductory instruction, not to the homily.

3) Does the permission given in the motu proprio to omit the Hour of Prime and recite only one of the three Little Hours extend to those who are obliged to choir, even if they are dispensed from choral recitation? The reply was not unanimous, and the solution was referred to a plenary meeting.[4]

4) It was explained that when the liturgical Constitution and the motu proprio use the term "Ordinary," it includes major superiors of institutes of perfection.

5) It was decided that clerics who were given permission to use the vernacular in celebrating the Divine Office must use a bilingual edition containing the Latin and vernacular texts.

6) There was a lengthy discussion of Little Offices, the use of which is described as follows in the motu proprio: those using "a little office, structured like the divine office . . . shall be counted as celebrating public prayer with the Church." It was confirmed that the translations needed approval from the episcopal conferences; that the permission given in the motu proprio with regard to Prime and the Little Hours in the Divine Office could also be used here; that newly composed Little Offices must henceforward be submitted to the Holy See for approval.

7) Finally, there was discussion of the request of Cardinal Gracias, Archbishop of Bombay, to use the simplifications in the planned instruction on the occasion of the Eucharistic Congress in Bombay. Approval was given.

All these matters were presented to the Holy Father, who decided that the answers to the questions would be given in the instruction then being prepared.

III. General Meetings[5]

The general meetings of the Consilium corresponded to the plenary meetings of the various Roman agencies. There were two differences:

1) Plenary meetings ("plenary congregations") had legislative authority, though the Pope had to give his approval. The Consilium was an

---

3. See *Sacram Liturgiam*, no. V (*DOL* 20 no. 283).

4. Eight were for, four against.

5. For a list of the meetings and the schemas discussed at them, see *Not* 18 (1982) 468–72; in the same volume, nos. 195-96, there is a list of all the schemas composed by the Consilium and the SCDW (pp. 488–539).

organization for study, though one directly dependent on the Pope. Its conclusions were to be regarded simply as opinions—expert and important, but still only opinions—for the Holy Father's use.[6]

2) Only the cardinals and bishops who were members of an agency took part in that agency's plenary congregations. In the meetings of the Consilium, on the other hand, consultors and *periti* attended along with the members, although for reasons of space and smoother functioning, the *periti* were limited to the relators of the study groups and—depending on the subjects being discussed and the judgment of the cardinal president—to a few other specially qualified experts. All in attendance could speak: members by right, consultors if asked; only the members voted. This procedure allowed the Fathers to have the *periti* immediately available; when difficulties arose in the course of the discussion, it was possible to appeal directly to someone who could give an expert explanation.

During the week preceding a general meeting, there was a meeting of the relators, who studied the same material as a "court of the first instance," with a view to presenting their conclusions to the Fathers later on.

General Meeting I (March 11, 1964)[7]

The first general meeting of the Consilium was held in Rome on March 11, 1964, a few days after its creation. It was held at Santa Marta, in a corridor on the second floor.

Present were: Cardinals Lercaro, Agagianian, Giobbe, Confalonieri, Larraona[8]; Bishops Felici, Grimshaw, Young, Botero, Mansourati, Rossi, Hervas, Zauner, Rau, van Bekkum, van Zuylen, Boudon, Jenny, Volk, Guano, Kerveadou; Monsignor Valentini; Fathers Antonelli, Bevilacqua; and Abbot Gut.

Communications from the president. In his welcome to the meeting, Cardinal Lercaro emphasized the importance and sensitivity of the task en-

---

6. This applies to the work of the reform and to ordinances of a general character. But the Consilium also had competencies of its own in the administrative area—for example, to approve the acts of the episcopal conferences, to allow experiments, to enter into relations with bishops and episcopal conferences in order to regulate, guide, stimulate, and, if need be, correct the implementation of the liturgical reform.

7. Data on the first four general meetings are taken from the duplicated *Relationes* that were sent *sub secreto* only to the members and consultors of the Consilium. Four of these were issued during 1964. They were the humble beginnings of *Notitiae*. See also EL 79 (1965) 162-64.

8. After this, Cardinal Larraona did not attend the meetings of the Consilium. He was to be seen only at some of the papal audiences.

trusted to the Consilium and recalled the work done by those who in the sixteenth century labored for a general reform of the liturgy, especially Cardinal Sirleto. He then explained the letter of the Secretary of State (February 29, 1964) that established the Consilium and assigned it its tasks: (1) to suggest names of experts to the Pope; (2) to coordinate the work of the study groups; (3) to prepare carefully an instruction that would settle questions arising out of the motu proprio *Sacram Liturgiam* and define the competence of territorial ecclesiastic authorities, pending the completion of the reform; (4) to be vigilant in seeing to it that the liturgical Constitution was followed and applied according to the letter and the spirit of the Council; (5) to study proposals from the episcopal conferences and answer questions raised by the conferences. Cardinal Lercaro also communicated the contents of a previous letter from the Secretariat of State (January 13, 1964) that had to do chiefly with the organization of the work and of the study groups.

Report of the secretary. Father A. Bugnini, secretary of the Consilium, spoke on the following matters:

1) *Activity of the Consilium.* This had been thus far limited to internal organization: setup of offices, undertakings, work schedule.

2) *Psalter group.* This had been formed back on February 15 and was holding regular meetings twice a week. The first ten psalms were not quite ready; they would be sent to thirty experts in exegesis, philology, literature, liturgy, and chant. The same course would be followed for the other psalms.

3) *First schemas.* Pursuant to the letter of the Secretary of State, work had been begun on preparing the instruction for the application of the liturgical Constitution. Also in preparation were the rites of concelebration and of communion under two kinds.

Discussion. At the suggestion of the president, the report of the secretary was discussed under four headings:

a) Working method. Unanimously approved.

b) The instruction. The Fathers asked that it not be limited to giving practical norms; they emphasized the importance of doctrinal explanation and of instruction aimed at an authentic understanding of the liturgical Constitution.

c) Concelebration and communion under both kinds. The members supported the suggestion that these rites be prepared immediately.

d) The commission that would hold ordinary meetings was established.[9]

---

9. See p. 138.

The secretary informed the meeting that minutes had come in from the episcopal conferences of Australia, Southern Africa, Brazil, the Caribbean, Chile, Belgium, France, and Tunisia.

At the end of the meeting Cardinal Confalonieri was named vice-president of the Consilium.

General Meeting II (April 17–20, 1964)

The second general meeting was held at Santa Marta from April 17 to April 20, 1964. It was preceded by a meeting of the relators of the study groups on April 14–16. Twenty-nine members were present at the general meeting: six cardinals, nineteen bishops, four priests.

On the agenda were:

1) The rite of concelebration and of communion under two kinds. This was the Consilium's first schema.[10]

2) The second schema of the instruction for the application of the liturgical Constitution and of the motu proprio Sacram Liturgiam. The schema had four parts: theologico-pastoral, normative, regulatory, and practico-ceremonial.[11] Only the second and third parts were introduced. For lack of time the other two were simply sketched.

3) It was recognized that joint meetings with the Congregations for Seminaries and for Religious were needed for studying questions about liturgical instruction and formation in seminaries and the use of "Little Offices" and "breviaries for the faithful."

4) The greater part of the meeting was devoted to establishing criteria for approval of the decisions of episcopal conferences. The discussion was lively and echoed earlier discussions in the preparatory commission and in the Council hall on the relation between Latin and vernacular. The crucial point was the clarification in concrete terms of the phrase "parts belonging to the people" (SC 54), for which the vernacular was allowed at Mass. According to some of the Fathers, the entire Mass belonged to the people. Others emphasized the irreconcilability of such a view with the conciliar statement that Latin is to be kept. The problem of the Canon inevitably came up in this context, but the discussion was so lively that the president suggested leaving the problem of the Canon to the general reform. The meeting voted in favor of this proposal.

Another point that gave rise to extended discussion had to do with chant. To allow the vernacular in the sung parts of the Ordinary and

---

10. *Schemata*, no. 1, De concelebratione, 1. The schema had been sent for inspection to the members and consultors of the Consilium on April 2.

11. See p. 826.

Proper could lead to the abandonment of sung Masses and of Gregorian chant and polyphony. Insofar as these problems were problems of the language to be used, the Consilium approved the principle of a *gradual* application of the liturgical Constitution; gradualness would allow for local situations and preparation, matters on which the episcopal conferences should be the judges.

The criteria for approval of the acts of episcopal conferences were accepted unanimously. These norms can be summed up as follows:[12]

1. The experiments of which no. 40 of the liturgical Constitution speaks refer, not to existing rites, but to elements of local tradition and culture that may be introduced into public worship.

2. The principle that the vernacular may be used even in sung Masses is accepted; the melodies must be approved by the ecclesiastical authorities.

3. The readings can be done in the vernacular in all Masses; in sung Masses they can be proclaimed.

4. A rite is to be prepared for the proclamation of the readings facing the people.

5. The Our Father can be said by the faithful along with the celebrant; it can be in Latin or in the vernacular, recited or sung (using an approved melody).

6. Local authorities can decide that the vernacular may be used in acclamations, greetings, dialogues, orations (collect, prayer over the gifts, postcommunion prayer, and blessing of the people), in the chants of the Ordinary (*Kyrie, Gloria, Credo, Sanctus-Benedictus, Agnus Dei*), in the formulas *Ecce Agnus Dei* and *Domine, non sum dignus*, in the chants of the Proper, and in the prayers at the foot of the altar.

7. The vernacular is allowed in the celebration of the sacraments and sacramentals, except in the sacrament of orders, where it may be used in the addresses and admonitions.

8. Rubrical simplifications: the prayer over the gifts and the Our Father may be said aloud, while a decision on the other parts of the Canon is postponed; the formula for the distribution of communion may be "Cor-

---

12. Some procedural difficulties were already evident at this second meeting. Some of the Fathers who were especially expert in juridical matters did not fail to ask frequently whether this or that question proposed to the Fathers for their study did not exceed the competency of the Consilium. The disagreement arose especially in regard to some practical decisions planned for the instruction and to the authority competent to promulgate the document. Finally, in approving the schema of the instruction, the Fathers added: "pending the special approval of the Supreme Pontiff in matters beyond, or seemingly beyond, the competency of the Consilium." But they immediately felt the need for a set of regulations that would facilitate procedures in the Consilium.

pus Christi. Amen";[13] Psalm 42(43) in the prayers at the foot of the altar, the last gospel, and the Leonine prayers may be omitted.

9. In read Masses the Apostles' Creed may be used instead of the Nicene-Constantinopolitan Creed.[14]

These were the principal decisions made by the Fathers. They were presented to the Holy Father, who gave his approval on the following April 21 in an audience granted to the Cardinal President. Many of these decisions would subsequently be included in the instruction.

Finally, the Consilium asked the president for powers to study and approve the acts of the episcopal conferences, provided they were in accord with the established criteria.

General Meeting III (June 18–20, 1964)

The third general meeting took place at Santa Marta, June 18–20, 1964. The relators were not present, because they had held their own meeting, at Santa Marta, on April 14–16. However, the Cardinal President did admit the seventeen consultors who had been appointed for the ordinary meetings.

The agenda included:

Report of the secretary on the activity of the Consilium during the period since the last meeting. He mentioned the death of Monsignor Valentini on May 11 and the elevation of two consultors, Monsignor Fallani and Father Salmon, to the episcopate. He informed the members that forty-two episcopal conferences had submitted the minutes of their decisions on liturgical matters; nineteen had received approval. He brought them up to date on the joint meetings with the Congregations for Seminaries and Religious on questions that fell under the competency of these agencies and were to be dealt with in the instruction. He then reviewed the meetings of the study groups: two on the calendar, two on the Order of Mass, various others on the Pontifical and on chant (preparation of the *Kyriale simplex* and of some models for the *Graduale simplex*), others of group 12 on the prayer of the faithful, as well as the weekly meetings of the Psalter group.

---

13. The application of this decision was anticipated by the decree *Quo actuosius*, which the SCR issued on April 25, 1964: *AAS* 56 (1964) 337–38 (*DOL* 252 no. 2034); the decree contained only this point. Inasmuch as an organic plan was in preparation and the Congregation had been informed of it, the action, good in itself, was felt to be rather astonishing.

14. The Holy Father postponed the application of this decision; it was to be re-examined by the Synod of Bishops. In the end, the Nicene-Constantinopolitan Creed would remain in the Missal because of its doctrinal completeness and for ecumenical reasons. The Apostles' Creed would be allowed by special concession.

The instruction. A new draft was presented that had been completely reworked after the meeting of the relators. Instead of the earlier four-part division, it was thought preferable to follow the order of the Constitution on the Liturgy and combine directives of a doctrinal, pastoral, and practical nature. Special attention was given to the section on the norms to be followed by the episcopal conferences in their decisions regarding the liturgy. Conferences had not yet been established in the majority of countries, and there were as yet no set of regulations and no routines. Norms were therefore established for the convocation of the conferences, their voting, and the submission of their acts to the Holy See.

Schemas of the rites of concelebration and communion under two kinds had been finished and given their final touches after the preceding meetings. The Fathers asked that before being definitively approved, the two rites be allowed for experimentation so that there might be some practical evidence of their value.

Report on the Mass. Monsignor Wagner presented a first report on the meetings of the group charged with revision of the Missal and the problems this raised, especially in regard to the Order of Mass. This first report was an informal one.

Other matters. On June 19 the Fathers took part in an experimental concelebration conducted by the Benedictine monks of Sant' Anselmo in their abbey church on the Aventine. On the preceding day they attended a showing of a documentary film on the concelebration at Bologna on the occasion of Cardinal Lercaro's sacerdotal jubilee.

Since the meeting coincided with the first anniversary of the Pope's election, the Fathers of the Consilium sent him the following telegram of good wishes:

> The president and members of the Consilium for the Implementation of the Constitution on the Sacred Liturgy wish Your Holiness every blessing on this happy first anniversary of your elevation to the Chair of Peter, and they ask the Lord to render fruitful and ever more extensive the activity of Your Holiness' glorious pontificate in restoring and advancing the sacred liturgy. —Giacomo Cardinal Lercaro.

The Cardinal Secretary of State telegraphed the Holy Father's thanks for the good wishes and communicated his apostolic blessing; he also assured them that the Pope was asking divine help and light for the Consilium so that its labors and studies ''might proceed safely and bear the fruit it looked for.''

General Meeting IV (September–November, 1964)

This fourth general meeting of the Consilium was held during the third session of the Council and had to allow for the commitments of its members at the Council. The sessions were therefore held only in the afternoon hours and at various times and places: from September 28 to October 1 and from October 5 to 9 at Santa Marta; on November 16 in a room that the General Curia of the Salvatorians (Via della Conciliazione) kindly put at the disposal of the Consilium. The relators held their meetings from September 19 to October 1.

The subjects treated had to do almost exclusively with the Mass and the Divine Office.[15] There was a general presentation by the various study groups dealing with the Mass and the Office; they asked the Fathers to vote on the general approach being taken to the work and on some particular questions. The Fathers had questions especially about the use and distribution of the psalms in the various Hours of the Office; the appropriateness of keeping the entire Psalter or, on the contrary, omitting some psalms that are more difficult or that are imprecatory; the hymns; the schema for Vespers; whether the Office should be the same for all or whether it might be possible to have a special Office for monks or religious of the contemplative life. There was also a report from Monsignor Pellegrino on the patristic readings.

Problems with various parts of the Mass were explained: the Ordinary, readings, votive Masses, chants.

Approval was given to the *Kyriale simplex* and the chants to be included in the Missal; all these had been prepared by study group 25.

Professor B. Fischer gave an overall presentation of the work of the study group dealing with the sacraments and sacramentals.[16]

---

15. The Divine Office was discussed from September 28 to October 1; the Mass on October 5 and 6; the Ritual on October 9; and the prayer of the faithful on November 16.

16. In their overall presentations the relators would ask the members of the Consilium to vote on the main questions, since they might have various answers. For the most part, especially when there was question of technical problems or matters on which the scholars themselves were in disagreement, the Fathers felt unprepared to decide. They therefore expressed some reservations about the many votes that were anticipated, especially in matters of the Divine Office. The secretary had to assure them that the votes were simply "guidelines" that would be useful in tackling the work. This assurance, while calming consciences, caused some difficulties later on. It was a weapon that could cut both ways. When it became necessary to adopt a decision different from that earlier approved by vote, some resisted, appealing to the earlier vote, while others emphasized the freedom to raise earlier questions once more. It was another one of the shadow areas in the Consilium, another of those points that were both weaknesses and strengths, that depended on good will more than on juridical norms. The desire to do serious work that would meet pastoral needs and take account of growth in the consciousness of the ecclesial communities in the course of the

The session of November 16 was devoted to an inspection of the booklet that group 12 had prepared on the prayer of the faithful, and to a discussion of the introduction of the vernacular into the preface of the Mass. Both were approved by the Consilium.

First papal audience

On October 29 the Holy Father granted a special audience to the Consilium. Seven cardinals, twenty-five bishops, and about forty consultors were present. It was the Consilium's first meeting with the Pope. The Cardinal President thanked him for the special privilege he had given to the Consilium in allowing it to contribute to so important a task,

> even though as the work goes on we feel the pressures increasing daily. For we must thoroughly examine the rites and forms of divine worship and these are elements that through the centuries of the Church's history all Catholics, and especially we priests, have held dear. But a pastoral concern presses us to carry out this work as a sacred trust; the danger of harming souls forbids us to resist the holy principles of this work. Ours therefore becomes an "ecclesial" task and a sacred pastoral charge. We bear with the work because we think of it as God's will, clearly expressed in the decisions of the teaching Church by the documents of the Council.[17]

In his address the Holy Father urged the Consilium to work unflaggingly and confidently.

> You are well aware of our great esteem and constant concern to follow your work, which—and rightly so—we regard as so important. . . . Through your activity especially, the wise prescriptions of the Council will be received gladly and daily be more appreciated; little by little the Christian people will shape their lives according to that model.

The Pope then reminded the Consilium of its mandate: (1) to revise the Church's forms of worship so that they may better meet the needs of our time and be expressions of the Catholic faith that are worthy of the divine majesty, filled with the spirit of religious devotion, and at the same time brief, simple, clear, and authentic; (2) to keep in mind the pedagogical character of the liturgy so that it may be a school of truth and love for the Christian people; (3) to combine past and present in a harmonious way. "For the liturgy is like a mighty tree, the continual renewal of whose leaves shows its beauty; the great age of whose trunk, with roots

---

work enabled this body to retrace its steps when a better, clearer, more pastoral solution was presented.
17. *DOL* 80 no. 620.

deep and firm in the earth, attests to the richness of its life." The Pope ended by saying:

> Remember always that it is a magnificent task to offer to the praying Church a voice and, so to speak, an instrument with which to celebrate the praises of God and to offer him the petitions of his children. A task of this kind, for whose success heaven and earth conspire, is a work at once human and divine: human, because it depends on your skill, learning, and piety; divine, because the inspiration and action of the Holy Spirit cannot be absent from it. Without the Holy Spirit, nothing holy, nothing strong, nothing saving can be accomplished.[18]

In these concluding words the whole Consilium family saw a fine description of its vocation in the Church, a call to be answered perseveringly and in a spirit of faith.

General Meeting V (April 26-30, 1965)

The sessions were held in the meeting room of the Congregations in the Apostolic Palace, on April 26-30, 1965. Twenty members and forty *periti* were in attendance.[19]

At the beginning of the meeting Cardinal Lercaro sent the following telegram to the Holy Father:

> The president, members, and *periti* of the Council for the Implementation of the Constitution on the Sacred Liturgy, gathered for their fifth plenary meeting and rejoicing over the first steps in a liturgical reform that is meant for the building up of the Lord's flock, offer heartfelt thanks to Your Holiness, who by word and example lead the Church's pastors in this work. They offer their filial good wishes and humbly ask your Apostolic Blessing on themselves and their work. — Giacomo Cardinal Lercaro.

On April 28 the Holy Father answered with the following paternal message:

> The Holy Father wishes to reciprocate your devoted and pleasing homage and publicly to praise you [Cardinal Lercaro] and the members and *periti* of the Consilium, now gathered for your fifth plenary session, for the commitment you have shown in carrying out the responsibilities entrusted to you. He is most pleased with the abundant spiritual fruits produced by this commitment, and he asks the Lord to be present with you, make your labors fruitful, and bring new growth to the entire Church. As a pledge of heavenly blessings, the Holy Father bestows his Apostolic Blessing on you and the entire company of the Consilium. — Cardinal Cicognani.

---

18. *DOL* 81 nos. 621 and 624.
19. See *Not* 1 (1965) 99–104; *EL* 79 (1965) 245.

Cardinal Lercaro remembered Bishops Francis Grimshaw and Jesús Enciso Viana, who had died recently. He also mentioned the elevation of Archbishop Bevilacqua to the cardinalate. He sent a telegram to the new Cardinal, who was absent because of the serious illness that would in a short time bring him to his grave. Finally, he referred to the changes that had taken place in the Congregation of Rites and to the appointments of Father Antonelli as its secretary, Father Bugnini, secretary of the Consilium, as its subsecretary, and Monsignor Frutaz as a consultor.

Report of the secretary. The secretary of the Consilium gave the Fathers a broad survey of the work done since the last general meeting and of prospects for the future. The activity of the Consilium had borne fruit in various typical editions: *Kyriale simplex; Cantus qui in Missali Romano desiderantur; De oratione fidelium; Ordo Missae; Ritus concelebrationis et communionis sub utraque specie; Variationes in Ordinem Hebdomadae sanctae inducendae.*

He also spoke of the good relations between the Consilium and the other agencies of the Roman Curia, as well as of some continuing difficulties.[20]

Finally, he explained the plan to inaugurate the periodical *Notitiae* and outlined its purposes. The publication of duplicated pages informing the Consilium family and workers in pastoral liturgy about the preparation of the reform and the activity of the episcopal conferences and national liturgical commissions had shown the need for a better organized and more complete publication that would appear at regular intervals.

Study of the schemas. A good 113 schemas were submitted by various study groups to the Fathers for their examination. The schemas had to do with the calendar, the Office (distribution of psalms, biblical readings, patristic readings, hymns, chants), the *Graduale simplex*, the Ceremonial of Bishops,[21] the *Ordo Missae*, the anointing of the sick, the baptism of adults, and the instruction on sacred music.[22]

---

20. The difficulty at that time had to do with the teaching of liturgy in the seminaries, since word had come that the Congregation for Seminaries was preparing an instruction without consulting the Consilium. The Fathers unanimously asked the president to discuss the matter with the Holy Father. This was the beginning of a lengthy episode that lasted over ten years (see pp. 859ff.).

21. The reference here is to simplifications that were subsequently published in the motu proprio *Pontificalia insignia* of June 21, 1968 (*AAS* 60 [1968] 374–77; *DOL* 549 nos. 4447-56) and the instruction *Pontificalis ritus* of the SCR, likewise on June 21, 1968 (*AAS* 60 [1968] 406–12; *DOL* 550 nos. 4457-96).

22. The sessions, and their subjects, of General Meeting V were as follows: April 26: report of the secretary; April 27: calendar and distribution of psalms; April 28: biblical and patristic readings and hymns of the Office, and the instruction on sacred music; April 30: funerals, baptism of adults, chants of the Office, anointing of the sick, special questions.

Also submitted to the Fathers were some specific issues raised in various quarters in connection with the initial implementation of the reform. These included a request for further simplifications or the elimination of incoherences in the celebration of Mass;[23] a petition from the German and Swiss episcopal conferences to experiment with an *Ordo lectionum per ferias;* the need for norms for the publication of liturgical books by the conferences. The Consilium was informed of the decision of the Congregation of Rites regarding the parts of the rite of ordination that could be said in the vernacular, and of the request made to the Holy Father for the extension of the vernacular to the Divine Office and for the suppression of Prime in communities obliged to the choral recitation of the Office. Finally, the Consilium approved the proposal to prepare an instruction on worship of the Eucharist.

Other matters. At the first session the Fathers presented reports on the beginning of the liturgical reform in their countries.

On April 29 a group of Fathers was appointed to examine the manuscript of the *Graduale simplex,* since this was a rather technical affair and not easily understood by everyone. The next day the group reported that their response was positive. On April 30 there was a meeting solely of the Fathers, without the *periti.* The Fathers felt the need for some meetings by themselves so that they could freely express their thinking and their desires with regard to the work of the Consilium.[24]

The fifth general meeting ended at midday on April 30. At the last moment the Holy Father sent some copies of his book *Discorsi su la Madonna e su i santi* (Milan, 1965) to the Cardinal President for distribution to the members of the Consilium.

General Meeting VI (October–December, 1965)

This meeting took place partly in the meeting room of the Congregations in the Apostolic Palace and partly at Santa Marta, on October 18–26, November 22–26, and December 1, 1965.[25] Almost all the members were present, as well as the consultors involved in the schemas to be discussed.

---

23. Even though some were in favor, the request was postponed in order not to disturb the course of the reform that had already begun.

24. They evidenced a certain uneasiness at the sometimes overly erudite lectures of the *periti.* The latter were asked to limit themselves to clarifications of problems; the Fathers for their part were interested chiefly in the pastoral aspects and always paid close attention to these. This fact gives the lie to complaints too often heard that the reform was the work of technicians and that pastors were absent from the scene.

25. See *Not* 2 (1966) 3–5.

The Cardinal President mentioned the recent appointment of new members: Cardinal Conway and Bishops Hurley, Dwyer, Clavel Mendez, Enrique y Tarancón, Pellegrino, and Bluyssen.

The secretary's report dealt with further work on particular questions discussed at the previous general meeting: the schema of rubrical simplifications in the Mass (postponed by decision of the Holy Father); grant of a Lectionary for weekday Masses; publication of the parts that could be said in the vernacular in the rite of ordination; concession of the vernacular in the Office and of the suppression of Prime in communities obliged to choir; preparation of the instructions on worship of the Eucharist and on sacred music. Among the publications issued: the booklet for the celebration of Mass during the fourth session of the Council; the *Graduale simplex* (now being printed); the *De oratione communi seu fidelium;* and *Notitiae.* The secretary mentioned the work on the revision of the Propers, and the meetings planned for translators, presidents of liturgical commissions, and editors of periodicals.

Schemas. Eight schemas were discussed: *Ordo Missae,* baptism of adults, funerals, revision of the Psalter, ordination of bishops, priests, and deacons, Ceremonial for Bishops, Divine Office, instruction on sacred music.[26]

The schema on orders was presented for the first time, the purpose being to ascertain from the Fathers the direction in which the *periti* might proceed. The other schemas, however, the secretary pointed out, were definitive as far as the *periti* were concerned, so that if the Consilium approved them, they could be sent out for experiment until the next general meeting, which was scheduled for the end of April 1966. The Fathers were therefore asked to examine these schemas carefully.[27]

Other matters. Two episodes marked this general meeting: ·

1) *Ordo Missae.* Monsignor Wagner, the relator of study group 10, presented the complete schema of the *Ordo Missae,* accompanied by an extensive report. During the meeting Mass was twice celebrated in accordance with the new *Ordo,* first on October 20 in Italian,[28] and then

---

26. The order of the presentations and discussions was as follows: October 18: adult baptism; 19: adult baptism, *Ordo Missae,* Office; 20: experimental Mass (in Italian); 21: *Ordo Missae;* 22: experimental Mass (in French); 25: funerals; 26: vote on the *Ordo Missae,* revision of the psalms; November 22: episcopal ordination; 23: presbyteral and diaconal ordination; 25–26: instruction on sacred music; December 1: Divine Office, Ceremonial of Bishops.

27. Consideration was given to the timeliness of releasing three schemas for experimentation: adult baptism, funerals, *Ordo Missae.* The first two were approved, the third was put off.

28. *Celebrant:* Father Bugnini; *director of music:* Father Luigi Agustoni; *masters of ceremonies:* Monsignor Schnitzler and Father Franquesa. The choir consisted of students from the International College of the Servants of Mary and sisters from the Institute. Form A of the Roman Canon was used.

on October 22 in French.[29] Both Masses were celebrated in the chapel of the Maria Bambina Institute at 21, Via del Sant'Uffizio. Attendance at the experiments was limited to the Fathers, who immediately afterwards discussed their impressions in a room at the same Institute.

Unfortunately, the experiments became known. Some organs of the press reported on them and thus gave rise to complaints. The result was that work on the *Ordo Missae* was stopped until the Synod of 1967.[30]

2) *Divine Office.* The publication of material on the Divine Office in *Notitiae*, the introduction of the vernacular, and the abandonment of daily celebration of the Office by some priests—all these factors resulted in rather alarmist views reaching the secretariat of the Consilium with regard to the structure being planned. Some found it too monastic, insufficiently responsive to the real needs of the clergy involved in the care of

---

29. *Celebrant:* Prof. P. Jounel; *director of song:* Father Gélineau; *masters of ceremonies* and *choir,* as at the previous Mass. Form B of the Roman Canon was used.

30. The fragmentary information in the press elicited interventions even from scholars, especially in the French-speaking world, who were perhaps inspired by an interview with a member of the Consilium that appeared in *La Croix* for October 24, 1965.

Father L. Bouyer sent the Holy Father a lengthy statement on the Eucharistic Prayers and the revision of the Roman Canon; Mme. Noële Maurice Denis Boulet did the same, using Jacques Maritain and Cardinal Journet as her channel.

It is not surprising, therefore, that the Secretariat of State immediately took a hand in the affair. On October 25 Cardinal Cicognani, Secretary of State (No. 56539), wrote to the president of the Consilium: "I have the duty of informing you that since the Consilium is now studying the entire *Ordo Missae,* and in view of the evident sensitivity of the matter, His Holiness wishes to know what kind of revision is being undertaken—minor changes or substantial reforms—so that he may choose to provide guidelines before the conclusions of this study, which will be intended for publication, are submitted to him for his consideration."

The Secretary of State returned to the subject on December 10 (No. 56539): "I have the duty of letting Your Eminence know that in the meantime new expressions of lively concern have reached us regarding the projects for the reform of the *Ordo Missae.*

"In view of the exceptional importance of Holy Mass, which is a sacred and age-old patrimony of the Church, His Holiness wishes the Consilium to exercise great caution both in organizing experiments in this area and, above all, in proposing innovations; the Holy See must be given timely notice of everything, so that under the responsibility and authority of His Holiness, it may study any possible changes proposed for the rite of celebration of the divine sacrifice."

Finally, in transmitting Mme. Boulet's study of the Roman Canon (March 7, 1966; No. 66385): ". . . I hasten to tell you of His Holiness' desire that the Canon itself not be altered, at least for the time being; any possible change must therefore be submitted for explicit approval of the Holy Father, who, for his part, believes he must not introduce any changes into the Canon itself without previous documented and rigorous studies and then, should the occasion arise, only after consulting with the bishops.

"I am to tell you that, all things considered, it is perhaps better to leave the traditional text unchanged; this, however, does not mean that study of the subject is not to continue."

souls, and too remote from the laity. They found especially objectionable the distribution of the Psalter over a two-week period, the retention
of the imprecatory and historical psalms, and the burdening of Lauds and
Vespers in particular with excessive psalmody.

The Fathers first dealt with these matters on October 19 at a meeting
reserved to them. As they discussed the reasons pro and con, they found
themselves faced with a painful dilemma: to continue the work, which
was already at an advanced stage, along the line that had been chosen
or to issue new directives to the study group and make it change course.

The dilemma was not resolved that day. The question was taken up
again on December 1 at a meeting at which the secretary presented the
reasons urging reconsideration of the entire problem. Canon Martimort
gave the Fathers a report with the reasons offered by his group. The discussion was lively, due to the tension between tradition and the necessity of meeting present-day needs. It was finally decided to send the
Fathers a statement of the entire problem, together with a questionnaire
that they promised to answer.

Special questions. Two were brought up: adaptation of the liturgy of
the Mass to the sign language of the deaf, and the use of Esperanto at
gatherings of those who were developing this language. The response
to both was positive, pending approval of the Holy Father.

The meeting ended at midday on December 1. At that meeting all present, both members and consultors, received a numbered copy of the booklet *P. Giulio Bevilacqua Cardinale* as a gracious gift from the private secretary
of the Holy Father.

General Meeting VII (October 6–14, 1966)

The sixth general meeting took place at Santa Marta, October 6–14,
1966. It was preceded by two meetings of the relators, May 5–14 and September 19–October 1.[31]

Present were eight cardinals, thirty-two bishops, and Abbot Gut. Three
members were taking part for the first time: Alexander Kovács, Ambróz
Lazík, and Gerald Emmett Carter. The Cardinal President sent fraternal
good wishes to those members who were absent because of illness.

This was also the first meeting of the Consilium at which observers
from the non-Catholic ecclesial communities were present.

---

31. See *Not* 2 (1966) 312–13. Some of the information set down here comes also from
the report of the meeting that was sent to the members.

The meeting was marked by a great deal of hard work. The relators and Fathers put in fifteen days of intense labor, morning and afternoon. The reason was that the assembly was beginning to harvest the ripe fruit of the study groups, for these were now presenting the Fathers with complete or almost complete schemas.

In his customary report on the activity of the Consilium the secretary listed the main documents that had been submitted to the Holy Father since the last general meeting: on March 1, 1966, a complete report on the first two years of the Consilium's activity and on the work done and to be completed by each of the study groups; on May 21, the tenth and final draft of the instruction on sacred music; an exposition of the discipline governing use of the papal altar, which led to the motu proprio *Peculiare ius* (February 8, 1966); on December 2, 1965, the rite of funerals; on March 18, 1966, the rite for Christian initiation of adults (which the Pope, on June 20, allowed to be sent out for experimentation); on June 10, a report on the reform of the *Ordo Missae* and on all the problems connected with it.

Permission had meanwhile been granted for an experimental adaptation of the monastic Office, especially in mission lands; the rites for the closing of the Council had been prepared, as had the Mass for the celebration of the extraordinary Jubilee.

The secretary also reported on some difficulties that had been raised within the Consilium with regard to its participation in the publication of some documents, and he explained the nature of this participation.[32] The Consilium could not claim complete competency in liturgical matters, as could the conciliar commission, which was free to range throughout the field entrusted to it. The Consilium had to respect the competencies of the other agencies, and when the latter were acting according to their special competencies, it could offer its collaboration but could not impose its ideas.

---

32. The reference is to the publication of the instruction on the liturgy in seminaries (*DOL* 332 nos. 2672-2761), which was issued on December 25, 1965, "after consultation with the Consilium," and then immediately withdrawn because of the reaction of the bishops; to the instruction *In edicendis normis* of November 23, 1965, on the vernacular in the Office of monastic and religious communities (*DOL* 114 nos. 791-811); and to the decree *Cum, nostra aetate* of January 27, 1966, on editions of liturgical books (*DOL* 134 nos. 918-29); these last two documents were signed also by the president of the Consilium. Some members and consultors of the Consilium complained of not having been informed. In addition to explaining the competencies of the various agencies of the Curia, the secretary of the Consilium could only say that the president had acted in accordance with the delegated authority given to him by the Consilium itself at its second general meeting (April 1964).

On October 12 the Cardinal President spoke of another difficulty when he exhorted all the participants in these meetings to be very prudent in letting others know of the work. Some schemas still needed revisions, others required experimentation, and all had to be submitted to the supreme authority in the Church. All sorts of expectations were harbored, both by those who were anxiously awaiting the reform of the rites and by those who feared such a reform. Revelation of what was being done in the Consilium could give rise to untimely hopes or provoke hostile reactions.[33]

Papal audience. The Holy Father once again received the Consilium at an audience on October 13 in the Hall of the Consistory. In his homage to the Pope, the Cardinal President listed three things that gave this meeting with the Pope a special character: the evidence that the reform was producing spiritual fruits of active, conscious, devout participation by the laity in the liturgy, and doing so in part due to the contribution of the liturgical commissions that had now been established in all countries; the progress of the Consilium's various works, some of which were in the experimental stage (funerals; Christian initiation of adults), while others had been presented to the Pope; and, finally, the presence of the observers, which was a pledge of ever closer links and collaboration between the Churches.

The Pope answered with a heartfelt address that looked to the future:

> We welcome you . . . with respect and with pleasure and thank you for this visit that allows our person and our thoughts to share in your most worthwhile work. For that work you have our thanks. What could be more profitable for the Church in these days after the Council? What could do more to spark the fire of devotion in the Church's heart, to win for it the help of the Holy Spirit, to provide it with the power that attracts, that teaches, that sanctifies?

He then went on to give three guidelines for the work of the reform. First, there is need for religious prudence and an intelligent respect for existing ceremonies, so as to avoid hasty and unjustifiable changes. It

---

33. The entire Consilium, in fact, showed great reserve. It was impossible, however, that people in Rome should fail to notice so large a gathering and avoid indulging in conjectures, sometimes very odd, as to its business. For this reason it was decided to publish some information of the work of the general meetings. But the Secretariat of State was in all likelihood worried about reactions even to such communications. In fact, it refused its consent to an article written for *L'Osservatore Romano* on the work of the seventh meeting, "because information on the work thus far completed may increase the anxieties, the arbitrary actions, the failures of observance, and the impulses to freewheeling reform that are unfortunately already widespread" (October 26, 1966; No. 81405).

is necessary, secondly, to preserve the rich doctrinal, artistic, and spiritual content that has always marked liturgical prayer and given it "the heavenly gift or charism of being universal and lasting, the charism of being ever young. The liturgy deserves the adornment of such special gifts." Finally, the liturgy must be made accessible in its intelligibility, expression, and execution to the faithful generally. He continued:

> To match liturgical structure and language to pastoral needs, to the catechetical aims of liturgy, to the spiritual and moral formation of the faithful, to the desire for union with God, to the nature of the sign of the sacred that allows for comprehension and, by experience, perception of its religious power—that is your work. What practical knowledge and charity it demands of you who are the artisans of the new liturgy, the bearers of treasures hidden from us till now! For in the liturgy the aim is beauty and simplicity, depth and clarity of meaning, substance with brevity, the resonances of ages past joined to the voices of today in a new harmony. To you the Church of God confides this sublime undertaking.

The Pope then mentioned other tasks of the Consilium and distinguished its competency from that of the Congregation of Rites:

> Your own Consilium has a responsibility of vigilance during this period when new forms of divine worship are being tested and introduced in the different regions of the Church. You must check misguided attempts that may here and there appear and constrain those who follow their own preferences at the risk of disturbing the right order of public prayer and of occasioning doctrinal errors. Accordingly, it is for you to prevent abuses, to prod those who lag or resist, to stimulate energies, to encourage promising initiatives, to praise those deserving praise.

The Pope then made benevolent mention of the periodical *Notitiae* and of the schemas that had been presented to him, especially the instruction on sacred music and the exposition of the *Ordo Missae*, a matter "of such a serious and universal import that we cannot do otherwise than consult with the bishops on any proposals before approving them by our own authority."[34] Finally, he urged the Consilium to go on its way confidently: "Continue on with hard work and with trust; may you be helped by the conviction that you have our trust and our respect."[35] At the end of the audience the Pope conversed in a friendly way with those present and gave the Cardinal President a copy of the artistic edition of the Gospels in Italian that Father Bevilacqua had published.

---

34. This the Pope in fact did on the occasion of the first Synod of Bishops in 1967.

35. The Pope's address is in *DOL* 84 nos. 630-36. Cardinal Lercaro's remarks are in *DOL* 83 nos. 62(-29.

Schemas. Eleven subjects were discussed: the calendar, sacred orders, the whole problem of minor orders, the readings of the Mass, infant baptism, marriage, the Divine Office,[36] the Ceremonial of Bishops, the prefaces and orations,[37] the consecration of the oils, the instruction on the Eucharistic mystery.[38]

In discussing these various schemas, almost all now complete, which showed the great intelligence, perseverance, and sensitivity of the *periti*, the Consilium was roused to genuine enthusiasm and forgot the fatigue induced by its nearly uninterrupted labors. There was a pervasive sense of profound brotherhood, especially due to the presence of the observers; there was also a sense of lighthearted joy[39] and of admiration for the preparedness of the *periti*;[40] and there were some tensions.

Of particular interest were the questions that Father Vagaggini raised in his brilliant, clear exposition of the vast range of problems connected with minor orders and with the Scripture readings of the Mass. The chief need in the latter area was to come to a decision on the cycle of readings and on the structure of the liturgy of the Word in the Mass. The experts of the study group argued passionately for three obligatory readings on Sundays, the aim being to promote knowledge of the Bible among the faithful and to implement the Council's decision to open up the treasures of the Scriptures to them. Some of the Fathers objected that there was danger of making the Mass too long and especially that neither clergy nor faithful were adequately prepared for this greater emphasis on Scripture. In the end, the reasons given by the experts won the day.

---

36. This was a presentation of the structure of the Office as revised by the study group as a result of replies to the questionnaire that had been requested at the previous general meeting and sent to the members and consultors on December 16, 1965.

37. After his voluminous presentation of the work done on revision of the orations and prefaces of the Missal, the heart of the relator, Father Placid Bruylants, gave out. On October 18, shortly after returning to his abbey, Mont-César, he fell asleep for ever in the Lord. He was a further victim of the generous and persevering effort that the Pope had called for in restoring the beauty of the liturgy.

38. The order followed in the discussion was: October 6: episcopal, presbyteral, and diaconal ordination; 7: minor orders, calendar; 8: calendar (meeting of the members alone); 10: readings of the Mass; 11: infant baptism, marriage; 12: calendar, instruction on worship of the Eucharistic mystery; 13: Eucharistic worship, Divine Office; 14: Ceremonial of Bishops, blessing of the oils, orations and prefaces.

39. Affection was felt at the heartfelt plea of a Father that the memorial of the dedication of his titular church be kept in the calendar. To the valid arguments of the relator he answered: "But I'm asking for only a little memorial! After all, just a memorial!"

40. In response to the puzzlement of some Fathers at the adoption of the prayer in Hippolytus for the ordination of bishops and to the claim that this prayer displays an impoverished theology that does not do justice to Vatican II, Father Lécuyer gave a learned, extempore defense of the text, eliciting prolonged applause from the entire gathering.

There was a lively discussion of holy orders, the complete text and rubrics of which were presented by an unsurpassed master, Father Botte. At the beginning of the discussion some of the Fathers raised difficulties that were more emotional than scientific.[41] In face of the relator's incomparable mastery of the subject, the other participants in the discussion finally became somewhat shy.

One of the Fathers gave voice to the uneasiness felt during the discussion when, at the final session (October 14), he expressed his puzzlement in a written statement. After telling his admiration for the untiring work of the experts, he revealed the anxiety aroused in him by the discussion of orders.

> I recognize the distinguished relator's erudition, his reputation, and his mastery in the study of the very early liturgical documents. Learned and valuable work has been done in revising the Pontifical. But before the fruit of this work is presented to the Holy Father, there are some small but very important points that I want to bring before you. For some reason or other, the discussion of episcopal consecration has proved difficult.

The speaker went on to ask for reconsideration especially of the proposal to replace the prayer of episcopal consecration with the third-century prayer set down in the schema. According to this bishop, such a change ought not to be made unless the text now in use were completely inadequate and incapable of improvement. He repeated what the Holy Father had said in the previous day's audience about respect for tradition. In the view of this bishop, the current prayer was superior in its expression of the effects of the sacrament.[42]

---

41. In regard again to the prayer of episcopal ordination, one of the Fathers said it would be better to take the current prayer as a basis and retain its best ideas. But the relator replied firmly: "I am afraid the result would be a monster of epic proportions." Still another Father asked, with regard to the new prayer, "What does it mean to ask the ordinand: 'Are you resolved to build up the body of Christ?' " "Ask St. Paul," Father Botte answered, "since the wording is his." In the final redaction, however, he took the question into account and added the explanatory words: "Are you resolved to build up the body of Christ, which is the Church of God?"

The climax was reached when, despite the majority's enthusiastic acceptance of the introductory address, a Father said that the one now in the Pontifical was much superior. "Show it to me," said the relator. A Roman Pontifical was brought, and the Father began to leaf through it while the discussion continued. After a while, perhaps feeling compassion for the man in his laborious search, Father Botte said: "There's no use leafing through; you'll never find it because it does not exist."

42. The most serious disagreement came with regard to two phrases in the sacramental formula: (1) "Nunc effunde eam virtutem, quae a te est, spiritum principalem," as compared with the old: "Comple in sacerdote tuo ministerii tui summam"; and (2) the new "ut gregem sanctum tuum pascat," as compared with the lengthy digression in the cur-

But the schema passed. It was also approved without difficulty by the Congregation for the Doctrine of the Faith and proved satisfactory in its use by the Church. A calmer reflection on the venerable prayer from Hippolytus showed its complete agreement with the doctrine of Vatican II on the episcopate; the agreement is indeed a splendid example of continuity in faith.[43]

Meeting of the members alone

On the afternoon of October 8 there was a meeting solely of the members, for the purpose of discussing some internal problems. Several specific decisions were taken:

1) A consultor's mandate was to be for three years, and renewable. The *periti* themselves had had their attention called to this matter in a questionnaire circulated among them during the preceding months. The proposal was motivated by a desire to keep on bringing new talents into the work of the Consilium. For the same reason, it was asked that the presidents of the national liturgical commissions should become part of the Consilium during their term of office. This would have the twofold advantage of lending greater credibility to the bishop in charge of the pastoral liturgy of a country and of helping him to equip himself better for his office. Participation in the work of the Consilium would be, as it were, a "bath" of liturgical formation.

2) A set of regulations were to be prepared governing the internal functioning of the study groups and their meetings and discussion. Also to be prepared was a constitution that would prescribe the tasks, competencies, composition, and membership of the Consilium, regulate the course of its general meetings, and determine the tasks of the presidency, the presidential council, and the secretariat.

The purpose of this decision was eminently practical. As we saw earlier, however, the move was misinterpreted.[44]

---

rent text on the power of the keys and the power of governance. The puzzlement of the Fathers came from the difficulty in fully understanding the words "spiritus principalis" and "gregem pascat."

43. Even after the new rites were published, requests came in for the reintroduction of parts that had been eliminated; among these was the old formula of episcopal ordination, at least as an optional text alongside the new. But other, even more radical proposals were also subsequently made. Chief among these were a desire for another consecratory prayer for presbyteral ordination, one that would be clearer to the faithful and more in accord with New Testament teaching on priesthood, and a call for updating and completing the Introduction (the *Praenotanda*); see below, pp. 721-23.

44. See above, pp. 75-78.

3) With the intention, again, of expediting the work of the Consilium and relieving it of procedural and psychological difficulties, the bishops decided to establish a presidential council composed of seven members in addition to the president and vice-president. Its duties would be to handle more serious and urgent problems that might arise between general meetings, to assist the president, and to enable the Consilium to take part in more important decisions that would not be submitted to general meetings, such as the cosigning of documents with other agencies of the Curia.

The election of members to this council took place on October 11. Those elected were: Boudon, Pellegrino, Spülbeck, Enrique y Tarancón, Conway, Isnard, and Bluyssen. The Pope approved the establishment of the presidential council and confirmed the election.[45]

Conclusion

At the end of the final session (October 14), the Cardinal President expressed his deep gratitude to the members and *periti* for the work done and the generosity shown. He also thanked the observers for their participation.

In the name of the other observers, Professor Shepherd thanked the Consilium and the Holy Father for allowing them to take part in the work of the assembly. He also stated that they were fully satisfied with the careful and thorough study devoted to the problems.

Monsignor Pellegrino spoke for all present in wishing Cardinal Lercaro well on his coming seventy-fifth birthday and in congratulating him on the renewed trust expressed by the Holy Father in his leadership of the Consilium.

Presidential council

After the conclusion of this general meeting, the presidential council held its own first meeting on the afternoon of October 14. At this meeting a commission was established to draw up the desired regulations for

---

45. The presidential council held eight meetings in all: I. October 14, 1966; II. January 12-13, 1967*; III. April 15 and 19, 1967; IV. November 23, 1967; V. January 30, 1968*; VI. April 30, 1968; VII. October 3, 1968; VIII. April 23-24, 1969*.

Only three (the ones marked with an asterisk) were held at a time different from that of the general meetings. For this reason, and also because the activity of the presidential council was closely connected with the general meetings, I will henceforth record its meetings along with the general meetings. The general context and the progress of the council's work will thus become clearer.

the Consilium,[46] while Monsignor Bonet was given the task of preparing a draft constitution. The council also approved a schedule of meetings for 1966–67 and some changes in the relators of the study groups.[47]

In the period between this general meeting and the next, the presidential council met a second time on January 12–13, 1967. It discussed the principal problems of the moment: relations with the agencies of the Holy See; the need of informing them about the work of the reform; delegation to the episcopal conferences and the national liturgical commissions of permission to allow experimentation with the rites prepared by the Consilium; the liturgical situation in the Netherlands, where the pontifical "mission" had just completed its visit; permission to use the vernacular in the Office. These and other matters were discussed with a view to publication of a general decree granting concessions now regarded as necessary for the progress of the reform. The discussion at this point was still of a simple "List of questions to be handled in the general decree." When developed, the list would become the instruction *Tres abhinc annos*.

Also studied was the first draft of a constitution, introduced by Monsignor Bonet. There was a lively discussion of a request from monastic communities in mission countries that they might make adaptations in the Divine Office. The Congregation of Propaganda Fide was in favor, the Congregation for Religious more reluctant. Some of the members of the presidential council would likewise have preferred to wait until the Consilium should have completed its work. In the end, the decision was for granting the request, with the understanding that the basic elements of the Office as set forth in the Constitution on the Liturgy were to be maintained.

General Meeting VIII (April 10–19, 1967)

This meeting was held April 10–19, 1967, partly at Santa Marta, partly in the Apostolic Palace. Nine cardinals, twenty-eight bishops, and Abbot Gut took part.[48] The relators had already met April 3–8.

In his greetings to the assembly, the Cardinal President called to mind the death of Father Placid Bruylants and the appointment of new members: Archbishop Gordon Gray and Bishop Leo de Kesel, who was replac-

---

46. For the members of this commission see above, p. 76, n. 9.
47. The following relators were appointed: Father Jounel, calendar (1); E. Lengeling, Scripture readings in the Breviary (4); A. Hänggi, special rites during the liturgical year (17); J. Lécuyer, penance (23bis).
48. See *Not* 3 (1967) 138–46.

ing Bishop van Zuylen, the latter having voluntarily surrendered his position in favor of the president of the Belgian liturgical commission.

Archbishop Simon Lourdusamy of Bangalore also took part in this meeting as the representative of Cardinal Gracias. The substitution had been unilaterally arranged and decided by the Cardinal, but the president decided that Archbishop Lourdusamy could take part in the sessions.

In his report the secretary mentioned the approval or new structuring of duties in the study groups that had occurred in the final months of 1966; the publication of the instruction on sacred music; the presentation to the Holy Father of the definitive version of the instruction on Eucharistic worship, the general decree on some simplifications or concessions, the drafts of a motu proprio on the use of pontifical insignia, and drafts on holy orders and the calendar. He also brought up a twofold problem that had become pressing in recent months: on the one hand, the rise and spread of personal and sometimes aberrant initiatives in the celebration of the liturgy, and the urgent call for indults and experiments; on the other, the poisonous campaign against the liturgical reform (there was to be an echo of this at the meeting itself).

April 10 was the vigil of the feast of St. Leo the Great. At the beginning of the session the president sent the Pope a message of filial homage and respect (prepared by Monsignor Schnitzler). It said:

> In the radiance of the feast of St. Leo the Great, the Council for the Implementation of the Constitution on the Sacred Liturgy hails Pope Paul VI, the Holy Father who rules in love and is reforming the sacred liturgy. It thanks him for the task he has so confidently entrusted to it, and it expresses the gratitude of all for the fruits already reaped: a more lively faith, a stronger hope, a more fervent and fuller participation in the celebration of the paschal mystery. It receives with thankfulness the teaching he gives in word, writing, and regulation.
>
> May the Lord preserve you, Holy Father, and enlighten and guide you, so that, following the example of St. Leo the Great, you may reform the sacramentaries and reaffirm the sacraments that bring peace.

The next day, Cardinal Cicognani, Secretary of State, responded in the name of the Holy Father:

> The Holy Father is grateful for, and deeply moved by, the sentiments of respect and reverence that you have so lovingly sent him for the feast of St. Leo the Great in the name of the members of the Consilium. He sends his regards in turn and prays for the light and strength of the divine Paraclete on the work of the Consilium, in order that with unwearying care it may promote and spread the honor of God, the beauty of holy Church, and the good of souls. With fatherly kindness he imparts to you the Apostolic Blessing.

Schemas. The agenda called for the presentation to the Fathers of a number of schemas requiring their comments: the Divine Office (general structure, based on directives given at the preceding meeting; various parts of the Office: distribution of the psalms; biblical, patristic, and hagiographical readings; hymns; chants); complete schema for the *Ordo Missae* and, in particular, four new Eucharistic Prayers and nine new prefaces; infant baptism; marriage; penance; reports to be given to the Synod of Bishops; draft of a constitution for the Consilium.[49]

In order that the Fathers might have a concrete grasp of the new structure for the Office, a little volume was prepared that contained the complete Office for a week; this was used in common and private prayer throughout the week of the meeting.

Special attention was paid to the schemas on the Mass and the Divine Office, the intention being to present them to the Synod of Bishops. Something unexpected at this meeting was the presentation of four new Eucharistic Prayers that had been prepared by the study group with the assistance of some further experts appointed by the president. In General Meeting V, the question had been raised of revising the Roman Canon, but neither the *periti* nor the Fathers were entirely convinced that changes should be made in this venerable text. The matter had been presented to the Holy Father, who decided, at an audience granted to the Cardinal President on June 20, 1966, that "the present anaphora is to be left untouched; two or three other anaphoras should be composed, or sought in existing texts, that could be used during certain defined seasons." As a result of this decision, three schemas were prepared: the present second and third Eucharistic Prayers and the Anaphora of St. Basil, which was thought suitable for its intrinsic value and because it would be especially useful in certain circumstances, such as the unity octave.

Because of practical difficulties in adopting the Anaphora of St. Basil, the relators subjected themselves to a kind of forced labor during their meeting and prepared the fourth Eucharistic Prayer, in the style of the Eastern anaphoras.

Special attention was paid to the words of consecration; the matter was subsequently submitted to the Synod of Bishops.[50]

---

49. The order of the discussions was as follows: April 11: Divine Office; 12: rite of the Mass; reports for the synod; infant baptism; 13: infant baptism; penance; marriage; 14–15: new anaphoras; 17: constitution; Mass; Divine Office; 18: rite of Mass without a congregation; 19: Mass.

50. The schema of the new Eucharistic Prayers (including the prayer of St. Basil, on which the Fathers' vote was almost equally divided: 15 for, 16 against), together with the schema of the new prefaces, was presented to the Holy Father on May 3, 1967, along with an extensive report.

Support for the Cardinal President. The meeting opened in an atmosphere of interior, spiritual suffering. During the days before the meeting, a defamatory book had been widely advertised in Rome and elsewhere,[51] which for a while achieved an undeserved international fame due to its poisonous attack on the liturgical reform and on the conciliar renewal generally. Some Roman newspapers had repeated the slanderous innuendos.[52] The president of the Consilium was portrayed as a "Luther resurrected."[53]

On April 17 the Consilium determined to let the president know of its fraternal solidarity with him. Bishop Boudon, a member of the presidential council, spoke in the name of all:

> I take it upon myself to speak in the name of all the members of the Consilium.
>
> We wish to assure His Eminence Cardinal Lercaro of our affectionate attachment and our complete support. The incidents in which his person and work have been attacked have awakened profound resonances in the heart of each of us.

---

51. Tito Casini, *La tunica stracciata* (Florence, 1967).

52. The matter appeared all the more serious because in an article against the elimination of Latin from the liturgy, *L'Osservatore Romano* seemed to approve Casini's theses, though this was not its intention.

53. The Cardinal was dismayed. He asked the Holy See to express immediately its regret for the article in *L'Osservatore Romano*. The request had no result; when another unworthy article was published in the Roman newspaper *Il Messagero* on April 14, the Cardinal interpreted this frontal and shameless attack as an underhand maneuver by Roman conservative circles, and he immediately left for Bologna. The next day the presidential council met and decided: "We can no longer remain silent about this situation. We must express our support of the president."

That same day Cardinal Confalonieri, vice-president of the Consilium, had an audience with the Pope in his capacity as prefect of the Congregation for Bishops and was able to speak directly with the Pope and decide what was to be done. On his return he informed the presidential council and sent a telegram to Cardinal Lercaro in the name of the Consilium: "The Consilium, especially at this time, expresses its sentiments of deep devotion and renewed determination to collaborate with you in the work of liturgical renewal that has been entrusted to us by the Holy Father and that is of such vital importance to the Church. It eagerly awaits Your Eminence's return on Monday to complete important work and to join in presenting His Holiness with our unanimous filial homage." As a matter of fact, thanks to the Deputy Secretary of State, Archbishop Dell'Acqua, a note was prepared for the Vatican daily, while it was also planned that in his address to the Consilium at the end of its general meeting the Pope would publicly express his confidence in the organization and its president. The Italian text of the address was in the Pope's own handwriting.

On receiving these assurances, Cardinal Lercaro returned to Rome and resumed his position as president of the Consilium, a position filled during his absence by the vice-president, Cardinal Confalonieri.

The liturgical reform has been willed by the Second Vatican Council. The Constitution on the Sacred Liturgy lays the foundation for it and defines its principles. The decisions of the Holy See and the episcopal conferences are responsible for the first implementations of it.

For these reasons the Consilium vigorously and sadly objects to writings, whoever their authors may be, that attack a reform which is producing such abundant fruits in Christian life. These writings slander those to whom the Holy Father has entrusted the task of implementing the reform.

This statement was greeted by prolonged unanimous applause from all present.

The Cardinal, who was obviously moved, responded in a steady voice and with noble words. He reaffirmed his confidence in the work and teaching of the Council; his filial devotion to the Pope, who had summoned the members of the Consilium to implement the reform under his own direct and august leadership; and his gratitude to the Consilium, which day after day, with unwearying toil and in a spirit of unremitting service, was carrying out the will and intention of the Council and the Pope, and had won respect and hopeful expectation from the bishops of the entire Church. He ended by saying: "In this same spirit we shall persevere in our labors and with the grace of God complete the work that we have begun, not by our own choice but by decree of God himself."

Papal audience

On the last day the Pope came to the meeting room and gave a brilliant address. His visit was an exquisitely sensitive expression of appreciation for, and trust in, the work of the Consilium. This appreciation and trust were further emphasized in his words to the assembly:

The Consilium fully deserves to receive renewed expression of our high esteem and confidence and its members our encouragement. For we know the men who make up this body and their qualifications, men outstanding for their knowledge and love of the liturgy. We know how massive is the material the Consilium must face, how serious and diverse are the questions it must bring to resolution, how rapid the pace it must set if it is to accomplish its assigned task in a reasonably short space of time.

We know, as well, the primary considerations that are the groundwork for a task so difficult and so demanding of prudence. . . . But even if there have in fact been misjudgments and defective application regarding some new measures, nevertheless we feel obliged to express our gratitude and general approval. We have, then, a shining occasion not only to praise and encourage its strenuous work, but also to urge the clergy and the laity to appreciate its merits and to promote its effectiveness.

We cannot, however, veil our disturbance over some facts, incidents, and preferences that without any doubt are not favorable to the success the Church expects from the hard work of the Consilium.

The first fact is the unjust and irreverent attack published recently against Cardinal Lercaro, the illustrious and eminent President of the Consilium. Obviously we do not agree with this publication, which surely in no one inspires piety nor helps the cause it pretends to advance, namely, that of preserving the Latin language in the liturgy. Latin is an issue certainly deserving serious attention, but the issue cannot be solved in a way that is opposed to the great principle confirmed by the Council, namely, that liturgical prayer, accommodated to the understanding of the people, is to be intelligible. Nor can it be solved in opposition to another principle called for by the collectivity of human culture, namely, that peoples' deepest and sincerest sentiments can best be expressed through the vernacular as it is in actual usage. Setting aside the whole question of the use of Latin in the liturgy, harmed rather than helped by the above-mentioned publication, we wish to express to Cardinal Lercaro our regret and our support.

The Pope then mentioned other reasons for distress: the arbitrary introduction of personal preferences into the liturgy and a tendency toward "desacralization." He then expressed confidence in the future. For, in fact,

the genuine prayer-life of the Church has renewed vigor in the communities of the faithful, a thing of beauty and a sign of high hope to anyone burning with love for Christ, in an age so confused yet full of earthly vitality.

Carry on your work peacefully and cheerfully. "God wills it," we can truly say, for his own glory, for the life of the Church, and for the salvation of the world.[54]

Presidential council. The presidential council met on April 15 and 19. At the first meeting it was concerned chiefly with the situation created for the Cardinal President. Among other problems, it discussed the turmoil caused in the Church's liturgy by an exaggerated desire for uncontrolled novelty. It studied the problem that had arisen with regard to the revision of the Psalter; the establishment of the Commission for the Neo-Vulgate had made the whole matter a subject of discussion once again. The commission was claiming the right to revise this book of the Bible as well as the others and had expressed its intention of making the Pian Psalter the basis of the revision. It was decided to write a letter to Cardinal Bea asking for clarifications.

Another subject discussed at this meeting of the presidential council was translations. The Fathers expressed their desire that criteria be elaborated for determining how texts might be adapted in translation. The main

54. *DOL* 86 nos. 638-40.

difficulty in this area was the translation of the Roman Canon. It was proposed that a special study group (32bis) be given the task of drawing up an instruction on the subject. Another point raised was the need of adapting the Mass to particular groups, especially children.

The Taizé community had asked that it might use the text of the third anaphora. It was decided to report to the Holy Father that the presidential council was in favor of granting the request, but without publicity.

General Meeting IX (November 21–28, 1967)

This meeting was held at Santa Marta, November 21–28, 1967, while the Synod of Bishops was being celebrated. Thirty-eight of the forty-eight Fathers and five observers were present. The relators had met November 14–20.[55]

The Cardinal President remembered Cardinal Ritter, whom the Lord had called to his eternal reward; the appointment of Cardinal Cody; the elevation of several members—Pellegrino, Felici, and Gut—to the purple; and the election of Father Weakland, a consultor of the Consilium, as Abbot Primate of the Benedictines.

A letter was sent to the Holy Father in place of the usual telegram:

> All the members of the Consilium, gathered in Rome for the work of their ninth general meeting, regard it as their first duty and their joy to send to Your Holiness an expression of their devoted filial attachment.
>
> First of all, they wish to tell Your Holiness that, in obedience to the letter and spirit of the documents of the Second Vatican Council, they regard it as their goal to examine with religious respect both what has been handed down and the legitimate pastoral demands of our time, so that in the reform of the sacred liturgy tradition and innovation may be harmoniously combined.
>
> Furthermore, the members and *periti* of the Consilium assure Your Holiness that they intend to study with great openness and readiness what the Fathers of the recent Synod had to say about the liturgical reform generally and about each area of it, and what they asked should be investigated more thoroughly.
>
> From all that the Fathers said either in the meeting hall or in writing, and especially in the *modi* attached to their votes, the members of the Consilium will endeavor to extract whatever can best and most satisfactorily promote the dignity of divine worship, the understanding of the sacred texts, and the active, conscious participation of God's people.
>
> The members, *periti*, and advisors of the Consilium offer their fervent wishes for Your Holiness' complete restoration to bodily health; they also

---

55. See *Not* 3 (1967) 410–17.

pray the Lord that he would deign to give continued strength and vigor
to you, his Vicar on earth, so that you may ever more diligently promote
a many-faceted renewal of the Church in the name of the Lord.

On November 24 (No. 108031) Cardinal Gaetano Cicognani, Secretary
of State, wrote to express the Holy Father's thanks for the kind thoughts
and good wishes presented to him; the Cardinal conveyed the Pope's
continued interest in the work of the Consilium, at whose meetings he
was "always present through his paternal affection and esteem, and especially through his prayers, in which he asked almighty God for abundant light and help."

Since the Pope was still convalescing from a recent operation, it was
thought inappropriate to request an audience.

Report of the secretary. The secretary mentioned the publication of the
second instruction, which had been studied at various meetings and in
the presence of the Holy Father. The need of preventing abuses and aiding the episcopal conferences had made its publication advisable. In general, it had been well received, although there were some complaints with
regard to its timeliness; there had even been an echo of these at the
Synod.[56]

The instruction on Eucharistic worship had also been published, as
had the *Graduale simplex*. In the case of the latter, many pages already
printed had to be changed at the last minute because there were those
who did not want any mention made of the "psalmist." The episcopal
conferences were now asking permission to translate the *Graduale*.[57] The
secretariat was also very busy with the translation of the Roman Canon.
The Holy Father had asked that the translations be "faithful and literal,"
but in fact practically no liturgical commission was observing this criterion. Approval of the definitive texts had therefore been put off until the
Commission for the Doctrine of the Faith approved a translation. This
had recently been done for the French text, which could now serve as
a model for other translations.

The presidency of the Consilium had sponsored a second referendum
at the request of the Supreme Pontiff. It was intended to counter an inquiry conducted by the Consociatio Internationalis Musicae Sacrae, which

---

56. The secretary recorded the words of a Father who "invoked the shade of Doctor
Martin Luther, horror-stricken by the ceremonies of the Church, as if the Apostolic See
had followed in his steps when it simplified the rites of the Mass" (but perhaps the Father's
intention was simply to commemorate in his own way the 450th anniversary of the Protestant Reformation!).

57. At this meeting the norms for the translation of the *Graduale simplex* were studied;
these were subsequently communicated to the episcopal conferences on January 10, 1968.

published the results in the January 1967 issue of its journal, *Musicae Sacrae Ministerium*. According to this poll, the reform was a catastrophe for the Church.[58]

Among the activities listed by the secretary was the formation of two groups: 12bis for the *preces* in Lauds and Vespers, and 32bis for the translation of liturgical texts into the vernaculars. In addition, the schemas for the readings from Scripture had been printed and sent to eight hundred experts,[59] and a volume of hymns had been readied.[60]

The Consilium had been collaborating in the preparation of rites for the creation of new cardinals, the opening of the Synod, liturgical celebrations at the World Congress of the Apostolate of the Laity, the visit of Patriarch Athenagoras I, and the canonization of Blessed Benildus of the Christian Schools.[61]

The secretary went on to discuss an event of great importance for the liturgical reform: the Synod of Bishops.[62] The results of the latter had not,

---

58. More careful investigation showed that this poll had been taken chiefly among the faithful of the United States and by Gomer De Pauw in November 1964; it had come somewhat belatedly to the knowledge of *Musicae Sacrae Ministerium*.

59. *Ordo lectionum pro dominicis, feriis et festis Sanctorum* (pro manuscripto; Vatican Polyglot Press, 1957. 474 pp.).

60. *Hymni instaurandi Breviarii Romani* (Libreria Editrice Vaticana, 1968. 328 pp.).

61. The renewal was gradually making its way even into the functions of the papal chapel, which, step by step, were being transformed into true sacred celebrations with participation of the congregation. This brought the reform into the very heart of the Curia and elicited varied reactions. One such came from a distinguished person on the occasion of the canonization of Blessed Benildus. By order of the Holy Father, the liturgy of canonization had been slightly changed. The person in question, ignorant of the real background, attributed the change to the "arbitrariness" of the secretary of the Consilium, who at that time was also in charge of papal ceremonies. The regrettable episode even got into the newspapers.

62. The Consilium gave the Synod a general report on the reform, the work in progress, and, more particularly, the Mass and the Divine Office. In the volume sent in advance to the Fathers, *Argumenta de quibus disceptabitur in primo coetu generali Synodi Episcoporum, Pars I* (Vatican Polyglot Press, 1967), the following sections are to be found: "De statu instaurationis liturgicae" (25–32); "De laboribus Consilii" (32–38); "De Ordine Missae" (40–48); "De Officio Divino" (49–56); "De sacramentis" (57).

During the Synod the Cardinal President of the Consilium gave two reports: *Relatio de sacra liturgia* (Vatican Polyglot Press, 1967. 17 pp.) and a *Supplementum ad relationem "de Sacra Liturgia"* (10 pp.), in which he presented four "papal queries" on which he asked the views of the Fathers; see *Responsiones Em.mi Card. Iacobi Lercaro, Relatoris, ad animadversiones circa quaestiones "de sacra liturgia"* (18 pp.); *De sacra liturgia. Exitus manifestationis sententiae cum recensione modorum propositorum circa quaesita in "supplemento" relationis contenta* (10 pp.); *De sacra liturgia. Exitus manifestationis sententiae cum recensione modorum* (16 pp.). Also distributed to the Fathers of the Synod were the volume containing the *Ordo lectionum* for Mass; the *Graduale simplex*; a duplicated pamphlet for the celebration of the normative Mass, which was celebrated in the Sistine Chapel on October 24, 1967; and a "Specimen divini Officii

at first sight, been favorable, despite initial enthusiastic reports. Several factors—the absence of experts, an incomplete grasp of the problems, confusion between arbitrary experiments and those controlled by the Consilium, the campaign of slander conducted by various organs of the press—had clearly had a negative influence on the Synod. Nonetheless, the secretary concluded, there would have to be a careful and serious effort to study the *modi* and proposals of the Synod, since the reception and outcome of the reform obviously required that the presentation of the new rites take into account the actual situation in much of the Church and the need for an adequate preparation and formation of both clergy and faithful.[63]

Study of schemas. Most of the meeting was spent in a study of the *modi* submitted by the Synod on the Divine Office and the Mass, with special attention to the "papal requests" and the words of consecration. In addition, there was an initial discussion of the work done by group 12bis on the *preces* to be introduced into Lauds and Vespers (a novelty in the Roman Office) and of some other matters not previously touched on, such as the organic connection of the Mass with an Hour of the Office and of the Hours among themselves, and commutations and dispensations. Other schemas presented were those on confirmation, the prefaces, marriage, Holy Week, the chants of the Mass, the consecration of virgins, and the rite for the admission of non-Catholics to full communion with the Catholic Church. There was also a first report on the work of group 32bis, which was dealing with the translation of the liturgical books into the vernaculars and the principles to be used in the translation of the *Graduale simplex*.[64]

On November 24 there was a meeting of the presidency and the relators who were serving as section chiefs, for the purpose of programming future work.

---

pro diebus a 12 ad 18 novembris 1967." For the treatment of the liturgy at the first Synod of Bishops, see "De liturgia in prima Synodo Episcoporum," *Not* 3 (1967) 353–70.

63. In his report to the consultors the secretary became more specific, urging them to avoid both an excessive radicalism in the revision of the rites and an excessive vagueness. He asked them, therefore, to remove some of the "pro opportunitate" phrases they were putting into the rites. In saying this the secretary was simply making known to them the desire of the Pope as expressed to him at an audience.

64. The order followed was this: November 21: confirmation; 22: *modi* regarding the Divine Office; 23: specific questions regarding the Office: organic connection and commutations; 24: *modi* on the Mass; *Graduale simplex* (translation); rite of admission to full communion with the Catholic Church; 25: marriage; 27: Holy Week; 28: consecration of virgins and religious profession.

Presidential council

This met on November 23 and discussed chiefly the following points:

1. Relations with the Protestants. The World Council of Churches had sent an invitation to take part in a colloquium on the sacraments of baptism, confirmation, and the Eucharist, to be held in April 1968; the colloquium was to be in preparation for the assembly at Uppsala. Some names were therefore suggested for presentation to the Secretariat of State, and Cardinal Pellegrino was appointed to pay a courtesy visit to the Secretary.

The Lutheran World Federation had sent an invitation to a meeting on penance, while a Presbyterian publisher had asked permission to publish the Consilium's order of Sunday readings. Since this order had not yet been definitively determined, it was decided to wait before deciding on an answer.

2. Many areas were experiencing difficulty with regard to the celebration of Mass by foreign priests, since frequently there was no Latin Missal to be had. It seemed necessary, therefore, to prepare a *Missale itinerantium* (a "Missal for Travelers").[65]

3. A question of special importance was how to handle the publication of the Divine Office. The sheer amount of material already drafted made it clear that publication would be difficult. If the two-year cycle of biblical readings were adopted, each of the two planned volumes would have to be about 5100 pages in length!

The problem was a thorny one. A return to a four-volume Breviary (with each volume still quite lengthy) might discourage the clergy. The alternative, however, was to undertake a new revision of the material already prepared and thus to postpone completion of the work. But the bishops were urging the need of speedy publication because of the increasingly worrisome abandonment of the Breviary by some of the clergy. One suggestion was to publish the biblical readings in a separate volume, but this too had its disadvantages. The decision was postponed.

4. Support for the secretary. During the celebration of the Synod the conservative press and flysheets surreptitiously distributed had not failed to fire their darts at the secretary of the Consilium. At the preceding meeting the president had been the target; now it was the secretary's turn. The presidential council unanimously deplored the attack and expressed

---

65. The proposal would bear fruit, after the publication of the Missal, in the norms set down by the Congregation for Divine Worship regarding the inclusion of a Latin appendix in vernacular Missals (November 10, 1969; *Not* 5 [1969] 442; *DOL* 210 nos. 1753-56) and the subsequent publication of the *Missale parvum* (Vatican Polyglot Press, 1970), which has had three reprintings and an updated edition.

its solidarity with the secretary of the Consilium. It wrote a letter to the Pope in which it said:

> Having noted the material recently published, especially during the Synod of Bishops, against the secretary of the Consilium, Father Annibale Bugnini, and the work he has been doing, the members of the presidential council of the Council for the Implementation of the Constitution on the Sacred Liturgy use the occasion of the ninth general meeting of the Consilium to assure Your Holiness with all due respect of the full confidence which the presidential council and the Consilium as a whole have in the secretary's work. He deserves praise for the way in which he has played his part in the restoration of the sacred liturgy.[66]

Conclusion of the meeting

The Cardinal President ended these days of intense toil by thanking God that the work assigned to the Consilium was proceeding safely and expeditiously. He noted that while there was still a long road to travel, the principal landmarks in the reform were already beginning to stand out clearly. He thanked all for taking part in the discussions "with a praiseworthy freedom that was equalled only by the love which inspired it," and he appointed April 1968 for the next meeting.

General Meeting X (April 23–30, 1968)

This meeting was held in the hall of the Palazzo S. Marta from April 23 to April 30, 1968, immediately after the meeting of the relators (April 14–22). Thirty-five members, some consultors, and five observers were present.[67]

This was the first general meeting at which Cardinal Benno Gut presided. He had been appointed president of the Consilium on January 9, 1968.

The meeting began with an address of affection and gratitude to the absent Cardinal Lercaro, who was now president emeritus and still a member of the Consilium and of its presidential council.

---

66. This letter, dated November 28, 1967, carries the signatures of Cardinals Lercaro, Confalonieri, and Pellegrino and Bishops Spülbeck, Boudon, Isnard, and Bluyssen. At an audience a few days later, on December 1, the Holy Father showed the letter to Father Bugnini, read it aloud, and added: "I add my voice to theirs."

The fifth meeting of the presidential council was held on January 30, 1968; it discussed the continuation of the work, especially on the Mass, and approved the agenda for the next general meeting.

67. See *Not* 4 (1968) 180–84. Among the observers, Dr. Eugene L. Brand participated for the first time, replacing Pastor Friedrich Wilhelm Künneth (see p. 200).

Cardinal Gut thanked those present for the good wishes they had sent him on the occasion of his appointment, and he assured them that the Consilium would continue to work in the same spirit and with the same methods as in preceding years. He greeted in particular the new members: Father Hänggi, who had recently become Bishop of Basel, and Abbot Weakland. He also remembered Bishop Hallinan, who had been called home to the Father's house.

The following telegram was sent to the Holy Father:

> The tenth general meeting of the Council for the Implementation of the Constitution on the Sacred Liturgy wishes to express to Your Holiness its sentiments of filial respect and to affirm its fidelity to the desires of Your Holiness as it continues with its work. Seeing the progress already made, it offers heartfelt thanks to the Lord, for it hopes that the reformed liturgy with its new youthfulness will contribute to the spiritual growth of the Christian people and to the reunion of all human beings in a single family in Christ, the King of peace, the Head, and the Teacher.
>
> Holy Father, may your Apostolic Blessing strengthen us in our determination.

The next day brought a reply from Cardinal Cicognani, Secretary of State:

> The Supreme Pontiff is greatly comforted by the remembrance and respectful homage of the Consilium as it celebrates its tenth general meeting under the presidency of Your Eminence. He takes delight in your labors, your commitment, and your resolutions. He invokes heavenly light and aid upon your meeting so that the liturgical reform already begun may advance safely along the road it has entered upon and may reach the goal desired by the Second Ecumenical Council of the Vatican. In gratitude for the homage rendered, and as one constantly united to you in the bonds of love, he ratifies his desires and prayers with the Apostolic Blessing which he cordially bestows on you.

Report of the secretary. The secretary of the Consilium began as usual by first sketching the present situation in the Consilium. He recalled the appointment of its new head and the meeting of the presidential council during the previous general meeting. He then went on to describe the work that had been accomplished:

The following had been presented to the Holy Father: the new anaphoras, which, like the Way of the Cross, had had fourteen "stations";[68] holy orders;[69] the rite of marriage. The General Calendar had

---

68. May 3, 1967: first presentation to the Holy Father. June–July 1967: examination by the Congregation for the Doctrine of the Faith and the Congregation of Rites. July 13: difficulties regarding the words of consecration. September 28: memorandum on the formulas of

been sent to the interested Congregations on December 5, 1968, for their examination, but no answer had as yet been received.

The question of participation by consultors of the Consilium in the meetings of the World Council of Churches and the Lutheran World Federation had been taken up with the Secretariat of State and the Secretariat for Christian Unity.[70]

Also sent to the Holy Father were: a plan for the promulgation of the new Order of Mass (January 16, 1968) and for the application of some points approved by the Synod (chants of the Mass; use of the Apostles' Creed; new anaphoras); the formation of a joint commission to deal with minor orders.

---

consecration. October 12: question referred to the Synod. December 10: report to the Holy Father. January 16, 1968: a plan is proposed for beginning use of the new anaphoras. January 22: request for inclusion of the words "Mysterium fidei" and for a special rubric on the manner of uttering the Lord's words. January 24: new request, along with a letter of Father Bouyer. January 28: request for an accompanying instruction. February 8: new presentation of drafts with norms for use. February 15–16: further difficulties and a reply. March 19: new presentation and entreaty. March 23: further request for an instruction. March 25: the Consilium sends its answer regarding an instruction and the text of "Pastoral Guidelines for the Episcopal Conferences" (see also pp. 460ff.).

69. After the agencies concerned had submitted their observations in November–December 1967, a joint commission was established to study the emendations (February 1–2, 1968) and the revision of the rubrics (February 5). On February 8 the new, definitive text was given to the Holy Father, who replied on February 19 with further observations. On February 29 the Holy Father asked that the text of the apostolic constitution be prepared; this was given to him on April 9, together with an answer to his observations of February 19. The rite was used for the first time, with permission of the Holy Father, at the episcopal ordination of Monsignor Hänggi, a consultor of the Consilium.

70. A meeting of representatives from the Consilium and from the World Council of Churches was held in Geneva from April 28 to May 1, 1968; see Not 4 (1968) 206. Its purpose was to give and receive a detailed description of the liturgical work of the Faith and Order Commission (the "spiritual" arm of the World Council) and the reforms thus far achieved by the postconciliar commission of the Catholic Church.

The representatives from the Consilium were: E. Lengeling, A.-G. Martimort, J. Lécuyer, C. Vagaggini, P. Jounel, and G. F. Arrighi. Cardinal Pellegrino was present for the second half of the conversations. The representatives from the World Council were: Professor Th. Taylor (president), Professor Shepherd, Frère Max Thurian, A. van der Mensbrugge, Professor von Allmen, Professor Briner, Vitaly Borovy, and Lukas Vischer.

The undertaking was a sound one and the results satisfactory. Everything pointed to a promising future, but that future was not to be. The meeting remained "one of a kind."

The undertaking then moved from the official sphere to the private and came under the egis of the Societas Liturgica, an organization of Catholic and Protestant students of the liturgy who held an annual meeting for joint study and prayer and continued the valuable dialogue begun at Geneva by some periti from the Consilium in the spring of 1968.

Father Lécuyer represented the Consilium at a meeting of the Lutheran World Federation on penance.

Finally, the secretary came to the main point of the meeting: the study of the directives and observations of the Holy Father on the Order of Mass and on the Divine Office.

A report on the votes and views expressed at the Synod of Bishops and on the replies given at the ninth general meeting of the Consilium had been presented to the Holy Father on December 1, 1967. On December 3, in an audience granted to the secretary, the Pope gave some directives on the Mass; these had been passed on to the relevant study groups on December 6, 1967, and on February 26, 1968. They were discussed again in a second audience on January 3, 1968. Next came the experiments in the Capella Matilde. Finally, on January 22, the Pope communicated his observations, which had to do with: (1) the beginning of the Mass: the penitential act and sign of the cross; (2) the formularies of the offertory; (3) the place of the words ''Mysterium fidei''; (4) the structuring of the part of the Mass after the Our Father, which included the rites of the fraction and the greeting of peace.

For the Divine Office the Holy Father preferred a pastoral solution: ''It seems better to choose psalms more adapted to Christian prayer and omit the imprecatory and historical psalms (while allowing that the latter may be appropriately used on certain occasions).''[71]

The secretary reported that both problems had caused difficulties within the Consilium itself. The first skirmish had occurred in the preliminary meetings of the groups and the relators. The secretary's report therefore concluded with this exhortation:

> I dare urge, and with some insistence, that the clear and precise wishes of the Holy Father be cheerfully accepted. There is no doubt about the mind of the Supreme Pontiff. The schema for a new Order of Mass was sent to him three times, and each time he studied it carefully. Then came the Synod, and the response of the bishops was not unanimous. The votes in the Synod went to some extent contrary to what the Consilium wanted, and that is something else the Supreme Pastor had to take into account. Therefore he decided to gain personal experience of the new Order by means of three celebrations. Having carefully considered all the evidence, he made his mind known in writing. . . . The views of our supreme President must therefore be the criterion for our work and for the balanced decisions reached at our meeting.

---

71. The Holy Father's reply was forwarded to the groups concerned in January 1968.

Discussions

In view of the sensitivity and difficulty of the subject matter, two sub-commissions were established for the Mass and for the Office; each included members and consultors.

Even so, the discussion was not unexacting, and this meeting may be said to have been marked by a certain tension. On the one hand, the secretary, who knew beyond a doubt the thinking of the Pope and had presented it to the members and consultors, wanted it to be respected. The members and consultors, on the other hand, proposed to study the question anew and once again present all the difficulties to the Pope, always, of course, with deference to his final judgment. They offered various arguments for doing so: "The developments of the age call for quick revisions and changes"; "There is nothing against making a humble appeal"; "In so important a matter it is not insulting the Pope to ask him to explain his thinking more clearly"; "The Holy Father is presenting not a decision but an invitation to study." There were some witticisms about the fact that in his note the Pope did not distinguish between a sung Mass and a said Mass and used such imperatives as "examine," "see." But this was his customary polite way of presenting his observations.[72]

---

72. A certain punctiliousness of the *periti* found support, oddly enough, in Fathers who were usually quite unreceptive to the reform. At other meetings these Fathers were distinguished by their calls to respect for tradition, but now, when faced with recourse to the Pope for changes that "go beyond or seem to go beyond the competency of the Consilium," they became defenders of untenable opinions. It may be that even here they were acting in good faith. One "jurist," however, found acceptable only such words as the Pope addressed to cardinals. But the secretary was not a cardinal or even . . . a bishop! Others showed more good sense and experience when they pointed out that the Pope could use whomever he wished for communicating his will; there had been instances of this, for example, during the Council.

The secretary nonetheless found himself isolated. Even the Cardinal Prefect, who was having his first experience of directing so large and varied an assembly, did not know where to take a stand, even though he was personally in favor of unconditionally accepting the Holy Father's wishes. The secretary therefore had no choice but to let the discussion move forward of its own weight. But the capacity of human beings to adapt to circumstances is truly astonishing. Therefore, there were not lacking those who after the meeting found a way of informing the Secretariat of State that it should not let pass the opportunity of telling the secretary of the Consilium that it had heard complaints of his somewhat "harsh and authoritarian" conduct of the meeting, and asking for explanations of this behavior.

In replying on June 18, 1968, the secretary explained the facts and then added: "A complex organization of two hundred persons, who are laboring at one of the most demanding reforms of the Church, accepts certain unwritten conventions by friendly agreement as they struggle with problems full of contradictions and displaying a variety of aspects depending on the countries, peoples, and continents represented by the participants in a general meeting. This complex organization of 12 cardinals, 36 bishops, and 150 *periti* is headed in the-

After the meeting an extensive report was prepared for the Holy Father on the work done and on the replies of the Consilium to each question, along with a report from the two groups dealing with the Mass and the Office. An appendix contained the remarks and judgment of the secretariat.

Another subject of lively discussion came up in the study of the schema on penance. The members had already voted at the eighth meeting against having several formulas of absolution. Now, however, the study group offered three formulas for discussion. This irritated some Fathers who wanted not only a single formula but one that would be based on the formula presently in use and be declarative in form.

There was also discussion of the General Instruction of the Roman Missal, the structure of the Office as a whole and of its several parts, the structure of confirmation, Holy Week,[73] the litanies of the saints, the rite of admission to full communion with the Catholic Church, and the instruction on translations.[74]

Presidential council

The presidential council met on April 30, after the general meeting, and was given more detailed information on the practices currently being undertaken with a view to approval of the new anaphoras and on the rite of holy orders. In regard to the latter, the Secretariat of State still

---

ory by a cardinal, but in practice by a secretary who in dealing with the assembly has two tasks that do not always meld harmoniously: on the one hand, to carry out the decisions of the Consilium and, on the other, to communicate the Pope's thinking to the Consilium and win acceptance of it there. It is to the honor of the Consilium that in a situation so incoherent from a constitutional viewpoint, the organization has proved so vital. Its success also shows the efficacy of a collegial and, we might say, 'democratic' system. The surprising thing is that instead of degenerating into sheer tumult, the Consilium has been able to regulate itself and accomplish so much important work."

Since the Cardinal President's effort had met with defeat, the Pope was asked to receive the Consilium at an audience during its next general meeting. And in fact he did receive it on October 14 of this same year. As he moved around greeting the bishops one by one, he came to a certain Excellency; here he stopped, beckoned to the secretary of the Consilium, and said: "Your Excellency, when I offer some of my own thoughts, I do not intend to impose anything; I simply express a desire and am happy if the Consilium is willing to give it courteous consideration. In turn, I welcome gratefully all the suggestions that reach me. I intend to impose nothing but simply to offer my own ideas as humble suggestions."

73. The report was presented by Monsignor Pascher, who had replaced Bishop Hänggi as relator of the group.

74. Order followed in the discussion: April 23–24: confirmation; 25: readings for Mass and GIRM; 26: GIRM, Divine Office, and penance; 29: litanies of the saints, penance, Mass; 30: Holy Week, instruction on translations.

insisted that the hymn "Come, Holy Spirit" be introduced. The council accepted the secratary's suggestion that it be included among the songs to be sung during the anointing.

The council asked that the Consilium study the problem of adapting and composing texts as a way of channeling the arbitrary exercise of creativity; that it retain the memorial of Our Lady on Saturday in the calendar; and that despite all the objections, it study the question of having two other formulas of sacramental absolution, at least for use in cases of general absolution.

The council also took a look at how the discussions had gone at the general meeting just concluded. Some Fathers expressed a concern that some of those at the general meeting were monopolizing the podium, and they insisted that steps be taken to prevent this.

General Meeting XI (October 8–17, 1968)

The eleventh general meeting was convened at Santa Marta on October 17, 1968. The relators had held their meeting from October 1 to 7.[75] Present at the general meeting were thirty-two Fathers (six cardinals, twenty-six bishops, the Abbot Primate of the Benedictines) and six observers.

Presidential council

This time the council convened at the beginning of the general meeting. Since the problems connected with the rite of Mass and with the Divine Office which had caused some contention at the previous general meeting were still unresolved, it was thought appropriate to begin by hearing the advice of the council. Also taken into consideration were some observations made after the publication of the rite for the ordination of bishops and of the new Eucharistic Prayers. The Fathers asked that the old prayer for the consecration of bishops be retained and that in the Eucharistic Prayers the words of consecration be standardized, some rubrics simplified, and some expressions corrected.[76]

Finally, the council approved the program of future work, especially in regard to the publication of liturgical books that were now almost ready:

---

75. See Not 4 (1968) 348–55.

76. See the Consilium's declaration, signed by the secretary on November 6, 1968, prescribing that in translations the words of consecration were to be made uniform in all the Eucharistic Prayers and that at the mention of the bishop's name the phrase to be used by bishops themselves, "and me, your unworthy servant," be inserted, at least in editions of the Canon for use by bishops. See Not 4 (1968) 356; DOL 245 nos. 1964-65.

the calendar with the litanies, the readings for Mass, the rite of Mass along with the General Instruction of the Roman Missal, baptism, confirmation, penance, holy orders, matrimony, funerals, readings of the Office.[77]

Sessions

At the outset there was a commemoration of Romano Guardini, who had died recently.

In his welcoming speech the Cardinal President had a special greeting for Bishop Lazík, who was attending a general meeting for the first time.

The secretary's report was brief. He mentioned the recent fortunes of the new Order of Mass (which had been sent to the cardinals of the Roman Curia); the presentation to the Pope of the General Instruction of the Roman Missal; the formation of a joint commission (from the Consilium and the Sacred Congregation for the Doctrine of the Faith) for the study of the calendar. He also listed the documents published since the preceding meeting: the Eucharistic Prayers, described by someone as "the finest gift given to the Church this year"; the constitution *Pontificalis Romani*, which approved the new rites for the ordination of deacons, priests, and bishops (these rites were to be published very shortly); the motu proprio *Pontificalia insignia* and the instruction of the Sacred Congregation of Rites on the simplification of the pontifical rites. The secretary also spoke of his personal experience of concelebration at the Eucharistic Congress in Bogotá, at which some new rites were used experimentally.

Schemas. This meeting began the study of several schemas: (1) The Mass: some final questions were taken up before proceeding to the compilation of the complete Missal: votive Masses, chants, prefaces, and prayers; (2) Divine Office: the schema of a general instuction was presented, and there was a discussion in particular of the binding character of the Office; (3) baptism of children: the complete rite with all its parts was presented; (4) Holy Week; (5) religious profession; (6) blessing of an abbot; (7) funerals: the revisions to be made after experimentation, and completion of the rite by providing a funeral for children; the Office of the Dead; funerals at a crematorium; (8) celebration of Mass with small groups; (9) penance.[78]

---

77. The program would be followed except for confirmation and penance, for which a longer wait than expected was required.

78. The schemas were studied in the following order: October 8: chants of the Mass, orations, and prefaces; 9: Masses for various occasions, penance; 10: blessing of an abbot,

Particular questions

On October 9 and 14 there were meetings attended only by the Fathers or members. At the first the subject was once again the Order of Mass. The Holy Father had asked that it be sent for study to the prefects of the Roman Congregations. Their observations had been sent to the Pope on June 24, 1968. On September 22 the Pope sent the Consilium some new observations. These still had to do with the usual questions: the sign of the cross at the beginning of Mass; the *Kyrie* to be obligatory; formulas for the offertory, with the Pope asking that the phrase "which we offer to you" be included; retention of the *Orate, fratres* (otherwise "a precious pearl would be lost"); the insertion of the prayer "Domine Iesu Christe" in the rites of peace.

All these points had been discussed at the preceding general meeting. The Pope was coming back to them in his usual sensitive manner: "I ask you to take these observations into account, with freedom and balanced judgment." His words were obviously an invitation to accept his views, but the opinion prevailed which saw in them an invitation to study the problems once again, while always freely and willingly accepting the Pope's final judgment. As a result, the several points were discussed and voted on once again.[79] The Fathers also unanimously approved making the words of consecration in the Roman Canon identical with those in the new Eucharistic Prayers.

At the meeting on October 14 three subjects were discussed:

1) *Mass with small groups.* On several occasions the view had already been expressed that there should be adaptations made in Masses celebrated with small groups, especially in families (a phenomenon that was becoming more common, and not always without arbitrary adaptation). On September 5, 1968, the Consilium had asked the Holy Father for permission to deal with the problem. On September 23 the Secretariat of State communicated the permission and determined that any steps taken should be taken in agreement with the Congregation for the Clergy. This decision was questioned, and the reply was favorable to the Consilium, provided a distinction was made between the celebration of Mass with

---

religious profession and consecration of virgins; 12: Divine Office; 14: Mass with special groups; 15: baptism of children; 16: Holy Week, funerals; 17: funerals, penance, Mass with special groups.

79. This is how the Fathers voted: *sign of the cross:* 17 yes, 13 no, 1 yes *iuxta modum* (= "with qualification"—only in read Masses); *prayers of the offertory:* 12 yes, 14 no, 5 *iuxta modum* (instead of the words "we offer," find others to express the ordering of the gifts to the Eucharist); *retention of the "Orate, fratres":* 14 yes, 15 no, 1 blank; *prayer for peace:* 26 yes, 3 no, 2 *iuxta modum* (provided the prayer before communion be omitted).

small groups and Masses in homes. The Secretariat also gave some guidelines on the questions of permission (the judgment of the bishop), the day (not on Sundays), delegation of the pastor, observance of the Eucharistic fast, and acceptance into the group of all who desired to attend.

The debate in the Consilium was a comprehensive one. At the end it was decided that the group should prepare a schema; this was in fact presented to the general meeting on October 17.

2) In connection with this same problem, and in order to ensure the dignity of the celebration and the use of sacred vestments, a model "chasuble for use without an alb" was displayed. It had been made in a Dutch abbey and pleased everyone.

3) "Requests." Urged on by the need of giving the episcopal conferences the authority to regulate the liturgical reform so as to combat impatience and increasingly frequent personal initiatives, the Fathers decided to send the Holy Father a letter containing some requests. They asked for the speedy publication of the new Order of Mass; some revisions in the Roman Canon so that comparison with the new Eucharistic Prayers might not lead to its neglect; faculties for the episcopal conferences to allow adaptations in the liturgy of the Word for Masses in various settings: with children and young people, in the missions, with small groups, at congresses and extraordinary celebrations; to allow communion under two kinds with the permission of the Ordinary; to permit timely adaptations in the new rites of baptism, confirmation, anointing of the sick, and funerals; to allow those episcopal conferences that requested it the use of a four-week Psalter in the recitation of the Divine Office so that they might meet the present crisis in recitation of the Breviary.

Penance. Another serious problem occupied the attention of the Fathers at this meeting: the problem of the plurality of sacramental formulas for penance. This had already been taken up at two meetings; in the judgment of some, however, the discussion had not been comprehensive enough and the vote was unclear. The presidential council, following upon various requests from episcopal conferences, decided to remit the question to the Consilium.

Discussion began on the second day but was immediately blocked by the more energetic Fathers, who insisted that there should be no going back to questions already decided. They even went so far as to request the minutes of the preceding meetings. The discussion was therefore put off until the final day of this general meeting. Meanwhile, two cyclostyled pages were distributed in which the facts were set down.

On one side of the argument, it was pointed out that the earlier vote had been on the question of whether there should be alternative formulas for use "according to the judgment of the priest," whereas it was now proposed to leave the choice to the judgment of the episcopal conferences. On the other side, there was pressure to abide by the earlier vote.[80] The debate was a lively one, and the discussion lengthy.[81] The alternatives were to extend the meeting or to postpone discussion until the next meeting in order to have time for reflection. The Fathers unanimously accepted the second alternative. A further reason may have been that after ten days they were weary and in a hurry to return home.

Papal audience

On October 14 the Holy Father received the Consilium in the Hall of the Consistory. To the Cardinal Prefect's address, in which he paid homage and recalled the principal recent publications, especially the Eucharistic Prayers, the Pope replied: "The new rites and the new prayer forms introduced into the liturgy have added to the splendor of the age-old and beautiful sacred patrimony of the Church and we observe with joy a new flowering in divine worship everywhere because of a more lively participation of the faithful."[82]

For this he thanked not only the Lord but the Consilium and the episcopal conferences, and exhorted them to continue the revision of the liturgical books. The Pope then turned to aspects of the liturgical renewal that he had touched on in previous addresses: fidelity to Catholic teaching, majesty, simplicity, beauty of form, respect for the patrimony of the past and for the ecclesial and hierarchic character of the liturgy, the necessity of advancing gradually while taking into account the degree of preparation of the faithful, and the preservation of the special Roman character of the liturgy. At one point in his address the Pope referred to tendencies that were a cause of "anxiety and pain."

> We refer, first of all, to the attitude of those who receive with bad grace whatever comes from ecclesiastical authority or is lawfully commanded. This results at times even in conferences of bishops going too far on their own

---

80. As some pointed out, this was not a very sound argument. At that same meeting the members had gone back for at least the second time to questions on the Order of Mass. Then, too, there was the work on the Divine Office, which had changed direction three times, despite preceding votes. Furthermore, it had always been said that the votes were to serve as guidelines.

81. As often happens in such cases, some individuals spoke repeatedly in an effort to make their own view prevail. Finally one colleague said: "I didn't come all this distance just to hear one individual talk!"

82. See *Not* 4 (1968) 335–47 and *DOL* 92 nos. 669-74 (the two quotations are from 669 and 672-73).

initiative in liturgical matters. Another result is arbitrary experimentation and the introduction of rites that are flagrantly in conflict with the norms established by the Church. Anyone can see that this way of acting not only scandalizes the conscience of the faithful, but does harm to the orderly accomplishment of liturgical reform, which demands of all concerned prudence, vigilance, and above all discipline.

A cause of even greater worry is the behavior of those who contend that liturgical worship should be stripped of its sacred character and who therefore erroneously believe that no sacred objects or ornaments should be used, but that objects of common, everyday use should be substituted. Their own rashness leads some so far that they do not spare the sacred place of celebration. Such notions, we must insist, not only distort the genuine nature of the liturgy, but the true meaning of the Catholic religion.

In simplifying liturgical rites, formularies, and actions, there must be care not to go further than necessary and not to neglect the importance to be given to liturgical "signs." That would open the way to weakening the power and effectiveness of the liturgy. To remove from the sacred rites whatever today seems repetitive, obsolete, or pointless is one thing; it is something else to strip the liturgy of the signs and splendor that, if kept within their proper bounds, are needed for the Christian people to perceive rightly the hidden realities and truths concealed under the veil of external rites.

It was above all this part of the address that drew the attention of journalists, who misunderstood it. For this reason, when the Italian text was published in *L'Osservatore Romano*, it was preceded by the following note:

On the morning of October 14, in the Hall of the Consistory, the Holy Father received the cardinals, members, and experts of the Council for the Implementation of the Constitution on the Sacred Liturgy, which had just ended its eleventh general meeting.

The Italian text that we are publishing here will dissipate some confusion created by part of the press at the publication of the Latin text, despite the latter's transparent clarity. Some have seen in the address references to "liturgical deviations," "admonitions," "rebukes to sectors of the European episcopate," and "rebellious sons." In point of fact, the vision of liturgical renewal that shines out in the address of Paul VI is straightforward, serene, and logical. It is the same vision as in the past; those who have before them the Pope's other authoritative interventions in this field, for example, the four addresses of preceding years, will see that there is no break in the continuity of thought or in the continuous effort to achieve a healthy balance between the various ways of expressing worship of God: liturgical piety and private piety, individual actions and communal participation in the liturgy, must all have their turn and be combined.

Here and there the tendency to cliquishness has raised its head; the Pope, however, does not condemn the warm and lively piety that inspires certain prayer groups, provided such groups do not cause harm to the Christian community in its most authentic manifestations, namely, as parish and diocese. Every form of legitimate and authorized liturgical action must tend to strengthen and increase the holy connection uniting the people of God at prayer. Otherwise it turns into a dry branch that withers and dies.

The Pope has also called attention to another point that is of vital importance for the present liturgical renewal: the role of the episcopal conferences. The Constitution on the Liturgy and subsequent decrees provide that these organizations, which are of such basic importance for the life of the Church, are to have a special role to play in the cultic action of the local Christian communities. The rubrics and norms to be found in the new liturgical books will give further practical form to these constitutive decrees.

Some uncertainties of interpretation during the prolonged wait for the new rites have at times hastened the recourse to idiosyncracies. The Pope paternally exhorts groups and individuals to act in such a way that the entire ecclesial community may be assured of an orderly and full life in the area of divine worship. The Pope's words have no other purpose than that; on the contrary, they repeatedly call attention to the difficult but effective work of the Consilium, its spirit of self-sacrifice, and the dedication with which experts and bishops, united by a common ideal and working in perfect harmony with one another and full agreement with the thought and will of the Pope, are bringing to completion one of the most splendid and magnificent reforms known to the history of the Church.[83]

Conclusion

On the late afternoon of October 17 the work of the meeting ended with some words from the secretary, inspired perhaps by the impact the meeting had had without and within. He ended by saying:

> This eleventh meeting has been peaceful and calm; for this, too, we should thank the Lord. As a matter of fact, all our meetings have been marked by peacefulness, even if we have not all been of the same opinion—which is hardly surprising! Indeed, the absence of disputes and divergences of opinion show a lack of freedom or commitment or vitality. The three last-named characteristics are those we have desired and still desire for our hardworking Consilium. The Consilium is, of course, a young and modest organization; it has no desire to be compared with the great agencies of the Roman Curia, which we esteem and venerate.

---

83. *L'Osservatore Romano*, October 19, 1968; *Not* 4 (1968) 340–41. The one-sided focus of the journalists had perhaps another cause as well. A press agency had claimed that the doors of the Consilium had been closed to Bishop Bluyssen; a statement of the Bishop before leaving the Netherlands had perhaps given rise to this notion. As a matter of fact, the pastoral problems faced by Bishop Bluyssen and their repercussions in Rome were of a quite different character, and he regularly attended the meetings of the Consilium and was present at the papal audience of October 14.

When the history of this liturgical renewal is written, reliable and honest historians will have to acknowledge that one of the greatest reforms of the Catholic Church was carried on under the flag of mutual trust, fraternal harmony, good will, and the shared ideal of reaching our unwavering and well-defined goals. We have no constitution, no set of rules, no written law. We wanted these things but did not get them; all things considered, that, too, is perhaps a sign of our vitality and spirituality. Everything is done with mutual trust and in full harmony. Should we be surprised that difficulties sometimes arise? In any case, we have always overcome them and shall continue to overcome them to the satisfaction of all.

We are pressed on every side—by time, by friends (in a benevolent spirit), by others near and far. We have nonetheless done our work methodically and with constancy and shall continue it to the end. As a result, the people of God shall have regained a rich and overflowing fountain of grace, and the entire holy Church shall find delight in it. I say "the entire Church," for it is our ultimate, firm hope that all who bear the Christian name will be reunited in joyous harmony around the table of the Lord and in the sacred signs, as children of the one God and Lord.

General Meeting XII (November 10–14, 1969)

On May 8, 1969, the Congregation for Divine Worship came into being. According to the constitution of the new agency, the Consilium became part of it as a "Special Commission for Completion of the Liturgical Reform." It was under this new name that the Fathers gathered at Santa Marta, a year after their previous meeting. This was but the second time in five years of life that the general assembly met only once in a calendar year. The reason for this unusual situation was that it had been impossible for the study groups to prepare the needed material before the meeting scheduled for April 1969.[84] In addition, the secretariat was laboring under the burden of work required by the printing of the schemas that were gradually reaching completion.

It must be noted, however, that during the long interval between general sessions several important meetings had been held: one was a meeting of the presidential council in April; three were concerned with the Roman Missal (one of them lasted an entire month), five with the sacraments, and eight with the Divine Office.

---

84. The April general meeting was replaced by the eighth and final meeting of the presidential council (April 23–24), which concerned itself chiefly with the present status of the work and with the program to be followed in promulgating the new liturgical books, especially the calendar, the rite of Mass, the Missal, the biblical readings for Mass, and the baptism of children.

The twelfth general meeting took place on November 10–14 (while the relators met earlier, on November 4–8).[85] Present were forty-two Fathers (ten cardinals, thirty-one bishops, and the Abbot Primate of the Benedictines) and thirty-seven experts.

The feast of St. Martin was the inspiration for the telegram (drafted by Monsignor Schnitzler) that was sent to the Pope:

> The members and experts of the Special Commission for Completion of the Liturgical Reform, gathered for their twelfth general meeting, express their sentiments of filial devotion and love for the Successor of Peter on this feast of the holy bishop Martin. Know, Holy Father, that we have spared no effort in order that the people of God may develop an ever fuller faith in the sacred liturgy and that the entire human family, gathered in common prayer, may approach the Father with confidence. May your blessing descend on this meeting and all its labors for the reform of the "work of God"; may it strengthen us to help the people of God always to participate in the sacred mysteries with lively faith and active love.

A few days later a reply came by way of Cardinal Villot:

> The Supreme Pontiff gratefully accepts the homage of the Special Commission for the Completion of the Liturgical Reform, for he knows that this Commission is inspired by a determination to labor tirelessly, and he hopes for a happy outcome and abundant fruits from this meeting. As proof of his good will, he cordially grants his Apostolic Blessing to you and to all of the participants.

The Cardinal Prefect recalled the establishment of the new Congregation; greeted in particular the new members of the Commission: Cardinals Baggio and Willebrands and Bishops Byrne, Kabangu, and Otčenášek; and urged all to pray for the deceased members: Bishop Lazík and that much loved and valiant fellow worker, Monsignor Bonet.[86]

In his opening report the secretary of the Congregation reviewed the abundant liturgical publications that had made 1969 a memorable year: *Ordo celebrandi Matrimonium* (March 19); *Calendarium Romanum* (May 9); *Ordo Missae* and *Institutio generalis Missalis Romani* (April 3); *Ordo lectionum Missae* (May 25); *Ordo baptismi parvulorum* (May 15); *Ordo exsequiarum* (August 15). In addition, there were documents and instructions on the proper use of the new books: instruction on translations (January 25); instruction on editions and use of the new Lectionary (July 25); extension of the *vacatio legis* for the rite of baptism for children (July 10); in-

---

85. See *Not* 5 (1969) 436–41.

86. The relators decided to remember their esteemed and beloved colleague in a special way with a concelebration in the holy cave at Subiaco on November 8.

struction on the interim adaptation of particular calendars for 1970 (June 29); instruction on the gradual implementation of the apostolic constitution *Missale Romanum* (October 20); instruction on Masses with special groups (May 15).

All this activity had also elicited criticism of the reform and especially of the continual "trickle" of instructions from the Consilium and then from the Congregation. The secretary of the Congregation observed that

> the situation is a consequence of any reform. The decrees published by the Congregation of Rites during the first years of its existence—1587 to 1600—numbered 157; but there were 487 from 1600 to 1614, the year in which the last of the liturgical books, the Roman Ritual, was published. The decrees issued in the first years after the reform of Pius X numbered 54. It must be admitted that by comparison the present reform displays a noteworthy and laudable modesty.

The secretary announced further publications in the immediate future: the Roman Missal, the rites for the consecration of virgins and religious profession and for the blessing of an abbot or abbess.

In addition, he anticipated an intensification of efforts to explain and support the reform—more specifically, the publication of a reference book for episcopal conferences, national liturgical conferences, and bishops; a collection of the documents of the reform and their sources; a collection of studies of the new liturgical books.

The secretary concluded with a further proposal:

> The Consilium was an organization established by Paul VI, who was constant in support of it and always esteemed and favored our work. The Consilium has now been transformed into the Congregation for Divine Worship. This series of events was marked by struggles and challenges, but it will remain a bright beacon in the history of the Church. Would it not be appropriate that this phase of the Church's history and renewal be permanently commemorated by a marble or bronze memorial that the members of the Consilium would erect *ad perpetuam rei memoriam* in the new premises of the Congregation?

Schemas. The schemas presented and studied[87] had to do with the sick: introduction, visitation of the sick, communion, viaticum, anointing of the sick, commendation of the dying; the baptism of children, which was definitively revised and readied after two years of experimentation in various parts of the world; the Divine Office, regarding which some secon-

---

87. The order followed in the work: November 10: Roman Gradual, detailed questions on the calendar; 11: penance, blessing of oils; 12: Divine Office; 13: Divine Office, blessing of oils; 14: anointing of the sick.

dary questions were raised. On the Divine Office, the main subject of discussion was the cycles for the biblical and patristic readings. It was decided to go with the two-year cycle for the biblical readings and the one-year cycle for the patristic, since it was impossible in the short time available to bring the two readings into harmony over a two-year period.[88] (This decision would, however, be revised for the biblical cycle, since the printing problem became insoluble and since a two-year cycle would perhaps be too burdensome for the majority.)

The problem of penance came up again; this time, however, the discussion was more serene, and two formulas were approved. There were some slight revisions in the calendar (the numerous suggestions for change that had come in from many quarters were rejected) and in the blessing of the oils. Finally, the Consilium took under consideration difficulties that had surfaced regarding some points in the General Instruction of the Roman Missal, especially no. 7; a declaration was therefore prepared that would explain the meaning and importance of that number.[89]

Finally, there was the election of the seven bishops whom *Regimini Ecclesiae* required to be assigned to each agency and whom the Pope allowed on this occasion to be elected by the members of the Consilium and chosen from within the Consilium itself.[90]

After the meeting the Congregation for Divine Worship moved its offices to the new location assigned it on the fourth floor of the Palazzo delle Congregazioni, at 10 Piazza Pio XII, near the Congregation for the Causes of the Saints. As the newspapers said at the end of their report, the two Congregations shared "archives, faith, tenacity in work, fraternal charity, and love for Holy Church."

General Meeting XIII (April 9–10, 1970)

The thirteenth general meeting was held in the Hall of the Congregations in the Apostolic Palace, on April 9–10, 1970. The consultors had held their own meetings in the assembly room of the Congregation for Divine Worship.[91]

Present were thirty members (nine cardinals, twenty-one bishops), thirty-two *periti*, and six observers.

---

88. At this meeting the title for the book of the Divine Office was chosen. Among the several names proposed, one received unqualified preference: *Liturgia* (or *Liber*) *Horarum*.

89. See *Not* 5 (1969) 417–18; DOL 204 nos. 1368–70.

90. See *Not* 6 (1970) 12; the names were given earlier on p. 81, n. 18.

91. See *Not* 6 (1970) 222–31.

After a speech of welcome from the Cardinal Prefect, the secretary gave a detailed report of the work accomplished since the previous general meeting. The major effort had been devoted to the preparation of the Missal. Opposition to the work had come in the form of pamphlets published against the new Order of Mass, which was accused of being heretical. This flood of opposition required a careful revision of the entire General Instruction; this was done in collaboration with the Congregation for the Doctrine of the Faith. The accusations proved to be unfounded. In order to eliminate all doubts, the Holy Father ordered the preparation of an introduction that would bring out the doctrinal continuity between Trent and Vatican II, the ties with tradition amid a legitimate evolution of forms, and the criteria applied in the compilation of the new Missal. Since publication of the Missal had been delayed for the reasons indicated, the section containing the Chrism Mass was extracted and sent to all the bishops through the episcopal conferences. — In the Divine Office the *preces* had been revised, and the volume containing the patristic and hagiographical readings had been published.

After explaining the work presently in hand, the secretary gave some figures for the six years of work accomplished by the Consilium. He called to mind the members and *periti* who "have gone before us in the sign of faith": Cardinal Bevilacqua, Bishops Grimshaw (Birmingham), Hallinan (Atlanta), and Bekkers (s'Hertogenbosch), Father Bruylants (Mont-César), Cardinal Ritter (St. Louis), Bishop Nabuco (Rio de Janeiro), Cardinal Bea, Bishop Lazík (Trnava), Monsignor Bonet, beloved friend and invaluable fellow worker. According to the chronicler, these were "ten companions, now standing like so many candles in the Lord's presence and acting as patrons of our labors."

Finally, after discussing the imminent work on the structural organization of the Congregation, the secretary ended by thanking all those who had so generously devoted themselves to erecting the great edifice of the liturgical reform.

Schemas. Three subjects in particular were discussed: the reform of the Martyrology; confirmation (especially the questions of age and matter); the blessings. Also studied were a schema on the extension of the permission to receive communion under two species and, regarding the Divine Office, the still unresolved problems of obligation and of the organic connection of the hours with the Mass or of the hours among themselves.

On the afternoon of April 9 there was a solemn inauguration of the new quarters of the Congregation for Divine Worship. A commemorative plaque was unveiled, as was a bust of Pope Paul VI, the gift of the members of the Consilium.

This event brought the end of the meeting and at the same time the end of the Consilium. The Pope commemorated the latter fact on the following day in the audience he granted to the members and consultors: "The Consilium comes to an end after its outstanding service." But the Consilium's dedication, its goal, and its spiritual enthusiasm for continuing the work remained in the new Congregation.

Papal audience

On April 10, in the Hall of the Consistory, the Pope received the entire Consilium for the last time. Henceforth the Consilium would be known as the Special Commission for the Completion of the Liturgical Reform.

Cardinal Gut, the prefect, paid homage to the Pope in an address that deserves to be cited in full.

> Holy Father. For the fifth time we come together before you during our plenary sessions devoted to reform of the liturgy and this is the last session at which we will all gather as members of the Consilium.
>
> In these last six years we have lived through a remarkable period in the Church's history. It has been a period of hard and difficult work, not without problems; it has at times been marked by controversy; its passage has been measured by wise and often courageous experimentation. It is a period of history that has been at once serious and happy, bringing joy to the spirit.
>
> Looking back over the course we have traveled, we gladly offer thanks to you, Holy Father, for having been so kind as to choose us to devote our energies to the work of renewing the inmost life of the Church. This work brings to realization those things by which Vatican II has marked the Church and its structure with the spirit of genuine reform. That is a starting point from which the Church, entering on a new course pointed out by God, will advance toward more sublime and shining goals.
>
> Like a ship that after a long voyage nears the harbor, the reform of the liturgy is fast approaching its successful outcome. The soon-to-be-published Roman Missal as well as the divine office that we hope to be able to put in the hands of the people of God in a short time stand as the more notable achievements of the latest phase of the process.
>
> Thirteen plenary and innumerable particular sessions, three hundred sixty-five schemata prepared for the plenary sessions, many other kinds of documents, including constitutions, decrees, instructions—this sums up the work done. By their silent but assiduous and dauntless work the fifty Fathers, cardinals and bishops, and the one hundred fifty *periti*, chosen from all parts of the world, have given a new form to the Church's *lex orandi*, in which the whole of God's family is raising a beautiful chorus of celebration.

Future historians will have the advantage of archives full of priceless records should they wish to reconstruct the development of the individual reformed rites or examine their texts, deriving from tradition or newly composed, or evaluate the particular reformed rubrical and pastoral norms. Then it will be utterly clear how conscious of their responsibility before God and the Church the members of that institution were in doing their work. It is the institution that you, Holy Father, with such foresight created on 3 January 1964 and that will be remembered in history as "the Consilium."

Further, we are happy to acknowledge that you have made our fervent wish come true when you initiated the Congregation for Divine Worship. This new agency will continue to guide along the same course the work of liturgical reform so happily begun.

Finally, we wish to thank you because you have continually supported, favored, and guided our work. There have been days not only of calm, but days also when the seas surged around the prow and imperiled the fragile ship. Your strong hope, your encouragement, your enlightening words, above all your faith in the good work begun have constantly supported us. For this reason the reform of the liturgy that has taken its name from you stands clearly and in fact as your work and will be counted as one of the brightest jewels in the history of your pontificate.

Now the Consilium or special commission for the completion of the liturgical reform is dissolved and gives way to a new congregation. Nevertheless we deeply desire that this family which has worked together in shared joys and sorrows may not be dissolved. May it always remain united so that all the members in their own Churches will stand always at the forefront, leading the liturgical reform, which promises such great benefits in the Church.

We promise you our service to the Church all the days of our lives. At the same time we ask your fatherly blessing on us so that through sacrifice and the praise of God, our humble work also will serve to bring about the sanctification of the faithful and the unity of believers and in all things will do honor to God.[92]

In his allocution the Holy Father likewise referred to the work done by the Consilium, to the accomplishments already realized and those in course of completion, and to the principles that had inspired them: to help the people of our time draw fully from the source of the divine mysteries and to preserve as far as possible the heritage and patrimony of the Latin Church. He then expressed his desire for the future of the new Congregation: that it would bend every effort to see to it that the liturgical reform was wisely carried out and given religious respect, while avoiding all arbitrariness. "The liturgical reform will achieve fulfillment through

---

92. *DOL* 98 nos. 688-89.

loyalty to the will of the Council; in a cause so holy because it involves divine worship and the spiritual life, we must preserve, safeguard, and promote without reserve unity and harmony of spirit."[93]

IV. PLENARY MEETINGS

Plenary Meeting I (November 10-13, 1970)

The first plenary meeting of the Congregation for Divine Worship was held November 10-13, 1970. The *Consulta*, or meeting of consultors, had taken place November 3-6, with nineteen consultors in attendance.[94] Twenty members were present for the plenary meeting; the others said they were prevented from coming. The plenary meetings of the Congregation differed from the general meetings of the Consilium in that the former had a smaller number of members in attendance and the consultors were not present. It would have been desirable to have the latter present, since this had proved so useful during the discussions of the Fathers. But the reply of the Secretary of State was negative.[95] The only non-members present were the relators for the several schemas.

In his greetings the Cardinal Prefect, Benno Gut, announced that the Pope had confirmed the election of seven bishops as members of the Congregation; this election had been held during the twelfth general meeting of the Consilium. The Lord had already called one of them, Bishop Spülbeck, to his eternal home; Bishop Kisberk, a Hungarian, was ap-

---

93. *DOL* 99 nos. 690-91.
94. See *Not* 6 (1970) 388-94.
95. To the request of the Congregation, the Secretariat of State replied as follows on June 30: "Regarding the participation of the consultors along with the members: You are well aware that the general regulations of the Roman Curia distinguish between a plenary meeting and a meeting of consultors (arts. 110ff.) and prescribe that the group of consultors is to be called together a few days before the plenary meetings (arts. 126 and 127). We have reviewed the reasons you offer, but we believe it best to accept the opinion of experienced men who think that, all things considered, it is inadvisable not to follow the detailed prescriptions in the recent set of regulations. The presence of the consultors would excessively limit the freedom of the cardinals and bishops in voting. On the other hand, it is appropriate that the consultors and experts meet before the members do and prepare the material to be studied by them; for these two different authorities should be equally free in their own area of competence—the consultors on the one hand, and, on the other, the members, who make decisions, even if these depend on the approval of the Supreme Pontiff.

"We offer these considerations for the prudent judgment of His Eminence, the Cardinal Prefect, and your own [the secretary's] and ask you to follow willingly the universal norms set down in the regulations. If, however, in a special case it were desired to have the members and consultors meet together, this office would raise the matter with the Holy Father whenever such a request might reach us."

pointed in his place. The Cardinal Prefect also mentioned the death of Bishop Emilio Guano and the appointment of other members: Cardinals Bengsch, Wojtyla, Dearden, Marty, and Tabera.

On the agenda were the rites for minor orders, the dedication of a church, and the anointing of the sick; and the second report on blessings. Monsignor Jounel was relator for the first two, Father Gy for the last two.[96]

Minor orders. This was a first and provisional schema. The details were to be defined after the Congregation for the Sacraments had decided on the elements required by law. The Fathers were satisfied with the structure and the formulas proposed. But they also offered *vota* to be presented to the competent authority.[97]

The sick. The schema begun in 1965 reached completion in 1969 with the collaboration of theologians, pastors, and physicians from various countries. Account was taken not only of what was said at Vatican II but of the many and varied necessities introduced by the care of the sick in our day. The first deliberations on the schema took place in the Consilium in November 1969. It was from there that the suggestion came of including the rite of commendation of the dying in this schema.

Dedication of a church. This was the first report on this rite. The Fathers approved the relator's exposition as a set of guidelines.

Blessings. Second report; very interesting and received with satisfaction. Not all difficulties were resolved, but all were on the way to solution.

Plenary Meeting II (March 7–11, 1972)

The second plenary meeting took place March 7–11, 1972, at the Congregation for Divine Worship.[98] The meeting could not be held in 1971 because of a change of prefects. Cardinal Gut had died peacefully on December 8, 1970. The following February 20 Cardinal Arturo Tabera Araoz was appointed prefect, but because of commitments in his diocese, he did not take up his charge until some months later.

The consultors had met January 25–28, 1972.

Sixteen Fathers were present at the plenary meeting. The Cardinal mentioned the secretary's election to the episcopate and the appointment of Cardinals Antonio Samorè and Paolo Bertoli, the prefects respectively

---

96. November 10: discussion of minor orders; 11: the ritual for the pastoral care of the sick; 12: dedication of a church; 13: blessings.

97. See below, pp. 745–46.

98. See *Not* 8 (1973) 118–34.

of the Congregations for the Sacraments and for the Causes of the Saints, as members of the Congregation for Divine Worship.

The plenary meeting followed the plan set down in the regulations. After the presentation of a schema by a relator, each Father read his opinion; the question was then proposed, a short discussion followed, and a vote was taken.

Six subjects, discussed in the following order, were on the agenda:

1) *Naming of the bishop in the Canon* (relator: Cardinal Pericle Felici). Numerous requests had recently come in for permission to mention in the Eucharistic Prayer the names of Ordinaries who were not bishops. The question was not simply a juridical one but rather liturgical and pastoral. A bishop is named in the Canon not only or primarily to do him honor, but because of the communion of love and to make clear who is the steward of the grace of the High Priest and around whose altar the people gather to celebrate the Eucharist. But some sectors of God's people are not at all times led by a bishop; they have Ordinaries who bear titles other than that of bishop. Permission to name such Ordinaries in the Canon has therefore frequently been given by the Congregation of Rites and the Congregation of the Propaganda. Rome was now being asked to give a universal answer to the question.[99]

2) *Eucharist* (relator: Bishop Boudon). The subject here was the part of the Ritual that dealt with worship of the Eucharist outside Mass. The schema brought together and reorganized all the material scattered in various documents, especially in the instruction *Eucharisticum mysterium*, and supplied a careful synthesis of doctrinal principles and of practices.

3) *Blessings* (relator: Father Gy). This was the third report on the subject. The main issue was determination of the role of the laity in blessings. Some model blessings were also presented. After stating some general principles, both doctrinal and liturgical, the schema intended to offer some fifteen models for the more common blessings; on the basis of these, the episcopal conferences could then prepare their own rituals.

4) *Rites in Book II of the Pontifical* (relator: Monsignor Jounel). The rites in Book II that were still to be reformed were studied. Monsignor Jounel's presentation was schematic, but it gave a precise idea of how this book was to be structured. It was to contain major blessings which of themselves were reserved to the bishop as head of the diocesan community and the one in charge of it, but which in special circumstances could be delegated to a priest.

---

99. This was done in a decree of the SCDW on October 9, 1972: *AAS* 64 (1972) 692–94; *DOL* 247 nos. 1970-74. See *Not* 8 (1972) 347–49, 349–52.

5) *Ceremonial of Bishops* (relator: Monsignor Schnitzler). The relator described the history of the Ceremonial of Bishops, the need of it today for a worthy performance of the episcopal liturgy, and the character of the revised book. This was to bring together in one place all of the ceremonial legislation of the new liturgical books, but adapted to the episcopal liturgy; it was also to give spiritual and doctrinal guidelines so that the full meaning of the episcopal liturgy might be understood.

6) *Eucharistic Prayers* (relator: Monsignor Lengeling). This was the most carefully studied, thorny, and sensitive part of the plenary meeting. The relator sketched the history of the handling of the material from the preparatory commission to the conciliar commission and on to the Consilium.

Creativity freely exercised at the very heart of the Eucharistic liturgy was a phenomenon to be found everywhere in some degree and was of concern to both the Holy See and the bishops. Requests came in almost daily asking for the denunciation of abuses, for clarifications and interventions, for greater freedom, or for a supply of other texts from the center of the Church. A detailed examination of the whole phenomenon was called for. With the consent of the Holy Father, a study group had been set up which, through detailed research and at frequent meetings, conducted a radical study of the phenomenon of creativity in this area, approaching it from the theological, pastoral, and historical viewpoints. It now offered its conclusions to the Fathers of the Congregation. The Holy Father had been kept fully informed at every step and after every meeting of the group.

The problem was a difficult one for the further reason that it involved the competence of other agencies that would eventually have to be consulted, once the Fathers of this Congregation had expressed their views. But everyone else also wanted to express a view; this included the Congregation for the Doctrine of the Faith. Members of the Congregation who also belonged to the Curia were thus somewhat forewarned.

For these reasons the various documents, along with the guidelines that the Holy Father eventually gave to the Congregation for Divine Worship, were distributed at the beginning of the discussion.[100]

Plenary Meeting III (November 21–24, 1972)

The third plenary meeting was held in the assembly room of the Congregation for Divine Worship from November 21 to November 24, 1972.

---

100. See below, p. 471, n. 31.

Nineteen Fathers attended.[101] The consultors had met from the seventh to the tenth of the same month.

There were three topics on the agenda: the rites for the institution of lectors and acolytes and for admission as candidates for ordination as deacons and priests and for embracing celibacy; the rite of penance; the Directory for Masses with Children.

Cardinal Tabera opened the meeting with a lengthy report on the work of the Congregation: publication of the *Ordo cantus Missae*, the Lectionary for Mass, and the four volumes of the *Liturgia Horarum*. He announced the proximate publication of the *Ordo unctionis infirmorum*, the document *De sacra communione et de cultu mysterii Eucharistici extra Missam*, and the *Ordo Paenitentiae*. He also mentioned that work on the Ceremonial of Bishops and the Martyrology had reached an advanced stage.

He dwelt on the *Collectanea documentorum instaurationis liturgicae* that was now being prepared and ended by stressing the importance of personal contacts that he had had with the episcopal conferences, especially during his travels in Latin America.

Schemas discussed

Rite of admission and institution of lectors and acolytes. The Fathers had already studied this rite at their first plenary meeting. Since then it had followed the usual route. It was being brought up again here simply for examination of the opening exhortations, which had been completely revised.

Rite for embracing sacred celibacy. This rite was being presented for the first time; the Fathers were to examine its structure and the texts. The discussion, especially of the structure, was lively; the goal was to decide on how the decision to accept celibacy "for the sake of the kingdom of heaven" was to be expressed. There was a great deal of emphasis on the preservation of a traditional element that was dear to many: the step forward taken at the subdiaconate. The consultors had proposed two alternative forms: a verbal acceptance in the form of a reply to a question of the bishop or the expression of the decision by the step forward. But on this latter proposal the Fathers were clearly divided in their views.[102]

With regard to the obligation to celebrate the Liturgy of the Hours, it was asked that the text of the bishop's question on this subject be more clearly worded, so as to make indisputably clear the need of prayer in the life of ordained ministers.

---

101. See *Not* 9 (1973) 44–46.
102. See below, p. 750.

Penance. After the publication of the "Pastoral Norms for General Absolution" by the Congregation for the Doctrine of the Faith (June 16, 1972), the *Ordo Paenitentiae* had been completely revised. One point specifically proposed to the Fathers was the adoption of the term "reconciliation." The presentation of this schema to the plenary assembly before it had been studied by other concerned Congregations caused some wrangling over procedure. A circular letter was to be sent explaining the nature of the present discussion and the impossibility of proceeding otherwise due to a lack of time. In the period between the publication of the norms and the plenary meeting, it had been impossible both to effect a radical revision of the schema and to consult all the agencies concerned. The examination of the revised schema at the plenary meeting (the circular would say) was an informal one and in no way forestalled the observations of the other agencies. — In point of fact, however, according to the practice of the Curia, plenary meetings were not informal examinations or study sessions; they came to decisions which were to some extent binding on the other agencies.

Directory for Masses with Children. The Fathers' attention was drawn to three points: (a) elements of the Mass that could be simplified or omitted in Masses with children; (b) adaptations to be made in Masses with adults when children were also present; (c) technological aids to be used in due measure in celebrations with children.

Letters to the presidents of the episcopal conferences. At this plenary meeting the Fathers were presented with a draft of a letter that the Cardinal Prefect was proposing to send to the presidents of the episcopal conferences. Similar letters had been sent several times, beginning in 1965, for the purpose of keeping the bishops *au courant* with the work of the Congregation and of signaling some weaker areas in liturgical discipline. After an extended debate on the value, juridical status, need, and appropriateness of this kind of letter, the view of the more traditionalist members, who were against the practice, prevailed; the bishops, on the other hand, were unanimously for it. The Cardinal Prefect concluded that he must do without this very useful means of dialogue with the conferences. Thus law throttled the spirit, and there was no more talk of letters to the conferences.

This was the last plenary meeting. Another was scheduled for the end of 1973, to coincide with the tenth anniversary of the approval of the Constitution on the Liturgy, which it was thought desirable to commemorate in a special way. But the Secretariat of State would not permit special commemorations of the anniversaries of conciliar documents. Meanwhile, in addition, Cardinal Tabera became prefect of the Congregation for Religious, and the plenary session was postponed indefinitely.

On the other hand, as the Congregation for Divine Worship proceeded with its work, it did hold some "ordinary" meetings, some of them jointly with other agencies, in order to discuss particular matters, as, for example, the declaration on concelebration and the notification on the Liturgy of the Hours in some communities.[103]

The final ordinary meeting was held on June 19, 1975, when the suppression of the Congregation for Divine Worship had already been indicated. The subject was the request from the Netherlands and Belgium for some Eucharistic Prayers of their own. I have already dealt with this subject and shall return to it later on.[104]

---

103. See below, pp. 565–66.
104. See above, p. 94; and below, p. 266, n. 13; pp. 484–86.

13

Observers at the Consilium

A distinguishing mark of the meetings of the Consilium was the participation of observers from non-Catholic ecclesial communities. They were a congenial addition; relations were fraternal and peaceful. Outside of the Consilium, however, it gave a handle for insinuations and for interpretations that were arbitrary and sometimes malicious.[1] I shall describe how observers came to be present and what limits were placed on their participation.[2]

At the audience of December 2, 1965, Cardinal Lercaro, president of the Consilium, gave the Pope a statement in which he said that some members of the Anglican communion who were involved in the revision of that Church's liturgy had let it be known by indirect channels that they would be interested in following the work of the Consilium at close hand.

The Cardinal noted that a reciprocal knowledge of the researches and schemas of the two Churches would not be a bad thing. It might even serve as a positive help to rapprochement of the two Churches. This was more readily true, he added, for some parts of the liturgy. For example, if a common schema for the Psalter in the Divine Office and for the readings in the liturgy could be worked out, it might be a spiritual and psychological help to union.

---

1. Those in particular who were opposed to any reform of the Mass took advantage of the observers' presence to claim that the reformed Mass was Protestant. One of their main arguments was that Protestants had had a hand in the revision. Further grist for their mill was a photograph taken at the end of the Consilium's work, for which the Holy Father, as a sign of fraternal good will, posed with the observers.

2. See *Not* 10 (1974) 249–52.

Other confessions also were showing interest in the liturgical reform now going on in the Roman Church.

On December 14 the Holy Father sent a positive answer. The Consilium was asked to join the Secretariat for Christian Unity, the Secretariat of State, and the Congregation for the Doctrine of Faith in establishing suitable norms.

Between December 1965 and August 1966 there was an exchange of views and information between these several agencies and the Consilium, and between the Secretariat for Christian Unity and the various interested ecclesial communities, for the purpose of determining the appointees and the modalities of their participation. The list of observers as finally approved by the Secretariat of State and the Congregation for the Doctrine of the Faith read as follows on August 23, 1966:

The Anglican communion appointed the following on July 1:

1. Reverend Canon Ronald C. Jasper, D.D., of London, president of the Liturgical Commission of the Anglican Church in England.

2. Reverend Doctor Massey H. Shepherd, Jr., of California, professor at the Church Divinity School of the Pacific.

On August 12 the World Council of Churches appointed:

3. Professor A. Raymond George, a member of the Methodist Conference and Director of Wesley College at Headlingley (Leeds), England.

On August 12 the Lutheran World Federation appointed:

4. Pastor Friedrich Wilhelm Künneth of Geneva, secretary of the Commission for Worship and Spiritual Life. In 1968 he was replaced by:

5. Reverend Eugene L. Brand, a Lutheran from New York.

Lastly, the Taizé community chose:

6. Frère Max Thurian, subprior of the community.

The idea was suggested of inviting a representative of the Orthodox Church to be an observer, but this was not pursued.

What was the role of the observers at the Consilium? Simply to "observe." Their attitude at the meetings of the Consilium was one of great reserve and unobtrusiveness. They never took part in the discussions, never asked to speak.

They were the first to arrive at the meetings, the last to leave the hall. They were always affable, polite, sparing of words, and ready to engage in a friendly way in any conversation that might be requested.

Only on one occasion did the Consilium decide to ask for the views of the observers as a group. This was during the discussion of the problem of cycles of readings in the celebration of the Eucharist. The question here was whether, having opted for a three-year cycle of readings, the Consilium should retain the one found in the Roman Missal or develop an entire new three-year cycle from scratch.

A group headed by Cardinal Bea chose the first solution. Their strongest reason was the ecumenical one: the traditional order of readings at the Eucharistic celebration was followed in many non-Catholic ecclesial communities, the Lutherans in particular. It seemed imprudent, therefore, to throw away the tie between the confessions.

The second solution was the one favored by the study group in charge of work on the Lectionaries (with Father Vagaggini at its head). It was beyond doubt that the majority were for this second solution. But to make certain that this approach truly respected the thinking of the other ecclesial communities, it was decided to hold a joint meeting of the five observers and the *periti* of the Consilium.

The two parties met on the afternoon of October 8, 1966, at the Palazzo S. Marta. On October 10, at the beginning of the plenary meeting, Canon Jasper, an Anglican, read a statement saying that the observers:

a) could not offer any decision, since none of them could speak for the ecclesial community to which he belonged;

b) did not want ecumenical considerations to hinder the abandonment of the traditional Lectionary. They, too, in fact were hoping for a similar revision and were waiting on the results achieved by the venerable Roman Church;

c) suggested that the new Roman Lectionary be used experimentally for a certain period and that meanwhile timely agreements be reached on a Lectionary acceptable to the Roman Church and the other ecclesial communities.

This was the only intervention the Fathers requested and the observers agreed to; it was marked by great courtesy, respect, and prudence.[3]

---

3. The only area in which a study group looked to any of the observers for information on the experience of their Churches was in regard to the *preces* in the Divine Office. Since these were something new for the Roman Church, whereas the Taizé community was already using them, study group 12bis availed itself of the opportunity for a friendly consultation with the very competent Frère Max Thurian.

On the other hand, there was no basis for the claim that the third Eucharistic Prayer had been composed in collaboration with the Protestants. *Not* 10 (1974) 252 made this clear: "The draft of the schema that was to be the basis for the third anaphora was completed in three months' work (summer of 1965) in the abbey library at Mont-César (Louvain) by one of the Consilium's most capable consultors, now a member of the International Theological Commission and a man whose exceptional competence in theology and rare knowledge of the liturgy are recognized by all. The schema was then examined carefully and honed at intervals by the study group charged with the reform of the rite of Mass. The names of those in the group are to be seen in the Directory of the personnel of the Consi-

When the work of the Consilium came to an end, some of the observers asked that they might also attend the plenary meetings of the Congregation for Divine Worship, but the request was not granted by the competent authority.

---

lium. Further changes were made when the schema was passed on to the Fathers of the Consilium (General Meeting VIII, April 1967).

"After all this, the schema was studied by other interested and competent agencies of the Holy See. It was from this four-stage sifting that the text of the third Eucharistic Prayer emerged which was finally approved by the Holy Father, Paul VI, and introduced into the Roman Missal.

"Any other scenario is the product of imagination, prejudice, or malicious innuendo, and has no basis in fact."

B. Encouragement of a Pastoral Approach to the Liturgy

14

Letters to the Presidents of the Episcopal Conferences

As the Consilium proceeded with its revision of the liturgical books, it felt the need of establishing a direct and active relationship with the outside world, and especially with those on whom the Church's liturgical life depended in one degree or another: the presidents of the episcopal conferences and liturgical commissions, scholars, institutes, and publications of a liturgical and pastoral kind.

The Holy Father acknowledged such an obligation when, in the audience of October 13, 1966, he reminded the Consilium that its task was to guide "the broad and multiform reform efforts inspired by the Constitution on the Liturgy" and to keep a watchful eye on experimentation, correct deviations, "prevent abuses . . . prod those who lag or resist . . . stimulate energies . . . encourage promising initiatives . . . praise those deserving praise."[1]

Contacts were of several kinds. The Consilium had an opportunity for repeated direct dealings with the presidents of the episcopal conferences whenever the moment came to confirm a decision of theirs or their translation of a liturgical book. On these occasions there was a sometimes intense and lengthy dialogue that helped the Consilium gain a detailed knowledge of local situations. The information thus gained was supplemented by bulletins and the press.

Furthermore, as the work grew more detailed, there was an increasing need for a personal, on-the-spot understanding of problems. Cardinal Tabera, for example, took part in the meetings of the liturgical

---

1. See *Not* 2 (1966) 305–6; *DOL* 84 nos. 630–36 (at 634, par. 1).

commissions of the German-speaking world, then in those of the English; finally, he visited almost all the countries of Latin America.[2]

The secretary of the Consilium, for his part, went to the Netherlands on three occasions[3] and took part in liturgical meetings of the bishops of Mexico. The presence of a representative of the Consilium and, later, of the Congregation for Divine Worship came to be looked for wherever important meetings of a pastoral kind were held. Unfortunately, this activity had to be limited because of economic or bureaucratic difficulties, among other things.[4] Most of the time the various countries had to be satisfied with direct contacts in Rome on the occasion of *ad limina* visits and attendance at meetings of the Congregations and the Commissions and, in the earlier years, of the Consilium. The problems of liturgical reform came up at the Synod of Bishops on two occasions: at the first meeting of 1967, when they were raised at a majority of the sessions and held the attention of the Fathers; and in 1974, when Cardinal Knox reported on the state of the reform, its program of future activity, and its main problems.[5]

In addition to these occasional reports, which were not always prepared much in advance, the Consilium tried to establish direct contact with the episcopal conferences and liturgical commissions in several ways that deserve to be recalled here: letters to the presidents of the episcopal conferences, meetings, and the periodical *Notitiae*.

I. General Letters

One of the first actions of the newly formed Consilium was to establish contact with the presidents of the episcopal conferences in a letter

---

2. See *Not* 8 (1972) 31, 345; 9 (1973) 304.

3. See above, p. 106.

4. At the beginning, the fact that the Cardinal President resided in Bologna and the necessity of keeping tabs on the work of the groups and of organizing meetings did not allow any planning for special trips. Furthermore, the chancy juridical status of the Consilium made such activity inadvisable.

5. The experience of the Synod of 1967, on which such hopes had been set, was negative. The results of it were disconcerting by reason of the gap between the reports prepared for the episcopal conferences and the reactions and voting at the Synod. Henceforth there would always be a certain hesitation in dealing with the liturgy, and liturgical questions were no longer raised. Only at the Synod of 1974 did Cardinal Knox succeed at the last moment in giving a report that had not been planned but was requested by the participants. Many bishops found it odd that at a meeting devoted to evangelization and at which almost all the addresses made reference to the liturgy and popular religion, no word was being heard from the agency in charge precisely of this sector of the Church's life. See *Not* 10 (1974) 355–62, and in the following pages the main statements made regarding the liturgy.

of March 25, 1964.[6] Conferences of bishops did not yet exist in all countries; the Consilium was certainly one of the first postconciliar bodies to concern itself with them.[7]

The intention was to communicate with the conferences in an authoritative but, as it were, unofficial way by means of letters that would keep them informed of the ongoing work of renewal, rectify inaccurate or incomplete interpretations of documents and decrees, correct abuses, give suggestions or guidelines for the implementation of the Constitution and revised rites, or prepare the way for the acceptance of these.[8]

The letters are expository in style, being as it were a dialogue between the president of the Consilium and the pastors of the Christian communities. They were a new kind of contact between a central agency of the Church and the episcopates, and they pleased and did a great deal of good. At a time of transition to a new legislation and a new spirit, a time when much tact was needed, the letters served as a guide and gave assurances that the pastors would be proceeding along the right lines.

The letters were composed in Italian and translated into French, English, Spanish, Portuguese, and German; they were then duplicated and sent. The secretary of the Consilium was completely responsible for the work. Letters were readied when it was thought that there were problems worth bringing to the attention of all the bishops. These letters played an auspicious part in the first years of the Consilium's existence. The initial letter, dated March 25, 1964, was followed by three more on general problems, the last being dated June 21, 1967; here the series stopped. In the ensuing years, contact with the bishops took the form chiefly of the transmission to them of the new liturgical books successively published and of instructions and other documents.

First Letter

The first letter was sent on June 30, 1965, a few months after the official beginning of the liturgical reform.[9] That beginning was described as the day when "the entire Church was empowered to sing the glory of

---

6. *DOL* 79 nos. 615-19.

7. The other agencies of the Curia also made use of the early files on the conferences.

8. Whenever a liturgical book, document, or instruction was published, a copy was sent to the papal representative in each country as well as to the president of the episcopal conference and the president of the national liturgical commission. In the beginning the copies were sent directly to these several addressees; then, by order of the Secretariat of State, they were sent via the papal representative.

9. *Not* 1 (1965) 257-64 (the letters are always in French in *Not*); *DOL* 31 nos. 407-18.

God in the languages of the faithful.'' For the sake of ''a more fruitful liturgical life,'' the Cardinal Prefect issued these guidelines:

1. The new liturgical norms have been drawn up with a certain flexibility so that they can be adapted in a timely way. But this adaptation cannot be left to the judgment of each individual; it is rather the responsibility of those to whom the Church entrusts this task.

2. The sense of brotherhood and of the community as a family should not be allowed to obscure the hierarchical aspect of the Church's life, which requires a harmonious and disciplined cooperation with the bishop, the episcopal college, and the Vicar of Christ. This holds especially for experimentation. The faithful want to be the true people of God and true children of the Church; consequently, they want to take part in the liturgy of the Church and not in one arbitrarily excogitated by the priest. Obedience is a bond of unity and does not throttle variety.

3. The Consilium works tirelessly, but the general reform of the liturgy requires time and patience. A task done in such a manner as to ensure seriousness and validity would be compromised by untimely and harmful innovations. Those who think they have new ideas, suggestions, and useful proposals are asked to make them known to the Consilium, which will study them with the closest attention.

4. Legislation not formally declared obsolete remains in force. No one should go beyond what has been established in the Constitution on the Liturgy, the instruction *Inter Oecumenici*, and the decrees of the bishops. As for experiments, the Consilium will grant permission for them case by case and in writing, for times and places carefully defined and put under the control of the ecclesiastical authorities. Any other form of presumed permission is declared to be an abuse.

There are, however, two attitudes that are equally harmful to the renewal: undisciplined action and inaction.

5. One of the rediscovered treasures of the Roman Church is concelebration; the latter is not to be regarded as an easy way of overcoming the practical difficulties of individual celebration but must be seen in the light of its true doctrinal value as a manifestation of the unity of the sacrifice, the priesthood, and the entire people of God in the sacred service. Concelebration is worth promoting in cases in which it is truly advantageous for the clergy and the faithful. Care must be taken that it is not practiced at the cost of the faithful by excessively reducing the number of Masses made available to them.

6. It is desirable that in new churches the altars be built to face the people; in existing churches the change is to be brought about gradually.

Temporary altars can be used, provided that they have dignity and beauty.[10]

7. The tabernacle should be given a place that is central, worthy, prominent, and easily visible to those entering the church. In large churches it can be placed in a chapel set aside for the purpose. Artists, under the guidance of the priest, can suggest the best solution for the reservation of the Sacrament, provided it accords with the dignity of the latter.

Some of the solutions proposed or adopted for the placing of the tabernacle on the altar that faces the people are not satisfactory: tabernacles permanently inserted into the altar table or retracted automatically;[11] tabernacles located in front of the altar on a pedestal or on a little altar lower than the altar of celebration; tabernacles built into the wall of the apse or placed on an existing altar, with the celebrant's chair located in front of this.[12]

8. The liturgical renewal has rightly given primacy to the mystery of redemption. But the veneration of the Blessed Virgin Mary and the saints

---

10. The beginning of the liturgical reform was accompanied by a renovation of sacred buildings to make them more expressive of the nature and style of the revised celebrations. In particular, there was a generally felt need of celebrating the Mass on an altar facing the people. The shift, however, brought various drawbacks in its wake: the construction of artificial little altars that lacked dignity, the depreciation of the consecrated main altar, two altars close together, overly hasty adaptations of structures possessing artistic value. The Consilium did not devote any special documents to this problem, but it did bring it up on various occasions, reminding its readers of the respect due to the laws of art, the need of dignity, the need of study in connection with the commission of works of sacred art. In addition, it endeavored to form a mentality through frequent articles and photographs in *Notitiae*, along with about twenty interventions in various situations and various parts of the world from 1965 to 1975.

11. The use of things mechanical also made headlines at the beginning of the liturgical reform. There was the fuss, for example, about the "offertory machine" at Ferrara. This was a machine that allowed the faithful to make a host drop untouched into baskets, which were then taken to the altar at the time of the offertory. It was a clever way of letting the people express their participation and of consecrating as many hosts as would be needed at the celebration, while at the same time safeguarding hygiene. But some journalists discovered the ingenious device and spread word of it; in the process, however, they misrepresented its function and spoke of it as though it were a machine for the automatic distribution of communion. Here again the Consilium had to intervene; it dealt with the matter in general terms in a short piece entitled "Mécanique et liturgie," *Not* 3 (1967) 3–4; *DOL* 38 nos. 443-44.

12. This solution was allowed, provided that there was enough space between tabernacle and chair so that the celebrant did not hide the tabernacle. Guidelines for the tabernacle were given when *Notitiae* was still a duplicated flysheet intended for the use of the members and consultors of the Consilium and of the liturgical commissions. Another question regarding the tabernacle would arise later when various places began to use tabernacles with transparent doors; see "Tabernacolo di vetro," *Not* 7 (1971) 414.

is a logical complement of this mystery and a crown set upon it. There should be a healthy balance in regard to sacred images—an avoidance of both excessive clutter and exaggerated bareness.

9. The liturgical movement is entering a new phase of maturity. It was originally promoted and supported by limited organizations and religious families. Now, however, the Church has taken it over and made it directly dependent on itself. We must adapt to this new situation and collaborate generously with the hierarchy.

Second Letter

The second letter was issued on January 25, 1966, only six months after the first.[13] The fervor that all the Christian communities were bringing to the reform had created further difficulties, especially in practical relations between the promoters of the liturgical movement and the bishops, the Latin language and the vernacular, the *schola cantorum* and popular songs. These were the main points handled in the letter.

1. Every effort must be made to establish a harmonious collaboration between liturgical centers and the hierarchy. Before the Council the centers operated with a certain freedom, and they deserve praise for having brought the liturgy to the attention of the Church. Now, however, they must learn to situate themselves in a new perspective. It is the task of the hierarchy to promote and regulate the liturgy, and the centers that play one or other role in this area must acknowledge the authority of the bishops and collaborate with them. On the other hand, the bishops must know how to make use of the liturgical centers and support and go along with them in their undertakings.

2. It is only right that the Ordinaries should consider the eventual possibility of having some Masses celebrated in Latin in certain churches, especially in large cities and in places much visited by tourists; these celebrations should follow a fixed and published schedule. This will facilitate participation by foreigners and help those who have difficulty in taking part in celebrations using the local vernacular.

3. In bilingual areas the bishops must see to it that each language is respected and that its speakers have celebrations available in their own tongue.

4. Some people think that in the reform the *scholae cantorum* have lost their function; they have therefore abolished them. This is a mistake. If we want the people to sing, they must have the support of a choir, which can on occasion perform pieces proper to it.

---

13. See *Not* 2 (1966) 157–61; *DOL* 32 nos. 419-29.

5. While taking into account local mentalities, traditions, and sensibilities, the music of the Church must retain its sacred character as well as its beauty and dignity, both in its chant and in its sound.[14]

6. An altar facing the people facilitates participation, but it is not indispensable. If one is to be used, several factors must be taken into account, for example the architecture of the church as a whole and of the sanctuary in particular, and the dignity and harmonious arrangement of the elements of the sanctuary area. Special care should be taken with regard to the location of the tabernacle, in accordance with guidelines already given.

7. The final point has to do with the liturgical ministry of women at the altar. In some places such a ministry has been introduced, at times with a somewhat comical effect (female altar-servers wearing surplices). The letter states that according to the legislation presently in force, such a ministry is not allowed.[15]

---

14. The first compositions for liturgical celebrations in the vernacular were beginning to make their way. These were at times banal; at times they echoed the secular musical environment: jazz and beat music, use of such musical instruments as the guitar and drums. Work was still being done on the instruction on sacred music, amid the hostility of traditionalist musicians. This was the first call for consideration of something that needed extensive study.

15. There was nonetheless to be an evolution. Requests came chiefly from communities of women and places where it was not easy to find a layman capable of proclaiming the readings in the vernacular, especially in mission countries. A statement regarding these cases was presented to the Holy Father on April 21, 1966. On June 6 the Secretariat of State replied (No. 73588): "The Holy Father has deigned to decree that this favor may be granted in places where true necessity requires it only for the readings and the leading of the singing; it is to be done outside the sanctuary, by well-known women of adequate years and moral way of life, preferably religious women." Individual concessions were granted in these precise terms. Then the requests became more widespread, and the GIRM made the concession universal but without changing the conditions: no layman available; a suitable woman; office exercised outside the sanctuary (see the GIRM, ed. of 1970, no. 66).

The third instruction (*Liturgicae instaurationes*) of September 5, 1970, no. 5, introduced a further small extension when it said that women could proclaim the readings, the intentions for the prayer of the faithful, and the admonitions from a place from which they could be easily heard with the aid of modern technological means (this was a roundabout way of saying they could go to the lectern). The instruction added that more detailed dispositions regarding place were to be given by the episcopal conferences. In the second edition of the Missal (1975) all the casuistic detail has disappeared, and it is said simply that the episcopal conferences can allow a capable woman to proclaim the readings and the intentions for the prayer of the faithful and can determine in greater detail the place from which this is to be done (no. 70). Thus there was a slow evolution that took in account the varying degrees of maturity and sensibility to be encountered in different places.

Third Letter

This was sent on June 21, 1967, two months after the eighth general meeting of the Consilium and the audience granted by the Holy Father on April 19.[16] The letter reflects the climate in which these two events took place. It mentions at the beginning the Pope's invitation to optimism and hope, since "the first results of the liturgical reform are, in certain respects, truly encvouraging and full of promise." It also mentions the Pope's reminder of the Consilium's responsibility for giving the Church's worship a liturgical form marked by truth, beauty, and spirituality. The Pope had rebuked the detractors of the liturgical reform, but he had also shown concern at manifestations of arbitrariness.

After recalling the recent publication of three important documents—the instructions on sacred music and on worship of the Eucharist and the second instruction on the application of the liturgical Constitution—the Cardinal President asks the close cooperation of the liturgical commissions in making known the legitimate aspirations, needs, and desires of the people of God. He then turns to the following points:

1. *Experiments.* Some of the rites prepared by the study groups of the Consilium have been allowed for experimental use: the catechumenate and funerals of adults. Other rites for experimental use will follow. In order that the experiments may be carried out with the proper guarantees and under uniform direction, it has been decided to give the national liturgical commissions responsibility in this area. It is a sensitive task, and one of the most important entrusted to them, in regard both to the carrying out of the experiments and to the collection of observations and suggestions that will help in preparing the definitive rites.

2. *Arbitrary experiments.* Alongside these legitimate experiments, others are to be found that are entirely arbitrary; they create confusion and are reason for concern. Priests allow themselves to alter liturgical actions and texts according to their personal tastes or the desires of one or the other group of the faithful. The bishops are reminded of their responsibility to put a stop to these innovations that are being introduced under pretext of experimentation and adaptation.

3. *Adaptations.* These are foreseen by the Constitution but must follow the procedure sketched out in it: preparatory work of the experts; approval by the episcopal conference; petition to the Holy See, which determines the modalities of experimentation with the proposed adaptations; and use in specific circumstances for a limited period. It is fitting,

---

16. See *Not* 3 (1967) 289-96; *DOL* 41 nos. 477-86.

however, that the conferences wait until they have in hand the projects now being developed by the Consilium.

4. *Local Church and universal Church.* The sense of the local Church is happily being revived and developed, leading to a better understanding of the liturgical assembly as a visible, efficacious sign of the Church. But this attention to the local Church must not obscure its connection with the universal Church. In an age of intense development of the communications media, when news spreads with astonishing rapidity, no group is isolated. Thus the liturgical celebration, too, has a worldwide dimension. Fidelity or arbitrariness quickly becomes known to all and exerts a positive or negative influence. Each community that celebrates the liturgy of the Church must remain in communion with the entire Church.

5. *Joint commissions.* A single official translation must be prepared for all countries speaking the same language. Joint commissions are therefore to be established, consisting of experts and bishops from all the countries involved. Every text produced by these commissions must be submitted for examination by the bishops, whose right it is to approve it. The observations of the bishops must be considered by the experts in the joint commissions. Each conference is then to send the approved translations to the Consilium. After its confirmation has been received, each conference will decide when to publish the translations.[17]

6. Now that permission has been given to use the vernacular in the Canon of the Mass and in the ordination rites, literal and faithful translations must be prepared. Interim translations of the Canon from existing missalettes are not allowed.[18]

A Letter Never Sent

The events of the subsequent years led to a suspension of the letters to the conferences. The memory of the welcome given to them and the good they did remain, however, as does a sense of nostalgia.

In 1972, as a result of the Cardinal Prefect's visits to Latin America and some countries of Europe, it was thought desirable to send a letter similar to those formerly sent by the president of the Consilium, in order

---

17. The principle of a single translation had already been established in 1964. While awaiting the determination of more detailed norms in an instruction on translations, general criteria were given for the functioning of the joint commissions, criteria that would make it possible to respect the authority of the bishops of each country in approving texts and their publication. But the path of the joint commissions would itself not be an easy one.

18. But in the face of necessity this principle was mitigated in the interim period; see above, p. 108.

214 PART I: THE MAIN STAGES

to take stock of a situation the prefect had encountered almost everywhere.

The first point made was the need for methodical, penetrating, intelligent instruction that would be marked by great faith and love and would be addressed to all categories of persons: children, young people, adults, priests, and religious. It would explain the biblical and liturgical meaning of the various signs, the texts, and the overall structure of the rites.

The letter then moved on to the importance of the liturgical commissions in ensuring the orderly development of a liturgy-based pastoral practice, as well as the importance of translations, adaptation, and creativity.

Next came particular problems caused by some liturgical books: the preparation of particular calendars, national, diocesan, and religious; in the Missal the translation of the antiphons; the distinction between altar book and pulpit book; the translation of Sacred Scripture; and the use of missalettes.

With regard to the Liturgy of the Hours, consideration was given to the request for a different structure and for replacing the patristic readings with readings from modern authors. There was an exhortation to continue the effort of preparing good texts and music for singing. The conferences were urged to set aside special times of the year for prayer intentions (a replacement for the Ember Days); it was emphasized that these intentions should always include prayer for priestly and religious vocations.[19] A final paragraph mentioned some shadows on the scene, namely, the rather frequent abuses on the right and on the left.[20]

All these subjects would continue to vex the path of reform in the years ahead. A timely intervention might perhaps have given helpful correction and guidance. But the planned letter had to be submitted to the third plenary meeting of the Congregation for Divine Worship, where fear and juridical quibbling throttled the initiative. The letter remained in the archives.[21]

---

19. The spirit behind this provision, which was also dear to the heart of Pope Paul VI, who more than once urged it upon Archbishop Bugnini, is recalled in Not 9 (1973) 273; see also 5 (1969) 405.

20. On the one side, there were certain rather widespread abuses; on the other, there was the resistance of Christians saddened and confused by the changes and of others who were nostalgic for the "Missal of St. Pius V" or for Latin. With regard to the latter groups, the letter said: "The best solution seems to be pastoral firmness combined with fraternal understanding and the effort, made by some conferences, to 'catechize' these little groups in a timely way and with all patience." And again: "Patient dialogue and charity have overcome resistances and anxieties." The letter also exhorted bishops to consider with pastoral charity the requests of groups desirous of having celebrations in Latin, especially if these groups are numerous.

21. See above, p. 197.

II. PARTICULAR INTERVENTIONS

The Consilium and the Congregation for Divine Worship engaged in dialogue with the episcopal conferences on many other occasions in order to settle particular points, especially regarding translations, the joint commissions, and the preparation of particular calendars. These will be discussed in the chapters devoted to these matters. I shall dwell here on some interventions called for by special subjects or circumstances.

1. *Inquiries.* Immediately after March 7, 1965, in order to learn how the faithful were in fact receiving the liturgical reform, the Consilium asked for the expert views of the presidents of the liturgical commissions. The first reports were read by the Fathers present at the general meeting of April 26, 1965. Beginning with its second issue, the periodical *Notitiae* published the replies from each country.[22]

In view of the catastrophic picture of the results of the reform as seen by its opponents,[23] a second questionnaire was sent by the Consilium on June 15, 1967. It asked:

1) What are the advantages and disadvantages of the liturgical reform?

2) Has attendance at Mass on Sundays and weekdays increased or decreased?

3) What of participation in the other rites of the liturgical year, especially those of Holy Week, and what of the frequent reception of the sacraments?

4) Is the vernacular an aid to active and conscious participation by the faithful?

5) Do the singing and the common responses favor participation by the faithful?

6) What are the reactions of the faithful especially to the vernacular, adaptations of the sacred space, and simplifications in rites and furnishings?

These questions all referred to points made in the attack by the periodical *Musicae Sacrae Ministerium.* The responses, which were quite specific and often accompanied by detailed statistics,[24] would serve to refute the often unfounded rumors and would at the same time make known the expectations of the people of God and its pastors.

On several occasions the Consilium asked for the views of *all* the bishops, for instance, on the reform and various particular matters dur-

---

22. *Not* 1 (1965), beginning on 109.
23. See above, pp. 168–69.
24. Published in *Not* 4 (1968) 15ff.

ing the first Synod of Bishops, and again on the structure of the Divine Office and on the manner of distributing holy communion.[25]

2. *New anaphoras.* When the three new Canons were published, the Consilium sent the conferences a letter, dated June 2, 1968, "to assist catechesis on the anaphoras of the Mass."[26] It urged the conferences to have confidence in the ongoing work of reform and to cooperate in implementing it in a gradual, orderly way that would take into account the capacity and preparation of the faithful. It renewed the exhortation to wait upon the results of the Consilium's work before venturing upon proposals for adaptation.

The guidelines for a catechesis on the anaphoras singled out the basic points to be made that would help the faithful understand the Eucharistic Prayer: overall meaning, structure and essential parts, reasons for the variety of texts, characteristics of the Roman Rite, suggestions for use.

3. *Music.* Almost all the letters sent by the president of the Consilium mention sacred music. An important point in this area is the Council's recommendation that the faithful also learn to sing some Gregorian chants in Latin. To encourage the heeding of this conciliar wish, the Congregation for Divine Worship, with the consent of the Holy Father, prepared a small volume containing a minimal repertory of Gregorian chants;[27] this was sent to all the bishops of the world at Easter 1974.

The prefect of the Congregation accompanied the Holy Father's gift with a letter[28] in which he emphasized the liturgical role and importance of singing as fostering a more intense expression of the festive, communal, and fraternal dimensions of the celebration. Musicians and poets were urged to continue their efforts to compose popular songs in the vernacular that would be worthy of the praise being offered to God as well as of the liturgical action and the religious realities being expressed.

This new flowering that the Church expects from the liturgical renewal must not, however, lead to forgetfulness of the treasures of the past and, in particular, of Gregorian chant, which has for so many centuries accompanied the celebrations of the Roman Rite, nourished the devotion of the faithful, and reached such a point of perfection that the Council could speak of it as the chant "distinctive of the Roman liturgy" (*SC* 116)

---

25. These several points will be taken up further on.

26. See *Not* 4 (1968) 146–55; *DOL* 244 nos. 1945-63.

27. *Iubilate Deo* (Vatican Polyglot Press, 1964), 11 x 16 cm.; 54 pp., with four plates from liturgical manuscripts in the Vatican Library. The little book has two parts: chants for Mass and various other chants (Eucharistic songs; hymns and antiphons in honor of the Blessed Virgin; the *Te Deum*, etc.).

28. See *Not* 10 (1974) 123–26; *DOL* 523 nos. 4237-42.

and a priceless heritage of faith and art. The knowledge of at least a few chants from this traditional repertory and the preservation of these alongside songs in the vernacular will create a bond of communion between past and present, facilitate participation at international meetings, and lead to an esteem for all artistic values. The bishops are therefore urged to see to it that the faithful learn the Gregorian chants contained in the little book.[29]

4. *Special letters.* The letters thus far mentioned were concerned with topics of interest to the entire Church. But the Consilium also frequently addressed the problems or difficulties of particular Churches. It is not possible here to survey all the Consilium's activity in this area. In implementing the Constitution and the liturgical reform, every nation displays traits shared with other countries but at the same time also has its own road to travel, its own difficulties to overcome, and a development of its own to undergo. Only two letters dealing with particular countries were made public; one was addressed to the Italian Episcopal Conference and the other to the Council of Latin American Episcopal Conferences (CELAM).

The first of these two letters[30] dealt exclusively with the situation of liturgical music in the Italian liturgical renewal. Due to the opposition of some composers and the lack of a worthwhile heritage in this area, liturgical songs in Italian were not being written. As a result, in the beginning all liturgical celebrations involved reading alone, to the great detriment of participation. Repertories of songs were gradually compiled, due chiefly to the initiative of individuals and some bishops. But there was a felt need for a stimulus from an authority which is able to direct, choose, and guide and which will promote the establishment of at least a minimal repertory so that the faithful can join together in singing at national or regional gatherings.

The letter was thus intended to inspire the creation of a new musical patrimony, ensure a minimum of singing at every celebration, and give new status to associations of musicians, the *scholae cantorum*, the *pueri cantores*, and parish organists. To this end it called for the renewal of the St. Cecilia Association[31] in the service of popular liturgical singing. Fi-

---

29. The response of the bishops was everywhere positive and at times even enthusiastic; see G. P., "Iubilate Deo," *Not* 11 (1975) 47ff.

30. The letter was dated February 2, 1968, and took as its starting point the answer to the second questionnaire on the liturgical reform. For the letter see *Not* 4 (1968) 95–98; *DOL* 512 nos. 4198–4206.

31. Despite this invitation, which was inspired by the Pope, the St. Cecilia Association did not greatly change its attitude and even distanced itself from the Consilium and the

nally, the letter also called attention to the need of forming readers and leaders of the assembly and of cultivating a sense of artistic beauty and dignity in both liturgical gesture and liturgical furnishings.[32]

The second letter, addressed to the Council of Latin American Episcopal Conferences, was written after Cardinal Tabera had returned from his trip to Latin America. It singled out the directions to be taken in pursuance of the liturgical renewal.[33] The main point made is that once the new rites and new liturgical rites have been introduced, steps must be taken to help the people to grasp them and understand their spirit. The bishops must inspire and animate the liturgical ministry; to this end they must be familiar with the situations, needs, and requirements of their people and see to their instruction.

Another important point is the establishment of well-organized and effective liturgical commissions. Where lack of personnel makes this unfeasible, recourse can be had to existing interdiocesan organizations. In this situation, however, a specialized personnel must be trained with the help of the Liturgical Institute at Medellín. A sizable body of teachers and students ensures fruitfulness and the ability to face up to the problems of the South American continent.[34]

Relations with the Netherlands is a subject deserving special treatment. The liturgical situation there developed more rapidly than elsewhere, and news coming from the Netherlands sometimes had a deleterious influence on other countries. Only a patient, unremitting dialogue, filled with the spirit of understanding, enabled the bishops to regain responsibility for the liturgy and regulate it with the help of prudent norms and the publication of all the liturgical books.[35]

Congregation for Divine Worship, while also raising some polemical points regarding the reform and the generous efforts of musicians whom the Association did not find acceptable.

32. On the problem of sacred song and new compositions, see P. Damilano, "Nuovi orientamenti della musica liturgica," *Not* 8 (1972) 187; (AB), "Cantate al Signore un nuovo canto," *Not* 11 (1975) 161.

33. Letter of November 8, 1972: *Not* 8 (1972) 365–69; *DOL* 54 nos. 534-37.

34. An earlier letter to the presidents of the episcopal conferences of the Spanish-speaking countries had resolved old difficulties between Spain and the Latin American countries in regard to the translation of the liturgical books. The Holy See (October 29, 1972) allowed Spain and CELAM to proceed independently and gave responsibility for the Latin American countries to the Liturgy Section of CELAM; see *Not* 8 (1972) 38–40.

35. See above, p. 106, on the missions to the Netherlands; instruction on the sacred liturgy, issued by the Dutch episcopate after the second visit to the Netherlands in 1966; "Déclaration de l'Episcopat Néerlandais à propos de la Lettre circulaire sur les Prières eucharistiques" (December 11, 1973), issued after Archbishop Bugnini's third visit: *Not* 10 (1974) 127; see also "Commissio mixta pro interpretatione textuum liturgicorum lingua neerlandica," *Not* 10 (1974) 224.

15

Conferences

From the outset the Consilium sought to form close ties not only with the presidents of the episcopal conferences but with all who were more directly involved with the liturgy. It felt the need of joining forces, agreeing on goals, and working cooperatively. To this end it organized conferences for the various categories.

I. CONFERENCE OF TRANSLATORS OF LITURGICAL BOOKS (NOVEMBER 9-13, 1965)

The first reference to this undertaking was in a note which Cardinal Lercaro sent to the Pope on October 1, 1964, and in which he stated the purposes of such a gathering: "1) to promote a common orientation in the work of translation; 2) to establish some criteria and limits; 3) to group together, under the principal languages, the largest possible number of countries speaking the same tongue; 4) to promote reciprocal help among all those working in the same field."

Regarding the organization and date of the conference, the Cardinal wrote:

> The conference is to be organized by a committee composed of some members [bishops] and consultors of the Consilium, chosen for their competence in the several branches of sacred science that come into play in the undertaking.
>
> The best time for the conference would seem to be March–April 1965, that is, when the [liturgical] commissions are into their work and already have some experience of its demands and difficulties.

The Pope gave consent, but there was not enough time to organize a conference in the spring, and it was put off until the fall.

At their fifth general meeting (April 1965), the Fathers of the Consilium expressed satisfaction with the proposal, discussed its various aspects, and appointed an organizing committee.[1] A new date was set: November 9–13, 1965, during the fourth session of the Ecumenical Council.

The president of the Consilium wrote as follows of the conference to the presidents of the liturgical commissions on April 15, 1965:

> The purpose of the congress is to combine and compare the experiences, difficulties, and ideas of all who are working on the translation of the liturgical books and thereby to establish some general criteria for carrying out the work, especially that of rendering the new liturgical texts in the vernacular.
>
> Only those really "involved" will be able to take part in the conference, that is (a) the presidents of the national commissions or their delegates; (b) the members of the commissions; (c) the scholars who are working on the translations; (d) some parish priests; (e) laypersons (men and women) who are working on the translations; (f) some exegetes and composers.
>
> All these individuals will have to be appointed by the president of the liturgical commission.

The president's letter also outlined the program and urged all to send helpful suggestions and information to the Consilium secretariat.[2]

The conference, which was held under the authority of the Consilium, took place in the Palazzo della Cancelleria. In attendance were 249 experts (69 bishops, 167 priests and religious, 13 laypersons) from 69 countries and five continents, all officially appointed by the presidents of the national liturgical commissions.[3]

Cardinal Lercaro opened the conference with warm greetings: "We all form a single family that is closely united in the mystery of the altar . . . and that has now gathered around, as it were, a single table for study and meditation, so that together we may more confidently carry on the great work we have begun."[4]

The Cardinal spoke of the importance and compelling need for the study and research to which the conference was dedicated. He reminded

---

1. See *Not* 1 (1965) 203–6, 273–76.

2. The approach was taken in order to let the congress retain its spontaneity by freeing it from bureaucratic complications that would only have been a useless burden on it.

3. See the account of the meeting in *Not* 1 (1965) 393–98.

4. See *Le traduzioni dei libri liturgici, Atti del Congresso tenuto a Roma il 9–13 novembre 1965* (Vatican City: Libreria Editrice Vaticana, 1966) 23.

his hearers that the periods following upon councils have been notable for very fervent efforts at renewing and advancing Christian life. What then, he asked, was to be the distinguishing note of the period following upon Vatican II? The answer is the more active, devout, and conscious participation of God's holy people in the liturgy and thus in the authentic and perennial sources of holiness: "The more the faithful enter into the liturgy, the more the life of heroic sanctity will flourish in the Church, especially among the laity."

Another point emphasized by the Cardinal was that the theme of the congress reflected a tricky and sensitive aspect of the liturgical renewal. The actual text, especially in the reformed liturgy, is the basis of a dignified and worthy celebration and of an effective participation by the faithful. Translations must therefore have their basis in the sacred books, the liturgical texts, and venerable tradition. A language must be developed that is modern but not oblivious of tradition. Such a combination is beset with difficult problems because of a lack of experience in this area as well as, at times, a lack of suitable tools. Nonetheless, we must create new liturgical languages that satisfy contemporary requirements, do justice to the special character of peoples, and at the same time are permeated with a sense of the sacred.

The same theme was taken up and developed in the brilliant opening lecture of Bishop Boudon, president of the conference, on the conditions for an authentic and pastoral translation.

There followed seventeen papers by great masters of the international liturgical world, among them Martimort, Pascher, Matéos, Tilmann, Bruylants, Roguet, and Gélineau.

Also of great interest were the reports read at the several forums (one for each language area) on the difficulties encountered by translators of the liturgical books in the various countries.

On November 10, in the Sala Clementina, the Pope gave an audience to the participants, addressing them first in Latin and then in the vernacular (Italian) in order, as he said, "in this context, too, to acknowledge the theme of the congress."

> We fully approve the purpose for holding this meeting. The translation of those texts into the vernacular languages is a matter of such great discernment, importance, and difficulty that it seems achievable only through an exchange of views by all concerned . . . .
>
> The translations published here and there prior to promulgation of the Constitution on the Liturgy had as their purpose to assist the faithful's understanding of the rite celebrated in Latin; they were aids to people untrained in this ancient language. The translations now, however, have be-

come part of the rites themselves; they have become the voice of the Church.[5]

Since the conference was a gathering for study, no *vota* were formulated; the president did, however, summarize the principal points that emerged in the various papers, while repeating some ideas of the Holy Father in his address to the participants.[6]

The principal liturgical books already published in the vernacular were on display in the Sala della Cancelleria. Another exhibition of liturgical books, ranging from the oldest codices of Sacramentaries, Antiphonaries, Breviaries, Lectionaries, Pontificals, and Missals down to the first translations into the vernacular (there was an Italian *Exsultet* from the twelfth century and a Chinese Missal of Paul V) was mounted in the rooms of the Vatican Library and under the auspices of the latter.

The program was to include an evening devoted to popular liturgical songs, Western and Eastern, which were to be performed in one of the Roman churches (San Ignazio or S. Andrea della Valle were suggested) by the national colleges of the city. But the growing hostility of Roman circles opposed to any innovation of liturgical music led to the cancellation of the event, to the great disappointment of the international world, which found certain local attitudes incomprehensible.

II. MEETINGS WITH THE PRESIDENTS
OF THE NATIONAL LITURGICAL COMMISSIONS

There was constant communication with the presidents of the national liturgical commissions. The Consilium decided to hold meetings with them on two occasions when a large number of them were in Rome.

The first took place at Santa Marta on October 26, 1964. This was the initial contact between the Consilium and the presidents. The secretary explained the structure of the Consilium, the organization of its work and its study groups, the anticipated schedule, and the responsibility of the liturgical commissions.

Father Braga explained the recently published instruction *Inter Oecumenici* on the implementation of the Constitution on the Sacred Liturgy. In his address he singled out the innovations it introduced into the celebrations and especially into the Mass. Above all, however, he tried to bring out the spirit of the instruction, the objective realities being high-

---

5. *Ibid.*, 11.
6. *Not* 1 (1965) 395–98; *DOL* 113 nos. 786 and 787.

lighted in the new organization of the rites of Mass (the distinction between the liturgy of the Word and the liturgy of the Eucharist, the specific role of each minister, and so on), and the function of the liturgical commissions.

The meeting was a genuinely enthusiastic one. The bishops felt at home, helped with their concerns, inspired in their work. They voiced a desire to meet again and continue the dialogue.

A second meeting became possible in the following year, on November 17, 1965. Many of those present had taken part in the conference on translation.

After a brief greeting from Cardinal Lercaro, the secretary of the Consilium read a lengthy paper that was meant to stimulate a fraternal dialogue, a valuable and useful exchange of views. The salient points of his communication had to do with the situation of the moment and referred to the problems that had been, or were presently being, studied by the Consilium.

1) *Task of the liturgical commissions.* Their function is not only to watch and see that the decrees of the Holy See are faithfully applied but also and above all to promote a liturgy-based pastoral practice. Many things are left to the initiative of the bishops and their organizations. These have the duty of intervening tactfully and prudently, but also fearlessly when serious abuses are found.

2) *Liturgical centers and periodicals.* There is need for explanation and "catechesis"; to this end the bishops make use of periodicals. These must be dependent on, and obedient to, the hierarchy, even those that previously acted independently because they came into existence through the initiative of some eager individual or some religious body and were supported by the good will and sacrifices of a few. They must now become instruments in the bishops' hands for the apostolate, for pastoral action, and for spiritual conquest.

The periodical *Notitiae* is fully at the disposition of all, and free use may be made of it. Its emphasis is not so much on matters rubrical as on liturgical catechesis, the liturgical spirit at work in the rites, and the liturgical life as a source of Christian life.

Liturgical centers and periodicals are acquiring a new importance. The Pope mentioned this point in his address of November 10:

> Since the whole liturgy is subject to the regulation of the hierarchy, in every nation the individuals, groups, and especially the principal national institutes for the care and promotion of liturgy, as well as all periodicals having the same purpose, should be wholly dependent on the hierarchy.

The competent authority has the right to determine the means and establish the rules for this close relationship.[7]

The reference is to centers that engage in external apostolic activities, such as institutes, schools, liturgical weeks, and, above all, popularizing periodicals. The bishops are to determine the most suitable way of being present to these works through a delegate, a reader, or the appointment of the editor. The Consilium intends to draw up a list of all the periodicals dealing with this area.

3) *A single liturgical text for the language used in most places.* Now that Latin has been abandoned, at least in large measure, unity has given way to a plurality of languages. It is appropriate, however, that speakers of the same language use the same text everywhere. The Consilium has already communicated its thinking on this subject, and it has been well received.[8] Joint commissions have already been established for the main international languages (French, English, Spanish), and it is gratifying to see how these have set to work with good will.

4) *Editions of liturgical books:*

a) Liturgical editions must be marked by dignity. This holds for editions in the vernacular which in the future, like the Latin editions of the past, will be declared "typical" for the various episcopal conferences.

b) A bilingual text—Latin and the vernacular—is obligatory in all editions of the Missal, the Liturgy of the Hours, and the Pontifical. The Latin text is not to be put in an appendix but alongside the vernacular (in two columns or on facing pages) so that clerics can have the Latin before them for purposes of comparison and for use should the need arise.

c) The national liturgical commission is to appoint the commission's official publishers. In countries that already have "publishers to the Holy See," it is preferable to turn to them and make use of their equipment and experience in the effort to produce dignified liturgical editions. The regulations regarding the percentage to be paid to the Holy See for rights over the Latin text remain in force.

d) The commission is to appoint someone responsible for overseeing liturgical editions. Before granting the decree of publication, he must make sure that the edition meets all the requirements of textual integrity and propriety.

e) The commission is to see to it that there is no competition among

---

7. *DOL* 113 no. 789.

8. See the letter to the presidents of the episcopal conferences of countries speaking the same language, October 16, 1964: *Not* 1 (1965) 195–96; *DOL* 108 no. 764.

publishers. Two copies of every publication are to be sent to the Consilium for its archives.[9]

5. *Experiments.* This is the sore spot at the moment. The liturgy is evolving, the old rites still in use display their clashing elements, and people are not patient enough to wait for the new rites. Arbitrary experiments must be prevented. Experiments that the Consilium is able to allow are under the authority of the bishops.[10]

6) *Special Propers.* This area is another that cannot be left to improvisation; it is therefore necessary to show good will and prepare the needed translations, especially for Propers of the Mass.[11]

On these points a useful conversation began among those present, but it turned into a storm of requests addressed to the president and the secretary. From these a series of problems emerged that were in many cases specifically local but were always very interesting. The discussion showed clearly the fervor with which the liturgical renewal was spreading and becoming real almost everywhere among the clergy and the Christian people.

III. RELATIONS WITH THE DIRECTORS OF LITURGICAL PERIODICALS

On the occasion of the publication of the first instruction, the Consilium called all the directors of liturgical periodicals to a meeting in Rome. It realized how important and substantial their collaboration was in the formation of public opinion.

1. *First Meeting*

This took place at Santa Marta on November 13–14, 1964. The purpose of the meeting was expressed in the letter of invitation:
   a) to explain the activity and programs of the Consilium;
   b) to make clear the spirit guiding the liturgical reform;
   c) to strengthen the role of the communications media in the reform;
   d) to establish a better understanding and mutual support among those working in the same field in the same part of the world.

---

9. Anticipated here were some norms that would be contained in the decree on editions of liturgical books; the decree would be published by the Congregation of Rites and the Consilium on January 27, 1966: see *Not* 2 (1966) 172–74; *DOL* 134 nos. 918-29.

10. See the declaration on liturgical experimentation: *Not* 1 (1965) 145; *DOL* 29 nos. 404-5.

11. On June 2 the president of the Consilium had sent to the presidents of the episcopal conferences and the superiors general of religious an instruction on the translation of Propers belonging to dioceses and religious families: *Not* 1 (1965) 197–98; *DOL* 111 nos. 767-75.

After the Cardinal President had greeted the participants and thanked them for coming, the planned reports began:

1) *Report of the secretary.* After expressing disappointment at the absence, for financial reasons, of representatives from the Third World countries, the secretary of the Consilium explained the latter's organization and activity. He then spoke of the following: the preparation of the rites for concelebration and for communion under both kinds (in the experimental stage); the instruction *Inter Oecumenici,* published on September 26; the confirmation of the acts of the episcopal conferences; the difficult and laborious work of translation; editions of the liturgical books in the vernacular, with insistence on these being dignified and beautiful; and, finally, the principle of gradualness in the preparation and application of the liturgical reform. He ended by saying:

> Let there be no rupture, no wall between the Consilium and others working for the same cause with their knowledge and inquiries, their popularization and other activities. Even if all are not materially enrolled in the Consilium organization, all belong to it. You are among our most important collaborators and, as the Cardinal President put it, you are all members of the Consilium family. Journals and periodicals are a valuable and indeed indispensable aid in the restoration of the liturgy, since they deal extensively with questions of a pastoral and liturgical kind and gather the suggestions that are, as it were, stones for the building of this temple of the Lord that is the sacred and divine liturgy.

2) *Collaboration of periodicals in the liturgical reform.* This paper was given by Father Schmidt. After recalling that before the Constitution on the Liturgy came into existence the liturgical periodicals had prepared the ground with the publication of scientific studies and the discussion of pastoral problems, the speaker went on to consider the role of the liturgical press after the conciliar document. There is a profound connection between the liturgical press and the Consilium, if for no other reason than that almost all the consultors and advisors of the Consilium publish in the liturgical periodicals. The problems dealt with by the one are therefore the problems dealt with by the other, and vice versa. This fact also plays a positive part in relations between the center and the periphery. From these general considerations Father Schmidt drew some practical conclusions:

a) After the promulgation of Consilium documents, the press should endeavor to make them known to the Christian people, explaining and presenting them in a favorable light. There may well be elements that at first sight displease and prove disappointing to expectations; the reasons for the solutions adopted must therefore be given.

b) Liturgical formation is still a pressing need. The work begun years ago must be continued. The liturgical reform is not welcomed by all, for it brings change to things people find dear and challenges deep-rooted mentalities and valued traditions. There is need for instruction, guidance, and exhortation.

c) A principal task faced by the new liturgical books is to harmonize tradition and the needs of our day. The latter will not always be familiar to scholars; there is need, therefore, for wide-ranging sociological, religious, and historical analysis. The liturgical press must facilitate contact between liturgical science and the other sciences, between tradition and the contemporary situation.

3) *What do those in charge of the communications media expect from the Consilium?* This subject was discussed by Father Godfrey Diekmann. Because the liturgical reform is so important for the progress of the people of God, they must be kept accurately and completely informed. To this end Father Diekmann made the following suggestions:

a) Good translations in the principal languages should accompany publication of the documents.

b) Abundant explanatory documentation should be provided to show the value of the document being published, the theological and pastoral principles at work in it, its historical evolution, and the fruit hoped for. A commentary by a qualified person and an official of the Consilium would be very welcome.

c) This documentation should be sent to all the communications media and sent directly, not by way of official agencies, in order to avoid the danger of selectivity and delay.

d) It would be very helpful if the press were given advance notice of the publication of a document so that it might prepare public opinion and create an anticipation that will ease the way for the document.

e) In the Consilium itself there should be persons really knowledgeable about the problems and questions of the communications media. The latter can then have recourse to them at any time and receive the needed help. Something similar is required in the national liturgical commissions.[12]

---

12. Although Father Diekmann's suggestions were a bit on the idealistic side, the Consilium kept them in mind and implemented them as far as possible. Especially at the time of the publication of the first documents, before bureaucratic complications began to play a part, an extensive program was prepared for the press: document printed in Latin, translation into the principal languages (a sufficient number of duplicated copies), a press conference, an explanatory article written by the secretary or other qualified person. Then some difficulties hindered ready action: difficulties raised against the translation done in Rome,

4) *Presentation of the instruction* Inter Oecumenici by Father Braga. His address had three parts: the nature and method of the instruction; its most important innovations; collaboration of the directors of liturgical journals to make the instruction effective.

The directors, by reason of their background, were urged to cooperate with the liturgical commissions in forming the clergy, seminarians, and Christian people; in preparing aids (celebrations of the Word of God; schemas for the prayer of the faithful; practical directories for the instruction of Mass servers, ministers, cantors); in explaining the vernacular translations of the texts; and in effecting a coordination with other areas, especially the scriptural, catechetical, musical, and artistic.

2. Second Meeting

This was held concomitantly with the conference of translators on November 14, 1965, at Santa Marta; about eighty persons attended, which was more or less the same number as at the previous year's meeting. The aim of the program was: (1) to bring the participants up to date on the work of the Consilium; (2) to emphasize collaboration in disciplined research and in a prudent response to dangerous experiments that hurt the common cause; (3) to seek the support of the periodicals for Consilium productions that would be published in the near future.

A dialogue followed that was at times animated, "polychromatic," and lively, but never overheated. There was a unanimous request for more information from the Consilium; for informing the press before new rites were promulgated so that articles and studies might be prepared in time; for polling the people through the periodical press so that the rites might be correctly adapted, pastoral, and practical (it was clear that even the directors of periodicals thought that the "workers" of the Consilium were all scholars and ignorant of the pastoral arts).

Cardinal Lercaro presided at the meeting and as usual gave the participants complete freedom to speak, make requests, discuss, and even criticize. At the end he promised all that the Consilium would do everything it could to accept such legitimate requests as were compatible with the regulations governing procedure and secrecy that were imposed on workers in the agencies of the Holy See. He invited all those present to

---

even though by native speakers of the language; captiousness and factionalism on the part of some journalists or other participants in the press conference. The articles prepared by the secretary of the Consilium and later of the SCDW had better luck; they appeared punctually in *L'Osservatore Romano* as each document or liturgical book was promulgated, and were extensively reprinted in other organs of the press.

continue this fruitful, fraternal collaboration by their writing in their periodicals.

3. *Difficulties*

These meetings were very useful for establishing bonds of fraternal collaboration with the liturgical journals. This is not to deny that there were at times different views on the two sides and that the Consilium had to take a sometimes strong position against certain periodicals, whether for proposals that were too advanced and debatable[13] or for hostility to the reform. In particular, an attack launched by Roman composers led to an intervention of the Consilium not long after the second meeting with the editors of periodicals.

The first shot was fired in an editorial of the *Bolletino Ceciliano* entitled "La colpa è tutta dei musicisti!" (It's all the musicians' fault).[14] It was a defense of traditional music and an attack on the promoters of the reform. In support of this outlook, a new journal was started, *Capella Sistina*,[15] which in its very first issue made a direct attack on the Constitution on the Liturgy. Reaction was not long in coming, and a sharp debate ensued that was made even more bitter by the eminence of the persons engaged in it.[16]

On January 25, 1966, the secretary of the Consilium asked the Secretariat of State to send a letter to the editors of Italian periodicals, informing them of the plot that was afoot. The next day an affirmative answer arrived, with some corrections in the Pope's hand. The letter was sent on January 29, 1966, "to the editors of journals dealing with the liturgy, sacred music, and pastoral activity in Italy." It was signed by A. Bugnini, secretary of the Consilium, and read as follows:

> For the purpose of rendering more harmonious and effective the efforts all are making to carry out the liturgical renewal which, in Italy as elsewhere, is now progressing in such a promising and consoling way, I gladly accept the duty of calling certain points to your attention:
> 1. Journals dealing with the sacred liturgy, sacred music, and pastoral care play a very important role in promoting the success of the liturgical

---

13. There was extensive correspondence with, for example, *Paroisse et Liturgie* and the *Rivista de Pastorale liturgica*.

14. *Bollettino Ceciliano*, no. 4 (April 1964) 3–16; see below, p. 886.

15. The first number was that of January–March 1964.

16. Such Italian newspapers and periodicals as *Il Messagero, Il Tempo, Il Borghese, Lo specchio*, and *Candido* took a hand, as did, in private, ecclesiastics and composers who bombarded higher authorities with "memoranda."

renewal. They must therefore faithfully follow the norms set down by the Holy See and the sacred hierarchy.

2. It is therefore desirable that periodicals dealing with liturgical problems develop to a greater extent the exegetical, explanatory, ascetical, and pastoral aspects of the liturgy, while avoiding barren disputes, especially those directly personal in nature, which in the end only confuse clergy and faithful.

3. In interpreting the liturgical Constitution, they are to follow the official documents that explain or implement it. This means chiefly the instruction of September 26, 1964, and the more recent instructions on the language to be used in the Office and the Mass by religious communities (*AAS*, 1965, 1010–13) and on the liturgical formation of clerics (Sacred Congregation for Seminaries, December 25, 1965), as well as the decrees of the Italian Episcopal Conference. It will also help to keep in mind, as sure guides, the responses and documents published in *Notitiae*, the monthly journal of the Consilium.

4. Editors of journals, in particular, are urgently asked to drop any attacks on sacred music and the vernacular and instead devote themselves more fervently to a serious and balanced study of the liturgical Constitution with its great possibilities for pastoral application. They will thus give positive guidance to clergy and faithful for a wise use of the patrimony of the past and a timely development of the same in the approved forms.

It must honestly be said that the request was accepted by the liturgical periodicals, which made an effort to respond to the letter, but not by the musical world.

As a matter of fact—to cite but the most strident example—the editor of *Cappella Sistina*, while professing unqualified fidelity to the norms of the Holy See, filled two editorial pages of the issue following the above-cited letter with a baffling attack on the liturgical renewal. Fortunately, the attack was one-sided and did not last long, since the journal soon ceased publication.

IV. CONFERENCE OF THE SECRETARIES OF THE NATIONAL COMMISSIONS

This meeting, which was organized by the secretariat, was held February 25–26, 1971, on the premises of the Congregation for Divine Worship. Sixteen persons attended, from England, Austria, Portugal, Brazil, Canada, France, Germany, Switzerland, Spain, Hungary, Italy, the Netherlands, and the United States. Secretaries in other countries expressed solidarity but were unable to come, usually for financial reasons.

The occasion for the meeting was the publication of the *Liturgia Horarum*. This was regarded as a major event and one to be displayed in the best possible light. The meeting itself, however, dealt with a much broader range of problems that covered the entire ongoing reform and raised questions regarding the immediate future.

The secretary of the Congregation spoke of the work already accomplished and of the work still to be done, of publications expected shortly, and of the questions of greater importance that were arising in the various countries with regard to the translation of the liturgical books and the progress of the liturgy.

A comparison of ideas and situations in the different countries showed how extensive were both the convergences and the divergences among the peoples making up the universe that is the Church.

Contact among the secretaries was therefore most useful both for the Roman agency that must daily be responsible for promoting the liturgical worship of the Church and for those in attendance, since the latter were here able to become acquainted with one another, some for the first time, and to compare problems.[17]

At the end of the meeting there was a unanimous feeling that it should be repeated at least annually, but with the participation of those who had not been able to come to the first meeting, especially the secretaries from Latin America, Asia, and Africa. This desire, at least as formulated, remained just that—a desire. The meeting in fact was not repeated. There would indeed be such meetings at the continental level, but by the free choice of those involved. In Europe, for example, the secretaries of the national commissions met every two years to deal with their common problems; on two occasions the Congregation was represented by an official.[18] CELAM organized similar meetings for Latin America; ICEL (International Commission on English in the Liturgy) did the same for the commissions of the English-speaking world.

This final kind of meeting, like the others that have been discussed, unfortunately had to be abandoned, despite the fact that it promised to be a powerful force for unity and guidance.[19] The chief reason was the expense involved, which the central administration itself was unable to handle. A further reason was the fact that the Consilium, now that it had been raised to the status of an agency, had to align itself with the other agencies and adopt an attitude in which undertakings of this kind could at best be occasional but never institutionalized.

All these varied meetings were nevertheless a proof of the vitality and fresh energy of the Consilium, which had in a short time succeeded in

---

17. See *Not* 7 (1971) 133.

18. See *Not* 9 (1973) 341; 11 (1975) 249.

19. A second meeting was planned for January 23–25, 1973, but after a discussion of the subjects for the meeting (October 18, 1972), there was no follow-up.

rousing the forces operative in the liturgical sphere and winning the respect even of those who kept their distance and were not well disposed toward the ecclesiastical bureaucracy.

16

Translations

The problem of translation was the first and most troublesome of the liturgical reform. A good many of the Consilium's communications to the episcopal conferences during the opening years of its activity dealt with this matter. In addition to the conference on this subject, which I recalled in the preceding chapter and which was rather a study session, there were many other interventions by the Consilium.

1. *Joint Commissions*

On October 16, 1964, the president of the Consilium wrote to the presidents of those episcopal conferences whose language was one of the most widely used (English, French, Spanish, Italian, Dutch, and German):

> As the centuries-old unity of liturgical language gives way and the various vernaculars are coming into use alongside Latin, we must see to it that the spiritual and pastoral effectiveness of the liturgy is not imperiled. Transition to a new state of things should come about with the deliberateness and prudence required.
>
> The Consilium accordingly wishes to make known its mind on the special issue of vernacular versions in regions using the same language: in these regions uniformity is to be maintained in texts for vernacular celebration of the liturgy.[1]

Above all, this uniformity would make it possible to combine forces and engage in a serious work of translation. The Pope authoritatively

---

1. *Not* 1 (1965) 194–5; *DOL* 108 no. 764.

made this thinking his own when he spoke to the participants in the conference on the translation of liturgical books: "First, it seems right to recall the norm . . . . Especially in countries of a common language, uniformity should be preserved in the liturgical texts, and multiplicity of versions, harmful to gravity and dignity, should be avoided."[2] In order to carry out these directives, joint commissions were established in each of the major language areas, with each of the conferences concerned sending its representatives, both *periti* and bishops.

It was easy enough for the French-speaking[3] and German-speaking[4] countries to set up such a joint commission. The English-speaking countries, too, established an "International Commission on English in the Liturgy" (ICEL) with its headquarters in Washington, D.C., and provided it with a capable staff. There were indeed some difficulties, essentially literary in character, that put England in one camp and the rest of the English-speaking world in another, and for a while the English hierarchy provided its own translations. Eventually, however, an agreement was reached with which all professed themselves satisfied.[5]

When it came to Dutch or, more accurately, the language of some of the Low Countries, things got more difficult. The dioceses of the Netherlands and the Flemish-speaking dioceses of Belgium found collaboration difficult because of certain linguistic peculiarities separating the two areas, but chiefly because of the special liturgical situation in the Netherlands. The Dutch were unwilling to engage in translating the Roman liturgical books but preferred to give rein to local free creativity. After great efforts the work finally received a decisive impulse from the third visit of the secretary of the Congregation for Divine Worship, which had for its chief purpose to promote publication of the liturgical books.[6]

As for Spanish,[7] linguistic differences between Spain and the Latin American countries proved burdensome. Difficulties were raised especially by Argentina, which was going ahead on its own and translating all the pre-reform liturgical books. It was also difficult to secure capable and available people in Latin America. As a result, this part of the world was handed texts that had been almost completely prepared and published in Spain, and it felt a kind of "colonial" dependence in this sphere

---

2. See *Le traduzioni dei libri liturgici* (p. 220, n. 4) 13–14; *DOL* 113 no. 788.

3. See *Not* 1 (1965) 190–91, 364; 11 (1975) 182–85.

4. *Ibid.*, 2 (1966) 190.

5. *Ibid.*, 1 (1965) 308, 339; 2 (1966) 191, 341; 3 (1967) 15, 117; 4 (1968) 128, 355; 5 (1969) 20; 6 (1970) 56, 272; 10 (1974) 21, 348; 11 (1975) 31, 245.

6. *Ibid.*, 10 (1974) 206, 224.

7. *Ibid.*, 2 (1966) 135, 192, 341, 364; 3 (1967) 21; 11 (1975) 68.

as in others. Economic and commercial factors also played a role in the Spanish-speaking world as in the other linguistic areas.

Analogous difficulties arose between Portugal and Brazil when it came to translation into Portuguese. A further factor here was the greater energy and dynamism for change that distinguishes the language of the former colony from that of the mother country.

Outside Italy itself, translation into Italian concerned only a single region of Switzerland—the canton of Ticino, which never voiced any difficulty about accepting the texts prepared in Italy or seeing to some on its own account.

Despite all the efforts made, these difficulties eventually led the Holy See to relax the principle of a single translation for all liturgical texts. The difficulties were real; the diversity of situations was likewise real and could not be overlooked. It was decided that a distinction ought to be made among types of text and that uniformity is more appropriate in texts that are recited or sung by all than in those that are sung or proclaimed by one person. Therefore, first for Portuguese,[8] then for Spanish,[9] and finally for all,[10] it was decided that a single translation is required:

1) for all the parts belonging to the congregation (acclamations, responses, dialogues);

2) for the entire rite of Mass;

3) in the Office, for the psalms, hymns, and *preces* of Lauds and Vespers;

4) for the sacramental formulas.[11]

For all other texts a single translation is recommended but not obligatory.[12]

---

8. November 12, 1968: *Not* 6 (1970) 84.

9. August 5, 1969: *ibid.*

10. See the instruction on translation (January 25, 1969), nos. 41-42, in *Not* 5 (1969) 11-12; *DOL* 123 nos. 878-79. The instruction of October 20, 1969, on the gradual carrying out of the apostolic constitution *Missale Romanum*, no. 4, requires a single translation only for the Ordinary of the Mass and the parts belonging to the congregation; see *Not* 5 (1969) 420; *DOL* 209 no. 1736. The general decree for all languages dates from February 6, 1970: *Not* 6 (1970) 84-85; *DOL* 126 nos. 888-92.

11. The specification of the sacraments is found in a circular letter sent to the Spanish-speaking countries by the Cardinal Prefect of the SCDW on November 20, 1972, in which the parts requiring a uniform translation are listed in detail: *Not* 9 (1973) 70-71; *DOL* 129 nos. 901-3.

12. Another communication (dated October 29, 1971) of the prefect of the SCDW to the Spanish-speaking countries clarifies further the relations between Spain and CELAM. Two distinct entities are recognized; the Latin American countries are advised to follow CELAM; each country is allowed, however, to adopt the books either of CELAM or Spain, as its episcopal conference thinks best. See *Not* 8 (1972) 38-40; *DOL* 128 nos. 894-900.

2. Instruction on the Translation of Liturgical Texts

In order to facilitate the work of translation, the Consilium sent guidelines for the translation of the Roman Canon[13] and of the *Graduale simplex*[14] to the presidents of the episcopal conferences and national liturgical commissions. It was still felt necessary, however, to establish more detailed and complete principles that would apply to every type of translated work. The presidential council entrusted this task to a special study group, which began its work in April 1967[15] and presented its results at the eleventh general meeting of the Consilium (October 1968).

The principles and norms were approved by the Consilium and given to the Holy Father for his consideration. The letter sent to him along with the instruction explained the character of the document. It was said that the norms were not binding in the same degree as a liturgical book; they were rather a working tool that brought together in a systematic form the general and particular regulations issued by the Consilium during the previous five years.

The Holy Father studied the text carefully. The original was written in French; the secretariat of the Consilium had then translated it into the various languages. The Pope received the Italian version. The translation was not first-rate, and the typing was rather poor due to haste. As a result, the Pope made corrections not only of the substance but of the language and style, and kindly listed all the errors in the typing, thus serving as a proofreader. A text so extensively corrected by a Pope had never been seen before—forty-seven notations in eleven pages.[16] There were even a few that were facetious—something we do not associate with the papal style.

On December 29, 1968, the Pope wrote on the file: "Seen. A bit long; there are a few revisions, but it can be issued." This was followed by a note to the secretary of the Consilium.

The document was thus published under the aegis of the Consilium, in French, on January 25, 1969, with the title "Instruction on the translation of liturgical texts for celebrations with a congregation."[17]

---

13. August 10, 1967: *Not* 3 (1967) 326; *DOL* 118 nos. 820-25.

14. January 23, 1968: *Not* 4 (1968) 10; *DOL* 120 nos. 831-34.

15. See above, p. 167.

16. The Pope asked that the title be changed from "Norms" to "Instruction." In no. 5 the final words, "and the people, through the Spirit in the Church, answer their Lord," were added by the Pope (*DOL* 123 no. 842).

17. Text in *Not* 5 (1969) 3-12; *DOL* 123 nos. 838-80. There is no Latin version of the document, nor was the instruction published in the *Acta Apostolicae Sedis*.

The instruction has forty-three numbers, which are divided into an introduction and three main sections. The purpose of the document is stated in no. 3: "Although these [liturgical] translations are the responsibility of the competent territorial authority of each country, it seems desirable to observe common principles of procedure, especially for texts of major importance, in order to make confirmation by the Apostolic See easier and to achieve greater unity of practice."

1) *General principles*

A liturgical text is a medium of spoken communication, but to the believers who celebrate the liturgy, the word is itself a mystery: Christ speaks to his people, and the people respond to their Lord. Moreover, when they speak, the Church speaks: "Liturgical translations have become . . . the voice of the Church" (no. 6). In liturgical communication three points must be considered:

a) *What is being said* in the original text. Translators must identify the content of the message and give it a new form that is both accurate and agreeable. They must apply the scientific methods of textual and literary criticism that the experts have developed.[18]

b) *The addressee* of the text. The language used must be accessible to the majority of the faithful, including children and uneducated folk. It must not, however, be "common" in the bad sense but must be beyond blame from the literary standpoint.[19]

c) *The manner and form of expression* are integral elements in oral communication. The literary genre of any text depends on the nature of the ritual action. It is one thing to utter an acclamation, another to offer a petition or proclaim or read or sing.

2) *Particular considerations*

The instruction analyzes some concrete cases from Sacred Scripture or the liturgical books in order to show how the principles laid down are

---

18. The instruction is here saying that translations should not always be word for word, since this can obscure the overall sense of the message. In Latin an accumulation of words reinforces the meaning, as, for example, the series "ratam, rationabilem, acceptabilemque" in the Roman Canon; in modern languages, on the other hand, such a use of three adjectives may have the opposite effect. In his observations the Pope warned against "arbitrary and subjective manipulations" of the original and gave a "humorous example: the translation of 'mea culpa' by a modern man of letters who follows the principles set down: 'It was I; yes, it was I; there is nothing more to say.' "

19. Note of the Holy Father: "The Italian translation of the Mass is not quite perfect when measured by this standard (*dovunque* instead of *dappertutto, mai* instead of *non mai,* and so on)."

to be concretely applied. It specifies that the euchological formulas for the sacraments, consecratory prayers, anaphoras, prefaces, exorcisms, and the prayers accompanying actions (imposition of hands, anointings, signs of the cross) must be translated integrally and faithfully, without variations, omissions, or insertions.

A freer translation is acceptable for the presidential prayers of the Mass, as is their amplification, since the meaning is expressed with excessive succinctness in the Latin text. Other texts should be adapted to fit their genre: singing, acclamations, dialogue.

3) *Committees for translating*

The third part of the instruction deals with organizing the work of translation at the national or international level. Task forces are to be formed that comprise experts in the various disciplines. Before a translation is definitively approved, there should be a period of experimentation.[20]

For countries using the same language, the translations are to be done by a "mixed" or joint commission. But the texts intended for several countries must be responsive to the needs and mentality of each country; each conference must therefore have time to study the text and point out needed corrections. If it is not possible to produce a single text that is acceptable to all, the conferences that have special linguistic needs may modify the base text, but they should use suitable devices for calling attention to these variants.[21]

The instruction ends with this extraordinary expression of openness (no. 43):

> Texts translated from another language are clearly not sufficient for the celebration of a fully renewed liturgy. The creation of new texts will be necessary. But translation of texts transmitted through the tradition of the Church is the best school and discipline for the creation of new texts so "that any new forms adopted should in some way grow organically from forms already in existence" (SC art. 23).[22]

---

20. The final sentence of no. 40: "Otherwise, it [the authority] should give the task to a new committee which is more suitable, but also composed of qualified people," were added by the Pope.

21. There are, however, texts that ought to be completely identical; the Consilium was to list these in detail.

22. Nor is the statement to be interpreted as incidental, especially since it had originally been preceded by another number which spoke of the need for a "periodic" revision of the texts but which was deleted by the Pope with the marginal notation: "Does this need saying?"

3. *Interim Translations*

By pointing out that translations ought to be tested before being definitively approved, the instruction on translation was in effect allowing interim translations. The Consilium's position caused puzzlement and protest in some circles; some conferences even forbade "interim" translations.[23]

The Consilium allowed them for the following reasons:[24]

1) Revision, study, and agreement take a good deal of time. In order not to impose a lengthy, compulsory, and impatient wait on the clergy and, at the same time, not to hinder the work of revision, the bishops asked that interim translations be allowed.

2) Interim translations make it possible:

a) to determine, on the basis of wide consultation, whether a text that seems complete, crystal clear, and literarily unexceptionable on the work table is equally so in practice (in use, in being understood by the people, in being easily delivered);

b) to prevent, in case the official publication is unavoidably delayed, the proliferation on every side of texts, translations, and experiments that would afford the press a basis for speculation and scandalmongering and give rise to endless criticism and complaint, thus causing a great deal of spiritual distress;

c) to advance the preparation of the faithful, which is so necessary and which all the documents of the reform emphasize.

The prolonged wait that some regions had to endure in connection, for example, with the Eucharistic Prayers, sometimes caused difficulties for zealous priests who had quickly begun to instruct the faithful in the reform; on the other hand, the delay caused others to postpone any pastoral action, and so they found themselves unprepared when the new texts did finally arrive. An interim translation prepared by the national liturgical commission was thus an aid both to pastoral government and to the legitimate needs and aspirations of the clergy.

Experience showed the validity of this approach. Almost all the conferences regarded it as a real blessing, because the interim texts roused interest and prepared public opinion—and, even more, the souls of the faithful—for the introduction of the definitive texts.

The Consilium, however, was also concerned that the interim translations be dignified and accurate and that they not remain indefinitely in use. It requested the approval of the Holy See for them, since they

---

23. This was the course taken by, for example, the Italian Episcopal Conference.
24. See the article of A. Bugnini in *Settimana del clero*, no. 38 (October 5, 1968).

were texts for official public use in liturgical celebrations. It was thought that the interim translations would be needed for from six months to a year, except for special cases that would be examined as they arose.[25]

4. *Integrity of the Liturgical Books*

Faced with the riches of the revised liturgical books, which contain extensive instructions and a wide choice of biblical and euchological texts, the temptation to reduce the content of the translations and keep only the indispensable minimum was strong, at least in some countries. Various Roman interventions insisted on the necessity of integral translations: the vernacular liturgical books must contain everything found in the Latin typical edition.[26] More particularly it was explained that:

a) The two general instructions, of the Missal and the Liturgy of the Hours, and the doctrinal, pastoral, and rubrical introduction to each rite must be translated; otherwise there is no way of grasping the spirit behind the reformed rites.

b) All the rubrics must be included; they may be amplified but not reduced. They are a necessary help both to a correct celebration and to an understanding of the structure of the rites.

c) The appendix to the Missal may not be printed as a separate booklet but must be included in the Missal so that it can be easily found and used by those unfamiliar with the vernacular of a given Missal. It must not be translated, for this would defeat the purpose for which it is required.

d) The hymns, responsories, and antiphons of the four weeks of the Psalter belong to the structure of the revised Office and must be translated in their entirety. Other optional texts may be put in an appendix.

e) The texts offered for optional use that are found in all the new liturgical books should be included in the vernacular editions, for they are one of the riches produced by the reform.

f) The printed book must contain the declaration of its agreement with the Latin typical edition.[27]

g) All the liturgical books, and especially the Missal, must include the melodies for the celebrant and ministers. They are to be included in the body of the Missal and not in a separate booklet, unless the edition of

---

25. The declaration on interim translations is in *Not* 5 (1969) 68; *DOL* 124 nos. 881-83.

26. Declaration on the translation of new liturgical texts: *Not* 5 (1969) 133; *DOL* 125 nos. 884-87.

27. *Not* 9 (1973) 153–54.

the Missal is one intended for several countries that have different musical traditions.[28]

5. *Translation of the Sacramental Formulas*

Meanwhile difficulties arose that were to make even more arduous the already demanding and complicated work of translation. On October 11, 1972, eight members of the International Theological Commission wrote directly to the Pope of their concern "for the unity and integrity of the Catholic faith," which was being imperiled by certain translations they regarded as "inadequate and even seriously defective on essential points of the Catholic faith." The letter also cast doubt on the operation of the Congregation for Divine Worship, which, it claimed, had relied too much on local authorities and had not carried out the revision with the required strictness.

While the dispute raged between these theologians and the Congregations for the Doctrine of the Faith and for Divine Worship,[29] another "incident" worsened the situation, namely, the challenges to the English translation of the sacramental formula for confirmation, which had been approved by the Congregation for the Doctrine of the Faith and confirmed by the Congregation for Divine Worship. The translation was charged with departing too much from the Latin original. Thus began a long and laborious process that after years of toil, consultations, and alternative texts ended in the adoption of the initial, already approved formula.

Meanwhile, the Congregation for the Doctrine of the Faith, which was itself now being challenged, stated on May 23, 1973, that it was simply granting a *nihil obstat*; it also insisted that

> normally a literal translation of a formula is required that follows the Latin even in sentence structure. If this is absolutely impossible either for lack of a term that corresponds exactly to the Latin or because of difficulty in structuring the formula according to the genius of the vernacular in ques-

---

28. SCDW, Note on the music for inclusion in vernacular editions of the Roman Missal (May 1975): *Not* 11 (1975) 129–32; *DOL* 538 nos. 4811-16.

29. The letter was given to the Pope on October 25. The next day the Cardinal Secretary of State passed it on to the SCDW (No. 220575). The Congregation saw in it an underhand maneuver, a lack of the spirit of cooperation, a set of baseless accusations, and a recourse to a superior without having first inquired of those being accused. It therefore wrote a rather haughty letter to the eight signers (January 19, 1973), reminding them, among other things, that liturgical abuses were not the only ones around and that they perhaps originated in turn in abuses in doctrinal and moral theology. It is not hard to see that the Congregation's action displeased some and caused hard feelings.

tion, then stylistic changes are allowed, provided always that the substantial content of the formula is maintained.

On July 20, 1973, the Secretariat of State (No. 237.808), while deciding that the formula was to be restudied, also transmitted a decision of the Holy Father: "In the future it will be well to reserve to the Pope the approval of the liturgical formulas for the sacraments." The Congregation for Divine Worship communicated this decision to the presidents of the episcopal conferences[30] and also set down some regulations:[31]

1) Translations of the sacramental forms into the principal modern languages (English, French, German, Spanish, Dutch, Italian, Portuguese) will be prepared by the Congregation for Divine Worship, in agreement with the episcopal conferences concerned.

2) The vernacular forms must not only be completely correct theologically but must also agree fully with the Latin text that has been prepared with the greatest care by the competent Roman agencies.

3) For languages other than the principal ones mentioned, the translation will be prepared by the liturgical commissions. The episcopal conferences, however, after approving it, must submit it to the Congregation for Divine Worship for its confirmation. The submitted translation is to be accompanied by explanations of each word in a language used internationally. If the translation is not literal, the reasons for the changes must be explained.

The decision was not well received. Most saw it as derogating from the right of the conferences to approve vernacular liturgical texts. A commentary in *Notitiae* sought to dissipate these suspicions and restore trust.[32] It stated in strong terms that the dialogue between the Congregation and the conferences would continue without interruption and that the Congregation would make no decisions without the collaboration and assent of the bishops.

This new decree greatly retarded the process for the approval of formulas. The review conducted by the Secretariat of State on behalf of the

---

30. Circular letter to the presidents of the episcopal conferences on the translation of the forms of the sacraments: *Not* 11 (1973) 37-38; *DOL* 130 nos. 904-8.

31. These regulations repeat those already given to Archbishop Bugnini by the Congregation for the Doctrine of the Faith on August 2, 1973: "In the case of languages with which people in Rome are presumably unfamiliar, the liturgical commissions in question must provide accurate translations in more accessible languages and indicate whether the translation of the essential formulas is not literal and what the reasons are for the departure from the Latin text. Only under these conditions will this agency be in a position to pass a doctrinal judgment that can be transmitted to the Congregation for Divine Worship, which will then consider asking the approval of the Holy See."

32. *Not* 11 (1974) 39.

Holy Father was finicking and did not consistently follow the same criteria, these being sometimes excessively strict, sometimes mild. The Congregation for Divine Worship had to act as a buffer between the Secretariat of State, with its demands, and the conferences; it had to send texts and then send them again with new criteria added, not always with success. The history of the approval of some sacramental forms is a long one, and not always one to be proud of.

On the other hand, there is an undeniable advantage in careful supervision when this is in the hands of competent persons. The objective sensitivity of the subject matter made such attention desirable. But the process was not an easy one. The Congregation for Divine Worship prepared a new letter on the question, with the intention of further clarifying the precise juridical procedure to be followed in the submission and approval of the texts of the sacramental formulas. The process was frequently hindered by a failure to observe these formalities. This letter, revised over and over again, was finally published by the Congregations for the Sacraments and for Divine Worship, with the addition of a restrictive introduction on the kinds of language to be accepted into the liturgy.[33]

The same preoccupation with doctrinal exactitude inspired the declaration of the Congregation for the Doctrine of the Faith on the meaning to be assigned to translations of the sacramental formulas.[34] After reminding its readers that the translation of a sacramental formula must faithfully reflect the original Latin text but that it may at times appear to depart from the Latin because of the exigencies of a given vernacular, the Congregation states that in case of doubt the vernacular text is to be interpreted in light of the meaning of the Latin.

This declaration was likewise not well received in the liturgical world. It seemed to downgrade vernacular liturgical texts, as though they were

---

33. The letter on the use of the vernacular in the liturgy was dated June 5, 1976: *Not* 12 (1976) 300–302; *DOL* 133 nos. 911-17. It was in this context, too, that the problem of "dialects" arose. It is obvious that the dialectal idioms of a language cannot have a right to acceptance in the liturgy. Here again there was some exaggeration by speakers of dialects. On the other hand, there are indeed minorities that have a language of their own with its literature, grammar, and published works. It is not always easy to distinguish clearly between a language and a dialect. Even more serious, however, is the problem of new mission lands. In many places, at least as long as the majority of the population have not received an elementary schooling, recourse must be had to tribal linguistic expressions. For this reason, at the beginning of the reform many such expressions were accepted into liturgical use by the bishops. The letter of June 5, 1976, calls for some centralization, but it also accepts the decisions of the bishops as valid.

34. January 25, 1974: *Not* 10 (1974) 395; *DOL* 131 nos. 909-10.

incapable of expressing theological concepts with the same accuracy and completeness as Latin. It also seemed to have forgotten the statement of Pope Paul VI that when the vernaculars are taken into the liturgy, they too become "the voice of the Church."

For this reason the commentary in *Notitiae* carefully defined the scope of the declaration by stating that the spoken languages share the status of Latin as true and proper liturgical languages. "The purpose of the declaration is to ensure the identity of the sacramental sign amid a variety of forms and linguistic peculiarities."[35]

6. Publication of Liturgical Books

The publication of liturgical books was also the subject of various interventions.

Competent authority

The Congregation for the Doctrine of the Faith tackled the subject in a decree of March 19, 1975, from which the following regulations emerge:[36]

1) Liturgical books can be published in Latin only with the consent of the Holy See. The edition must give the name of the Ordinary of the place, who guarantees "conformity to the approved edition." The episcopal conferences can entrust this responsibility to the liturgical commissions.

2) Liturgical books in the vernacular are to be promulgated by the president of the conference after confirmation by the Holy See. The vernacular edition is the "typical" edition and must include the decree of promulgation, which indicates the date on which use of the book can begin and the date and protocol number of the decree of confirmation by the Holy See. If the confirmation is an interim one, this too must be explicitly stated.

3) Diocesan and religious Propers, whether in Latin or in the vernacular, are published after confirmation by the Holy See and with the permission of the Ordinary. The decree of confirmation by the Holy See must

---

35. *Not* 10 (1974) 397. The commentary was by Benoît Duroux, O.P., a staff member of the Congregation for the Doctrine of the Faith who was assigned to handle problems of a liturgical kind.

36. Decree *Ecclesiae Pastorum* on the vigilance of bishops with regard to books: *AAS* 67 (1975) 281–84; *Not* 11 (1975) 99–100 (excerpt); *DOL* 140 nos. 935-37 (excerpt). The guidelines as cited here are to be found more in the commentary than in the text of the decree, which is rather vague. It seems that between the time when the document was drafted and the time of its publication, some years passed during which liturgical legislation became more detailed.

be included, as must the Ordinary's statement that the text agrees with the original.

4) Vernacular editions that follow the typical edition and are for use either on the altar or by the faithful can be published with the permission of the episcopal conference to which the translation belongs. This permission, as well as the assurance of the Ordinary of the place in which the book is printed that it agrees with the original, is to be stated.

5) Prayer books for private use can also be published only with permission from the local Ordinary.

Ownership

In and of themselves, liturgical books are juridically a form of international laws and as such cannot be claimed as literary property. They are in fact considered to be in the same class as legislative documents. But the Holy See has always defended their inviolability with special regulations and has claimed ownership of the Latin liturgical books, in order, among other things, to safeguard their dignity and proper appearance. Once the liturgy was put into the vernaculars, it became necessary to bring things up to date in this area. The Congregation of Rites, in agreement with the Consilium and the Administration of the Patrimony of the Holy See, did so in a decree on January 27, 1966.[37]

1) Typical editions. The Latin falls under the authority of the Holy See and is its property; the vernacular belongs to the conference of bishops.

2) Publishers. In each country the national conference is to decide on the publishers of liturgical books; the latter are to follow the established norms without exception and must see to it that their publications are beautiful and easy to handle.

3) On the financial side, publishers are to reach timely agreements with the conference of bishops for the vernacular text and with the Administration of the Patrimony of the Holy See for the Latin text.[38]

4) Conformity with the typical edition, whether for the Latin text or for the vernacular text, must be declared by the Ordinary.

Closely connected with the question of ownership is the problem of the author or authors of the translations and of the new liturgical texts. In a semi-official declaration the Congregation for Divine Worship stated

---

37. SCR, decree on editions of liturgical books: *Not* 2 (1966) 169–71; *DOL* 134 nos. 918-29.

38. This regulation worked out as might be expected: some conferences were accurate and faithful in their accounts, others were less so. For this reason, the SCDW wrote a letter dropping the percentage due to the Holy See and asking instead for a one-time contribution to the expenses involved in the work of reform.

what the Consilium had on various occasions constantly laid down as
its own principle that the translations and new liturgical texts should remain anonymous. The names of the authors are not to be given in printed
liturgical books.[39]

Bilingual liturgical books

The instruction of September 26, 1964, had decreed that Missals and
Breviaries in the vernacular must also contain the Latin text. The same
regulation was repeated in the decree, mentioned above, on the publication of liturgical books.[40]

The Secretariat of State, which had perhaps been informed of failures
to comply, asked the Consilium on July 13, 1967, to issue a new document stating the principle that "Missals, whether for weekdays or for
Sundays, must always have the Latin text alongside the vernacular translation, though the Latin may be printed in a smaller type." As a result
of this letter, the regulation was repeated in the letter to the presidents
of the episcopal conferences on the translation of the Roman Canon.[41]

This principle, valid in itself, came up against enormous difficulties:
the resultant excessive size of the liturgical books; technical problems,
especially in certain countries that do not use Latin characters in printing. In these cases the Latin text ended up being printed illegibly. The
Holy Father therefore dispensed from the original principle and decided
simply that an appendix to the vernacular Missal should contain a section in Latin that would include the Ordinary of the Mass, the Eucharistic Prayers and their prefaces, and some Mass formularies for the liturgical
seasons and for various occasions.

A communication to the presidents of the episcopal conferences urged
that all churches should possess a copy of the Missal in Latin, and all
sanctuaries the Latin texts of Masses proper to the place.[42]

---

39. *Not* 6 (1970) 153; *DOL* 139 no. 934.

40. See SCR, instruction *Inter Oecumenici,* nos. 57 and 98 (*DOL* 23 nos. 349 and 390);
SCR, decree on editions of liturgical books, no. 5 (*DOL* 134 no. 923). Furthermore, the decrees
of confirmation issued by the Consilium always ended with a reminder to print the Latin
text along with the vernacular.

41. August 10, 1967, no. 5: *Not* 3 (1967) 327; *DOL* 118 no. 825.

42. November 10, 1969: *Not* 5 (1969) 442–57; *DOL* 210 nos. 1753-56. This communication
was accompanied by a booklet containing the Mass texts to be included in the appendix.
These were also printed by the Libreria Editrice Vaticana in a volume, several times updated, that sold well. It proved handy and useful especially for priests who were traveling:
Missale parvum ad usum sacerdotis itinerantis (Vatican Polyglot Press, 1971ff. 174 pp.).

17

Notitiae

As the structure of the Consilium gradually became more complex and as the agency became more organized and turned into an extensive "family," the need was felt of promoting unity by keeping the various parts informed of its internal life and the progress of its work. Alongside the drafts for study (the schemas), other papers were gradually issued as means of communication: *Quaestiones tractandae*, on the problems to be discussed outside the setting of the study groups; *Relationes*, intended only for members and consultors and having for their primary purpose to report on the meetings, but also conveying information on the internal life of the agency[1]; *Res Secretariae*, for general communications and the acts of the secretariat, among which the secretary's reports on the general meetings were of special interest; and, finally, *Notitiae*.

Like the others mentioned, *Notitiae* consisted originally of duplicated sheets sent to the members and consultors and also to the entire "peripheral" family, namely, those involved in the liturgical renewal, especially the presidents of the liturgical commissions and the editors of periodicals. The first number came out on December 10, 1964; the third and final number came out on March 13, 1965, and was of special interest, since it contained a short practical treatment of adaptation in the sanctuary and, in particular, of solutions, some good, some not to be followed, of the problem of locating the tabernacle.

In addition to information on the agency's work, *Notitiae* provided answers to questions asked of the Consilium, various kinds of data, and interpretations of points in the liturgical Constitution and later documents.

---

1. *Relationes* is to be regarded as the direct predecessor of *Notitiae*. It had four issues; the last, dated December 4, 1964, already had *Notitiae* as a subtitle.

Its value became clear when the first instruction (*Inter Oecumenici*) was published. These unassuming pages offered guidelines of a semi-official kind, answered difficulties commonly felt to be of greater importance, and provided guidance in the application of the reform. They proved to be both interesting and needed. At the meeting in October 1964, the editors of liturgical and pastoral periodicals asked that they be made available to the public.

Meanwhile, on March 4, 1965, Cardinal Cicognani, Secretary of State, asked the Consilium to keep the papal representatives informed of communications sent to the bishops. The presidents of the episcopal conferences and liturgical commission made a similar request for information on several occasions. It was motivated not only by a legitimate desire to be kept *au courant* with the reform but also by a need for direction in making their decisions.

It was thought, then, that the simplest and easiest way of conveying the desired information would be a periodical containing the guidelines, recommendations, and undertakings of the Consilium and the Holy See. The Cardinal Prefect presented the suggestion to the Holy Father during the audience of March 16, 1965. The Pope expressed enthusiasm for the project, saying: "A splendid idea! But the review, even if modest in size, must be perfect in its typography and accuracy."

The purpose of the new bulletin was stated in the first printed issue, which came out in April 1965:

1) to support the internal life of the Consilium;

2) to convey information about the activities of the Consilium to the national and diocesan liturgical commissions, the liturgical centers, and all those whose study, action, words, and writings were advancing the liturgical apostolate;

3) to let liturgical and pastoral periodicals know about the progress of the liturgical reform;

4) to announce and explain liturgical documents emanating from the Church's authorities, especially the Sacred Congregation of Rites;

5) to follow and support liturgical activity throughout the Church, call attention to undertakings of a more universal scope, provide tools, and keep the readers informed of innovations in the area of liturgy.

Thus, as its very title indicates, the new periodical was concerned with information rather than scholarship and formation. The same purpose also emerged clearly from the first printed issue, which was entirely devoted to a summary of the decrees of the episcopal conferences that had been confirmed by the Consilium from April 25, 1964, to April 13, 1965. Here an immense amount of work was presented in summary form in

96 pages; the figures show the extent of the coverage: 87 episcopal conferences, 121 countries, 187 decrees, 205 languages allowed into the liturgy, plus 29 decrees for regions or dioceses and 11 for religious families.[2]

From that time on, the periodical followed the work of reform step by step, reporting documents of the Holy See and informing readers about the work of the Consilium's general meetings and study groups, internal events (appointments, assignments, deaths, etc.), as well as the work of the national liturgical commissions. At times there were reports on the more limited documents of a particular conference or commission when these dealt with problems that might well be of interest to other regions or serve as models or provide suggestions. Although scholarship was not the periodical's aim, it did occasionally publish studies on one or another point when these served to throw light on especially important aspects of the reform. In particular, the replies to questions, though explicitly "unofficial,"[3] ended up being taken as authoritative; they were reprinted in journals and contributed not a little to creating a certain uniformity of interpretation that was of value to all. This was, in fact, the purpose the Consilium hoped to accomplish.

The volumes of *Notitiae* will be an inexhaustible source of information on the history of the postconciliar liturgical reform, with regard both to the activity of the central agencies of the Church and to the application of the reform in the local Churches, although the latter information can obviously not be taken as complete. Of special value are the reports that the Consilium asked the individual episcopal conferences to supply on the beginnings of the liturgical reform and its progress; these were published in 1965 and 1967. They take the pulse of the Church, as it were, in the area of liturgy and at the same time make the voice of the periphery heard with its desires, aspirations, and expectations.

The Pope himself, who had favored the undertaking and was the periodical's first eager reader, did not fail to point out its merits, not only in his letters to the Secretariat of State in response to the annual presentation of the bound volume to him but also in an address to the Consilium on October 13, 1966:

> We note with pleasure that your brief but valuable commentaries, published in *Notitiae*, are already fulfilling a needed function. This small collection of commentaries has value for another reason, for which we gladly

---

2. See *Not* 1 (1965) 96.

3. The heading "Documentorum explanatio" was preceded by this note: "Solutions offered are not official but simply provide guidance. Official replies, if needed, will be issued by the competent authority in the *Acta Apostolicae Sedis.*"

honor the Consilium: the spread throughout the Church of information and new points related to liturgical practice, thus serving to influence others by good example and to encourage at once a legitimate variety in ways of liturgical expression and a unity in essentials that we must always treasure in the Church's liturgical life.[4]

The information was given openly and straightforwardly, but the periodical did not fail to call attention, as need arose, to deviations or incorrect interpretations of the renewal. The periodical's manner was such that it would later win the nickname "the open Congregation" for the Congregation for Divine Worship.

The Consilium's example was immediately followed. Within the Curia imitations quickly arose in the form of other periodicals with very similar titles: the *Nuntius* of the Congregation for the Doctrine of the Faith, although only one issue appeared and nothing more was heard of the venture; the *Information Service* of the Secretariat for Christian Unity; the *Communicationes* of the Pontifical Commission for the Revision of the Code of Canon Law; and the *Nuntia* of the Pontifical Commission for the Code of Oriental Canon Law. Abroad, too, the newly organized liturgical commissions also began publication of their own bulletins, often modest in size but very useful at the national level.

Everything in *Notitiae* that dealt with the activity of the Consilium and the Congregation for Divine Worship, as well as with the early days of the Congregation for the Sacraments and Divine Worship, is listed in the general indexes.[5]

CONCOMITANT UNDERTAKINGS

The Consilium and later the Congregation for Divine Worship had always been keenly desirous of providing the liturgical reform with a series of scientific, pastoral, and spiritual studies that would lead to a better understanding of the new rites and help clergy and faithful to absorb the riches of the renewal in a more than superficial way. The Holy Father had the same desire, and on various occasions exhorted the secretary to such an undertaking. He would say: "You've done a splendid work; the liturgical reform is the Church's delight. The formulas old and new, the pastoral instructions, the renewed rites, and the rubrics form a priceless patrimony. It would be a fine thing if the same *periti* who worked on the

---

4. *DOL* 84 no. 634 (par. 2).

5. *Not* no. 113 (1975): *Indices generales annorum 1965–1975* (= Vols. 1–10) (Vatican City, 1976. 241 pp.). The volume is divided into three sections: acts of the Holy See; decrees, confirmations, concessions; alphabetical index of names and topics. The volume was prepared by the SCDW and published by the "divine worship section" of the SCSDW.

reform would write some good commentaries for popular consumption, in which they would not only describe the historical, juridical, and structural aspects but also show the spirit at work in the liturgical reform and bring out the ascetical and pastoral value of the renewal."

The suggestions were good and wide-ranging, but for various reasons not much could be done. There were, however, some productions that deserve to be mentioned.

a) *"Documenti e sussidi di* Notitiae"

This collection was planned almost as soon as the periodical began to appear and the reform was in its first stage. Five volumes varying in kind and enduring value were published:

—*Verso la riforma liturgica,* edited by A. Bugnini (Vatican City, 1965; 205 pp.). This was gotten together in a few days' time at the wish of the Holy Father, who wanted to make a gift of it to the Roman clergy during his annual meeting with the Lenten preachers in 1965.

—*De oratione communi seu fidelium* (Vatican City, 1966; 182 pp.). The purpose of this volume was to educate readers regarding the innovative "prayer of the faithful" that was being introduced into the Mass.

—*Dialogo con Dio. Reflessi liturgici nel discorsi di Paolo VI* (Vatican City, 1965; 140 pp.). The Holy Father Pope Paul VI not only kept in close personal contact with the work of the liturgical reform, but he was also its first catechist in his meetings with the faithful, as this volume proves. Passages on the liturgy from later addresses of the Holy Father would be signaled in the issues of *Notitiae.*

—*Le traduzioni del libri liturgici. Atti del Congresso tenuto a Roma il 9–13 novembre 1965* (Vatican City, 1965; 140 pp.).

—*Canon Missae pro Concelebratione.*

b) *Documents of the Liturgical Reform*

On November 10, 1969, at the twelfth general meeting, the secretary of the Congregation for Divine Worship suggested publication of a collection of all the documents concerning the liturgical reform, beginning with the Constitution on the Liturgy. This work was somewhat delayed by more urgent tasks, especially the publication of the Missal and the Liturgy of the Hours. The undertaking was mentioned in a report to the Pope on May 27, 1971: "We would like to collect all the documents on the liturgy from the Council on. This would be a useful tool not only for students and specialists but also for bishops and episcopal conferences, which often cannot get their bearings amid all the new legislation that has come out during these years."

After a few tentative beginnings, the work was handed over to Dr. Reiner Kaczynski, a staff member of the Congregation; he had the constant assistance of the secretary and the other members of the secretariat. The editing and printing, which called for a sizable commitment, was entrusted to the Marietti publishing house. In fact, when the Secretariat of State approved the launching of a collection of studies that would explain the liturgical reform, it also accepted the proposal that the financing and distribution be entrusted to some interested publisher, thus relieving the Holy See of any financial burden (January 24, 1973; No. 225753).[6]

In June 1975 everything was practically ready for the printer when the Congregation for Divine Worship was suppressed. But, despite some delay due to bureaucratic complications caused by the new situation, the work went on to completion. The book came out in the spring of 1976, still under the sponsorship of the Congregation for Divine Worship and with an anonymous preface that was dated "June 1975" and retained the substance and form it had had on that date. The volume was the final great undertaking that marked the silent departure of the Congregation for Divine Worship from the Church.[7]

The volume covers a period of ten years, from December 4, 1963, to December 2, 1973. The first document is the constitution *Sacrosanctum Concilium;* the last is the *Ordo Paenitentiae.* Thus the book does not contain all the documents of the liturgical reform, and in fact is presented as the first volume of a series that is to be continued. It does, however, contain the second edition of the *Missale Romanum* (March 27, 1975) and the *Graduale simplex* (November 22, 1974). There are 180 documents in all. The majority were published by agencies directly involved in the liturgical reform; also included, however, are conciliar texts and documents from other Roman agencies that deal with, or make reference to, the liturgy. Among these—to mention but the most important—are the regulations concerning the obligation of Sunday Mass, mixed marriages, the diaconate, indulgences, the Eucharistic fast, and penance.

The documents are given in chronological order and in the language in which they were originally published; this means that most are in Latin and a few in the vernaculars. For each there is a brief notice stating the

---

6. The book was offered to the Libreria Editrice Vaticana, but it too said it could not accept the burden.

7. *Enchiridion documentorum instaurationis liturgicae* I (1963–1973), edited with an index by Reiner Kaczynski of the SCDW (Turin: Marietti, 1978. 1224 pp.).

Notitiae, which had meanwhile become the journal of the SCSDW, gave the book a somewhat detached review in its *Bibliographica* section: 12 (1976) 290–91.

agency from which it came, the date of publication, the names of its signatories, the official edition, the translations into the principal languages, the more important commentaries, and an essential but very useful bibliography. With regard to the liturgical books, the rites themselves are not given but only the decrees of promulgation, the introductions, and the other legislative data.

In addition to the notes that are part of a document, the compiler provides others that include everything published by way of official or unofficial interpretation of doubtful points; he also lists alterations made in the texts. The most interesting example here is the General Instruction of the Roman Missal, which, while remaining unchanged in its substance, went through four editions (1969, 1970, 1972, 1975), with alterations in each; all these are listed.

In explaining doubtful points, the compiler falls back, for the most part, on the commentaries in *Notitiae*. The reader is thus given the entire situation for each text and its variants. With this background, it is possible to see the progress of the reform and the need of supplementing or refining certain points in the light of later publications, new questions, or a better grasp of the role liturgy plays in the life of the Christian community.

Room is given not only to official documents but also to the interventions in which the Consilium and the Congregation for Divine Worship endeavored to start, stimulate, guide, and correct the application of the reform, the translations, and the use of the liturgical books (including the obligation attached to each). The volume also includes the addresses of the Holy Father and the letters of the Consilium to the episcopal conferences.

The analytical index (934 entries, 22 pp.) was achieved by classifying about fifteen thousand file cards. While the documents themselves are printed in chronological order, the index makes available all the material on a given subject and facilitates a complete and direct consultation of the documents, while also showing how maturity in the various areas of the reform was achieved gradually. This gradual maturation is proof that the reform was a vital thing, for it was achieved in and through human beings.

The *Enchiridion* is a working tool, a means of consulting the documents, and itself a document concerned with history. That history was written by men of faith who labored solely for the good of the Church. Above all, however, it was a history written by God, who made use of human beings but at times also acted independently of them and despite them.

c) *Directories*

In order that each person in the Consilium might know the individuals working in the agency and be able easily to contact them, a directory was needed that would give the addresses of each as well as other information helpful in understanding the organizational structure.

In 1964, therefore, a first list was published that included only the members and consultors.[8] A second edition appeared in 1967. It lists not only the members and consultors but also the individuals belonging to the presidential council and the secretariat, the advisors, the observers, and all the study groups.[9] It does not include some groups, because these were established only later on. An appendix lists the secretariats of the mixed or joint commissions in countries using the same language; it also lists the international liturgical institutes.[10]

Meanwhile, the always frequent communications with the liturgical commissions had broadened the field of action. The members of these commissions came to be regarded as in some sense part of the Consilium because of their activity in the operational phase of the liturgical reform. Consequently, the third edition of the directory, which was published by the Congregation for Divine Worship, includes not only the members and consultors and secretariat of the Congregation but the names and addresses of the presidents and secretaries of the national liturgical commissions, the liturgical centers, and the liturgical periodicals of each country. At the end of the directory there is also a list of the mixed commissions for translations and of the institutes for liturgical study.[11] The preface states that the directory "has thus opened the door to all who are doing the same work in the various countries. It is intended as a means of union, harmony, and mutual knowledge and understanding."

---

8. Consilium, *Elenchus Membrorum, Consultorum, Consiliariorum, Coetuum a studiis* (Vatican City, 1964).

9. Consilium, *Elenchus Membrorum, Consultorum, Consiliariorum, Coetuum a studiis* (Vatican City, 1967. 70 pp.).

10. Both editions of the *Elenchus* were for private distribution. They contained this note: "The *Elenchus* is for private use. It has been the policy of the Consilium since its beginning that the names of the consultors and participants in the study groups should be made available only to the members. The *Elenchus* is therefore published *solely* for the use of those working in the Consilium."

The reason for this relative secrecy has been stated several times: to ensure peace and a respect for the principle that liturgical texts, belonging as they do to the entire Church, should remain anonymous. And, in point of fact, the system followed in the work was such that no one could possibly assign authorship of a text or of the structure of a rite.

11. SCDW, *Elenco dei membri e consultori. Commissioni-Centri-Istituti-Periodici di liturgia* (Vatican City, 1972. 94 pp.).

IV. Trials and Tribulations of the Reform

18

Experiments

I. Unauthorized Experiments

By accepting the principle of adaptation, the Constitution on the Liturgy opened the way to some extent to experimentation. It speaks explicitly of the usefulness and even the necessity of experiments preliminary to adaptation of some rites, and says that the episcopal conferences can allow such experiments to "certain groups suited for the purpose and for a fixed time" and with authorization from the Apostolic See (*SC* 40; see 44). Such experimentation was to be an orderly, temporary, and limited procedure under the control of two authorities—the Holy See and the bishops.

There were those, however, who began to take a different approach, which might be summed up more or less in this way: Private persons, whether singly or in groups, should conduct liturgical experiments from among which the hierarchy may then choose whichever best meet the needs of the people. In addition, there was a certain impatience; this made it difficult to accept the idea that it was not permissible to anticipate or experiment with what the liturgical Constitution allowed and that implementation of the Constitution must wait upon the lawful decisions of the Church.

As a result, the pretext of "experimentation" was frequently used as a ready justification for personal vagaries. Some individuals, perhaps not entirely in good faith, even claimed to have permission. All this appeared on the scene rather quickly, as can be seen from the fact that in the second issue of *Notitiae* Father Bugnini was forced to ask, in the title of a signed note at the end of the issue, "Where are you headed, liturgy?"

In the note he said: '' We are not infrequently astounded by writings, photographs, and conferences on liturgical subjects. They bring to mind the words of Job: 'The hairs of my body stood on end.' '' And he ended thus: "Where are you headed, liturgy? Or, rather, where are you taking the liturgy, you liturgists and pastors? The sure, luminous, broad, and spacious way of reform is that laid down by the Church and its Supreme Shepherd; any other leads astray."[1]

The problem was continually being raised by the Consilium at meetings with the presidents of the national liturgical commissions and with the editors of periodicals, as well as in general[2] and special letters. The problem also showed up, as we saw earlier, in addresses of the Holy Father—in the one to the participants in the conference on translation on November 10, 1965, and in all the addresses to the Consilium. The Pope's tone was often sad and pained when he spoke of those who attack the sacred character of the liturgy and act on their own initiative, contrary to the principles laid down in the liturgical Constitution.[3]

The Consilium found itself forced at times to speak out publicly because of the publicity given to certain writings or actions. The articles in Notitiae often took stock of situations and rebuked arbitrary activities.[4] These self-willed ventures were to be found in various areas, and it would be difficult to cover the whole range of cases, especially since serious violations of discipline were usually the work of isolated individuals and clearly the product of eccentric minds. The more common extravagances had to do with—the free composition of texts, including the Eucharistic Prayer; the substitution of secular readings for biblical ones; celebrations outside a sacred place (homes, meeting rooms, refectories); use of ordinary bread; rejection of the vestments; use of noisy music unsuited to a sacred action; dialogue homilies that at times became discussions rather than a listening to the Word of God; ritual eccentricities.

---

1. Notitiae, no. 2 (February 1965). This was a cyclostyled issue, not numbered with the printed series.

2. See especially the general letters of June 30, 1965, no. 4 (Not 2 [1966] 259; DOL 31 no. 413), and June 21, 1967 (Not 3 [1967] 290-92; DOL 41 nos. 480-81).

3. See especially the addresses of April 19, 1967 (Not 3 [1967] 127-28; DOL 86 nos. 638-40) and October 14, 1968 (Not 4 [1968] 344-45; DOL 92 nos. 669-74).

4. See, e.g., "Liturgiae degradatio," 6 (1970) 102; "Quaestiones ex Hollandia," 6 (1970) 41; "Autenticidad, no ibridismo," 6 (1970) 72; "Rinnovamento nell'ordine," 7 (1971) 49; " 'Myricae,' " 11 (1975) 196; "Quonam sensu Liturgia renovari debet?" 9 (1973) 288. To be added are the interventions of the bishops; e.g., Algeria, "De quelques anomalies dans les célébrations liturgiques," 11 (1975) 145-47; France, "Notificatio circa celebrationem Missae," 11 (175) 112-18, with a commentary by the SCDW, and see 12 (1976) 445-46; "Lettres des Evêques flamands sur la liturgie," 12 (1976) 195-202.

In honesty it must be admitted that the reports of liturgical abuses were often exaggerated. Sometimes the celebrations were in perfect order but made use of the possibilities of adaptation that were allowed by the liturgical books but were unknown to unprepared or prejudiced observers. On the other hand, it cannot be denied that real abuses occurred and that they did harm to the faithful and to the reform generally. The Consilium and the Holy Father himself made this point on a number of occasions. And as a matter of fact, the claim, even if it be but a pretext, of those who are unwilling to accept the liturgical reform is based precisely on abuses which are deliberately exaggerated as proof that the reform is a bad thing and unacceptable and that it even causes the lack of discipline.

In any case, no honest observer can say that the agencies in charge of the reform shared responsibility for the abuses because they remained silent.

II. STATEMENTS ON EXPERIMENTS

In addition to the points already made, mention ought to be made of some more important and authoritative interventions in the matter of experimentation.

1. *Declaration of the Consilium (June 1965)*

When the phenomenon of abusive experimentation made its appearance, the Consilium determined to say clearly that such actions could not be justified by an appeal to its example or positions. It was necessary to explain the meaning and limits of experimentation, to distinguish experiments permitted by the authorities from those that were self-willed, and to state whether the presumed special permissions claimed by some really existed.

This was the purpose of the declaration of June 1965:

> There are occasional reports of liturgical innovations here and there at variance with either the rubrics now in force or with the Constitution or Instruction on the Liturgy. The innovators commonly claim that they have obtained a faculty or indult from the Consilium, authorizing liturgical experimentation.
>
> The Consilium declares that, except for the indults granted from 3 July 1964 to 14 April 1965 for concelebration and communion under both kinds, it has issued no general indult of any kind authorizing experimentation.[5]

---

5. Even permissions for concelebration and communion under both kinds were given case by case to those requesting it and were accompanied by a decree specifying modali-

A reminder is hardly necessary that according to the Constitution art. 40, no. 2, such a faculty is to be granted by the Holy See solely to territorial ecclesiastical authority; concession for experimentation is made only: a. within specified groups; b. to those qualified; c. for a fixed period.

If in the future the Consilium permits experiments, then, it will forward the faculty always to the territorial ecclesiastical authority, always in writing, and with a statement of the conditions and limits within which the experiments are allowed.

When, therefore, rites, ceremonies, or initiatives of any kind are seen to conflict with prevailing liturgical laws, they are to be regarded as "personal" and individualistic, and as such repudiated by the Constitution and the Consilium.[6]

2. Declaration of the Congregation of Rites and the Consilium (December 29, 1966)

In December 1966 the French weekly *Paris Match* published some photographs of home Eucharistic celebrations that violated all the liturgical regulations. The Holy See thought this an opportune occasion for rebuking such erratic and willful celebrations through a public statement by the two agencies in charge of the liturgy:

> For some time now certain newspapers and magazines have been providing for their readers reports and pictures of liturgical ceremonies, especially celebrations of the eucharist, that are foreign to Catholic worship and quite unbelievable. "Family eucharistic meals" followed by dinner are celebrated in private homes; there are Masses with novel and improvised rites, vestments, and texts, sometimes with music of an altogether profane and worldly character, unworthy of a sacred service. These travesties of worship, springing from mere private initiative, tend inevitably to desacralize the liturgy, the purest expression of the worship the Church offers to God.
>
> Appeal to pastoral renewal as a motive is completely ruled out; renewal develops in an orderly way, not haphazardly. All the practices in question are at odds with the letter and spirit of Vatican II's Constitution on the Liturgy and harmful to the unity and dignity of the people of God.
>
> Pope Paul VI said on 13 October of this year: "Diversity in language and newness in ritual are, it is true, factors that the desire for reform has introduced into liturgy. Nothing is to be adopted however that has not been

ties, time, and conditions. Another permission had been given to the presidents of the national liturgical commissions on December 21, 1964, to have experimental concelebrations of the Mass in accordance with the guidelines set down in the instruction *Inter Oecumenici*. Here again the permission was accompanied by very detailed instructions and the warning that it would be better not to have concelebrations at all than concelebrations with inadequate preparation.

6. *Not* 1 (1965) 145; *DOL* 29 nos. 404-5. See also "Expériences liturgiques," *Not* 2 (1966) 345.

duly approved by the authority of the bishops, fully mindful of their office and obligations, and by this Apostolic See. Nothing should be allowed that is unworthy of divine worship, nothing that is obviously profane or unfit to express the inner, sacred power of prayer. Nothing odd or unusual is allowable, since such things, far from fostering devotion in the praying community, rather shock and upset it and impede the proper and rightful cultivation of a devotion faithful to tradition."

While deploring the practices described and the attendant publicity, we urgently invite Ordinaries, both local and religious, to watch over the right application of the Constitution on the Liturgy. With kindness but firmness they should dissuade those who, whatever their good intentions, sponsor such exhibitions. Where these occur, Ordinaries should reprove the abuses, banning any experiment not authorized and guided by the hierarchy and not conducive to a reform in keeping with the mind of the Council, so that the noble work of renewal may develop without deviation and produce those results in the life of Christians that the Church expects.

We add the reminder that apart from those cases envisioned by liturgical law and therein precisely defined, celebration of Mass in private homes is unlawful.[7]

3. *Third Instruction*

After the publication of the revised Roman Missal, the Congregation for Divine Worship deemed it opportune to speak to some aspects of the liturgical renewal. It did so in the third instruction on the orderly carrying out of the Constitution on the Liturgy, in which it dealt with, among other things, experimentation:

> Any liturgical experimentation that may seem necessary or advantageous receives authorization from this Congregation alone, in writing, with norms clearly set out, and subject to the responsibility of the competent local authority.
>
> All earlier permissions for experimentation with the Mass, granted in view of the liturgical reform as it was in progress, are to be considered as no longer in effect. Since publication of the *Missale Romanum* the norms and forms of eucharistic celebration are those given in the General Instruction and the Order of Mass.

---

7. *Not* 3 (1967) 37–46; *DOL* 35 nos. 433-34. As was said at the press conference, the Holy See did not issue this criticism with one or other country in mind; the phenomena in question were widespread, even if the journalists and photographers of *Paris Match* referred to local situations in France and the Netherlands. The declaration was intended as "a red warning light to both clergy and faithful, showing avenues closed to good intentions and excessively daring initiatives" (*Not*, p. 41).

The conferences of bishops are to draw up in detail any adaptations envisioned in the liturgical books and submit them for confirmation to the Holy See.

Should further adaptations become necessary, in keeping with the norm of the Constitution *Sacrosanctum Concilium* art. 40, the conference of bishops is to examine the issue thoroughly, attentive to the character and traditions of each people and to specific pastoral needs. When some form of experimentation seems advisable, there is to be a precise delineation of its limits and a testing within qualified groups by prudent and specially appointed persons. Experimentation should not take place in large-scale celebrations nor be widely publicized. Experiments should be few and not last beyond a year. A report then is to be sent to the Holy See. While a reply is pending, use of the petitioned adaptation is forbidden. When changes in the structure of rites or in the order of parts as set forth in the liturgical books are involved, or any departure from the usual, or the introduction of new texts, a point-by-point outline is to be submitted to the Holy See prior to the beginning of any kind of experiment.

Such a procedure is called for and demanded by both the Constitution *Sacrosanctum Concilium* and the importance of the issue.[8]

III. EXPERIMENTS AUTHORIZED BY THE CONSILIUM

The Consilium had authority to determine the "conditions required for the application of the Constitution now in process of testing. The Consilium will thus have a basis for deciding what forms may be best for definitive and authoritative approval by the Congregation of Rites."[9] This statement of the Secretariat of State was confirmed by the Holy Father in his address to the Consilium on October 13, 1966.[10]

After the particular cases involved in the preparation for the decree of March 7, 1965, on concelebration and communion under both kinds, the Consilium also obtained permission from the Pope to allow experiments with the rites definitively approved by the Consilium and submitted to the Pope himself with a view to such experimentation (June 2, 1965; No. 48628).

Without such testing, the renewed rites, which at times had been extensively revised, ran the risk of remaining theoretical. Faced with both risks and advantages, the Consilium, fortified by the authority of the supreme shepherd, made its choice. The risks were foreseen and taken into

---

8. SCDW, instruction *Liturgiae instaurationes* (September 5, 1970), no. 12: *Not* 7 (1971) 24–25; *DOL* 52 no. 530.

9. Letter of the Secretary of State, January 7, 1965: *EDIL* 379; *DOL* 82 no. 625.

10. *Not* 2 (1966) 307–8; *DOL* 84 no. 630.

account; therefore, these authorized experiments were not at all to be confused with uncontrolled experimentation.

Because of the difficulty of knowing which groups were best suited for carrying out experiments, and in order to bring the authority of the bishops more directly into play, the Pope decided that permission to experiment with the rites prepared by the Consilium should be granted through the presidents of liturgical commissions selected by the Consilium itself or which had asked for permission. In *every* case two decrees were issued: one to the president of the episcopal conference of the country concerned, and the other to the president of the national liturgical commission, who was also given a set of "Regulations for experiments" and a questionnaire to be used in making his report. The conferences thus had all the information needed for distinguishing what originated in the Consilium and was under their direct control, and what was the result of personal initiative.

But the question of experiments also bulked large in the reports on the liturgy that were given at the first Synod of Bishops. For this reason, when the Cardinal President of the Consilium replied on October 26, 1967, to the statements of the various bishops, he dwelt at length on, among other things, the matter of experimentation, explaining the procedure followed and the regulations in force.[11]

a) *Procedure*

A concern of the Consilium from the very beginning has been that before being definitively sanctioned, the new rites should be experimentally used in various places and groups in order to determine their value. This was done with concelebration; it is now being done with the catechumenate for adults and funerals; it will shortly be done for the baptism of children and marriage. Regions are chosen in which by and large the various religious and social conditions of the world are to be found; this includes the young Churches in mission countries.

The Consilium recognizes two kinds of experiments.

The first, which is proposed by the Consilium itself, has to do with schemas that its study groups have carefully researched and suitably scrutinized.

The procedure is as follows: The Consilium gives each national commission permission to organize experiments, according to set regulations, in places and groups that are varied and suitable; the commission is obliged to submit in time a detailed report of the results, the difficulties met,

---

11. Synod of Bishops, *Responsiones Em.mi Card. Iacobi Lercaro, Relatoris, ad animadversiones circa quaestiones "de sacra Liturgia"* (Vatican Polyglot Press, 1967; 9 pp.). The "Normae de experimentis peragendis" are in an appendix to the booklet (pp. 17–18).

and the suggestions that spring from the experience. All this will help in revising, correcting, and improving the schema in its definitive form.

The second kind of experiment is proposed by the episcopal conferences or by others with the consent of the competent authority; these experiments are then studied and permitted by the Consilium in accordance with article 40 of the Constitution. This kind of experiment is concerned chiefly with the adaptations found to be necessary or appropriate in a given country, in order that the liturgy, while displaying the substantial unity of the Roman Rite, may also be in harmony with the character and traditions of each people. Experiments of this kind are carried on under the responsibility of the conferences or religious families. An example: In some monasteries of Africa and Madagascar, whose members are predominantly natives, experiments are being carried on in the organization of the Divine Office.

The Consilium is not averse to this second kind of experiment and gladly grants permission, but only in writing and provided several things are made clear: the limits of the experiment, the authority that controls it, and the capacity of the experimenting group. The Consilium trusts that these experiments will furnish information of use in perfecting the rites in their definitive form. The experience of the Church as a whole and of the dioceses and religious families is a very great help in reforming the liturgy.

b) *Regulations for Experiments*

1. The rites composed by the Consilium are submitted for experimentation in various regions via the national liturgical commissions or via competent individuals appointed by special mandate.

2. The national commissions either directly or through an institute of pastoral liturgy or a liturgical center (*SC* 44) choose, with the consent of the local Ordinary, some dioceses or parishes or suitable groups (depending on the nature of the experiment) that verify the pastoral conditions for achieving the purpose of the experiment.

3. In each diocese in which an experiment is conducted, someone is appointed, again with the consent of the local Ordinary, to see to the pastoral and ritual preparation in that place and, bearing in mind the concrete circumstances, to decide on that which the *Ordo* leaves to the determination of the conferences of bishops (in this matter he will, if necessary, consult the local Ordinary). The collaboration of the laity in all this will be very profitable.

4. It will be appropriate and, in the case of more important experiments, even necessary for those in charge to gather, under the sponsorship of the national liturgical commission, and together study the rite, decide on conditions and means, and provide in advance for everything that can promote the success of the experiment.

If necessary, such meetings will be repeated during the course of the experiment.

5. The national commission and the national center are to provide and prepare the aids and practical guidelines that are to be given to pastors, even during the course of the experiment. In the experiments, such musical aids as are needed should be provided by experts in this area.

6. The rite to be used is the one sent by the Consilium with the decree giving permission. It will be the responsibility of the national commission to make copies of the rite and distribute them, with the aid, if necessary, of the mixed commissions that are in charge of the vernacular translations.

7. Various settings should be chosen for the experiments: for example, urban or rural parishes, a university or working-class setting, schools, communities.

8. Experiments are not to be conducted at congresses or major celebrations, since these by their nature are too public. Nor is anything to be written about them in newspapers or periodicals or said of them on radio or television.

9. In any experiment all the formulas or forms of the rite are to be used.

10. After each celebration the judgment of the faithful regarding the intelligibility and effectiveness of the various parts is to be asked by means of appropriate questionnaires or at meetings.

11. Every three months the person in charge must collect the reports of the experiments conducted and send them on to the national liturgical commission; the reports are to give the circumstances, the opinion of the participants, the difficulties met, the outcome, and any suggestions. If possible, the report should include some photographs.

12. Twice a year the national liturgical commission in turn must send the Consilium a report on the experiments conducted; these must include the data just listed and any suggestions. If the Consilium thinks it appropriate, it may ask for a final summation on the experiments before proceeding to a definitive edition of the rite.

Despite the extreme caution shown in the procedure and despite explanations and interventions of various kinds, the occurrence of abuses under the pretext of "experimentation" was not entirely eliminated. At least, however, it could not be said that the proper course was not made clear. There were, of course, some who turned a deaf ear to instructions, but there were also some, even in positions of responsibility and authority, who refused to understand the actions of the Consilium and the Congregation for Divine Worship and chose instead to distort their position and hold them responsible for abuses.[12]

If the bishops had been given more scope for action, even within set limits, they might have been able to stem the abuses more effectively.

---

12. See above, p. 94, on the ordinary meeting of June 19, 1975.

But this is sheer guesswork. In any case, it would have been unthinkable at the time to give them this greater scope.[13]

---

13. At the same ordinary meeting of June 19, 1975, the question was discussed of helping the bishops of two conferences in their efforts to handle a difficult situation at the end of a lengthy process of meetings and persuasion. Yet the only thanks the SCDW received for its action was to be accused of "yielding to arrogance and pressure" and of "excusing the bishops instead of rebuking them."

19

Adaptation

The ideas of experiment and adaptation are closely linked. Adaptation is a necessity if the liturgy is to be the action of all God's people and, while maintaining its essentials everywhere the same, to be integrated with the reality of each people and each nation. It is the principle of adaptation that accounts for the rise, down the centuries, of the Church's varied rites and the diversity in its song, vestments, and building styles, and in its ways of expressing the same ideas and showing God praise, adoration, and obedience. This same principle justifies the use of all human languages in worship of the Lord. Adaptation has its place in all areas of the Church's life—theology, catechesis, spirituality. As Pope Paul VI said to the African bishops:

> The liturgy is a living example of this [adaptation]. And in this sense you may, and you must, have an African Christianity. Indeed, you possess human values and characteristic forms of culture which can rise up to perfection such as to find in Christianity and for Christianity a true superior fullness and prove to be capable of a richness of expression all its own and genuinely African.[1]

As far as the liturgical reform is concerned, the main problems of adaptation, which were acknowledged in the liturgical Constitution,[2] have hardly been tackled as yet. A decisive approach to them will be the task of the third phase of the reform, once the general revision of the liturgi-

---

1. Address to the Bishops of Africa at Kampala, July 31, 1969: *Not* 5 (1969) 346; *DOL* 44 no. 490.
2. See *SC* 37-40, which are, as it were, the Magna Carta of adaptation; see also nos. 24, 62, 65, 68.

cal books has been completed,[3] since the latter provide the basic structure, the foundation that is being laid in accordance with the data of tradition, the guidelines given in the liturgical Constitution, and the pastoral needs of today's faithful. The revised books cannot of themselves satisfy the needs of all peoples. Therefore, in compliance with the liturgical Constitution (no. 39), they always contain an introduction pointing out the adaptations that are left to the responsibility of the episcopal conferences or the minister.

But, in addition to possibilities of adaptation that can be signaled in the liturgical books, "in some places and circumstances . . . an even more radical adaptation of the liturgy is needed." And in fact

> even in the liturgy the Church has no wish to impose a rigid uniformity in matters that do not affect the faith or the good of the whole community; rather the Church respects and fosters the genius and talents of the various races and peoples. The Church considers with sympathy and, if possible, preserves intact the elements in these peoples' way of life that are not indissolubly bound up with superstition and error. Sometimes in fact the Church admits such elements into the liturgy itself, provided they are in keeping with the true and authentic spirit of the liturgy (SC 37).

This has been the constant tradition of the Church as it has striven to safeguard unity and, at the same time, to achieve a real incarnation in the various cultures.

During the years after the Council, the first efforts at adaptation were focused almost exclusively on the translation of the liturgical books and the search for a language that could express the realities of the faith and interpret the liturgical texts both accurately and in a suitable way.

As the liturgical reform took hold, however, the need was gradually felt for a more thoroughgoing adaptation. The sense of need was intensified by the very introduction of the vernaculars, since the new texts had to be matched by an appropriate musical, symbolic, environmental, and cultural setting if it were not to resemble a person wearing an ill-fitting garment.

---

3. See the report of Cardinal Knox, prefect of the SCDW, to the Synod of Bishops in 1974: *Not* 10 (1974) 358–59; *DOL* 100 no. 697. The SCDW showed that it was itself following this path by making provision, after the reform of the liturgical books, for special situations and problems: for example, the Directory for Masses with Children; the publication of three Eucharistic Prayers for celebrations with children; instruction on the celebration of Mass with special groups; circular letters on the Eucharistic Prayers. Also under consideration was the publication of a *Lectionarium parvum* for use in special missionary situations; this never appeared.

The bishops discussed the matter at the Synod of 1974;[4] in some places studies were undertaken that are still awaiting continuation.[5] I shall dwell briefly on what has been accomplished during the first fifteen years of the liturgical reform. No one should be surprised that all the cases discussed concern Third World countries in which adaptation to the culture and genius of the various peoples has proved to be more necessary and not to be postponed.

1. *Imitation of foreign models and anxious search for a new way, both being regarded as the way to greater pastoral effectiveness*

Some missionary Churches have imported from countries of Western culture liturgical practices that are suitable in the country of origin but utterly out of place in missionary countries. Conversely, we have seen centers of Mediterranean culture importing from Asia or Africa usages and customs that are native to those peoples but completely out of place in a European ecclesial and social setting.[6]

This sort of thing is now less frequent; it resulted from impulses at work in the immediate postconciliar period. As the reform has achieved its goals through the publication of new rites, a mature liturgical consciousness has developed and the more outlandish oddities have disappeared.

2. *Start of a more thorough adaptation through use of local ritual elements*

In 1967 Thailand asked permission to replace the kiss of peace at Mass with the Thai gesture of peace, which consists in touching the altar or Book of the Gospels with hands clasped and touching the forehead.[7]

In 1968 the Pakistan episcopal conference approved eight adaptations in the ceremonies of the Mass: a bow instead of a genuflection; the more frequent use of incense; the use of perfumed water on solemn occasions; the use of local music and instruments; various modifications in the rite of marriage.[8]

---

4. See *Not* 10 (1974) 363ff.

5. See "Le fondement biblique de l'adaptation liturgique," *Not* 11 (1975) 24; A. Botero Alvarez, "Principios para la adaptación litúrgica en las culturas nativas," *ibid.* 11 (1975) 384–90; "Africanizatio liturgiae," *Not* 7 (1971) 105–6.

6. At the same time an adaptation was begun that was simpler and more immediately needed—the adaptation of sacred music and art. Workshops were set up for the production of sacred vestments using designs adapted to local mentalities and usages, and institutes of art were established, such as the one that the Scuola di Arte Sacra of Milan opened and operated in Burundi. See "Instrumenta musica africana in liturgia," *Not* 5 (1969) 119–20.

7. *Not* 3 (1967) 341.

8. *Ibid.*, 4 (1968) 331.

In 1969 it was India's turn. The adaptations carefully considered by the national commission (headed by Archbishop Simon Lourdusamy of Bangalore) had to do with the posture to be adopted during Mass (sitting or standing), genuflections, a profound bow ("panchenga pranam") during the penitential act, the kissing of objects, the rite of peace, the use of incense, the sacred vestments, the corporal, the use of oil instead of candles, the preparatory rites of the Mass, spontaneity in the prayer of the faithful, and the enrichment of the offertory gifts.[9]

On January 20, 1970, Bishop Loosdregt, president of the episcopal conference of Laos-Cambodia, asked permission to transfer the feast of All Saints and the Commemoration of the Faithful Departed to September 15 and October 15, respectively, because it is on the latter date that Cambodians, in accordance with age-old tradition, hold their celebrations in honor of the dead ("Prachum Ben"). The request was granted on January 26, 1970.[10]

In 1972 Bishop Loosdregt asked permission to replace all genuflections with a profound bow; kisses with a bow and hands clasped to the fore-

---

9. This adaptation (along with the one in Zaire) was perhaps the most extensive and carefully worked out in the entire first decade after the Council. A special Eucharistic Prayer was also planned. The adaptations followed the normal course. They were discussed in the episcopal conference, and every bishop was left free to introduce them or not. The petition to Rome was forwarded by the president of the conference, Cardinal Valerian Gracias, Archbishop of Bombay and a member of the Consilium. The decree of consent was dated April 25, 1969: see *Not* 5 (1969) 365–66 (with a detailed commentary on each point: 366–74); *DOL* 43 no. 489.

An experiment using the "Indian Mass" was conducted at Rome on February 15 in the hall of the Pontifical Urban College of the Propaganda Fide. The entire Indian colony was present, and Archbishop Lourdusamy celebrated. Fragrances, flowers, incense, vestments, lights, songs, ceremonies, and gestures all made a positive impression on the participants; see *Not* 6 (1970) 89. Later on there were some objections, especially to the use of the Eucharistic Prayer (see *Not* 9 [1973] 77), which had not been authorized, and there were objections from some, both ordinary Christians and bishops, who regarded the Indianization of the liturgy as a baneful Hinduization. In March 1970 the conference of bishops re-examined the entire project and decreed as follows:

1) The adaptation was not obligatory. The bishops or the regional conferences were free to introduce it in whole or in part.

2) Where it was introduced, the changes were to be made gradually, depending on the degree of preparation of the faithful.

3) Pastoral preparation of the people and instruction regarding the reasons and significance of the adaptation were to precede the actual introduction of the new rites; see *Word and Worship* 3 (1970) 192–93 and *Not* 6 (1970) 282. But the debate continued, and despite the support of Cardinal Parecattil, president of the conference, the adaptations had to be suspended at the beginning of 1976. Influences from outside India itself played a part in the suspension; see N. Manca, "Polemiche sulla liturgia indiana," *Mondo e Missione*, April 1976, 228–30.

10. *Not* 6 (1970) 97.

head; the striking of the breast at the *Confiteor* with a bow; the extension of the arms, for example, at the *Dominus vobiscum*, with joined hands.

In 1974 he requested a further series of ritual adaptations. Kneeling, which in the Laotian tradition is done while resting on the heels, would be reserved to the celebrant at the beginning of Mass, during the penitential act, and at communion. Sitting, in the two forms used, would be the posture of the celebrant throughout the liturgy, including the Eucharistic liturgy, except during the gospel and the penitential act. Prostration: in greeting the cross and after the consecration or, preferably, after the doxology that ends the Eucharistic Prayer.[11]

3. *Adaptation extended to the texts and to local cultural and cultic expressions*

The adaptations thus far described, though external and peripheral, could not fail to pave the way for further steps involving the adaptation of rites, formulas, and texts.

A mini-program of careful and prudent adaptation could be seen in the letter of February 27, 1974, from the liturgical commission of Laos/ Khmer Republic: "We have been proceeding by stages: adaptation of the calendar (1971) and some gestures of the celebrant (1972). We are aware that there is yet much to be done to organize the texts and rites in a way that will more clearly express the sacred realities they signify and that will, as far as possible, enable our Christian people to understand them more readily and take part in them more easily."

The texts or spoken part of the liturgy, in which the sensibility and soul of a people find expression, are thus the subject of the final stage of liturgical adaptation. This is the hardest, most demanding, and most sensitive part of the entire process. It determines the authenticity and sincerity of the vital forces at work in the Church.

In October 1969, Japan was the first country to launch out in this area. All the adaptations requested had to do with liturgical formulas. The exclamation "The word of the Lord!" at the end of the readings did not sound right in Japanese. Therefore, let the reader bow to the sacred book and the congregation respond "Thanks be to God"; or else let the minister say "Praise to you, O Christ" after the gospel, and the congregation repeat the same words.

The congregation's prayer "Suscipiat" in response to the celebrant's "Orate, fratres" should be replaced by a silent prayer, since it is very difficult to translate the "Suscipiat" into Japanese.

---

11. Laos/Khmer Republic, "Adaptation de certaines attitudes du prêtre dans la célébration de l'Eucharistie," *Not* 10 (1974) 391–92. For Vietnam: *Not* 9 (1973) 73–74.

The "Domine, non sum dignus" should be replaced by John 6:68-69: "Lord, to whom shall we go? You have the words of eternal life. You are the Christ, the Son of God." The reason is that all attempts at a tolerable translation of the "Domine, non sum dignus" have been unsatisfactory.

Finally, the formula "Sanguis Christi" at communion under both kinds should be omitted, since it sounds excessively materialistic to a Japanese.[12]

These were modest changes, but they were already in the vital area of the liturgy; the roads were now open in every direction and would lead even to the very heart of the liturgy, namely, the Eucharistic Prayer. The four anaphoras of the Roman liturgy are certainly the products of Latin sensibilities and culture. Some asked, therefore: Why should not every people be able to sing their faith in a way expressive of their own genius, even at the supreme moment of worship?

Steps, even if still timid, have been taken in this direction. I shall point out the more important ones.

1) *India.* There has been an attempt to compose texts in the "Indian" style for Masses for local feasts: anniversary of the Republic, Independence Day, harvest feast, feasts of Christ the Light and Christ the Wisdom of God.[13]

When I speak of an Indian "style," the reader should not think simply of the literary form; the Indians also had the very substance in mind. It was precisely here that the problem became very serious and demanding. The pastoral theologians of India were asking themselves whether the Hindu scriptures might not be used in expressing Christian religious thought, thereby giving Christian prayer an Indian face. The more diligent and prudent students of the problem rightly pointed out that before any use of the Hindu scriptures in the Christian liturgy, there ought to be a careful, multi-year study by philosophers and theologians in order to determine whether and in what way Catholic dogma can be expressed in the language of the Hindu scriptures.

A congress was even held at Bangalore to discuss this very subject. It was organized by the Indian National Center for Scripture, Catechesis, and Liturgy and was attended by theologians, biblical scholars, liturgists, people in pastoral positions, and some bishops. Also present were representatives of the Secretariat for Non-Christians and the Congregation for Divine Worship. The representative of the latter had not a few

---

12. See "Aptatio liturgica in Iaponia," *Not* 6 (1970) 67.
13. *Not* 9 (1973) 76; 10 (1974) 100.

reservations to make regarding various statements at the congress. An especially sensitive area was the use of non-biblical readings; the Congregation had always been intransigent when it came to the exclusive use of the Hebrew and Christian Scriptures in the Eucharistic liturgy.

2) *China*. On February 15, 1972, which was the Chinese New Year's Day, the ancient rites in honor of the dead ancestors were celebrated in all the Catholic churches of Taiwan. This was the first time that these ceremonies, allowed in the sixteenth century by Father Matteo Ricci but then condemned as superstitious in the bull *Ex quo singulari* of Benedict XIV, were not only permitted by the Church but even ordered by the local ecclesiastical hierarchy. This adaptation was of special importance both because of the historical background and because of its doctrinal implications. The obstacles from both points of view were surmounted by means of a careful study of Chinese customs and traditions in the light of the teachings of Vatican II.

This same spirit found expression in the commentary that the Chinese episcopate issued to the faithful, explaining that the rites in question were not only free of superstition but also gave an effective stimulus to family solidarity and to the preservation of advantageous national traditions.

The theological significance of this religious act was summed up as follows by Father Thaddeus Hang, professor at the University of Fu Jen: "This is an act both of worship of the God who gives life and of veneration of the ancestors who have transmitted that life to us and thus enabled us to share in a way in the divine life."

Thus after 230 years of debate and exclusion, one of the major obstacles that hindered the integration of the Christian community into the Chinese community was removed.[14]

A comparable adaptation was the decision to have a Mass or a liturgy of the Word to mark the feast of "Ching Ming" (around April 5), on which the Chinese remember the dead.[15]

3) *Zambia*. For over a year (1969–70), at meetings of priests and laity, the various diocesan liturgical commissions of Zambia discussed ways of making the Eucharistic celebration more meaningful to the Bantu

---

14. In the first year only four bishops followed Cardinal Yu Pin's example. A good many Christians resisted: the young because they were opposed to restoring usages in which they no longer believed; older people, along with the missionaries and Protestants, because they regarded these practices as superstitious and pagan.

15. *Not* 8 (1972) 14.

peoples. The result of this study was a cyclostyled work entitled "Normative Mass for Zambia," a collection of principles and regulations that were to be the basis for experiments that would be carried out under the direction of the local Ordinary and his diocesan liturgical commission.

The adaptations here are many. Some of them are ritual: omission of the kissing of objects, since this action is meaningless in the Bantu mentality; bow in place of genuflection; use of incense in the penitential act (incense is used in some regions to purify the air); dialogue homily interspersed with refrains; offering of the gifts by the entire congregation.

Other adaptations go beyond the ritual level but reflect the influence of teaching at the European institutes. For example, the mingling of some water with the wine is omitted because it has no biblical basis; the Lavabo is omitted as meaningless (Africans wash only before eating).

The *Orate, fratres* is used in place of the prayer over the gifts or vice versa. The commingling is abolished.

Finally, some steps show a desire to carry the study to a deeper level, for example, the request to the experts to compose presidential prayers that relate to the readings, or the exhortation to poets to compose prefaces and Eucharistic Prayers that are "in harmony with African sensibilities."

4) *Congo (Brazzaville)*. The episcopal conference of Congo approved a schema for adaptation of the liturgies of the Mass and marriage.[16]

As regards the Mass, the schema stopped at the liturgy of the Word: "On some occasions we would like to see the meaning of God's word conveyed in a form adapted to local conditions."

The structure of the Mass is substantially identical with that of the Roman Missal, except that the penitential act is placed after the homily. Some details, however, are noteworthy.

The celebrant goes to the altar, solemnly carrying the Book of the Gospels, which is a highly ornate volume. He then carries it to the ambo and incenses it. This incensation replaces the incensation of the altar. After greeting the people, the celebrant explains the reason why they have gathered, namely, to celebrate the faith together; at this point, therefore, the Creed is recited.

The liturgy of the Word follows. Then there is an examination of conscience in the form of the Lavabo, during which the *Kyrie* or a penitential psalm may be sung.

---

16. This did not get beyond the "proposal" stage, since the dialogue begun with the Congregation for Divine Worship was not carried forward.

Next comes the penitential act (described as an "absolution of sins," in a rather ambiguous context), which is followed by a song of thanksgiving (for example, the *Gloria*).

Marriage: the most significant detail here is the exchange of cups and the drinking of the wine contained in them. A carafe of wine is placed on a table visible to all. At the prescribed moment the bride rises, fills a cup with wine, and presents it to the celebrant as to the head of the Christian family. She then kneels before the celebrant, surrounded by her family. A dialogue between the two ensues, in which the celebrant ascertains that the bride is freely and permanently accepting the promised bridegroom. Then the celebrant drinks from the cup before the entire congregation. The bride takes the cup once more and carries it to the bridegroom. The latter then approaches the celebrant and there is a second dialogue, like the one with the bride. The cup is finally placed on the altar; the remaining wine will be used in consecrating the Eucharist.

5) *Zaire*. This conference turned its attention immediately to the Mass. Its first call (April 20, 1970) was for research with a view to creating an African and Zairian framework for the Order of Mass.

After three years of patient study, a rite was ready that was approved on November 2, 1972, by the standing committee of the bishops and then published with "explanatory" photographs and a series of interesting slides taken in the pilot parish of St. Alphonsus in Mabete-Kinshasa (40,000 Catholics). The booklet containing the schema for the Mass[17] also gives the criteria and principles behind it. This information shows that careful research paved the way for the rite. The principles at work werethese: fidelity to gospel (biblical) values; fidelity to the inner nature (structure) of the liturgy; fidelity to the African and Zairian religious genius and cultural heritage.

A rite characterized by this threefold fidelity is profoundly catholic, that is, universal, and promotes participation by the people (a dominant theme in the liturgical reform of Vatican II).

The distinctive points of the rite are these:

—At the beginning of the celebration there is a "litany" containing six invocations, but with typical developments.

—The readings in the liturgy of the Word are framed by extensive teachings and acclamations.

—The penitential act, using formulas more fully developed than those in the Roman Missal, follows upon the homily and Creed.

---

17. *Vers une Messe africaine* (Kinshasa, 1974).

—At the offertory, the bread and wine are presented by the congregation with appropriate formulas.

—The Eucharistic Prayer, freshly composed, follows the traditional pattern, but acclamations of the assembly are more frequent and the language reflects Zairian reality.

These rites serve as a framework for lively and joyous gestures, dances, decorations, singing, and music, all of which spring from the Zairian soul.[18]

In conclusion, it can be said that adaptation has only begun and that thus far there have been only quite limited efforts. The process is difficult due to the material itself and to the spiritual, psychological, and cultural situation of those concerned. We have seen that no attempt at adaptation has been exempt from internal disputes. Careful study—theological and liturgical but also sociological, ethnological, and contextual—is an absolute necessity. In addition, before instituting adaptations there must be careful and lengthy instruction of the people.

The need for adaptation is felt everywhere, since Christianity is not an adjunct of any particular culture or cultural form. It must be able to adapt itself in forms appropriate to all civilizations and help the latter to purify and sublimate themselves. Today more than ever there is an awareness that Christianity must not let itself be perceived as a foreign religion, even in its external forms.

The coming years will make many demands on the Church in this area. Adaptation is necessary if the Church is to maintain itself in many countries; it will also ensure this permanence. When all peoples pray and sing in their own language and in harmony with their own genius, and when they offer God a worship which is a sincere and authentic expression of the Christian faith and which springs from the depths of the native strengths, only then will it be possible to say that Christ has truly encountered human beings on their earth and in their flesh and soul.

---

18. The SCDW allowed some experiments to be conducted according to the norm of SC 40, in some specific locales and for a certain period. Meanwhile the standing committee was to continue its study, jointly with the Congregation. The latter explained the problem to the Holy Father on April 10, 1974, and then examined it conjointly with some representatives of the Congregation for the Doctrine of the Faith. The SCDW forwarded some difficulties to the liturgical commission of Zaire, especially regarding the penitential act, the rite and gesture of peace, the Eucharistic Prayer, and some other less important details. But the dialogue did not continue. Instead, the rite spread through many dioceses, giving rise to divergent views and appraisals. Some bishops forbade its use. A further difficulty was that, due to the government's ban on their meetings, the episcopal conference as such could not discuss the project, at least in its initial phase and during the preparation of the rite.

20

Opposition

The path of liturgical reform has been marked not only by experimentation and adaptation but also by opposition. While some indulged in uncontrolled experimentation, to the detriment of the faith and the sacredness of worship of the Lord, others took a hard stand on the past and launched a systematic attack on the reform. Among the latter, well-known names were to be found—writers, literary people, composers, educated and cultured men and women. In many cases they were far removed from Christianity and even openly hostile to it; their only desire was that the Church should protect a cultural heritage; they were uninterested in its mission of bringing human beings to Christ.

Also to be taken into account is the support given by others from the middle classes and the financial world who saw in the new liturgy a dangerous kind of democratization. It was perhaps they who provided the financial support for an expensive campaign, supplying funds that could have been better spent in the cause of God's reign. But the liturgical renewal is not the only concern of the traditionalists; in fact, it is the very image of the Church which the Council yielded that they cannot accept.[1]

1. *Una voce*

The Constitution on the Liturgy had hardly been approved when a group of the faithful organized themselves as an association for the de-

---

1. Y. Congar, *La crise dans l'Eglise et Mgr. Lefèbvre* (Paris, 1976). [English translation: *Challenge to the Church: The Case of Archbishop Lefèbvre*, trans. Paul Inwood (Huntington, Ind., 1976).] It is impossible to cite the entire extensive literature on the subject; I shall limit myself to a few sources.

fense of Latin. The name they chose was significant: *Una voce*. The association came into existence in France on December 19, 1964, in the crypt of a Paris church. Similar groups immediately sprang up in many countries: France, Germany, Italy, Norway, Spain, Uruguay, New Zealand, England, Scotland, Switzerland, Austria, Belgium, the Netherlands, and Sweden, as well as in several other countries of Latin America. Its purpose was "to preserve Latin and Gregorian chant, as well as sacred polyphony, in the Catholic liturgy, in accordance with the conciliar Constitution *Sacrosanctum Concilium*." On January 7, 1967, the various associations combined to form an international federation with headquarters in Zürich. Its president was Dr. Erich M. de Saventhen. Its first general secretary was Paul Poitevin, but when he realized the extremist bent of the association, he eventually resigned his position and even began to oppose the group. The vice-president was Duke Filippo Caffarelli.

As we have seen, the defense of Latin and Gregorian chant, which was the initial purpose of the association, was not neglected in the Church's documents on the reform.[2] If the vernacular came to be used more extensively, even in monastic communities, this was because it satisfied a conscious and widespread need. In all honesty, however, it must be acknowledged that in some regions those responsible for local pastoral practice showed an intransigency that prevented the recognition and toleration of particular sensibilities.

2. *Organization of the "Counterreform"*

Some groups remained faithful to their original purpose and were content with having Mass celebrated in Latin; this was true, for example, of the Association for Latin Liturgy.[3] Others, however, took a hard and fast stand against any and all renewal. *Una voce* brought together the discontented, those opposed to all of the conciliar innovations; for these, opposition to the reformed liturgy—which was the most evident and decisively implemented result of the Council—became a catalyst.

The movement started by *Una voce* spread and fragmented into a plethora of small groups with the most varied names; their publications became so numerous that it is almost impossible to list them all. In 1971 an Italian newspaper listed twenty national *Una voce* associations, as well as national organizations of Christian Civilization (International Committee for the Defense of Christian Civilization, which was formed in West

---

2. See above, pp. 111–13.
3. See *Not* 11 (1975) 26–28.

Germany in 1956 by a group headed by Konrad Adenauer) and over a hundred other lesser groups and associations.[4]

Among the groups that were especially active, and virulent as well, were: Christian Civilization; *Vigilia Romana*, with headquarters in Rome; in France, *Courrier de Rome, Forts dans la foi, Itinéraires, Le combat de la foi* (founded and directed by Abbé Coache), *La contre-reforme catholique au XXe siècle* (Abbé Georges de Nantes), and the movement led by the *Fraternité S. Pie X* and the seminary at Ecône (both of them founded by Archbishop Marcel Lefèbvre).

In France the opposition soon came into the open and displayed intense hostility. The original instigator was Abbé Coache, who called for massive disobedience to the decrees of the bishops and the Holy See. In 1969 and 1970, in direct opposition to the local authorities, he organized great gatherings of the faithful at the castle of Alaincourt (parish of Montjavoult) for the feast of Corpus Christi. Though apparently intended as tributes to the Most Holy Eucharist, these gatherings were in the true and full sense expressions of dissent.[5] The Abbé was therefore suspended from his ministerial functions by the Bishop of Beauvais and put on trial by the Roman Rota.

The United States had its own Catholic Traditionalist Movement, founded by a priest, Gommar A. De Pauw.[6] It conducted a poll among

---

4. See *Lo specchio*, no. 22 (May 30, 1971); P. Fernandez, "Diez años de la renovación litúrgica (1963–1973)," *Phase* 415–32.

5. Dissent is unfortunately the characteristic trait of this opposition, even in the more strident expressions of it by Archbishop Lefèbvre and his followers. "They turn their celebrations into means of protest and proclamations or gestures of disobedience and even defiance. My God, can this be? Is this to be regarded as a way of 'eating the Lord's supper' (1 Cor 11:16)?" (Congar [n. 1], 39). For example, no. 11 (March 1, 1970) of *Le combat de la foi* (the newspaper of Abbé Coache's association) contains the following exhortation: "If an important occasion arises for your family or some of your friends, for example, a wedding or a funeral, know that *you have a strict right* to a celebration entirely in Latin (except for the epistle and gospel) and a traditional Mass (Mass of St. Pius V). The documents of the Council and the Holy See give you authorization for it. If the local clergy refuse, *do not stop insisting;* demand the true Mass, in Latin and in the Gregorian form; if they continue to refuse, phone your bishop and let him know that if he does not satisfy you, *you will immediately appeal to the Sacred Congregation of Divine Worship in Rome* (by telephone in case of a funeral). If you phone, ask for the Vatican exchange and request it to call Cardinal Gut or the secretary of the Congregation for Divine Worship." The one or the other is to be asked to send a telegram to the bishop. See also "La Messe à Rome," *Itinéraires*, June 15, 1975, which is a cry of victory because Archbishop Lefèbvre had celebrated the Mass of St. Pius V at Rome: "This Mass was celebrated by Mons. Lefèbvre, along with all the members of the *Fraternité sacerdotale S. Pie X* and the participants in the Credo pilgrimage."

6. De Pauw's association was banned by Cardinal Shehan of Baltimore; its president, suspended from his ministerial functions, sought incardination in another diocese. During

the Catholics of the United States at the very beginning of the reform[7]
and collected signatures on printed and mimeographed flysheets, which
were sent to the Pope or the Roman Congregations with the request for
a return to Latin and the preconciliar liturgy.

Another group very active in the United States was The Remnant,
which published a journal of the same name. Among other ideas, it had
the unusual one of printing birthday greeting cards depicting the elevation of the "traditional" Mass and containing a printed greeting: "I wish
you every happiness and blessing on your birthday, and I ask you to help
restore the beautiful Latin Mass of Pope St. Pius V, the Mass which we
learned to know and love." A fair number of these cards also reached
the Congregation for Divine Worship.

The point needs to be made that in the United States and especially
in England, and more generally in countries with a strong Protestant
majority, the introduction of the vernacular into the liturgy meant to many
the loss of one distinction between Catholics and Protestants and of a
sign of their attachment to Rome in the face of Protestantism. For these
people, the psychological effects of the reform were quite serious. For
some, the reform meant the collapse of a world and the practical acceptance of views until then regarded as heretical.

As these associations became organized, the liturgical reform was
proceeding apace. The year 1967 saw the publication of the second instruction on the application of the liturgical Constitution, which contained
some simplifications of the Order of Mass; the instruction on worship
of the Eucharistic mystery; the instruction on sacred music; the first Synod
of Bishops, which took up the question of the liturgical reform of the Mass;
and the first translations of the Roman Canon. All these actions showed
that Rome intended to continue on the path it had taken. This elicited
in turn a very bitter response from those who saw in it a new attack on
tradition. Their influence among the Fathers of the Synod was decisive,
causing them to change their view of the reform, at least to some extent,
and to trouble their study of what was set before them.

There were also manifestations of extreme intolerance. The most violent came from a rather well-known Italian writer, Tito Casini, a fervent
Catholic who had drawn inspiration from the liturgy for some of his better publications. Casini wielded his pen with typical Tuscan acidity in
defense of Latin. His book *Tunica stracciata*[8] is an exasperated cry of

---

the first Synod of Bishops, he threatened to go into schism; on March 2, 1968, he held a
demonstration against the liturgical reform on Fifth Avenue in New York City.

7. During the winter of 1964 and from August 1 to September 15, 1965.

8. Tito Casini, *La tunica stracciata. Lettera di un cattolico sulla "riforma liturgica"* (Rome,

"Betrayal!" This is in fact the word that recurs more often than any other in his little work. The title already conveys the message: Those in charge of the reform have unhesitatingly torn the seamless robe of Christ, the robe of the Church's unity and of the Tridentine faith, and have sided with the Protestant Reformers. The book unsparingly names individuals,[9] especially Cardinal Lercaro, whom Casini portrays as a new Luther.

The worst aspect of the whole business was that the book had a preface by Cardinal Antonio Bacci, a famous Latinist, who, while acknowledging some exaggerations in the book, justified it with an appeal to the example of the saints: "In my opinion, these pages, which remind us of the even more fearless writings of St. Catherine of Siena, may lead to the correction of some ideas and thus do good." He saw the book as being also a kind of roadblock thrown up against certain extremes: "Eucharistic suppers, beat Masses, rah-rah Masses, Masses of the longhaired folk, and similar rubbish." The Cardinal, like Casini, made no distinc-

---

1967). On the whole affair see L. Bedeschi, *Il Cardinale destituito. Documenti sul "caso" Lercaro* (Turin, 1968), especially 37–54 (with extensive bibliographical information).

9. These personal attacks became habitual among the opponents of the reform. Y. Congar (n. 1) noted as characteristic of these opponents that they "gave their enemies contemptuous labels and never withdrew them; they included everything they hated in a term expressing passionate and unnuanced rejection; they claimed to be in the right, even if this required them at times to act like pettifogging lawyers; they were convinced that the wicked were plotting and that a conspiracy of 'Jews and Masons' or Communists had breached the Church's walls and was operating within it, fomenting an internal rebellion" (p. 19).

The description is perfect. These people respected no one and gave no one credit for good faith. With a disregard that was neither human nor Christian, they indulged in utterly defamatory charges that in the civil sphere would have been the basis for indictments for slander. The authors of the reform were called "Lercarians" or "Bugninists" and described as continuing the devastation wrought by Hannibal (reference again to the secretary of the Consilium), destroyers of the faith, "the liars of Santa Marta," and "the Protestants of Rome" (R. Capone in *Candido*), and always, in addition, "Masons." With astonishing "simplicity," Archbishop Lefèbvre wrote in his *Lettre aux amis*, no. 10, March 27, 1976 (the *Lettre* is the quasi-official organ of the *Fraternité sacerdotale S. Pie X* of Ecône): "When we learn in Rome that the man who has been the soul of the liturgical reform is a Mason, we may think that he is not the only one. The veil covering the great mystification that has been worked on clergy and faithful is undoubtedly beginning to lift."

The charge that Archbishop Bugnini was a Mason quickly got into the newspapers. The baffling suppression of the Congregation for Divine Worship, the sending of its secretary as pro-nuncio to Iran, and the scattering of his principal fellow workers would all help give credit to the disgraceful slander. The series of affronts makes a lengthy and amusing story. For example, while attending a meeting of traditionalists in Rome, a woman recognized the secretary of the Consilium, was filled with a holy anger, and attacked him in St. Peter's Square with scorching words and spat in his face. He received many letters, more or less anonymous, that were filled with unquotable insults and, in one case, even threatened him with death.

tion between arbitrary activities rejected by the authorities and legitimate pastoral needs. From this point on, and through the years ahead, the liturgical reform was condemned as the cause of all aberrations in the Church; no other cause of these was acknowledged.

Neither the surprise expressed by many Catholic newspapers nor a ringing rebuke from the Pope himself[10] had any effect. Casini even produced a second book, in which he challenged and ridiculed those opposed to him;[11] he followed this up with still others in the same vein that said nothing new worth noting but simply repeated the same accusations over and over. The only thing new about them was the added venom and the added insults.[12]

On the feast of Corpus Christi, 1967, *Una voce* sent the Pope a petition, signed by, among others, educated non-Catholics and expressing "alarm and amazement" at the liturgical reform. It asked that "alongside the communal liturgy in the vernacular that is now everywhere obligatory (despite the limits set by the liturgical Constitution), the Latin Gregorian Mass, which is the form proper to the Roman Rite, be firmly assured of a continued place."[13]

The admission of the vernaculars into the Canon of the Mass marked a further step in the opposition. An Italian priest won notoriety for himself with duplicated materials and then with privately printed pamphlets.[14] These booklets, too, trampled on good sense and reason. Their very

---

10. See *DOL* 86 no. 639 and above, p. 166.

11. T. Casini, *Dicebamus heri. La tunica stracciata alla sbarra* (Florence, 1967).

12. Idem, *Super flumina Babylonis. Lettere dall'esilio* (Florence, 1969); *L'ultima Messa di Paolo VI. Sogni di una notte d'autunno* (Florence, 1970); *Dall'esilio alle catacombe. Ricorso a Maria* (Florence, 1970); and, finally, *Nel fumo di Satana. Verso l'ultimo scontro* (Florence, 1976). The last-named book ends in this way: "*Our Mass*, supreme expression of our worship, which the smoke of Satan seeks to hide and thus take from us at the end of a reform (led by a Bugnini who has at last been shown to be the Mason we always suspected him of being) that lacks only this for its victory to be complete and its reign unchallenged" (p. 150).

The same tone was to be found among the Roman composers, especially after the publication of the instruction on sacred music. This was all the more surprising, since the whole debate seemed to be a domestic squabble. We have already seen something of this business (see above, p. 229). See also C. R., "Le innovazioni nella musica sacra provocano polemiche anche in Vaticano," *Il Tempo*, March 7, 1967; L. Calo, *Presente e futuro della musica sacra*, which contains nothing less than the lectures, entirely directed against the reform, which the author gave on Vatican Radio!; D. Celada, *Arcobaleno Beat* (Rome, n. d.), a combination of charges and pornography; P. Santucci, *La Rèpubblica di Pilato* (Bologna, 1973), another savage, free-swinging book full of insults.

13. *Il Messagero*, June 17, 1967.

14. Clemente Belluco, *Stabilire quale è "la formula precisa della Consacrazione Eucaristica"* (n. d.; 25 pp.). In an article entitled "La 'formula precisa della consacrazione eucaristica.' Un opuscolo venenoso" (*Palestra del clero* 52 [1973] 803–17), Father Gabriele Roschini re-

style betrays a writer of unbalanced mind and a common slanderer who respects no one.

Instead of helping to throw water on the fire, some reputable students of the liturgy and the sacred sciences fanned the flames, showing that they did not understand either the tact required by the situation or the pastoral goals of the reform.[15] The point of absurdity was reached when some individuals, taking advantage of their reputations, managed to get articles published even in *L'Osservatore Romano*. Thus, on January 15, 1969, the latter gave space to a lengthy article of Hubert Jedin entitled "Storia della Chiesa e crisi della Chiesa." The liturgy is here listed first among the causes of the present crisis and depicted as responsible for "violent opposition," "chaos," and dangerous experimentation. Here was a primarily negative vision of the reform, with nostalgic regrets for the lost Latin language, which had been a "bond of unity," and for the "immortal creations of our sacred music." Jedin also pointed out the defects of the translations, especially those in German.[16]

---

plied "not in order to convince Don Belluco (who does not seem disposed humbly to accept the truth) but to put the clergy and faithful on guard against his snares." Belluco's pamphlet is described as "elegant in its typography but utterly erroneous in its content and deplorable in its manner (full of vulgar insults directed at the Church, the Pope, the Italian Episcopal Conference, Cardinal Lercaro, and Monsignor Bugnini)" (p. 803).

As was to be expected, Don Belluco responded with another pamphlet: *Lettera aperta al Direttore della Rivista "Palestra del clero"* (n. d.; 20 pp.). Other publications of Belluco: *Lettera aperta a P. Rotondi* (n. d.; 12 pp.); *Taccuino di "appunti"* (n. d.; 98 pp.), which is an open condemnation of the Council.

15. See L. Bouyer, *La décomposition du catholicisme* (Ligué, 1968). [English translation: *The Decomposition of Catholicism*, trans. Charles Underhill Quinn (Chicago, 1969).]

16. On January 29, 1969, the secretary of the Consilium wrote Professor Jedin a lengthy letter in which he pointed out the contradictions in the latter's article and the one-sided way in which he reported facts. "As a good historian who knows how to weigh both sides and reach a balanced judgment, why did you not mention the millions and hundreds of millions of the faithful who have at last achieved worship in spirit and in truth? Who can at last pray to God in their own languages and not in meaningless sounds, and are happy that henceforth they know what they are saying? Are they not 'the Church'?"

As for the "bond of unity": "Do you believe the Church has no other ways of securing unity? Do you believe there is a deep and heartfelt unity amid lack of understanding, ignorance, and the 'dark night' of a worship that lacks a face and light, at least for those out in the nave? Do you not think that a priestly pastor must seek and foster the unity of his flock—and thereby of the universal flock—through a living faith that is fed by the rites and finds expression in song, in communion of minds, in the love that animates the Eucharist, in conscious participation, and in entrance into the mystery? Unity of language is superficial and fictitious; the other kind of unity is vital and profound."

The secretary also makes this observation, which is valid for the entire "liturgical counterreform": "You have failed to grasp one of the most important elements in the liturgical 'restoration': the *pastoral*, which Vatican II sought and pursued. Here in the Consi-

Among the activities of the traditionalist associations that deserve mention because of the attention given to them were three international pilgrimages, also known as "marches on Rome." The first took place on the feast of St. Peter in 1970; there were Masses at the Colosseum and in some acquiescent Roman churches, a pilgrimage to the tomb of St. Pius V in Santa Maria Maggiore and the tomb of St. Peter, and a prayer vigil in the Piazza S. Pietro during the night of June 28–29. All these activities were intended to strengthen fidelity to the traditional Mass and the Catechism of St. Pius X and to promote rejection of the translations and ambiguous interpretations of Sacred Scripture. About five hundred people took part.[17]

The other pilgrimages were held at Pentecost in 1971 and 1973, with more or less the same program of events. Especially at the time of the first pilgrimage, there was a demand that the Holy Father receive the participants, but the request was fruitless.

3. The "Heretical" Mass

The promulgation of the new Order of Mass and General Instruction of the Roman Missal by the apostolic constitution *Missale Romanum* of April 3, 1969, caused traditionalist groups to focus their efforts on preserving the Tridentine form of the Mass, or the "Mass of St. Pius V." Their request could even be regarded as quite legitimate when seen as a psychological and spiritual need of faithful who were accustomed to the kind of celebration they had known and loved since childhood and who were ill at ease with the new rite. But the petitions made had a serious drawback: they criticized the Missal of Paul VI as heretical and Protestant and claimed that the Mass of St. Pius V was the only authentic Mass.

On September 25, 1969, Cardinals Alfredo Ottaviani and Antonio Bacci sent the Holy Father a letter and a *Breve esame critico del "Novus Ordo Missae"*;[18] this critique was, they said, "the work of a select group of theologians, liturgists, and pastors of souls." In their letter they wrote:

---

lium we are not working for museums or archives, but for the spiritual life of the people of God. . . . The present renewal of the Church is serious, solid, thoroughgoing, and *safe*, even if it also brings suffering and opposition. It has not focused its attention on a *single* 'echo' (and one that is truncated and deformed in the bargain) of a historical event and drawn catastrophic conclusions from it. Do you not think, Professor, that historians too ought to search historical events and discover signs of God in them?"

17. See G. Rospigliosi, "La manifestazione dei cattolici tradizionalisti. Riconfermano la fedeltà al messale e al catechismo," *Il Tempo*, June 19, 1970.

18. *Breve esame critico del "Novus Ordo Missae"* (Rome: Fondazione "Lumen gentium," n. d.; 32 pp.). News of the incident created a sensation and found its way into many

When we look at its new underlying and implied elements (though they are admittedly susceptible of divergent interpretations), the new Order of Mass represents, both as a whole and its details, a significant departure from the Catholic theology of the Mass as formulated at the twenty-second session of the Council of Trent. That Council definitively established the norms for the rite of Mass and erected an impassable barrier to any heresy that might attack the integrity of the mystery . . . . The recent reforms have made it quite clear that new changes in the liturgy can lead only to a total disorientation of the faithful, who are already showing signs of impatience and an undeniable lessening of faith. Among the better clergy all this takes the concrete form of a painful crisis of conscience to which we have countless daily testimonies . . . .

In this time of painful wounds and increasing dangers to purity of faith and the unity of the Church—a situation that finds a daily, sorrowful echo in the addresses of the common Father—we therefore urge and implore Your Holiness not to take from us the possibility of continuing to draw upon the fruitfulness and integrity of the *Missale Romanum* of St. Pius V, whom Your Holiness has so greatly extolled and whom the entire Catholic world so venerates and loves.

The "critical study" singled out the points that were to be obsequiously repeated by the traditionalists in their opposition to the Missal of Paul VI.

1) The Mass is now regarded, not as the sacrifice of Christ, but as a "supper" and "memorial" rather than the unbloody renewal of the sacrifice of Calvary. "Even the formula 'Memorial of the passion and resurrection of the Lord' is inaccurate, since the Mass is the memorial solely of the sacrifice, which is redemptive in itself, whereas the resurrection is simply the subsequent fruit of it" (pp. 8–9).

2) The real presence is at least tacitly denied, and the word "transubstantiation" is absent. Rubrical simplifications (in the matter of genuflections, purifications, etc.) are a further sign of this new attitude.

3) "The formulas of consecration are now spoken by the priest as parts of a historical narrative and no longer as *expressing a categorical and affirmative judgment uttered* by the One in whose person the priest acts (for he says 'This is my body,' not 'This is the body of Christ')" (pp. 16–17). According to the authors, in the second Pauline acclamation—"When we eat this bread and drink this cup, we proclaim your death, Lord Jesus, until you come in glory"—"the several realities of immolation and eat-

---

newspapers; see R. G., "La nuova Messa 'eretica' e 'profanatoria,' " *Il Messagero*, October 30, 1969.

ing, real presence, and second coming of Christ are presented with a maximum of ambiguity" (p. 17).

4) The communal character of the new Mass gives an equivocal picture of the priestly office because it does not make clear the "subordination" of the common priesthood to the hierarchic priesthood. "The true role of the priest disappears"; he is *"president* or *brother* rather than *consecrated minister* who celebrates *in the person of Christ"* (p. 19).

5) Protestant teaching has found its way into the new Order of Mass. This assertion is frequently repeated in the illustrative notes and explicitly in the text: the new Order of Mass "would on many points satisfy the most modernist Protestants" (p. 5); the priest is obviously "no more than a Protestant minister" (p. 19). The second Eucharistic Prayer "immediately scandalized the faithful by its brevity"; the authors go so far as to say, among other things, that this prayer could be used with a completely serene conscience by a priest who no longer believes in transubstantiation or the sacrificial character of the Mass and that it could therefore readily be used in a celebration by a Protestant minister (p. 24).

6) The new Order of Mass contains "elements that are *spiritually and psychologically destructive . . .* both in the text and in the rubrics and instructions" (p. 23). "It is clear that the new Order *no longer intends to reflect the faith of Trent. But the Catholic conscience is for ever bound to that faith.* The promulgation of the new Order therefore compels a true Catholic to make a tragic choice."

Cardinals Ottaviani and Bacci show a little more sensitivity when they write: "When a law shows itself to be truly harmful, subjects who realize this have not so much a right as a duty to approach the legislator with filial confidence and ask him to abrogate the law."

The "short critical study" reaches precisely that conclusion. It thus provides the basis not only for the open disobedience to Pope and bishops that would subsequently be so vociferously demonstrated, but also for the extremes that would be reached in the "counterreform." *Il Messagero* of October 30, 1969, had no trouble in seeing this.

> For the two elderly cardinals (who accept the conclusions reached by the authors of the study) the abandonment of the traditional liturgy and its replacement by the liturgy approved by Paul VI "is clearly an incalculable error—to use no harsher language." What term would the authors of this letter use if they were asked to avoid euphemisms? Would they not say "heresy" instead of "error"?

That is precisely what others were to do.

It is impossible to understand how Cardinal Ottaviani could have signed a pamphlet marked not only by one-sidedness but by ignorance of theology. After all, despite his well-known traditionalist views, he was an intelligent man and had the education required by his office. As prefect of the Congregation for the Doctrine of the Faith, he approved the instruction on worship of the Eucharistic mystery, the document on which the General Instruction of the Missal largely depends. In addition, he approved the new Eucharistic Prayers! And how could he have failed to see that his opposition was an attack on papal authority?

There is no need here of showing that the objections raised were unfounded.[19] The Holy Father replied to the appeal of the two cardinals by writing personally to the Congregation for the Doctrine of the Faith on October 22, 1969. He enclosed the documents sent to him and requested that the Congregation conduct "a careful examination of the criticisms raised." He also ordered that "the Sacred Congregation for Divine Worship not proceed with the definitive publication of the *Ordo Missae* and the *Institutio generalis Missalis Romani* until the Sacred Congregation for the Doctrine of the Faith has decided whether the criticisms in question require a revision of these important liturgical texts."[20]

After a group of theologians in the Congregation had studied the objections, Cardinal Šeper was able to write to the Secretariat of State on November 12, 1969, that "the pamphlet *Breve esame* . . . contains many superficial, exaggerated, inaccurate, biased, and false statements." The study led only to a few not strictly necessary revisions in the General Instruction of the Missal, especially in no. 7. In order to confirm and explain the continuity in the doctrinal and liturgical traditions, as well as in catechetical instruction, an "Introduction" was added to the instruction. The instruction itself, however, was found to be in full conformity with the teaching of the Church on the Eucharist.

Despite this outcome, the Cardinal's action became the basis for the attack on the orthodoxy of the new Order of Mass and against the Missal

---

19. Many capable writers have demonstrated this. I shall mention only well-known theologian C. Vagaggini, O.S.B., "Il nuovo *Ordo Missae* e l'ortodossia," *Rivista del Clero Italiano* 50 (1969) 688–99. There was dissent even in circles not at all favorable to the reform; see Renié, "Le nouvel *Ordo Missae* serait-il hérétique?" *Chévalier* (Supplément à *Magistère-Information des Chévaliers de Notre-Dame*), nos. 24-25 (1974–75) 11–15, and no. 26 (1975) 5–10. There is also the valuable little book of Guy Oury, O.S.B., *La Messe de S. Pie V à Paul VI* (Solesmes, 1975; 128 pp.), which examines the main objections of the opponents and shows them to be entirely lacking in validity and foundation; see also A. Richard, *Le mystère de la messe dans le nouvel Ordo* (Paris, 1970); A.-G. Martimort, "Ma cos'è la Messa di San Pio V?" *L'Osservatore Romano*, August 30–31, 1976, reprinted from *La Croix*, August 26, 1976.

20. Letter of the Sacred Congregation for the Doctrine of the Faith, October 25, 1969 (Prot. No. 2747/69).

of Paul VI generally. A leaflet distributed during the first traditionalist pilgrimage of June 28–29, 1970, had this to say:

> We know that the infallible and irreformable teaching of the Council of Trent on the Holy Sacrifice of the Mass has been betrayed in the new rites: by the imposition of the vernacular, by the fraudulent watering down of the consecration of the chalice, and by the translation into the vernacular which has destroyed the Catholic doctrine on justification as defined by the Council of Trent. The Mass is no longer the bloodless renewal of the sacrifice of Calvary, but an assembly; the hierarchical and sacral priesthood has been eliminated and replaced by a president of the assembly . . . .
> We know that the entire liturgical reform amounts to a real disavowal of transubstantiation and the real presence of Christ in the Eucharist.

One of the organizers, a Mrs. Gerstner, supposedly said that the "Montini" Mass is "heretical" and that if the Pope "regards us as rebels that is not our fault."[21]

Noël Barbara, a priest, said in his *Lettera al Santo Padre il Pontefice Paolo VI*: "How can we respect a reform in which six Protestant pastors played a part, men whom you received at the end of their work (and with whom you were photographed) as a token of thanks for their collaboration?"

Also worth citing are the words of Dominican Th. Calmel: "I unhesitatingly acknowledge the authority of the Holy Father. I claim, however, that any Pope in the exercise of his authority can abuse that authority. I maintain that Pope Paul VI has abused his authority in an exceptionally serious way by approving a new rite of Mass that is no longer Catholic."[22]

The traditionalist sector put together an increasingly intense campaign aimed at showing the new Missal to be "heretical," "ambiguous," and "a denial of the most authentic Catholic tradition and a concession to centrifugal tendencies that seek to have Catholics adopt ceremonies of a Protestant kind."[23] Malicious use was made of the presence of non-

---

21. Agenzia Ansa, *Informazioni religiose*, July 4, 1970, p. 6.

22. Noël Barbara, *Lettera al Santo Padre il Pontefice Paolo VI* (Rome: Giovanni Volpe Editore, 1970) 8 and 4.

23. See "La nouvelle Messe est équivoque," *Forts dans la foi, Supplément* to no. 30, p. 7. See, too, the motion passed at the November 1970 meeting of four traditionalist organizations in the United States (The Latin Mass Society, Legionary Movement, *Una voce*, and the Catholic Traditionalist Movement), reported in *Notiziario* (of the Italian *Una voce* movement), no. 4 (January 1971) 5. It is impossible to list all the articles and pamphlets that conveyed the same ideas. Many appeared in the journal *Itinéraires* (and *Itinéraires supplément*) and in *Forts dans la foi*; no. 122 (1969) of *La pensée catholique* is entirely devoted to the new Order of Mass. Other publications: Salleron, *La sovversione nella Liturgia* (Rome: Ed. Volpe; 128 pp.); P. Tilloy, *L'"Ordo Missae." L'unità nell'eresia* (Rome: Ed. Volpe; 140 pp.); Vinson,

Catholic observers in the Consilium; this presence supposedly showed that the texts of the Missal of Paul VI are "worlds removed from the dogmatic purity and integrity of the earlier texts and have been composed in a strange collaboration with six Protestant pastors; the purpose was at least to lessen the abyssal distance separating Roman Catholic doctrine from that of the innovators who were condemned by the 'dogmatic' Council of Trent."[24]

The same groups saw to it that on November 30, 1969, the day on which the new Order of Mass went into effect, the waters of some famous Roman fountains were stained red. A leaflet explained the symbolism by citing Exodus 7:19 and adding: "Romans, today, November 30, 1969, the new Reformers have decreed the death of the Holy Mass as celebrated for centuries throughout the world! A cry of indignant protest arises from the City that is the center of Christianity! The waters of Rome run red just as the waters of Egypt were transformed into blood!"

That same day the secretary of the Congregation for Divine Worship received a drawing that showed Luther crying, "I have conquered!" It was accompanied by a black-bordered note that said, among other things:

> November 30, 1969: Day of mourning for the Catholic Church. — A multitude of Catholics are today mourning the deceased Catholic Church, whose religion will henceforth stand beside Luther's, due to the changes and desecrations in it, which include even tampering with the substance and form of the divine sacrifice of Christ. Souls are confused, and there is a frightening increase in defections from Catholic truth and in religious indifference and atheism.
>
> Let the promoters of these changes, the men in charge of the Congregation for Divine Worship, consider the seriousness of the situation and their own resultant responsibilities.
>
> Today, November 30, 1969, it is not only Luther but neo-Protestant pastor Bugnini who conquers.

The note ended with: "Get thee behind me, Satan!"

La nouvelle Messe et la conscience catholique (pro manuscripto; 33 pp.); James F. Witheu, O.S.J., *The Great Sacrilege* (Rockford, Ill., 1971); G. De Nantes, *Lettere* (Rome: Ed. Volpe, 1969); D. Celada, "La mini-messa contro il dogma," *Lo Specchio*, June 29, 1969; "Tout restaurer dans le Christ" Association, *Parce, Domine, parce populo tuo* (1975; 32 pp.), containing revelations of Christ the King from 1964 to 1974; same Association, *Note explicative. La Messe falsifiée ou les trahisons dans l'Eglise* (1975; 22 pp.).

24. From the Christian Civilization document at the meeting on "Orthodoxy and Orthopraxis" that the *Chiesa viva* organization sponsored at Rome in 1974; see "Per il ripristino del rito tridentino," *Realtà politica*, October 26, 1974, p. 3.

The ideas poured out by the press of every persuasion are reflected here as in many other letters sent to the Holy See. Here is another example, dated January 3, 1973:

> We are a group of priests of Paris who have abandoned the Protestant (or Protestantized) Mass of Paul VI and are again celebrating the Roman Catholic Mass of all times (the so-called Mass of St. Pius V).
>
> We are celebrating this holy and true Mass in private premises in Paris for hundreds of the faithful who have left their parishes because they can no longer accept the falsified Mass.
>
> The Tridentine Mass (which is really not Tridentine but in substance the same Mass celebrated from the time of Christ and St. Peter to John XXIII) is the sure, Catholic, intact, pure Mass.
>
> The faithful know this. They have the *sensus fidei*.
>
> They know that the "mass" of Paul VI is really a lie; that it is really the "mass" (or rather the supper) of Thurian, Smith, George, Konneth [sic], and Sephard (!), those five Lutheran/Calvinists who are the authors of this falsified Mass. When the bishops impose the new Mass, they are abusing their authority. It is better to obey God rather than men.
>
> We have chosen obedience to God and to truth.
>
> We refuse obedience to the ambiguities and lies of the new Church. (Signed by the Abbé Descamps, 32, rue de Babylone, Paris; dated and sent from Rome.)

4. *The Challenge to Papal Authority*

This letter is an obvious rejection of ecclesiastical authority. The question is often asked how devout persons, attached to tradition, could maintain that an apostolic constitution, one of the most solemn of papal documents and one that comes close to involving papal infallibility, could sponsor and even impose a liturgical book not in conformity with Church doctrine.

The opponents felt the difficulty and got around it by sophistries.

1) Someone spread the idea that the apostolic constitution *Missale Romanum* was a forgery. The claim was based on a difference between the text published by the Vatican Polyglot Press in *Ordo Missae*, 1969, and the text that appeared in the *Acta Apostolicae Sedis*. In the first of these two publications, the apostolic constitution does in fact lack some lines establishing the *vacatio legis*. But this was a secondary point that could be, and in fact was, established by a decree of the Congregation of Rites. Furthermore, the official text is the one in the *Acta*.

2) The majority of opponents took their stand on a comparison between the final words of the bull *Quo primum* of St. Pius V and those of the apostolic constitution *Missale Romanum*. The stern words of the former,

establishing *in perpetuum* the form of the celebration of Mass and threatening serious penalties for those who dare to introduce changes, supposedly make the Missal of St. Pius V irreformable. But this thesis cannot be maintained on either historical or doctrinal grounds.[25]

3) According to others, the Pope was forced to sign the document. This claim was perhaps an inference from, of all things, the good faith and ingenuousness—misused by ill-intentioned people—of Cardinal Benno Gut, president of the Consilium and prefect of the Congregation of Rites. This good Cardinal, a candid soul and a lover of monastic life and liturgy, was deeply disturbed and affected when told of some abuses in the area of liturgy. When questioned about these abuses, he showed his grief and concern. Someone took advantage of it by twisting his words and still more his meaning. He supposedly said: "Many priests have simply done whatever they pleased. It was often impossible to put a stop to these unauthorized actions because the situation had gone too far. Then the Holy Father, in his great goodness and prudence, yielded, often against his will."[26]

The Cardinal was obviously speaking of the Pope's response to abuses; of this there could be no doubt for those who knew Cardinal Gut. For him the Pope's word was absolute law, even on occasions when he himself could not understand the reasons for a step. To see the Cardinal as challenging the Pope's action or even criticizing it is to offer him a serious insult. As a matter of fact, he suffered much from the whole business.

4) In support of the thesis just discussed, it was also said that in private the Pope celebrated Mass according to the old Missal. This utterly strange notion was attributed this time to the secretary of the Congregation for Divine Worship. He never received an answer to his repeated requests to know when he was supposed to have made the statement.[27]

---

25. See the exhaustive article "La mise en application du nouveau Missel Romain. Etat de la question," *La Documentation Catholique*, no. 1614 (August 1972) 731–34, and in *Not* 8 (1972) 337–42.

26. *La Documentation Catholique*, November 16, 1969.

27. The claim was spread by the spiritual father of the seminary at Ecône, first in a duplicated "dossier" and then in print: L. M. Barrielle, *La Messe catholique est-elle encore permise?* (Montigny, n. d.; 48 pp.). On p. 19 the author writes: "Referring to the signing of the new Order of Mass by Paul VI, Monsignor Bugnini supposedly said: '*It took endless efforts to extort this signature from him. Now he [the Pope] continues to use the Order of Mass of St. Pius V for his private Masses!*'" (italicized words are in bold print in the original). Archbishop Bugnini twice wrote to Father Barrielle (March 23 and April 27, 1974), asking him for the names of his sources and the circumstances and place in which these words were supposed to have been spoken; he received no answer. Bishop Hänggi of Basel also tried to find out, but in vain.

It was not too difficult to guess who the rumormongers were. In any case, the whole thing was very odd. It is, after all, the Pope's public acts and not his private life that is authoritative.[28]

5) According to still others, the Pope did not intend to impose the new Missal but simply to permit it. Cardinal Ottaviani himself supposedly said in an interview:

> The traditional rite of Mass according to the Order of St. Pius V has never, to my knowledge, been abolished. Therefore, in order especially to ensure the purity of the rite and the understanding of its communal dimension by the congregation, the local Ordinary would, in my humble opinion, do well to encourage the continued use of the rite of St. Pius V, while not denying that the Mass as recently revised substantially retains its essential unity of structure, as the ordinary faithful can see.[29]

The Cardinal's statement here is strangely at variance with what had been said in the *Breve esame critico!* In any case, the final words of the apostolic constitution *Missale Romanum* leave no doubt. It is the Pope's intention that the new Missal should, even if only gradually, completely replace the earlier Missal.[30]

6) The most specious contrivance, however, is the distinction between "Montini" the person and "Paul VI," the man in authority. The Christian Civilization document mentioned earlier claims that

> a very clear and providential distinction between "Peter" and "Simon" belongs to the very substance of the dogma of papal infallibility:
>
> —between Peter who must alone *guide* his brethren, *help them by word and example* and thus *confirm* them in the faith by his teaching . . . which, if it is to be valid and binding, must be proposed within the limits and under the conditions of safety and authenticity laid down by the First Vatican Council;
>
> —and Simon, the fearful individual who despite his enthusiasm could be a stumbling block for Jesus, went to sleep in Gethsemane, and denied his master.[31]

---

28. The Pope expressed his mind clearly in several addresses, concerned especially with the Mass, on November 19 and 26, 1969, and August 22, 1971: see *Not* 5 (1969) 412, 221; 9 (1973) 297; *DOL* 211 nos. 1757-59; 212 nos. 1760-64.

29. *Carrefour*, June 9, 1971.

30. For challenges in the juridical area, see "Consultation, temoignage et voeu sur le nouvel *Ordo Missae*," *La pensée catholique*, no. 122 (1969) 44–47, written by a group of traditionalist canonists; L. Salleron, "La loi de l'Eglise en matière liturgique," *ibid.*, no. 134 (1971) 10–24; Fidelis, "Les deux Messes," and G. Romains, "A propos de l'intention de la validité," *Courier de Rome*, no. 123 (October 15, 1973); Neri Capponi, "Alcuni considerazioni giuridiche in materia di riforma liturgica," *Archivio Giuridico* 190, no. 2 (1976) 147-73.

31. "Per il ripristino di rito tridentino," *Realtà Politica*, October 26, 1974, p. 3.

Using this specious argument, some groups went so far as publicly to accuse the Pope of heresy and to ask Paul VI to reject the work of "Montini."

The signal was given here by Abbé Georges de Nantes, who wrote in November 1972:

> The Pope must be deposed, because Paul VI incarnates in his person the violation of God's law by the reformers. It must be done before he can introduce disorder into the manner of electing his successor and thus pave the way for chaos.
>
> I have therefore decided, with the agreement of our Circle leaders, who met on October 1, and of my brothers in religion, to lay at the feet of His Holiness Pope Paul VI a *libellum accusationis*, a bill of charges listing heresy, schism, and scandal and requiring that he pass solemn sentence and infallible judgment on his own actions.[32]

And, in fact, in April 1973 a delegation of sixty persons from France, led by the Abbé himself, came to Rome to hand the indictment to Pope Paul VI. There were stormy press conferences and scuffles with the Italian police as well as with the papal police who barred the way to the papal apartments. From the Abbé's own description, it seems that despite all precautions one of his followers managed to make his way into the offices of Bishop Giacomo Martin, prefect of the Pontifical Household, and left the indictment with him, and that Bishop Martin immediately sent it back to the hotel where the Abbé was staying.[33] The indictment was published in several languages and distributed free in St. Peter's Square, preferably to clergymen.[34] This and similar actions pass judgment on themselves; it was thought that the proper response was patience, forbearance, and understanding.[35]

---

32. *La Contre-Réforme catholique au XXe siècle*, no. 62 (November 1972) 16. (This is the periodical of the Abbé de Nantes' association.)

33. The incredible adventures of the "descent" on Rome to secure an indictment of Pope Paul VI are told by Abbé Georges de Nantes himself. His quasi-diary for April 9–11, 1973, in which the pathetic, the humorous, and the grotesque are intermingled, is in *La Contre-Réforme catholique au XXe siècle*, no. 67 (April 1973).

34. *Liber accusationis in Paulum sextum*. A notre Saint Père le Pape Paul VI par la grâce de Dieu et la loi de l'Eglise Juge Souverain de tous les fidèles du Christ. Plainte pour hérésie, schisme et scandale au sujet de notre Père dans la foi, le Pape Paul VI, de l'Abbé Georges de Nantes (St. Parres les Vaudes: Maison Saint Joseph, 1973. 102 pp.). Anyone patient and persevering enough to read these pages will see a man on the brink of madness.

35. The Sunday celebration in the Salle Wagram, organized by Father Ducaud-Bouget, caused special tension and attracted unusual attention. The efforts of Cardinal Marty to reach an understanding were rendered fruitless by the elderly priest's uncompromising rejection of the Pope's authority to legislate in matters liturgical. In "A propos de la salle

The opposition became more serious and worrisome, however, when Archbishop Marcel Lefèbvre became its champion. All attention was soon focused on him as he became leader of the opposition to the conciliar renewal and to the Council itself. He had founded a "brotherhood of priests" (*Fraternitè sacerdotale*) and a seminary at Ecône in Switzerland; its members were to exercise their ministry according to the preconciliar liturgy. Their activity and that of Archbishop Lefèbvre himself in various dioceses of France, Switzerland, England, and Italy soon began to sow confusion and uneasiness among the faithful. In response to petitions from bishops, the Holy See arranged for an apostolic visitation of Ecône by a committee made up of Cardinals Garrone, Tabera, and Wright. They decreed:

1) the immediate dissolution of the *Fraternité sacerdotale S. Pie V*;

2) the closing of the seminary in Ecône;

3) a prohibition against clergy and faithful giving aid to the work of Archbishop Marcel Lefèbvre.[36]

The decree was, of course, not accepted, and a period of open disobedience and opposition began which displayed its full virulence in the "manifesto" or profession of faith that Archbishop Lefèbvre issued on November 21, 1974, and published in *Itinéraires*. In it he states his refusal to heed

> the Rome that has clearly shown itself to be neo-Modernist and neo-Protestant in tendency at Vatican II and in all the postconciliar reforms that originated in the Council. All these reforms have helped and are still helping to demolish the Church, ruin the priesthood, destroy the sacrifice and sacraments, put an end to religious life, and promote Teilhardian naturalistic teaching in universities, seminaries, and catechetics, though this teaching derives from liberalism and Protestantism and has frequently been condemned in the solemn teaching of the Church.
>
> No authority, even the highest in the hierarchy, can force us to abandon or water down our Catholic faith that has been clearly expressed and professed by the magisterium of the Church for nineteen centuries. . . . We choose what has always been taught, and we close our ears to the destructive novelties now found in the Church.

And, with more direct reference to the liturgical reform:

Wagram," *Présence et dialogue* (Paris), January 9, 1975, the Cardinal told of all he had done to settle matters. Father Ducaud-Bouget published his side of the story in *Lettre a un Cardinal*.

36. See Jean Madiran, "Les mesures 'sauvages' illégalement prises contre Ecône," *Itinéraires. Supplément-Voltigeur*, no. 29 (June 15, 1975) 6–8; Jean Anzevui, *Le drame d'Ecône (Historique, analyse et documents)* (Sion: Valprint, 1976); Y. Montagne, "*Il Vescovo sospeso.*" *Mons. Lefèbvre* (Rome: a cura del Centro di Ecône, n. d.); Y. Congar (see note 1).

It is not possible radically to change the *lex orandi* without also radically changing the *lex credendi*. The new Mass is matched by a new catechism, a new priesthood, new seminaries, new universities, and charismatic, pentecostal churches—all of them opposed to orthodoxy and constant teaching.

This reform, which derives from liberalism and Modernism, has poisoned everything; it is born of heresy and ends in heresy, even if all of its acts are not formally heretical. It is therefore impossible for a conscientious, believing Catholic to accept this reform and submit to it in even the smallest degree.

The only response possible for those who are faithful to the Church and Catholic teaching and who wish to be saved is a categorical rejection of the reform.

Thus began the disobedience, the public demonstrations, the protest celebrations, the ordination of priests, and the resultant suspension of Archbishop Lefèbvre from his priestly functions. The correspondence between the Pope and the Archbishop is a full one and displays, on the one side, a paternal concern and determination not to provoke the break-off of relations, and, on the other, the stubbornness of a man who is convinced that he alone is "faithful" to Christ and the Church. The Lefèbvre and Ecône affair ceased to be of limited interest and became a major event in all the newspapers. But no bishop followed him.[37]

5. *Attitude of the Holy See*

Not all traditionalist groups accepted the extreme conclusions of the most fanatical. Some limited themselves to petitioning that "in the future, as in the past, the so-called Tridentine Order of Mass (in the form published in the *Rubricarum instructum*) may have its place among the legitimate and universally recognized rites for the celebration of Holy Mass."[38] These groups regarded the Holy See's rejection of the petition

---

37. Even those who were opposed to the reform and therefore in agreement with some of Lefèbvre's positions would not follow him in his extreme stands.

38. Letter of Dr. Erich de Saventhen, president of the *Una voce* International Federation, to Cardinal A. Tabera, August 31, 1971; idem, Letter "Ai Padri del Sinodo," October 23, 1971. The same view—that the "Tridentine rite" should be regarded as a special one that had a right to exist alongside others—also found support in monastic circles. Especially conspicuous was the French abbey of Fontgombault, which for a long time insisted that a liturgy better adapted to contemplative monks was needed no less than a more pastoral liturgy for the faithful. The Abbot of Fontgombault also had the idea of reviving the ancient rite of Cluny; in this he was supported by the Cistercian Abbot of Hauterive. The SCDW was not opposed in principle; it simply asked for a description of the rites and texts, but never received it. The abbey continued instead to use the Tridentine rite, thereby eliciting reactions from the local bishops. Neither the interventions of his religious superiors nor those of the SCDW nor those of the Apostolic Nuncio in Paris succeeded in making the Abbot of Fontgombault change his mind.

as excessively harsh. As a matter of fact, despite good intentions, the dialogue proved difficult because of the intransigence of some and the continued misinterpretation by others of statements issued.[39]

It must be acknowledged in all honesty that the Roman authorities were even too understanding and patient. No steps were taken against the campaign of defamation that was carried on publicly in the press, even when polemics led to the vilest insinuations and vulgarities. The Holy Father himself put up with those who publicly accused him of heresy. Even when confronted with high-level actions like that of Cardinals Ottaviani and Bacci, he ordered that they be given consideration and that a "careful examination" of the liturgical books be made in the light of their accusations.

The Holy See was not even opposed to giving lenient consideration to the legitimate requests of certain groups of individuals. Thus elderly or sick priests who had difficulty in accepting the new rite of Mass or the new Liturgy of the Hours were allowed to continue using the old rites in private celebrations and with the permission of the Ordinary.[40]

Contrary to what has sometimes been asserted, consideration was also given to groups of the faithful who had the same difficulty in coming to grips with the new order of things. As a matter of fact, when the Congregation for Divine Worship was preparing the notification of June 14, 1971, it gave lengthy thought to granting the use of the old Missal in certain cases. There was a tendency to take a lenient view of the matter and to trust in good sense and the persuasion that the good cause of the reform would not be harmed thereby.[41] But the manifestations of intoler-

---

39. See, e.g., "Unicuique suum . . . ," *Not* 9 (1973) 48. To the request for a *single* celebration of Mass according to the "Tridentine" rite, in a specific place and under specific circumstances, the SCDW gave a benevolent answer, telling the petitioner to approach the local Ordinary, who would exercise pastoral prudence and judge whether the concession was appropriate and "would bring with it no danger of dividing or troubling the community of the faithful." The petitioner took advantage of this reply to spread the word that it was possible to ask the Ordinary for the habitual celebration of the Tridentine Mass. The inference was false and abusive.

40. See SCDW, instruction on the gradual carrying out of the apostolic constitution *Missale Romanum* (October 29, 1969), nos. 19-20: *Not* 5 (1969) 423; *DOL* 209 nos. 1750-51; SCDW, notification on the Roman Missal, the book of the Liturgy of the Hours, and the calendar (June 14, 1971), no. 3: *Not* 7 (1971) 215; *DOL* 216 no. 1772.

41. The first schema of the notification, which was sent to the members and consultors of the Congregation on April 5, 1971, had the following provision in no. 4: "When asked in cases of real need by special groups which, for the formation of its members or because of age or custom or other reasonable consideration, wish to participate at times in a Mass according to the rite and texts of the old Missal, local Ordinaries can allow it for Masses celebrated solely for the group in question and in Latin, provided that the request is motivated by true piety and there is no danger of introducing doubt, disturbance, or harm into

ance led to a decision to hold the line more firmly. If there had not been the danger of seeming to approve the opposition between the Tridentine and Pauline Missals, as though the former, unlike the latter, were a symbol of orthodoxy, the Holy See would certainly have taken a more lenient attitude.

All of this can be seen in a subsequent letter (June 29, 1973) from the Congregation for Divine Worship to the Secretariat of State on the subject of the attitude to be taken toward requests from traditionalist groups:

> Opposition to the "new" Mass has given rise to a bitterly disputatious campaign of attacks on the Pope and the Church, on the Council and ecclesiastical institutions. It has opposed the Mass of Pius V to that of Paul VI, calling one the expression of true faith, the other heretical. Once the problem is located on this doctrinal level, any yielding would be harmful to faith and discipline.
>
> On the other hand, when special cases arise in which the moving force is not polemical and doctrinal, a concession can be granted to celebrate the old Mass, not as "the Mass of Pius V," but simply as a liturgical formulary no longer in use, just as in some cases the Congregation has allowed the celebration of Mass according to the Mozarabic rite.
>
> Concessions thus understood are to be granted by the Holy See at the request of the local Ordinary, in order to avoid all disturbance and division.

It was thought that the campaign being conducted by more fanatical traditionalist groups would gradually die out. This did not happen, and so any concession became impossible.

The only known concession had been made earlier by direct intervention of the Holy See. At an audience of October 29, 1971, Cardinal Heenan had told the Pope of the discomfort of groups of converts and of elderly people who wanted to be able to celebrate Mass according to the old rite on special occasions. The next day the Pope wrote to Father Bugnini in his own hand:

> I pass on to the respected Father Annibale Bugnini, secretary of the Congregation for Divine Worship, the enclosed letter of Cardinal John Heenan, Archbishop of Westminster, which was followed by a verbal request at an audience on the 29th of this month. I ask you, in agreement with the Cardinal Prefect, to give the due answer before the Cardinal leaves Rome at the end of the Synod.

---

the community of the faithful." The members and consultors, except for two, asked that this number be removed. While recognizing that it represented an act of understanding, they also took into account the attitude of individuals asking for the concession and the difficulties it would create for bishops; they therefore regarded such a concession as harmful to the liturgical reform and the pastoral efforts of the bishops to apply it.

The Congregation must have already drawn up instructions for such cases. . . . In any event, I think, in agreement with the Cardinal Archbishop, that a favorable answer, cast in the proper formulas, should be given to the first request, and to the second as well, wherever special circumstances justify the concession. The Cardinal who is making the petition deserves every respect and confidence.

My thanks, prayers, and blessing. Paul VI, Supreme Pontiff. October 30, 1971.

Thus on November 5, 1971, permission was granted to individual bishops of England and Wales "to permit some groups of the faithful to participate on special occasions in a Mass celebrated with the rites and texts of the earlier Roman Missal that was published by decree of the Sacred Congregation of Rites on January 27, 1965, as modified in the instruction of May 4, 1967."

The requests had to be inspired by true devotion, and the permissions given in a way that would not bring harm to the community of the faithful. Since the Eucharist is a bond of unity, the concession could not be allowed to become a cause of disunity.[42]

6. *A Binding Missal*

In their propaganda against the new Roman Missal, traditionalist groups not only brought doctrinal accusations but argued that use of the book was optional and not obligatory. Bishops asked the Holy See on a number of occasions to clarify this point not only against the traditionalists but for the peace of conscience of many of the faithful.

At a plenary meeting on November 15, 1972, the Congregation for Divine Worship asked itself whether it might not be time to seek a juridical answer from the Pontifical Commission for the Interpretation of the Conciliar Documents. This recourse was proposed as indeed not necessary

---

42. The concessory letter urged that prudence and reserve be exercised in granting the faculty and that any grant not be given too much publicity. This perhaps displeased Cardinal Heenan, who wanted to publish the concessory letter. The English bishops would, in fact, show prudence and skill in using the faculty for the spiritual good of some groups of the faithful while continuing the liturgical renewal for the community as a whole; see the regulations they set down when the English translation of the Missal was published: "The New English Missal," *Not* 11 (1975) 143–44.

It seems that when Cardinal Heenan died, attempts were made to declare the indult no longer operative. It is certain that the concession, which the Pope granted in view of the special situation and mentality in England, caused difficulties: for the Holy See and the bishops of other countries, who were urged to obtain the same faculty; for the Congregation for Divine Worship, which the most intransigent rebuked for the grant; for its secretary, since the Pope had decided to turn to him rather than to the prefect.

but certainly useful in explaining matters to the faithful who were look-ing for an answer to doubts raised about the legitimacy or the binding character of the new Missal. The step was, however, judged to be inop-portune, since it would seem to suggest that the doubts had a solid foun-dation, whereas in fact the apostolic constitution *Missale Romanum* was perfectly clear, and would consequently be an insult to the authority of the Pope. For this reason the Congregation on December 29, 1972, sent the following response to the Secretariat of State, which had sent the ques-tion to the Congregation:

> No declaration will ever "convert" those who are determined at any cost to gain permission to use the Missal of St. Pius V. The leaders of this movement are not acting in good faith but with an ulterior purpose.
>
> The apostolic constitution *Missale Romanum* and its juridical intention are perfectly clear.
>
> Such a declaration would undermine the authority of the Pope, since everyone knows of the campaign of accusations against him by that sector of the Church, which continues to charge him with heresy and to label the Missal as heretical and Masses celebrated according to it as invalid, thereby dissuading the faithful from participating in them.
>
> The objection to the Missal would only be extended to all the reformed books, since the principle that is the basis and source of the challenge makes such an extension inevitable.

But on August 31, 1973, Monsignor Sustar, secretary of the Council of European Episcopal Conferences, insisted on a statement being issued as to whether the Mass of Pius V was unconditionally prohibited. After a new study of the question, it was decided that a response would be opportune. The text of an answer was proposed to the Secretary of State, who at that time was signing important documents of the Congregation for Divine Worship. On October 15, 1973 (No. 243874), the Secretary of State replied to the secretary of the Congregation that "in view of the delicacy of the subject, which is under such attack, it seems appropriate that Your Excellency should reply to the petitioner, in an entirely per-sonal form and in an unofficial letter bearing no protocol number." What was wanted was a clarification that would offend no one.

On October 17, 1973, the secretary of the Congregation explained mat-ters to Monsignor Sustar as follows:

1. The "Missal of Pius V" was definitively abrogated by the apostolic constitution *Missale Romanum*. One need only read the final paragraph.

2. In view, however, of the time needed to do translations, the new Missal was introduced only gradually. The Order of Mass went into ef-fect on November 30, 1969, and was to be in use everywhere in the Church by November 28, 1971. The episcopal conferences are to decide when the

other parts of the Missal go into effect. When a conference determines the date on which a vernacular text must be put into use, the corresponding Latin text becomes obligatory at the same time.[43]

3. Therefore the date for the obligatory use of the new Missal in its entirety is not the same for the whole Church but differs in different countries and linguistic regions, according to the decision of each episcopal conference.

But it was not enough to clarify the thought of the Holy See in a private letter to a single conference. Therefore, in light of the difficulties that some groups were causing local bishops, the problem had to be reconsidered. The Congregation proposed to the Secretariat of State that it turn to the Pontifical Commission for the Interpretation of the Conciliar Documents, the reason being that a quite precise juridical response from Rome would be useful to bishops, enabling them to set down regulations on the subject.

On June 10, 1974, the Secretariat of State responded by asking the Congregation to draw up a short statement. Recourse to the Commission was regarded as inopportune for the reason, among others, that a response favorable to the reform would be interpreted as "casting odium on the liturgical tradition." Once again, the desire was to avoid offending anyone.

A first and somewhat extensive schema was prepared on September 18, 1974, and the Secretariat of State was asked to shorten it. The final text was approved by the Holy Father on October 28, 1974, with the words "Suitable. P[aul]," and was published as a notification from the Congregation for Divine Worship.[44] The document explained that when the bishops decide on the introduction of the vernacular Missal, whether in whole or in part, it becomes obligatory in both its Latin and its vernacular forms. Dispensations allowed for elderly sick priests can be granted only for Masses celebrated in private. Ordinaries cannot grant permission to use the old Missal in Masses with a congregation. Under no pretext can this be allowed.[45]

The notification represented a further clarification, but it did not suffice to do away with the difficulties. Some found ways of splitting hairs

---

43. See the instruction on the gradual carrying out of the apostolic constitution *Missale Romanum* (October 20, 1969), nos. 7 and 10: *Not* 5 (1969) 418–23; *DOL* 209 nos. 1739 and 1742.

44. Notification on the obligatory nature of the Roman Missal of Paul VI (October 28, 1974): *Not* 10 (1974) 353; *DOL* 219 no. 1784.

45. The people I have in mind here held the contrary view, basing it on the Constitution on the Liturgy, no. 4, which calls for respect for all rites.

over it; others considered it an act of persecution. Documents, no matter how solemn, are ineffective against bad faith. People will find all kinds of justifications to defend their actions against those in authority.[46]

---

46. To the cited documents of the Holy See must be added those of the bishops. See "Communiqué de l'Episcopat français à propos du Missel Romain" (November 14, 1974), *Not* 11 (1975) 16–18 and 12 (1976) 81–83, with the letter of the Cardinal Secretary of State on the new Missal; "Die Liturgie der Kirche nach der Ordnung der Kirche," *Not* 12 (1976) 159–61; "Die Einheit der Kirche wahren!" *ibid.*, 442–44; "*Lettre des Evêques flamands sur la liturgie,*" *ibid.*, 195–202.

Part II

Sections Common to the New Liturgical Books

21

The Calendar

I. History

The liturgical calendar is the basis on which the celebrations of the Mass and the Liturgy of the Hours are organized. For this reason, the study group in charge of revising the calendar was put first in the list of Consilium committees (study group 1).[1]

Presidency of this group was reserved to the secretariat of the Consilium, "at least," according to an explanatory note, "until the final, decisive stage of the work is reached. When that point comes, this group will have to decide on dropping or keeping certain feasts and on the rank to be assigned to feasts, and will thus directly impinge on the sensitivities of individuals, associations, dioceses, and religious families." The guidelines for the revision of the calendar were set down in Chapter V of the Constitution on the Liturgy; several criteria determine the structure of the liturgical year:

> The liturgical year is to be so revised that the traditional customs and usages of the sacred seasons are preserved or restored to suit the conditions of modern times; their specific character is to be retained, so that they duly nourish the devotion of the faithful who celebrate the mysteries of Christian redemption and above all the paschal mystery (no. 107).
>
> In celebrating this annual cycle of Christ's mysteries, the Church honors with special love Mary, the Mother of God, who is joined by an inseparable bond to the saving work of her Son (no. 103).

---

1. *Relator:* secretary of the Consilium; *secretary:* A. Dirks; *members:* R. van Doren, J. Wagner, A.-G. Martimort, P. Jounel, A. Amore, H. Schmidt. In 1967 P. Jounel was appointed relator for the group.

The Proper of Seasons shall be given the precedence due to it (no. 108).

By celebrating . . . [the] passage [of the martyrs and other saints] from earth to heaven the Church proclaims the paschal mystery of Christ achieved in the saints (no. 104). Lest the feasts of the saints take precedence over the feasts commemorating the very mysteries of salvation, many of them should be left to be celebrated by a particular Church or nation or religious family; those only should be extended to the universal Church that commemorate saints of truly universal significance (no. 111).

With these criteria as the basis, the study group began its work[2] and produced seventeen schemas.[3]

1. *First Report to the Consilium (1965)*

The first meeting on the revision of the calendar took place on January 23, 1965, at the offices of the Consilium. All the consultors were present and set themselves to studying the schema "de tempore," which P. Jounel had prepared. After lively discussion it was agreed to send the consultors and other *periti* a new schema in the form of a questionnaire that would ask for new suggestions (February 12, 1965).

On March 16, 1965, the first schema on the Proper of Saints was sent to the consultors of study groups 1 and 17.

The two schemas were examined on April 1 and 12. On April 25, at the first general meeting, Father Dirks gave the first report to the Consilium. After open discussion the Fathers approved the following points as guidelines for the work:[4]

1) The liturgical year begins on the First Sunday of Advent;

2) January 1 has three objects: the Name of Jesus, the commemoration of Our Lady, and the beginning of the civil year.[5]

---

2. The group profited especially by the *Memoria sulla riforma liturgica*, the longest part of which was devoted to the calendar, and by the third appendix, of which I spoke earlier (see Chapter 1, pp. 7-8).

3. Introductory schema (Jounel) (*de tempore*), January 19, 1965; Schema 1 (*Proprium de tempore*), February 12, 1965; Schema 2 (*de tempore*), March 15, 1965; Schema 3 (*ordinatio anni liturgici*), March 30, 1965; Schema 4 (*de tempore; lineamenta de sanctis*), April 10, 1965; Schema 5 (*decisiones Consilii*), May 10, 1965; Schema 6 (*de sanctis*), December 3, 1965; Schema 9 (*de sanctis*), April 5, 1966; Schema 10 (*calendarium*, 2 addenda), August 1, 1966; Schema 11 (*de calendario generali*, 1 addendum), September 22, 1966; Schema 12, March 1, 1967; Schema 13, April 18, 1967; Schema 14, August 14, 1967; Schema 15, November 3, 1967; Schema 16, November 27, 1967; Schema 17, December 14, 1967.

4. See "Principia seu criteria ad Calendarium instaurandum," *Not* 1 (1965) 150-52.

5. The liturgy of January 1 was always a composite liturgy, that is, various rites had been combined on that day: the Motherhood of Mary, the octave of Christmas, the Circumcision, the Name of Jesus, New Year's Day, day of peace. The liturgical expression of all these commemorations could not but be composite and unparalleled in the liturgical

3) The season known as Septuagesima loses its penitential character (the three Sundays become Sundays in Ordinary Time,[6] but by and large the present texts will continue in use);

4) The season of Lent begins on the First Sunday of Lent.[7] The imposition of ashes can be done, depending on the judgment of the episcopal conferences, from Ash Wednesday to the Monday after the first Sunday;

5) The Sacred Triduum begins at evening Mass on Holy Thursday[8];

6) The octave of Pentecost is suppressed;[9]

7) The feast of the Ascension can be transferred to the following Sunday if the episcopal conferences so decide;

8) The feast of the Trinity remains as and where it was;[10]

9) The principles proposed for the revision of the feasts of the saints are approved "as a norm for further work."

---

year. All the themes of the day found benevolent supporters in the Consilium. It was agreed that the Gallican theme of the Circumcision should be completely eliminated. The Name of Jesus is recalled in the gospel for the octave of Christmas; it was thought that the prayer of the faithful should be used for recalling New Year's Day, although some of the Fathers would have liked to see it mentioned in the texts of the Mass. The view prevailed that January 1 should be once again the feast of the Motherhood of Mary, which goes back to the origins of the Roman liturgy and links Rome with the East, where on December 26 Our Lady is "congratulated" (Mansourati). In the texts of the Mass, too, the Marian feast is given primacy, although other themes are mentioned.

6. There was disagreement on the suppression of the Septuagesima season. Some saw these weeks as a step toward Easter. On one occasion Pope Paul VI compared the complex made up of Septuagesima, Lent, Holy Week, and Easter Triduum to the bells calling people to Sunday Mass. The ringing of them an hour, a half-hour, fifteen, and five minutes before the time of Mass has a psychological effect and prepares the faithful materially and spiritually for the celebration of the liturgy. Then, however, the view prevailed that there should be a simplification: it was not possible to restore Lent to its full importance without sacrificing Septuagesima, which is an extension of Lent.

7. A strictly penitential rite on Sunday would be a contradiction. Leaving the imposition of ashes on the preceding Wednesday was one way of adhering to tradition, but it had the drawback of keeping the association with Mardi Gras. The Pope would subsequently have the decisive word on the matter.

8. Some would have liked to see the Sacred Triduum identified strictly with Good Friday, Holy Saturday, and Easter Sunday, to the exclusion of the Last Supper. Others pointed out that the Supper could not be separated from the Passion (Jenny). The Supper *is* the paschal mystery, "a covenant in my blood; a new law" (Martimort, Wagner, Vagaggini, Pascher, Guano).

9. Here again there was disagreement. The suppression was accepted with the expectation that the formularies of the octave would be used during the nine days of preparation for Pentecost. On this point again there were changes of mind, but the decision of the Fathers finally prevailed.

10. The proposal was accepted after heated discussion. Suppression would be an impoverishment (Vagaggini, Wagner). It is a summary of the work of salvation (Hänggi). Various suggestions were made for transferring the feast to another day or combining it with another feast, for example, the Baptism of Jesus (Pascher, Martimort).

The relator stated some principles concerning the celebration of saints' feasts. Care must be taken that their cult continues but also that priority is given to the mysteries of Christ. In order to harmonize these two requirements:

a) Let the universal calendar retain or introduce feasts of saints from the various parts of the world in order to bring out the universality of holiness in the Church and to keep the Roman calendar from being a Mediterranean calendar. Examples of saints to be introduced are the Japanese, Canadian, and Ugandan martyrs, and the protomartyr of Oceania.

b) The number of feasts that do not commemorate an event or mystery in the life of Christ, or a saint, is to be reduced.

c) Several saints may be commemorated on the same day, with celebrants left free to celebrate any one of them in the Office and the Mass.

With regard to the various categories of saints it was proposed that:

a) All the apostles and evangelists, who are the foundation of the Church, are to be kept in the universal calendar.

b) Of the ancient martyrs, those are to be kept who are universally venerated or possess a universal interest for the life of the Church; a selection of the others is to be made that will be representative of all classes of the clergy and the faithful.

c) The principal Doctors are to be kept in the universal calendar; the others are to be evaluated case by case.

d) Saints of general interest because of their type of spirituality or apostolate are to be kept in the general calendar.

2. Second Report (1966)

These various guidelines were followed with good results. The work in this area was speeded up so that other groups could begin or continue their own work on a more secure basis.

At this point it seemed appropriate to entrust the two parts of the calendar to two different *periti*: the Temporal to P. Jounel, and the Sanctoral to A. Amore.

At the seventh general meeting of the Consilium, the two men set forth the general structure of the new calendar (October 1966).

Two special points were discussed: the feast of the Holy Family and the terminology to be used in ranking liturgical days.

a) Holy Family

This was an idea-feast that Pope Leo XIII had introduced into the already complicated maze of the Christmas season, and only with difficulty could it be given an appropriate place in a system governed by the new criteria. The effective celebration of the three "epiphanies" (Magi, Baptism of Jesus, Cana), especially in view of the fact that in some countries Epiphany is celebrated on the Sunday after January 6, left no room for the feast of the Holy Family. On the other hand, this feast had undeniable pastoral advantages and fitted nicely into the Christmas season from the viewpoint of the ideas it conveyed.

Various suggestions were offered for its date: Sunday between January 1 and 5; third Sunday after Epiphany; May 1. The choice went finally to the Sunday within the octave of Christmas because, even if it is out of place chronologically, "it highlights the mystery of the incarnation whereby the Son of God acquires a fully human place in the family" (Guano) and because the feast of Christmas reunites so many families around the domestic hearth. On both accounts the feast serves as the basis for timely pastoral reflections.

b) *Liturgical terminology*

The terms "solemnity," "feast," "commemoration," and "memorial" were suggested for indicating the rank of liturgical days. The suggestion was discussed at length but was not favored by all. The group was asked to study the matter further. The main difficulty was with the noun "commemoration," which could be confused with the "commemorations" of the old rubrics. By the time the question came up again before the Consilium, the term "optional memorial" (*memoria ad libitum*) had been invented.

The Consilium gave general approval to the two reports, and the study group went on to a final draft of a complete calendar. At the eighth general meeting (April 10–19, 1967), this draft was definitively approved.

3. *Examination by the Curia*

After leaving the Consilium, the schema had a long way to travel before its official publication.

On April 18, 1967, Cardinal Lercaro presented it to the Holy Father at an audience; the latter decided that it should be submitted to the Congregation for the Doctrine of the Faith and the Congregation of Rites.[11]

---

11. The successive stages were as follows: April 18, 1967: presentation to the Pope, who ordered that the schema be studied by the Congregation for the Doctrine of the Faith and the Congregation of Rites (July 19, 1967, No. 102097); December 5, 1967: the schema is sent to the two Congregations; May 18, 1968: the Pope sends a sheet of observations; May 27, 1968: reply and observations of the Congregation for the Doctrine of the Faith; June 6, 1968:

The Congregation for the Doctrine of the Faith issued a lengthy four-part reply and, contrary to its usual practice, explained the reasons why the Fathers decided as they did. They had studied the schema at two plenary meetings (February 21 and May 22, 1968). They decided, moreover, that to oversee the practical carrying out of their decisions, a joint commission should be formed with representatives from the Congregation and from the Consilium.

Meanwhile, the Holy Father had sent his own observations regarding Ash Wednesday and the memorials of some saints. The joint commission examined these, along with those of the Congregation.[12]

The remarks of the Congregation were under four headings:

1. *General considerations.* The elimination of numerous devotion-feasts that have been established by recent Popes, or the reduction in the rank of their celebration, is seen as a danger to religious practice.

The principle that the liturgy of the season should take precedence over the cult of the saints should be harmonized with the psychological and pedagogical considerations that underlie the sanctoral and with ecumenical and traditional motifs.[13]

2. *Proper of the Seasons.* Advent is a time not only of joyous expectation but of penance.[14] Ash Wednesday should be the beginning of Lent, as in the past.[15] The octave of Pentecost may be abolished, provided the

---

joint commission of that Congregation and the Consilium; June 21, 1968: reply of the Congregation with some minor clarifications; July 19, 1968: presentation to the Pope of the schema as corrected after the meeting of the joint commission; July 26: approval by the Holy Father; April 2, 1969: presentation of the galley proofs to the Pope; April 13, 1969: approval for printing. On the last-named occasion the Secretariat of State said that the Pope would announce the publication at a consistory on April 28 and that the presentation to the press would be made on May 9. Meanwhile the motu proprio *Mysterii paschalis*, which would promulgate the new calendar, was being prepared. The motu proprio was given to the Pope on February 18, 1969, along with the decree of the Congregation of Rites. It was then revised by Monsignor Tondini and published together with the calendar.

12. The participants from the Congregation were Archbishop Paul Philippe, Father Luigi Ciappi, Monsignor Gilberto Agustoni; from the Consilium, Fathers Bugnini, Braga, and Neunheuser. The meeting was held at the Palace of the Congregation.

13. It was explained, in regard to the suppression of recently instituted feasts, that the intention was not to cast doubt on the validity of the magisterium's action but rather to be faithful to liturgical principles. For these feasts, even a short time after their institution, had little following in many regions. As for the cult of the saints, this was ensured by the inclusion, for special reasons, of some saints in the general calendar, while the others were left to local celebration.

14. The aspect of interior renewal as an element in repentance was to be brought out in the readings.

15. The Pope insisted that the first four days of Lent not be eliminated: "It would admittedly be difficult, and even questionable, to introduce them for the first time in our day;

Masses of these days are used for the days between Ascension and Pentecost. Let the practice of transferring external solemnities to Sundays be cut back; this includes those of the Virgin and the saints. The feast of Christ the King ought to keep its social dimension and be celebrated in October as in the past.

3. *Proper of the Saints.* The following feasts of Our Lady should continue to be obligatory: Our Lady of Lourdes, Our Lady of the Rosary, the Motherhood of Mary (October 11), the Queenship of Mary (May 31), the Presentation of Mary (November 21), the Immaculate Heart of Mary, Our Lady of Sorrows, and the Name of Mary, as well as the feasts of St. Gabriel the Archangel, the Guardian Angels, and the Doctors of the Church.[16] The Visitation should continue to be celebrated on July 2.

The revisers should attend not only to the universality of a cult but also to the influence of a person or of the work he or she began in the Church (for example, the founders of religious orders and congregations). An excessive autonomy of the local Churches can be harmful to the Church's universality.

4. *Specific points.* Optional memorials should be reduced to a minimum, because they lend themselves to use as "a convenient system for leveling down," that is, for celebrating the ferial Mass and neglecting the cult of the saints.[17] The calendar should remain open to further saints' feasts.

The Congregation's study had been a careful one and not without pastoral sensitivity, even if it was tinged to some extent with nostalgia for the past and with fears, although both were expressed courteously and with respect for work that the study group had carried out with so much expertise and care. These qualities also marked the atmosphere of the joint commission's meeting, with the result that agreement was quickly reached (even though in the process many requests of the Congregation were effectively denied).

---

but now that they have been accepted by all the peoples who follow the Roman Rite, it is not a good idea to suppress them, especially if the rite of the imposition of ashes is to be observed on the Wednesday before the first Sunday, as is now the case." Ash Wednesday continues, therefore, to be the beginning of Lent.

16. The Pope asked that some saints be given an obligatory memorial. All the requests were accepted, but the Consilium reserved the right to study the cases of some saints whose feasts regularly occur in Lent and for whom an obligatory memorial was therefore impossible, for example, Sts. Perpetua and Felicity and St. Patrick.

17. The principle of the optional memorial proved, on the contrary, to be effective and acceptable. It made it possible to increase the number of saints in the calendar and the number of requests for inclusion that are made to the Church; it also gave places and individuals ample room for choice.

The feast of Christ the King was accepted as proposed by the Consilium.

With regard to the Marian feasts it was decided that:

Lourdes should be an optional memorial;

Rosary: obligatory memorial;

Motherhood of Mary (October 11): transferred to January 1, the traditional day. In the Office there is to be a commemoration of Ephesus.

Queenship of Mary: obligatory memorial on August 22, as complement and crown of the Assumption.

Visitation: transferred to May 31.

Immaculate Heart: optional memorial, close in date to the solemnity of the Sacred Heart of Jesus (the following Saturday).

Presentation of Mary: the old date, November 21, is to be kept, but the feast is to be given the larger meaning it has in the Eastern vision of it: Mary's total dedication to God from the very beginning of her existence.[18]

Our Lady of Sorrows: obligatory memorial on September 15, after the feast of the Holy Cross.

Name of Mary: suppressed, since it is included in the feast of her Nativity.

Angels: Gabriel, Michael, and Raphael are to be honored together on September 29; the Guardian Angels remain an obligatory memorial on October 2.

Doctors: it is impossible to celebrate all of them, since they are so numerous (thirty), for that would create an imbalance in relation to other categories of saints. The Consilium's suggestion was accepted: that there be obligatory memorials for the "principal Doctors" of East and West, that is, those who more than others exerted a truly decisive influence on the life and teaching of the Church (for example, Thomas Aquinas, Francis de Sales, Alphonsus Liguori). On the other hand, there is no difficulty about yielding to the desire that the title "Doctor of the Church" be appended to the relevant names in the calendar.

Agreement was reached on elevating to the rank of obligatory memorials the celebrations of twenty-three saints that had been proposed as optional memorials in the draft calendar. This change also satisfied the

---

18. The proposal was made to suppress this feast because it was founded on legend, but this argument was countered by an appeal to the basic inspiration at work in the feast. The Pope explicitly requested its retention: "Let it be retained for ecumenical reasons, but let it have the same tonality it has in the Eastern liturgies; that is, let it express the unreserved surrender of the Virgin to God. Some texts from the Eastern liturgies might be used."

"desire to increase the number of the saints," which some thought rather low.[19]

4. *Papal Approval and Publication*

The Pope accepted the results of the agreement between the Congregation and the Consilium. In his letter of approval, the Secretary of State wrote:

> Having learned with satisfaction of the work completed and the conclusions reached by the joint commission, the Holy Father has charged me to communicate to Your Eminence his supreme approval of the draft calendar presented to him earlier but with the changes introduced into it at the suggestion of the Congregation for the Doctrine of the Faith. He expects, too, that the new group of saints assigned an obligatory memorial instead of an optional will all be added to the original list.[20]

The Pope announced the publication of the new calendar at a consistory on April 28, 1969; on the same occasion he announced the publication of the new Order of Mass and the establishment of the new Congregation for Divine Worship. At the consistory he had this to say of the new Roman calendar:

> In the new General Roman Calendar you will notice that the liturgical year has not been altered radically. Rather the criterion for its revision was that the elements making up the individual parts of each liturgical season would give clearer expression to the truth that Christ's paschal mystery is the center of all liturgical worship. Further, to the extent possible, the General Roman Calendar has retained the celebration of the saints' "birthdays," but in such a way that for the whole Church those saints have been chosen who seemed to be the most important both historically and as examples. Other saints of less general significance were left to be honored by the local Churches. There has also been care to ensure the historical truth of the elements pertaining to the saints' lives and feasts. The purpose of all these measures has been to bring out clearly that holiness in the Church belongs to all parts of the world and to all periods of history and that all peoples and all the faithful of every rank are called on to attain holiness, as the Dogmatic Constitution *Lumen gentium* has solemnly taught [see nn. 39-42].[21]

---

19. Here is the list (the asterisks indicate saints proposed by the Pope): Sts. Timothy and Titus, the disciples of St. Paul; Sts. Francis de Sales,* Agatha, Scholastica, Polycarp,* Perpetua and Felicity,* Patrick,* John Baptist de la Salle, Philip Neri,* Justin, Anthony of Padua, Aloysius Gonzaga,* Martha,* Clare,* Alphonsus,* Monica, Therese of the Child Jesus, Charles Borromeo,* Josaphat,* Elizabeth of Hungary, Cecilia, Lucy, John of the Cross.*

20. The reference in this last sentence is to the saints marked with an asterisk in the list in note 19.

21. Paul VI, address to a consistory (April 28, 1969): *DOL* 93 no. 676.

The motu proprio *Mysterii paschalis*, which promulgated the new calendar, was dated February 14, 1969,[22] but was not published until May 9, along with the calendar itself.[23]

The document begins by reminding readers that the Second Vatican Council had placed the paschal mystery at the center of the annual cycle of liturgical celebrations. It then recalls the liturgical activity of Pius X and John XXIII as they gave Sunday its former vitality and pre-eminence once again, and the liturgical reforms by which Pius XII restored the Easter Vigil to its original splendor. These developments were steps leading gradually to a new structuring of the liturgical year on its traditional foundations.

This renewal could not but affect the veneration of Our Lady and the saints, since she and they are so closely linked to the paschal mystery of Christ. The motu proprio ends by decreeing that the new calendar is to go into effect on January 1, 1969, in accordance with norms to be issued by the Congregation of Rites.[24]

These norms, which were prepared by the Congregation and the Consilium, were published along with the calendar and accompanied by a decree dated March 21, 1969. The norms were provisional and were to be valid until the publication of the revised Missal and Divine Office.[25]

---

22. Paul VI, motu proprio *Mysterii paschalis* (February 14, 1969): *DOL* 440 nos. 3754-57. There is a little story behind the date. On that day in Rome, in the Basilica of St. Peter, Pope Paul VI, the Czechoslovakian bishops, and many Czechoslovakian pilgrims, whether from the mother country or from other parts of Europe and America, were solemnly celebrating the eleventh centenary of the death of St. Cyril, Apostle of the Slavs. February 14 was the actual day of the saint's death, and the new calendar transfers the annual celebration of Sts. Cyril and Methodius from July 7 to that day. On that day in February 1969 the new calendar of the Roman Church was being inaugurated, although the bishops and congregation were not aware of the fact.

23. *Calendarium Romanum* (Vatican Polyglot Press, 1969. 180 pp.). In addition to the motu proprio *Mysterii paschalis*, the decree of the SCR, and the General Norms for the liturgical year and the calendar, the volume contains the General Roman Calendar, the interim calendar for 1970, and the Litany of the Saints. In the second, unofficial part of the book there is a lengthy commentary on the calendar; the historical, liturgical, and pastoral reasons for changes are given, and there is a comparison of the new calendar with the old.

24. *DOL* 440 nos. 3754-57.

25. The decree *Anni liturgici ordinatio* of March 21, 1969, is in *DOL* 441 nos. 3758-66. A notification from the SCDW, dated May 17, 1970 (*DOL* 443 no. 3828), put off the introduction of the new calendar for another year, since publication of the relevant liturgical books (Missal and Breviary) was still incomplete. See also the notification of the SCDW, dated June 14, 1971 (*DOL* 216 nos. 1769-77). To facilitate preparation of provisional calendars, the SCDW also published the draft calendar for 1971 (*Not* 6 [1970] 284). An instruction of the SCDW on the interim adaptation of particular calendars was issued on June 29, 1969 (*DOL* 480 nos. 3991-94).

The new calendar and the General Norms were presented to the journalists on May 9, 1969, at a conference by P. Jounel, who had been the principal author of the work. His presentation was brilliant and lively. Despite this, the publication of the calendar elicited rather negative reactions among the lay journalists and in the Catholic press generally. Commentators focused on the sensational and what might be used for propaganda, instead of seeking objective truth and providing a calm evaluation of the work and the new norms. Journalists looked for saints who had been "eliminated," "disqualified," "reduced to second rank," and so on. Those of the clergy and faithful whose view of worship and religion generally had been devotion-oriented were disconcerted, although the confusion was also due in part to surprise and a lack of preparation.

Others lamented the omission from the new calendar of their patron saint or the saint of their own region, diocese, or nation. Thus feelings were touched that resulted in an unfavorable reception of the new calendar.[26]

5. *New Revisions*

Before the new calendar was finally introduced into the new Missal and the new Liturgy of the Hours, some further revisions were made. In the meantime, groups, nations, and religious families endeavored to have the case of "their" saint restudied.[27]

The representations made to the Congregation for Divine Worship were carefully studied at its twelfth general meeting.

1. *Most Precious Blood*. Requests concerning this feast were more numerous than for any other: 367 petitions that it be restored.[28]

The study group dealing with the calendar pointed out that although this feast had been dropped as a celebration obligatory for the universal Church, references to the Precious Blood were still in the Roman Missal, especially on the Fridays of the Easter season[29] and in the votive Mass of the Precious Blood, which had been enriched with more readings.[30]

---

26. See *Not* 5 (1969) 294–303 on the press conference, the reactions, etc. See also A. Bugnini, "Il nuovo Calendario," *L'Osservatore Romano*, May 14, 1969; *EL* 83 (1969) 160–201.

27. This explains why the preparation of the calendar was conducted in such secrecy. The subject was an explosive one. The secrecy hurt the preparation and reception of the calendar, but it also cut down on polemics. For the same reason, the Congregation refused, even later on, to accept requests for the introduction of new celebrations into the calendar, since to accept even a few would have brought down an avalanche of them.

28. Twenty-seven requests from bishops, 111 from associations, 220 from priests and faithful; the requests were from Italy (253), the United States (101), the Netherlands (3), France (3), Canada (3), Austria (2), and Germany (2).

29. See *Missale Romanum*, pp. 180, 181, 196.

30. See *Ordo lectionum Missae*, pp. 337–38.

It was suggested by several that explicit mention of the Precious Blood might be made in the calendar at the Solemnity of Corpus Christi.[31] "Solemnity of the Body and the Blood of Christ" had been one of the early titles of the feast and would be quite appropriate now that communion under two kinds had been restored. The Consilium accepted this proposal.[32]

Dioceses and religious families were free, of course, to include the feast of the Precious Blood in their special calendars. The same did not seem appropriate for the universal Church.

2. *Holy Family*. It was decided that in years in which Christmas fell on a Sunday and in which there was therefore no Sunday within the octave, the feast of the Holy Family should be celebrated on December 30.

3. *St. Cajetan and St. Dominic*. By peaceful agreement among the Dominicans and Theatines, it was settled that the celebration of their respective founders should be held on August 7 for St. Cajetan and August 8 for St. Dominic.[33]

4. *All Souls on November 2*. Requests came from various quarters that the commemoration of all the dead might be celebrated on November 2 even when this fell on a Sunday. The relator observed that he saw no difficulty with this, inasmuch as many of the formularies of Masses for the deceased had a paschal character. White vestments could be used. For pastoral reasons and because of the paschal vision of Christian death, the Consilium voted in favor.[34]

5. *A few other requests* were studied, but with negative results. They are included here for the sake of completeness.

a) *St. Nicholas*. The secretariat had asked the *periti* to conduct a radical review of the place of this saint. The study group presented its point of view as follows:

—The cult of St. Nicholas appeared sporadically in the West in the eleventh century and then spread in a rather noteworthy fashion once the relics were transferred to Bari (1087) and in virtue of the legend associated with his name. In the calendar of St. Pius V, the feast was a semidouble; it became a double in 1670 under Clement X. In the East only the Byzantine and Coptic Rites celebrate it. The only thing known about

---

31. See the article of Monsignor R. Masi in *L'Osservatore Romano*, June 5, 1969; L. Ciappi, "Santissimo Corpo e Sangue di Cristo," *Not* 6 (1970) 275–78.

32. See "Variationes in Calendarium Romanum inductae," *Not* 6 (1970) 191; 11 (1975) 309.

33. See *Not* 6 (1970) 192.

34. The situation was left somewhat anomalous, since the Mass was to be for the deceased but the Office was to be of the Sunday, except for parts of it that are celebrated with the congregation, such as Lauds and Vespers.

St. Nicholas is that he was a bishop of Myra in the fourth century. Not even his name appears in the Hieronymian Martyrology.

—In the first plan for a revision of the calendar, the feast of St. Nicholas was proposed as an optional memorial; no one in the Consilium raised any objections. The reason was certainly that no one could claim that this saint enjoyed any truly universal importance.

—One of the principles governing the revision of the calendar was that no saint's cult could be made obligatory if there was not historical evidence of his or her name, place, and date of celebration. The higher authorities in the Church decided to make exceptions for Sts. Cecilia, Agatha, and Lucy, who were honored at Rome in the time of St. Gregory the Great. If a further exception were made for St. Nicholas, the door would be opened to a new conception of the revised calendar, and the very basis on which the revision was being made would be threatened.

—The optional veneration of a saint does not mean a "second-class cult" (see *Calendarium Romanum*, p. 81); there are equivalent cases in the Eastern liturgies.

The secretariat of the Congregation appended the following lines to the relator's note:

> While I appreciate what the relator says, it must be acknowledged that the judgment passed by the Consilium on the universality of this saint's cult is perhaps a bit hasty. There is no denying that both the East and the West— and by "West" I mean the entire world of Western culture, the Americas and Australia included—extensively honor St. Nicholas (some statistics show 2000 churches in France and Germany, 400 in England, and 40 in Ireland, to mention only a few countries). It is proposed, therefore, that St. Nicholas be made an obligatory memorial.

In the discussion on November 10 Monsignor Mansourati pointed out that the feast of St. Nicholas is well known in the Syro-Antiochene Rite; Cardinal Confalonieri added that this might be an ecumenical argument for preserving the feast. Monsignor Wagner noted that the Northern countries would evidently like to have an obligatory memorial, but was the same true of the other Churches? Bishop Rau (Argentina) said that the feast was not popular among his people. Cardinal Pellegrino added that the feast is not known in Northern Italy and that it would be difficult to introduce it there. Cardinal Willebrands: "The feast is also known in Russia, but the ecumenical argument does not seem sufficient; it is enough that the feast be retained in places where there is a true cult. Nicholas belongs to folklore more than to anything else." Bishop Guano: "I see no reason for changing our position, even if St. Nicholas is venerated in the maritime regions."

The vote taken yielded 2 votes for an obligatory memorial and 32 for an optional.

b) The bishops of Poland asked that at least one of the Polish saints (Casimir, Stanislaus, Hedwig, John Cantius) have an obligatory memorial and be named in the Litany of the Saints, so that "at least once a year the entire Church might recall how much Poland has suffered for its fidelity to the gospel."

The secretariat proposed that St. Hedwig be given a higher rank. All agreed on the insertion of St. Stanislaus in the litany, but the vote on a change of rank in the calendar was negative (23 to 11).[35]

c) Other requests had to do with Sts. Catherine of Alexandria,[36] George, Christopher, Barbara, Januarius, Lucy, Louis IX, Balbina, Bibiana, and Joseph of Cupertino, and Our Lady of Lourdes. For all it was asked either that they be included in the calendar or that their optional memorial be made obligatory.

The cases were studied and voted on individually; the decision was that no change should be made.[37]

II. Content

1. *Proper of the Seasons*

There was a certain amount of reorganization here for the purpose of properly emphasizing the cycle of celebrations dealing with the mystery of salvation.

---

35. The request of the Polish bishops was fully explained by Bishop Jop of Opole. It was supported by Bishop Hervás (Spain). Others said that the request might be accepted, provided that every country would have a representative in the calendar. Monsignor Mansourati took advantage of the occasion by asking that St. Ephraem, the only Doctor who was a deacon, might also be considered. Pope John Paul II raised the feast of St. Stanislaus to the rank of an obligatory memorial on May 8, 1979, on occasion of the ninth centenary of his death; see *Not* 15 (1979) 235 and 308.

36. The case of St. Catherine brought several protests, especially from the East. Admittedly, she entered the Roman calendar at a rather late date (thirteenth century), and nothing certain (except for her name) is known of her—too little to give her a place in the calendar when many others are more deserving. But perhaps two factors might have tilted the balance in her favor: the evidence of the cult, which in the East goes back at least to the fifth century, and the widespread devotion of Eastern Christians, both Catholic and Orthodox, to the patroness of the great monastery on Mount Sinai. In these respects she may be compared to St. Cecilia, whose situation is more or less the same but who has been kept in the calendar "because of the devotion of the people to her" (see *Calendarium Romanum*, p. 59).

37. Later on, other requests came in or those already mentioned were renewed. There was a movement in favor of introducing a celebration of Mary as Mother of the Church. It was in fact allowed only for particular calendars, usually on the Monday after Pentecost.

Advent takes on a note of joyous expectation of Christ's twofold coming—his second coming and his coming at Christmas. The first of these two comings is emphasized especially in the first two weeks, the second during the days from December 17 to December 24.

The Christmas season, which ends on the Sunday after Epiphany, shows some differences from the past. The feast of the Name of Jesus is suppressed, since the naming of the Lord is commemorated on January 1, which becomes the "Solemnity of Mary, Mother of God." The feast of the Holy Family is transferred to the Sunday within the octave of Christmas, while the feast of the Baptism of the Lord is assigned to the Sunday after Epiphany.

The Septuagesima season is suppressed, and the three Sundays making it up become Sundays of Ordinary Time.

Also suppressed as a title is "Passiontide." The whole of it now becomes, even externally, a part of Lent.

Lent begins on Ash Wednesday and ends on Holy Thursday. It has two aspects, penitential and baptismal. The former is emphasized especially during the first two weeks by means of appropriate readings and of euchological texts that have been suitably revised, and the second aspect during the following three weeks. The readings and prayers used in antiquity on the third, fourth, and fifth Sundays have been restored (the Sundays of "the Samaritan," "the Man Born Blind," and "Lazarus"). The final two weeks are dominated by preparation for the celebration of the passion.

The Easter Triduum begins at evening Mass on Holy Thursday. It is not a preparation for Easter, but rather the celebration of the Christian Pasch: the passion, death, and resurrection of Christ.

The Easter season lasts fifty days, beginning with the Easter Vigil and ending with Pentecost Sunday. This is attested by the ancient and universal tradition of the Church, which has always celebrated the seven weeks of Easter as though they were a single day that ends with the feast of Pentecost. For this reason, the octave of Pentecost, which was added to the fifty days of Easter in the sixth century, has been abolished.[38] How-

---

A beautiful Mass was also composed; it is a votive Mass in the second edition of the Missal. But no further changes were accepted for the celebrations in the General Calendar.

38. This suppression, which was agreed upon only after some discussion, subsequently caused confusion and second thoughts. Perhaps the abrupt passage from the Solemnity of Pentecost to Ordinary Time made people very uneasy. In some areas Pentecost is continued into the following day, which is a feast, and the shift to Ordinary Time is smoother.

The suppression of the octave of Pentecost followed logically from consideration of the inherent structure of the Easter season. Pentecost is the octave Sunday after Easter. An octave of an octave is illogical. Scholars admitted this without difficulty: see I. Schuster,

ever, the days from Ascension to Pentecost with their appropriate texts are used as a time of expectation of the Holy Spirit.

The thirty-four weeks remaining outside the special seasons make up "Ordinary Time" (*tempus per annum*), which occurs partly before Lent, partly after Pentecost. The formularies are given as a single block in the Sacramentary but are to be used in the two stages just indicated. This period now includes the feast of Christ the King, which has been transferred from the last Sunday of October to the last Sunday of the liturgical year.

The various seasons derive their character in no small measure from the Scripture readings (for example, Isaiah in Advent, the Acts of the

---

Liber sacramentorum IV (ed. of 1926) 26; A. Chavasse, "Le cycle pascal," in *L'Eglise en prière*, ed. A.-G. Martimort (Tournai, 1961) 714; M. Righetti, *Manuale di storia liturgica* II (Milan, 1969) 316; R. Cabié, *La Pentecôte* (Tournai, 1965) 256. In 1948 the commission for liturgical reform that was established by Pius XII clearly looked forward to this solution of the problem as more consonant with the character of Pentecost and the origin of the celebration. The *Memoria sulla riforma liturgica* said: "In the beginning, of course, there was no octave, since the feast itself represented a terminus; it marked the end of the Easter season. Berno of Reichenau in the eleventh century says that in his day they were still debating the suitability of celebrating an octave of Pentecost.

"Looking back from our present vantage point, we can see that with the inclusion of a Pentecost octave the Easter season, originally fifty days long and ending on Pentecost, has been prolonged a further week, down to the Saturday after the fiftieth day (the real eighth day of the octave is lacking, now that the feast of the Trinity is celebrated on that day).

"All these concrete facts and liturgical data have led not a few scholars to ask whether it would not be more appropriate to return to the ancient and original practice, that is, to regard, and celebrate, Pentecost Sunday as the true and real end of the Easter season, as the true *pentekostē*, or fiftieth day, and therefore to have the courage to do away with the octave. A further advantage would be to relieve the summer period of the themes of Pentecost and restore its ancient form.

"Such a request is supported by history and by the meaning of the feast itself, and is therefore reasonable in theory. It is also argued that the disappearance of another privileged octave would leave more room for the celebration of current feasts, while the single-day celebration of Pentecost would make it stand out more clearly, for it would be seen as undoubtedly the end of the entire Easter cycle" (pp. 78–79).

To the question "whether it is agreed that Pentecost Sunday ought to be restored to its original character as the end of the Easter season through suppression of its octave," the Pian Commission replied at its meeting of February 14, 1950, by opting for suppression; the commission thought it sufficient to make some provision for Pentecost Monday and Tuesday in places where these two days were still feast days.

This was the constant view of the Consilium and of the joint commission of the Consilium and the Congregation for the Doctrine of the Faith.

As for devotion to the Holy Spirit, the euchological texts of the new Missal, and especially the Eucharistic Prayers, show beyond a doubt that references to the Holy Spirit are far more numerous now than in the past (160 to 64).

Greater emphasis ought to be given, however, to the week before Pentecost by way of a more intense preparation for the feast through meditation on the texts of the Missal and the Liturgy of the Hours.

Apostles and the Gospel of John during the Easter season, the baptismal and penitential pericopes of the Gospel during Lent, and so on) and from the first presidential prayer of the Mass. The number of the latter has been increased, so that each day of Advent, Lent, and the Easter season has its own collect.

The Ember Days are to be celebrated at times and on days to be determined by the episcopal conferences, provided that they are in harmony with the seasons and thus truly correspond to the purposes for which they were established.[39]

2. *Proper of the Saints*

The following goals determine the organization of the new calendar in its sanctoral section:

a) to assign to each saint as the day of his or her celebration the *dies natalis* or day of death, unless something prevents this. If there is in fact such a hindrance, then some other important day of the saint's career is chosen, for example, the day of episcopal ordination or of the translation of the relics or of the canonization;

b) to select saints of greater importance for the Church as a whole, while leaving the others to their local, national, regional, or diocesan cult;

c) to bring out the universality of holiness in both time and space. Thus, the numerous saints of antiquity and those from the Mediterranean world are now flanked by more recent saints (for example, St. Maria Goretti) and saints from other parts of the world (for example: the Nagasaki martyrs for the Far East; the martyrs of Uganda for South Central Africa; St. Peter Chanel for Oceania; the Canadian martyrs for North America; St. Turibius and St. Martin de Porres for South America; St. Columbanus and St. Ansgar for the several regions of Northern Europe).

d) An entirely new practice is the optional celebration of many saints listed in the calendar. Thus many saints whose chief significance is that they manifest the continual flowering of sanctity and who have a traditional cult, perhaps even a strong one, in certain areas are included in the calendar, but their celebration is not made obligatory for the entire Church.

A survey of the new calendar yields the following data:

a) Feasts of the Lord: the traditional ones, except for the Name of Jesus and the Most Precious Blood.

---

39. In an audience granted to Father Bugnini on November 6, 1971, the Pope would insist that the periods which replace the Ember Days be carefully determined by the conferences and that they be also days of prayer for ecclesiastical vocations. See above, p. 214, n. 19.

b) Feasts of Our Lady: in addition to the principal ones (Assumption, Immaculate Conception, Nativity, Annunciation, Divine Maternity, Presentation of the Lord in the Temple, Visitation), the following remain obligatory: Queenship of Mary (August 22), Our Lady of Sorrows (September 15), Our Lady of the Rosary (October 7), and the Presentation of Mary (November 21). Now optional are: Our Lady of Lourdes (February 11), Our Lady of Carmel (July 16), the Dedication of St. Mary Major (August 5), and the Immaculate Heart of Mary (Saturday after the feast of the Sacred Heart).

· c) For St. Joseph, the feast of March 19 remains obligatory; that of May 1 is now optional.

d) Angels Michael, Gabriel, and Raphael are joined in a single celebration (September 29), and the feast of the Guardian Angels is kept (October 2).

e) The traditional feasts of the apostles have been retained. But in addition to the feast of June 29, there is now only one other feast of St. Peter (the Chair of Peter on February 22) and one of St. Paul (the Conversion on January 25).

f) Of other saints not included in the preceding categories, there are 58 obligatory feasts and 92 optional ones.

g) Chronological distribution: 64 saints from the first ten centuries and 79 from the following ten; the centuries most heavily represented are the fourth (25), the sixteenth (17), and the eighteenth (17). Geographical distribution: 126 feasts of saints from Europe, 8 from Africa, 14 from Asia, 4 from the Americas, and 1 from Oceania.

The episcopal conferences, diocesan bishops, and religious families are to compile their particular calendars in accordance with the structure of the General Calendar.[40]

III. Special Questions

1. Holy Days of Obligation

Beginning in 1965, the Consilium took up the question of holy days of obligation. Not infrequently, national conferences asked permission of the Holy See to transfer to Sunday those holy days of obligation that fell on weekdays. Such transfers, however, had to be consonant with the principles set down in the Constitution on the Liturgy on the primacy and paschal character of Sunday and on the priority of the mystery of Christ over other celebrations (see nos. 102 and 106).

---

40. See below, pp. 570ff.

On May 12, 1965, the Consilium presented the Holy Father with a memorandum that was then adopted as a directive. Some of the principles set down in it became part of the General Norms for the calendar. Here is what the memorandum had to say:

A. *General Principles*

The practice regarding holy days of obligation that occur during the week must take into account the conditions under which Christians live in today's world—the demands of work, the minority status of Catholics.

The episcopal conferences should be given broad authority to determine what is best for the spiritual good of their faithful.

It is desirable that the bishops of the Eastern Churches come to an agreement with the competent authorities of the other Churches and Christian communities in the same region so that all the Christians of the area can celebrate the principal common feasts and the Lord's Pasch on the same day.[41]

B. *Suggestions*

a) Four feasts of the Lord should be celebrated annually by all the faithful of the Latin rite: Christmas, Epiphany, Ascension, and Corpus Christi.

Christmas is everywhere celebrated on December 25.

Epiphany is celebrated on January 6 and Ascension on Thursday the fortieth day after Easter. But the episcopal conferences can ask the Holy See's approval for always celebrating these two feasts on Sunday, which thus becomes the proper day for them. The liturgical norms will have to specify the manner of celebration.

Corpus Christi is celebrated on the Thursday after Trinity Sunday. But, again, the episcopal conferences can ask the Holy See for authority to transfer it regularly to the following Sunday or some other Sunday or some other more suitable day during the year.[42]

b) The episcopal conferences can ask the Holy See to do away with the obligation attaching to the other feasts listed in canon 1247 §1 of the 1917 Code: Octave of Christmas (January 1), St. Joseph (March 19), Sts. Peter and Paul (June 29), Assumption of the Blessed Virgin (August 5), All Saints (November 1), and the Immaculate Conception (December 8).

---

41. As part of its work in preparing the calendar, the Consilium also gave the Holy Father a paper (November 1964) on establishing a common date for Easter. The question was taken up and brought before the Secretariat of State; see *Not* 5 (1969) 391.

42. These suggestions were adopted by the General Norms for the Liturgical Year and the Calendar, no. 7 (*DOL* 442 no. 3773).

It is expedient to make it as easy as possible for the Christian people to "make holy" those feasts that may cease to be holy days of obligation.

In non-Christian countries, days habitually celebrated as festive during the week may be chosen as holy days of obligation, for example, Saturday in Israel and Friday in Islamic countries.

In like manner, some regions keep Saturday as a day or half-day of rest.

In some countries there are popular non-Christian feasts (New Year's Day, national festivals, harvest festivals) that can be christianized by celebrating some great Christian feast on the same day: for example, the feasts of St. Joseph, of the Apostles Peter and Paul, and All Saints. This last especially would doubtless achieve new brilliance if it were coordinated with the concrete exigencies of a particular culture.

2. Sanctification of Sunday

Along with the problem of holy days of obligation occurring during the week, the Consilium also took up the problem of the sanctification of Sunday. The problem in question was not the principle of the thing but the pastoral aspect. Present-day conditions of life for the faithful, social customs, tourism, the decline in the number of priests, and the decline in faith as well have turned the sanctification of Sunday into a serious problem.

Since the problem was primarily juridical and pastoral, it did not fall within the competence of the organizations in charge of the liturgy. But in a letter of April 21, 1971, which however did not arrive until June 22, the Congregation for the Clergy informed the Congregation for Divine Worship that it had sent a questionnaire to the episcopal conferences with a view to discussing the subject at a plenary session;[43] it asked the Congregation for Divine Worship for its views on the matter. The latter Congregation in turn queried its members and *periti* on three points:

1. *Sunday:* the time limits for applying the precept of the sanctification of Sunday. Might it be possible to assign some other day of the week for particular categories of persons or in particular circumstances?

2. *Holy days during the week.* In addition to what is already said in the General Norms of the calendar, might it not be possible to transfer some other major feasts and solemnities that cannot be celebrated during the week: for example, Christmas, the Octave of Christmas, St. Joseph, Sts. Peter and Paul, the Assumption of Mary, All Saints, and so on?

---

43. A letter had been sent to the presidents of the conferences and the papal representatives on February 28, 1971.

3. *Obligation*

a) Should the obligation to attend Mass on Sundays continue to be a serious one?

b) In places habitually without a priest, could the obligation not be satisfied by means of other celebrations, for example, a section of the Liturgy of the Hours?

c) Experiences and problems peculiar to the various regions.[44]

When the answers had come in, the Congregation for Divine Worship prepared a lengthy paper for the Congregation of the Clergy.[45] The emphasis was placed chiefly on presenting the theological, ascetical, and pastoral significance of Sunday; from this various practical conclusions were drawn.

On March 6 of the following year, a joint meeting was held that included the Congregations for the Clergy, for the Doctrine of the Faith, and for Divine Worship. At its conclusion it was decided that a document should be prepared which would contain a doctrinal section and a section of regulations; the composition of the first part was assigned to the Congregation for the Doctrine of the Faith, that of the second to the Congregation for the Clergy. In the following months the doctrinal section was prepared and delivered on May 25. But neither in its spirit nor in its letter did it harmonize with the regulatory section; suggestions were therefore made regarding it, which were accepted in substance.

At this point a lengthy correspondence began between the three Congregations, the Secretariat of State, and the episcopal conferences. The whole business became so entangled that the document was never published.

In the stage it had reached in November 1973, the document contained an introduction and five chapters: the nature and foundation of Sunday; the celebration of Sunday; the necessity of the Sunday celebration for the Church and its members; Sunday and the weekly day of rest; solemnities and feasts during the week. A regulatory section was to follow. The main difficulty that hindered publication of the document seems to have been the definition of the obligation.[46]

---

44. Questionnaire sent to forty individuals in various parts of the world, July 1, 1971.

45. The subsecretary was given the task of preparing this document. His draft was twice presented to the assembly of the Congregation, on September 25 and September 28. The task was then given to R. Kaczynski, who worked with G. Pasqualetti; their results were sent to the Congregation for the Clergy on October 13, 1971.

46. The most recent information available has to do with precisely this point. A letter of the Secretary of State to the Congregation for the Clergy stated that "with regard to the obligation of the faithful to take part in a possible liturgical assembly even when Mass cannot be celebrated due to a lack of priests, His Holiness wishes the question to be sub-

It is unfortunate that this study could not have been brought to a successful conclusion. It contained valuable guidelines both for the many communities that never assemble on Sundays because they lack a priest and for the reorganization of feasts that fall on weekdays.

---

mitted to the Sacred Congregation for the Doctrine of the Faith and that the episcopal conferences then be asked for their views'' (July 11, 1974).

22

The Litany of the Saints

The revision of the Litany of the Saints was combined with that of the calendar because of the close connection between the two. The study group therefore assigned the work to P. Jounel.

The Roman liturgy used to have three formularies for the Litany of the Saints:

—a lengthier one, used on Rogation Days;

—a second, shorter one, based on the first and used during the Easter Vigil and in the rites contained in Book II of the Pontifical;

—a third, even shorter, was used in the rite of the Recommendation of the Departing Soul to God (*Rituale Romanum*, tit. VI, cap. 7).

1. *Principles of the Revision*

The first two formularies were to be revised in accordance with the general principles set down in the Constitution on the Liturgy. It was therefore necessary:

—*to eliminate doublets*, especially such as would occur when the litany is recited in a rite connected with Mass;

—*to revise the text*, that is, to make a new list of saints that would be more universal in its inclusion of historical periods and parts of the world; to re-examine the various categories of saints; and to correct some formulas in the third part that were no longer in harmony with the spirit of the conciliar documents (for example: "that you would humble the enemies of holy Church"; "that you would restore to the unity of the Church all who have gone astray and lead all unbelievers to the light of the gospel");

—to facilitate the participation of the congregation by simplifying the invocations, which varied too much (for example, "pray for us," "deliver us, O Lord," "we beseech you, hear us");

—to allow more formularies: if there can be variety in readings, prayers, and songs, why not in the Litany of the Saints?;

—to grant to the episcopal conferences, or even to the individual bishops, the authority to adapt the text to local needs.

2. Elimination of Doublets

a) Doublets when the litany and the Mass are combined

The last part of the litany corresponds to the general intercessions or prayer of the faithful. Therefore, in Masses during which the litany is said, the last part of it is to replace the prayer of the faithful by including intentions having to do with the welfare of the Church and the world and with the persons or things with which the rite is concerned (for example, those being baptized at the Easter Vigil; ordinands; the church or altar being blessed; and so on).

The *Agnus Dei* certainly belongs to the structure of the Roman version of the litany. On the other hand, it used to be omitted in the litany said during the Recommendation of the Departing Soul. Furthermore, since the *Agnus Dei* has been part of the Order of Mass at least since the seventh century as a song accompanying the fraction, it seems that precedence should be given to the Order of Mass and that the *Agnus Dei* should be omitted from the litany when this is said during Mass.

b) Doublets within the litany

When the litany for the Recommendation of the Departing Soul was compared with the Rogation litany, it became clear that the first and simpler of these two formularies avoided doublets that had in many cases originated in a fusion of varied usages.

From "God the Father in heaven" to "Holy Trinity, one God": four invocations after the *Kyrie* that are not in the litany of the Recommendation. They are a duplication, as the tradition shows.

"Holy Mary": The Recommendation has but a single invocation of the Blessed Virgin; "Holy Mother of God" and "Holy Virgin of Virgins" were added in the tenth century. These do not represent a doublet in the full and proper sense, but they might well be omitted from the second formulary.

"Christ, hear us" and "Christ, graciously hear us" are two invocations that do not necessarily go together; they are not combined in the

Recommendation. The first appeared in the eighth century, the second only at the end of the thirteenth. They are an amplification of "Lord, have mercy; Christ, have mercy."

3. *Plurality of Forms*

Two basic schemas were adopted for the Litany of the Saints: a lengthier one for processions and more solemn supplications, the other for consecrations and blessings.[1]

The longer series contains four groups: I. Invocation of God; II. Invocation of the saints (Blessed Virgin, patriarchs and prophets, apostles and disciples of the Lord, martyrs, bishops and doctors, priests and religious, laypersons); III. Invocation of Christ; IV. Petitions for various needs; V. Conclusion.

In these groups varied texts may be chosen, depending on the sensibilities of the faithful and local needs.

The short schema contains the variants for baptism, ordinations, and the blessing of a church and altar.

The purpose of the Litany of the Saints is to offer supplications to God, Christ, and the saints. The literary expression, however, may vary not only from country to country but even within one and same community of the faithful.

In addition, therefore, to the possibility of choices in some parts, there is also permission to enlarge others by inserting the names of the saints proper to each community (patronal saints, titular saint, founder, saints especially venerated) or by adding special invocations according to needs and circumstances.

This kind of adaptation of the litany falls within the purview primarily of the episcopal conference, which can establish a general format for the entire region. For the same reason, each bishop can do the same for his own diocese. There may even be a more immediate adaptation by the pastor or the priest presiding at a celebration (names of the saints proper to that church or community, or other special invocations).

Two criteria should always be observed: the general format cannot be abbreviated lest the universality of the invocations be compromised; in printed texts additions should be indicated by typographical means so that the real character of these invocations will be clear.

---

1. These were published in the volume *Calendarium Romanum* (Vatican Polyglot Press, 1969), 33–39. The commentary, on which my own description here is based, is on pp. 159–62. Some revisions were subsequently made, as there were of the calendar; see *Not* 6 (1970) 375. The Fathers of the Consilium approved the drafts of the litanies at their general meeting of April 1968; see *Not* 4 (1968) 184.

4. List of the Saints

This is the part in which greatest scope is allowed to local usages and personal devotion. The original list had few saints' names; the litany of Louis the Pious (d. 839), on the contrary, contained 532 names (277 martyrs, 153 confessors, 102 virgins).

The recent revision was based on the data provided by the hagiographical sciences, so that legendary saints were excluded. In addition, the criterion of universality in space and time was always kept in mind; as a result, the more important Eastern saints are represented, as are more recent saints (previously the latest was St. Francis of Assisi), those of antiquity, and those of the Old Testament. Previously only the litany in the Recommendation included Sts. Abel and Abraham.

At the end of the list of saints the earliest litany had the invocation "All holy saints of God, pray for us." In the course of time this invocation was introduced at the end of each category of saints: apostles, martyrs, virgins, and so on. In the short version of the revised text, this generic or collective invocation is not repeated but occurs only once, at the end of the entire list of saints: "All holy men and women, pray for us."

In the long version, however, a variety of collective invocations have been kept: "All holy angels . . . ," "Holy patriarchs and prophets . . . ," "All disciples of the Lord . . . ."

23

Commons

One area which, like the calendar, applies to a variety of liturgical books, and especially the Missal and the Divine Office, is the Commons. These are sets of texts to be used for the various categories of saints. The choice of these texts fell to the study groups in charge of the Missal and the Liturgy of the Hours.

Study group 18, on the other hand, had the task of restructuring the classification, that is, of determining which Commons there were to be in view of present-day realities and sensibilities.[1]

The presidency of the Consilium provided the group with the following guidelines:

The current Common of Saints is a rather haphazard collection that lacks any real logical order. At present there are sixteen Commons, of which nine are complete; the others are sets of more or less extensive variants to be introduced into a preceding or following Common.

The desiderata with regard to the Commons can be summed up as follows:

a) *a more organic systematization.* The haphazard development of the existing Commons can be too sharply felt. First place should go to the Common for the Dedication of a Church (a feast of the Lord); next would come Our Lady and the other saints.

b) *greater concentration.* Simple variants might be included in the text of a given Common;

---

1. *Relator:* B. Neunheuser; *secretary:* G. Sobrero; *members:* E. Lengeling, H. Schmidt, F. Dell'Oro, R. J. Hesbert, B. Opfermann.

c) *better development*. The Common of the Saints should be broken down into new categories: a Common of Priests, a Common of Holy Mothers of Families, a Common of Widows, and so on.

On the other hand, there is also a felt need and desire for Offices that are more diversified. The repetition of the same texts, sometimes for three or four days in a row, becomes burdensome and does not help to devotion. Problems in this area should be carefully studied.

The group endeavored to set down main lines and general principles. It held two meetings at Turin in February and June of 1965, and others on the occasion of the meetings of the relators in Rome. At these sessions it worked out four schemas.[2]

The work done by this study group ran into difficulties, mainly (in many instances) because of the results reached by other groups, especially those working on the calendar, the Mass, and the Divine Office. As a result, its achievements never reached "maturity" and therefore never came before the Consilium, although they were discussed by the relators.

This situation became clear in connection with the very first schema, which was full of such phrases as "the question is not yet ripe for solution," "this point needs further study," and "the matter is complicated." The group did, however, propose to reduce the Commons to three: martyrs, confessors, and holy women, each having from five to seven subdivisions.

The second schema (no. 94) is a learned excursus, full of references to the Commons of the Saints in the Roman liturgical books down to Pius V. But the study, though displaying immense erudition, does not seem to shed any greater light on the new outlook being sought. The fonts have nothing to say with regard to the stagnant situation found in the Tridentine Missal.

Finally, in a report to a meeting of the relators that was held from May 2 to May 13, 1966, Father Neunheuser said that the classification of saints in the Commons should take into account (1) the divisions made in Scripture and the earliest liturgical tradition (for example, apostles, martyrs, virgins), and (2) the distinctions flowing from the categories suggested in *Lumen gentium* when it speaks of the people of God and the universal call to holiness.

This return to *Lumen gentium* was requested by the consultors in May 1966. According to Father Neunheuser (in the fourth schema, October 13,

---

2. Schema 66 (March 5, 1965); schema 94 (May 10, 1965); schema 153 (April 5, 1966); schema 196 (October 13, 1966).

1966), the consultors "referred us to *Lumen gentium*, where it speaks of the people of God generally, then of the hierarchy and the laity." Speaking of the universal call to holiness, the Constitution on the Church praises martyrdom as the "highest" gift and perfect continence as a "precious" gift in God's kingdom.

With the Scriptures, the early liturgy, and these passages of *Lumen gentium* as a basis, the study group proposed a new classification of saints that is better suited to catechesis and in harmony with the Council:

Apostles
Martyrs
Holy men (confessors)
—generally
—pastors
—religious
Holy women
—generally
—virgins

The purpose of this division was to bring out the characteristics shared by all holy men and women, so that the laity would no longer be "secondary saints" after bishops, abbots, and priests. For the same reason, it was not appropriate to compose a "Common of Laymen." The same holds for holy women. The charisms of the pastoral office, religious life, virginity, and so on, should rather be brought out by means of variants in the formularies.

The relator also had remarks to make on the various classes of saints.

Apostles: Since each of them has a proper Mass, the Common is of use only for the Office.

Martyrs: To be avoided is the distinction between one and several martyrs and between men and women and the separate classification of martyred popes. All that is needed is an appropriate selection of texts.

Confessors: The name sounds like something from archeology; in addition, it is equivocal both in the modern languages and in its early use, since it gradually changed its meaning. The reality to which the word "confessor" points is in fact complex, since the holiness of a bishop or priest is one thing, that of a religious or a layperson something else.

Virgins are prefigurations of the eschatological Church; therefore they cannot be simply intermingled with other holy women. But this distinction is sufficiently brought out in the special formularies.

Other categories of holy women do not seem necessary; it is enough to specify in the title the characteristic of the holy woman being venerated. Therefore, there is no reason for having widows as a separate class, especially since "widow" nowadays has a much different significance than it did originally. Much less is there reason for a class of women who are "neither virgins nor martyrs."

Three other Commons are being eliminated: supreme pontiffs, who ought to be commemorated among the bishops, martyrs, or confessors; doctors, whose numbers have been inflated and whose role cannot be specified as such in worship; and abbots, a classification that is well-nigh superfluous.

The best thing, said the relator in conclusion, would be to compile anthologies of texts and to indicate which are better suited for one or other type of saint. In the readings, for example, the point would be to list those suitable for apostles, for martyrs (with a further indication of those more appropriate for a bishop or a layman or a laywoman), for holy men (bishop, priest, deacon, religious, or layman), and for holy women (virgins, religious women, etc.).

The same process would also be applied to the songs, the prayers, the prefaces, and the blessings.

The Antiphonary would provide psalms, along with entrance and communion antiphons, but with authorization to choose other suitable texts in keeping with the general rubrics.

Finally, the Common of the Dedication of a Church should be placed first among the Commons, since a feast of dedication is a feast of the Lord. It should be followed by the Common of the Blessed Virgin.

In this schema the main lines of the Commons were clearly laid down. The particulars were to be determined in harmony with the work done by the other groups.

The definitive establishment of the Commons came at the time when the Missal was being compiled; it was based on the work of study group 18. The Commons included: Dedication of a Church, Blessed Virgin Mary, Martyrs, Pastors (popes, bishops, founders of Churches), Doctors, Virgins, Holy Men and Women (with special formularies for religious, those engaged in the works of mercy, and teachers).

Part III
The Missal

24

The Order of Mass

I. THE "NORMATIVE MASS"

The program for the revision of the Roman Missal provided for seven study groups, of which group 10 was assigned to study the Order of Mass. It thus became the group from which the others took their lead.[1]

The following directives were issued to this group:

1) The group is to implement article 50 of the liturgical Constitution: "The Order of Mass is to be revised in a way that will bring out more clearly the intrinsic nature and purpose of its several parts, as also the connection between them, and more readily achieve the devout, active participation of the faithful.

"For this purpose the rites are to be simplified, due care being taken to preserve their substance; elements that, with the passage of time, came to be duplicated or were added with but little advantage are now to be discarded; other elements that have suffered injury through accident of history are now, as may seem useful or necessary, to be restored to the vigor they had in the tradition of the Fathers."

2) The problems connected with the Order of Mass are among the most complicated and difficult of the entire liturgy; one reason for this is that

---

1. *Relator:* J. Wagner; *secretary:* A. Hänggi; *members:* M. Righetti, T. Schnitzler, P. Jounel, C. Vagaggini, A. Franquesa, P. M. Gy, J. A. Jungmann. Because of the complexity of the work, the group was expanded. Its composition in March 1967 was as follows: *relator:* J. Wagner; *prosecretary:* A. Franquesa; *members:* M. Righetti, T. Schnitzler, A. Hänggi, P. Jounel, P.-M. Gy, J. A. Jungmann, L. Agustoni, J. Gélineau, C. Vagaggini, L. Bouyer; *advisors:* S. Famoso and K. Amon, along with J. Cellier, F. McManus, V. Noè, H. Wegman, and J. Patino (these five in their capacity as secretaries of national liturgical commissions). See schema 218; *De Missali* 34 (March 1967), p. 111.

they have to do with the rite that is at the center of worship and that is supremely important from the pastoral standpoint. For this reason an effort has been made to have the two areas of history and pastoral care represented in the study group.

3) Although the Mass is a sensitive and complicated subject, it also has the advantage of being the most fully studied of all the liturgical rites. The literature on the subject is very extensive; the group will have to be fully cognizant of it. In any case, the individuals called to work in the group are for the most part writers internationally famous for their solid works on the Mass. It is enough to mention Father Jungmann and Monsignor Righetti.

4) As part of the work done by the preparatory commission, the scholars in charge of this area had produced complete plans for simplification and renewal. At the time, these were set aside because it was decided to include only guidelines of a general kind in the liturgical Constitution. All that material is now to be utilized.

5) Another valuable source that did not exist a few years ago is the critical editions of the sacramentaries and *Ordines;* with the aid of these it is possible to follow the present-day rites, and especially the Mass, from their birth to their manifold developments. Nowadays nothing eludes the historian and the critic. Therefore every change proposed is to be exhaustively documented.

6) Since the pastoral aspect of the rite of Mass is regarded as exceptionally important in the present reform, it seems appropriate that once the work of the "technicians" is complete, the "critical" pastoral sense of a sizable group of parish priests should have its say. These men are to be chosen from various countries and various types of parishes. Room is also to be made for some experiments (on the basis of article 40), these being limited to some "circles," churches, or parishes.

1. *First Phase of the Work (April 1964–October 1965)*

The group set to work in a decisive manner and in accordance with rigorous methods of research. The first meeting was held at Rome in April 1964. As a result of it, on April 17, at the second general meeting of the Consilium, Monsignor Wagner was able to present a report on the work that needed to be done. He asked for a reply to five questions; the answers adopted would indicate clearly the basis on which the schema of the reformed Mass was to be constructed.

The questions had to do with the norms governing the work; article 50 of the liturgical Constitution; the readings at Mass; the prayer of the faithful; communion under two kinds; and concelebration. I shall deal with the first two here and take up the others at their proper places.

1) *Norms governing the work*

The group was to base its activity primarily on the mandate given by the Council, while also taking into account the reports made by the conciliar commission in the Council hall. In addition, the group was to have before them:

a) the minutes of the preparatory commission, especially the *declarationes* on each article; although these possessed no juridical authority, they were greatly valued for an understanding of the text on which the Fathers voted;

b) the views of the bishops as contained in the acts of the antepreparatory commission of the Council;

c) the work of the commission established by Pius XII for the reform of the liturgy;

d) the works of the most qualified authors on the subject.

In principle, no door was to be closed to the investigators; their purpose, after all, was not to essay an archeological restoration but to see to it that "any new forms adopted should in some way grow organically from forms already existing" (*SC* 23).

The Fathers approved these norms.

2) *Problems connected with SC 50*

Article 50 of the Constitution on the Liturgy sets down six requirements: (1) that the distinctive character of each part, as well as their interconnections, appear clearly; (2) that a devout and active participation of the faithful be made easier; (3) that the rites be simplified; (4) that doublets and less useful additions be eliminated; (5) that worthwhile elements lost in the course of time be restored; and (6) that the substance of the rites be faithfully maintained.

The preparatory commission had drawn up a detailed explanation (*declaratio*) of this article. It began by recalling the need for a clear distinction between the liturgy of the Word and the liturgy of the Eucharist. It then went on to say that the parts of the Order of Mass that seemed in need of careful revision were the opening rites, the offertory, the communion, and the dismissal, all of which had acquired new elements when the Roman Rite was accepted in Gaul. There was need, for example, of:

a) reducing the number of signs of the cross, kissings of the altar, genuflections, bows, and other such gestures;

b) shortening and simplifying the prayers at the foot of the altar;

c) facing the congregation while proclaiming the readings;

d) allowing for participation of the congregation or its representatives in the offertory rite, at least on more solemn days (as in the Ambrosian

Rite); the prayers that accompany the offering of the gifts should bring out the aspect of oblation, and the prayer over the gifts should be said aloud;

e) increasing the number of prefaces and reciting the Canon aloud;

f) also saying aloud the embolism of the Our Father, as at the Good Friday liturgy;

g) improving the organization of the fraction;

h) removing the restrictions on communion of the faithful at some Masses;

i) shortening the communion formula to, for example, "The Body of Christ.—Amen," as in the writings of St. Ambrose;

j) ending Mass with the blessing and the dismissal, "Go, the Mass is ended."

While accepting these suggestions, the group formulated other worthwhile observations:

1. The point of departure for the reform should not be "private" Mass but "Mass with a congregation"; not Mass as read but Mass with singing. But which Mass with song—the pontifical, the solemn, or the simple sung Mass?

a) Given the concrete situation in the churches, the answer can only be: Mass celebrated by a priest, with a reader, servers, a choir or cantor, and a congregation. All other forms, such as pontifical Mass, solemn Mass, Mass with a deacon, will be amplifications or further simplifications of this basic Mass, which is therefore called "normative."

b) There must be a substantial sameness among all the forms of Mass with a congregation, with or without singing. For if, in fact, Mass without singing were made the model because, for example, of the vernacular, sung Mass would gradually fall into disuse.

c) A sharper differentiation can be made between Mass with a congregation and Mass without a congregation ("private" Mass). Mass with a congregation requires several areas (for the altar, for the lectern, for the presidential chair) and perhaps fewer formulas, since by its nature its celebration will take more time. Mass without a congregation, on the other hand, does not require these several areas and can have longer or more numerous formulas that may augment the devotion of the celebrant.

2. The number and length of the readings calls for special attention. Is it appropriate that there usually be three: prophet, apostle, and gospel?

3. The Canon raises many problems:

a) Should the number of signs of the cross be reduced?

b) Should the "Amens" be omitted, except for the final one of the congregation?

c) Should the entire Canon or the principal prayers or at least the final doxology be said aloud?

d) Should there not be acclamations of the congregation during the Canon, as in the other liturgies of the Church? Ought not the lists of the saints be revised to make them accord better with historical truth? Should not the other formulas be revised so that the faithful may more easily grasp their meaning?

4. The final part of the Mass should also be radically revised. Should the "last gospel" be eliminated? Should there be psalms and songs for the period of thanksgiving after communion? Should there be a variety of formulas for the blessing of the congregation?

Monsignor Wagner ended his report by saying that in this first phase of the work, the group has simply listed in summary fashion the problems that seem to call for closer study. There are doubtless other problems that ought to be faced by the study groups in charge of the various parts of the Mass.

The Consilium accepted in principle the general approach taken to the work on revision of the Order of Mass.

On April 17, 1964, a sturdy, powerful machinery was set in motion that in five years' time would bring the "new" Mass.

2. *Continuation of the Work*

The second meeting of the study group was held at Trier in Germany from May 8 to May 18 of the same year, and the third at Einsiedeln Abbey in Switzerland, June 5–7. The program for these meetings was pretty much the same as for the first, the procedure being as follows: With regard to any question, it was determined whether the group was in unanimous agreement; if it was not, an effort was made to overcome disagreements through discussion; if unanimity was still not achieved, the manner of conducting a further special study was decided on, and the problems to be submitted to the judgment of other experts were listed.

On June 17, 1964, the Consilium was brought up to date on the progress being made.

The fourth meeting was held at Fribourg in Switzerland, August 24–28, 1964; from the 26th to the 28th the study group met with group 15 ("on the structure of the Mass") and other experts specially invited. The material already discussed twice was here discussed a third time at a more inclusive gathering.

On October 4 and 5, 1964, the work thus far accomplished was again described to the Consilium at its fourth general meeting. Some norms were approved that the group was to follow in establishing the definitive Order of Mass:

1. The description of the rite of Mass was to be based on Mass with singing, a reader, at least one server, a choir or cantor, and a congregation.

2. The proper place for the liturgy of the Word is the lectern; the proper place for the liturgy of the Eucharist is the altar.

3. There is to be a single collect, a single prayer over the gifts, and a single prayer after communion.

4. There are to be three readings on Sundays and feast days.

5. In some circumstances and situations the Apostles' Creed may replace the Nicene-Constantinopolitan. It may be either sung or recited.

6. The final blessing may be sung.

7. The dismissal "Ite, missa est" is to be kept in the Latin text, but it may be translated in ways better adapted to the various vernaculars.

8. At the beginning of Mass, during the offertory, and during communion, songs adapted to the season and the particular sacred action may be sung.

Other questions had to do with the opening rites, the *Kyrie* and *Gloria*, the song between the readings, the prayers and rites of the offertory, the Canon, the reorganization of the communion rites, and the formulas for the dismissal.

Meanwhile, some of the points studied by group 10 and approved by the Consilium would be given practical application for the entire Church in the first instruction *(Inter Oecumenici)* and in the introduction, on March 7, 1965, of the new rites of concelebration and communion under two kinds.

Another report on the progress of the work was made to the Consilium in April 1965.

The sixth meeting of the group was held at Le Saulchoir (near Paris), June 8–23, 1965; also present were group 15 and some other experts individually invited. The purpose was to carry on discussions and experiments (behind closed doors) that would aid in improving the schema drawn up for the Order of Mass. It was clear that there was no further need for studies and theoretical discussions; the need now was for practical decisions, and these in turn required experimentation.

3. First Schema of the "Normative" Mass

The complete schema of the new Order of Mass was presented to the Consilium at its sixth general meeting. It was discussed for five days, during which two experimental celebrations were also held.[2] The schema in question was "the first schema of the normative Order of Mass," which was accompanied by a lengthy explanation that ended with eight sets of questions on which the views of the Father were requested.[3]

The Mass was called "normative" because, while there would always be several forms of celebration, this was the one that was to serve as the norm or standard for the others. According to the schema, the celebration begins with the singing of the congregation. The ministers make the sign of the cross in silence; this is followed by the celebrant's greeting and the penitential act, the *Kyrie*, *Gloria*, and collect. A point on which there was disagreement was the succession of three songs: opening song, *Kyrie*, and *Gloria*, which could make the early part of the Mass somewhat slow and heavy. It was suggested that the singing of the *Kyrie* be optional.

Next comes the liturgy of the Word with the three (optional) readings, homily, the Creed on holy days of obligation, and the prayer of the faithful. This last was declared to a structural and permanent element of the celebration, not to be omitted "from any celebration, even on weekdays and in private Masses, though in the latter the form is to be appropriately adapted."

The offertory begins with the washing of hands; it continues with the preparation of the gifts, which are brought to the altar, where the celebrant places them on the altar to the accompaniment of short formulas.[4]

After the prayer "In a spirit of humility . . . ," the celebrant immediately says aloud the prayer over the gifts; he then enters into the Eucharistic Prayer by beginning the dialogue before the preface.

The Roman Canon was the most sensitive and complex problem of all. On the one hand, respect for this prayer made the group hesitate to touch it; on the other, there were suggestions from experts and requests from pastors for a different and more logical organization of the Eucharistic Prayer. In order to achieve a resolution of the difficulties, it was proposed to experiment with three revised forms of the Roman Canon.

---

2. See above, pp. 151–52.

3. Schema 113, *De Missali* 14 (October 9, 1965); the schema occupies twenty-four pages, the report twenty-six, and the queries four more.

4. A passage from the *Didache* (with some adaptation) was proposed for the placing of the bread on the altar: "As this bread was scattered and, having been gathered, is now one, so may your Church be gathered into your kingdom." For the chalice: "Wisdom has built herself a house; she has mixed her wine and set her table. Glory to you through all ages" (Prov 9:1-2). The Fathers approved the formulas, with five nays for the formula for the bread.

Schema A

This consisted of the traditional Canon, including all the elements added to it over the centuries and not excluding even the most recent change—the addition of St. Joseph's name as ordered by Pope John XXIII. Some formulas, however, were to be corrected in accordance with the critical edition of Bernard Botte, that is, by omitting the so-called "Addition of Alcuin" ("for whom we offer to you or") in the memento of the living and the Amens which are scattered throughout the text but which, as the manuscript tradition shows, were inserted only during the Middle Ages.

Study group 10 was of the opinion that this traditional Canon, including the entire series of saints' names—despite the doubts of historians about some of them—could do good service in the future as it had in the past.

Schema B

This schema attempts to reduce, at least to some extent, the mass of interpolations that have been made in the original Roman Canon. In fact, the two mementos are shortened slightly; the series of saints' names are not completely omitted, but the two sets (one in the "Communicantes," the other in the "Nobis quoque") are combined into one, and only the names of biblical saints are kept. This was done out of a desire to adopt the suggestions long since made by experts in this area.

The group had not felt up to accepting suggestions that new lists of saints be drawn up that would exclude the local saints of the City of Rome and include others from all times and places.

Schema C

The content here is exactly the same as in Schema B, except that the two mementos and the "Nobis quoque" are combined into a single complex prayer. This new prayer is placed after the consecration, between the "Supplices" and the final doxology.[5]

---

5. The purpose of these revisions was to smooth the transition from the *Sanctus* to the consecration, in an attempt to recover, at least in this first part, the original grandeur and sublimity of the Eucharistic Prayer. The resultant union, in the "Te igitur," of "In primis quae tibi offerimus" and the "Communicantes" (which contains the list of—biblical—saints) is certainly an advantage, because it is the joining of two groups: those who "in terris offerunt" and the triumphant Church (Jungmann); this was something that Cardinal Schuster had long ago thought perfectly in harmony with the present Roman Canon.

These three schemas were discussed at great length. No one denied the difficulties

For the rite of communion the following sequence of actions was proposed: Our Father with its opening exhortation, the embolism, and the acclamation "Yours is the kingdom . . . " (in the form that would be kept in the definitive rite), the greeting and exchange of peace, the fraction during the singing of "Lamb of God." The priest then says quietly a single prayer, "Lord Jesus Christ, Son of the living God," and then immediately says "Behold, the Lamb of God . . ." and receives communion. His reception of the chalice is accompanied by the prayer, "What shall I give to the Lord . . . ."

Conclusion of the Mass: silence or singing after communion, prayer after communion, announcements, blessing, dismissal.[6]

The study groups asked for the views of the bishops on each point, and the latter gave substantial approval. This does not mean the bishops did not have their doubts. Their intention in approving was that the group should conduct experiments and then bring the subject up for discussion again. In some of the votes this point was expressly made: "Yes, for experiments." The Fathers were in agreement that the schema of the rite of Mass proposed to them should be the subject of experiment in suitable, controlled centers. These experiments were rendered impossible, however, by leaks to the press and the fright of bishops, faithful, and other experts. The Secretariat of State intervened several times, saying that no further steps were to be taken before informing the Holy Father of them in detail; such in fact had always been the procedure and intention of the Consilium.[7]

---

presented by the Roman Canon. Some, however, closed ranks against even the slightest revision or development of the Roman Canon (with the exception of the critical restoration of the text to the form it had before Alcuin tampered with it); their motives were historical and literary. On the other hand, all without exception urgently asked for the addition of a new canon to the existing Roman Canon.

The Fathers of the Consilium did not vote on the request for the introduction of a second canon, but limited themselves, in a secret vote requiring a two-thirds majority, to consenting to an experimental use of the three schemas.

6. In order to make the rites of preparation for communion less cumbersome, the other two prayers (one for the peace and unity of the Church, the other in preparation for communion) were suppressed. The part of the Mass that follows upon communion was discussed at length. Some regretted that the Roman Mass ended almost abruptly, with no pause for meditative prayer and for praise and thanksgiving for the gift received. It was suggested that the *Gloria* be moved to this point, but the group did not think this opportune. Others saw in the rapid conclusion of the Roman Mass a characteristic of the Roman Rite that ought to be preserved. The group found a compromise: "After communion and an optional exhortation depending on circumstances, a hymn or psalm or other prayer of praise is sung or recited."

7. See p. 152, n. 30.

It was agreed, however, that some time should be allowed to pass. Meanwhile the secretariat and those in charge of group 10 prepared a presentation to the Pope of the situation with regard to work on the Order of Mass; this report was submitted to the Consilium in October.[8]

At an audience granted to Cardinal Lercaro on June 20, 1966, the Pope expressed his mind on two points:

> a) [Penitential act:] The Kyrie, duly adapted, is to be used when there is no Gloria in the Mass; in order to avoid three songs in a row (Introit, Kyrie, and Gloria), the Kyrie is replaced in this case by another penitential formula; this formula is to be of a kind in which the congregation can participate (unlike the present prayers at the foot of the altar, in which only the celebrant and servers have a part).
>
> b) [Canon:] The present anaphora is to be left unchanged, and two or three others are to be composed or found for use at special limited times.

The way was thus opened to further studies on a basis authoritatively provided by the Pope himself.

The study group immediately began to put the Pope's regulations into effect. Contacts were maintained chiefly through correspondence during the summer of 1966. Meanwhile another stage was being anticipated—consultation with the bishops, for which advantage was to be taken of the Synod.[9]

II. The Normative Mass at the Synod of Bishops

At an audience on September 22, 1966, the Holy Father suggested that the liturgical schemas already prepared should be sent to the 1967 Synod of Bishops, and he asked the Consilium to contact the secretariat of the Synod in good time so that the texts might be forwarded to the conferences.

---

8. Schema 170, De Missali 23 (May 24, 1966), containing the schema of the normative Mass, with reasons given at each point to explain the solution adopted. The schema was accompanied by a "Memorandum on the activity of Group X (De Ordine Missae) and on the need, possibilities, and goals of the reform of the Ordo Missae in accordance with the conciliar decrees" (25 pp.), and by two pages of a "Note on the purposes and importance of the experiments." The memorandum and its adjunct are a lengthy report on the work completed and on the problems connected with the most difficult and controverted points. It shows the circumspection, conscientiousness, and extensive scientific study that marked the group's work. See J. Wagner, "Zur Reform des Ordo Missae. Zwei Dokumente," in the collective work Liturgia opera divina e umana. Studi sulla riforma liturgica offerti a S. E. Mons. Annibale Bugnini in occasione del suo 70° compleanno (Rome, 1982) 263–89 (the text of the "Memorandum" is on pp. 267ff.).

9. A reference to a possible consultation of the bishops may already be found in the March 7, 1966, letter of the Secretary of State.

He made the same point to the members of the Consilium when he received them in a special audience on October 13, 1966:

A second issue, worthy of your most intent consideration, is the *Ordo Missae*. We are aware of the work done and of how much learned and thoughtful discussion has taken place with regard to composing both a new missal and a liturgical calendar. The issue is of such serious and universal import that we cannot do otherwise than consult with the bishops on any proposals before approving them by our own authority.[10]

The vague wording of this announcement gave some credence to the idea that the Pope was intending to hold a special session, or "Extraordinary Synod," of the Synod of Bishops in 1968, solely for the purpose of discussing liturgical problems. This prospect was in fact a welcome one, so much so that at the end of the seventh general meeting of the Consilium (October 1966), the Cardinal President wrote as follows to the Pope:

Given the point that the work has now reached after the general meeting held October 6–14 of this year, if the intention is confirmed of having a special meeting of the Synod of Bishops to deal with questions of the liturgical reform, I can anticipate that we will have some schemas ready for sending to the parties concerned for the requisite prior study; specifically, the schemas on: 1) the *Ordo Missae*; 2) the general structure of the Office; 3) the *Ordo lectionum* for Mass on feast days and weekdays; 4) the rites of ordination (bishops, priests, deacons); and 5) some sacraments (baptism of adults, baptism of children, marriage) and sacramentals (funerals).

Some information on this point is needed so that we can decide on the order in which various parts of the work are to be done; it must also be kept in mind that the printing and sending of the pertinent texts will likewise require no small amount of time.

On November 15, 1966, the Secretariat of State communicated the Pope's decision that the most important schemas of the reform should be presented to the Synod of 1967.[11]

---

10. *DOL* 84 no. 636.

11. But at the audience of November 10, at which the Cardinal President presented the Pope with the above-mentioned explanation, the Pope had already said that the liturgy would be discussed at the Synod of October 1967. On that same day the secretary of the Consilium wrote to the relators in charge of the sections (Martimort, Wagner, Botte, Fischer, Gy) that they must set forth the principles and general structure of the reformed rites, together with some illustrative models. The Consilium would inspect their work at its general meeting in April 1967. The intention was to present the Synod with the rites of the Mass, the Office, child baptism, marriage, holy orders, the readings for Mass, the prefaces, and the calendar.

The material was prepared and sent to the members of the Consilium, who discussed it at length at their eighth general meeting (April 10–19, 1967). It was decided to compile a lengthy report on the work of the Consilium and then to explain to the Fathers only the key sensitive points in the reform of the principal rites, namely, the Mass and the Office.[12] As for the sacraments, it was not possible to do more than give a general description of the state of the work, since each sacramental rite was a special case, and it was therefore necessary to present either all or none of them. The material prepared was sent to the bishops, along with the other matters to be taken up at the Synod, so that the episcopal conferences might discuss them and their delegates might then report on their thinking.

On October 21, 1967, Cardinal Lercaro opened the synodal discussion of the liturgical schemas with a vigorous report. Immediately following this, a "Supplement to the Report on the Liturgy" was read, explaining the four new Eucharistic Prayers, the variants in the formulas of consecration, and the introduction of the Apostles' Creed into the Mass. These further liturgical matters were described as "Papal Queries." The Pope had decided to bring them up at the Synod after the booklet containing the subjects for discussion had been sent to the bishops; he did not wish to pass up the opportunity of having at least the *personal* views of the Fathers on these important matters.

That same day saw the first interventions on both the report and the supplement: nine Fathers spoke; on October 23, twenty-one more; on October 24, sixteen; on October 25, seventeen; or sixty-three in all. Nineteen Fathers expressed their views only in writing.

On Monday, October 24, the normative Mass was experimentally celebrated in the Sistine Chapel. The Fathers were given a booklet containing the chants and prayers of the Mass and of Eucharistic Prayer III, which was here used for the first time with the permission, and at the wish, of the Pope (letter of the Secretariat of State, October 17, 1967).[13]

The secretary of the Consilium celebrated in Italian; G. Pasqualetti was lector; the music was directed by Father Rossi, of the Ministri degli In-

---

12. See p. 169, n. 62.
13. The Mass was celebrated according to the schema presented to, and approved by, the Consilium in October, 1965, and then given to the Pope. Meanwhile, in order to decide how to implement the directives given by the Holy Father on June 20, 1966, the study group on the Mass had held special meetings in Innsbruck, Paris, and Louvain, and then general meetings at Orselina (January 24–30, 1967) and Nemi (March 8–12). The main subjects discussed were the new Eucharistic Prayers, special points in the rite of Mass, and preparation of the presentation to be made at the Synod. (See schema 218, *De Missali* 34 [March 19, 1967].)

fermi, professor of musicology and chant at the Barnabite Collegio Internazionale S. Antonio M. Zaccaria (Rome); the Barnabites also provided the altar servers.

The Mass was to be thought of as a Sunday Mass in a parish church, with the participation of a congregation, a small choir, a lector, a cantor, and two servers.

The readings were taken from the Nineteenth Sunday after Pentecost (Schema B) in the *Ordo lectionum;* in the new organization of the liturgical year, the Nineteenth Sunday would fall in approximately the second half of October. The chants were taken from the *Graduale simplex,* Schema IV, for the time after Pentecost. The entire Mass was prepared *solely* for this celebration.

It must be said flatly that the experiment was not a success and even that it had an effect contrary to the one intended and played a part in the negative vote that followed. Few of the Fathers were disposed and ready for the experiment; this was even more true of those who had grasped the value and essential character of the normative Mass. The majority of the Fathers entered the Sistine Chapel with their minds made up[14] and ill-disposed to the new Mass.

The ceremonies and chants had been worked out in the smallest detail, and as far as these were concerned the celebration went very smoothly. The setting, however, was completely unsuitable. In the first place, the Sistine Chapel lends itself to elitist, not popular, celebrations. Most important of all, the congregation was in a false position. The Fathers of the Synod had to imagine a fine assembly of ordinary people present

---

14. During the opening days of the Synod, the Fathers were enthusiastic about the reform and urged the conferences to hasten the time for promulgation of the new rite of Mass (see H. Fesquet in *Le Monde,* October 26, 1967). At the end of the discussions, however, there was a massive intervention by persons opposed to any reform and coming not from the periphery of the Church but for the most part from the Roman Curia. Because of their position, the latter seem to have made a strong impression and led others to see the liturgical reform as the source of some worrisome kinds of arbitrary action, as well as of excessively bold agitation for renewal in still other areas of religious and ecclesiastical life. Many of the Fathers heard alarm bells ringing when the very Secretary of State, Cardinal G. Amleto Cicognani, said his "Enough!" to liturgical changes, "lest the faithful be confused" (see his "I lavori del Sinodo Episcopale," *L'Osservatore Romano,* October 27, 1967). Some Fathers even ridiculed the reform, taking their cue from disputed points, such as song in the Mass, and eliciting laughter but also indignation, and creating a situation of bewilderment. Outside the Synod other groups were busy raising alarms, for example, *Una voce* in *Il tempo,* October 27, 1967; a vaguely defined conservative group that smuggled in some duplicated pages entitled "Fortes in fide" to the Fathers of the Synod; and the Bulletin C.E.D.I.C. Insults and defamatory accusations, directed especially against Father Bugnini, were not lacking.

in the hall, for it was with such a congregation in mind that the songs, rites, language, and tone of the homily had been chosen. Instead, the Fathers saw around them a gathering of illustrious Church dignitaries. The Italian language and the many sung parts were a further obstacle to participation.

The celebration must therefore have left many of the Fathers with the impression of something artificial, overly pedantic, and quite unparochial.[15] Some of them thought that such a Mass could not possibly be celebrated in a parish. The very term "normative" suggested, incorrectly, that all the parts sung in the Sistine Chapel would have to be sung always and in all circumstances in every parish. Other Fathers, accustomed to individual celebration, found this Mass to be impoverished by omission of the priest's private prayers. Still others, incited by the dogma of the real presence, looked with concern on any reduction in gestures and genuflections and on the lengthening of the liturgy of the Word. In short, the changes in the Mass seemed too radical.[16]

The vote on the four "Papal Queries" took place on October 24, and on the other eight (four on the Mass, four on the Office) on October 26. The outcome of the two votes was communicated to the Fathers on October 28.

During the debate on the liturgy, two press conferences on the subject were also held: one on October 22 by Archbishop George P. Dwyer of Birmingham, England; the other on October 25 by Cardinal Raul Silva Henríquez, Archbishop of Santiago, Chile.[17] Both prelates were members of the Synod and of the Consilium.

---

15. On October 26, Cardinal Heenan, Archbishop of Westminster, took the podium and accused the commission of technicism, intellectualism, and a lack of pastoral sense. Cardinal Lercaro immediately replied that forty-seven Fathers, almost all of them pastors of dioceses, and eighteen parish priests belonged to the Consilium.

16. The chief spokesmen for these objections were the representatives of the English-speaking hierarchies, who gathered at the English College on October 25 to agree on a common attitude that would be expressed in the voting. The attitude adopted was a negative one and displayed an obsession with singing in particular; it was claimed that people in the English-speaking world do not sing in church (the reference seems to have been solely to Catholic churches) and that the normative Mass should therefore be the read Mass. Another concern was to defend the Church's faith in the real presence.

17. See Not 3 (1967) 401; A. Bugnini, "Genesi e sviluppo del nuovo Ordo Missae," in V. Fagiolo and G. Concetti (eds.), La collegialità episcopale per il futuro della Chiesa (Florence, 1969) 514–33; "De liturgia in primo Synodo Episcoporum," Not 3 (1967) 353–70; "De Missa normativa," ibid., 371–80.

1. *Papal Queries*

The vote on these was taken on October 24. The presidency appointed three Fathers to sort the ballots: Joseph Kuo, a Chinese, Titular Archbishop of Salamis; Archbishop Enrico Nicodemo of Bari, and Archbishop John F. Dearden of Detroit. Father Bugnini, the Synod's special secretary for liturgy, acted as secretary. The ballots were sorted at Santa Marta on October 25 and 26.

The value of the vote taken on the "Papal Queries" was quite relative. For although some of the Fathers claimed to be speaking in the name of their conferences, this claim could not be accepted except in a broad sense, since the conferences had not known of these queries and therefore could not have taken a stand on them. In the final analysis, therefore, the vote could only be interpreted as an expression of personal preference.

I. *Should three other Eucharistic Prayers, in addition to the Roman Canon, be introduced into the Latin liturgy?*

Of the 183 Fathers voting, 173 said yes, 22 no, and 33 yes with qualifications (*iuxta modum*). The qualifications were:

1) The Roman Canon should always have the place of honor and be used on Sundays and more solemn feasts.

2) Very precise norms should be set down for the use of each prayer; the choice of prayer should not be left to the celebrant.

3) The new Eucharistic Prayers should be restricted to special. well-prepared groups.

4) Before use of the prayers is allowed, they should be submitted to the episcopal conferences for study, and the faithful should be carefully instructed in advance.

5) There should not be only three further Eucharistic Prayers, but a good many more; these should be taken from the Eastern liturgies. Furthermore, the episcopal conferences should be granted authority to compose others proper to them.

6) The Roman Canon should itself be revised to facilitate its use.

II. *Should the words "quod pro vobis tradetur" be added to the formula for the consecration of the bread in the new Eucharistic Prayers?*

Of the 183 Fathers voting, 110 said yes, 12 no, and 61 yes with qualifications. The qualifications were reducible to two:

1) The same very meaningful addition should be made in the Roman Canon as well.

2) The tense of the verb *tradetur* should be changed from future to present, in accordance with the parallel passages of Scripture: *datur, traditur, frangitur.*

III. *Should the words "mysterium fidei" be removed from the formula for the consecration of the wine?*

Of the 183 voting, 93 said yes, 48 no, and 42 yes with qualifications. In substance, the qualifications were these:

1) The words should also be omitted in the Roman Canon.

2) The words should not completely disappear from the liturgy but should be used as an acclamation after the consecration or in some other formula.

3) The verb *effundetur* should be put in the present tense, as in the parallel passages of Scripture, which read *effunditur.*

IV. *Should authority be given to the episcopal conferences to use the Apostles' Creed as well as the Nicene-Constantinopolitan Creed in the Mass?*

Of the 183 voting, 142 said yes, 22 no, and 19 yes with qualifications. The points made in the qualifications were these:

1) The concession should be made only by the Holy See and for those places in which the faithful are illiterate, or for carefully defined cases.

2) Care must be taken that it is really possible to use the two Creeds at all times and that the Nicene Creed be kept in sung Masses.

3) The Apostles' Creed should be allowed only for children's Masses and in the simpler kind of Mass, for example, on weekdays or similar occasions.

4) The formula used should be uniform throughout each country in order to facilitate the participation of the faithful.

5) The singing of the Apostles' Creed should be prohibited.

6) The Apostles' Creed should be the only Creed used everywhere.

2. *The Queries on the Mass*

On October 26 Cardinal Lercaro responded to the observations that the Fathers had made on the liturgy. He explained the principle of gradualness in implementing the liturgical reform and spoke of the freedom sought by the episcopal conferences, the experiments, the excessive simplification of the rites, the use of Latin, and relations between the Consilium and the bishops.

With regard to the Mass, the Cardinal raised six points. The most interesting had to do with the term "normative Mass," which had caused such confusion. He explained: It is a term for use during the period of study and designates the basic pattern of the Eucharistic celebration. Once the reform is implemented, the term will disappear, because each type of Mass will have its own proper name.

The schema for the normative Mass is the basis for the other forms. There are degrees of solemnity, the Cardinal continued, depending on the singing, the number of ministers, and other factors. Thus there can be a Mass of the utmost solemnity that is completely sung, and Masses of lesser solemnity, even to the point of being completely read or recited; in all cases, however, these Masses are distinguished by the presence of a congregation. No one unable to sing will be forced to sing, even though all are warmly urged to express their interior joy in song.

The other special forms of Eucharistic celebration will reflect the same basic schema: Masses for children, for beginners, for the sick. In these several cases there will be guidelines as to what is to be kept or omitted; in other cases, as to elements in which there is a choice. The Consilium has anticipated all these points and will set them down in precise norms as soon as the fundamental schema is approved.

When Cardinal Lercaro had completed his reply, the vote was taken on the four general queries regarding the Mass.

I. *Is the structure of the normative Mass acceptable on the whole?*

Seventy-one Fathers said yes, 43 no, and 62 yes with qualifications. The high number of qualifications became less striking in light of the vague formulation of the question and in light of the many detailed remarks made in the interventions. Here is a summary of the qualifications offered.

1. *On the general structure of the normative Mass:*

a) The read Mass and not the sung Mass should be normative; it is easier to celebrate a read Mass on Sundays and feast days.

b) The conferences should be free to make timely adaptations according to the requirements of regions and the traditions of their peoples.

c) The entire schema needs to be enriched, especially with signs of the cross, genuflections, and bows, in accordance with the desire and taste of many peoples.

d) The prayers said by the priest privately should be kept; in fact, their number should be increased so that he may have a choice available.

e) Nothing should be left to the discretion of the priest; everything should be clearly set down, and there should be no variations from one region to another.

f) The liturgy of the Word seems too long by comparison with the Eucharistic liturgy.

g) The conferences should have a good deal of freedom in choosing the readings and composing the prayers.

h) There should be more numerous moments of silence.

i) There should be no moments of silence, since these do not suit the mentality of modern men and women, wholly given over as these are to activity.

2. *Observations on the liturgy of the Word:*

a) The *Kyrie* should never be omitted.

b) The *Gloria* should be kept according to the rules now in force.

c) After the liturgy of the Word there should be a time of silence in order to accustom the faithful to meditating on the word of God.

d) The chants after the readings should be shortened or eliminated.

e) The general intercessions do not seem necessary at all Masses; they could be made after communion.

3. *Observations on the liturgy of the Eucharist:*

a) The offertory seems impoverished; therefore, keep the prayers and rites now in use, especially the mingling of water with the wine and the accompanying prayer.

b) The prayers to be said by the priest privately during the offertory should be obligatory.

c) The *Orate, fratres* and its answer should be kept.

d) The number of the saints mentioned in the Canon should be reduced.

e) The acclamation of the congregation after the consecration should be obligatory in all of the Eucharistic Prayers.

f) The present prayer before the sign of peace should be kept.

g) The short prayers before and after communion should be kept, at least in private Masses.

h) Communion under two kinds should be left to the discretion of the conferences and bishops.

i) The solemn blessing at the end of Mass should be reserved to bishops.

II. *Should all Masses have a penitential act which differs according to the liturgical seasons or to circumstances and in which the entire congregation participates?*

One hundred eight Fathers said yes, 23 no, and 39 yes with qualifications. The principal qualifications were these:

1. The penitential act should be short, well defined, uniform throughout the Church, and the same throughout the year (or at least there should not be too many formulas).

2. There should be more numerous formulas for the penitential act, from which the conferences or even the celebrant may choose.

3. The absolution after the penitential act is not to be a genuine absolution and should not be worded in such a way as to lead the faithful into error on this point.

4. It should be permitted to celebrate the penitential act before either the liturgy of the Word or the liturgy of the Eucharist.

5. The *Confiteor* should be kept. But there were several suggestions as to the form:

a) abbreviated, or said by priest and people together;

b) only the first part;

c) add the words ''and omission'';

d) the *Confiteor* should be the sole formula for the penitential act.

6. There should be a variety of formulas for the concluding prayer.

III. *During the period of experiment should there be three readings at Mass, so that after that period and in the light of pastoral experience, the problem of the number of readings can be settled with a better understanding of what is at issue?*

Seventy-two Fathers said yes, 59 no, and 41 yes with qualifications. The text set down in the volume of *Argomenti* provided that there should be three readings at Mass on Sundays and feast days. In their interventions various Fathers asked that this decision be set aside until after the experiments, since the experience derived from these would suggest the best path to follow. This tendency was also reflected in the *modi*.

1. *Experiments:*

a) These are not necessary;

b) only certain conferences should carry them out, or else they should be carried out in specified private places;

c) the experiments should not be too prolonged, for example, not beyond a two-year period.

2. *The use of two or three readings:*

a) The use of three readings should not be obligatory during the experiments but only later on, if the experiments prove favorable;

b) experiments should be conducted with both two and three readings;

c) three readings should be obligatory only in Masses for adults;

d) three readings should not be obligatory but only highly recommended; they should therefore be in the Missal, but with the option of choosing one of the first two;

e) it should be possible in the missions to have but one reading that is adapted to the occasion, and this even if it means departing from the established sequence;

f) at Mass without a congregation there should be only one reading; at Masses with a congregation, one, two, or three.

IV. *Should it be permitted to replace the antiphons at the introit, offertory, and communion with other songs if the conferences judge this good, and using texts approved by them?*

One hundred twenty-six Fathers said yes, 25 no, and 19 yes with qualifications. Not many observations were offered; the most important were the following:

a) a certain order must be kept in the new texts;

b) the texts must be approved by the conferences to make sure that they are appropriate for their intended purpose;

c) sung parts should be omitted unless sung by the congregation;

d) care must be taken that the traditional texts, so devotional and artistic, are not forgotten.

All these details show how disagreeable many of the Fathers found the path of reform. It is not easy to cut one's ties with age-old practices, open oneself to new horizons, and force oneself to accept the demands expressed in the signs of the times. That which may seem obvious in theory must come to grips in practice with armor-clad contingencies.

In addition, a unique international assembly such as a Synod shows the human variations amid which the Church lives, grows, and acts.

Among the qualifications opposing viewpoints are at times found side by side. For example, one man calls for more numerous moments of silence, but another calls for the elimination of all such moments; one asks greater freedom of action for the conferences, bishops, and individual celebrants, while another—and there were many—asks for rigid, specific, inflexible legislation.

An editor was left with the task of selecting and choosing from the mass of materials thus provided and of proceeding with extreme caution to build the house of prayer. It was the Consilium that had to undertake this task, which demanded responsibility, sensitivity, and prudence, and to do so in accordance with the guidelines provided by the Fathers.

When Cardinal Lercaro asked for the "replies" of the bishops, he said:

I wish to assure you that we will examine with the greatest care each and every one of your observations, since these will be the fruit of long and diligent pastoral experience. In a few weeks' time the Consilium will assemble for its ninth general meeting and will study your suggestions one by one, while keeping in view the entire work of the reform. Have confidence, therefore, in this Consilium that is made up of 47 Fathers, almost all of them pastors of souls in various parts of the world, and 180 experts of whom 18 are parish priests.[18]

The ninth general meeting was held in Rome from November 2 to November 28, 1967, and made the results of the Synod the focus of almost all its labors. The suggestions, the qualifications, the requests—all these were carefully studied and discussed point by point.

The result was a forty-page report, which the Cardinal President sent on to the Pope on December 10, 1967. In it the material was so organized that the Pope would have a bird's-eye view of the voting at the Synod and be able to grasp its importance and value.

With this purpose in mind, the Consilium offered three introductory observations:

1. The liturgical schemas had reached the conferences in time to be studied and voted on at their plenary sessions. The various speakers explicitly said as much. But in at least ten cases in which a conference had voted yes, or yes with qualifications, the delegate from that conference voted no. What was the value of the delegate's vote?

Given the system of voting at the Synod, in which no distinction was made between those voting in the name of a conference and those voting in their own name, it must be concluded that the voting in the hall was not representative; the votes expressed the thinking of the Fathers in the hall, not the thinking of the conferences. The 197 votes represented 197 Fathers, not the 2500 bishops of the Catholic Church.[19]

---

18. This was in reply to those who insisted that in their view the schemas presented were the work of scholars and university professors, not of pastors.

19. A characteristic of the voting on the normative Mass was the abstentions, which were as many as ten. Perhaps they expressed simply the uncertainty of the Fathers, who on the one hand were negatively influenced by certain external considerations and on the other were conscious of the truth neatly expressed in the Synod hall by Bishop Dwyer, who spoke in the name of the English episcopal conference: "It seems to us that we dare not reject what has been so carefully put forward by the Consilium, especially since the meeting of the hierarchy lasts only a few days, while the work of the Consilium has lasted for months and even years." Many, however, seem to have easily overcome their uncertainty and gone on to cast a negative vote in opposition to the views of the conference. In fact, when the time to vote came, Bishop Dwyer himself, after voicing the unanimous acceptance by the English hierarchy of the structure of the normative Mass, did not approve of it, as he himself said in the *Times* (November 1967).

2. The English-speaking segment of the Synod was decisively influenced by the fear that the intention behind the normative Mass was to do away with the read Mass (which is so important in English-speaking regions), to impose singing as a "monolithic part" of the Mass, and to make three readings obligatory.

3. The mainly negative and polemical attitude of the Curia played a major part, as can be seen from corrections introduced at the last moment into the text of interventions and from votes that were contrary to statements made in the original text.

The report itself offered a detailed study of the *modi* and ended with some points that the Consilium wished to bring to the attention of the Holy Father:

1. *Offertory:* Every "action" is to be accompanied by a formula. The text of these is to be offered at the tenth general meeting, which is planned for April 1968.

2. *Orate, fratres:* After considering the reasons pro and con, and with a view to giving prominence especially to the prayer over the gifts, the dialogue before the preface, and the Canon, the Consilium is not averse to doing away with the *Orate, fratres.* If it is thought appropriate to keep it, the formulas would be revised.[20]

3. *Penitential act:* Three formularies will be prepared, in one of which the *Confiteor* will be included.

4. *Readings:* The decision to make three readings obligatory would be an imposition that would be badly received. It is better to make the third optional, that is, to let celebrants choose one of the first two. The end might also be achieved by means of timely instruction and preparation.

5. *Changes in the formulas of consecration:* Some of the synodal Fathers, and the Consilium by a unanimous vote, have asked that the changes

---

20. The consultors (30 of them) were, with one exception, opposed to its retention; among the Fathers, 30 were opposed, 12 were in favor, 3 were in favor with qualifications (in favor of keeping only the first part, as an introduction to the prayer over the gifts), and 1 abstained.

The problem was discussed at length in the Consilium. The following arguments were offered in favor of retention: the formula is in current use and is one of those in which the congregation participates more fully; it is an expression of participation in the offering of the sacrifice; unlike other prayers of the offertory, this one does not anticipate ideas proper to the Eucharistic Prayer. Against retention: lack of uniformity in the way the Church uses the formula (said aloud in read Masses; said in a low voice in sung Masses); lack of congregational participation because of the difficulties in translating the formula in many regions; it detracts from the solemn dialogue of the preface; the difficulty of some ideas expressed in it ("my" sacrifice and "yours," as though these were two distinct and juxtaposed sacrifices); repetition of ideas already expressed during the prayer of the faithful in the intention for the congregation here gathered.

introduced into the formulas of consecration in the new Eucharistic Prayers be also introduced into the Roman Canon so that the formulas of consecration will always be identical in all the anaphoras. From a practical standpoint, the suggestion is impressive and persuasive.

Will it therefore be necessary to set aside the often repeated principle that the Roman Canon "cannot be touched"?

6. *New Eucharistic Prayers:* It is advisable that these be approved and promulgated as soon as possible. Great expectations have been aroused by all that was said at the Synod.

7. *Apostles' Creed:* According to the votes at the Synod and in the Consilium, it would seem appropriate to accept the suggestion that the Holy See grant the conferences that have requested it permission to use the Apostles' Creed in cases of special need.[21]

The Holy Father was asked to express his mind on these points in order that the work might go forward expeditiously.

The points gave rise to a lengthy series of discussions, postponements, and waits.

III. The Normative Mass in the Presence of the Pope

Because of an indisposition, the Pope had not been able to take part in the normative Mass celebrated by the synodal Fathers in the Sistine Chapel. On January 4, 1968, he therefore ordered the secretary of the Con-

---

21. This point had already been studied and given a favorable answer by the Consilium in April 1964, when it set down the criteria for confirmation of decisions of the episcopal conferences. The possibility of also using the Apostles' Creed had been accepted, especially with congregations made up chiefly of illiterate people, people of little education, and children. For theological and ecumenical reasons, the Pope had wanted the Nicene-Constantinopolitan Creed to be kept. But some conferences kept asking.

The question that the Consilium had raised with the Pope on September 18, 1967, was presented to the Synod, which showed itself in favor of the concession. The use of two symbols of faith would be a bond of union with the other Churches, since the Eastern Churches use the Nicene-Constantinopolitan Creed and hold it in great veneration, while the Western communities of the Protestant Reform use the other Creed. The Consilium therefore expressed the opinion that "the Holy See should grant this permission to episcopal conferences that ask it for special pastoral reasons."

The request was renewed once more in a letter of January 16, 1968, which also asked for action on two other matters approved by the Synod and restudied at the ninth general meeting (November 1967) of the Consilium: the new Eucharistic Prayers and Mass chants to replace those given in the Missal for the introit, offertory, and communion, in accordance with no. 35 of the instruction on sacred music. The outcome was that conferences requesting it were allowed the use of the Apostles' Creed, with the proviso that the Nicene-Constantinopolitan Creed be also printed in the Missals. The permission was given in a general way for Masses with children.

silium to organize three celebrations to be conducted in his presence in
the Capella Matilde of the Vatican.[22]

The next day Father Bugnini took a sketch of the program to the Pope.
The three celebrations had been chosen so as to give him the most complete possible overview of the forms of Mass that might be used in an
average parish, that is, one in which the priest had at his disposal a lector, a server, and a small choir. The three forms were: (1) a read Mass
with singing; (2) a completely read Mass; (3) a sung Mass.

Mass with no participation by a congregation was excluded, because
while the Consilium had made a first study of this form at its eighth general meeting (April 1967), the rite was not yet ready.

The Pope was also given a list of the participants. He had ordered that
there be an assembly of about thirty persons who would be representative of various social conditions. He would then complete this list with
such appointees as he judged opportune.[23]

---

22. The Pope gave this order at an audience to the secretary of the Consilium. At this
audience, held from noon to 1:00 P.M., the Pope and the secretary went over the file on
the results of the Synod and of the work done at the general meeting of the Consilium.
The details of the experiment were worked out on the following day, January 5, at another
meeting with the Pope. He first thought of conducting the experiments in his private chapel.
When the time came to discuss this point, he presented it in an affable manner to the secretary of the Consilium, reminding him of the works of art that adorn this chapel, especially
the Way of the Cross that begins with the Last Supper and ends with the resurrection.
But when all aspects were considered, and given the small size of the chapel, he thought
the experiment could not be properly conducted there and decided on the Capella Matilde.

23. The list of participants, prepared in accordance with the Pope's directives and completed and approved by him, was as follows: the Holy Father; Cardinal Amleto Cicognani,
Secretary of State; Archbishop Benelli, Substitute Secretary of State; Archbishop Ettore Cunial, administrative deputy for Rome; Bishop Canisius van Lierde, the Pope's sacristan;
Bishop Carlo Manziana of Crema; Archbishop Ferdinando Antonelli, secretary of the Congregation of Rites; Luigi Rovigatti, Auxiliary Bishop of Civitavecchia; Monsignor Mario Nasalli
Rocca di Corneliano, the Pope's chamberlain; Monsignor Pasquale Macchi; Monsignor Luigi
del Gallo Roccagiovine; Father Rembert Weakland, Abbot Primate of the Benedictines; Father Gabriel Brasó, Abbot General of the Subiaco Benedictines; Father Joseph Lécuyer,
C.S.Sp.; Father Annibale Bugnini, secretary of the Consilium; Father Carlo Braga, assis-
tant for studies of the Consilium; two priests of Rome, one a pastor and one an assistant
pastor; Mr. Rus Matteo, a university man; Mr. Marcello Olivi; Miss Ave Ribacchi, teacher;
Miss Maria Marinuzzi, clerk; Sister Alberta Ortolani, of the Sisters of the Holy Family (of
Bordeaux); Sister Concesi, of the Daughters of Charity.
Performance of the experiments:
Celebrants: C. Braga (first and third days); G. Pasqualetti (second day). Server: Antonio
Galuzzi, Barnabite. Choirmaster: Miguel Alonso, priest, organist of the Spanish Church in
the Via Monserrato. Singers: Vincenzo De Gregorio, Alberto Trombini, Giuseppe Cogotzi,
Daniele Ponzoni, Giovanni Sana, Giuseppe Ciliberti, and André Lietarert, Barnabite students.

1. *Performance of the Celebrations*

For each celebration the secretariat of the Consilium had prepared a booklet containing the songs, rubrics, and texts, including the Eucharistic Prayer. These were distributed on each occasion to each participant, along with paper for notes, a pencil, and a page containing practical guidelines for the celebration. Each participant was asked to write down any observations.

The celebrations took place in the Capella Matilde on the second gallery of the Apostolic Palace, at 5:30 P.M. on January 11, 12, and 13, 1968. At the beginning of each, Father Bugnini described the form of Mass that was to be celebrated.[24]

After the celebration on all three days there was a discussion in the Pope's private library. The participants, in addition to the Holy Father, were men specifically invited: Archbishop Cunial and Bishop Manziana and Fathers Weakland, Bugnini, and Braga. On the second and third days Archbishop Antonelli and Bishop Rovigatti were added.

First celebration: A read Mass with singing (January 11)

Celebrant: C. Braga
Lector: G. Pasqualetti

---

24. Each participant was given a set of the following directives, in cyclostyled form, for all of the celebration:

1. The normative Mass will be celebrated on all three days, but in three variations: first day, a Mass with singing; second day, a read Mass; third day, a sung Mass. The schema to be followed is always the same; the formulas of the Proper are different, as are some formulas of the Ordinary, such as the penitential act and the Canon.

2. Three forms of the penitential act are provided for the normative Mass. In the first it is combined with the *Kyrie*; in the second it includes the *Confiteor*; in the third it comprises an exhortation, versicle, and *Indulgentiam*. All three forms will be used: the first on the first day, the second on the second, and the third on the third.

3. There are three readings; after the first a responsorial psalm is sung; after the second, the Alleluia; the gospel follows.

4. Since each celebration is supposed to be a parish Mass for Sunday, the Creed will always be recited.

5. The prayer of the faithful changes daily, being taken from the Italian version of the Roman Missal for feast days.

6. The whispered prayers of the offertory accompany the several actions and are inspired by the Ambrosian Rite. The formulation of them is in part new.

7. Eucharistic Prayer: on the first day, the Roman Canon in the translation prepared by the Italian Episcopal Conference (not yet approved by the Consilium); on the second and third days, two new Eucharistic Prayers prepared by the Consilium.

8. When the celebrant says, "Give one another a sign of peace," those present exchange this sign.

9. All the participants are strongly urged to take part in the singing and the prayers said in common.

Server: A. Galluzzi

Present: All those invited

Formulary of Mass:

1) The presidential prayers were taken from the First Sunday after Epiphany in the translation in the Italian Missal.

2) The readings were those of the Third Sunday after Epiphany as found in the Consilium's Lectionary, Schema A. These were *not* included in the booklet, so as to get the participants to *listen* and thus make the experiment more alive.

3) The chants were taken from the *Graduale simplex,* but with melodies composed by Maestro Alonso so that the melodies might fit the Italian text. The introit: "The Lord is great," with Psalm 96: "Sing to the Lord a new song." Song between the first two readings: "The Lord is my light and my salvation," with some verses from Psalm 26. Alleluia verse: "The kingdom of God is at hand; be converted and believe in the gospel." Communion song: "We shall proclaim your reign, O Lord."

Of the other parts that might be sung: the *Kyrie* was linked to the penitential act; the *Gloria* and Creed were recited; the *Sanctus* and the Our Father were sung; and the *Agnus Dei* was recited.

The Roman Canon was used, in the translation of the Italian Episcopal Conference.

The celebration lasted thirty-eight minutes.

Second celebration: A Mass entirely read, with participation of a congregation (January 12)

Celebrant: G. Pasqualetti

Lector-server: A. Galluzzi

Present: All those invited and Cardinal A. Cicognani, Secretary of State

Formulary of the Mass:

1) Presidential prayers from the Roman Missal (Second Sunday after Epiphany).

2) Readings from the Third Sunday after Epiphany (Consilium Lectionary, Schema B).

3) Chants (all of them recited) from the *Graduale simplex.* Introit antiphon: "Let all the earth worship you, O God," and verses from Psalm 65, read by the lector. Song between the readings: "The ends of the earth," with verses from Psalm 97. Alleluia verse: "Praise God, all you angels." Communion antiphon: "Sing to the Lord a new song, Alleluia," with verses from Psalm 32.

Since the recitation of these texts did not fill the period for which they were intended, they were supplemented by short organ pieces.

Eucharistic Prayer IV was used, in the Consilium translation. By order of the Pope the celebrant gave the homily (eight minutes). Length of the celebration: thirty-seven minutes.

Third celebration: A sung Mass (January 13)

Celebrant: C. Braga

Lector: G. Pasqualetti

Server: A. Galluzzi

Present: The same as on the second day, minus Sister Concesi, and with the addition of Monsignor Piergiacomo De Nicolò, private secretary of the Cardinal Secretary of State.

Formulary of the Mass:

1) Presidential prayers from the Roman Missal (Third Sunday after Epiphany).

2) Readings from the Third Sunday after Epiphany (in the Consilium Lectionary, Schema C).

3) Chants from the *Graduale simplex.* Introit song: "O God, may we be mindful of your love," and Psalm 47. Song between the readings: "It is good to give thanks," and Psalm 91. Alleluia verse: "Blessed they who choose and draw near; they shall dwell in your halls." Offertory antiphon: "Blessed they who fear the Lord," and verse from Psalms 127 and 128. Communion antiphon: "Taste and see," and Psalm 33. After communion: "Praise God."

These parts of the Ordinary were sung: the *Gloria* (Maestro Alonso), the *Sanctus,* the acclamation after the consecration ("Whenever you eat . . ."), the Our Father, the acclamation "For yours is the kingdom," "The peace of the Lord," and "Lamb of God." The celebrant sang the opening greeting to the congregation ("The love of God the Father . . ."), the presidential prayers, the dialogue before the gospel and the ending "The word of the Lord," the prayer of the faithful, the preface, the doxology of the Canon, the embolism after the Our Father, and the dismissal.

4) Eucharistic Prayer III.

The homily lasted seven and a half minutes.

Since January 13 was the twenty-fifth anniversary of the death of Professor Giorgio Montini, father of Pope Paul VI, the Mass was said for him (the Pope was told of this in advance) and the special formula for a deceased person was included in the Eucharistic Prayer.

Since the appointment of Cardinal Angelo Dell'Acqua as Vicar General for Rome had been announced that same day, at the Pope's request a special intention for the new Vicar was included in the prayer of the faithful.

The celebration lasted fifty-two minutes.

After the celebration the Holy Father addressed a few words to those present, mentioning the sensitive character of the transition through which the liturgy was passing and the privilege that those present had of witnessing a "historical moment" and offering their "critical" judgment. He recalled the two main guidelines set down in the Constitution on the Liturgy: active and conscious participation and the need of a profound Christian life as the expression and result of a more perfect understanding of the liturgy and a more complete participation in it.

He then gave his blessing and allowed all present to kiss his hand.

2. Scrutiny of the Experiment

The round-table discussions that followed in the Pope's private library among the few persons invited were marked by great simplicity and frankness. Each participant was able to express his observations, some pertinent, others less so. These were all included in the points set down in writing and forwarded to the Consilium in the ensuing days.

The meeting lasted about an hour and a half on the first day, an hour on the second, and a half-hour on the third.

The laypersons invited by the Consilium expressed their mind at a meeting held at Santa Marta on the second day after each experiment.

3. Observations of the Pope

The most desired remarks were, of course, those of the Pope. He, too, put them in writing at an audience granted to Father Bugnini on January 22:

1) As far as possible, changes in the current form of Mass should be avoided.

2) Strive for a more organic and normal opening (sign of the cross and penitential act).[25]

3) The offertory seems lacking, because the faithful are not allowed any part in it (even though it should be the part of the Mass in which their activity is more direct and obvious) and because the offertory formulas are reserved to the celebrant and are said silently and in Latin.

The offertory should be given special prominence so that the faithful (or their representatives) may exercise their specific role as offerers.[26]

---

25. The rite used for Mass was the same as the one followed in the Sistine Chapel at the Synod, with some slight variations, especially in the offertory. The Mass began with the sign of the cross made in silence by the celebrant, while the congregation was singing.

26. The offertory rites were organized differently than in the original schema for the

4) The consecration: It seems we should approve the completion of the formula for the consecration of the bread through inclusion of Luke's words: "which is given for you. Do this in memory of me" (Luke 22:19) or those of St. Paul in his first letter to the Corinthians: "which will be given up for you; do this in memory of me" (1 Cor 11:24).

At the end of the formula for the consecration of the chalice, the words "mystery of faith" can be used as a concluding acclamation of the celebrant, to be repeated by the faithful (or to be followed by another acclamation of the faithful).[27]

5) There is need for a set of appropriate formulas for the greeting of peace. The third acclamation of the *Agnus Dei* should therefore not be changed.[28]

6) Authoritative persons are calling for the restoration of the last gospel, that is, the Prologue of John, after the blessing.[29] It could perhaps be assigned for private recitation by the celebrant after the blessing, before, or in place of, the "Trium puerorum," as a prayer of thanksgiving.

7) As already noted, the words of consecration are not to be recited simply as a narrative but with the special, conscious emphasis given them by a celebrant who knows he is speaking and acting "in the person of Christ."

4. *Observations of the Churchmen*

In general, their remarks focused on common objectives.

Penitential act. One man noted: "The introductory, or 'penitential,' part seems bare. People today, however, need to realize that if they are to

---

normative Mass. Their sequence was the one regularly followed in the celebration of Mass at that time: placing of the bread on the altar with a formula said in a low voice by the celebrant; mixing of water with the wine, with its formula; presentation of the wine, with its formula; the prayer "In a spirit of humility"; washing of the hands, immediately followed by the prayer over the gifts.

The texts differed from those found in the first schema for the normative Mass and were the product of a study undertaken by Professor Jounel at the bidding of the secretariat of the Consilium:

—Presentation of the bread: "Holy Father, accept this bread which we offer from the fruit of our labors, that it may become the body of your Only-begotten Son."

—Mingling of water with the wine: "Lord, by the mystery of this water and wine may we come to share the divinity of him who deigned to share our humanity, Jesus Christ, your Son and our Lord."

—Presentation of the chalice: "Lord, we offer you this cup that expresses the mystery of the unity of your people, so that it may become the blood of our Lord, Jesus Christ."

—Washing of the hands: "Create a clean heart in me, God, and renew in me an upright spirit."

27. The words "Mystery of faith" were simply omitted.

28. At all three Masses the *Agnus Dei* ended with "Have mercy on us." There was no prayer for peace.

29. The remark about the "last gospel" was made out of respect for some persons in positions of authority close to the Pope who still called for its retention.

approach God, they must free themselves from evil, which they feel to be an affliction, even if they do not always attribute it to sin." Others, however, found this part too lengthy: "I would like to see it short and simple," said one observer. All were of the opinion that the *Confiteor* should be said only once, by celebrant and congregation together (in the schema used for the experimental Mass the *Confiteor* was repeated, as in the old Missal).

Liturgy of the Word. All found it to be well organized. "There is no difficulty in assigning it a longer time than the time for the sacrificial action of the Mass. The importance of a rite is not in proportion to its duration but depends on the nature of the action itself." Three readings were felt to be generally suitable, "provided," said one observer, "that they are fairly equal in length." Another remarked: "Avoid selecting passages so short that the pedagogical and pastoral function of the readings will be forgotten." A third said: "In order not to isolate the readings and break them up too much, it would be helpful if the text of the intervening songs expressed and summed up what has been heard in the readings."

Offertory. First remark: "I do not see why the offertory is still in Latin and said in a low voice. An offertory that is more understandable (in language and gesture) would be more effective." Another made the point that "the rite should have an air of greater simplicity. It should be reduced to a simple offering of the bread and wine."

Several thought the *Lavabo* to be superfluous: "It should be kept only in Masses in which the celebrant must really dirty his hands, for example, by using incense. Eliminate it from other Masses."

Canon. One man said: "The new Canons are truly pleasing; no less pleasing is the idea of a participation of the congregation by means of acclamations in the course of the Canon itself. Another remarked:

> On the whole the anaphoras are good. One reason among others is that they are a good subject for pastoral instruction.
>
> I like the introduction of an acclamation of the congregation immediately after the consecration.
>
> Also good is the new formulation of the embolism, followed by a response of the entire congregation.
>
> I understand the desire to keep the traditional Roman Canon with its two long lists of saints. It must be anticipated, however, that it will be abandoned in practice, especially outside of Rome.

A parish priest remarked: "There are four 'Amens' too many; they interrupt the single prayer that is the Canon. This should be restored to its original unity and should end with the one 'Amen' of the 'Per ipsum.'

If it is judged necessary to keep these 'Amens,' why not at least have the faithful say them?"

Greeting of peace. This part of the Mass is one of the least "transparent." One observer said: "I anticipate a slight difficulty in regard to the 'fraction' and the 'peace'—two actions or gestures that deserve more careful study. I do not think it necessary to give much emphasis to the fraction; this is a symbol that has no great value for people of our day, whereas the latter do set great store, even humanly speaking, by the gesture of peace. It is time to give this a greater prominence."

Communion. "Why say the words 'Lord, I am not worthy' three times," said one observer. "Once would be more forceful and avoid the impression of a refrain."

The washing of the chalice at the altar was also criticized; as a knowledgeable liturgist observed, "This action is not performed in any other of the Liturgies."

Other criticisms had to do with the music and the texts for the three experimental celebrations. The music was generally felt to be inferior, and the texts "not worthy of their function." The two observations were quite justified; the only excuse was the quasi-improvised character of the music and texts due to the lack of time available for preparation of the experiments.

Finally, some observers said they were concerned about the excessive flexibility of the rubrics.

On the whole, however, the clergy were satisfied with the normative Mass. "I am very satisfied," one wrote; and another: "The normative is clearly in the line of the reform intended by Vatican II. The revision must be continued to completion." A third concluded: "My general impression is that the revision marks a notable improvement of the rite and the formulas by comparison with the traditional texts. The new ones seem better adapted to helping the faithful understand the mystery of the Mass; they seem to contain nothing that can cause dismay. I even have the impression that the concern for preservation has sometimes undermined the desire to renew."

5. *Observations of the Laity*

The four laypersons and the two sisters drew up a joint report that I shall reproduce here in its entirety, because it shows how much good sense and how constructive a critical mind the faithful can bring to bear when their interest is roused, and this even in quite specifically religious matters.

1) The general structure of the Mass is agreeable. One of our group spoke of the need of greater freedom in organizing the rites and selecting the texts in order to make the Mass more understandable, especially to certain groups of individuals.

2) But the need is felt for a greater trenchancy and animation that will stimulate interiority. It would be good to put some text, or say something, at the beginning and the end that expresses the purpose of the gathering: to celebrate the Lord's Supper, etc.

3) One member found the introductory part of the Mass a bit protracted. We were pleased with the penitential act. Some observations:

a) the first form (with the *Kyrie*) seemed too long and insufficiently expressive;

b) the repetition of the *Confiteor* in the second form was too much.

4) The principle of three readings is gratifying, but the need is felt for selecting readings that are accessible to all classes of people.

5) We do not see the reason for the "Lavabo" at the offertory. The symbolical meaning—purification—has already been satisfactorily expressed by the penitential act.

6) We liked the new anaphoras (though one person found the fourth somewhat long), as well as the acclamation of the congregation. But we thought that the acclamation, at least in the text used, did not lend itself to singing.

7) All of us thought there was an excessive fidelity to the Latin of the Roman Canon and to every detail of its content.

8) The rite of the commingling was not understood; it could even suggest the erroneous idea of consecration by contact.

The part after communion caused some perplexity. It does not seem to be well organized.

9) Some texts are not intelligible or say nothing to the contemporary mind. There seems to be too rigid a limitation to the psalms for the processional parts. Then, too, there are obscure expressions or expressions that can make a negative impression: "Holy God," "thrones and dominations," "Lamb" (a term that occurs at least five times).

The celebrations in the Capella Matilde were one of the many brilliant initiatives marking the pontificate of Pope Paul VI. This Pope wanted to see in person how things were going with the reform, but at the same time he wanted to secure the interest and consensus of the Roman world—the pontifical household and the Curia—no less than of others.

The celebrations showed that not everything was perfect, but they convinced all that the reformed rite was substantially valid. It was not an accident that in his closing remarks the Pope spoke of a "historical moment."

The next need was to win the consent of the Curia. At that same audience of January 22, the Pope decided therefore that once the schema had been revised in accordance with the observations submitted after the experiments in the Capella Matilde, it should be sent to the heads of the agencies. These had already voiced their opinions at the Synod and had generally been opposed to the schema. "Therefore," said the Pope, "the schema, with the corrections required by the Synod, must be sent to them, and they must be asked anew for their views. We must win them over and make allies of them."[30] First, however, the texts had to be revised.

6. "The Pope's Wishes"

Everything now suggested that the work would soon be completed. At that same audience of January 22, the Pope, with the secretary of the Consilium, had studied a formal statement sent to him on January 15 setting out a program for the introduction of the new rite of Mass;[31] this introduction was planned for December 1, 1968.

That same day, January 22, Father Bugnini wrote to the relator of study group 10, which was meeting at Orselina, and communicated the Pope's views, asking him to introduce the requested changes. What the Pope wanted was, in substance, six things:

1. *Beginning of the Mass.* The Pope wanted every Mass to begin with the sign of the cross said aloud by the celebrant, with the reply of the congregation.

2. *Penitential act.* The threefold schema proposed seem overly complicated. The Pope would prefer a single schema using the *Confiteor* if possible.

3. *Offertory.* There should be a single set of formulas that will express the idea of an offering of human toil in union with the sacrifice of Christ. There should also be active participation of the congregation, at least when there is no singing. In the latter case, the priest recites the formulas in a low voice.

---

30. To the objection that the rest of the Church was solidly convinced of the rightness of the reform, the Pope replied: "That is not enough; the Curia must also be convinced; otherwise—you know the Roman saying—one Pope approves and another disapproves, and I don't want anyone coming along after me and restoring everything to the present *status quo.* You saw, didn't you, what happened when St. Joseph's name was introduced into the Canon? First, everyone was against it. Then one fine morning Pope John decided to insert it and made this known; then everyone applauded, even those who had said they were opposed to it." "And if the response is still negative?" "Don't worry," the Pope said in conclusion, "I have the final say."

31. The program determined the stages for bringing the work to an end in the various areas; a period of experimentation from May to September; the convocation of the directors of the national centers and liturgical commissions with a view to preparing the faithful; and the introduction of the new Order of Mass on the First Sunday of Advent, 1968.

4. *Words of consecration.* In all the Eucharistic Prayers there should be a rubric before the consecration reminding the priest that the words of consecration are not to be uttered "in the manner of a narrative" but "clearly and distinctly as required by their nature."[32]

5. The words "mysterium fidei" are to be spoken by the priest before the acclamation of the congregation.

6. The rites for the greeting of peace must be better organized.

But the experts immediately expressed some difficulty about accepting these suggestions. As a result, a tenth general meeting of the Consilium was held (April 23–30, 1968), at which the problem was placed on the agenda for the sessions of both the relators and the bishops.[33] The whole matter caused some dismay, since the Pope seemed to be limiting the Consilium's freedom of research by using his authority to impose solutions. Least convinced of all were the experts who saw not a few difficulties in reducing the Pope's wishes to practice.

A special committee of Fathers and consultors was elected; it was made up of Cardinal Silva Henríquez, Bishops Hurley, Boudon, Spülbeck, and Guano, Abbot Weakland, and experts Agustoni, Gélineau, Jounel, Schnitzler, Vagaggini, and Wagner.[34]

Of the six points raised by the Pope, four were chosen for discussion that seemed to call for more extensive consideration: the beginning of the Mass, the penitential act, the offertory, and the words "mystery of faith."

But first the committee wanted to secure the consent of the plenary gathering: Were all in agreement that the Pope should be told of the difficulties caused by the introduction of what he wanted? The vote showed little disagreement, with 26 of 28 saying that he should be told.

What were the difficulties raised by the study group against the adoption of what the Pope wanted? Let us examine them:

---

32. The Pope's wishes as expressed on the sheet dated January 22 had given the impression that he wanted to add "Do this in memory of me" after both consecrations. In a circular letter of February 26, the secretary of the Consilium explained that it was enough to say these words only once, after the consecration of the wine.

33. The study group had meanwhile composed a new schema for the "Order of Mass with a Congregation" (*Schemata*, no. 281, *De Missali* no. 47; March 21, 1968) in which (almost all) the desired corrections had already been introduced, but in order that they might be discussed at the next general meeting.

34. This event did not pass off with complete tranquillity. It was clear that some maneuvering was going on that was not entirely ineffective. It seems, for example, that the special committee appointed by the Consilium was the result of a "secret" agreement reached at a limited gathering of German and French *periti* at the French College on April 23. One Father publicly protested, seeing in this an attack on the freedom and independence of the Consilium.

1. *Beginning the Mass with the sign of the cross*

a) This would be an innovation contrary to the entire liturgical tradition. Today only in read Masses does the celebrant bless himself as he begins the prayers at the foot of the altar. In sung Masses only the servers join him; the congregation pays no attention, since they are singing the introit or *Kyrie*. The Pope is asking, therefore, that a practice followed in read Masses and originating in the personal devotion of the priest be transferred to every type of Mass, including the most solemn.

b) If a Trinitarian formula is used in greeting the people, there would be two Trinitarian formulas in a row; there would be a doublet, contrary to the provision of the liturgical Constitution.

c) The Eastern Churches do not have it, except for the Byzantine, where the priest does sign himself, but in silence.[35]

2. *Penitential act.* Pastoral considerations urge the use of different formulas so as to lend a bit of variety to the prayer.[36]

3. *Offertory.* Let there be a new redaction of the formulas.[37] But the experts asked again that the priest be free not to say the prayers aloud, even when there is no singing. The reason: to give the faithful an opportunity to recollect themselves in some moments of silent prayer after the liturgy of the Word. The experts also pointed out that the acclamation of the people did not fit in with the structure of the offertory and that it duplicated their participation through their "Amen" at the prayer over the gifts.[38]

4. *Mystery of faith.* If the words were said by the celebrant before the acclamation of the congregation, (a) this would be an innovation not found

---

35. A more probative argument, which someone pointed out during the discussion but which was not included in the report, was the difficulty that arises when the Mass begins with singing, as ought to be the case in every Mass with a congregation. If the entire assembly sings, it seems discordant to end the song and begin the Mass with the sign of the cross, as though it had not already been begun with the congregational song. But since there was as yet no experience to go by, the argument perhaps did not seem persuasive.

36. The Pope would subsequently accept this suggestion.

37. The new redaction yielded substantially the formulas later approved and put into use. In the schema, which was then submitted for study to the prefects of the curial agencies and to the Holy Father, the phrase "which we offer to you" ("quem/quod tibi offerimus") was lacking. The Pope was the one who added it. This formula, which was the same for the bread and the wine, was judged appropriate by the committee, because it expresses God's generosity, human collaboration through work, and the destining of the gifts for the Eucharist, while not promoting an erroneous understanding of the meaning of the offertory. This meaning is clearly different from the meaning of the sacrifice of Christ's body and blood.

38. In his letter of February 26, the secretary had suggested the adoption for this purpose of the acclamation in the *Didache:* "Blessed be the Lord for ever." — The *Orate, fratres* was not included in this schema either.

in the liturgical tradition; (b) it would alter the structure of the Canon at an important moment; (c) it would change the meaning of the words in question, since they are no longer connected with the consecration of the chalice.

If the words are to be kept, the report said, they should be connected either with the formula of consecration of the wine or with the acclamation.

The vote taken by the Fathers in the plenary assembly supported the thinking of the special committee. Therefore, the report, worded by the relator of group 10, was sent to the Holy Father on May 10, 1968.[39] He read it, studied it carefully, and then gave his definitive answer on September 15, along with his remarks on the replies sent by the Cardinal Prefects of the curial agencies.[40]

IV. Critique by the Prefects of the Curial Agencies

The Consilium's report was studied by the Pope and then discussed with the secretary of the Consilium at an audience on May 18, 1968. The Holy Father had made his own remarks, noting in the margin the points that he found obscure.

The time had come to ask the views of the prefects of the curial agencies. The schema for the new Order of Mass was sent to them on June 2; it was the same as the one submitted to the Pope, containing the rite of Mass with a congregation and the rite of Mass without one. In addition to the prefects, the presidents of the secretariats received the schema. Of the fourteen cardinals involved, two did not reply, seven sent observations, and five said simply that they had no remarks to make or were "very pleased" with the schema.

The Consilium combined the observations and sent them to the Pope on July 24, along with a statement of its own in which it said:

> 1) All the cardinals expressed their appreciation, sometimes in highly complimentary terms, for the gesture of collaboration in which the Curia was asked to express its views on such a sensitive and important matter.

---

39. The booklet also included a section containing the observations of the secretariat on each point, as well as a report on the meeting (which also covered the other subjects discussed).

40. For practical purposes the Pope would remain firm on his views, except for the penitential act. This shows that before adopting these positions, he had reflected on them at length. It must be acknowledged after the fact that from the pastoral standpoint, the Pope's positions were very positive; he had a correct grasp of the real situation.

2) The opinion requested was primarily personal, but more than one of the cardinals thought it appropriate to ask the entire Congregation for its views.

3) None of the replies is negative, nor do the remarks have to do with the overall structure of the rite or of any of its essential parts. Some of the remarks reflect, moreover, the fact that the respondent had before him only the schema for the Order of Mass, in which the rubrics are necessarily given in summary form. A more extensive and detailed description of the rite will be given in the General Instruction to be placed at the beginning of the Missal.

4) The desire is expressed by many that the rubrics be explicit and unconditional, leaving no freedom for the celebrant or for a timely selection that takes into account the various concrete situations. This desire will, it seems, be largely satisfied by the further prescriptions that will be included in the description of the rite in the General Instruction. On the other hand, it seems that a certain degree of flexibility in nonessential parts should not be excluded.

The Pope had this file examined by two *periti* of his choice: Bishop Carlo Colombo, a theologian, and Bishop Carlo Manziana of Crema. Bishop Colombo submitted his views on August 15, 1968.

1) It is difficult to appraise the pastoral and spiritual import of the revised Order of Mass: a liturgical text reveals its true value only after lengthy experience of it. A great deal will depend, moreover, on how the new Order is implemented.

No one should be surprised, then, if there is a period of difficulty and groping before the new, pastorally satisfactory form is achieved. Older people will have more difficulty in coming to grips with a new liturgy that is not always adapted to their sensibilities. We will have to see, therefore, whether the young, who can adapt more easily, will find in it the spiritual food that their elders found in the old Order.

2) Meanwhile, some remarks made the cardinals deserve attention:

a) The observation . . . that *the formulas are unduly impoverished:* it is in fact the case that a certain time is required for the mind to acquire the proper religious mood, and some formulas that prolong the time of prayer can help to this end (for example, the prayers of the priest before communion);

b) the remark repeated by several that formal changes have been made in the present text for which they see no compelling need: it would seem better, in fact, not to change a few words in a formula or rite unless such a change is needed in order to give expression to some real new value;

c) they do not understand why the names of Our Lady, St. Michael, St. John Baptist, and the Holy Apostles Peter and Paul are omitted from the first part of the *Confiteor* at the beginning of Mass. These names are in fact a magnificent witness to the communion of the Church on earth with the Church in heaven (something very timely today). In addition, they express our belief that our sins not only offend God but lessen (or squander) the supernatural patrimony left to the Church by past Christian generations (the social dimension of sin, recalled by the constitution *Lumen gentium*, no. 11);

d) for the same reason the request seems reasonable that the names of Our Lady and Sts. Peter and Paul (and perhaps St. Andrew, and St. Ambrose for the Ambrosian churches) not be dropped from the embolism after the Our Father.

e) I myself do not understand why there should be a single *Confiteor* said jointly by celebrant and congregation. In the present form of Mass (the old Order), the *Confiteor* is evidently a personal, nonsacramental penitential act, and this precisely because it is reciprocal. In the new form it can much more readily be assimilated to the act of contrition *by which one disposes oneself for sacramental absolution* (especially if we take into account that the formula of absolution has varied in the course of time and has at times taken a deprecatory form). The fear [expressed by . . .] is not entirely without a basis.

Bishop Manziana's analysis (submitted August 31) was even more detailed and showed him to have a fine knowledge of the subject.

It seems to me important that a good number gave a favorable reception to the text set before them.

In general, their objections focus on changes in formulas without a proportionate justification, on the greater number of occasions for intervention by the congregation, and, finally, on what they see as excessive freedom of choice. My answer would be that long centuries of liturgical immobility have given us an exaggerated conception of changelessness and singleness of formulas as desirable; this is a view that was certainly foreign to the early liturgy. In any case, if the territorial conferences were afraid that formulas *ad libitum* would beget confusion, they could determine the selection.

I have the impression that during these years of experimentation with the new liturgy, the people have gotten used to changes and to variety in formulas. It is necessary, of course, to avoid abuses and especially that individual priests not act arbitrarily (Cardinal Bevilacqua is afraid that even bishops may act arbitrarily!).

Masses with a congregation and private Masses

This distinction, which some find unacceptable or do not correctly understand, seems to me timely both for pastoral reasons and because it encourages priests to celebrate with suitable formulas when no congregation is present.

Beginning of the celebration

This is one of the most debated parts of the new Order and, I may add, most debatable. Nevertheless, when I recall the first drafts, this one seems to me to be a better text. The difference, at the introit, offertory, and communion, between Masses with singing and Masses without singing seems justified to me on the grounds of greater "authenticity."

As for the sequence: sign of the cross, kissing of the altar, and greeting of the people—this gives me a sense of surfeit.[41]

The remarks on the *penitential act* cancel each other out: some find it too short, others fear that, given certain trends toward communal or general absolution, it may be confused with the sacrament of penance . . . . All things considered, I think the formulas read well, including those provided for *ad libitum* use in the appendix.

With regard to the *Kyrie eleison:* Cardinal Seper would like it recited always and at every kind of Mass. There is no denying that the variation in the number of the invocations causes some difficulty; on the other hand, saying it or not saying it according to circumstances has no drawbacks.

Liturgy of the Word

Another complaint (Šeper): Why not answer all readings with "Thanks be to God"? But then it would be necessary to end every reading with "This is the word of God" or "This is the word of the Lord," lest confusion be created when "Thanks be to God" is said in direct response to words . . . of condemnation in a reading! Cardinal Bea is of the opinion that the formula "Through the words of the gospel may our sins be wiped away" should not be dropped.

Many of the cardinals wanted details on the unspecified acclamations after the gospel. A selection of formulas might be offered.

Offertory

This part of the Mass is especially criticized both because of the change of formulas and because of the formulas proposed . . . . In my view, they are successful and remove the equivocal impression that the offertory rite is a "little Canon"; they are further explained by the prayer over the gifts. The collaboration of human work with creation is a *disposition for sacrifice.* If the newer prayers over the gifts are insufficiently expressive, they can be revised.

With regard to the formula for mixing water with the wine: . . . it is to be noted that the present formula is a Christmas oration which in its full form is not suitable for the action. The preparation of the altar for the sacri-

---

41. The Pope had been giving special attention to the organization of this part of the Mass; in the margin at this point he lightly penciled in a question mark.

fice, *after* and not during the prayers of the faithful, allows room for singing and for an offertory procession, if there is to be one.

Consecration

Some regard "The mystery of faith!" as too isolated an acclamation, and they fear that the acclamations of the congregation may cause difficulty for lack of participation . . . . All things considered, I think the present solution should be kept.

From the embolism to the communion

With regard to the embolism after the Our Father: Some want the phrase "from all evils, past, present, and future" to be kept, while they regard the reference to the parousia as a useless duplication. Nor do they appreciate the acclamation of the congregation. I think that we should rather bear in mind the ecumenical value of this acclamation (Bea). Furthermore, the reference to the parousia rescues the embolism from a kind of "horizontalism."

Regarding the greeting of peace: I agree with Cardinal Bea that the prayer "Lord Jesus Christ, who said . . . " should not be omitted in Masses with a congregation.

I point out, too, that while the phrase "Offer each other a sign of peace" (to be said as circumstances permit) may not be classical Latin, it is used in the Ambrosian Rite.

It will be necessary to define more clearly the manner of exchanging peace among the faithful . . . but I would not play down the gesture in view of its profound evangelical meaning.

I have some reservations about the formulas "May this holy commingling . . . ," which does not seem to me very felicitous.

The cardinals have reservations about replacing "my soul" with "me" in the formula for the priest's communion . . . but I note that the changed formula is an ancient one to be found in the Roman Pontifical for the communion of a newly ordained priest.

Some are displeased by the substitution of a "prayer over the people" for the final blessing. . . . I admit that I would be puzzled if I did not remember how in early times the congregation was dismissed during the penitential season (Lent).

Liturgy of the Word and Eucharistic liturgy

The repeated concern over the disproportion between the liturgy of the Word and the liturgy of the Eucharist (with the latter being shorter) does not seem to me to be justified. Given the close connection between the two that is called for in the liturgical Constitution and the instructions, and given the fact that the texts are easily understood, the liturgy of the Word prepares the way for, and illumines, the "mystery of faith," while the sacred silence or singing after communion makes the encounter of the faithful with the sacramental Christ an especially devout and recollected one.[42]

V. THE FINAL STAGE

1. *New Study by the Pope*

The Pope took a more personal approach. He had repeatedly read the Order of Mass, annotating it at every point and filling the pages of the schema with red and blue signs. Thirty-four of the 104 numbers were glossed. Then, on September 22 he penned this note: "I ask you to take account of these observations, exercising a free and carefully weighed judgment."

These observations were once again brought to the Fathers of the Consilium for discussion at their eleventh general meeting (October 8–17, 1968). This time they studied them at sessions at which they alone were present, and then they gave the Holy Father their replies to each point, while adding further wishes of their own.

Sign of the cross. In view of the difficulties raised by the experts, the secretariat of the Consilium had looked for a middle way: Make the sign of the cross aloud when there is no opening song. But the Pope was in-

---

42. In their response to the replies of the Cardinal Prefects, Bishops Colombo and Manziana obviously took into account only such remarks as were worthy of attention. In the midst of the good grain there was also chaff; this only showed how long the road of reform is, and especially of a religious reform.

For example, one critic said of the greeting of peace: "If this rubric is preceptive and not optional, I do not see how it is to be carried out. In the case of a closed and educated community (a seminary or convent), there is no problem. But if several hundred or even several thousand people are attending a Mass and not arranged in some orderly manner, how is the rubric to be obeyed? Such a rubric supposes a congregation of well-educated, serious people. Among the 'masses' of the faithful it can easily become ridiculous." Subsequent experience showed that these fears were groundless. The greeting of peace, which takes only a few moments, is one of the pearls of the new rite of Mass and is greatly appreciated by all (see *Not* 10 [1974] 397).

Some other objections. "The distinction between a Mass with a congregation and a private Mass seems neither necessary nor timely. The formulary for Mass with a congregation can be used in only a very few parishes, because most parishes do not have an adequate personnel." "The celebrant tells the people to exchange a sign of peace; this is a formalized gesture that smacks of the stereotyped." Will not the revival of the procession with the gifts at the offertory ensure "a procession of little old ladies? Or that the gifts will be extravagant and eccentric?" "I do not understand what the 'acclamations' after the gospel are or might possibly be. A text must be supplied if we are not to see and hear all sorts of things."

Nor were rubrical anxieties lacking. "On which side of the altar is the chalice to be placed?" "How are the chalice and paten to be arranged?" "Which is to be held in the right hand, and which in the left?"

sistent: "It is appropriate that the formula 'In the name of the Father . . .' be said aloud by the priest and that the congregation respond."

The vote of the Consilium was still indecisive (17 in favor, 13 against, 1 yes with a qualification: only at read Masses). But the secretariat presented the Pope with a revised version of the rubric that expressed the thinking of the Pope himself, that is, that Mass is always to begin with a sign of the cross made by all, with the priest speaking the words and the congregation answering.

Kyrie, eleison. The Pope had made three notations. The rubric said that the *Kyrie* is to be said "unless it has already been used." The reference was to the third form of the penitential act, in which the *Kyrie* follows some short invocations. The Pope asked: "Is it not better to omit it?" Once the point was explained, the Pope did not insist.

The second question of the Pope was: "Why not nine invocations as in the past?" The response was that the General Instruction of the Missal would explain things more clearly: A simple form would be allowed, consisting of *Kyrie, Christe,* and *Kyrie* as a dialogue between celebrant and congregation but there could also be a fuller form with three repetitions of each invocation, especially when the existing musical forms are used.

The Pope's third notation: "Why omit it 'when the *Gloria* is said'? The *Kyrie* is part of the penitential introduction to the Mass, whereas the *Gloria* is a hymn with an entirely different spiritual tone. It does not replace the penitential litanic invocation but bursts out after it, as though inspired by renewed confidence in the possibility of conversing with and praising God."

On this point the secretariat continued to call for permission to omit the *Kyrie* when the *Gloria* is said, in order not to slow down the beginning of Mass with too much singing and because the *Kyrie* can be, and in fact is, used in the prayer of the faithful. The Pope's wish was followed, however.

Liturgy of the Word. The Pope remarked:

> It is a good idea to end the Scripture readings with the words "The word of God" (or: "The word of the Lord").
>
> It also seems right to keep the acclamation of the people, which echoes the words of Scripture: "Thanks be to God" after the first and second readings, and "Praise to you, O Christ" after the gospel. The same for the priest's formula: "By the words of the gospel may our sins be wiped away."
>
> The acclamation [after the gospel]: Specify which ("Praise to you, O Christ" or some other).

All these directives were accepted.

Offertory. The Pope noted that the formulas used in offering the bread and the wine

> are two fine euchological utterances, but they do not express any intention of offering if the phrase "which we offer to you" is removed from the two formulas; without it they are not offertory formulas. The phrase seems to be what gives the gesture and words their specific meaning as offering. However, I leave the decision as to their retention or removal to the collegial judgment of the Consilium.

After lengthy discussion the collegial judgment of the Consilium took this form: 12 for retention of the phrase, 14 against, and 5 in favor of finding an expression that would refer to the presentation of the elements for the sacrifice, but without using the term "offer." This was the word that caused difficulty, since it seemed to anticipate, or at least detract from the value of, the one true sacrifice of the immolated Christ that is expressed in the Canon.

The phrase suggested was kept, since it could ease the difficulties earlier pointed out in the translations. The Italian version, for example, has: "which we present to you." Almost all the languages followed the same line.

With regard to the offertory, the Pope also asked: "Is it necessary to shorten and thus mutilate the prayer, 'O God, who wonderfully ennobled . . .'?" The reply to this was the one given in the observations of Bishop Manziana, and the text remained as it was.

Orate, fratres. The Pope asked: "Should the *Orate, fratres* be removed? Is it not a beautiful, ancient, and appropriate dialogue between celebrant and congregation before beginning the prayer over the gifts and the sacrificial liturgy? Its removal would be the loss of a pearl."

Here again the reasons were given, and they were such that the Consilium once again asked itself whether the *Orate, fratres* should be kept. The result: 15 against retention, 14 for, 1 in favor provided some phrases were altered, 1 abstention. The prayer was therefore kept.

Eucharistic Prayer. The Pope said:

> I agree with the scriptural addition "which will be given up for you."
> I agree with transferring the words "Mystery of faith" to the end, after the consecration of the chalice ("Do this in remembrance of me").
> "Through him and with him and in him": Would it not be better to read: "Through Christ and with Christ and in Christ"? The result in the vernaculars would be clearer and more dignified.

It was decided to leave the traditional wording in the Latin text and allow freedom in translating the phrase into the vernaculars.

Communion rite. The Pope asked: "Why omit the 'Let us pray' before the Our Father?" The implied suggestion was not accepted, because "Let us pray" is an invitation to prayer, but such an invitation is already contained in the exhortation that precedes the Our Father.

The Pope: "It should be asked whether the embolism ought not to be left as it now is." This suggestion, too, was not accepted, because it did not seem appropriate to repeat intercessions made a few moments ago in the Eucharistic Prayer.

The Pope: "At this point [= after the embolism] the prayer to Christ, 'Lord Jesus Christ,' which is a prayer for the peace and unity of the Church (and the world) should be kept." The directive was clear and specific and was readily accepted.

After the celebrant's greeting of peace, at the exhortation "Let us show one another a sign of peace," the rubric said this was to be done "as circumstances allow" (*pro opportunitate*). The Pope noted: "Remove the 'as circumstances allow.' "

This was a call to further reflection. The words were retained because there are cases in which it is not suitable to have the sign of peace. In such circumstances the exhortation "Let us show one another a sign of peace" would be formalistic and unauthentic.

The Pope asked that "the words 'most holy' be removed" from the formula for the commingling of the body and blood of Christ. They were removed.

At the "Lord, I am not worthy," the Pope asked: "Should they be said three times? once?" It was decided that they should be said only once.

At his own communion the priest says: "May the body of Christ preserve me . . . ." The Pope asked: "Would it not be better to retain the old formula, 'May the body of Christ preserve my soul . . . '?" In response, it was said that the suggested formula, which is already used in the Mass of ordination, seems more complete and accurate—not the soul alone but the entire human person is destined for eternal life. The new formula was kept.

Final blessing. The Pope observed: "It does not seem appropriate to omit the blessing and replace it with a prayer over the people; if the latter is to be said, it should follow a 'Let us pray' and precede the blessing."

In answer, it was pointed out that in the liturgical tradition the prayer over the people is in fact a true formula of blessing and dismissal. It seemed appropriate to revive it in the reform, just as it seemed pastorally advantageous to revive, at least in some circumstances, other formulas of solemn blessing known as the "Gallican blessings."

However, since this conception would not be readily grasped in many circles, given the now universal use of the blessing with the Trinitarian formula, it was proposed that the latter be kept even when the rite provides for another formula of blessing as well. This was done.

The Pope: "Even if another liturgical action follows, the blessing should not be omitted." But the omission of the blessing in that situation seemed quite natural and was in fact already in practice. The Consilium therefore insisted that the new rubric remain.

Mass without a congregation. On this rite the Pope had a few remarks, which generally were the same as those he had made on Mass with a congregation. In particular, he found it extreme that the prayer of the faithful should always be said and that at the beginning of Mass the celebrant should greet the server.[43]

2. Changes in the Roman Canon

The file sent to the Pope on October 24, 1968, after the eleventh general meeting of the Consilium, contained not only the responses to the papal wishes that I have just outlined but also a letter to the Pope with the wishes expressed at that meeting regarding the implementation of the reform, and a statement on the Lord's words in the formula of consecration. Both the letter and the statement were introduced and annotated by the secretariat of the Congregation.

The request that concerns us here[44] is the one having to do with the Roman Canon. The second *votum* expressed the desire that the Roman Canon might be made attractive to celebrants even after experience of the new Eucharistic Prayers. With this end in view, it was asked that they be allowed to omit the repeated "Through Christ . . . " at the end of the various prayers, shorten the list of saints in the *Communicantes*, and omit entirely the list in the *Nobis quoque.*

The secretariat of the Congregation supported this request and suggested that in the first list the saints from Andrew to Cosmas and Damian be put in brackets, and in the second list those from Ignatius to Anastasia. A rubric would indicate that the names in parentheses might be omitted.[45] The secretariat made the same suggestion for the "Per Christum" conclusions of the prayers, except in the final prayer, where

---

43. The Pope would make this point again on the page proofs of the Order of Mass.
44. On the requests contained in the *vota* see above, Chapter 12, p. 181.
45. The Pope insisted that St. Andrew, brother of St. Peter, be likewise always named; he would also have liked to see the name of St. Ignatius kept, but he subsequently agreed that it could be put in parentheses.

this ending forms a bridge to the conclusion of the Canon as a whole. If this suggestion were adopted, the text of the venerable Roman Canon would remain unaltered, and yet it would be made easier to use in Masses with a congregation.

With regard to the Lord's words at the consecration, the note of the secretariat had this to say:

> As we look forward to the publication of the revised Order of Mass, which will necessarily contain all four Eucharistic Prayers, it seems advisable to accede to the request from many quarters that the Lord's words in the two formulas of consecration be made the same in all the Canons and in every celebration. This uniformity will help the celebrant, especially in concelebration, where it will ensure an unhesitating and dignified enunciation of these formulas that are at the heart of the Mass.

In order to achieve this uniformity it is necessary:

a) to add the words "which will be given up for you" to the formula for the consecration of the bread in the Roman Canon;

b) and to remove the words "The mystery of faith" from the formula for the consecration of the wine.

These changes were made without opposition. There were two other variants that the Holy Father was asked to approve:

c) the insertion of the words "all of you . . . of it" ("ex hoc/eo omnes") into the formula of consecration in the three new Eucharistic Prayers.

These words have no precise counterpart in the biblical text. Matthew alone has "[Drink] of it, all of you" (26:27) for the wine; Mark has a similar phrase in connection with the wine, but as part of the narrative: "they all drank of it" (14:23). But the use of "ex hoc omnes" for the wine and the addition of a parallel "ex eo omnes" for the bread is a traditional liturgical procedure, a procedure of a kind found at work in other parts of the liturgical prayers in the Canon.

The Canon cited by St. Ambrose in his *De sacramentis* already has both expressions, although with a small difference in the second ("ex hoc omnes" for "ex eo omnes").

The Consilium therefore decided (19 in favor, 1 against) to follow the tradition as set down in the text of the Roman Canon.

d) The substitution, in the Roman Canon, of "Do this in memory of me" for "As often as you do this, you will do it in memory of me." The latter of these two is liturgical, that is, it is found as such only in the liturgical tradition and not in the biblical sources. The second is found as such in Luke (22:19) and in Paul (1 Cor 11:24).

The second text seemed preferable as being easier and at the same time more biblical. The change was approved unanimously by the Consilium.

The Pope agreed to these requests regarding the Roman Canon and uniformity in the words of consecration.

The Pope's observations and the work done by the Consilium at its eleventh general meeting were, as it were, the final bricks for the building. On November 6 the Pope decided to go over the whole schema in detail with the secretary of the Consilium in order to see what use had been made of the various observations and to make any final decisions on questions referred to him by the Consilium. At the end of the session he wrote on the booklet containing the schema: "I approve in the name of the Lord. Paul VI, Pope. November 2, 1968."

Only on January 17, 1969, however, did the Secretariat of State communicate this formal approval to Cardinal Gut, along with a handwritten letter of the Pope, which read:

Wednesday, November 6, 1968
7:00–8:30 P.M.

Together with Father Annibale Bugnini, I have once again read the new Order of Mass compiled by the Council for the Implementation of the Constitution on the Sacred Liturgy, now that observations on it have been made by myself, the Roman Curia, the Congregation of Rites, and the participants in the eleventh general meeting of the Consilium itself, as well as by other churchmen and members of the laity. After careful consideration of the various changes proposed, many of which have been accepted, I give the new Order of Mass my approval in the Lord. Paul VI, Pope.

VI. Publication of the Order of Mass

Since the preparation of the entire Missal would take more time, it was decided that, as requested by the members of the Consilium, a separate booklet should be published containing the apostolic constitution *Missale Romanum*, the General Instruction of the Roman Missal, the Order of Mass, the prefaces, and the four Eucharistic Prayers.

The page proofs of the booklet were sent to the Pope on March 11, 1969. On April 10 he gave them his approval, but made a few more changes.

1) In the introductory rites the greeting "Dominus vobiscum" rather than "Dominus tecum" should be kept, even when Mass is being celebrated without a congregation, since the Eucharistic sacrifice is and must always

be a communal action, and the celebrant is addressing a congregation, even when this is represented by a single individual.[46]

2) For the same reasons, the "Orate, fratres" prayer is to be said at a Mass without a congregation; no. 222 of the GIRM is to be altered accordingly.

3) On the other hand, when "for serious reasons" Mass is celebrated without a server, it will be appropriate to omit the greetings and the final blessing.

4) It will be necessary to change no. 266 of the GIRM on the relics of the saints to be enclosed in an altar when it is being consecrated. The relics must indeed be subjected to a rigorous investigation, but once they are acknowledged and declared to be authentic, they are to be kept, no matter how small.[47]

5) The various colors of the liturgical vestments should be retained (see no. 307), and their use throughout the Church should be regulated by detailed norms, while allowing that when special circumstances make it advisable to change the traditional practice, the Holy See may grant privileges or allow exceptions to the universal norms.[48]

The Pope announced publication of the new Order of Mass at a consistory on April 28, 1969:

> The Church has an innate need to pray that finds its preeminent expression in the Eucharistic sacrifice. That need is the abiding, pure source for all liturgical norms . . . . That is the context of the new Order of Mass. After the long and laborious work to simplify the rites for the beginning of Mass, the offertory, the sign of peace, and the breaking of the bread, the Order of Mass should be seen as the culmination of the new structure of the Mass desired by the conciliar Fathers and designed to assist the faithful to take an ever more conscious and active part in the Eucharistic sacrifice.[49]

On May 2 the apostolic constitution *Missale Romanum* (dated Holy Thursday, April 3, 1969) was presented in the press room. On that same occasion the booklet containing the Order of Mass was made public.[50]

---

46. In accordance with the principle of truthfulness, the retention of "Dominus tecum" was allowed.

47. Justice was done to this observation by adopting a generic statement which urges that the traditional custom of placing relics in the altar be kept, provided their authenticity is certain.

48. This principle was likewise accepted (see no. 308). The traditional practice of the Roman Rite is there set down, but followed by a statement that the conferences may petition the Holy See for adaptations to the needs and mentalities of their respective peoples.

49. DOL 93 no. 675.

50. *Ordo Missae* (Vatican Polyglot Press, 1969. 174 pp.). It contains the decree of the Congregation of Rites, the apostolic constitution, the Order of Mass with a congregation and without a congregation, the prefaces, and the four Eucharistic Prayers.

1. *Apostolic Constitution* Missale Romanum[51]

In this document Pope Paul VI promulgated the new Roman Missal and to some extent gave anticipatory approval to those parts of the Mass that were not contained in the Sacramentary (for example, the Scripture readings) or were still being readied.

The constitution notes that the current reform brings to completion the work begun by Pius XII with his restoration of the solemn Easter Vigil and Holy Week. The basic principles set down by the liturgical Constitution give the entire Missal a greater degree of clarity and homogeneity. The Pope here signals the essential things to be noted in this new Order of Mass:

1) the General Instruction, which brings together the new norms for the celebration of the Eucharistic sacrifice;

2) the Eucharistic Prayers, anaphoras, and prefaces, all of which have been increased in number after the example of the Eastern liturgies, in order to give greater variety to the Church's prayer and to render the formulas more complete and richer in theological, scriptural, and liturgical content;

3) the formulas of consecration, which have been restored to a purer form, reflective of the biblical sources;

4) the prayer of the faithful and the penitential rite or rite of reconciliation with God and our brothers and sisters at the beginning of Mass;

5) the new organization of the readings and a larger number of readings, so that the more important parts of the Old and New Testaments will be read at festal Masses;

6) general revision of all the other texts and prayer formulas.

When Pius V promulgated the "Tridentine" Missal in 1570, his intention was to provide the Christian people with an instrument of liturgical unity and an outstanding expression of the Church's authentic religious worship. In like manner, Paul VI, while acknowledging the legitimate variety and adaptations that characterize the new Missal, expects "that the faithful will receive the new Missal as a help toward witnessing and strengthening their unity with one another; that through the new Missal one and the same prayer in a great diversity of languages will ascend, more fragrant than any incense, to our heavenly Father, through our High Priest, Jesus Christ, in the Holy Spirit."[52]

---

51. The General Instruction was prepared by P. Jounel, revised by the Congregation for the Doctrine of the Faith, and given its stylistic form by Monsignor Tondini.

52. The phrase "ascend, more fragrant than any incense" ("quovis ture fragrantior ascendat") is from Monsignor Tondini; it was left in out of deference for this man who had proved

2. *General Instruction of the Roman Missal*

This is the document that precedes the Order of Mass and describes the celebration and its meaning, both as a whole and in its several parts. The treatment is at once doctrinal, pastoral, and rubrical. Its eight chapters are the product of assiduous labor by a study group headed by Father Braga.[53] I shall survey it briefly.

1) *Importance and dignity of the Eucharistic celebration*

The Eucharistic celebration is the center of Christian life and the high point both of the work by which God sanctifies the world and of the worship which human beings offer to the Father. It is necessary, therefore, that the celebration of Mass be so arranged that ministers and faithful, each playing their proper part, may participate in it in a more fruitful way. This goal will be reached if the faithful are enabled to participate consciously, actively, and fully.

Finally, since the Eucharistic celebration, like the liturgy as a whole, involves the use of sensible signs, it is necessary to select carefully and

---

so courteous and understanding, even though it is a mannered phrase that does not fit the style of the document. The apostolic constitution is in *DOL* 202 nos. 1357–66; citation from no. 1365.

53. See *Not* 5 (1969) 148–58; G. Fontaine, "Institutionis generalis Missalis romani concordantia verbalis," *ibid.*, 304–22. The General Instruction underwent some revisions after its first publication. The first number to be revised was no. 7, because of the attacks by conservative groups after publication of the Order of Mass; they thought that this number gave an incomplete and defective definition of the Mass, and they objected to the term "Lord's Supper." The Congregation for Divine Worship felt obliged to issue a declaration on November 18, 1969, in which it explained the character of the General Instruction and of no. 7 in particular (*DOL* 204 nos. 1368–70). For the moment, no. 7 was expanded in order to facilitate acceptance of it; see *Not* 5 (1969) 417–18.

When the Missal was published in 1970, further clarifications were made of some expressions, even though the Congregation for the Doctrine of the Faith found the text to be doctrinally accurate; see "Variationes in 'Institutionem generalem Missalis romani' inductae," *Not* 6 (1970) 177–90. When the Missal was reprinted, and again when the second edition was published, further revisions were made which were required in order to harmonize the text with the liturgical books and other documents published after the General Instruction; see "Variationes in 'Institutionem generalem Missalis romani' inductae," *Not* 9 (1973) 34–38; 11 (1975) 298–308.

For completeness' sake I must add that while the Order of Mass had been sent to the prefects of the curial agencies, the General Instruction had not. The Consilium presented the fruit of its various labors to the Holy Father, and he decided on each occasion what further steps were to be taken, as we have seen. In the case of the General Instruction, he did not ask that it be studied by the other curial agencies. After its publication and the protests it elicited, especially from the Congregation for the Doctrine of the Faith, the Secretary of State ordered that all the schemas be examined by that Congregation; this was regularly done. (See also below, p. 601, n. 7.)

arrange properly those forms and elements provided by the Church that will promote the participation and spiritual well being of the faithful.

2) *Structure, elements, and parts of the Mass*

This is one of the key chapters of the document. It describes the celebration not only from a rubrical and ceremonial viewpoint but also, and even more, from a doctrinal viewpoint. Attention is focused on the nature and significance of the various elements found in the celebration: the word of God, presidential prayers, singing, external postures, silence. Each is introduced and explained, because this is a necessary condition for any practical applications.

A description of the parts of the Mass follows: introductory rite, liturgy of the Word, Eucharistic liturgy, concluding rite.

To be noted in particular is the wide range of possibilities offered for singing. This allows both the full preservation of the traditional patrimony (Gregorian and polyphonic) and, at the same time, a genuine openness to new musical creations for new texts.

Thus, for the entrance song, in addition to the texts in the Roman Gradual and the *Graduale simplex*, it is possible to use other texts that are liturgically adapted to the season or feast and are counterparts of the old texts. They are to be approved by the episcopal conference. The same holds for the offertory and communion songs.

All these songs accompany an action. It is therefore possible to allow a certain flexibility, especially with an eye on the heritage of popular song in the various countries and the various modern languages. This means in turn that the texts must be to some degree adaptable to new and different musical requirements.

The document prescribes how each "sung" text is to be handled when the Mass is actually a Mass with singing and when the Mass is simply read. The entrance and communion antiphons, for example, are to be sung or read for their value in showing the meaning of the celebration and feast. The offertory antiphon, on the other hand, may be omitted if it is not sung, because it then loses its value as accompaniment to a procession and to the offertory rites; if it is simply read it would create a textual overload of this part of the celebration.

Because of their importance, the songs between the readings receive special attention. The Alleluia must be sung if its note of exultant praise is to be expressed; therefore, if it is not to be sung, it *may* be omitted. The same holds for the verse that accompanies the Alleluia or replaces it during penitential periods.

On the other hand, all the parts of the Ordinary must be recited if they are not sung.

The sequences for the feast of Corpus Christi, the Mass of the deceased, and the feast of Our Lady of Sorrows are optional. In Latin they are marked by poetic beauty; when translated into the vernaculars, they lose a good deal of their value. The sequences of Easter and Pentecost, however, are to be kept. The episcopal conferences have authority gradually to provide translations and new musical compositions to go with them.

It is to be noted, finally, that in this chapter rubrical notations of a general kind are combined with a doctrinal and pastoral treatment. It is clear that this complex whole must be kept in mind for a correct and effective arrangement of the celebration.

3) Offices and ministries in the Mass

In the assembly that gathers for Mass, each person has the right and duty of participation. Each participant carries out his or her own function, thus accomplishing that, and only that, which falls within his or her competence. This premise having been laid down, the General Instruction describes the offices and ministries of those in holy orders and the members of the people of God, as well as some special ministries. Three points deserve mention because they are innovations:

a) The episcopal conferences may allow the readings, except for the gospel, to be done by a woman when no authorized minister or qualified layman is present.

b) If several ministers of the same degree, especially deacons, are present, they may all take an active part in the celebration by dividing the various functions among them. As far as deacons are concerned, this permission had already been given in the instruction of the Congregation of Rites on the episcopal rites; the permission is here made more general.

c) If members of chapters or communities obliged to have a conventual Mass as part of the choral Office attend such a Mass, they may receive communion at it even if they must for pastoral reasons celebrate Mass themselves.

4) The different forms of celebration

This chapter describes the ceremonies of the several forms of celebration: first, Mass with a congregation; then, Mass without a congregation. The description is followed by some general rules for communion under both kinds.

The basis for the description of Mass with a congregation is a celebration not overly lacking in the external solemnity provided by singing and the presence of ministers. This form of celebration is possible in an ordinary parish if the pastor is seriously committed to good liturgical services.

To the description of the ordinary form of Mass celebrated by a priest alone is added a description of what a deacon is to do, if one is available, in the exercise of his functions.

When the rite of concelebration was promulgated, it included permission for diocesan priests to concelebrate with their bishops on the occasion of diocesan synods, parish visitations, and congresses. The permission is here extended to religious in their relations with their Ordinary on comparable occasions. This is meant to develop a sense of union with the hierarchy through the celebration of one and the same Eucharist.

Mass without a congregation is described at length, even if succinctly, with the variations peculiar to it.

Also taken into consideration are Masses celebrated without a server. It is said, however, that such celebrations are not allowed "except out of serious necessity." Logically enough, in such Masses there are no greetings or responses; also omitted are the *Orate, fratres* and the final blessing.

With regard to communion under both kinds, the text simply summarizes current practice, disciplinary and rubrical.

Among adaptations foreseen as possibly required in different cultures is the replacement of the kiss given to the altar or Book of Gospels by some other sign of veneration that is more consonant with a local situation.

5) *Arrangement and furnishing of churches for the Eucharistic celebration*

The purpose of this chapter is to bring together the regulations for the arrangement of sacred places in connection with the Eucharistic celebration: the general arrangement of the church, the sanctuary, the altar and its furnishings, the celebrant's chair, the ambo or lectern, the place of the congregation, the place of the choir. After this come some regulations having to do less directly with the celebration: the reservation of the Eucharist, sacred images, the surroundings of the church.

a) If the Eucharist is celebrated outside a sacred place, especially if for only a single occasion, a suitable ordinary table may be used. In fact, a movable altar no longer need have a sacred stone in it.

b) There has been a change in the definition of a fixed and a movable altar; the difference no longer derives from the form of consecration or blessing, but from the physical movability or immovability of the altar itself.

c) It is preferred that the table of a fixed altar be of natural stone, in keeping with the tradition of the Latin Church; but the episcopal conferences can allow the use of artificial stone (composites, cement, and so on) or other materials, provided these are solid. Altars not made of stone are still to be found today in some places.

d) A movable altar, on the other hand, can be made of any material that is suitable and worthy of the purpose for which it is intended, for example, metal, wood, and so on.

e) Every altar, fixed or movable, can be consecrated. A movable altar, however, may be simply blessed. The point is to emphasize the importance of a fixed altar as a permanent part of the sacred building.

f) The relics to be placed in or under the altar need not be those of a martyr, but they must be certainly authentic.

6) Requisites for celebrating Mass

This chapter brings together the regulations regarding the material of the sacrifice (bread and wine), along with the principal solutions of difficulties caused by defects in the material. It also describes the furnishings required for the celebration (sacred vessels, vestments).

a) The number of *altar cloths* required for the Eucharistic celebration has been reduced to one.

b) While the principle still holds that the *sacred vessels* should be made of some noble material, greater choice is now allowed in light of the situation and differing value-systems of the various countries.

Chalices and other sacred vessels destined to contain the blood of Christ should have a cup made of a nonporous material. Other sacred vessels that will contain only the consecrated hosts may be made not only of metal but of other worthy and prized materials, such as ivory or hard and valuable woods.

The gilding of the inside of sacred vessels is required only if the metal used is subject to rust. Otherwise, the gilding is not required, especially if made of metals more precious than gold.

The shape of the vessels is generally left to the artist, but the latter must take into account the liturgical use of the vessel and the genius of the various cultures and peoples.

c) The *vestments:* The episcopal conferences may allow, in addition to the traditional materials, natural fibers peculiar to various regions or even artificial fibers judged to be in keeping with the dignity of the person and action for which they intended.

The colors to be used may likewise be decided by the conferences, which may accept or modify traditional usage or adopt new usages that are in keeping with the mentality and traditions of the different countries. However, the approval of the Holy See is required for innovations.

The episcopal conferences may also modify the form of the vestments, always with a view to special local situations.

7) *Choice of the Mass and its parts*

The rubrical norms governing the use of the calendar to be followed in choosing and arranging the Mass are repeated here, but in a broader and more pastoral form. They serve the priest as a guide in choosing among the various formularies so that he will be able to organize the celebration in a way that promotes the active participation of the faithful and is to their spiritual advantage.

Since the calendar for any given day contains numerous optional memorials of the saints, the possibility must be allowed of a wider choice of the several parts of the Mass—from the presidential prayers to the readings and even the Eucharistic Prayer—for one and the same celebration.

This chapter of the General Instruction, therefore, has two parts: the first having to do with the choice of the Mass to be said on the various types of liturgical days; the second having to do with the choice of the various parts of the Mass formulary.

8) *Votive Masses and Masses for the dead*

An effort has been made to sum up in a few paragraphs the extensive and complex legislation in the code of rubrics. It seemed excessive and indeed useless to offer a developed casuistry that in practice is not helpful either to the celebration or to the minister.

The new rubrics leave a wider margin of freedom to the priest in charge of the parish or the celebration. Also given is a broader permission for the use of votive Masses; one reason for this is the new calendar itself, which has a greater number of days on which votive Masses may be celebrated.

3. *Effective Date of Use*

The decree of the Congregation of Rites determined that the new Order of Mass was to be followed beginning on November 30, 1969, the First Sunday of Advent.[54]

It thus became necessary to make preparations for it. The months from May to November 1969 were marked, throughout the world, by an intense work of preparation in the various national and diocesan centers, in parishes, and in religious institutes.

---

54. The decree was dated April 6, 1969 (*DOL* 203 no. 1367).

First of all, the texts had to be translated and published. In this area the joint commissions had the most to do. The various language areas—French, Spanish, English, Italian, and Portuguese—quickly produced in their respective tongues an Order of Mass that was elegant in style and sumptuous in presentation.

Some countries had already managed to publish the new Lectionary, either in its entirety or for Cycle B, which would be used for the 1969–1970 liturgical year.[55] Other countries were still waiting to undertake a task that required time and the availability of persons and means; these continued to use the "old" Missals for the prayers and to take the needed readings from editions of the Scriptures that had been approved for liturgical use.

The period of preparation was also an intense one for study meetings, national, regional, and general "weeks," and specialized groups. Press, radio, television—use was made of them all, especially in countries that had an active, efficient liturgical secretariat, in order to prepare the Christian community to enter consciously into the liturgical climate of the "new" Mass.[56]

It is understandable that all this interest in the liturgy should have given rise to pastoral and rubrical problems that bishops and priests submitted to the Holy See either directly or through the episcopal conferences.

The Congregation of Divine Worship sent its answer in the form of an instruction on the gradual carrying out of the apostolic constitution *Missale Romanum* (October 20, 1969).[57]

---

55. The *Ordo lectionum* was officially published on May 25, 1969, but the volume was not in fact available until the beginning of the summer.

56. The work of preparation not only caught the interest of the clergy and the faithful but also, for obvious reasons, gave rise to bitter attacks, regrets, and unfounded accusations against the conduct of the reform and against the orthodoxy of the new rite of Mass; see above, pp. 284ff. The Pope himself, as was his custom, instructed the faithful in order to prepare them to welcome the new rite of Mass; see *DOL* 211 nos. 1757-59; 212 nos. 1760-64.

57. *DOL* 209 nos. 1732-56.

25

The New Roman Missal

It was thought that with the Order of Mass now published, the entire Missal could be published before Advent of 1969. The controversies that accompanied the work, however, and the successive examinations and critiques of it delayed the final version. Furthermore, the review of all the texts by the Congregation for the Doctrine of the Faith and the discussion of the Congregation's observations required more time than anticipated. As a result, the Roman Missal did not see the light until 1970.

On March 11 of that year the Holy Father gave definitive approval in his own hand: "I approve in the Lord. March 11, 1970." The book was then officially published with a decree of the Congregation for Divine Worship, dated Holy Thursday, March 26, 1970,[1] and was ready for May 17, the day on which the Pope celebrated the fiftieth anniversary of his own priestly ordination and ordained 278 priests, to whom he gave as a gift a copy of the new Missal that he was promulgating.

Four centuries earlier, almost to the day, in obedience to the mandate given him by the Council of Trent on December 4, 1563, Pius V on July 14, 1570, issued the bull *Quo primum,* by which he gave the Church of the Roman Rite the Missal "revised by decree of the Sacred Council of Trent."

Both Missals sprang from the reforming will of a council and from the principles laid down by it. Both took the same sources as their starting

---

1. *Missale Romanum ex decreto Sacrosancti Oecumenici Concilii Vaticani II instauratum auctoritate Pauli Pp. VI promulgatum* (Vatican Polyglot Press, 1970). The decree of the Congregation for Divine Worship is in *DOL* 213 no. 1765. The Missal was reprinted in 1972 and went into a second edition in 1975.

point: "the tradition of the Fathers,"[2] but the end result was quite differ-ent. The commission appointed by Pius V and presided over by Cardinal Guglielmo Sirleto had rather limited tools at its disposal: the codices of the Vatican Library and the current editions of the Missal, which had been printed for the first time a century earlier (1471). The work nonetheless had the merit of giving the Church a single, sure basis for its prayer, a basis purified of many transitory, imperfect elements. But the commis-sion's vision of the tradition was necessarily limited; it was also condi-tioned by the positions taken by the Protestant Reformers.

The Consilium, on the other hand, was able really to go back to the origins. It had access to the various forms of the Church's euchological riches; it had the advantage of numerous studies and could reflect with greater tranquillity on the pastoral needs of the faithful.

I. DOCUMENTS

The Missal begins with the apostolic constitution *Missale Romanum* (April 3, 1969) and the part of the motu proprio *Mysterii paschalis* (Febru-ary 14, 1969) that has to do with the Missal.

Next comes an Introduction that had not yet been written when the Order of Mass was promulgated. It is quite lengthy and focuses on three points: (a) the history of the Roman Missal, especially from Trent to Vati-can II; the purpose here is to explain the changes introduced in accord-ance with the guidelines set down by the latter Council; (b) the theological and even ritual fidelity of both Missals to the teaching of the Church; there is continuity in one and the same faith with regard to the sacrificial value of the Mass, the real presence of Christ in the Eucharist, the hier-archical character of the ministerial priesthood, and the links between this priesthood and the priesthood of the faithful; and (c) the norms fol-lowed in the reform.

In addition, the concept of tradition is clearly defined: it covers not only recent aspects of the Church's life but includes whatever is valid in the various periods of history. Tradition needs to be located in the historical context of each age, so that while remaining faithful to doctri-nal principles, it also adapts itself at the level of practical implementa-tion. This is the case, for example, with the use of the vernacular in the

---

2. See the apostolic constitution *Missale Romanum* (*DOL* 202 nos. 1357-66); C. Braga, "Il nuovo Messale Romano," *EL* 84 (1970) 249-74, 401-31; (AB), "Paulus Episcopus plebi Dei," *Not* 6 (1970) 161-68. — The motu proprio *Mysterii paschalis*, to which reference is made in the next paragraph of the text, is in *DOL* 440 nos. 3754-57 (this was the motu proprio ap-proving the General Norms for the Liturgical Year and the Calendar).

liturgy and with communion under both kinds; the latter was refused by Trent for reasons then valid but is now allowed in the quite different historical and pastoral context of Vatican II. The same holds true for the use, with timely adaptations, of the euchological treasures of the past. Some statements in the Missal have been changed in order to adapt their theology to the language of Vatican II. Now, as then, the Holy Spirit assists the Church, not changing its substance but readjusting its form.[3]

The Introduction was written as a result of the attacks made and the apprehensions voiced after the publication of the Order of Mass; these had cast doubt on the orthodoxy and legitimacy of the reform.[4] The Congregation for Divine Worship thought initially of issuing a more solemn document, a motu proprio that would be a follow-up on the apostolic constitution *Missale Romanum*. It was the Pope's keen intuition that suggested the idea of an Introduction. This would be a kind of plain, instructional introduction to a full understanding of the General Instruction, in which every reader, "whether catechist or professor of theology, would find answers that might prove useful when they saw the actual direction taken by liturgical worship as a result of the new Missal."[5]

After the Introduction comes the General Instruction,[6] which has been revised in accordance with the criteria applied in the Introduction, that is, to make clearer and more explicit some expressions that might cause

---

3. See A. Pistoia in *EL* 84 (1970) 241ff.

4. This response to attacks was announced beforehand in the declaration *Institutio Generalis Missalis Romani* of the Congregation for Divine Worship (November 18, 1969), which accompanied the reprinting of the *Ordo Missae*. This short statement not only explains the nature of the General Instruction and guarantees its complete orthodoxy but also announces that in order to allay anxieties, any needed clarifications will be included. The document is in *DOL* 204 nos. 1368-70.

5. Guidelines given to Father Bugnini by the Pope at an audience on February 14, 1970. The Pope added that the Introduction must contain a defense of the continuity of the new Missal with the preceding tradition and, of course, its dogmatic identity with the old Missal. Furthermore: "The Introduction must begin with some striking phrase—perhaps 'Go and prepare the passover . . .' from Mark or from Luke, or 'A large room prepared. . . .' The point is to show that what the Lord commanded, the Church does in the Mass." In fact, the Introduction begins in Latin with "Cenam paschalem . . . Christus Dominus cenaculum magnum, stratum."

The Pope then ordered that the text be sent to the Congregation for the Doctrine of the Faith and the Congregation for the Sacraments; this was done. He also ordered that (1) in the General Instruction there should be a reference to individual thanksgiving; (2) one of the formulas "Corpus tuum" or "Quod ore sumpsimus" be recited during the purification of the sacred vessels (the second was kept); (3) the prefaces for the Trinity and Pentecost be retained in the collection of prefaces; (4) no. 7 should be stylistically improved in agreement with Archbishop Philippe; and (5) the Missal should come out at Easter.

6. See pp. 386ff.

difficulty.[7] Special attention was given to no. 7, since this had been the object of an especially bitter attack. The attackers had not taken into account that this number gave a simple *description* of the general liturgico-ritual structure of the Eucharistic celebration. The number has its place, in fact, in the chapter dealing with the "Structure, Elements, and Parts of the Mass." In a desire for clarity and for the sake of charity rather than from any doctrinal need, the text was nonetheless more carefully worded and made more complete.[8]

The introductory section of the Missal also includes the General Norms for the Liturgical Year and the Calendar, as well as the liturgical calendar itself, divided by month.

II. THE SACRAMENTARY

The text of the Missal proper begins at this point. By good use of technical and typographical devices, each page of the Latin book usually contains the entire formulary for a Sunday or feast, that is, the entrance and communion antiphons, the three presidential prayers, and, if there is one, the proper preface. The readings are given in the Lectionary. Thus a division and clear distinction is definitively made between Sacramentary and Lectionary. The former is the book for the altar, the latter the book for the lectern. One contains the euchological and sacramental formulas, the other the word of God.

1. *Euchological Riches*

The new Missal has eighty-one prefaces and sixteen hundred prayers, or more than twice as many as in the old Missal. Almost all the texts of the old Missal have been used, revised if need be to harmonize them with the reform and the teaching of Vatican II.[9]

In addition, extensive use has been made of all the very rich and splendid euchological treasures of the Church that are contained in the manuscript collections, the liturgies of East and West, and the particular rites. In cases where there were no models to follow in meeting new needs

---

7. A list of the changes is given in *Not* 6 (1970) 177–90.

8. A similar desire for clarity determined the correction of articles 48, 55d, and 60.

9. On the sources of the new or revised euchological formulas of the Missal and on the principles followed in the revision, see A. Dumas, O.S.B., "Les sources du Missel Romain," *Not* 7 (1971) 37, 74, 94, 134, 276, 409; idem, "Pour mieux comprendre les textes liturgiques du Missel Romain," *ibid.*, 6 (1970) 194–213; A. Franquesa, O.S.B., "Las antífonas del Introito y de la Comunión en las Misas sin canto," *ibid.*, 213–21.

(for example, the prayer for nonbelievers on Good Friday or some Masses for various needs and situations), the experts employed their own talents and charism.

The reduction in the number of saints' feasts has meant a quantitative reduction in the part of the Missal reserved for the sanctoral. On the other hand, every celebration has at least one proper presidential prayer (the collect). Effective texts from the preceding repertory have been kept; those of suppressed feasts have been used; set or stereotyped or vague phrases have been avoided in favor of others which are more specific and which better catch the spiritual features of the saint being celebrated.

The work of chisel and file was done by study group 18bis. This was not the original intention, but as early as the first general meetings it was realized that a work requiring so much research, harmonization of texts, and creativity could only be brought to completion by a group of careful, sensitive specialists with a good knowledge of the Church's euchological sources, both Eastern and Western.

The director assigned for this group was Father Placide Bruylants, a Benedictine of Mont-César (Louvain), known everywhere for two solid volumes on the prayers of the Missal and for his *Concordance verbale du Sacramentaire Léonien.*[10]

The group worked first on the prayers of the temporal cycle. These were all reviewed and revised at a meeting in Louvain, April 5–11, 1965. By mid-June of the following year, the prayers for the celebrations of the saints were also ready, at least for those saints who would certainly be kept in the universal calendar. A complete and definitive redaction had to wait, however, until the calendar was completed. The same was true of other areas—votive Masses, Commons, and so on.

All this represented, however, only a kind of first-stage work, a testing of the water, because the Consilium had not yet set down the criteria to be observed. It was unable to do this until the seventh general meeting (October 6–14, 1966).

The relator had given the Fathers a thick booklet of sixty-nine pages with the corrected text of the prayers and prefaces and with an explanation of the criteria followed in the revision.

While appreciating the work that had been done, the Fathers got no further than a discussion of the principles at work. They put off an examination of the texts to a further meeting and promised that in the interim they would set down their remarks on the texts and send them in.

---

10. *Secretary:* G. Lucchesi; *members:* A. Rose, W. Dürig, H. Ashworth, G. A. Gracias, A. Dumas. At the death of Father Bruylants, A. Rose became relator.

The principles, formulated in short statements and put to a vote, were unanimously accepted. For practical purposes, this is what they said:

> The criteria to be applied in the revision are these: The number of texts is to be increased so as to avoid the many unnecessary repetitions found in the present Missal; the texts are to be revised in the light of the originals in order to restore a fullness of meaning, including theological meaning, that has sometimes been altered; expressions that have now lost most of their meaning (for example, the reference exclusively to bodily fasting in the prayers of Lent) are to be replaced, as opportunity allows, by others more in keeping with modern conditions.
>
> The number of prayers can be increased not only by taking texts from the sacramentaries but also by composing new ones through shrewd centonization that uses and combines in a suitable way elements from various prayers found in the sacramentaries.
>
> With regard to the prefaces: The common desire has been accepted of having proper prefaces for all the seasons of the year, the Sundays of Ordinary Time, and the principal solemnities. A revision of the existing texts is to be made with a view to restoring the original literary form of each, especially in cases in which the expression of thanksgiving, so characteristic of these formularies, has been dropped.

Unfortunately, Father Bruylants did not live to see the fruits of his labor, for he was struck down by a heart attack on October 18, 1966. But the group continued to work along the lines he had established. The Consilium discussed its work again at the eleventh general meeting (October 8, 1966), focusing especially on the nature of the presidential prayers, on the details of the three "orations" (presidential prayers), on their endings, and on the blessing of the people at the end of Mass. The work received its final form by the time the Missal was to be put together, thanks to the valuable collaboration of Father Braga and in conjunction with the Congregation for the Doctrine of the Faith.

2. Commons

The problem of the structure of the Commons was studied by group 18.[11] In the Missal the Common of the Dedication of a Church[12] is followed by those of the Blessed Virgin (six formularies), the martyrs (ten

11. See above, pp. 331ff.

12. In the second edition of the Missal, the Common for the Dedication of a Church contained the Masses for the anniversary of a dedication. The Masses for the dedication itself were put among the Ritual Masses; in the English Missal they are in Appendix VIII. See Not 11 (1975) 318.

formularies, plus three sets of more specialized prayers), pastors (twelve, including founders of churches, missionaries), doctors (two), virgins (four), and holy men and women (twelve, some adaptable to all classes, others meant for particular categories: religious, teachers, mothers of families, those who worked with the underprivileged).

3. *Masses for Various Needs*

> For well-disposed Christians the liturgy of the sacraments and sacramentals causes almost every event in human life to be made holy by divine grace that flows from the paschal mystery. The eucharist, in turn, is the sacrament of sacraments. Accordingly, the Missal provides formularies for Masses and prayers that may be used in the various circumstances of Christian life, for the needs of the whole world, and for the needs of the Church, both local and universal.[13]

These formularies are divided into three categories:

a) *Ritual Masses*, which are those connected with a sacramental rite or a special blessing. If these rites are celebrated within the Eucharist, it is appropriate that the Mass should have special texts so that the entire celebration—Eucharist and other sacrament—may be homogeneous.

A further argument for having proper texts is the fact that, as history, especially the history of the Eastern Church, teaches, all the sacraments, and their anniversary celebrations, are connected with the Eucharist: the election of a pope, the ordination of a bishop and a priest, religious profession, marriage.

Precisely because the Eucharistic liturgy and the other sacramental liturgies are so closely connected, the ritual Masses were prepared along with the liturgical books for the various sacraments. This explains why some ritual Masses were lacking in the first edition of the Missal and had to be added in the second.[14]

b) *Masses for Various Occasions*. From its very beginnings the Roman liturgy has linked the needs of the Church, human beings, and the world with the Eucharistic celebration as the center of the entire work of redemption. Within limits the liturgy also embraces individual, local, and temporal needs. Masses celebrated in these various situations bring the

---

13. See GIRM 326.

14. For the election or enrollment of names (catechumenate); blessing of an abbot or abbess; twenty-fifth and fiftieth anniversaries of religious profession; dedication of a church and an altar. There is no Mass associated with the sacrament of penance, the celebration of which has always been separate from the celebration of the Eucharist. There is, however, a Mass for reconciliation among the Masses for various needs; see *Not* 11 (1975) 315–37.

Eucharist closer to human life and make Christ a participant in its principal events. Among these situations and occasions are the spiritual and material needs of the Church (for example, the union of Christians, the missions, councils and synods, congresses) and of the faithful (for example, sickness, war, drought, national feasts).

There is need, of course, for restraint and a sense of balance in order not to undermine the unity, universality, and coherence of the liturgy and to safeguard the preeminence of the celebration of the mystery of Christ, Our Lady, and the saints.[15] In any case, many specific situations do not call for special Masses; all that is needed is to make use of the general intercessions and of the other adaptations possible at any celebration of the Eucharist. Nor is the Mass the right occasion for every kind of preaching or instruction on special themes. On the contrary, the treatment of such themes should rather be adapted to the mystery of salvation and its unfolding in the course of the liturgical year.

At the same time, however, once the criteria of restraint are applied, the use of Masses for special occasions is of pastoral value, especially now that there are many more days for which no particular celebration is appointed. The Missal divides these Masses into four categories. It will be worthwhile running through the list.[16]

For the Church: for the universal Church (5); for the pope (2); for the bishop (2); for the election of a pope or bishop; for a council or synod (2); for priests; for the celebrant himself (3); for the ministers of the Church; for priestly vocations; for religious; for religious vocations; for the laity; for the unity of Christians; for the spread of the gospel (2); for persecuted Christians; for pastoral or spiritual meetings.

For civil needs: for the nation or city; for those who serve in public office; for the congress; for the president; for the progress of peoples; for peace and justice (2); in time of war or civil disturbance.

For various public needs: beginning of the civil year; for the blessing of human labor (2); for productive land (2); after the harvest; in time of famine or for those who suffer from famine (2); for refugees and exiles; for those unjustly deprived of liberty; for prisoners; for the sick; for the dying; in time of earthquake; for rain; for fine weather; to avert storms; for any need (2); in thanksgiving (2).

For particular needs: for forgiveness of sins; for charity; for promoting harmony; for the family; for relatives and friends; for our oppressors; for a happy death.

---

15. See (AB), "Messa a tema," *Not* 11 (1975) 350ff.
16. If there is more than one formulary, the number is given in parentheses.

c) *Votive Masses*. These are devotional Masses in honor of the mysteries of the Lord, the Blessed Virgin, and the saints. The early sacramentaries and the medieval tradition have transmitted a large number of such
Masses. Some were in response to needs now past and no longer felt
or needs that were too specialized. The Roman liturgical tradition also
had the "Alcuin Masses" for each day of the week; these were dear to
many priests. Later on, Masses were established for specific days of the
week (first Friday, first Thursday, first Saturday) or for certain days of
the year (in thanksgiving for the various harvests). A careful selection
has preserved what is truly worthwhile, and the list has been further enriched, but without linking Masses to a particular day of the week or year.

They include Masses of the Holy Trinity, the Holy Cross, the Holy
Eucharist, the Holy Spirit, St. Joseph, the Blessed Virgin (especially on
Saturday), the angels, all the apostles, St. Peter, St. Paul, a single apostle,
and all the saints.[17] To this series have been added the Masses of the Sacred Heart, the Holy Name of Jesus, and the Precious Blood, the latter
two having lost their special day in the calendar of the universal Church.

Finally, there are *Masses for the Dead*, with five formularies for general
use and fourteen for more specific occasions. In all of them the Christian
sense of death is located within the hope of resurrection and of the final
meeting with the Father.

These various Masses were compiled by study group 13,[18] which on
October 6, 1964, had presented the fourth general meeting of the Consilium with a panoramic view of the problems raised by the votive Masses.
The group itself had met earlier in Rome to decide on its working method.
Since this group, too, had to await the results of the work of other groups
(calendar, Missal, Pontifical), it was decided that until January 1, 1966,
each member should examine the various sources for everything that
might prove useful. The group experienced some obstacles because of
suggestions that came in meanwhile from all sides and were aimed at
retaining elements that the consultors felt bound to eliminate in accordance with the norms established for their work.[19]

Things went on in this fashion until the eleventh general meeting, at
which the new relator, Father A.-M. Roguet, explained the definitive organization of this entire sector (October 8, 1968). The subdivision was

---

17. As a result of numerous and insistent requests, Masses for Mary as Mother of the
Church and for the Holy Name of Mary were included in the second edition of the Missal.

18. *Relator:* H. Schmidt; *secretary:* D. Balboni; *members:* B. Neunheuser, H. Ashworth,
F. Dell'Oro, J. Llopis Sarrió, R. J. Hesbert. In 1966 A.-M. Roguet became relator and J. B.
Molin secretary.

19. See the reports on the group's work in *Not* 2 (1966) 80–83; 4 (1968) 349.

then proposed which in fact entered the Missal. The task of the group was to limit the selection of Masses to themes that were truly essential, universal, and important, and to resist requests demanding the inclusion of Masses with the most diverse motifs, some of them utterly trifling and highly personal.

4. *Some Special Rites*

The liturgical year contains days on which the celebration of Mass includes special elements: the blessing and procession of candles on February 2 (feast of the Presentation of the Lord in the Temple); the blessing and giving of ashes on Ash Wednesday; the venerable rites of Palm Sunday, Holy Thursday, Good Friday, and the Easter Vigil during Holy Week.

The task of examining these rites and suggesting their revision was entrusted to study group 17.[20] The group focused its attention chiefly on the most demanding part of its work, namely, Holy Week. This had already been the subject of study and revision in 1951 and again in 1954. Needed now was a further updating of the whole week so that it would be in harmony with the style of the restored liturgy. Once again the group had to be concerned to save elements dear to the tradition and the devotion of the faithful without at the same time overburdening the liturgy of these sacred days. The group began with a careful theological, historical, and pastoral study of the entire matter, with a view to restoring the rites to their authentic original form and making them pastorally more effective.

The group developed five schemas in a row as the fruit of meetings held in Milan (September 1964) and Rome (September 1966). On three occasions these schemas were studied, discussed, and finally approved by the Consilium at its fourth (November 27, 1967), tenth (April 30, 1968), and eleventh (October 16, 1968) general meetings, after having been discussed by the relators before each of these meetings.[21]

5. *General Intercessions (Prayer of the Faithful)*

An appendix to the Missal contains a number of sample formulas for the general intercessions at Mass. They are intended chiefly for the use

---

20. *Relator:* P. Borella; *secretary:* A. Nocent; *members:* J. Pascher, P. Jounel, J. A. Miller, F. Kolbe, R. Falsini, J. Gaillard. In 1965 M. Righetti was appointed relator and F. Vandenbroucke secretary. A. Hänggi was subsequently appointed as a second relator; when he was made Bishop of Basel, he was replaced by Monsignor Pascher.

21. See *Not* 4 (1968) 352-53.

of someone celebrating without a congregation or who does not have at hand the pertinent volume approved by the episcopal conference.

The restoration of the general intercessions, or prayer of the faithful, was ordered in the Constitution on the Liturgy: "By this prayer, in which the people are to take part, intercession shall be made for holy Church, for the civil authorities, for those oppressed by various needs, for all people, and for the salvation of the entire world" (no. 53).

The instruction *Inter Oecumenici* (September 26, 1964) started the implementation of this decree by establishing very general norms (no. 56).

Group 12 was given the task of studying the problem in depth and coming up with a modern version of a type of prayer that goes back to the early Church.[22]

During the first half of 1964, the consultors and advisors made a careful study of the nature and purpose of the prayer of the faithful, and of its place in the Mass.[23] The relator and his secretary also visited the Liturgical Institute of Trier in order to consult its extensive collection of books on the subject and to acquire useful information about the functioning and experience of this prayer in the German-speaking countries (May 15-16, 1964).

On November 16 of that same year, a report was read to the Fathers of the Consilium on the general criteria for this prayer, along with six sample formulas.[24] The report and the formulas were unanimously approved. The text of the prayers, corrected and extended, was published on January 13, 1965.[25] At that same meeting the Fathers had been asked whether they agreed to a possible enrichment of the models to be offered for the use of the episcopal conferences. The unanimous response was an encouragement to advance along this line.

Fathers Molin and Ramos, two specialists on the subject, worked on these new formulas at San Cugat, near Barcelona, during April 1965. The

---

22. *Relator:* A.-M. Roguet; *secretary:* J. B. Molin; *members:* B. Opfermann, R. Beron, C. Vagaggini, P. Ramos, C. A. Bouman.

23. For some years liturgists had been debating the best title for this part of the Mass: "prayer of the faithful," "common prayer," "universal prayer" (or "general intercessions"). In the definitive edition of the General Instruction the title "universal prayer" was adopted as best expressing the nature of the prayer, which is open to all the needs of the Church, the world, and human beings.

24. This had been discussed at a meeting of group 12 with the group working on the Order of Mass (Freiburg, August 27-28, 1964).

25. *De oratione communi seu fidelium. Eius natura, momentum ac structura. Criteria atque specimina ad experimentum Coetibus territorialibus Episcoporum proposita* (Pro manuscripto). The first printing was quickly sold out. A reprinting was put off for a year.

resultant text was sent to study group 18bis ("De orationibus") for stylistic revision.

The second meeting of group 12 was held at La Houssaye-en-Brie, near Paris, July 24–28, 1965. Also present was Father Bruylants, who reported on the thinking of his group. In this way a collection of fifty-four schemas or formulas was made ready; the formulas were arranged according to the liturgical seasons and feasts, and in harmony with the *Graduale simplex*.

Between August 1 and November 11 these formulas were studied, revised, and polished by Latinists A. Lentini, G. Lucchesi, and A. Coppo, C.M.

The Pope approved the project on February 1, 1966. As a result, the work of the group was published, by authority of the Consilium, on April 17, 1966.[26]

Some introductory remarks explained that the book was intended as a service to the episcopal conferences and that the formulas were not obligatory but were meant only as samples that the competent territorial authorities could use as models in preparing texts better adapted to local mentalities and needs. For the same reason, the Latin text was accompanied by a French version. It was clearly intended that the vernacular formulation should be made in a free manner, account being taken of the special character of each language.

A practical directory explained the importance, nature, structure, and criteria used. The guidelines were sometimes quite detailed, but they were also indispensable, since the conferences were faced with the task of introducing a form of prayer from scratch. All were concerned that the right approach be taken from the start so that there would be no need of correcting mistakes later on.

The book had an enthusiastic reception and was translated and used in various countries. It contributed greatly to train others in the style proper to this type of prayer. Numerous texts and handbooks were published[27] that led to a reintroduction into the Roman liturgy of a precious stone that had been lost and then recovered in all its splendor.

---

26. *De oratione communi seu fidelium. Natura, momentum ac structura. Criteria atque specimina Coetibus territorialibus Episcoporum proposita* (Vatican City: Libreria Editrice Vaticana, 1966. Pp. 182). The volume was part of the collection "Documenti e sussidi di *Notitiae*."

27. Various formulas were also published in *Notitiae*, always as examples and for instructional purposes. See also "De oratione communi seu fidelium," *Not* 1 (1965) 366–68.

6. *Songs*

Another appendix of the Missal brings together the essential melodies for singing the greetings, acclamations, prefaces, and Eucharistic Prayers, the solemn intercessions on Good Friday, the *Exsultet* at the Easter Vigil, and the blessing of water for baptism. A simple and a solemn melody are given for a single preface; the other eighty-one are to be modeled on these.[28]

In 1972 a decree of the Congregation for Divine Worship gave the status of "typical" to the edition of the *Ordo cantus Missae*[29] which study group 25 had prepared. This volume regulates the use of the melodies in the *Graduale Romanum* in accordance with the new organization of the Missal and the Lectionary. It also gives the adaptations to be made in the *Graduale simplex* as a result of the publication of the new liturgical books for the Mass. The melodies (except those already in the Missal) are given for the singing of the Order of Mass and, in an appendix, for the singing of the new Litany of the Saints (based on the melody in the Vatican edition). The volume is intended for those who want to continue singing the Mass in Latin, using the classical Gregorian melodies but in the spirit and form of the new liturgical books. Credit for the work belongs not only to study group 25 but also to the tenacity and talent of the Benedictine abbey of Solesmes, which carried it forward with constancy, great effort, and self-sacrifice.

This brought to a conclusion the work of revising the Roman Missal. The new Missal represents the work of twelve study groups and of many scholars, pastors, and experts, known or, in many cases, unknown. It was an ecclesial work done in a spirit of sincere dedication, intelligently, and at the cost of personal sacrifice. By his apostolic authority Pope Paul VI gave the result of their work to the Church as the form of its prayer and the rule of its faith.

---

28. In 1971 the monks of Solesmes published the prefaces with the Gregorian melody in full in a volume entitled *Prefationes in cantu* (Solesmes, 1971. 215 + IV pp.). Adaptation to the melody required the inversion of some words in the text; permission for this was granted by the Congregation for Divine Worship on November 22, 1971; see p. 3). The book was very successful.

29. The decree was dated June 24, 1972 (*DOL* 534 no. 4275). The volume: *Ordo cantus Missae* (editio typica; Vatican Polyglot Press, 1972). The Introduction (translated in *DOL* 535 nos. 4276-4302) contains three short chapters: "Reform of the Graduale Romanum," "Rites to be followed in singing the Mass," and "Use of the Ordo Cantus Missae." See the commentary of J. Claire, "L'Ordo Cantus Missae," *Not* 8 (1972) 221-26.

The Lectionary of the Roman Missal

I. EXPERIMENTAL LECTIONARY FOR WEEKDAYS

The compilation and publication of the Lectionary of the Roman Missal was preceded by the use of more limited lectionaries for weekday Masses (*Ordo lectionum per ferias*). These had a providential twofold effect: they educated the faithful to a taste for Sacred Scripture on a broad scale, and they yielded valuable guidelines, based on experience, for the compilation of the definitive set of readings.[1]

The desire for a greater variety in the readings was stimulated by the introduction of the vernaculars. Repetition of the same readings—especially on weekdays, when the Scriptures of the preceding Sunday were read over and over, and in the Commons—created boredom and did not promote prayer. A variety of plans was therefore called for.

1. *The German Plan*

Once the vernacular was introduced, the German Church found itself impoverished as far as Scripture readings were concerned. As a matter of fact, at an earlier date, on the initiative of Cardinal Michael Faulhaber, Archbishop of Munich and Freising, and with the consent of the Ordinaries of the German diocese, it had become the custom at Mass

---

1. Study group 11 was engaged in making suitable preliminary studies for the compilation of new cycles of readings. The shift from the existing annual cycle to a system of multi-year cycles was a major innovation. The arguments offered by the experts for cycles of one, two, three, or even four years were theoretical, since there was no experience on which to base a fully valid solution.

that while the celebrant was reading the appointed pericopes in Latin, a lector read in German other pericopes on which the homily was then preached. However, this practice ceased once permission was given to read the epistle and gospel in German.

On November 6, 1964, therefore, the episcopal conference asked Rome that on ordinary Sundays of the year and on second- and fourth-class weekdays that lacked their own readings the multi-year cycles of readings already in use in various dioceses or published in *Liturgisches Jahrbuch* might be used experimentally.[2] When the request was presented to the Holy Father on December 17, 1964, he answered that "discussion of this matter should be postponed" (January 4, 1965). Similar requests came from the Swiss (January 15, 1965) and Dutch (March 28, 1965) episcopal conferences.

These petitions were studied at the fifth general meeting of the Consilium (April 1965). The Fathers showed themselves in favor of the experiment. The Consilium regarded it as an excellent means of quickly securing valuable information for a future judgment, since the experiment would involve peoples who differed in culture, preparation, and mentality. In addition, the experiment would facilitate the organizational work involved in producing an official set of Scripture readings for Mass.

At an audience on May 12, 1965, Cardinal Lercaro brought the matter up once more to the Holy Father, who now acceded to the requests of the episcopal conferences of Germany, Switzerland, and the Netherlands.[3]

In order that the experiment might be conducted in an orderly manner and not be prejudicial to the future work of the Consilium, the latter laid down the following conditions:

1) The readings of the new Lectionary could be used at Masses of the third and fourth class that had no proper readings of their own; in addition to the series of readings from the Gospels, the first year of the cycle was to have another New Testament reading, the second year an Old Testament reading.

2) These readings could also be used in Masses for the dead, except on November 2.

3) The use of the permission to experiment was optional and left to the responsibility of each bishop.

4) A detailed report was to be made on the advantages and disadvantages of the system.

---

2. See *Not* no. 13 (1963) 133–39.
3. Letter from the Secretariat of State, June 28, 1965 (No. 36624).

5) The experiment was to end once the Lectionary for the universal Church was published.[4]

The announcement of the permission roused great interest, and a number of other conferences asked if they might join in the experiment.[5]

2. The French Plan

After Germany, France too drew up a plan that was approved for experiment, on the same conditions, on April 20, 1966.[6] The readings were published by the Centre Nationale de Pastorale Liturgique in pamphlets entitled *Lectures pour les Messes de semaine*.

This Lectionary was based on the principle of the continuous reading (*lectio continua*) of books of the Bible; the purpose of this was to make the faithful aware of the main lines of the economy of salvation. Once this principle was followed, however, it was no longer possible to correlate the two readings.

The first reading was taken now from the New Testament, now from the Old, a shift from the one to the other taking place every two or three weeks. Since only a small part of the Old Testament could be read, preference was given to the Law and the Prophets. The readings were generally short. For the gospel, the passages peculiar to a given evangelist were chosen, but parallel passages were included (though not more than two for the same event or parable).

The songs between the readings were chosen for their relevance to one of the two readings, preferably the first.[7]

The French system was adopted in the French-speaking countries but also by some others.

3. The Consilium Plan

The set of readings prepared by the Consilium was presented to the conferences that had not asked for permission to use the German or the French plan.[8]

---

4. See "Ordo lectionum per ferias," *Not* 2 (1966) 6–7; "Quaedam quaestiones circa usum Ordinis lectionum per ferias," *ibid.*, 3 (1967) 13–14.

5. Each conference could present a plan of its own. In general, however, one of three was adopted: the German plan, with the addition of a set of pericopes for weekday Masses with children; the French plan; or the Consilium plan. The German plan was in two volumes entitled *Perikopenbuch für die Messfeier an Wochentagen* (Einsiedeln–Freiburg–Salzburg, 1966).

6. See *Not* 2 (1966) 168.

7. See "Plan d'ensemble du Lectionnaire férial français," *Not* 2 (1966) 169–71; L. Deiss, C.S.Sp., "Le psaume graduel," *ibid.*, 365–72.

8. "Ordo lectionum per ferias a Consilio propositus," *Not* 3 (1967) 9–12.

It followed the calendar then in use, even for those parts that it was foreseen would be changed, such as Septuagesima, Passiontide, the Ember Days, and the octave of Pentecost. The general principles governing the Lectionary had been approved by the Consilium at its general meeting of October 1966, along with the schemas for the weekday readings of Advent, Christmas, Epiphany, and the Easter season.

After general information the schema gave the list of pericopes for the various seasons of the liturgical year. This order of readings was the one that, with suitable changes suggested by experiment, would be adopted three years later as the usage of the Roman Rite.

The new system of readings for weekdays reached the entire Church in one or other of the three plans just described[9] and was met with very lively interest. One proof of this is the many publications aimed at helping the faithful to understand and meditate on the Scriptures read each day in the liturgy of the Mass.[10]

4. *Special Lectionaries*

Relish for the Sacred Scriptures also created a desire to have a variety of readings for particular circumstances. Some schemas were prepared that were handed from one conference to another and, after approval by the Consilium, were widely used. Ten series were approved for the following Masses: Sacred Heart of Jesus, the Blessed Virgin at the Marian shrines, confirmation, sacred orders, marriage, the dead, funerals of adults and children, the unity of Christians, children and adolescents, and the summer camps of the scouts.

The list of these sets of readings was published in an issue of *Notitiae* that was immediately sold out. Some of the sets were especially full; that for the Blessed Virgin had seventy-eight numbers, that for the scouts eighty-eight.[11] The word of God was on its way to reconquering the people of God.

II. Lectionary for Mass

Study group 11 was given one of the most difficult tasks of the entire reform: the reorganization of the readings for Mass.[12] This was the most

---

9. There are some statistics in *Not* 2 (1966) 372: 22,000 copies printed in France; used in all the parishes of the diocese of Lugano, in 15,000 churches of Spain, and 20,000 of Italy.

10. See *Not* 3 (1967) 112.

11. See *Not* 4 (1968) 41–88. To be added is the set of readings published later on "for the sick," in *Not* 6 (1970) 13–21.

12. The group initially included: *relator:* G. Diekmann; *secretary:* G. Fontaine; *members:*

important part of the work of restoring esteem and appreciation of the word of God in the liturgy, an area that the Catholic Church had undoubtedly neglected somewhat in recent centuries.

1. Goal

The Constitution on the Liturgy orders that "in sacred celebrations there is to be more reading from holy Scripture and it is to be more varied and apposite" (no. 35.1). This principle is subsequently applied to the Mass: "The treasures of the Bible are to be opened up more lavishly, so that a richer share in God's word may be provided for the faithful. In this way a more representative portion of holy Scripture will be read to the people in the course of a prescribed number of years" (no. 51).

These prescriptions were concerned primarily with Sundays and feastdays. A new system of readings had therefore to be designed that would take into account the existing cycle, the findings of comparative liturgy, and the needs of today's faithful.

2. Principles

These were set forth by the relator, Father Diekmann, at the second general meeting of the Consilium (April 1964).[13]

The basic principle is that "the mystery of Christ and the history of salvation" must be presented in the readings. Therefore, the new system of readings must contain the whole nucleus of the apostolic preaching about Jesus as "Lord and Christ" (Acts 2:36) who fulfilled the Scriptures by his life, his preaching, and, above all, his paschal mystery and who gives life to the Church until his glorious return.

The new Lectionary must make clear:

—that the Church is today living out the mystery of salvation in its entirety, the mystery that found its complete form in Christ and that must also be completed in us;

H. Schürmann, P. Jounel, P. Massi, E. Lanne, H. Kahlefeld. In November 1965, J. Féder was added. In June 1965, Father Diekmann asked to be replaced because of commitments at the national level (United States) and because of the difficulties of attending frequent team meetings abroad; C. Vagaggini replaced him as relator. G. Fontaine remained secretary; at the end of 1964 he had given up his work as director of the liturgical movement in Canada in order to be completely at the disposal of the Consilium. As close collaborator of Father Vagaggini, he became one of the creators of the Lectionary for Mass. The original group was subsequently expanded to include other members, finally numbering seventeen, all chosen from an international field in the areas of liturgy, Bible, catechetics, and pastoral care. The added members were: A. Rose, A. Nocent, A.-M. Roguet, K. Tilmann, H. Oster, J. Gaillard, H. Marot, and L. Deiss.

13. G. Diekmann, "De lectionibus in Missa," Not 1 (1965) 333–37.

—the mysteries of faith and the principles governing Christian life, which are then to be explained in the homily;

—that the entire Old Testament is presupposed in the Lord's preaching, his actions, and his passion;

—that attention to the central theme, the Lord's Pasch, must not lead to forgetfulness of other themes, for example, the coming of God's reign;

—finally, that the liturgical year provides the ideal setting for proclaiming the message of salvation to the faithful in an organized way.

Father Diekmann explained the first outlines made by the study group for the reform of the Lectionary, and the Consilium then approved some guidelines:

> 1) On Sundays, first- and second-class feasts of the Lord, and holy days of obligation, the Mass is to have three readings, though it will be permitted to drop the first (prophet) or the second (apostle) depending on the special circumstances of the congregation.
>
> 2) Even in a system of readings covering a three- or four-year period, there is always to be a one-year cycle of readings for some Sundays and principal feasts, so that the same passages will always be read on these days.
>
> 3) The tradition is to be kept of having certain books of Scripture assigned to certain seasons of the year.
>
> 4) In distributing the readings from Sacred Scripture, the principal part, both of the Old and the New Testament, is to be assigned to the Missal, while the part assigned to the Breviary is to be looked upon as a kind of complement to the readings in the Missal.

The work began immediately and ran the following course:

Schema 1	(principles)	October 1, 1964
Schema 2	(report)	August 20, 1965
Schema 3	(report)	October 2, 1965
Schema 4	(problems)	November 20, 1965
Schema 5	(OT pericopes)	December 11, 1965
Schema 6	(NT pericopes)	December 22, 1965
Schema 7	(questions)	March 31, 1966
Schema 8	(report)	May 4, 1966
Schema 9	(minutes)	May 16, 1966
Schema 10	(principles; list of pericopes)	July 25, 1966[14]
Schema 11	(report)	September 19, 1966
Schema 12	(weekdays of Ordinary Time)	September 27, 1966
Schema 13	(report)	October 5, 1966
Schema 14	(minutes)	October 17, 1966

---

14. Minority report on the question of whether there should be a three-year or a four-year cycle of readings; see below, p. 417 (*Schemata*, no. 184: *De Missali* 26).

Schema 15	(weekdays of Ordinary Time)	October 28, 1966
Schema 16 & 17	(experimental weekday Lectionary)	November 9, 1966; 1967
Schema 18	(order of readings)	1967[15]
Schema 19	(corrections)	April 6, 1967
Schema 20	(additions)	November 16, 1967[16]

3. Collection of Materials

A first substantial labor was to gather together the "building materials." This work proceeded along four lines:

1) Father Fontaine made a systematic collection of the biblical passages used in the various liturgies, ancient and modern, Western and Eastern, both in the Catholic Church and in the non-Catholic ecclesial communities:

—in the Western liturgies: Roman, Gallican, Ambrosian, Spanish, and Italian (North and South Italy);

—in the Eastern liturgies: ancient liturgy of Jerusalem, Nestorian, Jacobite, Syro-Catholic, Syro-Malancar, Syro-Chaldean, Syro-Malabar, Jacobite of India, Maronite, Armenian, Coptic, and Byzantine;

—in the liturgies of the Reformed Churches: Anglican of England and India, Reformed Church of France, Lutheran Church of the Scandinavian countries, Old Catholic Church of Germany—all down to our day.

This work of comparative liturgy summarized eighty years of scholarly research. In over fifty splendid comparative tables, these workers of the liturgical reform had managed to show how the Bible had been used in the Eucharistic celebration over the course of eighteen centuries. Their labors made it possible to identify constants and variants, and thus pointed out a sure path that the new organization of readings might follow. Their work also made it possible for "sound tradition" to be "retained," while yet allowing "the way [to] remain open to legitimate progress" and "any new forms . . . [to] grow organically from forms already existing" (SC 23).

2) In 1965 thirty-one Bible scholars[17] were given the task of selecting from all the books of the Old and New Testaments the passages that they

---

15. This was the schema printed "pro manuscripto" for purposes of consultation; see below, p. 419.

16. Completion of the *Ordo lectionum* in the sections on the Commons, the votive and ritual Masses, and the sanctoral; see below, p. 423, n. 22.

17. *Genesis, Exodus:* L. Alonso-Schökel, S.J.; *Leviticus, Numbers, Deuteronomy:* H. Cazelles, P.S.S.; *Judges:* P. Rossano and T. Matura, O.F.M.; *Joshua:* R. MacKenzie, S.J.; *Ruth:* P. Rossano and T. Matura, O.F.M.; *1-2 Samuel (1-2 Kings), 1-2 Kings (3-4 Kings):* T. Matura, O.F.M., and P. Beauchamp, S.J.; *1-2 Chronicles (1-2 Paralipomena):* A. Brune, O.P., and P. Beauchamp, S.J.; *Ezra, Nehemiah (1–2 Ezra):* A. George, S.M.; *Tobit:* T. Federici; *Judith, Esther:* A. Barucq, S.D.B.; *Job:* L. Alonso-Schökel; *Proverbs:* H. Duesberg, O.S.B., and F. Vattioni; *Ecclesiastes*

regarded as best suited for liturgical use. They were also asked to say for which liturgical season or feast they thought the various passages were best adapted, and to mark divisions and, possibly, omissions. The guideline given them was to choose passages that they judged easily understandable by the people and best suited for conveying a grasp of the economy of salvation.

The list produced by this group of scholars was sent to about a hundred catechetical experts or pastors. The responses yielded some twenty-five hundred slips containing useful aids for the selection of passages, their division, and their liturgical utilization.

3) In addition to setting up this work of collecting materials, the secretariat organized a series of studies that would facilitate use of the material:

H. Schürmann, plan for revision of the pericopes now used

J. Feder, selection of Sunday readings for mission countries

E. Lanne, the Byzantine Lectionary

H. Marot, the Anglican Lectionary

P. Borella, the Ambrosian Lectionary

J. Matéos, the Syriac Lectionaries

J. Pinell, the Spanish Lectionaries

A. Chavasse, plan for the Lenten Lectionary

A. Nocent, plan for an Advent and Christmas Lectionary (to January 13 inclusive)

J. Gaillard, plan for a Lectionary for the Easter season

P. Jounel, details of the Scripture readings in the Neogallican Missals

A.-M. Roguet, corrections in the present pericopes

P. Gy, plan for reform of the period after Pentecost

Monks of Encalcat: list of the principal Marian readings

(Qoheleth): H. Duesberg, O.S.B.; *Song of Songs*: A. Feuillet, P.S.S.; *Wisdom, Ecclesiasticus (Ben Sira)*: H. Duesberg, O.S.B.; *Isaiah*: J. Guillet, S.J., and P. Auvray, C. O.; *Jeremiah*: R. Tournay, O.P.; *Ezekiel*: P. Auvray, C. O.; *Daniel*: T. Matura, O.F.M.; *Hosea*: E. Osty, P.S.S., E. Beauchamp, O.F.M., and G. Rinaldi, C.R.S.; *Joel*: G. Bressan, F.D.P., G. Rinaldi, C.R.S., and I. Trinquet, P.S.S.; *Amos*: E. Osty, P.S.S., E. Beauchamp, O.F.M., and G. Rinaldi, C.R.S.; *Jonah*: A. Feuillet, P.S.S.; *Micah*: A. George, S.M.; *Habakkuk*: T. Matura, O.F.M.; *Zephaniah*: A. George, S.M.; *Haggai*: T. Matura, O.F.M.; *Zechariah, Malachi*: G. Rinaldi, G.R.S.; *1-2 Maccabees*: R. MacKenzie, S.J.; *Matthew, Mark, Luke*: H. Schürmann; *John*: D. Mollat, S.J.; *Acts*: J. Dupont, O.S.B.; *Romans*: S. Lyonnet, S.J.; *1-2 Corinthians*: R. Schnackenburg; *Galatians*: F. Mussner; *Ephesians*: P. Benoit, O.P., and F. Vattioni; *Philippians, Colossians*: P. Benoit, O.P., and X. Léon-Dufour, S.J.; *1-2 Thessalonians*: B. Rigaux, O.F.M.; *1-2 Timothy, Titus*: R. Schnackenburg; *Hebrews*: C. Spicq, O.P.; *James, 1-2 Peter*: T. Matura, O.F.M.; *1-2 John*: I. de la Potterie, S.J., and T. Matura, O.F.M.; *Revelation*: T. Matura, O.F.M.

4) Finally, the members of the group were asked to draw up preliminary schemas. The work was distributed as follows:

—Sundays of Advent: A. Nocent
—Weekdays of Advent: G. Fontaine
—Sundays and weekdays of the Christmas season: P. Jounel
—Sundays after Epiphany: A. Nocent
—Sundays and weekdays of Lent: G. Fontaine
—Sundays and weekdays of the Easter season: J. Gaillard
—Sundays after Pentecost: A. Nocent

4. Discussion at the Seventh General Meeting (1966)

Two whole years of study and meetings (fourteen of them, held in various parts of Europe) made it possible to see more clearly the direction to be taken in the new Lectionary.

Another major help was the experience derived from experiments under way in many countries with the weekday Lectionaries that had been drawn up by the various episcopal conferences.

In May 1966 the entire set of problems raised by the research and study done on the Scripture readings were examined by the relators of the Consilium (Schema 8). Finally, at the seventh general meeting of the Consilium (October 1966), Father Vagaggini was able to present the body with a fully developed, ninety-three-page comprehensive plan for the new organization of the readings at Mass. This was the result of long and persevering work in the biblical, liturgical, and pastoral areas. As a matter of fact, the many lists in the booklet had been made possible solely by the tables which Father Fontaine had drawn up and in which the Consilium was given a splendid bird's-eye view of the various systems followed in the readings at Mass over the centuries. This demanding preparatory work was indispensable if the new system of readings was to have a surely and reliable basis.

Three points in particular that emerged from the very lively discussion deserve to be noted:

1. *Obligation of three readings.* In 1964 Father Diekmann had suggested that of the three readings, the first or the second should be optional. The Fathers had accepted the suggestion, but Bishop Jenny had asked that the decision not be final and that after a suitable period of experimentation, the question might again be presented to the Consilium. Two years later, first at the meeting of the relators (May 11–12, 1966) and then at the general meeting of the Consilium (October 10, 1966), Father Vagaggini proposed that the three readings be made obligatory. His reasons were these:

—the fulfillment of the Council's desire that "a more representative portion (*praestantior pars*)" of the Scriptures be read to the people;

—a return to the purest and earliest tradition as attested by St. Augustine and St. Ambrose and still found in various liturgies (Ambrosian, Gallican, Spanish);

—three readings are needed in order to see the unity of the two Testaments and of the entire history of salvation;

—if one of the first two readings is left optional, experience shows that the Old Testament passage will regularly go unread, as is the case among the Ambrosians, Syrians, Chaldeans, and Armenians.

In response to these arguments, the *periti* maintained that:

—the faithful are not yet prepared to listen to three readings; it is necessary to proceed gradually;

—nor do the clergy have sufficient training in the Bible; therefore, let the use of two or three readings be left to the judgment of the rector of the church.

The Fathers, however, were more optimistic. If two passages are read in one church and three in another, the faithful will be confused (Rossi). The whole subject is important for ecumenism: only by a habitual three readings will Catholics rediscover the Scriptures (Pellegrino). This is a unique opportunity to re-educate the people in the Bible (Hervas). We bemoan the absence of the Old Testament (for example, the Psalms) from our spirituality; we must see to it that the faithful once again acquire a taste for the Old Testament; the Council wants the history of salvation to be the basis of theology and Christian life; therefore three readings should be obligatory (Volk). The Old Testament is not difficult to understand if it is studied along with the New (Bea). Let us not waste this unique opportunity, if one of the readings can be omitted, all will inevitably omit the first, and thus the Old Testament will no longer be read (Jenny). And finally Cardinal Pellegrino noted: "A priest coming to celebrate in another church will never know which readings will be used and how to prepare his homily."

After this heartfelt and passionate defense, the Fathers voted to accept the three readings as obligatory. Thus October 10, 1966, proved to be a day of special "good omen" (*dies faustus*), a day full of promise and hope for the pastoral life of the Church.

2. *Should the present cycle be kept or abandoned?* Some members suggested that the Lectionary presently in use be kept intact and serve as one of the cycles, out of respect for tradition and for ecumenical reasons, since most of the Churches issuing from the Reformation use the traditional Lectionary. The ecumenical argument was given great weight in the dis-

cussion, but Father Vagaggini demonstrated, ably and skillfully, that it was in fact weak. He did so by showing, evidence in hand, what the real situation was:

a) In 1965 the Anglican Churches, headed by the "London Group," proposed to abandon the traditional cycle and establish a new Lectionary with a two-year cycle.

b) In 1962 the Anglicans of India, Pakistan, Bermuda, and Ceylon drew up a new list of readings for Sundays and feasts as a supplement to the Prayer Book.

c) In Germany the Evangelische Michaelsbrüderschaft has added a list of twenty-eight optional pericopes to the traditional Lectionary.

d) The Lutheran Church of Germany follows the traditional Lectionary, but for preaching it uses a Lectionary compiled in 1945. In 1953 the Lutheran Liturgical Conference of Germany accepted the possibility of a further reform of the Lectionary.

e) The Lutheran Church of Switzerland and Denmark use both the traditional Lectionary and another that is optional.

f) In 1953 the Reformed Church of France adopted a new Lectionary with three readings and three cycles.

g) The Old Catholics follow the traditional Lectionary, but have adopted an optional three series of other readings; they thus have four cycles in all.

The group's dealings with the secretariats of the various Protestant confessions show that all profoundly desire a revision of the Lectionary and look with sympathy on this undertaking of the Catholic Church.

The members of the group and the relators are of the opinion that the Consilium must not without good reason consider itself bound to the old Lectionary: (a) this is the first time in the history of the Church that the opportunity has arisen of revising it, and this in hitherto unparalleled favorable circumstances and with hitherto unavailable tools; (b) if the old Lectionary, whose defects everyone knows, is retained as one of the annual cycles, there will be major differences between that cycle and the others; (c) changes in the calendar and the addition of an Old Testament reading necessarily require changes in the other readings; (d) only the Lutherans of Germany want to hold on to the old Lectionary; the other Churches are searching for new paths and waiting for the Catholics to do the same; (e) it would be very desirable for all Christians to have a single Lectionary, but if such a goal is ever reached, it will take a long time; meanwhile, the Roman Church will be in danger of losing a great and sure good.

In order to have further evidence of what the relator had said about the position of the non-Catholic ecclesial communities, a meeting of the consultors and the observers was held on October 8. The observers read a statement in the public assembly in which they asked the Roman Church not to consider itself obliged for ecumenical reasons to abstain from revising the Lectionary. They also expressed the wish that the revised Lectionary be allowed experimentally for a rather lengthy period (six to nine years) in order that the various Christian confessions might examine it during that time.[18]

The vote that followed found the Fathers expressing an approval that was unanimous with a single exception.

3. *A three-year cycle or a four-year cycle?* The third problem that greatly concerned the Consilium in the fall of 1964 was the number of cycles in the Lectionary. The language of the liturgical Constitution (no. 51) had been vague: "in the course of a prescribed number of years" ("inter praestitutum annorum spatium"). The *periti* were convinced from the outset that a two-year cycle would be insufficient. The various systems devised by the non-Catholic confessions all required three or four years.

It was also in terms of "three or four?" that the experts approached the system to be used by the Catholic Church. In three years it would be possible to read "a more representative portion of holy Scripture" (*SC* 51). In addition, a three-year cycle would have the advantage of being geared to the Synoptics, with one of the first three Gospels being assigned to each year. In a four-year cycle, on the other hand, it would be necessary to fall back on very short pericopes (*logia Domini*) or passages of little catechetical value.

Group 11 decided, with the practical approval of Schürmann and Kahlefeld, who had been arguing for a four-year cycle, to develop a triennial system. If it turned out that valuable passages were thereby neglected, the group declared itself ready to turn to the other system. In order that there might be no residual doubts, the minority was asked to prepare a report in which they would defend their viewpoint to the Consilium.

The vote that followed the discussion on October 10, 1966, yielded the same results as the vote on the preceding question: "All approve, with one exception."

In this way the Roman liturgy acquired a three-year cycle of readings for Sundays and feasts, that is, for the days when the Christian community truly gathers for common prayer. The result was that the faithful could recover an understanding and taste for the word of God, after cen-

18. See above, pp. 200–201.

turies of neglect and abandonment had caused the fresh and authentic stream of that word to be lost in rivulets and ravines.

5. *Report to the Pope*

In the report on the eleventh general meeting, which was given to the Holy Father on November 10, 1966, the relator of group 11 summed up as follows the end results of the long and complex development of the Lectionary for Mass.

1) *Sundays and feast days.* Sundays and feasts will have three readings: Old Testament, apostle, and gospel. Not only will the number of passages read be increased, but there will be a broader vision of the history of salvation, which will be seen from its earliest foreshadowings to its fulfillment.

—The three readings will be obligatory. If one is left optional, it will be regularly omitted, to the detriment of a progressive introduction of the faithful to the knowledge and love of the Scriptures. The overall length of the three readings will usually not be significantly greater than that of the present two readings.

—The Lectionary for feasts will be arranged in a three-year cycle, so that the same passage is read every third year. This will also mean a greater variety in subjects for the homily.

—In keeping with tradition, some books will be read during specified periods; for example, the Gospel of John during the second part of Lent and during the Easter season; the Acts of the Apostles during the Easter season.

—On the Sundays of Ordinary Time one of the three Synoptic Gospels will be read in each year of the cycle; there will thus be a Matthew year, a Mark year, and a Luke year. It will be possible in this way to bring out more fully the characteristics of each Gospel. The parts of John that are not read in the other seasons of the year will be used in the Mark year, since Mark is the shortest of the Synoptics.

—Except in Advent and Lent, there will be a semi-continuous reading of each Gospel. The other readings will be harmonized more or less closely with the gospel, so that as far as is feasible, there will be a thematic unity that will ease the preacher's task.

—In this selection of passages, those will be omitted that require a complex exegetical or literal explanation before any spiritual application is possible. This does not mean, however, the exclusion of all texts that may be somewhat difficult, simply because they are difficult; the homily, after all, has for one of its functions to explain the meaning of the sacred text in its context.

—For some readings that would be very long if read in their entirety (for example, the stories of the Samaritan woman and the man born blind), the Lectionary will indicate how the passage may be shortened in a way that retains the essential parts of the pericope. In a limited number of cases, moreover, an alternate optional reading will be given that has the same meaning; the celebrant can choose it if he thinks it fits better with the concrete situation of the congregation before him.

2) *Weekday readings.* A further expansion of the knowledge of Scripture will be made possible by the series of weekday readings, which will be independent of the festive Lectionary. Each day will have its own reading from Scripture at Mass, just as it does in the Office. It will thus be possible on weekdays to avoid repetition of the Sunday readings and of the same readings in the Common of the Saints.

The principles governing the organization of the ferial or weekday Lectionary are the following:

—For the weekdays of Advent, the Christmas season, Lent, and the Easter season, there will be a one-year cycle for both readings.

—For the weekdays of Ordinary Time, the gospel will be arranged according to an annual cycle; the first reading, on the other hand, will follow a two-year cycle, with alternating weeks of Old Testament and New Testament passages.

—In the case of some books, the arrangement of the readings will take tradition into account (for example, Isaiah in Advent; the Acts of the Apostles and the Gospel of John during the Easter season); the others will be read according to their order in the canon of the Bible.

—These weekday readings will be used at Masses of the third and fourth class, which do not have readings of their own.

6. *Consultation*

In accordance with these principles, the group drafted a Lectionary. It was decided that it should be published *pro manuscripto* and made the subject of a lengthy questionnaire distributed to scholars and people engaged in pastoral care.

As a result, the *Ordo lectionum pro dominicis, feriis et festis sanctorum* was published in July 1967. The 474-page volume became the subject of extensive deliberation on the part of all the episcopal conferences, the participants in the first Synod of Bishops, and some eight hundred experts on Scripture, liturgy, catechesis, and pastoral care, who were appointed by the episcopal conferences.

On the basis of 460 responses received (300 pages of general remarks and 6650 file cards on the various texts), the system was radically revised in January 1968: passages regarded as too difficult were eliminated; missing passages were added; the division into verses was improved; the readings for the Sundays of Lent and some major feasts were changed. The most important changes were made on the occasion of the tenth general meeting of the Consilium (April 1968). The part of the Lectionary for the special seasons was reviewed at three meetings held at Laveno near Milan (January 29–February 2), Saint-Odile near Strasbourg (March 4–8), and Neuilly-sur-Seine (April 1–5, 1968).

It was the *periti* to whom the international questionnaire had been sent who suggested that on the major solemnities alternative passages be provided at least for the gospel, without the feast thereby losing its characteristic tonality.[19]

The final meetings, held in the winter of 1968–69, were devoted to the other parts of the Lectionary: sanctoral, Commons, ritual Masses, and Masses for various needs. The special Lectionaries that had been compiled for the period of experimentation facilitated the work in these areas.

7. *Papal Approval*

In May 1969 the proofs for the Lectionary were given to the Pope, who sent the following handwritten note of approval to Cardinal Benno Gut, prefect of the Congregation for Divine Worship:

> In the very limited time allowed me, I have not been able to get a complete and detailed grasp of this new and extensive *Ordo lectionum Missae.*
>
> But because of the confidence I have in the skilled and devout individuals who spent a long time compiling it, and because of the trust I owe to the Congregation for Divine Worship, which has examined and corrected it with such expert care, I gladly approve it in the name of the Lord.
>
> The feast of St. John the Baptist, June 24, 1969.
>
> Paul VI, Pope

8. *Publication*

The new system of readings was promulgated for the entire Church on Pentecost, May 25, 1969, by decree of the Congregation for Divine Worship.[20] From the typographical standpoint, the volume, which ap-

19. See *Schemata,* no. 286 (*De Missali* 49), April 6, 1968.

20. Decree: *DOL* 231 no. 1842. — *Ordo lectionum Missae* (Vatican Polyglot Press, 1969. 434 pp.). See *Not* 5 (1969) 237, 240–45 (= *Praenotanda*); G. Fontaine, "Commentarium in Ordinem lectionum Missae," *ibid.,* 256–82; idem, "Le Lectionnaire de la Messe au temps de l'Avent," *ibid.,* 7 (1971) 304–17; see also A. Bugnini's article in *L'Osservatore Romano,* May 14, 1969, and G. Fontaine in *EL* 83 (1969) 436–51.

A second edition of the *Ordo lectionum Missae* was published in 1981. In this edition the

peared at the end of June, was truly an *editio princeps:* 500 pages in large format (21 x 39 cm.). This unusual format was chosen precisely because of the many six-column tables, which required a great deal of space.

The volume contains: (1) a general introduction, which gives the principles behind the choice of readings, the overall organization for each season of the year, and the practical regulations for translation into the vernaculars; (2) the Lectionary proper, subdivided into six parts: seasonal Proper (Sundays, feasts, and weekdays); Proper of the Saints, arranged according to the new calendar; Commons; ritual Masses; Masses for various occasions; and votive Masses; (3) the volume ends with a full index of all the passages and verses of the Bible that have been used or cited.[21]

9. Festal Lectionary

For Sundays and feasts three readings are given; the finest passages from the Old and New Testaments are read. The three readings represent a return to the authentic early tradition as attested for Rome until the fifth century and maintained subsequently at Milan and in the East by the Armenians (three readings), the Copts (four readings), and the Syrians (six readings). The episcopal conferences, however, have authority in their own territories to allow only two readings. The major feasts have their own readings.

Harmonization of the three readings or continuous reading of a book of Scripture? This is one of the crucial issues that disturbed not a few of those who were effecting the reform. For some years priests had been complaining about the disparity among the Sunday readings and asking for the texts to be more homogeneous. But any homogeneity had been difficult to achieve with the old system, and the commentators and the missalettes for the people did their best to show how each reading of a Mass was independent of the other.

Praenotanda were greatly expanded, and readings were added for the sacramental rites published since 1969 and for the new Masses included in the second edition of the Missal (1975). See "De editione typica altera Ordinis lectionum Missae," along with the decree of the Congregation for the Sacraments and Divine Worship (January 21, 1981), and the *Praenotanda*, in *Not* 17 (1981) 357–409; and "Variazioni della editio typica altera," *ibid.*, 410–62. The decree and the new introduction ("Prologue") are translated in the second edition of the *Lectionary for Mass* (Collegeville, 1986), iii–iv and 1–41 respectively.

21. The *Ordo lectionum Missae* contains only the lists of pericopes. The actual texts were published in full, in Latin, later on: *Lectionarium* I. *De tempore ab Adventu ad Pentecosten* (Vatican Polyglot Press, 1970. 892 pp.); II. *Tempus per annum post Pentecosten* (1971. 964 pp.); III. *Pro Missis de sanctis, ritualibus, ad diversa, votivis et defunctorum* (1972. 972 pp.). See "Il lezionario latino della Messa," *Not* 8 (1972) 246–48.

More specific requests came in that the Scripture readings should deal with the great themes of Christian life, which might then provide the subject of the homily. Some even suggested that each Sunday in Ordinary Time be devoted to a special catechetical theme: a Sunday on faith, another on hope, another on love of God, and so on.

But a rigid and artificial thematization decreed by a program of instruction on abstract subjects was impossible, and the Consilium unanimously rejected it. The liturgy has its own more natural and flexible way of achieving unity in the Mass. It seemed unnatural and forced to impose the same homiletic subject on the entire world on the same day. Teaching should flow in a humanly more varied and diversified way from the living word and be an echo of that word. For this reason a middle way was chosen: the Old Testament reading and the gospel generally display an accord based on objective elements within the readings.

Outside the main liturgical seasons, an effort is made to have a semi-continuous reading of the New Testament letters and the Gospels in two independent cycles. It is semi-continuous because it is not possible to read the entire New Testament on Sundays. Some difficult passages and passages of lesser importance have therefore been moved to the weekday Lectionary or the Divine Office.

10. *Weekday Lectionary*

This displays three characteristics:

1) Apart from Sundays, solemnities, and some special celebrations, the Lectionary never has more than two readings: the first from the Old or New Testament, and the second from the Gospel. No weekday, even Ash Wednesday, has more than two readings.

2) In the special seasons of the liturgical year, there is a one-year cycle of weekday readings. In the thirty-four weeks of Ordinary Time, on the other hand, the first reading follows a two-year cycle; the gospel readings always form an annual cycle. This system allows the reading of a larger number of passages.

3) The weekday Lectionary, which is entirely independent of the festal Lectionary, is based on the principle of the semi-continuous reading of the sacred books. The more important books are read extensively; characteristic passages are selected from the others.

In Advent and Lent the Old Testament readings and the gospels are generally harmonized. During the Christmas and Easter seasons the two readings form two independent series.

11. *Lectionary for the Saints*

Two sets of readings are given—one for the Proper and one for the Common. In the former, special, suitable texts are given for each saint, or else the celebrant is referred to the Common.[22] Solemnities have three readings, feasts and memorials have two. Proper texts in the strict sense are those that refer directly to the saint being celebrated; in practice, only these passages are obligatory (for example: St. Mary Magdalene on July 22; St. Martha on July 29).

Each category of saint included in the Commons is provided with a rather extensive selection of readings from the Old and New Testaments. The selection is especially abundant in the inclusive Common of Holy Men and Women (sixty-one passages); more appropriate passages are indicated for some of the categories under this comprehensive heading.

12. *Masses for Various Occasions*

Finally, there is a very abundant selection of readings for the ritual Masses, the Masses for special occasions, and the votive Masses. At a later date, further enrichments were made, since at the time when the Lectionary was published, not all of the sacramental rites had yet been completed and promulgated.

13. *Songs Between the Readings*

In order that the chant or song after the readings might be really a response to the word of God just heard, the entire system of chants was revised. The responsorial psalm that follows the first reading is chosen in function of that reading and completes it. The verses of the psalm are grouped in stanzas of equal length in order to facilitate its singing by the psalmist or cantor. The refrain, which consists of the most characteristic and meaningful verse of the psalm, explains why this psalm has been chosen.

Sundays and weekdays have their own special psalm. But two complementary lists are also supplied. The first gives a certain number of refrains that may be used during a particular season in place of the re-

---

22. The care expended on the revision in this area can be seen from Schema 327 (*De Missali* 59; November 16, 1968), in which, in the case of each saint with readings of his or her own, a detailed analysis is made to see whether the selection is legitimate and pastorally useful or, on the contrary, is connected rather with an unimportant episode in the saint's life or with a mere legend. The analysis takes into account the older Missal and any diocesan, local, or religious Propers in which the saint is assigned special readings. Further details in this regard are given in the *Praenotanda* of Volume III of the *Lectionarium*.

frain assigned to each day. This facilitates the singing of the refrain by the congregation. Thus, the cantor sings the psalm proper to the day, while the congregation frequently repeats the same refrain or refrains.

The gospel is usually preceded by a different type of song, one normally comprising two parts: a refrain of the congregation (usually an Alleluia, which is replaced by a different formula of praise during Lent). This acclamation precedes and follows a verse, which is a proper one in the case of solemnities but taken from a common repertory in other cases. Many of these verses are from the gospel, for which the song is a preparation. For this reason, and because of its paschal character, this song is sung standing.

14. *Initial Use*

The Congregation for Divine Worship was also concerned about the use to be made of this monumental opus that is the Lectionary for Mass. On July 15, 1969, it therefore issued a suitable instruction in which it provided the episcopal conferences with some guidelines.[23]

1) The First Sunday of Advent (November 30, 1969) is appointed as the first day on which the new Lectionary may be used along with the new Order of Mass. But the use is optional; it becomes obligatory when the episcopal conferences determine the date on which the vernacular Lectionary is to be placed in use in each country.

2) The considerable number of the readings will require that the new Lectionary be published in several volumes. The conferences will decide how to distribute the material among the various volumes in order to facilitate their liturgical use.

3) Provision must be made first for publication of the volumes with the readings for Sundays and feasts, beginning with the volume containing the readings of Year B, that is, the cycle used in the 1969–70 liturgical year.

4) Until the new weekday Lectionary is published, the systems presently being used in almost all countries may continue in use.

5) For the same reason, continued use may be made of the Roman Missal for the Proper and Common of the Saints, the votive Masses, and the Masses on various occasions until the new Lectionary is ready.

Other guidelines had to do with the translation and printing of Lectionaries in the vernacular.

---

23. *Instructio de editionibus apparandis et de usu novi Ordinis Lectionum Missae* (July 25, 1969): *Not* 5 (1969) 238–39; *DOL* 233 nos. 1879-77. See also "De textibus biblicis in editione latina Missalis romani et liturgiae horarum," *Not* 9 (1973) 39–40.

The preparation of the biblical Lectionary for Mass was one of the pillars of the liturgical reform. As Pope Paul VI wrote, the Church expected that the Lectionary would

> arouse among the faithful a greater hunger for the word of God. Under the guidance of the Holy Spirit, this hunger will seem, so to speak, to impel the people of the New Covenant toward the perfect unity of the Church. We are fully confident that under this arrangement both priest and faithful will prepare their minds and hearts more devoutly for the Lord's Supper and that, meditating on the Scriptures, they will be nourished more each day by the words of the Lord. In accord with the teachings of the Second Vatican Council, all will thus regard sacred Scripture as the abiding source of spiritual life, the foundation for Christian instruction, and the core of all theological study.[24]

---

24. Paul VI, apostolic constitution *Missale Romanum: DOL* 202 no. 1362.

27

Masses with Special Groups

While the liturgical reform was still in its early stages, the Congregation of Rites and the Consilium had to intervene in connection with the celebration of Mass in private homes. The press was giving wide publicity to the practice and suggesting that scandal was being given.[1]

The phenomenon became even more marked in the ensuing years. Among other things, ecclesial groups committed to the apostolate and evangelization were being formed, and their work involved at times the celebration of the Eucharist. The human setting (the young; apostolic groups), the place, the homes, the parish halls, the oratories—all these made it easy or even obligatory to introduce peculiarities into the celebration itself. A distinction may be made between Masses celebrated in homes and Masses celebrated with special groups.

I. Precedents

1. *Mass in the home.* Mass in this setting was connected with domestic events such as the birth of a child or anniversaries—all of them occasions on which the family invited relatives, friends, and neighbors to celebrate with them. In families that were more spiritually developed, the family feast became a religious one and included at times the celebration of the Eucharist.

---

1. See the declaration *Da qualche tempo* repudiating arbitrary liturgical innovations (December 29, 1966): *AAS* 59 (1967) 85–86; *DOL* 35 nos. 433-34. The declaration was explained to the press on January 4, 1967; see *Not* 3 (1967) 37f.

The phenomenon of the home Mass was more often connected with the work of evangelization as organized by pastors or associations for the family. People living in the same apartment house or neighborhood would take part. Proximity, friendship, the occasion, and the suitable time (usually the evening) made such meetings possible even for those who did not regularly attend church. The practice proved to be a very effective pastoral tool.[2]

Examples of meetings of this kind were those of *Domus Christianae* (belonging to the Citadella Cristiana di Assisi) or the "family gatherings" held throughout Colombia in preparation for the International Eucharistic Congress of 1968. Every Wednesday six thousand meetings were held in homes, presided over by as many "dialogue leaders," who had been suitably prepared by the various parishes. From the pastoral point of view, this was the most fruitful activity of the entire congress. The meetings were lengthy. Sometimes they ended with the celebration of Mass, or at least Mass was regarded as desirable and was requested.

These meetings, which were organized and regulated by the hierarchy, were very useful in grass-roots evangelization and were imitated by others. For example, meetings of this kind were held by the "Family Movement," which extended throughout Latin America.

In the English-speaking world (Great Britain, United States, Australia), periodic family meetings have been a longstanding practice under the heading of "Family Social Action." They are held weekly, and if a priest is present, Mass is celebrated.

2. *Masses for groups.* These, too, were connected with the evangelizing and instructional activities of youth groups, Catholic Action, the scouts, and similar associations. The pastoral activity of such groups underwent an extensive development after the Council, motivated by the difficulties met in evangelization and by new advances in pedagogy. The request was made that the group meetings might end with Mass.

---

2. See the collective work *La casa luogo dell'incontro con Cristo* (Assisi: Cittadella, 1968). At the Second General Conference of the Latin American Episcopate (Medellín, 1968), the bishops were handed a booklet entitled *El desarollo de la comunidad cristiana por medio de la liturgia doméstica*, composed by "a team of married people in the Movimento Familiar Cristiano." The assembly of bishops discussed the problem but left the issuance of regulations to the local Ordinaries.

On the occasion of its own Fifth Latin American Encounter (Santiago, Chile, September 22-29, 1969), the same organization published a *Folletto litúrgico* containing various items for the liturgical celebration and prayer and, in particular, Masses to be celebrated during the Encounter. Also included were a *Misa penitencial*, a *Liturgia doméstica*, and a *Misa Panamericana*. The contents were analyzed and critiqued in *Not* 6 (1970) 74-76.

At the same time a more specialized phenomenon, "youth Masses," came on the scene. This, too, had its phases of extensive growth, euphoria, and opposition.[3] The Masses in question were attended primarily by young people, often with their families. The intense participation and the dynamic, lively character of the celebration were impressive, deriving as they did, not from any eccentricities or extravagances, but simply from songs and music that respected the sensibilities of the young; from lively homilies which the priest had prepared during the week in collaboration with the young people and which were sometimes followed by interventions of these same young people; from the voicing of spontaneous intentions during the prayer of the faithful; and, finally, from the handclasp at the greeting of peace.[4]

As a rule, the structure of the Mass was as usual; it was only the external form that made it seem so different. This unusual outward form required, of course, that the priest in charge be himself a balanced person and have some liturgical training, which was not always the case. Oddities could and did occur that inevitably worried bishops and the Consilium, which heard echoes of such happenings from all over the world. A timely intervention of the Holy See was thought necessary in order to regulate matters before they went too far.

---

3. The starting point of the development may have been a "Youth Mass" composed by Maestro Giombini and performed for the first time in the Sala Borromini (Rome) on April 27, 1966. It was simply a piece of music performed by the entire Oratorio Filippino and was not intended immediately for use in worship; it was also an attempt at using modern music for the Mass.

The following period saw a multiplication of songs composed in the same style, which were, however, used in Masses with youth groups. At Rome the Youth Mass celebrated in the domestic chapel of the Marianum (Servants of Mary) received wide attention; it was subsequently celebrated in the parish church of the Canadian Martyrs and then in the chapel of the Collegio Leoniano. Others gradually followed the example. Some elements of this Mass, especially the music and songs, came to be used in almost all parishes, at least at Masses attended chiefly by young people. A connected problem, and one sometimes felt intensely, was the use of guitars and other musical instruments at Mass.

Here and there bishops attempted to intervene with guidelines; other bishops asked the Holy See for guidelines. In 1970 the Italian Episcopal Conference published regulations for youth Masses. The French concerned themselves with the problem at a broader level and took up the question of Masses with special groups at its plenary meeting in Lourdes (December 10-12, 1968). On January 15, 1969, after consulting the bishops, the Centre National de Pastorale Liturgique issued a "confidential" note on the celebration of Mass with small groups. See *Il Canto dell'Assemblea*, no. 16 (1968); *Phase* 48 (1968); *Art Sacré*, 1968 (fourth quarter).

4. All these things are now taken for granted, but at the time, when the transition was under way from an unyielding fixism to a degree of spontaneity, they attracted attention. Some people thought them a desecration. There were in fact reasons for confusion, especially with regard to the character of certain spontaneous interventions.

The original intention was to wait for the publication of the official liturgical books and then take up special problems of this sort. But, faced with the spread of home Masses and Masses for special groups, the Consilium judged that it should not delay any longer in handling the problem and should act now to avoid the danger "of being faced with situations that had reached the crisis stage, without having the time required for a calm examination of the matter and perhaps even being too late to apply any remedy." It was in these terms that the secretary of the Consilium wrote to the Secretariat of State on September 5, 1968, asking permission "to institute a study of 'Masses in a family setting' " and to take up the matter at the Consilium's meeting the following October.

The secretary had recently returned from the Eucharistic Congress in Bogotá, where he had become aware of how far the phenomenon had gone in Latin America. In addition, on his return he had found awaiting him a letter from Cardinal Pellegrino, dated August 14, 1968, which said:

> Some of my reading in recent days, together with requests that have come to me, have made me aware of a problem that must certainly be concerning you: the problem of "Mass in the home." I have thus far refused such requests, both because I do not think they are allowed for in the present law (except for the sick) and because it seems to me that the participants would need the kind of adequate theological, liturgical, and spiritual preparation which I cannot think is often to be found. It is easy, however, to anticipate that such requests will become more frequent. On the other hand, there seem to me to be objective reasons for allowing the practice, provided always that the requirement of attendance at the Sunday liturgical gathering is honored.
>
> Do you not think it would be advisable for the Consilium to pay urgent attention to this problem and issue the needed directives as soon as possible? Otherwise I fear that arbitrary practices will spread and it will be difficult to stem easily foreseeable abuses. It is my hope that others better prepared than I have anticipated me in this request and that the guidelines I suggest have already been adequately worked out.

As a matter of fact, requests of the same kind had also come from other bishops.

II. Study of the Problem

The permission to study the problem came from Cardinal Cicognani, Secretary of State, in a letter of September 18, 1968 (No. 123619), in which he said that the study should be undertaken conjointly with the Congregation for the Clergy. He added:

> It seems impossible in principle to allow the practice of Mass in private homes, and this for several reasons: abuses and arbitrary practices can eas-

ily arise; there will be an inevitable change in the Church's sense of community, with the larger community being replaced by the small clique; the hierarchic and unifying aspect of the Eucharist will be lost (see, for example, the Letters of St. Ignatius of Antioch to the Philadelphians, chapter 3; to the Ephesians, chapter 5; to the Trallians, chapters 2 and 3, and so on); there will be a danger of keeping ministers and faithful from serving and being present to the Christian people.

In this very sensitive matter it will therefore be necessary to impose limits and a discipline that will prevent the drawbacks listed.

On October 11, 1968, the Congregation for the Clergy submitted its opinion (Prot. No. 120242/I), which was substantially in favor of having two coexisting forms of Eucharistic celebration: in the churches and in special groups, provided that in the latter case a dignified place was chosen and that partiality and favoritism were avoided. It proposed that some guiding principles be issued for the episcopal conferences, and it suggested some conditions:

1) Authority to celebrate the Eucharist in private homes is reserved to the diocesan bishop; for the permission to be given, "a room must be available that is not used as a bedroom and that is suited for the celebration of Holy Mass."

2) No permission is to be given for holy days of obligation.

3) If the celebrant is not the local parish priest or one of the latter's regular assistants, the priest who is asked to celebrate and who has obtained the bishop's permission is also obliged to inform the pastor of the place. The latter is then to make a report on it and submit any remarks on the proper performance of the celebration. No general permissions are to be given, but only permission for single cases or for a limited number of celebrations, and the recipient is obliged to submit a report.

4) During his homily the celebrant should mention the permission received and "make it his concern to keep those present united, even psychologically, with the universal and diocesan Church."

5) The Eucharistic fast is always to be observed.

6) When a bishop grants the permission, he should ensure that the gatherings are not held late at night.

7) Access to the place of the liturgical celebration must never be refused to anyone who reasonably asks to participate, especially at meetings of family groups.

The entire problem was set before the Fathers of the Consilium at their closed meeting on October 14, 1968. They discussed it at length, bringing to bear the experiences of their own countries and, in some cases, the directives already issued there. It was finally decided to establish a small study group;[5] this group drew up a first, very brief draft and submitted it on the last day (October 17, 1968) of the eleventh general meeting.[6] This schema set forth the general principles to be kept in mind and gave some guidelines for possible adaptations and simplifications. The Fathers engaged in the discussion had some difficulty in distinguishing between Masses in private homes, which, according to the information available, was the most widespread practice, and Masses for special groups. The Fathers asked for clarification on this point.

In the next schema the generic title "small groups" included the various possible gatherings: family groups and associations, groups making a retreat, or other homogeneous groups. General principles were laid down that emphasized the need of communion with the parochial, diocesan, and universal Church, and repeated the broad lines of the instruction *Eucharisticum mysterium*. The suggestions of the Congregation for the Clergy were also included, and guidelines were given for the carrying out of the ritual. Here is a summary:

a) Introductory rite: If a meditation on Scripture or a period of spiritual instruction is followed by Mass, the opening rites are limited to a brief exhortation, the penitential act, the prayer of the day.

b) Liturgy of the Word: There can be a single reading (if so, it is the gospel), selected from those listed in the Lectionary.

c) Prayer of the faithful: This may be adapted to the group, but the universal intentions should never be omitted.

d) Communion: may be administered under both kinds.

e) Other adaptations thought to be necessary are to be examined by the episcopal conferences and submitted to the Holy See.

It was also urged that the celebration, and the furnishings as well, be noble and dignified.[7]

On January 20, 1969, the schema was discussed by a joint committee representing the Congregations of Rites, the Sacraments, and the Clergy.[8]

---

5. *President:* R. Weakland; *members:* J. Wagner, P. Jounel, F. McManus, J. Patino, P. Visentin, J. Cellier.

6. *Schemata,* no. 320: *De Missali* 57 (October 16, 1968).

7. A comparison of these guidelines—which were simple, general, sensitive to situations, careful to safeguard the dignity and sacral character of the celebrations, but also open to healthy adaptation—with the definitive guidelines finally issued shows the restrictive development that took place.

8. *Participants:* Cardinal Gut, president of the Consilium and prefect of the Congregation of Rites; Archbishop F. Antonelli, secretary of the same Congregation; Monsignors G. Casoria and L. Vetri, for the Congregation of the Sacraments; Monsignors Bovone and Rossetti, for the Congregation of the Clergy; and Fathers Bugnini and Braga, for the Consilium.

On January 28 it was sent, after slight modifications, to the Secretariat of State.

On February 8 the Pope granted an audience to the secretary of the Consilium and there gave him a memorandum containing a series of general requests regarding Masses for special groups.[9] Meanwhile, perhaps on the basis of the same set of requests, the Secretariat of State sent a questionnaire to the papal representatives.[10] The reports of the latter confirmed the extent and frequency of the problematic practice but certainly did not help to a suitable solution, since they gave extreme descriptions of some abuses or liberties taken.[11]

As a result, on March 9 (No. 132121) the Secretariat of State replied that in the planned document some principles needed to be reasserted

---

9. "It would be advisable to collect and summarize the information available on the celebration of Mass in 'spontaneous groups,' as they are called, in order to gain clarity on several points: the general characteristics of the phenomenon; who are promoting it; what typical forms it takes and which ones are most imitated; the role of the priest; the music and songs; the tendency of some lay promoters to do the preaching; the tendency to improvise the prayer of the faithful; whether and how communion is distributed; what sacred vestments and furnishings are used; whether the liturgical books prescribed by the Church are used; and, finally, whether it is necessary to remind people of certain principles and set down some regulations."

On February 27, 1969, Father Bugnini replied to each point in a seven-page statement, in which he explained the phenomenon, its manifestations, its positive side and its weaknesses, and its dangers. He concluded by suggesting two remedies: the speedy publication of the instruction, and "a request to the bishops that they would pay close attention to these activities, either directly or through a capable, dynamic priest, with a view to regulating then, correcting them in a timely fashion, and guiding and giving a sense of unity to the celebrations." As far as the agencies of the Holy See were concerned, he suggested that they ought to proceed in a united way "by sharing information and, where necessary, taking counsel *together.*"

10. The Secretariat did this in a letter of February 27, 1969. Some of the reports submitted by the papal representatives were shared with, among others, the Consilium.

11. Since both the phenomenon and certain irregularities were facts, some reasoned as follows: "If a law is passed approving home Masses, it will provide its opponents with an occasion for seeing who can vilify it most." The Consilium, on the other hand, believed that in this matter the Holy See should issue rules that would suitably regulate this religious manifestation and turn it into an instrument of the apostolate (see Cardinal Gut's letter to the Secretariat of State, March 12, 1969).

On February 10-11, 1969, a meeting was held at Assisi on "La Messa nelle *Domus.*" The secretary of the Consilium had an opportunity to learn of the ideas being circulated, some of them really eccentric. At his insistence, the promoters of the meeting sent the participants a letter calling attention to certain points: (1) the celebration of Mass in homes should not be added to, or replace, the celebration of the parish community; (2) furthermore, unleavened bread and the texts of the Missal and Lectionary are to be used; (3) exaggeration should be avoided in teaching, and the existing liturgical regulations should be obeyed. At the same time, however, the possibility was allowed of developments in some areas: dialogue homily, prayer of the faithful, greeting of peace. See *Not* 5 (1969) 328-29.

and some guidelines should be made more specific "in order to avoid confusions and abuses."[12] But then, as a result of the negative opinion issued by the Congregation for the Doctrine of the Faith (which the Secretariat had asked to comment),[13] the reply ended by saying: "The August Pontiff wishes that publication of the instruction already submitted to him be postponed, and that meanwhile the Consilium reply case by case to requests submitted to it and give provisional guidelines and directives."

A few days later, however, on March 28, a further letter said that the Pope,

> after seeing the data presented by Reverend Father Bugnini on this problem,[14] has decided that a provisional instruction should be issued that will reply to the various requests in this area and take steps against the troublesome practices encountered here and there. This provisional instruction is to be sent to the papal representatives and the episcopal conferences and is to be in force until the definitive guidelines are established by the publication of the new Order of Mass and by possible instructions from the Congregation for the Doctrine of the Faith.
>
> The text already prepared by the Consilium and submitted to this body by Your Eminence along with your letter of January 28 can serve as the ba-

---

12. The principles and regulations were set forth in a typewritten note of the Holy Father (it was unsigned, but the accompanying letter described it as "authoritative"). It said:

"1) Emphasis is to be placed, even if only briefly, on the social and communal character of the sacrifice of Holy Mass.

2) A paragraph on music is to be included which prohibits rhythms, sounds, and songs that are not in keeping with the character of the liturgical ceremonies and do not help increase devotion and recollection.

3) Not to be allowed:

a) that Masses with a group should become so habitual as to alienate the faithful from their respective communities;

b) that communion be received under two kinds, unless this is in accordance with concessions presently granted;

c) that Mass be celebrated in a private bedroom;

d) that changes be made in the usual Order of Mass, for example, by reducing the liturgy of the Word to a single reading."

13. The Congregation for the Doctrine of the Faith had expressed a negative judgment for two reasons. The first was that the text had been presented to it in "quasi-transitional and temporary form" that was to be valid until definitive and comprehensive regulations should be published in the General Instruction of the Roman Missal. The Congregation believed that such a document "would be received with indifference, like many other documents of the same type, thus prejudicing the effectiveness" of the regulations in the future instruction. (But the Consilium had never spoken of the regulations as transitional.)

In addition, the Congregation reserved to itself the right to pass "a more concrete judgment on the entire question" after it had studied the new Order of Mass and its accompanying General Instruction.

14. The reference is to the letter of February 27 (see note 10).

sis for such an instruction. In the introduction, however, it will be necessary to bring out the preeminence of the community Mass, as has already
been said in the Note sent to you on March 9.

The Secretariat returned the draft of the instruction, now containing
some notes of the Holy Father, along with two handwritten pages from
him in which he explained more fully the annotations he had made in
the margin of the text.[15] The letter from the Secretariat ended by saying,
rather oddly, that "it would be wise to consult the Italian Episcopal Conference, which has been commissioned to study the question" and that
the new text should be drawn up "with the greatest possible care."

The new text, revised in accordance with the guidelines received, was
sent to the Secretariat of State on March 30. It was now a "provisional"
instruction. Despite the limitations set upon it, the instruction was conceived along broad lines. There were even a few new elements, for example, regarding the exhortations and interventions of the celebrant and
especially regarding participation in the homily. These were phenomena
often associated with these celebrations, and were frequently the subject
of questions put to the Consilium. It seemed reasonable to take a middle-
of-the-road position, especially in regard to the homily. This was a point
that would continue to be the subject of debate in the coming years and
would never be satisfactorily resolved. The Consilium proposal was as
follows:

> If the celebrant think it appropriate, after the homily *he may invite* some
> of those present to offer a few brief and suitable thoughts. But he must see
> to it
>   1) that these interventions, which can serve to make participation more
> lively and personal, are prepared in advance;

---

15. One page contained general reflections and said: "It is true that the faithful should
be trained to become part of the ecclesial community and to appreciate the liturgical celebration presided over by one who has authority to gather (*convocare*), guide, instruct, and sanctify
the people of God. But it is also true that when aiding the special groups under discussion,
we must avoid fostering any tendency to apartness, to the formation of a "little Church,"
and to a sense of being in a privileged position; the aim must rather be to take advantage
of the group's homogeneity, the element of friendship, and the mutual edification of those
making up the group, in order to promote a deeper spiritual life."

The specific observations written in the margin of the text and repeated on the other
sheet were these: "5. Is the Mass in question composed according to arbitrary standards,
or is it a Mass according to the Missal? — With regard to communion under two kinds:
Is this appropriate? [Later it was absolutely prohibited; see also *Not* 5 (1970) 49.] —With
regard to the sacred furnishings: Should not more detailed regulations be given? (Is an altar needed? with a sacred stone? a chasuble, etc.? candles, etc.?) — No celebration in a
bedroom."

2) that they are thoughts which fit in with the word of God that has been heard or with the homily or with the liturgy of the day;

3) that the various interventions, including the homily itself, are finished in a reasonable time and do not get spun out to a tedious length, thus disturbing the balance of the celebration as a whole;

4) that he himself recapitulates at the end and relates what has been said to the spirit of the liturgical celebration.[16]

At this point, for practical purposes, the dialogue came to an end. On April 27, 1969 (No. 136944) the corrected text was sent to the Secretariat of State and approved by the Holy Father. The prefect of the Congregation for Divine Worship was asked "to see to it that copies are prepared for sending to the papal representatives and the bishops of the various countries."

The text had been entirely revised not only in its content but in its form as well. What the Consilium had phrased in positive terms had now become negative.[17] On May 17 the secretary of the Consilium submitted four pages of observations in which he listed points that could have a wrong sound or could seem to be, or actually be, in opposition to the other documents of the reform or to faculties already granted the bishops. On May 9 (No. 136944) the Secretariat of State sent back "changes that can be introduced into the document," but only four of the secretary's points had been accepted. The letter from the Secretariat even prescribed the formulation to be adopted.

The instruction was promulgated in cyclostyled format on May 15, 1969, the feast of the Ascension of the Lord.

---

16. Unfortunately, not only were the Consilium's suggestions not accepted, but they were replaced by a heavy-handed statement: "The faithful are not to speak out in the form of reflections, exhortations or other expressions of that kind," except, of course, for the leader or commentator and for interventions in the prayer of the faithful. The homily was also the subject of a reply issued by the Pontifical Commission for the Interpretation of the Decrees of Vatican Council II on January 11, 1971: *AAS* 63 (1971) 329–30; *DOL* 215 no. 1768.

17. Here are just a few examples. The description of the various kinds of special groups became a list of cases in which "celebration of the Eucharist may be allowed." The simplification of the introductory rites was eliminated. The reference to the authority of the episcopal conferences to look for other possible adaptations needed in their region was gone. A reference to the absolute prohibition against giving communion by placing the host in the recipient's hand was included, even though it was known that this problem was currently being studied. (In fact, the instruction *Memoriale Domini* on the manner of giving communion, which permits the method just described, was published on May 29, 1969, only fourteen days after the publication of the instruction!)

III. Reception of the Instruction

Unfortunately, the document was not well received. Numerous protests came from the bishops. Bishop Boudon, secretary of the liturgical commission of the French episcopate, wrote to the Secretariat of State, complaining that the document instituted "prejudicial restrictions on several guidelines in the General Instruction of the Roman Missal." Liturgical commissions and bishops in various countries also made their reactions known. On August 4, 1969, the Secretariat of State asked for the Consilium's views on the matter. On September 9 it responded with the following realistic analysis of the situation:

> The Instruction on Masses with Special Groups that was sent to the episcopal conferences on May 15, 1969, has unfortunately not had a good reception, despite the fact that it had been so eagerly awaited.
>
> The bishops were expecting that the document would make it easier for them to cope with the increasing demands for such celebrations.
>
> What they found in fact was regulations that are restrictive in relation to the General Instruction of the Mass. At times they perceive a less keen pastoral sense manifested here.
>
> The document had not even been given considerable publicity. France and Belgium have not officially published it, hoping that at least the less acceptable points would be reviewed; they have sent their remarks on the document to this Sacred Congregation.
>
> The Spanish conference has published the document, but rather resentful letters have come from that quarter.
>
> In Italy the conference has sent this "reserved" document on to the bishops, but only a few diocesan bulletins have called attention to it.
>
> Elsewhere the document has met with silence.
>
> The Congregation for Divine Worship thinks it appropriate that in such a situation the instruction should be published in the *Acta Apostolicae Sedis*, especially since the Holy Father has authoritatively cited it in a recent address. In order that the text may be in complete harmony with the other documents of the liturgical renewal now in progress, we have *revised* certain points, thereby also satisfying the express wishes of the bishops.

The corrected text was therefore returned for publication in the *Acta Apostolicae Sedis*. The revisions did not affect the substance of the document as a whole.

On November 21, 1969 (No. 147021), the Cardinal Secretary of State wrote that "after learning the views of the Congregation for the Doctrine of the Faith, the Holy Father acceded to the request . . . and gave his approval for publication."[18]

---

18. It was published not now as a provisional document but as a set of permanent regulations in *AAS* 61 (1969) 806–11; *DOL* 275 nos. 2120-33.

The Consilium and the Congregation for Divine Worship have always regarded this document as having normative force for the celebration of Mass with special groups. It must be said, however, that the document was still found to be unsatisfactory and that requests continued for a new set of regulations that would be more complete and more sensitive to the situation and to pastoral needs. The instruction of May 15, 1969, was in fact intended primarily as a call to full respect for the liturgical norms governing the celebration of Mass, even when this takes place in homes or in groups. It must be admitted, however, that the situation in these settings is different from celebrations with parish congregations and in churches. This consideration provided the point of departure for the study done by the Consilium, which was convinced that "a pure and simple reminder of the traditional discipline would be ineffective."[19]

Other considerations, however, and interventions from other quarters won the day!

---

19. Letter of Father Bugnini to the Secretariat of State, accompanying the presentation of the schema (January 28, 1969).

28

The Directory for Masses with Children

When the bishops spoke on the liturgical reform at the first Synod of Bishops (1967), different ones made known the desire of their respective episcopal conferences that the Mass might be specially adapted for celebrations with children. In his response Cardinal Lercaro said that "there is certainly no question of establishing a special rite but rather of deciding which elements are to be kept, shortened, or omitted and of selecting more suitable readings."[1]

The General Instruction of the Roman Missal sets down "the general guidelines for . . . the eucharistic celebration" and leaves it to the episcopal conferences "to lay down norms for its own territory that are suited to the traditions and character of peoples, regions, and various communities."[2]

Not only were requests made for adaptations; some liturgical commissions went ahead on their own and issued regulations for Masses with children. In other instances adaptations were made by individual priests or planned by catechists.

I. HISTORY

At its meeting on March 10, 1971 (the first at which Cardinal Tabera presided), the Congregation for Divine Worship decided to write to the presidents of the national liturgical commissions, asking for their thoughts

---

1. See "De Liturgia in prima Synodo Episcoporum," *Not* 3 (1967) 368.
2. GIRM 6 (*DOL* 208 no. 1396).

on the problem and for information on any relevant undertakings in their countries, any relevant publications, and any suggestions being made. The letter was sent on March 15 to 109 commissions; 58 replied.

A first report on the material received was given to the Congregation at its meeting of October 15, 1971, by G. Pasqualetti. The situation differed widely in the various countries, ranging from a minimum of adaptation in songs, prayer of the faithful, homily, and gestures, to radical solutions which sought to make the basic parts of the Mass—liturgy of the Word, liturgy of the Eucharist—clear to children and which therefore eliminated whatever, in the judgment of catechists, made these parts too complicated for children. Collections of texts had also been received: experimental Eucharistic Prayers, presidential prayers, lectionaries.

The situation in regard to participation also differed from country to country:

> —In some places Masses are celebrated specifically for children only during the week or on some special occasion. The celebration has an educational purpose and is meant to help children more readily understand and take part in the Sunday celebration of the community.
>
> —Elsewhere, however, the liturgy of the Word at the Sunday celebration of Mass is conducted in two separate locales: in church for the community and somewhere else for the children, who then assemble with the community for the liturgy of the Eucharist.
>
> —There are also cases, not considered in the replies, in which the congregation for a Sunday Mass consists chiefly of children, though some adults are present. This is usually the case at "children's Masses," as, for example, in Italy.

The report therefore suggested that Mass with children not be considered as simply another Mass with a special group. It should rather be looked at specifically as a Mass at which only children are present or at which they are in the majority.

A genuine adaptation called for:

1) *A more simple structure.* Three basic elements ought to catch the child's attention: the hearing of the word, the Eucharistic Prayer, and communion. Some freedom is needed in regard to the other elements that provide the setting for these three.

2) *Texts adapted to children.* In general, it is desirable that there be a greater freedom in selecting the texts and that these be written in a language accessible to children.

a) *Readings:* A request made by almost everyone was that there might be *a single reading*, and that recourse be allowed to paraphrases of the Bible or to translations made specifically for children.

b) *Presidential prayers:* It should be permitted to adapt these, or simply to compose new ones, in accordance with the themes, language, and mentality of children.

c) *Eucharistic Prayer:* Some should be composed that are adapted to children, or else a basic pattern should be provided that a celebrant might then use to construct a Eucharistic Prayer.

3) *More active participation.* Children find it difficult to concentrate for a lengthy period on any text. They need to be more active:

—through verbal expression of one or other kind, even during the Eucharistic Prayer;

—through the use of audiovisual aids, especially during the liturgy of the Word and the homily;

—through suitable bodily actions.

The report ended with some suggestions:

1. The Church is looking for a kind of *directory* for Masses with children, one that will suggest concrete ways of adaptation that the episcopal conferences can then develop more fully.

2. It would be good to list the parts of the Mass that can never be omitted even in Masses with children and those in which greater freedom can be used.

3. If the principle of freedom in choosing texts is accepted, then at the present time:

a) Let a Lectionary for Masses with children be compiled, even if only by way of guidelines, and at least for the major seasons. This will ensure that these celebrations do not wholly ignore the annual commemoration of the mysteries of redemption and that the essentials of the biblical message are presented. If the choice of texts is left entirely to the celebrant or other person in charge, without any guidelines being given, there is a danger that some individuals will fasten their attention on marginal points meaningful only to them and on the purely human and subjective aspects of the Scriptures, and that instruction will be disorganized and ineffective. It must be added that celebrations of the word that follow a "theme" are sometimes not celebrations at all but catechetical instructions.

A directory should also say something about the use of paraphrases of Scripture.

b) At least some control over the other texts should be assigned to the national and diocesan organizations in charge of the liturgy and catechetical instruction.

4. Some guidelines should also be given for Sunday Masses in which the participants are to a great extent children accompanied by adults. Some possibilities to be considered:

—the liturgy of the Word celebrated in a place apart for the children;

—or, if children and adults celebrate the entire Mass together, thought should be given to the omission of some parts and to the number of readings.

5. It would be advantageous to set up two study groups: one for the Lectionary and the other for questions concerning the Order of Mass.

The Fathers of the Congregation accepted the content of the report, in which the main problems were already set forth, along with possible solutions. It was decided, however, to set up only one study group for the entire problem.

Initially a limited group was formed that was quasi-provisional in character and had no specific appointees. It met in Rome on March 15, 1972, for an initial contact.[3] The only result of this meeting was a two-part decision:

1) to classify all the material that had been sent in to the Congregation and to prepare a representative selection from it;[4]

2) to launch a second inquiry among a limited number of experts. This was done by sending the material received from the various countries on the rite of Mass, together with a questionnaire drawn up by Professor Fischer and containing twenty-two queries (three general, nine on the liturgy of the Word, ten on the liturgy of the Eucharist). The documentation resulting from this inquiry (sent out on April 25, 1972, solely to ex-

---

3. Present were B. Fischer, who was looked upon as relator; G. Pasqualetti, R. Kaczynski, Professor S. Cavalletti, and Sister Marisa Fasciani of the Daughters of the Church. The subsequent makeup of the complete group was as follows: *relator:* B. Fischer; *secretary:* R. Kaczynski; *members:* A. Haquin (Belgium), E. Matthews (England), V. Pedrosa (Spain), H. Rennings (Germany), B. Violle (France), S. Cavalletti (Rome), and Sister Marisa Fasciani. This was the first time that a study group included two women (S. Cavalletti and Sister Marisa) and had a very large majority of members not connected with the Congregation. The members were chosen for their specific competencies and as representatives of various regions and educational methods.

4. The material was patiently sorted and organized by Sister Marisa Fasciani. The result was five booklets: Rite of Mass (77 pages); Lectionary (39); Texts of the Eucharistic Prayer (87); Thematic Masses (134); General observations (35). The first booklet, which was organized according to the successive rites of the Mass, also contained the guidelines issued by the national ecclesiastical authorities, as well as concrete examples from Canada, France, Germany, Haiti, Malaysia, New Zealand, and the United Sates. This first booklet was the only one photocopied and sent to the experts for consultation.

perts chosen by the Congregation or suggested by the presidents of the liturgical commissions) was likewise organized and collected in a booklet.[5]

This was the basis for the discussion at the first meeting of the study group, which was held in Rome, June 21–22, 1972. The group went over the twenty-two questions of this second questionnaire. I shall list them, along with the results of the discussion.

1. Forms of participation: The actions performed and the place where the celebration is held are very important.

2. Adaptation of the prayers: This seems necessary, but care must be taken to avoid moralizing and a classroom approach.

3. Paraphrases of the acclamations: To be avoided.

Liturgy of the Word

4. Use of a single reading: Should be allowed; a nonbiblical reading may not be substituted for the biblical, but can at most serve as an introduction to it.

5. Special Lectionary: It is decided to leave this to Father Fontaine.[6]

6. Translations of the Bible that are adapted to the child's capacity for understanding: Paraphrases are to be excluded; not to be excluded are simpler translations approved by the bishops for catechetical use.

7. Use of dramatization: Should be allowed.[7]

8. Use of audiovisual aids: This is a possibility that ought to be allowed within precisely defined limits; any use made must be prudent and careful.[8]

9. Paraphrases of the sung *Gloria* and Creed: In these songs a formal, but not a literal, identity is the important thing. Permission should be given to use the Apostles' Creed or the renewal of baptismal promises from the Easter Vigil.

10. Participation of the children in the prayer of the faithful: Advantage should be taken of this.

11. Postponement of some parts (for example, the penitential act) until after the homily: This should be allowed.

---

5. The replies had come from twenty countries and from priests, laypersons, and religious men and women. The booklet was seventy-five pages in length, and to it were added forty-eight letters that came in after the assigned date (namely, June 1, 1972).

6. Eventually the difficulty of preparing a Lectionary for the entire world was realized. It was therefore decided to leave the Lectionary to the episcopal conferences.

7. This point was not accepted by the Congregation for the Doctrine of the Faith.

8. Nor was this point accepted, despite the emphasis put on it. The Congregation was planning a document on the entire problem of audiovisual aids, but it was unable even to sketch out a respectable piece of work. The problem of audiovisual aids was discussed again as a result of a request from Australia for Masses celebrated with groups of deaf-mutes. Technicians and laypersons experienced in the field of audiovisual aids were also asked for help. But the work was continually put off and nothing came of it.

12. Possibility of omitting the penitential act: Yes, in view of the fact that the introductory rites are burdensome for children.

12bis. Homily: This is extremely important. It should be carefully prepared, adapted to the celebration and to the children's understanding; it is to be given by capable individuals, and use is to be made of audio-visual aids and dialogue.

Liturgy of the Eucharist

13. Simplification of the offertory texts: The best solution would be to recite them in a low voice.

14. Eucharistic Prayer: The fourth in the Missal seems to be the best one for children; if used with them, the second and third need to be expanded. But a change in the present Eucharistic Prayers does not seem to be the answer to the problem.

15. Composition of new Eucharistic Prayers: It seems better to grant permission for this to the episcopal conferences.

16. Introduction of further acclamations into the Eucharistic Prayer: This seems suitable.

17. Our Father: The text must be the same in all Masses and never omitted.

18. Omission or shortening of the embolism: The parts between the Our Father and the communion can be omitted or shortened or lengthened; not all at the same time, however, but now one, now another.

19. Rite of peace: Great freedom should be allowed.

20. "Lamb of God": Permission should be granted for also using other songs with the same meaning.

21. Adaptation of the texts immediately preceding communion: Various models should be supplied, or there should be a clear statement of how they may be adapted.

22. Adaptation of the dismissal rite: The blessing should be a fixed part, but first a few words should be said to the children.

During the discussion it was added that the document should deal with some other points: gestures of the priest; silence; age of the children whom the document has in mind; religious education generally; non-Eucharistic liturgies for children; persons taking part; singing. These are points that would be considered in the opening section of the document.

Preparation and Discussion of the Directory

A *first schema* of a directory was drawn up by the relator and the secretary, with the help of H. Rennings, on the basis of the ideas that surfaced during the study group's discussion. It is dated July 11, 1972, and already displays the structure to be seen in the definitive document; it has fifty-two numbers (the final document would have fifty-five). It was

sent to the study group and thirty-four experts and revised, in the light
of their observations, at the second meeting of the study group (October
2–4, 1972).

The *second schema*, which resulted from that meeting, is dated October 7. It was sent to the members and consultors of the Congregation
with a view to discussion at the Congregation's third plenary meeting.
The consultors went over it on November 9 and accepted it in substance.
The only point that gave rise to a lively discussion was the use of audiovisual aids. The Fathers then discussed the schema on November 23. Their
acceptance was likewise not only favorable but enthusiastic. Ten votes
were taken, the result being unanimously affirmative in nine cases; with
regard, however, to the proposal that nonbiblical texts might be used
simply in explaining the reading from Scripture, there were four votes
against and nine for.

The *third schema*, with the corrections introduced at the plenary meeting, is dated December 1, 1972, and was sent for study to the Congregations for the Doctrine of the Faith, the Clergy, and the Evangelization
of Peoples. Their replies were substantially favorable, but the Congregation for the Doctrine of the Faith raised objections to three points that
it wanted changed:

> a) It is not appropriate that a layperson give the homily after the gos-
> pel . . . . A layperson could address the children *before* Mass.
> b) The suggestion about using audiovisual aids would bring the Mass
> down to the level of a school broadcast.
> c) With regard to the timeliness of new anaphoras: It will be necessary
> to adhere to the decisions of the Congregation for the Doctrine of the Faith
> on whether it is expedient to give the episcopal conferences authority in
> this area.[9]

On the basis of the various observations, the schema was revised once
again by the secretariat of the Congregation and sent to the Holy Father
on May 3, 1973. But the secretariat did not accept the three wishes of the
Congregation for the Doctrine of the Faith, and it sent the Pope, along
with the directory, a lengthy explanation of the reasons why it thought
these wishes ought not to be honored. The secretary of the Congregation discussed the entire document with the Pope at an audience on September 13, 1973.

On October 4 the Pope sent in his own observations. Some had to
do with matters of style, others with four specific points: the reasons for

---

9. That is, whether it is expedient to grant no authority at all; see below, pp. 474 and
479. The reply was dated March 23, 1973.

thanksgiving that the children were to express after the dialogue of the preface; the use of slides;[10] the placing of the penitential act after the homily; and special Eucharistic Prayers. The Pope showed himself opposed on all these points that the schema included. His wishes were followed. The secretariat insisted, however, on the need for special Eucharistic Prayers, in view of the requests that had come in from individual bishops and from conferences; a list of these was sent to the Pope on October 15, 1973. It insisted, that is, on the request, made as early as May 3 of that year, for the creation of one or two Eucharistic Prayers for children that would be offered to the entire Church. Such a creation would satisfy the wishes expressed by the conferences and would solve a difficulty generally felt.

On October 23 the Secretary of State sent a handwritten note of the Holy Father that read as follows: "I have seen the text of the 'Directory for Masses with Children' which the Congregation for Divine Worship sent to me, along with the page bearing the protocol number 688/73, dated October 15, 1973, and I gladly approve it. Paul VI, Pope. October 22, 1973." The accompanying letter of the Secretary of State said among other things that the Congregation was authorized to draw up two or three Eucharistic Prayers for children, for use by the entire Church.

On November 19 the Cardinal Secretary of State, having received the page proofs of the document, wrote: "The Supreme Pontiff has given his consent for printing this document." The document was printed with the date November 1, 1973, and was made public on December 20 of that year.[11]

II. CONTENTS

The Directory consists of an introduction and three chapters. The intention is not to give a detailed description of the rite of the Mass, since this is already to be had in the General Instruction of the Roman Missal,

---

10. The reference to slides was removed; left, however, was what was said about the value of visual experience for children. Children must be trained to attend to the signs that the Church uses in the liturgy—adoration of the cross; Easter candle; procession with candles on February 2—and to the things in the celebration that shed light on the mysteries of God. Pictures painted or otherwise prepared by the children themselves can be used to illustrate the homily or the intentions in the prayer of the faithful (see nos. 35-36). Analogous considerations apply to bodily gestures—processions, genuflections, standing—even if the explicit reference to dramatization (which is a particular form of gestural expression) has been removed from the document.

11. The instruction is in *DOL* 276 nos. 2134-88; see also the commentary of R. Kaczynski in *Not* 10 (1974) 22-28.

but only to set down basic principles that complement, as it were, the General Instruction and adapt it to a particular situation. The purpose is, therefore, to indicate the means and methods of educating children to understand the Eucharistic mystery and take a full and conscious part in it so that they will eventually be able to participate in the Eucharistic celebration of the community. This last is the ultimate end in view. Mass geared to children is not an end in itself but seeks the eventual full participation of children in the Eucharistic community of adults. The Directory is aimed at children of catechetical age, those who have not yet reached pre-adolescence.

The first chapter deals with the training of children for the celebration of the Eucharist. It speaks of the indispensable role of the family, of the Christian community that helps the family in its educational mission, and of catechetical instruction in school and in the parish. It wants the children to gain an understanding, through the rites and prayers of the meaning of the Eucharistic celebration. An important role in the liturgical and Eucharistic training of children belongs to celebrations that introduce them to an understanding of important elements of the Mass, such as the greeting, silence, praise, and thanksgiving.

The second chapter is concerned with Masses for adults in which children also take part. The witness given by adults who live and express their faith fully plays an indispensable and primordial role in the formation of children. Therefore, if children at Mass have their parents and other family members at their side, the spirituality of the family will be greatly fostered (no. 16).

The most important practical conclusion from these principles is that children must not be allowed to feel neglected. Children are here divided into two categories: those who are still unable or unwilling to participate in the Mass (these can be kept in an appropriate place apart and brought into the church for the blessing at the end of Mass), and those who are able to take an active part. Some account at least must be taken of their presence by speaking more directly to them in the exhortations and at some point in the homily too (no. 17). Ways should be sought of involving them more directly and assigning them some task. At times it can be helpful to celebrate the liturgy of the Word with them in a separate place and then have them rejoin the community for the liturgy of the Eucharist.

Chapter 3 is the longest and deals more specifically with Masses for children in which adults also take part. Although the Directory is still addressing itself to children, it is no longer dealing with Masses solely for children. The presence of at least some adults has an educational purpose and is necessary.

Once again, some principles of religious pedagogy are mentioned, dealing especially with education to an understanding of the signs used. This kind of formation should precede the celebration and concern itself with the human values that underlie the celebration: standing in unison, greetings, the readiness to hear and respond and to ask and receive forgiveness, the experience of symbolic actions, the idea of a feast and of a banquet shared by friends. The instruction should then turn to the religious application of these values in the celebration of the Eucharist and to the meaning of the gestures and signs used in this celebration.

Precisely because Mass with children is an educational preparation for Mass with the community, it is preferably to be celebrated during the week and not on Sunday. Furthermore, the structure proper to the Mass should be respected, so as not to put an excessive emphasis on the difference between Mass with children and Mass with the community. Some rites and texts may never be adapted: the acclamations and responses of the faithful, the greetings of the celebrant, the Our Father, the Trinitarian formula of the final blessing. It is also recommended that the children gradually learn the Nicene-Constantinopolitan Creed, even if the Apostles' Creed be used in Masses in which they take part.

The Directory explains the responsibilities of the celebrant, on whom largely depends the creation of a certain atmosphere among the adults present and among the children themselves. The children are to be given various active roles: preparation of the church and the altar, singing and the playing of musical instruments, proclaiming the readings, asking questions during the homily, offering intentions during the prayer of the faithful, and bringing the gifts to the altar. All these activities are ordered in turn to the most important kind of participation, namely, the interior. The Directory therefore offers practical guidelines with regard to the place of the celebration, the texts, the singing and music, the gestures, the visual elements, silence, and the various parts of the Mass (introductory rite, liturgy of the Word, presidential prayers, and communion rite).

The Directory is concerned less with solutions of concrete cases than with principles and guidelines, exhortations and motivations. It shows how the reformed liturgy can be wisely and profitably adapted to the real situations of believers, so as to facilitate their joyous, conscious, active, and devout participation in the divine mysteries. Then they will grow in faith and proclaim Christ to others.

29

The Eucharistic Prayers

I. New Eucharistic Prayers

1. *Return to Authentic Tradition*

Once euchological pluralism and rubrical flexibility had been rediscovered after centuries of fixism, it was unthinkable that a monolithic approach to the Eucharistic Prayer should long endure.

a) This was true first and foremost on *historical* grounds: the exclusive place given to a single Eucharistic Prayer was not original. The liturgical history of the first four centuries shows a high degree of adaptability at this point in the Mass. The Eastern Rites, which are the most faithful echoes of that original tradition, all have several anaphoras: there are eighty in the Western Syrian Rite, fourteen in the Ethiopian, three in the Byzantine, and three among the Nestorians.[1]

In the West, the Mozarabic Rite has a Eucharistic Prayer in which the formulas, except for the account of institution, vary daily. In the Ambrosian Rite the Canon has about eighty prefaces, as well as variants within the Canon for Holy Thursday and the Easter Vigil. The Roman Canon itself originally had a large number of variable texts; thus while the Missal used until 1968 had only 14 prefaces, the Leonine Sacramentary (fifth century) had 267 and the Gelasian (sixth century) 184. The same is true of variants in the *Communicantes* and *Hanc igitur*, which had been reduced to five and two respectively in the Missal before the reform of Vatican II.

---

1. See A. Hänggi and I. Pahl (eds.), *Prex eucharistica. Textus e variis liturgiis antiquioribus selecti* (Spicilegium Friburgense 12; Fribourg, 1969).

Consequently, the decision to add other Eucharistic Prayers to the Roman liturgy was not an "intolerable audacity" but a return to authentic tradition and a rejection of the deplorable impoverishment that had been a typical result of centuries of liturgical decadence.

b) Historical investigation was echoed by *literary criticism*. I mean that when the Roman Canon and other very old prayers "canonized" by centuries of liturgical tradition were subjected to a careful conceptual and stylistic analysis in light of the general principles of Vatican II and the comparative history of anaphoras, they revealed "numerous and serious . . . . defects and limitations of structure."[2]

In 1965 Karl Amon proposed a new form of the Canon. Other models followed, not all of them showing desirable caution or done by competent people. Some of these "restored" Canons circulated among the clergy and were used in celebrations; others remained within the community and were used only in certain circumstances.

The study group dealing with the Mass initially attempted a revision of the Canon, but with uncertainty and trepidation. Even this attempt immediately roused concern outside the group and brought attacks.[3] When the Consilium presented the Pope with an explanation of the work being done on revision of the rites of Mass (May 25, 1966), it said:

> If the time comes to reopen the question of composing a new Eucharistic Prayer (in view of the difficulties that mark the present Roman Canon from a pastoral standpoint), study group 10 would be honored to be allowed to work up some models. In that case it would also feel obliged to see to it that any new prayer still displayed the Roman genius, so that the Roman Mass would continue to be faithful to the spirit of the Roman liturgy.

Cardinal Lercaro did in fact once again submit the problem for papal consideration at the audience granted to him on June 20. In the memorandum that the Cardinal prepared for that occasion he said:

> Any projected revision of the text of the Eucharistic Prayer faces numerous and sensitive problems; but then so does the retention of the prayer in its present form present difficulties. Especially if said aloud, the Roman Canon would become burdensome due to its very changelessness and to some elements that are too narrowly local, such as the lists of the saints (in regard to which historical criticism also raises objections not easily answered).
>
> The Canons suggested by various sources tend to be revisions of the text with a view to curtailing the elements just mentioned and relocating

---

2. See C. Vagaggini, *The Canon of the Mass and Liturgical Reform*, trans. edited by P. Coughlan (Staten Island, N.Y., 1967) 107. The Italian original was published in 1966.

3. See above, p. 152, n. 30.

other intercessory prayers (*Memento, Communicantes, Nobis quoque*) so as to make the Eucharistic Prayer more of a single unit that includes the preface, *Sanctus* and anamnesis. But revisions are always dangerous, especially when they mean tampering with texts that have so venerable a tradition behind them.

It seems more expedient to leave the traditional text of the Canon untouched and to compose from scratch one or more Eucharistic Prayers that would be added to the traditional Canon and used as alternatives to it, even if only for the purpose of having a greater variety of texts.

The Pope's decision was brief and to the point: ''The present anaphora is to be left unchanged; two or three anaphoras for use at particular specified times are to be composed or looked for.''

On the basis of this decision, the study group immediately set to work. Its first step was to ask for views and concrete proposals. The files were kept by A. Franquesa, who stayed in Trier for three months as a guest of Monsignor Wagner. Meanwhile C. Vagaggini conducted a more penetrating study of the subject; in three months of intense work in the library of the Abbey of Mont-César (Louvain) during the summer of 1966, he studied questions relating to the Roman Canon and composed two models of new Eucharistic Prayers, which he presented to the group for discussion.[4]

2. *Preliminary Questions*

The group began by trying to respond to two basic problems:

1) Adoption of existing texts, as suggested by the Pope, who said that anaphoras should be ''looked for'' in the traditional treasury of prayers. The anaphoras that stood out were the anaphora of Hippolytus (third century) and the Alexandrian anaphora of St. Basil; both would blend in well with the other texts of the Latin liturgy.

---

4. Father Vagaggini's work and its accompanying documentation were published in the book cited in note 2. It was the basis for the new Eucharistic Prayers of the Missal. The variants it shows in comparison with the definitive text in the Missal were the fruit of the discussion and cultural contributions of the *periti* and the Fathers of the Consilium. Study group 10 (on the Ordinary of the Mass) had been enlarged and now included: J. Wagner, A. Franquesa, T. Schnitzler, A. Hänggi, P. Jounel, L. Agustoni, P. Gy, J. A. Jungmann, J. Gélineau, L. Bouyer, H. Wegman, L. Ligier, F. McManus, B. Botte, C. Vagaggini, G. Gellier, G. Patino, S. Famoso, and A. Lentini. The need was recognized of appointing subcommittees within the group, each having its own relator and dealing with a single Eucharistic Prayer. The relators: for Eucharistic Prayer II, P. Jounel; for Eucharistic Prayer III, C. Vagaggini; for Eucharistic Prayer IV, J. Gélineau and C. Vagaggini; for Eucharistic Prayer V (the Alexandrian anaphora of St. Basil), L. Bouyer.

2) The Pope had also allowed the "composition" of new anaphoras. The group endeavored to establish general criteria in response to certain questions: What is meant by the "Roman genius" that is to be preserved? Which are the essential elements of a Eucharistic Prayer both in general and specifically according to the Roman style? Using the results of this discussion, the group then went on to compose six schemas, one of which was adopted as a base model. During the meeting at Nemi the group achieved a final determination of the criteria and schemas to be set before the Consilium. The following are the salient points that were substantially respected in the texts finally approved:

a) *Common structure*

Anaphoras form a special genre with specific requirements as to structure, themes, and style. Some of these requirements must be met in every anaphora. Only within relatively narrow limits can the variations be allowed that account for the special characteristics of individual anaphoras or groups of anaphoras.

The three new anaphoras have a substantially identical structure:

I. Preface (changeable in Eucharistic Prayers II and III, unchanging in IV).

II. Transition from the *Sanctus* to the consecratory epiclesis (very short in II, short in III, lengthy in IV).

III. Consecratory epiclesis.

IV. Account of institution.

V. Anamnesis and offering of the divine Victim.

VI. Prayer for acceptance of the offering and for a fruitful communion.

VII and VIII. Commemoration of the saints and intercessions (or: intercessions and commemoration of the saints).

IX. Doxology.

The main difference between this structure and that of the Roman Canon is that in the new anaphoras the commemorations of the saints and the intercessions are all placed together in the second part, between the prayer for the acceptance of the offering and the doxology, whereas in the Roman Canon they come partly before the account of institution (second part of the *Te igitur*, the *Communicantes* and *Hanc igitur*), partly after it (*Nobis quoque*).

The grouping of the intercessions in the second part of the anaphora (as, for example, in the Antiochene tradition) makes it possible to give the new Eucharistic Prayers a more marked forward movement and a much greater clarity.

At the same time, however, the specifically Roman character of the structure of the new prayers is sufficiently preserved by having a single (consecratory) epiclesis before the account of institution; of all the characteristics of the Roman tradition that might be mentioned, this is the most typical (in the Roman Canon, the *Quam oblationem*).

b) *The principle of variety*

It seems proper that while respecting the laws that every anaphora must obey, the new anaphoras should also have their own spiritual, pastoral, and stylistic characteristics that would distinguish them both from one another and from the Roman Canon. This kind of variety seems needed if the Roman liturgy is to have the greater spiritual and pastoral riches that cannot find full expression in a single type of text.

As far as possible, therefore, concepts, words, and phrases from the Roman Canon have been avoided in the three new anaphoras, and things found in one of the three have not been repeated in the other two.

c) *Why three?*

The reason is that only by having three did it seem possible to introduce into the part of the Roman liturgy the spiritual and pastoral riches required today.

There seemed to be a need, first of all, for a very short anaphora displaying very simple and clear lines. To this end, and to the extent allowed by the common structure described above, the group kept before it as a model the anaphora of Hippolytus, the oldest of those that have come down to us. The result is Eucharistic Prayer II.

It was also thought necessary to have an anaphora of medium length and clear structure, in which the transitions from part to part would leap directly to the eye. This could be used with any of the traditional Roman prefaces as well as with any new prefaces that might be composed; it would be stylistically compatible with them. The result: Eucharistic Prayer III.

Finally, there seemed to be a need for an anaphora in which the account of institution would be preceded by a leisurely but still summary exposition of the entire economy of salvation. To this end the preface had to limit itself to praising God in himself and for creation in general and the creation of the angels in particular. Then, after the *Sanctus* and before the consecratory epiclesis, the anaphora would run through the economy from the creation of the human person down to Christ and Pentecost. All this means that in such an anaphora the preface cannot change from feast to feast but must remain always the same. The result: Eucharistic Prayer IV.

d) *The account of institution*

After careful study and lengthy discussion of the entire problem, the formulas of the Roman Canon were retained, with two changes: after "This is my body" the words "which will be given up for you" were added, and in the formula for the consecration of the wine, the words "the mystery of faith" were dropped. These changes were motivated essentially by considerations of completeness and pastoral clarity. The following explanation was given:

1. *In the Scriptures* there is no single formula but rather four different ones.

1 Cor 11:24-25: "This is my body which will be given up for you. Do this in memory of me." There are variant readings for *tradetur* (will be given up), namely, *frangitur* (is broken) and *frangetur* (will be broken). For the wine: "This cup is the new covenant in my blood. As often as you drink it do it in memory of me."

Luke 22:19ff.: "This is my body which is given for you. Do this in memory of me . . . . This cup is the new covenant in my blood, which will be shed for you."

Mark 14:22ff.: "This is my body . . . . This is my blood of the new covenant, which will be shed for many for the forgiveness of sins."

Matthew 29:19ff.: "This is my body . . . . For this is my blood of the new covenant, which will be shed for many for the forgiveness of sins."

There are evidently no sentences completely the same in all four authors who report the words of institution.

2. *In the liturgy*, therefore, it is necessary either to choose one of these texts in preference to the other three or to create composite formulas.

From the beginning the liturgical tradition chose the method of composition. But in the process two common tendencies manifested themselves in the consecration of both the bread and the wine: one was to compose formulas that were as complete as possible by taking into account, after the manner of a diatessaron, the details found in the several New Testament writers; the other tendency was to formulate the consecrations of the bread and of the wine so that they were parallel in their details. The result of these common tendencies was a very great variety of formulas in the liturgies both of the past and of the present time.

3. With regard to *the formula for the consecration of the bread in the Roman Canon* ("For this is my body"), which was also received into the Ambrosian Canon for Holy Thursday:

—It is an isolated phenomenon in the liturgical tradition both past and present. The Mozarabic Rite adds "which will be given up for you" (we do not have precise knowledge of the Gallican tradition). All the others add something: "which is given *or* given up *or* will be given up for you," "which will be broken *or* is broken *or* is broken and distributed for you."

—It is in itself notably incomplete from the viewpoint of the theology of the Mass. For, taken by itself, "this is my body" says only the real presence and does not express the sacrificial character of the rite. In the Roman Rite, the sacrificial nature of the first consecration must be inferred from the context.

—Many bishops and pastors throughout the world, to say nothing of liturgists and theologians, have asked that to the words "For this is my body" there be added "which will be given up for you," as in the Vulgate of 1 Cor 11:24. It would be no small disappointment if this request were not honored in the new anaphoras.

4. *The addition "the mystery of faith"* in the formula for the consecration of the wine in the Roman Canon:

—is not biblical;

—occurs only in the Roman Canon;

—is of uncertain origin and meaning. The experts themselves disagree on the precise sense of the words. In fact, some of them assign the phrase a quite dangerous meaning, since they translate it as "a sign for our faith";

—interrupts the sentence and makes difficult both its understanding and its translation. The French, for example, have been forced to repeat the word "blood" three times: "This is the cup of my blood, the blood of the new covenant, mystery of faith, blood shed . . . ." The same is true to a greater or lesser extent in the other languages.

Once again, many bishops and pastors have asked that in the new anaphoras the addition "mystery of faith" be dropped.

All this explains the course followed in the new anaphoras with regard to the words of consecration.

e) *The other details in the account of institution*

It has been thought expedient to favor variety in the new anaphoras. This is a way of introducing into the Roman anaphoras the greater spiritual and pastoral, not to say theological, riches which find expression in the various details to be found at this point in the biblical and traditional sources and which cannot be expressed in any single text.

f) *Acclamations of the congregation in the new anaphoras*

In the three new anaphoras, it is expected that there will be an acclamation of the congregation after the consecration and elevation of the chalice. The practice is native to the Eastern Churches, but it seems appropriate to accept it into the Roman tradition as a way of increasing the active participation of the congregation.

Regarding the exact form of the acclamation, the rubric says that it can use "these or similar words approved by the territorial authorities." Since the acclamations are to be said, or even sung, by the congregation, it is necessary to leave enough freedom for them to be adapted to the requirements of the various languages and musical genres.

g) *Changeable formulas (embolisms) to be introduced into Eucharistic Prayers II and III in Masses for the dead, after baptism, for marriages, and so on*

In the Roman tradition special formulas (in the *Hanc igitur*) are introduced into the Canon of the Mass for the three above-mentioned special intentions; these formulas expressly commend to God the persons for whom the sacrifice is being offered. The sacramentaries likewise have several special forms of the *Hanc igitur* for the deceased and for spouses.

The new anaphoras do not have the *Hanc igitur* of the Roman Canon (in any case, the *Hanc igitur* would of its nature be a formula for use only in particular circumstances). It is expected, however, that there will be special formulas to be introduced when Eucharistic Prayer II or III is used in Masses for the dead, for the baptized, for spouses, and so on.

The formula for the deceased is given after the texts of Eucharistic Prayers II and III.[5] By means of it, these two new anaphoras take on the tone proper to the occasion, and greater prominence is given to the great Christian truths that show us how to view death.

Eucharistic Prayer IV cannot be used in Masses for the dead because these Masses have a preface proper to them, whereas the preface in Eucharistic Prayer IV is always the same.

h) *Tradition and novelty*

In the new anaphoras, more than elsewhere, care has been taken to be true to article 23 of the Constitution on the Liturgy, which urges that "sound tradition" and "legitimate progress" be combined.

The traditional character of the structure common to the three new anaphoras is clear from the fact that it is substantially that of the Roman Canon, except for the place assigned to the intercessions and the commemorations of the saints. As a matter of fact, however, in the tradition

---

5. This was the only one published along with the Eucharistic Prayers. Other texts for baptism, confirmation, sacred orders, and religious profession would come into use when the various sacramental rites were published.

of the universal Church the position of the intercessions and of the commemorations of saints in the Eucharistic Prayer has varied greatly. The
position given them in the new anaphoras is that found in the Antiochene
tradition. It is this resolution of the problem that gives the new anaphoras
the clarity everyone wants them to have.

The traditional character of the concepts and images in the new
anaphoras is demonstrated by their biblical origin and their use in the
liturgies and the Fathers. This is a point that can be readily documented.

An effort has been made to make the new anaphoras contemporary
by simply emphasizing, among the biblical and traditional elements, those
which are most responsive to the concerns of today's men and women
and which they can most easily understand.

An effort has also been made to keep the rhythms (*cursus*) of the Roman
euchological style, especially in Eucharistic Prayers III and IV.

Comparative length of the new anaphoras: II is about one-third as long
as the Roman Canon, III is a little more than half as long, and IV contains about 150 fewer words than the Roman Canon.

3. *Eucharistic Prayer II*

The aim was to produce an anaphora that is short and very simple
in its ideas. The anaphora of Hippolytus was therefore taken as a model.
But, although many thoughts and expressions are derived from Hippolytus, Eucharistic Prayer II is not, as it were, a new edition of his prayer.
It was not possible to retain the structure of his anaphora because it does
not have a *Sanctus* or a consecratory epiclesis before the account of institution or a commemoration of the saints or intercessions. All these developed after Hippolytus and could not now be omitted in a Roman
anaphora. In addition, various ideas and expressions in the anaphora of
Hippolytus are archaic or difficult to understand and could not be taken
over into a contemporary anaphora.

4. *Eucharistic Prayer III*

The intention here was to compose an anaphora of medium length
that would be clear in its structure and in which the transitions from section to section would be immediately perceptible. In addition, as I said
above, it could be used with any of the traditional Roman prefaces or
any new preface and would be compatible with them in its overall style.

1) In such an anaphora, praise of God and thanksgiving for the
wonders he has accomplished in the economy of salvation would therefore be limited to changeable prefaces and not expressly mentioned again
after the *Sanctus*.

As a result, the prayer after the *Sanctus* in this anaphora is seen as simply a transition to the consecratory epiclesis. In this prayer, the economy of salvation, which has been described in the preface, is simply summed up in a very general phrase, as in the Gallican tradition. This general phrase, which is meant to aid the transition to the consecratory epiclesis, refers to the sanctifying work of the Holy Spirit, one fruit of which is the gathering of the Church for the purpose of worshiping God.

2) Express mention is made of the Holy Spirit in the consecratory epiclesis. The offering of the gifts is not repeated, but there is a reference to the offering of them already made in the prayer over the gifts. There is a reference, finally, to the Lord's command to celebrate the Eucharist; this effects a natural passage to the subsequent account of institution: "cuius mandato haec mysteria celebramus. Ipse enim . . . (at whose command we celebrate this eucharist. On the night . . .)."

3) As in a good many anaphoras, the anamnesis explicitly says that we await the Lord's glorious return. The sacrificial character of the offering here being made is unequivocally affirmed (the words used, "sacrificium vivum et sanctum—holy and living sacrifice," occur in, for example, the anaphora of Theodore of Mopsuestia). It is also clearly stated that what we offer is first and foremost Christ himself. That this offering includes the offering of ourselves is stated in the next prayer: "Ipse nos perficiat munus aeternum—May he make of us an everlasting gift to you."

4) The prayer for the acceptance of the sacrifice and for a fruitful communion expresses two thoughts: acceptance of the Church's offering and the gift of the Spirit in communion. This prayer is thus linked to the earlier one asking that the gifts may be consecrated by the action of the Holy Spirit. Among the fruits produced by the gift of the Spirit two are expressly mentioned: the unity of the Mystical Body and the spiritual sacrifice in which the Church learns to offer itself together with Christ. The prayer ends with the idea of a heavenly inheritance; this in turn leads naturally to a commemoration of the saints.

5) The commemoration of the saints is introduced, as just noted, by mention of the heavenly inheritance that we hope to share with them. The same thought occurs in the Roman Canon (in the *Nobis quoque*) and in the Byzantine anaphora of St. Basil. The list of the saints is deliberately restrained.

6) The intercessions for the living and the dead for whom the sacrifice is being offered also display restraint. Both intercessions move into a universalist perspective; the intercession for the dead embraces all human beings who, even if with a wholly implicit faith, have died in peace with God. This approach reflects the outlook of Vatican II.

5. *Eucharistic Prayer IV*

The aim here was to produce an anaphora that, while remaining in the Roman tradition, would have room to develop the total picture of the economy of salvation on a much broader scale than in the other anaphoras. Of the three new Eucharistic Prayers, it is the one that approaches most closely to the Antiochene type. The details found in this anaphora are a logical consequence of the approach taken.

1) In order to remain in the Roman tradition at least as regards the essential point, this anaphora, too, has a consecratory epiclesis before the account of institution.

2) In order to include a general summary of the entire economy of salvation:

a) the anaphora works through the economy not only in the preface but after the *Sanctus;* this entails a notable lengthening of the prayer between the *Sanctus* and the consecratory epiclesis. In addition, explicit mention is made of Pentecost and the sanctifying action of the Holy Spirit after the ascension of Christ;

b) the preface contains only praise and thanksgiving to God as seen in himself and for the work of creation in general and the creation of the angels in particular. After the *Sanctus* the summary exposition of the economy continues with God's work from the creation of human beings onward. The preface is therefore unchangeable, and this anaphora cannot be used in Masses that have their own proper preface;

c) from the consecratory epiclesis on, the structure is substantially the same as in Eucharistic Prayers II and III.

3) With regard to the style, it is enough to note that:

a) it is more markedly biblical in its images and language. This is in keeping with the overall approach taken in the anaphora, since the latter is characterized by a broader exposition of the economy of salvation and since such an exposition is better done in the language of the Bible itself;

b) the perspectives controlling the exposition of the economy of salvation are chiefly those that are of greater concern to contemporary men and women and can be more readily understood by them.

6. *Alexandrian Anaphora of St. Basil*

There was a strong movement among scholars and people in pastoral care to introduce the Alexandrian anaphora of St. Basil into the Roman liturgy so that a typical and noble example of the Eastern tradition might be available for use in the Western Church. Two arguments were given:

1. Now that the liturgy was being reformed, many in the Latin Church wanted a Eucharistic Prayer that would contain:

a) a generous expression of thanksgiving for the entire economy both of creation and of redemption;

b) the clear presence of all the essential elements of the traditional Eucharistic Prayer;

c) a formula that is both biblical and adapted to the requirements of catechesis.

All these elements are beautifully united in the Alexandrian anaphora of St. Basil.

2. The introduction of this text into the Western liturgical tradition would be of great value for ecumenism, since no text is so popular in the East. It is used in the Coptic Church and all the Byzantine Churches, both Greek and Slavic. It is also used in the Catholic Church by the Ukrainians, Melkites, and Copts. In the past it was used in almost all the Eastern Churches: in Armenia, Georgia, Syria, and so on.

No anaphora is more complete and yet at the same time more simple. It follows this pattern:

a) thanksgiving for creation (down to the *Sanctus*);

b) thanksgiving for the whole history of salvation;

c) words of consecration (connected with thanksgiving in reference to the Pauline "mystery") in the most summary of all the New Testament formulas;

d) full anamnesis of the work of redemption, along with the offering of the divine sacrifice; the language used is in complete harmony with Sacred Scripture;

e) epiclesis in its oldest form, in which the Holy Spirit is invoked in order that the gifts may be consecrated and the offerers may be sanctified and led, as a single body with a single spirit, to the full enjoyment of God's kingdom and the glorification of the entire Trinity;

f) short but universal intercessory prayer that all may be made one in the building up of Christ's body and God's people;

g) great recapitulatory doxology.

Objections were raised, however, against the introduction of this anaphora into the Roman liturgy. There were two main objections:

1. The consecratory *epiclesis* comes after the consecration instead of before it as in the *Quam oblationem* of the Roman Canon.

Response:

a) This creates no difficulty from the theological standpoint. This text and many others of the same tradition have been accepted by the Church for use by the Easterners. In addition, there are numerous testimonies of supreme pontiffs that not only acknowledge the complete orthodoxy of these texts but also proclaim the complementarity of the Eastern and Western traditions regarding the Eucharist. To deny or call into doubt that the Eastern liturgies have equal status with the Western would be to deny or cast doubt on these solemn papal statements.

b) Not only were Eucharistic Prayers of the same type common in the past even in the Latin Church (the Old Gallican liturgy and the rites of Spain and Ireland), but they remain in use even today (with the consecratory epiclesis after the words of consecration) wherever the Holy See permits the Mozarabic Rite.

2. Where is the *elevation* to be placed?

Response:

It would be best to locate the showing and adoring of the sacred species at the end of the Eucharistic Prayer, because in the anaphoras of this Eastern tradition the full expression of the Church's intention in using the words of Christ is not complete until that point. To say this is not to prejudge the question of the theological value of the epiclesis as such; rather, the location of the elevation at the end would make it clearer that the intention of the Church in using Christ's words (the same words it uses in the Roman Canon) is expressed in the total prayer of which the words of consecration are an inseparable part.

The anaphora was presented to the Consilium on April 15 by Father Louis Bouyer, who was not only the relator but had also prepared the text. Father Vagaggini presented a minority report.

The result of the vote: 15 yes, 16 no. Since the numerical difference was so small, the president proposed to leave the decision to the Holy Father.

The presidency of the Consilium, for its part, was in favor of accepting this Alexandrine anaphora into the Roman liturgy, at least for use in certain circumstances, such as the Unity Octave, ecumenical days, and so on.

7. A Long Journey

The schema was now scrutinized first by the presidential council and then by the Fathers at the eighth general meeting (April 1967). After being approved by these bodies, it was given to the Pope on May 3. The schema also included nine new prefaces.[6] The letter accompanying the document told the Pope that it was being forwarded "not without some

---

6. *Schemata,* no. 226: *De Missali* 37 (May 1, 1967).

emotion." This, it said, is a work "to which our best experts—theologians and liturgists—have devoted heart and mind with unparalleled generosity for several months. Next to the instruction on worship of the Eucharistic mystery, which we regard as our best pastoral and regulatory document, these new anaphoras reflect the heart of the Consilium in the euchological area."

In his letter Father Bugnini then went on to make suggestions for the continuation of the work:

> In my opinion, these prayers should be given for timely review to the Sacred Congregation for the Doctrine of the Faith. His Eminence Cardinal Alfredo Ottaviani has promised me that if he receives them in the near future, he will do all he can to have them studied before the summer holidays. This timely examination is very important if we are to be able to answer possible requests from episcopal conferences. These requests involve other important matters connected with permission for experimental use of the anaphoras (this is true of the Netherlands[7]).
>
> The Holy Father may decide to have the texts examined by other agencies as well; the Congregation of Rites would certainly be one of them. I await instructions as to what Your Holiness thinks appropriate.

The Pope ordered the schema sent to the Congregation for the Doctrine of the Faith and the Congregation of Rites,[8] which gave it their approval. After a flattering appraisal of it,[9] the Congregation for the Doctrine of the Faith added three pages of appropriate observations and gave its

---

7. As a result of Father Bugnini's visit to the Netherlands (see above, p. 106), a special committee was set up to examine some anaphoras sent by the liturgical commission. Several meetings made it clear that it would be difficult to obtain approval for these; the Consilium therefore suggested that the Dutch wait for the new Eucharistic Prayers then being composed. To this end, a Dutchman, H. Wegman, was included in the study group.

8. The decision was communicated on June 7 in a letter from the Secretariat of State (No. 98582): "It is advisable that in this matter the Consilium proceed in agreement with the Congregation for the Doctrine of the Faith and the Congregation of Rites." Also asked was a speedy report on the work, "during the present month, if possible." The schema was sent to the Congregation for the Doctrine of the Faith on June 12 and to the Congregation of Rites on June 10; the latter examined it July 6–8 and sent back remarks dealing only with details.

9. "In view of the importance of these texts, which are meant to accompany the central action of the Eucharistic sacrifice and which contain the words of consecration, this Sacred Congregation has studied the documentation submitted to it with special care. It has therefore been able to perceive and appreciate the careful and serious preparatory work done by the Consilium and set forth with arguments in the reports accompanying the proposed liturgical texts." The Congregation asked that in addition to the correction of some expressions, the prayers be subjected to a stylistic revision; it cautioned that "terms ought not to be used that may give rise to doctrinal inaccuracies in the vernacular translations."

nihil obstat for the three Eucharistic Prayers and the prefaces, but deferred its approval for the Alexandrian anaphora of St. Basil.[10]

Meanwhile, as was his custom, the Pope had annotated the copy sent to him and had written a page of observations in his own hand.[11] The responses of the two Congregations were then sent to him on July 10, and three days later he sent his own response via Cardinal Cicognani (No. 99893): "You are authorized to prepare a booklet that is to be given to the Fathers of the coming Synod; all things considered, however, it is advisable that the formula of consecration not be changed."

This last decision caused no little difficulty after all the work of the experts, the approval given by the Consilium, and the pastoral expectations that had been aroused. On September 28 the Consilium therefore returned to the subject; it explained the reasons why it had introduced changes and asked that at least the new Eucharistic Prayers have the text that it had approved. This was granted (October 12, 1967; No. 106059):

> The Roman Canon must remain unchanged, since it seems best not to introduce any changes into that text. There is no difficulty, however, about taking into consideration the suggestions made by the experts for the three new Canons. But these changes, together with all the other parts of the reform, must be submitted to the judgment of the Synod.

---

10. "In view of the vote taken by the eminent Fathers of the Consilium and the necessity of prefixing an adequate study of the complex problem of the epiclesis, and in view also of the difficulties that could arise from an unconditional permission to use this Eucharistic Prayer: let the matter be postponed for the time being *(pro tempore dilata)*." The difficulty remained even when the question was raised again at the urging of the Congregation for the Eastern Churches, and nothing more was done (see above, pp. 132–33).

11. These observations were given to Father Bugnini at an audience on July 5. They had to do with some expressions that did not seem to be quite clear. In particular, the Pope expressed his preference for ending the anaphora with "through Christ, with Christ, and in Christ."

He also asked "whether it is really expedient to leave some degree of freedom for adaptations or local tastes" with regard to the acclamations after the consecration. The rubric said: "in these or similar words," while the explanation said: "It is necessary to leave a sufficient margin of freedom for adaptations to the demands of the several languages and the various musical genres." The Pope, however, decided at this same audience that "a set of acclamations (five or six) after the consecration be prepared for the anaphoras." He feared that if the initiative were left to the episcopal conferences, unsuitable acclamations would be introduced, such as "My Lord and my God" (which, however, had been suggested by the Congregation for the Doctrine of the Faith!).

He also expressed his wish that the booklet containing the Eucharistic Prayers be given to the Fathers of the Synod and that the Fathers experiment with the new rite of Mass. The little book containing the prefaces of the Roman Missal and the new prefaces, along with the Roman Canon and the new Eucharistic Prayers, was in fact made ready, and the page proofs were sent to the Pope on October 9. The idea was to present it to the Fathers of the Synod as a gift from the Pope. But the book remained in the page-proof stage.

The third prayer was also used in the experimental "normative Mass" celebrated for the Fathers of the Synod.[12]

The response of the Synod was largely favorable to the introduction of new Eucharistic Prayers.[13] Once the Pope had received the report on the results of the Synod and on the experiments in the Capella Matilde, in which the new Eucharistic Prayers were used, it seemed that publication would now be imminent. But new problems arose that delayed publication. The business was further complicated by the usual interferences and a request for an instruction that would accompany the promulgation of the new Eucharistic Prayers.[14] Once the problems were resolved

---

12. This, too, caused some difficulties. On October 10 the booklet containing the Mass to be celebrated experimentally at the Synod was sent to the Secretariat of State. No. 4 read: "The text for the Canon of the Mass is the one composed for Switzerland, since the Italian Conference has not yet decided on any text." The same statement was repeated on the first page of the booklet. But on the seventeenth of the same month the response came back from the Secretariat of State: "Permission is granted to proceed as outlined, with provision also for experimenting with a new anaphora." This in fact is what was done, using the third anaphora in the text already submitted to the Pope and with the words of consecration as initially adopted and allowed in the letter of the Cardinal Secretary of State on October 12. The Secretariat of State had not been closely following the whole sequence of events and was surprised to see the third anaphora being used, but it was satisfied with the explanation given.

13. See above, p. 351.

14. After a request for expeditiousness on January 24, the Secretariat of State said on January 28 (111.527) that there were no objections to proceeding with the plan for introducing the new rite of Mass. The first stage of this plan called for the publication of the new Eucharistic Prayers on February 1. But the Secretariat added: "But before you proceed to the publication of the 'Prayers,' which, as you are well aware, entails the preparation of a suitable instruction, I would be grateful if you would kindly let me know who will be authorized to use them and under what conditions." It was assumed that the reference here was to regulations for the use of the new anaphoras, to be included as an introduction to the book.

In response, the definitive text of the book was sent on February 8. It included: (1) at the beginning, the regulations for use; (2) before the consecration a rubric was inserted on the way in which the Lord's words were to be spoken, as suggested by the Holy Father on January 22; (3) the words "the mystery of faith" were placed after the Lord's words, as an introduction to the acclamation of the congregation; (4) to avoid difficulties, the Roman Canon and the prefaces found in the Missal were removed, leaving only texts that were new; (5) juridical approval was included in the form of a decree of the Congregation of Rites, signed also by the president of the Consilium.

Everything seemed clear, but the material sent was not what was wanted. On February 15 the Secretariat of State sent a copy of a letter, "from a person of authority, regarding the Italian translation of the Roman Canon," which asked that consideration be given to whether, in a further edition, the formula of consecration in the Roman Canon should be made the same as in the new anaphoras. This question, too, had already been answered on January 15: it was expedient that this uniformity be introduced for the entire Church simultaneously "when the new Order of Mass is published, so as not to create difficulties

and the instruction had been prepared, definitive approval was at last given on April 27, 1968 (No. 111.527).

The new texts were promulgated by a decree of the Congregation of Rites, dated May 23, 1968, which also determined that the prayers could be used beginning on August 15, feast of the Assumption, in that same year.

On June 2, Cardinal Gut, president of the Consilium, sent copies of the book to the episcopal conferences, along with a letter and guidelines for instruction of the faithful on the Eucharistic Prayers.[15] In the letter he expressed the feelings of all:

> The publication of the new Eucharistic Prayers for the Roman liturgy, truly as a new canticle placed on the lips of the praying Church by the Holy Spirit, gives me the welcome opportunity of communicating for the first time as president of the Consilium with Your Excellency and, through you, with all the venerable bishops, clergy, religious and faithful of your country, especially with those who wholeheartedly dedicate themselves to the progress of an intelligent, orderly, and dynamic renewal of the liturgy in the spirit of the Council and the postconciliar documents.

In addition to the new Eucharistic Prayers, the book contained eight new prefaces: for Advent (2), the Sundays of Lent (1), the Sundays of

---

for those episcopal conferences that have already introduced translations of the Roman Canon.''

Only on March 23, after repeated requests for speed, was it explained that what was wanted was an instruction to accompany the new Eucharistic Prayers; that it was not clear under what conditions these prayers were being allowed; and that the answer regarding the uniformity of the words of consecration was not regarded as a real answer. The instruction was then prepared and sent to the Secretariat of State on March 26, along with a new explanation of all the points said to have not yet been clarified: conditions, uniformity of the Lord's word, manner of approval.

The matter was thus finally settled in God's good time. But the delay had become painful because outsiders were holding Cardinal Benno Gut, the new president of the Consilium, responsible for the delay in publication, when the responsibility was not his at all. In fact, he and Father Bugnini had had a meeting on March 7 with Archbishop Philippe and Monsignor Agustoni of the Congregation for the Doctrine of the Faith at which definitive agreement was reached on the entire book containing the Eucharistic Prayers.

15. *Preces eucharisticae et praefationes* (Vatican Polyglot Press, 1968. 54 pp.). In addition to the text, the book included the melody for the parts that can be sung. Documents: Congregation of Rites, decree *Prece eucharistica* promulgating three new Eucharistic Prayers and eight prefaces (May 23, 1968): DOL 241 no. 1930; Congregation of Rites, Norms for the use of the Eucharistic Prayers I-IV (May 23, 1968): DOL 242 nos. 1931-41; Cardinal Benno Gut, letter *La publication* on the new Eucharistic Prayers (June 2, 1968): DOL 243 nos. 1942-44; Consilium, guidelines *Au cours des derniers mois* to assist catechesis on the anaphoras of the Mass (June 2, 1968): DOL 244 nos. 1945-63. — Presentation to the press was made by C. Vagaggini by appointment of the Secretariat of State.

Ordinary Time (2), the Eucharist (1), and two common prefaces. These provided variety and at the same time satisfied, at least provisionally, desires expressed with regard to the Eucharistic celebration.[16]

II. THE CIRCULAR LETTER *EUCHARISTIAE PARTICIPATIONEM*

Even before the new Eucharistic Prayers were published, it was clear that Eucharistic Prayers were being composed without restriction in many places. The problem had already been faced in the Netherlands, and Rome had begun an examination of some texts submitted by the Netherlands liturgical commission. As a result of this uncontrolled production, over a hundred models were in circulation, some of them clearly deficient. Their translation into other languages only made the problem more difficult.[17] In an attempt to stem the flood, the Dutch bishops took the initiative by selecting eleven texts, publishing them along with the Order of Mass,[18] and allowing their use (November 11, 1969). The bishops of Flemish-speaking Belgium did the same but limited the texts to five (November 1, 1969). They had been preceded by the bishops of Indonesia, who had given their approval to ten formularies (October 24, 1968).

It was hoped that the publication of the new Eucharistic Prayers would eliminate or at least lessen the problem. This did not happen. The bishops felt torn between two opposing forces: the necessity of establishing observance of liturgical legislation and the need for more extensive adaptation. When the Congregation for Divine Worship called upon the German Episcopal Conference, on December 18, 1970, to brand as illicit the use of the Eucharistic Prayers printed in the book by A. Schilling, the conference replied:

> Priests and faithful have been told on a number of occasions that only lawfully approved texts may be used; another statement would produce no results . . . .
>
> The primary reason why privately composed texts are being used is that when said in the vernacular, the Eucharistic Prayer needs to display a greater

---

16. Nine prefaces had been planned, but because of difficulties raised by the Congregation for the Doctrine of the Faith, the preface for the feast of the Apostles was removed and its publication deferred until the publication of the new Missal. The texts had been prepared by study group 18bis. The Consilium had gone over them together with the Eucharistic Prayers.

17. See A. Schilling, *Fürbitten und Kanongebete der Holländischen Kirche* (Essen, 1968), which quickly went through many printings (eleven by the end of 1971).

18. See Netherlands Liturgical Commission, *Missaal I. Ordo Missae* (Hilversum, 1970). Some of the texts had been published for study purposes and as literary exercises, but once they were printed in journals, people yielded to the temptation of using them.

variety than it presently has. Some priests also claim that they use these texts because they are better understood, less ponderous theologically, and more attuned to the language and culture of our times than are the four Eucharistic Prayers of the Roman liturgy . . . .

Many are persuaded that the most effective way of preventing the use of unauthorized Eucharistic Prayers is the official introduction of other approved texts in addition to the present four. The liturgical commissions of the German-speaking countries have set up a study group to deal with all questions regarding the Eucharistic Prayers . . . . When the moment is ripe, the episcopal conferences will submit texts to the Holy See in accordance with article 40, 1 of the liturgical Constitution.[19]

Meanwhile, having received approval from the Congregation for the Doctrine of the Faith (June 19, 1970), the Congregation for Divine Worship on June 26, 1970, approved an adaptation of the Eucharistic Prayer for use in Masses with deaf-mutes.[20] Similar concessions were given to the Philippines for experimental use of a Eucharistic Prayer in First Communion Masses;[21] to Switzerland for an adaptation of the Roman Canon and of Eucharistic Prayer IV in Masses with children;[22] and for a Eucharistic Prayer for Masses with children[23] and another for Masses with Aborigines[24] on occasion of the International Eucharistic Congress in Melbourne.

---

19. A movement following the same pattern could be seen in the African Church as well. In 1968 there was an unsuccessful effort to introduce the Ethiopian Anaphora of the Apostles and then to adapt the Roman Canon. The episcopal conference of Zambia asked for, among other adaptations, a Eucharistic Prayer that would better reflect the African mentality (August 24, 1970). The Congregation for Divine Worship answered: "You may look into the possibility of a Eucharistic Prayer for the African peoples. But before any experimentation the texts, like other projects of a similar nature, must be submitted to the Congregation for an examination in which experts on things African will play a part" (January 15, 1971). The news had immediate effects, with the bishops of Burundi telling their clergy, in a letter of March 12, 1971, that the Congregation for Divine Worship was willing to approve Eucharistic Prayers adapted to the circumstances of regions and particular groups, provided the texts were submitted to it. This was a broad interpretation of the Congregation's intentions and inevitably had wearisome consequences.

20. June 26, 1970; the same concession was made *ad interim* to Australia on March 14, 1972. For the texts allowed by the Congregation for Divine Worship, see Ph. Béguerie and J. Evenou, *Eucharisties de tous pays* (Paris: Centre National de Pastorale Liturgique, 1975).

21. March 16, 1971.

22. December 6, 1971.

23. November 1, 1972; reviewed and approved by the Congregation for the Doctrine of the Faith. A Eucharistic Prayer for the congress itself was also requested but not granted.

24. December 7, 1972, approved by the Congregation for the Doctrine of the Faith. Its use was extended after the congress, with the permission of the Secretariat of State (May 30, 1973; No. 232821).

Other petitions for approval were unsuccessful. Meanwhile the situation was becoming increasingly worrisome. Therefore, at an audience on May 27, 1971, the Congregation for Divine Worship told the Pope:

> The problem cannot be ignored, because it is becoming too widespread. It is difficult to say what the best solution would be. One thing that can be said is that many of these compositions have arisen due to ignorance of the Roman Missal or to preconceptions or to inadequate theological instruction.
>
> On the other hand, it also seems necessary to study the problem from all sides, that is, to take into consideration the needs and the reasons for the phenomenon. This Congregation thinks such a study should be made. We hear that the Liturgical Institute of Paris has collected and studied over two hundred Eucharistic Prayers. Many publications offer new Canons.

The Congregation concluded: "If the Holy Father agrees, the Congregation would like to undertake a systematic collection of all the existing material and study it . . . so that it may have a clear grasp of the dimensions of the problem and be able to tackle it with greater clarity and on a solid basis."

A reply came on June 22 (No. 184899): "Given the extent of the indiscriminate use of unapproved Eucharistic Prayers, the Holy Father wishes that a careful study be made of the problem in all its aspects, in order to find a solution that will remedy this serious situation of undisciplined liturgical practice." The reply emphasized that "a detailed investigation of the situation and a thorough study of the question" should be made.

After the necessary negotiations, a special study group was appointed on September 17, 1971.[25]

1. *Work of the Study Group*

The *first meeting* of the study group dealing with Eucharistic Prayers was held October 21–23, 1971. At this meeting the group made a first survey of the problem and possible solutions to it. It was decided to conduct a further investigation of the situation in countries not represented in the study group itself and to prepare studies on specific points.[26] After

---

25. *Relator:* E. J. Lengeling; *secretary:* R. Kaczynski; *members:* C. Braga, P. Coughlan, P. Farnés, J. Gélineau, P. Gy, J. Rotelle, D. Sartore, P. C. Vriens, J. Wagner.

26. J. Gélineau: forms of congregational participation; P. Farnés: the communion of saints; J. Wagner: literary genre and epiclesis; S. Marsili: concept of "anamnesis" and offering; L. Ligier: relation between Jewish *berakah* and Eucharistic Prayer; F. Sottocornola: intercessions; K. Amon: *Sanctus*; P. C. Vriens: contemporary relevance of the Eucharistic Prayer.

this meeting, as after the others, a full set of minutes was prepared and sent to other qualified persons for their observations and suggestions.

The minutes were, of course, sent to the Pope. The Secretary of State replied on December 18, 1971:

> I am happy to inform you that the Holy Father, to whom I submitted the booklet as quickly as possible, has expressed his lively satisfaction at the broad approach taken to the question, as was indeed necessary if the situation was to be accurately grasped and timely remedies proposed.
>
> At the same time His Holiness has commented that in his opinion the problem is not to be resolved either by avoiding every increase [in the number of Eucharistic Prayers] or by following the path of total permissiveness, which might open the door to improper and arbitrary actions, confuse the faithful, and call into the question the very validity of the Eucharistic sacrifice. The need rather is to see whether and how formulas of suitable language and content can be found in the vast liturgical treasury and also to compose new formulas with the utmost literary and theological care—all of this under the supervision of the episcopate and with the carefully granted approval of the Congregation.

The *second meeting* was held November 24–27 of the same year. The discussion was based on the statements requested after the previous meeting. The relator[27] and secretary then drew up a first schema, which was sent on December 18 to the study group and to thirty-six *periti* and eighteen consultors of the Congregation.[28]

---

27. Meanwhile two requests had come in, from the dioceses of Münster and Limburg, for permission to experiment with the new Eucharistic Prayers. The reason given was the present serious violations of discipline. The Congregation discussed the matter at length at one of its plenary meetings and finally came down in favor of the grant. In this it was motivated solely by respect for Professor Lengeling, who would be in charge of the experiments. The experience would also be of value to him personally, in view of the work of the study group. The permission was granted to both dioceses on November 9, 1971 *ad interim*, that is, until the study group should have finished its work on the Eucharistic Prayers. As a matter of fact, after a positive evaluation by Professor Lengeling, the grant ended on November 13, 1972.

28. The schema, which remained substantially the same in later redactions, was about a hundred pages in length and had six chapters: I. The problem of the Eucharistic Prayers, from the schema for the Constitution on the Liturgy to 1972; II. Situation regarding Eucharistic Prayers of private origin; III. Reasons for the use of privately composed Eucharistic Prayers; IV. Evaluation of privately composed Eucharistic Prayers; V. Possible solutions to the problem; VI. Guidelines for preparing and evaluating Eucharistic Prayers.

Chapter VI had six subdivisions: A. General observations (theological, ecumenical, liturgical, pastoral); B. Nature of the Eucharistic Prayer (a presidential prayer; praise of God and thanksgiving, crowned by the doxology; petition; anamnesis; Trinitarian structure); C. Essential elements (thanksgiving; petition, words of institution; anamnesis; doxology); D. Elements for completeness (remembrance of the sacrifice; epiclesis; communion with the Church); E. Elements "necessary because of their appropriate and constant presence"

The *third meeting* (January 25–26, 1972) was given over to a study of the answers received. During the next few days (January 26–28), the consultors of the Congregation held their own meeting; they were joined by the members of the study group dealing with the Eucharistic Prayers. The discussion was rather lively, due in part to opposition from some reputable consultors. At the end four questions were put to a vote:

1. *Should the number of Eucharistic Prayers in the Roman Missal be increased?*
Yes: 10; no: 3; yes with reservations: 4.

2. *Should a larger number of Eucharistic Prayers be allowed in regions in which the episcopal conferences think it advisable?*
Yes: 12; no: 0; yes with reservations: 5.

3. *Is the solution proposed in no. 39 a) of the schema acceptable?* (That is, that the Congregation for Divine Worship should prepare models of Eucharistic Prayers, with the possibility of adapting them to some small extent.)
Yes: 8; no: 8; yes with reservations: 1.

4. *Is the solution proposed in no. 29 b) acceptable?* (That is, that the Congregation should set down guidelines in accordance with which the episcopal conferences can pass judgment on or compose new Eucharistic Prayers.)[29]
Yes: 8; no: 5; yes with reservations: 4.

The result was substantially positive.[30] But in its letter (February 2)

(singing of the *Sanctus*; mention of the angels before the *Sanctus*; communion with the saints; intercessions); F. Possible or even desirable elements (thanksgiving for creation; request that the Church's offering be accepted; "actualization"; gestures, modes, and forms of participation).

The schema ended with an appendix of eleven chapters containing reports on studies done or requested by the study group; some texts of new Eucharistic Prayers in French, Dutch, and German; the study group's evaluation of these texts.

29. Chapter V of the schema, on possible ways of damming the stream of free creativity, examined four possible solutions: tolerance; unqualified prohibition; new Eucharistic Prayers to be prepared by the Holy See; new Eucharistic Prayers to be prepared by the episcopal conferences. There was hesitation about having the Holy See prepare new texts, because it was not certain that ways could be found of meeting local needs; if these needs were not met, the phenomenon would persist. The study group inclined toward the fourth solution and suggested two approaches, which were put to a vote of the consultors. The first approach differed from the third solution only in that it offered greater possibilities of choice and adaptation. The second approach was like that adopted for the prayer of the faithful by publication of the little book *De oratione communi seu fidelium*. The group showed itself clearly in favor of this second approach, which it regarded as the only really possible and effective solution. But this solution was also the one that elicited the strongest opposition, as we shall see.

30. Unfortunately, the consultors, who were a minority and isolated in addition, were not polled. An anonymous booklet entitled *Observationes de opportunitate an importunitate*

of thanks for the documents on the *second* meeting of the study group, the Secretariat of State went on to say:

> It is my duty to inform you that the documents submitted do not seem entirely in keeping with the guidelines sent from this Secretariat in its letter of September 18 (No. 199130). When His Holiness admitted the timeliness of further study in this area and even the possible composition of new formulas "under the supervision of the episcopate and with the carefully granted approval of the Congregation," he did not mean that the Holy See should be content simply to provide guidelines for the composition of anaphoras and then to approve texts submitted for its consideration, thus opening the way to a perhaps endless number of Eucharistic Prayers.
>
> On the other hand, we realize that the mind of the Supreme Pontiff was made known to Your Eminence only when the experts had already completed the work of their second meeting. It is therefore quite possible that they did not take it into account at their third meeting, held at the end of January.

The Secretariat of State had come to see that the rhythm of work in the study group differed from its own and that this gave rise to difficulties. As a matter of fact, by the time this letter of February 2 arrived, the group had already revised the schema (it was dated February 1, 1972) and had sent it to the members of the Congregation. The haste had been dictated, among other things, by the need of allowing the Fathers adequate time to study the entire extensive documentation in preparation for their plenary meeting to be held in March.

Meanwhile the new schema, together with a report on the work, had been sent to the Holy Father, who discussed it at an audience (February 28) with the secretary of the Congregation (whom he had ordained a bishop on February 13). The Pope explained his thoughts, which he had also typed out and given to the secretary. He said:

> I once again strongly urge the Congregation for Divine Worship to try to control the tendency to multiply Eucharistic Prayers.
>
> The Congregation is reminded that several other Congregations—for the Doctrine of the Faith, the Discipline of the Sacraments, the Clergy (especially the pastoral aspect of the matter), and the Bishops—also have competency in this area.

Preces Eucharisticas novas conficiendi was circulated almost everywhere. It was sent to representatives of the Curia and the members of the Congregation. The Cardinal of Berlin responded by sending all the members his vote against the introduction of new Eucharistic Prayers. Expressions of concern poured in from the nunciatures in Bonn and the Netherlands. Consultors Rose and Martimort sent their "vote" against the view of the Congregation for the Doctrine of the Faith. This became a weapon for that Congregation and a serious injury to the Congregation for Divine Worship.

The Congregation should keep in mind the principle of the correspondence between the *lex orandi* and the *lex credendi*.

It should set a proper value on liturgical uniformity in the Latin Church, especially at the present time, in which movements of the faithful from one region to another are so frequent and extensive.

There should be no yielding to the arbitrary inspirations of some learned individuals or literary people or charismatics, when the communities of the faithful want regularity in liturgical formulas and a certain intangible sacredness in the Eucharistic Prayers said by their priestly minister.

The episcopal conferences are not to be given permission to introduce new Eucharistic Prayers unless these have at least been first carefully reviewed by the Holy See, and unless permission is first given on each occasion and for specific reasons.

Changes of any kind in the sacramental words are not to be tolerated; moreover, the faithful retention of the essential parts of the anaphora, as prescribed by tradition for official worship, is always required.

The possible introduction of peculiarities judged timely in special circumstances may be discussed for other parts of the rite of Mass but not for the Eucharistic Prayers.

2. Discussion at the Plenary Meeting

During the last two days of its second plenary meeting (March 7–11, 1972), the Congregation for Divine Worship studied the schema for the Eucharistic Prayers.[31] Five propositions were put to a vote:

1. *In view of the present situation regarding the development and use of Eucharistic Prayers, should competent authority take some steps to increase the number of these prayers?*

Yes: 13; no: 0; yes with reservations: 3.

2. *Is it enough that the Holy See should prepare some new Eucharistic Prayers?*

Yes: 2; no: 12; yes with reservations: 2.

3. *Is it enough that the Holy See should provide some models to be adapted by the episcopal conferences?*

Yes: 0; no: 16; yes with reservations: 0.

---

31. The Fathers were also given an account of the entire history of the study of the problem, together with the instructions successively received by the Secretariat of State. The latter had recommended that the contents of the letter of February 2 be made known to the plenary meeting of the Congregation for Divine Worship, lest the Fathers, "in ignorance of the real thinking of His Holiness, proceed along the path traced out by the *periti*, although this is not fully in conformity with the directives given to them," and lest they "adopt the conclusions approved by the consultors, inasmuch as the entire approach taken to the problem may make them regard these conclusions as the only possible solution of the problem."

4. *Should the episcopal conferences be able to compose new Eucharistic Prayers that satisfy criteria set down by the Holy See and are then submitted to the latter?*

Yes: 11; no: 3: yes with reservations: 2 (provided the vote of the conferences is consultative).

5. *Are the guidelines set down in Chapter VI for preparing and evaluating Eucharistic Prayers acceptable?*

Yes: 9; no: 2; yes with reservations: 5 (the essential parts must always be present; one of the epicleses and the *Sanctus* are necessary elements; further thorough review is needed).

A report on the plenary meeting was sent to the Secretariat of State on April 12, accompanied by a request from the Cardinal Prefect that he might be allowed an audience at which he could explain in person the particulars of the problems discussed at the plenary meeting. On the problem of the Eucharistic Prayers, the report had this to say:

In light of all the fine work done by the *periti* and of the lively discussion at the plenary meeting—a discussion sealed by the votes of the Fathers (some of which were truly valuable for their balance and content)—the Congregation ventures to make the following suggestions.

1. As a matter of principle, it seems that changes and variety in the Eucharistic Prayers and, more generally, in the Order of Mass should be very firmly rejected. The reasons:

a) those involved in pastoral care at the *parochial* level emphatically call for a degree of stability, and their voices, we think, should be heard;

b) liturgists and pastors must be persuaded to enter more thoroughly into the liturgical renewal and to take advantage of the copious euchological material in the Missal and other liturgical books.

2. The Congregation might prepare *embolisms* for various feasts or "occasions," to be inserted into the four Eucharistic Prayers (these embolisms would have the same function as the proper *Communicantes* and *Hanc igitur* of the past).

3. It would be a help to approve the fifth Eucharistic Prayer—the "Anaphora of St. Basil"—that was proposed and requested two or three years ago by a plenary meeting of the Congregation for the Eastern Churches.

4. Another possibility is some new Eucharistic Prayers for various feasts or various circumstances, to be prepared by this Congregation.

5. Only in extraordinary circumstances, and then case by case, should episcopal conferences that have the personnel and means for the task be given permission to prepare any new Eucharistic Prayers. The conference must first request authorization and then prepare the text, which must be subjected to close study by the competent agencies of the Holy See.

6. These regulations should be set forth clearly in an instruction, as was done for communion in the hand. No. 5, however, which admits the pos-

sibility of the conferences being allowed, case by case, to prepare new Eucharistic Prayers, should be turned into a footnote. Even the typographic format will thus make it clear that such permission is to be something utterly exceptional.

These suggestions represented a balanced solution that took into account the real situation, the work done by the group, and the various reactions expressed in the votes at the plenary meeting.

The audience granted by the Pope to the Cardinal Prefect took place on April 20, but a response was issued only a month later (May 23). The reply said:

> It is not expedient that the Congregation publish the acts of the study committee containing the guidelines for the composition of anaphoras; the Congregation should also prevent its *periti* from making them public. On the other hand, it may with all due haste, and in collaboration with the agencies concerned, draft an instruction containing the regulations and guidelines in this matter.

3. *Final Phase*

The instruction was drafted by the relator and secretary of the group during the summer months and sent to the study group on September 8, 1972. The group held its *fourth* and final meeting on September 25-26, in a somewhat "disheartened" atmosphere. It worked hard, however, and the schema for the instruction was sent to the Holy Father on October 7.

The accompanying letter singled out the following points, among others, that were made in the instruction: the emphasis on the need of using to the full the vast possibilities offered by the new Roman Missal; the reminder of the traditional structural elements of a good anaphora; and, finally, the decree (in its last number, 39) that only in truly extraordinary circumstances, and then case by case, could the episcopal conferences ask the Holy See for permission to prepare a new anaphora and, permission having been received, furnish the text and submit it for the study and approval of the Apostolic See. After mature study and careful reflection, this seemed to be the best, if not the only, realistic way of dealing with the difficult question and providing the bishops with a strong instrument of pastoral government.

On November 17 the Cardinal Secretary of State let it be known that he had sent the text on to the Congregation for the Doctrine of the Faith "with a request that it act as quickly as possible." The judgment of this

Congregation was negative.[32] The Cardinal Secretary of State made this known on January 11, 1973.

> The Congregation for the Doctrine of the Faith has given a negative answer regarding the timeliness of granting the episcopal conferences permission to redact new anaphoras. Its prohibition must be accepted.
>
> In the judgment of the Holy Father, the Congregation must therefore inform the episcopal conferences of this decision. It should urge them to put an end to "experimental" Eucharistic Prayers, to regard as authorized by the Church only the Eucharistic Prayers in the Missal, and to cultivate in this matter a sense of respect for a uniform discipline common to the entire Latin Church.
>
> The Holy See does not unqualifiedly exclude the possibility that it might in special circumstances authorize the use of a new anaphora; in such cases, however, the matter both of its preparation and of its promulgation should be agreed on in advance with the Holy See.
>
> With regard to the many unapproved Eucharistic Prayers already in use in some countries, it will be necessary eventually to decide on the steps to be taken.
>
> His Holiness has also called attention once again to the need of exercising moderation and discernment in regard to Masses for special categories of the faithful (for example, the "Mass with children" now being studied), so as not to multiply special forms of worship when the existing regulations seem to allow sufficient room for adaptations and for the introduction of special prayers into other parts of the Mass outside the anaphora.

This reply came like a cold shower after a year and a half of hard and intelligent work. A short circular letter (a page in length) containing the thoughts of the reply just cited was then drafted and sent to the Secretariat of State (January 20, 1973). The Secretariat was now surprised in its turn. In fact, it sent the following answer:

> The substance of the letter is fine, but it needs to be milder in form, and the doctrinal and pastoral reasons for the decision should also be given.
>
> In fact, as far as is possible, the regulations should be set forth in a positive way by making more abundant use, for example, of the positive elements in the projected instruction and by laying greater emphasis on the

---

32. In the meantime, others made their voices heard in opposition to approval of new Eucharistic Prayers: a group of theologians on the International Theological Commission (October 11), a French archbishop, and those consultors of the Congregation for Divine Worship who had cast a negative vote at the study sessions. All these put pressure on the Supreme Pastor or denied their own knowledge and insight! When the Congregation for the Doctrine of the Faith examined the instruction, it did not take into account the extensive work of the study group but took its stand on the two "votes" sent to it by the two consultors of the SCDW who had declared themselves opposed (see n. 30).

part dealing with the possibility that the Holy See, which reserves to itself all permissions in this area, may in particular cases authorize the compilation and use of new anaphoras.

The Secretariat then asked that a new draft be prepared (January 31, 1973).[33]

4. *The Circular Letter*

The secretariat of the Congregation now summoned a small group[34] and came to an agreement with it on the redaction of the definitive document. The draft was sent to the Pope on March 10. The letter accompanying it described the contents, which, apart from some small alterations, were to remain unchanged.

The document took the form of a declaration and dealt with a number of points, beginning with the reform of the Missal and the reasons for undertaking it (nos. 1-2). The Missal has not yet been everywhere translated (no. 2), yet a greater degree of adaptation, especially in the Eucharistic Prayers, is already being requested (no. 4). The Congregation for Divine Worship and other agencies concerned have studied the problem and submitted their conclusions to the Holy Father. It is not thought expedient to grant the episcopal conferences a general permission to prepare and approve new Eucharistic Prayers. The need is rather for instruction of the faithful (no. 5). The approved prayers are the four in the Roman Missal; no others may be used without the permission and approval of the Apostolic See. The conferences and individual bishops must try to persuade priests to follow Church discipline. In particular cases, the Holy See, which reserves to itself all permissions in this area, will grant authorization for the compilation and use of new anaphoras or will itself compose others (no. 6).

---

33. The thinking of the Congregation for Divine Worship was that the Church was faced "with a widespread phenomenon which, it seems, cannot be handled by simply prohibiting it or by ignoring it, but only by channeling it so that the Holy See can still be in control." The secretary expressed this view to the Pope at an audience on December 21, 1972. The Pope then stated his decision: " 'No' to any further experiments. The Holy See *reserves to itself* the authority to prepare new Eucharistic Prayers in particular cases."

34. The group was made up of: B. Fischer, E. J. Lengeling, J. Wagner, P.-M. Gy, G. Agustoni, C. Braga, and R. Kaczynski. It met at the home of the secretary on March 1. Three schemas were composed, with Father Braga doing the editing. Lengeling was not present; recent events had prostrated him. After being attacked abroad on occasion of the publication in German of eleven Dutch Eucharistic Prayers (see A. Schilling, *Elf Eucharistische Gebete* [Essen, 1972]), and seeing the work of the study group of the Congregation going for naught, he began to feel the exhaustion that would result in the beginning of heart trouble at the end of March.

The meaning and application of this decision is then explained (nos. 7-10). Until the recent reform, the Roman tradition (unlike other traditions) had a single unchanging Canon, which, however, was variable in its preface, *Communicantes*, and *Hanc igitur*. The reform has extended the variability by increasing the number of changeable parts of the Roman Canon and adding three new Eucharistic Prayers. The Eucharistic Prayers give expression to the Church's unity and the objectivity of liturgical prayer (no. 11).

Also pointed out are the possibilities of adaptation in the celebration of the Eucharist (nos. 12-16): selection of formularies and texts, preparation of teachings (no. 13); the introductions (no. 15); the homily (no. 15); the prayer of the faithful (no. 16).

Finally, the document urges respect for the various ways of uttering liturgical texts (no. 17) and also for silence as part of the liturgy (no. 18). The document ends with the wish that priests would devote themselves to the education of the faithful (no. 19).

On April 18 the following answer was received:

> I hasten to tell you that the Holy Father has carefully studied the draft and, after making some minor changes, has approved it, and to return the definitive text to you with revisions and corrections in form and Latinity.
>
> I advise you, in addition, that it seems better not to call the document a "declaration" but to keep the name and form of a "circular letter" to the presidents of the episcopal conferences. I am charged as well to express to Your Eminence and all those who have worked on the preparation of the text the gratitude and satisfaction of His Holiness.

After approval had been given to the page proofs, the circular letter *Eucharistiae participationem* to the presidents of the episcopal conferences, on the Eucharistic Prayers, was published on April 27, 1973, and made known on June 14.[35]

III. SPECIAL EUCHARISTIC PRAYERS

In the ensuing years it was the duty of the Congregation to see that the provisions of the circular letter were fully carried out. It did so by intervening to call attention to and suppress abuses and by keeping faith with the promise made in no. 6 that the Holy See would in special cases grant authorization to compile and use new anaphoras. On the first point it met with resistance abroad, on the second with resistance in the Curia.

---

35. *DOL* 248 nos. 1975-93. See *L'Osservatore Romano*, June 14, 1973; *Not* 9 (1973) 193-200. This entire issue (no. 84) of *Notitiae* is given over to a commentary on the circular letter and to studies of the Eucharistic Prayers.

The first country to ask for a special Eucharistic Prayer was Switzerland on the occasion of its synod;[36] the second was the Netherlands for its "Pastoral Colloquium" of November 1, 1974;[37] the third was Brazil for the National Eucharistic Congress at Manaus.[38] All three requests were granted with the approval of the Holy Father and after a doctrinal review by the Congregation for the Doctrine of the Faith.[39] Other requests, as, for example, for the centenary of the Cathedral of Strasbourg and for Indonesia, were turned down.[40]

a) *Masses with children and Masses of reconciliation*

There were many requests for Eucharistic Prayers adapted to the language and mentality of children and for others on the occasion of the

---

36. Permission to prepare a special Eucharistic Prayer for the Swiss Synod was given by the Holy Father on February 14, 1974 (No. 251806). The text was then prepared, scrutinized by the Congregation for the Doctrine of the Faith, and approved by it with minor observations on July 20, 1974 (Prot. no. 19/72), and then by the Holy Father (August 5, 1974; No. 263878). The decree of the Congregation for Divine Worship was dated August 8, 1974 (Prot. no. 1972/74).

This was a single prayer, but with variations, according to four themes, in the preface and intercessions. To facilitate celebration, the variations were printed along with the fixed parts, thus giving the impression of four Eucharistic Prayers. This surprised the Congregation for the Doctrine of the Faith and brought rebukes from it, even though it had given its approval and had also approved the variable parts. The same anaphora was then granted to Luxembourg (November 6, 1974; Prot. no. 2255/74), Austria (January 2, 1975; Prot. no. 2471/74), and Strasbourg (April 15, 1975; Prot. no. 463/75), in each case with the Holy Father's approval.

37. The concession was limited to the opening of the colloquium. The text was corrected by the Congregation for Divine Worship, which added the consecratory epiclesis and the commemoration of the dead. The grant was then made on August 19, 1974 (Prot. no. 1852/74), after the *nihil obstat* had been obtained from the Congregation for the Doctrine of the Faith on July 5 (Prot. no. 272/74) and the Pope had given his approval on August 16 (No. 264810).

38. Three prayers had been requested, but only one was granted (after corrections) by the Congregation for Divine Worship in a decree of November 11, 1974 (Prot. no. 272/74); the Holy Father had given authorization on February 12, 1974 (No. 250354), and the Congregation for the Doctrine of the Faith had given its *nihil obstat* on August 13, 1974 (Prot. no. 213/72).

39. As is clear from the information given above, the law and the several competencies involved were respected in each case.

40. After the failure of the request for an Indonesian Eucharistic Prayer, the Holy Father allowed the Indonesian Liturgical Commission to submit a special anaphora for funeral Masses. The text, however, was never approved.

On the other hand, the German-speaking episcopal conferences used the authorization granted by the circular letter (nos. 9-10) to prepare new special prefaces and embolisms for insertion into the approved new Eucharistic Prayers. They submitted various of these in connection with the German translation of the new Missal, which was confirmed on December 10, 1974; see Ph. Béguerie and J. Evenou (n. 20), 96–116.

celebration of the Holy Year, which had begun in the local Churches in 1974. In order to avoid private undertakings, which were being considered even by some national or international liturgical commissions, the Congregation for Divine Worship decided to take the initiative. It had already dealt with the subject of Eucharistic Prayers for children when it was preparing the Directory for Masses with Children. At that time, however, the question had been put off at the insistence of the Congregation for the Doctrine of the Faith.

On May 3, 1973, it asked the Pope for permission to prepare one or two formularies for Masses with children, and he granted it. The letter sent by the Secretariat of State (October 23, 1973; No. 245165) said: "After reflecting on the note requesting Eucharistic Prayers for children and studying the observations and suggestions made by the same Congregation, the Supreme Pontiff has authorized the Congregation to prepare two or three formularies for the entire Church."

A short time later, with regard to a request having to do with the Holy Year:

> His Holiness has considered the reasons given and has decided to accept the proposal. He therefore commissions Your Excellency [Archbishop Bugnini] to have a draft prepared on the basis of the guidelines you have set down, and to submit it for his examination.
>
> In communicating this decision, may I suggest that since this is an anaphora granted on the occasion of the Holy Year, it be given a special title under which it may then be made part of the Missal (October 29, 1973; No. 243972).

A special study group was set up;[41] it held three general meetings. At the first, which took place November 13–15, 1973, it was decided to compose three Eucharistic Prayers for Masses with children and two for the Holy Year;[42] the guidelines for these were also determined. The texts

---

41. The group included: B. Fischer, L. Agustoni, Ph. Béguerie, P. Coughlan, A. Haquin, G. Pasqualetti, R. Kaczynski, V. Pedrosa, H. Rennings, D. Rimaud, J. Gélineau, and A. Dumas. For Masses with children: *relator:* B. Fischer; *secretary:* R. Kaczynski. For the Holy Year: *relator:* D. Rimaud; *secretary:* A. Dumas.

42. Existing models were used as a basis: for the first prayer for children, a Belgian-Dutch text; for the second, one of the prayers prepared by the committee for French liturgical texts; for the third, a text prepared by Germans.

The same was done for the Holy Year prayer. The original intention was to prepare a single prayer. But concrete requests then came in from various episcopates, and in order to satisfy them, it was thought expedient to prepare two texts that would embody different perspectives. The first uses and develops the major lines of biblical thought on reconciliation. The second starts rather with the concrete experience of people today and interprets it in the light of faith.

were prepared in French and German during the following days and were then translated into English, Italian, and Spanish. They were then sent for examination to forty-nine experts around the world, these being chosen by the members of the study group itself.

The second meeting was held January 16–18, 1974, with two "observers" from the Congregation for the Doctrine of the Faith in attendance.[43]

The third meeting was attended only by the men chiefly responsible for the redaction of the prayers (Fischer, Gélineau, Rennings, and Rimaud), the observers from the Congregation for the Doctrine of the Faith, and Abbot Egger, from the Secretariat of State, who had seen to the Latin text of the five Eucharistic Prayers.[44]

After this meeting all five prayers were gathered into a booklet, together with an introduction, and sent to the Congregation for the Doctrine of the Faith on March 7, 1974. A barely favorable reply came back on May 10.

> Given the doctrinal confusion presently existing in matters liturgical, this sacred Congregation voices its lively concern at the multiplication of Eucharistic Prayers, for this foreshadows and encourages other requests of the same kind, which it will be difficult to refuse.[45]
>
> Inasmuch as the Holy Father has commissioned the Congregation for Divine Worship to draft some Eucharistic Prayers, we have voted in favor of approval of one new Eucharistic Prayer for each of the two categories suggested, that is, one for children and one for the Holy Year; use of the latter is to be limited to the Holy Year.
>
> We also suggest that the two new Eucharistic Prayers, if and when approved, not become part of the Missal. There are various reasons for this; for example interest in the Eucharistic Prayer for children is not likely to last. The prayers are therefore approved for the time required and for the occasions on which they may be useful.

---

43. The secretary of the Congregation for Divine Worship had asked for their attendance: "It would be quite helpful if the two theologians who will subsequently have to examine the texts on behalf of the Congregation for the Doctrine of the Faith could attend our meetings as observers" (December 16, 1973). The suggestion was accepted, and on January 7, 1974, Archbishop Hamer sent the names of the two observers: Fathers Benoît Duroux and Marcellino Zalba. Their collaboration was really useful and cordial.

44. Abbot Egger's presence had been requested of the Substitute Secretary of State on January 19. As on other occasions, he proved to be an intelligent, courteous, and cordial co-worker.

45. In its reply the Congregation for Divine Worship pointed out that the circular letter gave the episcopal conferences the right to ask for other Eucharistic Prayers in special circumstances. It added that "the Congregation for Divine Worship is firmly convinced that the requests for Eucharistic Prayers and the manifestations of arbitrary creativity can be restricted *only* if the Holy See itself seeks to *anticipate them* by offering worthwhile texts that meet various needs and circumstances." But this idea was never really accepted.

The reply asked, finally, that the principle in no. 8 of the Introduction, which granted a certain freedom in translating, be revised and that it emphasize rather fidelity to the original.[46]

On May 15 the matter was resubmitted to the Secretariat of State. It was pointed out that the proposed Eucharistic Prayers had been based on guidelines received from the Holy Father and the Secretariat of State itself, after these two authorities had carefully considered the requests of the bishops and the possibilities of meeting them that were offered by current liturgical law. The regulations set down by the Pope were reviewed, and the document ended by asking:

1. that approval be given to at least two Eucharistic Prayers for children and two for the Holy Year;

2. that the approved texts be included in the Missal as an appendix;

3. that except for the sacramental formula, a translation be permitted that is freer and more in tune with the mentality of the faithful of the language in question.

The reply that came back was that the Congregation for Divine Worship should follow "the rules set down by the Congregation for the Doctrine of the Faith" (June 3, 1974).

On June 20, however, the secretary of the Congregation for Divine Worship was received in audience by the Pope, who discussed the affair. He did not show any great enthusiasm for the Eucharistic Prayers for children, but in view of the situation, on the one hand, and "the unanimity of the Congregation for the Doctrine of the Faith," on the other, he urged Archbishop Bugnini to "consider how he might carry matters through." In the end, he himself was ready, if necessary, "to open doors hitherto closed."

The next day, the Cardinal Prefect of the Congregation for Divine Worship submitted the new suggestions in mature form:

---

46. But the principle established with regard to translations was likewise in conformity with a recent decision of the Pope. When Indonesia submitted its request for a special Eucharistic Prayer on grounds of the difficulty of understanding the four in the Missal, the Secretariat of State answered as follows on April 27, 1974 (No. 256930): "The Holy Father . . . made the point, first of all, that inquiries should be made as to whether the difficulty of understanding the anaphoras now in use may not be due to an excessively literal translation and whether it might not be overcome by a translation more attuned to the language of that country."

Number 8 of the regulations said that the Eucharistic Prayers are "rather to be radically rethought in order to cast them in a form more effective for liturgical use in the particular vernacular. Lexical departures from the Latin text, which will be greater in the non-Western languages, should cause less difficulty than in other liturgical texts previously published, since for the first time the Latin texts will never be used in a liturgical celebration" (the reference here is especially to Eucharistic Prayers for Masses with children).

1. I think it better, in regard to both series of formulas, not to publish them for the Church at large but to tell the episcopal conferences that the Congregation can grant one Eucharistic Prayer for children and one for the Holy Year.

2. I would leave to the conferences the selection of the formulary from each of the two series, because the formularies will reflect a variety of mentalities and embody different structures. It is therefore probable that each conference will incline to the formulas it considers more in tune with the character of its faithful.

3. From the selection made by the conferences, the Congregation, which must then approve the vernacular version, will be able to see which formulas find greater favor.

4. The prayers for children have been composed by an international group and have been examined and emended by persons qualified in the areas of pedagogy and child psychology.

5. Requests can be made, especially of conferences far removed in mentality from the European way of expressing things, for possible corrections, additions, or substitutions that are more in keeping with the "genius" of their peoples.

6. Since the celebration of the Holy Year is almost at an end in the dioceses, the two prayers for the Holy Year might be given the title: "Eucharistic Prayer for Reconciliation" and be accompanied by the following rubric: "This Eucharistic Prayer may be used in special celebrations of reconciliation and repentance, especially during Lent and on the occasion of pilgrimages and spiritual gatherings."

No answer was received until October 26, 1974,[47] but this time it was favorable. Here are the Holy Father's decisions:

1) The five texts [three for Masses with children and two for the Holy Year] which Your Eminence submitted for His Holiness' approval, are authorized for experiment for a period of three years, that is, until the end of 1977, but they are not to be published officially or included in the Roman Missal.

2) The five anaphoras may, however, be sent to the presidents of those episcopal conferences that have asked or will ask for them; they are to be

---

47. Meanwhile (on September 5) the Congregation for the Doctrine of the Faith sent an addendum to its letter of May 10, that is, to the decision of the ordinary meeting of April 24: "The observations of the consultors' meeting and the ordinary Wednesday meeting are herein communicated and called to the attention of the Congregation for Divine Worship; a small committee is to be set up to determine whatever modifications are thought necessary." There is no way of knowing whether this communication reflected a previous oversight or was a result of the statement sent to the Pope by the Congregation for Divine Worship. The observations were accepted; the texts were corrected and sent back to the Secretariat of State.

accompanied by a letter that will not only repeat what has been said in no. 1, above, but will also make it clear that each conference may select and use only one of the three prayers for children and one of the two for Masses "of reconciliation," in accordance with the rubric suggested by your Congregation in its letter of June 21, 1974.[48]

3) The translation of the texts chosen may be rather free and even depart somewhat from the Latin text; it must however retain the sense of the Latin and translate the formula of Eucharistic consecration faithfully and literally.

4) It will also be necessary to determine when the Eucharistic Prayer for children may be used, namely, when the majority of those present are children or when the Mass is being celebrated specifically for children. Also to be specified is the age group signified by the term "child," namely, those who are obliged to attend school, which means in practice to about the end of the twelfth year.

5) The Eucharistic Prayer based on the theme of the Holy Year may likewise be used for the period specified in no. 1, in Masses on penitential occasions.

These points were made on the first page of the booklet containing the five texts and the regulations for their use. This was published in cyclostyled form on November 1, 1974, and sent to the episcopal conferences that had requested the Eucharistic Prayers contained in it.[49]

Requests poured in from almost all countries, and the new Eucharistic Prayers came into experimental use for a period ending, theoretically, in 1977.[50]

b) *The Netherlands and Belgium*

On April 22, 1975 (No. 279711), the Secretariat of State sent the Congregation for Divine Worship some "directives and guidelines for deal-

---

48. It was difficult for the conferences to accept this arrangement, since they would have trouble in making their choice. The first conference to complain was the French. After a new statement from the Congregation for Divine Worship (January 2, 1975), the Secretariat of State (January 26, 1975; No. 272908) sent word that the Holy Father was allowing France to use all of the Eucharistic Prayers for children, while decreeing "that the concession was valid only for the Church of France, which had specifically requested it, and that any requests from other episcopates would be considered case by case." See *Not* 11 (1975) 5, n. 3.

This decree was made known to the joint commissions in order that they might take it into account in organizing the work of translation.

49. With the permission of the Secretariat of State, the concession was published in *Not* 11 (1975) 4–12, along with a statement of the regulations for obtaining permission to experiment and with the introductions to each of the Eucharistic Prayers.

50. At the end of 1977 the permission was extended to 1980 and then indefinitely; see *Not* 13 (1977) 555–56; 17 (1981) 23.

ing with questions and requests falling within the Congregation's competency, with special reference to Eucharistic Prayers.''

The Holy Father wishes, above all, that in all its examinations of practices the Congregation follow the prescribed course with all its stages, namely, plenary meeting, meeting of consultors, and the ordinary meeting of the cardinals.

In this context it must also be remembered that the consultors who are called upon are to be selected from among those who are provided with the proper letter of appointment and are listed in the Pontifical Yearbook (*Annuario Pontificio*).

When the decision to be made concerns requests for, or texts of, new Eucharistic Prayers or translations of sacramental formulas, the matter must be investigated jointly by this Congregation and the Congregation for the Discipline of the Sacraments. First, therefore, a study must be conducted by a committee of consultors from both Congregations; then there must be an ordinary joint meeting of the cardinals present in the Curia, in accord with normal practice, and they must be given a position paper on which they can express a reasoned judgment.

If the vote of these representatives of the two agencies is positive, the question or the texts are to be passed on to the Congregation for the Doctrine of the Faith, in order that it in turn may study those aspects of them that fall within its competency. If different views from those of the first two Congregations should emerge, they can be discussed by a joint committee of persons from the three Congregations.

Furthermore, when the matter under discussion is Eucharistic Prayers, His Holiness has ordered the following norms to be applied:

1) Only the four anaphoras contained in the Missal are to be regarded as official and definitive.

2) No other Eucharistic Prayers besides the recent ones for children are to be allowed for any special categories of persons: the sick, for example, or workers, refugees, ordinands, and so on. Instead, reference can be made to these in the homily and the prayer of the faithful.

3) New Eucharistic Prayers will be considered only for special occasions, that is, for events of limited duration that ought to be acknowledged and accepted from time to time by the Holy Father.

4) Supplementary anaphoras approved for special circumstances cannot be included in the Missal but must be printed in a separate booklet so that their temporary nature will be clear.

5) When new Eucharistic Prayers are being scrutinized, they must be certified as having all the parts listed and described in no. 55 of the General Instruction of the Roman Missal. In particular:

a) the epiclesis in the Latin liturgy must always precede the consecration;

b) the formulas of consecration must always be those of the anaphoras in the Roman Missal;

c) the terms used must reflect the sacrificial nature of the Mass and, after the consecration, the real presence;

d) mention of the Blessed Virgin Mary, Mother of God, must never be omitted;

e) explicit mention must always be made of the Pope and the local bishop.

As he issues these regulations, the Supreme Pontiff wishes to assure the Congregation of his deep esteem and good will for it. He has often praised its diligent work and he hopes that the procedure just described will promote a more organized handling of questions and thus bring to bear in a more advantageous way the Congregation's already vast experience and meritorious service of the Church.

The intention was that the Congregation should adhere strictly to the juridical procedure of the Roman Curia. There were those, however, who saw the action as a way of preventing possible concessions of further Eucharistic Prayers.[51]

Meanwhile, a request had come in from the bishops of Belgium, who wished to use the publication of the Missal in Flemish as an occasion for regularizing the situation of the five Eucharistic Prayers that they had allowed in 1969. Their idea was to publish in a separate booklet the Eucharistic Prayers for Masses with children and Masses of reconciliation and the five local Eucharistic Prayers. They asked the approval of the Holy See for this.

---

51. Here is a typical example. The third Eucharistic Prayer for Masses with children allowed for changeable embolisms. Some of these were suggested, while it was left to the conferences to compose others of the same kind (see Introduction, nos. 8 and 25; DOL 250 nos. 2006, 2023). The Swiss Conference submitted some of these on March 25, 1975, and asked for approval of them. They were sent for expert study to the Congregation for the Doctrine of the Faith, which replied on September 11, 1975 (meanwhile the Congregation for Divine Worship had been amalgamated with the Congregation for the Sacraments). The reply said: "Since a study of this text shows that the new embolisms submitted introduce further changes into the already approved Eucharistic Prayers for children, this Congregation is of the opinion that in accordance with the directives communicated by the Secretariat of State to the then Congregation for Divine Worship in letter No. 279711 of April 22 of this year, the request must be refused." But the letter cited did not say this; furthermore, there was question of something already granted when the third Eucharistic Prayer for children was allowed.

On January 30, 1975, the Congregation for Divine Worship had also submitted a document that it regarded as very explicit, it had to do with current legislation in the matter of Eucharistic Prayers and was to be sent to the episcopal conferences to help them see their way more clearly in a confused situation. The purpose was a good one, but the Secretariat of State feared that the document would lead to increased requests for Eucharistic Prayers for special circumstances, and it therefore refused to approve the document (April 4, 1975). The clarifications proposed can be found, in part, in Not 11 (1975) 114–18.

The Holy Father, to whom the matter had been presented, decided that it should be studied by a joint committee of consultors from the Congregations for Divine Worship and the Discipline of the Sacraments and then by an ordinary joint meeting of the same Congregations.

The joint committee met on May 21, 1975, and favored the grant, but it also pointed out the need for a radical revision of the texts. The ordinary joint meeting of the two Congregations was held on June 19, 1975. A position paper was prepared that included the "official sheet" of the Congregation for Divine Worship, the minutes of the joint committee meeting, the votes of the consultors, and the texts of the Eucharistic Prayers that had been submitted. At the same time, the similar situation in the Netherlands was considered. The Congregation for Divine Worship, in keeping with the circular letter and in order to help bishops seriously committed to a regularization of the liturgy in accordance with the norms of the Holy See, said that it favored the grant of two or three duly revised texts.

As we have already seen, the result of this ordinary joint meeting was entirely negative. Cardinal Šeper, who was publicly opposed to the liturgical reform, began the meeting with an indictment of what he regarded as abuses and surrenders in the area of liturgy. This opening intervention set the tone of the entire meeting. The majority of the cardinals were for a complete denial of the request, giving as their most cogent reason that the concession would open the door to abuses and an endless multiplication of anaphoras.

On June 28, 1975, the secretary of the Congregation for Divine Worship, who had been attempting for ten years to bring order into the liturgical situation in the Netherlands, sent the results of the ordinary joint meeting to the Pope, along with the written texts of the cardinals' statements. At the same time, he felt it his duty, with the consent of the Cardinal Prefect, to express his own views. He asked:

> 1) That Belgium be allowed one of the five anaphoras requested, after it has been revised in accordance with the norms and the schema for the Instruction of the Roman Missal. This would not be included in the Missal but would be printed in a separate booklet, along with the five granted *ad interim* for Masses with children and Masses of reconciliation.
>
> 2) That use of the Eucharistic Prayer already granted for the Dutch Pastoral Colloquium be permitted until the end of 1977, without being included in the Dutch Missal.

On July 8 (No. 285866), in a letter to the secretary and in another to the prefect of the Congregation for Divine Worship, the Secretariat of State let it be known that the Holy Father had accepted Archbishop Bugnini's suggestions, despite the negative opinion of the ordinary joint meeting. He did so "in view of the pastoral arguments contained" in the secretary's letter and "of the work" the secretary had done "to settle the difficult situation in which the episcopates of Belgium and the Netherlands found themselves."

This was the last good news. On the following day Cardinal James Knox visited Archbishop Bugnini and told him that his role and that of the Congregation were ended.

The road traveled by the reform in this sensitive and vital area of the liturgy had been long and wearisome.[52] The problem of the Eucharistic Prayers represented the climactic point in a dangerous but necessary dialogue. The Congregation for Divine Worship had acted out of a profound conviction that

> a plurality of liturgical texts is harmful if uncontrolled; but it is a positive and enriching ascetical instrument if it is controlled, properly prepared, and well directed, as is the case with formularies that are proposed, studied, and approved according to a process that has yielded good fruit.[53]

It can be said, speaking generally, that the Congregation for Divine Worship took seriously—and not in a merely rhetorical fashion, still less boastingly or opportunistically—the task assigned it by Pope Paul VI in October 1966, when he told it "to prevent abuses, to prod those who lag or resist, to stimulate energies, to encourage promising initiatives."[54] It always believed that the best means of preventing abuses was to *anticipate* them rather than repress them; to give the bishops and episcopal conferences adequate means of promoting a pastoral liturgy rather than sending them anachronistic "decisions" that are neither heeded nor obeyed.

It believed in the mandate of which the Pope, in the still vital years of his pontificate, constantly reminded it, while at the same time assuring it of his trust and good will and personally following step by step each stage of the reform.

---

52. In order to complete the picture of the discussion of the Eucharistic Prayers, I must remind the reader of another intervention of the Congregation for Divine Worship, which had to do with the name of the bishop to be mentioned during these prayers. The point was discussed at the second plenary meeting of the Congregation (see above, p. 194); the decree settling the matter was dated October 9, 1972 (*DOL* 247 nos. 1970-74).

53. From the letter of the Congregation for Divine Worship in connection with the questions raised by the request of the Brazilian Episcopal Conference for a Eucharistic Prayer (April 1975).

54. Address to the members and *periti* of the Consilium, October 13, 1966 (*DOL* 84 no. 634).

After a difficult and sometimes painful career, this Congregation ended its existence. It had sprung into being due to a sudden impulse, and it disappeared from the scene due to an equally sudden impulse. Such are God's mysterious ways! But the Congregation will never regret having fought a good fight, having done its duty to the point of sacrifice, and not having proved false to the commission given to it—even though struggles without and faintheartedness within (''foris pugnae, intus timores'' is how St. Paul puts it) forced it to lower its sails.

Part IV

The Liturgy of the Hours

The General Structure of the Liturgy of the Hours

The work of revising the Divine Office was entrusted to eight study groups, one of which was charged with coordinating the entire work and also proposing a general structure for the Office as a whole.[1] To a large extent, this group decided the approach to be taken by the other groups in their own work.

I. First Phase (1964-1965)

The task of developing the structure of the new Office was a rather wearisome one. In a first phase, the approach taken was to update while leaving the structure of the existing Breviary substantially untouched. This seemed to be the approach most conformed to the decrees of the conciliar Constitution.

The first report on this work was presented by A.-G. Martimort at the second general meeting of the Consilium, on April 19, 1964.[2] According to the relator, the Council had set down four principles governing the

---

1. This was group 9: *relator:* A.-G. Martimort; *secretary:* V. Raffa; *adjunct:* I. Oñatibia; *members:* representatives from all the other groups (some of these were members only for a time), namely, P. Jounel, J. Pascher, E. J. Lengeling, M. Pellegrino, U. Neri, F. Nikolasch, J. Rotelle, G. Raciti, A. Amore, A. Lentini, P. Visentin, S. Famoso, A. Dirks, J. Gribomont, A. Rose, and I. Rogger.

2. All the groups together produced about eighty schemas. Basic among these are eight general reports submitted to the Consilium by group 9 and dated: April 17, 1964 (6 pp.), September 14, 1964 (17 pp.), December 1, 1965 (2 pp.), October 8, 1966 (30 pp.), March 15, 1967 (16 pp.), September 28, 1967 (19 pp.), April 17, 1968 (18 pp.), and October 31, 1969 (7 pp.). I shall refer to these as to basic stages on the way to a definition of the general structure of the Liturgy of the Hours.

reform of the Office: (1) fidelity to the past and sensitivity to the conditions in which the pastoral clergy are now living;[3] (2) the person praying should be able to draw spiritual life from the texts of the Office; (3) the faithful should be able to participate fruitfully in the recitation of the Office; (4) the Hours of the Office are to be prayed at their "true" and appropriate times.

With these principles as the point of departure, the relator listed in the form of thirty-three "questions" the problems connected with the main points of the new Office: structure, cycles of psalms, biblical and patristic readings, calendar, sanctoral, and celebration of the Office. In light of this general survey, the Fathers gave the green light to set in motion the complex machine that was the groups charged with reforming the Church's prayer of the Hours.

The second report (October 1, 1964) went to the heart of the various problems. Twenty-one questions were submitted to the Fathers for their vote.[4]

The picture was filled in at the next general meeting—the fifth (April 1965)—when further votes were taken on points submitted by the various study groups.[5]

The resulting definitive picture can be sketched as follows:

Lauds: five psalms (25 in favor; 5 wanted three psalms, 1 three psalms and a canticle). Also approved was the transfer to Lauds of the prayers found in Prime (or similar prayers) for the sanctification of the day's work; these were, however, to be optional.

Vespers: five psalms, with the option of omitting two in celebrations with a congregation. The Consilium gave the group the go-ahead to look into the possibility of adding New Testament canticles to Vespers. The option of a longer biblical reading in celebrations with the people was allowed, as was the introduction of general intercessions.

Matins: three psalms for the clergy and active religious, two readings (one from Scripture and one from the Fathers) which would be of about the same length as the readings in the present Matins.

Terce, Sext, None: three psalms.

Compline: three psalms.

Distribution of the Psalter: the entire Psalter is to be recited (150 psalms over a two-week period). It was expected that a special selection would be made for Lauds and Vespers.

---

3. It was precisely the difficulty of reconciling these two requirements that caused all the rethinking and revisions that we shall be seeing.

4. See Schema 31: *De Breviario* 10 (September 14, 1964).

5. See Schema 95: *De Breviario* 26 (May 22, 1965).

The discussion brought two tendencies to light. One, which was represented by the majority of the members of the Consilium and of the consultors charged with the revision, was the concern not to shorten the Office. The other focused on the difficulties of religious and faithful; its representatives felt that a simpler structure was needed for them. Some at the meeting warned that more attention was being given to private recitation than to the celebration of the Office with the people, but the majority could only regard this perspective as unqualifiedly "ideal."

In fact, the Fathers voted for the possibility of adapting Lauds to celebration with the people, but the study group came down on the opposite side, since it regarded this participation as doubtful. On the other hand, it did call for the preparation of two schemas for Vespers: one for celebration with a congregation and another for choir or private recitation.[6] The Consilium, however, was opposed to having two forms of Vespers. The same was true of Matins, for which the group proposed a special, fuller form for contemplatives. The Consilium did not take a final stand but sent the problem back for further study.

1. The Problem of the Psalms

Study group 3, which was in charge of the distribution of the psalms among the various Hours of the Office,[7] had presented the results of its studies at the same meetings.[8] The various plans for distribution of the psalms obviously depended on the shape to be taken by the several Hours of the Office. Meanwhile, however, there were some questions to be tackled.

1) *Length of the psalms.* A shortening of the psalmody was a desideratum for all the Hours. A lengthy psalmody may be well enough for monks (though some questioned even this), but it is not consonant with the spirituality of the clergy. This principle, which was set down by Pascher in his report, found the Fathers of the Consilium in agreement; accepting a suggestion of Cardinal Confalonieri, they decided that the sections of

---

6. See Schema 31: *De Breviario* 10.

7. *Relator:* J. Pascher; *secretary:* A. Rose; *members:* A. Paredi, B. Fischer, J. Pinell, H. Schmidt, and V. Raffa.

8. The first schema (July 19, 1964) sets forth the problem and offers two plans for distribution of the psalms. These were simply initial suggestions. The second schema (September 28, 1964) also tackles problems of principle with a view to the general report to be made to the fourth general meeting of the Consilium. A third schema, drawn up for the Fathers of the Consilium, is dated April 26, 1965. New schemas, based on decisions of the Consilium, are dated May 31, 1965, and June 22, 1965. The final schemas (March 7, 1967, and September 20, 1967) follow upon the final decisions reached by the Consilium.

psalmody should be from eight to twelve verses in length. Longer psalms would have to be divided into several sections.[9]

2) *Integrity of the Psalter.* This was the most serious and trickiest problem of all. When the secretariat of the Consilium had given this study group its commission, it had said: "There are two main questions: (a) Should all the psalms be used or only a selection (for example, eliminating the imprecatory psalms or using them only on certain occasions during the year)? (b) Over how many weeks should the Psalter be distributed?"

In the meeting hall of the Council itself, seven Fathers, among them Cardinals Bacci and Ruffini, had urged that the imprecatory psalms be eliminated from the Church's prayer of the Hours. Many felt the difficulty of using these psalms for prayer. The question was raised at the fourth general meeting of the Consilium. Monsignor Pascher asked whether it was really certain that the liturgical Constitution (no. 91) called for all of the psalms to be used in the weekly cycle. Could not the imprecatory psalms be used in some other way? The group dealing with the general structure of the Office said it was in favor of using all the psalms in the ordinary course of the Office, lest the revised Breviary venture into uncertain waters. The Fathers opted for this solution (21 against 4) and decided that the entire Psalter should be kept.[10]

---

9. A two-week cycle of the psalms for all the Hours would require 336 segments, whereas the entire Psalter and seven canticles would yield only 273 segments of about ten verses each. Sixty-three more would be needed. To meet this difficulty, it was suggested that the psalms of Lauds and Vespers follow a one-week cycle, those in the other Hours a two-week cycle. This solution was adopted for the time being. G. Castellino was asked to study the division of the psalms into segments, according to the principle approved by the Fathers. On the group's work, see J. Pascher, "De psalmis distribuendis," *Not* 1 (1965) 152.

10. Some of the Fathers noted that, according to the liturgical Constitution, all the psalms were to be included in the regular cycle. All of them are God's word, and no psalm may be deleted. Others, including the president, Cardinal Lercaro, pointed out that, without violating the intention of the Constitution, use of the imprecatory psalms could be limited to certain seasons of the year when they are interpreted as prophetic rather than as imprecatory; it does not seem necessary to include them in the weekly Psalter.

A Father from Eastern Europe said: "Our special circumstances require that the entire Psalter be used. Afflicted as we are by a very difficult external situation, we need expressions suitable for use *contra diabolum*" (Spülbeck). Cardinal Confalonieri offered a conciliatory approach: "Keep all the psalms but shorten them, removing the imprecatory verses." Others: "If there is no obligation to read the whole of Sacred Scripture, why not apply the same criterion to the psalms?"

Finally, Canon Martimort made several points: "(a) It would be difficult to find an objective criterion for selecting psalms; only a few verses need to be eliminated from several; (b) if some psalms were reserved for certain seasons, they would only become the more burdensome; (c) the psalms are prayed not in our own person but 'in the person of Christ

2. Second Thoughts

After the meeting of April 1965, several members and consultors made known to the secretariat of the Consilium their serious doubts about the revision of the Divine Office and the approach being taken to the work. Meanwhile some reports of the study groups had been published in *Notitiae*, and these too raised questions. Requests were also received to experiment with an organization of the Office notably different from that planned by the Consilium. In some religious communities experiments were already being made with the consent of superiors. Others expressed concern that the Office was being excessively shortened.[11] Still others repeated difficulties already raised within the Consilium itself.

Meanwhile, on the other hand, a preferred approach to the Divine Office was already becoming visible. Many religious women who were revising their regulations were opting for making the Office their community prayer. For some months now the Congregation for Religious had likewise been taking this approach and not allowing the use of "Little Offices" but urging religious communities to introduce the Divine Office.

The secretary of the Consilium presented this entire range of problems at a meeting limited to the Fathers on October 19, 1965, during the sixth general meeting of the Consilium. He asked the Fathers to settle on answers, since eight study groups were dealing with these problems and could not work in a void. It was because of these unresolved questions that the subject of the Office had been excluded from the agenda of the sixth general meeting.

The secretary also presented a summary of the main proposals: (1) The basic times for daily prayer, at least for the diocesan clergy and for religious clergy involved in pastoral activity, should be morning, noon, and evening. (2) The nocturnal aspect of Matins should be retained only for the vigils of the great feasts, of Sundays, and in other special circumstances. On other days, Matins should rather be an obligatory, long *lec-*

---

and the Church'; therefore an effort is always required if they are to be a life-giving food for the soul."

11. Fear that a reduction in quantity would in the course of time lead to less prayer gave rise to discussion and became a pretext for opposing the new Liturgy of the Hours. See C. Vagaggini, O.S.B., " 'Sit brevis oratio' e la riforma liturgica," *Not* 4 (1968) 380; "Contemplazione e Ufficio divino restaurato," *Not* 5 (1969) 398; Sr. Chiara Augusta, O.S.C., "Pregare di piu o pregare meglio?" *Not* 8 (1972) 161. The Congregation for Divine Worship had to intervene in this area in order to help communities of contemplative life to appreciate the riches and potentialities of the Liturgy of the Hours; see its notification *Universi qui Officium* on the Liturgy of the Hours for certain religious communities (August 6, 1972): DOL 432 nos. 3728-35. See "Adaptation de la Liturgie des Heures à l'Office de certaines Communautés religieuses," *Not* 10 (1974) 29.

tio divina. (3) It is desirable that there be fewer psalms recited in each Hour so that the recitation may be unhurried, meditative, and marked by appropriate moments of silence. (4) If this principle is accepted, then the Psalter should be covered over the period of a month, with the imprecatory psalms being omitted and put off to a more appropriate time, and with the historical psalms being used rather as readings. (5) The minor Hours should be structured in such a way that certain psalms are not neglected by those who celebrate only one of these Hours.

The stakes were high. Those of the clergy who found the general approach to the Office to be overly static, "monastic," and lacking in pastoral interest were in danger of gradually abandoning the Church's official prayer or turning to individual, arbitrary experiments.

A lively discussion ensued. Some of the Fathers objected that it was dangerous to go back over decisions already taken, because "everything could be called in question again." Another remarked that it was not prudent "to abandon the certain [i.e., tradition] for the uncertain." But Bishop Boudon stressed the point that "priests do not find their real prayer in the Office; they find it in the Mass. The structure of the Office does not meet the expectations of the majority. If, then, the general organization of the Breviary remains as it was, even the people will not participate." The debate focused on these two approaches. The president came to the conclusion that there was need to consider and decide whether to continue along the line already taken or to issue new guidelines.

The president decided to take the matter up again with the Fathers and consultors; meanwhile, he brought the relator up to date on the difficulties.[12] As a result, after a month and a half of reflection, the problem came up before the Consilium again on December 1. Canon Martimort read a closely argued two-page statement defending the position of the study group. He answered the objections and asked that no decision be made before the group had a chance to study the problem thoroughly (fourth report).

The statements made by the Fathers did not add much to what had come out in the preceding discussions. On the one hand, there were those more attached to tradition: it is not the Consilium's role to seek new paths; its task is simply to apply the liturgical Constitution; we may not depart from tradition! On the other hand, it was necessary to provide the clergy and faithful with something vital and solid: there is need for a Breviary for priests trained after the Council; the Breviary is the prayer of the Church, but as a matter of fact it is now reserved to certain categories

---

12. The president reported this to Canon Martimort in a letter.

of persons; we must provide for the laity as well; the Office should also be a source of personal prayer, whereas in fact many priests do not find food for their prayer in the Breviary.

Cardinal Lercaro summed up as follows: The Constitution sets certain boundaries we may not cross:

a) the Office is to keep its traditional structure as a prayer "of the Hours";

b) the entire Psalter is to be used, but its distribution is not prescribed.

c) "truth of the Hours": Matins should be adapted to any time of day and lend itself to meditation; outside of choir one of the Little Hours may be chosen for recitation, but things must be so arranged that psalms are not lost. Thought must also be given to parish communities.

Monsignor Bonet suggested sending all the Fathers a questionnaire to which they would respond in writing after having gotten the views of other bishops and priests.

The suggestion was accepted. The secretariat of the Consilium sent the questionnaire on December 16, 1965,[13] and Canon Martimort communicated the results at a meeting of the relators (May 2–13, 1966).[14] Twenty-four of forty-seven Fathers replied, as did twenty-three *periti*. On the more important issues, about two-thirds came down for a more or less traditional approach, while one-third wanted a more radical reform. The fact that only half of the Fathers sent in replies was a source of puzzlement.[15]

3. *Intervention of the Pope*

The question was a serious one and a matter of dispute. The Cardinal President decided to tell the Pope about it at an audience on March 18, 1966. He presented to the Pope, and discussed with him, a broad exposé of all the problems dealt with in the questionnaire sent to the members

---

13. Schema 135: *De Breviario* 32 (December 16, 1965). The questionnaire contained nineteen questions concerning five subjects: I. Participation in the Divine Office: If various categories of persons are to have access to this prayer, is it enough to prepare a Breviary that is normative for the entire Church but can be adapted to various needs and groups, or is it better to prepare various forms of the Office for the various categories? II. Adaptation of the structure of the Office to contemporary needs. III. Length and number of the psalms in the various Hours. IV. The entire Psalter in the regular cycle; question of the imprecatory psalms. V. Question of the three Little Hours: retain all three or have one between Lauds and Vespers?

14. Schema 167: *De Breviario* 38 (May 30, 1966).

15. Perhaps the time allowed for the replies was not adequate for the bishops; they were asked to respond by January 20, 1966.

and consultors of the Consilium. The Pope in turn made his own thinking known to the relator in a letter of April 5, 1966. These were the salient points:

Matins. Readings are to be the main element as far as length goes, and a wide selection of biblical, patristic, and hagiographical texts is to be provided. It seems preferable that the psalms be interwoven with the readings; the responsories are to be kept (this had been expressly requested by others before the Pope), and in the form they take in the Office of Corpus Christi, that is, with the Old and New Testaments being combined.

Lauds and Vespers. Provision is to be made for participation by a congregation; there is to be permission to recite only three psalms and a fairly lengthy reading.

Prime. Some elements of this—the offering and sanctification of the day's work—are to be incorporated into Lauds.

Psalms. A selection of the better ones is to be made; the imprecatory psalms are to be used only during certain seasons of the year to which they are better adapted; the historical psalms can be used as readings.

Little Hours. Since only one Hour is obligatory outside choir, and since choral recitation of one after the other contradicts the "temporal truth" or "truth of the Hours," which is a basic principle governing reform of the Office, consideration should be given to the proposal that there be a single "middle" Hour between Lauds and Vespers. It would mark a pause at the end of the morning's work and the beginning of the afternoon's.

Cardinal Lercaro raised this point at the meeting of the relators.

4. Back to the Consilium

Toward the end of July 1966, by way of preparation for the seventh general meeting of the Consilium in the fall of that year, Canon Martimort sent his fellow workers a lengthy statement of forty dense pages; it was the most extensive of all those he wrote on the subject. In it he dealt with five basic problems: the imprecatory and historical psalms; the question of three Little Hours or only one; the structure of Lauds and Vespers; the question of one or two Breviaries; the retention or exclusion of choral elements.

The report was based on the answers received to the questionnaire of December 16, 1965, on wishes and suggestions received directly by the relator and on documents concerning the Divine Office in non-Catholic communities.

The report displays an astonishing wealth of historical and liturgical information. Each point is thoroughly discussed in the light of the pastoral situation and in the setting of the conciliar documents. Especially noteworthy is the treatment of the imprecatory and historical psalms. The main emphasis here is on how the non-Catholic ecclesial communities have handled this problem.

a) *Anglican Church.* This Church daily celebrates Morning Prayer (Matins) and Evening Prayer (Evensong) according to the Order of 1662, with the modifications and variants introduced into the Elizabethan edition by the 1928 Book of Common Prayer. The Psalter is distributed over a month's time, but bishops have authority to depart from the established distribution on certain days; one psalm (57) is completely omitted, and verses that may be omitted are printed in square brackets.[16]

b) *Reformed Church.* The praying of the psalms was highly esteemed in the sixteenth century; subsequently, however, it fell into neglect, especially in the nineteenth century, and was revived beginning in 1943, when R. Paquier and A. Bardet proposed an Office on the Anglican model in their book *L'Office divin de chaque jour* (3rd ed., 1961). Some psalms are used more frequently than others; twenty-one are omitted completely,[17] while another eight are shortened.[18]

c) *Taizé community.* The psalmody in this renowned center of Protestant worship has undergone a significant development:

---

16. Psalm 13: the verses lacking in the Hebrew (Rom 3:10-19).

54, v. 16 ("Veniat mors super illos . . .").

67, vv. 21-23 (= 22-24) ("Verumtamen, Deus, confringe capita . . . ut intingatur pes tuus in sanguine").

68, vv. 23-29 ("Fiat mensa eorum . . . cum iustis non inscribantur").

108, vv. 5-19 (= 6-20) ("Constitues super eum . . . animam iustorum").

136, vv. 7-9 ("Memor esto, Domine . . . ad petram").

139, vv. 9-10 (= 10-11) ("Caput circuitus . . . non subsistent").

140, vv. 7-8 (= 6-7) ("Absorpti sunt . . . secus infernum").

17. Psalms 36, 48, 49, 51, 52, 57, 63, 77, 80, 81, 82, 86, 93, 94, 105, 107, 113B, 126, 127, 128, 136.

18. Psalm 9, vv. 5-11 ("Inquinatae sunt . . . in finem").

17, vv. 8-16 ("Commota est . . . irae tuae").

17, vv. 32-51 ("Quoniam . . . " to the end of the psalm).

44, vv. 11-16 ("Audi, filia . . . ").

54, vv. 10-22 ("Praecipita, Domine . . . et ipso sunt iacula").

72, vv. 4-11 ("Quia non est . . . in excelso").

88, vv. 20-38 ("Tunc locutus es . . . in caelo fidelis").

108, vv. 5-19 ("Et posuerunt . . . qua semper praecingitur").

131, vv. 12-18 ("Si custodierint . . . sanctificatio mea").

An analysis of these omissions shows that some of them eliminate parts that are directly messianic or otherwise dear to Christian devotion. The omissions are therefore not motivated by the difficulties the passages cause for Christian prayer.

—In a first distribution of the Psalter over a six-week period, five psalms were omitted,[19] two were abridged,[20] and two very short psalms (116 and 133) were used as introductions to morning and evening prayer on Sundays.

—In a second phase, marked by the massive presence of young people of every mentality and degree of preparation, it was decided that there should be greater selectivity. Some psalms were excluded because they were regarded as "war songs," others because of excessively harsh wording, and still others because they are historical or geographical.[21] But some of the omitted psalms were used on certain feasts,[22] and others were salvaged for use in responsories or in the formulas introducing the Hours.[23] Some verses were omitted from nine psalms.[24]

After presenting the results of research into the other Christian confessions, Canon Martimort offered his own theological and pastoral reflections, which tended to show the dangers of an arbitrary selection. In his conclusion he suggested that the Consilium should follow the example of the Anglican Church, that is, it should keep the entire Psalter in the Office but indicate by suitable signs or rubrics those psalms for which substitutions could be made or in which verses might be omitted. The relator lacked the courage to enter upon a new path. Therefore he did not give much weight to the thinking of the Pope on the new proposals

---

19. Psalm 57, 78, 82, 127, 132.

20. Psalm 108, vv. 1-21 ("Deus laudem . . . libera me").

    136, vv. 7-9 ("Memor . . . ad petram").

21. Psalms 5, 7, 9, 10, 11, 13, 14, 16, 19, 20, 27, 34, 35, 36, 40, 43, 44, 48, 49, 51, 52, 53, 54, 55, 57, 58, 59, 63, 68, 72, 73, 74, 75, 77, 78, 81, 82, 86, 93, 104, 105, 107, 108, 119, 121, 126, 127, 128, 132, 134, 139. There are fifty-two psalms in all, among them some of the longest in the Psalter.

22. Psalms 5, 20, 75, 86, 126, 127.

23. Psalms 5, 27, 40, 44, 54, 58.

24. Psalm 3, vv. 8-9 ("Quoniam . . . benedictio tua").

    17, vv. 36-51 ("Et disciplina tua . . . in saeculum").

    62, vv. 10-12 ("Ipsi vero . . . iniqua").

    65, v. 15 ("Holocausta medullata offeram tibi cum incenso arietum/offeram tibi boves cum hircis").

    109, vv. 5-7 ("Dominus . . . exaltabit caput").

    136, vv. 7-9 ("Memor esto . . . ad petram").

    138, vv. 19-22 ("Si occideris . . . facti sunt mihi").

    140, v. 10 ("Cadent in retiaculo eius peccatores/singulariter sum ego donec transeam").

    149, vv. 7-8 ("Ad faciendam vindictam . . . sanctis eius").

I may add the tradition of the German Calvinists, who exclude some psalms from the regular psalmody and use them instead as Old Testament readings during the first week after Epiphany: Psalms 9 (second part), 49, 54, 57, 63, 72, and during the Easter season: Psalms 17, 36, 48, 67, 77, 81, 87, 88, 93, 104, 105, 113B, 126, 127.

(thinking passed on by Cardinal Lercaro); the result was a loss of time and a waste of energies. Yet even this, perhaps, was providential, since the relator's approach helped to produce more mature views on the character and purpose of the Office; these mature insights had not yet been achieved and were having difficulty in emerging.

II. SECOND PHASE (1966–1967)

1. *A New Approach*

Group 9 met in Genoa, September 6–8, 1966, and worked out a new approach to the structure of the Divine Office. This was presented at the seventh general meeting of the Consilium (October 1966) and at the preceding meeting of the relators. The group's report was of a more detailed kind; it proposed the fundamental elements in the structure of the new Office in the form of one general question and eighteen specific ones, on which the Fathers were asked to vote.[25]

On the following November 10 a report was submitted to the Pope on the entire work of the seventh general meeting. The relator explained the situation regarding the Office. In it he outlined an approach that would in substance be the one finally adopted. He described it as follows:

> The basic problem which we face today and which the present report attempts to deal with and resolve is this: How is the Divine Office, while continuing to be the prayer chiefly of the clergy and religious, to be also accessible to the faithful, so that they may find in it, not something that is, as it were, a concession to them, but rather the exercise of a function that truly belongs to them as members of the praying ecclesial community?

The relator then went on to review the several points:

1. Until the time when the faithful lost an understanding of the liturgy and a taste for it, the most authentic liturgical tradition distinguished a part of the Office that was more specifically "ecclesial," that is, intended for solemn communal celebration, and a part that was more directly reserved to clerics and religious. The first of these two parts included Lauds and Vespers as a public, official prayer of the entire community; the solemnity with which these two Hours are still celebrated is a sign of their "ecclesial" character. The second part, which was intended as an official practice of continual prayer and was therefore reserved to clerics and re-

---

25. Schema 185: *De Breviario* 40 (September 19, 1966), for the relators; Schema 194: *De Breviario* 41 (October 8, 1966), for the members. The results of the voting are given in the report on the work of the seventh general meeting (*Res secretariae*, no. 25 [October 28, 1966]).

ligious, included nocturnal prayer (Matins) and the Little Hours, by which the successive phases of the day were to be sanctified.

Today an effort is being made, in accordance with the spirit of the liturgical Constitution, to revive this participation of the faithful in the basic segments of the Office. This participation will never become very widespread, but it can become a reality at least in non-clerical communities and in groups that are better prepared, especially during meetings and retreats. It can also become a reality in parishes more given to a full and energetic participation in the liturgy.

For this reason, the general structure of the Office provides that the principal Hours, namely, Lauds and Vespers, be so organized that they can, with slight modifications, be celebrated either by a community or by a priest alone.

It is important that there be but a single form of these Hours. For if abridgements are made when the people are present, the impression will be given that the Office is in fact a purely clerical affair and that popular participation is, as it were, reluctantly allowed and requires simplification of the Office to bring it down to the level of the congregation.

2. Lauds and Vespers are therefore to have three psalms, plus a hymn and a concluding canticle from the New Testament.

Furthermore, if a congregation is present, the "little chapter" may be replaced by a longer reading and a homily.

Finally, Lauds will end with elements taken from or inspired by the present Hour of Prime; these have to do with the offering or sanctification of the day's work. Vespers, on the other hand, will have general intercessions (prayer of the faithful) that will focus on some general intentions of greater importance for the life of the Church and the particular celebrating community.

3. The psalmody will be enriched by some New Testament canticles that will become part of the psalmody at Vespers, just as Old Testament canticles are already part of the psalmody at Lauds.

4. The part of the Office intended primarily for clerics and religious includes Matins, the three Little Hours (Terce, Sext, None), and Compline.

a) As prescribed in article 89c of the Constitution on the Liturgy, Matins is to have only three psalms but longer readings (from Scripture and the Fathers) than at present.

b) The three Little Hours are to be kept in the Breviary, with the understanding that those who are not obliged to choir and therefore have permission to celebrate only a single Little Hour may nonetheless read all three of these Hours.

There is, therefore, to be an Hour with psalms that vary from day to day and with elements (hymns and perhaps prayers) proper to the various times of the day; this Hour must be recited by those who decide to celebrate only one of the Little Hours.

In addition, there will be two other Hours containing unvarying psalms (taken from the Gradual Psalms), for those who wish, or are obliged, to say more than one Little Hour. The system of unvarying psalms comes from the Psalter of the monastic Office.

c) Compline will be substantially organized as at present, with psalms that vary from day to day and are appropriate for the time and purpose of this part of the Office.

5. An especially difficult point in the general organization of the Office is the use to be made of the Psalter—more specifically, its distribution and whether all the psalms are to be recited or only a selection of them.

The Fathers have accepted the suggestions made in the report given to them; these suggestions seek to reconcile the age-old tradition of the Church in this area with demands inspired by contemporary sensibilities.

a) The Constitution on the Liturgy decreed that the Psalter be distributed over a longer period than is presently the case; it will therefore follow a four-week cycle. This much longer cycle is required by the reduction of the number of psalms in the various Hours and by the new elements being introduced. Another factor taken into account is the permission to celebrate the Office in the vernacular both in private and in public (when the people are present and taking part); celebration in the vernacular calls for a little more tranquillity and takes a little longer.

b) Another problem arises from the character of certain psalms which contains expressions that are extremely harsh and offensive to modern sensibilities. These are the "imprecatory" psalms.

There are two opposing views on this matter. One group, appealing to the constant tradition of the Church, demands that these psalms be retained in the regular cycle of psalms; they need only be interpreted according to their authentic meaning and thus properly understood. The other group is equally insistent that these psalms be either omitted entirely or used only in certain circumstances. In response to these opposing demands, a middle way has been chosen, one already being followed by some non-Catholic communities in the revision of their liturgical books.

As far as possible, then, these psalms will be used in Hours destined for celebration chiefly by the clergy. In addition, the more objectionable verses will be set off by suitable typographical devices and may be omitted in celebrations with a congregation. If the objection is to an entire psalm (there may be one or two such), a rubric will explain that another psalm may be substituted.

c) The historical psalms (those that recall events in the life of the Old Testament people of God) will also be kept in the regular cycle of psalms, but care will be taken that they not be said one after another in the same Hour and that as far as possible they be read in Matins, that is, during the Hour in which readings will be the main constituent.

d) Concerning the use of the psalms in general, care will be taken in distributing them to ensure sufficient variety (by alternating psalms with different kinds of contents), to divide them in a logical manner rather than by simply counting verses, and to consider not interrupting the flow of psalms with the *Gloria Patri* simply in order to obtain a certain number of "stanzas." The overall length of the psalmody, and not the number of psalms, will be decisive.

6. The fact that the Office may be celebrated both in choir, or in common, and privately has also raised the question of whether it is better to keep or omit those parts that are proper to a public celebration and are therefore known as "choral elements." Some of these certainly have an intrinsic value even in individual recitation and will therefore be kept. Specifically:

a) Versicles serving as invocations; for example, "O God, come to my assistance."

b) Responsories, especially after Scripture readings, which help in understanding the text that has been read, or connect the reading with the history of salvation, or help in effecting a transition from the Old Testament to the New or in turning the reading into a prayer.

c) Antiphons, which help in understanding the psalm they enclose, either in its literal meaning or in the special meaning given it by the context in which the Church uses it on a particular feast or during a particular celebration.

d) Hymns, at least those in the traditional repertory whose content is still applicable today. The episcopal conferences may, however, be given authority to replace these hymns, in the vernacular celebration of the Office, with others, traditional or new, that are native to the language in question and have a comparable doctrinal and ascetical content.

7. In a second stage of the work, once the basic general structure of the Roman Office is securely established, adaptations to communities of contemplative life (especially regarding the nocturnal celebration of Matins) will be studied.

Following these guidelines, which have emerged from the discussion and votes of the general meeting of October 1966, the group appointed to establish the general structure of the Breviary will be able to proceed to decisions on many other details that are needed for a more complete and clear organization of the public prayer of the Church.

The same study group, in collaboration with the other groups, hopes to present to the Fathers at the next general meeting a concrete schema, all parts included, for Lauds and Vespers of a single week. This will enable them to evaluate with greater assurance, and on a concrete basis, the practical results of the principles they have accepted.

The secondary study groups, those in charge of the various sectors of this large subject, will then be able to undertake their work on a solid basis. This holds especially for the groups more directly and fully concerned, namely, those dealing with the distribution of the Psalter and with the selection of biblical and patristic readings.

Once these results are obtained, it will be possible to satisfy a desire expressed in many quarters that some experiments, at least with the principal Hours of the Office, be carried out in suitably prepared circles. The remaining difficulties were now few, the most worrisome being the problem of the imprecatory and historical psalms. It was a problem that still had an eventful history ahead of it.

2. *Specimen of a Week*

The promised book containing a sample week of the Office was prepared by the group and distributed to the Fathers when they gathered for their eighth general meeting (April 10–19, 1967). It was a substantial volume of 250 pages containing not only the Psalter arranged according to a four-week cycle but also the full wording of the Office for a week. The Fathers were to celebrate this Office during their meeting so that they would "be able to discuss the entire problem with greater ease and clarity" and come to suitable conclusions.

The structural elements of the Office as set forth in the fifth report of the study group corresponded faithfully to what had been said in the report of November 10. The sixteen questions submitted to the Fathers touched rather on matters of detail that were certainly useful but were also so narrow as to be somewhat burdensome to the Fathers. The latter were interested in the general approach rather than in the minutiae that are the delight of experts.

The approach was substantially acceptable. Some revisions, however, would still further facilitate the prayer of the Hours. The secretary of the Consilium made himself the spokesman at this point, both in his own name and on the basis of impressions gathered from others. He wrote

about them to Canon Martimort on May 8, 1967. Some of his suggestions were accepted, others were not, but it is worth listing them all here.

1) In my opinion, the readings in the Office of Readings should run to
about 150 words.

2) Throughout the Office, the psalms should not be more than ten to
twelve verses in length, in accordance with the first rule proposed by Cardinal Confalonieri. Long psalms and long readings are wearisome. The praying
soul wants moments of pause, and the interruption of the psalmody by
the *Gloria Patri* offers mind and soul just such moments of rest. On the other
hand, the assignment of a special antiphon to each section of psalm seems
of doubtful value.

3) I therefore think it useful, for practical purposes and in the interests
of simplification, that the Office of Readings, Lauds, and Vespers should
always have three psalms (entire psalms or sections as noted earlier), but
in the manner that you have proposed for the canticles and for the distribution of the Psalter.

4) To the Middle Hour and Compline, on the other hand, I would have
assigned a single psalm and one easily memorized. This is my reason: for
many the Middle Hour will be their noonday prayer; this will certainly be
the case with communities of priests or religious. Furthermore, the Middle
Hour will become part of the prayer that every good priest—and all religious communities—make before dining. At the present time, the usual
prayer in such communities consists of the "Come, Holy Spirit," an examination of conscience, some other elements, and the *Angelus*. If the Middle
Hour is included, it can eliminate some of these components but not all,
nor would a total elimination be advisable, since the examination of conscience at midday is an excellent ascetical practice, and the *Angelus* is a prayer
in general use. If, then, the Middle Hour is short—a single psalm—the combination will be possible; otherwise the two prayer practices will be difficult to harmonize.

That is why I am in favor of a single psalm for the Middle Hour. When
priests see . . . three verses, three little chapters, and three prayers for this
short Hour, their reaction will be that love of tradition has made us lose
sight of real life.

If the day is divided into three parts—morning, midday hours, and
afternoon—and not into six, this is not the fault of liturgists, but neither
is it the fault of the priests or faithful who read the Breviary. Why not accept the real situation and put aside the pretense of still living in the fourth
century?

As for Compline, my reasons for inclining to a single psalm are these:
(1) people are tired by evening, and their prayer must be short if it is to
be fruitful; (2) in communities the evening also brings some exercise reflective of the spirit of that community, as well as preparation for the next day's
meditation; these are facts that must be taken into account.

5) Next, I doubt the value of the invitatory unless it is connected (as it logically should be) with the Office of Readings. If one begins his prayer in the morning with Lauds, nothing should be added to it; after Lauds come Mass and meditation.

3. *At the Synod of Bishops*

The new approach taken to the Office was presented to the 1967 Synod of Bishops. On October 26 a vote was taken on four questions regarding it.[26]

1) *Psalms.* The Fathers were asked whether they were in favor of keeping all the psalms, including the imprecatory and historical psalms, in the regular four-week distribution of the Psalter.

Response: Yes: 117; No: 25; Yes with reservations: 31.

Among the reservations was a request that the three psalms which are wholly imprecatory be omitted from the ordinary cycle and placed among the Hours that are not obligatory for all, or that they be said by those who have a good knowledge of the Scriptures and can read these psalms in the correct way and with spiritual profit.

2) *Lauds and Vespers.* The structure proposed—hymn, three psalms (canticle), reading (short or long), canticle (*Benedictus, Magnificat*), *preces*, Our Father, collect, and conclusion—was accepted by the Synod with 144 in favor, 7 against, and 23 in favor with reservations.

The reservations asked that only Lauds and Vespers be obligatory; that outside choir the hymns and responsories be omitted; that the prayers of Prime be used in Lauds, since they are well suited as prayers for the sanctification of the day and for the offering of one's work.

3) *Little Hours.* One obligatory Hour with psalms taken from the current Psalter; the other Hours to be optional, except for those obliged to choir, and to have fixed psalms.

The vote on these guidelines: 141 in favor, 13 against, 20 in favor with reservations.

The reservations asked that the Little Hours not be obligatory; that they be reduced to one; that the short responsories be suppressed.

4) *Office of Readings.* Three psalms, a reading from Scripture, and another from the Fathers (or hagiographers). The readings to be chosen with an eye on the readings at Mass, so that the entire New Testament and a good part of the Old will be read in the course of a year.

The Synod's response: 129 votes in favor, 7 against, 28 in favor with reservations.

---

26. For bibliography on the Synod see above, pp. 169–70, n. 62.

The reservations covered a broad spectrum: the Office of Readings should not be obligatory; it should not be too short; it should never lack psalmody; there should be a psalm before each reading; the readings should be left to the choice of the priest or the judgment of the Ordinary; the New Testament should be reserved to Mass; precise rules should be drawn up for commutations and dispensations.

4. *Final Decision of the Pope*

The results of the discussion at the Synod were carefully examined at the ninth general meeting of the Consilium.[27] The acts (forty pages of foolscap) were sent to the Holy Father on December 10, 1967. In the report to the Pope the president added the following note regarding the imprecatory and historical psalms, which were a critical issue in the organization of the Office and conditioned the continuation of the work:

> A majority of the Consilium has decided that all the psalms should be retained in the regular cycle for distribution of the Psalter.
>
> It is necessary, on the other hand, to be objective and state that the number of those who want the regular cycle to contain only a selection of psalms, with the imprecatory and historical psalms being restricted to certain times of the year, has notably increased in recent years.
>
> The spiritual discomfort caused by expressions of anger and revenge, even when the exegetes have properly situated them in the development of revelation, is felt especially by the younger people and by those who say the Office in the vernacular. Pope John XXIII himself several times expressed the wish for a selection of the more beautiful psalms and those psalms that are important in the perspective of Christian revelation.
>
> The reason for the discomfort and the desire for selectivity is that a psalm is a formula for prayer and the text should promote prayer. Certain expressions of anger, hatred, and cursing can be correctly understood only if one has a good training in Scripture; even then, however, their use does not facilitate union with God and praise of him. The same is true in some degree of the historical psalms, which are devoted by and large to the "wonderful works of God" but in their wording are cold and dry for purposes of prayer.
>
> The use of technical devices—square brackets or asterisks telling those praying that they may omit certain verses—is only a partial solution of the problem. It will be difficult to avoid the impression, already mentioned by many, that these verses or entire psalms are being kept in the Breviary be-

27. At the same meeting, after discussion of the synodal votes and reservations, the regular report of the study group on the Office was given (the sixth report in the series). It brought nothing new, being provisional and marking time, since the great question of the psalms was still unresolved.

cause of formalism rather than necessity. It is not really agreeable to have them set off by typographical devices and omitted when the Office is celebrated with the faithful; in fact, the end result is to call all the more attention to them.

The secretariat humbly requests that in light of all these considerations, the Holy Father would deign to express his thinking on the subject.

The distribution of the psalms has already been made for the four weeks and the feasts on the assumption that the entire Psalter is to be used in the regular cycle.

If, therefore, it is decided that a selection of psalms is to be made even for the ordinary cycle, it will be necessary to restudy the entire distribution; this, however, would not entail insuperable difficulties.

The Pope expressed his mind in a handwritten note to the secretary of the Consilium on January 3, 1968: "In my view it is preferable that a selection be made of psalms better suited to Christian prayer and that the imprecatory and historical psalms be omitted (though these last may be suitably used in certain circumstances)."

At its meeting on January 30, 1968, the presidential council took cognizance of these guidelines established by the Holy Father and decided to pass them on to Canon Martimort in a letter to be hand-delivered by Bishop Boudon. In this letter, dated January 30, 1968, Cardinal Gut wrote:

After studying the minutes of the Synod and of our ninth general meeting last November, the Holy Father has deigned to make known to us in writing his thoughts on the question of the psalms. I send you a photostatic copy of the Pontiff's handwritten note.

At its meeting of January 30 the presidential council gratefully acknowledged that the Holy Father had deigned to decide a question so long debated, and it asked His Excellency Monsignor René Boudon to bring this letter to you.

The Holy Father's decision will discomfit the group that has done such fine work on the distribution of the psalms, but I am sure that it will make the needed revisions with its customary generosity, even if also with no little sacrifice.

May the Lord generously reward and bless your work and that of your collaborators, a work carried out amid such great difficulties but doubtless, for that very reason, also destined to bear no little fruit for the holy Church of God.

The study group met again on February 28 in the Abbey of Santa Maria della Castagna near Genoa. For the occasion, Canon Martimort composed a further report on the problem of the historical and imprecatory psalms (February 20, 1968).

As a result, the problem came up again at the tenth general meeting of the Consilium (April 23–30, 1968). The material to be studied was extensive, for the (seventh) report on the Office included the reports of the other groups working on the Breviary. It dealt with the components of the individual Hours, the celebration of saints' feasts, the way of organically linking Office and Mass and one Hour of the Office with another, and commutations. Since this report dealt with more or less technical details, it was studied by a limited group of Fathers and consultors, appointed by the presidency.

Monsignor Bonet also presented some general principles that were intended to serve as a basis for drawing up norms on obligation. For the first time a program (four parts, twenty-eight chapters) was proposed for the General Instruction for the Office, a document that would become one of the most illustrious in the postconciliar liturgical literature.

The question of the historical and imprecatory psalms was once again discussed at length. The arguments were more or less the same: traditional use of the entire Psalter; danger of admitting subjectivism if a selection of psalms were made; exclusion of the historical psalms would mean a loss of knowledge and appreciation of the history of salvation; possibility of omitting the imprecatory verses and of substituting other psalms for the imprecatory psalms.

The Fathers for the most part sided with the group and asked that the matter be once again submitted to the Pope; they would abide completely by his final decision.

Three questions on this matter were proposed to the Fathers for a vote:

1) Should Psalms 57, 82, and 108 be retained in the Psalter, with permission to substitute others for them?

24 in favor; 5 against; 1 blank ballot.

2) Should the imprecatory verses in other psalms likewise be retained in the official text, once again with permission to omit them?

18 in favor; 7 against.

3) Should the verses that may be omitted be marked as such in the text itself?

20 in favor; 7 against.

In his report to the Pope (May 10, 1968), the relator presented the arguments of the group and the votes of the Consilium. The secretary added his own "Observations," in which he expressed his views on the several arguments and concluded as follows:

1. There is no reason for holding to the principle that the entire Psalter be used, any more than we call for the integral use of the other sacred books, including even the New Testament.

2. Since the study group in charge of the distribution of the Psalter has, without excessive difficulty, sought and found a solution along the lines set down by the Holy Father, it seems appropriate to adopt it. It provides for:

a) the omission of Psalms 57, 82, and 108 from the ordinary cycle of the Psalter on the grounds that they are "imprecatory," and their replacement by other psalms (in the solution suggested by the bishops, the substitution would be simply optional);

b) the omission of some of the harsher "imprecatory" verses in other psalms. The omission would be indicated by listing, at the head of the psalm, the verses actually used, as is done for the other parts of Scripture;

c) the utilization of the three "historical" psalms (77, 104, 105) in the ordinary cycle of the Psalter only during certain periods of the year in which there is a more intense focus on the mystery of salvation (for example, in Lent and Advent). Such a solution would be easy to implement, since these psalms would be printed only in the volume of the Breviary being used at that season.[28]

The position taken by the secretary was accepted by the Pope at an audience granted to him on May 18, 1968. The papal action thus closed the long period of quest for the definitive structure of the new Office.[29] At the general meeting of the previous April, the relator had said: "We have reached the point in our work at which no new problems are arising, and we are faced only with difficulties of detail. All that remains is to implement the decisions taken."

---

28. At the meeting in Genoa, the group still stuck to its position but also looked for an alternative solution in line with the guidelines given by the Pope. This alternative solution provided that the three imprecatory psalms (57, 82, 108) and verses of a similar character in other psalms be completely omitted from the Psalter. The omission of verses was to be signaled by listing, at the head of the psalm, the verses actually included (just as the omission of verses is signaled at the beginning of the biblical readings). The historical psalms (77, 104, 105) were to be limited to the seasons of Advent, Christmas, and Lent.

The group also asked that in the General Instruction for the Breviary there be a statement that the omission of these texts was not motivated by doubts about their intrinsic adaptability to Christian prayer but rather by pastoral considerations, since in our day many persons, especially among the ordinary folk, find it difficult to use these psalms in their prayer.

29. In addition to the exclusion of the three imprecatory psalms already listed and to the assignment of the historical psalms to the seasons of Advent, Christmas, and Lent, the following verses were also omitted:

Psalm 5, vv. 2-10, 12-13.

20, vv. 2-8, 14.	62, vv. 2-9.
27, vv. 1-3, 6-9.	68, vv. 2-22, 30-37.
30, vv. 1-17, 20-25.	78, vv. 1-5, 8-11, 13.
34, vv. 1, 2, 3c, 9-19, 22-23, 27-28.	109, vv. 1-5, 7.
39, vv. 2-14, 17-18.	136, vv. 1-6.
53, vv. 1-6, 8-9.	138, vv. 1-18, 23-24.
54, vv. 2-15, 17-24.	139, vv. 1-9, 13-14.
55, vv. 2-7b, 9-14.	140, vv. 1-9.
58, vv. 2-5, 10-11, 17-18.	142, vv. 1-11.

The various other study groups now began preparing the material for the printing of the liturgical book that would henceforth regulate the Church's prayer.

III. Final Phase (1968–1972)

At the two remaining general meetings (the eleventh and the twelfth), the final questions of detail were discussed, including some of importance, such as the systematization of Compline, vigils, the obligation attaching to celebration of the Office by priests and religious who were bound to it, the substitution of another prayer for the Office (commutation),[30] and the organic link between Office and Mass.[31] In the relator's

---

30. It is up to the diocesan or religious Ordinary to dispense from recitation of the Office in individual cases or to allow fulfillment of the obligation by means of other prayers; see SC 97 (DOL 1 no. 97); motu proprio *Sacram Liturgiam* VII (DOL 20 no. 285); motu proprio *Pastorale munus* 26 (DOL 103 no. 733); instruction *Inter Oecumenici* 79 (DOL 23 no. 371). The rubrics of the Office itself provide for the case of those participating in the celebration of the evening Mass on Holy Thursday, the liturgical action on Good Friday afternoon, and the Easter Vigil.

There was discussion of two points. The first was whether to list other actions, of the kind just mentioned, that dispense a person from recitation of the corresponding Hour (e.g., the rite of ordination, the blessing of a church or altar, the consecration of virgins and religious profession, funerals, or other exceptional celebrations).

The second was whether it would be appropriate to list some preferred forms of commutation, so that the alternative would not always be the recitation of the Rosary. It was noted in regard to commutations that the nature of the Divine Office should be kept in mind, that is, that it is a prayer "of the Hours," and that the commutation should therefore not be universal, especially in regard to the most important Hours, which are Lauds and Vespers. Furthermore, the prayer that is to replace the Hour being commuted should be truly a prayer (not a simple reading or other action that is not a prayer) and should be recited in such a way that it really replaces the Hour being commuted. Various suggestions along this line were made. In the end, however, it was decided to say nothing, in view of the new way in which the obligation itself is formulated and of the danger of minimizing the importance of the Divine Office in the life of the clergy.

31. From the outset of the work, this concern made its way into almost all the schemas. The reason for the emphasis was the existing custom of having the conventual Mass preceded or followed by an Hour of the Office. Requests for a more organic connection were coming with increasing frequency from communities in which Mass immediately followed upon Lauds or, in some cases, Vespers. These communities saw in Mass and the Office a simple repetition of the same components: prayer, reading, intercessions.

The study group adverted to the problem as early as 1964 but did not tackle it until November 1967. It then studied the ways of organically linking an Hour of the Office with the Mass and came up with appropriate guidelines. It rejected, however, the linking of one Hour with another, since such a connection would be contrary to the principle of *veritas temporis*. It considered only the special case of the Office of Readings being connected with Midnight Mass on Christmas and of the same Office (which may be celebrated at any time of the day or night) being connected with another Hour (see the General Instruction 99 [DOL 426 no. 3529]).

final report (his eighth) on November 12–13, 1969, the Latin terminology to be used was settled: *Laudes Matutinae* (Morning Praise) for *Laudes* (Lauds), and *Liturgia Horarum* (Liturgy of the Hours) for *Breviarium* (Breviary) as a name for the Office as a whole.[32]

The preparation of the material, its review by the competent agencies of the Holy See, and the printing of the volumes would still take time. Meanwhile, there was need to prepare clergy and faithful and to sensitize them to the coming changes. The need was met by various undertakings.

1. Consultation of the Bishops

In December 1968 the Pope decided to send all the bishops of the world and religious superiors general a specimen of the new Office, together with an extended description of its structure and the criteria and principles at work in it. A short volume was prepared that contained the description and two Offices—one for a weekday (Monday of the fourth week of Ordinary Time) and one for a saint (St. Ignatius the Martyr, whose feast was at that time still being celebrated on February 1).[33]

The bishops were asked to join with their presbyteral councils and other qualified priests and laypersons in studying the principles and Offices. Religious superiors were asked to do the same. Any eventual observations were to be sent to the Consilium on the enclosed forms. The Holy Father approved the book in galley form on January 17, 1969 (No. 130550), and it was sent off on January 29.

Eight hundred seventy-three individuals and institutions replied; the forms received numbered about five thousand. The vast majority expressed satisfaction with the work. But the Offices also gave the impres-

---

32. On this occasion various titles were suggested: *Liber Officii Divini* (Book of the Divine Office), nine Fathers; *Liber Precum* (Book of Prayers), three; *Liber Precum Sacerdotalium* (Book of Priestly Prayers), one; *Officium Divinum* (Divine Office), two; and *Liber Liturgiae Horarum* (Book of the Liturgy of the Hours), sixteen. Titles containing "Office" were rejected for the reason that the word is too indefinite and has traditionally been used for other liturgical actions as well, including the Mass. On one point there was unanimity: the title should bring out the "hour" element that is characteristic of this prayer. A simple *Liber Horarum*, however, had too much of a medieval ring and lacked elegance. In the end, *Liturgia Horarum* prevailed. The term "liturgy" shows that the Office is an authentically liturgical action; the addition "of the Hours" pinpoints one of the specific characteristics of this liturgical action.

33. *Descriptio et specimina Officii Divini iuxta Concilii Vaticani II decreta instaurati* (Vatican City, 1969; 80 pp.). See "Descriptio Officii Divini iuxta Concilii Vaticani II decreta instaurati," *Not* 5 (1969) 74–85.

sion of being overly "monastic" and not adapted to private recitation.[34] A specific request was that some points, especially the principles governing obligation, be more clearly set down.

The results of the inquiry were the subject of a lengthy report to the Pope (January 2, 1970), in which the more important replies were given.

2. Experimental Psalter

One of the most urgent requests emerging from the consultation of the bishops was to "move quickly." The bishops were not only anxious to have something new and more accessible both to clerics in pastoral service and to the faithful; they were also concerned about a quickly spreading phenomenon—the abandonment of the Divine Office by some of the clergy.[35]

For this reason, at their meeting in Lourdes, November 2-9, 1968, the French bishops had insisted that the Holy Father be asked for permission to use the texts prepared by the Consilium, even before publication of the typical or normative edition. At another time a request of this kind would not have been even considered, but now necessity, and the climate of collaboration and understanding that had been achieved with the national liturgical commissions, made the request successful.

On January 3, 1969, the Consilium presented its views to the Secretariat of State. It outlined the situation at the moment: the preparation of the Liturgy of the Hours was still quite incomplete, especially in regard to

---

34. The same difficulty was raised within the Consilium itself. The clergy were used to "private" recitation of the Office and to looking upon the latter as a prayer reserved to priests. Elements that still gave the impression of being "monastic" were simply, it was said, parts retained with a view to celebration with the people or to communal celebration by priests and religious (the kind of celebration it was desirable should become increasingly common).

35. A basis for this worry was provided by a questionnaire circulated among the French clergy in the fall of 1967 and passed on to the Consilium by the Centre National de Pastorale Liturgique. A glance at two of the questions will be enough in the present context: (1) What use do you make of the Breviary? Replies: "I rarely use the Roman Breviary, preferring the Taizé Breviary or the Little Office of the Brothers of Father de Foucauld"; "I rarely say Matins, preferring a few pages of Scripture"; "I say Lauds and Vespers almost every day, but with a single psalm, a long reading, and some meditation"; "I have eliminated the responsories, little chapters, hymns, versicles, and the reading in the second nocturn"; "I omit the Office completely on Sundays and Thursdays because of pastoral duties."

2) What kind of Office would you like to see? Replies: "One that is a real invitation to prayer, one that can be a truly personal prayer"; "One with fewer 'Hours' and fewer psalms"; "One with Hours that follow the rhythms of life"; "One with a selection of Scripture readings"; "One from which all the 'monastic' elements are removed"; "An Office promoting vital, adapted prayer, not one recited because we must."

the texts of the antiphons and responsories and the patristic and historical readings; the biblical readings, however, were ready. Furthermore,
the consultation of the bishops was now in progress, and it would be
better to wait for the results of this. In order to satisfy the pastoral need
felt by the French episcopate, permission could be given to publish the
Psalter in French in the four-week arrangement planned by the Consilium. The concession was to be temporary and by way of experiment,
under the responsibility of the episcopal conference, until the publication of the Latin typical edition. The old Breviary was to be used for the
parts of the new that were not yet published.

On January 27 the Secretariat of State replied to the president of the
Consilium as follows: "The matter is left to the prudent judgment of the
Congregation of Rites and the Consilium, which are familiar with the present situation in the liturgical reform and will see to it that any concession
not prejudice the participation of France in the reform itself; the concession is to be under the control of the French episcopate."

The Holy Father discussed the matter with the secretary of the Consilium at an audience on January 31. He decided that the grant could be
extended to all the French-speaking episcopal conferences. That same day
Cardinal Gut put his signature to some guidelines for implementing the
grant; the next day he signed the letter of concession.[36] The Centre National de Pastorale Liturgique in Paris immediately set to work and was
able to send a manuscript to the Consilium on May 26 for its final *nihil
obstat*. This was given on June 19, 1969, with the stipulation that nothing
was changed as to the obligation of clerics and religious to recite the Office.[37]

On the following July 4 the little book appeared under the title *Prière
du temps présent*, with a preface by Bishop Boudon, president of the French-
language liturgical commission, and a "charismatic" presentation; it was
in pocket-size format and invitingly youthful in appearance.[38] At the back
of the book was a questionnaire addressed to "the baptized, religious,
and priests" and asking them to make known any suggestions, impressions, and assessments they might have (and the French would surely
have plenty of these).

---

36. The regulations for carrying out the plan are also set down in a letter from the Secretary of State to Cardinal Joseph Lefèbvre, president of the French Episcopal Conference
(February 8, 1969; No. 129926).

37. The Congregation for the Clergy, which had authority in this area, was asked for
its views. It decided that no change in the obligation should be made, since this was a matter that concerned the entire Church (July 22, 1969).

38. *Prière du temps présent. Le nouvel Office Divin* (Paris: Desclée De Brouwer/Desclée et
Cie./Lebergerie-Mame, 1969; 592 pp.).

On the whole, the book met with widespread and encouraging approval; the size of the sales is evidence of this.[39] A good many priests recovered their taste for and fidelity to the prayer of the Hours. Among the things they liked about the new Breviary were the balanced structure of the morning and evening Offices; the improved distribution of the psalms; the introduction of New Testament canticles; and the intercessions. Along with these positive assessments came some criticisms or requests: a greater range of choices in the scriptural and patristic readings; the need for a broad law setting the Office in its context rather than for fixed rubrics; greater harmony between Mass and Office, in order to unify the spiritual life; reduction of the obligation to the key Hours, namely, Lauds and Vespers; formulation of the obligation so as to stress conviction rather than external imposition.[40]

Some communities of contemplative life also wanted to join in the experiment.[41] The large number of copies sold showed that some of the laity, too, were adopting the prayer of the Hours.

The success of the French publication encouraged other countries to follow France's example. Within a few months' time, the Netherlands, Spain, Germany, England, and Brazil had an experimental edition in their languages.[42]

There were those who feared that this partial new Office, which was limited to the Psalter, would weaken interest in the rest of the new Office. In fact, it created a more intense desire for the complete Liturgy of the Hours.

---

39. Two printings were soon sold out—50,000 copies in July and 100,000 in October.

40. The first reactions were gathered together by the Centre National de Pastorale Liturgique in a cyclostyled document, "L'expérimentation du novel Office Divin," which was sent to the Secretary of State, among others; on December 11, 1969, the Secretary asked for the views of the Consilium.

41. See "Contemplazione e Ufficio Divino restaurato," Not 5 (1969) 398–402.

42. The Consilium secretariat prepared a text of the four-week Psalter and sent copies of it to the secretariats of the joint commissions for the use of those who, like France, might request it. To my astonishment, no official move was made in Italy. Publications undertaken by private individuals did appear (the one produced by the LDC was especially well received) but did not have the approval of the authorities, so that doubts were raised about their validity. Someone thought the Consilium secretariat had unjustly favored the French and neglected everyone else, and wrote to the Pope to this effect. It was not difficult to prove that Italy had received the manuscript at the same time as everyone else. More than this, at the bidding of the Pope, the secretary of the Consilium urged the secretariat of the Italian Episcopal Conference to embark immediately on an experimental edition of the Office. Unfortunately, this move elicited a lively reaction, and the suggestion, though phrased very diplomatically by the Pope himself, was not accepted.

3. Obligation

The final question to be answered before the official publication of the Liturgy of the Hours was that of the obligation incumbent on certain categories of persons to celebrate it.

A first approach to the obligation of ordained ministers (deacons, priests, bishops) to recite the prayer of the Hours was contained in the little volume *Descriptio et Specimina Officii Divini* (no. 67). The statement contained here was the result of discussions and decisions in the Consilium.[43] The obligation of priests in regard to the new Office differed for the various parts of it: serious for Lauds and Vespers, with even the time of day being prescribed (Lauds before midday; Vespers before midnight), and substantial for the Office of Readings (the sense being that a protracted neglect should be considered serious). Only a general reference was made to the other Hours: "Priests are daily to recite the Divine Office, at the true time for each Hour." No reference was made to deacons. The statement was obviously incomplete.

Once observations and remarks on the book of samples had been received, the final text was composed and sent on March 30, 1970, to the Holy Father and the Congregations for the Doctrine of the Faith, the Clergy, Religious, Catholic Education, and the Evangelization of Peoples. The obligation was worded as follows:

> 1. All priests and others who have received from the Church the mandate to celebrate the Liturgy of the Hours should recite the full sequence of Hours each day, observing the true time of day.
> 2. [Lauds and Vespers] should not be omitted except for a serious reason.
> 3. Protracted omission of [the Office of Readings] is to be regarded as a serious fault.
> 4. They will also treasure [the Middle Hour and Compline].

The Congregations for Catholic Education and the Evangelization of Peoples declared themselves completely satisfied; on August 25, 1970, the Congregation for the Doctrine of the Faith gave its *nihil obstat* (No. 640/70), and this for the entire text of the General Instruction of the Liturgy of the Hours.

The Congregation for Religious sent a rather annoyed reply. It took a somewhat casuistic approach and asserted that the liturgical books have no authority "to legislate with regard to those who are or are not obliged to recite the liturgical Hours" and that, generally speaking, it was "in-

---

43. The text was the work especially of Monsignor Bonet, who presented it at the eleventh general meeting of the Consilium. This was the final contribution of an unforgettable friend, who was called on August 6, 1969, to the glory reserved for faithful workers.

clined to regret the perhaps excessive shortening of some parts of the
Divine Office and the excessive elasticity of the obligation to recite it"
(April 2, 1970). The Congregation for the Clergy, which was the Congregation most directly concerned, insisted that the obligation of daily reciting the entire Office be described as serious with regard to the substance
of the prayer.[44]

The Congregation for Divine Worship accepted the proposed statement of obligation but stressed that it thought there should be a grada-
tion in the obligation for the several Hours. Therefore it consented to the
insertion of the following sentence: "The substantial observance of this
obligation is a serious matter."

The secretary of the Congregation discussed the problem with the Holy
Father at an audience on July 8, 1970. The Pope wanted the obligation
of celebrating the Divine Office to be presented in persuasive terms, with
an emphasis on the substantial obligation. A new text was redacted with
this in mind and presented to the Secretariat of State on July 11.[45] This
text now had to be reviewed. The sentence "The substantial observance
of this obligation is a serious matter" was removed, in order to avoid
endless casuistry and because the words "recite the full sequence of Hours
each day" seemed sufficient to express the daily obligation (they were
considered to be the equivalent of the words "they are obliged [*tenentur
obligatione*]" in canon 135 of the 1917 Code). The obligation of reciting
the Office of Readings was stated in positive terms.[46]

After reviewing the text, the Secretariat of State approved it on October 3, 1970, and it became part of the General Instruction of the Liturgy of the Hours (nos. 29-32).[47]

---

44. The text proposed was: "Clerics in holy orders . . . are obliged to celebrate the Liturgy of the Hours in its entirety every day. The substantial observance of this obligation
is a serious matter."

45. "Priests and others . . . should recite the full sequence of Hours each day, observing *as far as possible* the true time of day. *The substantial observance of this obligation is a serious
matter.*" The words "as far as possible" were added in response to a request from the Congregation for the Clergy, which feared that the clergy might otherwise be embittered, since
to make the proper time of day part of the obligation would create an impossible situation
for the clergy in the pastoral ministry.

Lauds and Vespers "should not be omitted except for a serious reason." Office of Readings: "Repeated omission should be regarded as a serious fault" ("protracted" seemed
too broad a term). Middle Hour and Compline: "they will treasure. . . ."

46. "By means of the Office of Readings, which is above all a liturgical celebration of
the word of God, let them daily fulfill the duty of receiving the word of God into themselves so that they may become more perfect disciples of the Lord and experience more
deeply the unfathomable riches of Christ."

47. No reference was made to the necessity of "oral recitation," though this was re-

As here presented, the obligation is grounded in spiritual motives and is expressed in a positive way. It is viewed from an ascetical standpoint that is moral rather than juridical, although not therefore less binding. The recital of the Divine Office by priests and others to whom it is especially entrusted should be inspired by an awareness of their priesthood or their consecration to God and not by a burdensome sense of externally imposed obligation.

Despite this positive approach, there would be second thoughts and requests for new "declarations" regarding the character of the obligation in an attempt to install a new casuistry. But the text was not altered in the definitive publication of the General Instruction,[48] and the Pope spoke of obligation as follows when promulgating the new Liturgy of the Hours:

> Those who are in holy orders and are marked in a special way with the sign of Christ the Priest, as well as those consecrated in a particular way to the service of God and of the Church by the vows of religious profession, should not only be moved to celebrate the hours through obedience to law, but should also feel themselves drawn to them because of the intrinsic excellence of the hours and their pastoral and ascetical value.[49]

---

quested by some. *Notitiae* explained that such a recitation was not required in private celebration; see *DOL* 426 no, 3449 R1.

48. The only clarification introduced was in no. 31b (*DOL* 426 no. 3461) for religious obliged to choir; it is said that they are bound to the daily celebration of the entire choral Office; outside of choir, however, their particular law applies. This clarification was requested by the Congregation for Religious (April 29, 1971).

49. Apostolic constitution *Laudis canticum* (*DOL* 424 no. 3428).

31

Composition of the Liturgy of the Hours

The new Liturgy of the Hours was promulgated by Pope Paul VI in the apostolic constitution *Laudis canticum*, which was dated November 1, 1970, but was not published until February 1971.[1]

The new Office comprises four volumes. This format itself caused difficulties requiring time, calculations, and revisions for their resolution. The bishops of the Consilium had always shown themselves to be practical-minded men. They wanted the book containing the Liturgy of the Hours to be "handy" and not to have the drawbacks of technical complexity, large size, and high cost. At the final general meeting of the Consilium (April 1970), they had urged that publication be speeded up and that the book be no more than two volumes in length. The extent of the material, however, was an obstacle to a two-volume format.

A first problem was the cycle of Scripture readings, which was originally planned as a two-year cycle.[2] In view of the practical difficulties this entailed, it was finally decided to include only a one-year cycle in the books containing the Liturgy of the Hours and to leave the two-year cycle to a Supplement.[3]

---

1. See *Not* 7 (1971) 146. A good many articles marked the publication of the several volumes of the *Liturgia Horarum*. Here are a few: A.-G. Martimort, "L'*Institutio generalis* de la nouvelle *Liturgia Horarum*," *Not* 7 (1971) 218-40; P. Jounel, "La Liturgie des Heures dans le renouveau de Vatican II," *Not* 10 (1974) 310-20, 334-43; articles of A. Bugnini in *L'Osservatore Romano* for March 13 and 14, 1971, June 24, 1971, October 22, 1971, and January 1, 1972; and the collective work, *Liturgia delle Ore. Documenti ufficiali e studi* (Turin–Leumann, 1972. 568 pp.).

2. See above, pp. 171 and 188, and below, pp. 534-36.

3. The "Supplement" was the projected fifth volume containing the various optional

Even with this reduction, however, a two-volume Office would have been unwieldy. One volume would have had to contain the Psalter, the Ordinary, and the Commons, a second the readings; there would have been no gain in clarity, nor would the books have been any easier to use. In the Psalter all the proper elements would have had to be included one after the other: the antiphons and hymns for Advent, the Christmas season, Lent and Eastertide, and Ordinary Time. The person praying the Hours would have had to search out the correct item with notable inconvenience. Even then each of the two volumes would have had over two thousand pages. A person obliged to move about from place to place would have had to take along both of these sizable tomes. For these reasons the choice was finally made of a much handier four-volume edition in which each volume would be complete and self-contained.[4]

The four volumes were published one after another in a real tour de force involving the secretariat of the Congregation, the Vatican Polyglot Press, the correctors of the page proofs, and the binder.[5] Technical problems made it impossible to keep to the established schedule.[6] Each volume was examined by the Congregation for the Doctrine of the Faith[7]

---

elements. The SCDW left it in proof form, and nothing more was heard of it. The episcopal conferences can adopt a two-year cycle in their own editions of the Liturgy of the Hours if they think it advisable.

4. The four-volume plan was approved by the Secretariat of State on August 22, 1970. Here is the arrangement of the four volumes in the Latin edition: I. Tempus Adventus; Tempus Nativitatis (1304 pp.); II. Tempus Quadragesimae; Tempus Paschale (1800 pp.); III. Tempus per Annum, Hebdomadae I–XVII (1644 pp.); IV. Tempus per Annum, Hebdomadae XVIII–XXXIV (1614 pp.). All volumes in duodecimo format, 11 x 17 cm., printed in red and black on India paper.

The episcopal conferences have authority to arrange the contents differently, and in fact various attempts at a different arrangement were made, but in the end the arrangement adopted by the SCDW proved to be the handiest. Some guidelines were issued in this area: SCDW, Note *Liturgiae Horarum interpretationes*, on vernacular editions of the Liturgy of the Hours, January 15, 1973 (*DOL* 434 no. 3739); see A. Bugnini, "Circa editionem libri *Liturgiae Horarum*," *Not* 7 (1971) 411.

5. A circular letter (March 27, 1971) from the secretary of the Consilium to the relators of the study groups, the correctors of the proofs, and the Latinists gave the tight schedule that would have to be followed in order to complete the entire publication in 1971.

6. Despite good will and perseverance, the volumes did not appear on the planned dates. Volume I was ready in July 1971; Volume II at the end of December 1971; Volume III in April 1972; and Volume IV in July 1972. Thus it was not possible to avoid falling back on the old "Breviary" for the days from January 10 to February 15, 1972, since Volume III was not yet ready; see "Communicatio circa la pubblicazione della *Liturgia Horarum*," *L'Osservatore Romano*, November 25, 1971.

7. To facilitate the reading, the volumes were sent to the Congregation in page-proof form and therefore as the material became available from the printer (October 1970; October–November 1971; April–May 1972). After approving the General Instruction, the Congrega-

and by the Latinists of the Secretariat of State and then approved by the Pope.[8]

The first volume contained the official documents: the decree of the Congregation for Divine Worship,[9] the apostolic constitution *Laudis canticum*, and the General Instruction. The distribution of the material was the same in all four volumes: Proper of the Seasons; Ordinary, with four-week Psalter; Compline for one week, with supplementary psalmody; Proper of the Saints; Commons; and, in an appendix, the various introductory formulas for the Our Father, and shorter *preces* for Lauds and Vespers.

I shall here review the various parts comprising the Liturgy of the Hours, which was the fruit of the labors of the several study groups.

I. GENERAL INSTRUCTION OF THE LITURGY OF THE HOURS

This document is acknowledged to be one of the most important, if not the most outstanding, of the entire postconciliar liturgical reform. It is truly a theological, pastoral, ascetical, and liturgical treatise on the prayer of the Hours, on the importance of this liturgy, and on its component parts. It is a directory that serves not only for the celebration of the liturgy but for meditation on it. The document is the work of a group of experts who themselves had been meditating for years on the texts that feed the prayer of the Church.

After being approved by the Consilium, the instruction was studied by the Congregations for the Doctrine of the Faith, the Clergy, Catholic Education, Religious, and the Evangelization of Peoples.[10] It was then

---

tion assigned one of its trusted consultors to examine the texts and agree on corrections with the SCDW.

8. Volume I: proofs sent on December 12, 1970, for examination and approval together with the apostolic constitution and the General Instruction; delivery of the printed volumes, June 22, 1971. Volume II: proofs sent on June 19, 1971; approved, July 3, 1971; delivery of volume, October 20, 1971. Volume III: proofs sent on October 29, 1971; approved, November 20, 1971; delivery of printed volume, December 29, 1971. Volume IV: proofs sent on May 10, 1972; approved, May 27, 1972; delivery of printed volume, June 1972. (The copies sent to the Pope were bound by the Vatican Press as soon as the printing was complete; therefore they preceded the issuance of the other copies, which were bound in Vicenza.)

9. The decree of the SCDW was dated April 11, 1971 (*DOL* 427 no. 3715).

10. The Congregation for the Doctrine of the Faith gave its *nihil obstat* on August 25, 1970. A joint meeting was then held on November 12 to handle corrections; the group included Archbishop Philippe and Father B. Duroux from the Congregation for the Doctrine of the Faith, and Father A. Bugnini and Canon Martimort from the SCDW. The other congregations either voiced their complete approval (Catholic Education, Evangelization) or sent remarks dealing chiefly with the character of the obligation (Clergy, Religious).

sent to the Holy Father on March 3, 1970. He examined it carefully during the months of July to September 1971, and finally gave his approval.[11]

Since several months would still elapse before the document could be officially published in the first volume of the *Liturgia Horarum*, the secretariat of the Congregation for Divine Worship thought it would be a good idea to make the text known in a semi-official way in order that the clergy and faithful might prepare themselves for the new Liturgy of the Hours and that any criticisms, observations, and suggested changes might be submitted. The plan was presented to the Pope and received his approval. The instruction was therefore published in a separate booklet on February 2, 1971.[12] This publication provided an excellent opportunity to prepare people to accept the new organization of the Church's official prayer.[13]

The document contains five chapters and 284 numbers.

Chapter I: Importance of the Liturgy of the Hours in the life of the Church. This chapter is the most doctrinal of all and gives the entire treatise its tone. The opening statement, that public and common prayer is one of the Church's primary duties, is the basis for a presentation of the Liturgy of the Hours in the light of the example of Christ and the early Church. By means of this liturgy the Church continues the priestly office of Christ, praising God and sanctifying human beings by sanctifying time. In this liturgy the Church communes with and participates in the heavenly prayer of praise and supplication, of listening and responding; it is therefore both the summit and source of pastoral activity.

---

11. The Pope communicated his observations at an audience granted to A. Bugnini on July 8. He asked that the prayer "Aperi, Domine" be recommended before private recitation; he found the number of *ad libitum* to be excessive; he thought that the psalms which may be substituted for Psalm 94 in the invitatory should be listed. He then made some other minor points. The approval given and observations made by the Pope at this audience were officially communicated by the Secretariat of State on July 11 and 14 and August 10. On September 2 the Secretariat sent on the corrections submitted by the Latinists and asked that no. 251, on readings from modern authors, be revised in accordance with the directives given by the Congregation for the Doctrine of the Faith (see below, pp. 543–44).

12. *Institutio generalis de Liturgia Horarum* (Vatican Polyglot Press, 1971. 11 x 17 cm. 94 pp.). The secretary of the SCDW had also taken steps to have the document explained by commissioning Father Roguet to write a popular book that appeared in Italian under the title *La Liturgia delle Ore* (Milan: Ancora, 1971). This book was also published in other languages.

13. The final text of the General Instruction of the Liturgy of the Hours is also in *DOL* 426 nos. 3431-3714. The differences between the text published on February 2, 1971, and the definitive text are minimal and almost entirely stylistic; see F. Dell'Oro, "Variazioni alla *Institutio generalis de Liturgia Horarum*," in *Liturgia delle Ore* (n. 1), 87–95.

At the end of this chapter the document considers those to whom the Liturgy of the Hours is entrusted, namely, the entire Church, even if in varying ways. It is entrusted in a special way to certain members of the Church: deacons, priests, bishops, religious, and canonical communities. The nature of the obligation is described.

Chapter II: Sanctification of the day by the various liturgical Hours. This chapter deals with the various Hours: Lauds and Vespers, Office of Readings, Terce, Sext, and None (Middle or Daytime Hour), and Compline. The characteristics of each are explained. The chapter ends with the regulations for organically combining the Mass and the Office or the Office of Readings with another Hour.

Chapter III: The different elements that make up the Liturgy of the Hours. Here again the description of each element—psalms, antiphons, canticles, readings, responsories, intercessions, prayers, hymns, silence—includes rubrical prescriptions but also, and more importantly, spiritual and ascetical reflections.

Chapter IV: Various celebrations throughout the year. Considered here are the mysteries of the Lord (Sunday, Easter Triduum, Advent, Christmas, and the other seasons); the saints; the arrangement of the celebration according to the rank of the day: solemnities, feasts, memorials. Especially useful are the remarks on the option to choose texts while taking into account the calendar and the characteristics of the various liturgical seasons.

Chapter V: Guidelines for celebration of the Office in common. The roles of the participants are described, as is the course of the celebration. The chapter and the document as a whole end with an inspired discussion of sacred song: its importance in the celebration of the Office, its spiritual significance.

II. PSALTER

1. *Psalms*

The question of the distribution of the psalms throughout the Office has already been dealt with at length. The work of the study group in charge of the distribution had been linked with that of the group dealing with the overall structure of the Office, since the distribution depended closely on this structure. A good deal of very careful work went into assigning psalms adapted to the characteristics of the various Hours, liturgical seasons, and feasts, while at the same time taking into account both the tradition and the spiritual good of the faithful.

Special attention was paid to the peculiar character of Sunday as the weekly memorial of the resurrection, and of Friday as the day of Christ's passion and death.[14]

The same group also dealt with the elements of the Office that help to an understanding of the psalms and to their Christological interpretation, namely, the captions and the quotations. The former indicate the genre and literal meaning of the psalm as shown by the tradition; the latter, which are taken from the New Testament or the writings of the Fathers, help to a prayer based on the plenary sense (*sensus plenus*) of the psalm, that is, its meaning as referring to Christ and the Church.

2. *New Testament Canticles*

The New Testament canticles are another new element in the Office; they come after the two psalms of Vespers and are arranged in a one-week cycle. The question of introducing them had been raised at the fourth general meeting of the Consilium (October 1966) by the relator of the group in charge of the distribution of the psalms. He justified his suggestion by an appeal to the tradition of other Rites and to their usefulness in understanding the psalms. The introduction of a New Testament canticle effects a passage from the psalms, which speak prophetically of Christ, to the reality of the mystery of Christ.

---

14. Here, by way of example, are the psalms chosen for the four Sundays of the Psalter (numbering according to the Vulgate for the Latin Psalter):

Office of Readings. Sunday 1: Psalms 1, 2, 3, in accordance with the earliest tradition. Sunday 2: Psalm 103, the song of creation; Christ's resurrection and their own baptism turn human beings into a new creation. Sunday 3: Psalm 144, in which the Church exults in the glory of Christ's resurrection. Sunday 4: Psalm 23, which proclaims the entrance of the Lord into the heavenly Jerusalem.

Daytime Hour. Sundays 1 and 3: Psalm 117, a song of deliverance. Sundays 2 and 4: Psalm 22, which sings of the sacraments of Christian initiation (paschal character), and Psalm 75, which is interpreted as referring to the resurrection by reason of vv. 9-10: "the earth feared and was still when God arose to establish judgment."

Vespers. The first psalm on all the Sundays is Psalm 109, which by very ancient tradition begins the psalmody of Vespers, being interpreted as referring to the victory Christ has won by his suffering; its regular occurrence is not likely to beget boredom. On Sundays 1 and 2 the second psalm is 113A-B: the Exodus from Egypt is a type of resurrection and baptism. On Sunday 3 the second psalm is 110, an Alleluia psalm celebrating the redemption (see v. 9: "He sent redemption to his people"), and on Sunday 4 it is Psalm 125, "When the Lord restored the fortunes of Zion," which describes the passage from tears to joy (v. 4 is interpreted as referring to the resurrection of Christ and the baptized).

Compline. On all Sundays the scheme is the traditional one: Psalms 4, 90, and 33, which are typical expressions of trust in God.

Biblical studies have shown that the canticles scattered throughout the New Testament writings are hymns to Christ in the true and proper sense of the term. In literary form they are psalms of praise: they begin with a call to praise and then go on to state the reasons for the praise: *"Praise the Lord, all you nations . . . for he has proved his mercy."*

The Fathers of the Consilium unanimously accepted the suggestion, and this favorable attitude never changed. The result was the introduction of nine New Testament canticles into the reformed Office.[15]

3. *Latin Text of the Psalms*

The revision of the Psalter that was made during the pontificate of Pius XII and published in 1945 had been welcomed because it restored intelligence and vitality to the praying of the psalms in Latin. But there had also been criticisms. The most objective of these seemed to be the ones focusing on the language used: the Latin seemed overly classical at the expense of "Christian Latin." On this point corrections or at least improvements seemed necessary. The Constitution on the Liturgy therefore decreed: "The work of revising the psalter, already happily begun, is to be finished as soon as possible and is to take into account the style of Christian Latin, the liturgical use of psalms, including their being sung, and the entire tradition of the Latin Church" (no. 91).

The task was entrusted to study group 2, which was formed in agreement with Cardinal Bea, toward whom it always showed special regard.[16] The group was, after all, dealing with a work to which he had devoted a number of years at the special request of Pius XII. He declared himself

---

15. There are seven canticles for the weekly cycle in Vespers: Eph 1:3-10; Col 1:3, 12-20; Phil 2:6-11; Rev 4:11 and 5:9-10, 12; Rev 11:17-18 and 12:10b-12a; Rev 15:2-4; and Rev 19:1-7. 1 Pet 2:21-24 is used on the Sundays of Lent, and 1 Tim 3:16 on the solemnities of the Lord's Epiphany and Transfiguration. Further canticles would have been welcome, possibly for the four Sundays of the Psalter, but they could not be found. 1 Cor 13:1-7, the famous "hymn to charity," was initially suggested but rejected because it is not strictly in the genre of hymns. The prologue of the Fourth Gospel was likewise proposed but rejected, again on grounds of its literary genre. The same for the Beatitudes.

Twenty-six Old Testament canticles are used in Lauds. Those found in the old Breviary have been retained, and twelve new ones have been added. They are distributed throughout the four weeks of the Psalter.

16. *Relator:* P. Duncker; *secretary:* J. Gribomont; *members:* G. Castellino, B. Wambacq, R. MacKenzie. A. Lentini was nominated Latinist; he let it be known that he would gladly review the texts at Montecassino, but could not accept the appointment if he were required to attend the weekly meetings of the group. But a Latinist who could take an active part in the work was needed; K. Egger was therefore appointed in November 1964. In February 1964 Abbot P. Salmon was added as a regular member; he attended only seven or eight meetings until June of that year and for the rest was content to keep abreast of the work via his fellow religious, J. Gribomont.

in favor of a study group, but also said he thought only finishing touches were needed. He acknowledged that the Latin of his version was overly classical and needed to be brought closer to the style of the Fathers and the liturgy (January 21, 1964).

The group held its meetings in the house of the Vincentian Missionaries at San Silvestro on the Quirinal, where the secretary of the Consilium also resided. The locale was chosen because it was central.

A first, informal meeting was held on February 6, 1964; the secretary of the Consilium took the chair and outlined the program for the work. He then asked the views of each on procedure. J. Gribomont said that the Gallican Psalter should serve as the textual basis for carrying out the wishes of the Constitution on the Liturgy (nos. 90-91) for the Latinity of the new translation and consistency in translating Hebraisms, and, finally, for the sake of the "spiritual transfiguration" in which the Old Testament is gradually illumined by revelation.

R. MacKenzie observed that since the Office would be celebrated in the vernaculars, the revision of the Latin Psalter would be of service primarily to monks; it would be advisable, therefore, to take as a working basis the Gallican Psalter, a venerable monument that is to be revised only with great caution.

Don Castellino remarked that the Gallican Psalter contains a wealth of history and traditions; it would be enough to revise it in places where its rendition of the original text is defective.

P. Duncker was inclined rather to start with the Pian Psalter, which all the critics valued for its fidelity and intelligibility. Only its Latinity was debated. However, he would gladly go along with the other experts.

B. Wambacq was absent but sent a verbal message that he would prefer to start with the Pian Psalter.

Agreement was reached on a program for the work, and it was decided to meet twice a week. J. Gribomont was elected secretary.

The inaugural meeting of the group was held on February 14 at the house of the Benedictine Sisters at S. Priscilla and in the presence of Cardinal Giacomo Lercaro.

On February 15 the group received an official summons to hold its first working session on March 5. The members were sent the text of the first seven psalms in the critical edition of the Vulgate, in order that they might prepare corrections of them.

Guidelines

The guidelines on which the revisors had agreed in principle were approved at an audience with the Holy Father on February 14:

The text of the Vulgate is to be *kept:* (a) when it faithfully renders the Masoretic text; (b) when it illumines and transfigures the meaning of the original text in the light of revelation.

The text of the Vulgate is to be *changed:* (a) when it departs from the correct interpretation of the original text; (b) when it translates idiomatic Hebraisms in too servile a manner.

Since the purpose of the study group was to complete the revisory process already happily begun, it seemed an obvious step to take as a basis not only the "Gallican" Psalter (the Vulgate) but also the Psalter with the corrections, emendations, and restorations of the *hebraica veritas* that had already been made by the Pontifical Biblical Institute. A further reason for proceeding in this manner was that the "Pian Psalter" had already been in the hands of the clergy for some twenty years, and a sudden and radical change would be counterproductive. Nor could the group afford to ignore the fact that the Pian Psalter was a good version of the original, was more intelligible than the Vulgate, and had been applauded by the majority of Catholic and non-Catholic exegetes. The "revision" to be undertaken had to be one that would not seem an exegetical step backward in comparison to the Pian Psalter. Two other safeguards were included in the working plan:

a) the text produced by the study group was to be sent for examination to a group of specialists in exegesis, Eastern languages, philology, Christian Latin, and liturgy. A new redaction would then be produced on the basis of their observations; this new version would once again be sent out, and so on, until a text acceptable to the majority of the experts was obtained;

b) once this acceptable version was established, there would be a period in which it would be used experimentally by some abbeys in public celebrations, by some religious families that recite the Office in common, and "by ten or so priests who recite the Office privately."

Two months later, on March 31, the first twenty-five psalms were sent to thirty experts all over the world, who had been selected by the group. The remarks of these experts were then studied by all the members of the group.[17]

---

17. The most active revisors were: Cazelles, Schildenberger, Tournay, Villegas, Cordero, Dalton, Kilpatrick, Diez Macho, and Ryan. Next came Bieler, Camps, Cerfaux, Lentini, Mohrmann, Pellegrino, Schwegler, and van der Ploeg. Some revisors sent in observations only on the first group of psalms sent to them: Botte, Bullough, Charbel, Coppens, and Marrou. No signs of life came from Guano, Hurley, Kalilombe, Norberg, and Panikkar.

At the end of January the first revision was complete. P. Duncker was then asked to report on the work done to the seventh general meeting of the Consilium.

After a few references to the approach taken to the work, Father Duncker stressed the two guidelines which had been set down at the beginning and which had been refined and adapted to particular cases:

> At times, although the Gallican Psalter gives a good rendition of a Hebrew word, another more readily understandable Latin word is substituted for the sake of clarity.
>
> We have made an effort to translate the meaning of Hebrew words with greater accuracy than is done in the Gallican Psalter.
>
> The same Hebrew word is rendered by the same Latin word, at least throughout a given psalm. Therefore, a Latin word that corresponds to different Hebrew words in one and the same psalm of the Gallican Psalter is used for only one of these Hebrew words, and another Latin word is used for the other(s).
>
> In choosing such new Latin words, an effort has been made to adopt others that are found elsewhere in the Psalter or in the other books of the Vulgate or in the Psalter *iuxta Hebraeos*.
>
> Special attention has been paid to the use of tenses and moods.
>
> An effort has been made to keep the poetic coloring of the Hebrew text; this accounts for the adoption or retention of such words as: *arx, rupes, scutum,* and *turris* in place of *firmamentum, adiutor, protector,* and *susceptor*.
>
> When the original text is clearly corrupt, we have adopted the Pian text or some other that seems better.

Finally, the relator touched on the revision made by the thirty experts: "Their remarks are many and varied, but in general seem to approve the text proposed to them. Some claim that the version departs excessively and needlessly from the Gallican Psalter; others would like a closer adherence to the Hebrew and a greater clarity in the Latin used. Their observations create difficulties for the final redaction."

To sum up: the majority showed that they wanted a clear, easily understandable Psalter, based on the Vulgate but closer to the original text, especially since all the translations into the vernaculars would be based on the original text. The Consilium approved the report. Encouraged by this approval, the study group continued its work.

Difficulties

After corrections had been made in the first twenty-five psalms on the basis of the observations received from the experts, Father Duncker sent the text to Cardinal Bea for his personal review. His judgment was the one most eagerly awaited, and in a sense the one most feared.

No answer came until March 31, 1967, when the Cardinal wrote to Father Duncker:

> I am sincerely sorry that I have to say I am not fully satisfied with the text I have examined; I do not think it is one that can be submitted to the Holy Father. I shall not specify my reasons here, since I give detailed reasons in the enclosed document.
>
> In my opinion, the study group will have to revise these psalms once again in light of the enclosed observations, especially those having to do with the group's attitude toward the Pian Psalter.

Some remarks of a general character were followed by three closely written pages of very detailed remarks, which showed how carefully Cardinal Bea had gone through the text.

The study group was surprised by some of the Cardinal's remarks on matters of principle, since it had reached agreement with him at the outset on the guidelines to be followed in the revision; these guidelines had now been considerably altered. Father Duncker realized this and asked the Cardinal for a meeting so that the group might not continue doing work that would be useless. He wrote to Cardinal Bea on April 10, 1967:

> When we began our work three years ago, we gave much thought to the method to be followed. After a great deal of discussion and differences of opinion, we reached agreement that we should take as our point of departure the text of the Vulgate rather than that of the Pian Psalter, while at the same time making the Latin text more faithful to the original and also clearer. In accordance with this viewpoint, henceforth shared by the entire group, we drew up guidelines to be followed; these were officially submitted to the Holy Father on February 15, 1964, and sent on to Your Eminence on December 13, 1965.
>
> We think that we have faithfully followed these guidelines, although in the course of our work hesitations and differences of opinion have arisen regarding their concrete application.
>
> I first spoke publicly of these difficulties in my report to the cardinals and bishops of the Consilium on October 15, 1965, and then to Your Eminence, who had been appointed president of the Neo-Vulgate Commission, to which our study group was assigned.[18]

---

18. The Pontifical Commission for a New Edition of the Vulgate had been established on November 30, 1965. Cardinal Bea was called upon to be its president. In agreement with him, the president of the Consilium asked the Secretariat of State if contacts might be established between the new commission and the study group charged with the revision of the psalms. When the Secretariat had replied that "there is no difficulty about proceeding as you indicated" (February 26, 1966; No. 66084), Cardinal Lercaro asked Cardinal Bea to send to the relator of the study group "any instructions needed to ensure that the definitive version of the Book of Psalms, on which the group has been working with great gener-

At that time I sent Your Eminence our Latin text for the first eight psalms; after you had sent us your authoritative observations, Your Eminence granted me an audience at which we discussed them and you gave me further explanations, while leaving us full freedom to apply them in accord with the agreed views of our group.

Since then we have continued our second revision of the Latin text of the psalms and have reached Psalm 73.

We have done our best to take your observations into account, as we have the guidelines established at the beginning and approved by papal authority. In addition, the observations of the thirty or so experts to whom our first revision was sent have urged us to a greater fidelity to the text of the Vulgate, to which we are also bound by the guidelines of the Neo-Vulgate Commission, as recently approved and prescribed by Your Eminence. Finally, we know that our work will have to be judged by a committee within the Neo-Vulgate Commission.

Now, the most recent observations of Your Eminence give us the impression that the direction of our work must be altered to a remarkable degree, and we find ourselves in a real quandary.

After sending this letter, Father Duncker had an interview with the Cardinal on April 22, 1967, at which he discussed other technical details. After this clarification the work continued,[19] and on May 2 Father Duncker sent the Cardinal five more psalms that had been revised in accordance with the latter's most recent observations. But the Cardinal continued to find things that were not right. On May 17, therefore, the relator wrote to the Cardinal:

Up to the present we have done our best to follow the guidelines originally set for our work and have tried to provide a Latin text that is a kind of compromise between, on the one hand, the Gallican and Pian Psalters and, on the other, the divergent views of the members of our study group. This work includes a second revision of the first half of the Psalter (seventy-five psalms), in which we have taken into consideration the various obser-

---

osity, skill, and dedication for two years, may follow the same guidelines as the revision of the other sacred books" (March 6, 1966). As a matter of fact, the relator met repeatedly with Cardinal Bea. Evidently, either understanding between the two was not easily reached, or suppositions were not brought into the open, or the new Commission did not look kindly on the work of the study group, even though the latter was trying to be faithful to the guidelines set by the Commission.

19. After this interview Father Duncker made the following notation, among others: "Our study group is not dependent on the Neo-Vulgate Commission but is still part of the Consilium. However, since Cardinal Bea has been told by the Holy Father to see that our Latin text is not overly different from the Latin text being prepared for the other books of the Neo-Vulgate, the Consilium will not be able to use our text until it has won Cardinal Bea's *placet.*"

vations of the experts to whom our work was submitted; it also includes a first revision of the second half of the Psalter. The work has required two hundred meetings of about two and a half hours each, to say nothing of the time each of us has had to devote to the task in private.

Now the "most recent clarifications," in which points *a* and *b* are explained only by a few examples that Your Eminence gave us at the last interview granted to me, seem to undermine the work thus far done, and this to such a degree that the new revision you call for will occupy us for a long time to come.

As a result, those among us who regard themselves as most responsible for the changes made in the text of the Vulgate are seriously asking themselves whether they are the persons best fitted to continue the work under present conditions.

The last sentence shows the state of mind that had been created. When the moment came for deciding on a definitive text, the difficulties became even more acute. Furthermore, the opposition within the Neo-Vulgate Commission, to which nonetheless five members of the study group belonged, was solidifying. It was becoming quite clear that the technical agreement reached in 1966 could only be the first step to a complete transfer of the work into other hands. Cardinal Lercaro therefore wrote to Cardinal Bea on June 12:

The further development of the situation has made it clear that a further step is perhaps now advisable: to put the Neo-Vulgate Commission in charge of the work of revising the Psalter. I hereby ask Your Eminence to see to it that the entire work, organizational, redactional, and financial, of revising the Psalter is taken over by your pontifical commission.

The answer came quickly. Cardinal Bea wrote to Cardinal Lercaro on June 17, 1968:

I am well aware that this decision was made solely in the interests of the speedy execution and successful outcome of the work desired by the conciliar Constitution on the Sacred Liturgy. The decisive point seemed to be the need of bringing the revision of the Psalter into line with the revision of the Neo-Vulgate as a whole. Since this is the situation and since Your Eminence leaves me no alternative, it seems to me that I cannot refuse this labor as well. I shall therefore take steps to establish timely contacts with the study group as soon as work begins again after the summer break.

Meanwhile the Consilium's decision was communicated to the members of the study group on June 13, 1967:

After careful study of all aspects of the problem, it has seemed opportune and even necessary to reach a new arrangement regarding the group.

Cardinal Bea has therefore been asked to make work on the Psalter part of the more comprehensive work on the Vulgate. He accepted this proposal. As of now, therefore, study group 2 is no longer part of the Consilium.

From March 5, 1964, to June 3, 1967, the group had met 207 times, or two to three times a week on the average during the academic year. From September 22 to October 14, 1965, it met daily.

Thus this study group ceased to exist, without blame but also without glory, after hard work done with ceaseless generosity and in an atmosphere of brotherly harmony. Six scholars of the first rank had dealt with one of the most important tasks of the reform, and had done so under concentrated fire from opposite sides. They succeeded only in turning the soil and opening the way to a comprehensive solution of the problem. But in difficult undertakings even the courage to tackle the job is highly meritorious.[20]

III. Biblical Readings

When study group 4 was assigned the task of choosing Scripture readings for the Office,[21] the presidency of the Consilium asked it right at the beginning to answer certain questions: "Should there be one cycle or several? A *lectio continua* or selections? A fixed set of selections or freedom of choice, at least during Ordinary Time? Should the readings of the Office be dealt with separately, distinctly and independently of those of the Missal, or should the two sets be interrelated?"

There were precedents that had to be taken into account. When Cardinal Bea was commissioned by Pope Pius XII to prepare a new Latin version of the entire Bible, he had drawn up a complete plan for a new set of selections from Scripture; this contained passages of greater spiritual importance and those that more directly presented the history of the people of God. In this plan more abundant use was made of the New Testament. Another plan had been compiled by the liturgical commission that Pius XII established in 1948.[22]

Both in the responses to the questionnaire sent to the bishops in 1956–57 on the reform of the Office and in the suggestions made on oc-

---

20. The Book of Psalms was the first published by the Neo-Vulgate Commission: Pontifical Commission for the New Vulgate Edition of the Bible, *Liber Psalmorum* (Vatican Polyglot Press, 1969; 178 pp.). This is the text used in the volumes of the Latin *Liturgia Horarum*.

21. *Relator:* A.-G. Martimort; *secretary:* E. Lengeling; *members:* P. Salmon, P. Grelot, C. Wiéner, G. Diekmann, O. Heiming, M. Du Buit, A. George, P. Dornier. In 1967 E. Lengeling was appointed relator and A. Rose secretary.

22. SCR, *Memoria sulla riforma liturgica* (Vatican Polyglot Press, 1948), 219–53.

casion of the preparation for the Council, there were requests for a quantitative and qualitative increase in the readings from Scripture. These desires subsequently found expression in the Constitution on the Liturgy, which decreed that Matins "shall be made up of fewer psalms and longer readings" (no. 89c).

The study group met for the first time on December 17, 1964, in Paris; it met again on February 20 and June 7, 1965, and January 29, 1966. At their fifth general meeting the Fathers of the Consilium established two guidelines: (a) no day without readings from Scripture; (b) the Bible readings of the Office are to complement those of the Mass.[23] This second guideline conditioned the work of the study group, since it seemed more prudent to wait for the results of the work being done on the Mass by its sister study group.[24] But this dependence also created difficulties, which were resolved at the eighth general meeting of the Consilium (April 1967), when three proposals of the group were approved:

a) the readings in the Office, which are generally longer, can be partially identical with the usually shorter readings of the Mass, provided they are read in a different season or year;

b) the New Testament, except for the Gospels, can be read in the Office;

c) in addition to a one-year cycle for the seasons of Advent, Christmas, Epiphany, Lent, and Easter, a two-year cycle, containing readings from the Old and New Testaments, can be organized for the thirty-four (or thirty-three) weeks of Ordinary Time.[25]

The Synod of 1967 also discussed the problem. One of the four questions on the Office that were submitted to the Synod asked whether to accept the principle of complementary interdependence between the Scripture readings of the Office and those of the Mass. The response was for the most part affirmative.[26]

With these ideas as the basis, the group prepared a general plan. First of all, about fifty exegetes were asked which parts of the Scriptures they

---

23. A.-G. Martimort, "De lectionibus biblicis Breviarii," *Not* 1 (1965) 206–9.

24. A memorandum of October 20, 1966, says: "When the Consilium has determined a definitive list of readings for Mass, study group 4 will be able to proceed with its work and decide (1) whether the readings of the Office should follow a one-year or a multi-year cycle; (2) which books should be read during the various seasons of the year; (3) whether, and according to what pattern, the New Testament should be read during the Easter season, as has been the tradition in all the Rites; (4) which readings to propose, and according to what pattern, for the other Hours of the Office."

25. See "Ordo lectionum biblicarum Officii Divini," *Not* 5 (1969) 88.

26. See "De liturgia in I Synodo Episcoporum," *Not* 3 (1967) 362.

thought might be best set before priests in order to feed their devotion and deepen their understanding of the mystery of salvation.

Since it was quite likely that the whole of the New Testament would be read at Mass, the exegetes focused their attention on the books of the Old Testament. Passages were chosen with the idea that each should have a self-contained sense or tell a complete story and should be about as long as the three readings together of the former Breviary.

With these ideas as guides, lists were drawn up containing 170 readings judged to be of the greatest importance, 180 that would be useful but not necessary, and 60 of dubious usefulness. Of these 427 readings, 44 would, at least partially, be read also at Mass. In drawing up their lists, the exegetes also kept in mind: (a) short readings that might be used as *capitula;* (b) responsories adapted to each reading and calculated to harmonize Old and New Testaments in the two parts making up each responsory.

In early January 1969 the general plan of Scripture readings for the Office was ready and was published *manuscripti instar.*[27] The book was sent to 750 exegetes, liturgists, and pastoral workers throughout the world. It provided an annual cycle for the seasons of Advent-Christmas, Lent, and Easter, and a two-year cycle for Ordinary Time. Replies were to be sent in by May 15. Five questions were asked:

1) What about the length of the passages?

2) Do you like the distribution, in general, of the books of Scripture?

3) Do you think the plan promotes understanding of the Bible and *lectio divina?*

4) What of the relationship between the two sets of readings—those of the Mass and those of the Office?

5) What do you think of the responsories?

By the end of May over twelve hundred replies had come from about two hundred experts. Their answers to the questions were for the most part positive, except for the second one. On this point many were satisfied, but others, including some religious communities that had tried the new arrangement, offered numerous criticisms. Here are the main ones:

1. Some passages that are very important for the history of salvation and Christian spirituality, especially in Exodus and Isaiah, are not to be found at all.

---

27. Consilium, *Ordo lectionum biblicarum Officii Divini* (manuscripti instar; Vatican Polyglot Press, 1969; 362 pp.). Especially important for an understanding of the group's work and the approach it took is the Introduction published in *Not* 5 (1969) 85–99.

2. The Old Testament is not sufficiently represented (28 percent) to carry out the intentions of Vatican II.

3. The special seasons have only a one-year cycle and will therefore become monotonous; this is true especially of the Easter season, throughout which the Book of Acts is to be read both in the Office and in the Mass. The special seasons should also have a two-year cycle of readings.

4. Another point of criticism was the omission of some verses in the course of a reading or at the beginning or end of a passage.

5. Also criticized was the inverted order in which some chapters were read, even though there were supposedly scholarly reasons for the inversion, and the insertion of parts of the prophetic books into the ongoing reading of the corresponding historical books.

Group 4, headed by Professor Lengeling, girded itself for another reorganization of the readings, one that would have two complete cycles covering the entire year. The new plan was ready on November 6, 1969. Two hundred new responsories were also composed. But difficulties remained, due now to technical considerations to which I have already referred. For in practice the material prepared by the various groups formed an imposing mass that would require very large and cumbersome volumes.

The presidency of the Consilium decided that the amount of material must be reduced by eliminating elements not indispensable and putting these in a supplementary volume that would nonetheless be part of the typical edition. But the problem created by the two-year cycle of biblical readings remained, and it was decided to create an annual cycle by selecting from the two-year cycle the parts best suited to each liturgical season. The annual cycle thus developed was included in the typical edition of the *Liturgia Horarum*.[28]

The General Instruction retains the regulations for a two-year cycle (nos. 143-52), this being regarded as preferable, and makes only a few references to the one-year cycle (no. 152).[29]

In Advent Isaiah and the other messianic prophets are read. The passages are arranged, not according to the sequence of chapters or to chronology, but so as to develop several major themes: judgment, the Day of the Lord, repentance, and the promises of salvation.

---

28. A complete list of the readings in the annual cycle was published in *Not* 7 (171) 393–408; 8 (1972) 265–69. The list for the two-year cycle: *Not* 12 (1976) 238–48, 324–33, 378–88.

29. The vernacular editions of the Office have likewise generally adopted the one-year cycle. But the point of reference remains the complete two-year cycle, the one-year cycle being an abbreviated form of this.

From December 17 on, the prophecies of salvation in Second Isaiah are read.

Christmas season: the Letter to the Colossians and some passages from Isaiah. The former was chosen because it situates the incarnation within a comprehensive vision of the mystery of Christ and the history of salvation.

Lent: during the first four weeks Exodus, Leviticus, and Numbers; during the last two weeks the Letter to the Hebrews and passages from Jeremiah, Lamentations, and Hosea.

Easter season: Revelation, First Letter of Peter, Letters of John.

Ordinary Time: the most important passages from the Old and New Testaments that are not in the Missal are read. In the first year of the two-year cycle, the books of the Old Testament are organized according to the history of salvation; the prophets are therefore intermingled with the historical books. In the second year, after the reading of Genesis (before Lent) the history of salvation picks up again from the end of the Exile to the time of the Maccabees. The later prophets and the sapiential books (Esther, Tobit, and Judith) have their place in this sequence. The Letters of the Apostles are distributed in a way that takes into account both the readings in the Missal and the chronological order in which the letters were written.

1. *Relation of Mass and Office*

Longer and more difficult texts, and even entire books, are read in the Office. This would not be possible at Mass. Given the difference in the cycles of Office and Mass, the different length of the readings, and the continuity of the readings within each service, it was not possible to achieve a harmonization, which many desired, between the readings of Office and Mass, either on Sundays or on weekdays. If the same books were to be read in both Mass and Office during the same period of time, it would have been necessary either to repeat the same passages or to choose passages of secondary importance. The two systems of readings are therefore simply complementary, in the sense that almost all the books of Scripture are read and meditated on in the combined Mass and Office.

2. *Short Readings*

When Lauds and Vespers are celebrated with a congregation, a longer reading may be used. The Consilium decided, however, not to compose a special cycle for such cases.

For the short readings (the *capitula*), on the other hand, four weekly series were prepared and included in the Psalter, so that there is a different reading for each day of the week. In addition, there are weekly series for Advent, Christmastide, Lent (two series), and Eastertide. There are also proper short readings for the solemnities and principal feasts. Finally, there is a weekly series for Compline.

The following guidelines controlled the composition of these series:

a) the existing short readings were kept when they seemed suitable;

b) passages of Scripture were chosen that express some specific idea or admonition;

c) an effort was made to respect the special character of each Hour;

d) the Roman tradition of not using readings from the Gospel in the Office was followed;

e) as a rule, the reading in the major Hours is a little longer;

f) the short readings in Vespers are taken from the New Testament;

g) since only one of the Little Hours is obligatory in recitation outside choir, the short readings for these Hours have the same tenor and are from the same sacred books.

IV. Patristic Readings

The task of developing a new cycle of patristic readings was given to study group 5.[30] In his first report (October 1, 1964) to the Fathers of the Consilium, Monsignor Pellegrino explained the program, guidelines, and state of the studies already made: "The work is quite difficult. It is not enough simply to tinker with the existing readings; what is needed is a radical revision of the entire material, because many readings in the present Breviary cannot be retained and because the treasury of Christian tradition contains vast riches to be offered to priests and faithful."

The essential norm for the selection of texts is their spiritual value for religious and laity, who look to spiritual reading for solid and substantial teaching, advice and assistance in leading a Christian life, and consolation and strength in their daily labors.

---

30. *Relator:* M. Pellegrino; *secretary:* I. Oñatibia; *members:* F. Toal, J. Quasten, W. Dürig, A. Olivar, J. Daniélou, J. Leclercq, and I. Ortiz de Urbina. In October 1965 Monsignor Pellegrino was appointed Archbishop of Turin, and his disciple, priest Umberto Neri, was named relator. A. Hamann and P. Serra Zanetti were added to the members. Don Neri was not able to join in the work for very long, since his labors in his community took all of his time. He was therefore replaced by I. Oñatibia in June 1967, and the latter in turn in 1968 by priest Franz Nikolasch, who was assigned to the Consilium for German-language matters. Nikolasch returned to Germany and passed the office of relator on to John Rotelle. The latter, however, also had to return home because of illness, and the work was continued by a team of two monks, Henry Ashworth and Gaetano Raciti.

It was necessary to abandon outdated readings, such as those attacking heresies, or based on now rejected hermeneutical, philosophical, or scientific principles, or too difficult and time-bound, or in any other way out of touch with, or no longer of interest to, the people of our time.

The need was rather for readings that bring out the vital meaning of the Scriptures, explain dogmatic, ascetical, and moral doctrine in a precise way, are linked to the given liturgical celebration, and are able to promote piety and the knowledge of God.[31]

It was anticipated that the work would be done in three stages:

—First, and most important, the gathering of many passages that satisfy the requirements just listed. The more abundant the material available, the easier the selection of appropriate passages.[32]

—Preparation of a specimen or sample of readings for some feasts or seasons of the year.

—Final selection of texts and their correlation with the structure of the calendar and the Office.

The Consilium approved three guidelines proposed by the relator:

a) The readings were to be taken from authors who always remained orthodox, but this would include some ecclesiastical writers who did not possess the note of holiness.[33]

b) Fully orthodox readings might also be chosen from the writings of authors who at times fell into errors of faith or expounded doctrines not completely Catholic (such men as Origen and Tertullian).

c) While most of the space would be given to the Fathers, some more recent ecclesiastical writers could also be represented, so that the Divine

---

31. This principle, while obvious, greatly complicated the choice of readings. In the *mare magnum* of passages selected, it was difficult to find readings that could be put into the modern languages and still be expressive when abstracted from the social, cultural, and philosophical framework in which they were originally written.

32. Precisely because of this abundance, and in view of the fact that there would not be room in the Divine Office for everything, the Consilium initially had the idea of compiling an optional patristic lectionary (see GILH 161). Such a lectionary, however, proved difficult to produce. It would therefore be left instead to the initiative of the episcopal conferences, thus also allowing the latter to select authors closer to the mentality and spiritual tradition of a given nation and to local sensibilities (see GILH 162). At the same time, however, it was anticipated that the fifth volume of the *Liturgia Horarum* would contain a second, optional cycle.

33. In the discussion some opposed this principle as being "contrary to the entire tradition" and a sign "honoring individuals on whom there was disagreement." The opposite experience of the Eastern Church was adduced: many of the texts used there are from authors who were not holy or even fully orthodox, and yet they are read in the liturgy. The same is true of the Dominican Breviary, in which, for example, there are passages from Origen.

Office would bear witness to the holiness, doctrine, and spirituality of all periods.

Monsignor Pellegrino also reported on the work already accomplished by the group: the complete works of 26 Fathers had been studied; 4 other Fathers had been partially studied; 2093 passages had been gathered, each the length of one to two columns in Migne.[34] Also ready was the specimen for Advent, which was subsequently sent to the members and consultors of the Consilium on January 25, 1965.[35]

Of the fifty-five individuals who received the specimen, nineteen responded. On the basis of these responses and the experience acquired during the first year of the work, Monsignor Pellegrino formulated eight questions, which he placed before the Fathers on April 25, 1965. The purpose of these was to define more clearly the plan, guidelines, purposes, and technical procedure for making selections from the Fathers.

The report was regarded as very satisfactory. The conclusions reached were summed up as follows:

a) The practice of centonization is to be abandoned, and readings are to be used in which there are no breaks and which display textual unity. It will be permitted, however, to omit, with great caution, some parts of a passage that are out of harmony with the life-style of our time.

b) To facilitate understanding of the readings, divisions, captions, and subcaptions will be introduced into the texts; texts are never to be omitted simply because of the difficulty that may attach to the Latin versions.

c) On occasion the reading of a work of great value may be continued for several days.

d) Instead of two patristic readings for each Office, one from the treatises and another from the homilies of the Fathers, there is to be a single lengthier reading.

e) For readings that are explanations of the Scriptures, texts may be chosen that are not commentaries in the strict sense.

---

34. See M. Pellegrino, "De lectionibus patristicis in Breviario," *Not* 1 (1965) 209–12.

35. The booklet of thirty pages contained eighteen passages, taken from the works of Cyril of Alexandria, Maximus of Turin, Caesarius of Arles, Cyril of Jerusalem, John Chrysostom, Tertullian, Justin, Ambrose, Maximus the Confessor, and Augustine. Critiques were to be submitted by February 25, 1966. The passages were rather wordy, because it was still thought that there would be three readings, as in the old Breviary. Only later on was it decided to have a single Scripture reading and a single patristic or hagiographical reading; this made it possible to read longer and more substantial texts, without having to break them up too much.

A second set of readings—for the weeks preceding the Passion—was dispatched on September 10, 1965.[36]

On September 18 Monsignor Pellegrino was appointed Archbishop of Turin and had to give up the leadership of the group; he did, however, become a member of the Consilium and continue to support and aid it with his advice. During the two years in which he had been relator, the program for the patristic readings had been determined and in no small measure carried out as well. At his departure he left almost the entire seasons of Advent and Lent supplied with readings; he left, in addition, a file of almost three thousand slips that would be a valuable source for those assigned to continue the work.

Father Umberto Neri took over direction of the group for two years. In July 1966 he was able to reap the first fruits of his labors when he sent out for criticism a volume of 137 pages containing patristic readings for various seasons. This was an anthology in which the items were not yet specifically assigned; it included writers from all periods, saints and non-saints. The authors were grouped alphabetically under ten headings: Christmas, Epiphany, Baptism of Jesus, Passion, Resurrection, Ascension, Pentecost, Common of Martyrs, Commentary on the First Letter of John, Commentary on Revelation 1–3.

The authors ranged from antiquity (Ambrose, Augustine, Leo the Great) to St. Bernard, Denis the Carthusian, Chromatius of Aquileia, Cardinal de Berulle, Cardinal Newman, and the Second Vatican Council.

It was thought necessary to give first place to the Fathers, in accordance with the wishes of the Council, but also to allow room for other periods and for modern authors, these to be chosen according to their theological and spiritual importance and with an eye on modern sensibilities. At its meeting of April 8, 1967, the Consilium approved this expanded range of selections.

At the beginning of the summer there was another change of leadership. Father Ignacio Oñatibia, a former student of Johannes Quasten and a professor in the seminary in Vitoria (Spain), was chosen to replace Don Neri, who had commitments elsewhere. It was not possible, however, for Father Oñatibia to keep on top of this kind of work from so far away, and the Consilium therefore gave Father Franz Nikolasch the task of keep-

---

36. All these readings were exclusively from the ancient writers: Justin, Origen, Cyril of Alexandria, Cyril of Jerusalem, Gregory of Nazianzus, Didymus of Alexandria, Pseudo-Macarius of Egypt, John Chrysostom, Asterius of Amasea, Maximus of Turin, Augustine, Leo the Great, and Caesarius of Arles. In the introduction it was noted that other readings would be taken from later writers, although still from those who held a place of honor in Christian antiquity.

ing au courant with it. But the latter had hardly begun to organize things and acquaint himself fully with the problems when he had to return to his own country.

Under the new relator, Father John Rotelle, O.S.A., the pace of the work picked up in October 1968. It was necessary, for one thing, to have greater continuity between meetings of the group. Two such meetings were held: one in November 1968 at Rome, the second in the following February at Orval, where Father Backaert had inaugurated a series of patristic editions that had been having a deserved success. It was an experiment to be held in high regard.

Father Rotelle planned the work to be done and assigned the parts of it to various scholars. The work being done on the periphery was brought together into unity at the center. First of all, he collected, organized, and classified all the abundant material that had been sorted out according to various methods by his predecessors in leadership of the group; he then distributed it according to the liturgical seasons, making shrewd selections as he went; finally, he sent it to fourteen experts, assigning no more than three or four pericopes to each, so that they might pass judgment on the value of the texts and the suitableness of the assignment. He asked them to examine the texts "carefully, even scrupulously, and in a very critical spirit"; to verify whether or not the author was a saint; to give an exact reference to a critical edition; and to suggest another text if they did not find acceptable the one proposed.

A final note reminded the readers that their study of the texts for Advent should be regarded as the final one; replies were requested by April 30, 1969. The material to be studied amounted to ninety-three pages of text. For each day (Sunday or weekday) a primary text was supplied, along with one, two, or three alternatives. The references given were those that appeared in the typical edition; each text also had a caption.

The work proceeded in an orderly and brisk fashion. Since the whole matter was so important, it was thought that in addition to the scholars whose expert judgment was being sought, others throughout the world should be consulted. This would be done by publishing the pericopes for the major seasons and the principal feasts. The Pope consented. The anthology was prepared and printed *manuscripti instar*; it was then sent to some hundred scholars and pastors whose names were provided by the national liturgical commissions and who were asked to offer criticisms and suggestions.[37]

---

37. SCDW (Special Commission for Liturgical Reform), *Lectiones Patrum et lectiones hagiographicae pro Officio Divino* (manuscripti instar; Vatican Polyglot Press, 1970; 424 pp.);

The introduction to the book outlined the criteria that had been followed in compiling the collection:[38]

a) The anthology contained in equal numbers texts from both Eastern and Western writers.

b) Although Christian antiquity had been given preference, there were some texts from medieval and even modern authors.

c) Moralizing passages had been avoided, and preference had been given to doctrinal selections that explain the truths of the faith and the concerns of Christian life and are more in conformity with the modern outlook and sensibilities.

d) It had been kept in mind that these texts would be read in the vernaculars; for this reason, some difficult pages of St. Hilary had been admitted, while others of St. Bernard had been excluded, because in translation these would have completely lost their spiritual savor.

e) Finally, great importance had been attached to pastoral value, that is, to the usefulness of the texts for priests in pastoral service, the intention being to provide them with a spiritual aid in their devotional life and their calling.

By the spring of 1970 half of the sheets containing remarks on the book had come in, but meanwhile a persistent illness had rendered Father Rotelle inactive, and he had to return to his own country for good. Once again the group was without a leader, and this at the critical moment. For while readings had now been provided for the major seasons, it was still necessary to distribute (and even, to some extent, to acquire) the material for the six months of Ordinary Time.

Meanwhile other details were being clarified, especially due to the intervention of the Congregation for the Doctrine of the Faith. As a result of its remarks on the volume of readings (March 9, 1970), a threefold distinction was made:

1) The readings for this part of the *Liturgia Horarum* can be drawn from all periods of the Church's history, but the technical term "patristic reading" is applied only to texts from the period commonly known as the period of "the Fathers of the Church." A more general terminology is therefore adopted for the readings in question: "Readings from the Fathers and ecclesiastical writers."

= Schemata 349: *De Breviario* 93. Included were the patristic readings for Advent, the Christmas season (to January 12), Lent, and the Easter season. Two series of readings were given for each of these seasons: one regular, the other optional. The hagiographical readings ran from November 30 (St. Andrew) to June 11 (St. Barnabas). There were 329 readings in all.

38. See "Lectiones patristicae et hagiographicae Breviarii," *Not* 6 (1970) 134–37; J. Rotelle, O.S.A., "De lectionibus patristicis in breviario," *Not* 5 (1969) 100; "Specimen lectionum patristicarum pro hebdomada I Paschae," *ibid.*, 102.

2) In the *official* volumes of the Liturgy of the Hours, texts from writers not recognized as saints are acceptable only for the period of the Fathers. For other periods only texts from the Magisterium (councils, popes), saints or blessed, and works regarded as Christian spiritual classics (for example, *The Imitation of Christ*) are admissible. Therefore, a number of passages suggested in the study phase, for example, from Dom Marmion, Charles de Foucauld, Romano Guardini, Thomas Merton, and others, must be eliminated.[39]

But there were also texts to be excluded from "the period of the Fathers." The Congregation for the Doctrine of the Faith asked that no use be made of Theodore of Mopsuestia, "well known for his errors in Christology," or of St. Cyprian's *De catholicae Ecclesiae unitate*, since "experts agree that there are defects in the saint's teaching on the primacy of the Roman pontiff."[40]

3) Greater freedom would be allowed in the optional lectionary to be compiled by the Holy See or the episcopal conferences, provided the authors included are "Catholic writers outstanding for their teaching and holiness of life."[41]

The continuation of the work, which had to be based on the remarks of the experts and the distinctions made by the authorities, now proved more difficult than might have been expected. It had been decided initially to compile one cycle of biblical and patristic readings for the major seasons and two for Ordinary Time. With this in mind, the patristic readings had been chosen to harmonize with the biblical readings. The biblical cycle, however, had been substantially changed by the decision to have a single cycle for the entire year, and the organization of the "reading from the Fathers" had to follow suit; the more extensive selection of texts would have to be left to the optional lectionary.

---

39. When the GILH was submitted for examination, the Congregation for the Doctrine of the Faith and the Secretariat of State returned to the subject and asked that "no passages from modern authors be included in the Office of Readings" (June 11, 1970, No. 161446; September 2, 1970, No. 163340).

40. Letter of March 9, 1970. The request was approved by the Secretariat of State (August 10, 1970; No. 165811), but details were added: "It seems fitting to exclude passages from Theodore of Mopsuestia, whose rehabilitation has not been fully accepted by modern scholars. On the other hand, the name of St. Cyprian should be represented in some manner, since he is honored by several citations from his works in the documents of the Council. If there are reasons for excluding the passage from the *De Ecclesiae catholicae unitate*, another passage from the same saint should be included among the patristic readings."

41. GILH 162. The Congregation for the Doctrine of the Faith added a further qualification: the writers "must be deceased": see "De lectionibus Patrum ad libitum in Liturgia Horarum," *Not* 8 (1972) 249–50 and again in 10 (1974) 323–24.

As a result of all these changes, the study group found itself faced with two difficult tasks: exegesis and harmonization.

Henry Ashworth, a Benedictine of Quarr Abbey, and Gaetano Raciti, a Cistercian of Orval, were enlisted to complete the work. For several months the two monks worked hour after hour, from morning to evening, in the offices of the Congregation for Divine Worship, reading, meditating, singing the psalms, and evaluating the various texts that their predecessors had collected but had as yet subjected to hardly any criticism. It was from this smithy, where prayer was splendidly wedded to toil and scientific expertise, that the patristic lectionary for Ordinary Time emerged.[42]

The many changes in the leadership of the group had not been a positive factor in the progress of the work, but they did perhaps improve its quality and render it more responsive to contemporary pastoral needs. Since the work was one of selection, it was inevitably influenced by subjective factors, tastes, sensibilities, and forms of spirituality. The internal travails of the group had the effect of bringing to maturity, under the ripening warmth of opposing views and laborious study, one of the most valuable parts of the Liturgy of the Hours.

V. Hagiographic Readings

The Constitution on the Liturgy had decreed that "the accounts of the martyrdom or lives of the saints are to be made to accord with the historical facts" (no. 92c). With this statement as its point of departure, the presidency of the Consilium set down the following initial guidelines for study group 6, which was to be responsible for the hagiographical readings:[43]

> (a) The readings are to be made to accord as faithfully as possible with the historical facts. (b) The Breviary is first and foremost a prayerbook, and in dealing with it we must respect the principle "in dubiis melior est conditio possidentis" [in doubt remain with the status quo]. Therefore, while it is permissible to qualify statements that are not certain by adding "it is reported" or "it is said" or "they say," it is not necessary simply to jettison everything that is not apodictically certain by the standards of historical criticism. It follows from this that even the Passions of the martyrs and

---

42. See the complete list of 596 readings for the Liturgy of the Hours in *Not* 10 (1974) 252–76.

43. *Relator:* B. de Gaiffier; *secretary:* A. Amore; *members:* J. Pascher, K. Baus, G. Lucchesi, and R. Volpini. A. Amore was later appointed relator, and Monsignor Cignitti was called upon to be secretary.

the Offices based on them (for example, St. Cecilia, St. Agatha, St. Clement, St. Andrew) are to be approached with great tact and circumspection.

The relator, Father de Gaiffier, director of the Bollandists, explained the historical problems at the second general meeting of the Consilium, in April 1964. What he offered was nothing more than the reflections of a superlative scholar on the *Passiones* of the martyrs.[44] A year and a half later (November 10, 1966) the notes sent to the Consilium by group 6 had this to say: "There has as yet been no special meeting of the group. The group is presently collaborating with group 1 (on the calendar) with regard to the historicity of the saints. It will begin its own proper work when the general lines for the structure of the Breviary have been decided."

At the beginning of 1967 Father de Gaiffier withdrew from the work for reasons of age and was replaced by A. Amore. The latter began by setting down the principles that were to regulate the work:

1) All legendary accounts are to be removed from the Breviary.

2) In the case of the saints of antiquity, if we possess genuine, trustworthy Acts, these are to be used for the hagiographical reading (as was done for St. Justin).

3) If such Acts do not exist, use a discourse or other work of a Father, even if it contains elements deriving from popular tradition. In a parenetic context such a discourse or other work provides a passage from which the reader can draw spiritual profit (this is the case, for example, with St. Hermenegild, St. Agnes, and St. Lawrence).

4) If the saint being celebrated has left writings, the reading can be taken from these (as for the feasts of St. Leo I, St. Ignatius of Antioch, and St. Cyprian).

5) For the medieval and modern saints, it will be necessary to start from scratch; rather than give a dry list of chronological data, we will place the emphasis on the spirituality proper to each saint, and thus on what will edify the person praying.

6) In all the readings two points are to be kept in mind: the spiritual profit of the reader and historical truth.

7) Since every feast of a saint is to have its proper presidential prayer (collect), the group will see to it that the most important aspects of the saint are made known to the relevant group so that they can find expression in the prayers.

The original program was thus extensively redefined. The hagiographical readings, even those made to accord with historical truth, disappeared almost completely. The idea now was that the saints should speak for

---

44. B. de Gaiffier, "De lectionibus historicis de textibus historicis,: *Not* 2 (1966) 77.

themselves or else that a selection should be made from a Father or ecclesiastical writer that could be linked to the type of life and spirituality
that each saint represented. At the same time, however, very short informative historical notices containing the important facts about the life,
activity, and place of the saint were to be placed at the beginning of the
reading.

In this work the group had the collaboration of the group dealing with
the patristic readings. But the secretary of the Consilium also wanted in-
put from those most concerned, namely, individuals specially connected
with a saint, experts on the subject, and the members of a religious family he or she may have founded. These persons were asked to offer the
reading or readings they thought would be best suited; these were preferably to be taken from the writings or letters of the saint. This consultation yielded the vast majority of the hagiographical readings in the Liturgy
of the Hours.

VI. Hymns

The Liturgy of the Hours contains 291 hymns that are the fruit of wide-
ranging and learned research. Ever since antiquity, hymns have been a
structural part of the Office—lyrical, popular compositions that express
the mystery being celebrated, the liturgical season, and the character of
the Hours. They are, as it were, joyous introductions to each Hour.

It was therefore decided that in the reformed Breviary, too, each Hour
of the Office should begin with a hymn. In the *Liturgia Horarum* the structure of these hymns is closely dependent on the Latin language in which
they were composed, and it is difficult to translate poetry conceived in
a given language into another. The General Instruction on the Office therefore grants the episcopal conferences broad faculties for choosing others
that are more in keeping with their languages. In the Latin edition the
hymns bear witness to the hymnodic treasury of the Church, to the liturgical tradition and Western culture. But they also provide cues or stimuli
for the creation of something similar in the vernaculars, while also, of
course, showing that hymns are an important and necessary element in
the liturgical celebration of the Hours.[45]

In the Psalter there are two series of hymns for each day of the week
at Lauds and Vespers; two hymns for each of the Little Hours; and twenty-

---

45. The Holy Father also intervened in behalf of this priceless element, urging the Consilium, via the Secretariat of State, that "the wealth and variety which the hymns give to
the Liturgy of the Hours not be lessened in any way" (January 4, 1974; No. 246412); see
Not 11 (1975) 15.

eight for the Office of Readings (fourteen for nighttime celebration and fourteen for daytime). In addition, there are special hymns for the liturgical seasons, the principal solemnities and feasts, some memorials of the saints, and the Commons.[46]

This large array of hymns was the work of study group 7 and especially of its relator.[47] The work was approached on the basis of the guidelines set down in the liturgical Constitution (no. 93):

a) *revision:* "To whatever extent may seem advisable, the hymns are to be restored to their original form"—a process rendered easier by the existence of fine critical editions;

b) *correction* of "any allusion to mythology or anything that conflicts with Christian piety";

c) *addition* of other hymns to be found in the hymnographic collections.

With regard to this last point, the relator observed in his report of November 10, 1966:

> It is sad to see that the very rich treasury of poetic songs, of which the Church is rightly proud, has been left in obscurity, never displaying the wealth of its precious stones either to churchmen or the laity. The group has therefore diligently and patiently selected from the abundance of ancient hymns a good number that it thinks suited for giving glory to God and stirring our devotion.

From May to June 1964, the relator outlined the work to be done and on October 1 made a report to the Fathers of the Consilium, who expressed a desire for some examples. He submitted these on April 29, 1965.[48]

Other schemas followed in which the texts of the hymns were accompanied by notes about the author, the date of the composition, the bibliography on each hymn, variant readings, and any questions the text might raise.[49]

---

46. When the time came to print the volumes, many other hymns were omitted for reasons of space, being regarded as excessive in number. They were to have a place in the fifth volume.

47. *Relator:* A. Lentini; *secretary:* I. Tassi; *members:* K. Egger, E. D'Anversa, G. Lucchesi, P. Bruylants, and L. Kunz. In 1967 S. Mazzarello and B. Borghini were added. The group did its work almost exclusively through correspondence.

48. See A. Lentini, O.S.B., "De hymnis Breviarii," *Not* 1 (1965) 213.

49. There were different schemas for the different parts of the Office: Office of Readings (nighttime and daytime), Lauds, Vespers, Little Hours, and Compline, for the seasons from Advent to Passiontide and from the Easter season to the feast of Corpus Christi, for the feasts of Our Lady, the feasts of Christ the Lord, and the Commons.

Once all the material had been gathered and revised in light of the criticisms and suggestions of the reviewers, it was thought that it might well be published. The Pope gladly gave his permission, and the Libreria Vaticana accepted the proposal. Publication made it easier for the experts to study the material and for the Consilium to get reactions regarding an area that is normally the preserve of a few specialists. Publication[50] was accompanied by permission to use the hymns experimentally, if so desired.

An extensive introduction explains the nature and history of hymns and states the criteria used in restoring the authentic original form. Next comes the collection of 296 hymns, classified according to the divisions anticipated for the new Office: four weeks of the Psalter, liturgical seasons, other feasts of the Lord, Commons (the old terminology is still used), feasts of Our Lady and of the saints. For each hymn there is a critical apparatus that gives the codices, sources, and variants.

The publication met with great interest, especially among those really competent in the field.[51] Some observations and criticisms came in and were used in preparing the final text[52] to be included in the Liturgy of the Hours. There are some notable differences between the 1968 volume and the *Liturgia Horarum*. Some hymns were set aside, and a good number of others were added.

> It is understandable that some hymns should have been eliminated: they were not well received because they were lacking in artistry or poor in content or because they seemed unprofitable or superfluous.
>
> The additions? There were several reasons for them. For example, after publication [of the 1968 volume] hymns were also assigned to the Easter Triduum and the Office of the Dead; the Commons were further subdivided in various ways; it seemed appropriate to assign separate hymns to the apostles and evangelists and also to the "Gospel" saints, that is, the saints mentioned in the New Testament (Mary Magdalene, Martha, Barnabas), for some of whom there was no suitable place even in the Commons; it was also thought proper to make concessions to modern ecumenism (therefore a hymn for St. John Chrysostom); and sometimes a hymn was required to replace one that had been removed.
>
> To meet all these needs, new hymns had to be composed when the old collections provided only texts that could not stand up to historical criti-

---

50. *Hymni instaurandi Breviarii Romani* (Vatican City: Libreria Editrice Vaticana, 1968; XXIV + 328 pp.). See A. Lentini, O.S.B., "Hymni instaurandi Breviarii Romani," *Not* 4 (1968) 99ff.

51. See A. Lentini, O.S.B., "Povera critica agli Inni della *Liturgia Horarum*," *Not* 8 (1972) 19–24, where mention is made of K. Egger, A. Ferrua, G. Lucchesi, A. Bendazzi, H. Hausberg, E. Briceño, and P. Fuentes Valbuena.

52. See *ibid.*

cism (this is the case with the old hymns for the apostles, which were based on historically doubtful hagiographical traditions) or that are alien to the mind of our time.

These, then, are the reasons why study group 7 had to take upon itself the difficult task of composing new hymns. These were carefully evaluated by all the experts involved in the reform of the Office; in keeping with the golden rule followed by the Consilium, the authors have not been named.[53]

There were thirty-five new hymns. Regarding the others, Father Lentini rightly said: "In light of the repeated consultation of the fifty-five volumes of the *Analecta hymnica* and so many other collections and works, it can be claimed that not only individual verses but individual words, including even simple monosyllables, have been the object of patient and careful study."[54]

Though done with such learning and conscientious application, the work did not go uncriticized when the *Liturgia Horarum* was published. I am thinking here especially of some Latinists who regretted the loss, at least in the better-known hymns, of the stylistic form created by Urban VIII and the Latinists of the Renaissance, which they regarded as more agreeable and fluent than the sometimes rough verse of the original text. There was some basis for the criticism,[55] but the manner of presenting it was mistaken.[56] Other criticisms were aprioristic and in-

---

53. See A. Lentini, O.S.B., "Hymnorum series in *Liturgia Horarum, Not* 9 (1973) 179–80. The following pages (181–91) give a complete list of the hymns in the four volumes of the *Liturgia Horarum*. For each the author and the use made of it are indicated. The notation "new" for a hymn is in fact a reference to Father Anselmo Lentini, the modest and able scholar who drew upon the poetic vein in monastic piety and the Church's tradition and was able to bring a modern voice into perfect harmony with the voice of centuries past. It is now evident that exceptions can be made to the rule strictly followed in the work of the Consilium and that history can be enriched with new gems which are in no way incompatible with the traditional treasury of hymns, either in artistic beauty or in solidity of content.

54. See A. Lentini, "Povera critica" (n. 51) 19.

55. The group had faithfully and intelligently followed the guidelines approved by competent authority. It had carried out its assigned task in a careful, scientifically reliable, and responsible way. Could it have acted differently? There were those, including some deserving of high esteem, who claimed that it could indeed have acted differently. But science has its own laws, and work that is scientifically serious avoids compromises and methodically follows the path laid out for it.

On the other hand, the results of scientific work can temporarily or on occasion be set aside to some extent for pastoral reasons. Thus the Latin typical edition of the *Liturgia Horarum*, which is intended primarily for the clergy, holds faithfully to the principle of including only critically accurate readings, whereas the little book *Iubilate Deo*, which was published in connection with the Holy Year and was destined for the masses of pilgrims, preferred to let traditional, familiar readings stand in several more widely known hymns, the purpose being not to create difficulties for the ordinary people. See *Not* 11 (1975) 160–62.

56. Father Lentini spoke in his own defense; see "Povera critica" (n. 51).

fluenced by factiousness and do not merit mention here. Experience has already provided an answer to them.

VII. CHANTS

In addition to the hymns, the Office contains other elements inherently linked to song: the antiphons, the responsories, and the verses before the psalmody, as transition from psalmody to readings, and as transition from readings to prayer. These elements carried a heavy mortgage, so to speak, because they were widely regarded as peculiar to the monastic or choral Office and therefore to be omitted in private recitation. As a result, it was felt that there must be a closer connection between readings and responsories.

The whole matter required careful study and was assigned to group 8.[57] By February 13, 1965, a broad schema had been prepared that included a couple of general questions: "Should the 'short' elements of the Office be kept in the new Breviary and, if so, in what form?" The schema was sent to many experts in various countries, who were asked to express their views in writing. A report on these views was drawn up for the fifth general meeting of the Consilium (spring 1965).[58]

The majority of the Fathers at this meeting approved the principle that the more important "short" elements, such as the antiphons and responsories, should be kept in the new Breviary, even when recited privately. They took this position not on purely historical grounds but for the sake of fostering devotion and not impoverishing the Office. The antiphons, for example, are a key to understanding the psalm or the meaning of a feast; the responsories interpret the reading and make it "personal" by bringing it alive and enabling it to touch the heart of the person praying.

On the other hand, all agreed that a careful revision was needed. The purpose of the revision would be to improve the choice of texts and adapt them better to celebration with the people. There was, however, no good reason for stripping the Office of valuable poetic elements which, as had been said in the Council hall, raise the soul to contemplation.

The group began its work by focusing on the antiphons and responsories. Some experts undertook a systematic scrutiny of the sources of the tradition with a view to finding texts that would be suitable and useful even today; others set about producing new compositions that would keep the psalms and Old Testament readings from seeming to be purely

---

57. *Relator:* P. Visentin; *secretary:* I. Rogger; *members:* E. Cardine, M. Pfaff, R.-J. Hesbert, I. Tassi, and D. Delalande. In 1967 Father Delalande departed and M. Sauvage was added.
58. See P. Visentin, O.S.B., "De cantibus Officii Divini," *Not* 1 (1965) 213–24.

Old Testament prayers and stories by bringing out their influence on the New Testament and making their Christological meaning clearer. At this point, of course, the difficulty that these texts should be singable immediately arose. It was thought best, however, not to sacrifice the conceptual value of these elements for the sake of making them singable, provided, of course, that they truly fostered prayer.

A year and a half later (autumn 1966), the relator described the situation as follows:

> The work done thus far has not been extensive, because we have to wait for the decisions and results of the work being done by various other groups. For example, we cannot prepare the antiphons until we know the definitive organization of the Psalter in the Office; nor can we choose the responsories until we know what the readings will be and until the calendar of feasts is finally settled.
>
> When we receive from other groups the new organization of the Psalter, the readings, and the calendar of feasts, our work will consist in adapting the text and melody of the antiphons and responsories to their respective psalms or readings.

Antiphons. Throughout the liturgical tradition, both in the Protestant communities and among Catholics, the psalms have been accompanied by antiphons. These help to bring out the literary genre of the psalm, turn the psalm into personal prayer, and possibly highlight something said in the psalm that is worthy of attention. Furthermore, provided arbitrary accommodations are avoided, the antiphons can be a great help for a typological interpretation or one relating the psalm to the feast as well as for a grasp of the objective meaning of the psalm. The antiphons lend variety to the recitation of the psalms and introduce a joyful note into it.

In the preparation of the antiphons:

1) The existing repertory was used, but recourse was also had to the manuscript sources when it seemed that the texts contained therein could help the person praying by providing a valid interpretation of the psalms and a correct Christological sense. This kind of antiphon had the advantage of being already provided with Gregorian melodies. They thus rendered a service both to the liturgy and to singing.

2) New texts were composed when existing ones did not satisfy the criteria being applied. In general, these new antiphons were taken from the New Testament and took into account the literary genre of the psalm, the liturgical season, and the hour of the day. Another criterion was also kept in mind: the possibility of easy translation into the vernaculars.

In these new texts the modern compiler used the same freedom exercised by his predecessors: he did not take over the text word for word but altered an expression or word here and there in order to adapt it to the purpose in view.

When, therefore, a psalm is repeated several times or divided into several parts, a number of antiphons were prepared in order to bring out the spiritual riches of the psalm, for these are not to be conveyed by any single concept but have various aspects.

Responsories. These retain their value even in individual recitation and in non-choral common recitation, because they supply new light for understanding the reading or locate the reading within the history of salvation or relate an Old Testament reading to the New Testament (as on the feast of Corpus Christi) or transform the reading into prayer and contemplation (for example, "Send your Wisdom, Lord . . . ") or, finally, by reason of their poetic quality lend variety and joy to prayer.

The "long" responsories that follow the first reading of the Office of Readings were composed by the group in charge of the Scripture readings and revised by the group in charge of the responsories; the latter group also undertook to compose the other responsories. The first responsory is always taken from Scripture and is meant to have some connection with the passage just read. The responsory after the patristic or hagiographical reading is a freer composition, but its intention is always to illumine the reading and turn it into prayer, even if it has not always been possible to connect it closely with the reading.

Short Responsories. In the Roman tradition these used to be found only in the Little Hours. The monastic tradition, on the other hand, had them in Lauds and Vespers as well. This was a more logical approach, since a responsory is a sung response to the word of God. Reading (long or short) and response should always go together; short responsories have therefore been included in Lauds and Vespers in the new Liturgy of the Hours. A further reason for the innovation is that the hymn now comes at the beginning of the Hour, whereas formerly it followed the reading and served as a song of transition to the *Magnificat* or *Benedictus.*

Various solutions were proposed for overcoming psychological difficulties (essentially those caused by the impression that the Office was being made too "monastic" in its structure):

a) The majority, appealing to monastic example, thought the responsories should be the traditional short ones, even in private recitation, because of their lyrical meditative quality and their poetic form and structure.

b) Others thought that this form is artificial in private recitation and would have liked to keep the responsory only when the Office is sung;

in addition, because of the difficulty of translating the responsories, they would have liked to see permission given to replace them with some other song.

c) Still others, finally, suggested that the responsories be replaced by something else: a verse expressing praise or festivity; a "short reading from the psalms," as at Taizé; a new composition, such as the troparies of the Greek euchologies;[59] or an acclamation of the people.[60]

In view of the pros and cons and the difficulties attaching to the several proposals, it was regarded as more prudent to keep to the traditional responsory, but with the following modifications:

—in public celebration the responsory or another appropriate song is to be obligatory;

—in private recitation the responsory is to be optional. In this way, said Monsignor Pascher, "those who like the responsories will have the opportunity to stop and meditate for a moment; those who do not like them will not be obliged to something they do not regard as effective." The proposal was agreeable to the Fathers, but with the provision that a statement be made that the responsory retains its value even in individual recitation and that permission be given to omit only the part that is repeated, unless the repetition is required for the sense.[61]

The study group concerned itself not only with these principal elements (antiphons and responsories) but also with the others of lesser importance: the verses that come after the psalmody in the Office of Readings and are intended to dispose the soul for listening to the readings; the verse after the short readings in the Little Hours. There were those who wished to eliminate these small items, but they are useful because they keep the transitions between the parts of an Hour from being mechanical and ensure that heart and mind "are in harmony with the words."

---

59. Cardinal Pellegrino, who was in favor of this idea, sent the relator a rich anthology of texts culled from the Byzantine liturgy. But a more careful study of the matter led to a rejection of the idea, since neither a lengthy composition nor a composition in the hymnic genre seemed appropriate, and a doxology would likewise have been out of place.

60. There is something of this kind to be found in Scripture after the addresses of Moses (Exod 19:7-8; Deut 5:32-33) and after the reading of the law (Ezra 10:12; Neh 8:5-8). The relator himself proposed some examples of similar acclamations that would be adapted to the various kinds of reading; after a reading about morality: "All that the Lord has spoken we will do (Exod 19:7-8). — Observe and do what the Lord has commanded you (Deut 5:32)"; after a reading about the wonderful deeds of God: "Great and wonderful are your works, O Lord! (Rev 15:3). — All that the Lord willed he has done (Ps 134:6)." The idea was an attractive one, but how could these acclamations be adapted to readings that vary so widely?

61. See GILH 47, 171, 172.

VIII. INTERCESSIONS IN LAUDS AND VESPERS

The Liturgy of the Hours contains both praise and petition; in the liturgical tradition of the various Churches we find prayer of praise joined with intercessory prayer. The presence of intercessions is already attested by Egeria, the pilgrim, in her description of the Morning and Evening Offices at Jerusalem, in which a "countless multitude" of children and other people took part.

The Roman Breviary retained only an unattractive, lifeless, standardized trace of the practice. The intercessions had gradually taken on a penitential character and were therefore reserved to certain days. In addition, they gave the impression of having been put together out of heterogeneous elements lacking in any logical order. For the most part, they were felt to be wearisome because of their fixed form and their lack of connection with real life. The end result was that a euchological element that had once been wonderfully effective was no longer attractive. A further result was that only a few references were made to the intercessions during the preparation of the Constitution on the Liturgy and at the Council itself, because they were regarded as something purely technical with which the experts would have to concern themselves during the reform of the liturgy. Even when the Consilium was organizing the work of the reform, no one thought of having a special group to prepare the intercessions.

The first reference to the intercessions came during the fourth general meeting of the Consilium (December 1, 1964), when the Fathers decided that some elements having to do with the sanctification of the day should be taken from the now suppressed Hour of Prime and given a place in Lauds and that general intercessions might be introduced, as an option, into Vespers when this was celebrated with a congregation.[62] There were further references, but always of a quite general kind, at the general meetings of 1965 and 1966.

For the eighth general meeting (April 1967), a sample of Lauds and Vespers for a week was prepared which contained sets of intercessions. Experience showed that these had to be improved and given greater va-

---

62. This proposal was likewise accepted only with some hesitation. Some commented that the prayers (*preces*) at Lauds "should be few"; "Lauds is already long enough, leave it alone. Put the other prayers into an appendix for private, optional use." Others said that "Lauds is already a set of *preces.*" With regard to the general intercessions at Vespers: "The whole of the psalmody is already an *oratio.* And if the faithful are not present, how is the rite to be carried out?"; "Psalmody is the important element in the breviary"; "It would be better to call it *supplicatio vespertina.*"

riety. At this point it was decided to establish a special study group, which was given the number 12bis.[63] The group undertook a careful historical, theological, and pastoral study of the intercessions; it then drew up guidelines and criteria to be followed in preparing the needed schemas.

At the ninth general meeting (November 14–20, 1967), the Fathers approved the overall approach being taken. It was decided that intercessions should be supplied for a four-week Psalter and that additional series should be compiled for the major seasons (Advent-Christmas, Lent, Easter), the principal solemnities and feasts, and the Commons.

Planning was followed by execution, the compilation of the series being entrusted to the various members of the group.[64] Their work was then sent out for examination by about fifty experts and for experimentation in monasteries or prayer groups of various countries. From the observations sent in to the Consilium, it appeared that:

   a) everyone was for the idea of intercessions;

   b) they were in favor of short, simple formulas;

   c) they wanted greater freedom to introduce personal requests and greater attention to the needs of the praying community.

The group made the corrections and increased the number of intercessions in accordance with the suggestions submitted. The Consilium approved the revised intercessions in principle. They were published *pro manscripto* in a little book containing 1345 formulas that were distributed into a number of series as planned.[65] An editorial note stated: ''Everyone who reads this little work is urged to submit improvements in the language, emendations of the ideas expressed, and any omissions or substitutions they regard as appropriate.''

From this consultation emerged the final text, which was approved at the thirteenth general meeting (April 9–10, 1970) and included in the *Liturgia Horarum.*

---

63. *Relator:* V. Raffa; *secretary:* J. Patino; *members:* A.-M. Roguet, A. Morlot, and J. Gélineau. One of the observers was also involved in the work: Brother Max Thurian of the Taizé community, where the *preces* had been in use for some years. His unobtrusive and intelligent contribution was extremely valuable. For more detailed information on the work of the group, see V. Raffa, F.D.P., ''Le nuove *Preces* delle lodi e dei vespri,'' in the volume *Liturgia delle Ore* (n. 1), 615–45.

64. Advent: Gélineau and Patino; Lent: Raffa; Easter season: Morlot; Holy Week: M. Thurian; Ordinary Time: Raffa and Morlot.

65. SCDW, Special Commission for Completing the Liturgical Renewal, *Preces ad Laudes matutinas et ad Vesperas Officii Divini instaurandi* (*manuscripti instar;* Vatican Polyglot Press, 1969; 130 pp.; = Schema 248: *De Breviario* 92). See ''Preces ad Laudes matutinas et ad Vesperas,'' *Not* 5 (1969) 458.

Norms Followed in the Composition of the Intercessions. Each formulary begins with an introduction. At Lauds there are four intentions, at Vespers five. The fifth at Vespers is always for the deceased and replaces the verse "May the souls of the faithful departed . . . ," with which the Hours always ended in the old Breviary.[66]

The intercessions at Lauds have to some extent the character of the prayers in the old Hour of Prime, but they also broaden the scope of these and are adapted to the major seasons and principal celebrations. Their primary purpose is to dedicate the new day to God by invoking his help and blessing on the work that will fill the day and on the persons whom we shall meet.

The intercessions at Vespers are primarily for the needs of the entire people of God.

The intercessions are formulated differently than the general intercessions at Mass. They can be adapted to celebration with the people (by having the people speak a brief invocation) and to private recitation.

The episcopal conferences can adapt the intercessions provided and can also formulate new ones; it is also always possible to introduce more specialized intentions of the praying assembly.

It must be acknowledged that the intercessions are one of the most interesting, stimulating, and best-liked elements in the reformed prayer of the Hours, and that they contribute most to making it topical, fresh, and relevant to the life of everyday.

---

66. The disappearance of the "Fidelium animae" initially caused some spiritual uneasiness and elicited some complaints (which ended, however, after the printing), as though the Consilium had forgotten the duty of praying for the deceased. The criticism was groundless; it failed to take into account the more effective daily remembrance of the dead in the intercessions of Vespers.

32

Religious and the Liturgy of the Hours

If the liturgy is the summit and source for the entire life of the Church and for the spiritual life of Christians, it is all the more such for those who dedicate themselves wholly to the search for ''God alone'' and consecrate themselves entirely to the welfare of the Church. The Council clearly says as much to religious when it exhorts them to seek nourishment for their spiritual life in authentic and basic sources: Sacred Scripture, the liturgy, and, above all, the celebration of the Eucharist.[1]

It is natural, then, that religious, more than others, should have been interested in and committed to the liturgical reform, and especially to the reformed celebration of the Mass and Divine Office, which provide the daily tissue of their spiritual lives.

For the same reason religious also felt more intensely the desire for a greater freedom of expression. From the outset the Consilium received requests from religious for indults and concession. This caused a certain amount of conflict. On the one hand, the Roman authorities thought of religious as better prepared to understand the liturgy and therefore readier to preserve the treasures of tradition, including Latin and Gregorian chant. On the other hand, religious were expressing a keen desire to draw closer to the sources of the spiritual life by removing everything that was an obstacle, even if only for some members of their communities. The reasons adduced might indeed at times seem forced or simply pretexts, but it was impossible not to recognize the sincerity of religious, their longing for authenticity, and their desire to contribute out of their experience to

---

1. See the decree *Perfectae caritatis* on the Timely Renewal of Religious Life, nos. 6 and 15.

the new style of celebration, the formation of new musical repertories, and accurate and expressive translations.

Requests most often had to do with the Divine Office and came especially from communities obliged to choir.

I. THE HOUR OF PRIME

The Council had decreed that "the hour of prime is to be suppressed" (*SC* 89d). The decree was implemented in the motu proprio *Sacram Liturgiam*, which also gave permission to recite only one of the three Little Hours. But all this applied only to those not bound to choral celebration of the Office.

Requests immediately poured in from religious communities obliged to choir, asking that they too might be dispensed from Prime. The Consilium was in favor, both because Prime was a doublet of Lauds and because the conciliar decree set no limits to the suppression of this Hour.

Cardinal Lercaro presented the request to the Holy Father on March 16, 1965, and renewed it on May 12. An affirmative reply came on June 2. The grant was not made in an unrestricted way but was sent to the superiors general of the communities concerned.[2]

II. THE VERNACULAR

The most urgent and troublesome problem, however, was that of the vernacular. On March 16, 1965, the Consilium dutifully explained the situation in detail to the Holy Father:

> Until now the Consilium, in agreement with the Sacred Congregation for Religious, has granted no exception to article 101 of the liturgical Constitution, which deals with the obligation of "clerics" to use Latin in the Divine Office. The local Ordinary can dispense individuals but not the body of clerics.

---

2. See *Not* 1 (1965) 272. The first to profit by the indult were the Friars Minor (July 12, 1965); other concessions followed and were documented in *Notitiae*. The time came, however, when the Congregation for Religious asserted that this matter involved the discipline and constitutions of the religious communities, and claimed the right to intervene. All questions having to do with religious became more complicated because of differences of views, especially in the early years, between the Consilium and the Congregation for Religious. All the Consilium's proposals for responding to legitimate requests were opposed. Eventually there was a kind of definition of the areas for intervention: The Consilium could, in agreement with the Congregation for Religious, deal with the problems of communities of men but was not to concern itself in any way with communities of women, these being the exclusive domain of the competent Congregation.

But requests for the Divine Office in the vernacular are extremely numerous; they keep coming in daily, from both individuals and groups. The problems can be outlined as follows:

1. *Monastic communities and communities obliged to choir.* — These ask to recite in the vernacular at least the Hours celebrated with the faithful, for example, Sunday Vespers, daily Compline with the students of the boarding schools at some Benedictine and Premonstratensian monasteries, and the Hours in which the lay brothers take part.

2. *Communities with communal recitation of the Office* (oblates, missionaries, etc.). — These ask to recite certain Hours in the vernacular, such as Lauds and Compline, when these replace the old community prayers (acts of faith, hope, and charity, and litanies), since the entire community, including lay brothers and postulants, is present.

3. *Communities obliged to choir but in the service of a parish* or church much frequented by the faithful. — These ask to recite in the vernacular the part of the Office in which the faithful in fact take part. For example, at a Franciscan pilot-church in Brussels, which has a house of theological studies attached to it, the Cardinal Archbishop of Malines has asked that these religious celebrate Vespers in the vernacular in order to get the congregation involved in the singing.

4. *In mission countries.* — There are widespread requests from all the communities that say the Office in choir or in common, for example, the Benedictine monastery in Toumliline, Morocco, and the monasteries of the Congo. The chief reason is that young men starting in the monastic life have difficulty understanding and mastering Latin, and this in turn makes recruitment difficult.

5. *Special cases.* — Fifty-five abbeys, especially in the United States, joined by the Confederation of Religious Congregations, have asked to use the vernacular in the Divine Office, because fidelity to Latin has an important negative influence on recruitment.

6. In the new monastery in Port Harcourt there are four priests, two lay brothers, and numerous native postulants who do not know Latin. The Abbot General of the Benedictines recommends that the vernacular be allowed in this case.

7. Some Congregations, for example, that of the Holy Cross, have equal numbers of priests and lay brothers; in some cases, there are even more brothers than priests. They ask, therefore, that they may use Latin for the parts of the Office which they recite together.

8. For the *nocturnal Office*, requests have come in from a number of places to use the vernacular at least for the readings. It seems that on this point the Congregation for Religious is also in agreement.[3]

---

3. The Congregation for Religious said it was disposed to allow the vernacular in the readings of the night Office only for nuns (April 10, 1967). Even here it made distinctions:

After careful study of the problem, the Consilium's view is this: While the Church should adhere to article 101 of the liturgical Constitution, the requests for the vernacular are so numerous from every part of the world and many types of religious families that it should look with favor on these requests in certain cases. Specifically: the case of canonical Hours being said by any community:

1) when a good many of the faithful are taking part;

2) when Hours are being recited by an entire religious community in which there are a large number of lay brothers who must by Rule take part in the Office together with the "clerics";

3) when Hours of the Office replace other common prayers and the entire community is participating;

4) in the missions;

5) when priests are a minority or almost a minority by comparison with the community as a whole.

The Pope decided that the Consilium should consult the Congregation for Religious. It did so, and also asked for the views of the Congregation of Rites.

On May 12 it brought the problem to the Pope's attention once again. The Congregation for Religious, it told him, "has shown itself inclined rather not to change the existing situation." The Congregation of Rites and the Consilium, on the other hand, thought this an opportune time to make a distinction among religious communities: priestly, non-priestly, obliged to choir, celebrating the Hours in common, serving a parish or shrine where the faithful take part in the Office, at least at times (for example, Sunday Vespers). In view of the diversity in forms of life and in situations, the Consilium and the Congregation of Rites suggested that favor be shown to the requests:

1) of communities of women and non-priests (explicitly granted by the liturgical Constitution, article 101, 2);

2) communities obliged either by their constitutions or by custom to recite the Office in common;

3) perhaps (accompanied by a working agreement) communities of any kind that administer parishes or shrines or churches attended by large numbers of people, when in fact the Office is celebrated with the faithful.

"We do not see why the use of Latin should be abandoned by the Benedictine Cistercian nuns, who by their traditional vocation are dedicated to liturgical worship and who retain, and ought to retain, Gregorian chant, which is one of the greatest treasures of the Latin Church. We can more easily understand, on the other hand, that other nuns, such as the Carmelites, the Poor Clares, and others, should ask and be given the use of the vernacular in countries whose culture is remote from the Greco-Latin."

The Instruction In edicendis normis

The Pope approved this approach, which was the basis of the instruction *In edicendis normis* of November 23, 1965. The instruction came from the Congregation of Rites but also carried the signatures of the prefect of the Congregation for Religious and the president of the Consilium to show that the three agencies had collaborated on the document.[4]

The instruction considers various types of religious communities:

1. *Clerical religious institutes obliged to choir.* The choral Office is to be in Latin, in accordance with the liturgical Constitution (art. 101, 1) and the instruction *Inter Oecumenici.* But in the missions consideration must be given to the native monks, and the vernacular may be introduced there in accordance with article 40 of the Constitution. The judge in specific cases is to be the Congregation for Religious.

2. *Clerical religious institutes not obliged to choir.* They may say in the vernacular any parts of the Office in which the lay members participate in virtue of the constitutions. The general chapter is to act as judge.

3. *Clerical religious communities* of whatever kind that are engaged in the pastoral ministry in a parish, shrine, or much-frequented church. These can recite in the vernacular the parts of the Office that are celebrated with the faithful. The decision is to be made by the local Ordinary with the consent of the Congregation for Religious or the major superior of the religious community.

4. *Nuns.* These can ask permission to recite the Office in the vernacular, even in choir; but Latin is to be retained as far as possible where the Office has traditionally been celebrated in Gregorian chant. In mission territories more generous permissions may be granted in favor of native nuns.

Even when the Office is celebrated in Latin, the readings can be in the vernacular. The competent authority in this matter is the Congregation for Religious. Nuns who for any reason cannot take part in the choral celebration may use the vernacular in private recitation.

5. *Lay religious institutes.* The competent superior can allow the vernacular in private and communal celebration in accordance with the liturgical Constitution, article 101, 2. The judge in the matter will be the general chapter or general council.

6. *"Conventual" Masses*

a) Clerical religious institutes obliged to choir must keep to Latin, except for the readings;

---

4. Instruction *In edicendis normis* on the Language to Be Used in the Recitation of the Divine Office and the Celebration of the "Conventual" or "Community" Mass among Religious (November 23, 1965): *DOL* 114 nos. 791-811. See the commentary in *Not* 2 (1966) 86-94.

b) if the community is in charge of a much-frequented public church, it is to follow the regulations set down by the territorial ecclesiastical authority when the "conventual" Mass is celebrated "for the convenience of the faithful";

c) nuns may use the vernacular within the limits established by the local authority.

7. *"Community" Masses*

a) Clerical communities not obliged to choir may use the vernacular, within the limits established by the territorial authority, "several times a week";

b) lay communities may use the vernacular within the limits established by the competent territorial authority. They are to see to it, however, that the members of the institute also learn to recite and sing the Proper and Ordinary of the Mass in Latin.

But the gradual extension of use of the vernacular in the liturgy did not leave the religious communities indifferent. Even after this instruction, requests for new concessions did not cease. The worry these caused was reflected especially in the Pope, who was very much concerned to preserve the solemn celebration of the Divine Office in Latin and in Gregorian chant, especially by monastic communities. He remarked in an audience to the secretary of the Consilium that

> monasteries are like the lights one sees at night in the countryside or on mountaintops. They are a reminder, a sign of life and hope. Imagine looking out on the world and seeing a lamp lit wherever a monastic community lives and prays; you would see a world spangled with lights. Monasteries are earthly choirs from which praise of God rises constantly to join that of the angels. They are a force irrepressibly and irresistibly at work in the Church.

For this reason Pope Paul did not see himself able to abandon a centuries-old tradition that was the glory of monasticism. He thought this would be to surrender a mark of authenticity and identity.

It was this heartfelt concern that inspired the pontifical letter *Sacrificium laudis*, addressed to the monastic communities on August 15, 1966. The letter begins with a recall of the many requests made to the Apostolic See for dispensations from the use of Latin in the choral celebration of the Office and Mass and with a mention of the concessions made in the instruction of November 23, 1965. The Pope goes on to speak of the special vocation of monastic communities in the Church, namely, the solemn celebration of praise of God, and of the harm that would be done to the faithful and the Church if this vital expression of faith and converse with God were to be lost. He ends by urging all to think carefully about the problem.

> Out of our good will and high esteem for you we cannot permit something that could be the cause of your own downfall, that could be the source of serious loss to you, and that surely would afflict the Church of God with sickness and sadness. Even if you are reluctant, allow us to defend your real interests.
>
> The Church has introduced the vernacular into the liturgy for pastoral advantage, that is, in favor of those who do not know Latin. The same Church gives you the mandate to safeguard the traditional dignity, beauty, and gravity of the choral office in both its language and its chant.
>
> With open and untroubled spirit, therefore, obey the commands that a great love for your own ancient observances itself suggests, but that also a father's love for you proposes, and that concern for divine worship commends.[5]

This firm motivational reminder did not have any great success.[6] In view of new and urgent requests, the Consilium decided it was its duty to pass these on to the Pope, although it knew that in doing so it was not giving him any pleasure. At an audience granted to the secretary on January 15, 1967, he allowed the readings to be done in the vernacular, "even though," he remarked in tones of resignation, "it will only open the door!" He added: "We can expect a major assault by the Benedictines in September."[7]

The problem was subsequently more closely monitored by the Congregation for Religious. I do not know what steps were taken. This much, however, is certain: on June 6, 1967, the Secretariat of State authorized the Congregation for Religious to grant permission in particular cases for use of the vernacular in the choral Office, provided the community in question expressed its desire to do so in a free election by secret ballot. The Secretariat added: "In order that the Church may retain this rich

---

5. Paul VI, epistle *Sacrificium laudis* to Superiors General of Clerical Religious Institutes Bound to Choir, on the Celebration of the Divine Office (August 15, 1966): *DOL* 421 nos. 3402-10.

6. It must also be said that while the letter stresses the question of language, the entire context of this question must be kept in mind. The Pope was well aware of the difficulties many communities were experiencing in this area. But the problem of language was connected with the larger and more sensitive question of the dignity and solemnity of the liturgical celebration, which in some places left much to be desired because of improvisations, curtailments, and perhaps even slovenliness. The coming years were to prove the Pope right: young people with serious intentions would seek more serious communities.

7. The matter had been taken up by the presidential council on January 12, 1967; the council had favored the request.

patrimony of liturgical prayer, it is highly desirable that the communities which are allowed to recite the Office in the vernacular should continue to use Latin when the Office is sung in Gregorian chant."

The concession was simply an exemption from what had been established in the instruction *In edicendis normis.* Those, therefore, who would continue to follow the guidelines of the instruction and lovingly cherish the chant peculiar to the Roman Church were "greatly encouraged and praised."[8]

III. THE NOTIFICATION OF AUGUST 6, 1972

In some sectors of religious life, especially among the Carmelites, the desire was for a more abundant prayer. In the three-year period 1967–1969 the Consilium received twenty-nine requests from cloistered communities regarding the Divine Office: fifteen from Italy, ten from the United States, two from Spain, one from Israel, and one from Argentina. Some of these communities wrote several times with various requests: in 1967 for a special Office for contemplative orders; in 1968 for the retention of choral recitation, with more space given to the psalms.

The Consilium had itself raised the same problem from the beginning and had even reached the point of considering the possibility of a variety of Offices. The final solution adopted was to plan a *Roman* Office intended for the clergy engaged in pastoral activity and adapted to the normal conditions of life among the people of God. Another Office better adapted to those who have prayer as their exclusive activity was to be prepared with the help of those concerned.[9]

---

8. Concessions were not general but, as the letter from the Secretariat said, for particular cases, which were not few. In granting the dispensation, the Congregation for Religious asked, in addition to the recommendations in the cited letter, for the retention of Gregorian chant "on solemnities."

9. The president of the Consilium had also said this at the first Synod of Bishops. See Synodus Episcoporum, *Responsiones Em.mi Card. Iacobi Lercaro, relatoris, ad animadversiones circa quaestiones de sacra liturgia* (Vatican Polyglot Press, 1967) 15: "The reform of the Divine Office that the Consilium is presently carrying out in accordance with the liturgical Constitution affects only the office according to the Roman rite, with special reference to those engaged in pastoral activity, The reform of the Office in the other rites, for example, the monastic rite and the rites of other religious families, will be undertaken by those concerned, although they will follow the general criteria observed in the reform in the Roman rite. The Consilium will then review the revised Office and give its approval."

The SCDW would subsequently try on a number of occasions to prod the monastic orders into preparing their own reorganization of the Office, but with scant results. A note jotted down for the audience of May 27, 1971, reads as follows: "Efforts are presently being made to bring the four monastic families into agreement on adopting a single fundamental pattern and a single calendar for the Divine Office. This fundamental pattern should yield

While awaiting this permanent organization of the Office for monastic and contemplative communities, the Congregation for Divine Worship restricted itself to giving provisional guidelines and suggestions in the notification of August 6, 1972.[10]

Psalms of the Office of Readings: six psalms instead of three, the extra three being taken from the same day of the preceding or following week. In practice this would mean reciting the Psalter in two instead of four weeks.

Daytime Hours: the psalms of the Daytime Hour of the current week can be used for Terce, those of the preceding week for Sext, and those of the following week for None.

In addition to these adaptations, the notification emphasized the importance of certain general points for a more complete celebration: understanding the psalms and meditating on them; lending solemnity to the psalms by singing them; proper use of periods of silence; celebration of a vigil Office for Sundays and solemnities; use of psalm prayers at the end of each psalm;[11] use of special lectionaries adapted to the needs of the community and approved by the Holy See.[12]

IV. EXPERIMENTS

From the very beginning of the liturgical reform, special attention was paid to the celebration of the Divine Office by those communities that

---

a particular rite in the full and proper sense and not be a matter of simple variations on the Roman rite. At the same time, it ought to be somewhat broad and general so that it can be followed both by monastic communities of the purely contemplative life and monastic communities which combine a life of prayer with pastoral activities (*Perfectae caritatis,* no. 7)." Only in 1977 would the SCSDW be able to approve the *Thesaurus Liturgiae Horarum Monasticae* (see below, n. 18). But by then the communities of contemplative life had had a chance to savor the new Liturgy of the Hours and were content with it.

10. SCDW, notification *Universi qui Officium* on the Liturgy of the Hours for Certain Religious Communities (August 6, 1972): *DOL* 432 nos. 3728-35. See the commentary of Valentino Macca, O.C.D., in *Not* 8 (1972) 258–64. See also "Adaptation de la Liturgie des Heures à l'Office de certaines Communautés religieuses," *Not* 10 (1974) 39, which offers further suggestions. For the problems experienced by contemplatives in connection with the reform of the Office, see the bibliography given above, p. 495, n. 11.

11. The psalm prayers were to be officially published in the fifth volume of the *Liturgia Horarum;* individual communities, however, could ask the Congregation to approve provisional collections.

12. The adoption of the adaptations listed here required the consent of two-thirds of the community, to be given by secret ballot. The notification contributed to an appreciation of the Liturgy of the Hours and especially to its full celebration. At the practical level, there were no more complaints or special requests, except those indicated in the notification itself, that is, for proper lectionaries, psalm prayers, and two-year cycles of Scripture readings.

regard as sacrosanct the criterion set down in the Rule of St. Benedict: "Nothing is to be preferred to the Work of God." The requests coming from these groups were concerned not simply with the language to be used but with the very organization of the Office and the choice of texts.

A first request came from the communities of Cistercians in the missions. Toward the end of 1966, Abbot Louf asked for adaptations that would enable native members of such communities to participate more easily and fruitfully in the celebration of the Office. The Congregation of the Propaganda and the Congregation of Religious were asked for their views: the former favored the request, the latter was rather reluctant to make any concessions.

On January 12, 1967, the problem was then brought to the presidential council of the Consilium, which after some hesitation agreed to allow experiments under the following guideline: "All the elements of the Office that are foreseen in the liturgical Constitution are to be kept, but permission is given to shorten them."[13] With the permission of the Pope, this concession was made.

Once the concession became known, other communities (Trappists, Cistercians, and some from the Benedictine Confederation) asked permission to work up their own organizations of the Office. Permission to do so was given first to individual monastic Congregations that asked for it, and then to the entire Benedictine Confederation (December 29, 1968). The individual monastic Congregations and even individual monasteries were free to use in whole or in part the possibilities made available.[14] In practice, the permission was to construct the Office on the basis of a normative framework provided by the Consilium:

1. The monastic community is to gather for prayer at least three times a day.

2. The individual Hours of the Divine Office must consist of psalms, readings, hymns, and a prayer.

3. The readings from the Old and New Testaments, as well as those from the works of the Fathers, doctors, and ecclesiastical writers (see the liturgical Constitution, art. 92b), may be selected by the local superior, after he has heard the views of the community.

---

13. See above, p. 161.

14. The reason for the liberality shown in the concessions was the importance of the Office in monastic life and the reliance that could be placed on monks because of their spiritual and liturgical background. The experiments would also be of service to the Consilium in its work on the reform of the Breviary and on the compilation of the monastic Office, the necessity of which was realized.

4. The Daytime Hours and Compline (obligatory) can be recited outside of choir if this seems opportune.[15]

5. The Psalter may be used according to one of the following systems:

a) so as to recite from seventy-five to one hundred psalms each week;

b) until the new organization of the Psalter is published, the provisory organization granted by indult of the Consilium on December 13, 1967, may be used;[16]

c) use may be made of other plans for the distribution of the Psalter in which the entire Psalter, 150 psalms, is recited each week;

d) the Breviary is to be followed in full for Lauds, but Psalm 66 may be omitted (except on Sundays), and Psalm 50 may be recited in its entirety every day (omitting the first psalm during the first week, and the psalm immediately after Psalm 50 in the second week).

6. It is permitted to drop the recitation of the Our Father after the nocturns; at the end of the readings, the blessing of the reader and the conclusion "Tu autem" with its response may be omitted.

7. The litany may be extended at the end of the Hour.

These permissions are given for two years. . . . They are deserving of high praise who will continue to recite the entire Breviary in accordance with the Rule of the holy Father Benedict ("Nothing is to be preferred to the Work of God," Rule 43, 3), or who at least recite "the full complement of one hundred and fifty psalms . . . every week" (Rule 18, 23).[17]

The individual monasteries are to submit a report on their use of the permissions to the Abbot Primate at the time appointed by him; he in turn is to pass it on to the Consilium.

These permissions were later renewed. Meanwhile, the Congregation for Divine Worship kept urging the abbots that after a certain number of years of experimentation and after the publication of the *Liturgia Horarum*, they should come to some conclusion. But the assembly of abbots was in favor rather of continuing to experiment: the communities had shown they were at ease with the situation, and the continuation would provide surer data and more reliable studies. As a result, the Congregation for Divine Worship wrote as follows on July 8, 1971, to the Abbot Primate of the Benedictine Confederation and the procurators general of the Cistercians and Trappists.

---

15. Not necessarily by individuals apart but, as many requested, in common at the workplace, out of respect for "the truth of the Hours."

16. After the permission to omit Prime, various systems for distribution of the psalms were examined with a view to recovering the psalms lost with the omission of Prime and to obtaining a better arrangement of the Psalter. The Consilium had allowed experimentation in this area.

17. This paragraph was included at the insistence of the president of the Consilium, Cardinal Gut, O.S.B., who wanted to attest in this way his love for and fidelity to the Benedictine Rule and spirit.

1. It is the wish of this Sacred Congregation that after a period of experimentation the monastic order should finally come to a decision about the basic elements of the *Ordo Liturgiae Horarum*, in order that the entire monastic family may have a common basis for both the structure and the celebration of the Office.

2. On this common basis several forms of celebration may be built, provided that all the communities, depending on their character and the external works they may be engaged in, will indeed share a common basis in their celebration of the Divine Office.

3. The Sacred Congregation thinks that the monastic order should preserve certain distinguishing characteristics of their prayer: divided over time, recited in common, and marked by a certain length.

With regard to the Psalter in particular, the Congregation advises the development of three plans: one following the guidelines in the Rule of St. Benedict (with possible revisions); a second plan based on a week; and a third based on two weeks.

Plans based on a three- or four-week distribution of the psalms would seem to be alien to the spirit of the Rule.

An assimilation of the monastic Office to the prayer of the clergy involved in the pastoral life, as given in the *Liturgia Horarum* of the Roman rite, would deprive the spirituality of the Church of the characteristic note provided by the monastic orders.

4. Particular law may propose guidelines for implementing what is called for by the circumstances or needs of individual communities.

5. This Sacred Congregation will be grateful if the liturgical commissions within the three branches of the monastic family combine their forces in an effort to discover a common ground of understanding regarding the form that the prayer of the Office is to take.

Over two years were to pass before something began to take shape. Two difficulties in particular still remained.

There were some who wanted each monastery to be able to organize its own Office, even if according to a normative framework. Others proposed as one possibility that the structure of the Liturgy of the Hours in the Roman rite be adopted. The Congregation opposed both requests. It opposed the first because of the service that a common organization would provide to the three contemplative communities, to the monasteries that do not have the means or ability to determine their own organization, and to monks living alone or traveling. It opposed the second on the grounds that monastic prayer would then not be much different from the prayer of the clergy in the pastoral ministry and that in practice the monastic Office would cease to exist, having lost its identity.

In order to discuss this matter and the first proposals made by the Benedictine Confederation, the Congregation for Divine Worship sponsored a joint meeting of representatives from the Benedictine Confederation, the Cistercians, and the Trappists on February 24, 1974. The meeting helped these representatives to become acquainted with each other's problems and elicited a commitment from the monks to continue the work.[18]

---

18. Three years later, on February 17, 1977, the SCSDW approved the *Thesaurus Liturgiae Horarum Monasticae* for the Benedictine Congregation. The *Thesaurus* contains a directory for celebration of the monastic Divine Office, normative guidelines for the celebration, and the "treasure (*thesaurus*)" in the true and proper sense, namely, the Psalter in three arrangements:

a) as set down in the Rule of St. Benedict, with the omission of Prime and with its retention (as some monasteries requested);

b) as called for by the exhortation in the Rule that "the entire Psalter of 150 psalms be sung each week";

c) with the psalms being distributed over two weeks (two arrangements).

See "Thesaurus Liturgiae Horarum Monasticae," *Not* 12 (1977) 156–91.

The *Thesaurus* thus acknowledges a pluralism in the organization of the Office, while nonetheless observing some basic criteria which are practically those followed by the Consilium, but further developed or broadened (see *ibid.*, 188–91). It also accepts what there had earlier been an effort to avoid: the possibility of adopting the Liturgy of the Hours of the Roman rite, in the form of the adaptations suggested for contemplatives by the notification of August 6, 1972. But not all these adaptations are accepted: the suggestion regarding the Office of Readings is, but not the one for the Little Hours (see *ibid.*, 191, n. 9).

33

Diocesan and Religious Propers

A Christian community that celebrates the liturgy lives in a very specific historical and local setting, with its own usages, traditions, and saints. Its center is the bishop and the cathedral church. In many cases it venerates the saint or saints who evangelized or founded this Church, and it may possess outstanding relics. All this goes into the living reality of a Church and must be turned to the fullest possible account.

During the postconciliar liturgical renewal the reformers twice concerned themselves with the diocesan, national, and regional Propers and the Propers of religious families.

1. *Instruction of 1965*

The first intervention in this area was occasioned by the introduction of the vernaculars into the liturgy and came in the instruction of June 2, 1965.[1] This document was in fact less an instruction in the full and proper sense than a set of guidelines given by the Consilium to the presidents of the episcopal conferences and the superiors general of the religious communities with regard to the translation of any Mass Propers they might have.[2]

Six months were allowed for the work. The period was admittedly brief but was thought to be sufficient (1) because there was question

---

1. Consilium, Instruction *Popularibus interpretationibus* to Superiors General and to Presidents of the Conferences of Bishops on the Translation of the Propers Belonging to Dioceses and Religious Families (June 1–2, 1965): DOL 111 nos. 767-75.

2. There was as yet no question of translating the Office, except in particular cases, and therefore nothing was said of it at the level of guidelines.

primarily of Mass texts, and these were for the most part already found in the missalettes and would not require a great deal of time for their revision; (2) because it was urgent to have vernacular texts for the feasts dear to the people.

The guidelines given were very simple:

1) The use of the vernacular was permitted within the limits established by the episcopal conferences of each country.

2) The translation was to be approved by the respective Ordinaries in accordance with the norms of the instruction *Inter Oecumenici*.

3) The work of translation was to be done in accordance with the same instruction and its guidelines.

4) In each country it was required that as far as possible there be a single translation of any given text. Texts contained in liturgical books already approved and published in the vernacular were to be taken from those sources. Parts common to several dioceses of religious families were to be translated conjointly.

5) While a better translation was being produced, approval might be requested for texts contained in any of the more commonly used missalettes.

6) When a request for confirmation was submitted, it was to be accompanied by a short report on the criteria followed in the translation.

The work done in these circumstances might be used for only a few years; it nonetheless had the advantage of stimulating close consideration of proper celebrations and thus preparing for the more radical revision that would follow upon the publication of the new liturgical books for the entire Church.

2. *Instruction of 1970*

Once the General Roman Calendar was published, it became necessary to supply guidelines for the inclusion of particular celebrations in the calendar. This was all the more true since the General Calendar had notably reduced the number of celebrations of the saints contained in it and had left celebrations of less than universal appeal to local calendars.

On June 24, 1970, therefore, the Congregation for Divine Worship published the instruction *Calendaria particularia*,[3] which had to do not only

---

3. SCDW, Instruction *Calendaria particularia* on the Revision of Particular Calendars and of the Propers for Offices and Masses (June 24, 1970): *DOL* 481 nos. 3995-4045. This had been preceded by another instruction on interim adaptation: SCDW, Instruction *Decreto Sacrae Congregationis Rituum* on the Interim Adaptation of Particular Calendars (June 29, 1969): *DOL* 480 nos. 3991-94.

with the revision of particular calendars but also with the texts for the Mass and the Divine Office.[4] The instruction is thus of some general interest, inasmuch as it sheds light on the meaning of certain parts of the Mass and the Office, and gives guidelines not found in the typical editions of the Missal and the Liturgy of the Hours.

1) *Calendar.* Proper celebrations should not duplicate what is already contained in the cycle of the mysteries of salvation in the General Calendar. In addition, local calendars should be mindful of the seasons during which particular celebrations are not allowed, so that the mystery of Christ may stand out as it should.

A careful historical, theological, and pastoral study is to be done for each saint or blessed and each special celebration. A great deal of attention must be paid to historical truth. Saints of whom nothing, or almost nothing, certain is known or who no longer have any appeal to the devotion of the people, as well as celebrations introduced for special reasons that are no longer valid (for example, epidemics or disasters), can either be removed entirely from the calendar or grouped together in a common celebration.[5]

The instruction urged that joint commissions with a diocesan, regional, or national membership or with members drawn from the various religious communities be set up. There is to be consultation with the clergy and people concerned or with the members of religious institutes.[6]

---

4. The instruction was published even before the promulgation of the new *Liturgia Horarum* in order to keep the more zealous from doing useless work. Every liturgical reform has been followed by an adaptation of Propers: thus after the reform of Pius XI in 1914 and after John XXIII's *Codex rubricarum* in 1961. In both cases the Congregation of Rites, by means of a circular letter (in 1914) or an "Instruction on the Revision of Particular Calendars and the Propers for Mass and Office" (1961), had given directives for the revision of diocesan and religious Propers. The revision was done in some cases. Yet on occasion of this third revision within a little more than sixty years, workers were still faced with texts dating back to the Council of Trent. For justification of their lazy failure to carry out the two previous revisions, people had perhaps appealed to the First World War in the first case and the proximity of the Council in the second!

5. This principle proved very useful. It provided a means of highlighting the more important celebrations in particular calendars, while at the same time forgetting no one, especially since many saints could be grouped into categories (martyrs, missionaries, catechists, bishops, etc.). The new Proper of the Jesuits is a fine example; see P. Molinari, "Il nuovo calendario liturgico della Compagnia di Gesu," *Not* 8 (1972) 56–59.

6. The SCDW promoted collaboration among various dioceses and especially among religious families that celebrate the same feasts or are united by a common lifestyle (even if each has its nuances). With stimulus from the Congregation, wide-ranging and interesting work was done in preparation for a common calendar and common texts for the various Franciscan families and the Carmelites. Within a common framework each family added celebrations peculiar to it. See (AB), "Il culto del santi," *Not* 11 (1975) 83–87.

An example of organization on a regional scale is the revision of the calendars and Propers

Other norms in the instruction had to do with the selection of a day for the feast and with the rank to be assigned to the celebration; these were to be established according to guidelines set down in the General Calendar.

The titles accompanying the names of saints were to be those found in the General Calendar. But particular calendars might also use other titles traditionally associated with certain saints and indicative of their state of life: king or queen, father or mother of a family.

The work of compiling particular calendars was to be completed within five years from the publication of the Liturgy of the Hours.[7]

2) *Liturgical texts*. Not only the calendar but the texts to be used were to be revised in accordance with the criteria and style of the new Missal and the new Liturgy of the Hours. The directives given by the instruction in this area repeat those already contained in the two liturgical books, but with some clarifications:

The purpose of the *introit* of the Mass is to introduce the congregation to the meaning of the day's celebration. The text chosen should therefore be one which can be read (whenever it is not sung) and which the celebrant can use as the basis for a brief instruction (no. 40a).

The *communion antiphon*, on the other hand, should always have a connection, at least indirect, with the Eucharistic mystery.

The (presidential) *prayers* are the element most in need of revision, especially in Masses of the saints. In the past they were often crammed with biographical data that were not always certain. "Among the prayers,

---

of the dioceses of the Piedmont; see "Revisione del Calendari e Propri particolari delle diocesi del Piemonte," *Not* 11 (1975) 57–58. The twelve dioceses in the Midi apostolic region of France also made common cause: see "Il culto dei santi," *Not* 11 (1975) 85. Even the redaction of the annual calendars was profoundly transformed, becoming increasingly an expression of the communion among all the Churches of a region. Regional calendars multiplied, with directives for individual dioceses. In addition, the content of these calendars was enriched: they changed from simple, cold rubrical lists into directories in the true and proper sense, containing suggestions of a pastoral kind (meaning of the celebrations and liturgical seasons; spiritual preparation of the faithful; the possibilities offered by the liturgical books). See (AB), "Calendari," *Not* 10 (1974) 408–9; also *Not* 9 (1973) 151–54.

7. The five-year period begun by the publication of the GILH was to end in 1976. In February 1974, however, the SCDW asked for completion of the work, urging the parties not to wait until the last moment but to finish the work in 1974. The completion would be to the advantage of the celebration of the Holy Year in the local Churches and in the universal Church. See "De Calendariis particularibus atque Missarum et Officiorum Propriis recognoscendis," *Not* 10 (1974) 87–88; "De Calendariis et Propriis," *Not* 9 (1973) 284–87. The reason why the SCDW kept returning to the subject was not only its acknowledged importance but also the Church's experience with the reforms that the Congregation of Rites had called for in 1914 and 1961. There are things which, if not done immediately, remain forever undone.

only the opening prayer has direct bearing on the saint being celebrated. It is well to give prominence to the saint's characteristics, some aspect of the saint's spiritual life or apostolate, without resorting to trite phrases, e.g., about miracles or establishing a religious institute."

The prayer over the gifts and the prayer after communion, on the other hand, should refer directly to the Eucharistic mystery, and "any mention of the saint must be only incidental" (no. 40b).

Readings. The Old Testament is not read during the Easter season. If proper readings are chosen, the first must be followed by a proper responsorial psalm with a refrain enabling the congregation to participate. Only solemnities have three readings.

With regard to the *Office*, the instruction makes reference to the style (still not fully determined at this point) that should characterize a hagiographical reading: this is not to be a "panegyric" or a biography,[8] but a passage, possibly from the writings of the saint, that will convey his or her spiritual message and provide edification and spiritual food.

In 1973 a further possibility was opened up to national, diocesan, and religious Propers: they might make use of proper texts, that is, texts adapted to local needs and situations, even in the prefaces and the intercessory formulas of the Eucharistic Prayer.[9]

3. *Particular Rites*

Although the instruction *Calendaria particularia* did not deal with this point, it calls for mention here as part of the work done on revision of Propers. I am referring to the concern of some Churches and religious families that had not only celebrations proper to them but also ritual peculiarities that at times amounted to a particular rite in the full and proper sense: the Dominican, Carmelite (Jerusalemite), and Cistercian liturgies, the liturgy of Lyons, the Mozarabic liturgy.

The parties concerned had to reflect seriously on the appropriateness of preserving these peculiarities. These only increased the difficulties already involved in the publication of the liturgical books in the vernacular. But there was a more radical question as well: Was it worthwhile to

---

8. In some cases, e.g., the Servants of Mary, the Congregation allowed that after a reading from the Fathers or the writings of the saint, a further hagiographical reading from the tradition of the order might be included if desired. This can help the members to a knowledge of their own history and is pleasing to some. There were other initiatives, too, that aimed at emphasizing the cult and knowledge of an order's own saints. See, e.g., "Profili spirituali," from the Office of the Postulator of the Society of Jesus, in *Not* 11 (1975) 87.

9. See the circular letter *Eucharistiae participationem* (April 27, 1973) 8–10 (*DOL* 258 nos. 1982-84).

preserve these peculiarities? One laudable characteristic of the reform of the Roman rite was that the scholars working on it had surveyed the entire Latin tradition and taken whatever was of value in the other rites, although always in accordance with the basic requirements and criteria of the reform. Despite some nostalgic sense of loss, the majority of those involved ended by fully adopting the Roman rite.[10]

---

10. For the Dominican rite, see *Not* 8 (1972) 17–18; for the Carmelite, *Not* 8 (1972) 362; for the Cistercian, *Not* 5 (1969) 360.

In practice, the only rite that tried and succeeded in maintaining itself was the Ambrosian, although not without objections, especially from the clergy engaged in the pastoral ministry. See the approval of the Ambrosian Missal in *Not* 11 (1975) 45, and of the Liturgy of the Hours, *Not* 17 (1981) 539.

Interested parties and the SCDW undertook a special study with a view to retaining some peculiarities of the rite of Braga. The studies and further examination showed that the peculiarities were of little or no value, either instructional or cultic. The Congregation confirmed the choice of the great majority of those concerned and abolished the rite.

The case of the Cistercian rite, on the other hand, was a long drawn-out one, because the requests that came in went beyond what the Congregation intended to allow, and seemed concerned rather with recovering archeological elements in the ancient rite of Cluny. Moreover, the requests seemed to be pushed by a single abbey, that of Hauterive, and were not shared by the rest of the order.

In the case of both the rite of Braga and the Cistercian rite, any concessions had to do simply with rubrical details. See "Il rito bracarense e la riforma liturgica," *Not* 8 (1972) 145–50; on the Cistercian rite, *Not* 8 (1972) 62. Some peculiarities in Holy Week were approved for the Trappists: *Not* 8 (1972) 143, and *Not* 9 (1973) 122.

Part V

The Sacraments

34

The Roman Ritual

Two study groups, 22 and 23, were given the task of revising the rites contained in the Roman Ritual.[1] On March 15, 1964, they received the following guidelines from the presidency of the Consilium:

1. In the history of the liturgy, the Ritual has always been the "liveliest" book, that is, the one that most quickly reflects changes in ecclesiastical institutions. This is true especially of the sacramentals, which have constantly increased in number, and often in importance as well, in successive editions of this liturgical book.

The principles set down in the Constitution on the Liturgy also make it clear that the current revision of the Ritual will basically have to follow the same guidelines.

2. It must be kept in mind that the future edition of the Roman Ritual will serve as the basis for the redaction of particular rituals, in accordance with no. 63b of the liturgical Constitution.

3. Consequently, in formulating the rites of the various sacraments and sacramentals, the Roman Ritual will have to be mindful, in its gen-

---

1. Group 22 on the sacraments: *relator:* B. Fischer; *secretary:* X. Seumois; *members:* E. Lengeling, F. McManus, I. Oñatibia, B. Luykx, A. Stenzel, J. Lécuyer, and J. B. Molin. In 1967 L. Ligier joined as an additional secretary, and J. Cellier as a member.

Group 23 on the sacramentals: *relator:* P.-M. Gy; *secretary:* S. Mazzarello; *members:* J. Mejia, J. Rabau, J. Hofinger, F. Vandenbroucke, and D. Sicard. Subsequently added were A. Chavasse, B. Löwenberg, and K. Ritzer.

Although the two groups were distinct, they always worked together, dividing up among them the study of the several sacraments (for each of which others in the group were appointed as relators and secretaries). Special groups were also set up for penance, religious profession, the dedication of a church and altar, and the blessings.

eral arrangement and its rubrics, of the parts in which suitable local adaptations are permitted by the liturgical Constitution, either as a matter of general principle (nos. 37-40) or as a matter of specific recommendation (for example, the rites of Christian initiation, no. 65; marriage, no. 75; anointing of the sick, no. 77; funerals, no. 80).

4. In revising the texts and rites of the sacraments, an investigation will be required with a view to restoring authenticity and a correspondence between texts and the ceremonies they accompany (for example, in the rite of infant baptism).

5. But the area in which the most radical revision and new adaptation will be needed is the sacramentals. Article 79 of the liturgical Constitution expressly refers to this when it speaks of revising the present rites and adding new ones that are called for by new social structures and by the need for a deeper penetration of the Church into various areas of present-day life.

This kind of adaptation and openness to the new is required especially in mission territories, where people pay greater attention to the sanctification of the created order. Evidence of this is the explicit requests that come in from bishops in the missions.

6. Another point on which adaptation is called for in the Ritual is the need of determining in concrete detail which sacramentals can be administered by qualified laypersons, in accordance with no. 79 of the liturgical Constitution. With this is connected the need of compiling an *Ordo brevior* of baptism, for use by laypersons in special cases, particularly in the missions, when no priest is available (see SC 68).

7. The field of labor, being so much larger than others, has been broken up among two study groups—one for the sacraments and one for the sacramentals. Ample room is left, however, for exchanges among the members of the two groups, since they are dealing with closely related and complementary matters.

An effort was made to include among the revisors of the Ritual, more than in other groups, persons who had contacts with the missions or with other areas having similar problems. The reason for this is that the Ritual is the liturgical book most in need of adaptation to local usages and traditions.

Approach to the Work

At the sixth general meeting of the Consilium (autumn 1965), the two relators submitted a joint report in which they surveyed the work to be done and the main questions connected with each sacrament and sacramental, especially baptism, penance, anointing of the sick, marriage, and religious profession.[2]

The following points were made with regard to problems of a general nature:

1. *Relation Between the Future Ritual and Particular Rituals*

The liturgical Constitution provides that adaptations may be made in the particular rituals. The Roman Ritual, though complete in itself, will therefore have to serve as norm and model for the particular rituals (no. 63). Consequently, possibilities of adaptation and variation must be left open for the particular rituals, "provided the substantial unity of the Roman Rite is preserved" (no. 38). This, of course, is not something new. The Ritual, unlike the other liturgical books, was never binding on the entire Latin Church; this point was expressly made by Pope Paul V, who published the Ritual in 1614. In fact, some particular rituals—regional, national, diocesan—were in use down to a very recent time.

2. *Extent of Adaptations*

The liturgical Constitution looks upon rituals as the privileged place for adaptations.[3] Therefore, after a careful study of present-day pastoral needs, the new Roman Ritual will have to explain clearly the extent and possibilities of adaptation. This is something that cannot be settled a priori but only case by case and after careful study. If other needs should crop up in addition to those foreseen in the Ritual, local authorities will be able to fall back on no. 40 of the liturgical Constitution, as they do for other parts of the liturgy.

---

2. See B. Fischer and P.-M. Gy, "De recognitione ritualis romani," *Not* 2 (1966) 22–30. Groups 22–23 initially met at a rather steady pace: Galloro (September 1964), Cologne (December 1964), Le Saulchoir (June 1965), Galloro (September 1965), Mont Saint-Odile, Strasbourg (December 1965). There were also various meetings of the subcommittees. The first meeting of the entire group was devoted to a discussion of the general approach to be taken to the Roman Ritual. At the other meetings the subjects were the care of the sick, Christian death, the burial of the dead, adult baptism, marriage, and infant baptism. These will be discussed in their respective chapters.

3. "Within the limits set by the *editio typica* of the liturgical books, it shall be for the competent, territorial ecclesiastical authority mentioned in art. 22, §2 to specify adaptations, *especially* in the case of the administration of the sacraments, the sacramentals, processions . . ." (*SC* 39; italics added). Reference is also made to adaptations in the rites of baptism (65, 68), marriage (77), new sacramentals (79), and funerals (81).

3. Instructions to Be Prefixed to Each Rite

The liturgical Constitution attaches special importance to the instructions that are to open each section of the Ritual and even each rite (no. 63b). In this connection:

a) The pastoral instructions that have been the glory of the post-Tridentine reform are to be revised so that they will reflect the spirit of Vatican II and present-day pastoral circumstances. These instructions can provide the material for explanations of the celebration of the various sacraments.

b) Although primarily pastoral, these instructions can take note also of juridical norms governing the celebration of the particular sacrament.

c) The instructions should be included in particular rituals, but a suitable adaptation of them is not prohibited. What is done must, of course, receive proper approval from the Holy See.

d) The instructions should bring out the ecclesial character of the sacraments.

All this provided the pattern according to which the *Praenotanda* (Introduction) for each liturgical book were drawn up; these introductions are one of the enrichments characteristic of the reform of Paul VI.

4. General Norms

Like the other reforms, that of the Ritual was to follow the broad guidelines set down in no. 23 of the liturgical Constitution and, more generally, all the principles set forth in Chapter I of the Constitution on the priority of communal celebrations over individual ones, participation by the congregation, simplicity in the rites, reading of the word of God, brief comments, instruction of the faithful, and the elimination of all special honors for private persons.

After these basic considerations, which hold for the entire Ritual, the report reviewed the individual rites that were to be studied by the two groups, and called attention to the main questions. The Consilium could not but be satisfied with so intelligently conceived and so careful and promising a program, and it approved it unanimously.

The jobs to be done were then distributed among the two groups, and work on the individual sacraments began.[4]

---

4. The rites were composed and approved at various times during the period from 1968 (rite of marriage) to 1974 (rite of penance). Independent volumes were thus published whenever the revision of each rite was completed. The time for collecting all the rites together into a single volume had not yet come. The SCDW nonetheless began to reflect on this problem in 1972, for it felt the need of finally bringing together all the rites successively

published. The very fact that time passed between the publication of the various books meant that changes occurred in the style of the rubrics, the arrangement of the material, and the Introductions. The rubrical and juridical parts of the liturgical books published last were more careful and complete. The Introductions of the early books were scantier (e.g., the rite of marriage) or even entirely lacking (orders). Some sections of the Introductions were to be found in some books and lacking in others. Some guidelines were repeated for every rite. There were also rubrical differences for the same situation (e.g., the circumstances in which a proper Mass may be celebrated). All these inconsistencies were easily explainable but could not be allowed to remain when the rites were collected into a single volume. The SCDW had decided on a plan of action, but this was interrupted by the suppression of that Congregation. The following is what the SCDW had thought should be done:

1. provide Introductions for rites lacking them;

2. revise and complete the Introductions in which the doctrinal, pastoral, juridical, and ritual presentation is less developed;

3. revise Introductions that are overly full by eliminating anything that a present rereading shows to be superfluous and any repetition of ideas already expressed in other words, whether in the same rite or in others;

4. compose a General Introduction (*Praenotanda generalia*) to the entire body of sacramental rites; this would include everything which holds for more than one rite, thus avoiding the repetition of certain guidelines in each individual rite;

5. wherever possible, follow the same outline in the Introductions of the various rites;

6. revise the guidelines scattered throughout the descriptions of each rite, making them consistent among themselves and, if possible, with those in the other liturgical books, and completing them where something is lacking.

35

Christian Initiation of Adults

The Constitution on the Liturgy had called for preparation of a rite of adult baptism; it had also called for a catechumenate for adults, which would be "divided into several stages" and "sanctified by sacred rites to be celebrated at successive intervals of time" (no. 64).

The task was entrusted to group 22, with the aid of group 23. Among the members were theologians, historians, and two missionaries. Later on, the office of assistant relator was given to Jacques Cellier, founder of the first modern catechumenate in Europe.[1]

I. History

At its first meeting, which was held in the Jesuit house at Galloro (September 1964), the group decided that before studying the rite of infant baptism, it would work out the main lines of the ritual for the Christian initiation of adults.[2]

The first schema came before the Consilium on November 19, 1965, accompanied by a masterly presentation from Professor B. Fischer. The Fathers engaged in a lively discussion of the report. The discussion dealt not so much with the structure of the rite as with details and showed a certain lack of experience on the part of Fathers who did not come from mission countries and were not familiar with the catechumenate. Profes-

1. In the second phase, after the experiments, Professor Fischer continued as director of the group but asked J. Cellier, a priest, to take direct charge of the work. L. Ligier was added as a secretary more directly in charge of this rite.
2. The rite of infant baptism was published first because of greater pastoral need.

sor Fischer was so successful in clearing up difficulties that the problems he set down as calling for solutions were unanimously approved, apart from some minor dissents on one or other point.

The second schema, which made some improvements on the first, was discussed with the Fathers and consultors of the Consilium and then presented to the Holy Father by Cardinal Lercaro at an audience on March 18, 1966.[3] The Pope was asked to approve it for purposes of experiment. This schema[4] covered the entire rite of the catechumenate but did not include the *Praenotanda*, which were to be composed after the experiments, nor did it go into particular cases. It provided for four successive steps or stages:

I. A rite for the *beginning* of the catechumenate (*ad catechumenum faciendum*). This would be followed by the period of catechumenate, during which the catechumen acquires an ever fuller knowledge of the Christian mystery, joins in prayer and the hearing of God's word, and is sanctified by means of the minor exorcisms and the several blessings.

II. *Election* or enrollment of names. This marks the start of immediate preparation for the sacraments of baptism, confirmation, and the Eucharist, and usually occurs at the beginning of Lent.

III. *Scrutinies and presentations.* The major exorcisms take place during Lent, on the three "baptismal" Sundays on which the gospels of the Samaritan woman, the man born blind, and the raising of Lazarus are read. These rites mark a deeper intervention of divine grace to purify the souls of the catechumens and prepare them to receive the sacraments of Christian initiation.

IV. *Rites in preparation* for the sacraments; these take place on the morning of Holy Saturday.

These four stages are followed by celebration of the three sacraments of Christian initiation.

This celebration in turn is followed by a period that was given the somewhat surprising name of "mystagogy," a period in which the newly baptized are closely accompanied through the first stages of their life as Christians.[5]

---

3. Schema 147: *De rituali* 9 (March 18, 1966).

4. There was an extensive description of it in *Not* 3 (1967) 55–70.

5. Although the rite took as its starting point the *Ordo baptismi adultorum per gradus catechumenatus dispositi*, which the SCR had published in 1962 (see *AAS* 54 [1962] 315–38), its approach and spirit were completely new. The 1962 *Ordo* deserves credit for calling attention to the liturgical importance of the catechumenate, but in practice all it did was divide into sections the rite currently found in the Roman Ritual.

Given that background, it was natural that the Fathers of the Consilium should often

Since the schema was intended for experimentation, it contained an interesting appendix in three parts. These were entitled: "Pastoral Guidelines for Experiments," "Practical Guidelines for the Translation of the Rite,"[6] and "Directives for Drawing Up a Report on the Experiments."

The first impressions within the Consilium were echoed by those within the Secretariat of State, which on April 28, 1966 (No. 69020), forwarded some observations of Abbot Franzoni. In substance the Abbot

---

have had the impression of being confronted with something artificial and with revivals that seemed inspired by a taste for the past. Professor Fischer's presentation made it clear that this was not the case. It showed a profound knowledge of the history of the catechumenate, especially in the first centuries of the Church, but also of the contemporary situation, especially in mission countries. This was due above all to the contributions of Father Xavier Seumois, who had extensive experience not only of scholarship but also of missionary work.

Despite all this, the Fathers' fear of archeologism led them to challenge the terms "initiation" and "scrutinies," to regard as complicated the rite of entrance into the catechumenate, and to think of the presentations as artificial. Of the latter one Father said: "They already know the gospel and the creed!" The relator replied: "It is one thing to know them, another to receive them officially from the Church in a celebration in the presence of the community." Again: in the entrance into the catechumenate the celebrant asks the candidate's name. "What's the point of that? He already knows it!" said one Father. The relator answered: "True, but the statement of the name in the presence of the entire community enhances and personalizes the act being performed."

There was also trouble getting the term "initiation" accepted, whether by the Consilium or by the reviewers in the Curia. The most frequent objections were: "It smacks of archeologism"; "It is unintelligible"; "It is ambiguous" because reminiscent of ideas from the mystery cults. The study group insisted that the word be kept because it brings out very well the spirit of the catechumenate as a gradual introduction to the mystery of God and the Church, an introduction that is not simply intellectual but also concerns one's manner of life. Furthermore, the adjective "Christian" removes any likelihood of ambiguity; instruction will do the rest.

A further objection had to do with the celebrating priest being able to administer all three sacraments. Granting the priest the faculty to confirm would, it was said, strip the bishop of his prerogative as "ordinary minister" of this sacrament. One accomplished jurist said: "At least let it be clear that the permission to confirm is given by the bishop as ordinary minister and not by the law." Others thought it better to postpone confirmation for pastoral reasons, namely, to ensure a further study and understanding of the faith. This problem was to crop up again. But the group did not yield, for it wanted to ensure the unity of the three sacraments and to have the catechumen experience a complete Christian initiation; the group did, of course, leave open the possibility of acting differently in individual cases.

6. This was a very interesting section. The group realized that there would be difficulties in translating *electio, scrutinia, mystagogia,* and some other expressions in the liturgical texts. But it thought it better to retain in the Latin text terms now well known and consecrated by tradition and to stimulate a search for appropriate translations. It therefore composed this little "handbook" on the meaning of terms and expressions recurring in the rite, in order to make it easier to "rethink" them in other languages.

made two requests: (1) that the new order of infant baptism be compiled and sent out for experiment at the same time as the order of adult baptism; (2) that instead of introducing a rite that in parts was so long and complex (although optional reductions were allowed), there be "a simplified rite" that would be an obligatory basis for the celebration but would be accompanied by an extensive repertory of optional rites and formulas that could be inserted into the essential structure if this seemed good to the episcopal conference or the Ordinary or the parish priest.

There was a failure here to see that the structures of the two rites—for infants and for the adult catechumenate—are utterly different and that the catechumenate is not to be celebrated in its entirety on a single occasion but over a long period, which in some cases may be a matter of years.[7] The explanations that the Consilium issued (May 18) were not enough to dispel doubts. The Secretariat of State returned to the point on May 25:

> The plan changes a rite already recently modified and, what is more, looks forward to two further series of changes: those to be introduced after a period of experimentation and those that will be left to the judgment of local authorities. Of these last it must be asked whether in any case they will be prepared to make such changes.
>
> Furthermore, even if a new rite of infant baptism is to be introduced that will be specially adapted to the condition of the newborn, there seems to be no reason why it must be substantially different from the rite of adult baptism and why its introduction should not be put off.
>
> Finally, it seems advisable that especially in the area of the sacraments the liturgical reform should not give any signs of uncertainty and should not open the door to arbitrary actions.

The Pope nevertheless granted permission for experimental use of the rite. This was sent to about fifty catechumenal centers in Japan, Mali, Togo, the Ivory Coast, Upper Volta, Rwanda, Congo, Zaire, Belgium, Canada, France, and the United States.

At the end of 1968 the study group gathered to analyze the reports that had been sent to the Consilium on the experiments (Paris, December 30, 1968, to January 4, 1969). The material, with all its observations, suggestions, and requests, was very extensive. In general, all the reports praised the approach taken in the rite. The observations had broadly to do with four points:

---

7. Even the Fathers of the Consilium had the impression that the rite was overly complicated. It was explained that there would indeed be a simpler rite, as called for by the liturgical Constitution itself (no. 66), although this would have to be considered not the norm but rather an exception for special cases.

a) The *general structure*. It was pointed out that entry into the catechumenate is preceded by a period of evangelization, sympathetic welcome, and initial contacts, and that this must be taken into account. These preliminaries, it was said, are at the human level and are concerned more with a spirit of hospitality and cordial relations than with the liturgy proper; but some reference should be made to it, and the question should be raised whether these preliminaries themselves might be marked by some kind of rite.[8] On the other hand, the period of mystagogy was felt as liturgically empty, since the rite made no specific provision for it.[9] On a broader scale, the whole period of the catechumenate, which in some places lasted for years, was felt to be somewhat thin in content, whereas the period (from the election on) immediately preceding the administration of the sacraments, a period usually covering Lent, was excessively full.

b) *Relevance*. People had the same impression as the Consilium itself: there were some rites not adapted to the modern mentality (for example, the scrutinies, presentations, and exorcisms) or overly involved (such as the rite of introduction to the catechumenate) or artificial (the rite of election[10]) or not practicable nowadays (the dismissal of the catechumens after the liturgy of the Word).

c) *Prayers*. The exhortations and prayers sometimes used negative ideas to express conversion to God and the progressive purification of the catechumens. More effective texts were requested, as well as more extensive possibilities of adaptation and selection.

d) Role of the *catechists*. It was thought that they should have a larger role, even in the liturgical part proper, since they are the ones who in many cases bear most of the burden of catechumenal instruction.

---

8. This request came especially from Japan, which was more sensitive to problems of hospitality and of making people feel welcome, since this is the first step toward an interest in Christian teaching and life. The suggestion was accepted to the extent that a short section on the precatechumenate was included in the Introduction (I, A), but here only some pastoral guidelines are set down. A great deal of freedom is left, however, to the episcopal conferences to decide on the appropriateness of having precatechumenal liturgical celebrations and on the form these should take; these are matters that depend on different situations and mentalities.

9. Once again, the study group thought it better not to be more specific about rites during this period and to stick to pastoral exhortations with a view to making pastors aware that they must follow up on the newly baptized, especially during the early stages of their Christian lives. The rite does suggest that there be special gatherings, namely, ''Masses for neophytes,'' for which the texts of the Easter season Masses are well suited.

10. The group tried to streamline the rites and point out the adaptations that would be left to the initiative of the episcopal conferences or of the people in charge of the catechumenate, but it regarded the structure of the periods and stages as essential and not open to modification.

The study group took these observations into account and, as far as it could, simplified things, notably enriched the euchology, and completed the schema by adding all the parts and the *Praenotanda*.[11]

The new schema[12] was submitted for definitive approval at the twelfth general meeting of the Consilium. It was studied on November 13, 1969, after a careful presentation by assistant secretary L. Ligier. Ten days earlier it had already been studied at the meeting of the relators. The general vote on the schema was very positive.[13]

The document then began a lengthy journey of examination by the agencies of the Roman Curia; over two years went by before the process was completed. This delay was due in part to the fact that the rite also contained the essential part of the sacrament of confirmation. It was therefore necessary to wait upon the publication of the *Ordo confirmationis*, which itself was a long time in the works.

After the twelfth general meeting the secretary of the Consilium worked on preparing the rite for publication and seeing to its typographical format.[14] The printer's galleys were sent to the Congregations for the Doctrine of the Faith, the Sacraments, and the Evangelization of Peoples on October 30, 1970. When they came back,[15] a joint meeting was held of representatives from the interested Congregations, as requested by the Congregation for the Doctrine of the Faith. All the observations submitted had already been studied within the Consilium itself by a special committee,[16] which compiled a list of the qualifications and reservations and set down the thinking of the Congregation for Divine Worship on each

---

11. This work was accomplished especially at two meetings in the summer of 1969: at Douvres-la-Délivran and Arromanches in France (July 15–21) and at Luxembourg (September 10–14).

12. Schema 252: *De rituali* 36 (September 29, 1969).

13. The observations made focused mainly on details. It was asked that a correction be made in no. 76 (of the printed text), which seemed to suppose that the catechumen already had an adult faith. Bishop Nagae, who gave expression to Japanese sensibilities, insisted, as he had already done at the first presentation of the schema, that the anointings and, more generally, everything requiring a direct contact of the celebrant and the catechumen or baptizand be made optional. Another point that elicited renewed calls was confirmation. Some Fathers wanted this to be always administered by a bishop.

14. In this process an effort was made to achieve a more logical and handy arrangement of the abundant material and, at the same time, as called for by some consultors, even consultors of the group, to reduce the number of some optional texts, especially presidential prayers, in order to avoid monotony and an appearance of inflatedness.

15. The SCDF replied on February 22, 1971 (Prot. no. 3085/70), the Congregation of the Sacraments on April 20, 1971, and Propaganda Fide on November 5, 1970.

16. This committee met on April 30, 1971, and was comprised of G. Agustoni, P. Jounel, B. Belluco, L. Ligier, and G. Pasqualetti.

of them. This document was in turn the basis for the work of the joint meeting held on June 7, 1971.[17] The corrections proposed by the Congregation for the Doctrine of the Faith and the Congregation for the Evangelization of Peoples were to a large extent the same (this can be explained by the fact that the consultors called upon by the two Congregations were in some cases the same); the Congregation of the Sacraments limited itself to a minute comparison of the new *Ordo* with the prescriptions of the Code of Canon Law.[18]

In substance, the requests were these:[19]

a) the revision of some texts, especially of the *Praenotanda*, with a view to clarifying some expressions or making them more precise;

b) since the most serious hesitations had to do with the General Introduction on Christian initiation as a whole (already published with the rite of infant baptism), it was proposed that it be omitted. The suggestion was accepted in order to facilitate publication.[20]

c) greater specificity in the section on the conferral of the sacrament of confirmation;[21]

---

17. The participants for the SCDF were J. Lécuyer and G. Roschini; for the Congregation of the Sacraments, A. Magnoni and Sutter; for Propaganda Fide, X. Seumois and J. Lécuyer; and for the SCDW, A. Bugnini and G. Pasqualetti.

18. But the style of the Introduction was based on the style of the conciliar documents, especially *Ad gentes, Lumen gentium, Unitatis redintegratio,* and *Sacrosanctum Concilium.* In the final analysis, the Congregation of the Sacraments was satisfied with the inclusion, at the points it indicated, of such phrases as "non obstante," "abrogato in hoc casu," and "derogato can. . . . CJC."

19. The SCDF had distinguished between "observations," "proposals," and "suggestions for improvement."

20. These *Praenotanda* were regarded as displaying God knows what doctrinal defects. We shall see further on that the corrections finally required were minimal.

21. Once the possibility was accepted that the celebrating priest might administer all three sacraments, a complex casuistry developed that was due in part to the variety of situations envisaged in the schema itself: confirmation and first communion of baptized persons who had neglected or lost their faith; Christian initiation of children of catechetical age; etc. It was requested that in these cases, too, the priest might administer confirmation. Then the question arose: Can he also confirm other baptized Christians who may be present?

The Congregation of the Sacraments was in favor of allowing a priest who celebrates baptism, confirmation, and the Eucharist for an *adult* to confirm also any other adults present who had been baptized in childhood. It did not allow without qualification that the celebrant might do the same at the Christian initiation of a child. The SCDW, on the other hand, was more in favor of the second case because among the children sharing a common catechetical formation there could be some preparing for all three sacraments and others preparing only for confirmation and first communion.

The problem was resolved by allowing the priest to confer confirmation only as part of the sacramental action of Christian initiation for an adult or for a child that had reached the age of reason, to the exclusion of everyone else.

d) insertion of a section on conditional baptism, and the specification that a Catholic cannot act as godparent but can only be allowed as a witness.

Agreement was easily reached, and on June 23 the secretariat of the Congregation for Divine Worship sent the texts, corrected as agreed at the meeting, to the other interested Congregations. The texts in the printer's proofs and the corrected texts were given in facing columns.

After the approval of the corrected texts,[22] the definitive proofs were made and sent to the Pope on November 14, 1971. He gave his final approval on the thirtieth of the same month (No. 197901).

The volume was published, by decree of the Congregation for Divine Worship, on January 6, 1972, the Solemnity of the Epiphany,[23] under the title *Ordo initiationis christianae adultorum.*[24]

II. Contents

1. *Introduction*

This comprises sixty-seven numbers. Taken together with the general principles published in the *Ordo baptismi parvulorum*, they form a whole of ample proportions, the lengthiest in fact after the General Instructions of the Missal and the Liturgy of the Hours.

The initiation of catechumens (section I, nos. 4-40) takes place gradually and follows the course of their spiritual growth. The initiation includes four basic phases: precatechumenate, catechumenate, period of purification and enlightenment, and "mystagogy." These phases are accompanied by liturgical rites and contain three fundamental moments or steps: entry into the catechumenate, election, and the sacraments of bap-

---

22. SCDF, August 31, 1971; Sacraments, July 9, 1971; Propaganda, July 6, 1971.

23. Decree *Ordinis baptismi adultorum* (January 6, 1972): *DOL* 300 no. 2327; see *Not* 8 (1972) 87-95. In November 1970 the SCDW had suggested an apostolic constitution on Christian initiation that would consider the rites of all three sacraments together. It would contain, among other things, a determination of the matter and form of confirmation. It was noted that "serious problems, caused by the dechristianization of broad sectors of society and also by supposed requirements of a psychological and educational kind, have arisen today with regard to the appropriateness of infant baptism, the age of confirmation, and the age for admitting children to the Eucharist." The proposed constitution would have had to confront these difficulties and emphasize the importance of the three sacraments beginning in childhood. But the suggestion was not accepted, and the constitution eventually published concerned itself only with confirmation.

24. *Ordo initiationis christianae adultorum* (Vatican Polyglot Press, 1972; 185 pp.). The rite is in *The Rites of the Catholic Church* 1 (New York, 1983[2]) 13-181; there is a new translation of the Introduction in *DOL* 301 nos. 2328-2488.

tism, confirmation, and Eucharist. The three steps mark the three major stages of the catechumens' journey, from their first hearing of the word of God to an initial faith, and from this in turn to full commitment to Christ in the Church.

The ideal and normal moment for the administration of the sacraments of initiation is the Easter Vigil. The final stage of preparation, that is, the period of purification and enlightenment, thus coincides with Lent, and the neophytes' first experience of their new life coincides with the Easter season. In the liturgy of these several periods the catechumens find reminders and helps suited to their situation.

The celebration of Christian initiation at some other time of the year is not excluded.

Section II (nos. 41-48) deals with the ministries and offices of the persons involved in the initiation of the candidates.

The person primarily responsible is the bishop or someone he delegates. Next in order come the priests, deacons, catechists, sponsors, and those immediately responsible for the catechumens, that is, those who answer for them and guarantee their preparedness. But the Christian community also plays an important and irreplaceable part: it actively shares in the celebrations, concerns itself with the candidates, and joins them in an effort at conversion and renewal. For this reason the Introduction emphasizes several points:

a) The entire local community should show a concern for the new catechumens, follow along with them, and introduce them to the life of the community as part of their new experience.

b) The formation of the catechumens is not to be merely intellectual but a matter of living. Their deeper knowledge of God and Christ must be accompanied by an ongoing effort at the renewal of their lives, an effort that the Church accompanies and supports by sanctifying action and prayer—blessings, exorcisms, scrutinies, and so on.

c) All this requires that the sacred ministers, aided by the community authorities, catechists, and sponsors, acquire a direct knowledge of the catechumens so that they may accompany, encourage, and guide them and be sure that they deserve admission to the sacraments.

The Introduction ends, as usual, with a section on adaptations by the episcopal conference, the bishop, and the minister of the celebration. As a matter of fact, the organization of the catechumenate differs from region to region, depending on local requirements.[25] For this reason, a broad range of material is provided.

---

25. The liturgical Constitution also allows for a more radical adaptation that is linked

2. A Complete Catechumenate

The first chapter explains the organization of a full and proper catechumenate that contains all the phases and steps. This is the normal and therefore obligatory course. There are three main rites:

a) *Entry into the catechumenate.* The characteristic action here is a "signing" in which the candidates give themselves to Christ. They do not yet share in the sacramental life, but they are now members of the "family of God" (St. Augustine).

b) *Election:* the definitive summons—which may, however, come only after several years—when it is sure that the candidate is ready to receive the sacraments. The election usually takes place at the beginning of Lent.

c) *Sacramental initiation* through the three sacraments, which are usually administered during the Easter Vigil.

Intermediate rites: the periods between the three basic steps are marked by certain special rites: exorcisms and blessings, which give spiritual aid to those who are endeavoring to advance toward a full Christian life; the "scrutinies," which signify and mediate the action of the God who "searches (*scrutatur*) hearts" and penetrates and transforms them by his grace; the "presentation" of the Creed and the Lord's Prayer; and, in the final days, the rites of immediate preparation for the sacraments.

Sacramental initiation is followed by a period of deepening understanding and experience of the mystery; this period normally lasts for the entire Easter season.

---

to the cultures and social traditions of the various peoples. "It is lawful in mission lands to allow, besides what is part of Christian tradition, those initiation elements in use among individual peoples, to the extent that such elements are compatible with the Christian rite of initiation" (no. 65). This is a vast and difficult field. Many peoples have rites of passage to mark the most important moments in life. Missionaries have adopted divergent attitudes toward these, from absolute prohibition to dissuasion to the expectation of their spontaneous abandonment. The Council realized that there is here a possible vital link between Christianity and the cultures.

In addition to setting down the general principle, the *Ordo* sometimes makes suggestions. One is the adoption of a practice often found in initiations, namely, the taking of a new name and the explaining of this name's significance or meaning to the community. The *Ordo* allows for the adoption of a specifically Christian name or a local name with a Christian meaning, but also for the retention of the name the candidate already has, provided its meaning is not at odds with the Christian faith. This point in the *Ordo* (nos. 88 and 203) gave rise to a high-level dispute when the President of Zaire changed his Christian name and required the rest of the country to do the same. This, of course, was something different than envisaged in the *Ordo*, being a change from Christian names already assumed; the claim to have support in the *Ordo* was therefore groundless. A "semi-official" clarification was nonetheless requested; see "Significato di una rubrica," *Not* 8 (1972) 100–102.

3. Special Cases

a) *Simple Rite* (Chapter II). It is not always possible or necessary to have catechumens pass through all the normal stages and rites of the catechumenate. An *Ordo simplicior*, one that can be done as a single continuous action, provides for such cases. It is a simpler rite, containing only some of the elements from the rite accomplished in a series of steps and stages.

b) *Short Rite* (Chapter III). This is intended for use by laypersons—catechists or non-catechists—when the candidate is in danger of death. It can also be used by priests and deacons; these, however, are advised to use, as far as possible, the fuller "simple rite" of Chapter II.

c) *Guidelines for Preparing Uncatechized Adults for Confirmation and the Eucharist* (Chapter IV). The subjects here are adults who were baptized as infants. Their situation closely resembles that of catechumens, since, though they are baptized, they have not received their religious initiation. This chapter became the object, two years later, of a detailed official interpretation that determines which rites may be repeated and which not in a form of neocatechumenal religious instruction offered by modern religious institutions.[26]

d) *Rite of Initiation for Children of Catechetical Age* (Chapter V). The situation of a child differs from that of an adult because a child is still under the authority of its parents, who take part in the liturgical rites. In addition, the instruction and rites must be adapted to the age of the candidates. This rite represents the first time in history that such an effort of adaptation has been made.

---

26. SCDW, Reflections on the *Rite of Christian Initiation of Adults*, Chapter 4 (March 8, 1973): *DOL* 302 nos. 2489-98. See the commentary of G. Pasqualetti in *Not* 9 (1973) 278-82. This chapter gave rise to serious discussion even in traditionally Christian countries. Following the lead of their founders, the "neocatechumenal communities," as they were called, had already begun to put in place a type of Christian formation for the baptized that was modeled on the catechumenate. They ran into difficulties and often appealed for advice to the SCDW, which interested itself in the problem. The vicariate of Rome had also asked for a clarification.

The problem was this: What meaning is to be assigned to a "catechumenate" for the already baptized and, above all, to any rites that might accompany the spiritual formation of Christians? Such rites must in principle be understood as a reliving of what had once been sacramentally celebrated. It was also explained, however, that certain rites may not be repeated: the ephphetha, the anointings, the bestowal of a white garment. Some that may be repeated are the presentation and "giving back" or recital of the Creed, and the giving of a candle. The neocatechumenal communities deserve credit for having realized the importance of the spirit of the catechumenate in forming true Christians. The Pope himself intervened in the discussion; see *Not* 10 (1974) 228-29.

The final chapter (VI) contains various optional texts, including an extensive anthology of readings from Scripture.

RITE OF RECEPTION OF BAPTIZED CHRISTIANS INTO FULL COMMUNION WITH THE CATHOLIC CHURCH

An appendix to the *Ordo initiationis* contained a "Rite of Reception of Baptized Christians into Full Communion with the Catholic Church." Such a rite had been called for by the liturgical Constitution (no. 69b).[27] It was obvious that the groups dealing with Christian initiation should draw up this rite as well, but in close collaboration with the Secretariat for Christian Unity.[28]

A first draft was composed at Trier during the meeting of July 6-7, 1967. It was intended for the members of both study groups. The many observations made on it forced a radical revision of the entire text.[29] A second schema was then prepared, with contributions from three sources: Cardinal Bea, president of the Secretariat for Christian Unity, with whom the relator discussed the matter in person; the meeting of the relators of the Consilium (November 17, 1967); and Professor Feiner, a Swiss, who was approached through the Secretariat for Christian Unity.

The text to be submitted to the Consilium was drawn up at the end of December 1967 and in February 1968 at Le Saulchoir; it was then discussed and approved at the tenth general meeting (April 1968).[30]

The rite for the reception of baptized non-Catholics into the Catholic Church has been reduced to a minimum. It generally takes place during Mass, but the text also expressly says that any display of triumphalism and any publicity are to be avoided. There should be some link with a parish community, but at the same time it seems more appropriate that the ceremony should take place in the presence of only a few friends and relatives. If Mass cannot be celebrated, there is to be at least a liturgy of

---

27. Instead of the language used in the liturgical Constitution ("a new rite . . . for converts who have already been validly baptized; it should express that they are being received into the communion of the Church"), the Rite of Reception uses that of the Ecumenical Directory (May 14, 1967), which was in turn inspired by the Decree on the Eastern Churches: "into the full communion of the Catholic Church."

28. After a preliminary schema (July 1967), four others were composed: November 3, 1967; November 20, 1967; March 8, 1968; April 21, 1968.

29. Especially influential were a detailed study by Professor McManus and the remarks of Monsignor Gianfrancesco Arrighi of the Secretariat for Christian Unity. Also valuable was the collaboration of Adalbert Kurzeja, O.S.B., assistant to Professor B. Fischer at the Liturgical Institute of Trier.

30. See "Decima sessio plenaria 'Consilii,' " *Not* 4 (1968) 184.

the Word. In this case, the persons received should share the Eucharist with their Catholic brothers and sisters at the first opportunity.

A profession of faith is the only act formally required for reception into the full communion of the Catholic Church.³¹ Baptism is not to be automatically repeated. Should there be serious doubts about the validity of an earlier baptism, the reasons for a new, conditional baptism must be carefully explained; the bishop is to decide the manner in which the baptism is to be administered, and is to do the same for confirmation. For both sacraments there is to be a "sponsor."

In view of the great variety of situations, it will be up to the episcopal conferences to make appropriate general adaptations; in individual cases this is the responsibility of the local Ordinary.

The rite takes account of three cases:

a) *Reception within Mass* (Chapter I). The reception takes place after the homily. The celebrant addresses a brief invitation to the candidate, who then joins all present in reciting the Creed.³² At the end of the Creed the candidate adds: "I believe and profess all that the holy Catholic Church believes, teaches, and proclaims to be revealed by God." The celebrant then lays his hand on the head of the candidate³³ and says: "N., the Lord receives you into the Catholic Church. His loving kindness has led you here, so that in the unity of the Holy Spirit you may have full communion with us in the faith that you have professed in the presence of his family."³⁴ If the candidate is also to be confirmed, this sacrament is administered at this point by the priest who has been delegated to receive the profession of faith. The general intercessions follow, and all present greet the newly received person as a brother or sister.

b) *Reception outside Mass* (Chapter II) follows the same form but in the setting of a liturgy of the Word.

c) *In special cases* (Chapter II, no. 28) even the liturgy of the Word may be omitted, and the ceremony may be limited to the invitation,

---

31. The Secretariat for Christian Unity had decided (October 17, 1967) not to ask for any more than this.

32. The *Ordo* speaks of "the Nicene [-Constantinopolitan] Creed" because this is the one regularly used at Mass, but where permission is given, the Apostles' Creed may be used instead.

33. This is the oldest gesture and was still to be found in the Roman Pontifical (Part III: De reconciliatione). It goes back at least to Innocent I; see his second letter to Bishop Victricius of Rouen: " . . . that those coming from the Novatians . . . be received by a simple laying on of the hand" (PL 20:475B).

34. The formula is based on the rite of the Jacobite Syrians; see H. Denzinger, *Ritus Orientalium* I, 466.

profession of faith, and laying on of the hand. The invitation can take as its point of departure one or other passage of Scripture on the mercy of God and make reference to Eucharistic communion as the full sign of communion with the Church.

36

Infant Baptism

The Constitution on the Liturgy had ordered that a rite of infant baptism be prepared which would be "suited to the fact that those to be baptized are infants," would bring out more clearly "the roles as well as the obligations of the parents and godparents," and would provide for a variety of cases ("a very large number are to be baptized"; baptism to be administered by catechists in mission lands; baptism to be administered by anyone of the faithful when the person is in danger of death and no priest or deacon is available).

I. History

The work was neither easy nor quickly accomplished. For the first time in the history of the liturgy, a rite was to be prepared specifically for infants. The rite of infant baptism in the Ritual of Paul V (1614) was simply the rite of adult baptism, shortened so that it might be performed in a single celebration. The child was directly addressed and asked what it sought from the Church and whether it renounced Satan and believed, as though it were really capable of taking on obligations and responding to questions. The prayers spoke of progress in faith and Christian life; there were repeated exorcisms, which had their place in the ancient scrutinies but certainly did not reflect the condition of infants.

The work was done by study group 22[1] and took a rather long time to complete.[2]

---

1. See p. 579, n. 1.
2. These, in summary, were the stages in the preparation of the document: fourth gen-

In his first report to the Consilium, Professor B. Fischer restricted himself to setting before the Fathers some general principles showing the lines along which the group intended to work. These principles had to do with the possibility of regularly celebrating a liturgy of the Word at the beginning of the rite; with the value of making the giving of a name a solemn part of the rite; and with the need of adapting the formula of renunciation to modern conditions.

The Fathers were satisfied with the report and approved it. Two years were to pass, however, before the rite itself came back to them for approval. As a matter of fact, the group had decided to give priority to the rite of Christian initiation for adults as being the original and pivotal form of the sacrament of baptism.[3]

But the group did not forget infant baptism in the meantime. It discussed it at a meeting in Montefiolo (Rieti), in the residence of the Benedictine Sisters of St. Priscilla, November 14–15, 1965; together with group 23 at Mont Saint-Odile (Paris), December 27–30 of the same year; at Trier, January 31—February 2, 1966; and finally at Le Saulchoir (Paris), March 2–6, 1966. The result was a complete schema "for several children," which emphasized the communal aspect of baptism. The relators studied this text in May 1966. It was also sent to various theologians for their comments on doctrinal matters, especially in connection with the renunciations and the profession of faith.

This first schema was submitted to the Consilium at its seventh general meeting in October 1966. In April of the following year the Pope was given the complete schema, which now included the other rites (for a single child, for a large number of children, and so on) and had been corrected on the basis of observations made during meetings of the group in Verona and Trier. The final chapter and the Introduction were ready for the ninth general meeting of the Consilium in October 1968; the meeting focused its attention chiefly on the Introduction.

The preparation of the Introduction had likewise been begun as early as 1964, during two meetings of the group in Cologne and Trier. The group then waited upon further experience in order that the Introduction might reflect the spiritual requirements of the rite and the definitive approach taken in it. The final redaction of the Introduction was effected

---

eral meeting of the Consilium (October 9, 1964): first report, on general problems; seventh general meeting (the *periti*, September 29, 1966; the Consilium, October 11): first schema; eighth general meeting (relators, April 3, 1967; Consilium, April 12): second schema (complete); ninth general meeting (relators, October 3, 1968; Consilium, October 15): third schema, which received the definitive approval of the Consilium.

3. See B. Fischer, "De ordine Baptismi parvulorum," *Not* 4 (1968) 235–45.

during two meetings held in the summer of 1968 at Senonches (Paris) and the Abbey of St. Gertrude in Germany.

Before submitting the rite for final approval, the group felt the need of some experimentation, since this was a completely new structure. The experiments were conducted during 1968 in about twenty parishes, under the guidance of experts belonging to the Consilium. The locations were not many, but they were scattered throughout the world. The most interesting reports came from Africa (Rwanda and Togo), the United States, Belgium, France, Germany, and Italy. Reports from other regions were scantier due to lack of time, but they were no less important. The rite as a whole was found to be satisfactory, thus answering the fears of the Fathers.

The Fathers, in fact, found the rite to be pastorally effective and rich, but a bit "idealistic." This idealistic aspect was their main concern: "The rite is a fine one, especially in its liturgy of the Word, but how can poor missionaries do all this in addition to their work in the chapels of their mission areas?" This question, which was raised by Bishop Isnard (Brazil) and Archbishop Hurley (South Africa), sums up the chief remarks of the Fathers. Some of these therefore expressed a preference for having two rites: a short one and a solemn one.[4] The experiments, they said, had indeed validated the structure of the rite and the general principles embodied in it: the approach and the division into parts, a common celebration for several children, participation of the mother.[5] But they

---

4. In the new approach to the rite, the distinction between solemn and "private" baptisms (1917 Code of Canon Law, can. 737) ceases to hold. The sacramental celebration is in fact always an action of the Church, even if in cases of necessity some parts of the rite are omitted and the minister is a layperson. The Consilium always opposed the idea of preparing a "shortened" rite that could be used in ordinary circumstances; its reason was the by no means imaginary danger that there would regularly be reduced, simplified celebrations not truly signifying the first sacrament of faith. This new and different outlook, which was based not so much on juridical as on theological and pastoral considerations, subsequently gave rise to a somewhat prolonged controversy, especially with the Congregation for the Discipline of the Sacraments, which wanted to keep the distinction between ordinary and extraordinary ministers and between solemn and "private" celebrations.

5. Because the rite emphasizes the responsibility of the parents and reminds them of their obligation to raise their child in the faith, the mother's presence is desired. This went against the expectations of circles that had been trained to get the child baptized as soon as possible. The same speedy administration was also urged by the 1917 Code, can. 770.

The new rite sets down the general rule that "an infant should be baptized within the first weeks after birth" (Introduction, no. 8). This "delay" is required by the need of adequately preparing the parents and godparents so that the celebration of baptism will not be reduced to an administrative and conventional act but will have an effect on the family. In normal cases, that is, when there is no danger to the salvation of the infant, delaying baptism until the mother could take part was not considered to be against the regulation

asked that there be greater flexibility on certain points: the questions addressed to the parents and godparents, the general intercessions, the prebaptismal anointings, the formula for the profession of faith, and some of the postbaptismal rites.

After its approval by the Consilium, the rite was sent to the Holy Father on November 39, 1968. He studied it together with the secretary of the Consilium at an audience on January 19, 1969, and then wrote down a page of brief remarks.[6] The rite was examined by the Congregation of Rites on February 9, 12, 19, 20, and 24, and then sent on to the printer.[7] The Holy Father gave his final approval to the printer's proofs on May 10, 1969 (No. 138563). The *Ordo* was published by a decree of the Congregation for Divine Worship dated May 15, 1969.[8] It was the first liturgi-

---

in the Code nor against the will of the Congregation of the Holy Office, which had given the Bishop of Strasbourg an interpretation to this effect on March 20, 1958; see B. Fischer (n. 3 above), 236.

6. The Holy Father jotted down three points: "Nothing is said of original sin"; "Will not the baptism be delayed if the mother is expected to be present?"; "Godparents, canons 765-66."

7. The new rite had been approved by a letter of the Secretariat of State dated January 17, 1969 (No. 130.535). This said that the rite must be examined by the SCR. Since no other agencies were mentioned, the rite was not sent for examination to the SCDF and the Congregation for the Discipline of the Sacraments. These two agencies rightly raised the point, and from then on all rites were sent to these Congregations for criticism.

8. *Ordo Baptismi parvulorum* (Vatican Polyglot Press, 1969; 92 pp.). English translation in *The Rites of the Catholic Church* 1 (New York, 1983²) 183-283; new translation of the Introduction in *DOL* 295 nos. 2285-2315. The decree of the SCDW is in *DOL* 292 no. 2248. The decree of promulgation set September 8, 1969, as the date when the rite was to go into effect, but this had to be pushed back in order to allow the episcopal conferences time to prepare translations without rushing. On July 6, 1969, the SCDW set Easter (March 29), 1970, as the new date; see the decree in *DOL* 296 no. 2316.

In 1973, when the first printing was exhausted and a new one was planned, some unimportant corrections were introduced; see *Not* 9 (1973) 269-72. The SCDF also took the opportunity to study the entire text. The reason: the failure to have this Congregation review the text before its first publication had led to the rumor that it contained serious errors. The SCDF asked for alterations on only four points, all of which have to do with making more explicit the doctrine of original sin, which had perhaps been insufficiently emphasized in the General Introduction (on Christian Initiation). Here are the points at which changes were made: (1) In no. 2 of the General Introduction, the words "raised from their natural human condition" were replaced by "rescued from the power of darkness." (2) In no. 5, after "living word," the words "washes away every stain of sin, original and personal," were included. (3) In no. 1 of the Introduction to the Rite of Baptism for Children, the words "have or" ("cannot *have or* profess") were removed. (4) In the prayer of exorcism in no. 221, the words "from the power of darkness" were changed to "from the stain of original sin you now." See the decree of the SCDW (August 29, 1973) in *DOL* 293 no. 2249.

cal book published by the new Congregation and "a good omen for a long and happy life of fruitful labor."[9]

II. CONTENTS

The new rite contained two Introductions—a general one on Christian initiation and a more specific one on infant baptism. These were followed by the baptismal rites for several children, for a single child, for much larger groups of children, a rite for baptism administered by catechists, and a rite in danger of death. Then comes a rite for bringing to the church a child already baptized when in danger of death. Finally, there is an anthology of texts, both scriptural and euchological, for use as alternatives to those given in the body of the rite. The basic rite is that for the baptism of several children at once; this is then adapted to the various other situations.

1. *Introductions*

The General Introduction on Christian initiation explains the doctrinal and pastoral principles underlying all the rites of Christian initiation, that is, baptism, confirmation, and the Eucharist. These are followed by a description of the duties and ministries of those who play a part in the celebration of baptism, of the baptismal rites, and of the time and place for baptism. Suitable guidelines are given regarding the points that are to be further determined by the episcopal conferences or may be adapted by the minister of the sacrament.

In the second and more specific Introduction, the general principles are applied to the baptism of children. This application brings out the characteristics of the new rite, which may be summarized as follows:

a) Baptism *adapted to the real situation of children*. Children are indeed the subjects of baptism but their real condition is taken into account, and therefore they are not questioned as if they were capable of responding. They are directly addressed only when such an address is meaningful: when the minister declares their acceptance into the community or performs rites directly on them. The rite is therefore performed for the children, but the celebrant addresses the Christian community and gets them involved, especially the parents and godparents.

b) *Roles of the parents and godparents*. The emphasis in the questions, the exhortations, and the general intercessions is primarily on their duties. Moreover, it is now the parents and no longer the godparents who are

---

9. *L'Osservatore Romano*, June 19, 1969.

the focus of attention. It is the parents who bring the child to the font, make the sign of the cross on its forehead after the celebrant, profess their faith, receive the child from the font, and hold the lighted candle. Most importantly, it is they who accept the obligation of educating the child in the faith. This is their primary task.[10] The godparents flank the parents and, if the latter should be wanting, take over their task.[11] It follows that the pastor should be concerned not only with the worthy celebra-

---

10. This principle naturally led to pastoral reflection on the necessity of faith in the parents and on special situations. In some parts of the world, pagan parents and Christians in "irregular" situations (polygamy, concubinage, not practicing) ask that their children be baptized for reasons of social convenience. This question was raised especially by Bishop Bartholomew P. Hanrion, of Dapango in Togo, with reference to the Muslims of the region. The parents asking baptism had themselves not always received a Christian upbringing; yet if the children were not baptized, they would likely end up Muslims, since the parents were ashamed to be considered pagans. What was to be done in such situations?

After studying the entire question as presented by the Consilium, the SCDF on July 13, 1970, issued the following regulations in a reply to Bishop Henrion (*DOL* 297 nos. 2317-19):

1) In the case of infants of practicing Christian parents, the prescriptions of the Introduction to the rite of infant baptism are to be followed in the preparation of these parents for the baptism of their child.

2) In the case of non-Christian parents or Christian parents in irregular situations, they must be made to understand their responsibility, and the authorities must assess the value of the guarantees concerning the Catholic upbringing of the children. Such guarantees must be given at least by godparents or by some member of the family or by the Christian community. If the guarantees are sufficient, the child can be baptized, since it is baptized "in the faith of the Church." If the guarantees are insufficient, the child can be put down for baptism in the near future, and an effort will be made meanwhile to maintain pastoral contacts with the parents.

3) In the case of adults, the principles of the catechumenate as given in the *Ordo initiationis christianae adultorum* are to be followed.

All this meant that there would be a kind of infant baptism in stages, the stages reflecting the structure of the rite itself. That is, the infant is first presented to the Church and received by the Church; there follows a period in which guarantees are sought for its future rearing in the faith; finally, at what seems the most opportune moment, the actual sacramental celebration takes place. See L. Ligier's commentary on the reply: "Le Baptême des petits enfants (ex parentibus non catholicis)," *Not* 7 (1971) 64-67.

11. With regard to non-Catholic godparents, the General Introduction 10, 3 (*DOL* 294 no. 2259) accepts the rules set down in the Ecumenical Directory (nos. 48 and 57; *DOL* 147 nos. 1002 and 1011), which distinguishes between Christians of the separated Eastern Churches, who can be godparents, and Christians belonging to other non-Catholic ecclesial communities, who can be allowed only to be witnesses, along with the Catholic godfather or godmother. Some Fathers of the Consilium initially opposed this distinction as odious. On the other hand, it was obvious that the godparent had to share the faith of the Church. One Father commented: "The Orthodox would consider it scandalous to be put on the same level as the Protestants. Both have the faith indeed, but differently." After the problem had been discussed with the Secretariat of State, it was decided to stay with the regulations of the Ecumenical Directory. See "De patrinis christianis non catholicis," *Not* 7 (1971) 92-93.

tion of the sacrament but also with the spiritual preparation of the parents and godparents, seeing to it that they are aware of their responsibilities and the commitment they are undertaking for the Christian education of the child to be baptized.

c) *A communal celebration* is preferred to a private one and usually takes place in the parish church. In addition to the relatives, friends, parents, and godparents, the parish community should be represented. The community takes an active part by welcoming the new member, listening to the word of God, and professing its faith. It will be desirable to celebrate baptism at Sunday Mass now and then. Communal participation is a general desideratum that is repeated in all the liturgical rites.

The new rite also lays emphasis on baptism as the sacramental phase of incorporation into the people of God. This aspect is already mentioned in the opening rite[12] and finds expression again in the formula for anointing with chrism, which explains that the baptized child becomes a member of a priestly, prophetic, and kingly people. This dimension of baptism is also emphasized in the Scripture readings and the general intercessions.[13]

d) Baptism is the *sacrament of faith*. Children are baptized "in the faith of the Church," which St. Augustine also describes as "the faith of the parents." The questions asked of the parents and godparents are therefore very important, as is, above all, their profession of faith, in which the entire community joins.

e) *The paschal character* of the celebration is indicated by the festive nature of the celebration, white or colored vestments (depending on the practice of the various regions), the songs, the lighting of the Easter

---

12. "N., the Christian community welcomes you with great joy," says the celebrant at the end of the rite of reception. Even this text was queried by some. It was observed that the baptizand is entering the Church and not a particular Christian community. But, according to the teaching of *Lumen gentium*, every legitimately constituted Christian community is the one, holy, catholic Church of which a person becomes part via a particular community. Furthermore, the same approach is taken in the Eastern Churches. It is also of great pastoral value for concretizing the sense of belonging to the Christian community and of shared responsibility therein.

13. In some places the principle of communal celebration, preferably in the child's own parish church, came into conflict with usages and customs that gave priority to private, familial celebrations in hospitals and at certain shrines. There was an echo of the same outlook even within the Consilium. The majority, however, insisted that communal celebration is required on theological grounds; avoidance of it reflects a "familial self-centeredness" that must be overcome. In pastoral practice, the application of the principle required a wearying effort and expenditure of energy. See, e.g., for Rome: "Baptismus in valetudinariis," *Not* 7 (1971) 59–63; "Norme liturgico-pastorali per la celebrazione del Battesimo nelle Basiliche Patriarcali," *Not* 11 (1975) 75–82.

candle, and the preference for administration of the sacrament on a Sunday. It also emerges in the blessing of the water, the prayers of the exorcisms, the Scripture readings, and the general intercessions.

2. *Structure of the Rite*

This is the same in all the forms of infant baptism and has four parts: rite for the reception of the children, celebration of God's word, the baptism proper, and the concluding rites.

Reception of the children

This is the rite by which the children are received into the Christian community and become part of it. The parents ask the gift of baptism for their child and pledge themselves in the presence of the community to educate the child as a Christian.[14] The celebrant asks them what name they have given or wish to give the child. They thus have two choices: to give the name at the time of baptism or, having given it earlier, to make it known now to the Christian community. The choice respects the various practices now current or possibly to be adopted in the future.[15]

The climactic moment of these introductory rites is the signing of each child's forehead with the sign of the cross by the priest, parents, and god-

---

14. The second question to the parents is the classical one: "What do you ask of the Church for N.?" The traditional reply was "Faith." But it was observed that in this first contact with the parents, the more spontaneous and concrete reply would be "Baptism." This was therefore put first. Some Father insisted on the traditional reply ("Faith"); others made other suggestions for the reply. All these were therefore included as alternatives in the rubric: "Faith," "The grace of Christ," "Entrance into the Church," "Eternal life."

15. Different peoples have different traditions in this matter. Broadly speaking, all have their own customs when it comes to giving a child a name. Some bishops, e.g., Bishop Kovács of Hungary, said that at least in their countries the preferable course would be to have the name given during the rite, as a counterbalance to the solemnity that Marxist society attached to the giving of the name. Others supported the same course for different reasons. Archbishop Malula, on the other hand, asked that the determination be left to the episcopal conferences, since in Africa customs vary, as do the names to be given. The final text made room for both approaches.

On the question of "Christian" names see above, p. 592, n. 25. Especially after the reform of the calendar, timely publications appeared in various countries that ease the task of choosing a Christian name; see *Not* 8 (1972) 177–79. In Italian: C. Fruttero and F. Lucentini, *Il libro dei nomi di battesimo* (Ed. Mondadori, 1969); this is a careful and pleasant study of the more common names. In French: A. Vinel, *Le livre des prénoms selon le nouveau calendrier* (Paris: Albin Michel, 1962); a list with careful biographical data, the accuracy of which is ensured by the collaboration of Jacques Dubois, O.S.B., one of the best contemporary hagiographers. In English: *Saints' Names for Boys and Girls* (London: Catholic Truth Society, 1965); a modest publication containing a list of names with brief biographical information.

parents. The gesture signifies that the child belongs to the family of Christ. In the beginning some Fathers of the Consilium found that this "sign of the cross made by the parents is difficult to accept, being strange and new," but this was only a passing impression. In pastoral practice this action proved to be a felicitous gesture with rich implications. Before signing the child, the priest expresses the reception of these new members into the Christian community: "The Christian community welcomes you with great joy."

Celebration of the Word

Next comes the celebration of the Word of God, which may take place in the baptistery, if there is sufficient room there, or in the body of the church.[16]

This is the most striking novelty in the rite, and therefore there was no little hesitation about accepting it. Various difficulties were urged: the setting, the time, the commitments of the priest. Attempts were made to secure at least the possibility of exceptions, that is, to make the liturgy of the Word optional or to omit the homily.[17] The study group, however, stuck firmly to its position and allowed only that this liturgy of the Word might be reduced to a minimal form. After all, if baptism is indeed the sacrament par excellence of faith, and if this faith must be expressed by the parents, godparents, and community, then it must also be stimulated and stirred up by the word of God. There must therefore be at least one reading and a short homily.[18]

---

16. The rite allows the children to be taken to a separate room during the liturgy of the Word. This provision was made to meet the concern of some bishops and consultors that "crying infants will attract all the attention." But as J. Cellier had already remarked, if the loudspeaker system is a good one, there will be no problem. And experience has shown that it is better if the infants remain—after all, they are in fact the center of attention! Their removal detracts psychologically from the effectiveness of the instruction given to the adults. Furthermore, mothers have made it clear they want to keep the infants with them and that they have means of quieting them, though not perhaps with success on all occasions.

17. Some suggested that some homilies be included, as in the rites of ordination. But others noted that the Scripture texts provided are very numerous and that it is not possible to include homilies on all of them. The study group insisted on a homily, and rightly so: it is inconceivable that there should be a celebration of the Word without at least some minimal explanation of what has been read.

18. Even after the rite had been published, there were calls for the elimination of the liturgy of the Word. Even the SCDF twice asked that the homily be included "if opportune" (July 24, 1969; February 8, 1973). But the request was turned down, to the advantage of all, since the supposedly insuperable difficulties have proved to be quite superable.

The text of the rite (no. 44) lists five pericopes (four in the English rite), one of which is Mark 10:13-16: "Let the little children come to me." There were suggestions that this be removed as inappropriate, but experience showed that it is indeed useful, and it remained.

The liturgy of the Word is followed as usual by general intercessions, which end with a short litany containing five invocations: to the Blessed Virgin, St. John the Baptist, St. Joseph,[19] Sts. Peter and Paul, and all the saints. It is recommended, however, that the list be lengthened, especially by introducing the patron saints of the children.

The general intercessions and the litany lead into the prayer of exorcism and the prebaptismal anointing. In the early schemas of the rite, this part was extremely simplified in order to remove every expression that might strike the parents as repulsive. Discussion among the experts, however, led to a careful re-examination, doctrinal as well as pastoral, of each part of this rite.

The experts thought the exorcism and anointing should bring out the sanctification wrought by baptism through configuration with Christ, the deliverance of the children from "the power of Satan" so that they might become "temples of your glory," and the future course of the children, who are being made one with Christ so that throughout their lives they may struggle against the devil. "He is anointed as one who will have to do battle," says St. Ambrose. All these ideas found a place in the final formulation of the two prayers of exorcism and the text accompanying the anointing: "We anoint you . . . in the name of Christ our Savior; may he strengthen you with his power. . . . "[20]

Celebration of baptism

The third part of the rite begins with the blessing of the water. This blessing is always given. During the Easter season the water blessed during the Easter Vigil is used; the blessing in this case praises God for the benefits he bestows through the water. This is an effective form of instruction.

Renunciation and profession of faith. This is a very important moment because infants are baptized in the faith of their parents and the Chris-

---

19. St. Joseph was not included in the first schema. His name was added to the obligatory invocations at the insistence of a few devout prelates.

20. The episcopal conferences can for serious reasons allow the omission of the prebaptismal anointing. Some wanted to reduce "serious" to "sufficient" because of the different interpretations given to the exorcistic rite of anointing and the difficulty of understanding it when it is performed on infants. But respect for universal tradition and the meaning of the rite won the day, and the rubric was retained in its original form.

Later on there were objections from the opposite quarter, that is, that there were too few exorcisms; controversies arose about the Church's thinking in regard to the existence of the devil. But the rite does continue to be exorcistic. The reason for having fewer exorcisms in infant baptism than in the past is that the old rite was really a rite for adults. See SCDF, "Christian Faith and Demonology," *The Pope Speaks* 20 (1975) 209–33.

tian community. Two formulas are provided for the renunciation: the traditional one and a fuller one using a contemporary vocabulary that is more intelligible to people today than such words as "pomps" and "works of the devil."[21]

The profession of faith that is called for from the parents and god-parents receives the assent of the celebrant and the entire community: "This is our faith. This is the faith of the Church. We are proud to pro-fess it, in Christ Jesus our Lord. Amen."

Baptism in water immediately follows. The child is presented by the parents.[22] After the immersion the newly baptized child is anointed on the head with holy chrism. The prayer accompanying the anointing is the traditional one slightly revised. It mentions the child's deliverance from original sin and its rebirth to new life. Some would have liked to avoid any further mention of sin and to put the emphasis exclusively on the positive element of rebirth. But the removal of the mention of sin from a longstanding formula would have caused astonishment.[23]

The newly baptized child is then clad in a white garment. Some other color signifying a new creature is allowed if local usage requires.

The candle to be given to the parents is then lit from the Easter candle. The child has been "enlightened" by Christ, and the parents must help it keep the flame that Christ has lit in its heart always burning.

The final rite of this part is the *Ephphetha*, if the episcopal conference judges that it is to be included. There was a rather lively discussion about whether or not to keep this rite. The experts disagreed about whether it was appropriate to retain it, even in a new and non-exorcistic setting. The decision was finally left to the pastors involved in the experiments. They were in favor of keeping it. The *Ephphetha* in fact conveys an im-portant teaching: by reason of their baptism Christians are empowered

21. Some bishops in the Consilium had asked whether it was necessary to retain this renunciation of the devil. The response was that it is a very ancient practice; that it is needed to express the break with the devil and the movement to God; that it is the adult commu-nity that is committing itself. At the same time, however, the need was felt of having a formula more adapted to our time. Cardinal Pellegrino: "The renunciations should certainly not be eliminated. But I ask whether the formulas of Tertullian did not fit better with his own age. Would not a positive form be better today?" As a result, the second formula of renunciation was composed.

22. The discussion brought out the objection that the godparents might feel too cut off from the ceremony. It was insisted, however, that the emphasis must be on the primary responsibility of the parents. Any ruffled feathers of the godparents can be handled in the particular rituals.

23. One person observed: "There are too many progressivists opposed to this truth of the faith." Another: "It would be different if we were dealing with an entirely new text."

to hear the word of God, to open their mouths in praise of the Lord, and to take an active part in the liturgical assembly and the life of the Church.[24]

Concluding rites

From the baptistery the newly baptized children are carried in procession to the altar. The point of this rite is to foreshadow the completion of Christian initiation by confirmation and the Eucharist. The celebrant reminds the parents of this before all join in reciting the Our Father.[25]

The rite of baptism ends with the solemn blessing of the mothers, fathers, and all present. If customary, the blessing is followed by a procession to the altar of the Blessed Virgin,[26] where the children are consecrated to her.[27] In any case, it is appropriate that there be at least a closing hymn to Our Lady.

3. *Other Forms*

1. *For a single child.* After the rite for several children there is one for a single child. This differs from the preceding only in rubrical adaptations substituting the singular for the plural. This rite is provided simply for the convenience of the celebrant.

2. *For a large number of children.* This rite was prepared at the request of some Latin American bishops for the celebration of baptism at large shrines where, in addition to the regular celebrations on Sunday, priests must often baptize hundreds of children.[28] The overall structure remains the same as in the basic *Ordo*, but some rites are simplified. If there are

---

24. There was a similar discussion of another part of the ceremony that was eventually dropped: the "giving of salt," on which the attention of the faithful used to be so much focused. Some wanted to keep it as an optional rite (Martimort), but the experts could find no plausible explanation for it and, on the other hand, thought it unwise to substitute a different practice that would confuse the faithful.

25. This part, too, became clearer from schema to schema. "Why a procession to the altar if there is no Eucharistic communion?" (Canon Pilkington). "The child should be placed on the altar; otherwise the procession is likely to be simply a pious act and nothing more" (A.-M. Roguet).

26. It was the bishops who reminded the Consilium of local traditions of going to the Blessed Virgin's altar in procession. They also asked that there be some invocation of Mary. These requests led to the final rubric and the reference to the singing of the *Magnificat*.

27. Some experts thought the closing rites too long and asked that they be made optional. Others, however, noted that something should be provided and the conclusion not left entirely to improvisation.

28. On February 5, 1966, after repeated requests based on the pastoral situation, the Consilium allowed the Brazilian shrine of Nossa Senhora de Aparecida do Norte to use an *ordo brevior* of baptism in cases where a large number were to be baptized; the concession was to be valid until the publication of the new rite of baptism.

not enough ministers to perform them, the two anointings are omitted, but the accompanying formula is recited.

As a matter of fact, the Fathers were quite perplexed by this solution, especially for the postbaptismal anointing, since the latter is a rite that has been a constant part of the tradition and is basic for bringing out the priestly, prophetic, and kingly status of the baptized. They would have preferred that laypersons be allowed to perform the anointing. In the vote taken on October 15, 1968, the members of the Consilium were almost equally divided on omitting or keeping the chrismation, while two thirds were in favor of using laypersons to perform it if it were kept. But the decision of the Congregation for the Doctrine of the Faith was opposed to this.

3. *Rite for catechists.* The Constitution on the Liturgy had asked that a rite of baptism be drawn up which catechists could use in the absence of a priest or deacon (no. 68). The rite for use by catechists is the same as that for a large number of children, but with the omission of everything a layperson cannot do, such as the exorcisms, the anointings, and the blessing of the water.[29]

The Fathers of the Consilium called for laypersons being allowed at least to bless the water. They supported their petition by an appeal to article 79 of the liturgical Constitution, according to which some sacramentals can be administered by laypersons. The Fathers found it odd that a person able to do the more important thing, namely, to administer the sacrament of baptism, should be unable to do the less important, such as to bless the water.

The vote taken by the Fathers was unanimous, with one exception, that laypersons should be given authority to bless the water for baptism.

---

29. On July 13, 1965, Bishop E. Loosdregt, president of the episcopal conference of Laos-Cambodia, had asked the Consilium whether the episcopal conference could authorize catechists to perform actions regarded as priestly in the sacrament of baptism, namely, exorcism, anointings, and the giving of salt, candle, and white garment. A reply was postponed until publication of the new rite.

The Consilium in turn put the question to the SCDF, which gave a negative reply on March 6, 1968, on the grounds that any cases were sporadic and occasional, but also for doctrinal reasons: "The decision of this Congregation is also dictated by a lively concern that such concessions will tend to the gradual and unnoticed blurring of the distinction between common priesthood and ministerial priesthood, as though the difference were not essential but a matter of degree. The result would be the loss in the Christian people of an awareness and sensitivity to the distinction. This in turn would have extremely serious consequences; indeed some alarming effects of it are already discernible." The Congregation therefore decided that permission for such steps "not be left to the decision of the local episcopal conferences but be completely removed from the guidelines given in the new rite of baptism."

But the decision was suspended until such time as a general position should be reached on the application of article 79.[30]

4. *Baptism in danger of death.* This is a simple rite for use in cases in which there is time at most to gather a few friends and relatives and when,

---

30. This rite for catechists also had its subsequent history. On October 30, 1969, the Congregation for the Discipline of the Sacraments asked the Pope for the clarification of various points in the celebration of baptism: godparents, registration, time and place, and, in particular, the authorization of laypersons to administer baptism apart from danger of death. On December 31 (No. 152360) the Holy Father allowed such a study to be made, but the views of the SCDF and the SCDW were also to be sought.

It seems that the Congregation of the Sacraments had already discussed the matter at one of its plenary sessions. In more specific terms, the request was, first, for a determination of "the conditions (moral and, more broadly, canonical) under which 'prepared' laypersons (comparable to the 'catechists' of the mission lands) might be allowed to administer baptism with the rite described in Chapter IV of the new *Ordo*"; and, further, "how to decide on the granting of permission for the administration of baptism by one who is not, strictly speaking, a catechist, or, in other words, what is the unambiguous juridical form for deciding when there is a habitual lack of priest and deacon."

The SCDW communicated its thinking on these various points in a lengthy statement of February 3, 1970. With regard to laypersons being allowed to celebrate baptism, whether the concession was given in a general way or to individual bishops requesting it, the Congregation recommended "that there not be too many detailed qualifications that would in the end only make things more complicated and give rise to the kind of casuistry that has so often proved useless." The Congregation proposed that the decision as to whether there is a habitual lack of a priest or deacon be left to the local bishop.

The decisions (approved by the Holy Father) of the Congregation of the Sacraments were that authorization be given by that Congregation "after a request from the local Ordinary," and that the minister in such cases be chosen from the following groups in descending order: "seminarians, lay religious, religious women, simple laypersons." The granting of permission was to depend on four conditions:

"a) an ordinary minister of baptism (priest or deacon) must be habitually lacking in the locality. The judgment as to the habitual lack (physical or moral) of the ordinary minister everywhere or in a part of the national territory is left to the episcopal conference;

"b) the seminarians allowed to baptize must be taking at least the introduction to theology and be eighteen years old;

"c) the lay religious, men and women, must be at least eighteen years old and have made their first religious profession or accepted an equivalent obligation; they must also have received adequate training in catechetics;

"d) the laypersons must be twenty-one and have obtained from their own pastor a testimony to their moral life and religious practice; in addition to the needed training as catechists, they must have been sufficiently trained in the administration of baptism."

"Judgment on the suitability of the laypersons, who are preferably to be chosen from among the members of Catholic associations, is left to the Ordinary. It is appropriate, however, that the national episcopal conference establish basic standards of suitability that hold for the entire national territory." These guidelines were for places "outside mission territories."

It was impossible to be more detailed. No one knows what happened to this set of standards, which was never published. Someone, however, undoubtedly felt satisfied at having done his duty and providing remedies for possible serious abuses.

though the ordinary minister is lacking, there is someone present who is capable of leading the common prayer. The rite is extremely simple: general intercessions, prayer for the child, profession of faith, baptism, Our Father. The intention is that these essential elements should stir faith and feed common prayer, so that even in such a case, if time and other conditions allow, there may be a short but effective celebration.

5. Finally some instructions are given for *bringing to the church* a child already baptized. The case expressly considered is that of a child previously baptized in danger of death, but a rubric speaks of the adaptations needed for other cases. The point is made that because it has already received the sacrament, the child is already a member of the Church.

Confirmation

I. History

The path of reform for the rite of confirmation was a long and difficult one because of the many problems connected with the sacrament, the uncertainties, and the diversity in theological and pastoral thinking about it. There were, and remain, questions about the connection of confirmation with baptism, a connection that the liturgical Constitution had asked should be made to stand out more clearly; about the minister, the matter and form, the best age for reception; about the very meaning of the sacrament. The theologians, who had the added spur of pastoral needs, had interpreted the sacrament in a variety of ways: completion of baptism, sacrament of adolescence, of the apostolate, of the solemn profession of faith, of Catholic action. All these problems reared their heads, sometimes with passionate insistence, in the studies conducted by the Consilium and in the solutions proposed there.

1. *First Phase*

As early as the period when preparations were being made for the Council, some bishops had been asking that, above all else, answers be found to the question of the age for confirmation and the question of its minister.

The Consilium was asked to give its views on these points. On October 11, 1964, a special group was established to study the pastoral problem of the age for confirmation. Three questions were posed to the group:[1]

---

1. *Relators:* B. Fischer and P.-M. Gy; *members:* Cardinal G. Bevilacqua, M. Righetti, B. Botte, C. Vagaggini, J. A. Jungmann, and J. Delcuve.

1) Are there *theological* reasons that exclude, require, or recommend a specific age for the reception of confirmation?

2) Are there theological or pastoral reasons that exclude, require, or recommend a specific age for the reception of confirmation *in the Latin Church?*

3) Do *local traditions* or *special pastoral needs* urge a specific age in some regions?[2]

The intention was above all to establish a theological basis on which to tackle the pastoral problem. Father Gy and Professor Fischer presented the Consilium with a general report on the replies received from the experts who had been consulted. The conclusion to be drawn from these replies was by and large opposed to any change in the age for reception.

Meanwhile Father Jungmann, who, along with Cardinal Bevilacqua, had proved to be one of the most convinced proponents of adolescence as the best age for reception, was preparing an outline for a motu proprio.

In February of 1966 the Secretariat of State told the secretary of the Consilium that the Holy Father wanted a solution to the problem. On March 2 the secretariat of the Consilium put the question to four theologians, to whom it sent the report of Gy and Fischer and a statement of Cardinal Bevilacqua.[3]

At an audience on June 20, 1966, Cardinal Lercaro presented the Holy Father with a complete statement on the question of the age for confirmation. The Pope then expressed his own thoughts on the matter, which the Cardinal reported as follows:

> The Consilium is to draft an instruction on the sacrament of confirmation. After a doctrinal introduction, two directives are to be given and explained:
>
> 1) Confirmation is to be regarded as the sacrament of adolescence, preferably to be conferred at the point when Christians have completed their obligatory schooling and are entering upon their subsequent life.
>
> 2) The bishop is to remain the ordinary minister, and there are to be no requests for permission to let priests administer the sacrament.[4]

---

2. The list of questions was sent to the members of the group on October 15, 1964.

3. A reply was requested by March 20, 1966; the Holy Father was fully informed of the steps taken and had given his approval.

4. During the Council all bishops had been authorized to delegate some priests to celebrate the sacrament of confirmation in their absence; see *AAS* 54 (1962) 780. After the Council requests continued to come in for the same authorization. The Holy Father showed himself consistently reluctant in the face of requests for the renewal of privileges received at one time and of new requests; concessions were in fact made only from year to year, in expectation that the whole problem would be resolved by the new rite of confirmation; as a result, there was pressure to complete the rite.

For example, on March 21, 1964 (No. 20219), in response to a request from the Arch-

N.B. Look at the interesting studies that have appeared in two issues of *La Maison-Dieu*.[5]

Preparation of the document was entrusted to Father Vagaggini. The idea was to issue a motu proprio that would deal primarily with the age for confirmation, and then an instruction that would give pastoral guidelines for applying the pontifical document.[6] The motu proprio was prepared in accordance with the guidelines given by the Pope and was sent to him on January 20, 1967. In it the author established a pastoral context and then developed three essential aspects of the subject:

1. From the *theological* standpoint, there is no difficulty about postponing confirmation to the years of adolescence if there are sufficiently serious pastoral reasons for doing so and provided due precautions are taken. Confirmation is a distinct sacrament from baptism; at the same time, it completes and crowns baptism, in the sense that the gift received in baptism is intensified with a view to a more binding deputation to certain Christian duties. The baptized are filled with the power of the Holy Spirit, as the apostles were on the day of Pentecost, so that they may be faithful witnesses to Christ before the world. The relation between confirmation and the Eucharist is not to be understood to exclude the reception of first communion before confirmation.

In the administration of the sacraments the Church has the authority (provided only that it leaves the substance of the sacraments unchanged) to establish or alter what it thinks advisable, according to circumstances,

---

bishop of Lyons, it was said that "it would be better, in attempting to facilitate administration of confirmation in your vast archdiocese, to ask for another auxiliary bishop or to seek help from other bishops who might be resident in the territory." Again, on December 4, 1965, the Congregation of the Sacraments was asked to restudy "the matter, possibly bringing in the Consilium as well, with a view to highlighting in a felicitous way this aspect of the sacrament [i.e., administration by a bishop], which allows the individual believer to come in contact with the hierarchy of the Church at the very moment when he or she is becoming a conscious, militant Christian."

5. After the Pope had spoken to the Cardinal, the Secretariat of State communicated the Pope's thinking to him once again on July 16, 1966, in an unsigned typewritten memorandum that set down, sometimes in a somewhat lengthier form, the guidelines already noted down by the Cardinal. For example, the memorandum says of the nature of confirmation: "Confirmation must be seen to be a true strengthening of baptismal grace, that is, a commitment to the faithful profession embodied in a Christian life. There must therefore be an adequate preparation for this conscious, decisive act by which young persons make the baptismal promises their own, give their life a Christian orientation, profess their personal faith in a public way, and become active, militant members of the Christian community. The minister of confirmation is to be the bishop, the pastor and head of the community."

6. At an audience on September 26, 1966, it was suggested that the plan for a motu proprio be sent to the presidents of the episcopal conferences so that there might be more extensive consultation on it.

for the advantage of those who receive the sacraments and for the dignity of the sacraments themselves. As a matter of fact, history shows that there have been variations in the practice of this sacrament as different circumstances and different pastoral concerns have led the Church to emphasize now one, now another aspect of it.

2. Some pastors in the Latin Church are asking that confirmation be postponed to adolescence. In other periods of its history the Church has departed from its earliest practice and put off the administration of this sacrament to the age of reason or even later. Consequently, a further postponement to the beginning of adolescence does not imply the influence of some new theological principle. In certain situations the postponement can be a pastorally enlightened step taken for the sake of more effective instruction.

3. If, then, the individual episcopal conferences think it opportune for pastoral reasons, and if due precautions are taken, they may postpone the administration of confirmation to an age that they themselves shall define more closely.[7]

On May 25 of that year the Pope wrote down his own observations:

1. Not only the Code but Leo XIII should be cited, since his authority is invoked in support of the law that fixes seven as the age for confirmation. We are departing from that ruling, which was made, be it noted, at a time when first communion was still put off to the age of ten or twelve or fourteen.

2. Include an approval of the present regulations regarding the administration of confirmation by the parish priest to seriously ill children.

3. Something further should be said about the pastoral reasons for postponing confirmation to an age beyond seven (in order to give instruction adapted to adolescence [the solemn communion that is still customary in France has the same purpose]; to elicit from the confirmands a more con-

---

7. The plan of the document was modest and flexible. It did not go into disputed questions or support ambiguous theories. It did not even press the episcopal conferences for a change in discipline in regard to the age of reception. It was content to say only that there could be circumstances in which postponement might have a pastoral value, and it gave permission for such a postponement. Nor did it say anything of the Holy See's desire not to assign the ministry of confirmation to priests, for it intended to deal with this in a separate communication.

The document was in fact so respectful of the freedom of the conferences to make decisions in these areas that when it was presented to the Pope, there went with it a proposal to complete it not only by a practical instruction of a pastoral kind and by the reform of the rite itself but also by the possible creation of a sacramental that would be suited to the period of adolescence. This last could be used as an alternative in places where the authorities thought it better to keep the existing practice of confirmation at the age of seven.

scious act of faith and commitment through a renewal of baptismal promises now strengthened by the grace of the Holy Spirit; to remind all Christians more effectively that they must be strong and faithful, be witnesses, apostles, and missionaries, and so on).

4. The sponsor for baptism can serve again for confirmation, if this is helpful.

5. It would be advisable to publish, along with the motu proprio,

a) the new rite of confirmation (at present, among other things, the confirmand does not say a word, not even an "Amen," throughout the administration of confirmation!);

b) the instruction on confirmation. Many of the historical details on confirmation can be transferred here from the Motu Proprio, leaving only the regulatory part in the latter.

On February 21, 1967, the Pope was presented with a second draft of the motu proprio on the age of confirmation with the corrections suggested in his note.[8]

All the papers were sent back to the Consilium on July 24, 1967, with the opinions of the Congregation for the Doctrine of the Faith and the Congregation of Rites.[9] The file contained the definitive text of the motu proprio as corrected by Monsignor Tondini and prepared for the printer.

But nothing was done with the document. The adverse opinion of the Congregation for the Doctrine of the Faith made postponement advisable.[10]

---

8. It was suggested, however, that no reference be made to the letter *Abrogata* of Leo XIII to the Bishop of Marseilles, lest this entail an exegetical and theological interpretation of the meaning and authority of papal statements. As a matter of fact, Leo's letter did not impose the practice of confirmation at the age of seven; many bishops continued to ignore it; see A.-G. Martimort, "La Confirmation," in *Communion solennelle et profession de foi* (Paris, 1952), 194. It was suggested, therefore, that the motu proprio be published first and then the new rite of confirmation and the instruction, for reasons of time and also in order that the pontifical document might serve as a basis for the other two.

9. The SCR had replied on April 10, 1967, and shown itself in favor. The Congregation of the Sacraments was likewise in favor of the document (February 28, 1967). In the following year the views of the Italian episcopal conference were also requested (April 22, 1968); the conference replied on May 9. The problem had evidently not been forgotten.

10. The prefect of the Congregation for the Doctrine of the Faith wrote to the Cardinal Secretary of State on July 12, 1967: "The Fathers of this Congregation have studied the plan submitted to them and at their plenary session on Wednesday, July 7 of this year, have decided that the episcopal conferences should be given authority to decide, in light of the situation in each country, the age at which the sacrament of confirmation should be conferred and that therefore the publication of a pontifical document on the subject does not seem opportune at this time." The arrangement suggested by the Congregation for the Doctrine of the Faith was taken over into the Introduction to the new rite.

2. Second Phase: Preparation of the Rite

Revision of the rite of confirmation was entrusted to study group 20.[11] The first report on its work came at the ninth general meeting of the Consilium (November 1967). The schema there presented for discussion by the Fathers and consultors[12] took up some general questions: the mandate of the Council; confirmation as the second step in Christian initiation; the age of the confirmand; the minister; problems connected with the rite itself (imposition of hands, chrismation, sacramental formula). The report thus represented a panoramic exploration of the entire subject. The Fathers approved both the general approach taken and the following points in particular:

> Confirmation is to be celebrated during Mass or, in any case, with a liturgy of the Word; the Pope is to be asked to let bishops delegate priests for confirmation; priests may help the bishop with the chrismation; the godparent can be the same as for baptism, or if there is no godparent, the parents may present the confirmand.

At the next general meeting (the tenth in April, 1968), the group was able to submit the complete rite for examination by the Consilium. This, however, did not include the Introduction, which had to wait upon the determination of the various parts of the rite and the answer to pending questions.[13] The schema was approved as a whole and in its parts, and it was thought that it might be sent out for experimental use in some places in order to test its value. This was not possible, however, since the sacramental formula had been changed.

3. Publication

After this approval by the Consilium, the group redacted the complete text of the rite,[14] but another three years were to pass before it could be published. For at this point the rite began a long and wearisome journey, the stages of which are not easy to follow. The reason for the delay was the need of clarifying the questions of the minister, the matter and form of the sacrament,[15] and certain other details regarding which the

---

11. *Relator:* B. Botte; *secretary:* B. Kleinheyer; *members:* J. Nabuco, E. Lengeling, C. Vogel, P. Jounel, and J. Lécuyer. In keeping with the usual manner of the relator, the work was done almost exclusively by him and the secretary. Contacts with the other members of the group were maintained through letters and not by meetings in the proper sense of the term.

12. See Schema 240: *De Pontificali* 16 (September 17, 1967), discussed on November 20 with the relators and on November 21 with the bishops; see *Not* 3 (1967) 414.

13. The rite was discussed on April 20 with the relators and on April 24 with the bishops.

14. Schema 326: *De Pontificali* 19 (November 15, 1968).

15. To these might be added the problem of the age for confirmation, which came up

Congregation of the Sacraments in particular displayed a degree of juridical "punctiliousness."[16]

Further time was also required for preparation of the apostolic constitution, since the matter of the sacrament had to be determined and a new sacramental formula approved.[17]

The new *Ordo* was finally published by a decree of the Congregation for Divine Worship dated August 22, 1971; the apostolic constitution *Divinae consortium naturae* was dated August 15, 1971.[18]

---

at all the Consilium meetings on confirmation. The relator held fast to the principle that the sequence baptism–confirmation–Eucharist must be respected and that the tradition of the Roman Church on confirmation at the age of seven must be maintained. As we have already seen, the solution proposed by the SCDF would finally be adopted.

16. I shall list only the main stages of the long journey of the document through the Curia: November 30, 1968: document sent to the Pope, who replies on February 17, 1969, that it should be sent to the SCDF for "determination of the valid form." February 1, 1969: document sent to the SCDF. April 23, 1969: joint committee of the SCDF and the SCDW. December 9, 1969: new text sent to the SCDF. January 3, 1970: sent to Pope, who asks (January 14, 1970) for a new revision by the SCDF and the Congregation of the Sacraments and, in particular, "that a clear theological determination be made of several points: what form is to be regarded as essential for a valid sacrament; who may grant authority to administer confirmation; how this authority is to be given. For, once the new rite allows bishops to use the help of simple priests even in the rite of anointing with chrism, doubts and uncertainties may arise; it is therefore necessary to give careful answers to the questions listed above."

March 27, 1970: document dispatched once more to the SCDF and the Congregation of Sacraments, as well as to Propaganda. April, 1970: the thirteenth general meeting of the Consilium studies and approves the Introduction; see *Not* 6 (1970) 227. April 21, 1970: Introduction sent to the SCDF, Sacraments, and Propaganda. July 11, 1970: the SCDF gives its *nihil obstat* "on condition that the Consilium wait for the publication of the apostolic constitution and that it take acount of the points" made therein and on other occasions. July 17, 1970: joint committee of Sacraments and SCDW. December 18, 1970: new submission of the document to the Congregation of the Sacraments, and reply.

May 7, 1971: final *nihil obstat* of the SCDF. May 12, 1971: another joint meeting of Sacraments and SCDW. July 20, 1971: Pope is given the document as corrected after all the above meetings and after the apostolic constitution had been written. July 26, 1971: Pope discusses document at an audience with the secretary of the SCDW. August 4, 1971: Pope sends his approval (No. 191138).

17. This determination was the task of the SCDF, which asked for the collaboration of the SCDW (July 11, 1970). It was sent another schema, composed by P. Jounel, which considered all three sacraments of Christian initiation. This was not accepted, because the constitution was to limit itself to confirmation. Several meetings of the SCDF, Sacraments, and SCDW were held until the text was finally ready on March 31, 1971.

18. *Ordo confirmationis* (Vatican Polyglot Press, 1971; 52 pp.). The English form of the rite is in *The Rites of the Catholic Church* 1 (New York, 1983[2]) 307–54. There is a new translation of the Introduction in *DOL* 305 nos. 2510-28. The apostolic constitution is in *DOL* 303 nos. 2499-2508. The decree of the SCDW is in *DOL* 304 no. 2509. See the commentaries of U. Betti and G. Pasqualetti in *Not* 7 (1971) 332-46 and 347-51 respectively.

In addition to the apostolic constitution and the Introduction, the *Ordo* has five chapters. The first four give in succession the rite of confirmation during Mass, the rite outside Mass, the rite celebrated by an extraordinary minister, and the rite celebrated in danger of death. The last chapter is a collection of prayers and Scripture readings.

The structure of the rite is the same in all cases: liturgy of the Word, homily, renewal of baptismal promises, laying on of hands, chrismation, general intercessions, and at the end a solemn blessing. The rite is also very simple, so that it can be celebrated in a dignified way even if there is a large number of confirmands.

In view of the special character of this sacrament, it seemed appropriate to introduce a specific mention of the Holy Spirit into the baptismal promises, which are the principal way in which the connection with baptism is brought out.

The other euchological parts underwent only such revision as seemed to be required by the more linear structure of the new rite; the prayers were also, of course, revised in the light of textual criticism. As in the rite of ordinations, a homily that can serve the celebrant as an outline is provided.

Despite a certain loosening of the discipline in particular cases, the new rite as a whole highlights the person of the bishop and contact with him as successor of the apostles and primary minister of this sacrament. See especially the homily, the end of the general intercessions, and the mention to be made of the bishop when the minister is not himself a bishop (Introduction, no. 18). Likewise, when the bishop decides to let priests play a role in the celebration by helping him with the chrismation, they receive the holy chrism from his hands to indicate that he is the primary minister and they his assistants; they are thus true ministers of the sacrament but become such only by appointment from the bishop and in communion with him. In the absence of the bishop or someone else with authority to confirm, priests could not take this step.

II. The Main Questions

It will be appropriate here to call attention to the resolution of the main problems that bedeviled the entire preparation of the rite, delayed its publication, and perhaps influenced the preparation inasmuch as the delay kept the study group from having its work backed by experience and experiment.

1. *Sponsors*

It is advisable that the sponsor at confirmation should ordinarily be the same as at baptism; this will promote continuity in the educational task of the godparent and spur the god-parent's interest. Having the same sponsor will also underscore the close union between baptism and confirmation (Introduction, no. 5).[19]

2. *Minister*

The bishop is the *primary* minister of confirmation. Communion with the bishop as successor of the apostles must also be emphasized when the minister is not a bishop (Introduction, no. 7).[20]

Ordinary faculties (that is, authorization bestowed by law) for confirmation are given to certain groups of persons: those who, even though not bishops, do in fact govern dioceses; those who carry out the Christian initiation of adults; those who receive a convert into the Church; and those who carry out the Christian initiation of a child of school age.

The authorization to confirm in danger of death that is already given by the Decree *Spiritus Sancti munera* is broadened in response to numerous requests from bishops at the time of the Council.[21]

---

19. There is no prohibition against having a new and distinct sponsor or against the parents themselves presenting the confirmand to the bishop. More detailed regulations are left to the local bishop. The SCDW had suggested that an adult confirmand might present himself or herself without a sponsor because this better reflects the real situation and possibly because of psychological reasons (adults prefer to stand on their own and be the guarantors of their own decisions). The proposal was not acceptable to the Congregation of the Sacraments, but it is quite possible that adults may in fact not have sponsors, for the Introduction says that while "as a rule" there is to be a sponsor, it is up to the bishop to determine diocesan practice (no. 5).

20. There was some difficulty about the word "primary," some preferring the more juridical term "ordinary." But the term *originarius* ("primary") is used in *Lumen gentium* 26 and shows that the bishop's office makes him the "natural" minister of this sacrament.

21. The position proposed by the SCDW was broader and extended to "every priest." The Congregation of the Sacraments insisted, however, that the faculty be restricted to priests "who have the care of souls" and then extended to "any priest who is not disqualified by censure or canonical penalty."

When considering the question of the minister, the Consilium in its final schema had proposed a greater loosening of the present discipline. It said: "The bishop has the habitual authority to delegate priests to administer confirmation, even outside the danger of the confirmand's death, whenever the person's spiritual and pastoral welfare requires. Not infrequently there are very large dioceses in which it is not always easy to have the bishop appear at regular intervals to administer confirmation; this creates difficulties at the pastoral level and even at the strictly liturgical level" (Schema 326: *De Pontificali* 19, p. 3). On May 10, 1969, the SCDF wrote that at their meetings of March 26 and April 16 the Fathers of that Congregation had come to a *non expedire* decision regarding "the habitual authori-

When there are many confirmands or when other real necessities require it, the minister of confirmation may coopt other priests for the general imposition of hands (but only the principal minister says the prayer) and for the rite of chrismation. These others then become true ministers of the sacrament along with the principal minister.[22] The priests who can be allowed to celebrate the sacrament are described in detail.[23]

3. *Matter and Form*

The rite depends at this point on what is decreed in the apostolic constitution on the sacrament of confirmation: "The sacrament of confirmation is conferred through the anointing with chrism on the forehead, which is done by the laying on of the hand and through the words: Be sealed with the gift of the Holy Spirit."

This determination of the matter means that chrismation becomes the sacramental sign. But the apostolic constitution does not come out and say this in so many words because the tradition of the Latin Church had given pride of place to the laying on of hands, a gesture coming down from the apostles. The lengthy discussion of the matter of the sacrament

---

zation to be granted bishops for delegating priests to administer confirmation even outside the danger of death."

22. The Consilium had suggested this possibility in order to ensure the dignified celebration of the sacrament on those occasions when there are many confirmands and the ceremony takes a long time and becomes boring, with a resultant diminishment in the intensity of the sacramental experience. It also thought of the concession as a help in another part of the rite that takes a great deal of time and is complementary to the first. The above-cited letter of the SCDF says on this point: "As regards the minister of the sacrament, the Fathers of this Congregation agree with the concession given in the new ritual, whereby the priests present can help the bishop in the rite of chrismation. The Holy Father, too, has approved this part of the rite, but he also noted that the bishops should make use of this authorization *only rarely* and in cases of *real necessity*, since confirmation is an occasion for a direct encounter of the bishop with his faithful."

23. On this point, too, there were lengthy negotiations with the Congregation of the Sacraments, which insisted on a more specific description of the persons whom the bishop might make his associates, since the validity of the sacrament was at stake. First place in this list was given to those possessing some "dignity": vicar general, episcopal delegate, etc.

It was pointed out, however, that these persons do not usually accompany the bishop on his pastoral visits or confirmation journeys and that in many regions the bishop must make use of the priests available. Too restrictive a list would hinder the bishop rather than help him as is intended. Moreover, since it is the bishop who makes the choice on each occasion, there is no danger of an invalid sacrament. At least the list should be made nonexclusive by substituting *"expedit"* for *"necesse"* in no. 8. The suggestion was not accepted.

The only course left was to demand the widest possible range of persons who might become the bishop's associates, including the parish priests of the place and of the confirmands and priests who had been in charge of their instruction.

that went on especially in the Congregation for the Doctrine of the Faith was always conducted in a way that suggested that only the form and not the matter of the sacrament was being changed.

On the other hand, it was also thought necessary to remove doubts arising from the older rubric in the Pontifical, though it was only in 1725 that the latter was introduced into an extract from the Roman Pontifical; it subsequently appeared again in an appendix to the Pontifical that was published in 1888 under Leo XIII. This rubric prescribed a mini-laying on of the hand during the act of chrismation. This gave rise to not a few perplexities. The new apostolic constitution therefore intends to say that chrismation replaces the laying on of the hand, or, in other words, that the action of anointing the forehead is already by its nature a laying on of the hand.

The text of the constitution would have been clearer if the subsequent explanation (now given in the Introduction) had been retained; this said that the rite is made up of a laying on of hands and a chrismation, "but chrismation alone is required for a valid sacrament." This statement was removed, however, during the final revision made with the Holy Father on August 27, 1971, in order not to diminish the importance of the laying on of hands. In fact the point would be clarified later on.[24]

The position of the Consilium and the Congregation for Divine Worship had been clear from the beginning: assign equal value to the two actions—the general laying on of hands and the chrismation—and remove

---

24. See the reply of the Pontifical Commission for the Interpretation of the Decrees of Vatican II to a query on the essential sacramental gesture for confirmation (June 9, 1972): *DOL* 306 no. 2529. This explains that anointing with the thumb is sufficient, that is, that an anointing done in this form sufficiently expresses the laying on of hands. See the commentary in *Not* 8 (1972) 281–86.

Without taking a position on the sacramental value of the gesture, the Consilium's schema had laid a great deal of emphasis on a true and proper laying of hands on the confirmands by the bishop and his concelebrants. The schema said: "The laying on of hands continues to be the sacramental sign par excellence of the conferral of the Holy Spirit, as is clear from the entire tradition. The gesture is even further emphasized when the celebrant does it for each confirmand, at least when the number of confirmands is not large."

The possibility of a laying on of hands on each individual was discussed at length in the Consilium, because some saw this as a kind of priestly ordination. The decision was finally left to the further reflection of the study group; the group allowed it as a possibility. It was subsequently removed, however, and only a collective laying on of hands remained. In its own study of the schema, the SCDF came back repeatedly to this point as it sought to define the matter of the sacrament; it showed itself much concerned not to obscure the laying on of hands. For this reason the apostolic constitution itself adds that even though the collective laying on of hands is not required for validity, it should be regarded as very important, since "it contributes to the complete perfection of the rite and to a more thorough understanding of the sacrament" (*DOL* 303 no. 2507).

from the latter the laying on of the hand that was prescribed in the rubric of the former Pontifical: "the right hand being laid on the head of the confirmand."[25]

In any case, the apostolic constitution itself takes time to demonstrate by an analysis of history and documents (especially those of Innocent IV and the Council of Florence) that there is continuity between the apostolic tradition of the laying on of hands and the signing of the forehead with chrism. In both East and West the chrismation has now replaced the laying on of hands. It is more expressive and is itself in fact a form of laying on of the hand, since it is accomplished through contact of the hand with the forehead.[26]

The final determination of the sacramental matter by the constitution reflects the hesitation felt by the Congregation for the Doctrine of the Faith, which did not want to lose the reference to a laying on of the hand in the act of chrismation.[27] Be that as it may, the constitution as a whole

---

25. The first version of no. 9 of the Introduction had been quite clear: "The sacramental rite of confirmation consists in the laying of hands on the candidates with the prayer, 'All-powerful God . . . ,' and an anointing of the forehead with the words 'Receive the seal of the gift of the Holy Spirit.'

"Therefore, although in case of necessity, and in keeping with the usual interpretation of the rite, the chrismation with its accompanying formula is enough for a valid conferral of the sacrament, the laying on of hands is to be highly esteemed, since it was part of the apostolic rite and is part of the full sacramental sign."

26. See B. Botte, "Problèmes de la Confirmation," *Questions liturgiques* 1 (1972) 3–8; *Not* 8 (1972) 284.

27. In his letter of May 10, 1969, to the SCDW, Cardinal Šeper made known the decision of the SCDF: "What is laid down in canon 780 of the [1917] Code of Canon Law is to be maintained; accordingly, by the laying on of hands which is required for the validity of the sacrament is meant only the laying on which takes place in the act of anointing, as in the tradition." But the Pope then expressed a wish for further explanation. A theological committee was appointed which approved the text cited in note 25; the Pope then gave his own approval on June 26, 1970 (letter of the SCDF, July 11, 1970).

Subsequently, however, some Fathers of the SCDF voiced apprehensions and suggested some other formulations: "the anointing, which is necessarily accompanied by a laying on of the hand, is essential for the sacrament"; "an anointing which by its nature implies a laying on of the hand"; "the laying on of the minister's hand in the act of anointing." The intention was to bring out the fact that there was no change in the matter of the sacrament as described in canon 780.

The Pope also asked for a statement by the SCDW on the practice of the Eastern Churches (January 21, 1971). Finally, after another small committee (drawn from the Congregation for the Eastern Churches, the Congregation of the Sacraments, and the SCDW) had studied the matter, as requested by the Pope on January 27, 1971, this statement was chosen: "The sacrament is conferred by anointing with chrism on the forehead." But when the text of the apostolic constitution was being composed, the question was raised once again; the result was the formulation in the published constitution.

On the whole matter see C. Vagaggini, O.S.B., " 'Per unctionem chrismatis in fronte,

and the subsequent clarification of it make it clear that only the signing with chrism is required and is the essential matter of the sacrament.

4. *The Sacramental Formula*

It was universally acknowledged that the old formula: "I sign you with the sign of the cross and I confirm you with the chrism of salvation in the name of the Father . . . ," did not suitably express the meaning of the sacrament. The study group therefore made a careful study of the texts of the Western and Eastern traditions. They were looking for a text that would express the external action of signing, that is, sealing the initiation, and at the same time the effect of the sacrament, which is the giving of the gift of the Holy Spirit.

The formula that seemed best to meet the need is the one used in the Byzantine rite. It satisfies both requirements and at the same time has the value of brevity. The first Latin version of it was: "Accipe signaculum Spiritus Sancti, qui tibi datur." (A more literal version would have been "Accipe signaculum doni Spiritus Sancti"; "qui tibi datur" was chosen instead of "doni" in order to avoid a double genitive and simplify the work of translation into the vernaculars.) After subsequent reflection, however, and a certain amount of back and forth, the formula "Accipe signaculum doni Spiritus Sancti" was chosen as better expressing the effect of the sacrament, in which the gift received is the Holy Spirit himself. In this form it was then translated into the various languages.[28]

---

quae fit manus impositione.' Una curiosa affermazione dell'*Ordo Confirmationis* del 1971 sulla materia prossima essenziale della Confermazione," in *Mysterion. Nella celebrazione del mistero di Cristo* (Quaderni di Rivista Liturgica, nuova ser. 5; Turin-Leumann, 1981) 365–439.

28. See Botte (n. 26) and *Not* 8 (1972) 285–86. There was also some wavering on the sacramental formula. The first decision of the SCDF, expressed in its letter of May 10, 1969, was to change the text suggested by the Consilium: "The formula given by the Consilium for the words accompanying the anointing should be changed to read: 'N., receive the seal of the gift of the Holy Spirit.' " But the consultors of the SCDF and two cardinals had expressed a contrary view. They saw the danger that "gift" might be taken to mean "the gifts of the Holy Spirit," whereas what is meant is the gift which is the Holy Spirit himself. The replacement of "gift" by "who is given to you" seemed easier to translate, while its meaning could be more immediately grasped even by the uneducated.

The theological committee subsequently appointed went back to the formula suggested by the Consilium (letter of July 11, 1970). But the SCDF finally decided on January 13, 1971, that the sacramental formula should be "Receive the seal of the gift of the Holy Spirit" (letter of February 2, 1971); this is the formula finally approved by the Pope on February 15 of that year. In the letter of the SCDF informing the SCDW of its decision, the word "gift" was underlined, since there had even been discussion about whether or not simply to omit it. The joint committee had decided on February 23, 1970, that the word "gift" was needed in order to express the idea of the "giving" of the Spirit and also because its omission could give rise to doctrinally inaccurate translations.

Holy Communion

I. Communion Under Both Kinds

Communion under both kinds is a typical case of a liturgical practice which the Council restored to the Church but which was only gradually clarified and resolved. The gradualness should not be thought surprising. Laws regarding new forms of worship reach their ideal form only as souls become better prepared and disposed for the responsible acceptance of these new forms.

1. *The Liturgical Constitution*

The Constitution devotes only a short paragraph to the integral restoration among God's people of a rite that historically has been one of the most contested and controverted. Moreover, it touches on the subject only in passing, as it were, as though it were something that could be taken for granted, and it adds a first, illustrative list of three cases in which there should be communion under both kinds:

> The dogmatic principles laid down by the Council of Trent remain intact. In instances to be specified by the Apostolic See, however, communion under both kinds may be granted both to clerics and religious and to the laity at the discretion of the bishops, for example, to the ordained at the Mass of their ordination, to the professed at the Mass of their religious profession, to the newly baptized at the Mass following their baptism (no. 55).

The Constitution thus leaves it to the Apostolic See to determine the "instances." Those given here by the preparatory commission were artfully chosen, since all three are "ritual," that is, connected with a special rite, and therefore less likely to be opposed; furthermore, one concerns the clergy, another religious, and the third the laity.

2. *Preparation of the Rite*

During the discussion at the Council, not a few Fathers were opposed, on grounds both doctrinal and practical, to the restoration of communion under both kinds. The article was finally passed, however, and the Consilium subsequently entrusted preparation of the rite to the same group that was dealing with concelebration,[1] since the two rites were blossoms from the same stock.

The first schema,[2] which was composed by C. Vagaggini, began with a fine theological synthesis that was to serve as a source for instruction. Two ways of receiving communion from the cup were then described: drinking from it directly and intinction. There was an interesting final note: in order to overcome the repugnance, almost invincible today, against drinking from the same cup, the celebrant could pour part of the consecrated wine into another cup before drinking of it himself. But the note displayed a needless hesitancy. Experience was to show that the practice of receiving from the cup was everywhere accepted without any very great difficulty. The schema was sent to the twenty consultors on April 2, 1964, and was very well received. Reservations had to do chiefly with the limits placed on occasions for receiving under both kinds; the schema was regarded as not "generous" enough.

The second schema was found to be clearer and more practical. The doctrinal part was better laid out, the advantages of communion under both kinds being explained as follows:

a) the Lord's commandment is carried out more fully;

b) the Eucharistic sign displays its meaning more fully in the combined food and drink;

c) the importance of the blood in establishing the new covenant emerges more clearly;

d) the ecumenical value of the Eucharist is also made clearer.

A timid marginal note said that since the instances given in the liturgical Constitution were only examples, some consultors had asked that the new practice be extended to first communion, confirmation, and nuptial Masses.

---

1. See p. 123, n. 2.
2. The stages in the preparation were these: first schema, April 2, 1964; second, May 30, 1964; third, June 17, 1964; fourth, June 20, 1964; fifth, February 10, 1965. In the Consilium this rite was discussed along with the rite of concelebration.

Two further methods of receiving from the cup were added to the two given in the first schema: the use of a drinking straw ("cum calamo") and the use of a spoon ("cum cochleari"). It was suggested that the straw might be made either of some precious material (gilded silver) that could be regularly purified like the other sacred vessels or of some ordinary material that could be burned after use. With regard to the use of a spoon, it was noted that the priest "is not to touch the lips of the communicant." But it was not easy to use a spoon, and in fact the practice was abandoned after a few attempts. It does not appear ever to have been used for the communion of the faithful.

In the third and fourth schemas the doctrinal part was limited to two paragraphs. There was a lengthier statement of the requirement that catechists should explain the doctrine of the Council of Trent on the real presence of Christ in each species and on the authority of the Church with regard to the administration of the sacraments, "provided their substance remains unchanged" (salva eorum substantia). The "instances" increased from three to ten.

The definitive text (fifth version) was finally ready at the beginning of 1965 and was approved by the Holy Father. Initially it was made available by special decree in each case to such bishops as requested it. On March 7, 1965, the new rite was extended to the entire Church by a decree of the Congregation of Rites.[3]

The instances for its use, which the liturgical Constitution had said were to be "specified" by the Holy See, were eleven in number. Implementation was to be with the consent of the diocesan bishop, since this was a new discipline. The decree of the Congregation of Rites also emphasizes the need of carefully instructing the faithful and helping them to see that this new rite makes clearer the full sign of the Eucharistic banquet.[4]

---

3. *Ritus servandus in concelebratione Missae et ritus communionis sub utraque specie* (Vatican Polyglot Press, 1965) 49–78. There is a new translation of the Introduction in *DOL* 268 nos. 2105-7.

4. Communion under both kinds was allowed for:

"1. those ordained at the Mass of their ordination;

"2. the deacon and subdeacon exercising their ministries at a pontifical or solemn Mass;

"3. an abbess at the Mass in which she is blessed;

"4. those consecrated to a life of virginity at the Mass of their consecration;

"5. those professed at the Mass of their religious profession, provided they pronounce their vows during Mass;

"6. the bride and bridegroom at their wedding Mass;

"7. adults newly baptized at the Mass following their baptism;

"8. adults newly confirmed at the Mass of their confirmation;

3. *First Extension (1967)*

The instruction *Eucharisticum mysterium* reorganizes all the material in a more logical form and also notably increases the instances in which communion may be received under both kinds.[5] The eleven instances given in the 1965 rite become thirteen here. But this is misleading, for the instruction combines several instances in the rite under a single heading and then introduces six others:

No. 5: "to lay missionaries in the Mass at which they are publicly sent out on their mission and to others in the Mass in which they receive an ecclesiastical mission."

No. 6: "in the administration of viaticum, to the sick person and to all who are present when Mass is celebrated, with conformity to the requirements of the law, in the house of the sick person."

No. 8: "when there is a concelebration:

a. to all exercising a genuine liturgical ministry in that concelebration, even lay people, and to all seminarians present;

b. in their own churches, to all members of institutes professing the evangelical counsels and members of other societies in which the members dedicate themselves to God either through religious vows or oblation or promise, and also to all who reside in the house of the members of these institutes and societies."

No. 10: "to all groups making retreats, in a Mass celebrated especially for those actually participating; to all taking part in the meeting of some pastoral commission, at the Mass which they celebrate in common."

No. 12: "to the godfather, godmother, parents, and spouse of baptized adults, and to the laypersons who have baptized them, in the Mass of initiation."

No. 13: "to the relatives, friends, and special benefactors taking part in the Mass of a newly ordained priest."

4. *Second Extension (1969)*

The General Instruction of the Roman Missal takes over almost unchanged the rite of communion under two kinds with the list of instances

---

"9. baptized persons newly received into the full communion of the Catholic Church;

"10. those mentioned in nos. 3-6 at Masses celebrating their jubilees;

"11. priests who are present at major celebrations and are not able to celebrate or concelebrate; brothers who are present at a concelebration in a religious house" (*DOL* 268 no. 2105).

5. See SCR, instruction *Eucharisticum mysterium* on worship of the Eucharist (May 25, 1967), no. 32: *DOL* 179 no. 1261.

given in the instruction *Eucharisticum mysterium*. In no. 76, however, the General Instruction also gives the case of the conventual Mass at which all the members, both priests who have already celebrated or must celebrate later on and laypersons, may receive communion under both kinds.[6] Unlike the other cases listed above, this concession is made directly by the legislator with no reference to permission from the diocesan bishop.

5. *Third Extension (1970)*

Meanwhile the practice of communion under both kinds, more extensive instruction of the people, and active participation in the Eucharistic celebration were all spurring requests that the bishops be given broader authorization to deal with particular cases without having to appeal to the Holy See. As a matter of fact, back in June of 1968 the Congregation of Rites had already drafted a decree "extending the permission to receive communion under both kinds." The decree was studied by the Congregation at its meeting of June 18, but nothing came of it.

In the following year, as repeated requests came in from the episcopal conferences, individual bishops, and even the ordinary faithful, the Congregation for Divine Worship thought of reviving the dropped plan. At the same time, requests were also coming in from the episcopal conferences and from bishops and priests for a broadening of the permission to concelebrate or to receive communion twice on the same day.

On June 11, 1969, the Congregation for Divine Worship asked the Holy Father for permission to prepare an instruction that would allow priests to concelebrate in special circumstances even though they had already celebrated Mass for the faithful; these circumstances would be in addition to those already listed in no. 9 of the Introduction to the *Rite of Concelebration*. The Pope gave his permission on June 19 (No. 140582).

As the instruction was being drawn up, its object broadened to include further cases of communion under both kinds and repeated communions on the same day. The aim was to include in a single document

---

6. The text published in the *Ordo Missae* of 1969 was later revised. In the 1970 edition of the *Missale Romanum* the "community" Mass of religious or institutes of perfection is equated with the "conventual" Mass (GIRM 76). But in that number (76) the GIRM limits itself to speaking of concelebration by those who must also celebrate individually. Further on, however, in no. 242, the case of communion under both kinds for members of a community at the community or conventual Mass is added as a fourteenth instance to the list of thirteen given in *Eucharisticum mysterium*. (See the fourth edition of the GIRM in *DOL* 208 nos. 1466 and 1632.) The second edition of the Roman Missal in 1975 lists the same cases but takes into account the regulations included in the third extension (1970).

the replies to all the most urgent requests. The compilers were, however, going beyond their mandate.

The instruction was prepared by the secretariat of the Congregation. On December 22, 1969, the first schema was sent to thirty-six experts on sixteen national liturgical commissions.[7] On the basis of their remarks, a second schema was prepared (February 14, 1970). This was sent not only to some consultors but also to the Congregations for the Doctrine of the Faith, the Discipline of the Sacraments, the Clergy, Catholic Education, Religious, and the Evangelization of Peoples (March 4, 1970).

The result of the collaboration thus sought with the Curia was really quite disheartening. Cardinal Šeper showed himself utterly opposed.[8] The prefect of the Congregation of the Sacraments claimed competency in the matter and blamed the instruction for being too broad and unjustifiably so. The Congregation for the Clergy appealed to the Council of Trent, fearing that communion under both kinds would lead to deviations in dogma, while communion twice in one day was a novelty and therefore not acceptable; it was, in fact, a deviation springing from a mind insufficiently enlightened with regard, for example, to the indwelling of the Blessed Trinity in a soul in the state of grace.

The Congregation for Religious regarded communion under both kinds as simply a matter of greater solemnity and therefore saw no reason for extending it; it also feared negative doctrinal consequences with regard to faith in the real presence under each of the species, and it asserted its competency in regard to the reception of communion twice in one day by the members of religious and secular institutes. The Congregation for Catholic Education was in favor of the instruction and offered remarks only on details. Progaganda, finally, thought it was up to the episcopal conferences to make collective decisions in these areas.

Meanwhile a third schema was being prepared which was to be submitted to the Consilium at its thirteenth general meeting on April 9–10, 1970. But on April 10, as the session was beginning, the Substitute Secre-

7. See *Res Secretariae*, no. 42 (December 22, 1969): "Instructio de ampliore facultate sacram Communionem ministrandi sub utraque specie, necnon bis in eodem die concelebrandi vel communicandi." After a short introduction the three cases are considered separately.

8. The Cardinal said that he was writing as a pastor of souls, but the Congregation made his judgment its own (letter of Archbishop Philippe, March 23, 1970). He also sent his remarks to the Secretariat of State, "saying [according to the letter of the Secretariat to the SCDW] that they are the fruit of his concern at the great anarchy spreading abroad in the liturgical field." Therefore the Secretariat advised making no decisions without first referring the matter to the Holy Father (March 24, 1970).

tary of State telephoned to say that there was to be no discussion of the schema and no extensions of any kind.[9]

But the requests from the bishops, which went to the Secretariat of State, did not stop coming in.[10] Moreover, while this Secretariat was insisting that the current discipline not be changed,[11] the Pope was discussing the question with the secretary of the Congregation for Divine Worship at an audience on June 5, 1970. It was decided on that occasion to limit the instruction to communion under both kinds, this being a matter that certainly was in the competency of the Congregation for Divine Worship.[12] The Holy Father also gave guidelines for the preparation of the instruction: broader authorization could be given with regard to

> homogeneous pious groups—due precautions being taken—due reverence for the Blessed Sacrament a matter of conscience—avoid giving communion under both kinds to large masses of people—use the method which, given the character of the assembly, best safeguards and provides for veneration and respect for the Most Blessed Sacrament.

It was on this basis that the Consilium prepared the instruction *Sacramentali Communione*, which broadened the practice of receiving communion under both kinds. It was approved by the Holy Father on July 10, 1970 (No. 161443) and bears the date June 19, 1970.[13]

After five years of ripening reflection, this instruction radically resolved the problem of communion under two kinds. The Holy See had decided to decentralize the authorization for this form of communion and leave

9. The Cardinal Prefect of the Congregation of the Sacraments also hastened to send a copy of his observations to the Secretariat of State, which sent it on to the SCDW and asked whether it would not be advisable to accept the suggestion of the Cardinal Prefect and establish a joint committee "to study the timeliness and scope of a possible document on the subject" (April 6, 1970; No. 158705). There was not even time to consider the suggestion, since the letter from the Secretariat arrived after the telephone call ordering the postponement.

10. Among the most recent were, e.g., one from the bishops of Laos and Cambodia (May 20) and one from the Canadian bishops (May 22).

11. On May 21, 1970, Archbishop Benelli let it be known, "for your information," that the Holy Father had refused the Archbishop of Brasilia permission for communion twice in one day during the National Eucharistic Congress. The permission was refused "in order not to create a precedent that might render more difficult the observance of current discipline regarding holy communion."

12. The problem of concelebration was to be dealt with later (see above, p. 131, n. 14). The subject of communion twice in a day would be handled in the instruction *Immensae caritatis* of the Congregation for the Sacraments.

13. The letter of approval also ordered that the list of cases already allowed be removed from the document and published in *L'Osservatore Romano* for September 3, 1970. See SCDW, instruction *Sacramentali Communione*, extending the practice of communion under both kinds (June 29, 1970): DOL 270 nos. 2109-15.

its regulation to the episcopal conferences. More important, even in the cases previously allowed, communion under both kinds was now left to the judgment, not of the bishop, but of the Ordinary and therefore of the major religious superior.

The task of the episcopal conferences was to decide what the occasions of special importance for the spiritual life of a community or group of faithful were on which communion might be received under two kinds and what conditions had to be verified for such a reception. Ordinaries could then proceed on the basis of the guidelines received from the conferences; they were not, however, to grant permission indiscriminately but only in clearly defined circumstances.[14]

After setting down these general regulations, the instruction turned to three points of special importance that had caused hesitation and opposition to the entire plan within the Curia:

a) Everything is to be done with respect, dignity, and devotion. The instruction repeats this five times and always in unambiguous terms: "[Ordinaries] must have assurance that *all measures can be carried out* that will safeguard the holiness of the sacrament" (no. 4); "care must be taken that all is done with *proper reverence*" (no. 6); "the way of giving communion" is to be marked by *dignity, devotion, propriety*, and the *avoidance of the danger of irreverence*" (no. 6); it is necessary to "ensure the *reverence due to the sacrament*" (no. 6). (All italics in these citations have been added.)

b) Communion "from the chalice" is to be avoided when large crowds are receiving, since in such circumstances it is difficult to carry out the rite with respect, order, dignity, and devotion, even if there are many priests or deacons or acolytes "to present the chalice." The presence of a minister authorized to offer the chalice is indispensable. Com-

---

14. This instruction did not exclude any cases. But communion under two kinds at Masses celebrated in homes was already expressly prohibited by the instruction *Actio pastoralis*, on Masses with special groups, no. 7 (May 15, 1969) (see *DOL* 275 no. 2128). Therefore this was one case in which permission could not be given. Yet it was one of the occasions for which communion under both kinds was most often requested! The SCDW did not fail to raise the matter with the Holy Father. On September 18, 1974 (No. 265804) the Secretariat of State responded to the SCDW in connection with a request from the Australian episcopal conference by saying: "I am happy to tell you that in view of nos. 2 and 3 of the instruction of your Congregation on extending the practice of communion under both kinds and in view of Your Eminence's own favorable opinion, he has decided that the matter should be left to the good judgment of that episcopate.

"His Holiness thinks it appropriate that in granting this authorization the episcopal conference should establish guidelines for its use and that the president of the conference should then let the Holy See know, for its information and needed documentation, the decision made and the guidelines issued."

pletely excluded, therefore, is the possibility of the faithful going directly to the chalice for communion or passing the chalice to one another; such a procedure is alien to the liturgy, even at the "Supper" of the separated brethren.

If communion "from the chalice" is impossible for any one of these reasons, then communion "by intinction" is to be preferred; the sign is less expressive, but the method is safer.

c) Suitable and specific instruction must precede or be intensified, in order, first, that the faithful may be adequately prepared not only to carry out the rite with dignity but also to understand the deeper meaning of the new rite as the full Eucharistic sign, and in order, secondly, that by thus participating fully in the sacrifice, they may obtain more abundant fruits of devotion and spiritual profit.

Provision was thus made for a requirement of which the Church had become aware through the fuller and more conscious participation of the faithful in the liturgy. Intense faith and fervent charity will suffice to overcome any fears and to ensure the necessary gravity and propriety.

II. Communion Twice in One Day

The instruction *Inter Oecumenici* had allowed that communion might be repeated by those who attend the vigil Mass for Christmas or Easter and then the Mass on Christmas or Easter itself.[15] The second instruction, *Abhinc tres annos*, had extended this permission to those who participate in both the Chrism and Evening Masses on Holy Thursday.[16] Finally, applying the same standard as in the previous cases, the instruction *Eucharisticum mysterium* took up the case of those who receive communion at a morning Mass and then in the evening attend the Mass for a Sunday or holy day of obligation.[17]

But other cases of a like kind could arise. Therefore the projected instruction that I described above was to include an extension of the current discipline. It allowed for the possibility of receiving twice on the same day, not for reasons of devotion but because of participation in two different services.[18]

---

15. See no. 60 (*DOL* 23 no. 352).
16. See no. 14 (*DOL* 39 no. 460).
17. See no. 28 (*DOL* 179 no. 1257).
18. The planned extension was not broad or "anarchic," as some claimed. In fact, in addition to the cases already allowed, it provided for the possibility of communion twice in the same day: (1) for clerics and laity who provided some liturgical service at two different Masses on a Sunday or holy day of obligation; (2) at ritual Masses and on the occasions of spiritual gatherings or pastoral meetings.

The matter was submitted for examination by the Congregation for the Sacraments, which had competency in this area.[19] On December 18, 1971, at the insistence of the Secretariat of State, the Congregation held a first joint meeting with representatives of other curial agencies for an exchange of ideas. It turned out that only the Congregation for Divine Worship was in favor of the extension.[20]

Three years were to pass before a decision was finally reached in the instruction *Immensae caritatis*. This was composed by the Congregation for the Sacraments and touched on four points having to do with the Eucharist: extraordinary ministers, communion twice in one day, the Eucharistic fast, and the devotion and reverence to be shown the Eucharist when communion is received by taking the consecrated bread in one's own hand.[21]

The Congregation for Divine Worship had a part in the composition of the document. It would have preferred to provide only broad guidelines, such as was done when extending the permission to receive communion under both kinds. But, true to the manner of the Congregation principally responsible for it, the document was full of casuistry; this, however, was simply an explicitation and even a further extension of what the Congregation for Divine Worship had included in its own draft.[22]

---

19. On September 22, 1970 (No. 166983), in response to a request of this kind from the United States conference, the Secretariat of State wrote as follows to the SCDW: "The question is to be examined in collaboration with the Congregations concerned, establishing, if need be, a joint committee. It is therefore thought that you should send a copy of the letter from the Cardinal President of the United States episcopal conference to the Congregation for the Discipline of the Sacraments, which has received similar requests, so that it may be informed of this one; you should ask it to establish the necessary contact with your own Congregation so that together you may submit concrete proposals for a solution of the problem to the Holy Father." On November 27 (No. 171.988), with reference to a similar request, again from the United States, the Secretariat of State wrote that it had asked the Congregation for the Sacraments to "begin a study of the problem as soon as possible"; it again urged "quick collaboration so that a solution may be speedily found."

20. Present were the Cardinal Prefects: Samorè, Šeper, Rossi, and Wright; the secretaries: Palazzini, Lourdusamy, and Bugnini, with G. Pasqualetti. The arguments discussed were more or less those adduced in the consultation carried out by the SCDW. The group did not see the need of the concession, since the emphasis was rather on the dangers. All, however, were a bit embarrassed when confronted by the documents of the Council and the reform, since these justified the requests and made them worthy of consideration. Some may have come to realize that the SCDW had not been acting thoughtlessly.

21. Congregation for the Discipline of the Sacraments, instruction *Immensae caritatis*, on facilitating reception of communion in certain circumstances (January 29, 1973): DOL 264 nos. 2073-88. Commentary in *Not* 9 (1973) 168-73.

22. The concession was given for ritual Masses at which a sacrament is administered; Masses for the consecration of a church or altar, religious profession, or the conferral of

The instruction also dealt with the extraordinary minister of communion. The Congregation for Divine Worship prepared the rites for the exercise of this ministry; they were attached to the instruction. It will be worth our while to dwell on them for a moment.

III. Extraordinary Minister of Communion

At the beginning of 1966 the Congregation for the Discipline of the Sacraments had, with the approval of the Holy Father, prepared an instruction entitled *Fidei custos* on lay ministers of holy communion; it was not published.[23] On April 28, 1966, this document was sent to, among others, the Consilium, which felt obliged to offer some observations that it believed necessary to complete the document (May 17, 1966). These observations had to do chiefly with two points:

1) The instruction said that the mandate or mission to distribute holy communion should be conferred "by a more or less solemn rite." It was not clear, however, whether "rite" here meant a liturgical rite or simply a juridical deputation. In the Consilium's view, the conferral of so important and sensitive an appointment should take the form of a liturgical celebration; a further reason was to prevent arbitrary or eccentric local initiatives.[24]

2) The regulations given for the rite of distributing communion were very skimpy and did not take account of the guidelines given in the liturgical Constitution (no. 35, 4) and the instruction *Inter Oecumenici* (nos. 37-39). One needed regulation concerned places lacking a priest. Here,

---

canonical mission; Masses for the dead when news of the death is received, at the final burial, and on the first anniversary; the principal Mass in a cathedral or parish church on Corpus Christi; Mass on the day of a pastoral visitation; Mass on the occasion of the canonical visitation of a major superior and at other meetings at which the major superior presides; the principal Mass at Eucharistic or Marian congresses, whether international, regional, or diocesan; the principal Mass at any meeting, pilgrimage, or mission to the people; the administration of viaticum. Faculty is also given to all local Ordinaries to allow communion twice on the same day for a single occasion whenever they think it advantageous and legitimate in light of the principles of the instruction. This last faculty was in response to the request which the SCDW submitted to the Pope on December 19, 1972, and to which he agreed (January 2, 1973).

23. The text received the handwritten approval of the Pope: "Placet in Domino. P[aulus] 7-III-1966."

24. One such was an appointment that involved putting a stole on the appointee and saying: "Receive this stole, the symbol of your authority in the Eucharistic ministry, so that you may be a Eucharistic minister by word and example, in the name of the Father and of the Son and of the Holy Spirit." See *La Chiesa nel mondo*, no. 32 (1968) 36; *Revista Eclesiástica Brasileira* (December 1966) 979.

especially on Sundays, the distribution of communion should be situated within a liturgy of the Word. On Sundays this liturgy should include a reading from the epistle or gospel, a song, the reading of a homily, general intercessions, Our Father, act of contrition, communion, and a song or prayer of thanksgiving. On weekdays there should be at least a short reading (for example, John 6:56-58), the Our Father, and so on.[25]

The secretariat of the Consilium prepared two rites—one for the distribution of communion by an extraordinary minister and one for the appointment or institution of such a minister. The first of these[26] was sent to the Congregation for the Sacraments on October 26, 1966; the second to the Holy Father on February 3, 1967.[27]

The rite for the distribution of communion allowed for three forms. The first was for distribution as part of a liturgy of the Word, especially on Sundays and feast days, "so that despite the lack of Mass, the part of the Mass which is possible without a priest may be celebrated." The second was simpler and intended for weekdays. The third was even simpler (recitation of an Our Father) and meant for the occasional distribution of communion outside the appointed times. In its final form the rite has only a "longer" and "shorter" form, organized as indicated in the first proposals made on May 17, 1966.

The appointment or institution of an extraordinary minister was to be accomplished either during or outside Mass. After the liturgy of the Word, there is a brief address to the candidates, an invitation to prayer, and the blessing of the minister. The final version includes questions to the minister regarding his office and duties.

These two rites, which were logical and very simple, had to wait three years for approval. Only on April 30, 1969, did the Holy Father give his

---

25. These observations were also sent to the Secretariat of State, which replied on May 22, 1966 (No. 73041), saying that "the various parts that are to make up the celebration of the liturgy of the Word seem too complex for ordinary private use, though they might be more appropriate on solemnities or gatherings of the people."

26. "Ritus administrandi S. Communionem a ministro ex indulto Sedis Apostolicae facultatem habente, absente sacerdote vel diacono." There was a second version on November 25, 1968; a third on January 16, 1969 (Schema 336), with the title: "Ritus administrandi S. Communionem a ministro ex indulto Sedis Apostolicae facultatem habente"; and the definitive version in 1969.

27. "Ritus ad instituendum ministrum qui sacram Communionem distribuat, absente sacerdote vel diacono." A second version was produced on November 25, 1968; a third on January 16, 1969 (Schema 335), with the title: "Ritus ad deputandum ministrum qui ex indulto Apostolico Sacram Communionem distribuere valeat"; and the final text. The first schema was sent directly to the Pope, because it also provided that the appointed minister could receive communion under both kinds; this was appropriate in the circumstances, but the permission went beyond current practice and required the Pope's approval.

final approval; he also decided that these rites should be an integral part of the instruction *Fidei custos* and should be communicated, along with the instruction, "only to the episcopal conferences via the papal representatives." On this occasion the instruction itself was updated.

There were those who had difficulty understanding why a worthy distribution of communion, especially on Sundays and feast days, should have to be in the setting of, and prepared for by, a liturgy of the Word based on the liturgy of the day. There were others who thought that the liturgical appointment of the special minister was an overly solemn affair and gave the impression that a kind of minor order was being conferred.[28] They wanted a simpler rite. It may be that the idea of a permanent minister of the Eucharist troubled them and that they preferred a kind of temporary commission, bestowed without too much solemnity.

As a matter of fact, on June 21, 1969, the Secretariat of State asked the Congregation for Divine Worship to draw up a rite "that is simpler and shorter, which can be given to the bishops as an optional rite for bestowing the authority to distribute holy communion on a single occasion." The same request was repeated in September, with the addition this time of a request that the opinion of the Congregation for the Sacraments and the Congregation for the Doctrine of the Faith be sought.[29]

---

28. When the Pope had been given the schema on the appointment of extraordinary ministers, he remarked in a handwritten note: "Isn't this overly solemn? It seems to imitate the conferral of a sacred order. What if the appointment is made in private? What will be the procedure if the authorization to distribute communion is given in a community of women? Or to a woman religious? Would it not be advisable to make the authorization temporary and to have it cease in certain circumstances? It would be advisable to reach agreement with the Congregation of the Sacraments and the SCR." When the Consilium persisted because it wished to counter the multiplication of arbitrary rites, the Pope, via the Secretariat of State, reminded it of the above remarks and added that it should also consult the Congregation of the Clergy (October 29, 1968).

The three Congregations were consulted on November 30, 1968, and schemas 335 and 336 were sent to the Pope on January 21, 1969. With regard to the extraordinary minister, he once again objected: "The planned rite still seems too solemn and, more importantly, vague in certain respects. The main idea of the rite is acceptable, but there is need of defining who the persons are who can do the choosing and who the persons are who may be chosen. The latter should then be commissioned in a special ceremony, which should include a short instruction, a blessing, and a promise on the recipient's part" (March 3, 1969). On March 12 a new version was sent that included the corrections received. The Consilium asked that the persons involved not be determined too closely, because the situation was "gradually evolving." Approval finally came (No. 138080).

29. September 3, 1969, at the request of the French bishops. The liturgical commission of France had also prepared a rite. This became the basis for the rite composed by the SCDW, which was sent to the above-mentioned Congregations on September 15.

The Congregation for the Doctrine of the Faith was hesitant about the opportuneness of such a rite. It said that it was

> indispensable at least to require "real necessity" as a condition (this necessity might differ according to circumstances, times, and places), in order to prevent at least the grossest abuses that would certainly arise from the indiscriminate application of this concession; on the other hand, if the concession is used prudently, it can prove to be a real advantage in the pastoral ministry.[30]

This rite, which consists of a simple blessing after the *Agnus Dei* ("Today you are to distribute the body and blood of Christ to your brothers and sisters. May the Lord bless you, N. Amen"), was also approved, and the new permission to appoint a minister for a single occasion was included in *Fidei custos*.

This brought things down to the end of 1972, when the Secretariat of State let it be known that the Holy Father had approved the instruction *Immensae caritatis*. He was now asking the Congregation for Divine Worship to examine the new norms and, if necessary, adapt to them the current rites for the appointment of a special minister of the Eucharist, whether for a period or on a single occasion, and for the exercise of this ministry. Also to be added, if needed, were regulations for the manner of bringing the Eucharist to the sick.[31]

As a matter of fact, the instruction *Immensae caritatis* publicizes, updates, and extends the authorization in *Fidei custos*. It gives local Ordinaries the authority to appoint suitable persons as extraordinary ministers of holy communion when their help is made necessary by the lack of ordained ministers.

An appendix to the instruction contains two rites for conferring the mandate on extraordinary ministers. It also contains rubrical directives

---

30. October 10, 1969. The often-requested answer of the Congregation of the Sacraments had still not come. The rites were therefore sent to the Holy Father on October 24. Approval came on November 8; on November 10 the reply of the Congregation of the Sacraments finally arrived, a copy being sent also to the Secretariat of State. Further proceedings were therefore needed to deal with the revision of some details, the challenges to others, and the formulation of the text of authorization that was to be included in *Fidei custos*. The final text of the authorization was sent to the SCDW on December 20, and the rite could be given its definitive form.

31. December 24, 1972. The SCDW replied on December 29 and again on January 12, 1973. On January 12, and before that on January 10, agreement on the text was reached with the Congregation of the Sacraments. On January 23, 1973, the Secretariat of State sent word of the Pope's approval; the Pope had decided that the rites should be published in an appendix to the instruction. The latter was dated January 29, 1973, but was published only on March 23, 1973.

for their activity in distributing communion during Mass.[32] For other cases (communion outside Mass and to the sick) it refers to the appropriate ritual.[33]

IV. COMMUNION IN THE HAND

At the beginning of the liturgical reform there was a trend in some countries toward the distribution of communion by placing the consecrated bread in the hand of the recipient. The practice soon spread, and bishops and conferences found themselves appealing to the Holy See.

Initially there was strong opposition.[34] But the bishops found it difficult to suppress the new practice, and their requests continued, especially from Germany, the Netherlands, Belgium, and France. Because the requests were so insistent, the Holy Father decided to give permission for the practice to the episcopal conferences that asked for it; they were to take the necessary precautions and keep an eye on the practice.

The letter of the Secretary of State on June 3, 1968, said this among other things:

> His Holiness thinks the bishops should be reminded of their responsibility to anticipate by timely guidelines any undesirable consequences that may arise and also to control the indiscriminate spread of this practice, which in itself is not contrary to doctrine but is nonetheless debatable and dangerous. Therefore, when similar requests come in, they should be brought to the attention of the Holy See, and any authorization that may be granted should be made through the Congregation of Rites.

---

32. Rite of Commissioning Special Ministers of Holy Communion, in *The Rites of the Catholic Church* 2 (New York, 1980) 165–67. Rite of Commissioning a Special Minister to Distribute Holy Communion on a Single Occasion, in *ibid.*, 168 (also published in an appendix to the second edition of the Roman Missal). Rite of Distributing Holy Communion by a Special Minister, in *ibid.*, 169. The brief Introductions to the three rites are newly translated in DOL 343 nos. 2949-52.

33. See Section V of this chapter, pp. 661–63.

34. After the first visit to the Netherlands, the Consilium wrote to Cardinal Alfrink: "The traditional way of distributing communion is to be maintained" (October 12, 1965). At the end of the visit paid by the special commission to that country (see above, p. 106), the Consilium wrote: "The Holy Father grants the episcopal conference authority to let holy communion be distributed by religious brothers and by carefully chosen religious women in communities of women or by laypersons appropriately instructed and regarded as suitable for this sensitive and sacred function, if the Conference regards this step as necessary. The Holy Father does not, however, think it proper that the sacred host be distributed in the hand and then received by the faithful themselves in one or other fashion. He therefore urgently asks the Conference to issue appropriate regulations so that the traditional way of receiving communion may be everywhere restored." But this and other reminders had no effect.

Authorization was given to Germany and Belgium[35] by the Congregation of Rites.[36] Then, however, in response to lively protests from some persons, the Pope discussed the matter with the secretary of the Consilium at an audience on July 25, 1968, and decided to suspend the concession. He ordered Father Bugnini to tell the Cardinal Presidents of the Belgian and German episcopal conferences that they were "temporarily to suspend the publication and implementation of the indult."[37]

1. *Consultation of the Bishops*

In a memorandum of July 30, 1968, the Consilium reported on the carrying out of the order received and on the way of resolving the entire problem. "The problem is not exclusively liturgical but has strong pastoral and, even more, psychological ramifications. Worship and veneration of the Blessed Sacrament, as well as the very faith in the sacrament, will be not a little affected . . . unless the transition from the traditional way of receiving to the new one is gradually and carefully prepared for." The report concluded:

> Since this matter concerns the Eucharist, which is the very heart of the liturgy, and since any consequences will be rather significant, we propose the following:
>
> 1) that during the coming September the president of the Consilium should, at the bidding of the Holy Father, send a letter to all the presidents of the episcopal conferences with an extended explanation of the state of the question, giving the pros and cons;
>
> 2) that he should ask . . . each episcopal conference to discuss the problem and come to a decision in a free and secret vote. The minutes of the discussion and the outcome of the vote are to be sent to the Consilium as usual. The Holy See will thus have a more accurate grasp of the situation

---

35. The request had been made to the SCR, which on May 8, 1968, replied, "It is not expedient," not for doctrinal reasons but for the sake of discipline, since the Christian people were by and large not prepared for this change. The Secretariat of State communicated the concession to Germany in a letter of June 27, 1968, and to Belgium in a letter of July 3.

36. On July 6 to Germany and on July 11 to Belgium. Certain conditions were set down in the decree: (1) communion in the hand is not obligatory; (2) the authorization is given to the bishop; (3) communicants are to hold their hands crossed one over the other as they receive the host; (4) they are not to take the host into their mouths while walking; (5) if communion is received under both kinds, it is not permitted to place in the hand a host that has been dipped in the Precious Blood; (6) there should be appropriate instruction beforehand.

37. Word was sent that same day by telephone and the next day by a letter in which the reasons were given. A promise was also made: "A final decision will be made as soon as possible."

and be able to decide on the granting of the indult. Without this preceding discussion of the problem, there is danger of creating a thorny situation for the bishops and weakening the faith of the people in the Eucharistic presence.

In September, after receiving a request from the French conference, the Consilium decided to restudy the question, especially at a meeting of the secretaries of the Congregations concerned.[38] This was held on October 2, 1968, in the library of the Secretariat of State. The Consilium had prepared a state of the question, in which the now familiar points were made: the practice has started and is difficult to stop, and it seems preferable to regulate it; at issue is discipline alone and not dogma. The dangers: coexistence of two ways of distributing communion; weakening of worship of the Eucharist; danger of profanations; yielding to a practice imposed from below. There was agreement, however, that, as the Consilium had suggested, the views of the episcopal conferences be heard.[39]

The Consilium prepared a first draft of a letter to be sent to the episcopal conferences and submitted this to the Secretariat of State on October 18, 1968. The text was returned on October 22 with corrections and annotations by the Pope himself. The variants he introduced show the care and interest with which he had been following the whole matter. Here is the text:

Your Excellency,

The official documents published over the last four years on the implementation of the liturgical reform in accordance with the guidelines set down by the Second Vatican Council have brought the first revisions of the Eucharistic celebration in the form of rites and texts that are deemed easier to understand and more profitable. The Consilium is continuing its work along this line, in order that the new liturgical books may be published as soon as possible.

Problems often arise, however,[40] which are so important and urgent that their solution cannot be put off to the end of our work. One of the most sensitive and pressing of these has to do with the distribution of communion into the hands of the faithful.[41]

---

38. Suggested participants: the Secretariat of State, the SCDF, the Congregation of the Sacraments, the SCR, and the Consilium.

39. Participants in the meeting: Archbishops Benelli, Philippe, Violardo, and Antonelli, and Father Bugnini.

40. Original text: "Meanwhile (problems) arise"; corrected by Pope to: "(Problems often) arise, however . . . ."

41. Original text: "One such is the question of the distribution"; corrected by the Pope to: "One of the most sensitive and urgent . . . has to do . . . ."

For a few years now this practice[42] has been abroad, at least in some countries and regions. Recently some bishops and even some conferences have asked the Holy See for an official reply that will show them the approach they should take in this matter, since its impact on the ministry and on worship of the Eucharist requires their special attention.[43]

At the express mandate of the Holy Father (who evidently cannot but look with apprehension upon this possible innovation),[44] I have the honor of asking the conference of which Your Excellency is president for its fraternal cooperation. In this letter I propose to explain the state of the question,[45] the arguments pro and con, and, finally, the procedure by which the episcopal conference of your country may make its thinking known to the Holy See.[46]

STATE OF THE QUESTION

I

As far as the manner of distributing communion is concerned, the instruction *Eucharisticum mysterium* (May 25, 1967) limited itself to the posture of the faithful, who may receive either kneeling or standing (no. 34). For at least two or three years, however, some priests in some places have, without proper authorization,[47] been placing the Eucharist in the hand of the faithful, who then communicate themselves. This method seems to be spreading rapidly, at least in more educated circles and in small groups, and is finding favor among laypersons[48] and among religious men and women.[49]

II

The arguments given by *supporters* of communion in the hand are these:
1. Communion in the hand does not touch the dogma of the Lord's real presence in the Eucharist. It is simply a matter of ecclesiastical discipline

---

42. Original text: "This problem"; corrected by the Pope to: "This (practice)."
43. The words "since its impact . . . special attention" were added by the Pope.
44. The words in parentheses were added by the Pope.
45. The Pope changed the Italian words "lo stato della questione" to "lo Status quaestionis."
46. Original text: "its position on this question"; corrected by the Pope to "its thinking."
47. The words "without proper authorization" were added by the Pope.
48. Original text: "many laypersons"; corrected by the Pope to "laypersons."
49. At this point the original text contained a further sentence: "Perhaps the increasingly common practice of concelebration has kindled a desire to extend to the laity the rite used for the communion of the concelebrants." The Pope crossed this out and explained: "The rite used in concelebration came after the practice here under discussion."

which ecclesiastical authorities may therefore change for good reasons, as was recently done for communion under two kinds.

2. This method of receiving is not a real innovation,[50] but on the contrary was the only one used throughout the Christian world from the beginning until the ninth or tenth century. During the latter period the use of unleavened bread became general in the West, and this change seems in turn to have promoted the distribution of communion by placing the particle on the tongue.

3. Nor can it be said that reception of the host in the hand shows less respect for the Lord than reception on the tongue. On the other hand, the faithful, including children, readily understand that they are receiving the Body of the Lord into their hands and that they must treat the consecrated bread with the greatest respect.

4. The traditional way of receiving the host on the tongue seems infantile to our contemporaries; it is too like the way children are fed who cannot eat by themselves. Many adults now feel ill at ease in this public performance of an action that has no outward attractiveness and makes them resemble children.

5. More than in the past, our contemporaries are sensitive to considerations of hygiene. Some individuals are so nervous that it is difficult, when giving them communion, to avoid contact with their tongue and saliva. This in turn makes others reluctant to receive communion on the tongue.

6. In many places the faithful receive communion while standing, and priests of short stature have some difficulty in placing the host in the mouths of those who are taller. There is also danger of the host falling to the ground, especially when priests are obliged to distribute communion rapidly because of large numbers.

7. In some dioceses laypersons are allowed to distribute communion. It seems less appropriate for them to put the host on the tongue of the communicant.

8. In countries and regions where the new practice of placing the host in the recipient's hand has been introduced, it seems increasingly difficult, if not outright impossible, to halt the practice. This is evident from the efforts already made by bishops to reverse the trend, even when the authority of the episcopate and the Holy See is invoked. In periods of profound challenge, such as the present, it is desirable that authority not be flouted for maintaining a ban that it would have difficulty implementing. On the other hand, authority would be strengthened if the hierarchy were to provide detailed guidelines for regulating the new manner of communicating.

Now for the reasons *against* receiving communion in the hand:

1. It is an important change in discipline and is likely to confuse the many faithful who do not see the need for it and have never felt the old way to

---

50. The word "real" was added by the Pope.

be a problem. Many changes have already occurred in the area of the liturgy and the sacraments that have not yet been assimilated by the Christian people as a whole. The introduction of a new way of receiving communion would require serious catechetical preparation that could not be effected everywhere at the same time.

2. The new practice that has been introduced here and there seems to be the work of a small number of priests and laypersons who are trying to impose their viewpoint on others and force the hand of those in authority. To approve the practice would be to encourage these persons, who are never[51] satisfied with the laws of the Church.

3. The greatest thing to be feared is a lessening of respect for worship of the Eucharist. Reception in the hand will be regarded by many as a less worthy and respectful way of communicating. Will all communicants, including children, have washed their hands?

4. We must also ask with some anxiety whether the fragments of consecrated bread will always be gathered up and consumed with the full respect they deserve. If even now, when a communion plate is used, it is so easy for fragments to fall and be lost, what will the situation be when the host is placed in the hands of the faithful, not all of whom will have the sensitivity and alertness to gather up [52] the fragments carefully?

5. Is there not also reason to fear an increase in profanation and irreverence by persons of ill will or little faith? Once the Eucharistic bread is received in the hand, will not ill-prepared and inadequately instructed people end up putting it on the same level as ordinary bread or bread that has simply been blessed?[53]

6. If we yield easily on this point that is of some importance in worship of the Eucharist, there is danger that the boldness of overly daring "reformers" will turn to other areas and wreak irreparable harm on Eucharistic faith and worship.

III

This difficult situation calls for serious reflection, and it is the purpose of this communication to set all the bishops of the world thinking about it.

It is necessary to anticipate what the effects of such a change of discipline will be:

a) on priests and ministers of communion;
b) on the faithful;

---

51. The Pope changed the Italian "mai" to "non mai."
52. The Pope changed the Italian "nel raccoglierli" ("to gather up") to "di raccoglierli."
53. "As ordinary bread . . . blessed." This was the Pope's correction for the original: "as simple ordinary bread or the bread blessed in some rites of non-Catholic Churches."

c) on the way in which the bread is made (it will have to be denser in order to prevent its slipping from the hand as easily and also to prevent, as far as possible, the breaking off of fragments).

d) on material changes in the churches (the possible removal of communion rails).

IV

Since, then, the whole matter is so serious in itself and in its consequences, the Holy Father wants to know the thoughts of each bishop and of the episcopal conferences.

In the name of the Holy Father, therefore, and by his order, it is my duty[54] to communicate the following instructions to Your Excellency:

1. At the first meeting of the bishops of your country, please make this circular letter known to your colleagues. After mature study of the question, each bishop is to make known in a *secret* vote whether or not he is in favor of communion in the hand. The results of this vote are to be sent to the secretariat of the Consilium by January 31, 1969.[55]

2. If the episcopal conference of your country will not be meeting before December 31,[56] please make this letter known to the bishops as soon as possible; each bishop is then to mail you his vote. The results of this form of consultation are likewise to reach the secretariat of the Consilium by January 31, 1969.[57]

Only after this consultation will the Holy See make known to the bishops the decisions reached, along with appropriate guidelines and a method for proceeding in so sensitive and important a matter.

This letter with its state of the question was dated October 28, 1968. It was translated into the various languages and sent to the papal representatives, who were urged to "deliver the document, in person if possible, to the president of the episcopal conference and carefully to explain its purpose and the procedure called for. The Holy See regards it as very important to know the thinking of the individual bishops and the episcopate as a whole as freely expressed in a secret ballot after the mature reflection required by so serious a matter."

Enclosed with the letter was a copy of a ballot containing three questions that the bishops were to answer.[58] Three months were allowed for

---

54. Original text: "I am pleased"; corrected by the Pope to: "it is my duty."

55. The date in the original text was December 15, 1968. The correction was made by the Pope.

56. The original text had December 1.

57. The original text had December 15, 1968.

58. The ballot was the Pope's idea. He also reformulated the first question; the Consi-

the procedure, the final date for replies being January 31, 1969, as decided by the Pope. Forty percent of the bishops, however, had not yet replied by that date. In response, therefore, to a communication from the Secretariat of State asking for an extension of the consultation period because of distance and because of difficulties within some regions, the Cardinal President of the Consilium decided to wait another month before totaling the results of the questionnaire. On March 19 it was possible to compile a general report[59] that presented general information, a summary of the suggestions made, a collection of the more important suggestions, and some reflections on the results of the inquiry.[60]

2. *Result of the Consultation*

When totaled up on March 12, 1969, the consultation of the bishops yielded the following results:

Voters: 2136.

Question 1: *Do you think the petition should be accepted that in addition to the traditional way of receiving holy communion, communion in the hand be also allowed?*

Yes: 567; no: 1233; yes with qualifications: 315; invalid ballots: 21. Total: 2136.

Question 2: *Do you think the new rite should first be used experimentally in small communities with the consent of the Ordinary?*

Yes: 751; no: 1215; invalid ballots: 70. Total: 2036.

N.B. The total was short a hundred votes because the French episcopal conference did not take a vote on this question.

Question 3: *Do you think that the faithful, if given timely instruction, would be in favor of the new rite?*

Yes: 823; no: 1185; invalid ballots: 128. Total: 2136.

3. *Comments and Suggestions*

At this same period, a couple of hundred letters, some signed by a single individual, others by several persons, came in to the Consilium;

---

lium text had: "Do you think that in addition to the traditional way, the rite of communion in the hand should also be allowed?"

The Pope then added: "How is it to remain secret? Who will collect the ballots?"

59. A first report with partial results was given to the Holy Father on February 12. By February 28, one hundred conferences had replied. Only about ten were still lacking, and they were not among the most reliable.

60. The replies of the bishops were statistically tabulated and collected in a book of 130 pages that was given to the Pope on March 10, 1968.

more exactly, there were 237 letters with 419 signers. Almost all were from France and Belgium and seem to have been a kind of reaction to the press conference which Bishop Boillon held at the close of the plenary session of the French episcopate. This conference had had the not very happy idea of publicizing the consultation regarding communion in the hand, despite the clear instruction that the whole procedure was to be done "in secret."[61] The announcement elicited the first reactions; these were to become more numerous in the ensuing months, partly due to the efforts of some associations that organized a campaign to collect signatures. The letters were from persons at all levels of society; the signatories ranged from simple people to personalities in the world of education, law, and the arts.

The Consilium went through this abundant material and tried to summarize the comments and suggestions of the bishops, as well as the conditions they wanted met; sometimes complete texts were cited. Many of the comments insisted on the need for prior instruction, the responsibility of the conferences, and experimentation in small communities.

This synthesis, which carried the title "Qualifications," is interesting because it brings out the points to which the bishops were sensitive. For this reason, the report also gives the names, not of the dioceses or bishops, but of the countries from which the comments and suggestions came, on the grounds that knowledge of the countries would be more useful in forming a comprehensive idea of the situation. That is how the matter was presented even to the Holy Father.

Principles

The problem is not one of Christian life in the strict sense. It is probable that the spirit of obedience alone will not be sufficient to maintain the manner of receiving communion that has been traditional in the Latin Church; therefore the principle of communion in the hand should be accepted (Laos). — The new practice should be introduced gradually (Chile, India). — An instruction should be published that deals fully with the manner of distributing communion and brings together all the regulations issued: communion under both kinds, communion during Mass and outside Mass, communion of the sick in private, in hospitals, in extraordinary circumstances. The fact that the new rite is pleasing to educated people is a sign that it does meet certain needs (Italy).

---

61. The Pope was right when he asked, "How is it to remain secret?"

Conditions

The faithful should be asked and heard (Philippines, Congo).

There should be a very broad consultation of the faithful (Upper Volta).

Provided there is an almost universal consent (Mexico).

Only if requested by the majority of the laity (Canada).

Provided there is uniformity (Canada, Italy).

There should be freedom to receive either way, just as there is more than one manner of concelebrating (Canada, Italy).

The new rite should be allowed, not required (Canada).

Provided steps are taken to ensure reverence and cleanliness (Australia).

Do not abolish the present practice (Ivory Coast).

It is one more way in addition to the usual one (Canada).

Allow it where all the reasons for it are present and where at the same time all or almost all the drawbacks pointed out can be avoided (Mexico).

The new rite should become effective at the same time as the new structure of the Mass is introduced (Upper Volta).

Responsibility of the Hierarchy

The final decision should be left to the episcopal conferences (India, Pakistan, New Guinea, Congo, Central Africa, Italy, Germany).

Grant permission to the conferences that ask for it (Ireland).

If the principle is allowed, the episcopal conferences should decide on its practical application (Laos).

The episcopal conferences should be authorized to exempt certain categories of persons (Upper Volta).

The decision should be left to the episcopal conferences or the local Ordinaries (CELRA [Coetus Episcoporum Latini Ritus Regionum Linguae Arabaicae = Conference of Latin Rite Bishops of the Arabic-speaking Countries]).

The final decision should be left to the judgment of each bishop (Pakistan, Australia).

The Ordinary should always be consulted and give his consent (Mexico, Spain, India).

Under the strict supervision of the bishop (Mexico).

Provided it is used throughout the Church (Belgium).

Recipient of the Concession

Experiments should be conducted (Italy, Ireland).

Begin with small communities (Chile, Congo, Ivory Coast, Mexico, Vietnam).

To small, carefully prepared communities and religious congregations in urban areas (India).

Only to small communities as carefully defined by higher authority and with the consent of the local Ordinary (Italy, Spain, Mexico).

It should be allowed at most to (1) ordinands, beginning with the subdiaconate; (2) clerics serving Mass; (3) in extraordinary situations (Corpus Christi, Holy Thursday) in communities of clerics and religious (Italy).

Begin with seminaries (Italy).

To religious and committed laypersons (Canada).

To small groups of the faithful with the consent of the Ordinary (Canada, Portugal, Antilles, United States, India, Thailand).

To selected groups (Portugal, Ceylon).

Only to small groups and selected individuals, e.g., religious or laypersons during retreats (Philippines).

It may be allowed after thorough instruction to people of great faith during retreats and courses of spiritual exercises (Ecuador).

Begin with seminaries and religious communities, then small communities of the faithful, during retreats and courses of spiritual exercises (Colombia).

Communion in the hand is wonderful in intimate groups (Colombia).

This manner of communicating is fine for religious men and women and for special groups of the faithful (Colombia).

It would not work well when there are many communions or on patronal feasts, during missions, and on First Fridays (Mexico).

In certain regions and for certain groups for which the bishop deems it appropriate (Thailand).

If the practice is reserved to qualified people, it will evoke resentment of the Church (Ecuador).

Only at Masses attended by persons whose age is known, and then experimentally (El Salvador).

Only to adults (Congo).

When communion is distributed to persons with contagious diseases (El Salvador).

Not to children, the sick, or the elderly (Austria).

Not to children (Mexico).

There is danger of irreverence in the case of children (Sudan).

Permissible for adolescents and adults but not for children, at least before their profession of faith, because they may have dirty hands (Laos).

To children if the present rite is followed (Antilles).

Communion should be given on the tongue to children up to a certain age; thereafter there is no danger of infantile actions (Italy).

Only after the age of twelve (the age of confirmation); confirmation would thus be seen as the sacrament by which one enters a more mature period of life as far as obligations to the Church are concerned (Austria).

In What Circumstances

Establish the same norms as for communion from the chalice (Canada, Mexico).

Only when communion is distributed under both kinds, because then it will be justified by the extraordinary circumstances and considerations of convenience (Italy, Portugal, India, Ceylon).

Only at concelebrations and to those who can receive under both kinds (United States).

It would be preferable first to introduce the complete sign of communion, namely, communion under both kinds, and then to allow communion in the hand (United States).

Not when communion is distributed under both kinds (India).

To be allowed only once or twice a year, because if done regularly it will lessen respect; respect will increase if the practice is rare (Korea).

To be allowed only on solemn occasions (Thailand).

On special occasions (India).

Only by special grant on each occasion (India).

To be reserved to days of special importance, such as Easter and Holy Thursday (Colombia).

On special occasions (India).

Preparation of the Faithful

A human and catechetical preparation—which must be a slow process among peoples not yet fully evangelized—to ensure respect for the Eucharist (Ivory Coast, Korea, Pakistan).

Human and hygienic training.

Start with small communities (Ivory Coast).

Prior instruction and preparation (Austria, CELRA).

A great deal of instruction (Spain).

After careful, timely, and adequate preparation (Portugal, Antilles).

Suitable preparation (Chile).

First there should be serious, orderly, prolonged instruction, regulated by the hierarchy (Colombia).

After lengthy preparation (Canada).

Success depends on preparation; everything should be done under the direction of the bishop (Mexico).

Everything should be preceded by experimentation and instruction of the faithful (Venezuela).

Provided the experiments with the new rite in small communities and with the permission of the Ordinary yield positive results (Uruguay, Ivory Coast, United States).

A lengthy preliminary preparation is needed to train the people for the new rite so as to avoid scandal and a lack of respect (Ivory Coast).

The faithful must be instructed to consume the host or particle immediately so as to avoid profanations and irreverences (South Africa).

Account must be taken of the sensibilities of people with long Christian traditions behind them. Their lengthy training in deep respect for the Eucharist may make them reluctant to receive the host in their hands (South Africa).

Attitude of the Faithful

The new rite should be minutely regulated (Spain).

The episcopal conference should have authority to determine the manner of receiving communion in the hand, depending on the customs of various regions (Upper Volta).

The new practice should be everywhere the same. All bishops should issue the same guidelines and explanations (Spain).

Both ways of receiving should be authorized (CELRA).

Introduce it first into the cities, then into the countryside (India, Italy).

Communion should be given in the hand only to those who so desire (Portugal, CELRA).

Detailed regulations should be issued regarding when and where communion may be given in the hand (Mexico).

There should be a washbasin at the entrance of the church (Italy).

At least a profound bow should be prescribed before receiving the host (Austria).

The communicant should be standing firmly before the priest (Italy).

The faithful should receive the host with both hands extended (Cameroun).

The host should be consumed at the place of distribution (Germany, Congo).

Some parishioners might be assigned to keep a watchful eye on the procedure (Congo).

Place the host in the left hand; the person then covers it with the right hand and consumes it back at his or her place (Italy).

The faithful can receive the host in their hands at the altar rail (United States).

The host should be placed not on the palm but on two fingers (Italy).

The particle should not be passed from one hand to the other (Colombia).

Each person should consume the host after being given it and should then wash the hands over a basin of water placed near the altar, but without touching the water (Italy).

The faithful should have a corporal or small handkerchief on the hand (India).

The faithful should have clean hands, indicating purity of soul. They should carry a purificator on which the sacred host can be placed (Venezuela).

The hands should be clean, but hands that are calloused and blackened can indicate a greater participation in the sacrifice (Italy).

How are the hands to be purified? Is this even possible? A source of running water would be needed close by. Would it be enough to have a purificator with which the faithful could purify their hands? (Switzerland).

After communion the communicants should go off to one side where they can wash their fingers in some vessels of water and then dry them with towels, as concelebrants do (Congo Kinshasa [Zaire]).

Communion in the hand should not be given indiscriminately or when communions are numerous (Congo Kinshasa).

The celebrant should put the host not on the hand but on a small dish held by the communicant (Upper Volta).

It seems important that communion should be distributed by the president of the assembly. Can this be done by having the president hold a tray? (Canada).

The communicants should not take the host themselves (Spain).

The priest gives communion; the faithful receive it (Philippines).

The consecrated bread should be taken by each communicant directly from a large tray or from the ciborium (India, Philippines).

The hosts should be placed in baskets, but not in the kind of baskets used in everyday life (Italy).

It will be necessary to provide ciboria of a kind adapted to the new rite (Venezuela).

Communion in the hand should be only for adults and should be distributed by setting out a dish or row of dishes from which each person may take the Eucharist while the priest stands nearby (Congo, Colombia, New Zealand).

This way of taking communion for oneself makes respect for the sacrament more difficult than does reception on the tongue (Canada).

The rite can quickly be degraded if each person serves himself or herself from the tabernacle (India).

The Eucharistic bread ought to be made differently in order that fragments may not be left (India, Switzerland).

The bread of the hosts should be more cohesive in texture (Australia).

The bread should be baked like real bread so as not to leave fragments (Italy, CELRA, Mexico).

In hot regions unleavened bread is preferable because it keeps better (Congo Kinshasa).

Change the form of the host so that less time will be lost (Italy).

Principal Arguments for the Vote Against

The change could be interpreted as a desire of the Church to answer those who cast doubt on the real presence of Christ in the Eucharist (England).

There is need of putting a stop to certain initiatives (Canada).

This is not a good time for this innovation (England).

Why take a vote on what is a violation of discipline? Why not do the same for recitation of the Breviary, the practice of celibacy, and the use of the pill? (Argentina).

The concession would be the acceptance and legalization of a *fait accompli* (Argentina, Colombia).

The new rite would not help the simple faith of children and old people nor respect for the Eucharist (Argentina).

It would be a serious stumbling block for the rather sizable group of persons who come to church with little faith and because they are accustomed to the ritual; profanation would be very likely (Congo).

There would be serious danger of profanation (Argentina, Ecuador, India).

The rite would give scandal (Italy).

Sacrileges would multiply (Italy).

The wish to receive communion in the hand is often inspired by sentimentalism (Zambia).

Various people would not dare to receive for fear of being irreverent. The Eastern Church requires married people to show reverence by fasting for some days before communion and abstaining from the conjugal act (Yugoslavia).

Reception on the tongue is the mark of an infant? No, it was and is a gesture of politeness to offer a fellow guest a carefully prepared morsel. The new rite would mean a greater expenditure of time (Italy). The placing of the host on the tongue is a sacred gesture that distinguishes this food from others (Italy).

Given the present climate of rebellion, which is being fomented by not a few teachers, where will we call a halt? (Congo Kinshasa).

Sorcerers are attempting to get their hands on things holy. Will the new practice not make it easier for them? (Congo, Gabon).

What of the fragments? Communicants will have to lick their hands (Italy).

Fragments would be scattered (Portugal).

In underdeveloped regions people rarely have clean hands (Yugoslavia).

In some areas there is a great deal of humidity and people's hands are always moist (Argentina).

Many people have dirty, sweaty hands and do not wash because water is scarce (Portugal).

Children play while on their way to Mass and while waiting. Are their hands clean enough to receive communion? (Congo).

Mothers usually come to church with children in their arms; even at present infants try to take the host from the mother's mouth (Congo).

Mothers must often go out during Mass for hygienic care of their babies; will they receive communion in their hands without first washing them? (Congo).

If communion in the hand is permitted, people will soon want baker's bread. They will believe that the Eucharist is simply a blessed bread distributed on certain occasions (Cameroun).

This opens the way to all kinds of abuses. A priest recently distributed communion by giving some communicants a handful of hosts and telling them: "Share these with your brothers and sisters" (Cameroun).

Experiments in small communities will end by spreading everywhere (Colombia).

Among us the priests and all members of the clergy who are in the sanctuary receive communion in the hand; all others outside the sanctuary receive it in their mouths. We do not want to change this practice (Ethiopia).

Among us it is a sign of ill-breeding to receive food in the bare hand; the new rite is therefore not advisable (Congo).

Pastors must be patient and not arbitrarily impose their own outlook; we must advance with a sense of balance (Mexico).

It is advisable to wait a little longer (United States).

Wait two or three years (United States).

4. Results and Reflections

The Consilium ended its report with some considerations and suggestions:

The consultation shows:

1) that there is an absolute majority, though not a two-thirds majority, against the new practice;

2) that there is a disproportion between the various continents and the various levels of education and religious faith. The contribution of Europe and the Americas to the "yes" vote is clearly greater than that of Africa and Asia.

The English-, Spanish-, and Italian-speaking world is less in favor of communion in the hand than the French, German, and Dutch.

3) The problem of communion implies consequences and therefore cannot be looked at in isolation; it has a broader aspect that extends to the entirety of Eucharistic worship. It will be enough to mention the question of leavened bread, which might easily be introduced, and the connected problem of preservation; the questions of exposition and adoration, communion of the sick, and so on.

The matter must therefore be studied in all its aspects and consequences.

In light of these remarks, three solutions are possible:

1. Close the door to any concession.

2. Allow the practice of communion in the hand as well as the traditional reception on the tongue.

3. Take a definite but not closed position, as was done for communion under both kinds.

The *first* solution has the support of the absolute majority, would avoid the negative consequences it is feared communion in the hand would bring, and would have the support of a large part of the clergy and faithful.

On the other hand, a violent reaction may be anticipated in some areas and a rather widespread disobedience where communion in the hand has already been introduced.

The *second* solution would go against the majority of the bishops, would reward disobedience, and would have serious drawbacks.

The *third* solution, i.e., a compromise by which communion in the hand is allowed in some cases (e.g., as was done for communion under both kinds or, in some areas, for communion in the hand) would be in keeping with the line taken by the Council, since the latter allows for a plurality of forms in the area of discipline and relies on the responsibility of the episcopal conferences and the individual bishops.

It must be kept in mind, however, that any concession will inevitably lead to the practice becoming general.

Finally, with regard to procedure: It would be advisable that a decision in the matter be communicated to the bishops along with a pontifical document based on the consultation of the bishops and not simply with an instruction of the Congregation of Rites. There are two reasons for this: we are dealing here with a very important aspect of Eucharistic worship, and the practice of communion in the hand has spread rapidly in recent months.

For the latter reason, various bishops and apostolic nuncios . . . are urgently requesting a decision as soon as possible, lest any measures to be taken come too late.

5. *The Instruction* Memoriale Domini

After carefully studying the documentation, the Pope jotted down these observations in his own hand:

Spoke to Father Bugnini: He will draft a pontifical document in which:

1. the results of the consultation of the bishops will be summarized; and

2. the mind of the Holy See regarding the inopportuneness of distributing communion in the hands of the faithful will be reasserted, and the reasons for it (liturgical, pastoral, religious, and so on) will be given. The present practice therefore remains the rule.

3. If any episcopal conferences nonetheless think they ought to allow this innovation, let them appeal to the Holy See and then, if the requested permission is granted, follow the guidelines and instructions that will accompany the permission.

In addition:

"March 27, 1969: To the Council for Public Affairs for its information and its views (it must be kept in mind that the practice—or abuse—of distributing communion [in the hand] is already widespread in some countries and that the bishops—for example, Cardinal Suenens, and others—think it cannot be suppressed)."

On March 25, 1969, the Secretariat of State sent the Consilium all the documentation, including a repetition of the points made by the Pope. In obedience to these directives, the Consilium drafted the text of the instruction *Memoriale Domini*,[62] which was approved on May 29, 1969.[63]

The instruction first points out that the manner of celebrating the Eucharist and receiving communion has not been uniform throughout the history of the Church. Mention of the new requests and demands and the consultation of the episcopate is followed by the regulatory part of the document: bishops, priests, and faithful are urgently exhorted to follow the traditional practice in obedience to the judgment of the majority of bishops, out of respect for current liturgical law, and out of a concern for the common good of the Church.

Wherever the contrary practice has taken hold,

> in order to help the conferences of bishops to fulfill a pastoral responsibility often made more difficult by the contemporary state of affairs, [the Apostolic See] entrusts to the same conferences of bishops the duty and task of evaluating any possible special circumstances. This, however, is with the proviso both that they prevent any possible lack of reverence or false ideas about the Eucharist from being engendered in the attitudes of the people and that they carefully eliminate anything else unacceptable.

In these cases the episcopal conferences will first conduct a full study and discussion of the matter and then take a secret vote. The decision, which must be by a two-thirds majority, will then be submitted to the Holy See for its required confirmation, together with a full report on the reasons behind the decision.[64] Then "the Holy See will carefully weigh each case in the interest of the general good, the building up of all, and the increase in faith and devotion that comes from mutual example."

Along with the instruction, those requesting the indult received a letter explaining the regulations, conditions, and rite of the new manner of receiving communion.[65]

---

62. Three drafts were prepared by the secretariat of the Consilium with the help of Luigi Vassalli, a Sacramentine Father and editor of the periodical *La nuova Alleanza*. The second schema was sent to the Pope on May 12, 1969. He made some comments on it; the final text was then composed and sent to him on May 28.

63. SCDW, instruction *Memoriale Domini*, on the manner of giving communion (May 29, 1969): *DOL* 260 nos. 2054-61.

64. Authorization always depended, therefore, on the decision of the episcopal conference; see "De modo sacram Communionem ministrandi," *Not* 8 (1972) 343.

65. SCDW, Letter *En réponse à la démande*, to presidents of those conferences of bishops petitioning the indult for communion in the hand (May 29, 1969): *DOL* 261 nos. 2062-69 [but see next note with regard to no. 4 of this letter. — Tr.].

1. The new manner of giving communion must not be imposed in a way that would exclude the traditional practice. It is a matter of particular seriousness that in places where the new practice is lawfully permitted, every one of the faithful have the option of receiving communion on the tongue and even when other persons are receiving communion in the hand. The two ways of receiving communion can without question take place during the same liturgical service. There is a twofold purpose here: that none will find in the new rite anything disturbing to personal devotion toward the Eucharist; that this sacrament, the source and cause of unity by its very nature, will not become an occasion of discord between members of the faithful.

2. The rite of communion in the hand must not be put into practice indiscriminately. Since the question involves human attitudes, this mode of communion is bound up with the perceptiveness and preparation of the one receiving. It is advisable, therefore, that the rite be introduced gradually and in the beginning within small, better prepared groups and in favorable settings. Above all, it is necessary to have the introduction of the rite preceded by an effective catechesis so that the people will clearly understand the meaning of receiving in the hand and will practice it with the reverence owed to the sacrament. This catechesis must succeed in excluding any suggestion that in the mind of the Church there is a lessening of faith in the Eucharistic presence and in excluding as well any danger or hint of danger of profaning the Eucharist.

3. The option offered to the faithful of receiving the Eucharistic bread in their hand and putting it into their own mouth must not turn out to be the occasion for regarding it as ordinary bread or as just another religious article. . . . Their attitude of reverence must measure up to what they are doing.

4. As to the way to carry out the new rite: they must follow the traditional usage, which expresses the ministerial functions, by having the priest or deacon place the host in the hand of the communicant. The faithful should consume the host before returning to their place; the minister's part will be brought out by use of the usual formulary, "The body of Christ," to which the communicant replies: "Amen."[66]

---

66. In the original version of this number, the possibility was also allowed of recipients communicating themselves by taking the consecrated bread directly from the ciborium, although always with a minister standing by. But reactions to this regulation were numerous and lively. In this manner of reception the action was impoverished and lost much of its human and sacral character. This option was therefore eliminated in: SCDW, *Holy Communion and Worship of the Eucharist outside Mass* (June 21, 1973), no. 21 (*DOL* 266 no. 2099). See (AB), "De sacra communione 'distribuenda,' " *Not* 10 (1974) 308.

[N.B. In the text I have given no. 4 of the Letter *En réponse à la demande* as it stands in the Italian version of Father Bugnini. *DOL* 261 no. 2066 gives the "original" and official text: "As to the way to carry out the new rite: one possible model is the traditional usage,

5. Whatever procedure is adopted, care must be taken not to allow particles of the Eucharistic bread to fall or be scattered. Care must also be taken that the communicants have clean hands and that their comportment is becoming and in keeping with the practices of the different peoples.

6. In the case of communion under both kinds by way of intinction, it is never permitted to place on the hand of the communicant the host that has been dipped in the Lord's blood.

7. Bishops allowing introduction of the new way of receiving communion are requested to send to this Congregation after six months a report on the results of its concession.[67]

6. *Later Developments*

Many conferences adopted the new method of distributing communion. Where the practice was accompanied by appropriate instruction, it was accepted calmly and even favorably; abuses and arbitrary or secretive types of behavior were avoided. The respect shown to the Eucharist fulfilled the wishes of the Holy See. In other places, the practice was the subject of lengthy controversy. Some groups that were opposed to any and every reform exaggerated or even invented sacrileges or blew out of proportion such thoughtless behaviors as may have occurred.

The Congregation for the Sacraments wanted to take advantage of the publication of *Immensae caritatis* to introduce a section on "Devotion and Reverence Toward the Eucharist in the Case of Communion in the Hand." The statement said nothing new but simply repeated what was already said in the instruction *Memoriale Domini*. The Congregation for Divine Worship insisted that this part not be included. The reason was not that it did not treasure devotion and reverence for the Eucharist but that when removed from the context in which the entire problem of communion in the hand had been treated, the inclusion was likely to have an effect opposite to the one intended. That is precisely what happened. There were those who thought that in this document the Holy See was extending the new way of communicating to the entire Church without any new

---

which expresses the ministerial functions, by having the priest or deacon place the host in the hand of the communicant. Alternatively, it is permissible to adopt a simpler procedure, namely, allowing the faithful themselves to take the host from the ciborium or paten. The faithful should consume . . . . '' Father Bugnini seems to be changing the text of the letter in anticipation of the removal of the second alternative in *Holy Communion and Worship* . . . , no. 21. — Tr.]

67. The Consilium was against publication of the two documents, preferring that they be sent to the conferences along with the indult, whenever the latter was requested. The Pope, however, was adamant that they be published in *AAS* 61 (1969) 541–47.

requests being required; they thought the Church was setting aside the guidelines laid down in *Memoriale Domini*.[68]

It was because of this reaction that the Holy Father asked Archbishop Bugnini to write an article of explanation, which he himself corrected and which appeared in *L'Osservatore Romano* for May 15, 1973.[69] I shall cite its conclusion, since it sheds light on the spirit at work in this as in other reforms.

> Anyone willing to consider the matter calmly and objectively and without bias or prejudice must admit that the measure is reasonable, wise, prudent, and moderate. It is completely in the spirit of the Council, which favored and sometimes urged a pluralism of forms and cultural expressions. Since the measure has not only a disciplinary, cultural, and theological background but also pastoral implications, the Holy See decided to seek the views of the bishops; it followed up this consultation with a decision which reasserts the validity of the traditional practice but at the same time does not wound the large number of pastors who are going back to a practice that has equal standing in the history of the Church and can be helpful even today in certain circumstances.
>
> The measure does not represent a yielding to pressure, still less a concession to "rebels," but a gracious compliance of the Holy See with the

---

68. See the leading article in *Il Tempo*, April 22, 1973, which tendentiously urges this interpretation.

69. The Pope sent the following note to the secretariat of the SCDW: "April 24, 1973. Should not a correction be issued of what influential journalist Nino Badano says in *Il Tempo* for April 22 on the distribution of holy communion?

"a) How was it distributed in the early centuries?

"b) Since the new practice has begun as an abuse, who if not the episcopal conferences are to ask that this way of distributing the Eucharist be legitimated where the episcopal conferences desire? The authorization represents a gracious compliance of the Holy See with the responsible wishes of the local Church as expressed by their respective episcopal conferences.

"c) In Italy it does not appear that the episcopal conference has acquiesced in communion in the hand (this needs to be checked). There may be drawbacks, and the Holy See is the first to warn of them; see the words of the text, as well as the more explicit statement in the preceding concession (referred to in a note).

"The reasons? A more varied and less uniform discipline. The spirit of the article is certainly not meant to promote obedience to the Apostolic See (and this precisely out of devotion to the Blessed Sacrament)."

The title under which the article appeared in *L'Osservatore Romano*, "Devotion and Respect for the Blessed Eucharist in the Application of the Liturgical Renewal," was given it by the editors of the newspaper. That title did fit in with the caption that had been supplied for the article. But then the caption was changed, and the editors did not see that the new title was no longer appropriate. The article appeared under its original title, "Sulla mano come in trono," in *Not* 9 (1973) 289–95. [This article can be found in the English version of *L'Osservatore Romano* (June 14, 1973), as well as in *Origins* (August 16, 1973, pp. 140–42.)—*Ed.*]

responsible wishes of the local Churches as expressed by their respective episcopal conferences.

There may be unacceptable concomitants, and the Holy See has been the first to warn against them in the instruction and even more comprehensively in the letter of concession. We must not forget, however, that "negligences and profanations" or sacrilegious acts against the Eucharist have unfortunately occurred at all times and in all places no less than today. The causes of such actions are complex and must be calmly examined and studied. A more continuous, careful, and vigorous catechesis, as well as a more responsible human and religious maturity, must provide the basis on which the faithful are prepared for the new way of receiving communion in countries where the authorization has been granted. . . .

In conclusion, in the current liturgical reform devotion and respect for the Eucharist continue to be a focus of attention and object of concern for the responsible authorities, even if expressions and forms of worship may undergo changes so that they may be more in keeping with the changed circumstances and mentality of our time. Church and Eucharist are equally indispensable and to be revered.[70]

V. Communion Outside Mass and Worship of the Eucharist

Implementation of the liturgical reform in the area of the Eucharist required that the part of the Ritual of Paul V entitled "De Sanctissimo Eucharistiae Sacramento" and the part of "De processionibus" on the Eucharist be revised.

The initial intention was to produce a kind of instruction "on sacramental communion and worship of the Eucharist outside Mass," which would bring together and update all the extensive material dealing with the Eucharist. The work was entrusted to a study group,[71] which composed a schema containing a rather broad treatment of the subject. This was unsatisfactory, however, precisely because of its breadth and because the new treatment would have necessitated a lengthy and complex doctrinal study. It was thought preferable to base the treatment on documents already published and to make it a kind of synthesis of these.[72] The new

---

70. But not even these explanations appeased everyone. There were those who made it their mission to "make an impression" on the Pope by reporting "cases" of serious profanation. It seems that as soon as it was established the new Congregation for the Sacraments and Divine Worship sent a questionnaire to the episcopal conferences on the application of the concession. There were rumors that Rome wanted to withdraw the authorization. But the new way of receiving communion, which is really not new but the oldest way, has been well received in the Churches that have introduced it.

71. The group comprised V. Noè, B. Raffa, C. Michel Jean, L. Vassalli, I. Calabuig, and G. Pasqualetti.

72. The synthesis was the work of C. Braga.

schema was critiqued at the second plenary meeting of the Congregation for Divine Worship.[73]

The document was then sent to the Congregations for the Doctrine
of the Faith,[74] the Sacraments,[75] and Religious[76] for their examination.
The Secretariat of State likewise contributed several sets of remarks.[77] The
Secretariat also communicated the Holy Father's approval on July 18, 1973
(No. 238794). The liturgical book was officially published by decree of the

---

73. It was discussed on March 7, 1972; *relator:* Bishop Boudon. See "Secunda Congregatio
Plenaria," *Not* 8 (1972) 120-22. Practically all the members were in favor.

74. Sent on February 21, 1973, and approved on March 21, 1973, with some comments.

75. Sent on February 21, 1973; reply on March 29. Meanwhile the instruction *Immensae
caritatis* had been published, and many difficulties had been resolved. The most important
request from the Congregation for the Sacraments was that the decree of approval should
"explicitly state that all the regulations in the Code of Canon Law and in other pontifical
documents not abrogated or modified are still in effect."

The SCDW did not think it could go along with this request, since it had to respect the
procedure followed in the publication of all the liturgical books. Moreover, it had always
been held that regulations not affected by new legislation are still in effect. But then, at
the suggestion of the Secretariat of State, the SCDW published a note entitled "De habitu-
dine ritualis instaurati ad normas canonicas vigentes" in *Not* 9 (1973) 333. The note referred
to a document published by the Congregation for the Sacraments in 1938 regarding reservation of the Eucharist. As far as the new document on holy communion and Eucharistic
worship is concerned, the reference in no. 10 to the most recent document on the subject,
the instruction *Eucharisticum mysterium*, nos. 52-53, was regarded as sufficient.

76. Especially discussed with this Congregation was the problem of adoration in communities dedicated to this practice by their vocation; the result of the discussion was no.
90 of the new liturgical book. The Congregation for Religious asked the Secretariat of State
to see to it that the document avoided giving the impression "that community adoration
is preferred to private, thus creating uneasiness and division within religious institutes whose
constitutions call for continuous adoration of the Blessed Sacrament in their churches or
chapels" (letter of the Secretariat of State to the SCDW, July 18, 1973). The SCDW accepted
this legitimate request, but preferred to say simply that the alternative form of adoration
"is not excluded." The Congregation for Religious insisted on the document saying that
the alternate form "is also to be maintained and is highly recommended." The Pope thought
the request should be accepted. The opinion of the Congregation for Religious had been
asked on April 5, 1973, and it had replied on April 12.

77. May 14, June 4, and July 18, with final approval. Credit goes to the Secretariat of
State (which was implementing the comments of the Holy Father) for the formulation of
no. 6 on the various kinds of presence (the wording was intended to avoid the disputes
that had arisen over no. 7 of the GIRM), no. 21 on the manner of distributing communion,
and no. 90, mentioned in the preceding note.

A difficulty also arose within the SCDW at its final discussion of the printer's proofs.
The secretary insisted on some points that he regarded as connected with respect and veneration for the Eucharist, such as the use of a humeral veil at Benediction and the use of incense; he also had in mind various sensibilities that had found expression and ought to
be respected. His views were finally accepted.

Congregation for Divine Worship on June 21, 1973, the Solemnity of the Lord's Body and Blood.[78]

As I indicated a moment ago, the book contains nothing new from the doctrinal and pastoral viewpoints, but uses documents already published as its point of reference. It is on the basis of these that it regulates the rites of communion outside Mass and the various forms of Eucharistic worship.

The material is divided into two parts: the first deals with communion outside Mass, the second with the forms of public worship of the Eucharist.

A General Introduction is followed by four chapters, the first three of which deal with communion outside Mass, communion of the sick given by an extraordinary minister, and the various forms of worship (exposition, Eucharistic processions, Eucharistic congresses).

The fourth chapter contains an extensive collection of texts: a "lectionary" of fifty-one passages of Scripture; hymns, songs, and traditional responsories; and many prayers from the Roman Missal and old processional books.[79]

---

78. *De sacra Communione et de cultu mysterii eucharistici extra Missam* (Vatican Polyglot Press, 1973; 72 pp.). The rite is in *The Rites of the Catholic Church* 1 (New York, 1983²) 469–532. There is a new translation of the Introductions in *DOL* 266 nos. 2091-2103, and 279 nos. 2193-2226.

79. There are eight hymns (nos. 192-99), namely, those in the Office of Corpus Christ and some others with Eucharistic content. Here, for the first time in the liturgy, the critical text of two of these hymns is used: "Adoro te devote, latens veritas" (no. 198) and "Ubi caritas" (no. 199). The first of these two hymns has several variants from the text hitherto in use; they derive from the critical edition by Dom Wilmart in his *Auteurs spirituels du moyen âge latin* (Paris, 1932) 361–414.

There is only one change in the hymn "Ubi caritas," but it is a significant one. In the first verse, "Ubi caritas et amor" has been changed to "Ubi caritas est vera." The critical text was reconstructed by Karl Strecker, in *Monumenta Germaniae Historica (Poetae latini Aevi Karolingi)*, IV, II, 1, 526–29; see also E. Franceschini, "Dov'è carità e amore qui c'è Dio," *L'Osservatore Romano*, June 1, 1972. This information and the critical text for the typical edition were supplied by Monsignor Pietro Amato Frutaz, the very learned undersecretary of the Sacred Congregation for the Causes of the Saints. The *Orationes post Communionem* (nos. 210-19) were all taken, with one exception (no. 215), from the Roman Missal of 1970.

The "Prayers at Benediction of the Blessed Sacrament" (nos. 224-28) are almost all from the *Processionale Parisiense* of 1690. Formula 226 has been slightly adapted. Formula 228 is from the Roman Missal, with some revisions.

Reconciliation

I. History

The reform of the rites of penance traveled a rather long and tortuous road. Seven years were required to implement the few lines that the liturgical Constitution devotes to the subject: "The rites and formularies for the sacrament of penance are to be revised so that they more clearly express both the nature and effect of the sacrament" (no. 72).

1. First Stage (1966–1969)[1]

On December 2, 1966, a separate group was established to study the problems inherent in the sacrament of penance.[2]

Questionnaires on the sacrament were sent out in France, England, Scotland, the United States, Australia, and Africa,[3] and at the same time a collection was made of writings of various scholars on the subject. The inquiry brought to light a growing dissatisfaction with the sacrament of

---

1. For discussion of the subject see especially C. Braga, C.M., "Il nuovo *Ordo Paenitentiae*," EL 89 (1975) 165–76; F. Sottocornola, S.X., "Il nuovo *Ordo Paenitentiae*," Not 10 (1974) 63–79.

2. *Relator* of group 23bis: J. Lécuyer; *secretary:* F. Heggen and, from 1967 on, F. Nikolasch; *members:* Z. Alszeghy, P. Anciaux, C. Floristán, A. Kirchgässner, L. Ligier, K. Rahner, and C. Vogel. This group worked throughout the first phase; another replaced it in the second phase (see below, n. 20).

3. The inquiries in France (16 centers in Southern France and 104 parishes in the Paris region), in England (among 614 fifteen-year-old students in various schools), and in Scotland were conducted directly by the Consilium. The questionnaires filled out in the United States, Australia, and Africa were collected by *The Clergy Review* and sent on to the Consilium.

penance and a desire to restore vitality to it by means of a less mechanical and formal practice that would bring out more clearly the social and communal aspect of both sin and reconciliation. There was hope that the rite for individuals would be complemented by some form of communal celebration.

In its effort to shed light on the nature and effect of the sacrament, the group not only turned to worthwhile recent studies but also combed the conciliar documents,[4] from which it might derive the basic points to be kept in mind in the reform of the rite:

—Sin is by its nature both an offense against God and a wound inflicted on the Church.

—Sacramental reconciliation is reconciliation with both God and the Church.

—The entire Christian community works together for the conversion of sinners.

The study group held its *first* meeting at Rome, February 8–9, 1967; the purpose was to look at the main problems and draw up a program of work. Its reflections, condensed into the first report, were presented to the Consilium at its eighth general meeting (April 13, 1967; to the relators on April 4) in the form of a set of principles and alternative solutions.[5]

The question of a possible celebration of penance in communal form, with general absolution and without a prior individual confession, was immediately seen as a serious problem that would require thorough study. The discussion was long and excited. The Fathers ended by asking the group to prepare a schema for forms of celebration "in cases anticipated in the existing legislation." The Fathers did not take up doctrinal and disciplinary problems, which did not come within the competency of the Consilium, but everyone knew that concessions did exist and that their concrete application should not be made in just any manner but in a liturgical context that would ensure the efficacy of the sacrament.

Another important question discussed was the sacramental formula of absolution. Various possible solutions were suggested:

—retention of the present text, with some revisions;

—search for a new text to be taken from the rich treasury of early tradition, both Latin and Eastern;

—several optional formulas, one of which would be the revised present formula.

---

4. Especially *Lumen gentium* 11, *Presbyterorum ordinis* 5, *Christus Dominus* 30, and *Sacrosanctum Concilium* 109–10.

5. See "Octava sessio plenaria Consilii," *Not* 3 (1967) 146.

When the group asked whether it was to offer several optional formulas from among which the priest would be permitted to choose, the answer was negative.[6]

The group held its *second* meeting at Rome on May 10–11, 1967. Following the directives given it by the Consilium, it discussed reform of the existing rite of penance, attempted to compose a rite for communal celebration, and started a collection of texts for sacramental absolution in the Latin Church down to about the year 1000, a historical study of the evolution of the sacrament, and an investigation of general absolution.

In dealing with this last subject, the group assembled a rather voluminous documentation on the Tridentine decrees and their interpretation by theologians and moralists. In particular, it collected and studied the various replies from the Holy See to bishops, especially in the missions, regarding general absolution.

Researches were also conducted in the archives of the Roman Congregations involved in this problem. It turned out that during the First and Second World Wars and in various situations of serious necessity, the Holy See had several times given permission for general absolution without prior oral confession. The practice of the Congregations, especially when dealing with the great masses in mission countries and in Latin America, took as valid, and applied, the instruction issued by the Apostolic Penitentiary in 1944.[7]

The *third* meeting of the group took place on December 6–8, 1967, again in Rome. It produced the schema submitted at the tenth general meeting of the Consilium (April 7, 1978; to the relators on April 16 and 19).[8] This was a well-organized document that contained the principles for reform of the sacramental celebration, a historical section, and a ritual.

The well-documented historical exposé of the evolution of the sacrament showed the existence of varying traditions in the form and manner of celebrating the sacrament in both the Western and the Eastern Church. It also supplied extensive information on general absolution without prior confession; this information, when compared with the practice of the Holy See, made possible a clearer understanding of this sensitive area.

---

6. The vote was 15 for and 17 against; see Schema 222; "Status quaestionis circa plures formulas absolutionis sacramentalis," in Schema 356bis = *De Paenitentia* 11bis (October 31, 1961), and in *Res Secretariae*, no. 36 (October 11, 1968).

7. "Instructio S. Paenitentiariae circa sacramentalem absolutionem generali modo pluribus impertiendam" (March 25, 1944), *AAS* 36 (1944) 155–56.

8. Schema 279: *De Paenitentia* 6 (March 16, 1968); see "Decima sessio plenaria Consilii," *Not* 4 (1968) 183.

The ritual part of the schema provided a form for individual celebration of the sacrament and another for communal celebration with individual confession and absolution. There was as yet no rite for general absolution, but only a presentation of the problem.

The Fathers, by and large, accepted the schema. Their attention was focused chiefly on the sacramental formula, because of the conciliar decree that it should more clearly express the purpose and effects of the sacrament. The decree gave rise to two problems:

1) Should the declarative form ("I absolve you") of more recent tradition, which emphasizes the role of the minister, be retained, or should there be a return to the more ancient deprecative form, which brings out more clearly the action of God and Christ ("May he absolve you")?

2) Should there be a plurality of formulas in order to allow a choice depending on the variety of cases and needs?

After lively and excited discussion the Fathers approved modification of the existing form to make it more responsive to the requirements of the Council; they also approved the suggested text.[9]

The question of the possibility of several formulas proved to be more knotty. The vote taken in the previous year had been negative, but the rejection had been by a very small margin. Furthermore, the question in that vote had been whether there should be several formulas from which *the priest* might choose. Given the quite different situations in many countries, the group studying the problem of the formula thought it might present several formulas "from among which the episcopal conferences themselves might choose;"[10] they regarded this as a solution that did not contradict what had already been decided.

The discussion grew hot, with some maintaining there should be no going back to a question already decided, while others claimed that the subject was in fact new, namely, the possibility of a choice by the episcopal conferences. Since the discussion dragged on with no consensus in sight, the problem was set aside, and the meeting turned to an examination of the formula that was proposed as a third and that imitated the formula currently in use. The third formula was approved on April 29.[11]

At the eleventh general meeting the question of a plurality of formulas came up again (October 9 and 17, 1968; October 5 for the relators).

---

9. The text: "In the name of our Lord Jesus Christ and by the power of the Holy Spirit I absolve you from your sins and restore you fully to the peace of the Church." When possible, the prayer "May the passion of our Lord . . . " was to follow.

10. See Schema 279, nos. 29 and 28.

11. The result of the vote was 25 for, 1 for with qualifications, and 3 against.

The Consilium confined itself to approving the Introduction. But under pressure from various Fathers who wanted a decision on the possibility of having several texts for sacramental absolution, the presidential council decided to bring the question to the floor once again. It asked:

a) whether other formulas were to be allowed in addition to the one already approved, so that the episcopal conferences might choose from among them; and

b) if the reply to a were affirmative, which texts should be offered?

The discussion on October 17 developed the arguments pro and con; mainly, however, as a result of the piqued stubbornness of some, it centered on the legitimacy of dealing again with a matter already decided. It proved necessary, therefore, before any discussion of the substantive issue, to take a vote on "whether it was opportune to raise the problem of a possible second or third formula of absolution." The vote was affirmative,[12] but the ensuing discussion came to no conclusion. The Fathers decided to study the entire question again at the next meeting; they would then have time to go into it thoroughly.

The problem thus came up again at the twelfth general meeting (November 11, 1969; November 6 with the consultors). The study group gave a full report on the preceding stages of the discussion and on the arguments for and against.[13] The discussion that ensued showed a certain weariness with the whole business. Two groups were still at odds: those who spoke for the demands of the episcopal conferences, which favored a plurality of formulas; and those who regarded the problem as already settled and saw in a plurality of formulas a threat to unity and a source of confusion for the faithful and who would not allow the possibility of a deprecative formula, that is, one in which the direct statement "I absolve you" did not appear.

In the end those favoring several formulas won out, and two others suggested by the study group were approved.[14] This action ended the work of the study group. The schema still needed to be completed by some further elements, but the rite was substantially in place. It was

---

12. Here again with a very small gap: 17 for and 15 against.

13. Schema 356bis: De Paenitentia 11 (October 30, 1969).

14. Here are the texts:

1."Our Lord Jesus Christ sacrificed himself to the Father for us and gave his Church the power to forgive sins. May he, through my ministry, absolve you from your sins by the grace of the Holy Spirit and restore you to the perfect peace of the Church."

2. "Our Lord Jesus Christ reconciled the world to his Father by his passion and resurrection. By the grace of the Holy Spirit he forgives your sins through my ministry and restores you fully to the life of the Church."

reviewed and then sent to the Congregation for the Doctrine of the Faith on February 9, 1970.[15] The schema, however, never saw the light, although some use would be made of it.

This schema reflected the toil that went into its preparation, as well as the main concerns that occupied the attention of the group and the Consilium. It did not represent any real ritual and euchological enrichment. The most worthwhile part of it was the historical synthesis and the presentation of the criteria governing the revision. The Introduction was rather skimpy in dealing with such fundamental matters as the nature of the sacrament, the minister, and the parts of the celebration. The rite for individual celebration followed the current ritual, even in the prayers used, although with some timely alterations and simplifications. The schema did not, however, supply a true and proper rite for communal celebration of penance with individual confession and absolution, but said only that if a group was present, a suitable short liturgy of the Word could be organized to prepare the penitents, and a collective thanksgiving could be made at the end. The schema did, however, include a rite for collective absolution without prior individual confession.

With the passage of time and as a result of experience gained in dealing with other rituals, the Consilium realized the need of a greater enrichment in the prayers of the rite and the doctrinal and pastoral Introduction.

When the Congregation for the Doctrine of the Faith sent its reply to the schema (July 8, 1970), it was clear that this rite could not be published and that it was best to wait. The Congregation decreed that only the Introduction might be published, along with the rite for individual penance. The section on absolution with general confession needed to be revised in accordance with norms that would be given.

With regard to the sacramental formula: "There ought to be a single obligatory form of the sacrament. . . . The episcopal conferences can, if need be, propose other additional formulas that reflect the mentality of the various peoples."[16]

And with regard to the minister:

    a) there is need of emphasizing his role as pastor and judge;

    b) absolution is to be given by the confessor who has heard the confession;

---

15. Schema 361: *De Paenitentia* 12 (January 31, 1970).

16. The SCDF chose the first formula approved by the Consilium (above, n. 9), which resembled the current one and was declarative in form. Thus, after so many lengthy discussions, the two great questions of the plurality and the style of the sacramental formula were answered by those in authority.

c) the question of extending jurisdiction for confessions is to be studied conjointly with the Congregation for the Discipline of the Sacraments
and the Congregation of the Clergy. After this study the question may be
settled.

The reply contained other remarks on details having to do with the
place for confessions, the sacred vestments used, and the absolution of
censures. It was clear, then, that in the diminished form that remained,
the schema could not be published. It was necessary to wait for the
promised document on general absolution.[17]

2. Second Stage (1972-1973)

On June 16, 1972, the Congregation for the Doctrine of the Faith settled
the matter of general absolution by publishing a set of "pastoral norms"
for it.[18] This document sets down the doctrinal principles and practical
guidelines for this manner of celebrating the sacrament (it is a celebration intended only for truly exceptional cases).

On the previous May 31 the Secretariat of State had informed the Congregation for Divine Worship that "the pastoral norms for the sacrament
of penance are now ready and will be sent to your agency so that it may
adapt the rite it has prepared for general absolution in cases where this
may be given."[19]

---

17. The SCDW wrote to the Pope about this toward the end of May 1971. In a note prepared for an audience it said:

"The revision of the ritual part of the sacrament of penance has already been approved
by the SCDF. It cannot be published at present, however; there would be no advantage
in doing so, and many would be disappointed.

"Dissatisfaction with this sacrament has now become general: on all sides we see new
initiatives, studies, researches, study groups. Individual bishops and even episcopal conferences have published their own documents or are preparing them. Clarification from
the central authority is becoming increasingly necessary and is increasingly expected, if only
to avoid what are seen as abuses. We know nothing about meetings held on this subject
by representatives of the various Roman agencies. But the matter must be dealt with immediately, and a good number of persons expert in the field must be assigned to it in order
to enlighten pastors and faithful on this sensitive, complex, and vitally important subject
before it is too late.

18. SCDF, Pastoral Norms *Sacramentum Paenitentiae*, on general absolution (June 16, 1972):
AAS 64 (1972) 510-14; *DOL* 361 nos. 3038-51. See the commentary of M. Zalba, S.J., in *Not*
8 (1972) 317-26; and the address of the Holy Father to a general audience on July 19, 1972,
in *DOL* 363 nos. 3057-59.

19. The Secretariat of State thought that the rite of penance might be published simultaneously with the pastoral norms. The SCDW replied that it could not publish the rite
before Lent or, at the earliest, at the beginning of 1973. The Secretariat then insisted that
the SCDW publish at least the formula of absolution. But this did not seem at all appropri-

When the Consilium looked at the work already done in the light of the new pastoral norms, it became clear that the *Ordo Paenitentiae* would have to be radically revised, although the values and positive elements of the 1970 schema could be used. A new study group was therefore established which was completely different from the earlier one; the new group would do its work in the light of new directives and new requirements.[20]

The group labored in the summer of 1972 to prepare the Introduction and the rites. A first meeting, on the approach to be taken, was held on June 22 at the Congregation for Divine Worship. A second was held October 5-7 and produced the first schema. This was studied by the consultors of the Congregation (November 8-10, 1972) and then at a plenary meeting (November 21, 1972).[21] After being corrected in accordance with the observations submitted, the *Ordo* was sent on December 1, 1972, for

---

ate: a new formula could not be published without a solemn document approving it. Furthermore, to publish the formula of absolution apart from the rite of which it was to be a part would be an absurdity. The Secretariat agreed, therefore, that a note should be added to no. V of the Pastoral Norms, saying that once the new rite of penance was published, its sacramental formula was to be used, in the plural, whenever the faculty for general absolution was used.

20. *Relator:* P. Jounel; *secretary:* F. Sottocornola; *members* A. Gracia, P. Visentin, H. Meyer, K. Donovan, and G. Pasqualetti.

21. See "Tertia Congregatio plenaria," *Not* 9 (1973) 46. As I mentioned earlier (see above, p. 197), the discussion was not unaccompanied by feelings of resentment at suspected violations of areas of competency and at the failure to present the matter first to the agencies concerned. The secretary had to explain in a statement to all the Fathers (November 13, 1972) that the document was simply a draft for study, that the Congregations concerned were to have been consulted, and that this was not done simply for lack of time. The explanation did not suffice. The Secretariat of State observed (October 30, 1972; No. 220955) that "since this was a typical question involving several agencies, it would have been appropriate to produce the document conjointly before presenting it to the plenary meeting, and not to risk going beyond the competency of the study group. Since it was anticipated that the formula of absolution and even the very name of the sacrament were to be changed, collaboration with the other concerned agencies would seem to have been required from the very outset."

For his part, Cardinal Samorè, prefect of the Congregation for the Sacraments, expressed the hope (November 7) that "the new *Ordo* would be very respectful of competencies," and he spoke on this subject at length. There was an echo of this at the plenary meeting, which was therefore marked by a certain malaise; it ended with suspicion being cast on the entire work of reform. Cardinal Bengsch of Berlin was quick to send his remarks to the Secretariat of State. The latter passed these on to the SCDW on January 9, 1973, and emphasized that "they deserve close attention." But the Secretariat also sent the Cardinal's remarks around to the entire Curia. The Commission for the Code wrote that it had seen them and asked for the schema. At an audience on December 12, 1972, the Pope showed Archbishop Bugnini the petition of one person and the rather negative comments of another.

examination by the Congregations for the Doctrine of the Faith, the Sacraments, the Clergy, and the Evangelization of Peoples, and by the Apostolic Penitentiary and the Commission for the Code of Canon Law.[22] The schema was also submitted to the Pope, who sent in his remarks via the Secretariat of State.[23]

A joint meeting of the Congregations for Divine Worship, the Doctrine of the Faith, and the Sacraments was set up for January, 1973. It had to be put off, however, until March 2-3, after all the Congregations

---

22. Schema 387: *De Paenitentia* 14. The replies came in this order: SCDF, February 13 and 26, 1973; Sacraments: February 10; Clergy, January 31; Propaganda Fide, January 9; Apostolic Penitentiary, January 9 and 24. The last-named was asked again on April 3 and June 23 for its opinion of the text for the absolution from censures; its first reply came on April 11, and its final one on July 2.

This extensive consultation, the purpose of which was to respect all possible competencies, perhaps aroused curiosity and even resentment in those not consulted. In any case, the Secretariat of State asked on September 21, 1973, that the schema also be sent to the Congregation for the Eastern Churches, since its secretary had asked to see it. It was sent to him on October 11, and a reply came on the 30th, along with an "inconclusive lecture" from one of the consultors of that Congregation (in general, the Congregations sent or cited the views of those consulted. But the consultation in this case was so extensive that the views of some consultors of various Congregations were sent directly by the individuals themselves!).

The Commission for the Code, whose president was a member of the SCDW, also asked that it might examine the schema, since it "had seen" the remarks of Cardinal Bengsch (January 10, 1973). The schema was sent and a reply came on January 18, along with a letter from the Cardinal President that was devoted entirely to the matter of competencies and collaboration between the various agencies of the Curia. The Commission was then asked for its views on two points: the jurisdiction of the minister and the place for confessions.

23. The Holy Father laid special emphasis on the formulas for expressing repentance. The schema had suggested the Our Father. On January 15, 1973, the Secretariat of State wrote of this: "The Our Father does not seem to be a prayer sufficiently suited to expressing sorrow and the determination not to sin again, which the sacrament of reconciliation requires. What is needed is an act more directly expressive of 'contrition' and 'determination' and more directly related to the *metanoia*, or change of heart, proper to this sacrament. If you do not want to compose a new and suitable act of contrition, you might look in the Psalms and Gospels for short, suitable, and easily grasped sentences that are explicitly concerned with repentance, the plea for forgiveness, the invocation of mercy, and conversion of heart, such as all the penitential literature seems to require (see Luke 15:13; Ps 50; St. Ambrose, *De paenitentia* II, vii, 53)."

The same point was repeated in a letter of January 24, which was accompanied by "some examples of penitential prayers" that had been suggested to the Holy Father "by persons expert in this area." One suggestion was "A further Prayer of St. Ambrose before Mass," which was to be found in the Tridentine Missal in the section entitled "Preparation for Mass": "Remember, Lord, your creature. . . ." Further suggestions: "the first verses of the *Miserere*" and one of the first four prayers at the end of the old Litany of the Saints.

The Holy Father returned to this subject when the conclusions reached by the SCDF were submitted to him.

to which the schema was sent had submitted their observations.[24] At this meeting the participants worked through the observations. All the requests were winnowed out, divided into groups, and then re-examined during the following days by the delegates from the Congregation for Divine Worship and the Congregation for the Doctrine of the Faith.

In order to facilitate the speedy publication of this new liturgical book for which the Church was so eagerly waiting, the Congregation for Divine Worship decided to accede to all the requests, since these did not alter the substance of the rite but on the whole (there were eleven closely written pages from the Congregation for the Doctrine of the Faith alone) made the text leaner and reduced its vagueness.

On the other hand, the movement of the Introduction, which drew its inspiration from Sacred Scripture, was weighed down here and there by the insertion of expressions of a Scholastic kind. Thus the use of the word "reconciliation" was reduced to a minimum; the individual aspect of penance was emphasized at the expense of a broader vision of the Church as a community of forgiveness and reconciliation; the judicial function of the confessor was stressed. In general, the changes showed a keen concern to preserve individual confession and its pre-eminence over communal penance. The norms for jurisdiction and the place of confessions were also made more restrictive.[25]

When the galleys were being returned to the Congregation for the Doctrine of the Faith on May 21, 1973, the Congregation for Divine Worship insisted on two points:

1) It asked for a softening of the statement in no. 7a of the Introduction that according to God's will, "each and every grave sin" must be confessed. This, the Congregation said, seemed to cut short all further discussion and study of the Tridentine decree on this matter. The text

---

24. *Participants:* for the SCDF, B. Duroux and E. Lio; for the Sacraments, L. Vetri; for the SCDW, A. Bugnini, G. Pasqualetti, and the members of the study group.

25. Both for jurisdiction (see Introduction 9b) and for the place of confession (*ibid.*, 12) the text agreed upon with the Commission for the Code was adopted. The texts suggested by the SCDW had been worded more broadly. For jurisdiction: "All bishops of the Church, along with their priests, validly exercise the ministry of sacramental penance everywhere, unless they are prevented from doing so by some censure or interdiction. But in order licitly to absolve or hear the confessions of the faithful, they must follow the regulations established by the episcopal conferences for each region."

For the place of confession: "The sacrament of reconciliation is regularly celebrated in a church or oratory, in accordance with the regulations established by the bishops, and with respect for the customs and traditions of each region. The place intended for the celebration of penance must therefore be appropriate for confession and for carrying on a conversation with the minister."

proposed by the Congregation for Divine Worship was more nuanced: it called for an integral confession, but without deriving the need of this from the positive will of God.

2) The Congregation for Divine Worship had proposed that in the formula of absolution the essential words be introduced by an "and *therefore*," while the Congregation for the Doctrine of the Faith wanted this changed to "and *I* absolve you . . . ." The former seemed more appropriate because it better reflected the theology of the sacrament; it sought to bring out the fact that God forgives through Jesus Christ, who in turn acts in his Church. "And I," on the other hand, makes a distinction between two subjects, "God and I," so that the priest's action seems to be as it were added on to the first part of the formula rather than intrinsically connected with it. Many of the *periti* in the Congregation for Divine Worship strongly emphasized this point, because they regarded it as necessary for a proper understanding of the sacrament and as expressing a genuine liturgical sense that rejects any separation of the essential words from the context in which they are used.

But on June 19 the Congregation for the Doctrine of the Faith denied both requests. Regarding the second, it said: "The reasons given by the Congregation for Divine Worship are not convincing. The Congregation for the Doctrine of the Faith has serious reasons for keeping the formula as it is." When asked what these reasons were, the Congregation replied that it would make them known to the Pope.

In the same letter the Congregation expressed reservations about the schemas for penitential celebrations, which had been sent to it on April 30, 1973. After saying that there had as yet been no opportunity for it to study these at the meeting of its consultors and at its own regular weekly meeting, it added that it found some points in these celebrations to be "theologically debatable and unacceptable." It then proposed:

a) to replace them with another plan that would contain "only guidelines for the structure of the celebration" and, "in order to avoid any confusion," would say nothing about "a possible administration of the sacrament";

b) or "if the Congregation for Divine Worship thinks it appropriate, to prepare a little booklet [for these celebrations] that would be distinct from the volume containing the *Ordo* and would follow the normal course leading to approval, this approval to include that of the Congregation for the Doctrine of the Faith."

The Congregation for Divine Worship, however, thought that the sample penitential services needed to be published for pastoral reasons, namely, to keep penitential celebrations from developing in a disorderly way and to help such conferences as were inadequately provided with the means and personnel needed for developing services of their own.[26] The Congregation saw no danger of confusion, since the very division of the *Ordo* into chapters and the explanation given in the Introduction made it quite clear which celebrations are sacramental and which are not. It therefore rejected the first proposal of the Congregation for the Doctrine of the Faith and called for publication of the sample services in an appendix to the volume containing the *Ordo*. If, however, this proved impossible "because of the need of publishing the *Ordo* quickly in order to avoid abuses inevitably arising from prolonged delay," then, and only then, it would accept as a last resort the proposal that these sample celebrations be published separately.

The three points of disagreement were set before the Holy Father when the galleys of the *Ordo* were given to him on July 11, 1973.[27] He discussed the proofs directly with the secretary of the Congregation for Divine Worship at an audience on August 3. The Pope said he had read every word of the entire document. He repeatedly expressed his satisfaction with it; he also asked the names of the consultors who had shared in the work and gave the secretary some medals and rosaries to be distributed among them.

With regard to the three questions, he advised that for the first two the wishes of the Congregation for the Doctrine of the Faith be followed, while for the penitential celebrations he accepted the request of the Congregation for Divine Worship. The mind of the Holy Father was also expressed in a letter from the Secretariat of State, dated August 17, 1973 (No. 239667):

> After studying the new *Ordo*, the Holy Father asked me to convey to Your Eminence and to all who worked on the preparation of the text his sincere praises for the work done and, at the same time, to request that you accept the comments of the Congregation for the Doctrine of the Faith on no. 7a of the Introduction and on the sacramental formula. He also urges careful study of the notes he gave to Msgr. Annibale Bugnini at an audience on August 3.[28]

---

26. At an audience granted to the secretary of the SCDW on May 27, 1971, the Holy Father himself, while referring to the problem of general absolution and communal celebrations of penance, said: "The penitential celebrations must be carefully prepared. The SCDW is doing a very important piece of work. It might also consider celebrations for different categories: children, women, workers, and so on, at least for the period when Easter is approaching."

27. The decree of approval was also studied at a joint meeting with the SCDF on June 28 and was approved by the latter on July 11, with some corrections.

28. The points made by the Pope concerned chiefly: (1) no. 9 of the Introduction, in

As for the sample penitential celebrations, the Supreme Pontiff's view is that they may be published as your Congregation proposes, namely, as an appendix in the typical edition of the *Ordo;* they are informational and not preceptive.

It will therefore be necessary to revise this extremely important work very carefully and with a keen pastoral sense, even if the revision requires a further expenditure of time. You should, however, endeavor to have the work published before Lent of 1974.[29]

The Congregation for Divine Worship hastened to communicate the Holy Father's wishes to the Congregation for the Doctrine of the Faith. The latter, however, seized upon the Secretariat's statement about revision and decided to have "the consultors and eminent Fathers" of that Congregation study the sample penitential services.[30]

A reply on these finally came on November 23, 1973. It said that after five months the serious confusions and the theologically debatable and unacceptable points had not been cleared up at all. The Congregation insisted that there be a clear statement of the difference between celebrations of the sacrament of penance and non-sacramental penitential celebrations. It asked that no mention be made of a possible administration of the sacrament in connection with the penitential celebrations; it

---

which at the Pope's wish Matt 16:19 was cited; (2) no. 15: it was said there that the examination of conscience might be made using the Beatitudes as a basis; this was removed. The Pope remarked: "How can the faithful who are not instructed in the Scriptures derive an examination of conscience regarding their sins from the gospel passage on the Beatitudes?"; (3) no. 16: the text had the priest and the penitent making the sign of the cross at the beginning of the rite of confession. With a fine practical sense, the Pope noted: "The confessor too, for every penitent?" He then corrected the text so as to require only the penitent to make the sign; the confessor *may* make it if he wishes.

The Pope showed some hesitation regarding the optional reading of Scripture in the individual celebration of the sacrament. The reasons were explained to him, and he accepted them. He also asked: "With regard to the examination of conscience: Would it not be wise to present a preferred plan in the style of the catechism? The same for the act of contrition: a concise and accurate popular form should be provided." A text for the act of contrition was therefore prepared (*Ordo,* no. 92 [Rite of Penance, nos. 45 and 85-92]), as was a plan for the examination of conscience, which became Appendix III because the SCDF asked that it not be placed in the body of rite of sacramental penance and also that reference be made to it in all the sample penitential celebrations.

29. The secretary of the Congregation also communicated the results of the audience to the members of the study group on August 6.

30. Letter of September 25, 1973, in which the SCDF also asked for thirty-five copies of the page proofs of the "Specimina celebrationum Paenitentialium." The copies were sent on October 1; on the 31st the plans for the examination of conscience that the Pope had requested were also sent. At an audience on the previous Saturday, October 29, the Pope had asked the secretary of the SCDW to urge the SCDF to make haste. But the authorities of that Congregation replied that their "machinery has a rhythm that cannot be altered."

suggested some additions of a more concrete kind in the penitential acts and the litanic prayers. Finally, at the end of every formula there was to be a period of silence, at the beginning of which the celebrant was to exhort those present to call to mind their other personal sins (using the commandments of God as a guide). This pause would be followed by a final appeal to the mercy of God and a concluding prayer.

As the Congregation for the Doctrine of the Faith had required, the corrections were made on November 26 and 30 by a joint committee consisting of Fathers Duroux and Zalba from that Congregation and Archbishop Bugnini and Father Pasqualetti from the Congregation for Divine Worship. The Congregation for the Doctrine of the Faith then gave its unconditional *nihil obstat* on December 10, 1973, and the Secretariat of State conveyed the definitive approval of the Holy Father on December 19 (No. 247762).

The long journey was over. The volume was published by a decree of the Congregation for Divine Worship, dated December 2, 1973.[31]

II. Contents

The *Ordo Paenitentiae* contains an Introduction and three chapters giving the several forms of sacramental celebration: reconciliation of individual penitents; reconciliation of several penitents with individual confession and absolution; and reconciliation of several penitents with general confession and absolution. A fourth chapter supplies a collection of texts that may be used. There are also three appendixes. The first deals with absolution from censures. The second gives seven sample penitential celebrations (one each for Lent and Advent, two common celebrations, and one for each of three categories: children, young people, and the sick). [The English-language rite has two for Lent and three common, or nine in all.—*Ed.*] The third appendix suggests a form for the examination of conscience.

1. *Title*

The general title of the volume is *Ordo Paenitentiae, Rite of Penance*, because the book contains both sacramental and non-sacramental rites.

---

31. *Ordo Paenitentiae* (Vatican Polyglot Press, 1974; 122 pp.). The rite is in *The Rites of the Catholic Church* 1 (New York, 1983²) 337–445. There is a new translation of the General Introduction and the Introduction to Appendix II in *DOL* 368 nos. 3066-3109. In his addresses the Holy Father spoke on several occasions of the new rite and of the sacrament itself; see, e.g., *DOL* 369 nos. 3110-13 (April 3, 1974); 371 no. 3115 (February 26, 1975); 372 nos. 3116-18 (March 5, 1975); and 373 nos. 3119-22 (March 12, 1975).

The rite prefers the term "reconciliation" when speaking of sacramental liturgical actions. The reason for this is that sacramental penance is an action of both God and a human being, whereas the word "penance" puts the emphasis on the action of the human being. After all, it is God who first loved us and "through Christ reconciled us to himself" (2 Cor 5:18; see Col 1:20-22; Rom 5:11). "Reconciliation" was therefore quite properly used by the early Church to describe the sacramental act.[32] The Council of Trent likewise several times used the phrase "rite for the reconciliation of a penitent." The term thus draws attention to and leads to reflection on an aspect of sacramental penance that is basic to a proper understanding and renewal of this sacrament.

"Reconciliation" brings out the bilateral relationship of reciprocal encounter that is proper to all the sacraments. For in these God comes to meet human beings with the salvation that he gives through Christ acting in his Church; in that same Church and through the same Christ human beings accept God's gift of salvation.

2. Introduction

The Introduction has four sections:[33]

1. *Reconciliation of penitents in the Church's life.* This section explains how the Church exercises the ministry of reconciliation assigned to her by Christ. It then describes the nature of conversion, satisfaction, and absolution, and stresses the importance of frequent confession.

2. *Offices and ministries in the reconciliation of penitents.* This section describes the role of the Christian community in the celebration of penance and the dispositions required in ministers of reconciliation and in penitents.

3. *Celebration of reconciliation.* This section describes the several forms of sacramental penance. In recent centuries the Western Church has celebrated penance only in its individual form. The new rite, on the other hand, proposes three new and distinct rites for this sacrament: individual, communal with individual confession and absolution, and communal with general confession and absolution in accordance with the "Pastoral Norms" issued by the Congregation for the Doctrine of the Faith in 1972.

---

32. See, e.g., The Old Gelasian Sacramentary: L. C. Mohlberg, P. Siffrin, and L. Eizenhöfer (eds.), *Liber sacramentorum Romanae aeclesiae ordinis anni circuli* (Rerum ecclesiasticarum documenta. Series maior: Fontes 4; Rome, 1960), nos. 351, 354, 359, 363.

33. The Introduction as given in the Latin and in *DOL* nos. 3066-3105 has six sections. The two not listed here are entitled "Mystery of Reconciliation in the History of Salvation" and "Penitential Services"—*Ed.*

The three rites complement one another and make it possible to bring out better the various aspects of penance, depending on circumstances, and to adapt the sacramental celebration to the real needs of the faithful.

4. *Adaptations* to be made by the episcopal conferences or by priests celebrating this sacrament. It is up to the episcopal conferences to oversee the translation of the texts and to have new prayers composed, except for the formula of absolution. They are also to decide on the penitential gesture by which those who intend to receive absolution at a collective reconciliation are to manifest their conversion and sincere repentance. Finally, they are to set down more precise regulations regarding the jurisdiction of ministers, the place of confession, and the vestments to be worn. Individual bishops, in addition to being responsible for the discipline of penance in their dioceses, are to decide when general absolution may be given.

Priests are urged to determine the parts of the rite and the concrete modalities that are better suited on each occasion for the celebration of penance in its several forms, although they must always keep the basic structure of the rite and the formula of absolution and must follow the norms establish by the episcopal conference.

3. *The New Rites*

1. *Reconciliation of individual penitents.* The structure is the same as in the older rite but has been enriched and revised. The penitent is now welcomed; he makes the sign of the cross and is urged to trust in God's mercy. This opening rite is followed by a reading from the word of God (optional), personal confession, expression of repentance, prayer of absolution, praise of God's mercy, and dismissal of the penitent.

The various formulas put on the lips of priest and penitent are either taken from or thoroughly inspired by the Scriptures. The presence of God's word as read during or before the sacramental rite urges us to repentance and to proclamation of God's mercy. By means of it the power of God to save is proclaimed in the very midst of human sin. It is a highly significant innovation to have God's word present even in this manner of celebrating reconciliation.

The rite is easily adaptable to situations in which there are a large number of penitents. On the other hand, it also becomes possible, especially at times when there is less pressure, to have a true celebration that is spiritually rich and profitable.

The formula of absolution has been completely revised. The new formula shows that the reconciliation of the penitent brings with it the grace of forgiveness and peace (see John 20:19-23) and that this grace has its source in the mercy of God, who reveals his fatherly heart to the repentant sinner. It relates this moment of grace to the history of salvation, wherein God reconciled the world to himself through the death and resurrection of his Son. It emphasizes the work of the Holy Spirit in the conversion and sanctification of sinners. Finally, it calls attention to the ecclesial aspect of reconciliation, since this is effected through the ministry of the Church.[34]

Also to be noted is the restored gesture of the laying on of hands (or at least of the right hand), which accompanies the formula of absolution. This is a classical gesture from the ancient penitential liturgy. It signifies the giving of the Holy Spirit for the forgiveness of sins and also the penitent's reconciliation with God and the Church; the formula pronounced during this imposition of hands proclaims and effects the forgiveness and reconciliation.[35]

2. *Reconciliation of several penitents with individual confession and absolution.* This is a genuinely ecclesial celebration: the word of God urging human beings to repentance is read to the assembly; there is common prayer, a communal acknowledgement of sin, and a communal plea for forgiveness. The liturgical movement and the conciliar documents brought to light once more the community dimension of all liturgy. Critiques of the past as well as more recent studies had shown the rather negative side of traditional penance with its excessive individualism, not only ritual but also moral and psychological. It was desirable, therefore, that the

---

34. The formula originally approved (above, n. 9) was changed precisely because it was not Trinitarian and did not explicitly refer to the paschal mystery and because the words expressing reconciliation with the Church did not seem sufficiently clear. Furthermore, it did not seem appropriate for confessions of devotion, in which the penitent does not submit for the confessor's judgment any serious sins that imply a break with the Church.

35. The gesture had already been restored in the Ritual of Paul VI, which ordered that the confessor raise his right hand when giving absolution. Since this Ritual had for the first time ordered the use of a grill, it could ask no more than that the hand be raised. In the new rite the rubric says clearly: "The priest extends his hands over the penitent's head (or at least extends his right hand)" as he gives absolution (no. 46).

But what of the grill, which evidently prevents this action? Nothing is said of it. The new rite lays down no regulations regarding the place for celebration of the sacrament. Such regulations are more appropriately established by the episcopal conferences or by individual bishops, depending on the different religious and cultural traditions of the various peoples and on the rather disparate situations in which the sacrament may be celebrated. But at the time when the rite was being prepared, and afterwards, there were not lacking exhortations to prudence. The Congregation for the Sacraments and the SCDW sent a questionnaire to the episcopal conferences, asking what their practice was in connection with the new rite and whether any abuses had surfaced.

penitential rite should bring out more clearly the responsibility which human beings share in good and evil, the collective as well as individual awareness of guilt, and the ecclesial nature of reconciliation.

This new rite satisfies these requirements, for it locates individual confession and absolution within a communal preparation and conclusion. The purpose of this new rite is not simply pedagogical, that is, to help a group of persons to "dispose" themselves properly for the sacrament; it is also to have them join together in celebrating their conversion, in praising the mercy of God, and in realizing their shared responsibility in good and evil and on their journey back to God.

3. *General absolution.* This rite can be used in the cases allowed in the "Pastoral Norms" regulating this sensitive area. The rite follows the same pattern as the second rite just described. The difference is that in place of individual confession and absolution, an outward gesture is made by those who desire to be absolved (the episcopal conferences are to determine what the gesture is to be); a prayer of collective absolution is then said. In this case the prayer is fuller and richer, lending greater prominence to the sacramental words of absolution and helping the penitents to enter more deeply into the mystery of salvation, which is expressed much more concisely in the ordinary prayer.

4. *Penitential Celebrations*

After describing the importance and structure of these in the Introduction (nos. 36-37), the *Ordo* gives seven models for penitential celebrations that help promote, and give communal expression to, the commitment to ongoing conversion. These services can also be used as preparations for the celebration of the sacrament proper; this can be celebrated individually later on at the time most convenient for each individual.

These celebrations are most useful, however, in those increasingly common pastoral situations in which there is no priest available who can absolve penitents. Even in these situations, the faithful who fall into serious sin are, after all, bound to repent and be converted. Yet the lack of priests and therefore of the availability of *confession* has led to neglect of instruction on the far more important duty of *conversion*. The great value, then, of these celebrations which can be organized by a deacon, a catechist, or even a simple believer is quite clear. In them the hearing of God's word and common prayer foster the sincere repentance which, together with a desire for the sacrament of penance, already ensures the fruit of the sacrament, namely, forgiveness from God and reconciliation with him and with our brothers and sisters.

These celebrations are also quite useful for developing in children a penitential attitude in keeping with their age and condition; for helping groups and communities to an authentic renewal that is collective as well as personal; and also for promoting detachment from sin and true conversion among catechumens.

The sample penitential celebrations given in the appendix to the *Ordo* can help in composing formularies and structures better adapted to the requirements of various cultures and of different circumstances and situations. When episcopal conferences translate and adapt the new rite, they can already adapt the samples; priests in turn should try to adapt the models as they deal with their communities on each occasion.

5. *Essential Elements*

The reason why it took so long to produce a new rite was the goal envisaged: that the celebration of penance should make clear "the nature and effect" of the sacrament. The goal is in fact fully achieved both in the doctrinal and pastoral explanations of the Introduction and in the three possible ways of celebrating the sacrament. The essential points that must be kept in mind in an authentic renewal—a renewal that puts into practice what is contained in the Rite of Penance—may be summed up as follows:

—*the primary role of the interior dispositions* of conversion, sincere repentance, reparation for the evil done, and trust in the mercy of God the Father, all of which are stimulated by meditation on God's word and expressed in prayer;

—*the ecclesial dimension* that is present even in individual celebrations and by reason of which penitents know that they are being helped in their renewal by the entire Church and know too that their repentance is a reconciliation with both God and the brethren (see the introduction of the communal celebration of penance into the Church's liturgy);

—*the importance of the word of God* in enlightening the conscience and urging the person to conversion (see the introduction of the reading of Scripture even into individual penance, and the important place that this reading has in communal celebrations);

—*the true meaning of the confession of sin*, whereby penitents do not simply acknowledge their sinfulness in an abstract and generic way but also acknowledge responsibility for the various manifestations of evil in their lives (therefore the confession of serious sins is part of penance and remains necessary, even after general absolution, as a manifestation and completion of conversion within the Church).

—*reconciliation as a mystery* of the Father's merciful love which associates us with the victory of Christ and renews in us the gift of his Spirit; this vision of penance moves beyond a narrowly moral and psychological view of "confession" and brings out more clearly the properly *sacramental* dimension (see the new formula of absolution and the gesture of the laying on of hands).

—*the role of satisfaction or penance:* this needs to be rediscovered and its value understood through the assignment of more demanding but also better adapted acts of penance (see the Introduction, nos. 6c and 18).

—*the need of combining the confession of one's sin with a proclamation of God's mercy* in acts of thanksgiving and praise (see the concluding part of the celebration of penance whether individual or communal); this proclamation shows that even the sacrament of penance is an act of spiritual worship, a sacrifice of praise, and a proclamation of the Easter victory of Christ. In this context it can be appropriate to have the celebration of penance followed by the celebration of the Eucharist.[36] In any case, we must recover the festive aspect of the celebration of penance, an aspect inherent in reconciliation, since every reconciliation is a victory and manifestation of divine love within the history of the world.[37]

---

36. But the distinction between the rite of penance and the rite of Mass must always be carefully preserved. Despite the strict "affinity" between penance and the Eucharist, the sacrament of reconciliation is the only one that cannot be celebrated during Mass. This is expressly excluded in the Pastoral Norms for general absolution (no. 10). The reason for this is the concern to avoid any possible impression that the sacrament of penance is reducible to a moment in the Eucharistic celebration. Such an impression would lessen its importance in the minds of the faithful and detract from the prominence it ought to have. The authorities wanted to preserve the complete autonomy of penance, especially at a time when there is need of a radical renewal in the practice of this sacrament. This does not mean that the celebration of this sacrament may not be followed by Mass, just as any other liturgical action may.

37. See F. Sottocornola, S.X., "Il nuovo *Ordo Paenitentiae,*" *Not* 10 (1974) 78–79.

Rites for the Sick

Reform of the rites in which the Church devotes itself to sick Christians and shows them the concern Christ has for the sick was entrusted to the second group established for study of the Ritual.[1]

I. History

The group began its work in 1965. As I mentioned earlier, the two relators made a joint report to the Consilium on the overall program for the reform of the Roman Ritual.[2] Attention was focused chiefly on problems connected with the sacrament of the anointing of the sick, regarding which the liturgical Constitution had set down four points for study:

—Name of the sacrament: " 'Extreme unction,' which may also and more properly be called 'anointing of the sick,' is not a sacrament for those only who are at the point of death" (no. 73).

—Fitting time for reception of the sacrament: "Hence, as soon as any one of the faithful begins to be in danger of death from sickness or old age, the fitting time for that person to receive this sacrament has certainly already arrived" (no. 73).

---

1. Study group 23 (= second study group on the Ritual; see p. 579, n. 1). This group called upon the services of other specialists in this area, especially A. Chavasse and J. Didier. Also consulted were some professors on the Faculty of Medicine at Paris and Louvain and in Italy and Germany, as well as specialists in the pastoral care of the sick, especially at Lourdes.

2. See B. Fischer and P. Gy, in *Not* 2 (1966) 227-28.

—Preparation of a suitable rite for cases in which the three sacraments of penance, anointing of the sick, and viaticum are celebrated on the same occasion (no. 74).

—Number of anointings: this is to be reduced, and the accompanying texts are to be adapted to the varying conditions of the sick persons to whom the sacrament is being administered (no. 75).

The first need which the group saw and which it presented to the fifth general meeting of the Consilium on April 30, 1965, was for a new sacramental formula that would fully express the nature and effects of the sacrament. The existing formula brought out the negative effect of the sacrament, namely, deliverance from sin, but was less clear on the positive effect, namely, the spiritual and even the physical relief of the sick person.

The group therefore suggested that the matter be taken up with the Holy Father and that his permission be asked to produce a new version of the sacramental formula for the anointing of the sick. The Consilium agreed, and the problem was brought to the Holy Father on May 12, 1965. He immediately said yes to the Cardinal President at an audience granted him at that time, and then put his permission in writing on June 2, 1965.[3]

The work then continued within the study group. A great source of help in bringing the new rite to completion was the permission given on June 10, 1969, to experiment with a communal celebration of the anointing of the sick at the sanctuary in Lourdes.[4]

An almost complete schema was submitted to the twelfth general meeting of the Consilium (November 14, 1969; November 8 to the consultors). It was requested, among other things, that the rite of confirmation in danger of death and the rite of the commendation of the dying be added to the schema. In this way all the rites for the sick would be grouped together: visitation and communion of the sick, sacramental anointing, viaticum, continuous rite of anointing and viaticum, apostolic blessing with plenary indulgence at the moment of death, confirmation (if necessary), and commendation of the dying.[5]

---

3. Letter from the Secretariat of State, June 2, 1965 (No. 48627), which said that the Consilium should solicit "the criticism and views" of the Congregations of the Holy Office, the Sacraments, and Rites on the new formula.

4. See "La célébration communautaire de l'Onction des malades à Lourdes," *Not* 6 (1970) 22–24; list of Scripture readings, *ibid.*, 13–21; A. M. Théas, "Rapport sur la célébration communautaire de l'Onction des malades dans le Sanctuaire de Notre-Dame de Lourdes," *ibid.*, 24–33.

5. See "XII Sessio plenaria Commissionis specialis ad instaurationem liturgicam absolvendam," *Not* 5 (1969) 439–40.

The next year the complete schema was again examined and given final approval at the first plenary meeting of the Congregation for Divine Worship (November 13, 1970).[6] On December 3 of that year the text, revised once again on the basis of observations made, was sent to the Congregations for the Doctrine of the Faith, the Sacraments, the Clergy, and Propaganda Fide.[7]

Consultation of the curial agencies took so much time, however, that two full years were to pass before the rite was published. Of several factors at work, two especially contributed to this delay:

1) *Special problems.* In addition to the time needed for examination of the new sacramental formula, which was intended to express the effects of the sacrament in a more suitable way, there were two matters that had to be clarified in light of the teaching of the Council of Trent and Vatican II: the repeatability of the sacrament, and the subject who can receive it.

The Constitution on the Liturgy had said that the sacrament is administered to "infirmis periculose aegrotantibus," thus repeating the expression used in the Ritual of Paul V. Authors writing on the subject did not make a sharp distinction between "serious" and "dangerous" illness, but medicine had made it possible to distinguish clearly between the two. Serious illnesses that of their nature can lead to death (for example, leukemia or breast cancer) may be discovered several years before they enter their acute phase. At this early point there is certainly danger of death, but it is not immediate; moreover, there can even be a cure with the right treatment.

This situation has consequences for the repeatability of the sacrament. In the past it was allowed that the sacrament can be repeated in case of a new illness occurring after a cure.[8] Now, however, room must be made, on the basis of new data from medical pathology, for repetition during the same illness when the latter becomes more serious. The same must be said of an operation made necessary by a serious illness that would lead to death if the operation were not performed.

Consequently, when the Congregation for the Doctrine of the Faith sent its first observations on the proposals of the Congregation for Divine Worship,[9] it decided that

> because of innovations in the matter and form of the sacrament an apostolic constitution should be published; this is to be drafted by a joint com-

---

6. See "Prima Congregatio plenaria," *Not* 6 (1970) 389–99.
7. See Schema 374: *De Rituali* 41 (November 30, 1970).
8. See Council of Trent, Sessio XIV: *De extrema unctione,* cap. 2 (DS 1696).
9. June 25, 1971.

mittee consisting of one delegate from each of the following agencies: the Congregation for the Doctrine of the Faith, the Congregation for Divine Worship, the Congregation for the Discipline of the Sacraments, and the Congregation for the Clergy. Presidency of the committee is reserved to this Congregation.

In addition it had this to say about no. 9 of the schema:

> The Congregation for the Doctrine of the Faith is now conducting a study of the repeatability of the sacrament (and therefore of the subject who may receive it). It will make its conclusions known in due time. For the present it proposes that a balanced course be taken: the anointing of the sick is neither a sacrament for the dying nor a religious remedy for any and every illness.

After months of waiting, the Congregation for Divine Worship asked that the program be set in motion once more.[10] The answer given was that the work of the joint commission could begin only after the results were in from the study of the repeatability of the sacrament; the Congregation for the Doctrine of the Faith expected that this study would be completed before the end of 1971.[11] In fact, it was only on January 20, 1972, that Cardinal Šeper made known the results of the doctrinal study of repeatability.

The decision of the Fathers of his Congregation, which had been reached on January 12 and confirmed by the Pope on January 14, was worded as follows: "The subject of this sacrament is any one of the faithful who is seriously ill (*graviter aegrotat*) because of sickness or old age. The sacrament can be repeated if the sick person gets better after being anointed or if the condition becomes more serious during the same illness." But the wording was soon corrected by replacing *graviter aegrotat* with *periculose aegrotat*, "in order to avoid all ambiguity and any interpretation that may depart from the tradition."[12]

Only after this reply could the joint meeting of all the interested agencies be held at last on March 4, 1972, for the purpose of studying the ob-

---

10. October 22, 1971.

11. November 6, 1971.

12. Change approved by the Holy Father at an audience on March 3, 1972 (Letter of the SCDF, March 4, 1972). The SCDW returned to the point, but the SCDF stood by its decision, explaining that the term ought to be understood by reference to article 73 of the liturgical Constitution and to "the authoritative interpretation given at the Council by the relator, Bishop P. J. Hallinan, when the Fathers were to vote on it" (see *Acta Synodalia*, vol. II, periodus IIa, 568). According to this interpretation, "the expression 'dangerously ill' . . . applies, 'as the words themselves indicate,' to subjects whose illness is beginning to threaten their life" (letter of the SCDF, June 23, 1972).

servations submitted by each of them.[13] The meeting produced a more careful statement of the early numbers of the Introduction, ensuring that, as requested, they (especially nos. 5-8) would better reflect the teaching of the Council of Trent and Vatican II.

Difficulties had also been raised regarding the first part of the Introduction, which deals with the meaning of human sickness in light of the mystery of salvation. The Congregation for Divine Worship thought that this opening should not be changed, for it regarded this short section as a general introduction to all the rites for pastoral care of the sick and not solely to the sacrament of anointing.

Revisions were made especially in no. 19, which deals with communal celebrations; no. 21, on the blessing of the oils (the Congregation for Divine Worship had envisaged broader possibilities here); and no. 30, which deals with the relation between penance, viaticum, and anointing in cases of necessity (the Congregation for Divine Worship wanted an affirmation of the special place of viaticum as being of divine precept).

On March 14 the Congregation for the Doctrine of the Faith sent the text of the numbers that had been corrected on the basis of the observations received to all the agencies that had taken part in the meeting; it asked for their approval.[14]

Once these straits had been navigated, the group could tackle the preparation of the apostolic constitution. The basic text of this was prepared by the Congregation for Divine Worship and then examined on May 4, 1972, at another joint meeting with participants from the Congregations for the Doctrine of the Faith, Divine Worship, the Sacraments, and the Clergy.[15]

---

13. Participants: for the SCDW, Archbishop Bugnini, G. Pasqualetti, and P. Gy; for the SCDF, B. Duroux; for the Sacraments: Monsignor G. Cattani; for the Clergy: M. Simcic; for Propaganda Fide, T. Scalzotto. There were still other meetings with the delegate of the SCDF on March 11 and 14 and May 23.

14. On April 21 the SCDF replied with further observations on this new text; agreement was reached on these with the delegate of the SCDF. The SCDF finally gave its *nihil obstat* to the printer's proofs on November 16, 1972.

The replies of the other Congregations: Clergy, January 19, 1971, to the first draft; April 25 and May 2, 1972, after the joint meeting; Propaganda, January 8, 1971, to the first draft, April 24 after the joint meeting. I shall deal separately with the SCR.

15. The first schema, prepared by P. Gy, was sent to the SCDF on March 28, 1972. After the joint meeting, the text, regarded as final, was sent to the Secretariat of State by the SCDF on June 23 and came back, with corrections by the Latinists, on July 13. The Secretariat of State asked that the Congregation for the Sacraments be named in the document, since the SCDW was. But the SCDF opposed this, on the grounds that then all the other agencies that had collaborated in the work should also be named; this would mean, first of all, the SCDF itself (November 11, 1972).

2) *Conflict of competencies.* While this joint work was proceeding, the Congregation for the Sacraments issued a challenge, refusing to respond until "a point of order which it regards as of fundamental importance and needing resolution" was first settled, namely, the question of "competency in preparing the document" as well as of "the form of the document itself."[16]

Meanwhile that Congregation held a plenary meeting of its own on June 18, 1971, in order to answer a question asked of it by the Secretariat of State: May extraordinary ministers of holy communion also administer the anointing of the sick?[17] The Congregation found itself in a quandary, knowing as it did that the sacrament of the sick was presently being studied by the Congregation for Divine Worship. It nevertheless tackled the entire problem of the reform of sacramental discipline and ended up with proposals that dealt almost exclusively with the method followed in the work.[18] Only after this plenary meeting did the Congregation for the Sacraments submit its observations, on June 24, 1971.[19]

Now that all the obstacles had been surmounted and all the agencies involved had given their approval, the Congregation for Divine Worship was able to give the Pope the final printer's proofs of the *Ordo Unctionis*

---

16. Letter of December 7, 1970, in reply to the sending of the definitive schema. It asked that in order to settle this "point of order," a joint committee be convoked of the prefects, accompanied, if they thought it opportune, by their secretaries and possibly by others among their official collaborators. But the office of prefect of the SCDW was vacant, and a delay was necessary.

17. When the Secretariat of State informed the SCDW on May 4, 1970, of the question asked of the Congregation of the Sacraments, it also urgently recommended that "these two competent Congregations work closely together in the study of problems connected with the anointing of the sick . . . whenever there are 'mixed' matters in which it is not easy to distinguish the various competencies. In these cases it is in fact necessary that there be common agreement on the study of the matter in its entirety and in all its aspects, with the aid of frequent contacts and reciprocal sharing of information, so that conclusions acceptable to both interested parties may be reached more easily and more quickly." The SCDW replied on May 8 that it would do so, but that a little patience was needed, since the studies undertaken were not yet completed.

18. These conclusions were made known to the SCDW by the Cardinal Prefect of the Congregation for the Sacraments. They called for: (1) the preparation of an apostolic constitution; (2) a directory to be produced by all the agencies concerned; (3) a separate study by the SCDF of the problems falling under its jurisdiction; and (4) the same for the Congregation of the Sacraments. Also to be heard were the Congregations of Propaganda and the Clergy and the Commission for the Code (July 12, 1971). This is precisely what was being done. The SCDW was thus able to reply on July 21 and ask for the response of the Congregation for the Sacraments to the schema sent to it on December 3, 1970.

19. After the joint meeting of March, these observations were supplemented by others of lesser importance, which were sent on March 25, 1972. Definitive approval of the printer's galleys came from the Congregation of the Sacraments on October 21, 1972.

infirmorum eorumque pastoralis curae on November 17, 1972. On December 9 the Secretariat of State sent word of the Pope's approval (No. 222.937).[20]

II. CONTENTS

The *Ordo* begins with the apostolic constitution *Sacram Unctionem infirmorum*. An Introduction to the rite is followed by seven chapters that explain and present the rites and texts for visitation and communion of the sick; anointing of the sick; viaticum; the sacraments to be celebrated for a sick person in proximate danger of death; confirmation in danger of death; commendation of the dying; and a collection of optional texts.[21]

1. *Apostolic Constitution*[22]

The purpose of this document is to approve the more important changes introduced into the rite, especially the new wording of the sacramental formula. After explaining in a summary way the authentic meaning of the sacrament as attested down the centuries by the magisterium of the Church and the liturgical sources, the change in the sacramental formula is approved. The change has been made so that the formula will more clearly express the effect of the sacrament, which is to give to the sick the graces suited to their state. These are spelled out in the Letter of St. James (5:14-15), which has constantly been cited by the magisterium and the liturgical books: "The prayer of faith will save the sick man and the Lord will raise him up. If he has committed any sins, they will be forgiven him."

The new formula ("Through this holy anointing may the Lord in his love and mercy help you with the grace of the Holy Spirit. May the Lord who frees you from sin save you and raise you up") opens up two im-

---

20. *Ordo Unctionis infirmorum eorumque pastoralis curae* (Vatican Polyglot Press, 1972; 82 pp.). The rite is in *The Rites of the Catholic Church* 1 (New York, 1983²) 593-740. There is a new translation of the General Introduction in *DOL* 410 nos. 3321-61. The SCDW issued its decree of publication on December 7, 1972: *DOL* 409 no. 3320.

21. See A.-G. Martimort, "Le nouveau rituel des malades," *Not* 9 (1973) 66-69; P.-M. Gy, "Le nouveau rituel des malades," *ibid.*, 108-18.

22. Paul VI, apostolic constitution *Sacram Unctionem infirmorum*, on the sacrament of anointing of the sick (November 30, 1972): *AAS* 65 (1973) 5-9; *DOL* 408 nos. 3315-19. The apostolic constitution also set January 1, 1974, as the date on which use of the new rite must begin. The SCDW had asked that no expiration date be set for the old rite but that the formula by now customary in the liturgical books be used. But nothing could be done. As a result, the SCDW had to issue a special decree (January 10, 1974) extending the *vacatio legis*: *DOL* 411 nos. 3362-64.

portant perspectives. The first is that the grace bestowed is the work of the Holy Spirit, who continues to be invoked in the blessing of the oil of the sick as the God of consolation. The second is that the sacrament of anointing is a remedy for soul and for body. The sacrament is effective in the way that penance is, so that it can supply for penance when this is impossible; above all, however, it brings gifts of health, strength, and spiritual relief.[23]

The change in the formula is accompanied by two less important regulations having to do with the sacramental sign. The first concerns the number of anointings. Vatican II had expressed its desire that "the number of the anointings . . . be adapted to the circumstances" (SC 75). It was therefore necessary to find a middle ground between the multiplicity of anointings provided for in the older, medieval rite and the reduction of the sign to a single anointing in cases of necessity. For the future, then, the usual rite will have only two anointings—one on the forehead and one on the hands, accompanied by a single recitation of the sacramental formula. In case of necessity a single anointing on the forehead (with the formula) will always be enough; if the particular condition of the sick person requires, the anointing may be made on another part of the body.

The second pontifical decision is in response to a desire expressed by many episcopal conferences in missionary countries. In the past, olive oil has always been the obligatory matter for the anointing of the sick, because the Bible sees it as a sacramental symbol of healing and relief (Mark 6:12-13; James 5:14-15). Henceforth, however, it is permissible in case of need to use some other oil, provided it is derived from a plant.

Finally, the apostolic constitution introduces greater flexibility into the current discipline: the sacrament of anointing can be administered again to a sick person who has already received it, not only if the person becomes ill again after a period of convalescence (this was already allowed: Code of 1917, canon 940), but also if the danger to the person becomes greater in the course of the same illness.

---

23. The first part of the formula is taken from the Roman formula used from the thirteenth century on: "Per istam . . . misericordiam." The remainder of the text is inspired by the Council of Trent and the Letter of St. James: "Further, the reality (res) and effect of this sacrament are explained in the words: 'and the prayer of faith will save the sick man, and the Lord will raise him up; and if he has committed sins, he will be forgiven'" (Council of Trent, Session XIV, chapter 2: DS 1696, Neuner-Dupuis 1637). In formulating the Latin text, account has been taken of the correction introduced in the Neo-Vulgate, which has *allevet* for *alleviet*, a reading that is a better translation of the Greek *egerei*, which means "raise up, pull a person to his feet, get a person standing." Thus the formula aptly expresses both the spiritual and the material or physical meaning of the sacrament.

2. *Introduction*

The first part of the Introduction discusses the Christian meaning of sickness. Following the example and action of Christ, the Church makes its own the anxieties, hopes, and joys of human beings. It therefore encourages scientists in all their efforts to combat bodily disease. But it also points the way to the redemption and spiritual sublimation of sickness through conformity with Christ, who shared human suffering and still suffers in his members. When joined to that of Christ, suffering fills up what is lacking in his sufferings for the good of the Church and the salvation of human beings. In addition, in her concern for the sick the Church continues the mission of Christ, who went about this world doing good and healing every manner of sickness (see Mark 6:13).

The Introduction goes on to consider the sacrament of the anointing of the sick: its meaning, recipient, repeatability, sacramental formula, place and number of the anointings (all these points in accordance with the decisions published in the apostolic constitution). It then speaks of the minister and of the celebration itself, whether individual or communal. It deals successively with viaticum, the continuous rite in danger of death, and the part to be played by all (family members, priests, other Christians) in ministering to the sick. The Introduction ends in the customary fashion by indicating the adaptations that may be made by the episcopal conferences and by the minister of the anointing.

3. *Visitation and Communion of the Sick*

This is the subject of the first chapter [the first three in the English rite]. Guidelines of a pastoral kind are given for visits to the sick, reminding pastors of souls that they have a duty to help their suffering brothers and sisters make the time of sickness fruitful by union with the suffering Christ and by prayer.

Two rites are given for communion of the sick. The fuller rite includes a greeting, a reminder of baptism (possibly by sprinkling the person with holy water), a penitential act, a short reading from Scripture, the Our Father, communion, and a closing prayer. The shorter rite is intended chiefly for use in nursing homes and hospitals or places where there are several sick people: an antiphon (for example, "O sacrum convivium—How holy this feast"), the brief exhortation before communion ("Behold the Lamb of God . . ."), and a concluding prayer.

4. *Anointing of the Sick*

The second chapter [Chapter IV in the English rite] contains the rite of anointing to be used for those who are not in imminent danger of death.

It can therefore be used also for those who are not bedridden, that is, those whose disease has not reached the acute stage. It can also be administered to the elderly whose vital forces are in serious decline and to those about to undergo an operation because of a disease that by its nature endangers their life.

The ritual distinguishes three main forms of celebration: outside Mass, within Mass, and a communal celebration with several priests participating, all of whom impose hands and do the anointings. The gesture of the laying on of hands, even if not part of the sacramental rite proper, is even more emphasized in the new rite than in the old. It can also be done by other priests who may be present at the celebration of the sacrament for a single sick person. The gesture recalls that of the Lord Jesus, who used to lay his hands on the sick.

The communal celebration is not only consonant with a principle set down in the liturgical Constitution; it also provides opportunity for instruction toward a revitalized understanding of a sacrament that is not meant to be administered as it were stealthily in order to conceal from the sick person the imminence of his or her death.

It is now possible to bless the oil for the anointing during the sacramental rite itself. In this case the act of blessing acquires great prominence, especially during a communal celebration. The oil can be blessed at this time if the Ordinary of the place is the one who presides over the concelebration. In other cases the principle still holds that the priest must normally use the oil blessed by the bishop on Holy Thursday, but in case of necessity he can bless the oil during the celebration of the sacrament. This faculty makes it possible to deal with urgent or unforeseen difficulties.

The full celebration (in cases of urgent necessity the rite can obviously be reduced to its essentials) includes: greeting and opening instruction; penitential act (or confession); reading of Sacred Scripture (which may be shorter or longer, depending on circumstances); litany; laying of the hand on the head of the sick person; prayer over the oil (or blessing of it); anointing with the sacramental formula; prayer after the anointing (this, as the liturgical Constitution decrees, is adapted to the situation of the sick person: serious illness, old age, imminent danger of death, a dying person who has been unable to make a confession, and so on); recitation of the Our Father; and final blessing.

Any adaptations to be made will depend, of course, not only on the form of celebration that is chosen but also on external circumstances and the state of the sick person. The minister will therefore have to be very sensitive to all these points.

5. *Viaticum*

Chapter 3 [Chapter V in the English-language rite] highlights the importance of the viaticum that the sick take with them on their journey from this world to the Father. Configuration to Christ, so often expressed during this life by participation in the sacrament of the Lord's death and resurrection, acquires its ultimate meaning at the moment when the Christian is completing his or her own "passage" from this world to the Father.

It is expected, as a general rule, that viaticum will be administered during a separate celebration, that is, not in combination with the anointing of the sick. It can be administered during Mass, when possible, or outside Mass. In this second case the rite used will be, for practical purposes, that of communion of the sick, but with the addition of the plenary indulgence at the moment of death (bestowed after the penitential act) and of the exhortation to the person to renew his or her baptismal faith. Also suggested is a short litany before the Our Father.

6. *Continuous Rite*

Chapter 4 [Chapter VIII in the English-language rite] provides for cases of extreme necessity. The rite considered here is chiefly one in which penance, anointing, and viaticum are all celebrated on the one occasion. The *Ordo* reminds us that the continuous rite of anointing and viaticum is not to be regarded as normal but is intended for use when the sick person is unexpectedly placed in proximate danger of death. In other cases the sacrament of anointing should be administered at an earlier stage. Furthermore, in immediate danger of death viaticum is the more important sacrament; above all, therefore, the sick person must be given the opportunity to make his or her confession[24] and receive viaticum. After this the person is anointed if still alive (see the General Introduction, no. 30). — The chapter also contains the rite of Christian initiation of the dying.

---

24. This point was much debated at the meeting with the other agencies. Taking into account the nature, significance, and necessity of the several sacraments involved, and while allowing that in practice various situations and possibilities have to be considered, the experts of the SCDW had given priority to viaticum, which every believer is bound by divine precept to receive at the time of death; then to the sacrament of anointing, which has the remission of sins as one of its effects; and then to confession. It was also concerned not to have people regard the sequence penance–viaticum–anointing as normal, since that would only make them go on thinking that spiritual care of the sick should be put off until they were unconscious. But the SCDW agreed to take the practical viewpoint and allow precedence to be given to confession, at least a generic confession. It did, however, succeed in preventing the traditional sequence from being regarded as normal and in giving due prominence to viaticum.

A separate short chapter [Chapter VI in the English-language rite] contains the prayers for the commendation of the dying. It represents a revision and enrichment of the old "Rite of the Commendation of the Dying'; it also eliminates prayers regarded as overly harsh. This short chapter can also be of use to the faithful, who not infrequently find themselves at the side of a friend or relative at the moment when that person is passing to the Father.

This document—*Pastoral Care of the Sick: Rites of Anointing and Viaticum*—is more than an updating of the old. It also brings together in organic fashion all the activities that the Church performs in its effort to stand by the sick, support and help them spiritually, and accompany them as they complete their own paschal mystery in conformity to Christ.

41

Marriage

The sacramental rite of marriage was one of the first to be studied and the very first to be published. Some problems inherent in its celebration were raised and discussed by the Consilium shortly after it came into existence;[1] they were then resolved in the motu proprio *Sacram Liturgiam* and, more fully, in the instruction *Inter Oecumenici*.[2] Marriage is one of the most meaningful and important moments in the life of a Christian, and the reformers therefore felt it urgent to revise and enrich the rite of marriage so that it might more clearly signify the grace of the sacrament and the duties of the spouses.[3]

The liturgical Constitution (nos. 77-78) also sets down some guidelines pertaining to the ritual:

> Marriage is normally to be celebrated within Mass, after the reading of the gospel and the homily and before "the prayer of the faithful" . . . . But if the sacrament of marriage is celebrated apart from Mass, the epistle and gospel from the nuptial Mass are to be read at the beginning of the rite and the blessing is always to be given to the spouses (no. 78).
>
> The prayer for the bride [is to be] duly emended to remind both spouses of their equal obligation to remain faithful to each other (no. 78).
>
> "If any regions follow other praiseworthy customs and ceremonies when celebrating the sacrament of marriage, the Council earnestly desires that by all means these be retained" [Council of Trent]. Moreover, the competent, territorial ecclesiastical authority . . . is free to draw up . . . its own

---

1. See above, pp. 138–39.
2. See above, p. 57, and below, p. 834.
3. See *SC* 77.

rite, suited to the usages of place and people. But the rite must always conform to the law that the priest assisting at the marriage must ask for and obtain the consent of the contracting parties (no. 77).

I. History

The first steps taken in the reform of the rite of marriage established the following:

1) The celebration of marriage always takes place within a Mass or a liturgy of the Word.

2) The nuptial blessing is always given to the spouses, even during the closed times and even if one or both spouses are contracting a new marriage.

3) The rite is to take the following form: short instruction ("not a homily but simply an introduction to the celebration of marriage"), reading of the epistle, song, gospel, homily ("based on the sacred text"), celebration of the sacrament, prayer of the faithful using a text approved by the Ordinary of the place, and nuptial blessing.

4) The readings are to be in the vernacular. If no translation approved for liturgical use exists as yet, a text approved by the local Ordinary may be used for the time being.[4]

Meanwhile study group 23, in collaboration with group 22,[5] began its examination of the entire subject.[6] It held special meetings at Mont Saint-Odile (Strasbourg) in December 1965, at Le Saulchoir (Paris) in March 1966, and at Verona in June of the same year. In the following October it was able to present the Consilium with a first report on the general structure.[7] At the next general meeting (April 1967) it presented the first three chapters of the new *Ordo*[8] and, in November of that year, the complete schema in a final form that could be used for experimentation.[9] The most important and impressive of these experiments was the one conducted by Pope Paul VI himself at the International Eucharistic Congress

---

4. See the motu proprio *Sacram Liturgiam*, no. V (*DOL* 20 no. 283); instruction *Inter Oecumenici*, nos. 70-75 (*DOL* 23 nos. 362-67).

5. During the work other experts were called upon for particular problems: Bishop Carlo Colombo for theological questions, on the advice of the Secretariat of State, November 9, 1966; Monsignor Gianfrancesco Arrighi for ecumenical problems; Father Xavier Seumois for matters peculiar to mission lands.

6. See B. Fischer and P.-M. Gy, O.P., "De recognitione ritualis romani," *Not* 2 (1966) 228-29.

7. See "Septima sessio plenaria Consilii," *Not* 2 (1966) 312.

8. See "Octava sessio plenaria Consilii," *Not* 3 (1967) 145.

9. See "Nona sessio plenaria Consilii," *Not* 3 (1967) 412-13.

in Bogotá in August 1968. The Pope used the rite in marrying twenty-four couples with the enthusiastic participation of a huge crowd (August 23, 1968).

The schema was given its final revision after approval by the Consilium[10] and was sent to the Holy Father on March 23, 1968. The Cardinal Secretary of State, acting in the Pope's name, returned it to the secretary of the Consilium with papal approval in principle; the only proviso was that account be taken of some points made by Father Luigi Ciappi, theologian of the papal household.[11]

On May 6 the document was sent to the Congregation for the Sacraments, the Congregation of Rites, and the Congregation for the Doctrine of the Faith for their examination.[12] After these agencies had been consulted, the schema was once again sent to the Pope on January 15, 1969. The Pope spoke of it to Father Bugnini at an audience on February 8 and made final arrangements for publication.[13]

The Pope gave his approval to the printer's proofs on March 17, 1969 (No. 134485) and agreed that the decree of promulgation from the Congregation of Rites should be dated February 19, 1969, the feast of St. Joseph, husband of the Virgin Mary. The same letter said: "His Holiness wishes to express his satisfaction and gratitude to all who have in any way contributed to the production of the new *Ordo*; he hopes that when explained in suitable instructions it will help spouses better to understand the profound meaning, the inexhaustible spiritual riches, and the serious obligations of Christian marriage."[14]

---

10. Schema 280: *De Rituali* 27 (March 21, 1968).

11. The written answer was dated April 13, 1968 (No. 115949). On May 2 a response was made to the first observations of Father Ciappi, which came in fact from the Cardinal Secretary of State. These had to do with clarifications that were taken into account and with the problem of marriages between Christians who were no longer believers. This source was responsible for the addition of the following sentence in the Introduction, no. 4: "Children are the most precious gift of a marriage and contribute most to the well-being of the parents."

12. The Congregation for the Sacraments replied on June 12, 1968. The SCR studied the schema at its regular meeting, which was also attended by representatives of the Consilium. On December 13, 1968, the SCDF gave its *nihil obstat*, with the proviso that certain changes sent on the same occasion be made. The rite of marriage between a baptized and an unbaptized person was submitted on January 29, 1969, and approved on February 3.

13. Letter of the Secretariat of State, February 12, 1969 (No. 132122); the Secretariat returned the schema and in this letter told the secretary of the Consilium to act "in accordance with the explanations and directives given at the audience on the eighth of this month."

14. *Ordo celebrandi Matrimonium* (Vatican Polyglot Press, 1969; 40 pp.). The rite is in *The Rites of the Catholic Church* 1 (New York, 1983²) 551–90. New translation of the Introduction in *DOL* 349 nos. 2969-96. The decree is in *DOL* 348 no. 2968. On this decree see "A propos

II. Contents

1. *Introduction*

This document shows the disadvantages attached to being a firstborn. It was the first of the many Introductions to new liturgical books. With the help of experience, improvements were gradually made in the style, content, and scope of these Introductions. It should not be surprising, therefore, that this first Introduction does not have the fullness and completeness found in those of the liturgical books published later on.

The Introduction on marriage recalls the teaching of the Council; it then takes up the celebration of marriage during Mass and apart from the Eucharistic celebration, and the celebration of marriage between a Catholic and a non-baptized person.

Next come guidelines for the preparation of particular rituals, along the lines indicated in the liturgical Constitution. The formulas of the Roman Rite may be adapted or even supplemented (including "the actual words of consent"). One point, however, must remain unchanged: the priest is to ask and receive the consent of the contracting parties. After the exchange of rings, the crowning or veiling of the bride may take place if this is customary. If the joining of hands or the exchange of rings is contrary to local custom, the episcopal conference can allow these rites to be omitted and replaced by others.

2. *A Special Question*

During the compilation of the Introduction and rite, the group had to face a serious question that is topical today: whether or not faith is needed for a true and effective celebration of the sacrament. Pastoral workers were faced with the situation of non-practicing Christians who wished to marry but said that they no longer believed or even claimed to be atheists; they nonetheless wanted a religious wedding for quite a variety of reasons—family pressures, custom, current mentality, and so on.

After lengthy discussion the Consilium approved a principle suggested by the study group and to be included in no. 7 of the Introduction. It read as follows:

---

d'une 'Note' sur le droit liturgique du mariage," *Not* 6 (1970) 121. See also S. Mazzarello, "De novo Ordine celebrandi Matrimonium," *EL* 83 (1969) 251–57, and the article in *L'Osservatore Romano*, April 1, 1969. See also "Norme e indicazioni pastorali per la celebrazione dei Matrimoni [Rome]," *Not* 5 (1969) 56ff. Publication of the liturgical book had been preceded by publication of readings for marriage, prepared by France (*Not* 3 [1967] 118–20) and by the Consilium (*Not* 4 [1968] 61–63).

Pastors should first of all strengthen and nourish the faith of those about to be married, for the sacrament of marriage presupposes faith (see the liturgical Constitution 59). But if it is clear that both spouses reject the faith, then, even if they clearly have a serious intention of contracting a marriage, it is not permitted to celebrate the rite of the sacrament of matrimony.

When the schema was sent to the interested curial agencies, a lengthy note was attached to this article, explaining the reasons for so courageous a formulation or adoption of a position. The note had been written by Bishop C. Colombo and said:

If the sacraments presuppose faith (each in the way proper to it), then priests who are preparing engaged couples for marriage must nourish their faith and, if necessary, make an effort to revive it or even bring it into existence for the first time. Here, however, they must take into account a difficulty that is perhaps rare in regions that have remained more Christian but that is frequently encountered in dechristianized areas, namely, the existence of persons who were baptized in the Catholic Church but who have not only abandoned all practice but are publicly known as "non-believers" or formally tell the priest before the marriage that they reject the faith but nonetheless want their marriage celebrated in the church. One or both of the engaged parties may be in this situation.

The problem is a serious one and is regarded as such by both faithful and clergy. The faithful are scandalized (especially now that the liturgy is in the vernacular) to hear liturgical texts that express and presuppose faith being used even in the marriages of those who reject the faith. Non-Catholics ask whether the Church really regards its liturgy or even its faith as important. Priests are deeply disturbed at having to exercise their ministry in these conditions. It seems absolutely necessary, therefore, to use the revision of the rite of marriage as an opportunity for remedying this difficult situation.

When only one of the two baptized Catholics rejects the faith, while the other is a believer, it is recommended, in the interests of the believing party, that the sacramental rite be celebrated in a church and in accordance with the liturgical regulations. The following remarks, therefore, apply only to cases in which both parties reject the faith.

If the priest is completely unsuccessful in reawakening the faith of the engaged couple or bringing them to faith for the first time, it is desirable that they not be obliged "to observe the Catholic form of marriage" (see [1917] Code of Canon Law, can. 1099), since this would be contrary to their conscience (see the Declaration on Religious Liberty 2), which rejects the faith expressed in the liturgy of the sacrament.

It would seem wise in this case even to refuse the couple "the Catholic form of marriage," in order to avoid scandalizing the faithful and placing an obstacle to the evangelization of the non-baptized. In this case, two baptized Catholics who marry while both reject the faith would be in the same position as two baptized non-Catholics who reject the sacramentality of marriage; that is, *when such a marriage verifies all the conditions required for being a true marriage, it is also a sacrament,* even if the spouses are ignorant of its precise religious meaning.

At the same time, however, there is a clear difference between the situation of two baptized Protestants who deny the sacramentality of marriage and that of the unbelieving baptized Catholics: the former regard marriage as a religious act, while for the latter this religious meaning is completely missing.

As a result, it was proposed that the second part of no. 7 be worded as indicated above. But this second part was not approved either by the Congregation for the Doctrine of the Faith or by the Congregation for the Discipline of the Sacraments.[15] This left only the first part, which states the general principle that faith is necessary in the celebration of the sacraments. There was fear of forcing the issue too much by taking a drastic position and of thus losing an occasion for the Church's contact with her alienated children.

3. *Marriage During Mass*

The first chapter of the liturgical book gives the ordinary rite for marriage as celebrated during a Mass. The rite includes:

1. *Welcoming of the couple.* There are two possible places for doing this: at the door, with the procession to the altar, or at the altar. If the rite of reception is omitted, the wedding service begins immediately with the celebration of Mass. The welcome is meant as a sensitive human gesture that will bring the couple, their relatives, and their friends into an atmosphere of spiritual fellowship.

---

15. Father Ciappi, whom the Holy Father had assigned to examine the schema, had already shown himself opposed to the wording of no. 7. Among other things, he pointed out that "the Church always has an obligation to remind 'unbelieving Catholics' of their duties as *de jure* 'subjects,' even if they behave as though they were not such" (letter of Father Ciappi, May 3, 1968).

In remarks accompanying its grant of approval, the SCDF decided as follows with regard to no. 7 of the Introduction: "Leave out the entire number (unless the Consilium judges that the first part should be kept, namely, 'Priests should first . . . and demands faith'). The issue here is not simply ritual and liturgical, but involves very serious questions with which the Congregation is presently dealing and regarding which it will keep the Consilium informed at the appropriate time." The conclusion of the SCDF's study would be the one already communicated. And in fact it was reconfirmed in a letter of July 15, 1969, in which the thinking of the Holy Father was also made known: "It is a serious matter, especially from the pastoral and psychological viewpoints, to sever contact with the Church at the time of marriage; it does not seem advisable to close the doors of the Church to spouses, but rather to open them."

The flexibility displayed in the rubric reflects the opposing views expressed during the discussions within the Consilium. There were those who saw the rite as possibly giving rise to discrimination: for the wealthy, reception at the door of the church, with a great deal of pomp and ceremony; for the poor, reception at the altar. Others disliked the idea of a procession through the church and other possible drawbacks. All agreed that room must be made for a rite of reception, precisely in order not to lose an opportunity of immediately placing the couple and the assembly in the atmosphere proper to a sacramental celebration.[16]

2. *Liturgy of the Word.* This takes place in the usual manner. The celebrant is urged to give a homily "drawn from the sacred text[s]" of the Mass and explaining the mystery of Christian marriage, the dignity of conjugal love, the grace of the sacrament, and the responsibilities of the spouses. Some Fathers of the Consilium wanted a model homily to be offered, but it was decided to let the particular rituals provide this.

3. *Questions asked of the couple.* The rite of marriage proper is introduced by a short address of the celebrant in which he reminds the couple of the meaning of what they are about to do and invites them to express their intentions publicly in the presence of the Church. Then, in response to several questions, the couple express their intention to enter marriage freely and take on its responsibilities. A third question has to do with the acceptance of children and the determination to raise them as Christians.[17]

This part of the rite also met with some opposition in the Consilium. Some regarded it as formalism, on the grounds that it repeats what has already been done during the preparation for marriage. But the study group pointed out that the answers given do not simply reiterate obligations accepted during the premarital course, but are a solemn profession and acceptance of them in the presence of all. This public profession strengthens and intensifies the commitment the couple is taking on in the sight of God.

---

16. Even after publication of the rite, difficulties were raised on this point. Some took the suggestions as obligatory and went even further by introducing other details for which permission should have been obtained from Church authorities: adorning the altar with a table cloth, flowers, candles, and offerings from the couple; communion in the hand; drinking from the chalice. All these things might be good, but at times they reflected folklore rather than faith.

17. Some, even within the Consilium, wanted the words "from God" removed. They were kept, however, in order, as Bishop Colombo said, to bring out "human and Christian responsibility and docile reverence for God" in the acceptance of children (see *Gaudium et spes*, no. 50).

4. Consent. The priest then asks the couple to express their consent. The response to the celebrant's question might have been a simple "Yes," but it was thought better to assign a more complete formula that has been used since the Middle Ages in the English-speaking world: "I, N., take you, N., to be my wife (my husband). I promise to be true to you in good times and in bad, in sickness and in health. I will love you and honor you all the days of my life."[18] The formula is spoken by the contracting parties. In special situations, however, the celebrant may turn the formula into a question, to which the parties answer "I do."[19]

The priest then puts a seal, as it were, on the spouses' expression of consent: "You have declared your consent before the Church. May the Lord in his goodness strengthen your consent and fill you with his blessings. What God has joined, man must not divide."

This formula replaces the one in the old rite: "I join you in marriage," which was in use since the sixteenth century and was brought into the

---

18. The formula originally also had "in poverty and in riches" (*in paupertate et opulentia*), but the phrase was eliminated at the request of the Pope (letter of the SCDF, December 3, 1968).

19. This option had been expressly requested by the SCDF and also by the Holy Father. The remarks of the SCDF (December 13, 1968) said, among other things: "The formulas now traditional should be retained, and there should *always* be the option of using, *ad libitum et pro opportunitate*, the simple formula with the answer 'I do.' " Where this simple formula is used, there should also be the option of *complementing* it with the more complex formula of the new ritual (but the exchange of consents by means of the simple formula is always enough for validity)." But the norm for the sacraments should not be what suffices for validity. The Consilium therefore decided to give first place to the fuller expression of consent, while giving the celebrating priest permission to use the same text in the form of a question and allowing the episcopal conferences to decide that in their territory this interrogative form alone should be used (see no. 25). Moreover, the conferences always have authority to prepare a ritual of their own in which even the words of consent can be adapted or filled out (see no. 13).

The desire of the SCDF was thus fully satisfied, but this did not seem so to all. On July 9, 1968, Archbishop Benelli wrote to the secretary of the Consilium: "Some individuals in positions of authority have expressed puzzlement with regard to the new formula in the rite of marriage, since it lacks the traditional 'I do.' I would like to remind Your Reverence that the Supreme Pontiff told the Consilium to make it clear that use of the new formula should be optional. I ask whether this order has been obeyed. The Holy Father also added that a very short formula (a question and an answer in the form of the tradition 'I do') should be retained for the uneducated, the dying, and other situations in which circumstances make use of the formula inadvisable."

It was explained that these wishes had already been met by the guidelines in the rite. But disappointment remained at the disappearance of the "prophetic 'I do,' " which had become the focus of so much poetic reflection. Without this "I do," marriage no longer seemed marriage. And in many cases high-ranking personages who were asked to celebrate marriages in order to lend greater pomp to the "ceremony" voiced this disappointment.

Ritual by the Council of Trent. It came originally from the four-teenth/fifteenth-century Ritual of Rouen. In particular rituals, including some recent ones, it was altered or replaced. The Consilium therefore had no difficulty in accepting a different formula.

The experts argued at length over the juridical value of the formula. The intention in selecting this formula was not to settle the question of whether the Church is simply a witness to the consent given by the partners in a marriage or whether, on the contrary, the marriage requires the express intervention of the Church in the person of the priest who receives and confirms the consent.

5. *Rings.* The old Roman Ritual placed the blessing of the rings after the consent. Other rituals—the German, for example—put it before the consent, in order that the consent might be immediately followed by the giving of the ring, an action that is as it were the confirmation and visible sign of the consent. After extensive discussion and various suggestions, it was decided that the new *Ordo* should follow Roman usage.

Three formulas are given for the blessing of the ring. The one given in the body of the text has deliberately been kept very simple in order to shorten the time between the consent and the giving of the rings.

The bridegroom places the ring on his wife's finger with the words: "N., take this ring as a sign of my love and fidelity. In the name of the Father and of the Son and of the Holy Spirit." The bride then does the same for her husband.

This action is followed by the prayer of the faithful, in which the petitions are adapted to the occasion. At the offertory the spouses may bring the matter for the sacrifice to the altar. The preface is proper to the occasion, as is the *Hanc igitur* in the Roman Canon. The other Eucharistic Prayers have short intercessions to be included at the proper place. All these prayers are valuable as showing the connection of Christian marriage with the history of salvation and the Eucharistic sacrifice.[20]

6. *Nuptial blessing.* After the Our Father the celebrant solemnly blesses the spouses. In addition to the traditional formula for the blessing of the wife, which has been suitably revised and adapted so as to apply to both spouses, two other shorter formulas are provided. All three begin with

---

20. There were frequent requests for a special Eucharistic Prayer for the celebration of marriage; Sacred Scripture provides abundant suggestions for such a prayer. Some prayers of this kind were composed; unfortunately, some were even used, not always with happy results. The wish still exists, inspired by a desire to highlight the place of the mystery of Christian marriage in the history of salvation, which is a history of loving communion between God and his people. A Eucharistic Prayer for marriage was granted to Canada in 1982; see *Not* 18 (1982) 142.

an exhortation to prayer and a short period of silence, during which those present offer their individual prayers. This is followed by the priestly prayer of blessing.[21]

After the blessing come the prayer for peace and the greeting of peace. This, too, is characteristic of the rite of marriage according to the Roman usage. A twelfth-century rubric expressly says that this is the only day on which a husband may kiss his wife in church. Nowadays, of course, the greeting of peace has fortunately become a regular and characteristic part of the Eucharistic celebration and no longer causes surprise or astonishment. It is nonetheless appropriate to recall a tradition that makes the gesture especially meaningful on the day of marriage.

At the end of Mass, after communion under both kinds and the final prayer, there is a final solemn blessing that is adapted to the particular celebration, as it is in all ritual Masses.

4. *Marriage Outside Mass*

The rite of marriage outside Mass is described in the second chapter and follows the same format as a marriage during Mass: reception of the couple, liturgy of the Word, rite of marriage, prayer of the faithful, blessing of the spouses, Our Father, and final blessing. If the spouses wish to receive communion, they may do so after the recitation of the Our Father. In this event, communion is followed by a time of silence (or of suitable song) and the prayer after communion.

5. *Marriage of a Catholic and an Unbaptized Person*

The problem of the ceremony for a marriage between a baptized and an unbaptized person was brought to the Congregation for the Doctrine of the Faith by the Consilium on October 18, 1966, in the following terms:

---

21. The adaptation of the traditional text was made in accordance with the guidelines set down in the liturgical Constitution and with the explanation given by Archbishop Hallinan, relator at the Council for the chapter of the liturgical Constitution that deals with the sacraments: "As for adaptation: while avoiding radical changes, at least the part of the ancient blessing which speaks to the wife alone of conjugal fidelity is to be made to refer to both spouses."

When the Consilium studied the text as revised by the study group, there were those who regretted the disappearance of "Rebecca and her companions"; others wanted the reference to the Flood kept; still others found some expressions difficult to translate. Another request was for improvement of the Latin style, which some found "dry, untranslatable, common, and uncharismatic" (H. Schmidt). The Consilium stuck to the principle that only indispensable corrections were to be made.

The instruction *Matrimonii Sacramentum* allows that, when the proper dispensation has been granted, the marriage of a baptized and an unbaptized person may be celebrated in church. The future Roman Ritual will therefore have to prescribe the manner in which such a marriage is to be celebrated. As we set about preparing the rite, it seems appropriate that the precise theological nature of such a marriage be clarified. It seems that in some cases such marriages have been dissolved on the principle that they are not sacramental "even for the Catholic party." Does the Congregation for the Doctrine of the Faith think that the non-sacramentality of marriages in which one of the contracting parties is not baptized is sufficiently sure that the future Roman Ritual can take this for granted in determining the way in which these marriages are to be celebrated?

The Congregation answered on November 7, 1966:

In composing the texts of the Ritual for marriages between a Catholic party and a non-Christian party, it is neither necessary nor appropriate to give an implicit answer to the question of the sacramentality of such marriages. The group in the Consilium that has been charged with preparing these texts should, on the contrary, carefully avoid any expression that can be interpreted as taking one or other side on this point of doctrine.

The same Congregation gave its approval to the rite on February 3, 1969. It ordered, however, that the opening rubric be changed to say that the rite in this case may be celebrated in a church or some other suitable place, rather than that "the church is the preferred place in these cases."

The rite forms part of a liturgy of the Word. Nothing is said of the possibility of celebrating the Eucharist. The rite and texts follow the general lines of the pattern already described, but account is taken of the special situation of the spouses by avoiding expressions not applicable to both. One instance of such adaptation is the blessing of the spouses; this may also be replaced by a prayer of the priest. The rite may end with the Our Father and the final blessing.

Ritual guidelines are given for making the marriage part of a sacred celebration, but everything is very flexible and account must be taken of the situation of the parties concerned so as to offend no one.

The final chapter of the *Ordo* is a collection of biblical and euchological texts from which a selection may be made. The chapter provides extensive material for use not only in the celebration of the rite but in the preparatory instructions on marriage.

42

Holy Orders

Study group 20 (= *De Pontificali* 1)[1] took as its first order of business the revision of the rites of ordination.[2] The relator sought the written views of the members on the principles to be followed in the work and on its scope and organization. The members gave their opinions on the problems involved in the revision of all the ordinations. The first conclusion reached was that discussion of the rites for the sacrament of orders (diaconate, presbyterate, episcopate) should be kept separate from discussion of problems having to do with "minor orders." At the fifth general meeting of the Consilium (April 1965), the question of minor orders was entrusted to a separate group,[3] while study group 20 limited itself to holy orders.

I. History

Group 20 held a first meeting at Trier from August 3 to August 5, 1965, and a second at Rome on September 29, 1965. The group then began the preparation of actual schemas; these were to pass through a good seven redactions.

The first presentation of the main problems involved in the revision of the rites for all three holy orders was made at the sixth general meet-

---

1. *Relator:* B. Botte; *secretary:* B. Kleinheyer; *members:* J. Nabuco, C. Vogel, E. Lengeling, P. Jounel, and J. Lécuyer (subsequently added).
2. The same group subsequently took up the subject of confirmation.
3. See below, p. 727, n. 1.

ing of the Consilium on November 22–23, 1965.[4] The main lines to be followed were approved, as were the solutions of more specific questions.[5]

This first examination of the matter brought to light all the problems that needed to be resolved if the group was to be able to proceed. Some of these problems, however, were rather complex and demanding, and their resolution seemed to call upon competencies beyond those of the Consilium alone.

On April 21, 1966, Cardinal Lercaro therefore sent the Pope a memorandum in which he explained some especially important and demanding problems having to do with the rites of holy orders. He then asked the Pope to allow the Consilium to study these matters more fully with an untrammeled expression of views and only then submit everything "to the other agencies concerned." The following are the main points the Cardinal made in his memorandum:

The revision of the sacramental rites in the Roman Pontifical raises a series of problems that are very serious and sensitive not only from the viewpoint of ritual but also and above all because of their theological consequences. In fact, the rites in their structure and particular parts should also have a didactic function; they should therefore be clear in their organization and contain a series of gestures and words that express sure teaching.

The problem becomes even more urgent and sensitive where the rites of ordination are concerned, especially the three sacramental ordinations: episcopate, presbyterate, and diaconate. The ritual for these orders has been formed by successive contributions that reflect the doctrinal and cultural influence of the periods in which the rites and formulas were created. The formulas of ordination, for example, reflect the allegorizing mentality and spirituality of the early Middle Ages, containing as they do a whole series of references to personages, events, and rites of the Old Testament as applied to the new covenant. The gestures and several parts of the rite, for example, the *traditio instrumentorum*, the *traditio insignium*, and, to some extent, the taking of an oath of fidelity, reflect the influence of the feudal period, and so on.

Furthermore, each gesture is habitually accompanied by a formula, but the latter is not always in harmony with the objective meaning of

---

4. See "Sexta sessio plenaria Consilii," *Not* 2 (1966) 4.

5. See Schema 102: *De Pontificali* 5 (September 18, 1965), "De consecratione episcopali." The members of the Consilium were here asked for their views on twenty-two points. Schema 124: *De Pontificali* 6 (November 8, 1965), in which the members were queried on fifteen points relating to presbyteral ordination and twenty-five to diaconal ordination.

the gesture itself. For example: the laying on of hands (an essential part of the rite) at the consecration of a bishop is accompanied by the words "Receive the Holy Spirit," which are not the sacramental formula but, by reason of their placement and of the solemn moment at which they are said, end up by pushing into the background the real sacramental formula, namely, the ensuing preface.

Finally, it is necessary for the study group to keep before it the extensive doctrinal enrichment brought to this area by Vatican II, especially in its Constitution on the Church, when dealing with the episcopate and with the priesthood in general. In the present effort at renewal, the liturgy cannot fail to introduce this wealth of teaching into its formulas, which are intended not simply for the conferral of a sacrament but also for the instruction of the faithful through the rite. Nor may we set up an opposition between this renewal and the simple respect due to a text that is rich indeed, but rich rather by reason of its venerable age than of its authentic theological content.

The Cardinal then addressed himself in greater detail to several issues:

1. *Sacramental formulas.* In virtue of the apostolic constitution *Sacramentum Ordinis* of Pius XII, the sacramental formula for the conferral of holy orders in each of its three degrees is the entire preface, although only one part of this is said to be essential and indispensable.

But the three prefaces in the Pontifical no longer seem suited to their purpose, since they do not adequately show forth the true nature of priesthood to the full extent in which the Church now understands it. The Consilium should therefore adopt two resolutions. The first has to do with the episcopate: "In our opinion there should be a study of whether other texts may be substituted which better express the theology of the episcopal office." The second concerns the diaconate: "The Fathers have decided that there should be a study of how the consecratory preface may better express the theology of the diaconate in the light of the constitution *Lumen gentium.*"

A good starting point for the study of episcopal consecration would seem to be the text used for this purpose in the *Traditio Apostolica* of Hippolytus. This is still used for episcopal consecration in the Coptic Rite and, in a fuller version derived from the *Testamentum Domini,* among the West Syrians.

For the diaconate the formula has been tackled almost from scratch, using part of the current formula and completing it.

For the presbyterate the current formula seemed already a rich one, needing only the restoration of the original form it had in the sources and a few additions or revisions.

2. *The words "Receive the Holy Spirit."* These occur at the moment when the celebrant lays his hands on the elect during episcopal consecration. They also occur in a fuller form in diaconal ordination ("Receive the Holy Spirit for strength to resist the devil and his temptations, in the name of the Lord").

These words are not part of the sacramental formula and can lead to incorrect interpretations in catechetical instruction and in the understanding of the rite by the faithful. It seemed wise, therefore, to eliminate them, so that the imposition of hands is done in silence, as is already the case in the ordination of priests.

3. *Participation of co-consecrating bishops in the episcopal ordination.* According to the regulations in the old Pontifical, after the imposition of hands the co-consecrating bishops should "also recite the prayer *Propitiare* and the entire preface that follows; throughout the remainder of the rite they should likewise read in a low voice everything that the consecrating bishop reads or sings."

All this creates a disagreeable situation, since the words of the principal consecrator are continually accompanied by the murmur of the other two bishops as they recite the same formulas. It would seem more appropriate to adopt the practice of the Eastern Rites, in which only the principal consecrator says all the formulas, while the other bishops participate simply by imposing hands and by their intention. The verbal participation of the co-consecrators will therefore be limited to the essential formula, that is, they will sing or recite, along with the consecrating bishop, only the part of the preface that is determined to be the "essential part."

1. *Approval by the Consilium*

The Holy Father went along with these requests and had the Secretariat of State write as follows on June 8, 1966:

> Given the importance and sensitivity of the subject, every aspect of the problem must be carefully studied, with a keen pastoral and apostolic consciousness, before any changes are made in rites so ancient and impressive. Furthermore, the liturgical Consilium should attend carefully to the matter of agreement with the Congregation for the Doctrine of the Faith and the Congregation of Rites.

In that same letter the Secretariat of State had asked for the names of those who would comprise the study group for the revision of the rites of holy orders. After receiving this information, it replied on June 22: "We would like the following to be invited as members of the study group: Monsignor Marc Armand Lallier, Archbishop of Marseilles, Mr. Georges

Jouassard, Dean of the Faculty in Lyons, and Father Joseph Lécuyer."
All three were sounded out, but only Father Lécuyer actually became a
member.[6]

Meanwhile, in May of 1966 there was a meeting of the relators, who
were able to finish their study of the now complete schema for the three
rites.[7] After this was corrected on the basis of the discussion, it was
presented to the Consilium at its seventh general meeting in October
1966.[8] It was unanimously approved.[9]

2. *To the Curial Agencies*

After the meeting of the Consilium the schema, now further polished
and corrected,[10] was sent on April 8, 1967, to the Congregations for the
Doctrine of the Faith, the Sacraments, and Rites for their study and, on
April 19, to the Holy Father.[11] The corrections made in the schema as

---

6. The request caused some difficulty. Jouassard could not accept because of sickness.
Father Lécuyer had no problem accepting and was a valuable member. Archbishop Lallier,
on the other hand, wrote in rather negative terms, saying that in his judgment "so radical
a change" was premature; the letter, however, was signed not by him but by his secretary.
Father Botte, who had no tolerance for surprises or for having to work with "incompe-
tents" or "individuals who had to be given special consideration," quickly wrote a strong
and resolute letter to Archbishop Lallier's secretary and another to the secretary of the Consilium. In the latter he did not mince words but asked that a choice be made: "either him
or Archbishop Lallier." If the latter were to be part of the group, he himself would drop
out. He also expressed a wish that his decision "be made known, if you judge it appropriate, to those who suggested the candidates." But there was no follow-up and the little squall
passed.

7. Schema 150: *De Pontificali* 7 (April 5, 1966).

8. Schema 180: *De Pontificali* 12 (August 29, 1066), "De ordinatione diaconi, presbyteri
et episcopi."

9. To the final question: "Should the schema, corrected as the Fathers have indicated,
be presented to the Holy Father for approval?" Thirty-three said yes, and one handed in
a blank ballot. At the same meeting, final approval was given to the prayer of episcopal
ordination, taken from the *Traditio Apostolica* of Hippolytus (30 in favor; 3 against; 2 in favor with qualifications).

10. Schema 220: *De Pontificali* 15 (March 31, 1967). After an introduction, this schema
compared the new rites of ordination with the old. It then gave the complete rite for the
ordination of a deacon, of a priest, of a priest and a deacon in the same liturgical action,
and of a bishop. Next came the blessing of the pontifical insignia and two appendixes: one
on the prayer of episcopal ordination and the other containing the Scripture readings for
the ordination Masses. This schema was especially important because in addition to the
notes which drew upon history and the liturgical sources to justify the solutions adopted,
it also listed the decisions reached by the Consilium when the earlier schemas were submitted.

11. On July 19, 1967, the Secretariat of State transmitted a memorandum containing handwritten notes of the Holy Father and said that the Consilium could proceed with the usual
handling of the schema.

a result of this consultation show that no special or radical objections had been submitted but only suggestions for improvement of the texts.[12]

The completely positive answer from the Congregation for the Doctrine of the Faith was particularly pleasing and an occasion of both joy and surprise. The Consilium had been worried especially about the proposal to use the text from the *Traditio Apostolica* of Hippolytus for the prayer of episcopal ordination. Here is what the Congregation said (November 8, 1967):

> Their Eminences of the Congregation for the Doctrine of the Faith carefully examined the matter at their plenary session on Wednesday, October 11, 1967, and came to the following decisions:
>
> The new schema is approved with the following qualifications:
>
> 1) Number 89: In the questions asked of the candidate for the episcopal office, greater emphasis should be put on faith and its conscientious transmission; moreover, the candidate should be expressly asked about his determination to give obedience to the Roman Pontiff.
>
> 2) Number 96: The text of Hippolytus, duly adapted, is acceptable. Regarding the approach: the mind of the Cardinals is that liturgical innovations should be dictated by real need and introduced with all the precautions that so sacred and serious a matter requires.
>
> Once the changes listed have been made in the *Ordo*, it is then to be studied by a joint committee, in accordance with the august decision of the Holy Father.

The joint committee met on February 1-2, 1968.[13] The schema was then further polished and sent once again to the Holy Father.[14]

3. *Final Revision*

On February 19, 1968, the Cardinal Secretary of State sent Father Bugnini some observations of the Holy Father; these were made in summary form in the Pope's own hand. The remarks simply indicated points in the schema that caused him difficulty or on which he wanted further explanations; these explanations were given to him as follows on April 9:

1. The Pope's first request concerned a point of style: not to use the *plural of majesty* in the request that the consecrating bishop proceed to

---

12. See "Adnotationes ad schema n. 22 *De sacris Ordinibus* post animadversiones Sacrarum Congregationum Romanarum" (January 16, 1968), attached to schema 220.

13. Participants: for the SCDF, Archbishop Philippe and Monsignor G. Agustoni; for the SCR, Archbishop Antonelli, Monsignor Frutaz, and Father Melchiore da Pobladura; for the Sacraments, Monsignor Vetri; and for the Consilium, Fathers Bugnini, Botte, Lécuyer, and Braga.

14. Schema 270: *De Pontificali* 17 (February 1, 1968).

the ordination; that is, put the Latin verb in the singular, not the plural ("ordines" instead of "ordinetis"). — A very appropriate suggestion.

2. *"There is no formula accompanying the donning of the stole and dalmatic."* This represents a change from the current rite in the Pontifical. But the tradition on this point has varied greatly. In the West the formulas appear in the Pontificals of the late Middle Ages and reflect the period's allegorical approach, which has now become almost unintelligible. In the Roman Rite, the tradition originating in the *Ordines Romani* has members of the same hierarchic rank placing the insignia on the newly ordained, but without any formula. The action is simply a gesture indicating acceptance of the new member into the presbyteral and diaconal colleges; the meaning of the gesture is further clarified by the kiss of peace. Later on, when the vesting of each candidate was done by the bishop, the action was accompanied by a formula.

In the East the tradition varies: in some Rites it is the bishop who does the vesting while reciting a formula (for example, in the Alexandrian Rite and among the Syrian Jacobites); in others, the action is unaccompanied by words (for example, among the Nestorians and in the Greek Church).

The restored rite harks back to the earliest practice, according to which the vestments proper to a degree of orders were put on the newly ordained by some ministers of the same rank; in accordance with the same practice, the new rite has dropped the accompanying formulas. The action is now accompanied by the singing of an antiphon and psalm that underscore the meaning of what is being done. Singing lends an action greater intensity than a sometimes rather dry and juridical formula can, especially when the formula is repeated over and over for a number of newly ordained ministers. Moreover, if there is singing, then it seems neither useful nor appropriate to have formulas being said in a low voice; these would not be heard by the faithful and would create an unbecoming doublet in the celebration.

3. *New formula for the consecration of a bishop.* This matter was discussed during the Consilium's very first study of the schema at its sixth general meeting.[15] The current formula in the Roman Pontifical was regarded as completely inadequate for expressing the teaching on the episcopate given by the Second Vatican Council, especially in its Constitution on the Church.

The prayer in the old Pontifical has two parts. The longest, which runs from the beginning to the words "Sint speciosi" and from "Tribue ei"

---

15. See Schema 102 (*De Pontificali* 5) and Schema 220 (*De Pontificali* 15), Appendix I: "De oratione ordinationis Episcopi" (pp. 50–53).

to the end is of Roman origin and already to be found in the Leonine Sacramentary. The remainder is a Gallican interpolation that was introduced into the Gelasian Sacramentary. The Roman part develops a single theme: the bishop is the high priest of the new covenant. As Aaron was consecrated by an anointing with oil and the donning of vestments, so the bishop is constituted high priest by a spiritual anointing and the adornment of virtue. — All this is true, but excessively scanty now that we have the teaching of Vatican II on the episcopate. Nothing is said of apostolic succession, and almost nothing of the episcopal office, except for the words "Grant him the episcopal chair."

The Gallican part is simply a cento of scriptural citations that can be applied partly to the apostles, partly to all Christians. Here again there is no consistent teaching on the episcopate. In addition, the impression is given that a bishop is the successor of the Old Testament high priest rather than of Christ's apostles.

As a result, attempts to correct this prayer, to shorten it and make it more organic, proved vain. Therefore, while the group planned to retain the prayers of the Pontifical for priestly and diaconal ordination and simply to make any corrections or additions required by textual criticism (especially in the prayer of diaconal ordination), it decided to look to another tradition entirely for episcopal ordination. The patriarchates of Antioch and Alexandria still use two texts which, despite differences between them, are identical in substance and come from the same source, the *Traditio Apostolica* of Hippolytus.

This prayer is theologically rich; it expresses the traditional teaching on the bishop as not only high priest but also shepherd of Christ's flock, successor of the apostles, and recipient from Christ of the "Spiritus principalis."[16] If the three texts are compared—the one proposed by Father Botte and those used in the patriarchates of Antioch and Alexandria—it will be clear that the basic ideas and logical succession of these are the same in all, although expansions have been introduced into one or other of these texts, without, however, detracting from the beauty and intelligibility of the prayer. From the ecumenical point of view, therefore, the formula proposed bears witness to our unity with the Eastern Church;

---

16. There were difficulties in understanding, and readily translating into the vernaculars, the term "Spiritus principalis" in the ordination prayer. Father Botte therefore explained the meaning in an article, "*Spiritus principalis*. Formule de l'ordination Episcopale," *Not* 10 (1974) 410–11. In summary, the term expresses the gift that is characteristic of episcopal ordination: in the sacrament of ordination the bishop receives the Spirit of Christ as the Spirit who gives authority and establishes as head, so that the bishop may feed the flock entrusted to him.

in the very act of ordination the three very ancient Churches of Rome, Antioch, and Alexandria can be seen asserting the same teaching on the episcopal office.[17]

For these reasons both the Congregation for the Doctrine of the Faith and the Holy Father accepted the introduction of the proposed text.[18]

4. *Singing of the* Veni, Creator. In the rite hitherto in use, this hymn was prescribed while the consecrating bishop was anointing the head of the newly ordained bishop or the hands of the newly ordained priest. The proposal that this hymn be omitted disturbed the Pope. Here are the reasons for the omission.

Historically, the *Veni, Creator* (replaced in some codices by the sequence *Veni, Sancte Spiritus* and the alleluia verse *Veni, Sancte Spiritus*) was first used for this purpose in the Pontificals of the twelfth century and was introduced into the Roman liturgy via the Pontifical of William Durandus (second half of the thirteenth century).

The purpose of the hymn was to fill the time occupied by the rite. It accompanied an episcopal action that had its own formula; the end result was that it became an action in its own right, parallel to and, as it were, superimposed on the action being performed by the bishop. It served as a way of keeping the faithful occupied while the bishop was engaged in something unconnected with the hymn. In short, it was a phenomenon of a kind not rare in our liturgical past.

A further consideration: the hymn invokes the Holy Spirit, but the Holy Spirit has already been given through the laying on of hands and the prayer of ordination. The result is to give undue prominence to an action—the anointing of the head or the hands of the ordained—that simply "explains" what has already happened. This is another reason for omitting the *Veni, Creator*.

On the other hand, it is difficult to find a place where the hymn might be suitably introduced. The most appropriate point would be before the prayer of ordination, that is, before the action in which the Spirit is given. But the Litany of the Saints is said immediately before this prayer. If the

---

17. The text adopted is the Latin translation of the *Traditio Apostolica* of Hippolytus, corrected in accordance with Father Botte's reconstruction, which is based on the Eastern versions and especially on the Greek *Epitome Constitutionis Apostolicae*, since the text of this last was taken directly from the *Traditio Apostolica*.

18. But the text that had been abandoned continued to evoke feelings of tender nostalgia, especially because of its phrases regarding the "majesty" of bishops and its invocation of a curse on those who curse the bishop and a blessing on those who bless him. At various times there were insistent requests that the old prayer be retained, at least as an alternative.

Veni, Creator were to be sung while the Litany of the Saints is being recited, the result would be a most unfortunate doublet.

If a choice must be made between the *Veni, Creator* and the litany with a view to the participation of the faithful, the litany certainly seems preferable: it is the most traditional and venerable form of prayer in which the people can easily participate. In addition, the second part of the litany contains invocations specifically geared to the celebration now going on, whereas the hymn is an invocation of a very general kind, without any specific reference to the purpose of the rite.

Also to be kept in mind is the doctrinal approach proper to the liturgy, which in the consecration of persons does not usually call upon the Holy Spirit to come but rather asks the Father and the Son to send the Spirit. All the consecratory prayers now take this approach; it is therefore more consistent to ask the divine power to send the sanctifying Spirit.

But at an audience on April 24, 1968, the Holy Father had already said to Cardinal Lercaro: "Tell Father Bugnini to keep the *Veni, Creator* in the ordination rites." He had the Cardinal Secretary of State say the same thing in a letter dated the following day: "The August Pontiff wants the singing of the *Veni, Creator* to be retained, as he has already indicated. He appreciates the reasons given for its suppression, but he thinks it better to keep this hymn in which the entire assembly serves as a choir during the rite of ordination."

The *Veni, Creator* is therefore sung during the anointing of the hands of new priests[19] and at the beginning of the rite of episcopal ordination, after the gospel and homily.

5. *The* Te Deum. The new rite retains the hymn of thanksgiving, during which the new bishop passes through the church, blessing the faithful. The schema, however, offered two possibilities: to sing it immediately after communion, so that the entire celebration would end with the prayer after communion; or to sing it during the procession in which the new bishop and his fellow bishops make their way through the church to the sacristy at the end of the celebration.

The Pope's objection had to do with allowing the second alternative. The above-mentioned letter of the Secretariat of State (April 25, 1968) communicated the decision that "the *Te Deum* is to be sung in the place now assigned to it." As a result, the first of the alternatives was adopted exclusively.

---

19. In place of the *Veni, Creator,* Psalm 109 may be sung, with the antiphon "Sacerdos in aeternum Christus Dominus, secundum ordinem Melchisedech, panem et vinum obtuilt"; or some other appropriate song may be used.

4. *Approval*

On May 9, 1968, the Consilium sent the Pope the text with the changes he had asked for. It also sent Cardinal Lercaro's response to the draft of the apostolic constitution approving the new rites and texts.[20] On May 18 the Pope and Father Bugnini went through these documents, now full of the Pope's annotations and underlinings, and the Pope gave the secretary final instructions regarding publication. On the outside of the file he wrote: *"In voto Consilii*—approved." Final approval of the *Ordo* and the apostolic constitution was officially communicated on June 10, 1968 (No. 116427).

The rites for the ordination of deacons, priests, and bishops were thus published in an elegant volume. This was in fact the first book of the liturgical reform to be published. The Congregation of Rites decided that use of it should begin on Easter, April 6, 1969.[21] Meanwhile its use was allowed experimentally in particular cases.[22]

II. CONTENTS

The volume opens with the decree of the Congregation of Rites and the apostolic constitution *Pontificalis Romani.* These documents are followed by the rites for the ordination of deacons, of priests, and of both in the same celebration, and for the ordination of a single bishop (the usual case), a single deacon, a single priest, a single deacon and a single priest in the same celebration, and of several bishops at one time.

The book ends with two appendixes: the first gives the readings for the ordination Masses; the second gives the texts that can be sung, along with the musical notation for them: the *Hanc igitur* for the ordination of

---

20. At an audience on February 20, 1968, the Pope had asked the Consilium to prepare the text of the apostolic constitution. The first schema, prepared by J. Lécuyer, was submitted on April 6, 1968. The Pope decided to ask Cardinal Lercaro's opinion of it. After the Cardinal's examination and the revision by the Latinists, the Pope approved the constitution together with the rites of ordination.

21. Pontificale Romanum ex decreto Sacrosancti Oecumenici Concilii Vaticani II instauratum auctoritate Pauli PP VI promulgatum, *De ordinatione diaconi, presbyteri et episcopi* (Vatican Polyglot Press, 1978; 136 pp.). The rites are in *The Rites of the Catholic Church* 1 (New York, 1980), 44–108. The apostolic constitution, dated June 18, 1968, is in *DOL* 324 nos. 2606-12; see the commentary of J. Lécuyer in *Not* 4 (1968) 213–19.

22. Permission for the first experimental use of the new rite of episcopal ordination was granted by the Holy Father for the ordination of Bishop A. Hänggi, a consultor of the Consilium. The permission was requested by the secretary of the Consilium at an audience on January 4, 1968. On other experiments see A. Bugnini, "Il nuovo Pontificale romano delle ordinazioni," *L'Osservatore Romano*, December 7, 1968; "Quaedam iudicia de ritu ordinationum," *Not* 4 (1968) 210–23.

deacons, of priests, of both together, and of a bishop; the *Veni, Creator Spiritus*; the *Te Deum*. The music for other texts—antiphons, addresses, presidential prayers, and prayers of ordination—is given in the body of the book at the proper place.

The Introductions to these rites are very brief and limited to rubrical remarks.[23]

1. *Apostolic Constitution*

The apostolic constitution *Pontificalis Romani* briefly explains the Church's teaching on the nature and effects of the three degrees of the sacrament of orders, as this is set down in the conciliar documents, especially *Lumen gentium*. The document then recalls the apostolic constitution *Sacramentum Ordinis*, in which Pius XII determined the matter and form of diaconal and presbyteral ordination. Finally, it states what the matter and form of each order are in the newly restructured rites and texts.

The "matter" in all three cases is the imposition of hands; the ordaining prelate silently places his hands on the head of each candidate immediately before the prayer of ordination. All the consecrating bishops can impose their hands on the candidate at an episcopal ordination and are to join the principal celebrant in saying the essential words of the prayer of ordination. At the ordination of priests, the other priests present may impose their hands on the ordinands.

The apostolic constitution specifies the essential part of each of three prayers of ordination, which are the form of the sacrament. These precise definitions, which are needed in order to avoid controversy and scruples, should not make us forget that the sacramental formula is the entire prayer of ordination, as Pius XII said in his own apostolic constitution.

I spoke above of the prayer used in the ordination of bishops. The prayer of presbyteral ordination used in the past seemed rich enough to be retained, though some additions and revisions were made in order to restore the reading found in the earliest liturgical sources.[24] In diaconal ordination, the text in the old Pontifical still serves as a basis, but it has been altered and greatly enriched in order better to express the deacon's participation in the ministry of salvation; it has been brought into line with the teaching of Vatican II on the diaconate and at the same time has

---

23. See what was said above on pp. 582–83, n. 4.

24. This was the group's idea, and it was accepted by the Consilium. It was not, however, confirmed by experience. That is why there were requests for a different ordination prayer that would better reflect New Testament teaching on priesthood.

been made more faithful to the oldest sources, namely, the Verona (Leonine), Gregorian, and Gelasian Sacramentaries.

2. *Rite of Ordination*

The general structure is identical in all three rites of ordination. These are celebrated after the presentation of the candidates and the bishop's ensuing homily.

The ritual gives three sample addresses that the bishop can take as guides in composing his homily. These addresses, though not obligatory (since the bishop's own homily can replace them), are nonetheless very important. They are based on the teaching of Vatican II and explain to the ordinands and all present[25] the meaning of the order conferred and of the mission given to the newly ordained.

Next comes the examination of the candidates. Here the latter express their determination to accept the responsibilities attached to the service they are undertaking for the sake of God's people; they promise fidelity in the fulfillment of their office and obedience to their superiors (to bishops, religious superiors, the Pope). This examination is another novelty, and a very important one, not only because it lends solemnity and weight to the commitment the candidates are making in the presence of the Church but also because it provides a new opportunity for bringing out in a concrete way the responsibilities given in each order.

The bishop then calls upon all present to pray, and the Litany of the Saints is sung. This is succeeded by the main part of the ordination rite—the silent laying on of hands and the prayer of ordination. After this prayer the newly ordained deacons and priests are clothed in the vestments proper to their order; this is done by the deacons and priests present.

Next, the hands of new priests and the head of a new bishop are anointed. The words accompanying these anointings have been changed so that they no longer seem, as in the past, to express the conferral of a new power but simply spell out the gift and power already received through the imposition of hands and the prayer of ordination. A comparable change has been made in the formula that, a moment later, accompanies the presentation to new priests of a chalice and paten containing the material for the Eucharistic sacrifice. A deacon is presented with the Book of the Gospels.

---

25. Another novelty is the directive that ordinations be celebrated, if possible, on a Sunday or other feast day, so as to permit the largest possible participation of the faithful. This directive does away with the idea of special days for ordination (which meant that they were usually celebrated on weekdays).

The ordained then receive a greeting and kiss of peace from the ordaining bishop and the fellow ministers present.

At the ordination of a bishop, the anointing of the head with sacred chrism is followed by the presentation of the Book of the Gospels (which has been held on the ordinand's head during the prayer of ordination). He is then given a ring, the sign of fidelity to and communion with the Church; a miter (without any formula); and a pastoral staff. He is then enthroned in his episcopal chair if the ordination is being celebrated in the cathedral church of the diocese to which he has been elected;[26] otherwise he takes first place among the concelebrating bishops. The Mass then continues from the offertory.[27]

On the whole, the new ordination rites are simple, linear, sufficiently brief and easily understandable, and therefore suited to participation by the faithful.

Precisely in order to achieve brevity and, more important, clarity, some secondary rites or texts have been omitted that used to prolong the celebration without any great profit and, by drawing attention to peripheral elements, could give rise to misunderstandings about the real nature of the action performed.[28] In general, the reform of the rite has yielded a celebration which the faithful can more easily understand and in which they can more actively participate.[29]

---

26. See E. J. Lengeling, "De loco ordinationis Episcopi Ordinarii et de missa ordinationis," *Not* 10 (1974) 95–108.

27. The book containing the rite of ordination only gives the list of readings for the ordination Masses (see also *Not* 4 [1968] 57–60). There are no other proper texts for these Masses except for the *Hanc igitur* of the Roman Canon.

28. For example, the laying on of hands in the ordination of a deacon and a bishop was accompanied by the formula "Receive the Holy Spirit," which was not the actual sacramental formula but, because of its position and the solemn moment at which it was uttered, overshadowed the real sacramental formula. In like manner, the solemn blessing given to the bishop elect (who was wearing his miter and holding his pastoral staff) during the litany could give the impression that this was the moment of greatest solemnity; for this reason the action was eliminated. The words accompanying the anointing of the hands and the presentation of the sacred vessels to a new priest could suggest the idea that this was the real moment of ordination and of conferral of the power to celebrate the Eucharist, whereas in fact these were simply explanatory rites (rites symbolizing in detail what had already been done). The same remark holds for the rite performed on the newly ordained priests after communion; it gave the impression that the power to absolve from sin was being conferred at that moment.

29. But the changes, especially those mentioned in the previous note, did not immediately convince everyone. Some were of the opinion that the rite had been impoverished and was now less solemn and impressive. There were requests that the suppressed actions be restored, at least in some form, and some bishops continued to give the blessing with great solemnity during the singing of the Litany of the Saints.

It is to be hoped that after being stripped down and restored in accordance with the

III. A NEW UNDERTAKING

The reformed rites of ordination were generally accepted as satisfactory. Use of them, however, also brought to light some deficiencies. These were felt at two points in particular: the lack of an Introduction comparable to those in the liturgical books published later on and the ordination prayer for priests, which, it was objected, was not very meaningful, inasmuch as it focused more on Old Testament priesthood than on the priesthood of Christ.

For these reasons the prefect of the Congregation for Divine Worship wrote as follows to the Secretary of State on June 4, 1973:

> This Congregation has in mind to produce a uniform edition of all the reformed rites; it will follow an organic plan which we will submit at the proper time.
>
> Since the various rites were published whenever their redaction was complete, the terminology used and the formulation of rubrics likewise took shape only gradually. There is therefore a good deal of polishing to be done if the various books are to be brought into harmony.
>
> Especially in need of work is the volume containing the ordination rites for bishops, priests, and deacons. This was the first book to be published and completely lacks the "General Introduction" to be found in all the other rites.
>
> The undertaking seems an appropriate one, both to obtain uniformity and in order not to have to repeat the same guidelines and norms for each rite, as is now the case.
>
> Before we embark on the work, I would be pleased to know the Holy Father's thinking on the matter.

This letter never received an answer, although one was twice requested.

Meanwhile the Congregation decided to start upon the most important task—the preparation of an Introduction to holy orders. Professor Kleinheyer was asked to direct the operation. He agreed and consulted Father Botte. On January 7, 1974, a study group was formed[30] that held three meetings. The first took place in the offices of the Congregation on April 2-3 and discussed the first draft of an Introduction; this had been

---

criteria of the liturgical Constitution and the most professional historical and textual criticism, as well as with the most authentic teaching on holy orders, the rite will not end up being once more encrusted with additions that obscure its crystalline intelligibility.

30. *Relator:* B. Kleinheyer; *secretary:* R. Kaczynski; *members:* P. Gy, P. Jounel. J. Lécuyer, E. Lengeling, M. Lessi, A. Nocent, and F. Bär. A. Dumas and P. Coughlan were added later. The last-named was added in view of requests from the English bishops that some parts of the abrogated rite might be reintroduced into the new rite of presbyteral ordination.

composed by the relator and the secretary and had been sent to all members of the group.[31]

All the participants agreed that the group should not limit itself to the Introduction but should also deal with other matters that needed revision: for example, inclusion of the rite of acceptance of celibacy in the rite of diaconal ordination; a new redaction of the ordination prayers for priests and deacons. A change in the layout of the book was also proposed: the rite of episcopal ordination should come first (as in the Constitution on the Church), since this is the source of the others.

After this meeting the individual members continued with the work assigned to them,[32] and a second schema was prepared and sent out for study on May 16 and 18.[33]

The group held its second meeting on June 6–8, again in the offices of the Congregation; P. Gy presided, since the relator had been taken to the hospital for an operation. The meeting yielded a third schema,[34] which was discussed at the third meeting, October 10–11, 1974. Immediately afterwards the relator and the secretary put the finishing touches on the schema.[35] The report of the meeting gives some idea of what the finished work was like:

> At the most recent meeting of the study group for the second edition of the rite of ordination, the changes made in the text of July 20, 1974, were discussed; these included changes in the ordination prayer for priests and deacons. Next, all the approved changes were introduced . . . into the text of July 20. . . . With regard to the formula for the prayer of priestly ordination, it was decided to ask the Fathers at a plenary session for direction in this area. It has been pointed out that the style of the new prayer differs from that of the prayers now in use. A logical conclusion would be that the group ought also to offer new prayers for episcopal and diaconal ordination.

---

31. The schema of thirty-six pages was entitled: "On the second edition of the book *The Ordination of deacon, priest, and bishop*," and was dated March 14, 1974.

32. Relator and secretary for the general revision: M. Lessi; for the revision of the rubrics: E. J. Lengeling; for the address at the ordination of deacons; for the preparation of texts for the ritual Masses, the embolisms of the Eucharistic Prayers, and the solemn blessings: A. Dumas.

33. "De ordinatione episcopi, presbyteri et diaconi" (May 16, 1974). The schema had five chapters. It also contained the rites for admission to candidacy for ordination as deacons and priests, the texts for the ritual Masses, and, in an appendix, the songs.

34. "De ordinatione episcopi, presbyterorum et diaconorum" (July 20, 1974; 115 pp.). Concrete suggestions are given (by Father Gy) for the ordination prayers for priests and deacons.

35. The fourth and final schema was dated October 17, 1974.

But everything stopped at this point. The matter was a sensitive one, and the climate was not favorable. Then the Congregation itself was suppressed, and the material so laboriously and generously developed by the experts ended up in the archives!

Part VI

Blessings

43

Ministries

I. First Phase (1965–1966)

1. *Study of the Question*

At the fifth general meeting of the Consilium in April 1965, the Fathers expressed their wish that the problems raised by minor orders be studied in a limited group. A special committee was therefore appointed[1] that met in Livorno from July 1 to July 3 of that year. The secretary of the Consilium was also present at the meeting, but Father Botte, one of the members, was absent, pleading prior commitments. The meetings were held in the episcopal residence, while the members were lodged with the Vallombrosian Benedictine sisters of the town. In Father Botte's absence, Canon Martimort acted as president (Bishop Guano, the appointed president, was not always there due to precarious health). The discussion was keynoted by a report from Professor Kleinheyer on the theological and juridical problems connected with the subject. The following, in summary form, were the points discussed:

1) Down to the present time there have been five minor orders in the Latin Church: subdiaconate and the offices of acolyte, exorcist, lector, and porter.

2) These orders have been conferred only on those men who intend to proceed to the priesthood and who therefore have already taken on the duties of clerics by receiving first tonsure.

---

1. *President:* Bishop E. Guano; *members:* B. Botte, A.-G. Martimort, E. Lengeling, C. Vagaggini, J. Lécuyer, and B. Kleinheyer.

3) No ordination *per saltum* ("by a leap") has been allowed, that is, the reception of an order without having received those that precede.[2]

Minor orders have thus become transitional steps to the priesthood and are no longer effectively correlated with a real situation. In fact, the duties at one time assigned in minor orders are now exercised by laypersons and not by those who receive the orders. The offices are simply empty titles and contrary to the principle of "truthfulness" that is to be followed in the liturgical reform.

In order to do away with these inconsistencies and at the same time meet the needs of the present-day Church, a change in discipline is required. The committee proposed:

1) That these orders be conferred also on persons who do not intend to go on to priesthood but will actually exercise the offices attached to minor orders.

2) That the prohibition against ordination *per saltum* be revoked. There was no such prohibition at Rome down to the tenth century; until that time no Pope had received all the minor orders. The prohibition was introduced in order that candidates for the priesthood might be tested for a while. But even this reason is not valid today, since seminaries provide preparation for the priesthood and this preparation does not involve the exercise of the minor orders, which are often received all at once, as though they were simply a formality. Furthermore, these orders are by their nature permanent ministries and not steps to the priesthood or diaconate. In fact, they came into existence because the duties of the deacon were divided up among several persons. Therefore they need not all be received before the diaconate.

3) That some of these orders be opened to laypersons as well.

4) There are different opinions in the Church regarding the terminology used for these orders. Without wishing in any way to prejudge the solution of the problems being presented, the group expressed a wish that in the case of the "minor orders" the term "ordination" be changed to "institution."

5) The number of the minor orders has varied not a little in different periods of history and in the Churches of the East and West. They can, therefore, be more or less numerous.

With regard to the individual minor orders of the Roman Rite, the committee made the following observations and suggestions.

---

2. See the 1917 Code of Canon Law, canons 108, 118, 973, 974, 977, 1004, 2374.

Subdiaconate

The commitment to celibacy should find better expression and should be sanctified by an appropriate rite that will do honor to the commitment. Such a rite cannot be connected with the diaconate, because *Lumen gentium* allows for the possibility of married deacons, nor with the subdiaconate, because in the future the Church might also allow married subdeacons. The best solution seems to be the creation of a new rite for the profession of celibacy, to be celebrated at an appropriate time as judged by the episcopal conferences. Some parts of the rite *de clerico faciendo* might be used, while the emphasis is put on the positive aspects of consecration to God, in the spirit of the conciliar decree *Presbyterorum Ordinis*.

Next is the revision of the rite for the subdiaconate. The task of the subdeacon is to assist the deacon in the liturgy and in ecclesiastical functions. This order has existed in the Church since the third century and should not be abolished. On the other hand, it seems appropriate to omit from the rite the presentation of the book of epistles (a late addition to this liturgy), since a subdeacon is already a lector and has received this book.

Office of lector

Nothing should be said any longer of the blessing of bread and new fruits—an idea that came from the treatise *De officiis VII graduum*, a work of obscure origin and uncertain use. On the other hand, it is desirable that in accordance with the liturgical Constitution, the laity be empowered to give some blessings. The function of the lector in the liturgical assembly should be brought out more fully.

Office of exorcist

Since the holder of this office cannot exercise any specific function, there is no reason for its existence. It is an order peculiar to the Roman Church, but even here it was in abeyance from the fifth to the tenth century.

Office of acolyte

This order should be kept and should be conferred at an appropriate time so that it can be suitably exercised for a certain period. It could be conferred also on married men, young boys, and youths who will be permanent altar-servers. The episcopal conferences, of course, will have to set down appropriate guidelines. The reason for regarding the office of acolyte as the worthiest of the minor orders was its connection with the Eucharist: acolytes used to be ministers of communion.[3]

Office of porter

This task is now performed by sacristans. "Institution as porter" could once again be conferred on them.

New blessings for other ministries

The committee also considered the possibility of other special blessings that would give prominence to other ministries exercised in the Church and would seal the conferral of these with an invocation of the Lord's blessing and help. Such a blessing could be given to catechists in the missions. Further study is needed for other functions, such as commentator, cantor, and organist; attention must also be given to rites already in the Roman Pontifical, such as the blessing of cantors and psalmists.

The committee also raised the delicate question of blessings to be given to women for the exercise of tasks already entrusted to them, for example, sacristan, organist, and director of song. But the subject was barely touched and not discussed in sufficient depth.

When we look back across the years to the work done at Livorno, and especially to Professor Kleinheyer's report, we can see that it contained all or almost all the elements needed for solutions reached only eight years later, and even then not completely.

The principal conclusions were these: abolition of the orders of porter and exorcist; retention of the offices of acolyte, lector, and subdeacon, but with the last named being reduced to a "minor order"; rite of commitment to celibacy as an independent entity, not attached to any order; long-term blessings for other ministries exercised by laymen, with the possibility of conferring some of them on women as well. If the work had continued along these lines and in the same spirit of openness, so much time would not have been lost, at the expense of institutions worthy of all respect and veneration.

---

3. See the letter of John the Deacon to Senarius (sixth century), ed. A. Wilmart, *Analecta Reginensia* (ST 59; Vatican City, 1933) 176; Innocent I, letter to Bishop Decentius of Gubbio (416), in PL 20:556-57 and ed. R. Cabié, *Lettre du pape Innocent Ier à Decentius de Gubbio* (Bibliothèque de la RHE 58; Louvain, 1973); *Ordo Romanus XXIV*, ed. M. Andrieu, *Les Ordines Romani du haut moyen-âge* 3 (Spicilegium Sacrum Lovaniense 24; Louvain, 1951).

2. Presentation to the Consilium

After the Livorno meeting Bishop Guano asked Canon Martimort to draw up a detailed report for the Consilium; he was to furnish it with references to all the historical, juridical, and literary sources.[4] The material (ten headings, each ending with a question) was studied at the meeting of the relators in May 1966. The positions taken and the conclusions reached by the Livorno committee were accepted. Questions remained on matters which that committee had not resolved: conferral on women; establishment of new blessings for offices given to laymen. The relators took a somewhat rigid position on minor orders, saying that they should be conferred only on those who would permanently exercise the office bestowed. They wanted a rite of introduction to the clerical state to be celebrated for candidates for the priesthood.

One point not clarified, and even deliberately left aside, was the distinction between minor orders and "ministries" or blessings. The relators confined themselves to the field of operation already established by the Livorno committee, namely, to determine which "minor orders" should be kept and what other blessings should be instituted for those persons, laymen in particular, who exercise a liturgical service on a more or less permanent basis. Out of respect for the thesis of those who held minor orders to be part of the sacrament of orders, they did not envisage the prospect of a minor order being changed into a ministry. The difficulty of giving a definite answer for or against that thesis made it difficult to take clear positions, especially on the relations between minor orders and ministries, accessibility to women, and the obligation of candidates for the priesthood to receive the minor orders.

The same difficulty arose from a statement of Father Botte, the acknowledged "grand master" in the field of orders. In his view the subdiaconate and the office of lector should be kept as "minor orders." He prepared and distributed a closely written paper on the office of acolyte, in which he said in summary:

> The order of acolytes is a very ancient one in the Roman Church, having perhaps been established by Pope Victor in the second century. In 251 there were forty-one acolytes in Rome, and there were always acolytes there from then on; in the East, on the other hand, they were unknown, except in the Armenian Church, which took them over from the Latins. The other Western Churches likewise had no acolytes. The office of acolyte was further defined in the sixth century when acolytes sometimes suspended from

---

4. See Schema 164: *De subdiaconatu et de ordinibus minoribus* 1 (May 4, 1966).

their necks the little bags in which the priest placed the *fermentum*, and took them to the priests in the titular churches.

The office of acolyte is still needed today, but it is now held by unordained children and youths who serve at the altar. It has been suggested that the order be kept for seminarians. Others, however, think this violates the principle of truthfulness, since very many seminarians have been exercising the office for years by the time they receive the order. The conferral of it on them seems, therefore, to be meaningless. Nor is it appropriate to confer this order on children and youths who after a time will cease to serve at the altar.

The question, then, is whether it is right to retain an order that has all the same drawbacks as other orders whose suppression is proposed.

Canon Martimort's report, supplemented by Father Botte's study and the observations made at the meeting of the relators, was reworked by Father Vagaggini for presentation at the seventh general meeting of the Consilium (October 1966).[5] His report consisted of a preface and four parts: general principles; the minor orders to be retained and to be suppressed; a new discipline for the conferral of minor orders; rites to be provided for other ministries and offices in the Church. The whole thing was also put in the form of twenty-five questions. An appendix contained two rites: a rite for the appointment of a minister to distribute communion in the absence of a deacon or priest; a rite for the distribution of communion by an extraordinary minister.[6]

Each point was accompanied by an extensive historical, theological, and liturgical explanation and ended with a question. It will be worthwhile here to present the content of the questions in declarative form, so that the reader can have an idea of the breadth of the treatment. Independently of the value of the resolutions taken on that occasion, this overall vision of the problems was very important. The very lack of such a vision was to be the reason for the difficulties experienced in reaching a speedy and coherent solution of the problem.

---

5. Schema 178: *De ordinibus minoribus* 2 (August 15, 1966; 45 pp.); Schema 193: *De ordinibus minoribus* 3 (October 5, 1966). Schema 178 was first discussed among the relators; consequently, when it was presented to the Fathers, it was completed by Schema 193, which gives the position of the relators and on that basis re-evaluates, poses differently, or abandons some questions.

6. These rites were prepared by P. Jounel (the rite for commissioning the minister) and by B. Fischer and P. Gy (the rite for the distribution of communion), in consequence of the concession made in *Fidei custos*. The rites were presented to the Consilium for its study; they were then passed on to the Congregation for the Sacraments.

General principles

1. This study has been done in such a way as not to prejudge the solution of the underlying theological problem, namely, whether or not all these orders are degrees of the sacrament of orders. For this reason, the question of whether or not they may be conferred on women is also left unanswered.

2. The Church may abolish, change, or increase the number of the orders below the diaconate, as any given period needs or finds useful.

3. The reform of the minor orders should obey the principle of truthfulness. This means that if the ministry or liturgical office conferred by an order is no longer necessary or useful for the Church, or if the person ordained does not in fact exercise the office, or if the "class" or "order" into which the person is incorporated no longer exists except at some ideal level, then the ordination and accompanying petition for divine grace are no longer truthful.

4. A distinction must be made between an office and the associated minor order, in the sense that it is not absolutely necessary to receive the order in order to carry out the task envisaged in it. On the other hand, rites should be provided which in specific circumstances can authorize a person to exercise a certain office when it is not appropriate to confer a minor order.

All these principles were unanimously approved by the Consilium in a show of hands.

Minor orders to be retained or suppressed

5-7. The following can be suppressed: the orders of porter,[7] exorcist,[8] and acolyte.[9]

8. The order of lector: the report proposed that it be kept because the office of proclaiming Sacred Scripture in the liturgical assembly is so important and is once again held in high esteem in the liturgical Constitution and the liturgical reform. Historically, it was the first order to appear on the scene and has always existed in the Church. On the other hand, the report said that this order should not be connected with incorporation into the clergy, so that it may be conferred also on laypersons.

The discussion among the relators, however, emphasized the authority that baptism gives every believer to proclaim the word of God; it is not

---

7. 30 in favor, 4 against.
8. 33 in favor, 1 in favor with qualifications.
9. 26 in favor, 8 against.

advisable that lectors be in any way set apart from the rest of the faithful; after all, seminarians exercise this office long before they receive the corresponding minor order.

The request for suppression thus won the day and was brought before the assembled Fathers of the Consilium. The latter showed themselves in favor of suppressing the order of lector.[10]

9. The subdiaconate should be kept[11] as a minor order.[12] This order has existed in the Church since the third century and has been preserved in all the Eastern Churches. The duties of the subdeacon as assistant to the deacon are still useful. Like the diaconate, the subdiaconate might well be conferred on married men. The commitment to celibacy by candidates to the priesthood could be made on some other occasion.

New discipline for the conferral of minor orders

10. The Church should allow conferral of the subdiaconate on men who have no intention of going on to the diaconate and priesthood, or are not suited for these orders.[13]

11. It should be lawful to confer a single minor order on a person who will actually exercise it; on the other hand, those entering the diaconate should not be obliged to receive each and all of the minor orders.[14]

12. Laymen should be allowed to receive the minor orders.

Rites to be provided for other ministries and offices

13. The thirteenth question had to do with whether or not there should be a rite of initiation or admission for exercising any liturgical office. This question was not discussed at the general meeting of the Fathers, because it seemed superfluous.[15]

14-16. Because *Fidei custos* allowed for the possibility of authorizing suitable lay persons to distribute communion, the Consilium, after full

---

10. On suppression: 20 in favor, 14 against.

11. 25 in favor, 7 against, 1 blank ballot.

12. 31 in favor, 1 against, 1 blank ballot.

13. Approved by a show of hands.

14. The question was limited to whether the request should be made to the Holy Father that a man receiving the diaconate not be obliged to receive the subdiaconate: 23 in favor, 8 against.

15. This question, like part of the preceding, is connected with the question of becoming a cleric; in the past, minor orders could be given only to one who had received first tonsure. The Consilium decided to leave the problem of entrance into the clergy to the competent agencies.

discussion, decided that this authorization should be communicated to the ordinary faithful by means of a special blessing.[16]

17-21. Those who exercise a liturgical function without having received the corresponding minor order should be able to receive a special blessing, if the episcopal conferences so decide, and provided the blessing does not look like the conferral of a minor order. Schema 178 dealt in detail with the general question and with individual offices: lector (male or female), acolyte, and sacristan, as well as catechist, teacher of religion, and lay missionary.

Discussion with the relators brought out differences of opinion. Some were opposed to such blessings, seeing them as amounting to the establishment of minor orders reserved to the laity. Others maintained that in virtue of their baptism the laity already have the authority to exercise the functions listed; giving this exercise an official approval by means of a rite might well weaken the laity's consciousness of their baptismal commitments. Others, however, were in favor of the blessings because they could be of pastoral use, provided (as had been said) that the episcopal conferences judged them worthwhile and provided the impression was avoided of bestowing an authorization similar to that given in minor orders. Associations of lectors, cantors, sacristans, and so on were thought desirable and were urged; these can contribute to the spiritual and liturgical formation of the persons in question.[17]

Rites for seminarians

22. The final two questions referred to seminarians. Minor orders have hitherto been reserved to them and have been regarded as a pedagogical means of preparing them for the priesthood. Assuming that entrance into the clergy is to be associated with the diaconate, it was thought desirable to have a special rite in which, after a suitable period of testing in the seminary, the candidate would express his intention of going on to holy orders and as a result would henceforth be publicly regarded as accepting this way of life. But the suggestion was not accepted.[18]

---

16. 36 in favor. The same principle was declared valid also for the other persons envisaged in *Fidei custos*: clerics in minor orders (subdeacons), religious, catechists, superiors of communities of women: 36 in favor, 2 against, 1 blank ballot.

17. The outcome of the vote: readers (men and women): 28 in favor, 1 in favor with qualifications, 5 against, 2 blank ballots; acolytes, catechists, teachers of religion, lay missionaries: 29 in favor, 5 against, 2 blank ballots; sacristans: 20 in favor, 13 against, 1 in favor with qualifications, 2 blank ballots.

18. 22 against, 14 in favor, 1 blank ballot.

23. It was also thought desirable that the commitment of the diocesan clergy to celibacy be more fully emphasized by means of an appropriate rite; this would be celebrated before the diaconate, at a time to be established by the episcopal conferences. This request was likewise not accepted.[19] The reason was the disagreement over the nature of this commitment in the case of the diocesan clergy—is it a promise or is it a vow? A special rite might well suggest an inclination to the second alternative; this suggestion seemed impermissible.

All this vast labor never crossed the threshold of the Consilium to the outside world. The discussion reached a mature stage in the decisions of the Fathers,[20] but it stopped there. In fact, the discussion had hardly begun when some zealous "servant" falsely reported to the Pope that the Consilium intended to *abolish all the minor orders;* the "news" greatly disturbed him. In this situation it was thought that the minutes of the meeting, though fully documented and logically argued, would only increase the Pope's anxiety and send him into hibernation. Therefore, the report on the state of the Consilium's work (November 10, 1966) said only this: "Minor orders: Given the complexity of the subject and considering the fact that the Holy Father's approval is not urgently needed at this point in the overall work of the Consilium, a detailed report on the entire problem and on questions connected with it will be submitted at a later time."

II. SECOND PHASE (1967–1971)

1. *Intervention of the Secretariat of State (1967)*

Six months later the "Extraordinary Affairs" department of the Secretariat of State was charged by the Pope to study the question of the permanent diaconate; in the process it revived the question of minor orders.

A memorandum on the audience of April 12 had this to say:

"A serious question still awaits resolution: the question of the orders preceding the diaconate." The matter was in the hands of Msgr. Pio Gaspari, who had diligently informed himself of the work done by the Consilium. One of his notes says: "When it became clear that the problem as a whole was not yet completely ready for resolution, the Cardinal President thought

---

19. 18 against, 15 in favor, 1 in favor with qualifications, 2 blank ballots.

20. The results of the discussion and the voting may be found in "Relatio VII sessionis plenariae Consilii," *Res Secretariae* 25 (October 28, 1966).

it better to delay submitting a report on the work to the Holy Father." Then he adds: "Note: I understood from what was said that there was also some 'fear' of submitting these provisional conclusions."

From the same source it was learned that the Congregation of Sacraments had shown itself "in favor (memorandum of December 3, 1966) of retaining tonsure (which, however, may be replaced by another rite), minor orders, and the subdiaconate, as in the present discipline. Deacons must receive minor orders and the subdiaconate before the diaconate."

Finally, there was a handwritten note from the Pope: "Minor orders should not be abolished but conferred with improved rites." And again: "May 4, 1967: Minor orders must be retained, but their concept and functions must be developed, and they must be integrated into the preparation for diaconate and priesthood."

On the basis of these principles minor orders were kept even for permanent deacons.[21] The question now seemed "closed."

But the study group dealing with the Pontifical could not fail to have a continuing interest in a problem that concerned it directly. It took the matter up once more at a meeting in Paris (March 4, 1968). Father Lécuyer was instructed to communicate to the secretariat of the Consilium the following points, on which group 20 was in unanimous agreement:

1. It seems necessary to preserve the principle of truthfulness that the Consilium voted to apply to minor orders, that is, that minor orders should correspond to real functions in the Church.

2. The subdiaconate should be kept as a minor order, but its reception should not be linked in the future to celibacy or access to holy orders. It could therefore be conferred even on laymen who accept a permanent association with the functions exercised by deacons and priests, especially in the area of worship. Men would enter the ecclesiastical state (with its juridical rights and duties) only at the moment of the diaconate.

3. Contrary to the wish of the Consilium, the group would like to keep the order of lector; this would be conferred on Christians capable of giving catechetical instruction to children and catechumens and teaching religion at all levels. The title "lector" would thus be understood as equivalent to "teacher" (lector in theology, and so on). It could be conferred on laypersons not destined for holy orders (the question would then arise of its conferral on women). It would also be given to seminari-

---

21. See Paul VI, motu proprio *Sacrum diaconatus Ordinem* (June 18, 1967): *AAS* 59 (1967) 697–704; *DOL* 309 nos. 2533-46.

ans after several years of study (for example, at the end of the first year of theology).

The arguments for retaining the order of lector were chiefly the following:

a) The task of teaching Christian doctrine, especially as catechists, is important; it calls for a special canonical mandate that establishes a person in a permanent and specific function of the Church; it is desirable, therefore, that it be accompanied by a liturgical blessing.

b) The lectorate, like the subdiaconate, is an order that has always existed in the Church; this makes it unique among the four "minor" orders. If the lectorate is retained, the Western Church would have the same orders as the Eastern; this would be an aid to unity.

c) If this order is retained as part of the preparation of candidates for major orders, it would constitute an important stage in their formation. Since it corresponds to a real function in the Church (one that can be exercised even by those not continuing on to priesthood), the ordination as lector could have a value that seminarians regret not finding in the present minor orders. It would then not be simply one more order deserving of suppression. Above all, minor orders are in fact received in two stages, since seminarians receive only two minor orders in one ceremony.

A special liturgical place could be assigned to lectors in the ceremonies of adult baptism, confirmation, and first communion: they could present the candidates and serve as guarantors of their spiritual preparation.

4. There might be a liturgical ceremony that would replace tonsure and be reserved for entrance into the seminary. This ceremony would correspond to that marking the entrance of religious into the novitiate.

This statement, coming as it did from a qualified individual who enjoyed esteem in papal circles, seemed a profitable occasion for resuming the dialogue after a two-year interruption and for testing the waters. It was therefore sent on to the Secretariat of State. A month later (April 20, 1968; No. 109771) a reply came that unmistakably conveyed the thinking of the Pope:

1. Minor orders should, it seems clear, be retained for a number of reasons:

a) they enjoy a degree of antiquity;

b) they help introduce men into the clerical life because they are a spiritual preparation for major orders and an occasion for a personal, religious meeting between the ordaining bishop and the students who are to serve in the sanctuary;

c) they can give spiritual meaning and value to the religious service that laymen perform as lectors, catechists, sacristans, and so on.

2. It will, however, be necessary to restore the original meaning of minor orders by means of explanatory texts that better reflect the functions given to the ordained; for example, in the case of the porter, the custody and administration of the church, the understanding of sacred art, love of the external orderliness of the house of God; in the case of the lector, the importance of Sacred Scripture in the assembly of the faithful and of catechetical instruction; in the case of the exorcist, the healing of spiritual and bodily ills, that is, aiding the sick and the poor; in the case of the acolyte, knowledge of the objects and ceremonies belonging to sacred worship, and participation in liturgical celebrations.

3. If some parts of the liturgical texts are changed in this way and if minor orders recover their true spiritual and practical meaning, they will be an effective pedagogical tool for the formation of young men who are called to serve the Church in its worship.

2. *At the Congregation for the Sacraments (1968–1972)*

But the uneasiness felt by permanent deacons and seminarians at having to submit to minor orders soon made itself known.

On October 22, 1968, the Council for the Public Affairs of the Church told the Congregation for the Sacraments that the Holy Father had accepted, "as a favor, on this one occasion," a petition of the Bishop of Rottenburg that he might be allowed to ordain eleven married candidates as deacons without having first conferred minor orders and the subdiaconate on them. The letter went on to say:

> It is nonetheless the Holy Father's ardent wish that in anticipation of possible repetitions of such requests the matter be carefully studied in its various aspects, as its seriousness requires, and that guidelines be formulated as soon as possible which will enable us to give more appropriate answers in each case (these cases often being presented as "urgent"). I hasten to convey this information to you . . . so that your Congregation—in collaboration with the Consilium—may quickly draft a set of guidelines.

The two agencies immediately established contact. The Consilium made all its material available to the Congregation: a request from the French episcopal conference, Father Lécuyer's statement and the answer from the Secretariat of State, a request from Cardinal Suenens regarding the permanent diaconate and the Consilium's answer.[22]

---

22. In its letter, written after consulting the Congregation for the Sacraments, which had promised a "speedy resolution of the question," the Consilium urged patience, because "a solution will not be long delayed, it seems." Furthermore, since Cardinal Suenens spoke of a rite of commitment to the permanent diaconate that would replace minor orders, the Consilium asked for information about the structure and texts of this rite. This

The work dragged on and requests multiplied: France, Belgium, Germany, Austria, Switzerland, and Canada asked permission to do away with first tonsure and minor orders and to replace them with new liturgical rites that would more accurately express the spiritual values inherent in the functions entrusted to candidates for the priesthood. And because Rome did not answer or kept delaying, some conferences acted on their own responsibility and undertook their own reform. As a result, "while Rome is being consulted, Saguntum falls."[23]

In January 1970 a plenary meeting of the Congregation for the Sacraments was being planned on the problem of minor orders. The Holy Father had a memorandum drawn up on tonsure and the orders of porter and exorcist, the three rites "under impeachment." The memorandum said:

> *Tonsure:* this could be replaced by a request from the candidates: "I ask to be admitted, and so on," and a reply from the bishop: "I accept you and enroll you, and so on," together with an address of admonition and exhortation. — *Order of porter:* giving of the keys of the material church, along with an address on the meaning of the church as house of worship and of the assembly of the faithful, and on the duties of the ordained in regard both to the building (art, principles, and so on) and to the order to be followed in the assembly of the faithful. — *Order of exorcist:* bodily and spiritual care of the faithful in distress (charity, aid, and so on).

The Pope also manifested his desire that the Congregation for Divine Worship be consulted on the matter. The latter was therefore asked by the Congregation for the Sacraments to express "its opinion, with the utmost freedom, regarding the whole subject and each point of it, including even the manner of convoking the plenary meeting."

An answer was sent on February 5, 1970; in it Cardinal Gut said:

> A plenary meeting with the member bishops participating seems to me most appropriate; on this matter I have no particular suggestions to add. As for the problem itself, the thinking of this Congregation cannot be substantially different from that which in its time the Consilium voiced, nor

was a polite way of preparing him for a negative answer and for some form of collaboration. But the Cardinal Prefect of the Congregation for the Sacraments saw in this another intrusion into the competency of his agency.

23. In May 1969, Cardinal Döpfner obtained permission from the Holy See for the provisional replacement of tonsure with a liturgical rite that was to be given the same juridical value intended by the Code for a person entering the ecclesiastical state. It was as a result of this permission that the German episcopate during its plenary session at Fulda in September 1969 ordered its national liturgical commission to prepare a draft of a rite for acceptance among the diocesan clergy; it also decided to ask the Holy See for permission to prepare a rite for minor orders. Similar steps were taken in France.

from that of the three liturgists who were queried by this Congregation and who then prepared and directed the study of the problem within the Consilium. Nonetheless, in view of the opinions expressed by the other consultors and in view especially of the request from the French episcopal conference and of the entire file sent to me, I believe I can put as follows the present thinking of this Congregation:

1. It would seem advisable that candidates for the priesthood should be canonically admitted into the ecclesiastical state not by *tonsure* but by another rite (a blessing) celebrated by the bishop.

2. Minor orders might be reduced to two:

    a) the order of *lector*, with a rite that would bring out the service to be performed for the word of God and catechetical instruction;

    b) the orders of *acolyte* and *subdeacon* but combined into a single "order" or a blessing that explainstheir service to the Eucharist.

3) The commitment to celibacy should be made only by candidates for the priesthood, in a special rite preceding the diaconate.

In practice, then, there would be four rites, but only two would be "minor orders" or blessings constituting real steps toward the priesthood. The first and fourth of the rites described above would rather be personal gestures of "incorporation," unaccompanied by any real, concrete empowerment.

Meanwhile, a call came from Austria. On April 10, Archbishop Opilio Rossi, the Apostolic Nuncio, wrote to the Secretariat of State:

> Bishop Zauner tells me that in his diocese the candidates for tonsure and the minor orders are this year refusing to receive them in the traditional form, claiming that they are "absurd and not fulfillable" (*sinnwidrig und nicht vollziehbar*). They have, he says, even supplied a new form that they want the consecrating bishop to use. . . . The bishop would therefore be very grateful for an authoritative response to the urgent situation that faces him, and happy to see thus resolved a question that the Consilium, of which he was a member, presented to the Holy See two years ago, with its own views and suggestions.

When the Secretariat of State forwarded this case to the Congregation for the Sacraments (March 1, 1970; No. 155349), it also sent a copy of a petition on the same subject from the Swiss episcopal conference. This conference wanted authorization for an experiment in which it would omit the conferral of the orders of porter and exorcist and would change the rites for lectors and acolytes (something not granted to the German episcopate).

As Cardinal Villot wrote,

> all this makes it clear that we cannot continue to give purely procrastinatory responses to the episcopal conferences or individual bishops, asking them to postpone the conferral of minor orders, if need be, while awaiting a reply.

Therefore, while asking the bishops to await the new guidelines and rites now being prepared, we judge it necessary to give them certain authorizations by way of temporary exception, for example, to omit whatever in the rite of tonsure is peculiar to another age or culture (cutting of the hair, excessive emphasis on clerical privileges, and so on), or, in minor orders, to omit the instructions with their mention of offices often no longer existing and to replace these instructions with comments that emphasize the fundamental aspects of the orders.

I therefore ask Your Excellency to see to it, as quickly as possible, that a solution of this kind is composed (with the agreement of the Congregation for Divine Worship for the ritual part) and that a response along this line is sent to the Bishop of Linz, the Swiss conference, and other bishops who may present requests of the same kind. This office will appreciate being informed of the terms of the response.

Another communication from Archbishop Benelli (dated March 7; No. 155349) urged the prefect of the Congregation for the Sacraments immediately to assemble the representatives of the Congregations for the Clergy and for Divine Worship "for the purpose of presenting to the Father, by Monday, March 9, if possible, a fully worked out draft of an answer to the pontifical representative in Austria."

The meeting was held at noon on March 9. The atmosphere was marked by a sense of fear at having to launch a dangerous precedent and to take a position that might poison the climate of the plenary meeting on minor orders, now scheduled for the following month (April 17–18).

For his part, the secretary of the Congregation for Divine Worship pointed out the drawback of having different replacement rites in every country. He stated that his Congregation was ready to provide "within a few hours," that is, on the following day, a text for the conferral of tonsure and the minor orders of lector and acolyte. He stressed the point that this would be a new text and not a revision of the current rite.

The rites were ready the next day. And, in fact, instead of three there were five, including the rites for porter and exorcist, in order not to predetermine future choices. Within twenty-four hours the Congregation for Divine Worship had (temporarily) solved a problem that had been dragging on for years.

The rites were still for the minor orders of old, but they were new in their approach and terminology, the latter indicating the spirit in which they had been composed: "Introduction into the Clerical State," "Blessing of a Candidate for the Priesthood to Whom Care of the Church Building and the Assembly of the Faithful Is Entrusted," "Blessing of a Candidate for the Priesthood Who Will Engage in Works of Charity" (exorcist), "Draft of a Blessing for Conferring the Office of Lector," and

"Draft of a Blessing for Conferring the Office of Acolyte." The last two also had appendixes listing the most suitable readings.

The general schema was the one that would subsequently be adopted in the definitive forms, except for a few changes.[24] The conferral takes place after the liturgy of the Word and comprises the call of the candidates; instruction (a set of questions in the case of the "Rite of Introduction into the Clerical State"); summons to prayer; the blessing; and, if the rite includes this, the presentation of a symbol of the office to which the candidate is deputed (keys of the church, book of readings, paten or chalice or pyx).

The new rites could be allowed to those who requested them "for one occasion and as an experiment," and carried with them an obligation to submit a report. The Congregation for the Sacraments added that the concession was made "not without some concern and to the exclusion of every obstacle in the way of a future discipline of minor orders."

Preparation of the documents

After the plenary meeting of the Congregation for the Sacraments, the definitive phase of the work began. The plenary meeting had decided on:

—the abolition of tonsure and its replacement by a rite of admission to the clerical state;

—the retention throughout the Latin Church of the minor orders of lector and acolyte;

—the linking of the commitment to celibacy with the diaconate;

—the suppression of the subdiaconate;

—the retention of the distinction between minor orders, reserved to candidates for the diaconate and priesthood, and other blessings for the conferral of particular functions.

The Congregation for the Sacraments began to prepare the documents for the reform of the canonical discipline regarding admission to the clerical state and minor orders.[25]

---

24. Three of these rites (acceptance into the clerical state, commissioning as lector, and commissioning as acolyte) repeated the text of a schema prepared by some consultors of the SCDW for France; the others were composed by Father Braga during the night between March 9 and March 10.

25. On July 6, 1970, the Congregation for the Sacraments sent the first draft of the motu proprio to the SCDW. The latter noted that it was uninspired and excessively dry and juridical. For example, for the acceptance of celibacy it proposed a commitment in the presence of two witnesses.

The Congregation for Divine Worship readied the respective rites and on June 25 sent them out to be studied by about thirty consultors; it asked them to respond by July 20.[26] After this consultation the rites were sent to the Pope.

In a personal letter to the Secretary of State, it was pointed out that the consultors had confirmed the Congregation for Divine Worship in its conviction that the term "minor orders" should be abandoned and that each of the two rites should instead be given concrete, realistic names reflecting their true nature, namely, "Rite for the Institution of Lectors" and "Rite for the Institution of Acolytes." This change was made in the schema, but the Congregation for the Sacraments had earnestly asked that the name "minor orders" be restored. The reasons: the juridical schema used the name; the plenary meeting of that Congregation had kept it; and . . . if minor orders became blessings, they would no longer come under the authority of that Congregation. This is what "Monsignor Vetri reported in the name of His Eminence the Cardinal Prefect." It was decided to go along with the Congregation for the Sacraments, but the matter caused annoyance and complaints.

Meanwhile the Pope, too, made his mind known to the Congregation for the Sacraments (September 11, 1970) and the Congregation for Divine Worship. In his letter to the first he said, among other things:

> The two basic concepts, namely, the pedagogical and the canonical, should find suitable expression in both the document and the texts of the rite. The cardinal points of the reform are these: a rite of admission, replacing the ancient tonsure, which will appropriately mark the beginning of the canonical clerical state, and the name "minor orders" for the offices of lector and acolyte, the former connected with the liturgy of the Word, the latter with the liturgy of the altar and the sacrament.[27] The subdiaconate

---

26. The schema included a "Rite of admission among the candidates for diaconate or presbyterate," "Ordination of a lector," "Ordination of an acolyte," and "Changes in the rite of diaconal ordination." In the last it was suggested that a sentence on celibacy be included in the opening instruction and that two questions be asked of the ordinand—one on the acceptance of celibacy, the other on the celebration of the Liturgy of the Hours.

On July 30 the schema was also sent to Cardinal Samorè. His remarks of August 6 emphasized retention of the term "orders," the need of mentioning more clearly the duties attached to these orders, and the distinction between "orders" and any blessings that would replace them in the case of lay recipients. The general remark on the listing of the offices proper to each order pointed to a basic difficulty, since an effort was being made in the new "orders" to include all the functions of the orders that were being suppressed. The same tendency would continue to operate and would be the reason why the final documents would display less clarity.

27. The letter to the SCDW also emphasized the same ideas concerning the retention of the term "minor orders" and the nature of the offices of lector and acolyte. Added was

disappears, and its liturgical functions can be exercised by an acolyte or a deacon, but not by a layman.

As for the diaconate, His Holiness asks whether this might not be more appropriately handled separately, both because of its sacramental efficacy and because of its hierarchic and ritual importance [the plan had been to deal with everything in a single document]. If treated separately, the document would have two chapters: one on the diaconate that leads to the priesthood, the other on the permanent diaconate of married men. The former kind of diaconate is to be preceded not only by a specific course of studies but also by the two minor orders and an act or rite in which the future deacon commits himself to the observance of celibacy and the recitation of the Divine Office.

Specific regulations for the second kind of diaconate will be left to the episcopal conferences; this includes a decision on "whether or not the minor orders will have to be received."

3. *At the Plenary Meeting of the Congregation for Divine Worship*

While the Congregation for the Sacraments, in agreement with the Congregation for Catholic Education, was continuing to prepare the juridical document,[28] which would have to be sent out to the episcopal conferences for their examination, the Congregation for Divine Worship first aired its draft of the new rites at its plenary meeting of November 1970.[29] This meeting formulated some wishes for presentation to the Holy Father:

1. The term "cleric" should be applied only to holy orders: diaconate, presbyterate, and episcopate.

2. Incardination should take place in connection with the first degree of holy orders, namely, the diaconate.

3. The term "ordination" should be used only of holy orders, which are conferred by the laying on of hands. For the other orders the term "institution" is preferable. This change of terminology for "minor orders" is a return to the usage of the early Church: a lector is not ordained, "but is instituted when the bishop gives him the book; for he does not receive the laying on of hands" (Hippolytus, *Traditio Apostolica* 10-13).

---

a request that in the Latin text "*Ordo* admissionis inter clericos" be changed to *Ritus* admissionis" in order to avoid confusion.

28. Meanwhile "external" pressures were not lacking. On July 30, Cardinal Ottaviani wrote in favor of keeping the subdiaconate. On September 8, Cardinal Confalonieri urged the retention, "optionally, according to the prudent judgment of the diocesan bishop," of the minor orders whose suppression was planned; his reason: they were valuable as "a step-by-step preparation for service of the altar."

29. See "Prima Congregatio Plenaria," *Not* 6 (1970) 288; Schema 373: *De Pontificali* 25 (November 9, 1970).

4. The rite of admission among the candidates for the sacrament of orders should be of a spiritual and not a juridical kind. For religious it seems superfluous.

5. The episcopal conferences should be given broader authority to determine the rites that sanctify the assumption of a liturgical or nonliturgical ministry.

6. A joint commission of experts from the Congregations for the Sacraments, Christian Education, and Divine Worship should be formed to clarify the matter more fully.

After the plenary meeting the rites were polished still further and sent to the Congregation for the Sacraments, in order that it might pass them on for examination to the episcopal conferences, together with the draft of the motu proprio. But at this point another small controversy arose. On January 19, 1971, the Congregation for the Sacraments made two observations:

1. At the beginning of the ordination of lectors and acolytes the text says that these may be conferred by the bishop "or by his delegate." The text should read: "they are conferred by the bishop or the major superior of a clerical institute of perfection or by a priest of ecclesiastical rank who is delegated by either."[30]

2. A strong objection was raised against the rite for the ordination of acolytes, which had been approved by the plenary meeting of the Congregation for Divine Worship. The objection was that it "gave the unqualified impression that the acolyte is the ordinary rather than the extraordinary minister of the Eucharist." The Congregation for the Sacraments therefore called for a change in the wording of the instruction or homily: "you are to assist in distributing holy communion to the faithful, including the sick," and in the rubric that has the acolyte helping the celebrant in the distribution of communion, an office that acolytes have had throughout the tradition. The Congregation also asked that in the prayer for the blessing of an acolyte, the words "that they may worthily distribute the holy Eucharist" be removed.

Furthermore, at the express wish of the members of the Consilium, and after lengthy discussion, the rite included the presentation to the acolyte of a vessel containing the bread to be consecrated; the accompanying formula was: "Be a diligent and faithful steward of the Body and Blood of Christ, so that all will find the Lord's table always set." But in the view

---

30. In the final text the conferral of the two ministries would be reserved exclusively to the local Ordinary and the major religious superior; see the motu proprio *Ministeria quaedam* IX (*DOL* 340 no. 2934).

of the Congregation for the Sacraments, this contradicted the motu proprio and had to be removed; the rite should once again have the presentation of other "instruments" as the matter and form of the order, namely, the cruets and candle.

It was pointed out (January 19) that an acolyte is not a simple "altar server." The perspective in which this office has been seen historically is Eucharistic;[31] this is corroborated by the fact that the very draft of the motu proprio provides for the acolyte taking over the functions of the subdeacon. The rites and formulas used for his blessing should bring this out.

In order not to delay the consultation of the episcopal conferences, the requests of the Congregation for the Sacraments were accepted, but these were not yet satisfactory. It was proposed that the presentation of the vessel containing the bread to be consecrated should be accompanied by a different formula; this was then approved. Instead of "pro celebratione Eucharistiae," which seems inaccurate, the words "ad celebrandam Eucharistiam" were proposed. So, too, in the last part of the formula, which speaks of the acolyte's service being rendered to both the sacramental and the mystical body of Christ, it was proposed that the text read: "in order that you may worthily serve the table and the Church, which is the body of Christ." But the specification "which is the body of Christ" also had to be removed on the grounds that it was not juridical; the text was thus impoverished.

Final approval was sought from the Secretariat of State, at which time the viewpoint of the Congregation for Divine Worship was also explained. In practice, however, all the demands of the Congregation for the Sacraments were met (February 5, 1971).

At last the booklet could be printed and sent to the episcopal conferences along with the draft of the motu proprio.[32] Meanwhile the Pope's permission to use the rites experimentally made it possible to learn what practical difficulties they might occasion and to take steps to eliminate them.[33]

---

31. P. Jounel was asked to prepare a similar historical note on ordination as acolyte and on the acolyte's service as minister of the Eucharist; this too was sent to the Secretariat of State.

32. The entire text had been reviewed both by the Congregation for the Sacraments and by the Secretariat of State; the latter also had the Latin text corrected. There was also a note saying that the rites had been prepared in conformity with the juridical documents drawn up by the Congregation for the Discipline of the Sacraments. Otherwise there were no difficulties. Only later on, on March 5 (No. 180135), were some observations sent in.

33. On March 15, 1971, the Congregation for the Sacraments proposed that the concession take the form of two rescripts—one from that Congregation for dispensation from the

III. FINAL STAGE (1972)

On April 29, 1972, the Congregation for the Sacraments sent the text of the juridical documents as revised after consultation with the bishops. These documents now displayed a radical change of perspective: the "minor orders" of lector and acolyte had become "ministries" and were open to laypersons; they had to be received by candidates for the priesthood but were not connected with entrance into the clerical state (this was now associated with the diaconate). To enhance these two ministries, the Congregation for Divine Worship suggested on May 14 that lectors also have the task of instructing and guiding those charged temporarily with reading the word of God in church, and that acolytes do the same for those who serve in liturgical celebrations.

In this new vision acolytes should logically have assumed the function of extraordinary ministers of the Eucharist. There no longer seemed to be any difference between the two, but the suggestion of the Congregation for Divine Worship was rejected, and the inconsistency remained.

On July 22 a new message came with another innovation: the Congregation for Divine Worship was to prepare a rite for the public commitment to celibacy by candidates for the priesthood; this commitment was to be made before diaconal ordination. The message added: "This commitment is to be made in a rite that immediately precedes ordination. It hardly needs saying that in view of its importance, the rite should be a very meaningful one." But it was not clear what was meant by "immediately precedes ordination," nor how religious were to be handled, since they have already made profession of chastity.

Meanwhile, the two motu proprios, *Ministeria quaedam* on first tonsure, minor orders, and the subdiaconate,[34] and *Ad pascendum* on the order of diaconate,[35] were published on August 15, 1972.

The first, after surveying the history of ministries in the Church, sets down a thirteen-point discipline for the Latin Church: tonsure is abolished; entrance into the clergy is connected with the diaconate; minor orders are henceforth to be known as "ministries" and may be conferred

---

two omissible minor orders, the other from the SCDW for use of the new rite. In addition, the Congregation for Religious regarded itself as the competent authority in the case of religious, though not all of these, since some were under the authority of Propaganda. Four agencies involved in such a little matter! Fortunately, things were somewhat simplified by the decision that exemptions for religious should be given through the local Ordinary. This left the two decrees of the two Congregations.

34. *DOL* 340 nos. 2922-38.
35. *DOL* 319 nos. 2576-91.

on laypersons. In the Latin Church these ministries are those of lector and acolyte, and "in accordance with the ancient tradition of the Church" are reserved to men.[36] The document goes on to set down the requirements men must meet for admission to these ministries, the intervals between them, and the obligation of candidates for diaconate and priesthood to receive these ministries. The episcopal conferences can establish other ministries.

The second document, *Ad pascendum*, likewise first surveys the history of the diaconate and its conferral. In ten points it then establishes the juridical norms: in place of tonsure there is to be a rite for admission among the candidates for diaconate and priesthood; unless dispensed by the Holy See, candidates for holy orders must receive and exercise the ministries of lector and acolyte; the rite of admission is performed by the Ordinary of the candidate,[37] but religious are excluded, since they already have a rite of their own for incorporation into religious life; the intervals (not clearly defined) established by the Holy See or the episcopal conferences must be observed; a written declaration must be made by all, including religious, that the diaconate is freely and spontaneously received; the celebration of the Liturgy of the Hours is obligatory for deacons who are going on to priesthood; the parts of the Office to which permanent deacons are bound will be determined by the episcopal conferences; the public profession of celibacy must be made by all in a rite preceding ordination.

The new regulations were to go into effect on January 1, 1973. It was therefore necessary to supply the needed rites with the utmost speed; these were presented at the third plenary meeting of the Congregation for Divine Worship in November, 1972.[38]

In the rite of admission to candidacy for ordination as deacons and priests, the bishop's instruction was enriched by drawing on the conciliar documents *Presbyterorum ordinis* and *Optatam totius*. Furthermore, a general rubric was introduced in response to a request from several episcopal conferences that the rite might include some manifestation or gesture to accompany the verbal assent which the candidates give when asked whether they are resolved to embark on a formation that will enable them to give faithful service to Christ and the Church. The rubric allows the

---

36. See "Precisazione sul Motu Proprio *Ministeria quaedam*," *Not* 9 (1973) 16.

37. The members of the SCDW had wanted this faculty extended to the vicar general or the rector of the church and had approved a request to this effect being made to the Congregation for the Sacraments. But the proposal was not accepted.

38. See "Tertia Congregatio Plenaria," *Not* 9 (1973) 44–46.

candidates to express their resolve in forms determined by the conferences themselves.

The discussion centered, however, mainly on the rite of commitment to celibacy.

Even before the meeting, the schemas had been sent for study to the Congregations for the Doctrine of the Faith and the Sacraments. The latter, referring to the motu proprio *Ad pascendum*, pointed out that the rite of commitment should "precede" diaconal ordination and not be celebrated as the first part of the ordination. It wanted a distinct rite, to be celebrated before the readings, and offered a text of its own that included an instruction of the bishop, a manifestation of the resolve to embrace celibacy (this manifestation includes words and the gesture of stepping forward), and a prayer of blessing—in other words, a little rite within a larger rite.

This proposal seemed unacceptable to the Congregation for Divine Worship because it broke the unity of the celebration and, above all, gave the impression of discriminating between celibate and married deacons. A statement of Cardinal König, speaking in the name of the Austrian conference, urged that everything be removed that hinted at distrust of married deacons, as though they were second-class ministers.

The Congregation for Divine Worship proposed, therefore, that the profession of celibacy be made part of the ordination rite; a reference would be made to it in the bishop's homily, and the candidates concerned would make the profession before their examination by the bishop.

The meeting devoted itself then to two possible ways of expressing the acceptance of celibacy. One was the verbal statement "I am [resolved] *(Volo),*" in response to the bishop's question, which all agreed should be asked. The other form would retain the gesture of stepping forward, as used to be done in ordination to the subdiaconate. Half of the Fathers were for this gesture, half against. There was a desire to hear their views, inasmuch as various consultors and bishops had asked for the retention of this form. But the discussion was undermined by the decision of the Congregation for the Doctrine of the Faith, which asked that in every case the acceptance of celibacy be made "aloud."[39] In the final text, therefore, the first form (question and answer) was kept, but the episcopal conferences were allowed to add "some external sign."

---

39. On November 7, along with other remarks on the schema, the SCDF had this to say: "I inform you in particular of the wish of this Congregation that an explicit verbal acceptance by the candidate of a commitment to celibacy be prescribed by the Holy See for the entire Latin Rite and not only in places where the episcopal conference may wish to prescribe this form of acceptance" (Prot. no. 027/72).

Finally, a question was added to the bishop's examination of the candidates; it asked whether they were resolved on a life of prayer and the faithful celebration of the Liturgy of the Hours.

A tortuous journey[40] thus came to an end at last with the publication of the rites for the two ministries of lector and acolyte, for the admission of candidates to the diaconate and priesthood, and for the acceptance of celibacy. Publication came by a decree of the Congregation for Divine Worship, dated December 3, 1972.[41]

The institution of these ministries was another step that would spur the reflection of the Church and broaden it in the years to come. The Consilium had foreseen and clearly defined the end of the long journey as early as 1965, but the end nonetheless had to be reached step by step. This was not a unique case in the history of the liturgical reform. The passage through many hands and various agencies did not improve the end result, but simply delayed it and prevented the final documents from having the clarity and consistency that only a sure approach to a problem can yield.

Discussion of the ministries would continue in the years ahead, but without much clarity; the obscurity would be due in part to the uncertainties and reticences of the documents I have been examining here.[42] The fruit of so much effort was to give venerable rites a new content and to open up a new perspective: that of a Church that understands itself to be, and is in fact, wholly ministerial.

---

40. On December 12, 1972, the Secretariat of State gave its approval to the printer's proofs and asked that "arrangements be made to have the texts reach the episcopal conferences before the date when they go into effect." On December 20 the little book was sent to the pontifical representatives and the presidents of the episcopal conferences and national liturgical commissions.

41. *De institutione lectorum et acolythorum. De admissione inter candidatos ad diaconatum et presbyteratum. De sacro caelibatu amplectendo* (Vatican Polyglot Press, 1972; 38 pp.). The Rite for the Institution of Readers and Acolytes is in *The Rites of the Catholic Church* 2 (New York, 1980) 3–22. The Rite of Admission to Candidacy for Ordination as Deacons and Priests is in *ibid.*, 39–43. The commitment to celibacy is in *ibid.*, 52–53. See G. P., "Commentarium de nova disciplina et ritibus circa ministeria," *Not* 9 (1973) 18–33.

The suppression of the subdiaconate necessitated some changes in the General Instruction of the Roman Missal. See "Variationes in Institutionem generalem Missalis Romani inducendae," *Not* 9 (1973) 34–38, and *DOL* 206 nos. 1372-73 with the references given there.

42. See Chapter 44, especially pp. 757-62.

44

The Laity and the Liturgy

Vatican II confirmed the conception of the Church as the people of God, in which each member exercises offices and ministries according to the powers he or she has received and the gifts God has given.[1] From this conception has come a deeper understanding of the place that the baptized have in the Church and of their responsibility for its life and growth. At the same time, there is a recognition of some ministries that the baptized can exercise, not only in case of necessity when the ordinary minister is not available but as their inherent right in virtue of their baptism.

The liturgical reform has played an important part in this evolution by implementing the teaching of the Council in concrete ways. I need only mention the emphasis on active participation and the depiction of liturgical celebrations as involving "the whole Body of the Church," in which each person with an office performs all, but only, the parts pertaining to that office by the nature of the rite and the principles of liturgy.[2]

In this chapter, however, I am more directly interested in the specific responsibilities or presidential roles bestowed on qualified laypersons.

1. *Eucharistic Ministries*

As early as 1965 the Holy Office authorized the bishops of East Germany to depute laypersons to carry and distribute the Eucharist in places

---

1. See Vatican II, dogmatic constitution *Lumen gentium* on the Church, especially nos. 33–35; and Decree *Apostolicam actuositatem* on the Apostolate of the Laity, nos. 2–4.
2. See *SC* 26, 28.

where the faithful gather for the celebration of God's word but have no priest. The authorization was given "for a year and by way of experiment."[3]

Next came a broader concession in the instruction *Fidei custos*, and finally, in the instruction *Immensae caritatis*, the authorization to choose extraordinary ministers of the Eucharist. These individuals not only help in distributing communion but also have custody of the Eucharist, can carry it to the sick even as viaticum, and can expose the Blessed Sacrament.[4]

2. Sacraments and Sacramentals

The Constitution on the Liturgy had already decreed (no. 68) that a short rite should be prepared for the administration of baptism by laypersons; this rite was prepared.[5] Meanwhile lay catechists were given the function of presiding at the various meetings of adult catechumens and were allowed to participate directly in the sacramental celebration of baptism.[6]

Laymen can preside at the celebration of funerals,[7] the Liturgy of the Hours,[8] and penitential celebrations.[9] They can give spiritual aid to the sick[10] and be the qualified witnesses of marriages.[11]

3. Sunday Worship

The Instruction *Inter Oecumenici* took up the question of celebrations of God's word on Sundays and feast days when no priest is available

---

3. See R. Kaczynski, "De Liturgia dominicali sacerdotibus deficientibus celebrata," *Not* 8 (1972) 377.

4. See *Holy Communion and Worship of the Eucharist Outside Mass*, nos. 17, 20, 26–78, 91.

5. See *Rite of Baptism for Children*, nos. 20–22, 132–64.

6. See *Rite of Christian Initiation of Adults*, nos. 44, 48, 98–124, 278–94.

7. See *Rite of Funerals*, nos. 5, 19, 22.

8. See GILH 258.

9. See *Rite of Penance*, no. 37.

10. See *Pastoral Care of the Sick: Rites of Anointing and Viaticum*, no. 29. In this context the problem arose of the power of the laity to anoint the sick. Several requests to this effect were received. Some bishops, following the view of some theologians, gave the laity permission to administer the sacrament of the anointing of the sick. Even though the rite published by the SCDW expressly says that priests alone are the ministers of this sacrament, this was not enough to clear the air. The Congregation of the Sacraments was expressly commissioned by the Pope to study this problem, but attention shifted to another subject (see above, p. 689).

11. The rite did not provide for this, but the Congregation for the Sacraments gave permission for it to those who requested it, along with a suitable ceremony that had been prepared by the SCDW.

to celebrate the Eucharist. A layperson may preside at these celebrations and read a homily chosen by the bishop or parish priest.[12] This was a providential encouragement to provide for the very numerous scattered communities that lack a priest and therefore the celebration of the Eucharist, but nonetheless regularly gather on Sundays. Henceforth efforts would increasingly be made, especially in mission countries and in countries of Latin America but of Europe as well, to bring communities together on Sundays around the word of God and to prepare ministers who would direct these celebrations.[13]

In this context the need was felt, especially in some regions, for clarification on the question of authorizing laypersons to preach. There was no real doubt, of course, as to whether they could preach at celebrations of the word. The question concerned rather the homily during Mass. The homily is rightly regarded as an integral part of the liturgy of the Word, but at times there can be no homily because the celebrating priest does not know the language of the people or is elderly or sick or does not feel capable of properly exercising his office.

In 1970 the German-speaking dioceses requested permission to allow laypersons to preach the homily during celebrations of the liturgy of the Word, even when a priest is present, and, in special cases, even during the celebration of the Eucharist. When the request was first submitted, the Congregation for Divine Worship was asked for its opinion on the matter, and it expressed this opinion as follows:[14]

---

12. See the instruction *Inter Oecumenici*, no. 37 (*DOL* 23 no. 329).

13. Many of these undertakings were subsequently collected by the SCDW. It is not possible to mention them all. In addition, the Secretariat of State sent three issues of *Culto Dominical*, which the bishop of the diocese of Rio do Sul, Brazil, had left with the Holy Father at an audience on March 25, 1972; see R. Kaczynski (n. 3). These various undertakings showed good will, but they also went to extremes at times.

One example: in November, 1972, the foundress of a community of religious women in Kerala presented the SCDW with the experiment and prayerbook (*Common Prayer Book of Dinasevana Sabha*) of her community. The sisters, who were often without a priest, recited the entire Mass, including the Canon and words of consecration. This type of thing quickly showed that some guidelines had to be given, as well as better aids for such situations. The sisters then asked that they might do something more for the sick to help them spiritually. There was often no priest to administer the sacrament of the sick, or a priest who might be there was paralyzed by fear of contact with the lepers.

14. Its reply was dated July 20, 1970, and was addressed to the Congregation for the Clergy, to which the Austrian episcopal conference had applied. As a result, an ordinary joint meeting of the Congregations for Bishops and the Clergy and the Council for the Laity met on October 7, 1970. The SCDW was simply informed; the old mentality that saw the homily as having little to do with the liturgy and as belonging rather to the Church's preaching activity was still at work, so that the SCDW was regarded not as competent in this area but as simply "interested." The decision, which was communicated to Cardinal König on

1. "A sharp distinction should be made between the celebration of the word of God and Mass." In the first case the Congregation saw no "substantial reasons why laypersons could not take part in explaining the word of God. But "when a priest or deacon is presiding at the celebration of God's word, it does not seem proper to exclude them completely from a share in the homily; the priest or deacon should at least introduce and end the homily, so as not to diminish his presidential role."

2. With regard to laypersons preaching during the celebration of the Eucharist, caution was advised. The Congregation for Divine Worship was opposed to "the homily regularly being preached by a layperson, with the priest, as it were, completely removed. There can, however, be special cases in which, because of the scarcity of clergy, laypersons can be appointed to exercise this pastoral office in place of priests who are advanced in years or suffer ill health but have no other priest or a deacon to help them. In these situations the bishop can appoint a layperson to give the homily, lest the faithful be deprived of instruction. These must, however, be regarded as exceptions and decided case by case."

3. "As for the liturgical forms to be used should it be decided to grant this authorization, this Congregation thinks that no special guidelines should be laid down and that the matter should be left rather to the episcopal conferences, which will decide on the basis of the sensibilities and needs of each region."

These suggestions were not accepted. But the problem cropped up again three years later when the president of the German episcopal conference submitted a new request.[15] The Congregation for Divine Worship was once again asked for its opinion, which did not differ from the one it had given earlier. Confronted now by need, the Curia showed itself more understanding, but it insisted nonetheless that in these cases

---

February 19, 1971, allowed laypersons to read a homily "assigned by the bishop or the parish priest" only at celebrations of the word when there was no priest or deacon present, or one might be present but was "physically or morally hindered" from giving the homily. Meanwhile, on January 11, 1971, the Pontifical Commission for the Interpretation of the Documents of Vatican II decreed in a reply that the homily cannot be given by anyone except a priest or deacon: *AAS* 63 (1971) 329-30; *DOL* 215 no. 1768.

15. The episcopal conference had approved a regulation covering permissions that might be given for lay preaching. This regulation stated clearly that such permissions were to be "exceptions," but it did not make any distinction between Mass and celebrations of the word; see *Amtsblatt für das Erzbistum München und Freising*, 1971, no. 3, pp. 94–97. This decision was then adopted by the Synod of the Dioceses of the Federal Republic of Germany and included in its document on lay participation in preaching ("Die Beteiligung der Laien an der Verkündigung"), which the Synod appoved at its meeting of January 3–7, 1973. Meanwhile, the Nuncio and the Congregation for the Clergy became aware of the situation. The result was the request submitted to the Holy See on February 22, 1973.

the homily should be given outside the liturgical action proper, that is, before or after Mass.

After noting that the office of preaching belongs to the ordained minister "not only in virtue of his ordination but also in virtue of a special mandate from the Church" (see the 1917 Code of Canon Law, can. 1342, 1), the Congregation for Divine Worship concluded that the prohibition against lay preaching seems to be a disciplinary principle and that it should be looked at in the light of historical circumstances.

On the other hand, if we look at the matter in the light of Church teaching, we must bear in mind the statement of the Council: "Christ . . . continually fulfills his prophetic office . . . also through the laity, whom he has made his witnesses and endowed with understanding of the faith (*sensu fidei*) and the grace of speech."[16] The laity "have, moreover, the capacity of being appointed by the hierarchy to some ecclesiastical offices with a view to a spiritual end,"[17] and "have to supply the sacred services, to the extent that they can, when there are no sacred ministers."[18] It seemed, in light of these statements, that a bishop could give a theologically prepared layperson a "canonical mission" for preaching. The Congregation went on to say:[19]

> The explanation of God's word by laypersons can be done on various occasions. Usually, however, communities gather for Sunday Mass; other celebrations are infrequent and intended for the most part for special groups. When, therefore, well-trained laypersons are available, it should be possible for them to be assigned the office of preaching, even during Mass.
>
> Having laypersons give a sermon before the celebration of Mass does not seem a suitable solution. The distinction would not be understood, and if this solution were adopted, it would disrupt the logical order of the celebrations: the explanation that applies God's word to the concrete situation of the hearers has its proper place after the proclamation of the word itself.
>
> Therefore, in cases in which for good reasons there would be no explanation of the word of God or the explanation given would be defective and therefore harmful to the faithful, it would be preferable that an able, though unordained person should exercise this office ("The salvation of souls is the supreme law"). This is in no way intended to lead to a separation of the ministry of the word from ordination or to lessen priests' sense of responsibility for this ministry that has been given to them. The intention

16. See *Lumen gentium*, no. 35 (*DOL* 4 no. 152).
17. *Ibid.*, no. 33 (Flannery 391).
18. *Ibid.*, no. 35 (*DOL* 4 no. 152).
19. The request for the SCDW's opinion was dated March 9, 1973. It replied on April 2, after consulting some theologians and discussing the matter at length in one of its meetings.

is rather to provide by every available means for the building up of the community, so that "in every way Christ may be proclaimed" (Phil 1:18).

The Congregation for the Clergy acceded to Germany's request on November 20, 1973.[20]

The problem, however, was widespread, and the need was for guidelines valid for all. The Directory for Masses in which children take part contained a promise that such guidelines would be given,[21] but in fact they were never published.

4. *Catechists*

Catechists played a classical role in the first phase of evangelization, when all communities were new and usually lacked a priest. Nowadays they are the right arm of the missionary or pastor. Their role and importance have been on the increase ever since the practice began of giving the laity special functions, such as those already mentioned. In normal circumstances, who are more suitable and available than catechists for distributing communion, presiding at prayer, preaching, celebrating one or other sacrament, burying the dead, and visiting the sick? This is why the motu proprio *Ministeria quaedam* points to them as an example of ministries that may be adopted by the episcopal conferences.

A special study was needed that would more carefully and completely define what a "catechist" is and what the tasks are that may be entrusted to this minister. Several essays were made, and there was even a more thorough study by the Committee on Catechesis and Catechists of the Congregation for the Evangelization of Peoples.[22] But no conclusion was reached.

---

20. The Congregation for the Clergy had also asked the SCDW for its views on the draft of the document in which the concession was granted. The SCDW submitted its observations on October 4, 1973.

21. Number 24 of the Directory for Masses with Children says: "With the consent of the pastor or rector of the church, one of the adults may speak to the children after the gospel, especially if the priest finds it difficult to adapt himself to the mentality of children. In this matter the norms *soon* to be issued by the Congregation for the Clergy should be observed" (*DOL* 276 no. 2157; italics added). [See *DOL* 344 nos. 2953-63. — Tr.]

22. *Catéchistes en Afrique, en Asie et en Océanie. Etude synthétique* (Rome, 1972). The last paragraph of this study says: "It is desirable that consideration be given to the possibility of officially recognizing the present 'canonical mandate' as establishing a ministerial order of catechists and conferring on them the ordinary authority to bless, distribute communion, preside at Sunday worship, and so on." Something along these lines was done by the institution of the Mukambi, or community leader, in Zaire; see the bulletin of the DIA Office, Kinshasa, March 4, 1975.

On October 12, 1972, the Congregation for the Evangelization of Peoples sent the SCDW a "Plan for a Ritual for the Catechists of New Caledonia," and the SCDW suggested some

The reason for the failure seems to be the same as the one that explains why other studies, as well as requests from the episcopal conferences for the establishment of special ministries in addition to lector and acolyte, did not come to very much: the lack of clarity of ministries.

The basic approach that guided the Consilium in its original study of minor orders in 1965 was that a complete overview should be made of the questions involved and the powers needed for the ministries of the laity, while at the same time consideration should be given to the pedagogical requirements of candidates for the priesthood. But as the discussion proceeded, these two things got mixed up, and in the end no clear picture emerged of the relationship in which the laity stand in regard to the ministries the Church can establish. Even the opening up of the offices of lector and acolyte to the laity smacks of the mentality that for centuries had linked these two ministries with the clergy and seminary training. Now they could be bestowed on men not going on to the priesthood, but not on women. And yet in practice women perform the work of catechists, distribute communion, help the sick, direct prayer, and celebrate baptism. Obviously, the whole subject called for further thought.

5. A New Study of Ministries

At the beginning of 1974 the Congregation for Divine Worship submitted two papers to the Secretariat of State: one clarifying the problem of ministries,[23] the other on the need for reflection on the Sunday celebration in places lacking a priest, with a view to providing some guidelines and aids.[24]

In regard to the first problem, the following points seemed in need of rethinking: "the nature of ministries; the rite for their institution; the minister; relations between candidates for the diaconate and for the priesthood, on the one hand, and the ministries, on the other; extraordinary ministers of communion and the ministries."

The following reflections and suggestions were offered on each of the above points:

1. In reflection on the nature of ministries, there should be no departure from the traditional practice which the Church followed for centu-

---

improvements. But the SCDW was also increasingly convinced of the need of drafting a directory containing broad guidelines, which the conferences could then use as a model for directories adapted to their local situations.

23. February 18, 1974.

24. January 22, 1974. Here the SCDW suggested that a study group be formed for a thorough examination of the problem in all its aspects. An affirmative answer came on February 4, 1974.

ries in minor orders, namely, that every new ministry should be directly connected with a specific role in the liturgy.

There is nothing to prevent laypersons instituted for some ministry to be also given offices and functions in the service of the community. It does not seem possible, however, to institute ministries which (as in some requests from Italy and the United States) are concerned solely with caritative work (helping the sick, the very poor, or disoriented families) or even with the teaching of religion. Such workers might, however, be given a special blessing.

2. It seems appropriate to prepare a structured rite for new ministries, based on the rites already published for acolytes and lectors, while leaving the episcopal conferences wide room for adaptation.

3. The regulation giving only Ordinaries authorization to confer ministries seems too narrowly drawn. In particular, the Ordinary ought to be able to delegate the parish priest; one important reason for this is that the rite of conferral should be celebrated in the presence of the community for which the ministry will be exercised.

4. The obligation of candidates for diaconate and priesthood to receive the ministries of lector and acolyte, unless the Holy See dispenses them, should be toned down once other ministries are in existence. It would seem inappropriate to oblige men to receive these two ministries if they have already been instituted in some other ministry and have exercised an office that makes demands beyond those imposed on lectors and acolytes—for example, the office of catechist or community leader. The bishop could be given the authorization to dispense.

5. Ministries exercised by laypersons are by their nature functions inherent in baptismal priesthood and not linked to the sacrament of orders. For this reason women should not be barred from them. Also to be kept in mind is the fact that to a large extent women already exercise such ministries as catechist, leader of song, and the charge of sacred places.

6. The ritual structure and the functions given in the rite of appointment as extraordinary minister of communion (published along with the instruction *Immensae caritatis*) do not differ essentially from those of the acolyte. The two rites have created two categories of individuals "authorized" to distribute communion. The first of the two should therefore be replaced by a ministry in the proper sense.

7. The Congregation suggests a global solution of the question and the creation of three further ministries (in addition to those of lector and acolyte). With the addition of these three, provision would be made for all universal needs. There would be persons:

—*in charge of an ecclesial community (catechist)*. The focus would be on the duty of leading a Christian community when there is no priest or deacon. It would be this person's task to preside at such liturgical actions as can be celebrated in the absence of ordained ministers.

—*in charge of service of the altar and Eucharist (acolyte)*. This minister would be responsible for service at the altar, assistance of the deacon, the distribution, custody, and exposition of the Eucharist.

—*in charge of the service of the word (lector)*. This minister would be responsible for reading the word and preparing the faithful for the sacraments.

—*in charge of singing and sacred music (cantor)*. This person's task would be to lead the liturgical assembly in song (psalmist, organist, choir director).

—*in charge of the sacred place (sacristan)*. This ministry supposes some religious and cultural training and an ability to get along with others. It commits the person to loving care of the church, the careful preparation of celebrations, and a habitual readiness to serve the faithful as collaborator with the priests.[25] The sacristan could also help in the parish office.

6. *Draft of a Directory for Lay Ministries*

The Secretariat of State authorized a study of the problem of Sunday celebrations without a priest, and to this end all the national liturgical commissions were consulted. In this consultation the entire problem of ministries was also raised, and the correspondents were asked to make known any undertakings at the local level, any existing publications, and their opinion on ministries that might be given to laypersons and on celebrations that such laypersons might conduct.[26] The consultation brought to light several different situations and attitudes:

a) In some countries there was a tendency to oppose liturgies at which non-ordained persons presided; this was especially true where Catholics co-existed with other Eastern Rites (Ethiopia, Greece, Turkey) or lived under totalitarian governments (Hungary, Poland).

b) Other countries had not yet experienced the problem, since they had a wealth of clergy (Algeria, Luxembourg, Malta, Vietnam). The same situation might be supposed in countries that did not reply to the questionnaire, such as Italy and the United States.

---

25. See *Notiziario della Conferenza Episcopale Italiana*, no. 8 (October 15, 1973) 168.

26. The letter was sent on April 26, 1974. By the appointed date, May 31, thirty-six commissions had replied. A new request was sent out on October 18 to the liturgical commissions that had failed to respond, and twenty-six more replies came in.

c) Great interest was expressed by areas that felt an urgent need of priests: Latin America, Africa, and Asia.

The majority of the answers mentioned the matter of Sunday celebrations, which was the central theme. A number of correspondents also sent material on this specific point.[27]

Meanwhile, the secretary of the Congregation for Divine Worship asked Father Braga to examine all the documentation that came in and to begin planning a document. What the secretary had in mind was a kind of directory, like that for Masses with children, but also including some sample Sunday celebrations.[28]

The first draft was ready on January 4, 1975, and was sent to twenty-one experts in eighteen countries for their examination.[29] The responses and the suggestions made served in composing a second, better-structured draft, which was then studied on May 16 by some consultors who happened to be in Rome.[30] They reconfirmed its value and suggested only some corrections. The third draft was ready on May 20, 1975, and was sent to thirty-seven other readers, who were asked to reply by September 10, 1975. The intention was to submit the document to a plenary meeting that the Congregation expected to hold in the final months of the year.[31]

---

27. The following sent materials: Brazil, Cameroons, Dominican Republic, East Germany, Guinea, India, Zaire. Others reported that their liturgical books or prayerbooks contained specific guidelines. For example, in the prayerbook for the faithful of Lithuania (published in 1968), there is an instruction on how the faithful can baptize in danger of death and celebrate funerals and how parents can bless their children. The missal in the Guerzé language of the diocese of N'Zérékoré (Guinea) contains a chapter on "Sunday celebrations without a priest" (confirmed on May 31, 1974).

28. R. Kaczynski acted as secretary. This was an unusual group, in the sense that despite attempts to establish it, as allowed by the Secretariat of State, it never got off the ground. The intention was to have Father Paul Brunner, S.J., then in Germany, as relator, but when the request was sent, he had just gone back to the Philippines. Some episcopal conferences on the various continents were asked to please appoint a representative as a member of the group. CELAM approved Alvaro Botero; India, Paul Puthenandady; and the United States, Daniel Coughlin. Tanzania replied but gave no concrete information. As a result of these practical difficulties, the group was never formed.

29. The countries consulted were Brazil, Canada, Chile, Colombia, Dominican Republic, France, Germany, India, Indonesia, Italy, Peru, Philippines, Rwanda, Switzerland, Thailand, United States, Upper Volta, and Zaire.

30. The consultors were C. Braga, R. Kaczynski, B. Fischer, H. Gräf, and P. Jounel.

31. Some replies came in despite the suppression meanwhile of the SCDW. It seems, however, that the material was simply deposited in the archives, and the planned directory became a closed chapter, even though the problem did not. In fact, it was taken up anew by a special committee of the new SCSDW. Despite the fact that this was a single Congregation with two sections and that it had been established precisely in order better

The "Directory for Some Ministries to Be Exercised by Laypersons" contained forty-six numbers: a preface, three chapters, and a conclusion.

The first chapter set forth in summary form the general principles governing lay ministries (nos. 4-17). The second dealt with the laypersons who exercise any ministry in the liturgical community (nos. 18-26); guidelines were given for the choice of ministers, their training and formation, and their formal institution. The third chapter discussed the liturgical actions that laypersons can perform (nos. 27-45). This final chapter had eleven sections, which dealt with Sunday celebrations; celebrations of the word of God; distribution of communion and Eucharistic worship outside Mass; baptism; marriage; penitential celebrations; spiritual care of the sick; the Liturgy of the Hours; sacramentals; devotions.

The picture was complete, and suitable suggestions were given. But events caused the draft to remain only a proposal.

---

to coordinate the work being done in the two areas, the section on the Discipline of the Sacraments claimed competency. Various schemas were prepared and were even discussed at the plenary meeting of the new Congregation (November 22, 1976; see *Not* 12 [1976] 461), but nothing came of them.

45

Religious Profession

In the past the Roman Ritual did not have a rite of religious profession. The Council therefore decreed in its liturgical Constitution that "a rite of religious profession and renewal of vows shall be drawn up with a view to achieving greater unity, simplicity, and dignity. Apart from exceptions in particular law, this rite should be adopted by those who make their profession or renewal of vows within Mass" (no. 80).

There was a great variety of traditions and rites for religious profession—some restrained, others redundant and rich in elements that stir feeling but often rather empty of content and anachronistic. In any case, the Council had given expression to a more mature theology of religious life and had brought out the close connection between this way of life and the mystery of Christ and the Church. These were factors that had to exert a significant influence on the rites of religious life.

I. HISTORY

The work was assigned to study group 20bis,[1] which started by consulting about fifty experts in the problems of religious life (February 1966). The group then held three meetings on May 4, October 1, and December 7, 1966, at the offices of the Consilium. It worked simultaneously on the several rites of religious life: consecration of virgins, profession of religious men, and profession of religious women.

---

1. *Relator:* A. Dirks; *secretary:* I. Calabuig; *members:* B. Fischer, B. Botte, P.-M. Gy, B. Neunheuser, J. E. Enout, and Fathers Elio Gambari and Dorio Maria Hout as representatives of the Congregation for Religious.

The group worked up several general schemas for religious profession[2] and sent them out to 102 superiors general of men and 150 superiors of women and abbesses for their review. The most important experiment was the one conducted under the supervision of Cardinal Ildebrando Antoniutti at the International Religious Congress in Bogotá (August 24, 1968).

At its eleventh general meeting (October 10–11, 1968), the Consilium reviewed the two schemas for the profession of religious men and of religious women (the relators had reviewed them at their own meeting on October 1). It approved the schemas in general and in their details. An explicit vote was taken on two points. The first had to do with the guideline which said that the making of temporary profession during Mass is a "laudable practice" (*laudabiliter*). The guideline was in accord with what the Council had said; according to the Fathers of the Consilium, it also respected divergent traditions. The *laudabiliter* was approved.[3]

The other point had to do with the homily. The schema allowed that in special cases the exhortation to the candidates for profession could be delivered by the superior, even if he or she was a layperson. Despite some strong opposition, the Consilium decided to go along with this permission,[4] but the provision was eliminated from the final, approved text because of opposition from the Congregation for the Doctrine of the Faith and the Congregation of Religious.

After approval by the Consilium, the curial agencies began their review. The first to be consulted was the Congregation for Religious (January 23, 1969), which replied with a long list of observations (March 4, 1969). These were weighed at a joint meeting of participants from the Consilium and the Congregations for Religious and Rites on March 24, 1969. Some of the observations had to do with the general guidelines being followed in the liturgical reform; others reflected the impression of a certain prolixity which, it was feared, would obscure the essential thing, namely, the act of profession. The correction of the texts proceeded in an atmosphere of ready agreement. On July 8, 1969, the Introduction was also sent to the Congregation for Religious. After its reply (July 6) and

---

2. These were schemas 268, 274, 292, 300 and 310, 342, and 343.

3. 22 in favor, 6 against, 1 blank ballot. Despite the one-sided vote, the final text of no. 5 of the Introduction took the various possible situations into account. For this reason the *laudabiliter* was dropped and the text says that temporary vows "*may* be taken within Mass." Thus if any religious family prefers to take them during some other liturgical action or during the conventual chapter, it is free to do so.

4. The question read: "May a lay superior be allowed in certain circumstances to give the address at a religious profession?" The vote was 21 in favor, 7 against, 1 in favor with qualifications.

the explanatory response of the Congregation for Divine Worship (September 12; 9 pages of foolscap), the Congregation for Religious gave its approval on October 8.

Meanwhile the schemas had also been sent to the Holy Father (March 29, 1969). In the reply received from the Secretariat of State on June 4, 1969, the only request made was to specify that if there was to be a blessing of the religious habit, it should be done by the priest.

On November 28 the printer's proofs were also sent to the Holy Father. The reply (December 9; No. 151.237) included a copy of a letter sent to the Holy Father by the president of the International Union of Superiors General. In it he spoke of the disappointment felt by some superiors on learning that the rite in preparation did not allow the "promise" (which would replace temporary profession) to be likewise made during Mass. He went on to say: "This arrangement would elicit strong reactions and thus detract from the prestige that a document from an agency of the Holy See should have." The reference was to the instruction *Renovationis causam* of the Congregation for Religious, which allowed (no. 34) for replacing temporary vows with a promise or other form of commitment. The Pope asked that for these cases the new rite of religious profession should include "a short ceremony, to be celebrated even during Mass."

On October 16, 1969, the Congregation for Religious also requested such a ceremony, but added that "the rite should take place outside Mass." The Consilium took the same view of the matter. The reason: these commitments are indeed ordered toward perpetual profession, but they are not themselves a true and proper religious profession which, because of the oblation signified, is associated in a special way with the Eucharistic sacrifice.[5]

In deference, however, to the wish expressed by the Holy Father, a rite of promise that could be celebrated even during Mass was prepared; various ways of carrying it out were indicated. This rite received the approval of the Congregation for Religious (January 5, 1970) and the Congregation for the Doctrine of the Faith (January 13, 1970), which had previously (November 17, 1969) given its *nihil obstat* (along with some observations on details) to the schemas as a whole (Prot. no. 2556/69).

When the rites had thus made their way through the Curia, they were published on February 2, 1970, the feast of the Presentation of the Lord, by decree of the Sacred Congregation for Divine Worship.[6]

---

5. See *Lumen gentium*, no. 45; *SC* 80.
6. Rituale Romanum ex decreto Sacrosancti Oecumenici Concilii Vaticani II instauratum auctoritate Pauli PP. VI promulgatum, *Ordo professionis religiosae* (Vatican Polyglot Press,

II. Contents

The volume opens with an Introduction that explains the nature and meaning of religious life, the stages by which religious consecrate themselves to the service of God and the Church, the adaptations that individual institutes can make, and the rubrical norms for the use of the rites and of the Mass on the day of profession.

Next comes the description of the rites and the texts for profession, first for religious men, then for religious women. Each takes account of the principal stages on the journey of consecration to God in religious life: introduction to religious life; temporary profession, perpetual profession, and renewal of vows. The Scripture readings and alternative texts are then given.

1. *Introduction to Religious Life*

The reference is to the rite that marks the beginning of the novitiate. This used to be the clothing, which, especially in families of religious women, was a very solemn occasion. Nowadays the habit is regarded as the external sign of interior consecration and is therefore given on the day of profession. A further consideration is that the giving of the habit at the beginning of a period of testing might jeopardize the necessary freedom of the novice. Entrance into the novitiate is therefore now marked by a matter-of-fact ceremony in which only the religious community takes part; in form it is a celebration of the word of God.

2. *Temporary Profession*

This is the act of self-donation to God that is made at the end of the novitiate. But it is still provisory and part of the period of testing. The Introduction therefore prescribes that these vows may be taken within Mass (or during some other liturgical action), "but without special solemnity" (no. 5). The rite itself is quite simple; the reason is that the sign of total consecration to God is had only in perpetual profession.[7]

1970; 126 pp.). In English: *Rite of Religious Profession* (Washington, D.C.: International Committee on English in the Liturgy, Inc., 1974). There is a new translation of the Introduction in *DOL* 392 nos. 3230-48. See the commentary of I. Calabuig in *Not* 6 (1970) 113-26. See also "Utrum professio religiosorum ab episcopo vel a sacerdote, qui celebrationi eucharisticae praesidet, recipi possit," *Not* 11 (1976) 62-64 (translated in *DOL* 392, R1); "Missa in XXV et L anniversario professionis religiose," *Not* 11 (1976) 317.

7. Even the Fathers of the Consilium had difficulty in the beginning with this distinction between temporary and perpetual profession. In particular, some of the members who belonged to religious families insisted on the spiritual principle that the religious must al-

In accordance with ancient custom, after their profession religious are presented with objects that symbolize the nature and spirit of the religious family to which they belong. The rite mentions only the rule and the habit (the veil for religious women). When the rites are adapted, other signs may be used, but restraint should be exercised.

3. *Perpetual Profession*

Full solemnity is reserved for perpetual profession because of the seriousness and inherent solemnity of the act itself. The rite is celebrated during Mass and is incorporated into it in a harmonious way, so that the entire celebration forms a single whole. Like all other rites of blessing or consecration, it takes place after the liturgy of the Word. In the past there were a variety of practices in particular rituals: profession might be made between the readings (before the gospel), after the gospel, at the offertory, or before communion in the presence of the Most Blessed Sacrament. The last-named was the practice most widespread in religious families from the sixteenth century on.

Those who adopt the new rite must respect the position assigned to it within Mass. But, in view of the phrase "apart from exceptions in particular law" in the liturgical Constitution (no. 80), the retention of other particular traditions is not banned, especially for monks.

When the rite was being planned, there was a great deal of reserve with regard to the practice of making profession just before communion in the presence of the Most Blessed Sacrament. The planners would have liked to abolish the practice because it is not consonant with a true understanding of the liturgy. But here again, respect for the liturgical Constitution caused them simply to ban it for new religious families. Those that already follow the practice in virtue of their particular law are urged to abandon it of their own accord (Introduction, no. 15).

The following parts make up the rite of perpetual profession:

a) Calling of the candidates; this may be replaced by the candidates' request to make perpetual profession in the religious family that they have entered to become part of.

b) Homily, based on the readings and explaining the meaning of religious life and the part it plays in the sanctification of the individual and the welfare of the Church and other human beings.

---

ready have the intention of consecrating himself or herself completely to God. The point, however, was that the liturgical sign differs in the two types of profession. This principle is repeated when the Introduction speaks of adaptations (see no. 14c).

c) Examination in the form of four questions addressed to the candidates regarding their resolve. The first brings out the connection between religious profession and baptism; the second, between religious profession and the closer following of Christ; the third, between religious profession and the principal factor in religious life, namely, perfect love; the fourth is concerned with the apostolic aspect of religious life.[8]

d) Litany of the Saints, with special intentions related to religious life and the need for vocations; for these the help of God, the Blessed Virgin, and the saints is asked.

e) Act of profession. Here the rite reaches its climax: in the presence of the assembly the candidates each read the formula, written if they wish in their own hand, sign it, and place it on the altar to show that their self-oblation as religious is united to the offering of Christ in the Eucharistic sacrifice.[9]

f) Prayer of blessing of the newly professed. In order to allow for varying sensibilities, the rite offers four texts for this blessing—two for religious men and two for religious women. The structure is the same in all, and it is the classical structure of prayers of consecration in the Roman liturgy. The prayer, which is addressed to the Father, briefly recalls the history of salvation in the Old Testament and then the Son's saving work that is now continued in the Church; finally, it asks the Father to pour out the Holy Spirit on the newly professed, the Church, and all humankind.

g) At the end, the now complete incorporation of the professed into their religious family finds expression in words and in the greeting of peace. There may also be a presentation to the newly professed of particular insignia proper to the religious family. The rite makes no suggestions

---

8. An effort is made in the rite to strike a balance between the contemplative and the apostolic aspects of religious life. Both are always present in every form of consecrated life, even if the one or the other predominates according to the nature of the particular religious family. While the rite was being composed, contrary fears were expressed: of overemphasizing the contemplative aspect (superiors general) or the apostolic aspect (Congregation of Religious).

9. The Congregation for Religious had to step in and clarify this point because some people got the impression that individual religious could compose their own formula of profession. On the contrary, the formula must be approved for each institute by the Congregation for Religious and must be substantially identical throughout the institute, since the duties and rights flowing from profession are identical. This does not mean that the candidates for profession may not, with the agreement of the superior, add personal expressions of their resolve at the beginning and end of the formula, provided these expressions are restrained, clear, and consistent with the solemnity of the step they are preparing to take. This is the meaning of a reply issued by the Congregation of Religious on February 14, 1973, and published in Not 9 (1973) 283 (= DOL 393 nos. 3249-51).

here for religious men; in the case of religious women, it suggests the possibility of presenting them with a ring, which expresses the permanent spousal commitment to Christ.

4. *Renewal of Vows*

The rite also gives guidelines and texts for the renewal of vows when this has a juridical value and is prescribed by the constitutions. The rite is restrained, dignified, and celebrated within Mass.

It is not possible, however, simply to ignore the fact that in some religious families there is also a "devotional" renewal of vows. This may be given some prominence when done communally on certain occasions, such as the titular feast of the institute, or on special occasions, such as the twenty-fifth or fiftieth anniversary of vows.[10] The Introduction reminds religious, however, that the practice of doing at Mass what belongs to private devotion is not to be encouraged. Some other liturgical action is to be preferred for these devotional renewals, except in the special cases mentioned.

5. *Texts*

The fifth chapter of the rite provides a series of Scripture readings for the rites of religious life, as well as other texts for the rite of the presentation of insignia, for the general intercessions, and for the prayer of blessing of religious men and women.

6. *Rite of a Religious Promise*

This is the rite for those who take advantage of the faculty granted by *Renovationis causam* (January 6, 1969). Three forms are offered:

a) In the first, the promise (or other form of temporary commitment) is emitted during the celebration of the word of God; great freedom is allowed in arranging the parts of the rite and in the choice of texts.

b) In the second, the promise is made during some part of the Divine Office (especially Lauds or Vespers), between the psalmody and the gospel canticle. This form lays special emphasis on the connection between the Liturgy of the Hours and the promise of a life consecrated to the praise of God. This would seem to be the preferable form.

c) In the third form the promise is made during Mass. From the liturgical viewpoint, this does not seem to be the most appropriate form, if for no other reason than that it can lead to a confusion of promise and

---

10. The second edition of the *Missale Romanum* has a Mass suitable for the twenty-fifth or fiftieth anniversary of religious profession; see *Not* 11 (1975) 317.

religious profession. If this form is used, there is a strong emphasis on the plea for divine help (which comes abundantly from the mystery of the altar), in order that the candidate's resolve may intensify and mature until it becomes a true and proper consecration through religious vows.

7. Appendix

The Appendix provides some models for composing the formula of profession, and four formularies of ritual Masses: one for the Mass of first profession, two for the Mass of perpetual profession, and one for Mass on the day of the renewal of vows.

The Mass of perpetual profession also has special texts for the *Hanc igitur* of the Roman Canon and for the intercessions to be included in Eucharistic Prayers II, III, and IV.

8. Adaptations

The rite offers wide room for adaptations. In fact, while keeping its essential structural line and its texts, this rite should have details that reflect the spirituality, manner of life, and tradition of the various religious families. The privileged places for giving expression to these are the Scripture readings, the homily, the request that the religious may make his or her profession, the examination, the Litany of the Saints, the formula of profession, the presentations, the songs accompanying the various actions, and the alternative texts of prayers.

The Congregation for Divine Worship realized, however, that especially in the period when the new rite was first coming into use, there was danger of distorting its character or impoverishing and reducing its content. The Congregation therefore took the step of sending out guidelines for the translation (to be made by the episcopal conferences and their liturgical commissions) and for the adaptations that each religious family was to undertake. In practice, the religious families were very respectful of the rite and its contents; they found that it fully met their expectations, and they limited themselves to introducing various details by adding some sentences, mentioning the saints special to the institute, and listing the presentations to be made.[11]

---

11. On July 15, 1970, the SCDW sent a letter to the presidents of the national liturgical commissions on the translation of the rite of religious profession; this translation, like that of any other liturgical book, was to be made, not by the individual religious families, but by the committees appointed by the episcopal conferences, which must then approve the text; see *Not* 6 (1970) 317-18. That same day the SCDW sent a letter to the superiors general of the religious institutes on adaptations. This letter was accompanied by more detailed guidelines on the same subject; see *Not* 6 (1970) 318-19 and 319-22.

46

Funerals

The reform of the rite of funerals was in the hands of study group 23,[1] which took as its point of departure no. 81 of the liturgical Constitution: "The rite of funerals should express more clearly the paschal character of Christian death and should correspond more closely to the circumstances and traditions of various regions." Number 82 then prescribes a revision of the rite for the burial of infants and the provision of a special Mass for the occasion.

The group also had to take into account the changed conditions of society and the variety of usages and traditions, and to produce a flexible rite that can be adapted to different situations.

I. History

Because of its importance and urgency, this reform was given priority. A schema was ready in 1965 and could be presented to the Consilium at its fifth general meeting (October 25).[2] This first schema already displayed the structure that would be seen in the definitive rite; it lacked only the part for the funerals of children. The Fathers of the Consilium approved it for experimentation. On January 20, 1966, it was submitted to the Holy Father, along with the guidelines for experimentation. Both

---

1. See above, p. 579, n. 1.
2. See P.-M. Gy, O.P., "Ordo exsequiarum pro adultis," *Not* 2 (1966) 353–63.

were approved on January 25 (No. 62793), and experiments could now be undertaken.[3]

On the basis of the reports that came in toward the end of 1967 and the beginning of 1968, the group was able to complete its work by introducing any needed changes and revisions. Experience had now shown that some parts of the rite were fully effective, while others needed polishing. The evaluations sent in were by and large positive, and the experimenters felt that the new rite helped to a deeper understanding of the paschal character of Christian death, though some difficulties had been encountered in the understanding of individual parts and in the use of certain psalms.

The work in its entirety was submitted once again at the eleventh general meeting of the Consilium (October 16–17, 1968).[4] The new schema was not only better organized; it also contained the hitherto missing parts, and specifically the rite for the funeral of children, including children who had died unbaptized but whose parents were intending to have them baptized. There were also guidelines for the funerals of those who had chosen to be cremated.

The question of these last two categories of persons was sent to the Congregation for the Doctrine of the Faith for its study on February 6, 1969.[5] The Congregation approved the texts submitted to it (March 11, 1969) and asked only that the 1963 instruction of the Holy Office on cremation be cited and that the final paragraph of no. 15 of the Introduction be changed so as to "bring out better the permissive rather than prescriptive character" of the celebration at the crematorium.[6] The Holy Father

---

3. See "De experimentis Ordinis exsequiarum," *Not* 3 (1967) 155–64, 269.

4. See "La XI sessione plenaria del Consilium," *Not* 4 (1968) 353–54.

5. The Congregation had already repeatedly concerned itself with the problem of the funerals of children who had died unbaptized but whose parents had been intending to have them baptized.

6. The decision of the SCDF said:

"1. With regard to funerals for those to be cremated: The norm proposed is approved, but with two corrections: the text should refer to nos. 2 and 3 of the 1963 Instruction from which the norm has been taken, and the final paragraph of this number [15] is to be changed to read: 'The rites usually held in the cemetery chapel or at the grave may in this case take place within the confines of the crematorium and, for want of any other suitable place, even in the crematorium room. Every precaution is to be taken against the danger of scandal or religious indifferentism' [*DOL* 416 no. 3387].

"2. With regard to the funerals of children who die unbaptized: The norm and prayers proposed are approved."

Definitive approval was given to the printer's proofs on September 9, 1968, with some minor observations. Among the latter, one concerned the reference to non-scriptural readings possibly being used at the wake. This practice was criticized as unsuitable "for promoting

gave his approval to the new rite and its publication (January 31, 1969, and September 19, 1968).

The volume containing the rites for funerals was published by a decree of the Congregation of Rites dated August 15, 1969.[7]

II. CONTENTS

After an Introduction and a first chapter that deals with the vigil for the deceased (the "wake"), the new *Ordo exsequiarum* gives three plans for the funerals of adults, a rite for the funerals of children, and a series of optional texts.

1. *Introduction*

In addition to describing the various kinds of funerals and the possibilities of adapting the rites to local usages and customs, the Introduction emphasizes the point that a Christian funeral is a celebration of the paschal mystery of Christ as accomplished in his faithful followers. The need to bring this out was one of the main concerns guiding the reformers.

To this end they drew from the treasury of the euchological tradition texts that would best express this aspect of funerals. At the same time, they got rid of texts that smacked of a negative spirituality inherited from the Middle Ages. Thus they removed such familiar and even beloved texts as the *Libera me, Domine*, the *Dies irae*, and others that overemphasized judgment, fear, and despair. These they replaced with texts urging Christian hope and giving more effective expression to faith in the resurrection.

These changes explain the closer and more organic connection between the funeral and the Eucharistic celebration in the new rite, the restoration of the Alleluia, and the abandonment of the color black for another which, in the judgment of the episcopal conferences, will inspire a calmer

---

the eminently sacred character of the wake and because it may stimulate individuals to eccentric experiments in the choice of secular texts."

7. *Ordo Exsequiarum* (Vatican Polyglot Press, 1969; 92 pp.). The rite is in *The Rites of the Catholic Church* 1 (New York, 1983²), 743–818; new translation of the Introduction in DOL 416 nos. 3373-97. See the commentary of S. Mazzarello in *Not* 5 (1969) 431–35. See also L. Brandolini, "Il nuovo *Ordo exsequiarum*," *EL* 84 (1970) 129–48; A. Pistoia, "Elementi dottrinali per i bambini," *ibid.*, 160–68. *Notitiae* gives further details regarding the celebration of funerals during the octaves of Christmas and Easter: 6 (1970) 263; Masses for the dead: 4 (1968) 145; funerals during the Easter Triduum: 11 (1975) 288; the commemoration of the deceased in special circumstances, as at the cemetery on All Souls' Day: 7 (1971) 318-19. See also the presentation of the French edition of the funeral ritual in *Not* 8 (1972) 333–34, and the list of Scripture readings: 4 (1968) 64–67.

approach to sorrow and suggest a hope that is illumined by the paschal mystery. The same perspective is to be seen at work in the directive that the Easter candle be placed near the coffin.[8] Finally, in accordance with the general principles governing the reform, the rite urges the participation not only of the family, friends, and relatives of the deceased but of the entire community. The community thus shares the lot of each brother or sister and gives witness, as a community, to its faith in the resurrection.

All these changes, operating within a new and better-adapted ritual structure, have contributed to give a new look to the celebration of funerals.

2. *Prayer Vigil at the Home of the Deceased*

The old Ritual said nothing about a wake or prayer vigil, at least not as a liturgical action, even though the vigil had been customary for some time in one form or another, at least in some places.

The prayer vigil was part of the ancient liturgy of funerals; some of the Fathers, Western as well as Eastern, attest to it as early as the fourth century. The elements that gave structure to this vigil were readings, songs, and prayers (preference being given, of course, to the psalms).

The new rite recognizes the pastoral value of the prayer vigil and makes it part of present-day funerals. The rite provides a basic, if flexible, structure for the vigil. It opens with an introductory explanation and the recitation of an appropriate psalm, a prayer for the deceased, and, if desired, another for the consolation of the sorrowing relatives. After this there

---

8. In an outstandingly courageous move, the guidelines and simplifications proposed in the *Ordo exsequiarum* were applied even to the funerals of cardinals. A renowned member of the Consilium broke the ice: "I thought it a kind arrangement of divine Providence that on the occasion of Cardinal Bea's funeral, the Vatican Basilica put aside the ostentatious and artificial trappings of mourning that used to mark the funerals of cardinals, and restored truth, simplicity, and liturgical beauty to the celebration, in keeping with the authentic Christian sense of death. The bier, set humbly on the ground with the Easter candle—so tall and solemn, so joyous and lightsome—beside it, was an eloquent reminder of essentials, an invitation, a sign of deep faith in Christ as sole light and resurrection and life. No longer did a hundred candles burn around the gorgeous catafalque; but in their place how many souls sunk in reverent prayer surrounded the one flame, themselves so many torches afire with gratitude and hope, so many hearts burning with affectionate love!": *Not* 4 (1968) 361-62 and, on p. 333, a photograph of that first funeral, which made such a deep impression, especially on the prelates present. Some of them felt the earth giving way beneath them. What a fine invitation to thoughts of death! See also *Not* 7 (1971) 3, on the funeral of Cardinal Gut. On those occasions booklets with the funeral liturgy were distributed. Even this elicited objections and appeals: see "De oratione 'Deus, apud quem omnia morientia vivunt,'" *Not* 8 (1972) 15-17.

are one or more readings from Scripture, a homily, and general intercessions. The Our Father or other suitable prayer serves as a conclusion.

3. *Three Forms for the Celebration of the Funeral*

In view of the wide variety of situations in various regions and of usages already to be found in particular rituals, the new rite provides three ways of celebrating the funeral proper. The three are differentiated by the place in which the funeral rite principally takes place: the home of the deceased, the church, or the cemetery.

a) The *first form* has three stations: the home of the deceased, the church, and the cemetery, with processions from each to the next. This first form is basically that of the ancient Roman Rite, the main lines of which were adopted in the Ritual of 1614. With the needed modifications it can still be used in rural Christian communities and communities in small towns. Moreover, since the parts that make it up (especially the two processions) are not strictly obligatory, at least not in their traditional form, this first form can also be used in other environments. This is all the more true since a deacon and, under certain conditions, a layperson can preside at the stations in the home of the deceased and in the cemetery.

This first form usually includes the celebration of Mass. Should pastoral reasons make this impossible, there is nonetheless an obligatory station in the church, where a liturgy of the word of God is celebrated and there is a final commendation and farewell to the deceased.

b) The *second form* has only two stations: in the cemetery chapel and at the grave or tomb. In this case, the body is brought directly to the cemetery, where the liturgical celebration takes place.

This celebration has two parts. First, after the celebrant's greeting, there is a celebration of the word, ending with the final commendation and farewell. Next there is the procession to the grave or tomb, during which appropriate psalms are sung, and the interment proper (which includes a short prayer of the celebrant's choice), the prayer of the faithful, and finally, if customary, a suitable song.

In this second form of funeral there is no place for Mass. This may be celebrated before or after the funeral, even (with the permission of the Ordinary) in the home of the deceased.

c) In the *third form* the liturgical action takes place entirely in the home of the deceased. In certain circumstances and in some places this form may have its advantages. The new rite has not thought fit to specify its elements in any rigid way but has limited itself to giving general guidelines and suggesting that in organizing the rite, use be made of what is provided in the first two forms; this holds especially for the liturgy of the Word and the final commendation and farewell.

In special circumstances the Ordinary of the place can, even in these cases, allow Mass to be celebrated in the home of the deceased.

The three forms of celebration are marked by flexibility, so that in one and the same region any of the three forms can be used either in its entirety or by choosing the most suitable parts, depending on circumstances.

4. The Final Commendation

In all three forms there is a rite of final commendation. This may take place at the end of the Eucharistic celebration in the church or at the end of the entire liturgical action, that is, at the graveside. It replaces the old "absolution." It is not a rite of purification but a true and proper "farewell" or *valedictio* in which the Christian community confides one of its members to the heavenly Church at the moment of interment.

This is a ritual action that originated in paganism but has deep human roots and can therefore be pastorally important. It was for this reason that the Roman liturgy took it over while also transforming it and enriching its meaning. It has a Byzantine counterpart in the farewell kiss given to the deceased, of which Simeon of Thessalonica speaks in a well-known passage (cited in the Introduction, no. 10).

In the new rite of the commendation there is an opening exhortation that explains its meaning. This is followed by some moments of silence, during which the celebrant may sprinkle and incense the body, as the responsory *Subvenite* ("Saints of God, come to his [her] aid") is sung. The antiphon *In paradisum* ("May the angels lead you into paradise . . .") is sung as a conclusion.

These various elements are not rigidly determined. The episcopal conferences may make substitutions, especially for the songs, provided only that the new songs express a real, authentic "farewell" and that the assembly can join in the singing.

In this context two other guidelines must be kept in mind. The first allows that, after a brief silence (the silence that follows the celebrant's exhortation), a relative of the deceased may say some words of farewell. The second limits the rite of farewell to celebrations in which the body is actually present; the very nature of the rite requires this.

5. Funerals of Children

These are celebrated according to one of the forms already described (if the form is used in the region) but with texts appropriate to the situation. The color of the vestments is to be festive and paschal. Mass may now be celebrated for the children, and readings and prayers that are suited to the condition of the children and the sorrow of the parents are suggested.

The Ordinary of the place can allow a funeral service even for children who died unbaptized but whom their parents were intending to have baptized. The funeral is preferably to be held in the home of the deceased child, but it may also be celebrated according to the rite customarily followed in the region.

6. Collection of Texts

The collection of texts from which a selection may be made occupies no small part of the volume. This extensive repertory of Scripture passages, euchological texts, and psalms provides the Christian community with ample material for reflection and for a wide range of pastoral uses.

In this collection the psalms have a prominent place. The Introduction to the rite reminds us that in its funeral celebrations the Church has always fallen back on the psalms to express its sorrow and nourish its hope.[9] The collection includes some psalms that are propitiatory in tone, but it also includes many that express hope or bring out the paschal character of death. Those who experimented with the new rite felt the abundant use of the psalms to be something of a hindrance; among other things, they pointed out the difficulty people have in understanding the psalms. The *Ordo* took this into account by allowing freedom in the use of the psalms and the substitution of songs inspired by them. Meanwhile, however, the people must be gradually made better acquainted with this privileged source so extensively attested in the patristic and liturgical traditions.

A prudent criterion is also at work in the choice of prayers, namely, that our thoughts must be focused not exclusively on the "souls" of the deceased but on the deceased as total human beings, and therefore on the body that is called to share in the resurrection of Christ and on the living relatives and friends who are left behind in sorrow.

The result is a rich repertory that allows freedom to adapt to circumstances and customs and makes it possible in every case to turn death into a true celebration of the paschal mystery of Christ, a celebration bathed in hope, solicitous for the sorrow of the survivors, and concerned to act as an effective form of instruction.

---

9. The original text of no. 12 of the Introduction was even stronger: "The Church has no more powerful . . . or effective" tool than the psalms. The language was toned down at the suggestion of the SCDF.

Blessings of the Ritual and the Pontifical

I. Blessings of the Ritual

1. *First Phase*

Study group 23 was also in charge of revising the part of the Roman Ritual that contains the blessings. A first report on the subject was presented to the Fathers of the Consilium at their twelfth general meeting, April 9–10, 1970.[1] It raised a complex set of problems and endeavored to take into account both the spirit of the Ritual and the variety of situations. On the one hand, the modern mind likes to stress the abilities of human beings and urge them to devote themselves to combating evil and producing things that make human life ever easier. On the other hand, blessings are a powerful means of educating Christians against the danger of attributing a mistaken autonomy to human beings and creation over against the Creator. The need, therefore, was to recover the authentic meaning of blessings. To this end the group determined the doctrinal and practical norms that were to guide it in its work. These may be summarized as follows:

1. According to Sacred Scripture and the tradition of the Church, a prayer of blessing includes acknowledgment and thanksgiving for benefits received from God and a petition for the needs of human beings. The finest example of this style is to be seen in the texts now used in the Roman Missal for the presentation of the gifts at Mass: these texts proclaim the

---

1. See "XIII sessio plenaria Commissionis specialis ad instaurationem liturgicam absolvendam," *Not* 6 (1970) 288; P.-M. Gy, "De benedictionibus," *ibid.*, 245–46.

goodness of creatures and the providence of the Creator; they acknowledge that the gifts come from his hand and ask that they may serve the spiritual good of human beings.[2]

2. God's blessing is invoked first and foremost on human beings. Only secondarily is he asked to bless the things that aid human beings in attaining their end.

3. The Church has always been on guard to prevent the superstitious use of blessings. The same vigilance is needed today.

4. The Constitution on the Liturgy asks that provision be made for having laypersons administer some blessings (no. 79).

5. Blessings can be differentiated as:

a) *constitutive* (of things or persons): these are the blessings that make a person or thing sacred by destining a thing for use in worship or consecrating a person to a special state. These blessings should be reserved to ordained ministers;

b) *invocative*, which can be performed by laypersons in the absense of a priest or deacon;[3]

c) blessings more properly to be left to the laity: these are the blessings having to do with family life (for example, the blessing of children by their parents and blessings at table).

6. With regard to the blessings to be included in the new Ritual, the relator pointed out that initially (in addition to the blessing of holy water) the Ritual of Paul V contained only seventeen common blessings and eleven "reserved" blessings that were more directly concerned with worship. The Ritual left a great deal of freedom in this area to particular rituals. From the latter, whether diocesan or religious, many blessings subsequently made their way into an appendix of the Roman Ritual, where they formed a collection of widely varying value and dubious usefulness.

After the meeting of the Consilium a smaller group[4] continued the work of preparing the Introduction and a selection of blessings. The results

---

2. The Constitution on the Liturgy says that blessings (sacramentals) are "sacred signs bearing a kind of resemblance to the sacraments; they signify effects, particularly of a spiritual kind, that are obtained through the Church's intercession" (no. 60).

3. Later on, on December 3, 1974, the Pontifical Commission for the Interpretation of the Decrees of Vatican Council II issued a reply regarding the blessings that a deacon can give. It explained that a deacon is authorized to give only those blessings explicitly allowed him by the liturgical books; see *DOL* 320 no. 2592.

4. This group consisted of P.-M. Gy, B. Fischer, E. Lengeling, S. Mazzarello, and H. Wegman.

of this group's work were submitted for examination at the second plenary session of the Congregation for Divine Worship (March 8, 1972).[5]

The Introduction dealt briefly with the nature of blessings, the minister, the celebration, and the adaptations to be made by the episcopal conferences. Seventeen blessings were then offered as models to serve the episcopal conferences in preparing their own rituals.[6] The structure of the celebration allowed for various possibilities, depending on the participants (a group or a single individual) and on the character of the blessing itself. By way of a general pattern, the text of one blessing was provided; it was preceded by a list of some more appropriate passages from Scripture that could be used *ad libitum*. Also emphasized was the importance of gestures, such as the laying on of hands, the sign of the cross, and the sprinkling with holy water (the appropriate gesture being chosen to fit the case).

2. *Second Phase*

The Fathers gave approval to the work done. But a closer reading showed that the material was too skimpy to merit publication when judged by the schema presented at the plenary session of the Congregation. The Introduction needed filling out, and the model blessings had to be enlarged. This need seems to have been felt especially by some regions that were pressing for the new ritual of blessings. Some countries, such as Brazil and Mexico, went ahead and prepared their own rituals of blessings. Other benedictionals were composed by private individuals. With the help of their experts, the German-speaking countries did some fine work on the blessings.

All this showed a felt need and at the same time a change of mentality. In years past, the influence of trends toward secularization and dechristianization had urged a (perhaps) excessive caution; now the impulse was to be bolder in this area.[7]

At the end of 1974, therefore, a new study group was appointed which adopted the norms already approved and continued the work while broadening it and filling it out. Beginning in January 1975, the new group

---

5. See "Secunda Congregatio Plenaria," *Not* 8 (1972) 122–24.

6. The seventeen blessings selected were of or for a child, a family, espousals, the anniversary of marriage, a sick person, the elderly, meals or food, a house, an automobile, "for any purpose," a crucifix, stations of the cross, a church bell, a cemetery, a rosary, a devotional object, and holy water.

7. I am aware that the Congregation for the Sacraments and the SCDW gave Germany permission for some of these activities "on an experimental basis."

met once or twice a week at the offices of the Congregation for Divine Worship.[8]

After the discussion of the general norms and guidelines, a first text of the Introduction which filled out the earlier one was composed. The Introduction was to be given its final form when the rest of the work had been completed.

A list was then drawn up of fifty blessings to be composed. In the final redaction of the benedictional, these were to be grouped under the three following headings:

I. Christians in their family life.[9]

II. Christians at worship and in the several forms of consecrated life.[10]

III. Christians at work and in the life of society.[11]

At the end there was an appendix containing blessings *ad omnia*, for any need, and for thanking God for favors received.[12]

With regard to the ministers of blessings, the principle to be followed was that laypersons could perform the blessings of family life; priests or deputed laypersons, those of parish or public life; and the bishop, those that have a special relation to the diocese.

The basic form of blessing was to be the communal form, which could be adapted to the cases of individuals. The communal form was to have these parts:

---

8. See *Not* 11 (1975) 168.

9. Among others: blessing of a new home, annual blessing of homes, blessings of a family, children, spouses, infants, handicapped elderly people, the sick, a woman after childbirth, engaged couples, and meals.

10. Blessing at the end of a catechetical session or a meeting for reflection on God's word; opening of a monastery, religious house, or seminary; clerical or religious garb; departure for the missions or on some other ecclesiastical mission; liturgical vestments, furnishings, sacred vessels, or musical instruments for use in worship; the investiture of altar servers or boy choristers; pilgrims at a sanctuary; offerings for the Church and the poor; holy water, stations of the cross, rosary, scapular, devotional objects, water or other elements used in honoring the saints.

11. Blessing before a journey or a long absence from home; blessing of animals, the cornerstone of an important building, the opening of a hospital or rest home, the opening of schools or universities, cultural, artistic, scientific, or sport centers, meeting places, centers of social communication, workplaces, tools of technicians or workmen, welfare organizations, means of transport, rural areas and fields, fruits of the earth, products of craftsmen and industrial workers.

12. The group worked under the direction of the secretary of the Congregation. Its members were G. Pasqualetti, V. Macca, D. Sartore, A. Pistoia, and G. Gilbert Tarruell. The work of preparation was divided up as follows: G. Pasqualetti: opening rites, instructions, and conclusions; V. Macca: general introduction and part of the intercessions; A. Pistoia: part of the intercessions; D. Sartore and G. Tarruell: the prayers of blessing.

1) *Opening rites:* song, sign of the cross with the words "In the name of the Father . . . ," and greeting (varying according to the blessing).

2) *Instruction* (a sample text was given). Its purpose was to explain the authentic meaning of the blessing.

3) *Reading* of a short passage from Scripture. The text of one or two more important passages was given; other, optional passages were simply cited.

The reading might be followed by the singing of a psalm or other suitable text and a short homily.

4) *Intercessions* modeled on those in the Liturgy of the Hours or on the general intercessions of the Mass.

5) *Prayer of blessing,* several formulas of which were given.

6) *Conclusion,* this again with texts that varied as the particular blessing required.

The Introduction also allowed for the possibility of Mass being celebrated, at least for some blessings. Emphasis was also placed on the use of gestures, as the nature of the case required.

After putting together in this way all the parts to be found in each blessing, the group went over them again one by one and prepared a second complete schema that was to be sent to a number of liturgists, Scripture scholars, and men in the pastoral life for their examination. The total work was thus half completed on July 11, 1975.

What the Congregation for the Sacraments and the Congregation for Divine Worship did with the material no one yet knows.

II. BLESSINGS OF THE PONTIFICAL

The reform of the rites in the Roman Pontifical was initially assigned to two separate study groups: group 20 or *De Pontificali* I, which was to deal with the first book of the Pontifical, and group 21 or *De Pontificali* II, which was to deal with the second and third books. In practice, each group completed only part of its task.

The first book of the Pontifical contains the consecrations and blessings of persons. The study group completed its work on the rites for sacred orders and confirmation. Special groups were established for the other blessings of persons.

The second and third books contain the principal blessings of things (ordinarily performed by the bishop) and the ceremonial for some important events of the year (blessings of the oils) or for special occasions (synods, councils, visitation of parishes). The members of the group assigned to this area[13] collaborated in various revisions of the pontifical rites but did not do much as a group. During May and October of 1965 they held three meetings in the offices of the Consilium, at which they laid the foundations of their work on the rite for the blessing of the oils, but accomplished nothing more.

The reason for this situation was the distance separating the members, the advanced age of the relator, and the connection between various rites in these books of the Pontifical and the Roman Ritual. This connection made it necessary to wait; then when the opportunity presented itself for continuing the work, it was assigned to other groups, as we shall see.[14]

---

13. *Relator:* J. Nabuco; *secretary:* R. Volpini, later replaced by A. Franquesa; *members:* P. Borella, G. Schiavon, S. Famoso, Th. Bogler, P.-M. Gy (added later on).

14. The reform of the rites in Book II of the Pontifical will be considered below in Chapter 50 (p. 792) in connection with the rites for the dedication of a church and an altar (see *Not* 8 [1972] 124–29). The reform of Book III, which deals with synods and provincial councils, will be taken up below in Chapter 53 (p. 818), on pontifical ceremonial.

48

Blessing of an Abbot and an Abbess

In the course of the centuries these ancient monastic rites in the Roman Pontifical have undergone changes in response to changing civic and social conditions. They now had to be looked at anew in the light of new and different situations. Their purpose is to shed light on the task given to those who are established as heads of the monastic family.

I. History

The blessing of an abbot had lost sight of the spiritual dimension of this office and had put the emphasis on things lending pomp to the occasion; as a result, the blessing aped the rites of episcopal consecration. An abbot was now seen as an administrator rather than as the father of a family. Clarity required that the stress be put on the real function of an abbot and that everything be avoided that might cause the blessing to be confused with the ordination of a bishop.

The work of revision was done by A. Nocent, who consulted and was aided by other persons in the monastic world. His draft was presented to the Consilium at its eleventh general meeting[1] and at its twelfth as well. It was approved without any difficulty. The Fathers laid even more emphasis on simplification by making optional the presentation of the pontifical insignia, miter and ring. The original rite for the blessing of an abbot consisted in a prayer of blessing and the presentation of the Rule. Subsequently the "presentation of a staff" was introduced, the staff being

---

1. See "La XI sessione plenaria del Consilium," *Not* 4 (1968) 350. The two meetings were held in October 1968 and in the fall of the following year.

regarded not as episcopal but as purely monastic. Later still the ring and miter were added.

A careful study was made of the oldest euchological texts.

After its approval by the Consilium, the schema was sent to the Congregations for Religious and for the Doctrine of the Faith; they in turn approved it.[2] It was then submitted to the Holy Father,[3] who approved it for publication.[4] The rites were published by a decree of the Congregation for Divine Worship, dated November 9, 1970.[5]

II. CONTENTS

The *Ordo* contains, in addition to the decree of the Congregation, an Introduction and the two rites for the blessing of an abbot and an abbess. At the end there is a list of Scripture readings that may be used in the ritual Mass.[6]

Since this is a pontifical rite, the Introduction imitates the style adopted for the Introduction to the rite of sacred orders. The Introduction is therefore quite skimpy and almost exclusively concerned with rubrics. Here again there is no thorough presentation of the spiritual and doctrinal meaning of the blessing of an abbot or abbess.

The rite takes place after the liturgy of the Word and is very simple. After the abbot-elect has been presented by the religious who elected him, he is questioned about his duties to the monastic community that he is to direct spiritually as its father. The Litany of the Saints is then said; this is immediately followed by the prayer of blessing. There is, of course,

---

2. The schema was sent on June 2, 1970. The Congregation for Religious gave its approval on June 18, asking only that the final question addressed to an abbess be changed to read "Will you encourage your sisters . . . ," so that it would be more in accord with the decree *Perfectae caritatis*, no. 7.

The SCDF gave its approval on September 12, 1970. It sent on, without calling for its implementation, the wish of a consultor who wanted the blessing of an abbot or abbess to be given by the bishop of the diocese or some other bishop, whereas the SCDW allowed another abbot to give it, with the consent of the local Ordinary. The Pope approved the position of the SCDW (see Introduction, no. 2).

3. October 7, 1970.

4. Letter from the Secretariat of State, October 19, 1970 (No. 169586), which also says that the Holy Father had accepted the proposal of the SCDW that an abbot be allowed (with the consent of the local Ordinary) to confer the blessing on an abbot or abbess.

5. *Ordo benedictionis Abbatis et Abbatissae* (Vatican Polyglot Press, 1970; 32 pp.). Translated in *The Rites of the Catholic Church* 2 (New York, 1980) 115-31; there is a new translation of the Introductions in *DOL* 399 nos. 3277-91.

6. The texts for the ritual Masses were published in the second edition (1975) of the *Missale Romanum*.

no laying on of hands. Four different texts are given for the prayer of blessing.

The new abbot then receives the Rule and (optionally) a ring and miter. Finally, the celebrant gives him a pastoral staff, while saying a prayer that brings out its meaning: "Take this shepherd's staff and show loving care for the brothers whom the Lord has entrusted to you; for he will demand an account of your stewardship."

The new abbot concelebrates the Mass. If he receives the blessing in his own abbatial church, he takes possession of his chair and presides over the celebration, unless the one who blessed him is a bishop.

Also considered in the ritual is the case of an abbot who has jurisdiction over a territory. In this case there are some variants in the rite which point up this pastoral mission to the part of Christ's flock that has been entrusted to him. Thus, after communion the *Te Deum* is sung while the new abbot passes through the nave of the Church and blesses the faithful. Otherwise the *Te Deum* or some other song is sung as the concelebrants return to the sacristy.

The rite for the blessing of an abbess follows the same pattern, with the necessary adaptations. After the liturgy of the Word, the chosen candidate is presented and is asked about her resolve to govern the monastery in a way that seeks the spiritual good of the religious and about her obedience to the Roman Pontiff and the bishop of the diocese. After the Litany of the Saints has been sung, the prayer of blessing is recited (three texts are given). The new abbess then receives the Rule; she also receives a ring, unless she already received one at the time of her profession.

49

Consecration of Virgins

I. HISTORY

In accordance with no. 80 of the Constitution on the Liturgy, the venerable rite for the consecration of virgins was entrusted for revision to study group 20bis, the same group that prepared the rites of religious profession.[1] Six general schemas were composed,[2] and the rite was studied by the relators and Fathers of the Consilium at their eleventh (November 20 and 28, 1967) and twelfth (October 1 and 10–11, 1969) general meetings. Together with the other rites of religious life, it was sent out for review by the superiors general of the religious orders of men and women and by abbesses; some monasteries also made experimental use of the new rite. The response of these men and women was a very positive one.

The Fathers of the Consilium, on the other hand, while approving the schema, were dealing with material rather unfamiliar to at least the majority of them. Some voiced their bafflement, especially at the title ''consecration of virgins,'' which they claimed was quite unintelligible to people today. But the title was kept because it is traditional and because translations into the vernacular would be able to handle any problems that might arise.

Others thought that in view of the contemporary re-evaluation of marriage, the rite excessively exalted virginity. In response, it was admitted that the ancient liturgical texts on virginity are sometimes rather unintelligible and would have to be revised; on the other hand, they cannot be

---

1. See above, p. 763, n. 1.
2. Schemas 173, 207, 214, 247, 254, and 305.

allowed to give the impression that the Church has less esteem today
than in the past for consecrated virginity as an act of complete and perpetual spousal self-giving to God and neighbor and an eschatological sign
of the kingdom of heaven and the presence of God's love for the world
and of Christ's love for the Church.

Once the schema had been discussed by the Consilium and the necessary changes had been made, it was sent for examination to the Congregation for Religious (January 23, 1969), which replied on March 4. Its
observations were studied at the joint meeting on March 4, 1969. The Congregation for Religious wrote as follows on the consecration of virgins:

> We do not see the necessity of having a consecration of virgins as an
> independent rite after religious profession. It may, however, be continued
> where it is already in use, but it does not seem appropriate to extend it
> to other religious institutes or monasteries. In these other cases it would
> seem more suitable to have a "consecration" (not a "consecration of vir-
> gins") introduced into the rite of religious profession, as is already pro-
> vided for in the two schemas.

The study group, however, had already composed a prayer of blessing to be introduced into the rite of perpetual profession; it regarded this
prayer as needed for the spiritual and ecclesial enrichment of the rite.
At the same time, it maintained that the ancient rite of the consecration
of virgins must be kept, in accordance with the directive in the Constitution on the Liturgy. It added: "The Consilium has excluded every suggestion that one of the rites is superior to the other; it regards them as
parallel, but reflecting different traditions."

In his report at the Council, the relator, Archbishop Paul Hallinan of
Atlanta had said: "Another change in this article [no. 80], a change not
yet submitted to a vote, has to do with the desired restoration of the rite
of the consecration of virgins, the goal being that this ancient practice,
adapted to modern circumstances, should be used more widely and frequently."[3]

If, then, the rite were limited to the few monastic families that have
authorization for it and have traditionally practiced it, the reformers would
seem to be going against the will of the Council and maintaining distinctions that smack of privilege. The report of the Consilium study group
added:

> We do not understand, therefore, on what theological grounds the con-
> secration of virgins is not allowed to religious women in the active life, even

---

3. Sacrosanctum Oecumenicum Concilium Vaticanum II, *Emendationes a Commissione Conciliari de Sacra Liturgia propositae*, VII, caput III, 18.

though these are in fact the ones most like the virgins of the early Church. We are rather sure that not many congregations will adopt the consecration of virgins, but we do not think it a good idea to refuse them a priori the right to practice it.

The schema composed by the Consilium provided, therefore, that the rite might be used by nuns, religious families that wish it, women living in the world, and members of secular institutes. The Consilium thought that the explanations it gave had settled the matter. But when the Congregation for Religious received the page proofs (May 14, 1970), it refused to allow the consecration of virgins to be used by religious women, but limited it to nuns.

Use of the rite was thus restricted to nuns, persons living in the world, and members of secular institutes. This limitation required a radical revision of the entire schema, which was finally submitted once again on June 16, 1970, and received the *nihil obstat* of the Congregation for Religious on June 17.

Meanwhile, the whole matter was of concern also to the Congregation for the Doctrine of the Faith[4] and the Holy Father.[5] Once their approval was obtained, the rite was published on May 31, 1970, the feast of the Visitation of Mary.[6]

II. Contents

The volume contains an introduction, three chapters, and an appendix.

The first chapter gives the normal rite of the consecration of virgins. The second gives the rite when it is celebrated along with religious profes-

---

4. The schema was sent to the SCDF on February 4, 1970, and approved by it on April 25, 1970 (Prot. no. 313.70). The SCDF suggested some changes that would make the text more precise. In particular, it asked that the consecration be allowed only to those who "have never married in a religious or merely civil rite or lived in public or flagrant violation of chastity." This norm was inserted into the Introduction, nos. 3 and 4, with the exclusion, however, of the phrase "in a religious or merely civil rite," as requested by the Congregation for Religious (May 23, 1970) and accepted by the SCDF (June 11, 1970).

5. The schema was first sent to him on March 29, 1969; he gave his approval on June 4, 1969 (No. 139686), asking only that the litany "show a better balance between the number of invocations of the saints generally and the invocations of holy virgins." The printer's proofs were sent to him on May 14, 1970; he replied that the publication could proceed (June 26, 1970).

6. Pontificale Romanum ex decreto Sacrosancti Oecumenici Concilii Vaticani II instauratum, auctoritate Pauli PP. VI promulgatum, *Ordo consecrationis virginum* (Vatican Polyglot Press, 1970; 65 pp.). Translation in *The Rites of the Catholic Church* 2 (New York, 1980) 132-64; new translation of the Introduction in *DOL* 395 nos. 3253-62. See "Circa Ordinem Consecrationis virginum," *Not* 7 (1971) 107-10; A. Bugnini, "L'*Ordo consecrationis virginum*," *L'Osservatore Romano*, September 7-8, 1970.

sion. Nuns can in fact make religious profession and receive the consecration of virgins in one and the same celebration. But the acts can also be separated; the rubric warns against repeating the same actions in two celebrations (for example, in a religious profession the prayer of blessing is omitted if it has already been used in the consecration of a virgin).

The third chapter gives suitable passages for the Scripture readings and alternative prayers. The appendix provides a model for the formula of religious profession, as well as Mass texts for the day of the consecration of virgins.

The rite bears witness to the love that the Church, both Eastern and Western, has always had for consecrated virgins. Attestations of this love go back to a very early period and are quite abundant: the depiction of the "veiling of a virgin" in the catacombs; patristic literature; the sacramentaries (especially the Verona, or Leonine, Sacramentary with its prayer of consecration, "Deus castorum corporum); and the Roman Pontificals. In the Roman Pontifical still in use at the time of the Council, the rite was solemn and prolix, complicated and full of pomp, with many repetitions and outdated elements, as well as texts that are real treasures of liturgical literature and tradition. The few families, usually cloistered, that used it had adapted it in their own rituals. Meanwhile, the type of consecration that had been the predominant one in antiquity had entirely disappeared, namely, the consecration to virginity of women living in the world, outside any organized form of communal religious life.

The revision of the rite is faithful, of course, to the general guidelines that the liturgical Constitution set down for the reform of all the rites. In addition, it emphasizes both the spousal aspect of total consecration to God and also the ecclesial aspect: consecration for the benefit of the Church and in the service of love for the brothers and sisters. The texts are taken from the rich heritage of liturgical prayer or else are new compositions; in either case, they are adapted to the modern mentality, without however derogating from the Church's lofty view of virginal consecration in its relation to the mystery of God and of the Church.

The celebration of the rite takes place within Mass after the liturgy of the Word and follows a simple, linear pattern: call of the candidates, examination of their resolve to consecrate themselves wholly to God in virginity for the service of the neighbor, Litany of the Saints, renewal of intention (regarding chastity or religious profession), prayer of consecration, and presentation of the ring or veil or other traditional insignia denoting consecration. At the end of Mass a solemn blessing is given to the consecrated virgins.

The rite is always celebrated by the local bishop.[7] He is also the one who decides whether this consecration may be allowed to women living in the world.

---

7. On this point, too, the schema proposed by the Consilium had allowed for greater flexibility: ordinary faculties to celebrate the rite were granted not only to the bishop but also to the abbots and superiors general of the monastic orders on which the candidates are dependent and, by delegation from these authorities, even to priests. But on June 11, 1970, the SCDF asked that in accordance with ancient and unchanging tradition, the celebration of the rite be reserved to the bishop.

50

Dedication of a Church and an Altar

The rites for dedicating places of worship to God are among the most important in Books II and III of the Pontifical. They have undergone extensive amplification over the centuries, acquiring a luxuriant multiplicity of signs that has made it almost impossible for the faithful to understand the rite and take part in it. The celebration requires a great deal of time—another factor that has prevented the people from participating. Despite all this, the dedication of a new place of worship—a house of assembly for the community and a sign of God's presence among his people—is not only theologically meaningful but has always been a joyous occasion for the people, who see in a new church a sign of their own growth as a Christian community.

I. History

Since the group charged with revising Books II and III of the Pontifical had for various reasons been unable even to begin the work in any systematic way, a special study group, 21bis, was appointed in 1970.[1] It was asked to turn first to the rites for the dedication of a church and an altar, and only then to move its attention to the other rites of the Pontifical.

---

1. *Relator:* P. Jounel; *members:* I. Calabuig, A. Rose, and D. Sartore. In the beginning D. Sartore served as *secretary;* the office was subsequently filled by I. Calabuig, who both in this area and in the rites of religious life was chiefly responsible for the work accomplished and for the new texts. By arrangement with the secretariat of the SCDW, Father Calabuig was actively aided by Professor Rosella Barbieri.

At the first plenary session of the Congregation for Divine Worship (November 1970), the group presented its initial report on the dedication of a church.[2] The work continued despite difficulties. A careful theological, historical, and pastoral study had to be made in order to answer several questions: which of the often venerable and impressive signs in the Pontifical could be kept as being still meaningful; what structure the celebration should have; and what new elements were to be introduced. The most important decision reached was agreement that the proper liturgical locus for the dedication is the celebration of the Eucharist. It is this last that had to receive the greatest emphasis; within it there should be a discreet presence of the traditional elements of the rite: sprinkling with holy water, rite of incense, and rite of illumination.

At the second plenary session (March 1972), all the rites in the second and third books of the Pontifical were ready for submission to the members of the Congregation.[3]

As a result of numerous and insistent requests, the rite for the dedication of a church was sent to many bishops for experimental use. This allowed for confirmation of the proposed rite and, at the same time, answered a much felt pastoral need—a dedication that can be celebrated with the full understanding and participation of the Christian community because it displays the same simplicity of ritual that marks the other reformed liturgical actions.

After being approved at the plenary session of the Congregation, the rites were set up in printer's proofs to facilitate examination of them.[4] They were then sent to the episcopal conferences, centers for liturgical studies, and a large group of experts. Answers were to be received by November 15, 1973.

The volume contained an Introduction and the following rites:

I. Rite for laying the cornerstone or beginning work on the construction of a church.

II. Dedication of a church.

III. Dedication of an altar.

IV. Blessing of a church.

V. Blessing of a movable altar.

VI. Inauguration of a place intended for liturgical celebrations and other uses.

VII. Blessing of a chalice and paten.

---

2. See "Secunda Congregatio plenaria," *Not* 8 (1972) 124–29.

3. *Ibid.*

4. *Ordo dedicationis ecclesiae et altaris deque aliis locis et rebus Deo sacrandis* (printer's proofs; Vatican Polyglot Press, 1973; 173 pp.).

VIII. Blessing of a new cross to be displayed for the veneration of the faithful.

IX. Blessing of a bell.

X. Blessing of a cemetery.

XI. Public supplication when a church has been the place of a serious offense.

XII. Crowning of a statue of the Blessed Virgin Mary.

As a result of the remarks received from the conferences and other sources, the texts were revised once more, and some additions were made. Two of these should be noted:

1) Many cases were adduced in which a church was dedicated only after a period (sometimes of years) during which it had already been in use out of necessity or for some other reason, or in which old churches were inaugurated again after a complete restoration. It was asked that some suitable celebration be provided for these occasions. The study group therefore prepared a "rite for the dedication of a church already in general use for sacred celebrations."[5]

2) Others saw profit in having a rite for the inauguration of a baptistery, since the latter plays an important part in the life of a Christian community.

After this the new rites were studied by the various curial agencies, especially the Congregation for the Doctrine of the Faith (which examined the entire set of rites) and the Secretariats for Christian Unity and for Non-Christians, which took under consideration the special but not unusual situation in which one and the same place of worship is used by various Christian confessions or is even shared by Christians and non-Christians. This situation seemed to call for doctrinal, pastoral, and liturgical clarifications.

Agreement was reached on all points, so that the Congregation for Divine Worship was able to send confidential copies of the entire work to the international translation committees, in order that these might begin their work while the Latin original was making its way through the publication process. The final printer's proofs were just ready to be sent to the Pope for his definitive approval when suddenly the Congregation for Divine Worship was suppressed.

---

5. The occasion for preparing such a rite was the reopening of an ancient church dedicated to "Our Lady of the Fields," which had become unusable and was restored by the efforts of Archbishop A. Bugnini, as a gift to his native place, Civatella del Lago (Tierni), at the time of his episcopal ordination. The new rite was used at the dedication on June 30, 1974, and the result was a truly popular liturgical feast.

II. PUBLICATION

Two years passed during which nothing further was heard of the work. Then, by a decree dated May 29, 1977, the Congregations for the Sacraments and Divine Worship published only a part of the complete work: the rites for laying the cornerstone of a church, for the dedication and blessing of a church and an altar, and for the blessing of a chalice and paten,[6] or, in other words, Chapters I–V and VII of the list given above, along with the first addition. No one knows why these parts were chosen for publication. The rest was put off . . . to another time.[7] Furthermore, the Introduction, and especially the doctrinal part that explains the meaning of the dedication of a church and altar, was seriously mutilated, at times in a clumsy way.

The structure, however, remained, and the texts contained in the schema of the Congregation for Divine Worship were kept. I shall limit myself to the rites actually published and indicate briefly their essential elements.

1. *Dedication of a Church*

This takes place during the first Eucharist celebrated in the new church. It takes the form of rites and prayers expressing the intention to dedicate the building to God as the home of the Christian community. This community is understood as the people of God assembled around its pastors and as the body of Christ that draws its nourishment from the table of the Word and the table of the Eucharist and that celebrates herein the praises of God and the sacraments of salvation.

---

6. Pontificale Romanum ex decreto Sacrosancti Oecumenici Concilii Vaticani II instauratum, auctoritate Pauli PP. VI promulgatum, *Ordo dedicationis ecclesiae et altaris* (Vatican Polyglot Press, 1977; 162 pp.). Translated in *The Rites of the Catholic Church* 2 (New York, 1980) 185–293; new translation of the Introductions in *DOL* 547 nos. 4361-4445. See I. Calabuig, "L'*Ordo dedicationis ecclesiae et altaris*. Appunti per una lettura," *Not* 13 (1977) 391–450.

7. By a decree of March 25, 1981, the SCSDW published an *Ordo coronandi imaginem beatae Mariae virginis* (Vatican Polyglot Press, 1981; 36 pp.). See *Not* 17 (1981) 246–67; I. Calabuig, O.S.M., "Significato e valore del nuovo *Ordo coronandi imaginem beatae Mariae virginis*," *ibid.*, 268–324. The rite allows for three cases: crowning during Mass, during the celebration of Vespers, and during a liturgy of the Word. An appendix gives the music for the antiphons. The rite is simple: prayer of blessing and thanksgiving, crowning, intercessions, conclusion.

This liturgical book possesses an undeniable value and meets some special needs while at the same time properly directing them. Some people found its publication rather surprising. As was anticipated, it would have made a better impression had it been simply one entry in a new Benedictional.

The material building is a sign of the Church as people of God. This Church becomes visible when the Christian community gathers with its ministers and the local bishop to inaugurate a place of worship that it wanted and has built. If possible, the people go in procession to the new church; there they and the individuals who worked on the building of the church hand it over in symbolic fashion to the bishop; its doors are solemnly opened and the community enters.

The bishop takes possession of the presidential chair. He then blesses the water that will be used in sprinkling the faithful, the altar, and the walls of the church. This sprinkling has taken on a new meaning: in the old rite it was regarded primarily as a purification; now it is a reminder of baptism and a call to conversion.

After the singing of the *Gloria* and collect, the inauguration begins at the ambo, the place where the word of God is proclaimed and where the book of the Scriptures is solemnly enthroned.

The homily is followed by the most expressive actions in the rite of dedication: the invocation of the saints and the deposition of their relics beneath the altar;[8] the prayer of dedication;[9] the anointing of the altar and church walls by the bishop, who can be helped by other priests as at a concelebration; lighting of the incense on the altar and incensation of the altar; preparation of the altar and lighting of it and the church.

The Eucharistic liturgy has a proper preface. After communion the place where the Eucharist is to be reserved is inaugurated by solemnly bringing the Blessed Sacrament there. The entire celebration ends with a solemn blessing.

The same rite, with texts adapted to the different situation, is used for the dedication of a church in which the sacred liturgy has already been celebrated.

2. Dedication of an Altar

The characteristic moments in this dedication (which is performed, as always, during Mass) are: sprinkling of the faithful and the altar after

---

8. The relics of the saints are placed beneath the altar and not in the table; the latter is not to be incised. Furthermore, the relics are not to be in the form of small "fragments" but are to be "meaningful," that is, of sufficient size; otherwise the rite is to be omitted. The relics are carried into the church in the entrance procession.

9. This point was also the subject of lengthy discussion. Initially the study group thought that the preface of the Mass should serve as the prayer for the dedication of the church. But then the celebration would have been deprived of a characteristic element and one of great importance and instructional value. Therefore the decision was reviewed, and the prayer of dedication was retained.

the greeting and opening address; then, after the homily, the Litany of the Saints, deposition of relics, prayer of dedication, anointing, lighting of incense, lighting of the altar. This Mass likewise has its proper texts.

3. Blessing of a Church and an Altar

The rites here are extremely simple. At the blessing of a church, there is no solemn entrance. The sprinkling of the faithful, the altar, and the walls takes place after the greeting and opening address.

After the homily and the general intercessions, there is a prayer of blessing. If the altar is to be dedicated, the dedication is performed at this point, as described above.

The blessing of a movable altar takes place after the prayer of the faithful, using a special formula. The blessing can be given by any priest, whereas the dedication of a church or an altar and the blessing of a church are reserved to the bishop or to a priest whom he delegates.

4. Blessing of a Chalice and Paten

This blessing, which the Roman Pontifical used to reserve to the bishop, can now be given by a priest. The rite has been very much simplified; the sacred vessels are no longer anointed with chrism.

The blessing can be performed during Mass (which is recommended) or outside Mass. It consists of a prayer which, if the ceremony takes place within Mass, is said before the presentation of the bread and wine.

If the blessing is given outside Mass, it should be part of a celebration that includes a greeting, a reading, the blessing, general intercessions, the Our Father, and a closing prayer.

51

Blessing of the Oils

The Chrism Mass, during which the bishop blesses the oils, is also an occasion for giving expression to the close links that bind clergy and faithful to the pastor of the local Church.

I. HISTORY

Some revisions were made in this celebration as early as 1955,[1] but they were marginal. Another indication of the attention being given to this celebration was the permission granted the faithful of receiving communion both at this Mass and at the evening Mass on Holy Thursday. The next step was the early publication of the part of the Roman Missal containing the Chrism Mass, including the renewal of priestly promises and commitments.[2] Finally, there was the publication of the little book containing the blessings of the several oils.[3]

The material, prepared by the second study group on the Pontifical (*De Pontificali* II), was reviewed at a meeting of the relators in the spring of 1966. They judged that it was not yet ready for presentation to the Consilium. Consequently, only the principles on which the relators were in

---

1. See above, p. 116.
2. See above, p. 118.
3. *Ordo benedicendi oleum catechumenorum et infirmorum et conficiendi chrisma* (Vatican Polyglot Press, 1971; 18 pp.). It was published by a decree of the SCDW dated December 3, 1970. The rite is translated in *The Rites of the Catholic Church* 2 (New York, 1980) 302-12; new translation of the Introduction in *DOL* 459 nos. 3861-72. The decree of the SCDW is in *DOL* 458 no. 3860.

agreement were set before the Consilium at its seventh general meeting on October 14, 1966. These principles were the following:

1. The oil of catechumens is to be used only for catechumens and not on other occasions.

2. The blessing of the oil of catechumens and oil of the sick and the consecration of chrism are ordinarily to take place on Holy Thursday. But where distance or other causes make it difficult to bring the clergy together on that day, the blessing can take place close to (before or after) Easter.

3. In some circumstances priests may be allowed to bless the oil of catechumens and oil of the sick, even at times other than Holy Thursday.

Some years were to pass before the schema reached completion and all its details were worked out: the moment for the blessing, the rite, the texts. The delay was not due solely to the study group; the group had to await the results of studies conducted by other groups with an interest in this rite.

The final presentation and definitive approval of the rite came at the twelfth general meeting of the Consilium on November 13, 1969.

The texts were then sent for examination to the Congregation for the Doctrine of the Faith on February 26, 1970. That Congregation gave its *nihil obstat*, along with some observations on the formulas and the minister, on July 9.

On September 9 the rite was presented to the Pope, who gave his approval on September 22 (No. 168960). He too sent some observations on the minister, especially in connection with the oil of the sick. These were discussed, along with the schema *de infirmis*, at the first plenary session of the Congregation for Divine Worship on November 12, 1970. The conclusions reached were submitted to the Pope on November 25, and he sent his reply on January 21, 1971 (No. 172942).

II. Contents

The Introduction is skimpy. The first two numbers highlight the importance of the blessing of oils as manifested by the role of the bishop in it and by the part played by the oils themselves in the sacramental ministry of the Church. The Introduction then goes on to deal with the matter of the blessing, the minister, the day appointed for it, and its place in the liturgical celebration.

Matter. Previous legislation required the use exclusively of olive oil; this meant that in some parts of the world the oil had to be imported, with the considerable difficulties this entailed. In 1968 the Congregation for the Doctrine of the Faith had already granted permission for the use of a vegetable oil.[4] This regulation, which at the time was seen as a concession to be granted to those applying for it, was made universal in the rite of blessing.

In the past, chrism was made by mixing oil with balm. The point was that chrism should be a perfumed oil. The same result could, however, be obtained by using a variety of aromatic substances, and this principle was introduced into the new rite (no. 4).

Minister. According to a very ancient tradition that became universal in the Church from the fifth century on, the consecration of chrism is an action reserved to the bishop.

On the other hand, the oil of catechumens—the use of which is left to the judgment of the episcopal conferences—can also be blessed by priests who are preparing *adults* for baptism. Some steps in this preparation may involve anointing with the oil of catechumens. In order to make clear the meaning of this anointing (its purpose is to call down upon the baptizands the power of God that will enable them to renounce evil), the priest can bless the oil just before he uses it.

In cases of special urgency or true necessity,[5] the oil of the sick may likewise be blessed by the celebrating priest. It can also be blessed by

---

4. Letter of July 29, 1968. The Latinists then translated "vegetable oil" as "oil derived from plants."

5. There were rather lengthy negotiations on this point. When the SCDF gave its *nihil obstat*, it demanded that the text proposed by the Commission for the Revision of the Code be adopted, and this became part of the Introduction, no. 8: the ordinary minister of the blessing is a bishop or a priest who has an indult from the Holy See and is equivalent in the law to a bishop; in case of "true necessity" any priest may bless it. When the Holy Father gave his approval, he too asked that there be a clearer statement of when a priest may bless the oil of the sick (and the oil of catechumens).

On September 25, 1970, the SCDF was once again asked whether the expression "true necessity" might not be toned down. On October 25 the SCDF answered that the reasons for the stand taken by the Fathers of that Congregation "were pastoral rather than doctrinal: too long a rite, too long a retention of blessed oil which was not needed, danger of laxity in leaving the judgment of opportuneness to simple priests." The SCDF then exhorted the Consilium to regard these reasons as "sufficiently serious." It added, however, that the SCDF did not itself have any (doctrinal) objection, "since from the doctrinal standpoint there is no objection to giving this faculty to priests."

The matter was then taken up at a plenary meeting of the SCDW, which called for a broader formulation that would allow priests to bless the oil of the sick "in case of necessity or when pastoral considerations urge it." The SCDW had in mind the catechetical value of blessing the oil during the actual celebration of the sacrament of the anointing of the sick. The rite of blessing, it said, was not too long, since it consisted of a single prayer; nor did the SCDW see any danger of laxity, since only a priest convinced of the "necessity" would perform the blessing; finally, the oil left over could be burned.

The view of the Fathers was presented to the Pope on November 25, 1970, along with

one who, though not a bishop, is the equivalent of a bishop in the government of a territory.

Date of the blessing. The blessing of the oils has traditionally taken place on Holy Thursday morning. There are two reasons for this. The first is that the sacraments in which the holy oils are to be used are the fruit of Christ's paschal mystery and give human beings a participation in that mystery. The second is that Holy Thursday is also the anniversary of the institution of the priesthood: this gathering with the bishop reminds each priest of the enthusiasm, the grace, and the commitment that were his at his ordination. The blessing of the oils provides an occasion for renewing the fraternal ties existing among men who are united by the same sacrament and the pastoral mission of sanctifying souls.

In many parts of the world, however, distance or the pastoral duties of Holy Week make it difficult for all the priests to gather for the Chrism Mass on Holy Thursday. In these cases the bishop may choose some other day, provided it is "close to Easter."

Rite. This has been greatly simplified. Emphasis is now placed on the procession with the gifts, at which not only the bread and wine but the oils to be blessed are brought to the altar.

There is but a single prayer for the blessing of the oil of the sick and another for the oil of catechumens.

There is likewise but a single prayer for the consecration of the chrism, but it is lengthier. During it the concelebrating priests show that they are taking part in the consecration by extending their hands over the chrism as the bishop recites the most important section of the formula.

Two texts are provided for the consecration of the chrism; one is the traditional text (with occasional revisions), the other a new composition. Both locate this sacred action in the mystery of salvation by invoking symbolic biblical incidents in which God's action was mediated by oil. The new composition is more clearly Christological and focuses on Christ's present-day saving action and on the sacramental ministry of the Church.

Place of the blessing in the celebration. The oil of the sick is blessed before the end of the Eucharistic Prayer, while the oil of catechumens is blessed and the chrism is consecrated after communion. After lengthy discussion among the consultors and members of the Consilium, two options

---

the response of the SCDF. But a reply came back on January 21, 1971, that "after hearing the views of the other agencies which had an interest in the matter, His Holiness expressed his opinion that, all things considered, it would be better to remain with the formula proposed by the SCDF, namely, that simple priests can bless the oil only 'in case of true necessity.' " That is how the regulation in the Introduction ended up.

were finally introduced into the new rite: to perform the blessings at the traditional moments just described or (according to the pattern henceforth followed by all other blessings that take place during Mass) to bless the oil of the sick and the oil of catechumens and consecrate the chrism (in that order) after the liturgy of the Word.

At the end of Mass the oils are carried in solemn procession to the sacristy. There the bishop instructs his priests about "the reverent use and safe custody" of the oils, these being a sign of the union existing between the diocesan Church and its bishop as well as a means of keeping the risen Christ alive in souls.

Part VII

Simplification of
Pontifical Rites

52

Papal Chapel

I. PLAN OF REFORM

On February 13, 1965, the Secretariat of State sent the Consilium a plan for the reform of the papal chapel; it was the work of P. Jounel and A.-G. Martimort. A formal note stated that "the plan was requested by the Holy Father."

The plan, which had been carefully annotated by the Pope himself, dealt with two points in particular.

1. *Need of Reform*

A reform of the celebrations in the papal chapel was regarded as urgent for the following reasons:

a) *The teaching of the Council on bishops* and on their relations with the Pope made even less acceptable the role played by some bishops in papal celebrations: "to assist at the throne," to hold the book and the candlestick, to act as masters of ceremonies or, in the case of cardinals, as deacons and subdeacons.

b) *The modern mentality* rejects a blending of court etiquette and religious rites. The atmosphere of the "court," however, plays too large a role in papal ceremonies: Roman nobles and patricians, diplomats, and members of old families, all given special places; armed guards and other court dignitaries taking part in the entrance procession; the washing of the Pope's hands being done by dignitaries and servants. The "chair of Peter," it was said, had become a "throne."

c) *Television* is featuring papal ceremonies with increasing frequency. Some medieval customs are thus carried beyond the Roman setting to peoples of other religions and to non-believers, where they give rise to divergent and not always laudatory interpretations. The Pope should be seen by all as the successor of Peter and the servant of the servants of God, and not as a medieval prince. Television requires exemplary behavior on the part of all who take part in the papal liturgy, and especially of the masters of ceremonies; their exposed position displays with pitiless clarity every move they make.

2. Directing Principles

a) *Suppression of time-honored customs.* The functions now exercised by bishops are to be given back to clerics of appropriate rank. If laypersons play a role, it is to be because of their baptism and not because they are members of the papal court. Singers should be given a place of honor and not be hidden away behind a grill. The entrance procession is to be simplified in terms of both its participants and its pomp. The papal litter is a necessity if the Pope is to be seen by the throng, but it has a serious drawback because it symbolizes a type of human exaltation that is incompatible with the modern mentality. Some other more appropriate method must be found. The washing of the Pope's hands should be done by the regular servers. The "tasting" can simply be eliminated.

b) *Adaptation to new liturgical legislation.* The papal liturgy is still what it was in the fifteenth century. It must now give an example of renewal according to the spirit and letter of Vatican II. Pope John XXIII did so by celebrating "dialogue" Masses. We must continue along this line.

Pomp. The original simplicity and dignity of the altar must be restored by removing the clutter from it—candlesticks, reliquaries, miters, tiara. There are now two thrones (one is enough) but no ambo for proclaiming the word of God! The choir should be placed between the assembly of the faithful and the presbyterium (sanctuary), in accordance with no. 97 of the instruction *Inter Oecumenici.* The sacred vestments should be restored to their original simplicity by getting rid of the lace and fringes and the embellished surplices that make their wearers look like "extras on the stage."

The *musical repertory* of the Sistine Chapel is still what it was before St. Pius X. Gregorian chant does not hold sway there as the "peculiar and principal form of singing in the Roman Church." The sacred silence from the consecration to the Our Father that is called for in the instruction of September 3, 1968, is not observed. The silver trumpets drown out the words of consecration that are being said aloud at the concelebration.

Communion is routinely not distributed to the faithful. Secondary rites that have acquired high visibility should be simplified: for example, the entrance procession should be accompanied by singing. The singing of Terce, the vesting of the cardinals, and their obeisance to the Pope should all be done elsewhere, for example, in the vesting room.

Other rites lend themselves to erroneous interpretations. Thus seven acolytes accompany the Latin-speaking deacon when he goes to sing the gospel, but only two accompany the Greek-speaking deacon. This may suggest that the Latin Rite is superior to the Greek, though the Constitution on the Liturgy recognizes the equal rank of all the Church's Rites.

As in the early Church, the Pope should at times concelebrate with other bishops and cardinals. This would serve as a unique manifestation of unity in the priesthood and in the episcopal office.

The Consilium carefully studied this statement by experts and then, on February 18, 1965, sent the Pope a note on the "reform of the papal chapel." It repeated the reasons adduced in the Jounel-Martimort statement and suggested that a study group be appointed that would include "our best liturgists and some papal masters of ceremonies, who would work under the direction and authority of the Consilium."

This last clause was extremely important. The papal chapel has its own "forms," which cannot be ignored. This is something not always taken into account by persons living in other parts of the world, who tend to strike dramatic attitudes without adverting to concrete circumstances. The secretariat must therefore act to keep things in balance. Meanwhile, the Consilium suggested, the position of prefect of papal ceremonies should be left unfilled; a "delegate" might be appointed, provided he be someone in full accord with the Consilium who would gradually implement the results of the studies of the appointed group (always, of course, with the prior approval of the Holy Father).

On the following day the Pope approved of the plan, and on February 22 Archbishop Dell'Acqua let the Consilium know of the Pope's desire that the rites of the papal chapel should be revised and updated.

As a result, study group 39 ("de ritibus Cappellae Papalis") was appointed.[1] On March 9 the group held its first meeting, which the Cardinal Prefect of the Consilium also attended. It decided on the main lines of the investigation and divided up the areas to be studied. It held its

---

1. *Relator:* A. Bugnini; *members:* J. Nabuco, A. Terzariol, J. Wagner, P. Borella, T. Schnitzler, A.-G. Martimort, P. Jounel, A. Franquesa, and C. Braga. Since the work of the group dealt directly with papal celebrations, it was not presented to the Consilium but was submitted directly to the Pope.

second meeting on May 3–4, 1965, again in the offices of the Consilium. The meeting produced "General Guidelines for a Revision of the Rites of the Papal Chapel," which were submitted to the Pope on June 10. In this document the original Jounel-Martimort report was taken as a guide. The concrete suggestions made there were amplified with greater attention to particular situations: for example, the need of providing a special place for the members of the papal household and chapel who do not take an active part in the rite; revision of the "uniforms" of the various personages in the papal household; reduction in the number of the guards appointed to keep order; arrangement of the place of the celebration; the course followed in the papal functions.

On June 18 the Secretariat of State made known the "approval in principle" of these "guidelines" and asked the Consilium to proceed to "the examination of concrete proposals." From that point on, the group held periodic meetings during the fourth session of the Council (October–December 1965).

Meanwhile, the several members of the group tackled the limited areas assigned to them and compiled the first schemas. The group produced a dozen schemas in all, dealing with special points or the various celebrations in which the Holy Father takes part.

II. First Results: The Liturgy at the Council

On May 3, 1965, a further report was sent to the Pope: "Remarks and Suggestions Regarding the Celebration of the Sacred Liturgy at the Second Vatican Council." The following points were discussed:

1) *Prayers before and after* the conciliar meetings. These were: the *Adsumus*, the *De profundis* at the death of one of the Council Fathers, and the *Agimus* and *Angelus* after the meeting.

It was pointed out that the recitation of the *Adsumus* usually amounted to a widespread murmur without rhythm or order. It was suggested that the prayer be simply omitted, since the celebration of Mass needs no complementary intercessions. If its retention was desired, then the text should be reprinted with dashes to indicate the pauses and facilitate communal recitation. In the margin of the report the Pope indicated his preference for this solution.

The *De profundis* was recited after the *Adsumus*. It was suggested that news of a death be made public before Mass or at the commemoration of the deceased in the Canon. The remembrance of the dead person would thus come at its natural place and would be in the context of the Eucharist. The suggestion was accepted.

Regarding the other prayers, it was observed simply that the custom of adding a triple *Gloria Patri*, the *Angele Dei* and the *Requiem* to the *Angelus* is primarily an Italian one. It would be preferable in an international assembly to keep to the simple traditional form of the *Angelus*. The Pope noted in the margin that the Consilium should do "what seems best."

2) *Enthronement of the Book of Gospels*. This could be improved in three ways:

a) The songs should be truly "select," that is, adapted to this sacred action. A number of the Church's liturgical families have truly marvelous songs for welcoming the gospel; these can be borrowed without reserve.

b) The participants in the little procession should be arranged not in a straight line but in the form of an X, with two candle-bearing acolytes in front, the bishop by himself in the center with the Book of Gospels, and two honorary masters of ceremonies bringing up the rear.

c) The Book of Gospels that is thus solemnly carried in should actually be used for reading the gospel at Mass. At the present time, it is kept in a safe like a precious stone and carried in procession like a relic, but it remains silent. Let us make it speak. If the gospel is the symbol of Christ, let us listen to what the Lord is saying to us today.

It was therefore proposed to celebrate the enthronement of the Book of Gospels before Mass as prescribed in the Ceremonial of Bishops for a pontifical Mass and to read the gospel of the day's Mass from it.

3) *Mass at the Council*. Four points were considered:

a) *Texts*. According to the "Rite for the Celebration of a Council," the votive Mass of the Holy Spirit was to be celebrated daily. But this regulation suffered numerous exceptions, depending on the wishes of the celebrant or the master of ceremonies. At times the celebrant's private devotions took precedence over consideration for the assembly, as, for example, when the Wednesday Mass of St. Joseph was celebrated. When there was no plausible or valid reason for such peculiarities, they elicited astonishment or disgust.

But the daily celebration of the Mass of the Holy Spirit could also prove a drawback to devotion over the long haul. It was therefore suggested that as a rule the Mass of the day be celebrated and that the Mass of the Holy Spirit be reserved for ferias and minor (third class) feasts. In order that the same texts might not be used repeatedly for this Mass, the study group would prepare a number of formularies (four were here provided as examples).

b) *Ceremonies*. It was desirable that the Mass celebrated at the Council should serve as a model, but unfortunately it did not always prove to be exemplary. According to the report,

> the main reason for this is the fact that there is no one in direct charge of the celebration, no one to prepare the material side of the ceremony and the service and to direct its execution. As long as the master of ceremonies changes daily and people belonging to the Basilica are put in charge of the material preparation, it seems impossible to avoid the drawbacks that everyone regrets.
>
> We are therefore unanimous in humbly offering a first concrete suggestion: that one person be put in charge of the sacred functions celebrated in St. Peter's in connection with the Council; his task will be to coordinate all the required elements—material preparation, ceremonies, service, singing, celebrants, direction of the participation of the Council Fathers, communion of the faithful, and so on.
>
> With regard to Mass servers: it seems appropriate to use four young seminarians from each of the Roman colleges in turn. It would be an honor and source of enthusiasm for them and would ensure dignified service.

c) *Participation*. Participants in the conciliar Mass included bishops, experts, officials, auditors, some of the faithful, and observers. But, as the report observed:

> Lay participation is almost non-existent; only with difficulty can the laity get to communion. At the present time the auditors, male and female, can receive communion at the Council Mass, but the faithful must receive in the Chapel of the Blessed Sacrament.
>
> If communion were open to all and were properly organized, hundreds of the faithful could receive in a few minutes' time. More importantly, this assembly would exemplify the truth that the faithful should receive communion at Mass.
>
> The same can be said of seminarians and children when they are invited to sing: they too should be able to receive communion.
>
> Participation of the Fathers and the faithful in the responses and dialogues should be supplemented by some songs for community singing. A dialogue Mass supposes a small number of participants; as the number increases, song becomes more necessary.

d) *Singing*. The situation had improved but was not yet satisfactory. The sung texts seemed to be chosen more for their beautiful melodies than for words adapted to the sacred liturgy. Some motets had no connection at all with the liturgical moment at which they were sung. The music (usually polyphonic) and the Gregorian extracts were not suited for singing in the Council hall. Here again it was desirable to give an example of how Mass should be sung with all participating and with songs taken, not just from any collection whatsoever, but from a collection called for by the rite itself.

In order to implement these several proposals, the Consilium suggested a suitable booklet.

On July 8 the report was sent back with the note: "The proposals seem to be, in principle, worthy of approval." But the note went on to say that it seemed better to allow only participants in the Council (auditors and possible observers) to receive communion, lest the ceremony run on too long, and that the Sistine Chapel choir should be alerted in good time to prepare the songs.

On July 15 the secretariat of the Consilium asked some members of the Papal Chapel group and of group 25 (songs of the Mass) to come to Rome and organize the work.[2] These individuals met at Santa Marta on July 21, 1965. They produced a booklet that was distributed to the Fathers of the Council at the beginning of the final session (September 14, 1965).[3] It contained an Introduction, Rite of Celebration, Calendar, and Mass formularies.

The Introduction provided useful guidelines on the Mass to be celebrated as well as on the various ways of participating, with or without singing. The singing was to be done in a variety of ways in order to bring out the riches and flexibility of the Church's musical treasury. To this end, some parts were taken from the *Graduale simplex* (then on the press), in order that the Fathers might see its nature and usefulness shown in practice.

The Rite of Celebration ordered that the enthronement of the Book of Gospels be done before Mass, during the singing of the introit. This procession replaced the prayers at the foot of the altar. On these occasions there was to be a five-minute, written homily, and the prayer of the faithful.

The Calendar listed the Masses to be celebrated from September 14 to December 8. It did not, of course, take into account the possible post-

---

2. These were J. Wagner, A.-G. Martimort, and A. Terzariol for group 39, and L. Agustoni and E. Cardine for group 25. The summer was certainly not a propitious time, and the work to be done was not small. Here again the consultors of the Consilium showed their readiness to help.

3. *Missae in quarta periodo Concilii Oecumenici Vaticani II celebrandae* (Vatican Polyglot Press, 1965; 119 pp.). See *Not* 1 (1965) 330–33. A note on page 2 cautioned that the booklet had been compiled for the fourth session of the Council and that therefore the Masses contained in it could not be used for celebrations outside the Council hall. After the Council not a few requests came in asking to use these schemas and calling for publication of the *Graduale simplex*, one of the most obvious and appreciated innovations.

ponement of meetings or the possible introduction of other celebrations or other rites.

The section on Mass formularies supplied the euchological content of the little book: seven Masses of the Holy Spirit, the Ember Mass, Masses for Advent and for the feasts of Our Lady, the Apostles, the Martyrs, and the Confessors; responsorial psalms; two schemas for the singing of the Ordinary of the Mass; six schemas for the general intercessions; an extensive collection of readings from the Acts of the Apostles and the Gospel of John and for the weekdays of Advent. Finally, it gave the prayer *Adsumus*.

This little book had the distinction of improving the conciliar celebrations, making participation more extensive (it reduced the number of those who read their Breviaries during Mass), and familiarizing the Fathers with certain aspects of the liturgical reform while at the same time making them look forward to it and helping them understand it better.

4) *Close of the Council*. The results of the Consilium's work were so positive that it was asked to join the office of papal ceremonies and the general secretariat of the Council in preparing the rites for the conclusion of the Council itself.[4]

III. Papal Altar

The study group also presented a report on revision of the norms governing use of the papal altar. The report took into consideration the privilege the Pope enjoyed of being the only one to celebrate at the main altar in the patriarchal basilicas of Rome. This privilege was originally connected with the oneness of the priesthood and of the Christian sacrifice. It is this idea that explains the custom of reserving to the bishop the use of the main altar of cathedral churches; the reservation symbolizes the unity of the diocese in faith and in allegiance to a single pastor around a single altar. The privilege was confirmed at the period when altars for individual celebration began to multiply. In order to keep this multiplicity of celebrations from obscuring the original oneness of priesthood and sacrifice, the decree of the Council of Auxerre was universally accepted: "It is not permitted to have two Masses celebrated on the same altar on the same day, nor for presbyters to celebrate Mass at an altar at which the bishop has already celebrated that day."

---

4. See *Ordo concelebrationis et Methodus servanda in publica sessione Concilii Oecumenici Vaticani II (die 7 decembris 1965)* (Vatican Polyglot Press, 1965; 42 pp.), which also contained the *Ordo ad absolvendum Concilium* (36–42); and *Ordo et Methodus servanda in concludendo Concilio Oecumenico Vaticano II (die 8 decembris 1965)* (Vatican Polyglot Press, 1965; 52 pp.). See "Ordo ad absolvendum Concilium Vaticanum II," *Not* 2 (1966) 19–28.

The original meaning of the privilege was gradually overshadowed by a juridical interpretation: The altar at which the bishop celebrates cannot be used by others out of "reverence" for him. The practice gradually disappeared outside Rome, but at Rome it became further accentuated by reason of the unique dignity of the Supreme Pontiff. The result was the privilege attached to the papal altar in the patriarchal basilicas: without the Pope's express permission, no one else could celebrate at an altar at which he customarily celebrated; the prohibition was not limited to a given day but extended to every circumstance.

As the first documents of the reform appeared with their emphasis on the altar as the central point to which the attention of the entire assembly is spontaneously drawn, people began to feel the incongruity of the strict discipline connected with the papal altar. In St. Peter's Basilica celebrations took place at the altar of the Cathedra, but this did not face the people. In the other basilicas a small movable altar was set up in front of the papal altar, but this only detracted from the dignity of the celebration and from the dignity of the papal altar itself.

It was therefore suggested that the current legislation be mitigated. The Pope accepted the suggestion, and a new discipline was established in the motu proprio *Peculiare ius* of February 8, 1966.[5] After a short historical survey of the papal privilege in the patriarchal basilicas of Rome (St. Peter, St. John Lateran, St. Mary Major, St. Paul Outside the Walls, and St. Lawrence), the Pope decreed:

1. The papal privilege is to remain as in the past on days on which the Pope himself celebrates. This will happen most frequently in St. Peter's Basilica.

2. Those who may otherwise use a papal altar are: a cardinal archpriest in his own basilica or his vicar or a bishop delegated by him; in St. John Lateran, the cardinal vicar of Rome or a bishop he delegates; in St. Paul, the abbot of the basilica; in St. Lawrence, the commendatory abbot; in all the basilicas, a bishop leading a large pilgrimage. Other concessions may be made by the person in charge of the basilica when he thinks it necessary due to large gatherings on the faithful, solemnities, or sizable pilgrimages.

This change in the law contributed not a little to more dignified celebrations in the patriarchal basilicas of Rome (so often the goal of pilgrimages and gatherings of the faithful) and to notably improved participation.

---

5. Paul VI, motu proprio *Peculiare ius* on the use of the papal altar in the Roman patriarchal basilicas (February 8, 1966): *AAS* 56 (1966) 119–22; *DOL* 544 nos. 4337-43. See the commentary of A. Franquesa in *Not* 2 (1966) 204–8.

IV. Oversight of Papal Ceremonies

If the other proposals made, especially in regard to the "papal Mass," were to be implemented, it would be necessary:

a) to simplify the principal rites in the Ceremonial of Bishops and to make known the basic lines of the new Rite of Mass;

b) to review and revise the "external" practices of the papal court and household with their pomp and circumstance;

c) to make a thorough study of the oral and written sources.[6]

With regard to the first point, the Consilium undertook a first simplification of papal rites and insignia.[7]

Pope Paul VI himself turned his attention to the second point in the well-known measures taken in his motu proprio *Pontificalis domus*, which notably reduced the baroque pomp of the papal court and household.[8]

The thorough study envisaged in the third point was hampered somewhat by the persons involved. The prefects of papal ceremonies had always been jealous protectors of the precious archives containing the written ceremonials and diaries of prefects from the Middle Ages to our own times. But Paul VI got around this difficulty by establishing on May 25, 1968 (No. 117543) "an administrative commission for the prefecture of papal ceremonies, which shall have for its purpose to apply the norms of the conciliar Constitution on the Liturgy to the papal ceremonies and to revise the regulations governing the prefecture itself."[9] It was understood that "the papal masters of ceremonies currently in office are to depend on the commissioner in everything pertaining to the conduct of their office."

The delegate[10] was also given the task of managing papal ceremonies and deciding on the person who was to direct the actual celebration of these.[11] This proved to be another duty laid upon the Consilium in the person of its secretary. But the experience could be valuable for the liturgical reform as a whole, and the secretary was unwilling to let the opportunity slip.

---

6. These three difficulties were raised in a letter to the Secretariat of State on January 8, 1966.

7. See below, pp. 820–21.

8. See Paul VI, motu proprio *Pontificalis domus* (March 28, 1968): *AAS* 60 (1968) 309.

9. A. Bugnini, secretary of the Consilium, was appointed commissioner; the vice-commissioners were Father Gabrielo Brasó, O.S.B., and Monsignor Virgilio Noè, who also served as secretary of the group.

10. At the suggestion of the appointee himself, the commissioner was instead called "delegate," in order to make the role of the commission less "offensive."

11. Letter from the Secretariat of State, June 15, 1968 (No. 117543).

His first job was to become informed of the situation, atmosphere, and practical implementation of papal ceremonies. None of the three commissioners had adequate knowledge in this area. The delegate thought it his duty to approach the problem experientially. This had the advantage of creating a new outlook and gradually introducing a new style of celebration and participation, as desired from the beginning in the studies submitted to the Holy Father. But the course was a difficult one, due to resistance from outside the commission and to a divergence of sensibilities within the commission itself (in fact, a bare month later, on June 25, 1968, Father Brasó expressed his vexation).

The commission remained in existence for fifteen months (May 25, 1968 to September 1969); this was not enough time for serious research and testing. In addition, the work of the Consilium, especially on the *Ordo Missae*, was taking shape. The delegate therefore had to limit himself to the material preparation of celebrations which daily became more numerous due to the urgent undertakings that marked these most brilliant years in the pontificate of Paul VI. Nonetheless, this rather short period of time saw reforms that created a new style and laid the foundations for the entire subsequent development. I shall mention only a few accomplishments:

a) The regulations governing the work of the papal masters of ceremonies were reviewed, updated, and revised; these individuals were also required to be adequately trained in the liturgy generally and in the area of ceremonial in particular. A suitable period of apprenticeship was established, and outdated privileges were abolished or at least reduced in number.

b) The papal Mass was changed to reflect the new *Ordo Missae*. In particular, there was a better distribution of functions (as foreseen in the General Instruction of the Roman Missal) and an increased participation of the congregation by means, among other things, of popular songs and the easier Gregorian of the *Graduale simplex*. In order to make this participation possible, the practice was introduced of printing suitable booklets for each celebration; these became customary. All this was only a beginning, courageous indeed but also prudent, since it meant encroaching on the longstanding privileges, customs, and competencies of a number of bodies and categories of persons.[12]

---

12. For example, altar servers were provided by the "chapel clerics," that is, twenty presbyteral prelates, of all ages, living in Rome or outside it, who were summoned for various celebrations by the office of the Camera Apostolica (section for civil ceremonies). These men usually showed up, unprepared, at the moment of the celebration.

The suggestion that seminarians from the ecclesiastical colleges of Rome should take

c) Another aspect of this simplification, which aimed at restoring linearity and a sense of the sacred to papal celebrations, was the dismantling of the baroque structures that "adorned" the funerals of cardinals.[13]

d) A similar revision, accomplished at the cost of humiliation and recrimination, was made in the rites of canonization, another papal ceremony of great importance in the life of the Church,[14] and in the rite for the creation of new cardinals.[15]

---

turns serving was one of the first ones made, but at the time it was not accepted. Even a modest degree of "declericalization" ran into no little difficulty. Nor did the commission get the cantors of the Sistine Chapel to exchange the cassock and surplice for a more suitable secular garb. It did, however, succeed in having the first readings and general intercessions read at papal Masses by laymen in secular clothing. The last layman who proclaimed the readings while wearing amice, cassock, and cincture was a rather elderly and corpulent professor in the celebration of Corpus Christi at Ostia Lido in June 1968. The sight of him thus garbed and walking with difficulty stirred mirth rather than recollection, especially among his many high school students who were in attendance.

13. See what was said above on page 774, note 8, about the funeral of Cardinal Bea. The thing that in the past had made the greatest impression and roused the interest of various groups had been a huge catafalque erected at the crossing of Sts. Processus and Martinianus in the Basilica of St. Peter. It was three meters high, with a false coffin on top, while the real coffin was pushed under the catafalque on a trolley. Roundabout stood a hundred tall candles that were new for each cardinal's death. This ostentatious and highly unrealistic funeral apparatus was done away with. Many people were very surprised to see a coffin sitting on the bare pavement; criticisms were many and there were even lampoons. On the other hand, the prayer of those present was fervent and heartfelt. It was this intense prayer, so fervent and so joyous even amid sadness, that lent the funeral its true solemnity. Those closest to the dead man felt this deeply. At the end of the celebration, Bishop Willebrands, secretary of the Secretariat for Christian Unity, and Father Arrupe, General of the Society of Jesus, approached the delegate in charge of papal ceremonies and thanked him: "This was a marvelous funeral; such a ceremony pleased us greatly." Once the ice was thus broken, future funerals were in the same style.

14. See above, p. 169, n. 61; "De ritu canonizationis," Not 5 (1969) 292–93.

15. As early as the beginning of 1964, the Pope had asked the Consilium to study this matter. The schema, composed by Monsignor T. Schnitzler, was sent to him on May 13, 1964. It proposed bringing out the spiritual meaning of the cardinalate by taking the action by which cardinals are created and making it part of a liturgical rite, while at the same time avoiding everything that might suggest a new "holy order" or a "sacrament of the cardinalate." The schema went on to propose a rite that would be: (a) intrinsically liturgical and conducive to devotion; (b) Christological; (c) ecclesial, since the focus was faith in the Church and in the authority of Blessed Peter; and (d) organized in accordance with the principles of Vatican II, that is, involving concelebration, participation of the people, a profession of faith, a promise of fidelity to the Church and the Roman Pontiff, and the presentation of the ring.

The schema reflected the time at which it was composed. Its main proposals were nonetheless gradually implemented, chiefly in the development of two celebrations for the creation of cardinals: the presentation of the cardinal's biretta, which took place during a

The entire work was one of stripping away and making a fresh start. Indeed, *mutatis mutandis*, this describes what the years before the publication of the reformed liturgical books were for the Church as a whole. Once the books were published, there was a foundation laid on which papal ceremonies could once again be marked by the deep spirituality, lively participation, and exemplary stature they are now acknowledged as having. All could now see that their vigor and special atmosphere are due, not to external pomp and ritual complexity, but to the presence of the high priest and supreme shepherd of the Church. The ardor with which Paul VI applied the liturgical reform to himself and the faith with which he celebrated were certainly the strongest stimulus for other bishops to make themselves truly responsible for the liturgical life of their dioceses and to be the chief celebrants therein.

---

celebration of the word; and a concelebration with the Pope, in the course of which the new cardinals received their rings and titles. See ''Impositio bireti rubri et assignatio tituli Cardinalibus nuper electis,'' *Not* 5 (1969) 289.

53

Episcopal Ceremonial

I. First Phase

The liturgical book containing the ceremonial to be observed in liturgical functions at which bishops preside was the last to emerge from the usages and customs that led, via the medieval ceremonial of the papal court, to the *Ordines Romani* and the sacramentaries. Some parts of the Ceremonial of Bishops had long since been outmoded. But the remaining parts likewise called for thorough revision, since they reflected to an excessive extent the culture and social order of the sixteenth and seventeenth centuries, when the book acquired its definitive form.

Although the work in this area could not be completed until the publication of the other liturgical books, since these had to be followed in the episcopal liturgy, the Consilium believed that it should immediately undertake a first revision of the more urgent sections. For at the outset of the reform many bishops were already asking that the pontifical rites be simplified by suppression of details that were out of step with the doctrinal, pastoral, and psychological situation of our time. The early documents of the reform laid emphasis on the importance of the liturgy celebrated by the bishop, since he is the shepherd and high priest of his people. Celebrations centered around the bishop, with their variety of functions and ministers and the participation of the entire people of God, are the supreme manifestations of the Church. But the embodiment of this ideal was rendered difficult by a number of regulations and rites which had to be followed in episcopal celebrations and which detracted from their simplicity and made them difficult to understand.

For this reason the study group assigned to episcopal ceremonial[1] began its work immediately. It met in Rome on November 7, 1964, and September 29-30, 1965. In February 1965 it sent a questionnaire to various consultors who were experts in the rubrical, juridical, and pastoral areas and asked for their views.[2] The questions asked were also raised at the fifth (April 28, 1965), sixth (December 1, 1965), and seventh (October 14, 1966) general meetings of the Consilium.[3] The Consilium went along with the experts on questions to which they had given unanimous answers. Those questions on which the experts had disagreed were sent back to the study group for further reflection. The principle to be followed was that elements that were useless or had fallen into desuetude were to be abolished, especially if they reflected the customs of the princely courts of past ages.

In connection with this first simplification of episcopal ceremonial, it seemed appropriate to act also on no. 130 of the liturgical Constitution, which required that "the use of pontifical *insignia* be reserved to those ecclesiastical persons who have either episcopal rank or some definite jurisdiction." The matter was a tricky one, since it directly affected many individuals who had been given privileges, often in acknowledgment of services they had rendered the Church. Regulations for this area had been published in the apostolic constitutions *Inter multiplices* of Pius X and *Ad incrementum* of Pius XI. Any change in this entire complex arrangement would therefore have to come in the form of a new papal document. For this reason, at the seventh general meeting of the Consilium the relator submitted drafts of a decree on the simplification of episcopal rites and a motu proprio on the use of episcopal insignia.

The schemas met some opposition in the Consilium because of the unpopularity that was bound to attach to these documents, especially the one on insignia. It was suggested that prelates and clerics who enjoyed these privileges without being bishops should be asked to renounce them of their own accord. But there was no consensus on this. After the meeting, which approved both schemas, these were published on June 21, 1968, one in the form of a motu proprio, the other in the form of an instruction from the Congregation of Rites.

---

1. *Relator:* A.-G. Martimort, who was joined by C. Braga; *secretary:* A. Cuva; *members:* J. Nabuco, G, Schiavon, P. Borella, S. Famoso, and H. Hombach.

2. Their views were collected in Schema 72: *De usu Pontificalium* 1 (March 31, 1965). The opinions are those of A.-G. Martimort, S. Famoso, P. Jounel, T. Schnitzler, A. Terzariol, G. Schiavon, J. Rabau, A. Franquesa, R. Pilkington, and L. Buijs.

3. See Schemas 85 and 128.

1. *Motu Proprio* Pontificalia insignia[4]

As I pointed out above, this rather short document applied no. 130 of the liturgical Constitution, using "truthfulness" as its criterion. Episcopal insignia are symbols of the bishop's rank and his office as shepherd of God's people. The symbolism is falsified when the person displaying the insignia of episcopal rank is not in fact a bishop. The insignia are therefore reserved to:

a) bishops;

b) persons exercising a real jurisdiction over a part of the people of God, but only within the territory assigned to them: abbots and prelates *nullius*, apostolic vicars and prefects, apostolic administrators;

c) abbots who govern a monastery, but only therein. Abbots who have left office and titular abbots may continue to use the insignia within the Congregation, but only with the permission of the abbot in charge;

d) those who represent the Supreme Pontiff in carrying out a mandate: papal legates, apostolic nuncios or delegates.

Prelates who already enjoy special privileges may continue to use them for the remainder of their lives, but these privileges will not be given to prelates in the future. The same norm applies to clerics who already enjoy such privileges through membership in a college, for example, canons of certain cathedrals.[5]

2. *Simplification of Pontifical Rites*[6]

The instruction *Pontificalis ritus*, which was issued by the Congregation of Rites, has five chapters:

1) *Priests* and *ministers* who assist a bishop during celebrations. The principle of truthfulness is applied to them: they must exercise the func-

---

4. See Paul VI, motu proprio *Pontificalia insignia* on the use of pontificals (June 21, 1968): *AAS* 60 (1968) 374–77; *DOL* 549 nos. 4447-56. And see S. Famoso, "Commentarium ad Motu Proprio *Pontificalia insignia*," *Not* 4 (1968) 307–12. A further simplification of vestments, coats of arms, and similar things would be effected in the instruction *Ut sive sollicite* of the Secretariat of State (March 31, 1969): *DOL* 551 nos. 4497-4532. These provisions were applied to canons, holders of benefices, and pastors in the circular letter *Per Instructionem* of the Congregation for the Clergy (October 30, 1970): *DOL* 552 nos. 4533-37.

5. In summary, the pontifical insignia in question were miter, staff, ring, pectoral cross, dalmatic, gloves, shoes, sandals, pallium, gold pitcher, canon, seven-branched candelabrum, archiepiscopal cross, seat or faldstool.

6. Congregation of Rites, instruction *Pontificalis ritus* on the simplification of pontifical rites and insignia (June 21, 1968): *DOL* 550 nos. 4457-96. See S. Famoso, "Commentarium ad Instructionem de ritibus et insignibus pontificalibus simplicioribus reddendis," *Not* 4 (1968) 312–24; see also *EL* 82 (1968) 345–58.

tions and wear the vestments proper to their rank. Priests are therefore no longer to serve as "assistant deacons."

2) The bishop's chair is the *cathedra*, which is the sign both of his pastoral office and of the diocese united under his teaching and government. It must therefore appear as such and not take the form of a throne with a baldachin or have so many steps as to place the bishop at an excessive height.

3) *Vestments* and *insignia*. Their use is simplified. Buskins, sandals, and gloves are made optional; the tunicle is abolished; use of the dalmatic is limited, being required only at certain more important episcopal celebrations: ordination of a bishop, conferral of holy orders, pontifical blessings, and so on. Also abolished is the cushion for kneeling and the candle. There is to be but a single processional cross and a single miter—plain or ornate—in the same celebration.

4) *Things abolished or changed:* the bishop vests, not at the altar, but in the sacristy; the Book of Gospels is solemnly carried in procession by a deacon and then placed on the altar, while the book of epistles is placed on the ambo; genuflections to the bishops are omitted; the washing of the bishop's hands is done by acolytes and not by members of the bishop's household; the prior tasting of the bread and wine is abolished. Use of miter and staff is reduced. This section of the instruction also introduces an important innovation: when a bishop takes part in a Eucharistic celebration but does not himself celebrate Mass, he may preside over the entire liturgy of the Word and give the final blessing.

5) The final chapter decrees that the norms set down in the instruction apply in due measure to prelates who, though not bishops, enjoy the privilege of certain pontifical insignia.

II. Second Phase

In the years that followed, not much was said of episcopal ceremonial, since there were other problems that had to be resolved first. The work was finally resumed in February 1971 by a new study group.[7] The group submitted its results to the second plenary meeting of the Congregation for Divine Worship.[8] Meanwhile it gave thought to a liturgical book that would not simply regulate episcopal ceremonies but be a kind of ceremonial for the use of all ministers of the Church. But the traditional view prevailed of setting forth in a special book the peculiarities of celebra-

---

7. The study group held its first meeting February 8–13, 1971; see *Not* 7 (1971) 133. *Relator:* T. Schnitzler; *secretary:* P. Marini; *members:* A.-G. Martimort, V. Noè, and P. Jounel.

8. See "Secunda Congregatio Plenaria," *Not* 8 (1972) 129–32.

tions at which a bishop presided, the reason being that these are especially important in the life of the diocese. The purpose of this special book is to help those in charge of these ceremonies to understand their spirit and meaning and to embody this spirit and meaning in an exemplary celebration.

The work of the study group was published in printer's proofs at the beginning of 1975 and sent to bishops, masters of ceremonies, liturgists, and consultors of the Congregation for Divine Worship. Replies were requested by June 30, 1975.[9] The book contained an Introduction, eight sections, and an appendix.

The Introduction briefly sketches the history of the *Caeremoniale Episcoporum* and its continuing importance.

The first section deals with episcopal liturgy in general, its importance and significance for the local Church, the tasks of bishops, and the cathedral church. The section then sets down general norms that apply to all episcopal celebrations: vestments and insignia, expressions of reverence, incensation, precedence, use of holy water.

The second section is devoted to the Mass, and especially the "stational" Mass of the diocesan bishop.

The third deals with the Liturgy of the Hours when the bishop takes part in it.

The fourth reviews the principal celebrations of the mysteries of the Lord during the liturgical year: Christmas, Presentation of the Lord, Lent, Ash Wednesday, Chrism Mass, Easter Triduum, and so on.

The fifth and sixth sections deal respectively with the sacraments and sacramentals.[10] The seventh reviews the most important moments in a bishop's life: election, ordination, enthronement, imposition of the pallium, transferral to another see, death and burial, interim without a bishop (*sedes vacans*), anniversaries.

Finally, regulations are set down for certain special acts of government: plenary and provincial councils, diocesan synods, pastoral visitations, installation of new pastors.

The appendix deals with the vestments of bishops, cardinals, other prelates, and canons.

---

9. *Caeremoniale Episcoporum, ex decreto Sacrosancti Oecumenici Concilii Vaticani II instauratum auctoritate Pauli PP. VI promulgatum* (printer's proofs; Vatican Polyglot Press, 1975; 248 pp.).

10. This section also deals with the blessings that had already been prepared and with the rites for the dedication of a church and an altar (not yet published). It also deals with blessings, referring to the first schema prepared by the group.

Part VIII

Special Documents

Instructions on the Carrying Out of the Liturgical Constitution

A. FIRST INSTRUCTION: *INTER OECUMENICI*

I. HISTORY

After the liturgical Constitution itself, the instruction *Inter Oecumenici* of September 26, 1964, was the first document of fundamental importance for the postconciliar liturgical reform. It took six months and a series of schemas to produce and was discussed at length in two general meetings of the Consilium.[1]

1. *Beginnings*

The first approach to the instruction anticipated that it would have three parts: (a) pastoral, containing the most important doctrinal principles on which the instruction of the faithful was to be based; (b) regulatory; and (c) ceremonial, describing in a general way the carrying out of the rites that would have to be changed due to certain innovations, such as facing the congregation during the proclamation of the readings.

---

1. The following schemas were produced:
   March 13, 1964: Schema 1: *Instructio* 1.
   April 14, 1964: Schema 4: *Instructio* 2.
   May 22, 1964: Schema 10: *De Instructione* 3.
   June 17, 1964: Schema 13: *De Instructione* 4.
   June 21, 1964: Schema 17: *De Instructione* 5.
   August 31, 1964: Schema 27: *De Instructione* 6.

On March 14, 1964, the Consilium sent some of its consultors a first sketch of the second part, which it regarded as "the most important," along with a general outline of the entire document, including juridical elements to supplement the motu proprio *Sacram Liturgiam*. This first document was the work of E. Bonet. Once the replies, requested by March 28, had come in,[2] a smaller group reworked the document.[3] It became immediately clear that the draft was inadequate as it stood; it lacked the pastoral spirit and was too restrictive in comparison with the liturgical Constitution.

Father Vagaggini then sketched out a new draft of the instruction and submitted it to the general meeting of April 17-20, 1964. In this new version the instruction was to have an introduction and four parts:

a) Introduction: need for the instruction; competency of the Consilium.

b) Pastoral section, with an explanation of the value of the liturgy for the pastoral activity and spiritual life of the Church.

c) Juridical section, with an interpretation of some articles in the liturgical Constitution, especially those dealing with the territorial ecclesiastical authority that was to make decisions in liturgical matters.[4]

d) Elements of the reform that could be introduced immediately.[5]

e) Innovations in the area of ceremonial.[6]

2. *The Foundational Schema*

In Father Vagaggini's draft the original schema of seven pages had become a real theological, liturgical, and pastoral treatise of twenty-seven pages. The Consilium found it excessive and decided that the doctrinal

---

2. The schema was sent to: H. Jenny, P. Paventi, A.-G. Martimort, B. Neunheuser, H. Schmidt, L. Buijs, F. McManus, J. Wagner, G. Brasó, and M. Noirot.

3. The committee consisted of E. Bonet, A. Dirks, I. Tassi, H. Schmidt, and D. Grasso.

4. In this section (which would become nos. 23-25 of the published instruction), account was taken of the observations sent in by the papal representatives in response to a letter from the Consilium (March 25, 1964).

5. These were then to be decided on and formulated in agreement with the study groups in charge of the various areas of the reform, in order not to prejudice their work and future decisions.

6. This schema (the second) was entitled "A general outline of an instruction on the Constitution on the Sacred Liturgy and the motu proprio of January 25, 1964, and a draft of the second, normative part and the third, regulatory part of the same instruction." The title was a descriptive one and useful, in this study phase, for giving the Fathers an idea of what the document as a whole would be like. As the title indicates, only the second and third parts were developed; for the others there was simply a statement of what they were to contain.

section should be reduced to essentials; it appointed Bishop Jenny to prepare a draft, which was then reworked by Father Vagaggini. The second and third parts were regarded as substantially satisfactory. Monsignor Famoso was to work on the ceremonial section.

The discussion made it clear that the Fathers preferred to abandon the division into three or four parts and to follow instead the order of the chapters in the liturgical Constitution, listing under each heading the liturgical innovations and ceremonial changes.

As a result, a third schema was produced that was chiefly, indeed almost exclusively, the work of Fathers Vagaggini and Braga. This was sent to the members and consultors of the Consilium on May 22; it received its definitive critique at the general meeting of June 18–20, where the Fathers by and large were satisfied with it.

On June 2 the Consilium met at Santa Marta with representatives from the Congregations for Seminaries and Religious in order to study the parts in which they could claim competency. The meeting was a fruitful one. The only part that ended up being sacrificed was that dealing with seminaries; this was rather lengthy, but at the wish of the representatives from the Congregation for Seminaries it was reduced to a minimum.[7]

3. *Presentation to the Pope*

The draft was submitted to the Holy Father by Cardinal Lercaro at an audience on June 21, 1964. In presenting the text, the Cardinal told the Pope of the Consilium's desire that the document be published "as soon as possible" (in July, if feasible) and that it take effect on the First Sunday of Advent (November 29).

At an audience granted to Cardinal Larraona, prefect of the Congregation of Rites, on July 1, the Pope ordered that the Congregation study the draft of the instruction, as well as the rites for concelebration and for communion under two kinds. These documents were examined in a series of fourteen meetings with Cardinal Larraona presiding and Archbishop Dante, Father F. Antonelli, Monsignor Ferraro, and Monsignor

---

7. Those present were: from the Congregation for Seminaries, Monsignor Anglés, Monsignor Noirot, and Father Stickler; from the Congregation for Religious, E. Gambari and D. Hout; from the Consilium, E. Bonet, H. Schmidt, and C. Braga. The text agreed upon was then sent once again to the delegates so that it might reflect the desires of the two Congregations. The Consilium also took up with the Congregation for Religious questions regarding the Divine Office, and specifically the regulations referring to religious and their superiors (nos. 78-89 of the published instruction). To deal with this matter, there was another joint committee consisting of A. Franquesa and C. Braga from the Consilium and E. Gambari and D. Hout from the Congregation for Religious.

Frutaz in attendance. The reply of the Congregation of Rites was sent to the Holy Father on July 23; it was thirty-four pages long.

The more important observations were summarized in the accompanying letter from the prefect of the Congregation of Rites.

1. First and foremost, prudence was urged. This was a concern that would recur frequently in the other observations on details. Two reasons were given: the difficulty of the material and the fear of showing favor to people here described as "bold," "given to exaggeration," and "fanatical."

2. Fear that some points in the reforms introduced by the instruction could prejudice the future general reform.

The Consilium would show that the fear was groundless. As a matter of fact, the elements of the reform that were introduced in the instruction were those which—as the studies undertaken, the critiques by the study groups, and the concrete plans for reform developed as early as the period of the preparatory conciliar commission all showed—could be regarded as accepted by all liturgists and practitioners of pastoral liturgics as having a solid doctrinal and historical foundation and as useful in promoting the active participation of the faithful. Other reforms that were not yet solidly grounded and needed further investigation were not included, despite requests from various quarters; such were, for example, the offertory formulas, the rite of the fraction, and the concluding rites of the Mass.

3. A critique in principle of the *gradual* application of the reform; the Congregation of Rites claimed that "many of the clergy and laity are tired of this multiplication of partial changes, while everyone is looking for the promised reform of the Mass and the Breviary."[8]

4. Finally, the most important remark: the instruction goes beyond "the Constitution in its spirit and perhaps in its letter as well," especially regarding the vernacular in the liturgy. The prefect's letter read:

> The Constitution provides for liturgical use of the vernacular, but only within limits. It speaks of a "suitable place" for the vernacular in the Mass (art. 54) and its "extended use" in the sacraments (art. 63), while remaining faithful to the principle set down in art. 36, 1, that Latin is to remain the proper language of the Latin liturgy. Unfortunately, there are bold tendencies at work here and there to make the vernacular in fact the basic language and Latin an exception. When the instruction touches on these and

---

8. This was a strange remark to come from the Congregation of Rites, which shortly before (April 25) had issued a decree changing the formula for distribution of communion, even though this was to be included among other changes in the projected instruction.

similar problems, it should be worded in such a way as not to give even the impression of favoring any other trends [diverging from the Constitution].

These basic observations were followed by remarks on the several numbers of the instruction, some of these remarks being of a juridical kind, others having to do with the points already made. In particular, the Congregation of Rites asked for removal of the permission for the faithful to receive communion during the Chrism Mass and for using the Apostles' Creed in vernacular Masses with a congregation. It manifested bewilderment at celebrations of the word of God; of these it said:

> In Catholic countries such celebrations must be carefully regulated because they can easily create an atmosphere smacking of Protestantism. In order to obviate this impression and to bring these celebrations to a fruitful conclusion according to the spirit of the Church, they might suitably close with Benediction of the Blessed Sacrament. It would be enough to add at the end of no. 36 of the instruction: "It is preferable that these celebrations of the word of God end with Benediction of the Blessed Sacrament."[9]

These various remarks, it was said, were "dictated by a sincere desire to cooperate as closely as possible with the full, joyous, and fruitful application of the Constitution."[10]

Finally, the Congregation suggested a pompous formula of approbation that emphasized its own authority in the area: "which [Congregation] in the name of the Vicar exercises ordinary authority in the liturgical life of the Church." Paul VI added in his own hand: "The signature of the Cardinal President of the Consilium is also required."

The Holy Father ordered that the observations of the Congregation of Rites be reviewed first by Bishop Manziana, then by the Consilium; the latter replied on September 2 with a booklet of about forty pages.

4. *Final Text*

The booklet of the Consilium was accompanied by a new text of the instruction (sixth draft), which incorporated changes made after the critique of the Congregation of Rites. These changes were quite insignificant improvements and corrections, for the substance of the remarks submitted by the Congregation of Rites could not be accepted. With regard to the vernacular in particular, the Consilium pointed out that the

---

9. The Pope put two question marks and two exclamation points after this final observation, then drew two lines through the entire last sentence.

10. The Pope also put a question mark alongside this statement. The margins of his copy ended up with thirty-two question marks in all.

instruction simply codified the norms for approval of the acts of episcopal conferences which the Consilium itself had already issued in April and which the Holy Father had confirmed; the concessions contained in the instruction had therefore already been granted to many conferences.

Two additions were made: one after no. 18 (therefore no. 19 of the final version), which reminds pastors of their duty of training the faithful in the liturgy and obtaining their active participation, especially when the laity in question are involved in Catholic associations; the other after no. 34 (therefore no. 36 of the final version) regarding certain simplifications of ceremonial. In addition, the permission to use the Apostles' Creed was removed; although its value for participation and instruction was acknowledged, the Nicene-Constantinopolitan Creed was alone to be used "for the time being, while the Consilium conducts further studies."

On September 16 the Holy Father received Cardinal Lercaro in an audience and discussed the instruction with him. He gave the president of the Consilium a little sheet of paper on which he had set down his own wishes in brief form: "Nicene Creed—Canon in Latin—Communion of the faithful at the Chrism Mass?—Age for confirmation[11]—tabernacle on the altar—formula: Approved."[12]

On the eighteenth of the same month the Secretary of State wrote to the president of the Consilium with reference to the audience, saying that the Pope

> thinks it advisable to proceed quickly to publication of the instruction on carrying out the liturgical Constitution, in order that it may go into effect at the beginning of Lent next year. In undertaking the printing of the instruction, the Consilium should as far as possible take account of the observations offered by the Congregation of Rites, and it should send the pertinent page proofs to that Congregation, so that they may discuss jointly the points still in dispute. Your Eminence will therefore kindly see to it that the final text of the document is submitted in good time to Holy Father for his approval; after that it can be promulgated using the formula proposed by the Consilium.

A meeting with the Congregation of Rites was held in Cardinal Larraona's apartments on September 22, 1964. In addition to Cardinal Larraona himself, E. Dante, F. Antonelli, and A. P. Frutaz represented the Congregation of Rites, while the Consilium was represented by Cardi-

---

11. The Pope introduced a short marginal note on confirmation alongside the remarks of the Congregation of Rites on no. 63 (no. 64 of the final text). What he wrote was: "Preferred age for administration of confirmation."

12. "Formula" refers to the formula of approval that was suggested by the Consilium and became part of the published text.

nal Lercaro, A. Bugnini, and C. Braga. All the remarks originally submitted by the Congregation of Rites were compared with the replies given by the Consilium, and agreement was reached. As a result, slight changes were made in the text. The most notable were the addition in no. 57 of the requirement that vernacular Missals also have the Latin text and the removal of the permission for the faithful to receive communion at the Chrism Mass.

The members of this group were in agreement in asking the Holy Father that the text be immediately printed in a special booklet and distributed to the bishops in the Council hall.

The results of this meeting were sent to the Secretariat of State, along with the page proofs, on October 3, 1964. On October 8 the Cardinal Secretary of State wrote to Cardinal Larraona that "you may immediately proceed to publication of the document, dating it September 26. It is also advisable to give a copy of it to each Council Father" (No. 30455).[13]

5. *Taking Effect*

The Consilium had expected that the new instruction would take effect on the First Sunday of Advent, 1964. The Congregation of Rites insisted, however, that it not take effect until March 7, 1965, the First Sunday of Lent.

Once the instruction was published, various episcopal conferences asked permission to anticipate and begin implementation on the First Sunday of Advent. The Consilium submitted these requests to the Holy Father, who asked the opinion of the Congregation of Rites. On November 23, 1964, the Congregation answered that it was not a good idea, since the texts of the rubrics had not yet been submitted, discussed, and approved by the competent authorities. "If this anticipation is allowed, there will be great confusion, with each episcopal conference following its own judgment." The Pope confirmed this opinion, jotting his comment in the margin of the letter from the Congregation of Rites: "This is how requests are to be answered."

Meanwhile, at an audience on October 1, 1964, the Holy Father arranged with Cardinal Lercaro that the Consilium was to examine and give timely answers to any queries that might arise about the instruction. On October 20, Cardinal Lercaro sent word of this arrangement to the Cardi-

---

13. Sacred Congregation of Rites (Consilium), instruction (first) *Inter Oecumenici* on the orderly carrying out of the Constitution on the Liturgy (September 26, 1964): *AAS* 56 (1964) 877–900; *DOL* 23 nos. 293-391. See P. Bruylants, "Bibliographia circa Constitutionem et Instructionem de sacra Liturgia," *Not* 2 (1966) 142-52 (for the instruction: 150-52).

nal Prefect of the Congregation of Rites and asked that the current practice might be continued of exchanging pertinent documents.

On October 26 Cardinal Larraona replied, assuring Cardinal Lercaro that in keeping with the esteemed arrangement made by the Holy Father, any queries on the instruction that might reach the Congregation of Rites would be speedily sent on to the Consilium. He added: "As for the exchange of documents: this is something I regard as very useful, and I therefore ask that the queries which reach the Consilium be also made known to this Congregation."

II. CONTENTS

The instruction comprises an Introduction that recalls the essential doctrinal principles and explains the nature of the document, and five chapters that follow the order of the chapters in the Constitution on the Liturgy.

1. *General Norms*

The first lengthy chapter of the conciliar document, in which the major themes of a liturgically inspired pastoral practice are set forth, is matched in the instruction by a sizable set of general norms that apply the Constitution to the practical order (Chapter I). The principles have to do with the following matters:

1) *Formation of the clergy and liturgical education of the faithful*. Teachers of liturgy in seminaries must be specially prepared for their work, just as is required in other disciplines. As soon as possible, institutes of pastoral liturgy are to be established. The time allotted to the study of liturgy in the seminaries is to be extended, and the method of teaching is to be adapted as needed. Liturgical celebrations are to be carried out as perfectly as possible; this applies to ceremonies, singing, exercise of the various liturgical functions, the dignified artistic arrangement of sacred places.

Above all else, careful attention is to be paid to the formation of the seminarians in a liturgical spirituality that is centered on the Eucharist. On Sundays there is to be a sung Mass with the participation (sacramental, if possible) of the entire seminary household; on the principal solemnities any priests not involved in the pastoral ministry may concelebrate. It is recommended that on feast days the seminarians take part in the Eucharist celebrated by the bishop in the cathedral. Clerics are to be initiated to a love and understanding of the Divine Office by singing or reciting Lauds in the morning and Vespers and Compline in the evening;

superiors and professors are to join the seminarians in these liturgical actions. This liturgical approach to the spiritual life of the seminarians does not hinder, but on the contrary strengthens and nourishes, the other manifestations of the devotional life. — What is said of seminarians applies, with the needed adaptations, to candidates for the religious life.

In speaking of liturgical education, the instruction has a closely written paragraph on the faithful (no. 19), especially those who are members of Catholic associations and have a special responsibility to share more fully in the Church's life and assist pastors in developing the liturgical life of the parish family.

2) *Competent authority in liturgical matters*. The instruction devotes twelve articles to the tasks, constitution, methods, and decisions to be made by the episcopal conferences in matters liturgical.

3) *Abolition of "classes"*. Individual bishops and episcopal conferences are urged to take timely steps to implement the conciliar decrees regarding the avoidance of preferential treatment of persons in worship.

4) *Simplification of some rites*. Almost all bows to the choir are abolished; the number of incensations is reduced; kissing of the hand and objects is to be omitted.

5) *Celebrations of the word of God*. These are warmly recommended on the eve of feasts and in places where a priest is rarely to be had.

6) *Translations of liturgical texts*. These must be made by individuals who are skilled in the various branches of knowledge involved: theology, liturgy, Sacred Scripture, literature, and music. There is also a statement on the use of vernaculars for immigrants, national churches, and ethnic minorities.

7) Finally, detailed regulations are given for the establishment and operation of national and diocesan *liturgical commissions*.

2. Mass

The Mass is simplified in several of its parts in order to facilitate direct participation. The most important points are these: the celebrant no longer says privately the parts of the Proper that are sung or recited by the congregation or the choir; he may recite or sing the parts of the Ordinary (*Kyrie*, *Gloria*, Creed, and so on) along with the congregation; Psalm 42 is omitted from the prayers at the foot of the altar; the prayer over the gifts and the final doxology of the Canon are said or sung aloud; all may join the celebrant in saying or singing the Our Father in Latin or in the vernacular; the embolism (the prayer "Deliver us, Lord" after the Our Father) may also be said or sung by all. The final gospel is suppressed, as are the prayers that Leo XIII ordered to be recited after Mass.

The readings are proclaimed facing the congregation, either from the lectern or from the edge of the sanctuary; the reading may be done by the celebrant or a competent minister or an appointed reader.

The prayer of the faithful, or universal prayer, is a "priceless jewel" that the liturgical reform has given back to the "holy people" of God; the formularies are those already in use or others established by competent authority.

The episcopal conference of each nation is to determine which parts of the Mass may be said in the vernacular.

3. Sacraments

The instruction allows almost complete use of the vernacular. The rites of some sacraments are partially simplified (for example, baptism and the anointing of the sick). In the administration of confirmation, it is decreed that if the bishop cannot celebrate the Mass, he is to be present already vested for confirmation and is to give the homily; he confers the sacrament using a single sign of the cross after the chrismation. In the sacrament of matrimony, the nuptial blessing is always to be given to the couple, even in the "closed times" and even if the marriage is a second or third for one or both of the spouses; if the sacrament is administered outside Mass, the instruction prescribes that it be made part of a liturgy of the Word.

4. Divine Office

The motu proprio *Sacram Liturgiam* of January 25, 1964, had already dealt with some problems of the Divine Office. The instruction now gives further specifications: secular priests bound to choir may use the permission to omit Prime and to say only one of the Little Hours, except on those days when the choral Office is in fact celebrated; in this case anyone prevented from participating must say privately all the Hours that his colleagues say in common. Those in mission territories, however, may be dispensed from this by the Ordinary of the place ("not by his vicar general or delegate").[14]

The faculty of dispensing or commuting or permitting use of the vernacular is extended to the major superiors of non-exempt clerical institutes or societies of clerics who live together without vows.

---

14. See no. 78c, which was based on decisions of the Congregation for the Propagation of the Faith; Cardinal Agagianian submitted these to the Holy Father on June 16, 1964, and then took them to the Consilium, in order that there might be "a general statement on recitation of the Divine Office by religious in the missions."

Special attention is given to "Little Offices" and to the recitation of the Office by religious men who are not priests and by religious women. If a "Little Office" is to be declared suitable for serving as the prayer of the Church, it must be made up of psalms, readings, hymns, and prayers and pay some degree of attention to the times of the day and to the liturgical year.

5. *Art and Liturgy*

This is the last subject discussed in the instruction. The renewed liturgical awareness of the faithful and their active participation in worship call for a complete revision of the principles governing the functional aspect of the construction of sacred buildings. The instruction limits itself to a few indications, but these provide sure guidelines for architectural programs and suppose a well-defined basic plan for the building.

Thus the main altar should be freestanding so that the celebrant and others can easily walk around it; it should be so situated that it is the focus of the congregation's attention. The sanctuary should be large enough to allow the easy performance of the sacred rites; the celebrant's chair should be in full view of the congregation over which he "presides." Minor altars are to be few in number and located in chapels that are somewhat set apart from the main body of the church. At the discretion of the local Ordinary, cross and candlesticks may be placed near the altar (instead of on it).

The Blessed Sacrament is to have a place of honor apart but need not be reserved on an altar: depending on custom or in special cases (which must be approved in each instance by the bishop), the tabernacle can be located apart from any altar, provided the place is "special and properly adorned."

Each church should have one or two ambos (lecterns). The choir and organ should once again serve as a link between altar and congregation. The baptistery is to be located in a place suitable for communal celebrations. There should be an adequate number of benches or chairs for the faithful, and these should be arranged so that those present can see what is going on and follow the sacred function; on the other hand, no places are to be reserved for private persons. Rectors of churches are to provide properly located and effective loudspeakers.

Finally, "churches and chapels, all sacred furnishings and vestments shall bear the mark of genuine Christian art, including the contemporary" (no. 13c).

B. SECOND INSTRUCTION: *TRES ABHINC ANNOS*

The application of the first instruction, with the resultant changes in the rite of Mass, the sacraments, and the Divine Office, was favorably received. At the same time, however, these very changes caused people to feel more keenly the lack of logic still found in some details and the need of taking steps to eliminate it. The details in question were indeed marginal, but the obvious inconsistency they displayed led individuals to go their own way, at the cost of discipline in matters liturgical.

I. HISTORY

The Consilium took up the problem at its fifth general meeting in April 1965. There were requests that there be but a single collect in a Mass; that collects ordered by the bishop be eliminated and replaced by special intentions in the prayer of the faithful; and that the nuptial blessing of a new wife be given before the "Pax Domini," because it did not make a good impression to have the blessing immediately followed by the prayer "Deliver us, O Lord, from every evil . . . . " Another inconsistency was to have the dismissal before the final blessing, with the result that the celebrant often found himself blessing the backs of the departing faithful. A reorganization of the concluding rites was needed.

In the area of the sacraments, the request considered by the Consilium was that the vernacular be used in the rite of ordination, just as in the other sacramental rites.

These more needful changes, which it was intended should be the object of a decree, were sent on to the Congregation of Rites for examination, and there they remained. Study of them was not begun again until the fall of 1966. Meanwhile other problems were being urgently and insistently brought to the Consilium, such as requests for the vernacular in the Canon of the Mass and the use of cycles of readings in ferial Masses. The projected decree was expanded and submitted to the presidential council of the Consilium in January 1967. By now the Secretariat of State also wanted such a decree,[15] and the draft was sent on to it on February 6, in order that the Consilium might learn "which points it would be preferable not to touch on and which, on the contrary, should be included."

---

15. On January 24, 1967 (No. 88520) the Secretariat of State passed on to the Consilium the requests presented at an audience by Archbishop Louis Levesque, president of the Canadian Episcopal Conference. The Consilium's reply was that these requests were answered in the planned general decree.

On March 8 (No. 92517) the Secretariat of State decided that the decree should be examined at a regular meeting of the Congregation of Rites, which was to be attended by Cardinals Larraona, Lercaro, Giobbe, and Bea, and by the secretary and two subsecretaries of the Congregation.[16] After considering the reasons pro and con, the meeting (held on March 31) came out in favor of the draft.

On April 25 the Pope summoned Father Bugnini and communicated his own observations to him:

1) With regard to the timeliness of publishing the decree, the Pope relied "on the good judgment of the Congregation of Rites and the Consilium."

2) The title "Decree on Some Changes . . . " seemed "rather unfortunate, since it is not sufficiently informative and specific."[17]

3) Call to observance of liturgical norms: the Pope himself in a handwritten note sketched the contents of this reminder:

> Fundamental principle of Church discipline, clearly reasserted by the liturgical Constitution, which decrees etc. Ordinaries, whether of dioceses or of religious Orders, should be alert in seeing to the observance of this norm, which holds such an important place among the decrees of Holy Church; and sacred ministers and all the faithful should willingly conform to it, both for their own edification and salvation and for the sake of spiritual harmony and the good example that every praying community in God's Church should give, being mindful of the Apostle's words: "God is not a God of confusion but of peace" (1 Cor 14:33).[18]

4) The principle at work in the decree should be to allow simplifications and norms that do not introduce any changes into the structural development of the rite.[19]

5) The Pope asked orally that use of the ferial Lectionary be granted not only for Masses of the saints and votive Masses but also for Masses "that have no strictly proper readings of their own."

Once corrections were made in accordance with the wishes of the Holy Father, the text received his approval. On the letter in which the secretary of the Consilium submitted the text he wrote: "I have seen it. Ap-

---

16. The last three mentioned were Archbishop F. Antonelli, secretary; Monsignor Frutaz and Father A. Bugnini, subsecretaries.

17. The title was therefore changed to "Second Instruction on the Carrying Out of the Constitution on the Sacred Liturgy." The new title showed more clearly the continuity with the previous document.

18. The final part of the Introduction was inspired by this note of the Pope.

19. On the basis of this principle, the Pope asked for the elimination of no. 13 of the draft, which placed the rite of the fraction after the greeting of peace and during the singing of the *Agnus Dei*.

proved. May 2, 1967." The next day, May 3, the approval was also officially communicated in a letter from the Secretariat of State (No. 95184). The document was published on May 4, 1967.[20]

II. CONTENTS

The second instruction represented a further step in implementing the reform and preparing the Church to receive the new Missal and new Liturgy of the Hours. It brought a noteworthy simplification especially to the celebration of Mass. Once Mass began to be celebrated facing the congregation and the vernacular was introduced into the Canon, difficulties arose. The introduction to the instruction explains that among the many requests submitted by the bishops, only those were being granted that were based on valid pastoral considerations and were in accord with the definitive decisions that could be expected to result from the ongoing work of reform. Finally, the introduction urges everyone to obey the laws of the Church in matters liturgical.

The regulations in the instruction deal chiefly with the Mass and the Divine Office. I shall briefly describe the most important ones.

1. *Mass*

Greater variety is allowed in the choice of texts: on weekdays, instead of the presidential prayers of the preceding Sunday the prayers of any Sunday in Ordinary Time may be used or those of votive Masses or Masses for various needs and occasions. Outside Lent and third-class days, it is permitted to celebrate the Mass either of the Office of the day or of the commemoration (that is, of one of the saints remembered on that day).

The readings of the ferial Lectionary, if this is adopted by the episcopal conference, can also be used in Masses without a congregation and in the vernacular.

There is but a single collect in a Mass. In some circumstances, especially in ritual Masses, a second may be added but under a single conclusion.

Prayers for special needs and other obligatory prayers (for example, the prayers for rulers that are said in some cathedrals) are to take the form of special intentions in the prayer of the faithful.

---

20. Sacred Congregation of Rites (Consilium), instruction (second) *Tres abhinc annos* on the orderly carrying out of the Constitution on the Liturgy (May 4, 1967): *AAS* 59 (1967) 442–48; *DOL* 39 nos. 445–74.

The instruction then introduces a notable simplification in genuflections, kissings of the altar, and signs of the cross over the gifts. It allows the faithful to receive communion twice on Holy Thursday: at the Chrism Mass and again at the Mass of the Lord's Supper. It introduces either a time of sacred silence or a song of praise after communion. It reorganizes the concluding rites so that the blessing is given just before the dismissal.

Other details have to do with nuptial Masses and Mass celebrated by a blind priest. The latter had in the past been forced almost always to use the same formulary; the instruction provides for his spiritual good by allowing others, even laypersons, to do the readings and recite the entrance, offertory, and communion antiphons.

As for vestments, the maniple becomes optional; concelebrants, except for the principal celebrant, may wear only an alb and stole.

2. *Divine Office*

The instruction sets in motion a simplification intended to promote congregational participation.

When an Office has three nocturns, one alone may be recited (three psalms and three readings).

At Lauds and Vespers with a congregation, three psalms may be recited or sung, together with a lengthier reading from Scripture and the inclusion of a prayer of the faithful.

In the Office and Mass for the Dead, the color used may be violet or some other that fits in with the customs and sensibilities of the various peoples. The responsory *Libera me, Domine* in the rite of farewell over the coffin or grave may be replaced by another from Matins of the Office of the Dead.

3. *Vernacular*

The final section of the instruction represents the end of a long journey. The final barriers to use of the vernacular in the liturgy are broken down, as the vernacular is allowed in the Canon of the Mass, throughout the rite of ordination, and in the readings of even the choral Divine Office.

C. THIRD INSTRUCTION: *LITURGICAE INSTAURATIONES*

The third instruction for carrying out the liturgical Constitution was quite different in content and style.

As the reform advanced, so did the number of reports increase that were sent to the Consilium from all sides on the arbitrary activities of individuals and groups. The result was a sizable file on which the secretary of the Consilium had written: "Abuses to be eliminated." The various documents issued by the Consilium, as well as the letters sent to the presidents of the episcopal conferences and the addresses of the Holy Father, had all included admonitory reminders of discipline and of the need to proceed in an orderly manner. Despite this, there were continual demands, especially from the Curia, which exaggerated the abuses, for a more drastic course of action. The Consilium and subsequently the Congregation for Divine Worship were held responsible for the violations of discipline. There was a call for more resolute action in areas in which arbitrary actions were causing more serious harm.

The Consilium's view was that it ought not to take a stand in a special document until the basic liturgical books had been published.

I. HISTORY

On February 18, 1968, the Consilium wrote as follows to the Secretariat of State:

> We are . . . preparing a short but strongly worded instruction that is to be published at the same time as the *Ordo Missae*. The emphasis in it will be on ten or so areas (all covered in the General Instruction of the Roman Missal) that are subject to the greatest abuses; these abuses will be brought to a firm and unyielding halt (we are thinking, for example, of the kind of bread used, explanations given during the Ordinary of the Mass, the choice of readings and other texts, communion in the hand, servers [female], vestments, and so on).
>
> The instruction is to be sent only to the *bishops* in an effort to get them involved and let them know clearly the mind of the Holy See on what is permissible and what is not. . . .
>
> Thus, while the new rubrics will make legitimate allowance for most pastoral needs, the instruction is meant to set up a needed barrier against arbitrary actions and subjective interpretations; the "good will" of bishops, priests, and faithful will thus be supported and given a solid basis for judgment and action.

A first draft of this instruction, in Italian, was sent to the Congregation for the Doctrine of the Faith on July 12, 1969. The Congregation's reply was dated July 7 (obviously August 7 was meant). It contained these requests:

1. With regard to Mass: when the texts are said to be inviolable, it should be emphasized that all are equally important and that among them the Eucharistic Prayer holds the supreme position.

By reason of its sacredness this prayer is unchangeable not only at the formula of consecration (where there is danger of invalidating the celebration of the Eucharistic sacrifice) but throughout, although sufficiently broad provision has been made to meet the requests for variation that have reached the Holy See from many quarters.

2. A way should be found of exhorting bishops to exercise their ministry not only by "teaching" but by "correcting" as well. "They should also have recourse to penal remedies when there is no other cure for the obstinate rejection of discipline by some priests, whose attitude of insubordination in so sensitive and sacred an area can only cause harm to themselves and souls."

3. In the introduction there should be an emphasis on the connection between liturgy and faith: an attack on the integrity of the one is an attack on the integrity of the other.

There were other remarks on details. The Congregation looked askance on speaking of the Mass as "the Lord's Supper" or "the Memorial of the Lord"—"terms popular in Protestant theology." It thought it advisable to use alternately the several traditional terms—Mass, Eucharistic sacrifice, and others—in order to prevent false interpretations of the sacrificial nature of the action and in order also to retain terms consecrated by use and now dear to the faithful. Instead of "Eucharistic bread," for example, the document should speak of "consecrated species," "sacred species," or "consecrated bread."

The Congregation also asked that the document urge the use of the traditional host for pastoral and practical reasons, and that it lay stronger emphasis on the exclusion of explanations during the Eucharistic liturgy. Furthermore, "there should be a clear condemnation of the tendency exemplified by those who use the liturgical renewal as a means of 'desacralization' or interpret it as a manifestation of the 'secularization' of the world."

In order to facilitate acceptance of the regulations for vestments at Mass, the draft referred to the granting of the use of "a chasuble-alb." But neither did this please the Congregation.[21]

The above lengthy discussion of the Congregation's reply makes it clear that the Consilium had no great freedom of movement. A calm, well-documented presentation of the various points, in which the Church's discipline would be reasserted in language that might facilitate acceptance of it, was regarded as too feeble.

---

21. The concession was given later on (May 1, 1971); see *DOL* 553 nos. 4538-41.

On September 6 the schema was submitted to the Holy Father. In his reply of November 8 (No. 148620), he picked out three other points: The Holy Father

> expressed his view that, contrary to what is said in no. 2a, no type of dialogue should be introduced into the homily; as for the bread to be used in the Mass, it would be better to retain the small hosts that are now used everywhere. . . . With reference to no. 12, the Supreme Pontiff observed that it is now time to put an end, if possible, to experiments. He gave his approval of everything else.[22]

The text was corrected once again and . . . set aside until publication of the Missal.

On May 16, 1970, a new version of the document was submitted to the Holy Father. The previous schema had been corrected as desired, and there were three additions: a paragraph on sacred song was introduced (no. 3c); in no. 3e, on the choice of Scripture readings at Masses for special groups, a clause was added: "as long as they come from an authorized Lectionary"; no. 12, on experiments, was revised in accordance with the mind of the Pope, and no. 13, on the anonymity of liturgical texts, was added.[23]

---

22. The Pope thus made it impossible to include some innovations in the instruction, along with the calls for a return to discipline. In its published version, no. 2a, on the homily, reads: "The congregation is to refrain from comments, attempts at dialogue, or anything similar." The text originally proposed read as follows:

> When the preparation, abilities, and spiritual benefit of the participants make it advisable, a form of dialogue can at times be used in the homily, *provided* that this dialogue be always under the control of the priest. He may therefore invite some of those present to offer some very brief reflections. But he must see to it:
> 1) that these interventions, when thought necessary, are prepared in advance;
> 2) that they are connected with the word of God that has been heard or with the homily or with the liturgy of the day;
> 3) that the several interventions, including the homily itself, occupy only a reasonable amount of time and not be dragged out, for this would undermine the balance of the celebration as a whole;
> 4) that he himself recapitulates what has been said and brings the dialogue to an end by connecting it with the spirit of the liturgical celebration.

23. The Holy Father gave his approval on May 20, 1970 (No. 161.106). On May 29 the Secretary of State transmitted to the Consilium still further observations of the SCDF. It was one of these that led to an addition in no. 13, paragraph 2: after the statement that liturgical prayer must appear to be "the work of the whole people of God," the phrase "in all their orders and ministries" was added in order that the principle set down in GIRM 58, which is here cited, may be correctly understood. The same Congregation asked for a statement (in no. 6d) that the priest or other qualified person must distribute communion and that the practice of the communicant taking the host directly from the ciborium is forbidden. The Congregation was asked to suggest a formulation; it replied on June 17, sug-

Other corrections were introduced after the publication of the instructions *Memoriale Domini,* on the manner of distributing communion, and *Sacramentali Communione,* on extension of the permission to distribute communion under two kinds.[24]

On October 2, 1970 (No. 169084) the Holy Father gave final approval for the printing of the document. The instruction was published by the Congregation for Divine Worship on September 5, 1970.[25]

The instruction was not well received. It was to be expected, of course, that a document urging a return to discipline would not be warmly greeted. In this case, however, the reactions were stronger than anticipated. The meaning of the document was distorted, and the values it urged were not understood. The general interpretation was that it represented a "brake" on reform and a return to the preconciliar situation, and that in it Rome was showing its determination "to do away with and repress all initiative."[26] This was a difficult time.[27]

The points reaffirmed in the instruction were certainly valid and important; the position taken was balanced and was continued in later years. The Congregation for Divine Worship therefore defended the document, referred to it, and insisted that the episcopal conferences, liturgical commissions, and liturgical periodicals make it known and explain it properly.

It must also be admitted, however, that the document would have had a better reception if the style had been different (except in the introduction): less harsh, more persuasive, more expansive in giving the reasons for admonitions, and also a little more open on certain points. In addition, it would have been more effective. But, as we saw above, this more relaxed approach was not possible. On the other hand, even though it

gesting the statement that in the absence of another priest, deacon, or acolyte, "the celebrant is to follow the rite described in GIRM 245."

24. The list of ministers of communion included acolytes. This elicited concern, but the text was left unchanged.

25. Sacred Congregation for Divine Worship, instruction (third) *Liturgicae instaurationes* on the orderly carrying out of the Constitution on the Liturgy (September 5, 1970): *AAS* 62 (1970) 692–704; *DOL* 52 nos. 509-31. See *Not* 7 (1971) 9–26; *EL* 84 (1970) 460–68.

26. See G. P., "La terza Istruzione mortifica l'iniziativa," *Not* 7 (1971) 85–88. The same volume of *Notitiae* published a number of articles, reactions, and explanations of the instruction: S. Maggiolini, "Una *Instructio* e il suo sottofondo teologico," 27–31; A. Iniesta, "En torno a la tercera Instrucción," 114–17; G. Oury, O.S.B., "Le Missel et la IIIe Instruction," 247–53; G. P., "La Musica sacra nella *Instructio tertia*," 294–98.

27. A further reason for discontent and surprise was the fact that, unlike the other documents, this one had not passed through the usual course of "readings" by experts, relators, and members. Few persons had been consulted, and therefore few were kept abreast of the developing instruction. But this was in fact a different kind of document, one that involved the responsibility of the central authority.

met with a somewhat humiliating reception, the document had to be published; it was necessary to say something about the points raised, and the pressures being brought to bear from within the Curia and from outside were many, strong, and justified.

II. Contents

The most positive part of the instruction is the introduction. Here the document reminds the readers of the reason for its existence, the work of reform already accomplished, the resistances met with, and the disordered efforts at progress. It then appeals to the bishops to meet their responsibilities, reminding them of their duty to direct, stimulate, discipline, and at times reprove, while always showing, patiently and by example, the proper way of implementing the liturgical renewal. If they act in this way, they will ensure that "the whole Body of the Church may be able to move ahead single-mindedly and with the unity of charity in the diocese, the nation, and the entire world. Such efforts of the bishops are the more necessary and urgent because the link between liturgy and faith is so close that service to the one redounds to the other."

The liturgical commissions are similarly exhorted. Their special task is to acquire accurate information on the religious and social situation and the spiritual needs of their region and to suggest how these needs may be met with the help of the possibilities available in the reformed liturgical books. In order to help the bishops and the commissions in this work of appraising the local situation and spirit and of understanding the demands of the liturgy, the instruction recalls and explains certain principles.

1. *Value of the liturgical signs* that find expression in rites and prayers, gestures and words. These signs point to and reveal the mystery. In accordance with the norms set down in the liturgical Constitution, the reform has brought about a certain simplification, a reduction in superfluous elements. It is not possible to go further in this direction. Even though an effort has been made to make the signs transparent and easily understandable, the mystery always remains. Some signs and gestures belonging to the world of the Bible will always need explanation if they are to be understood. Therefore:

a) Rites and signs may not be changed on the grounds that they are not understood. Instructors must undertake to explain them, and if one or the other causes difficulty in a particular culture, the episcopal conference will see to timely adaptations. It is not permitted to individuals to do this on their own.

b) The structure of the various celebrations must be respected, not because the rubrics prescribe it but for ecclesial reasons. This structure is the voice of the praying Church. A priest is a minister of the Church and therefore can carry out his ministry only in communion with and dependence on the hierarchy and as a service to God and his brothers and sisters. Private refashioning of the liturgy is an insult to the dignity of the faithful and opens the way to individualism. A priest who travels this path will not fulfill his cultic role as "faithful steward of the mysteries of God."

2. *Liturgy of the Word*. Special care must be given to this, for it is the first liturgical sign. In it God speaks to his people. It is therefore not permitted to replace God's word with readings from other books, whether sacred or secular, whether ancient or modern. The homilist is to be the priest. The liturgy of the Word and the Eucharistic liturgy form a single act of worship. Therefore it is not permitted to separate them and celebrate them at different times and in different places.

3. *Respect for liturgical texts* composed by the Church. Reference is made to the many possibilities offered, especially in the Mass, by antiphons and prayers, readings and songs. The document also mentions the instructions that the celebrant may give at the beginning of Mass, before the readings, before the preface, and before the dismissal. These are to be short, to the point, and prepared; they are not to be given during the Eucharistic Prayer.

Congregational liturgical song is to be promoted in every possible way. In accordance with the norms set down in the instruction on sacred music, the episcopal conferences can decide on special collections of songs to be used in celebrations; music and text must in all cases be dignified and adapted to the celebration. Similar determinations are to be made by the episcopal conferences with regard to the musical instruments used, so that the dignity and sanctity of the celebration and the sacred place will be safeguarded. *Liturgicae instaurationes* limits itself to urging that these instruments foster devotion, be limited in number, suited to the region and the culture of the congregation, and not too loud.

---

28. This was not an instruction on music and sacred song. Such an instruction had already been published and is referred to here as the basic document. The text of *Liturgicae instaurationes* was written with great caution, for the editors knew they were moving through a minefield. And in fact musicians immediately split into two camps. Some were quite satisfied; see, for example, P. Ernetti in *Bollettino Ceciliano* 65 (1970) 263: "We musicians should be really grateful to the lawgiver and thank him for giving us the essence and a strong and vigorous synthesis of an entire lengthy history of legislation concerning musical genres and instruments." Others, however, thought the instruction "weak" and "ambiguous" and open to "arbitrary interpretations"; thus R. B. Lenaerts in *Musicae Sacrae Ministerium* 8 (1970) 24–26. This was an unjust and sectarian judgment; see *Not* 7 (1971) 294–98. Yet this was the point that all the conservative musicians made with irritating insistence in the follow-

4. *Eucharistic Prayer*. This is the priest's prayer and may not be said aloud, in whole or in part, by others.

5. The *bread* for the celebration of the Eucharist must be wheaten and unleavened and baked in the traditional shape. The need for greater authenticity should be focused on the color, taste, and thickness of the bread rather than on its shape. Bakers of the bread are urged to ensure that it can be broken and divided and eaten without offending the sensibilities of the faithful.

6. *The manner of distributing communion; communion under two kinds*. The instruction refers the reader to the documents dealing with these matters; it adds that when communion from the cup is allowed, there is always to be a minister and the chalice is not to be passed from one communicant to another. Another reminder has to do with celebrations without a priest, at which God's word is proclaimed and communion is distributed.

7. *Liturgical duties carried out by women*. Women are not allowed to serve the priest directly at the altar. They may, on the other hand, proclaim the readings (except for the gospel), announce the intentions for the prayer of the faithful, direct the singing, play the organ and other instruments, read the commentaries, and attend to other functions in service of the congregation.[29]

8. *Sacred furnishings*. It is urged that these never be commonplace but noble, dignified, and artistic. Chalices and patens should be consecrated by the bishops, who will judge their fitness. It is not permitted, even for concelebrants, to celebrate in street clothes or with only a stole over cowl or cassock.[30] It is for the conferences to set down detailed regulations for the material and shape of vestments and of furnishings generally.

---

ing years; they completely forgot the instruction on sacred music to which *Liturgicae instaurationes* referred them for a complete and organic discussion of the subject.

29. Here again, contrary to the accusations leveled at the document, doors were not closed but rather opened. The traditional discipline of the Church governing service at the altar was indeed reaffirmed, but limitations on proclamation of the word of God were removed, and this only a few years after the GIRM. Women were no longer to read "outside the sanctuary" but from the place where they could be easily heard, that is, the ambo or lectern.

30. This is another point on which the Roman authorities always insisted. Tendencies elsewhere to celebrate without vestments or with vestments reduced to an almost irrelevant minimum were numerous and justified by various excuses. The Holy See never yielded in this matter. In order to handle the difficulties and suppress attempted abuses, it subsequently permitted the "chasuble without an alb" or, more properly, the "chasuble-alb." If this later concession had been made in the present document, as was planned, everything would have seemed more normal, understandable, and acceptable.

9. *Place of celebration.* As a rule the celebration must be held in a sacred place. In case of necessity some other place may be selected, provided it is worthy and excluding, if possible, dining rooms and refectories.

10. Bishops are urged once again to see to a fixed arrangement of the *sanctuary*. Temporary solutions that are unsuitable or in bad taste are becoming permanent (temporary altars knocked together; two altars, one near the other). Liturgical commissions must step in here.

11. *Liturgical translations.* The liturgical books are to be translated in their entirety. If a conference thinks it appropriate to add texts of its own, it should set these off by means of typographical devices. Such texts must be prepared with the great care and with the aid of theologians, Scripture scholars, and men of letters (whose names are to remain unknown). Liturgical books are the property of the entire ecclesial community. Legal ownership belongs to the episcopal conference.

12. *Experiments and adaptations.* The press laid great emphasis on this number of the instruction, interpreting it as putting "an end to all experimentation." In fact, the instruction was simply bringing clarifications. It said once more that the Holy See alone gives permission, in writing, for experiments. The point here was to answer those who claimed to have special permission to experiment. In addition, the instruction says that since the Roman Missal has now been published, no further experimentation with the Mass is permitted—a logical prohibition. On the other hand, the instruction speaks of adaptations possibly being needed and explains the procedure to be followed.

The instruction ends with a further exhortation to the unity which is required in the ecclesial organism and which gives this organism its effectiveness and authenticity. The liturgical reform sheds clearer light on the prayer of the Church as this flows from her age-old tradition, and presents it to the world as the work of the whole people of God. By their fidelity to tradition and their efforts to meet the needs of our age, pastors will prepare for "that flowering spring expected from this liturgical reform" (no. 13). If they are to do this, they must avoid everything secular and arbitrary that would seriously compromise the liturgical renewal.

Instruction on Worship of the Eucharistic Mystery

As a rule, encyclicals on matters of worship have been echoed in instructions or decrees of the competent Roman agencies, which endeavor thus to translate the doctrinal principles in the papal documents into practical norms.

Thus the encyclical *Mysterium fidei* of Paul VI (September 3, 1965)[1] was followed by an instruction on worship of the Eucharistic mystery, although the latter did not in fact depend on the encyclical for its origin.[2]

I. HISTORY

On May 12, 1965, Cardinal Lercaro sent the Pope a memorandum in which he said that as the liturgical renewal was progressing, practical difficulties regarding worship of the Eucharist were coming to light; the reason for this was that many rubrical and juridical norms were no longer in harmony with the new organization of the rites. Another source of concern was activities that gave the impression of a lessening in respect for the real presence of the Lord in the Eucharist. Therefore, said the

---

1. See *AAS* 57 (1965) 753–74; *DOL* 176 nos. 1145-1220.
2. The encyclical was published at a time when the first draft of the instruction was already being prepared; the drafters knew nothing about the encyclical. The unheralded publication of the latter was in fact rather disturbing to the drafters. Some of them read into it an advance determination of the line the instruction would have to take; others thought that the task entrusted to the Consilium was at an end. The fact was, however, that the encyclical and the instruction were two different undertakings that arose out of the same concerns; one was in the doctrinal field, the other was concerned primarily with the consequences and practical applications of doctrine.

Cardinal, "it seems a good time for the Consilium to draft an instruction that will harmonize in a suitable way the demands of the liturgical renewal and the demands of Eucharistic worship as seen in the light of the Church's authentic tradition."

The Pope told the Cardinal orally to "draw up a detailed outline of the liturgical points to be brought out." Meanwhile he sounded out the Holy Office, which answered that "such an instruction would seem especially useful at this time. As the Holy Office too is aware, the application of the Constitution on the Sacred Liturgy has given rise in various quarters to abuses that suggest the existence of real doctrinal deviations."[3]

Four consultors of the Consilium were charged with preparing a basic draft.[4] The first schema was ready on October 15, 1965, and was sent for study to about fifty consultors and experts on the subject. The same procedure was followed for four more of the eleven schemas that were produced.[5]

On August 5, 1966, the sixth schema was submitted to the relators, who discussed it at their meeting on September 21–22 of that year. Their remarks touched on almost all of the sixty-two numbers in the draft. The relators also suggested new points that had not been considered; they asked that something be said about the bread used in the Eucharist, to prevent or avoid unworthy ways of preparing it, and about television and radio broadcasts of the Mass, to which the Constitution on the Liturgy itself refers, if only to say that such broadcasts must be exemplary and under the supervision of the episcopal conferences.

The relators conducted a thoroughgoing discussion of the subject. With regard to the structure of the document, there was a lively debate over

---

3. Letter of June 16, 1965, sent on to the Consilium by the Secretariat of State on July 2, 1965.

4. Fathers Vagaggini and J. Tillard were put in charge of the doctrinal section, and S. Famoso of the juridical and rubrical applications. Father Vagaggini was the main author of the document.

5. Here is the series of schemas:

October 15, 1965: Schema 115: *De cultu eucharistico.*
November 16, 1965: Schema 123: *De cultu eucharistico* 2.
March 21, 1966: Schema 147bis: *De cultu eucharistico* 3.
April 30, 1966: Schema 159: *De cultu eucharistico* 4.
June 10, 1966: Schema 172: *De mysterio eucharistico* 6.
September 29, 1966: Schema 190: *De mysterio eucharistico* 7.
October 28, 1966: Schema 197: *De mysterio eucharistico* 8.
October 28, 1966: Schema 197: *De mysterio eucharistico* 8A.
February 7, 1967: Schema 205: *De mysterio eucharistico* 9.
February 23, 1967: Schema 208: *De mysterio eucharistico* 10.
March 23, 1967: Schema 217: *De mysterio eucharistico* 11.

whether the doctrinal summary at the beginning was advisable. The point was made that if some doctrinal principles are included and others not, this will cause difficulty; on the other hand, a complete synthesis of Eucharistic teaching takes time and is not one of the purposes envisaged for an instruction. In the end, all agreed on including the essential points of a catechesis on the Eucharist in the light of more recent documents, especially those of the Council.

The seventh schema, which included the corrections of the relators, was submitted to the Fathers of the Consilium at their seventh general meeting (October 1966). They took it for granted that the document should contain a broad synthesis of the sure principles of Eucharistic theology as found in the Church's magisterium and especially in the encyclicals *Mediator Dei* and *Mysterium fidei* and the documents of Vatican II.[6] What these documents chiefly bring out is the single vision that embraces all aspects of the Eucharist: sacrament, sacrifice, and real presence.

Under the guidance of the eloquent Father Vagaggini with his extensive theological and liturgical background, the members of the Consilium discussed all numbers of the instruction at length. The vote taken on the schema as a whole was unanimous and in the form of an enthusiastic show of hands. All the Fathers but one approved it and further expressed their mind in votes on two specific points: the daily celebration of Mass, and songs and prayers in honor of Our Lady and the saints during exposition of the Blessed Sacrament.[7]

Examination by the Curia

On October 31 the schema was sent to the Holy Father and, at the same time, to the members and consultors of the Consilium, who were to see to it that proper account had been taken of their observations in the correction of the text. The Holy Father sent some remarks on the text to Father Ciappi; he wrote that he did not think it appropriate to celebrate Mass "in a sick person's bedroom" when viaticum was given, and he ordered that the draft of the instruction be studied by the Congregation for the Doctrine of the Faith and the Congregation of Rites.[8]

---

6. See J. Lécuyer, "Concilii Vaticani II textus eucharistici," *Not* 2 (1966) 232–39.

7. See below, p. 858, n. 22.

8. Father's Ciappi's observations, which were supported by Cardinal A. Cicognani, Secretary of State, had to do with improvements in various phrasings but were chiefly concerned with the need of showing proper honor to the tabernacle. He wrote: "As can already be seen in many new churches (especially outside Italy), too radical an application of the liturgical Constitution can lead: (1) to an almost complete disappearance of sacred images, leaving

The remarks of these two agencies were considered at a joint meeting of the Congregation for the Doctrine of the Faith, the Congregation of Rites, and the Consilium[9] on January 19, January 31, and February 3, 1967.[10]

The definitive text was then submitted to the Pope on March 20, 1967. He replied on March 28 with a few "minor observations."[11] At the same time he asked in a note: "Should not the Congregation for the Sacraments be consulted? informed?" The text was therefore sent to this Congregation as well (April 4, 1967).

On April 14 the Secretariat of State informed the Consilium of some observations "which His Eminence Cardinal Larraona had sent to the Holy Father," and it enclosed a sheet with further handwritten observations of the Pope.[12]

On April 22 the Consilium sent the final text, corrected on the basis of all the remarks received, together with an explanation of its acceptance or rejection of the suggestions received from the Congregation of the

---

only the altar-table, the Bible, the crucifix, and, off in a corner (or in a wall), the Blessed Sacrament; (2) to a reduction in the number of faithful attending weekday Masses, because there are fewer Masses now that all priests are being urged to concelebrate; (3) to a reduction in the number of communions because of the many priests' objections to distributing communion outside Mass; (4) to a reduction in the number of people who adore the Blessed Sacrament, this being relegated to a corner and to a tabernacle that is not made attractive and may be hardly visible."

9. The SCDF had decided on this meeting in its reply of January 3, 1967. Its appointed delegates were Fathers A. Trapé and M. R. Gagnebet.

10. Archbishop Pietro Parente presided at these meetings. After them the SCDF gave its *nihil obstat* on February 16, 1967. The SCR conducted its own new study at its meeting of March 10, 1967. The corrections it called for were limited to making some expressions more precise. The only two more important changes were: the prescription that the words of consecration should be typographically distinct from the running text, and the recommendation that pastors exhort the Christian people to frequent communion (nos. 21b and 27).

11. The Pope's remarks had to do with various points in the instruction, which were then corrected; for example, no. 3e and no. 17, in which the celebration of marriage was added to the ceremonies to be avoided while another Sunday Mass was going on; no. 26, in which the recommendation that religious women take part in the parish Mass was extended to "small, non-clerical, religious communities." At the Pope's suggestion, no. 15 was canceled: it offered the possibility of a dispensation from the obligation of Sunday Mass for previously uninstructed adults who were preparing for first communion. The number read: "In certain circumstances, when baptized persons lacking adequate Christian instruction are being prepared for first communion, the territorial ecclesiastical authority may ask the Apostolic See for permission to suspend temporarily the obligation of Mass attendance for such persons, so that they may be better prepared for the Mass by means of suitable celebrations of the word of God." The Pope had remarked: "Is it really advisable to suggest in this way the expediency of suspending the obligation of Mass attendance? I think not."

12. A reply to these preceding "minor observations" was submitted on April 5, 1967.

Sacraments[13] or contained in the memorandum of Cardinal Larraona.[14]

On May 2 the Holy Father gave his final approval in a handwritten note that read:

May 2, 1967

—We have seen the new corrected and altered text;

—We have also seen the observations of the Congregation for the Sacraments and Cardinal Larraona, and the replies of the Consilium to them;

—We give our approval to the "Instruction on Worship of the Eucharistic Mystery," which has been submitted, by letter No. 618/67, on April 21, 1967. P.

The instruction was published by the Congregation of Rites on May 25, 1967.[15]

II. CONTENTS

The instruction, which is now the basic document on the regulation of worship of the Eucharist in accordance with the spirit of conciliar teaching on the Eucharist and of the liturgical reform, contains sixty-seven numbers and is divided into an Introduction and three parts.

The Introduction explains that the instruction is a practical document. For this reason not all aspects of the theology of the Eucharistic mystery have been taken into consideration but only those that influence, or are of interest to, the practical discussion that follows. Furthermore, the principles that are explicitly stated are not explained fully but only to the extent that they are sources from which practical norms flow. In other words, the doctrinal part is in the service of the normative.

The principle that unifies and inspires the entire document—a principle that is itself the fruit of theological reflection fostered by the liturgi-

---

13. The further observations reached the Consilium on April 14, along with some "Short notes."

14. The Cardinal's memorandum was based on an earlier schema; many of his remarks were therefore no longer relevant, since the text had already been corrected. He asked, among other things, that "in order to protect orthodox belief in the real presence, reception of communion while standing be allowed only as an exception" and that recitation of the Canon aloud be not permitted, since this would be the first step to the introduction of the vernacular into the Canon. These ideas were unacceptable. On the other hand, because of the Cardinal's observations the explanation of the place of concelebration in the life of priests and communities of priests (no. 47) was expanded in order to bring out more clearly the freedom of individuals to celebrate alone and the necessity of providing for pastoral needs.

15. SRC, instruction *Eucharisticum mysterium* on worship of the Eucharist (May 25, 1967): *AAS* 59 (1967) 539-73; *DOL* 179 nos. 1230-96. See the commentary of J. Tillard on the Introduction and Part I, *Not* 4 (1968) 261-70; of J. Lécuyer on Part II, 271-80; and of S. Famoso on Part III, 280-88.

cal renewal—is set down in no. 3e: "The celebration of the eucharist in the sacrifice of the Mass is truly the origin and the purpose of the worship that is shown to the eucharist outside Mass."

Furthermore, the Eucharistic mystery must be seen in all fullness: it is "at once and inseparably" the *sacrifice* of Christ and the Church, the *memorial* of the death and resurrection of the Lord, who said, "Do this in memory of me," and a *sacred banquet* at which, through communion in the body and blood of the Lord, the people of God share in the benefits of the paschal sacrifice, renew the covenant with God in the blood of Christ, and are given a foretaste of the blessings of the future kingdom (no. 3a).

Despite the limits it sets for itself, the doctrinal synthesis in *Eucharisticum mysterium* is truly one that can ground and direct understanding of the Eucharistic mystery as this finds expression in the celebration of Mass and in the forms of Eucharistic worship. The instruction has been universally appreciated, studied, and taken as the basis for catechetical instruction as well as for a full understanding of the Eucharistic mystery.

1. Part I: Pastoral Principles

Just as no. 3 of the introduction summarizes the theological principles regarding the sacrifice of the Mass, so Part I of the document expounds the principles of a pastoral kind that must be kept in mind when instructing the people about the Eucharistic mystery.

These principles may be briefly stated as follows:

1. The Eucharistic mystery is the center of the life of the Church, both universal and local. It is the culmination of God's action in sanctifying the world in Christ and of the worship that human beings offer to Christ and through him to the Father in the Holy Spirit.

2. The Mass, celebrated according to the Lord's will, "signifies and brings about the unity of all who believe in him"; the grace that it bestows tends to this concrete realization of unity.

3. The faithful should be given timely instruction on the principal ways in which Christ is present to his Church in liturgical celebrations; they should be instructed especially on the most important type of presence—his presence in the Eucharistic mystery.

4. The entire Mass is the supreme sacred action; instruction should therefore always lay great emphasis on the interdependence that exists between liturgy of the Word and Eucharistic liturgy.

Other points in the instruction to be given concern: the priesthood of the faithful and the ministerial priesthood; the place due the faithful in active participation in the Mass; the effects of the celebration on Christian life; the instruction to be given children in preparation for their first communion.

2. Part II: Celebration of the Memorial of the Lord

The instruction now turns to the Eucharistic sacrifice; here, and in the third part, are to be found the most interesting and new practical guidelines. I shall once again single out the most important points in summary fashion.

1. *Church as people of God and church as building.* The celebration of the Eucharist requires both of these elements.

The Church-as-people is the community of believers that is here and now united around the altar. They must experience themselves as a community. A mere assemblage of the faithful is not enough; they must experience themselves as one in common prayer and song. In liturgical celebrations (says no. 17) any division or scattering of the community must be avoided; for this reason two liturgical celebrations may not be conducted at the same time in the same church, for this would indeed distract and divide the congregation. Therefore, when Mass is celebrated with a congregation, especially on feast days, several Masses may not be celebrated at the same time, nor a Mass and a choral Office, nor may other sacraments (baptism, for example, or marriage) be administered while Mass is being celebrated, nor may an independent sermon be preached while Mass is going on.

Fine guidelines are also given for the church-as-building (temple), that is, the sacred place in which Eucharistic worship is practiced. "The becoming arrangement of the place of worship contributes much to a right celebration and to the active participation of the faithful" (no. 24).

2. *Celebration of the Eucharist on Sundays, feasts, and weekdays.* The instruction urges obedience to the precept that Sunday be kept holy, especially by participation in the Eucharist by the entire ecclesial community around its bishop in the cathedral or its local pastor in the parish church. Furthermore, in order to achieve an integral celebration of Sunday, "all measures are to be encouraged that are designed to make Sunday 'a day of joy and freedom from work'" (no. 25).

Three important points are to be emphasized with regard to the parochial celebration of the Eucharist:

a) celebrations taking place in other churches within the parish boundaries are to be coordinated with those in the parish church; this is a question of good order but also of communion;

b) small religious communities, whether of men or of women, are invited to take part in the parochial celebrations on Sunday;

c) rectors of churches are urged not to multiply the number of Masses in the parish at the expense of truly effective pastoral action.

In dealing with Sunday and festal Masses, the instruction faces and resolves another problem that the ever-growing international tourist movement has made urgently topical: that of Mass on Saturday evening or the vigils of great feasts as a way of satisfying the Sunday obligation. Where these evening Masses are allowed, the Mass of the Sunday is celebrated with everything proper to it, such as the homily, prayer of the faithful, color of the vestments, and so on. The faithful can receive communion at these evening Masses even if they have already received that morning.[16]

3. *Mass at meetings.* Mass in this setting should be seen as the supreme activity, the culminating point and point of convergence. This ought to be clear even externally from the order of the day. All this is simply an application of the principle that the Eucharist is the center of the entire life of the Church and each Christian.

4. *Celebration of Mass in the life of priest and bishop.* The daily celebration of Mass is strongly urged, because even if no congregation is present, the Mass retains its value and is offered for the salvation of the entire world.[17] Priests living in community should take part in the celebration of Mass in the way proper to them (*more sacerdotali*), that is, by concelebrating. This is the form of Eucharistic celebration proper to communities of priests. It is therefore favored, provided that each person is left free and that the obligation of providing for the needs of the faithful is met. Superiors of religious or clerical communities are urged to make concelebration easily available and to ensure its worthy accomplishment. Concelebration manifests the brotherhood that exists among priests and their unity in a single priesthood and a single sacrifice.

5. *Communion of the faithful.* As a rule this should take place during Mass. In special cases communion can be administered outside Mass; there should be a short liturgy of the Word in these cases. It is recom-

---

16. This point met with resistance within the Consilium. Some were afraid that the extension of this concession would mean danger of losing the meaning of Sunday. Various Fathers would therefore have preferred to handle the situation by means of special indults. But the situation itself was widespread, and the majority preferred to address it once and for all.

17. This article (no. 44) was voted on by the Consilium. It originally included a sentence that said: "This recommendation is not to be understood to mean that each priest . . . is obliged." The members were equally divided on whether this sentence should be included, and it was therefore removed; no. 44 ended up being almost entirely a citation from the conciliar Decree *Presbyterorum ordinis* on the ministry and life of priests, no. 13.

mended that there be a period of thanksgiving and silent prayer after communion, and that the Eucharist be taken to the sick and to those at a distance who cannot join the community; the value of viaticum is emphasized. The instruction also includes an extension of the permission to receive communion under both kinds, and it neatly resolves a little problem that had been debated for some years: How should the faithful receive—standing or kneeling? The custom of the Church, says the instruction (no. 34a), allows both practices. Persons should therefore follow the norms that may be laid down by the episcopal conferences. The important thing is that communion be truly a sign of brotherly and sisterly union among all who are invited to the Lord's table.

3. *Part III: Worship of the Eucharist Outside Mass*

The basic principle governing worship of the Eucharist outside Mass is this: The first and original purpose of reserving the sacred species is the communion of the sick, especially in the form of viaticum; secondary purposes are the distribution of communion to the faithful who have not been able to take part in the Mass, and adoration. Since Christ is really present, adoration and all the other forms of Eucharistic devotion are completely legitimate.

1. *Tabernacle.* The Eucharist is to be reserved in only one place in the church. There is therefore to be but a single tabernacle, and it is to be solid, secure, and located in a properly decorated place. The instruction says that, particularly in much-frequented churches, this place is preferably a special chapel that can also be used for marriages, funerals, and Masses during the week. In any case, it should be a place that fosters recollection and prayer.[18] The tabernacle can be placed on an altar or elsewhere. The instruction advises, however, that it not be on an altar at which Mass is regularly celebrated; this is in order that the various modes of Christ's presence may be shown forth successively in the celebration: in the minister, in the word, and, finally, in an unparalleled way in the Eucharistic species.

2. *Prayer in the presence of the Blessed Sacrament.* This kind of prayer leads to familiarity with Christ and to the opening of the person's heart to him. It also leads the person to realize that the presence of Christ in the Blessed Sacrament is the fruit of the sacrifice and leads to communion. As a re-

---

18. An excellent summary of the legislation and norms regulating the construction and location of the tabernacle is to be found in *Not* 8 (1972) 171–77, which reports on a directory published by the Irish Episcopal Conference; see also *ibid.* 7 (1971) 414–15.

sult, the person is inspired to self-surrender and to a close communion of heart with the dead and risen Lord.[19]

3. *Devotions and liturgical actions* should not be intermingled. Attention should be paid in particular to the conciliar decree that devotions be in harmony with the liturgy and the outlook proper to each liturgical season and that they educate Christians to understand and live the liturgy. Among the devotional practices that focus on the Eucharist, the instruction touches on the following:

a) *Eucharistic processions:* The instruction speaks only of those in the streets, not those that remain within the church.[20] Such processions may be useful, especially on the Solemnity of Corpus Christi, as a means of reviving faith and devotion. But they must be performed with dignity and decorum and without any danger of irreverence toward the Blessed Sacrament.

b) *Exposition of the Blessed Sacrament.* The more solemn form, which goes on for several days, can be used at moments and hours when participation of the faithful can be anticipated. Protracted exposition that no one or only a few people attend is meaningless.[21] Protracted exposition can be ordered by the bishop for special needs. In ordinary circumstances exposition is to be for only a short period. In this whole area the instruction introduces norms that have brought radical changes in age-old customs.

---

19. The expression "prayer in the presence of the Blessed Sacrament" replaced the old devotional phrase "visit to the Blessed Sacrament." To some of the consultors the old phrase still conveyed the idea of "going on pilgrimage to the Lord," but to the majority it suggested acts of courtesy and of consolation of the "divine prisoner"—ideas that have nothing to do with the doctrine of the real presence. "Prayer" therefore seemed the more appropriate term in the context.

20. The text of no. 59 originally contained an explicit prohibition of processions inside the church. But after the other curial agencies had studied the text, the prohibition was removed in consideration of the quite different situations in various countries. In some countries the civil authorities do not permit Catholics to engage in any kind of religious display outside their churches.

21. The so-called "Clementine Instruction on the Forty Hours" was hereby revoked. The pious practice of the "Forty Hours," which was so popular in the past, retains its value but needs to be updated in its form. It is not fitting to have continual exposition if there are not a sufficient number of adorers; the exposition can therefore be interrupted. The instruction also prohibits the celebration of Mass in the presence of the solemnly exposed sacrament; for this reason too, then, exposition must be interrupted. For a new approach to the Forty Hours in the diocese of Rome, see *Not* 6 (1970) 257-62.

The situation is different in communities whose vocation it is to devote themselves to perpetual adoration; see *Not* 4 (1968) 135, and also what was said above, p. 662, n. 76, in connection with the document on Holy Communion and Worship of the Eucharist Outside Mass.

Exposition solely for the purpose of having Benediction of the Blessed Sacrament is not meaningful; exposition becomes meaningful if the Benediction comes only at the end of a period of devotions. For this reason, short-term exposition must always be a time devoted to silent prayer, reading and meditating on the word of God, and communal intercession. Everything should be so organized that the faithful are intent upon Christ the Lord.[22]

c) *Eucharistic congresses.* All the manifestations organized on the occasion of a Eucharistic congress should be centered on the Mass and be a time for adoration, prayer, and meditation on the Eucharistic mystery in all its facets.

---

22. No. 62 of the instruction says that during exposition "everything should be so arranged that the faithful can *devote themselves attentively* in prayer *to Christ the Lord (Christo Domino vacent)."* In the draft the phrase read: "devote themselves solely (*unice vacent*)." The intention was to prevent the minds of the faithful from being drawn to other things and therefore to ban prayers and songs in honor of Our Lady (rosary) and the saints during the time of exposition. But in the revision conducted jointly with the SCDF the word "solely" disappeared. Not all the consultors adverted to this omission, and commentaries sometimes appealed to the "solely" to argue that during Eucharistic exposition there should be no prayers not strictly Eucharistic in character. Such commentaries certainly do reflect the spirit of the statement in no. 62; see *Not* 4 (1968) 133.

Similar considerations apply to the practice, widespread at one time, of preaching in the presence of the exposed Blessed Sacrament. Here again the principle applies: If the sermon is a meditation on the Eucharistic mystery, then it becomes an integral part of the devotional exercise and the two are quite compatible; if it is a sermon of a different kind, it is to be preached before or after the exposition. See *Not* 4 (1968) 135.

As for celebration of the Divine Office in the presence of the exposed Blessed Sacrament, this was originally rejected because it meant the mingling of two different liturgical actions (see *Not* 4 [1968] 134). Second thoughts followed, however, and the practice was allowed in the above-cited document on Holy Communion and Worship of the Eucharist Outside Mass, because "this liturgy [of the Hours] extends the praise and thanksgiving offered to God in the eucharistic celebration to the several hours of the day; it directs the prayers of the Church to Christ and through him to the Father in the name of the whole world" (no. 96; *The Rites of the Catholic Church* 1 [New York, 1983[2]] 511).

56

Liturgy and Seminaries

I. Instruction on Liturgy in Seminaries

The Constitution on the Liturgy had said that the ideal of full participation of the faithful in the sacred mysteries can never be completely realized unless pastors of souls are themselves first educated in the spirit of
the liturgy and unless they personally experience its efficacy and become
teachers of it (no. 14). Therefore:

> The study of the liturgy is to be ranked among the compulsory and major
> courses in seminaries and religious houses of studies . . . . clerics shall
> be given a liturgical formation in their spiritual life. The means for this are:
> proper guidance so that they may be able to understand the sacred rites
> and take part in them wholeheartedly; the actual celebration of the sacred
> mysteries and of other, popular devotions imbued with the spirit of the
> liturgy (nos. 16-17).

The Consilium therefore looked upon liturgical formation in the seminaries as one of its primary tasks. A good deal of space was given to the
subject in the first drafts of the instruction *Inter Oecumenici*. In the final
text, however, only three numbers (11-13) remained, and these contained
guidelines that were very broad and marginal as far as spiritual formation was concerned. The Congregation for Seminaries had removed the
topic for its own consideration and had promised to publish suitable
guidelines as soon as possible. And in fact at the beginning of the reform
(March 7, 1965), a first communication from that Congregation set down
some firm points of reference for seminaries; shortly after, the Congregation prepared an instruction proper.

1. *First Phase (1965)*

On June 26, 1965, the Substitute Secretary of State, Archbishop Angelo Dell'Acqua, sent the secretary of the Consilium a typewritten copy of an instruction, with a request that it be quickly reviewed. On June 30 the Consilium submitted eight pages of observations.

It remarked, in general, that "the document contains no heresies and can perhaps be emended and made *tolerable,* but it reflects an outdated mentality; it is utterly alien to the conciliar outlook." The distance between the two mentalities was reflected especially in the language of the document, which was completely preconciliar. The major themes of the liturgical Constitution had been passed over. The liturgy was seen as prefigured in Mosaic worship and not as the exercise of the priesthood of Christ and the presence of the paschal mystery.[1] The celebration of the liturgy in seminaries was viewed chiefly as an "exercise" in view of the future ministry. But the following points, above all, caused difficulty:

1) The lengthy, bombastic introduction, which brought out the esthetic aspect of the liturgy.

2) The restrictive guidelines for use of the vernacular, which was allowed, as an exception, once a week. The same restriction was applied to sacred music. Latin was even prescribed for the prayer of the faithful.

3) The instruction was accompanied by a program of studies that was impervious to everything new; for example, the full concept of the assembly, of Sunday, of the parochial liturgy. Seminarians were allowed to take part in the parish liturgy only in their final year of training, and then only once or twice a month.

4) More importantly, the program of studies did not take into account the authority granted the episcopal conferences of regulating this area in their seminaries, as had been allowed for in the draft of the conciliar decree on seminary formation.

On August 17 the Congregation of Rites, which had assigned Canon Martimort to study the document, submitted observations that were essentially the same, even if differently nuanced. On August 15 Archbishop Dell'Acqua put the entire matter into the hands of the secretary of the Consilium, asking that Canon Martimort revise the instruction and that the final version be agreed on by Father Bugnini and Archbishop Staffa, secretary of the Congregation for Seminaries. Canon Martimort wrote a critique of almost every number of the document and then sent in a new and completely revised draft that used the former document as a basis.

---

1. The expression "paschal mystery" occurred only once and then in parentheses.

In mid-September the Congregation for Seminaries sent the Consilium a new version, which, it said, took account of all the observations. This was not in fact the case. A joint meeting was therefore held which was attended by a representative of the Congregation for Seminaries (Monsignor Renato Pozzi) and the secretary of the Consilium, as well as by two consultors (A.-G. Martimort and A. Dirks). The discussion went on for two and a half hours, but no conclusions were reached.

Meanwhile, since complaints had been made about the intransigence of the Consilium experts, the document was examined by four other consultors (Hänggi, Wagner, Lengeling, and Jounel). They offered suggestions for making the introduction acceptable and for correcting the failure to allow for the competency of the episcopal conferences.

On September 27 the observations of the Consilium were sent to the Congregation for Seminaries and to the Secretariat of State. After another fruitless meeting in December, the printer's proofs arrived shortly before Christmas. After the holidays an effort was made to obtain a meeting at which the observations of the Consilium could be presented, but the reply came back that everything had been printed. In fact the text had already been sent to the bishops at the beginning of January 1965.[2]

On January 7 Archbishop Staffa wrote in a letter accompanying a copy of the instruction:

> If I may, I would like to summarize in a special note the various excellences with which in my opinion the recent instruction is endowed: the balance that marks the various parts and inspires each regulation, as well as the lively sense of responsibility that is to be inculcated in the future ministers of the altar, who are called upon to draw daily from the pure springs of the Church's official prayer so that tomorrow they may effectively spread that prayer among the Christian people. We trust, therefore, that superiors and students will find in the document a very clear and healthily stimulating norm for forming others and themselves in the liturgical spirit so urgently promoted by the ecumenical Council.

Reactions

The instruction was ill-received. The bishops and the press quickly made their reactions known.[3] They saw in the document an attack on

---

2. Sacred Congregation for Seminaries and Universities, instruction *Doctrina et exemplo* on the liturgical formation of future priests (Vatican Polyglot Press, n.d.); subsequently published in *Seminarium* 1 (1966) 37–65; now in *DOL* 332 nos. 2672-2761. The concluding statement of the document says that the instruction was prepared "after consultation with the Consilium and with the approval of the Congregation of Rites"—a formula suggested by the Secretariat of State. The document is dated "Christmas, 1965."

3. The Consilium had warned of this reaction in its first reply of June 30: "If the docu-

the authority of the bishops, which had been ratified by the Council, and a spirit out of harmony with the liturgical Constitution and the instruction *Inter Oecumenici*. Therefore, before publishing it in the *Acta Apostolicae Sedis*, the Secretariat of State directed Archbishop Felici, president of the Pontifical Commission for the Interpretation of the Documents of Vatican II, to see how the situation could be rescued.

Archbishop Felici inquired of the Consilium, which explained the entire sequence of events and suggested two solutions (March 18, 1966):

1) To let the document remain an act of a Congregation and not to publish it in the *Acta*. In this case it would be necessary to send all recipients of the instruction a declaration that the instruction is simply a set of guidelines, in accordance with the Decree *Optatam totius*, for the bishops, who must send the Holy See a "Plan of Priestly Formation."

2) To publish the document in the *Acta*, but only after having radically revised it. This course would inevitably lead to comparisons, odium, and controversy. Therefore the Consilium favored the first solution.

2. Second Phase (1966–1967)

Archbishop Garrone, who had meanwhile become pro-prefect of the Congregation for Seminarians, tackled the problem of the instruction once again with a view to having it published in the *Acta*. He summarized the needed corrections under four headings (letter to the Secretariat of State, April 27, 1966):

1) Revision of the introduction.

2) Correction of no. 15 on the language to be used in liturgical celebrations in the seminaries.

3) Recognition of the right of the episcopal conferences to organize the teaching and lifestyle of the seminaries.

4) Correction of expressions here and there so as not to cite earlier documents when a matter is taken up in the conciliar Constitution.

He also provided a corrected text facing the published text.

Archbishop Garrone's file was sent to Father Bugnini by the Undersecretary for Extraordinary Ecclesiastical Affairs at the end of May 1966.

A committee made up of Fathers Vagaggini and Braga and chaired by the secretary of the Consilium studied the new version and proposed a series of changes. The text was now in three columns: the printed text, Archbishop Garrone's corrected text, and the text of Fathers Vagaggini

---

ment is issued in its present form, the reaction will be anything but favorable. The Church will receive poor and spotty results from a fine idea and a document that is in fact very necessary at this time. It will also perhaps have reason for uneasiness."

and Braga (which was based on Archbishop Garrone's). In addition to the revision of points already attacked more than once, the committee added new sections on music for vernacular celebrations, celebrations of the word of God, and devotion to Our Lady and the saints (not a word had been said on these subjects in the instruction), and made a reference to the simpler melodies of the *Kyriale simplex* and *Graduale simplex*. In addition, the committee polished and emended the diction of a good part of the instruction. Their work was sent on June 4, 1955, to the Council for the Public Affairs of the Church. It came back to the Consilium, this time via Archbishop Garrone, who asked (August 9, 1966) that the text be prepared for the printer.

Further revisions were made on August 11 and October 3–4, while at a meeting with Archbishop Garrone on September 2 agreement was reached on further details, especially no. 63, which referred to the program of studies.[4] Once the Latinity of the document had been revised by Abbot Egger, the definitive text was sent to Archbishop Garrone on October 21.

Other corrections were made at the end of October as the result of a critique by the Congregation of Rites, which also had to sign the document. In fact, it had been decided that the instruction should be signed by the prefects of the Congregation for Seminaries and the Congregation of Rites and the president of the Consilium.

But still nothing happened. On April 3, 1967, the Congregation for Seminaries submitted a variety of remarks on the "new instruction" and demanded that the Holy Father intervene once again to approve the new text: "Neither the approval of the Consilium, which is a consultative body and a study group, nor even that of the Congregation of Rites is enough."

It also claimed that only the signature of the authorities in the Congregation of Rites was required, since the latter was the sole agency of the Holy See with responsibility in matters liturgical, while the Consilium was "a consultative body and a study group."

In addition, the Congregation for Seminaries objected that the new document had become informational and experimental. For such a document neither the authority of the Pope and three agencies of the Holy

---

4. Here is the text: "In order more easily to apply the norm set down by the Council for teaching the sacred liturgy under its theological, historical, spiritual, pastoral, and juridical aspects, this Sacred Congregation for Seminaries and Universities will provide some 'Outlines' (*Lineamenta*) for a course; these guidelines are to be organized according to norms established by the episcopal conferences for the plan of studies in their territory, in accordance with no. 4 of the Decree on Priestly Formation." Fathers Braga, Vagaggini, Hänggi, and Jounel took part in this final revision.

See nor publication in the *Acta* seemed required: "Publish in the *Acta* an instruction that is experimental and therefore left to the decision of the episcopal conferences."

The Congregation also complained of the reduction and rewording of the introduction and the broadening of the regulations for the language to be used: "Here the use of Latin in liturgical celebrations is put on the same level as the use of Latin by the ordinary faithful, that is, it is reduced to a minimum. Given these principles, Latin will suffer the same fate it has in other areas (Divine Office, Eucharistic Benediction, funerals, etc.)."[5]

The end result was once again that obstacles could not be overcome and nothing was done.

3. *Third Phase (1970–1972)*

In new contacts between Cardinal Garrone and the Consilium, it was suggested that it was time to take up once more the matter of an instruction. This was at the beginning of 1969. A new, international study group was formed: Bugnini, Braga, Lengeling, Martimort, Bodigel (Rennes), Cabié (Albi), Tena (Barcelona), and Jounel. On January 24 these men were asked to respond to two questions:

a) Would an instruction on the seminaries be useful at this time?

b) If the text in hand (the 1966 instruction) was still regarded as sound, how could it be corrected and completed or changed?

The Consilium studied the answers on February 15, 1969, and communicated the results to the Congregation for Seminaries on January 17:

1) It was clear that opinion was *substantially negative* on publication of an instruction. This view was unanimous, with one dissenter (Lengeling).

2) This view was confirmed by the fact that the General Norms published for seminaries on May 20, 1968, gave no prominence to the liturgy and indeed mentioned it only in passing. What was to be gained, then,

---

5. The Congregation for Seminaries also said: "The Second Vatican Council (constitution *Sacrosanctum Concilium*, nos. 36, 1, and 101, 1) makes preservation of the Latin in the rites—all the rites—of the Latin Church *a general and basic norm* and envisages limited exceptions, due to special local circumstances, *only for the faithful* ('the use of the mother tongue . . . frequently may be of great advantage *to the people*')." And again: "In Rome, no less than in the principal centers of the West, the liturgical language was Greek until about the fourth century; Greek, however, was not the 'language of the people' in the various communities but rather the 'language of refinement' throughout the 'Ecumene.' Even in the Churches of the Eastern Rite the liturgical language was not the 'language of the people.' " This remark referred to *Lineamenta* no. 15, in which the professor of liturgy was urged to point out "how in the beginning the liturgical language was the same as the language of the people."

by emphasizing it in a special document? This would be to go on speaking two different languages, with neither side understanding the other.

3) In any case, a new text would have to be prepared. The 1966 text was almost completely unserviceable.

It was also noted with regard to the teaching of liturgy in the seminaries that the decrees of the Council remained almost a dead letter.

The secretariat of the Consilium also expressed the view that once the new liturgical books had produced a somewhat stable situation, "there would be an advantage in having a set of well-organized and sure norms for seminaries."

On January 10, 1970, the Congregation for Seminaries again asked the Congregation for Divine Worship whether it was opportune to issue guidelines, especially for the teaching of liturgy in the seminaries; it also asked for an opinion on the possibility of including something on the liturgical life in seminaries. At the same time it sent for study a list of questions to be dealt with in instruction on the liturgy. The matter stopped there. The right time, it was thought, had not yet come.

In November 1970, after repeated urgings from the Congregation for Seminaries, the secretary of the Congregation for Divine Worship reached an agreement with the Congregation for Catholic Education on the drafting of a new instruction. The steps to be followed were these: preparation of a basic statement; once the main lines had been agreed upon, development of a fundamental text in collaboration with some *periti;* critique of this by a larger circle; critique by the episcopal conferences.

The basic outline was drawn up by A. Nocent, studied by the Congregation for Divine Worship, and sent to the Congregation for Catholic Education, which was then invited to a joint meeting on February 22, 1971.

On February 19 Cardinal Garrone wrote to the secretary of the Congregation for Divine Worship: "I take advantage of this occasion also to thank you in my own name for the instruction on the liturgy which we have begun to study; it strikes me at a first reading as being excellent."

The same enthusiasm was shown by the officials of the Congregation at the meeting of February 22. They asked that an appendix also be prepared which would give guidelines for the programs to be following in teaching the liturgy. Furthermore, the French text would have to be translated into Latin. This was sent to the Congregation for Catholic Education on April 21, 1971, and a joint meeting was called for May 18.

The approach was new, open, modern, and sensitive to the inspirations and themes dear to contemporary youth. The document had three parts: spiritual formation, technical instruction, and practical directives for the celebration of the liturgy.

I. Starting from the ideal community described in the Acts of the Apostles, the instruction took as its basis the idea of the community that is supposed and formed by the liturgy, namely, a form of common life that finds expression especially in prayer, in teaching (Sacred Scripture, taste for the psalms), in a proper balance between devotions and liturgical life, and in liturgy as a school and exercise of close union with God, especially through the sacraments.

II. In regard to technical and intellectual instruction, a distinction was made between students in minor seminaries or religious schools and students in theological studies; appropriate directives were given for the gradual initiation of the former into the liturgical life and for the further understanding and fuller participation proper to the latter.

III. Under the heading of practical guidelines for celebration, the various areas of the liturgy were reviewed: celebrations of the word of God; Eucharist and Eucharistic worship; Divine Office; sacraments; Sundays and the liturgical year.

The enthusiasm of the first meeting (February 22) was quickly dissipated at the meeting with the representatives of the Congregation for Catholic Education. Unfortunately, the Latin text was not blameless and at various points did not adequately convey the meaning of the French original. But criticism went beyond these points to the entire approach. The instruction was found to be either too ideal or too negative in regard to influences on common life; unclear (for example, when it spoke of the various modes of Christ's presence, which—it was said—were not yet solidly established); or too detailed. The conclusion: "we do not like" the text.

The representatives of the Congregation for Divine Worship were dismayed. Their dismay was met by bitter and really ugly attacks, such as these words that the undersecretary let slip: "We composed an instruction and you knocked it down; now you have composed one and asked us to examine it. We have examined it, and now it's our turn to reject your instruction."

The relator himself wrote in bitterness: "I must honestly say that I did not like the tone of the meeting. I think the lack of respect shown me was clear; the way they ended up was offensive and displayed a lack of courtesy that did not speak well of the group; this was especially true of the words spoken. But let it go."

The end result was one more blind alley. The Cardinal Prefect of the Congregation for Catholic Worship kept insisting on a new text, until finally the Congregation for Divine Worship wrote to him on June 22, 1972:

After this past year's meetings between officials of our two agencies on the matter in question—meetings that achieved no practical result—we think it appropriate to ask Your Eminence to have the Congregation for Catholic Education compose a base text that we can then study jointly. The seminaries are today raising many questions of a kind that, at least in part, do not fit into our perspective.

It seems better, therefore, that the basic approach taken in the document be determined by the competent agency. The Congregation for Divine Worship will then very gladly make a careful and serious study of the schema offered to it.

4. *Fourth Phase (1974–1975)*

On July 6 Cardinal Garrone wrote as follows in response to the above-cited letter of June 22: "We wish to assure you that in keeping with your courteous invitation, we shall embark as quickly as possible on preparation of the document mentioned. We shall be careful to have it sent to your Congregation as soon as its basic lines have been determined."

Two years passed, and everyone thought no further step would be taken. But on July 6, 1974, the Congregation for Catholic Education sent a new text, of which it said:

We think this document addresses present needs in the formation of candidates for the priesthood . . . . It endeavors to reflect faithfully the principal official documents on the liturgical renewal by formulating timely guidelines on the way in which these documents are to be applied in the spiritual, pastoral, and theological formation of students during their stay in the seminary and in their future pastoral ministry. Every paragraph of the schema displays a concern to take into account the mentality of the students, the difficulties and tendencies widespread in the apostolate today, and, above all, the basic and absolutely necessary requirement that the entire liturgical renewal and all of pastoral practice in this area be grounded in clear ideas that are based on the magisterium of the Church and on dogma.

As required by its usual method and also in order to prevent the danger of subjective responses inspired by past experience, the Congregation for Divine Worship sent the text to twenty-one experts on July 18, 1975. On the basis of their answers a reply was sent to the Congregation for Catholic Education on October 16.

The tone of the document, it was said, and the treatment of the several parts were not in harmony with the documents of the reform. The liturgical books were only sporadically cited, as were the General Instructions of the Missal and the Liturgy of the Hours, and the introductions of the rite of concelebration and of the document on Eucharistic worship outside Mass. The spirit of the new rite of penance was not to be seen. On the contrary, the foundation for everything was the "Basic Plan for Priestly Formation," which was cited to the point of improbability. The impression given was that the conciliar documents and the liturgical books were cited in justification of the "Basic Plan." As a result, there was no understanding of the new discipline of minor orders or of incardination or of the ministries. Above all, however, the instruction was shot through with a negative spirit that hinted here and there at criticisms of the liturgical reform and emphasized a concern with abuses: "any capricious actions being carefully reported," "faithful observance." The language was preconciliar.[6]

On February 18, 1975, a new redaction was sent which was substantially identical with the preceding. In particular, the observations regarding the negative emphasis in the instruction were rejected,[7] as were those on the rite of penance, and on the unified vision of the Eucharistic mystery.[8]

The examination of the new text went on for several months, first in a limited group, then in a larger one, and finally in a twosome consisting of the secretary and Cardinal Prefect of the Congregation for Divine Worship. The result was ten pages of remarks according to which almost all numbers of the instruction needed to be redone. On the whole, this instruction was lacking from the viewpoint of the liturgical reform. The officials of the Congregation therefore advised the prefect to leave full responsibility for the document to the Congregation for Catholic Education and not to involve the Congregation for Divine Worship, since the latter could not give its backing to a document that contradicted the spirit of the reform. That is what the Cardinal Prefect finally told his colleague at a private meeting.

Once again the attempt to issue directives on the liturgy to seminarians had taken a "no thoroughfare" path.

---

6. Such Latin terms as "piae exercitationes," "congressiones liturgicae," and "rogationes orationis universalis" were still being used. The exhortation to study the texts in Latin was accompanied by an unfavorable judgment of translations, which, it was claimed, lost the full meaning and overtones of the original. Daily attendance at Mass during vacations was considered to be a sign that the students understood its value.

7. "Not to refer clearly and explicitly to errors and drawbacks found today in the liturgical life of seminaries and in the pastoral ministry would amount to stripping the instruction of much of its concreteness."

8. "The distinction [between Mass and communion] is obviously made solely for pedagogical reasons, in order better to bring out the importance of communion, which in a number of instances is unfortunately neglected by seminarians and thus in practice separated from the Eucharistic sacrifice."

The business pleased no one. The failure to produce an instruction on the liturgical renewal in seminaries meant a failure at one of the most important points in the liturgical reform. When the reform began, a great deal of confidence was placed in the new recruits to the clergy. The reformers deceived themselves into thinking that they were putting the new liturgy into the hands of the young, "new wine in new bottles." It did not turn out that way. The instruction that both sides desired and wanted and tried for could not be produced. Every time the ship seemed about to enter the harbor, it was inexorably driven back to the high seas.

A document containing some elements of the schemas here reviewed did appear some years later from the Congregation for Catholic Education, "after consultation with the Congregation for the Sacraments and Divine Worship."[9]

II. CONCELEBRATION IN SEMINARIES

There is a minor question that is of interest from the viewpoint of the implementation of the liturgical reform in seminaries—the question of concelebration. The issue has now been settled, but in the beginning it occupied several agencies for some time.

The problem arose out of a request from the Cardinal Archbishop of Seville, who, as delegate of the Spanish episcopate for the Pontifical Spanish College in Rome, asked the Holy Father that the priests of the college might concelebrate Mass daily (May 2, 1966). Two questions were involved—one of law and one of practice.

1) *Juridical problem.* At that time concelebration was allowed in certain cases, with the permission and according to the judgment of the Ordinary. The question was whether daily concelebration in seminaries came under that rule and who it was that could give the permission in Rome with its international and national colleges.

2) *Practical problem.* The question here was whether it was advisable to introduce daily concelebration into seminaries and colleges or ecclesiastical residences. Concelebration was still looked upon as something extraordinary, while the ordinary thing in the life of a priest was either Mass for a congregation or "private" Mass. There were many who thought daily concelebration would not be good training for the future life of a priest and for the apostolate; there was also a fear that concelebra-

---

9. Sacred Congregation for Catholic Education, instruction *In ecclesiasticam futurorum sacerdotum* on liturgical formation in seminaries (June 3, 1969): *DOL* 335 nos. 2779-2916. See A. M. Triacca, "A proposito della recente Istruzione sulla formazione liturgica nei seminari," *Not* 15 (1979) 621-39; and the entire fourth issue (October–December) of *Seminarium* 31 (1979).

tion might lead to some communities being deprived of the service regularly provided by the priests residing in the colleges of Rome.

On June 4, 1966, the Cardinal Secretary of State directed the Congregation of Rites to convene a joint plenary meeting with the Congregations for Seminaries and for Religious and the Consilium. For, "before coming to a decision on so important a matter, which will affect all the colleges and seminaries of the entire Church," the Holy Father wanted the question of principle to be discussed in its various aspects, especially the pastoral. He asked that guidelines be established that could go into effect for the following scholastic year. The Cardinal Prefect repeated his directive on August 29, 1966.

The Congregation of Rites asked for the views of the agencies invited to the joint meeting.

The Congregation for Religious was opposed to granting the permissions:

> Seminarians, it must be remembered, are preparing for the pastoral life and have to realize that duty will have them almost always celebrating Mass in parishes or in institutions where they will be celebrating individually. Frequent concelebration in seminaries will make it more difficult for young priests to master the rubrics for Masses with a single celebrant, and this will be a drawback in their pastoral ministry. The claim that they are gaining time for the community should not be a reason for concelebration. It is worth noting that Mass read by a single priest takes less time than concelebration by several.
>
> In some places concelebration has become almost a fad, and priests even ask permission to binate solely in order that they may take part in concelebrations.

The same Congregation asserted that "for theological and pastoral reasons, the emphasis should rather be on the value of Masses celebrated by individuals."

The Congregation for Seminaries, on the other hand, was in favor of the concession, provided certain conditions were met: it should be justified solely by spiritual considerations; it should not detract from service to the faithful; the taste for private Mass should also be cultivated.

The Consilium shared the view of the Congregation for Seminaries and called for the co-existence of the two forms of celebration.

The joint plenary meeting took place on October 22, 1966, in the Vatican Apostolic Palace. The majority of the cardinals present opposed the concession: 12 against; 4 in favor; 1 proceed cautiously.

On November 7, 1966, Archbishop Dell'Acqua asked the secretary of the Consilium for a draft statement of norms for concelebration in the seminaries and the ecclesiastical residences and institutions of Rome. The

Holy Father revised and completed the text; on November 11 the Cardinal Secretary of State sent it to the Congregation of Rites with a request to have it examined also by the Congregation for Seminaries, the Roman Vicariate, and the Consilium. The Consilium answered on November 27; its only comment was to advise the addition of a statement that "the present norms issued by the Holy Father for the diocesan clergy may be usefully followed by religious as well."

From that moment on nothing more was heard of these "Norms," for in the interval they had become—no one knows how—an "Instruction on the Concelebration of Mass in Seminaries, Colleges, and Ecclesiastical Institutions." This had been drafted by the Congregation of Rites and was sent to the Consilium for study on January 25, 1967. The Cardinal President of the Consilium sent the text to two bishops of the presidential council (Boudon and Bluyssen) and nine consultors of eight different nationalities. Their observations were passed on to Cardinal Larraona at the end of February 1967. The instruction was not well received by the *periti* of the Consilium, either because it seemed to be a superfluous document and an interference in an area that the liturgical Constitution left to the diocesan bishop and the Ordinary, or because of its narrowly juridical flavor and lack of any vision or even any pastoral and spiritual touch.[10]

The Congregation of Rites now changed the instruction back once more into "Norms for Concelebration in Seminaries, Colleges, and Ecclesiastical Institutions." On September 16, 1967,[11] the Secretariat of State sent both documents to the Consilium, which replied on September 26, pointing out that the "Norms" were useless because the Instruction on Worship of the Eucharistic Mystery (May 25, 1967) had already issued regulations in this area: "The faculty to concelebrate also applies to the principal Masses in churches and public and semipublic oratories of seminaries,

---

10. Among other things, this new instruction cited the Instruction on the Liturgy in Seminaries according to the version from the end of 1966, which had not yet been published.

11. On August 4, 1967, seeing that the Instruction on the Liturgy in Seminaries was not being published, the Consilium had asked the Secretariat of State to publish at least the "Norms for Concelebration in the Seminaries, Residences, and Ecclesiastical Institutions of Rome," which had been compiled the previous year and carefully revised, but never published. The Consilium thought these would be useful at the beginning of a new year, and it also suggested that they be made known to the presidents of the episcopal conferences, "with a strong recommendation" that they use these norms as a basis for regulating the matter in their regions. On September 14, 1967, the Secretariat of State wrote that "you may without further ado proceed to do as you suggested" (No. 104944). But on September 16 the Secretariat sent the instruction along with the "Norms for Concelebration" and asked for data on the rights of bishops, religious Ordinaries, and episcopal conferences in regard to the discipline of concelebration.

colleges, and ecclesiastical institutions, as well as in those of religious orders and societies of common life without vows" (no. 47).

What, then, was the sense of a further instruction "issued by the authority and command of the Supreme Pontiff"?

Furthermore, the instruction and "Norms" contained so many minute details and such an emphasis on disciplines, faculties, and observance that they seemed bent on restricting and limiting concelebration, whereas the Instruction on Worship of the Eucharistic Mystery exhorted superiors to facilitate and encourage concelebration "whenever pastoral needs or another reasonable cause does not demand otherwise" (no. 47).

The Consilium suggested, therefore, that there be a return to the original "Norms for Rome," which it regarded as surer and more effective.

> That document is shorter, but it takes a spiritual and pastoral approach, especially in the corrections and additions introduced by the Holy Father; this outlook is missing from the proposed instruction and Norms. The Roman Norms also give less the impression of the kind of accentuated juridical rigor that will not be well received today. On the other hand, the juridical side of the matter seems fairly well safeguarded by existing documents.

And in fact, the new "Norms" were issued by the Cardinal Vicar of Rome "in accordance with the august wish of the Holy Father."[12]

In this document a distinction is made between residences or colleges that accept only priests; seminaries, where all are clerics; communities of both priests and other clerics. Provision is thus made for a healthy balance. Concelebration in communities of priests is permitted daily, as long as conditions mentioned at the outset are satisfied: provision always made for the spiritual needs of the faithful of the diocese of Rome, esteem for and celebration of "private" Masses as well, participation of superiors, frequent explanation of the theological and ascetical value of concelebration.

In the case of seminaries, there is an emphasis on the need of having the students trained in and accustomed to all the forms of celebration, since "these bring out more clearly the varied functions of the liturgical assembly and foster the active participation of all the students." Finally, in institutions of both priests and clerics, provision must be made for the needs of both categories: "Concelebration can be more frequent, but not exclusive: the complete priestly formation of the clerics must be effectively ensured by their participation in the several forms of celebration."

---

12. L'Osservatore Romano, October 14, 1967; Rivista diocesana di Roma 8 (1967) 971–73; Not 3 (1967) 388–89. The Norms were to go into effect on November 1, 1967.

57

Veneration of Mary

The overall plan of reform called for giving special attention to the devotions practiced by the Christian people, once the majority of the liturgical books had been revised. Even as the reform was advancing, those involved in it could already see the urgent need of tackling this entire area, in order to bring it into harmony with the liturgy proper. Then the Congregation for Divine Worship began to take a serious interest in the problem, as is evidenced by a report on its activity during the year 1972:

> Now that the revision of the liturgical books is nearing completion, this Congregation wants the problem of devotions to be studied, especially the principal devotions that have our Lady and the Lord's passion for their object, but also the many others that are now practiced and are dear to the faithful. These must be preserved, in order that they may feed the piety of the faithful; at the same time, however, they must be brought into harmony with the reformed liturgy.[1]

Devotion to Mary, in particular, seemed to call for urgent consideration.

I. History

As far back as 1968 the Consilium had offered a set of readings for Masses and celebrations in honor of our Lady, especially in sanctuaries and places of pilgrimage.[2] The purpose had been to lend depth to Marian

---

1. "Sacra Congregazione per il Culto Divino," *Attività della Santa Sede* 1972 (Vatican City, 1973) 601.
2. See "Lectionaria particularia. II. In Missis quae in honorem B. Mariae Virginis celebrantur in locis peregrinationum," *Not* 4 (1968) 46–52.

devotion by showing it in the light of the Sacred Scripture and the conciliar documents.

After the revised calendar and Missal had been published, there were signs that people were failing to grasp the meaning of the Holy See's action. The reform was wrongly accused of causing a lessening of devotion to the Mother of the Lord. It was easy enough to show that the accusation was unfounded.[3] On the other hand, it was undeniable that after the Council people had some difficulty in assimilating its doctrine and vision of Mary and her role in the mystery of Christ and the Church. As a result, there was a crisis in devotion to Mary, though this was also due in part to the disappearance of older forms of veneration.

Meanwhile, individuals, associations, and other groups were asking the Pope or the Congregation for Divine Worhip to declare the rosary a liturgical prayer and to urge its recitation. Others were looking for a renewal of the form of the rosary or, on the contrary, strongly resisting the efforts at such a renewal that were being made here and there.[4]

When passing on one of these petitions on October 8, 1970 (No. 160.865/70), the Secretariat of State asked the Congregation for Divine Worship to "prepare a draft of a papal document" that would encourage "recitation of the rosary by families."

After studying this request, the Congregation answered by stating its growing conviction that such a subject should be treated within the much larger context of Marian devotion as a whole. Marian devotion in turn should be related to the liturgical reform, and the document should seek to give a new impetus to veneration of the Mother of God. This, it had often been said in recent years, had entered a period of crisis; in addition, trends were perceptible that were not entirely in accord with the statements of Vatican II.[5]

Father I. Calabuig, with the collaboration of the theological faculty of the Marianum (Rome), was commissioned to study the problem. In a report to the Pope (May 27, 1971), he said: "We are preparing a document on Marian devotion and on the rosary in particular. We were not able

---

3. See G. P., "La riforma liturgica e antimariana?" Not 8 (1972) 41–50.

4. See, e.g., E. M. Rossetti, Il Rosario rinnovato (Milan, 1972); idem, Il mistero della redenzione meditato con Maria (Bologna, 1971²). Similar efforts were being made in other countries to promote a revival of the rosary by updating it. But these efforts elicited numerous backlashes against what was regarded as an attempt to tamper with, destroy, and impoverish this prayer.

5. See the letter that the SCDW addressed to the Secretariat of State (September 12, 1972) when sending the first draft of the document.

to have it ready by May, but we do hope to present it to the Holy Father in good time for publication by October."

In fact, a preliminary draft was ready only by the following December; it had three parts:

1) Liturgical veneration of the Mother of God, with special reference to the reformed Roman liturgy;

2) Directives for making Marian devotion more transparent and vigorous;

3) The devout recitation of the rosary.

After being studied at the Congregation's meeting of January 1972, the draft was sent out for examination by the consultors and by twenty or so theologians representing various nationalities and tendencies (January 8, 1972). The consultation encouraged the drafters to continue as they had begun, for, with a single dissenting voice, the judgments of the consultors were highly favorable.[6]

On the basis of the suggestions received from the experts, a first schema of a papal document was prepared and sent directly to the Pope[7] on September 12, 1972. On January 13, 1973, the Pope sent the Congregation for Divine Worship, via the Secretariat of State, a page of notes on various points and of requests for improvements or clarifications. The Pope found the document to be on the whole "good and well done, but too long and somewhat verbose." He asked, therefore, that it be "shortened and in some areas simplified." The document should take the form of an "apostolic exhortation."

A second schema, shortened as the Pope had requested (45 pages instead of 56), was sent to him on March 14, 1973. On April 6 the Secretariat of State, acting in the Pope's name, sent a "Note on the Draft of an Apostolic Exhortation on Devotion to the Blessed Virgin"; it asked that "the observations herein contained be taken into account in the further revision" of the document.

The primary emphasis in the "Note" was on the rosary. And in fact the idea for the entire document had arisen out of requests that this practice be recommended and updated. For this reason the schema gave guidelines for renewal of the practice. It accepted the principle of a plural-

---

6. The general direction taken, the doctrine, the approach, and the division into parts were all found highly effective. Some of the judgments were: "a very beautiful and rich document," "truly excellent," "first-rate," and "I am very satisfied with it."

7. Since this was to be a pontifical document, the drafts were not sent to the consultors or members of the SCDW (except for the preliminary consultation on the plan of the document).

ity of forms and made its own the points on which there seemed to be agreement in the various proposals for reform that were based on studies of the origins of the rosary and on pastoral research. The document therefore distinguished three forms of the rosary:

a) The traditional form, while retaining the likewise traditional order of the mysteries or choosing a different order, but in any case keeping the division into joyful, sorrowful, and glorious mysteries.

b) A revised form that includes a short reading, period of reflection, Our Father (recited only once, at the beginning); recitation of the decades of Hail Marys, but including only the biblical part of this prayer (with possible mention of the mystery being meditated on after the name "Jesus"); the "Holy Mary, Mother of God" section is said only at the end of each tenth Hail Mary; then the "Glory be to the Father."

c) Celebration of the rosary in a public and communal form, structured as a celebration of the word of God, with readings, songs, homily, and a series of Hail Marys, but limited to a single decade.

On these various forms of the rosary the "Note" had this to say:

> The second and third forms ("revised form of the rosary" and "celebration of the rosary") cannot be called "the rosary," since this term refers precisely to a specific form that cannot be confused with any other. It is not possible to develop another pious practice that includes a homily, Scripture readings, etc., and that eliminates some prayers and introduces others, and still claim the right to call the resultant devotional exercise "the rosary." It is expedient, therefore,
>
> —that the rosary (in the form presently in use) be left untouched;
>
> —that in order to increase Marian devotion, the apostolic exhortation should suggest other pious practices, such as a "Marian Hour," gatherings for Marian prayer, and so on;
>
> —that these new devotions, however, not be presented as variants of the rosary, which, as was said a moment ago, should remain unique and unchanged.
>
> If the document were published in its present form, the faithful would conclude that "the Pope has changed the rosary," and the psychological effect would be disastrous. The reason is that the rosary is and remains the prayer of the "poor," the illiterate, the blind, the soldier pinned down in the trenches; in other words, it is the prayer of those who have a place of honor in the Kingdom of God. Any change in it cannot but lessen the confidence of the "simple" and the "poor."

The "Note" concluded: "The apostolic exhortation should not go into too much detail. It should recall principles (and the schema does this splendidly), give general guidelines, suggest some formulas, and then leave the episcopal conferences room to make needed adaptations. Such an approach would help to broaden and deepen Marian devotion and would increase esteem for the Holy See."

The third schema was a revision of the second in accordance with the "Note"; it was sent to the Pope on April 27, 1973. At a meeting with Archbishop Bugnini, the Pope gave him a further page of observations, dated June 5, 1973. He asked for the deletion of some paragraphs on the rosary and the removal also of a reference to a different order of the mysteries: "The rosary is to remain single in form and unchanged from what it now is. Let any new forms of Marian devotion that are proposed to the faithful take their place alongside the rosary."

In the fourth schema (June 12, 1973) all references to a revision of the rosary have disappeared; instead, mention is made of "exercises of devotion that are inspired by the rosary." The new schema again elicited observations from the Pope on nineteen points; he also sent observations from the Secretariat for Christian Unity on the ecumenical aspects of Marian veneration and from a consultor of the Congregation for the Doctrine of the Faith.

The fifth and final schema was sent to the Pope on November 4, 1973, together with a report on the "route" followed in preparation of the document and with a list of texts that had been corrected, omitted, or newly introduced. As a result of the Pope's most recent observations, changes had been made in terminology and style. In addition, three new paragraphs were introduced that focused on Mary as model of the individual prayer of Christians (no. 21) and on the theological importance (no. 56) and pastoral value (no. 57) of veneration of the Virgin; no. 6 was expanded to bring out better the importance of the celebration of the Annunciation and the Assumption; the exhortation to abandon the still widespread practice of reciting the rosary during liturgical celebrations was made more explicit (no. 48).

The suggestions of the Secretariat for Christian Unity were incorporated in their entirety, except for a few redactional alterations. Many of the observations submitted by the consultor of the Congregation for the Doctrine of the Faith were also accepted.[8]

---

8. But in its report to the Pope the SCDW did not fail to express its displeasure at an outlook based on preconceptions: "This Congregation cannot understand how a text such as the projected document on Mary, which everywhere breathes love for the magisterium of the Church and for the holy Fathers, can be regarded as a mouthpiece for a supposed 'North-European theology' and as an expression of disesteem for tradition. This preconception has roused in the presenter of these observations an attitude of distrust and suspicion that extends even to expressions in the document that clearly are joyous and heartfelt recommendations of devotion to the Blessed Virgin."

Approval. On December 31, 1973 (No. 249283) the Secretariat of State made known the approval of the Pope and sent the page proofs of the Latin and Italian texts;[9] on April 6, 1974, it sent two copies, signed by the Pope, of the apostolic exhortation *Marialis cultus.* The exhortation was dated February 2, 1974, but was presented to the public on March 25, 1974, by Father Jean Galot, S.J., in the pressroom of the Holy See.[10] On the following April 18 (No. 256656) Archbishop Benelli, Substitute Secretary of State, made known the satisfaction, gratitude, and blessing of the Holy Father on all who had collaborated in the preparation of the document. As a special sign of his gratitude the Pope gave Father Calabuig a chalice and Professor Rosella Barbieri a papal decoration.

II. CONTENTS

The exhortation *Marialis cultus* has an introduction, three parts, and a conclusion.

The *introduction* explains the purpose of the document and expatiates on the importance of veneration of our Lady in the Church. This devotion is regarded as a necessary and characteristic part of Christian piety. In fact, the singular place of the Virgin in the plan of salvation calls for a singular devotion. Every time Christians encounter Christ, they inevitably find Mary, his Mother, at his side, humbly serving him in his work of salvation. As a result, veneration of the Virgin also has God's glory as its purpose. The Pope thinks it a good time to discourse on some themes connected with veneration of our Lord, in order that this veneration may be strengthened in the hearts of the faithful and may develop in harmony with the renewal of the liturgy,[11] progress in doctrine, and the religious sensibilities of our contemporaries.

Part I, on veneration of the Virgin in the reformed liturgy, has two sections. The first examines the Marian significance of the revised liturgical books. These by no means weaken devotion to the Virgin, but on the contrary promote it by incorporating it more fully and organically into the celebration of the mysteries of Christ, bringing out its ecclesial sig-

---

9. Examination of the proofs entailed further work: some expressions were not properly translated; others in the Italian text had been unduly altered. The examination led to ten pages of remarks on the Latin text and six on the Italian.

10. The document is in *AAS* 66 (174) 113-68; *DOL* 467 nos. 3896-3945 (with omissions). See I. Calabuig, O.S.M., "La portata liturgica della Esortazione Apostolica *Marialis cultus,*" *Not* 10 (1974) 198-216.

11. The Holy Father had often insisted on speaking not of a decline or lessening of Marian devotion but rather of the need of developing it.

nificance, and acknowledging the unique place that belongs to this devotion in Christian piety. In the reformed liturgy, veneration of the Virgin finds expression in formulas packed with content and, not infrequently, with lyrical affectivity. At the same time, however, this veneration is not an end in itself; it springs from contemplation of the bond between Mary and Christ and of the manysided mission of Mary in the Church, and consequently aims at glorifying God for the wonders he has performed in her (see Luke 1:49) and at stirring up in the faithful an active commitment to the Christian life.

The document then quickly reviews the principal books of the reformed Roman liturgy and signals the place that the Blessed Virgin occupies in each of them.

It turns first to the Roman Calendar. If we consider the solemnities of the Mother of God, the Annunciation of the Lord, the Assumption, and the Immaculate Conception; the distinctive Marian tonality of the Advent and Christmas seasons; the other feasts and commemoration of our Lady, among them the ancient memorial of our Lady on Saturday; and if we add the Marian celebrations proper to the calendars of various nations or dioceses, it becomes clear that the Virgin is constantly present throughout the liturgical year.

The exhortation then looks at the two basic books for the celebration of the Eucharist: the Roman Missal and the Lectionary. In the first we find all the great themes of Marian doctrine and devotion that have been handed down by the tradition, as well as others that are the special object of attention in our day, such as the relation between Mary and the Church. In the Lectionary we find a notable increase in the number of Scripture readings that are of Marian importance; these have their place not only in Masses in honor of Mary but also in various Sunday Masses and in Masses accompanying the celebration of some sacraments.

The document then turns its attention to the Liturgy of the Hours, in which the Virgin occupies a large place in the hymns, readings, and intercessions. Finally, the exhortation refers to the other liturgical books (rites of baptism, religious profession, anointing of the sick, and so on), which all show the Church having recourse to the Virgin at key moments in Christian life.

In the second section of Part I, the document reflects on Mary as a model for the Church as a whole and for individual Christians in their life of worship and devotion. Mary is the Virgin who listens to the word of God, prays, and praises the Lord, and who communicates life as a mother and offers her Son while associating herself with his sacrifice. The worshiping Church makes these attitudes its own: the Church, too, listens to the word of God in the liturgy of the Word, praises the Lord unceasingly, and intercedes for the salvation of the world; it begets and promotes life in the sacraments and calls the faithful together to offer the Eucharistic sacrifice, which is the memorial of Christ's death and resurrection.

Part II of the document gives directives for the renewal of devotion to Mary. Pious exercises and devotions that have developed over the centuries sometimes need to be revised so that outdated elements may be replaced, new vigor may be restored to what is of perennial value, and room may be made for doctrinal elements that theological study has brought to light and the magisterium has proposed to the faithful. This revision must be both respectful of tradition and open to the legitimate demands of our contemporaries. The directives given in the document have for their purpose to see to it that Marian devotions display the following traits:

—they should manifest their deeper Christological tendency, that is, they should bring out the indissoluble bond existing between the Virgin and the divine Savior and her essential reference to him;

—they should place adequate emphasis on the pneumatological aspect, that is, the relation between the Virgin and the sanctifying Spirit;

—they should express the ecclesiological dimension, that is, the place of Mary in the communion of saints;

—they should place new emphasis on the biblical content by deriving from Scripture their inspiration, their themes, and the expressive power of their forms;

—they should show their harmony with the liturgical renewal by taking account of the style and rhythms of the sacred liturgy;

—they should respect the requirements of the ecumenical movement and become themselves a means to the reunion of Christians;

—they should take into account the sure findings of the anthropological sciences. In this area, special consideration is given to the relationship between Mary and the person and mission of women. Mary is a model not because of the kind of life she led in the society of her day but because of her faith, hope, and love, her obedience to the word of God, her fidelity to her mission, her charity that took the form of service, and her active collaboration with the work of salvation. These are universally valid and permanent values. Emphasis on these positive elements should be accompanied by an effort to eliminate certain defects that have at times crept into devotion to the Mother of God—a mindless credulity, a barren sentimentalism, a narrow-mindedness, an exaggerated image of Mary, and a reliance on legend.

Part III dwells on two devotional exercises on which the Holy See has spoken on various occasions: the *Angelus* and the rosary. There is an urgent exhortation to preserve the practice of the *Angelus* despite changes in society and the surrounding culture.

The rosary is treated at greater length. The document recalls the scientific and pastoral research which has been conducted on the rosary in recent years and which has brought out with greater clarity the primary characteristics of this devotion: its evangelical and Christological character (since it is from the gospel that the rosary takes the "mysteries" to be contemplated, that is, the salvific moments in the life of Christ) and its laudative, impetrative, and contemplative nature. Without its contemplative dimension, the rosary would resemble a body without a soul and would risk becoming a mechanical repetition of formulas.

The Pope not only confirms the value of this pious practice but also reviews the principal elements of it as these have been handed down in the tradition. Other exercises of devotion may draw inspiration from the rosary and develop one or the other of its elements in order to give a better understanding of its spiritual riches and a better appreciation of its value. — Some persons have asked that the rosary be declared a liturgical prayer. In response it must be said that while from various points of view the practice of the rosary is in full harmony with the liturgy, it must not be confused with it or added to it, as has happened at times in the past, but must rather retain its character as an exercise of devotion that can help us better understand and live the liturgy.

Finally, the Pope explains the value of family recitation of the rosary. For by engaging in common prayer, this "domestic Church" carries out its essential function as a praying community and finds in Mary the most splendid of models.

Part IX

Sacred Music and the Liturgy

58

Song and Liturgy

The problem of song was one of the most sensitive, important, and troubling of the entire reform. The Consilium, the Congregation for Divine Worship, and the Pope himself took every opportunity to recall the importance and role of singing in the liturgy. Without singing there can be no adequate expression of the people's participation, of their joyous entering into the paschal mystery of Christ, or of their sense of communion with one another.

But the change from Latin to the vernaculars meant the abandonment of forms held dear in the past and called for a creative process that would be neither easy nor short. Time and experience were needed, as well as artistic genius of a literary and musical kind.

In addition, two conceptions of the function of sacred song in the liturgy were now at work. One type of musician looked upon song primarily as an art-form and an adornment of the celebration. Liturgists and pastors, on the other hand, as well as musicians more conscious of pastoral needs, saw song as having a structural role and serving to give better expression to the mystery being celebrated; they saw it, therefore, as related to the character of the celebration, its several phases, and the requirements of its various parts. The former group regarded singing as primarily the task of specialists; the latter, on the other hand, while acknowledging the indispensable role of the *schola cantorum*, thought it wrong to take away from the congregation the possibility of expressing itself in communal singing.

Because of the specialized choirs, professional organizations, and "chapels" (i.e., choirs) devoted to music that were to be found in the holy city, Roman circles were more sensitive to the artistic side of the question and to the preservation of the values of the past than they were to the requirements of popular participation. As a result, the problem of singing and music turned out to be one of the trials of the reform. I have already mentioned it several times in these pages.[1]

1. *Preconceptions*

Readers might think that the uncomfortable dealings with the musicians and the difficulty of collaborating with them were due to a lack of care in carrying out the liturgical reform. In fact, however, the refusal of any dialogue preceded even the establishment of the Consilium and the beginning of its activity. The opposition of some musical circles was directed to the liturgical Constitution itself.

As early as April 1964 a Roman periodical published a bitter and sarcastic article with the expressive title "It's All the Musicians' Fault!"[2] Implementation of the liturgical Constitution had not even begun, yet here were individuals already talking of "innovators" bent on destroying the monumental accomplishments of sacred music. It was implied that these unidentified innovators were the ones responsible for the section of the liturgical Constitution on sacred music. The claim was made that the people were not attending church, and why? Because Palestrina was no longer being sung!

Another article of the same period, written in defense of the Sistine Choir, asserted:

> Opinions being broadcasted today in writings and in insistent calls for liturgical reforms have shown and continue to show an open aversion to everything that the Cappella Musicale Pontificia has jealously preserved as sacred down the centuries. For some time now, these opinions have been directed in an obsessional way (at least in the most ardent and fanatical holders of these views) against everything that the Cappella Musicale represents, everything that until today has been regarded as worthy of divine worship and has constituted the most important song of the Roman Church, namely, the Gregorian and polyphonic heritage.[3]

The future would see more writings in the same vein.

In fact, all this opposition to the magnificent choirs and the artistic music of the past did not exist at all, or at least it did not display the alleged tone and had no place in the intentions of those seriously concerned

---

1. See pp. 21–22, 216–18, 229–30, 282, n. 12, and p. 845, n. 28.

2. D. Bartolucci, "La colpa è tutta dei musicisti!" *Bollettino Ceciliano*, no. 4 (April 1964) 3–16. See above, pp. 229–30, on the steps taken by the Consilium in regard to periodicals dealing with liturgy, sacred song, and pastoral practice.

3. D. Bartolucci, "La Capella Sistina al Concilio," *Cappella Sistina*, no. 1 (January–March 1964).

with implementing the Constitution. The real reason for the rebellion against the reform was a refusal to allow that the people could sing. It was not to be tolerated, as was said in another account of "the present moment in sacred music," that "a group of seminarians and students from the religious orders" should "perform the liturgical songs in our place." The mentality at work may be seen in the following statement:

> In the case of a dialogue Mass, no one objects to the people singing their own songs, even to the exclusion of a choir (assuming that music is to be used).[4] In like manner, there should be no objection if the *schola* or choir continues to keep the musical heritage of the Church alive and unchanged in sung Masses; this is to the advantage of the people. The latter will always have ways of participating actively through their responses to the celebrant, the formulas that are theirs in the dialogues, the acclamations, and so on; a way can also be found of having them sing something at the offertory and communion; they can also end the rite with a suitable song. But the traditional repertory of the choir cannot and must not be touched. . . . This is not to say that there may not be special cases in which the entire congregation takes a fuller and even totally active part in the solemn liturgy by their singing . . . or that the mass of the faithful may not raise their mighty and ringing voice in the songs of the liturgy. . . . But these can only be exceptions and must not alter the principle that in the solemn liturgy the choir always keeps alive and preserves its traditional repertory.

On May 25, 1964, the Secretariat of State informed the Consilium of these reactions. It also sent statements by other musicians, both in Rome (Renzi, Virgili) and abroad (Séraphin, Berchten), and asked that the consultors of the Consilium should include "some choirmasters and heads of *scholae cantorum*, or famous composers, whose special experience will enable them to make a worthwhile contribution in the field of sacred music."

A list was sent on June 10.[5] Meanwhile, the Consilium had replied (May 29); it said among other things:

> The liturgical Constitution has not the slightest intention of making a clean sweep of the traditional musical genres. One need only read the docu-

---

4. In fact, these individuals would be constantly raising objections even in this area; see, e.g., "Il Convegno nazionale di Assisi," *Cappella Sistina*, no. 5 (January–March 1968) 91–98, where there is a warning against the "Gélineau disease" and an exhortation to preserve a united front against "the harmful activity of those who would like to reduce divine worship to a lifeless desert and, with a view to making it more accessible to the people, strip liturgical actions of the solemnity and splendor that musical art has given to them."

5. The list was approved on June 15, 1964, and the appointments were then made; the name of Monsignor Fiorenzo Romita, president of the International Federation of Little Singers, was added.

ment without preconceptions to see that it supports those genres and encourages them. Still less is it prejudiced against choirs. . . . The only thing
new in the Constitution is that for sound and unquestionable pastoral reasons it now bestows the rights of citizenship in holy Church on popular
religious song, which for that matter is widely recommended in the most
recent legislation. We can see no reason why this kind of singing cannot
be fostered and coexist peacefully with the traditional musical genres for
the glory of God and the fuller participation of the Christian people in the
worship of the Lord.

The reply went on to complain that periodicals and individuals connected with the Holy See were discrediting so important a document,
and one addressed to the entire Church, as the liturgical Constitution.

But the radical prejudice against any undertaking, by the Consilium
and other movements, for the fostering of popular sacred song remained
unchanged. Collaboration with the groups in question, though sought
and urged, was quite difficult, if not impossible. The situation becomes
clear if we consider the obstacles and opposition met in preparing two
of the most important Consilium documents on sacred music: the instruction *Musicam sacram* and the *Graduale simplex*. Among the many petitions
and counterobjections that came in during those years,[6] I select one that
nicely summarizes the prejudice and preconceptions: it is a statement
made by the president of the Istituto di Musica Sacra of Rome on May 20,
1966, and sent to the Consilium by the Secretariat of State on June 6:

> Everything that one reads and hears about the new reform of the litur-
> gical books for the Mass and the Roman Office enables one to foresee the
> artistic destruction that is coming; yet no one is concerned to stop it. It is
> a tragedy that is unfolding: all, and especially many of those in authority,
> complain and criticize and feel humiliated by what they see going on in
> the Church in the area of liturgy and the new music, but no one dares say
> a word. The liturgical Consilium, which the Holy Father established in order
> to direct and reorganize the new liturgy and its sacred music, does not re-
> gard anything in the artistic heritage of the Roman Church as worth sav-
> ing. Concerned as it is to create a liturgy for the people (as if papal Rome
> had for centuries had no understanding of this area), it seeks to create a
> tasteless singing that possesses neither soul nor art.

On the other hand, every effort was made to discourage sound and
honest attempts to produce effective musical creations, especially for

---

6. Here are a couple of examples. On June 7, 1965, the Secretariat of State forwarded
to the Consilium a "Memorandum on the Impoverishment of Sacred Music in Our Day"
from the Pontifical Institute for Sacred Music (12-page reply of the Consilium, June 19, 1965).
On June 19 came another memorandum from Bartolucci and Habel on "present problems
of sacred music and the new requirements of liturgical worship."

popular singing, that would respond to the new needs of the age and of the reformed liturgy. Here is an example. *Universa Laus*, an International Study Group on Song and Music in the Liturgy, was founded at Lugano in April 1966, with the approval of the Apostolic Administrator of that city. It had behind it seventy scholars of various countries, as well as five annual international meetings for the study of problems of music in the liturgy. On May 11 the Secretariat of State, acting in the Pope's name, sent a friendly letter of congratulations and encouragement. The year before, on the occasion of the Fourth Musical Study Week, held in Fribourg, Switzerland, the Consilium had sent the meeting a telegram via the bishop of the city; it regarded itself as encouraging an important and necessary activity.[7] In addition, *Universa Laus* had always kept the Consilium informed of its programs and had willingly accepted observations and changes.

There were those who found all this extremely annoying, for these various actions were interpreted as approval of *Universa Laus* by the Holy See, to the detriment of an association that the Holy See itself had established and officially approved: the *Consociatio Internationalis Musicae Sacrae*. The latter claimed, moreover, that *Universa Laus* was moving into the sphere proper to the *Consociatio*.

But *Universa Laus* had no intention of competing with the Roman *Consociatio*, whose activity in fact hardly anyone had even noticed up to this point; its only purpose was to work for sacred music and sacred song along the lines indicated by the liturgical Constitution. Here again time was wasted in claims and petitions. In a letter of August 20, 1966, the Consilium explained the whole affair to the Secretariat of State, as requested. It urged that there should be no misconception of what *Universa Laus* was doing; at the same time it advised that the position and competencies of the *Consociatio* be clearly stated. These two goals were accomplished through communications from Monsignor Overath on behalf of the *Consociatio* and from Father J. Gélineau on behalf of *Universa Laus*.

Someone took advantage of these, however, to create even more confusion by claiming that *Universa Laus* had been censured and should simply fade away. With authorization from the Secretariat of State, the Consilium published a clarification explaining the true status of the two organizations. *Universa Laus*, it said,

> is an autonomous and distinct organization, with clearly defined interests, which exists, lives, and works in the same way as the other musical associ-

---

7. The letter of the Secretariat and the telegram of the Consilium are in *DOL* 502 and 505.

ations confederated under the Consociatio. It too will be joined to the Consociatio at the proper time, in harmony of purpose and activity.[8]

The priests and laity who founded Universa Laus in their shared goals and their love of the liturgy have earned the Church's commendation. They may continue in holy joy the valuable work they have begun under the direction of the competent authority and in conformity with the Constitution on the Liturgy.[9]

With the passage of time and the replacement of old faces by new, resistances and tensions gradually eased. Some circles indeed always remained distrustful and inclined to malevolence. But the progress of the reform, the contributions of good composers to popular song, and the better balance struck between the needs and roles of the choir and the congregation paved the way for the solution of the problem that the Consilium had desired from the outset: mutual understanding, coexistence, and mutual support.

2. Labors of the Consilium for Music and Song

Questions of sacred music and song were entrusted to two different study groups: numbers 14 and 25; in addition, there was group 33, which had a supervisory role.[10]

1) Songs of the Mass

Group 14 was assigned the study of the various forms of singing in the Mass.[11] During 1964 the relator and secretary held meetings and corresponded with a view to establishing the general principles governing the relations between singing and the Mass. The entire group met in Rome in June 1964, in Fribourg, Switzerland, in August, and again in Rome in October. Meanwhile the first instruction on the application of the liturgical Constitution was being prepared, but any specific treatment of sacred music lay outside its scope. Events then suggested that there be a document on sacred music; the group offered its collaboration for this work. Then it had to wait for decisions on the structure and euchological texts of the Missal.

---

8. See "Doverosa precisazione," Not 2 (1966) 249–51. English text: Consilium, Necessary Clarification Nell'aprile scorso on Universa Laus and the Consociatio Internationalis Musicae Sacrae (October 1966), in DOL 507 nos. 4119-21.

9. But for this to happen, a change was required in the style, conduct, and even the statutes of the Consociatio. The Consilium would subsequently be asked to suggest the revision. But things would not change very much.

10. J. Beilliard was the relator of group 33, and its first members were Overath and Schmitt.

11. Relator: E. Moneta Caglio; secretary: J. Hourlier; members: R. Weakland, J. Beilliard, J. Percy, J. Smits van Waesberghe, P. Damilano, and H. Hucke.

Meanwhile, especially as use of the vernacular in the liturgy was extended, the situation changed completely. The principal role in choosing and adopting repertories of songs for celebrations in the vernacular had to be left to the episcopal conferences; a Roman group could only provide general criteria for passing judgment. The entrance and communion antiphons of the Missal were intended to be recited, not sung, and to inspire the creation of suitable songs in the vernacular.

As a result of all this, group 14 could do nothing but offer technical assistance.

2) *Reform of the books of Gregorian chant*

Group 25, for its part, was asked to revise the books of Gregorian chant for liturgical use.[12] Its role was to implement no. 117 of the liturgical Constitution, namely, to complete the typical edition of the books of Gregorian chant, prepare a more critical edition of the books already published after the reform of St. Pius X, and prepare an edition with simpler melodies for use in smaller churches. All this required research and adaptation.

In its program of work the group said:

> It seems appropriate to hand this task over to the Benedictine monks of the Abbey of Solesmes, which is especially equipped for the work, since it has on hand photographs of almost all the codices containing Gregorian notation. The Benedictines of Solesmes will be aided by qualified individuals from other schools, in order to ensure expert consideration of other trends in Gregorian interpretation.

To this group and its generous collaborator, the Abbey of Solesmes, are owing all the results achieved and already cited: *Kyriale simplex, Graduale simplex, Ordo cantus Missae,* and *Cantus qui in Missali Romano desiderantur,*[13] as well as the adaptation of all the Gregorian melodies found in the various liturgical books, especially the Missal and the Roman Pontifical.[14] At the fourth general meeting of the Consilium, the group presented a general report on the work to be done and on the most immediate task, which had been called for since the beginning of the liturgical reform;[15]

---

12. *Relator:* E. Cardine; *secretary:* L. Agustoni; *members:* M. Altisent, L. Kunz, J. Hourlier, J. Claire, and J. Harmel.

13. See above, pp. 119–22 and 405.

14. Especially deserving of recall is the work done on occasion of the publication of the volumes on the ordination of deacons, priests, and bishops, the consecration of virgins, and the dedication of a church. This group also produced the melodies for the "Missae in quarto periodo Concilii Oecumenici Vaticani II celebrandae" and for the little volume *Iubilate Deo.*

15. See Schema 34: *Libri cantus* 2 (September 10, 1964).

at the fifth general meeting (April 1965) it presented the *Graduale simplex;* and finally, at the eleventh general meeting (November 10, 1966), it presented its plan for the *Ordo cantus Missae.*[16] Unobtrusively and without much fanfare, and in presentations that were often modest and therefore not very showy and hardly intelligible even to the members of the Consilium, this group perform a very valuable and solid work.

3. *The Difficult Path of the* Graduale simplex

Among the various productions of group 25, the *Graduale simplex* was the one that had the most difficulty in securing approval.[17] After the fifth general meeting of the Consilium, the *Graduale* was submitted to the Congregation of Rites, which declared itself favorable but reserved final approval until it should see the page proofs. These were ready the next year, but at this point an intense, even if useless, campaign of opposition was launched.[18]

1) *Official nature of the publication*

On June 7, 1966, the Secretariat of State voiced a first uncertainty about the character of the publication, namely, whether it was or was not to be an official book. Cardinal Lercaro discussed the matter at an audience with the Pope and on June 23 wrote as follows to the Secretariat of State:

> It seems best to me that the *Graduale simplex* should appear under the authority of the Consilium and "for experiment," as is being done with the rite of concelebration. As long as the book has this kind of juridical status, it will always be possible to correct it, revise it, or even, should it prove less useful, abandon it. Since no organization with legal standing is involved, as the Congregation of Rites would be were it to issue the book by its decree, no harm whatsoever would be done.

The Cardinal suggested a formula of approval similar to the one on page 4 of the little book containing the Masses used during the fourth session of the Council.[19]

The Congregation of Rites did not share the Cardinal's view and proposed that the book appear under the egis of the Abbey of Solesmes.[20]

---

16. See Schema 359: *De Missali* 61 (November 5, 1969); see above, p. 405.

17. See above, pp. 120–22.

18. The Pope was kept constantly informed about the work: May 24, 1964; June 19, 1965; June 26, 1965.

19. The formula in question was: "The Masses in this Simple Gradual were prepared and approved for experimental use in sung Masses, especially in small churches, in accordance with the Constitution on the Sacred Liturgy, no. 117."

20. There were also some who proposed that the Simple Gradual appear under the ban-

But Father Cardine, who was the Abbey's authorized representative in Rome, categorically excluded this possibility (1) because the Abbey as such had not been involved in the book, but had simply allowed some of its monks to work on it in behalf of the Consilium; (2) because to attribute the *Graduale simplex* to Solesmes would jeopardize its success. At this point, rather than leave the *Graduale* to the Consilium, the Congregation of Rites agreed to sponsor it.[21]

This was made known to the Holy Father, who showed himself favorable (July 9, 1966). It was thought that now the road would be clear. But those who had promised to prevent the publication raised other difficulties.

2) *Nature of the* Graduale simplex

"Serious reservations" were voiced regarding the nature of the *Graduale simplex*. The Consilium had to submit a further statement on November 6, 1966. This was not enough: it also had to answer other objections. It will be worth seeing what these were, for they shed further light on the characteristics of the book, the criteria followed in composing it, and the difficulties and fears that were felt.

    I. "The musical forms of the Gregorian chant used in the Roman Mass would be destroyed."

    Answer: Not at all! The *Graduale simplex* does not replace any of the chantbooks presently used in the Roman liturgy but takes its place alongside them and sees to it that even the choirs of small churches, which until the pres-

---

ner of the Pontifical Institute for Sacred Music. But at a meeting in Chicago in August 1965, a spokesman for this view stated publicly that the Simple Gradual would never be published. In addition, as soon as Cardinal Lercaro learned of this new proposal, he immediately vetoed it and wrote to those in charge: "Sponsorship by the Institute would strip the work of any moral value; nor would the Holy See gain any prestige in the bishops' eyes."

21. The Congregation let this be known in a letter of July 2, 1966, in which it said, among other things: "It is our view that if the idea of publication by the Abbey of Solesmes is rejected, it should not be published by the Consilium, for two reasons: first, the goal of having the Holy See keep more or less aloof from the publication would be defeated since the Consilium, too, is an agency created by the Holy See and working in dependence on it; secondly, and more importantly, if the book were to be published by the Consilium, this would give credit to the already existing, even if erroneous, view that in matters liturgical there are two departments of government—the Congregation of Rites and the Consilium. If, on the other hand, the *Graduale simplex* is published by decree of the Congregation of Rites, as have all the other books prepared by the Consilium, the relative positions of these two groups would be maintained, namely, the Consilium as a study group that prepares the conciliar liturgical reform, and the Congregation of Rites as the institutional agency with authority in matters liturgical."

ent *have usually not sung the Proper* in sung Masses, can henceforth sing it and thus observe the prescriptions of liturgical law.

Therefore the *Graduale Romanum* and its offshoot, the *Liber usualis*, retain their full authority and will continue to be used as they have been down to the present where there are choirs or groups capable of singing these melodies in a dignified way.

II. "New forms would be introduced that are not adapted to the faithful and not in conformity with the art of the Church and with the liturgical renewal."

Answer: Not in the least! The melodies of the *Graduale simplex* are all in the present chantbooks. *None* of them is new. The manner of singing, in which one or more cantors alternate with the congregation, which sings a refrain verse, is the oldest and most traditional in the Church. Its use has shown how easy and possible this kind of singing is; the truth of this claim was seen at the fourth session of the ecumenical Council and can be seen every time the congregation responds to the chant with an easy verse, as often happens even in televised Masses. This manner of singing is completely in conformity with the Church's art, as is shown by the venerable tradition dating from the time of such Fathers as St. Ambrose and St. Augustine. It is also consistent with the liturgical renewal, since one of the reform's basic principles is the active participation of the faithful in both the actions and the singing of the sacred rites.

III. "The text of the Roman Mass would be changed" (that is, the introit, gradual, tract, alleluia, and offertory and communion verses would be changed and, in some cases, changed completely).

Answer: This is a logical consequence of the entire approach to the problem. The aim is to choose melodies that are both simple and authentic.

Simplicity cannot be achieved by curtailing the Gregorian neums, as has been attempted in some cases, with serious harm to the musical heritage; no Gregorianist would have accepted such a solution. Nor would any Gregorianist have accepted neo-Gregorian melodies, that is, new compositions for the texts of the Missal. We say nothing of the difficulties in using as refrains texts as long as the present antiphons of the Missal, especially the antiphons for introit and offertory.

Authenticity is maintained by selecting solely from the truly Gregorian repertory, either as contained in the typical editions already published or as derived from the manuscripts. In the second case, it is logically necessary to fall back on texts which, though different from those presently in use, are nonetheless similar and inspired by the same ideas of the liturgical season or feast. In general, it can be said, however, that the text of an antiphon derived from a psalm and lacking a simple melody in the Gregorian repertory will be found elsewhere as a psalm verse that is sung together with the antiphon.

Then, too, the fundamental criterion that governs the organization of the *Graduale simplex* must be kept in mind: the aim is not to provide a set of chants for every single Sunday and feast but to provide a set that can be useful for a liturgical season, with permission to use it several times during the same period. For the final Sundays after Epiphany and Pentecost, there is, in addition to a separate set of presidential prayers and readings for each Sunday, a set of chants that is repeated without change each Sunday.

In any case, what really gives a Mass its tone is not so much the songs as it is the prayers and readings. And if we want to lead the congregations and small choirs to the regular practice of the sung Mass, no other way is feasible. We cannot ask the people to learn a set of songs which, no matter how short and simple, is completely new each Sunday and feast day. The important thing, therefore, is that the chants maintain and underscore the concepts that inspire a season or feast rather than that the congregation be bound to a text proper to a particular melodic form with which it is closely connected.

The frontal attack managed to delay publication. Meanwhile, requests were coming in from all sides from bishops who had seen the usefulness of the melodies and texts of the *Graduale simplex* at the fourth session of the Council. They came from Spain, South Africa, the United States, New Guinea, and Hong Kong. Therefore the Consilium wrote to the Secretariat of State once again on March 21, 1967, and asked for authorization to allow the *Graduale simplex* for experiment to the conferences or individual bishops who had requested it. The delay in publication was seen as doing serious damage to the future of the sung Mass.

3) *Final Difficulties*

At last, on June 14, 1967 (No. 98848), the situation improved. The little craft that had ended up on the rocks was beginning to get moving again. The draft of the decree and the introduction were sent back to the Consilium with some changes.

1. The title had read "Simple Gradual for the Use of Small Churches and Small Groups" in order to cover all situations. For in fact there can be small churches that have a fine choir, capable of executing even the most complicated melodies of the Roman Gradual, while there can also be basilicas that do not have even the minimum personnel for a dignified sung celebration, partly because of the groups that succeed one another there.[22]

---

22. The ways things were going was so obvious that the Simple Gradual was used at Masses of the Council in St. Peter's Basilica, which is certainly not a "small church," nor were the assembled Fathers a "small group"! Given the possibility of a wide range of uses, the Consilium did not want to impose limitations.

The revisor for the Secretariat of State, however, removed the words "and Small Groups," on the grounds that "they are not found in article 117 of the Constitution, which is cited in the decree. Omission of the words will, among other things, help to prevent abuses leading to the practical elimination of the Roman Gradual and to avoid giving a further occasion for other heated and harmful controversies."

2. The revisor also asked for removal of the clause calling this a typical edition.[23]

3. On the other hand, he asked that a clause limiting use of the book be added to the decree: "in those places whose episcopal conferences or, as the case may be, individual bishops ask this Sacred Congregation for use of the book in sung Masses (including solemn Masses), in accordance with the instruction *Musicam sacram* (nos. 28-29)."

His justification was that "this addition is in accordance with the suggestion of the Consilium (March 21, 1967). The balance it introduces will do a great deal to calm the many authoritative persons who are opposed to the *Graduale simplex*, by showing how it has been conceived and how it is to be used."

In its reply of June 20, 1967, to all the points made by the revisor, the Consilium responded as follows to this one:

> It is not appropriate to adduce the Consilium's letter of March 21, 1967, because the writer of the notes is very well aware that for two years now the Consilium has been writing and petitioning to get the *Graduale simplex* afloat again. It has made *numerous* suggestions, down to the very recent ones, in which it has asked that the work might be given *at least* to the conferences, not because this is the best way to go about it, but in order to resolve an *unbelievable situation*. But if a juridical approach is taken to "publication," then to allow the book by indult is completely unacceptable.
>
> 2) The motu proprio *Pastorale munus* granted bishops faculties hitherto reserved to the Holy See; they were granted only because the bishops asked for them. Do you want to begin a new list of such faculties?
>
> 3) "To be granted only for *non-solemn* Masses" means that the solemn form of celebration will disappear completely in the parishes, because there will not be a choir capable of executing the "more ornate" melodies. But

---

23. The Consilium was of the opinion that for the sake of peace it should not insist on its position. In fact, the *Graduale simplex* would not carry the words "typical edition," and the decree would *allow its use* "unless some future legislation determines otherwise." The "otherwise" came about: in the second edition the book is not only said to be a typical edition but is without ado called "the second typical edition" (November 21, 1974)! By now everyone had forgotten that because of the lawyers' quibbles, the first edition had not been regarded as "typical." The favorable reception of the book had caused these subtleties to be forgotten.

this is to sacrifice doctrinal and pastoral values to estheticism pure and simple.

4) If the book is allowed for experiment, then the granting of it is a matter for the Consilium, not for the Congregation of Rites.

4. The most serious observation on the introduction, since it required the correction of several pages already printed, was the removal of the term "psalmist." This point had already been discussed when the instruction on sacred music was being prepared. The reason given by the Roman musicians was that "a personage thus conceived and having these functions will destroy the authentic forms of the Roman Gradual, in which the Gradual psalms and the tracts are always assigned to the cantors."

But, given the character of the new book, the situation here was different. There was no question now of the Roman Gradual but of a "simple" one. The Consilium therefore believed that the term "psalmist" could be kept.

When the Secretariat of State sent on the definitive text of the decree and of the introduction on August 2, 1967 (No. 102646) and ordered that it be published, it also sent a note approved by the Pope. It said:

1) The title finally adopted is *Graduale simplex in usum minorum ecclesiarum* (Simple Gradual for the Use of Small Churches) and ought to appear in its entirety on the cover or title page of the book.

2) The term "psalmist" is to be removed from *all* the pages of the printer's proofs on which it appears and is to be replaced by "cantor."

Thus the book was published by a decree of the Congregation of Rites dated September 1, 1967.[24]

---

24. SCR, *Graduale simplex in usum minorum ecclesiarum* (Vatican City: Libreria Editrice Vaticana, 1967. Pp. vii + 432). The decree of the SCR (September 3, 1967) for the first edition is in *DOL* 532 no. 4256; the decree for the second edition is in *DOL* 536 no. 4303. The introduction to the first edition is in *DOL* 533 nos. 4257-74. Changes made in the introduction in the second edition are given in *DOL* 537 nos. 4304-10.

59

The Instruction on Sacred Music

I. HISTORY

1. *Origin of the Document*

Discussion of the problem of sacred music and song began when the instruction *Inter Oecumenici* was being drafted. Study group 14 had begun to set down some guiding principles on the subject. It was thought, however, that the matter called for a broader and fuller treatment and riper reflection.

When *Inter Oecumenici* had been published and musicians saw no reference in it to nos. 112, 114, and 117 of the liturgical Constitution that would underscore the importance of sacred music, they began to raise their voices in protest. They appealed to the Secretariat of State, which wrote to the Consilium about the matter on December 22, 1964 (No. 34384). The failure to refer to sacred music in *Inter Oecumenici* was being interpreted as a "positive and deliberate exclusion of, among other things, polyphonic and Gregorian sacred music."

The Consilium pointed out (January 4, 1965) that the instruction was not intended as a complete and exhaustive commentary on or application of the entire liturgical Constitution, but simply as providing concrete norms on points that required these; there was no repetition in this document of what was perfectly clear in the liturgical Constitution. One need only note, the Consilium's reply continued, that of the 130 articles in the Constitution, only 31 are considered in the first instruction. The Consilium promised, however, that it would take up the subject of sacred music with the fullness it called for in a special instruction in which musicians of every trend would be asked to collaborate. Thus the idea of an instruction on sacred music, which was already in the air, took shape. The introduction of the vernacular into the liturgy hastened the fulfillment of this promise.

On January 25, 1965, the Consilium explained the situation to the Secretariat of State and suggested a document in which it would say: (1) that the limits set on the language spoken by the episcopal conferences required simply a general program; (2) that this program need not necessarily be applied to all Masses with a congregation; (3) that, as the rector of a church judged desirable, there could be Latin Gregorian chants, polyphony, and modern music; (4) that even in Masses in Latin there should be some minimum in the vernacular, for example, the readings, the prayer of the faithful, and some songs, as a way of allowing the lively participation of the faithful; (5) that at least the Creed and the *Sanctus* should be in Gregorian but should use a melody that the entire congregation could join in singing.

An answer came back quickly and was favorable.

On February 12 the first schema of the document was ready; it was prepared by the relator of study group 14, who used the thoughts already expressed at the meetings of the previous year.[1] In fourteen numbers it explained the situation in which sacred music found itself as a result of the adoption of the vernacular, and the necessity of preserving the Gregorian and polyphonic heritage while at the same time bringing new demands into harmony with what was valid in the tradition. The schema was sent to the consultors. Twenty-four of them responded: all found the text too short, weak, and lacking in incisiveness. They were unanimous in wanting the instruction to review and codify the entire current discipline on sacred music as it related to the liturgical constitution, just

---

1. The instruction required twelve schemas:
Schema 62: *De musica sacra* 1 (February 12, 1965).
Schema 84: *De musica sacra* 2 (April 26, 1965).
Schema 117: *De musica sacra* 3 (October 20, 1965).
Schema 122: *De musica sacra* 4 (November 15, 1965).
Schema 126: *De musica sacra* 5 (November 25, 1965).
Schema 131: *De musica sacra* 6 (December 1, 1965).
Schema 141: *De musica sacra* 7 (January 13, 1966).
Schema 143: *De musica sacra* 8 (February 3, 1966).
Schema 145: *De musica sacra* 9 (February 24, 1966).
Schema 155: *De musica sacra* 10 (April 21, 1966).
Schema (no number): *De musica sacra* 11 (November 21, 1966).
Schema (no number): *De musica sacra* 12 (February 2, 1967).

as the instruction of September 3, 1958, had done with regard to previous legislation.

This new approach yielded the second schema, which was written with meticulous care and resolute determination by Canon A.-G. Martimort; in it the fourteen numbers of the first schema became seventy-four.

2. The Instruction's Way of the Cross

The new schema was studied by forty consultors at a meeting of the relators in Rome on April 29, 1965. It was well received on the whole, although it seemed somewhat verbose at times. Now it had to be gone over with the musicians, among whom discontent was already rife.

On May 25, 1965, in agreement with the academic senate of the Pontifical Institute of Sacred Music, Monsignor Anglés had submitted a memorandum to the Pope on the state of sacred music; in it he complained that the musicians had not been consulted during preparation of the instruction. Another memorandum followed on June 7. It asserted that the Consilium was not listening to real musicians but was seeking the views only of those representing a "certain trend"; it also complained that the instruction Inter Oecumenici had allowed the entire Proper and Ordinary of the Mass to be in the vernacular. Furthermore, it is priests and not the laity who are calling for the sacrifice of Latin, and this, quite often, not for the good of the faithful or to foster the active participation of the people, but out of "a spirit of nationalism and due to an anti-Roman tendency"; the faithful, except for those who sing, understand nothing of liturgical texts sung in the vernacular; in a few months' time everything has been lost; non-Catholics are much more concerned about Gregorian chant than the Catholic Church is. After other complaints in this vein and accusations against the Consilium ("it is not very sensitive to the safeguarding of sacred music"), the memorandum asked the Holy See to intervene and prevent "the practical introduction of many abuses."[2]

The attack was really against the entire liturgical reform. It was not difficult, indeed, to rebut, one by one, all the claims made by the president of the Institute of Sacred Music. It was evident, nonetheless, that the time had come to bring the musicians into the committee that was to put the finishing touches on the text that the liturgists had drawn up as a basis for the instruction.

---

2. The Secretariat of State sent this letter on to the Consilium on June 7, 1965, "with the recommendation to study this serious and urgent question in an organized way, to appoint, if necessary, a special committee, whose names we would like to know, and kindly to inform this Office with all due haste of the Consilium's thinking and activity in this area."

In order to make the meeting go more easily, the secretariat of the Consilium thought it proper to take direct charge of the affair. The committee was made up of forty-three experts, half of them liturgists and half musicians;[3] the third schema was sent out to all of them.[4] Thirty-four replied, almost all favorable to the schema as a whole. Only three musicians were dissatisfied because in their opinion the schema did not sufficiently safeguard the treasury of sacred music, especially polyphony; they therefore rejected the schema in its entirety.

The observations received from the experts were used in preparing the fourth schema, and a meeting was called for November 15, 1965. This gathering, which was intended to promote a meeting of minds, proved instead to be the beginning of a complicated and endless "way of the cross" for the instruction.

The meeting was held in the Palazzo Santa Marta, in the presence of Cardinal Lercaro. In attendance were twenty-five liturgists and musicians; among the latter were Monsignors Anglés, Bartolucci, and Romita. After an explanation of the criteria followed in the instruction and of its general structure, each number was studied. During the three hours of the meeting, Monsignors Anglés and Romita did almost all the talking. Monsignor Bartolucci stayed for an hour and then asked to be excused for reasons of duty, but left his observations in writing. Monsignor Overath did not come, nor did he send his observations to the Consilium; instead, he wrote that he had sent them to "higher authority." Monsignor Anglés had a copy of them, however, and asked that they be read at the microphone from time to time so that all might hear them. This was done.

The other musicians, who represented all sorts of trends, and, of course, the liturgists stayed and listened; they were in agreement on the text that had been given to them. The arguments against the instruction were weak and at times captious.[5]

---

3. On March 27, 1965 (No. 25598) the Secretariat of State, "on orders from higher authority," suggested "the appropriateness of including in the Instruction on Sacred Music a commendation of the Federation of Little Singers and listening to the views of its president, Monsignor Fiorenzo Romita, on this matter."

4. The experts were: J. Wagner, A.-G. Martimort, A. Dirks, J. Percy, A. Hänggi, J. Gélineau, L. Agustoni, L. Buijs, H. Schmidt, L. Borello, L. Trimeloni, S. Famoso, P. Jounel, F. McManus, J. Smits van Waesberghe, A. Franquesa, E. Lengeling, J. A. Jungmann, E. Moneta Caglio, B. Neunheuser, P. Damilano, J. Hourlier, E. Cardine, T. Schnitzler, P. Gy, R. Falsini, R. Weakland, J. Beilliard, J. Harmel, J. Claire, L. Kunz, I. Tassi, C. Vagaggini, I. Anglés, F. Romita, M. Altisent, B. Fischer, E. Bonet, H. Hucke, D. Bartolucci, L. Migliavacca, J. Overath, and F. Schmitt. This list, with that of the persons consulted on occasion of the composition of the other schemas, was made known to the Holy Father; on November 24, 1965, the Pope sent word that he was satisfied with the selection.

5. Let one example represent all. The instruction began with the words "Ministeriale

Some changes were accepted, others were not because they reflected bygone ideas of sacred music and took as their ideal the music and singing of the musical "chapels" as well as polyphonic performances and concerts. The new problems raised for sacred song by pastoral liturgics were either ignored or barely touched on. This was precisely the pivotal point in all the questions raised later and the reason for all the time lost. But it also strengthened the conviction that the instruction was needed for the renewal of song and music in liturgical celebrations.

3. Within the Consilium

From the meeting of November 15 came the fifth schema,[6] which was sent to the consultors and members of the Consilium. It was then studied at the sixth general meeting of the Consilium in November 1965. The discussion was preceded by a report that briefly reviewed the history of the instruction thus far and dwelt on its essential pastoral purpose: to foster the participation of the faithful. The relator stated the principles and general criteria at work in the document and reviewed the role of music and song in the more important rites: Mass, Divine Office, sacraments and sacramentals, liturgical year, and pious exercises. The final sections of the instruction were devoted to language, the treasury of sacred music, the melodies for new texts, instrumental music, and, finally, the task of liturgical commissions and commissions on sacred music.

Discussion among the Fathers and experts focused on individual points, with special attention to the most important. There was full discussion of no. 36 (no. 32 in the final text), which allowed the chants of the Mass to be replaced by other songs approved by the episcopal conferences. The instruction restricted itself to confirming the indults granted

---

munus musicae sacrae in dominico servitio" ("the ministerial function supplied by sacred music in the service of the Lord"). Monsignor Anglés launched a lively attack on the text; J. Overath did the same in a closely typed page. Yet the words were taken unchanged from the liturgical Constitution, no. 112. When this was pointed out, Monsignor Anglés was dumbfounded. Monsignor Wagner also reminded him that in the schema of the conciliar preparatory commission, Pius X's words "ancilla liturgiae Musica sacra" ("sacred music is the handmaiden of liturgy") had been used at this point and that it was Monsignor Anglés who as a member of the conciliar commission had gotten the phrase changed to "ministeriale munus musicae sacrae," the very phrase that was now causing him difficulty.

6. *Relator:* C. Braga, who to the end would be the skilled supporter of the document. The groups of experts for the occasion consisted of the following: two musicians of the Roman tradition, I. Anglés and D. Bartolucci; two Gregorianists, E. Cardine and L. Agustoni; two canon lawyers, E. Bonet and F. McManus; two theologians, C. Vagaggini and H. Schmidt; two pastoral experts, J. Wagner and A.-G. Martimort; and two rubricists, A. Dirks and A. Franquesa.

to certain countries for this purpose. Those concerned in these indults, namely, the consultors and members from the German-speaking countries, supported retention of this number; others regarded it as unnecessary because it referred to particular cases; still others thought that the *Graduale simplex* would handle the situation. The majority, however, saw the pastoral advantage of having other songs besides the psalms for the Proper of the Mass.

The paragraph was put to a vote and accepted.[7] It would subsequently play a very important role, because the episcopal conferences would appeal to it as a basis for asking the same indult for their regions. The principle of songs in the vernacular would be extended to the entire Church in the reformed Roman Missal.[8]

The discussion ended with a positive vote on the schema as a whole. The observations gathered served in drawing up the sixth schema, which was regarded as the definitive text when it was sent to the members and consultors and to the Holy Father on December 1, 1965.

4. *The Musicians Behind the Scenes*

On December 29 the Cardinal Secretary of State returned the papers, along with a note

> in which are summarized the thoughts presented on the subject by the Reverend Msgr. Anglés; the "notes" in pencil are those of the Holy Father. With regard to the *Cappelle* [special choirs]: it seems a good idea to add some special norms declaring that there is no intention of overlooking them, for they represent a tradition and are the heirs of a priceless artistic and religious patrimony, and because they have a specific task of their own, especially in some locales and in special circumstances of the liturgical year. They must therefore continue to lead an honorable existence wherever appropriate, while at the same time coordinating their activity with activity regulated by the new liturgical norms.

The note contained nine pages of remarks that the man in charge of music at the Secretariat of State had transcribed; he also adorned them with anti-liturgical gibes of his own.[9] The remarks referred once again to

---

7. The outcome: 17 for; 7 against; 1 abstention.

8. See GIRM 26, 50, and 56i.

9. See, e.g., the introductory note: "(a) The instruction must be faithful to the letter and spirit of the liturgical Constitution; (b) it must avoid getting into controversy and supporting one or the other trend among students whether of liturgy or of music; (c) since this is an instruction on *music*, an appeal to a (misunderstood) 'good of souls' may not justify sacrificing or attacking the vast and lofty heritage of traditional music, whether Gregorian or polyphonic, which is by now a heritage of the entire human race. As you know, the

the opening words, "the ministerial function supplied by sacred music," for the writer saw in them the position of "one school of musicians" in whose eyes music is always "the handmaid of liturgy" and musicians are the servants of the liturgists; that position, it was said, denied music its dignity and autonomy.[10] Another remark asked that the expression "groups of singers," which included all possible categories, from larger groups to the most modest, be changed to "choirs."[11]

Another of the more serious challenges was to no. 9 (no. 16 of the final text), which had to do with the active participation of the congregation by means of song. Various degrees of participation were indicated: first of all, the acclamations, responses, and refrains, then the other parts of the Mass. The text recommended that when the congregation is not sufficiently trained to express itself in song, it should be gradually educated at least to participate in the simplest and most elementary parts. When the choir does part-singing, the congregation should never be deprived of the easiest parts of the Mass.

Here precisely is where the views of the two sides diverged: in the view of the liturgists the people must truly *sing* in order to participate actively as desired by the liturgical constitution; in the view of musicians, however, even "listening to good, devout, and edifying music . . . promotes 'active' participation."[12]

These and other observations[13] betrayed a mentality that could not come to grips with new pastoral needs. In any case, a good number of the observations were accepted; others could not be accepted without betraying the mandate the Consilium had received. The result was the seventh schema.

Holy Father wanted this instruction precisely to safeguard interests not protected by the [first] Instruction on the Orderly Carrying Out of the Constitution on the Liturgy, which gave rise to serious controversy."

10. The criticism was in error, but it was agreed to begin the instruction with the words *Musicam sacram* and defer the reference to "ministeriale munus" to no. 2.

11. "Coetus cantorum" ("groups of singers") was a polite way of recalling all those involved in sacred song. But the expression was accused of being "deliberately equivocal." This change was also accepted, though with little enthusiasm.

12. The musicians even invoked the authority of St. Thomas: "Although some may not understand what is being sung, they understand why it is being sung, that is, *for the praise of God*, and this is enough, even if the faithful do not strictly speaking sing in order to rouse their devotion." The Pope placed a large question mark alongside these arguments and interpretations.

13. Other observations referred to nos. 14 (agents of the celebration), 16 (conscious participation), 18 (training in music), 32 (degrees of participation in the singing), 36 (substitution of religious songs), 38 (gradual of the Mass), 39 (Ordinary of the Mass), 41 (singing of the priest), 54 (use of Latin), and so on.

The musicians received the new schema as they had received its predecessors. Their reaction can be learned from numerous letters of Monsignor Anglés to Cardinal Larraona, prefect of the Congregation of Rites.[14] The schema was also studied at a meeting of the Congregation of Rites.[15] As a result, the eighth, ninth, and tenth schemas saw the light in the first months of 1966. The most fully developed of these was the ninth, in which many numbers of the text were revised in order to meet the demands of the musicians. But the Consilium did not intend to yield on certain basic points, since they embodied the basic principles on which the liturgical reform was founded. It decided therefore to speak to the Holy Father of the matter in a well-documented and detailed memorandum dated March 18, 1966.

5. *Four Points Made to the Pope*

Here are the main points made in the statement to the Pope:

1) *Nature and character of the participation of the faithful*

The idea the liturgical Constitution has of this is very clear and does not agree with that of the musicians. According to the Constitution, participation must be conscious and active, internal and external, and find expression in acclamations, responses, psalmody, and songs (see nos. 14, 30).

The instruction points out that there are degrees in this participation: from a minimum of responses and more simple songs to the possibility of participation in all the singing. It allows that some parts of the liturgy can be performed by the choir, provided that the faithful are not com-

---

14. January 25, 1966: "I return the schema . . . with some observations: they do not intend to take the serious approach to this instruction that is alone worthy of a document of the Holy See." Further complaints: the musicians have not been consulted; the group is unwilling to accept St. Thomas' concept of "active participation."

January 29, 1966: "The man at the Secretariat of State who was expressly put in charge of this problem by the Holy Father has asked me to tell Your Eminence that it is urgently necessary for the Congregation to tell the Holy Father in writing . . . that the instruction cannot be published as it stands . . . and that another committee must be appointed that is composed of real musical experts if the thing is to come out right."

January 30, 1966: another exhortation to write to the Holy Father that a different document must be composed by different people.

February 1, 1966: still another memorandum with remarks on thirty-four points. Steps are taken to prevent us from seeing even the texts that have been changed. We do not agree, e.g., that the words *Musicam sacram* should open the document; another attack on the "ministeriale munus" idea.

15. On January 31 and February 3, 1966.

pletely excluded from participation in the singing. The rights and functions of both the congregation and the choir are thus sufficiently protected and coordinated. But it would be contrary to the Constitution to sacrifice the participation of the faithful by restricting it to the simpler responses and not allowing the congregation to express itself more fully in the songs of the Ordinary and Proper of the Mass.

2) *Language to be used in sung celebrations*

The entire work of the Council makes it clear that the principles set down for use of the vernacular refer to all celebrations, whether with or without singing. The Constitution never distinguishes these two types. In no. 113, for example, when speaking of a solemn sung celebration, it expressly says that as regards the language to be used, the norms given for the various parts of the liturgy (Mass, sacraments, Office, and so on) are to be followed. In like manner, the instruction *Inter Oecumenici* makes no distinction between read and sung Masses (no. 37).

It follows from this that:

a) It would be contrary to the Constitution to decree or even to hint that sung celebrations, especially of the Mass, should be in Latin.

b) It would be contrary to the pastoral benefit of the faithful (and would therefore be ill received by the bishops) to decree that only singing in Latin is to be allowed in cathedral and collegiate churches. Indeed, such churches of a diocese should serve as examples to the other churches in the matter of pastoral organization.

c) On the other hand, it is legitimate to insist on what the liturgical Constitution and the instruction of 1964 decree, namely:

—the use of Latin in specifically determined cases, such as the choral celebration of the Divine Office by clerics;

—the ability to recite and sing the Ordinary of the Mass in Latin, especially in certain circumstances.

The musicians, as represented by the observations of Monsignor Anglés, had asked:

—that the use of Latin in sung Masses be obligatory in seminaries, religious houses, and Catholic schools;

—that there be a reminder of the norm requiring Latin in the recitation of the Divine Office by clerics;

—that there be an explicit reference to the maintenance of Latin in sacred celebrations in accordance with no. 36, 1 of the Constitution.

The first of these wishes could not be granted, because it is contrary to the pastoral benefit of the faithful, inasmuch as it involves their active and conscious participation, even and above all in cathedrals and schools;

and because in other cases it is in opposition to norms which the Holy See has issued for religious and seminaries and which allow the possibility of celebrations in the vernacular.

Furthermore, how can clerics be trained for the vernacular liturgy that will occupy most of their ministry if they experience only celebrations in Latin? Singing is something that requires long practice, beginning in youth.

The second of the three requests was accepted.

The third was accepted in part. After saying that the language of liturgical celebrations is either Latin (by law, confirmed by the liturgical Constitution, no. 36, 1) or the vernacular (by decree of territorial authority), the instruction states that in choosing the language in each case, the capacity of the participants must be kept in mind, as must the norms established by competent authority.

3) The "treasure of sacred music" and its preservation

The Constitution on the Liturgy shows proper esteem for the value of the musical repertory, both Gregorian and polyphonic, when it says that "the treasure of sacred music is to be preserved and fostered" (no. 114).

The reference is to the musical repertory connected with the Latin texts of the liturgy. When, therefore, the Constitution allowed the introduction of the vernaculars, it necessarily anticipated that the preservation of this "treasure of sacred music" would be dependent solely on celebrations in Latin. The musicians, concerned as they were that the musical heritage be preserved in liturgical celebrations, saw themselves under attack in any norm that would allow singing in the vernacular.

In this part of the text, the instruction intends to make it clear that just as there are two forms of celebration, one in Latin, the other in the vernacular, in accordance with the norms established by competent authority, so the use of the musical repertory that is connected with the Latin text is for celebrations in Latin, although it is possible to use some parts of it even in celebrations in the vernacular.

In particular, the instruction provides that:

a) The more ornate Gregorian melodies are to be carefully used; it is permitted, however, to use the simpler melodies of the *Graduale simplex* and *Kyriale simplex* in smaller churches and wherever people are not in a position to make proper use of the more ornate forms.

b) Compositions in another musical genre, with one or more voices, are also to be held in honor and used when it is possible to perform them properly; they require, in fact, a choir that is especially well trained.

c) These musical compositions of the past (Gregorian and polyphonic), which were written for the Latin text, can also be used in vernacular celebrations, provided the combination of the two languages is suitable.

d) The parts of the musical repertory of the past that cannot be adapted to the new requirements of the reformed liturgy may be used in popular devotions and especially in celebrations of the word.

e) Study of the repertory of the past, and especially of Gregorian, should be the basis of musical training, even when the ultimate goal is the creation of new compositions.

4) Choirs

Although the conciliar Constitution emphasizes the collective participation of the entire congregation in the celebration, including the singing, it also acknowledges in a positive way the value of the choir both as helping to lead the singing of the faithful and as having its own role in the celebration. The effort to promote the active participation of the faithful has led in some places to the extreme step of doing away with the choir. The musicians have therefore insisted that the instruction bring out the importance of the choir, especially in preserving the "treasury of music."

The instruction deals with this point in more than one article:

a) *Name:* the text retains the traditional name, *schola cantorum*, while noting that modern languages may use some other designation that is more in keeping with the character of the language and with the reality of the body named;

b) *Duties:* to see to the worthy performance of the parts proper to it in accordance with the musical genre being used and to lead the singing of the faithful;

c) *Makeup:* men alone or men and women together or, in case of necessity, women alone, as already foreseen in the encyclical *Musicae sacrae* of Pius XII and in the instruction of September 3, 1958;

d) *Location of the singers:* the place of the choir should make it clear that this group is part of the congregation of the faithful, while at the same time facilitating its special role and the participation (including sacramental participation) of the singers; it should therefore be within view of the altar and, if possible, close to it;

e) *Training:* this should be not only musical but liturgical; it should be carried out with the collaboration of the associations for sacred music, especially those approved and recommended by the Holy See.

In setting down these norms, the instruction has in view the normal situation and therefore such choirs as one finds in the majority of churches. It decrees in fact that choirs are to be established at the major churches, and especially in cathedrals and seminaries; it urges their establishment even in smaller churches, especially for the purpose of leading the congregational singing. The great choirs, or *cappelle musicali*, which are an institution peculiar to certain great churches or basilicas, are considered separately; the instruction desires their continued existence under their own statutes, especially for the singing they do in certain special circumstances.

6. *Harmonization of Texts*

When the Pope received the tenth schema, he felt an obligation to get a better insight into the divergent points of view. He therefore asked the musicians to draw up a single text that would include their variants and to provide justification for their differences with the liturgists. When he moved to Castelgandolfo for the summer months, he took the two schemas, that of the Consilium and that of the musicians, with him and attempted himself to produce a single text by taking the best parts from each schema and jotting down his own reflections. At times he softened expressions by adding "as far as possible"; at other times he divided one paragraph into two; he also interspersed the text with frequent question marks. Every time he found the word "omitted" in the musicians' text, he asked "Why?" or else noted: "This can remain" or "This can be omitted." When the two texts were identical, he wrote "The same." All this shows how attentively he read everything, for not infrequently the differences between the two texts were very slight and would have eluded a hasty reader.

On November 21, 1966, he sent the results of his work to the Consilium with a request that it redo the text in accordance with the annotations in the margin. The hard work of collating the texts must have given the Pope a deep understanding of the document, for he refers to the latter in his address to the members of the Consilium on October 13, 1966:

> There are certain weighty issues . . . that require careful attention, our own included. One is sacred music, which engages the interest of both liturgical and musical experts. The topic needs thorough exploration, which will undoubtedly come about as, on the one side, pastoral experience and, on the other, the musical arts continue an exchange that, we hope, will progress amicably and profitably. An instruction guiding the interrelationship of music and liturgy will make their cooperation easier. We are confident that it will restore a new collaboration between those two sublime voices

of the human spirit, prayer and art. . . . Here we should like to remind you of what the conciliar Constitution decreed on music and liturgy, doing honor to both. It is enough to point out that the pastoral and community character marking liturgical renewal and intended by the Council requires the revision and refashioning of music and sacred song in regard to those qualities by which they are, as they should be already, conjoined to the actions of the rites. To each the way must be opened to gain new worth, as it were, and to be encouraged to claim in the field of art and religion a new glory: "Sacred music will be the more holy the more closely it is joined to the liturgical rite."[16]

But the dance of the back-and-forth was not over. As soon as the text put together by the Consilium (schema 11) at the Pope's request reached the man in charge of music at the Secretariat of State, he saw in it just one more trick to do harm to true sacred music. His "discoveries" were communicated to the Consilium on December 19; they were completed by others on December 27. There is no point in relating them here, since they kept going back over the same points as before.[17]

Despite the objections, the Pope stood by the balanced and carefully worded text of the Consilium. As a result, the latter could move forward without losing more precious time. After a new revision, including stylistic improvements, the twelfth schema was submitted to the Pope on February 9, 1967, and was published on March 5, 1967, the Fourth Sunday of Lent, or Laetare Sunday.[18]

The document was presented to the press by the secretary of the Consilium;[19] at his side was Father Lopez Calo, who during the preceding years had played a marked role in the campaign against what the liturgical Constitution had to say about sacred music. This press conference of March 4 saw further unpleasant incidents of protest, especially on the part of Monsignor Virgili, master of the Cappella Pontificia at St. John Lateran. He also sponsored a debate, in the pressroom of the Holy See, on the evening of March 6 in order to attack the newly published document. He was supported by the principal Roman newspapers, which were run by laymen and which railed against this new attack on tradition; their

---

16. DOL 84 no. 635.

17. The emphasis is on the Consilium not having followed the Pope's instructions, whereas the musicians did follow them. Father Gélineau is twice attacked, on the grounds that some points in the instruction depended on his ideas, as though the document was aiming to canonize these ideas.

18. SCR, instruction Musicam sacram on music in the liturgy (March 5, 1967): DOL 508 nos. 4122-90. See L. Agustoni, presentation of the document in Not 3 (1967) 81–86; notes on some numbers, 105–8; and see EL 81 (1967) 230–98.

19. See L'Osservatore Romano, March 4–5, 1967.

ideas, of course, were distorted and twisted the meaning of the instruction.[20]

This was the final act in the series of bitter attacks which accompanied the preparation of the document and which were a price that had to be paid in securing the welfare of the Church. In fact, this instruction remains one of the soundest documents of the reform; it opened the way for the progress made in subsequent years and supplied it in advance with balanced guidelines that were in harmony with the spirit of the liturgical Constitution and the authentic renewal of the liturgy.

II. Contents

The instruction contains sixty-nine numbers, which include a preface and nine chapters.

The preface explains the nature and scope of the instruction, which is to deal with some questions regarding the ministerial role of music in liturgical celebrations and with the active participation of the faithful, in light of the new situation that had arisen after the liturgical Constitution and its initial application.

1. *General Norms*

Liturgical celebrations take on a nobler aspect when they are celebrated with singing and when all present participate according to their rank and office. The sung form of the liturgy is the normal form. For a liturgical action is truer and more authentic when each person fills the role proper to him or her and when the varying character of the rites is respected. The liturgical action will therefore be more perfect when the parts calling for song are in fact sung. It is necessary, of course, to take the available talents into account when choosing the type of music. But the thing that gives the celebration its intensity is not so much the intrinsic value of the forms used as the exterior and interior participation of those present and the respect shown for the proper character of each part.

2. *Those with a Role in the Celebration*

The principle of "graduated" participation is introduced. Not all congregations can proceed in the same way, especially as regards singing.

---

20. See G. R., "Le innovazioni nella musica sacra provocano polemiche anche in Vaticano," *Il Tempo*, March 7, 1967; M. Rinaldi, "Un'istruzione sulla musica sacra che provocherà molte perplessità," *Il Messagero*, March 8, 1967; C. Atzeri, "Un compromesso che offende la tradizione," *Il Secolo*, March 10, 1967; Un Ghibellino, "Polemica sulla musica," *Lo Specchio*, March 19, 1967; D. Celada, "Musicam sacram," *Cappella Sistina*, March 1967.

Some have more talents available, others fewer. Nonetheless, the entire holy people of God, which is the active subject of the celebration, should be trained to take part in the singing, in degrees ranging from the minimum to the maximum. Congregations with fewer talents at their disposal can content themselves with the responses, acclamations, refrains, antiphons, and psalms. Some songs may be assigned to the choir alone, but the congregation should never be deprived of the possibility of taking some part in the singing. Those selecting the songs must keep in mind what is said about the character of the different parts of the liturgy: some (the *Sanctus*, for example) by their nature call for singing, and this is preferably to be done by the entire congregation.

The instruction also urges respect for moments of silence and the bestowal of care on the various kinds of choirs. The function of the latter is to support the singing of the congregation and to replace it at times, but never completely. Every church should have at least a small choir or, if even this cannot be had, at least one or two cantors who will lead and support the singing of the congregation. The spatial arrangement of the church should bring out the role of the choir, which is not to be cut off from the congregation but is to be an integral part of it; the choir's location should also facilitate the singers' full participation in the celebration, especially through reception of sacramental communion at Mass. The members of the choir should be trained not only in music but in liturgy as well; care must also be devoted to their spiritual and pastoral formation.

3. *Singing at Mass*

The distinction still remains between solemn, sung, and read Masses. In singing, too, there are different degrees of participation. In every Mass, therefore, there should be at least a minimum of singing. The simplest form of participation includes the greetings, presidential prayers, acclamations, preface and *Sanctus*, the final doxology of the Canon, the Our Father with its embolism, the greeting of peace, and the dismissal. At a second level, the chants of the Ordinary are added; at a third, those of the Proper and, if the structure of the language makes this advisable, the readings as well. A dialogue Mass, for example, may have some chants of the Ordinary or the Proper and some other, popular songs that are attuned to the liturgical season and the moment in the celebration.

The instruction calls special attention to the importance and role of the responsorial psalm (no. 33). It also introduces the principle that the chants of the Proper may be replaced by others approved by the episcopal conferences.

4. *The Divine Office*

In accordance with the principles already laid down, singing has a privileged place in the Office, for the nature of this prayer and the parts that compose it call for singing. But the principle of "progressive" solemnity is allowed in the Office as well, in the sense that one may begin by singing the parts that by their nature are more directly intended for singing, such as the hymns, versicles, and canticles. The faithful are urged to celebrate some Hours of the Office, Lauds and Vespers in particular, especially on Sundays and holy days.

5. *Other Celebrations*

Song lends greater pastoral effectiveness to other rites: especially the sacraments, which play a particularly important part in the life of the Christian community; the sacramentals; and the celebration of the mysteries of the Lord during the liturgical year, especially the Easter Triduum. Care must be taken, however, lest under the guise of solemnity forms of music are introduced that are unsuitable, profane, and out of keeping with the worship of God.

6. *Language*

In view of the new situation, the instruction pauses in this chapter to advise that:

a) the faithful learn to sing the parts of the Proper in Latin;

b) in large cities and places visited by tourists, there be churches appointed in which one or more Masses are celebrated in Latin;

c) the heritage of Gregorian and other genres of music from the past be maintained in celebrations in which Latin is still used, and to some extent also in vernacular celebrations; to this end, care must be taken to give seminarians and young religious a rounded training in music;

d) a new music heritage be established in the vernacular, one that satisfies the needs of sacred music. This new heritage should be such that not only choirs but smaller groups can use it; it must also promote the active participation of the entire assembly.

7. *Musical Settings for Vernacular Texts*

Translators must bear in mind the requirements of music and therefore see to it that the texts can be adapted for singing. Among the melodies for vernacular liturgical texts, those sung by the celebrant and sacred ministers are especially important; they must be approved by the episcopal conferences. The instruction gives guidelines for the technical preparation of those who have the difficult task of setting vernacular liturgical texts to music.

8. *Sacred Instrumental Music*

After asserting the special value of the organ and its place of honor in liturgical celebrations, the instruction lays down a general principle: It is for the episcopal conferences to issue more detailed norms regarding the instruments to be allowed in worship. In any case, the instruments used must be suitable for a sacred action and be such as to raise the mind to God and not distract it. These are some of the criteria the conferences must keep in mind as they make their choices. Players, like singers, must have not only technical ability but an understanding of the spirit of the liturgy and its parts.

9. *Commissions for Sacred Music*

The final two numbers urge the establishment at the diocesan and national levels of commissions for sacred music. These are to act in harmony with the liturgical commissions; in many cases it will be appropriate to combine them into a single commission made up of experts in liturgy and experts in music. This will facilitate the task of coordinating enterprises, collaborating with other associations, and promoting a liturgico-musical pastoral program.

Part X

Varia

60

The Liturgical Reform at Special Events

During the years when the reform was being implemented, special events of international significance were taking place in the life of the Church. These served both as acid tests of the reformed liturgy and as splendid occasions for making it better known to the faithful. The Consilium or the Congregation for Divine Worship lent their aid on these occasions and played a part in them.

I. International Eucharistic Congresses

1. *Eucharistic Congress of Bombay*

The thirty-eighth International Eucharistic Congress was celebrated in Bombay, India, from November 28 to December 6, 1965. The Consilium had been established only seven months earlier. Cardinal Gracias, Archbishop of Bombay, was anxious that the congress profit from the fresh breeze of renewal that could already be felt.

On February 24, 1964, the Cardinal had asked the Congregation of Rites:

1) for authorization to administer baptism and confirmation in solemn fashion during Mass, possibly with the new rite and with a new text, adapted to infants, of the Mass "on the occasion of baptism";[1]

---

1. In its response to Cardinal Gracias (April 25, 1964), the Consilium asked him why he was planning infant baptisms and not adult baptisms, which would have a greater impact. In his reply of May 7, the Cardinal explained that the choice was dictated by contingent factors, namely, the presence of Hindu and Muslim "zealots," who if confronted with

2) for permission to use the vernacular at Masses at special meetings. He enclosed with his request the text, in English and in Hindu, that had been prepared by the committee in charge of the congress, together with the melodies for the songs. The songs were taken from the booklet *Sing and Pray*, which had been prepared for training the people to sing during the congress;

3) for authorization to have some concelebrations with the priests in attendance.

The Cardinal's requests were sent to the Consilium, which had them examined by some consultors at the meeting of April 13. The consultors were in favor, except for the rite of baptism, since this certainly would not be ready.

In May the Cardinal sent a great bundle of papers containing the program, texts, and rubrics, and his intentions for the congress. The congress was planned along sacramental lines: November 29: *Statio orbis* ("Station: The World"); November 30: day of baptism and confirmation; December 1: day of first communion; December 2: day of Catholic priesthood; December 3: day of the Catholic episcopate; December 4: day of penance and reconciliation; December 5: day of marriage; December 6: day of triumph for the Eucharistic Christ.

The consultors of the Consilium passed a substantially positive judgment on the proposals, while making some suggestions for improvement. Their judgment was made known to the Congregation of Rites and to Cardinal Gracias, in order that he might make the needed changes (June 20, 1964).

Meanwhile, on June 26 the president of the Consilium submitted four special requests to the Pope:

a) to put the instruction *Inter Oecumenici* into effect a month before the congress, in order that the people might become familiar with the changes;

b) to have daily concelebration by groups of priests attending the congress;

c) to say the Mass of the Blessed Sacrament daily, with a single oration;

d) to include the broad lines of the rite of concelebration (not yet published) in the congress booklet.

The Pope agreed to all the requests; to the second he attached the condition that the number of concelebrants be limited (no more than twenty) and that someone be in charge of the rite.

---

adults being baptized would accuse the Church of "proselytizing," to the possible detriment of the congress.

The Congregation of Rites, for what came under its competency, also sent an affirmative response to the Archbishop of Bombay on July 5.

In his letter of thanks the Cardinal said: "You have truly kept your promise to do your best for India" (July 8, 1964).

The International Eucharistic Congress of Bombay, which enjoyed the much-desired presence of Paul VI, was thus the first occasion for experimenting on a large scale with the initial steps of the reform; the outcome was very successful. Moreover, after the congress the printed booklet became a guide and valuable aid in promoting the reformed liturgy in India.

2. *Eucharistic Congress of Bogotá*

The thirty-ninth International Eucharistic Congress was held four years later in Bogotá, Colombia, August 18–25, 1968. The program followed that of Bombay insofar as the sacraments were celebrated during the Eucharist.[2] All the texts for the celebrations were prepared by the local liturgical committee. The first submission of the committee to the Consilium ran into difficulties inasmuch as the commission had done its work without being acquainted with the Consilium schemas on the sacraments. The commission therefore asked the secretary of the Consilium to go there himself so that he could bring everything into harmony.

A novelty desired by this congress was the possibility of using, *ad experimentum*, the rites of baptism, confirmation, orders, marriage, and religious profession. The sacred orders of diaconate and presbyterate were conferred by the Holy Father, Paul VI, on a hundred candidates from all over Latin America. A very beautiful "missalette," prepared for this ordination by the Consilium and printed by the Vatican Polyglot Press, was given to the ordinands and to the bishops and priests present; it was used for some years at ordinations in Latin America.

The rite of religious profession, in which four hundred religious men and women took part, was presided over by Cardinal Ildebrando Antoniutti in the cathedral of Bogotá. It was a magnificent celebration. This was absolutely the first time that religious were exposed to a completely new rite. The Cardinal was enthusiastic over it and for the rest of his life remembered that event as the beginning of his "conversion" to the litur-

---

2. August 19: day devoted to ecumenism; August 20: day of Christian initiation: baptism, confirmation, Eucharist; August 21: day of penance; August 22: day of the sacrament of orders; August 23: day of the development and advancement of peoples; August 24: day of Mary, Mother and image of the Church; August 25: closing day of the congress.

gical reform, which until then had struck him as problematic, especially as it applied to religious life.

All the other rites were celebrated by Cardinal Lercaro with the mastery and spiritual unction that distinguished his words and gestures. His presence fostered a climate of prayer and a sense of the supernatural throughout the entire congress.

3. Eucharistic Congress of Melbourne

The fortieth International Eucharistic Congress was celebrated in Melbourne, Australia, February 18–25, 1973. The program and the texts for the celebrations were carefully worked out and prepared by the diocesan liturgical commission, in complete cooperation with the Congregation for Divine Worship.

At this congress the sacramental schema for the successive days was replaced by one focusing on various categories of persons: immigrants, children, the elderly, the sick and handicapped, the young, the aborigines, ecumenism, and the peoples of the world. Each was seen in terms of the general theme, "Love one another as I have loved you."

It is to the credit of the Australian liturgists that they did not seek out Australian peculiarities but rather made full use of the reformed liturgy, with emphasis on participation in the singing of the choir and the Mass, a careful preparation of the celebrations, and the interior spirit at work in each sacred ceremony.[3]

Especially worth noting:

Mass of the immigrants. It was not easy to organize a liturgy that would enable groups varying so much in mentality, custom, and language to be sensitive to one another. The goal was achieved by leaving the Proper and some hymns in Latin while having the readings and the intentions of the prayer of the faithful in the national languages (seventeen were chosen). Some traditional songs were sung in several languages; the rest were in English.

Children's Mass. This was the most moving event of the congress: 110,000 children, gathered in the great Cricket Ground stadium and singing and praying together on a day full of sunlight and color. It was a magnificent sight.

At the introit, responsorial psalm, and offertory, two groups of girls, clad in flowing robes, performed dances descriptive of the liturgical texts.

---

3. See "La Liturgia al 40° Congresso eucaristico internazionale" (Melbourne, 18–25 February, 1973), *Not* 7 (1973) 135–40.

The Mass had its own Eucharistic Prayer, which had been approved for this one occasion.

Mass of the young people. This celebration was marked by an intense interior and exterior participation but had only one peculiarity—the responsorial psalm. Here the psalm was replaced by a spoken chorus, with the invocation "Lord, help me to see!" as the refrain. Here is the text of the questions and statements:

> What do people gain from the efforts they make? (Eccl 3:9)
> Who knows if the human spirit mounts upward? (Eccl 3:21)
> Good Master, what shall I do to inherit eternal life? (Luke 18:18)
> Look, we have left everything and followed you. What are we to have, then? (Matt 19:27)
> A human being, whose life . . . is full of trouble (Job 14:1).
> Listen to my cry for help (Ps 5:2).
> Why love what is vain and chase after illusions? (Ps 4:2).
> Their deeds are corrupt and vile, not one of them does right (Ps 14:1).
> To Yahweh when I am in trouble I call and he answers me (Ps 120:1).
> How long, Yahweh, will you forget me? . . . Look down, answer me, Yahweh my God! Give light to my eyes (Ps 13:1, 3).
> Yahweh, to my heart you are a richer joy than all their corn and new wine (Ps 4:7).
> Your words, O lord, are spirit and life (see John 6:64).

Liturgy for the aborigines. This was carefully worked out by the bishops, missionary priests, and sisters who labored among the aboriginal tribes of Northern and Western Australia. The Mass was characterized by more frequent interventions of the congregation in the form of songs and refrains. There was but a single reading—the gospel story of the Last Supper; the content of the reading was simultaneously mimed, because in the aborigines' tradition a message is not simply read from a book.

There was a special Eucharistic Prayer composed by local missionaries and approved by the congress. Later on, the bishops working with the tribes obtained permission to use this Eucharistic Prayer regularly in Masses celebrated among the aborigines. In the preface each statement was underscored by an acclamation of the congregation. Expressions that recurred continually were "Heavenly Father!" and "Father, you are good!" The *Sanctus* was paraphrased: "Father, you are good! We are happy when close to the man Jesus, your only true Son. Father, you are good! Come, Lord Jesus, come and remain with us!"

The Our Father was preceded and followed by an antiphon that read: "You are our Father; you live in heaven and we speak to you. Father, you are good; you are our Father and you live for ever." Thanksgiving after communion was expressed in a "ceremonial" dance.

The Congregation for Divine Worship kept abreast of all the texts of the congress and reviewed them; it also saw to their examination by the other agencies of the Curia. Distance and the time of year (summer in Australia) made it difficult to keep a watchful eye on the congress, but the success of the endeavor justified the faith that had inspired it and the mutual understanding and trust that existed between these two widely separated parts of the world.

II. JUBILEES

1. Extraordinary Jubilee

At the end of the Second Vatican Council, as a crown upon the work, Paul VI proclaimed an extraordinary Jubilee in his motu proprio *Mirificus eventus* (December 7, 1965).[4] The Jubilee was to run from January 1, 1966, to May 29, the Solemnity of Pentecost, in the same year; it was later extended to December 8, 1966.[5]

The Jubilee focused on the Church, which was the major theme of the Council itself, and had for its center of celebration the cathedral church of each diocese. Its main point of reference was the bishop as father and shepherd of his flock. The same two themes—the bishop and the Church—were likewise the focus of the Mass texts prepared for the occasion. Thus the entrance song describes the Church as the Father's house in which God's family assembles. The riches acquired by the Church through the grace-filled event of the Council and the need that the faithful should draw upon them are expressed in the first presidential prayer, which is based on two texts in the Verona Sacramentary. The first reading describes the Church as splendidly represented by the new Jerusalem that comes down from heaven (Rev 21:2-7), while the gospel proclaims the Beatitudes as the law of God's new people. The preface, which is from the treasury of Ambrosian euchology, interweaves five images of the Church: queen, spouse, mother of the living, chosen vine, and holy city set aloft on a mountain.

The booklet of texts, prepared by the Consilium and promulgated by decree of the Congregation of Rites,[6] also contains the melody for the

---

4. Paul VI, apostolic constitution *Mirificus eventus*, declaring and promulgating an extraordinary Jubilee, 1 January–29 May 1966 (December 7, 1965): *AAS* 57 (1965) 945–51; *DOL* 484 nos. 4052-55 (excerpts).

5. Paul VI, motu proprio *Summi Dei beneficio*, extending the extraordinary Jubilee of 1966 (May 3, 1966): *AAS* 58 (1966) 337–41; *DOL* 489 nos. 4067-69 (excerpts).

6. *Missa pro Iubilaeo extraordinario* (Vatican Polyglot Press, 1966. 24 pp.). See SCR, decree *Extraordinarium Iubilaeum*, promulgating the Mass for the Jubilee of 1966 (January 6, 1966):

intentions in the prayer of the faithful, a list of proper songs and of sources to be found in the Roman Gradual, as well as simpler songs taken from the Simple Gradual, which was then in preparation.

The Consilium sent the little volume to the episcopal conferences on January 21, 1966, and let it be known that on this occasion each bishop was authorized to approve a vernacular translation of the liturgical texts without having to ask for confirmation from the Consilium; the reason was that the material for the celebration of the Jubilee had to be readied as soon as possible.[7]

2. Holy Year 1974-1975

With Holy Year 1975 coming up, the Secretariat of State asked the Congregation for Divine Worship to suggest an approach, themes, and liturgical and non-liturgical celebrations (February 14, 1972). The requested suggestions were submitted a month later (March 14, 1972). They had to do chiefly with the following points:

1) The Holy Year should focus primarily on themes of pilgrimage. This is the oldest aspect of a Holy Year (Polycarp and Abercius of Hieropolis, in the second century, already give it a privileged place), while the Jubilee indulgence dates only from the thirteen hundreds.

2) A preliminary theological, historical, and pastoral study should be made of the meaning of the indulgence.

3) A program of papal celebrations should be drawn up to ensure that they are in full harmony with the liturgical renewal, and of celebrations in the patriarchal basilicas and the catacombs with appropriate Masses from the new Missal.

4) Ways should be found of giving an appropriate spiritual and human welcome to pilgrimages at the basilicas so that these people will not feel isolated and bewildered.

5) The pilgrims should be taught a concern for the various aspects of the Church's life: instruction, missions, apostolate, liturgy.

6) Provision should also be made for the moral improvement of the Eternal City and especially for seriously implementing the liturgical reform in the basilicas and parishes of Rome; this includes the arrangement of the churches, sacred music, and the participation of the faithful.

Nothing more was heard of the matter until the announcement of the Holy Year, which was to be celebrated in two phases: in the local Churches

---

DOL 487 nos. 4064-65; the text of the Mass is in *Not* 2 (1966) 44-46. For the indulgences of the Jubilee: *DOL* 485 no. 4056; and 486 nos. 4057-63.

7. See *Not* 2 (1966) 43.

(1974) and in the Eternal City (1975). The Congregation was then asked
to lend its assistance in matters liturgical to the Central Commission for
the Holy Year. At the behest of the Secretariat of State, an official of the
Congregation, Father G. Pasqualetti, was to serve as liaison (May 12,
1973).[8]

On August 1, 1973, a study group was formed,[9] which met September 18–19, October 1, and November 15 of that same year. The group
concerned itself primarily with suggestions for the celebration of the Holy
Year in the local Churches. The suggestions were sent to the Central Commission on October 3, 1973, and included:

a) guidelines for the celebration of the Holy Year in the local
Churches and for the "Week of Reconciliation";

b) Lent and the Easter season of the Holy Year;

c) themes, based on the Sunday Scripture readings, for instruction
on the Holy Year, to be given during the liturgical year 1973–74;

d) desires regarding the preparation of the "environment" in Rome
with a view to the Holy Year.

The material under the first two headings was published by the Central Commission for the Holy Year.[10] The only changes made were some
revisions in the introduction and the inclusion of the commemoration of
the dead and of prayer for the Pope.

The instructional themes, on the other hand, were published in the
official Bulletin of the Holy Year. The wishes expressed under the fourth
heading stayed in the material collected by the Central Commission.

a) *The Holy Year in the local Churches*

This celebration was viewed, and presented, by the Congregation for
Divine Worship as a time of special effort to enter into the living plan
of the Father that is being brought to fulfillment through the Son and
in the Holy Spirit. The Congregation therefore outlined a spiritual journey in which the faithful would relive the "path of salvation" as

---

8. The matter seemed settled. But relations were neither easy nor clear. It was subsequently learned, from *L'Osservatore Romano*, that at its first meeting the Central Commission had established, among other commissions, one for the liturgy, headed by the
undersecretary of the Congregation for Divine Worship. Thus two poles were set up in
the same organization: one to do the work, the other to be the public representative.

9. The group was as follows: *relator:* G. Pasqualetti; *members:* P. Jounel, S. Famoso, A.
Dumas, G. Fontaine, R. Kaczynski, V. Macca, J. Gélineau, G. Agustoni, and P. Gillet,
representative of the Vicariate of Rome.

10. *Ordo Anni Sancti celebrandi in Ecclesiis particularibus* (Vatican Polyglot Press, 1973. 126
pp.). The introduction to the *Order for the Celebration of the Holy Year in the Local Churches*
is in DOL 493 nos. 4078-88. See "De celebratione Anni sancti," *Not* 9 (1973) 345–92.

proclaimed in the Creed and experienced in the liturgy, where it is fore-told during the time of expectation of Christ, implemented by him from the Incarnation to Pentecost, and made continually present and opera-tive by the Holy Spirit by means of the sacred liturgy. The Holy Year was to concentrate, not on isolated and perhaps distracting manifestations, but on the presentation of the mystery of salvation and on the celebra-tion of the basic sacraments—penance and the Eucharist. The aim was to induce a spirit of greater seriousness among the pilgrims, which would be a sign of, and a commitment to, a journey of interior renewal.

The means offered for carrying out this plan was the "Week of Recon-ciliation," which was perhaps the most original element and the one that most influenced the form taken by the Holy Year in the local Churches. There the Holy Year was marked precisely by the spirit of renewal and intense prayer—a spirit that subsequently also characterized Holy Year 1975.

The "week" was not understood strictly as a sequence of days, but rather as a series of phases or stages, to be accomplished in successive periods of time. During these periods the faithful sought to follow the way of conversion through listening to God's word, more intense prayer, and a journey comprising penance and Eucharist. Each of the seven themes of the "weeks" corresponded to a stage in a briefly sketched his-tory of salvation, which was then to be entered into more fully through the Scriptures and expressed in celebrations and meaningful rites that related to concrete life. All these were briefly indicated in the overall plan. The basic stages were the third, fifth, and seventh. In each of the seven stages, texts for Eucharistic or non-Eucharistic celebrations were assigned. Elements always to be found were the proclamation of God's word; com-munal prayers and songs; and the ritual factors of signs, symbols, ges-tures, and blessings (see the outline on p. 926).

The booklet, which was prepared by the Congregation for Divine Wor-ship, contained a little collection of texts, guidelines, and suggestions for adapting the material to various situations and groups. It also contained a special Mass for the Holy Year on the theme of reconciliation (this Mass was included in the second edition of the Roman Missal). Valuable pointers were then given for highlighting the central period of the year, namely, Lent and the Easter season, as well as a list of themes for in-struction and for weekly celebrations (these themes were linked to the themes of the Sundays of Lent and the Easter season).

This booklet, though prepared for a particular occasion, remains a col-lection of useful themes, with approved texts, for special times of intense spiritual endeavor: retreats, spiritual exercises, popular missions.

GENERAL PLAN FOR THE WEEK OF RECONCILIATION

Theme of the Stage	Liturgical Context	Form of Celebration	Rites	Pastoral Suggestions
I. Hope of the world; reign of God	Advent	Celebration of word of God	Nocturnal vigil; prayer based on the Our Father	Salvation proclaimed to the poor. Expectations of our world
II. The Word was made flesh	Christmas-Epiphany	Vespers; cel. of word; Mass	Enthronement of Scriptures; veneration of image of BVM	Manifestations of Spirit in world and Church
III. "Be converted and believe"	Lent	Call to conversion. (Mass)	Fasting; almsgiving; imposition of ashes	Divisions in the world. Conversion
IV. Through death to life	Easter Triduum. Baptism	Mass. Recall of baptism	Profession of faith. Procession to baptistery. Asperges. Way of the Cross	Demands of Christian life. Concern for the sick
V. Celebration of reconciliation	Sacrament of penance	Penitential celebration. Sacrament of penance	Penitential act. Confession of sins; examination of conscience	Meaning of conversion. Meaning of sin. Mercy of God
VI. The Church united in the Holy Spirit	Pentecost	Celebration of the vigil. Office of Readings. (Mass)	Vigil. Pilgrimage. Invocation of the saints	Local and universal Church. Holy Spirit as bond of unity
VII. Mystery of unity	Eucharist	Mass	Lord's Supper as sacrifice of praise and of communion	Eucharist as center of Church's life and bond of charity

When Mass is mentioned in parentheses, it is suggested for those cases in which no other celebration is possible.

b) *Holy Year 1975 in the Eternal City*

On November 17, 1973, the Central Commission was presented with the work done on the celebrations of the Holy Year. The material was published in the *Pilgrimage Book* (various languages); in it the liturgical material occupies most space.

The wishes voiced by the Congregation for Divine Worship had to do chiefly with creating an atmosphere of prayer in the Roman basilicas. The suggestions were as follows: the restoration of a worthily celebrated daily Liturgy of the Hours, this work being entrusted, if need be, to various monastic or religious families or the ecclesiastical colleges of the City; rescheduling Masses so as to avoid the distraction caused by the simultaneous celebration of Masses at the various altars of the basilicas; prohibition of visits by tourists during celebrations; making the guided tours of basilicas a means of instruction; the setting aside of some churches for prayer, including nocturnal prayer; celebrations for the young.

Another suggestion was that the venerable icon of Christ the Savior (known as the *Acheropita*, or "(image) not made by human hands"), which is kept in the *Sancta Sanctorum* of the Holy Stair, be exposed as it had been in the Lateran Basilica during other Holy Years. This exposition would help stimulate visits to this basilica. Also urged was a timely scrutiny of the relics exposed in the various churches of Rome, as well as an updating of the practice connected with the Holy Stair, in regard both to the place and to the liturgy celebrated there. "It must not be forgotten that at the Holy Stair the most venerated oratory in Rome, the *Sancta Sanctorum*, is still preserved. The practice of climbing the Holy Stair could once again be given the meaning of an ascent to the glorified Christ."

Some of these suggestions were implemented, others were not. With regard to the celebrations, the following proposals were made:

1) The Office of the Holy Year, or of Reconciliation, should be celebrated every evening at St. Peter's. This Office was patterned on Vespers, but it also contained special elements connected with the themes of the Holy Year: invocation of the saints' help, penitential prayer, profession of faith, rite of peace, prayer for the Church and the Pope.

In the model submitted, these various elements were logically interconnected: expression of communion with the saints (first part of the Litany of the Saints); liturgy of praise (psalmody); word of God; glorification of God after listening to his word (the *Magnificat*); intercession (second part of the litany); profession of faith; conclusion, using the rite of peace.

In the final version of the rite, however, this model was overloaded and made complicated: double opening, collect, responsorial psalm, four "concluding" prayers in the course of the celebration, petitions for the

Pope and then for the pastors of the Church. But for some unknown reason the Congregation was not asked to concern itself further with the outcome of the work it had submitted.[11]

2) Daily Mass in the basilicas; the Mass to be thematically attuned to the spiritual and historical associations connected with each basilica.

3) Pauses for prayer for those visiting the basilicas but not taking part in a liturgical action. In addition to the usual elements of a prayer service (Scripture reading, intercession, singing, prayer), various devotional prayers were also supplied, as requested by the Central Commission. These last, however, were not included in the printed book.

Special attention was paid to the problem of song. A liturgy that does not include song is lifeless; the joy attendant upon faith, forgiveness, and fellowship goes unexpressed. The need was to find a shared, international patrimony of song. A Latin repertory, taken from the book *Iubilate Deo*, was submitted, and it was proposed to launch a little collection of songs, in several languages, in which the same melodies would be used. But the Consociatio Internationalis Musicae Sacrae claimed competency in this area, with the result, of course, that nothing was done.

The Congregation also composed the Holy Year Prayer, which was then published by the Central Commission, and the Eucharistic Prayers on the theme of reconciliation.[12]

---

11. The first two translations of the texts, into German and French, were sent to the Congregation. The former had to be completely redone because it actually distorted the meaning; the latter had not adopted the official texts of the French-speaking episcopal conferences. There was insistence on this point. In response, the Congregation was no longer consulted.

12. See above, pp. 477ff.

Conclusion

"We Tried to Serve the Church"

My original intention was to end these recollections of events that are indelibly printed in my heart with an affectionate remembrance of those for whom "the blessed hope and expectation of the coming of the Lord" has now become a reality. With the passing of the years, however, the list of those who have gone before to the Father's house has become a very long one, and it is impossible to give even a short sketch of each of the departed.

There is one group, however, to which I must not fail to say a word of gratitude and admiration. They are the bishops, scholars, and laborers in the secretariat, who worked with such humility, faith, understanding, and perseverance to give a new face and a powerful voice to the Church's prayer by implementing the most extensive liturgical reform in the multisecular history of the Church.

Gratitude is owed, in the first place, to the cardinals who served as presidents and prefects:

—Cardinal Gaetano Cicognani, president of the preparatory liturgical commission of the Council, who brought the work to completion thanks to his wisdom, sincerity, prudence, and confidence.

—Cardinal Arcadio M. Larraona, who succeeded Cardinal Cicognani and was president of the conciliar commission that brought the Constitution on the Liturgy to the point of approval by the Council.

—Cardinal Giacomo Lercaro, whom the entire Consilium so greatly esteemed and venerated for his fatherliness, his openmindedness, his understanding of problems, and his profound sense of the liturgy, which he knew thoroughly and lived intensely. In his words, proposals, and

931

decisions were reflected the anxieties, problems, and difficulties with which the path of every pastor of the Church is strewn.

—Cardinal Benno Gut, who so knowledgeably and faithfully continued along the path of reform already begun. His native goodness, his simplicity and kindness, his manner of speech, so lively and always leavened by humor, shortened and, as it were, eliminated distances. We thought of him as a father and friend and sincerely mourned his death.

—Cardinal Arturo Tabera A., who believed in the rightness of the reform and committed himself to its advancement; he brought the Congregation for Divine Worship into closer contact with the episcopal conferences and the national liturgical commissions.

—Cardinal James Robert Knox, who directed the Congregation during its final difficult year of existence.

"Thanks to all of you, the Fathers of the Consilium, whose understanding, experience, and pastoral concern made the renewal of the liturgy possible.

"Special thanks to the experts, who carried the burden of the reform in their study and research; they were the architects, craftsmen, and specialized workers in the service of a work through which, down the centuries, the Church will fill her house with a song of love for her Lord.

"Thanks to you, the observers, who were constantly present at our meetings, attentive but unobtrusive, as though fearful lest your presence, which we greatly desired and found so pleasing, might exert pressure on us. We thank you for your example and for the hope that your presence nourished in our hearts: that we might see realized at last the unity of the family of Christ that is so clearly expressed in the signs and realities of the sacred liturgy and in the gathering of God's entire family in the Father's house, around his table."[1]

Above all else, there remains the memory of the spirit that inspired, supported, and guided our steps. That spirit is summed up in two statements, which I would like to cite here at the end of this work in which I have passed in review the stages of the arduous path we traveled.

The first statement is that of Cardinal Lercaro at the beginning of the second general meeting of the Consilium:

"The love of Christ has brought us together in unity": the love of Christ but also of his bride which is without spot or wrinkle: the Church, which is always his and which he ransomed with his blood.

1. From the report of the secretary to the Consilium at its final general meeting, April 19, 1970.

Her sweet voice, which the divine Bridegroom asks should echo in his ears! It is our task to bring harmony and guidance to her utterances so that they may be in full consonance with the will and wishes of the Bridegroom and become a suitable instrument of his action. Such is our duty and our right, entrusted to us in a supreme act of kindness by the Holy Father Paul VI, to whom, with immense good will and affection, we offer our full and complete filial devotion and whom we wish humbly to thank for the confidence he has placed in us.

You are all well aware of the salutary and saving efficacy of the sacred liturgy as the first and necessary fountainhead of the Christian spirit. You know, too, how necessary it is that the holy people of God should participate fully, consciously, and in a communal way in the liturgical actions. . . . I am addressing persons who do not simply know but who also love. . . .

This is our task; this is the Church's will for us. This is the purpose and raison d'être of the conciliar Constitution on the Liturgy, that truly blessed and ever to be praised gift of the Holy Spirit in response to the expectation, even to the hunger and thirst, of all the clergy and the entire Christian people. The purpose is that the clergy and people may at last attain to an authentic and deeper understanding of the sacred liturgy and may be allowed truly to taste it. The purpose is that the sacred rites, now made simpler and almost transparent, may more easily promote the understanding and participation of all. The purpose, finally, is that the Christian people, "a holy nation, God's own people," may exercise the right and duty it has acquired in baptism; that it may give full and solemn praise to the divine Majesty; and that in Christ and through Christ the fountain of sanctification and salvation may be opened to souls so that their hope of eternal life with God in the heavenly fatherland may grow ever stronger.

Our entire work is aimed at making it easier for all the children of God to come to grips with matters so holy, serious, and necessary, in order that they may taste how sweet the Lord is and how important it is for the family of God to share in these riches.

May the Lord grant that I and all of you may work generously and unceasingly, while preserving our unity of spirit and following the truth in love. Then at last the entire Church may be enriched by our work and rejoice in it.

May the Lord bring it to pass! May the Mother of God, who is the perfect image of the Church, support us with her intercession. She it was, was it not, who first intoned the song of divine praise: "My soul magnifies the Lord"!

Let us *pray*, dear brothers, for our work needs divine aid and light. Let us *work* together, brothers. Let us *love one another*, for when brethren live together with good will and joyfully, the Lord promises them blessing and life. Let us *love* God's holy Church and its splendor. Let us *endeavor* to raise our songs to the heavenly Jerusalem, where true joys dwell and where praise is unending.

May the Lord deign to bless us and our work, just as he gave King Solomon the wisdom to build the temple and filled David, the singer of psalms, with wisdom and understanding.

The other statement is by the secretary, first of the Consilium and then of the Congregation for Divine Worship, at the end of his service to the liturgical reform. On January 6, 1976, before leaving to be apostolic pronuncio in Iran, Archbishop Bugnini wrote a letter of farewell to his fellow workers and friends. In it he said, among other things:

> Before setting out for my new post in the service of the Church, I want to express my profound fraternal gratitude to those who for eleven and a half years lived and worked with me through the various stages of the liturgical reform, on the secretariat of the Consilium and then of the Congregation for Divine Worship, on the national liturgical commissions and the various joint commissions, and in the liturgical institutes and centers; to those who during the past half year have expressed toward me, in person or in writing, sentiments of affectionate friendship; and to all who have prayed for me.
>
> I carry all of you in my heart; to all I express my sincere thanks; I humbly pray to the Lord for all of you.
>
> At a great moment in its history, we tried to serve the Church and not to make the Church serve us. We were caught up in a work that reaches to the boundaries of the supernatural. As Pope Paul VI said to the Consilium on October 29, 1964: "It is a magnificent task to offer to the praying Church a voice and, so to speak, an instrument with which to celebrate the praises of God and to offer him the petitions of his children. A task of this kind . . . is a work at once human and divine."[2]
>
> "Builders" of the new "sanctuary," humble and trusting "cultivators" of "God's field," at times "unknown soldiers" in the good fight (even if not always victorious), we labored with generous dedication, freedom of spirit, loyal zeal, and prompt obedience for the liturgical renewal and the defense of the goals reached.
>
> Let us thank the Lord for having called us to this undertaking, which is destined to feed the fountains of grace and gladden the city of God.
>
> There remains the most difficult task: to see to it that the celebration of the "work of salvation," which we humbly served, fully inspires the life of the faithful and of the Church, which is so many-sided because of the number of peoples making it up and so varied in its expressions.
>
> I shall follow with unflagging interest the work of those who continue this marvelous and fascinating commitment to the Church. My prayer is that they will carry it on with docility of spirit, careful attention to the signs of the times and the voices of the people of God, clarity of purpose, and sincere dialogue with the brethren.

---

2. *DOL* 81 no. 624.

Appendix

Members and Consultors of the Organizations for Liturgical Reform

(The names are followed at times by some other basic information that will show the criteria at work in the choice of persons: nationality, office, date of appointment [= app.] and, if known, of death [= d.].)

I. COMMISSION FOR LITURGICAL REFORM

Established by Pius XII, May 28, 1948

PRESIDENTS

Micara, Cardinal Clemente, prefect SCR
Cicognani, Cardinal Gaetano (from 1953), prefect SCR

MEMBERS

Albareda, Anselmo, O.S.B.
Antonelli, Ferdinando, O.F.M.
Bea, Augustin, S.J.
Braga, Carlo, C.M. (from 1960)
Carinci, Msgr. Alfonso
D'Amato, Abbot Cesario, O.S.B. (from 1960)
Dante, Msgr. Enrico (from 1951)
Frutaz, Msgr. Amato Pietro (from 1960)
Löw, Joseph, C.SS.R.
Rovigatti, Luigi (priest; from 1960)

SECRETARY

Bugnini, Annibale, C.M.

II. Preparatory Conciliar Commission[1]

PRESIDENTS

Cicognani, Cardinal Gaetano, prefect SCR, d. 2-5-1962
Larraona, Cardinal Arcadio Maria, prefect SCR, from 2-22-1962

MEMBERS

Anglés Pamiés, Msgr. Igino (Spain, Rome)
Bevilacqua, Giulio, C.O. (Italy)
Borella, Msgr. Pietro (Italy)
Calewaert, Karel, Bishop of Ghent (Belgium)
Capelle, Abbot Bernard, O.S.B. (Belgium), d. 10-19-1961
Cattaneo, Msgr. Enrico (Italy)
Fallani, Msgr. Giovanni (Italy)
Gogué, Joseph, Archbishop of Basra (Iraq), d. 1-15-1971
Guardini, Prof. Romano (Germany), d. 10-1-1968
Hervás y Benet, Juan, Titular Bishop of Dora (Spain)
Jenny, Henri, Titular Archbishop of Salde and Auxiliary Archbishop
    of Cambrai (France)
Jungmann, Joseph Andreas, S.J. (Austria)
Kniewald, Prof. Carlo (Yugoslavia)
Landersdorfer, Simon Konrad, Bishop of Passau (Germany)
Malula, Joseph, Auxiliary Bishop of Leopoldville (Congo)
Martínez de Antoñana, Gregorio, C.M.F. (Spain)
Nabuco, Msgr. Joaquím (Brazil)
O'Connell, Canon John (Wales, Great Britain)
Pascher, Prof. Joseph (Germany)
Pizzoni, Giuseppe, C.M. (Italy), d. 1-22-1972
Quasten, Prof. Johannes (Germany)
Righetti, Msgr. Mario (Italy)
Roguet, Aimon-Marie, O.P. (France)
Rossi, Carlo, Bishop of Biella (Italy)
Schiavon, Msgr. Giovanni (Italy)
Zauner, Franz, Bishop of Linz (Austria)

SECRETARY

Bugnini, Annibale, C.M.

---

1. For the names and members of the various study groups, see pp. 15–16.

CONSULTORS

Botte, Bernard, O.S.B. (Belgium)
Brinkhoff, Lucas, O.F.M. (Netherlands)
Cannizzaro, Abbot Giovanni Bruno, O.S.B. (Italy), d. 3-14-1961
Cardine, Eugène, O.S.B. (France)
Chavasse, Msgr. Antoine (France)
De Lepeleere, Georges, SS.CC. (Belgium)
Diekmann, Godfrey, O.S.B. (United States)
Dirks, Ansgar, O.P. (Netherlands)
Dubois, Marcel, C.SS.R. (Canada)
Famoso, Msgr. Salvatore (Italy)
Fischer, Prof. Balthasar (Germany)
Gy, Pierre-Marie, O.P. (France)
Hänggi, Prof. Anton (Switzerland)
Hofinger, Johannes, S.J. (Austria)
Jones, Percy (priest) (Australia)
Jounel, Prof. Pierre (France)
Kahlefeld, Heinrich, C.O. (Germany)
Kennedy, Vincent, C.S.B. (Canada)
Klauser, Prof. Theodor (Germany)
Kowalski, Kazimierz, Bishop of Chelmno (Poland), d. 5-6-1972
Luykx, Boniface, O.Praem. (Belgium)
McManus, Prof. Frederick R. (United States)
Martimort, Canon Aimé-Georges (France)
Mejia Gómez, Jairo (priest) (Colombia)
Moneta Caglio, Msgr. Ernesto (Italy)
Muthappa, Francis, Bishop of Coimbatore (India)
Oñatibia, Ignacio (priest) (Spain)
Pfliegler, Prof. Michael (Austria)
Radó, Polycarp, O.S.B. (Hungary)
Schmidt, Herman, S.J. (Netherlands)
Siffrin, Peter, O.S.B. (Germany)
Spülbeck, Otto, Bishop of Meissen (Germany)
Vagaggini, Cipriano, O.S.B. (Italy)
Vigorelli, Valerio (priest) (Italy)
Wagner, Msgr. Johannes (Germany)
Walsh, Joseph, Archbishop of Tuam (Ireland)
Zakrzewski, Tadeusz Pawel, Bishop of Plock (Poland), d. 11-7-1961

III. Conciliar Commission on the Liturgy

PRESIDENT

Larraona, Cardinal Arcadio Maria

MEMBERS

Elected by the Council Fathers (10-20-1962)

Calewaert, Karel, Bishop of Ghent (Belgium)
D'Amato, Abbot Cesario (St. Paul's Outside the Walls, Rome)
Enciso Viana, Jesús, Bishop of Mallorca (Spain)
Grimshaw, Francis, Archbishop of Birmingham (England)
Hallinan, Paul, Archbishop of Atlanta (United States)
Jenny, Henri, Auxiliary Archbishop of Cambrai (France)
Jop, Franciszek, Titular Bishop of Daulia (Opole, Poland)
Lercaro, Cardinal Giacomo, Archbishop of Bologna (Italy)
Malula, Joseph, Auxiliary Bishop of Leopoldville (Congo)
Martin, Joseph, Bishop of Nicolet (Canada)
Pichler, Alfred, Bishop of Banjaluka (Yugoslavia)
Rau, Enrique, Bishop of Mar del Plata (Argentina)
Rossi, Carlo, Bishop of Biella (Italy)
Spülbeck, Otto, Bishop of Meissen (Germany)
Van Bekkum, Willem, Bishop of Ruteng (Indonesia)
Zauner, Franz, Bishop of Linz (Austria)

Appointed by the Pope

Albareda, Cardinal Anselmo (Spain, Curia), d. 7-19-1966
Bekkers, Willem, Bishop of 's-Hertogenbosch (Netherlands)
Dante, Enrico, Archbishop, Secretary of the SCR
Fey Schneider, Bernardo, Bishop of Potosí (Bolivia)
Giobbe, Cardinal Paolo, Datary (Italy, Curia)
Jullien, Cardinal André (France, Curia)
Masnou Boixeda, Ramon, Bishop of Vich (Spain)
Prou, Jean, O.S.B., Abbot of Solesmes (France)
Schweiger, Peter, C.M.F., Superior General (Germany)

SECRETARY

Antonelli, Ferdinando, O.F.M.

PERITI

Anglés Pamiés, Msgr. Igino (Spain, Rome)
Bonet, Msgr. Emmanuel (Spain, Rome)
Bugnini, Annibale, C.M. (Italy)
Cecchetti, Msgr. Igino (Congregation for Seminaries, Curia)
De Clerq, Charles (priest; Belgium)
Dirks, Ansgar, O.P. (Netherlands, Rome)
Egger, Abbot Karl, C.R.L. (Rome)
Ferraro, Msgr. Nicola (SCR, Curia)
Fohl, Jules, O.S.B. (Luxembourg)
Frutaz, Msgr. Amato Pietro (SCR, Curia)
Gagnebet, Rosario, O.P. (France, Rome)
Jungmann, Joseph Andreas, S.J. (Austria)
McManus, Prof. Frederick R. (United States)
Martimort, Canon Aimé-Georges (France)
Martínez de Antoñana, Gregorio, C.M.F. (Spain)
Masi, Msgr. Roberto (Italy)
Nabuco, Msgr. Joaquím (Brazil)
O'Connell, Canon John (England)
Overath, Msgr. Johannes (Germany)
Righetti, Msgr. Mario (Italy)
Salmon, Pierre, O.S.B. (Luxembourg, Rome)
Stickler, D. Alfons, S.D.B. (Italy)
Vagaggini, Cipriano, O.S.B. (Italy)
Van den Eynde, Damien, O.F.M. (Belgium, Rome)
Wagner, Msgr. Johannes (Germany)

IV. THE CONSILIUM[2]

PRESIDENTS

Lercaro, Cardinal Giacomo, Archbishop of Bologna, 3-2-1964 to
1-9-1968. Appointed a member of the Consilium on 1-13-1968
and a member of its presidential council and of the liturgical
section of the SCR on 10-4-1968

Gut, Cardinal Benno, 1-9-1968 to 5-8-1969 (appointed a member of
the Consilium on 3-3-1964, when he was Abbot Primate of the
Benedictine Federation)

MEMBERS

Agagianian, Cardinal Gregory Peter, prefect SC Propaganda Fide,
app. 3-3-1964

Antonelli, Ferdinando, O.F.M. (subsequently Titular Archbishop of
Idicra), SCR, app. 3-3-1964

Bea, Cardinal Augustin, president of the Secretariat for Christian
Unity, app. 3-3-1964, d. 11-16-1968

Bekkers, Willem, Bishop of 's-Hertogenbosch (Netherlands), app.
3-3-1964, d. 5-9-1966

Bevilacqua, Giulio, C.O. (subsequently a cardinal, 2-22-1965), app.
3-3-1964, d. 5-6-1965

Bluyssen, Jan, Bishop of 's-Hertogenbosch (Netherlands), app.
10-14-1965

Botero Salazar, Tulio, Archbishop of Medellín (Colombia), app.
3-3-1964, d. 3-1-1981

Boudon, René, Bishop of Mende (France), app. 3-3-1964

Byrne, Leo Christopher, Coadjutor Archbishop of St. Paul and of
Philadelphia (United States), app. 12-13-1968

Carter, Gerald Emmett, Bishop of London (Canada), app. 12-14-1965

Clavel Méndez, Tomás Alberto, Archbishop of Panama, app.
6-1-1965

Cody, Cardinal John Patrick, Archbishop of Chicago, app. 7-18-1967

Confalonieri, Cardinal Carlo, secretary SC Consistory, vice-
president, app. 3-3-1964

Conway, Cardinal William, Archbishop of Armagh (Ireland), app.
6-3-1965

De Kesel, Leo, Auxiliary Bishop of Ghent (Belgium), app. 2-2-1967

---

2. Members, consultors, and advisors are listed in alphabetical order; some basic information is given on each.

Dwyer, George Patrick, Archbishop of Birmingham (England), app. 6-1-1965

Enciso Viana, Jesús, Bishop of Mallorca (Spain), app. 3-3-1964, d. 9-21-1964

Enrique y Tarancón, Vicente, Archbishop of Oviedo (then of Toledo, Spain), created cardinal 4-28-1969, app. 6-1-1965

Felici, Pericle, Titular Archbishop of Samosata (Curia), created cardinal 6-26-1967, app. 3-3-1964

Fey Schneider, Bernardo, Bishop of Potosí (Bolivia), app. 3-3-1964

Giobbe, Cardinal Paolo, Datary (Curia), app. 1-13-1964

Gracias, Cardinal Valerian, Archbishop of Bombay (India), app. 3-3-1964

Gray, Gordon Joseph, Archbishop of Edinburgh (Scotland), created cardinal 4-28-1969, app. 2-2-1967

Grimshaw, Francis, Archbishop of Birmingham (England), app. 3-3-1964, d. 3-22-1965

Guano, Emilio, Bishop of Livorno (Italy), app. 3-3-1964, d. 9-26-1970

Hallinan, Paul, Archbishop of Atlanta (United States), app. 3-3-1964, d. 3-27-1968

Hänggi, Anton, Bishop of Basel (Switzerland), app. 2-2-1967

Hervás y Benet, Juan, Titular Bishop of Dora, Prelate of Ciudad Real (Spain), app. 3-3-1964, d. 6-6-1982

Hurley, Denis Eugene, Archbishop of Durban (South Africa), app. 6-1-1965

Isnard, José Clemente Carlos, Bishop of Nova Friburgo (Brazil), app. 3-3-1964

Kabangu, François, Bishop of Luebo (Zaire), app. 12-13-1968

Kervéadou, François, Bishop of Saint Brieuc (France), app. 3-3-1964, d. 1-8-1983

Kovács, Sándor, Bishop of Szombathely (Hungary), app. 12-14-1965, d. 12-24-1972

Jenny, Henri, Archbishop of Cambrai (France), app. 3-3-1964, d. 2-8-1982

Jop, Franciszek, Auxiliary Bishop of Opole (Poland), app. 3-3-1964, d. 9-24-1976

Larraona, Cardinal Arcadio Maria, prefect SCR, app. 1-13-1964, d. 5-7-1973

Lazík, Ambróz, Bishop, Apostolic Administrator of Trnava (Czechoslovakia), app. 12-14-1965, d. 4-2-1969

López de Moura, Agostino, Bishop of Portalegre-Castelo Branco (Portugal), app. 3-3-1964

Malula, Joseph, Auxiliary Bishop, then Archbishop of Kinshasa (Zaire), created cardinal 4-28-1969, app. 3-3-1964

Mansourati, Clemente Ignazio, Titular Archbishop of Apamea in Syria (Rome), app. 3-3-1964, d. 8-11-1982

Martin, Joseph Albert, Bishop of Nicolet (Canada), app. 3-3-1964

Nagae, Laurentius Satoshi, Bishop of Urawa (Japan), app. 3-3-1964

Otčenášek, Karel, Bishop, Apostolic Administrator of Hradec (Czechoslovakia), app. 4-2-1969

Pellegrino, Michele, Archbishop of Turin (Italy), created cardinal 6-26-1967, app. 10-14-1965

Pichler, Alfred, Bishop of Banjaluka (Yugoslavia), app. 3-3-1964

Rau, Enrique, Bishop of Mar del Plata (Argentina), app. 3-3-1964, d. 8-11-1971

Ritter, Cardinal Joseph Elmer, Archbishop of St. Louis (United States), app. 3-3-1964, d. 6-10-1967

Rossi, Carlo, Bishop of Biella (Italy), app. 3-3-1964, d. 2-29-1980

Rugambwa, Cardinal Laurean, Bishop of Bukoba, then Archbishop of Dar-es-Salaam (Tanzania), app. 3-3-1964

Silva Henríquez, Cardinal Raúl, Archbishop of Santiago (Chile), app. 3-3-1964

Spülbeck, Otto, Bishop of Meissen (Germany), app. 3-3-1964

Valentini, Luigi (Rome), app. 3-3-1964, d. 5-11-1964

Van Bekkum, Willem, Bishop of Ruteng (Indonesia), app. 3-3-1964

Van Zuylen, Willem Marie, Bishop of Liège (Belgium), app. 3-3-1964

Volk, Hermann, Bishop of Mainz (Germany), app. 3-3-1964

Weakland, Rembert, O.S.B., Abbot Primate, app. 1-25-1968

Young, Guilford, Archbishop of Hobart (Australia), app. 3-3-1964

Zauner, Franz, Bishop of Linz (Austria), app. 3-3-1964

SECRETARY

Bugnini, Annibale, C.M.[3]

CONSULTORS[4]

Agustoni, Luigi (Switzerland), Institute of Sacred Music, Milan; Gregorianist and parish priest; app. 5-11-1964

---

3. For the officials and others assigned to the secretariat, see p. 53, nn. 7-8.

4. The distribution of the consultors into study groups was indicated in the text under each heading. The list of study groups is given on pages 63-65.

Agustoni, Msgr. Gilberto (Switzerland), SCDF; dogma, law; app. 3-16-1966

Altisent, Miguel, S.P. (Spain); music; app. 5-11-1966

Amadouni, Garabed, Bishop and Apostolic Exarch of the Armenians of France; app. 5-11-1966

Amon, Msgr. Karel (Austria); liturgy; app. 3-16-1966

Amore, Agostino, O.F.M. (Italy), Antonianum, Rome; Church history; app. 5-11-1966, d. 12-17-1982

Anglés Pamiés, Msgr. Igino (Spain), president of the Pontifical Institute of Sacred Music, Rome; app. 6-17-1964

Ashworth, Henry, O.S.B. (England); patrology; app. 5-11-1966, d. 10-13-1980

Balboni, Msgr. Dante (Italy); pastoral liturgy; app. 5-11-1966

Bartolucci, Msgr. Domenico (Italy), director Sistine Choir; app. 6-17-1964

Beilliard, Msgr. Jean (France); music; app. 5-11-1966

Békés, Gerardo, O.S.B., Anselmianum, Rome; dogma; app. 5-25-1964

Bennett, Dr. Clifford (United States), director Gregorian Institute of America; music; app. 6-17-1964

Beron, Richard, O.S.B. (Germany); liturgy; app. 5-11-1966

Bogler, Theodor, O.S.B. (Germany); liturgy; app. 5-11-1966, d. 6-13-1968

Bonet, Msgr. Emmanuel (Spain), auditor of the Rota; law; app. 2-22-1964, d. 8-6-1969

Borella, Msgr. Pietro (Italy); liturgy, ceremonial; app. 2-22-1964, d. 8-30-1982

Borello, Luciano, S.D.B. (Italy); liturgy, catechetics; app. 5-11-1966

Botte, Bernard, O.S.B. (Belgium), Liturgical Institute, Paris; app. 5-11-1966, d. 3-4-1980

Bouman, Deacon Cornelius (Netherlands), University of Nijmegen; liturgy; app. 5-11-1966

Bouyer, Louis, C.O. (France); liturgy; app. 3-16-1966

Brinkhoff, Lucas, O.F.M. (Netherlands); liturgy; app. 5-11-1966

Bruylants, Placide, O.S.B. (Belgium); liturgy; app. 5-11-1966, d. 10-18-1966

Buijs, Louis, S.J. (Netherlands), Gregorian University, Rome; law; app. 5-11-1966

Calabuig, Ignazio, O.S.M. (Spain), Marianum, Rome; liturgy, Mariology; app. 3-16-1966

Cardine, Eugène, O.S.B. (France), Pontifical Institute of Sacred Music, Rome; Gregorianist; app. 5-11-1966

Castellino, Giorgio, S.D.B. (Italy), University of Rome and Lateran University; psalms; app. 3-3-1964

Cattaneo, Msgr. Enrico (Italy), Catholic University of the Sacred Heart, Milan; history of liturgy; app. 5-11-1966

Cellier, Jacques (priest; France); pastoral liturgy; app. 3-16-1966

Claire, Jean, O.S.B. (France); Gregorianist; app. 5-11-1966

Cuva, Armando, S.D.B. (Italy), Salesianum, Rome; law, liturgy; app. 5-11-1966

Dalmais, Irénée, O.P. (France), Catholic Institute, Paris; liturgy; app. 5-11-1966

Damilano, Pietro (priest; Italy); popular song; app. 6-17-1964

D'Anversa, Msgr. Evaristo (Italy); Latinist, hymns; app. 5-11-1964

De Gaiffier, Beauduin, S.J. (Belgium), Bollandist; hagiography; app. 5-11-1966

Dell'Oro, Ferdinando, S.D.B. (Italy); liturgy; app. 5-11-1966

De Urquiri, Timoteo, C.M.F. (Spain); liturgy; app. 3-16-1966

Diekmann, Godfrey, O.S.B. (United States); liturgy; app. 5-11-1966

Dirks, Ansgar, O.P. (Netherlands), Dominican Liturgical Institute, Rome; app. 2-22-1964

Dubois, Marcel, C.SS.R. (Canada); rubrics; app. 5-11-1966

Duncker, Pieter, O.P. (Netherlands), Angelicum, Rome; psalms; app. 3-3-1964

Dürig, Msgr. Walter (Germany), University of Munich; liturgy; app. 5-11-1966

Egger, Abbot Karl, C.R.L. (Italy); Latinist; app. 5-11-1966

Fallani, Giovanni (Italy), Titular Bishop of Parthenia, president of the Pontifical Commission for Sacred Art in Italy; app. 2-22-1964

Falsini, Rinaldo, O.F.M. (Italy); liturgy; app. 5-11-1966

Famoso, Msgr. Salvatore (Italy); liturgy, rubrics; app. 5-11-1964, d. 5-31-1982

Féder, Joseph, S.J. (France); Scripture; app. 3-16-1966

Fischer, Msgr. Balthasar (Germany), Liturgical Institute, Trier; app. 5-11-1966

Fontaine, Gaston, C.R.I.C. (Canada); liturgy, Scripture; app. 5-11-1966

Franquesa, Adalberto, O.S.B. (Spain); liturgy; app. 2-22-1964

Frutaz, Msgr. Amato Pietro (Italy), SCR; history; app. 5-11-1966, d. 11-8-1980

Gélineau, Joseph, S.J. (France); music, liturgy, catechetics; app. 6-17-1964

Gherardi, Msgr. Luciano (Italy); parish priest; app. 2-22-1964

Grasso, Domenico, S.J. (Italy), Gregorian University, Rome; pastoral theology; app. 5-11-1966

Gribomont, Jean, O.S.B. (France); Vulgate; app. 3-3-1964

Gy, Pierre-Marie, O.P. (France), director Liturgical Institute, Paris; liturgy; app. 2-22-1964

Hamman, Adalbert, O.F.M. (France); patrology; app. 3-16-1966

Hänggi, Prof. Anton (Switzerland), University of Fribourg; liturgy; app. 2-22-1964 (subsequently bishop and a member of the Consilium)

Harmel, Jean, O.Praem. (France); music, song; app. 5-11-1964

Hesbert, René Jean, O.S.B. (France); liturgy; app. 3-16-1966

Hofinger, Johannes, S.J. (Austria), director East Asian Pastoral Institute, Manila; pastoral liturgy; app. 5-11-1964

Hourlier, Jacques, O.S.B. (France); Gregorianist; app. 5-11-1964

Hucke, Dr. Helmut (Germany); music; app. 6-17-1964

Jones, Percy (priest; Australia), University of Melbourne; music; app. 5-11-1964

Jungmann, Joseph Andreas, S.J. (Austria), University of Innsbruck; liturgy; app. 2-22-1964, d. 1-26-1975

Kahlefeld, Heinrich, C.O. (Germany); liturgy; app. 5-11-1964, d. 3-5-1980

Kennedy, Vincent, C.S.B. (Canada), Pontifical Institute of Christian Archeology, Rome; archeology; app. 5-11-1964

Kleinheyer, Bruno (priest; Germany); liturgy; app. 5-11-1964

Kniewald, Carlo (priest; Yugoslavia), University of Zagreb, Yugoslavia; liturgy; app. 5-11-1964

Kolbe, Ferdinand (priest; Germany); liturgy; app. 5-11-1964

Kunz, Lucas, O.S.B. (Germany); liturgy; app. 5-11-1964

Lanne, Emmanuel, O.S.B. (Belgium), Greek College, Rome; Eastern liturgy; app. 5-11-1964

Laroque, François (France); parish priest; app. 5-11-1964

Lécuyer, Joseph, C.S.Sp. (France), Lateran University, Rome; theology; app. 5-11-1964

Lengeling, Prof. Emil (Germany), University of Münster; liturgy; app. 5-11-1964

Lentini, Anselmo, O.S.B. (Italy); Latinist, hymns; app. 5-11-1964

Ligier, Louis, S.J. (France), Gregorian University, Rome; liturgy; app. 5-11-1964

Lucchesi, Msgr. Giovanni (Italy); liturgy; app. 5-11-1964, d. 12-6-1981

Luykx, Boniface, O.Praem. (Belgium), Louvain University, Kinshasa; liturgy; app. 5-11-1964

MacKenzie, Roderick, S.J. (Canada), Gregorian University, Rome; psalms; app. 3-3-1964

McManus, Frederick R. (priest; United States), Catholic University of America, Washington, D.C.; liturgy, law; app. 2-22-1964

Martimort, Canon Aimé-Georges (France), Catholic Institute, Toulouse; liturgy; app. 2-22-1964

Martínez de Antoñana, Gregorio, C.M.F. (Spain); rubrics; app. 5-11-1964

Massi, Pacifico (priest; Italy); biblical exegesis; app. 5-11-1964

Matéos, Juan, S.J. (Spain), Oriental Institute, Rome; Eastern liturgy; app. 5-11-1964

Mazzarello, Secondo (Italy); parish priest; app. 5-11-1964

Mejia, Jairo (priest; Colombia); pastoral liturgy; app. 5-11-1964

Messiaen, Olivier (France); organist; app. 6-17-1964

Migliavacca, Msgr. Luciano (Italy), director Cappella Musicale, Milan; music; app. 6-17-1964

Miller, John, C.S.C. (United States), Notre Dame University, Indiana; liturgy; app. 5-11-1964

Mohrmann, Prof. Christine (Netherlands), University of Nijmegen; Christian Latin literature; app. 10-20-1964

Molin, Jean-Baptiste, F.M.C. (France); liturgy; app. 5-11-1964

Moneta Caglio, Msgr. Ernesto (Italy), president Institute of Sacred Music, Milan; music; app. 2-22-1964

Mundó, Ansgar, O.S.B. (Spain); app. 5-11-1964

Nabuco, Msgr. Joaquím (Brazil); liturgy, parish priest; app. 2-22-1964

Neri, Umberto (priest; Italy); patrology; app. 3-16-1964

Neunheuser, Burkhard, O.S.B. (Germany), Sant' Anselmo Liturgical Institute, Rome; liturgy; app. 2-22-1964

Nocent, Adrien, O.S.B. (Belgium), Sant'Anselmo Liturgical Institute, Rome; liturgy; app. 3-16-1964

O'Connell, Canon John (England); liturgy, pastoral theology; app. 5-11-1964

Olivar, Alejandro, O.S.B. (Spain); liturgy; app. 5-11-1964

Oñatibia, Ignacio (priest; Spain); liturgy; app. 2-22-1964

Overath, Msgr. Johannes (Germany), president Consociatio Internationalis Musicae Sacrae; music; app. 6-17-1967

Paredi, Angelo (priest; Italy); liturgy; app. 5-11-1964

Pascher, Msgr. Joseph (Germany), University of Munich; liturgy; app. 2-22-1964, d. 7-5-1979

Patino, Joseph, S.J. (Spain); pastoral liturgy; app. 3-16-1966

Paventi, Saverio (priest; Italy); missiology; app. 5-11-1964, d. 4-18-1977

Peeters, Dr. Flor (Belgium); organist; app. 6-17-1964

Pellegrino, Msgr. Michele (Italy), University of Turin; patrology; app. 5-11-1964 (subsequently a bishop and member of the Consilium)

Pfaff, Maurus, O.S.B. (Germany), University of Munich; liturgy; app. 5-11-1964

Pilkington, Canon Ronald (England); rubricist; app. 5-11-1964, d. 1-21-1975

Pinell, Jorge, O.S.B. (Spain), Sant' Anselmo Liturgical Institute, Rome; liturgy; app. 5-11-1964

Quasten, Prof. Johannes (United States), Catholic University of America, Washington, D.C.; patrology; app. 5-11-1964

Rabau, Canon Jean (Belgium); parish priest; app. 5-11-1964

Raes, Alphonse, S.J., prefect Vatican Library; app. 5-11-1964

Raffa, Vincenzo, F.D.P. (Italy); liturgy; app. 5-11-1964

Ramos, Emmanuel (priest; Spain); liturgy; app. 5-11-1964

Righetti, Msgr. Mario (Italy); liturgy; app. 2-22-1964, d. 7-8-1975

Rogger, Msgr. Igino (Italy); history, liturgy; app. 3-16-1966

Roguet, Aimon-Marie, O.P. (France), Liturgical Institute, Paris; liturgy; app. 5-11-1964

Romita, Msgr. Fiorenzo (Italy), president International Federation of Little Singers; app. 6-17-1964, d. 9-22-1977.

Rose, Canon André (Belgium); liturgy, exegesis; app. 5-11-1964

Rousseau, Olivier, O.S.B. (Belgium); Eastern liturgy; app. 5-11-1964

Salmon, Pierre, O.S.B. (Luxembourg), Abbot of St. Jerome Monastery, Rome (later Titular Bishop of Giocondiana); Vulgate, psalms; app. 3-3-1964, d. 4-28-1982

Sauget, Msgr. Joseph-Marie (France), Vatican Library; Eastern liturgy; app. 5-11-1964

Schiavon, Msgr. Giovanni (Italy); ceremonies; app. 5-11-1964

Schmidt, Herman, S.J. (Netherlands), Gregorian University, Rome; liturgy; app. 2-22-1964, d. 7-9-1982

Schmitt, Msgr. Francis (United States); music; app. 4-27-1964

Schnitzler, Msgr. Theodor (Germany); parish priest; app. 5-11-1964

Seumois, Xavier, P.A. (Belgium), Catechetical Institute of Rwanda, Butare; liturgy, missiology; app. 5-11-1964

Sicard, Damien (priest; France); pastoral liturgy; app. 3-16-1966

Smits van Waesberghe, Joseph (Netherlands); music; app. 5-11-1964

Sobrero, Giuseppe, S.D.B. (Italy); pastoral liturgy; app. 5-11-1964

Stenzel, Alois, S.J. (Germany); liturgy; app. 5-11-1964

Tassi, Ildefonso, O.S.B. (Italy), Lateran University, Rome; liturgy, music; app. 5-11-1964

Terzariol, Msgr. Adone (Italy); papal master of ceremonies; app. 2-22-1965

Tilmann, Klemens, C.O. (Germany); pedagogy; app. 3-16-1966

Toal, Msgr. Francis Martin (England); patrology; app. 5-11-1964

Trimeloni, Lodovico, S.D.B. (Italy); rubrics; app. 5-11-1964

Vagaggini, Cipriano, O.S.B. (Italy); liturgy; app. 2-22-1964

Vandenbroucke, François, O.S.B. (Belgium); liturgy; app. 5-11-1964, d. 8-18-1971

Van Doren, Rembert, O.S.B. (Belgium), Abbot of Mont-César; liturgy; app. 2-22-1964

Vigorelli, Valerio (priest; Italy); sacred art; app. 5-11-1964

Visentin, Pelagio, O.S.B. (Italy); liturgy; app. 5-11-1964

Visser, Johannes (priest; Netherlands), Urbanianum, Rome; moral theology; app. 5-11-1964

Vogel, Cyrille (priest; France), University of Strasbourg; liturgy; app. 5-11-1964, d. 11-24-1982

Volpini, Raffaele (priest; Italy), Vatican Secret Archives; app. 5-11-1964

Wagner, Msgr. Johannes (Germany), director Liturgical Institute, Trier; app. 2-22-1964

Wambacq, Benjamin, O.Praem.; Scripture, psalms; app. 3-3-1964

Weakland, Rembert, O.S.B. (United States), Abbot Primate; app. 5-11-1964

ADVISORS[5]

Alszeghy, Zoltan, S.J. (Gregorian University, Rome)

Anciaux, Paul (priest; Belgium)

Arrighi, Msgr. Gianfrancesco (Secretariat for Christian Unity, Rome)

Baus, Karl (priest; Germany)

Borghini, Bonifacio, O.S.B. (Italy)

Bourget, Laurance, O.C.S. (Rome)

Bullough, Sebastian, O.P. (England)

Camps, Guido, O.S.B. (Spain)

---

5. The Consilium made use not only of consultors appointed by the Secretariat of State but also of numerous other persons. The present list does not include all of them but only those who figure in the Consilium lists as "advisors," because they either became participants in study groups or were regularly asked for their views by one or other of these groups (e.g., the groups on the psalms or the Lectionary). Other experts on whom the Consilium or the SCDW called in connection with particular questions are named in the chapters dealing with these matters.

Cazelles, Henri, S.S. (France)
Cerfaux, Msgr. Lucien (Belgium)
Charbel, Antonio, O.S.B. (Brazil)
Chavasse, Antoine (priest; University of Strasbourg, France)
Cignitti, Msgr. Benedetto (Italy)
Coppens, Msgr. Joseph (Belgium)
Coquin, Malo, O.S.B. (France)
Dalton, William Y., S.J. (Australia)
Daniélou, Jean, S.J. (France)
Deiss, Lucien, C.S.Sp. (France)
Delalande, Dominique, O.P. (France)
Díez Macho, Alejandro, M.S.C. (Spain)
Dornier, Pierre, S.S. (France)
Du Buit, Michel, O.P. (France)
Dumas, Antoine, O.S.B. (France)
Enout, João Evangelista, O.S.B. (Brazil)
Floristán, Cassiano (priest; Spain)
Franceschini, Prof. Ezio (Italy)
Gaillard, Jean, O.S.B., Abbot of Wisques (France)
Gay, Claude, O.S.B. (France)
García Cordero, Maximino, O.P. (Spain)
George, Augustin, S.M. (France)
Gracía, Juan Antonio (priest; Spain)
Grélot, Pierre (priest; France)
Gülden, Joseph, C.O. (Germany)
Heggen, Franz (priest; Netherlands)
Heiming, Odilo, O.S.B. (Germany)
Hesbert, René Jean, O.S.B. (France)
Hombach, Raphael, O.S.B. (Germany)
Kalilombe, Patrick (priest; Malawi)
Kilpatrick, Prof. George (England)
Kirchgässner, Alfons (priest; Germany)
Leclercq, Jean, O.S.B. (Luxembourg)
Llopis Sarrió, Juan (priest; Spain)
Löwenberg, Bruno (priest; Germany)
Maertens, Thierry, O.S.B. (Belgium)
Marot, Hilaire, O.S.B. (Belgium)
Marrou, Dr. Henri Irénée (France)
Michel, Jean Charles, S.S.S. (France)
Murphy, Roland, O.Carm. (United States)
Noè, Msgr. Virgilio (Italy)

Norberg, Dr. Dag (Sweden)
Opfermann, Bernhard (Germany)
Ortiz de Urbina, Ignacio, S.J. (Rome)
Oster, Henri (priest; France)
Panikkar, Raymond (priest; India)
Pfab, Joseph, C.SS.R. (Germany)
Rahner, Karl, S.J. (Germany)
Rinaldi, Giovanni, C.R.S. (Italy)
Ritzer, Korbinian, O.S.B. (Germany)
Ryan, Dermot, S.M.A. (Ireland)
Saraiva, Msgr. João (Portugal)
Sauvage, Michel, F.S.C. (France)
Schildenberger, Johannes, O.S.B. (Germany)
Schürmann, Heinrich (priest; Germany)
Schwegler, Theodor, O.S.B. (Switzerland)
Serra Zanetti, Paolo (priest; Italy)
Skehan, Patrick (priest; United States)
Tillard, Jean, O.P. (Canada)
Tournay, Raymond, O.P. (Jerusalem)
Van der Ploeg, Servatius, O.P. (Netherlands)
Villegas, Bertrand, SS.CC. (Chile)
Weber, Robert, O.S.B. (Luxembourg)
Wegman, Herman (priest; Netherlands)
Wiéner, Claude (priest; France)
Ziegler, Msgr. Joseph (Germany)

V. Sacred Congregation for Divine Worship

PREFECTS

Gut, Cardinal Benno, 5-8-1969 to 12-8-1969 (date of death)

Tabera Araoz, Cardinal Arturo, 2-20-1971 to 9-15-1973 (app. a member of the Consilium on 8-15-1970), d. 6-13-1975

Knox, Cardinal James Robert, 1-25-1974 to 7-11-1975, d. 6-26-1983

MEMBERS

Cardinals[6]

Agagianian, Gregory Peter, prefect SC Propaganda Fide, d. 5-16-1971

Arns, Paulo Evaristo, Archbishop of São Paulo, Brazil, app. 7-3-1974

Baggio, Sebastiano, prefect SC Bishops, app. 5-8-1969

Bengsch, Alfred, Archbishop of Berlin, East Germany, app. 5-18-1970, d. 12-13-1980

Bertoli, Paolo, prefect SC Causes of Saints, app. 2-19-1972

Cody, John Patrick, Archbishop of Chicago, United States, d. 4-25-1982

Confalonieri, Carlo, prefect SC Bishops

Conway, William, Archbishop of Armagh, Ireland, d. 4-17-1977

Darmojuwono, Justinus, Archbishop of Semarang, Indonesia, app. 7-3-1974

Dearden, John Francis, Archbishop of Detroit, United States, app. 8-15-1970

Enrique y Tarancón, Vicente, Archbishop of Toledo, then of Madrid, Spain

Felici, Pericle, d. 3-22-1982

Giobbe, Paolo, d. 8-14-1972

Gracias, Valerian, Archbishop of Bombay, India, d. 9-11-1978

Gray, Gordon Joseph, Archbishop of Edinburgh, Scotland

Jubany Arnau, Narciso, Archbishop of Barcelona, Spain, app. 4-12-1973

Lercaro, Giacomo, d. 10-18-1976

Luciani, Albino, Patriarch of Venice, app. 4-12-1973; subsequently Pope John Paul I, d. 9-28-1978

---

6. The cardinals for whom no date of appointment is given are those who were members of the Consilium and automatically became members of the Congregation in accordance with the regulations set down in the apostolic constitution *Sacra Rituum Congregatio* of May 8, 1969; see DOL 94 no. 683.

Marty, François, Archbishop of Paris, France, app. 8-15-1970

Otunga, Maurice, Archbishop of Nairobi, Kenya, app. 7-3-1974

Pellegrino, Michele, Archbishop of Turin, Italy

Pignedoli, Sergio, app. 7-3-1974, d. 6-15-1980

Rugambwa, Laurean, Archbishop of Dar-es-Salaam, Tanzania

Salazar López, José, Archbishop of Guadalajara, Mexico, app. 4-12-1973

Samorè, Antonio, prefect SC Sacraments, app. 2-19-1972, d. 2-3-1983

Silva Henríquez, Raúl, Archbishop of Santiago, Chile

Willebrands, Johannes, president of the Secretariat for Christian Unity, app. 5-8-1969

Wojtyla, Karol, Archbishop of Krakow, Poland, app. 8-15-1970, subsequently Pope John Paul II

Bishops (selected by the members of the Consilium and confirmed by the Pope on January 5, 1970, except for Bishop Kisberk, who was appointed later)

Boudon, René, Bishop of Mende, France

Carter, Gerald Emmett, Bishop of London, Canada

Hänggi, Anton, Bishop of Basel, Switzerland

Hurley, Denis Eugene, Archbishop of Durban, South Africa

Isnard, José Clemente Carlos, Bishop of Nova Friburgo, Brazil

Kisberk, Imre, Bishop, Apostolic Administrator of Szekesfehervár, Hungary, app. 8-17-1970, d. 4-24-1982

Nagae, Laurentius Satoshi, Bishop of Urawa, Japan

Spülbeck, Otto, Bishop of Meissen, Germany, d. 6-27-1970

SECRETARY

Bugnini, Annibale, C.M., ordained Titular Archbishop of Diocletiana on 2-13-1972 by Pope Paul VI, d. 7-3-1982

CONSULTORS

Appointed 9-12-1969, unless otherwise indicated

Agustoni, Msgr. Gilberto (Switzerland, Rome)

Amalorpawadass, Simon (priest; India), app. 7-3-1974

Belluco, Bartolomeo, O.F.M. (Italy), d. 11-10-1982

Bernal, José, O.P. (Spain)

Braga, Carlo, C.M. (Italy)

Calabuig, Ignazio, O.S.M. (Spain, Rome)

Coughlan, Msgr. Peter (England, Rome), app. 7-3-1974
Dirks, Ansgar, O.P. (Netherlands, Rome)
Famoso, Msgr. Salvatore (Italy), d. 5-31-1982
Fontaine, Gaston, C.R.I.C. (Canada)
Gy, Pierre-Marie, O.P. (France)
Jounel, Msgr. Pierre (France)
Lengeling, Msgr. Emil (Germany)
Martimort, Msgr. Aimé-Georges (France)
Mpongo, Laurent, C.I.C.M. (Zaire), app. 7-3-1974
Neunheuser, Burkhard, O.S.B. (Germany, Rome)
Nocent, Adrien, O.S.B. (Belgium, Rome)
Patino, José, S.J. (Spain)
Rose, Canon André (Belgium)
Rotelle, John E., O.S.A. (United States), app. 4-15-1972
Schnitzler, Msgr. Theodor (Germany), d. 8-29-1982
Soberal Díaz, José Dimas (priest; Colombia, CELAM), app. 4-15-1972
Swayne, Sean (Ireland), app. 1-14-1975
Wagner, Msgr. Johannes (Germany)

Bibliography of Annibale Bugnini

ABBREVIATIONS

AC	*Annali della Carità*
AM	*Annali della Missione*
DC	*Documentation Catholique*
EL	*Ephemerides Liturgicae*
Not	*Notitiae*
OL	*Ora et Labora. Rivista Liturgica Benedetina*
OR	*L'Osservatore Romano*
ORD	*L'Osservatore Romano della Domenica*
RL	*Rivista Liturgica*

1939

"Il beato Giustino de Iacobis attraverso l'epistolario del Cardinale Guglielmo Massaia," *AM* 46 (1939) 340–50.
"Il Convitto ecclesiastico," *AM* 46 (1939) 380–85.
"Missioni," *AM* 46 (1939) 434–44.

1940

"Tracce vincenziane a Loreto," *AM* 47 (1940) 19–29.
"Albania," *AM* 47 (1940) 93–99.
"S. Vincenzo, consolatore degli afflitti," *AM* 47 (1940) 328–37.
"Contributo alla storia delle Compagnie della Carità," *AC* 11 (1940) 113ff.

1941

"Una lettera inedita del sig. Pedrini ai seminaristi di Roma," *AM* 48 (1941) 151–56.
"Il sig. Nicola Basili," *AM* 48 (1941) 185–211.

"Inedito del servo di Dio Felice de Andreis," *AM* 48 (1941) 262.
"Cent'anni delle Figlie di Carità a Piacenza," *AM* 48 (1941) 270–77.
"Cent'anni della Compagnia della Carità di Palestrina," *AC* 12 (1941) 47–56.

1942

"S. Leonardo e i metodi di 'missionare,' " *AM* 49 (1942) 76–82.
"In memoria di suor Santini," *AM* 49 (1942) 128–39.
"Sanctus Vincentius a Paulo magister orationis mentalis," *AM* 49 (1942) 181–86.
"Il Sig. Rocco Petrone, C.M.," *AM* 49 (1942) 327–36.
"La rinascita della 1ª Compagnia della Carità del Lazio," *AC* 14 (1942) 50–52.

1945

Ardens et Lucens (Rome, 1945ff.). Liturgical collection founded and directed by
　A. Bugnini.
"Manuali italiani di liturgia," *EL* 59 (1945) 334–44.
"La liturgia dei sacramenti al Concilio di Trento," *EL* 59 (1945) 39–51.

1947

"Verso una riforma del 'Martyrologium Romanum'?" *EL* 61 (1947) 91–99.
"Liturgia e pietà cristiana," *Il Monitore ecclesiastico* 62 (1947) 235–39.
"Liturgia viva," *OR* (November 3–4, 1947).

1948

Miscellanea Liturgica in Honorem C. Mohlberg (Rome, 1948). 2 vols. Planned and
　edited by A. Bugnini.
"Un ospite illustre a S. Silvestro al Quirinale," *AM* 55 (1948) 270ff.
"La versione 'piana' del Salterio," *EL* 62 (1948) 240–48.
"Sessio Liturgica Lovaniensis," *EL* 62 (1948) 409–13.

1949

La nostra Messa (Rome, 1949ff.). Twelve printings. English edition: *Our Holy Mass*
　(Manila, 1960). Indian edition: *Amchem Mis* (Pilar, Goa, 1961).
"Il Messale della Sainte-Chapelle," *EL* 63 (1949) 70–76.
"Per una riforma liturgica generale," *EL* 63 (1949) 165–84. Complete translation
　in *Bibel und Liturgie* (1949–50). Lengthy summaries in *Ecclesia* (Spain, 1950) and
　Liturgia (Silos, Spain, 1950) 76–83.

1950

Thirty entries on Vincentian topics, *Enciclopedia Cattolica*.
"I missionari di S. Vincenzo," *Ecclesia* (Vatican City, 1950) 210–15.

1951

De Solemni Vigilia Paschali Instaurata (Rome, 1951) 48 pp. First published in *EL* 65 (1951), Suppl. to no. 1.

Notte Santissima. Riti e preghiere della veglia pasquale (Rome, 1951).

"Il latino, lingua liturgica," *EL* 65 (1951) 24–27.

"Rationabilis,"' *EL* 65 (1951) 104.

"L'eucologio di Dêr-Balyzeh," *EL* 65 (1951) 151–70. On the same topic: "L' 'editio princeps' di un antico eucologio," *RL* 38 (1951) 104–8.

"Voti per una revisione del Messale romano," *RL* 38 (1951) 206–9.

"Easter-Eve Liturgy," *Theology Digest* (December 1951) 21.

1952

"La partecipazione dei fedeli alla Messa," in G. Brinktrine, *La S. Messa* (Rome, 1952) 308–21.

"Decretum de facultativa celebratione instauratae vigiliae paschalis ad triennium prorogata," *EL* 66 (1952) 90–98. Same topic treated in *Apollinaris* (1952) 381–96.

1953

Documenta Pontificia ad Instaurationem Liturgicam Spectantia 1903–1953 (Rome, 1953) 213 pp.

Cerimonia della veglia pasquale (Rome, 1953) 64 pp.

R. Barin, *Catechismo liturgico*. 4 vols. Tenth edition revised and updated by A. Bugnini, C.M. (Rovigo, 1953ff.).

"Editio VI post typicam Missalis Romani," *EL* 67 (1953) 46–61.

"Il 1° congresso italiano di Pastorale liturgica," *EL* 67 (1953) 62–69.

"Quaedam formulae italica lingua in administrando baptismo," *EL* 67 (1953) 148–54.

"De modis hostias offerendi in Missa," *EL* 67 (1953) 167–70.

"La 1ª Settimana Italiana di Pastorale liturgica," *EL* 67 (1953) 62–69.

"Praefari = Praefatio," *EL* 67 (1953) 247.

"III congressus internationalis studiis liturgicis promovendis," *EL* 67 (1953) 365–77.

"Le nuove norme sul digiuno eucaristico e le Messe vespertine," *Ecclesia* (Vatican City, 1953) 76–77.

"La prassi liturgica," *Enciclopedia del Sacerdozio* (Florence, 1953) 1041–62.

"I laici e la 'laus perennis' " *OR* (December 24, 1953).

1954

"Parva Breviaria fidelium," *EL* 68 (1954) 171–79. On the same topic: ""I fedeli e la preghiera liturgica," *RL* 41 (1954) 165–76.

"Domenica delle Palme, trionfo di Cristo Re," *RL* 41 (1954) 114–18.

"La communione dei fedeli al Venerdì Santo," *EL* 68 (1954) 253–56.

Enciclopedia Cattolica, entries: *Compieta, Confessore, Croce, Defensor civitatis, Defensor Ecclesiae, De Puniet de Parry, Ephemerides Liturgicae, Epistolario, Evangeliario, Lezionario, Martirologio, Omiliario, Ordines Romani, Passionario, Patrono, Pontificale, Quiñones, Rubriche, Sacramentario.*

"La Medaglia miracolosa nel culto e nella liturgia," *AM* 61 (1954) 297–316. Also published separately by Edizioni Vincenziane (Rome, 1954) 20 pp.

"Una particolarità del Messale da rivedere: la preghiera 'pro Iudaeis' al Venerdì santo," *Miscellanea Mons. Giulio Belvederi* (Rome, 1954) 117–32.

1955

La semplificazione delle rubriche (Rome, 1955) 121 pp. English edition: *The Simplification of the Rubrics* (Collegeville, Minn., 1955) 131 pp.

With I. Bellocchio, C.M., *De Rubricis ad Simpliciorem Formam Redigendis. Commentarium ad decretum SRC diei 23 Martii 1955* (Rome, 1955²) 100 pp. First published in *EL* 69 (1955) 113–207.

"Why a Liturgy Reform?" *Worship* 29 (1955) 561–69. Translation of the first chapter of *La semplificazione delle rubriche.* Also published in *The Catholic Mind* 54 (1956) 74–81.

"Carattere e importanza pastorale della semplificazione delle rubriche," *Palestra del clero* 34 (1955) 1122–30.

1956

With C. Braga, C.M., *Ordo Hebdomadae Sanctae instauratus* (Bibliotheca *EL,* Sect. hist. 25; Rome, 1956) 174 pp. First published in *EL* 70 (1956) 81–228.

"Direttorio della Messa letta," *EL* 70 (1956) 276–77 (on Cardinal Lercaro's *A Messa, figlioli!*)

"Officium et Missa in solemnitate S. Ioseph Opificis, Commento," *EL* 70 (1956) 355–68.

"De hebdomada sancta instaurata," *EL* 70 (1956) 414–29.

"Bibliografia generale," in an Appendix of *Dizionario pratico di liturgia romana* (Rome, 1956) 477–80.

1957

With C. Braga, C.M., *Cerimoniale della Settimana Santa* (Rome, 1957) 132 pp.

With C. Braga, C.M., "Ordinationes et declarationes circa Ordinem Hebdomadae Sanctae instauratum," *EL* 71 (1957) 81–86.

"Sussidi per la pastorale liturgica," *EL* 71 (1957) 123–29.

"Commentarium alla 'Declaratio circa dubium de forma paramentorum,' e al 'Decretum de forma et usu Tabernaculi' della SRC," *EL* 71 (1957) 438–45 (on the form of vestments and the form and use of the tabernacle).

"Palm-Zondag. Over de geest van de Goede Weekhervorming," *SSma Eucharistia* 49 (1957) 41–46.

"Semana santa," *La Milagrosa* 42 (1957) 99–102.

"Sacra Liturgia" (and the beyond in the liturgy), in the collective volume *L'Al di là* (Turin, 1957) 91–103.

"Vita sacramentale e liturgica," in the collective volume *La formazione spirituale nei seminari* (Rome, 1957) 169–203.

"Missa cum diacono," in *Miscellanea in onore di Mons. Domenico Mallardo* (Naples, 1957) 21–25. Translated in *Worship* 32 (1958) 459–63.

All the entries on Vincentian topics in the *Dizionario Ecclesiastico UTET.*

"A dieci anni dalla 'Mediator Dei,'" *Bollettino del Clero Romano* (Rome, 1957) 441–42.

"Parola di Dio e liturgia," *OR* (July 5, 1957).

1958

"La Madonna nella liturgia occidentale," in the collective volume *Mater Christi* (Rome, 1958) 115–63.

"Pio XII et la liturgia," *Tabor* 24 (1958) 1034–40. Also published in *Quaderni del clero* (Padua, 1959) 91–98. Latin version: *EL* 72 (1958) 375–83.

"Ombre e luci nel Movimento liturgico attuale," *Studi Cattolici* 2 (1958) n. 9, 75–76.

Some entries on liturgical topics in *Dizionario Enciclopedico TRECCANI.*

First Appendix of *Dizionario pratico di liturgia romana* (Rome, 1958).

"Il Santo Padre Giovanni XXIII e la Musica sacra," *Bollettino degli amici del Pontificio Istituto di Musica sacra* 10 (1958) n. 3-4, 1–2.

"La nuova edizione del 'Messalino romano per i fedeli,'" *OR* (May 14, 1958).

"Piccolo clero e vocazioni," *OR* (May 31, 1958).

1959

Messa comunitaria, ed. R. Spiazzi, O.P., and A. Bugnini, C.M. (Padua, 1959) 32 pp.

Documenta Pontificia ad Instaurationem Liturgicam Spectantia. Vol. 2: 1953–1959 (Rome, 1959) 116 pp.

Ceremonial da Semana Santa (Petrópolis, 1959).

"La liturgia è l'esercizio del sacerdozio di Gesù Cristo per mezzo della Chiesa," *Asprenas* 6 (1959) 1–15.

"La Messe del SS. Cuore di Gesù," in the collective volume *Cor Jesu, Commentationes in litteras encyclicas "Haurietis aquas* 1 (Rome, 1959) 61–94.

"Musica e liturgia," *Bollettino Ceciliano* 54 (1959) 101–2.

"Alcuni aspetti teologici della partecipazione attiva dei fedeli alla Messa," *Bollettino Ceciliano* 54 (1959) 226–33.

"La Liturgia," *La Rocca* (February 15, 1959) 13 (on the liturgy of Lent).

"Vespri a S. Pietro," *OR* (May 20, 1959).

1960

"Rinascita liturgica," *Il sinodo di Roma* (1960) 23.

"Ordo ad Synodum," *EL* 74 (1960) 121–28.

"Come è stato celebrato il Sinodo romano," *Palestra del clero* 39 (1960) 363–66.

"La Messa didattica," in the collective volume *Lo sviluppo storico delle forme della Messa* (Rome, 1960) 59–82.

"Il nuovo Codice delle rubriche del Breviario e del Messale romano," second Appendix of *Dizionario pratico di liturgia romana* (Rome, 1960).

"50 anni del Pontificio Istituto di Musica sacra," *Bollettino degli amici del Pontificio Istituto di Musica sacra* 12 (1960) n. 3-4, 1–4.

"Notula sulle 'Variationes in Missali et in Rituali Romano in precibus pro Iudaeis' della SRC," *EL* 74 (1960) 134.

"Commento alla lettera della Congregazione dei Seminari e delle Università cattoliche in occasione del 50° di fondazione del Pontificio Istituto di Musica sacra," *Bollettino degli amici del Pontificio Istituto di Musica sacra* 12 (1960) 2–4.

"Commentarium al 'Decretum de precibus post Missae celebrationem recitandis' della SRC," *EL* 74 (1960) 459–60.

1961

"Es verdad que los sacerdotes ya no quieren rezar?" *Boletín de Pastoral litúrgica* 1, n. 3 (1961) 4–8.

"La Messa, dramma sacro," *Il Collegio dei Lettori* (1961) 3ff.

Editor of the Italian edition, *Messale quotidiano dei fedeli*, of G. Feder's missal (Rome, 1961).

"Adnotationes alla Declaratio: Laudes non possunt anticipari nec in recitatione 'a solo,' " *EL* 75 (1961) 57.

"Armonia e dignità della Liturgia," *RL* 48 (1961) 253–56.

1962

"L'opera del Card. Gaetano Cicognani per il rinnovamento liturgico dell'ultimo decennio," *OR* (March 5–6, 1962). Also published in: *EL* 76 (1962) 130–33, and in *Bollettino diocesano di Faenza* 49 (1962) 52–56.

"Musica e Liturgia," *RL* 49 (1962) 13–19.

"Adnotationes alla lettera 'Iucunda laudatio' di Papa Giovanni XXIII e alla relativa allocuzione pontificia," *EL* 76 (1962) 63–68.

Preface to *Introduzione agli studi liturgici* (Liturgica 1; Rome, 1962).

"La Comunità [=Congregazione della Missione] e il rinnovamento liturgico attuale," *AM* 69 (1962) 345–58.

Liturgia viva (Milan, 1962) 480 pp.

"Nova sedes Instituti Liturgici Trevirensis," *EL* 76 (1962) 56–57.

1963

"De sacra liturgia in prima periodo Concilii Oecumenici Vaticani II," *EL* 77 (1963) 3–18.

"Breviary Reform," *Worship* 37 (1963) 221–26.

"Attualità della liturgia dal Concilio di Trento al Vaticano II," *Euntes Docete* 16 (1963) 181–98.

1964

" 'Consilii' origo, structura, actuositas." Lecture given at the Gregorian University, March 12, 1964. Mimeographed text, 13 pp.

"Il Motu Proprio 'Sacram Liturgiam,' " *OR* (March 2–3, 1964).

"La Costituzione liturgica. Che cosa c'è di nuovo per i fedeli," *OR* (April 19, 1964).

"Istruzione sull'attuazione della Costituzione. Terzo tempo della rinascita liturgica," *ORD* (October 25, 1964).

"La Liturgia culmine e fonte della vita della Chiesa," *Fede e Arte* 12 (1964) 6–11.

"Sei mesi di attività del 'Consilium ad exsequendam Constitutionem de sacra Liturgia,' " *OR* (September 23, 1964). Spanish translation in *Sal Terrae* 52 (1964) 684–97, and in *Phase* 4 (1964) 287–94.

"Corpus Domini oggi e domani?" *Annali dei sacerdoti adoratori* 64 (1964) 464–68.

"De voorbereiding van de Constitutie over de Liturgie," *Tijdschrift voor Liturgie* 48 (1964) 83–88.

"De sacra liturgia in secunda sessione Concilii Oecumenici Vaticani II," *EL* 78 (1964) 3–14.

1965

Verso la riforma liturgica (Vatican City, 1965) 206 pp.

"Il nuovo 'Ordo Missae,' " *OR* (January 1965); *DC* 62 (1965) 315–20.

"Per l'attuazione della Costituzione liturgica: Le 'Variationes' ad alcuni testi della Settimana Santa," *OR* (March 19, 1965); *DC* 62 (1965) 603–4.

"Per l'attuazione della Costituzione liturgica: Il rito della Concelebrazione," *OR* (March 28, 1965); *DC* 62 (1965) 714–22.

"Il secondo anno di pontificato di Paolo VI: I primi passi della riforma liturgica," *OR* (June 28–29, 1965).

"La musica sacra nel rinnovamento liturgico attuale," *La voce di S. Gioacchino* 9/5–6 (1965) 5–8.

"Viaggio in Olanda," *ORD* (November 14, 1965).

1966

"Instructio de lingua in celebrandis officio divino et missa 'conventuali' aut 'communitatis' apud religiosos adhibenda. Commentarium," *EL* 80 (1966) 156–64.

"I testi liturgici della Messa per il Giubileo straordinario," *OR* (January 21, 1966).

1967

"Introduzione alla Costituzione su la sacra liturgia 'Sacrosanctum Concilium,' " in the collective volume *Il Concilio Vaticano II* (Milan, 1967) 405–7.

"Textus conferentiae ad scriptores diariorum ac periodicorum habitae die 4 ianuarii 1967 a Rev.mo P. A. Bugnini, Subsecretario S. Rituum Congregationis pro sacra Liturgia et Secretario 'Consilii,' " *Not* 3 (1967) 39–46; *OR* (January 5, 1967); *EL* 81 (1967) 75–80; *DC* 64 (1967) 829–36.
"In margine alla 'Dichiarazione': Commenti della stampa," *ORD* (1967).
"Instructio altera," *OR* (May 7, 1967); *DC* 64 (1967) 894–98.
"Sulla Instructio altera," *Orientamenti pastorali* 2 (1967) 109–15.
"Qualche chiarificazione sulla 'Instructio altera,' " *OR* (May 24, 1967).
"Il 'Graduale simplex,' " *OR* (October 4, 1967); French: *DC* 64 (1967) 2050–56; Portuguese: *OL* 15 (1968) 117–21.
"Intervento del P. Bugnini in occasione del convegno sull' 'Eucharisticum mysterium,' " *Liturgia* 1 (1967) 34–37.
"L'Istruzione sulla musica nella Liturgia: Documento fondamentale per il rinnovamento liturgico," *Rivista di pastorale liturgica* 4 (1967) 241–48; *Caecilia* 71 (1967) 2–4 (review).

1968

"Da domani il canone della Messa in italiano; Riforma liturgica e carità pastorale," *L'Avvenire* (March 23, 1968).
"Lo spirito delle celebrazioni liturgiche," *Rivista diocesana Torinese* 50 (June 1968) 249–52.
"La XI Sessione plenaria del 'Consilium,' " *OR* (October 21–22, 1968); *Not* 4 (1968) 348–55.
"Il Convegno liturgico-pastorale: Il Canone della Messa," *Liturgia* 2 (1968) 108.
"Il P. Bugnini fa il punto sui lavori del 'Consilium,' " *Settimana del clero,* n. 25 (June 23, 1968).
"Ricordo del Cardinal Bea," *Not* 4 (1968) 360–62.
"Il nuovo Pontificale Romano delle Ordinazioni," *OR* (December 7, 1968).

1969

"Come ve el 'Consilium' la renovación litúrgica," *Pastoral liturgica,* nn. 1-2 (1969) 6–10.
"Un altro passo verso la restaurazione liturgica: L' 'Ordo celebrandi Matrimonium,' " *OR* (March 31–April 1, 1969).
"Sulla via della riforma liturgica: Il nuovo 'Ordo Missae,' " *OR* (May 9, 1969).
"La restaurazione liturgica in cammino: 'Ordo Baptismi parvulorum,' " *OR* (June 21, 1969); *DC* 66 (1969) 676–77.
"Sul cammino della restaurazione liturgica: Il nuovo Calendario," *OR* (May 14, 1969); *Not* 5 (1969) 298–303.
"La restaurazione liturgica in cammino: L'Ordo Lectionum Missae," *OR* (August 6, 1969).

"Ad un mese dall'introduzione del nuovo 'Ordo Missae,' " *OR* (October 31, 1969); *Rivista diocesana di Roma* 10 (1969) 1249–51.

"La Messa di sempre," *OR* (November 29, 1969).

1970

"Riforma liturgica in cammino: L' 'Ordo Professionis religiosae," *OR* (February 11, 1970).

"Riforma liturgica in cammino: Calendari e 'Propri' particolari," *OR* (August 22, 1970).

"L'Istruzione 'Sacramentali Comunione': precedenti e significato," *OR* (September 4, 1970).

"Riforma liturgica in cammino: L' 'Ordo Consecrationis Virginum," *OR* (September 7–8, 1970); *DC* 67 (1970) 873–75.

"De editione Missalis Romani instaurati: 'Paulus Episcopus plebi Dei,' " *Not* 6 (1970) 161–68; *OR* (May 13, 1970); *Gottesdienst* 4 (1970) 81–85; *RL* 58 (1971) 447–55.

"Questa è liturgia rinnovata," *Not* 6 (1970) 406–7; in English: *News Sheet, Westminster Cathedral* 4, n. 2 (1971).

1971

"Riforma liturgica: Tre nuove pubblicazioni: I. Ordo Benedictionis Abbatis, II. Missale parvum, III. Lezionario latino," *OR* (January 9, 1971); French: *DC* 68 (1971) 239–40; Portuguese: *Boletim Eclesiástico da Diocese de Macau* 69 (1971) 107–9.

"Problema liturgico: Gli Oli santi," *OR* (March 4, 1971); French: *DC* 68 (1971) 297.

"Riforma liturgica: La istituzione generale della Liturgia delle Ore," *OR* (March 13, 1971, and March 14, 1971).

"Riforma liturgica: Il primo volume della Liturgia delle Ore," *OR* (June 24, 1971).

"Riforma liturgica: Il secondo volume della 'Liturgia Horarum,' " *OR* (October 22, 1971).

"Temas sobre la reforma litúrgica: Siete años," *Phase* 11 (1971) 127–30.

Editor of Italian edition, *Messale della domenica*, of P. Jounel's missal (Rome, 1973).

"Dal Breviario alla 'Liturgia delle Ore,' " *La rivista del clero italiano* 52 (1971) 42–51.

"Dialogo con i lettori: 'Pregare costa': una precisazione distensiva del P. Annibale Bugnini, Segretario della S.C. per il Culto divino," *Settimana del clero*, n. 37 (1971) 2.

"Rinnovamento nell'ordine," *Not* 7 (1971) 49–52.

"Opportuno ordinamento. Norme per l'uso provvisorio dei testi nella celebrazione, specialmente cantata, della Messa e dell'Ufficio divino," *OR* (November 24, 1971); *DC* 68 (1971) 1112.

"Circa editionem libri 'Liturgiae Horarum,' " *Not* 7 (1971) 411–13.

1972

"Primo incontro con la Liturgia delle Ore," *OR* (January 1, 1972).
"Sacralità del luogo di culto," *Not* 8 (1972) 182–84.
"Quattromila a San Pietro," *Not* 8 (1972) 335–36.

1973

"Un altro passo nella riforma liturgica: 'Ministeri, candidati e celibato diaconale,' "
    OR (January 14, 1973).
"Rinnovamento nell'ordine" (circular letter on the Eucharistic Prayer by the Congregation for Divine Worship to the presidents of the episcopal conferences),
    OR (June 15, 1973; French: *DC* (1973) 613–14; Portuguese: *OL* 19 (1973) 316–19.
"Dieci anni," *Not* 9 (1973) 395–99.
"La Liturgia al 40° Congresso Eucaristico Internazionale," *Not* 9 (1973) 135–40.
"Quonam sensu Liturgia renovari debet?" *Not* 9 (1973) 288.
"Al centro dell'attenzione e delle preoccupazioni dell'autorità responsabile: Pietà
    e rispetto verso la SS. Eucaristia nelle applicazioni del rinnovamento liturgico,"
    OR (May 16, 1973); under the title "Sulla mano 'come in trono,' " *Not* 9 (1973)
    289–96; French: *DC* 70 (1973) 565–68; Portuguese: *OL* 19 (1973) 267–76; English:
    English edition of *OR* (June 14, 1973) and *Origins* (August 16, 1973) 140–42.
"A dieci anni dalla Costituzione liturgica: Progresso nell'ordine," *OR* (December 12, 1973).
"Ricordo del P. Fugazza," *AM* 80 (1973) 126–28.
"La figura del P. Salvatore Cenci," *AM* 80 (1973) 129–31.

1974

"Il nuovo 'Ordo Paenitentiae' " (interview on Vatican Radio), *OR* (February 9,
    1974); *DC* 71 (1974) 211–12.
"Calendari," *Not* 10 (1974) 408–9.
"Celebrare con decoro," *OR* (August 28, 1974); *Not* 10 (1974) 306– 7.
"De sacra communione distribuenda," *Not* 10 (1974) 308.
"Gli Osservatori al 'Consilium,' " *Not* 10 (1974) 249–52, 383.
"'Movimento liturgico' o 'Pastorale liturgica'?" *Not* 10 (1974) 137–38.
"Musica e . . . fantasia," *Not* 10 (1974) 302–5.
"Restaurare la linea autentica del Concilio?" *Not* 10 (1974) 217– 21; *DC* 71 (1974)
    730–32.

1975

"La riforma liturgica nelle missioni," in the collective volume *Problemi attuali
    della evangelizzazione* (pro manuscripto; Rome, 1975) 193–217.
"Il culto dei Santi," *Not* 11 (1975) 83–87.

"Cantate al Signore un canto nuovo," *Not* 11 (1975) 161–66.
"Messe a tema," *Not* 11 (1975) 350–52; *DC* 58 (1976) 242–43.
"Myricae," *Not* 11 (1975) 196–201; *Settimana del clero* (December 14, 1975) 5–6.
"Salmo responsoriale: recita o canto?" *Not* 11 (1975) 59–60.
"Tibi silentium laus!" *Not* 11 (1975) 279–82.
"Vita comune e Liturgia," *Not* 11 (1975) 22–23.

1976

"Nella sua dimora romana Eugenio De Mazenod rafforzò l'ideale di santità," *OR*
    (January 12–13, 1976).

1977

"La figura e l'opera del P. Emilio Rinaldi," *AM* 84 (1977) 227–39.

1981

San Vincenzo de Paul. Pensieri (Rome, 1981) 218 pp.
La Chiesa in Iran (Rome, 1981) 472 pp.

Index of Persons

Abercius of Hieropolis 923
Adenauer K. 279
Agagianian G. P. 81 140 834
    942 953
Agatha (St.) 313 317 546
Agnes (St.) 546
Agustoni G. 87 310 464 475
    589 712 924 945 954
Agustoni L. 119 151 337 370
    450 478 811 891 901 902 910
    944
Albareda A. 8 9 937 940
Alcuin 401
Alexander VI 114
Alfonzo P. 7
Alfrink B. 106 107 640
Alonso M. 360 362 363
Alonso-Schökel L. 412
Aloysius Gonzaga (St.) 313
Alphonsus (St.) 313
Alszeghy Z. 664 950
Altisent M. 119 891 901 945
Alvarez A. B. 269
Amadouni G. 945
Amalorpawadass S. 954
Ambrose (St.) 117 340 374
    382 415 540 541 607 672 894
Amon K. 337 449 467 945
Amore A. 305 308 491 545
    546 945
Anastasia (St.) 381
Anciaux P. 664 950
Andrew (St.) 374 381 543 546
Andrieu M. 730
Anglés Pamiés I. 16 21 22 827

900 901 902 903 905 938 941
    945
Ansgar (St.) 321
Anthony (St.) 313
Antonelli F. 8 27 30 60 106
    107 140 149 360 361 431 642
    712 827 830 837 937 940 942
Antoniutti I. 919
Anzevui J. 294
Arns P. E. 953
Arrighi G. 132 174 595 697
    950
Arrupe P. 816
Ashworth H. 397 401 538 545
    945
Asterius of Amasea 541
Athenagoras I 169
Atzeri C. 911
Augusta C. 495
Augustine (St.) 46 415 540
    541 593 604 894
Auvray P. 413

Bacci A. 281 284 286 296 494
Backaert 542
Badano N. 660
Baggio S. 82 91 186 953
Baker K. 92
Balbina (St.) 318
Balboni D. 401 945
Bär F. 721
Barbara N. 288
Barbara (St.) 318
Barbieri R. 792 878
Bardet A. 499

Barnabas (St.) 543 549
Barrielle L. M. 291
Bartolucci D. 886 888 901 902
    945
Barucq A. 412
Basil (St.) 133 163 450 457 458
    459 462 472
Baus K. 545 950
Bea A. 7 9 12 30 166 189 201
    375 376 415 526 529 530 531
    532 533 595 774 816 837 937
    942
Beauchamp E. 413
Beauchamp P. 412
Beauduin L. 6
Bedeschi L. 281
Béguerie Ph. 466 477 478
Beilliard J. 21 890 901 945
Békés G. 945
Bekkers W. 189 940 942
Belluco B. 589 954
Belluco C. 282 283
Bendazzi A. 549
Benedict (St.) 567 568 569 570
Benedict XIV 273
Benelli G. 360 632 642 703
    742 878
Bengsch A. 193 671 672 953
Benildus (Bl.) 169
Bennett C. 945
Benoit P. 413
Bernal J. 954
Bernard (St.) 541 543
Berno of Reichenau 320
Beron R. 403 945

968

Bertoli P. 193 953
Berulle P. de 541
Betti U. 619
Bevilacqua G. 15 16 17 19 55
    140 153 156 189 374 613 614
    938 942
Bibiana (St.) 318
Bieler L. 528
Bluyssen J. 105 151 160 172
    184 871 942
Bodigel 864
Bogler T. 783 945
Boillon P. 648
Bonet E. 54 55 68 76 161 186
    497 510 517 826 827 901 902
    941 945
Borella P. 15 16 24 402 413
    783 807 819 938 945
Borello L. 901 945
Borghini B. 548 950
Borovy V. 174
Botero A. 761
Botero Salazar T. 140 942
Botte B. 15 16 123 158 344 347
    450 528 613 618 624 625 707
    711 712 714 715 727 731 732
    763 939 945
Boudon R. 82 83 140 160 164
    172 194 221 370 436 396 509
    515 662 871 942 954
Bouman C. 403 945
Bourdarias J. 93
Bourget L. 950
Bouyer L. 152 174 283 337
    450 460 945
Bovone A. 431
Braga C. xxvii 9 15 19 53 102
    114 222 228 310 360 361 363
    394 398 431 467 475 661 664
    712 743 761 807 819 827 831
    862 863 864 902 937 954
Brand E. L. 172 200
Brandolini L. 773
Brasó G. 360 814 815 826
Bressan G. 413
Briceño E. 549
Briner 174
Brinkhoff L. 16 939 945
Broccolo G. 53
Brune A. 412
Brunner P. 761
Bruylants P. 157 161 189 221
    397 398 404 548 831 945
Bugnini A. xix xx xxi xxii
    xxvii xxix xxxi xxxii 5 6 9 14
    15 30 43 49 50 52 54 60 61
    82 89 90 91 92 93 106 107

112 123 141 149 151 172 214
    229 239 242 251 281 282 291
    297 310 315 321 349 350 351
    360 361 364 369 383 395 420
    431 432 433 437 461 462 464
    480 485 486 520 521 522 523
    590 635 641 642 656 658 659
    660 671 673 675 677 688 698
    712 716 717 794 807 814 831
    837 860 862 864 877 937 938
    941 944 954
Buijs L. 819 826 901 945
Bullough S. 528 950
Burchard John 114
Byrne L. C. 186 942

Cabié R. 320 730 864
Caesarius of Arles 540 541
Caffarelli F. 278
Caglio E. M. 890
Cajetan (St.) 316
Calabuig I. 53 661 763 766 792
    795 874 878 945 954
Calewaert K. 16 938 940
Callam D. xxxii
Calmel T. 288
Calo L. 282 910
Camps G. 528 950
Cannizzaro G. B. 15 16 27
    939
Capelle B. 8 15 27 938
Capone R. 281
Capovilla L. 91
Capponi N. 292
Cardine E. 16 119 551 811 891
    893 901 902 939 946
Carinci A. 7 8 937
Carter G. E. 82 153 942 954
Casimir (St.) 318
Casini T. 91 164 280 281 282
Casoria G. 431
Castellino G. 494 526 527 946
Catania E. 91
Catherine of Alexandria (St.)
    318
Catherine of Siena (St.) 281
Cattaneo E. 938 946
Cattani G. 688
Cavalletti S. 441
Cazelles H. 412 528 951
Cecchetti I. 941
Cecilia (St.) 217 313 317 318
    546
Celada D. 282 289 911
Cellier J. 76 337 431 579 584
    606 946
Cerfaux L. 528 951

Charbel A. 528 951
Charles Borromeo (St.) 313
Chavasse A. 15 16 320 413
    579 684 939 951
Christopher (St.) 318
Chromatius of Aquileia 541
Ciappi L. 310 316 698 701 850
Cicognani A. 49 52 99 106
    148 152 162 173 248 360 362
    429 462 850
Cicognani G. 9 12 14 15 22 24
    25 27 28 37 168 349 931 937
    938
Cignitti B. 545 951
Ciliberti G. 360
Claire J. 119 405 891 901 946
Clare (St.) 313
Clavel Méndez T. A. 151 942
Clement (St.) 546
Clement X 316
Coache (Abbé) 279
Cody J. P. 82 132 167 942 953
Cogotzi G. 360
Colombo C. 373 377 697 700
    702
Columbanus (St.) 321
Concesi (Sister) 360 363
Concetti G. 350
Confalonieri C. 20 26 81 140
    142 164 172 317 493 494 506
    745 942 953
Congar Y. 277 281 294
Conway W. 82 151 160 942
    953
Coppens J. 528 951
Coppo A. 404
Coquin M. 951
Cordero 528
Cosmas (St.) 381
Coughlan P. 53 449 467 478
    721 955
Coughlin D. 761
Cunial E. 360 361
Cuva A. 819 946
Cyprian (St.) 544 546
Cyril (St.) 314
Cyril of Alexandria (St.) 540
    541
Cyril of Jerusalem (St.) 540
    541

Dalmais I. 946
Dalton W. Y. 528 951
D'Amato C. 9 937 940
Damian (St.) 381
Damilano P. 218 890 901 946
Daniélou J. 538 951

Dante E. 9 30 72 126 128 827 830 937 940
D'Anversa E. 548 946
Da Pobladura M. 712
Darmojuwono J. 953
Dearden J. F. 193 351 953
Decentius of Gubbio 730
De Clerq C. 941
De Foucauld C. 544
De Gaiffier B. 545 546 946
De Gregorio V. 360
Deiss L. 408 410 951
De Kesel L. 161 942
Delalande D. 551 951
De la Potterie I. 413
Delcuve J. 613
De Lepeleere G. 939
Del Gallo Roccagiovine L. 360
Dell'Acqua A. 106 164 363 807 860 870
Dell'Oro F. 331 401 523 946
De Nantes G. 289 293
De Nicolò P. 363
Denis-Boulet N. M. 152
Denis the Carthusian 541
De Pauw G. 169 279
De Saventhen E. M. 278 295
Descamps (Abbé) 290
De Urquiri T. 946
Didier J. 684
Didymus of Alexandria 541
Diekmann G. 16 24 227 409 410 411 414 533 939 946
Díez Macho A. 528 951
Dirks A. 15 16 19 123 305 306 491 763 826 861 901 902 939 941 946 955
Dominic (St.) 316
Donovan K. 671
Döpfner J. 740
Dornier P. 533 951
Dubois J. 605
Dubois M. 16 939 946
Du Buit M. 533 951
Ducaud-Bouget 293 294
Duesberg H. 412 413
Dumas A. 396 397 478 721 722 924 951
Duncker P. 526 527 529 530 531 946
Dupont J. 413
Durandus William 715
Dürig W. 397 538 946
Duroux B. 244 479 522 673 677 688

Dwyer G. P. 151 350 357 943
Egger K. 67 479 526 548 549 863 941 946
Eizenhöfer L. 678
Elizabeth of Hungary (St.) 313
Enciso Viana J. 111 940 943
Enout J. E. 763 951
Enrique y Tarancón V. 82 151 160 943 953
Ephraem (St.) 318
Ernetti P. 845
Evenou J. 466 477

Fagiolo V. 350
Fallani G. 16 45 144 938 946
Falsini R. 123 402 901 946
Famoso S. 337 450 491 783 819 820 827 849 901 924 939 946 955
Farnés P. 467
Fasciani M. 441
Faulhaber M. 406
Féder J. 410 413 946
Federici T. 412
Feiner, J. 595
Felici P. 34 37 38 50 55 68 82 140 167 194 862 943 953
Felicity (St.) 311 313
Fernandez P. 279
Ferraro N. 827 941
Ferrua A. 549
Fesquet H. 349
Feuillet A. 413
Fey Schneider B. 940 943
Fischer B. 76 123 347 441 475 478 479 493 579 581 584 586 595 599 613 614 684 697 732 761 763 779 901 939 946
Floristán C. 664 951
Fohl J. 941
Fontaine G. 53 386 409 410 412 414 420 442 924 946 955
Franceschini E. 663 951
Francis de Sales (St.) 313
Francis of Assisi (St.) 330
Franquesa A. 114 123 151 337 396 450 783 807 813 819 827 901 902 946
Franzoni 586
Frutaz A. P. xxi 9 106 107 149 663 712 828 830 837 937 941 946
Fruttero C. 605
Fuentes Valbuena P. 549

Gabriel (St.) 311 312 322
Gabro J. 132
Gagnebet R. 851 941
Gaillard J. 402 410 413 414 951
Galluzzi A. 360 362 363
Galot J. 878
Gambari E. 763 827
García Cordero M. 951
García del Valle D. C. 53
Garrone G. 294 862 863 864 865 867
Gaspari P. 736
Gay C. 951
Gélineau J. 152 221 337 370 450 467 478 479 556 889 901 910 924 946
Gellier G. 450
George (St.) 318
George A. 412 413 533 951
George A. R. 200 290
Gerstner (Mrs.) 288
Gherardi L. 947
Gillet P. 924
Giobbe P. 30 51 81 140 837 940 943 953
Giombini 428
Gogué J. 15 16 938
Gracia A. 671
Gracia J. A. 951
Gracias G. A. 397
Gracias V. 81 125 139 270 917 943 953
Gräf H. 53 761
Grasso D. 826 947
Gray G. 81 82 161 943 953
Gregory of Nazianzus (St.) 541
Gregory the Great (St.) 317
Grélot P. 533 951
Gribomont J. 491 526 527 947
Grimshaw F. 140 148 189 940 943
Guano E. 140 193 307 309 317 370 528 727 731 943
Guardini R. 179 544 938
Guéranger P. 6
Guillet J. 413
Gülden J. 951
Gut B. 80 81 82 83 84 88 140 153 161 167 172 173 190 192 193 279 291 383 420 431 432 464 509 515 568 740 774 932 942 953
Gy P.-M. 15 16 31 76 90 193 194 337 347 413 450 467 475

579 581 613 614 684 688 690 697 721 722 732 763 771 778 779 783 901 939 947 955

Habel 888
Hallinan P. J. 173 189 687 788 940 943
Hamer J. 479
Hamman A. 538 947
Hang T. 273
Hänggi A. 15 16 76 82 161 173 174 177 291 307 337 402 448 450 717 861 863 901 939 943 947 954
Hanrion B. P. 603
Haquin A. 441 478
Harmel J. 119 891 901 947
Haug A. 90
Hausberg H. 549
Häussling A. xxxi
Hedwig (St.) 318
Heenan J. 297 298 350
Heggen F. 664 951
Heiming O. 533 951
Hermenegild (St.) 546
Hervás y Benet J. 16 140 318 415 938 943
Hesbert R. J. 331 401 551 947 951
Hilary (St.) 543
Hippolytus (St.) 450 452 456 712 714 715 745
Hofinger J. 16 579 939 947
Hombach H. 819
Hombach R. 951
Hourlier J. 119 890 891 901 947
Hout D. M. 763 827
Hucke H. 890 901 947
Hurley D. E. 82 370 528 600 943 954

Ignatius of Antioch (St.) 381 430 513 546
Iniesta A. 843
Innocent I 730
Innocent IV 624
Inwood P. 277
Isnard J. C. C. 82 160 172 600 943 954

Januarius (St.) 318
Jasper R. C. 83 200 201
Jedin H. 283
Jenny H. 15 16 19 140 307 414 415 826 827 938 940 943

John Baptist de la Salle (St.) 313
John Cantius (St.) 318
John Chrysostom (St.) 540 541 549
John of the Cross (St.) 313
John Paul II 318
John the Baptist (St.) 373 420 607
John the Deacon 730
John XXIII 14 23 26 29 33 39 44 55 69 290 314 344 369 508 573 806
Jones P. 16 939 947
Jop F. 318 940 943
Josaphat (St.) 313
Joseph (St.) 322 323 324 344 369 401 607 809
Joseph of Cupertino (St.) 318
Jouassard G. 711
Jounel P. xxxi 16 21 28 87 132 152 174 193 194 305 306 308 315 327 337 370 385 402 410 413 414 431 450 491 520 589 618 619 671 707 721 732 747 761 792 805 807 808 819 821 861 863 864 901 924 939 955
Journet C. 107 152
Jubany Arnau N. 953
Jullien A. 30 940
Jungmann J. A. 8 11 15 19 54 337 338 450 613 614 901 938 941 947
Justin (St.) 313 540 541 546

Kabangu F. 186 943
Kaczynski R. xxxi 252 325 441 445 457 475 478 721 753 754 761 924
Kahlefeld H. 15 410 417 939 947
Kalilombe P. 528 951
Kennedy V. 15 939 947
Kervéadou F. 140 943
Kilpatrick G. 528 951
Kirchgässner A. 664 951
Kisberk I. 192 954
Klauser T. 16 939
Kleinheyer B. 618 707 721 727 730 947
Kniewald C. 16 938 947
Knox J. R. 85 206 268 486 932 953
Kolbe F. 402 947
König F. 750 754
Kovács S. 153 605 943

Kowalski K. 16 21 939
Kronsteiner H. 121
Künneth F. W. 172 200 290
Kunz L. 119 548 891 901 947
Kuo J. 351
Kurzeja A. 595

Laboa S. 82
Lallier M. A. 710
Landersdorfer S. K. 938
Lanne E. 132 410 413 947
Laroque F. 114 947
Larraona A. M. 25 30 50 80 107 140 827 830 832 851 871 905 931 938 940 943
Lawrence (St.) 546
Lazík A. 153 179 186 189 943
Leclercq J. 538 951
Lécuyer J. 157 161 174 360 579 590 618 664 707 711 712 717 721 727 737 739 850 852 947
Lefèbvre M. 91 93 277 279 281 294 295
Lefèbvre J. 515
Legardien L. xxxi
Lenaerts R. B. 845
Lengeling E. J. xxxii 161 174 195 331 467 468 475 491 533 536 579 618 707 720 721 722 727 779 861 864 901 947 955
Lentini A. 67 83 404 450 491 526 528 548 549 550 947
Leo the Great (St.) 162 541 546
Leo XIII 34 308 616 617 623 833
Léon-Dufour X. 413
Lercaro G. xxviii 12 13 30 50 51 54 55 60 71 74 75 76 80 81 83 99 101 107 125 140 141 145 148 149 156 160 164 166 169 172 199 219 220 223 228 281 309 346 348 350 352 353 356 407 438 449 494 497 498 501 520 527 532 559 585 614 708 716 717 827 830 831 832 837 848 892 893 931 940 942 953
Lessi M. 87 721 722
Levesque L. 836
Levi V. 91
Lietarert A. 360
Ligier L. 132 450 467 579 584 589 603 664 947

Lio E. 673
Llopis Sarrió J. 401 951
Loosdregt E. 270 610
López de Moura A. 943
Louf (Abbot) 567
Louis IX (St.) 318
Louis the Pious 330
Lourdusamy S. 162 270 635
Löw J. 7 8 10 27 937
Löwenberg B. 579 951
Lucchesi G. 397 404 545 548
    549 947
Lucentini F. 605
Luciani A. 953
Lucy (St.) 317 318
Luther M. 164 168 281 289
Luykx B. 16 579 939 947
Lyonnet S. 413

Macca V. 566 781 924
Macchi P. 360
MacKenzie R. 412 413 526
    527 948
Madiran J. 294
Maertens T. 951
Maggiolini S. 843
Magnoni A. 590
Malula J. 16 30 605 938 940
    944
Manca N. 270
Mansourati C. I. 140 307 318
    944
Manzanares J. 87
Manziana C. 360 361 373 374
    377 829
Maria Goretti (St.) 321
Marini P. 53 821
Marinuzzi M. 360
Maritain J. 152
Marmion C. 544
Marot H. 410 413 951
Marrou H. I. 528 951
Marsili S. 31 90 467
Martha (St.) 313 423 549
Martimort A.-G. 15 19 54 74
    123 153 174 221 287 305 307
    320 347 470 491 494 496 497
    498 500 506 509 520 522 533
    534 617 690 727 731 732 805
    807 808 811 819 821 826 860
    861 864 900 901 902 939 941
    948 955
Martin (St.) 186
Martin de Porres (St.) 321
Martin G. 293

Martin J. A. 940 944
Martínez de Antoñana G. 16
    938 941 948
Martinianus (St.) 816
Marty F. 193 293 954
Mary Magdalene (St.) 423
Masi R. 316 941
Masnou Boixeda R. 940
Massi P. 410 948
Matéos J. 221 413 948
Matteo R. 360
Matthews E. 441
Matura T. 412 413
Maximus of Turin 540 541
Maximus the Confessor 540
Mazzarello S. 548 579 699 773
    779 948
McManus F. xxxi xxxii 16 24
    54 337 431 450 579 595 826
    901 902 939 941 948
Megivern J. J. 6
Mejia Gómez J. 16 579 939
    948
Merton T. 544
Messiaen O. 948
Methodius (St.) 314
Meyer H. 671
Micara C. 8 9 937
Michael (St.) 312 322 373
Michel Jean C. 661 951
Migliavacca L. 901 948
Miller J. 402 948
Mohlberg L. C. 678
Mohrmann C. 528 948
Molin J. B. 401 402 403 579
    948
Molinari P. 573
Mollat D. 413
Molteni 83
Moneta Caglio E. 890 901 939
    948
Monica (St.) 313
Montagne Y. 294
Montini G. B. 9 30 292 293
    363
Morlot A. 556
Mpongo L. 955
Mundó A. 948
Murphy R. 951
Mussner F. 413
Muthappa F. 16 939

Nabuco J. 16 189 618 707 783
    807 819 938 941 948
Nagae L. Satoshi 82 589 944
    954

Nasalli Rocca di Corneliano
    M. 360
Neri U. 491 538 541 948
Nervi P. 53
Neunheuser B. 123 310 331
    332 401 763 826 901 948 955
Newman J. H. 541
Niccolini P. 12
Nicholas (St.) 316 317
Nicodemo E. 351
Nikolasch F. 53 491 538 541
    664
Nocent A. 402 410 413 414
    721 784 865 948 955
Noè V. 82 337 661 814 821
    951
Noirot M. 826 827
Norberg D. 528 952

O'Connell J. 16 114 938 941
    948
Olivar A. 538 948
Olivi M. 53 360
Oñatibia I. 15 16 19 491 538
    541 579 939 948
Opfermann B. 331 403 952
Origen 539 541
Ortiz de Urbina I. 538 952
Ortolani A. 360
Oster H. 410 952
Osty E. 413
Otcenásek K. 186 944
Ottaviani A. 20 284 286 292
    296 461 745
Otunga M. 954
Oury G. 287 843
Overath J. 21 889 890 901 902
    941 948

Pahl I. 448
Palazzini P. 635
Palestrina P. G. 886
Panikkar R. 528 952
Paquier R. 499
Parecattil J. 270
Paredi A. 493 948
Parente P. 107 851
Pascher J. 16 19 83 221 307
    402 491 493 494 545 554 938
    948
Pasqualetti G. xxiv xxxi 53
    325 348 360 361 362 363 439
    441 478 589 590 594 619 635
    661 671 673 677 688 781 924
Patino G. 337 431 450 556 948
    955

Patrick (St.) 311 313
Paul (St.) 119 158 313 322 323
  324 373 374 401 487 607
Paul V 222 581 598 661 686
  779
Paul VI xxi xxii xxiv xxviii
  xxix xxx 37 38 45 50 51 54
  58 77 80 83 87 89 91 94 113
  162 187 189 202 214 251 284
  285 286 287 288 289 290 291
  292 293 297 298 300 307 313
  314 363 368 383 385 420 425
  445 486 520 564 680 690 697
  737 813 814 815 817 820 829
  848 919 922 933
Paventi S. 826 948
Pedrosa V. 441 478
Peeters F. 949
Pellegrino M. 82 146 151 160
  167 171 172 174 317 415 429
  491 528 538 540 541 554 608
  944 949 954
Percy J. 890 901
Perpetua (St.) 311 313
Peter (St.) xxi 23 284 290 322
  323 324 373 374 381 401 607
  813
Peter Chanel (St.) 321
Pfab J. 114 952
Pfaff M. 551 949
Pfliegler M. 16 939
Philip Neri (St.) 313
Philippe P. 310 395 464 522
  631 642 712
Pichler A. 940 944
Pignedoli S. 954
Pilkington R. 114 609 819 949
Pinell J. 413 493 949
Pistoia A. 395 773 781
Pius V (St.) xxv xxvii 214 279
  280 284 285 287 290 291 292
  294 297 299 316 385 393 394
Pius X (St.) 6 37 187 284 314
  332 806 819 891 902
Pius XI 573 819
Pius XII xxiii xxvi 6 7 9 23 34
  44 314 320 339 385 526 533
  709 718 908
Pizzoni G. 16 938
Poitevin P. 278
Polycarp (St.) 313 923
Ponzoni D. 360
Pozzi R. 861
Processus (St.) 816
Prou J. 940

Pseudo-Macarius of Egypt
  541
Puthenandady P. 761

Quasten J. 16 538 541 938 949
Quinn C. U. 283

Raas F. xxxi
Rabau J. 579 819 949
Raciti G. 491 538 545
Radó P. 16 939
Raes A. 949
Raffa V. 491 493 556 661 949
Rahner K. 664 952
Ramos E. 402 403 949
Raphael (St.) 312 322
Rau E. 140 317 940 944
Renié R. 287
Rennings H. 441 443 478 479
Ribacchi A. 360
Ricci M. 273
Richard A. 287
Rigaux B. 413
Righetti M. 8 16 320 337 338
  402 613 938 941 949
Rimaud D. 478 479
Rinaldi G. 413 911 952
Ritter J. E. 167 189 944
Ritzer K. 579 952
Rogger I. 491 949
Roguet A.-M. 221 401 403
  410 413 523 556 609 949
Romains G. 292
Romita F. 887 901 949
Roschini G. 282 590
Rose A. 397 410 470 491 493
  533 792 949 955
Rospigliosi G. 284
Rossano P. 412
Rossetti E. M. 431 874
Rossi A. 635
Rossi C. 16 140 348 415 938
  940 944
Rossi O. 741
Rotelle J. 53 467 491 538 542
  543 955
Rousseau O. 949
Rovigatti L. 9 360 361 937
Ruffini E. 494
Rugambwa L. 82 944 954
Rus R. 53
Ryan D. 528 952

Saigh M. 132
Salazar López J. 954

Salleron L. 292
Salmon P. 526 533 941 949
Salotti C. 7
Samorè A. 193 635 671 744
  954
Sana G. 360
Santolamazza D. 53
Santucci P. 282
Saraiva J. 952
Sartore D. 467 781 792
Sauget J.-M. 949
Sauvage M. 551 952
Scalzotto T. 688
Schiavon G. 16 783 819 938
  949
Schildenberger J. 528 952
Schilling A. 465
Schmidt H. 15 16 19 20 26 29
  31 32 54 76 226 305 331 401
  493 705 826 827 901 902 939
  949
Schmitt F. 890 901 949
Schnackenburg R. 413
Schnitzler T. 15 114 151 162
  186 195 337 370 450 807 816
  819 821 901 949 955
Scholastica (St.) 313
Schürmann H. 410 413 417
  952
Schuster I. 319
Schwegler T. 528 952
Schweiger P. 940
Senarius 730
Seper F. 88 287 375 485 624
  631 635 687
Serra Zanetti P. 538 952
Seumois X. 579 586 590 697
  949
Shehan L. 279
Shepherd M. H. 160 174 200
  290
Sicard D. 579 949
Siffrin P. 16 678 939
Silva Henríquez R. 82 350
  370 944 954
Simcic M. 688
Simeon of Thessalonica 776
Sirleto G. xxv 141 394
Sixtus V 42
Skehan P. 952
Slipyi J. 132
Smits van Waesberghe J. 21
  890 901 949
Soberal Díaz J. D. 955
Sobrero G. 331 949

Sottocornola F. 467 664 671 683

Spadini L. 90

Spicq C. 413

Spülbeck O. 82 160 172 192 370 494 939 940 944 954

Staffa D. 860 861

Stanislaus (St.) 318

Stenzel A. 579 949

Stewart C. xxxii

Stickler D. A. 827 941

Strecker, K. 663

Suenens L. 656 739

Sustar A. 299

Sutter 590

Svizzero L. 91

Swayne S. 955

Tabera Araoz A. 84 85 193 196 198 218 294 295 438 932 953

Tarruell G. G. 781

Tassi I. 548 551 826 901 949

Tautu G. 15

Taylor T. 175

Tena M. 864

Tertullian 40 539 540 608

Terzariol A. 807 811 819 950

Testacci B. 90

Théas A. M. 685

Theodore of Mopsuestia 457 544

Therese of the Child Jesus (St.) 313

Thomas Aquinas (St.) 904 905

Thurian M. 175 200 201 290 556

Tillard J. 849 852 952

Tilloy P. 288

Tilmann K. 221 410 950

Timothy (St.) 313

Tisserant E. 37

Titus (St.) 313

Toal F. 538 950

Tondini A. 310 385 617

Tournay R. 413 528 952

Trapé A. 851

Triacca A. M. 869

Trimeloni L. 114 901 950

Trinquet I. 413

Trombini A. 360

Turibius (St.) 321

Urban VIII 550

Vagaggini C. 15 16 19 54 55 76 123 157 174 201 287 307 337 370 403 410 414 416 449 450 460 464 495 613 615 624 627 727 732 826 827 849 850 862 863 901 902 939 941 950

Valentini L. 140 144 944

Van Bekkum W. 140 940 944

Vandenbroucke F. 402 579 950

Van den Eynde D. 941

Van der Mensbrugge A. 174

Van der Ploeg S. 528 952

Van Doren R. 305 950

Van Lierde P. C. 106 107 360

Van Zuylen W. M. 140 162 944

Vassalli L. 661

Vattioni F. 412 413

Venmann H. xxxi

Vetri L. 431 673 712

Viana J. E. 111 149

Victor (Pope) 731

Vigorelli V. 16 939 950

Villegas B. 528 952

Villot J. 85 186 741

Vincent de Paul (St.) 5

Vinel A. 605

Vinson 288

Violardo G. 107 642

Violle B. 441

Virgili L. 887 910

Vischer L. 174

Visentin P. 431 491 551 671 950

Visser J. 950

Vogel C. 618 664 707 950

Volk H. 140 415 944

Volpe G. 288 289

Volpini R. 545 783 950

Von Allmen J. 174

Vriens P. C. 467

Wagner J. xxxi 16 54 123 145 305 307 317 337 338 341 346 347 370 431 450 467 475 807 811 826 861 901 902 939 941 950 955

Walsh J. 16 939

Wambacq B. 526 527 950

Weakland R. 167 173 360 361 370 431 890 901 944 950

Weber R. 952

Wegman H. 337 450 461 779 952

Wiéner C. 533 952

Willebrands J. 82 106 186 317 816 954

Wilmart A. 663 730

Witheu J. F. 289

Wojtyla K. 193 954

Wright J. 294 635

Young G. 140 944

Yu Pin P. 273

Zakrzewski T. P. 27 939

Zalba M. 479 677

Zauner F. 59 121 140 741 938 940 944

Zerwick M. 110

Ziegler J. 952